KnobCtrl2 Demonstrates a second version of the ActiveX (OLE) control object. (Chapter 16)

Life Demonstrates an old game as a simple electronic simulation. (Chapter 31)

List Demonstrates using dynamically allocated arrays and virtual memory functions. (Chapter 19)

MacSock Demonstrates using the Winsock API for the AppleTalk protocol. (Chapter 22)

MapDemo Demonstrates methods of identifying regions within bitmap images based on mouse selection. (Chapter 30)

Modes Demonstrates standard and custom mapping modes for graphics operations. (Chapter 23)

Mouse1 Demonstrates tracking mouse movements with simple responses to mouse button clicks. (Chapter 5)

Mouse2 Demonstrates the standard mouse cursor shapes and how the mouse cursor can be changed by the application window or by other application conditions. (Chapter 5)

Mouse3 Demonstrates how an application can respond to mouse clicks and correlate the position information to screen/window coordinates. (Chapter 5)

Multimedia Demonstrates how applications use multimedia extensions. (Chapter 37)

NamedPipe Demonstrates how to use multiple processes with named pipes. (Chapter 15)

Nest Demonstrates nested exception handling. (Chapter 18)

OLE_Client Demonstrates the simplicity of creating an OLE (Object Linking and Embedding) client using MFC and the AppWizard. (Chapter 36)

PainText Demonstrates the basics of "painting" an application screen, simple font metrics, scrolling, and scrollbar message responses. (Chapter 3)

PainText2 Duplicates the PainText application using MFC. (Chapter 3)

Parry Demonstrates a simple OLE server with a distinctly paranoid nature. (Chapter 36)

PenDraw1 Demonstrates drawing mode operations and color interactions. (Chapter 24)

PenDraw2 Demonstrates drawing using standard shapes—arc, chord, ellipse, pie, and rectangle. (Chapter 25)

PenDraw Demon... polygo... polygon... multisided figures. (Chapter 25)

PenDraw4 Demonstrates using bitmapped brushes to fill shapes. (Chapter 26)

PenDraw5 Demonstrates retrieving and displaying bitmap images. (Chapter 26)

PenDraw6 Demonstrates using metafile operations to store and replay previously calculated drawing sequences and how to exchange metafiles between applications. (Chapter 33)

PieGraph Demonstrates how pie charts are created. (Chapter 25)

Popups Demonstrates using pop-up messages and menus. (Chapter 13)

Reg_Ops Demonstrates registry access operations for both reading and writing. (Chapter 17)

RPClient Demonstrates an RPC (Remote Procedure Call) client. (Chapter 22)

RPCServ Demonstrates an RPC server. (Chapter 22)

SendMail Demonstrates using the Winsock API and the SMTP protocol to send e-mail. (Chapter 21)

SVGA_Win Demonstrates a variety of color palettes. (Chapter 26)

Target Demonstrates using nondestructive overlays for graphics images. (Chapter 29)

Threads Demonstrates synchronizing multiple threads and exception handling. (Chapter 14)

Unwind Demonstrates using a filter function to modify variables that cause an exception and how to replay the code where an error would have occurred. (Chapter 18)

ViewPCX Demonstrates loading and viewing .PCX (Paintbrush format) images. (Chapter 28)

WebView Demonstrates using the Internet ActiveX Browser control. (Chapter 21)

WinHello Demonstrates the basic requirements of any Windows 98 application and introduces the Template.I include file. (Chapter 2)

WNetDemo Demonstrates using the WNet functions to map a network drive. (Chapter 22)

Windows® 98 Developer's Handbook™

Ben Ezzell
with Jim Blaney

SYBEX®

San Francisco • Paris • Düsseldorf • Soest

Associate Publisher: Gary Masters

Contracts and Licensing Manager: Kristine Plachy

Acquisitions & Developmental Editor: Peter Kuhns

Editors: Marilyn Smith, LeeAnn Pickrell

Project Editors: Alison Moncrieff, Michael Tom

Technical Editor: Doug Langston

Book Designer: Catalin Dulfu

Graphic Illustrator: Andrew Benzie

Electronic Publishing Specialist: Cynthia Johnsen

Desktop Publisher: Kris Warrenburg

Production Coordinators: Katherine Cooley, Eryn L. Osterhaus

Production Assistants: Beth Moynihan, Rebecca Rider

Indexer: Matthew Spence

Companion CD: Molly Sharp and John D. Wright

Cover Designer: Design Site

Cover Illustrator/Photographer: Gregory MacNicol

Screen reproductions produced with Capture and Paint Shop Pro.

SYBEX is a registered trademark of SYBEX Inc.

Developer's Handbook is a trademark of SYBEX Inc.

TRADEMARKS: SYBEX has attempted throughout this book to distinguish proprietary trademarks from descriptive terms by following the capitalization style used by the manufacturer.

The author and publisher have made their best efforts to prepare this book, and the content is based upon final release software whenever possible. Portions of the manuscript may be based upon pre-release versions supplied by software manufacturer(s). The author and the publisher make no representation or warranties of any kind with regard to the completeness or accuracy of the contents herein and accept no liability of any kind including but not limited to performance, merchantability, fitness for any particular purpose, or any losses or damages of any kind caused or alleged to be caused directly or indirectly from this book.

Library of Congress Card Number: 98-84006

ISBN: 0-7821-2124-1

Manufactured in the United States of America

10 9 8 7 6 5 4 3 2

To the unsung heroes of the cyber-revolution

As anyone over 20 should be able to remember—save some who are oblivious (i.e., already brain-dead) even to an avalanche—computers have changed our world… and will continue to change our world.

For the most part, the changes are to the good, but they are also not without frustrations even for the experienced and generally expert power users. These frustrations simply go with the territory. The more complex computers become, the more potential for frustration exists.

Some years ago—at a time when those who had personal computers were not only the first on their block but often the first in their town or city—it was possible to know everything about the computer… from the details of how to troubleshoot a power regulator chip to how to rewrite the BIOS. At that time, computers held few secrets for the knowledgeable in either hardware or software. And it was even possible to know both and to know them thoroughly. But that was an earlier age—a simpler age in every respect.

Today very little is simple. Operating systems are multitasking; applications are built by teams, not individuals; and interactions—which didn't exist in the past—are now the rule. No application stands alone, and complexity increases as the power of the number of interactions involved.

Which brings us to the unsung heroes of the cyber-revolution. They are only voices on a phone or sometimes in an e-mail note. But they are also our recourses of last resort. The faceless, unmet, but oh-so-essential tech support people who answer our calls for assistance with patience, with courtesy, and sometimes with stifled laughter. And, yes, even I occasionally must resort to such requests for assistance.

I applaud their patience and their courtesies… and, even more, their ready answers. Not that they are always right—these are mere mortals, not cyber-gods. But they are right more often than wrong and, even when wrong, are diligent in seeking the right response. They receive little credit and few thanks, yet we owe them much.

Therefore, I take this opportunity—publicly—to say thank you wholeheartedly and sincerely… and, hey, I'll be calling, you hear?

Tip: If you would like to know a few of the things these unsung heroes put up with, visit `http://www.techtales.com`… where the truth is too funny to be anything else.

ACKNOWLEDGMENTS

As an author, my role in creating this book consists of expending blood, sweat, and tears to try to find, test, and explain those topics that will be most valuable to the reader. As such, I must admit to the sole responsibility for any errors found herein and confess fully to any shortcomings you may perceive in this book.

However, simply writing the book is only one part of the task of producing this volume. There are a number of other individuals who have participated in this effort.

To wit, Jim Blaney, my co-author, definitely deserves credit for his efforts in covering important topics, for which I personally lacked the experience or the opportunity to investigate and develop appropriate examples. Jim's explanations of networking, cryptography, Internet, and security issues are valuable contributions, without which this volume would be lacking. He deserves and receives my sincere thanks for his participation.

Next, as always, a special thank you goes to Doug Langston, my tech editor, who has the valuable (however annoying) habit of raising questions that the author would probably prefer to dodge. Doug is a true Knight of the Royal Order of Nit.

Also a note of thanks to Marilyn Smith and Lee Ann Pickrell for their collective efforts at converting my pawky and sometimes disjointed prose into an intelligible and coherent whole. They are responsible in no small part for making this a readable and valuable book.

Mention also goes to Peter Kuhns for helping to put this project together in the first place and to Michael Tom (both at Sybex) for miscellaneous and often forgotten tasks. To both Peter and Michael, for their efforts in keeping a host of details out of my hair and letting me concentrate on writing, my very sincere thanks.

In addition, thanks are in order for a number of individuals whom I have not met and whose names I have not heard but whose efforts are obvious in the final product. Without their participation, you would be reading this—if at all—as a large stack of loose sheets of paper of uncertain organization. While every book is the responsibility of one person—the author—it is not the result of the efforts of a single person; preparing and publishing a book involves a host of individuals. To all of those involved, I thank you very much.

And last, to you the readers, my thanks for buying this volume, which I hope will prove valuable to you.

Ben Ezzell

And Ben, thanks to you for giving me the opportunity to work with you and to contribute to this book. Your expertise and sense of humor are noted and appreciated. I also thank Doug (for those reasons Ben mentions), Marilyn (for her speedy yet accurate editing), Peter, Michael, and the other folks at Sybex.

I also wish to thank my Mom and Dad, who gave me life, love, and an attraction to learning. Finally, I wish to thank my uncle, Duane Brummel, who helped me be a "ham," and who first introduced me to the world of computing with his amazing home-built computers.

Jim Blaney

CONTENTS AT A GLANCE

TABLE OF CONTENTS

Appendix

INTRODUCTION

Windows 98—like its predecessor, Windows 95—represents a distinct departure from both DOS and Windows 3.*x*. At the same time, Windows 98 is also a continuation of the familiar Windows 3.*x* environment.

The newer version of Windows is familiar because it offers essentially the same operations and features that have made earlier Windows versions popular. It also retains the capability to execute most existing Windows 3.*x* applications. However, programming for Windows 98 is quite different from programming for Windows 3.*x*. The differences between the old and new systems are far from cosmetic. Many of the most important changes are not readily apparent but still provide extremely valuable enhancements in operations.

Unlike Windows 3.*x*, which is simply a shell operating on top of the DOS environment, Windows 98 is itself an operating system and no longer restricted to the limitations of the DOS environment. Windows 98 is able to take advantage of the new CPUs, but it does not run on the older 8086/80286 systems.

This book will show you how to develop all types of applications to operate under Windows 98. The topics covered here range from the basics of handling keyboard and mouse input to advanced techniques for networking and Internet support. You will learn how to take advantage of the Windows 98 features and functions to create programs that look and perform the way that you want.

Who Should Read This Book

Regardless of your previous programming experience and whether you are an expert or a novice, this book offers you a single comprehensive guide to application development for the Windows 98 operating system.

For programmers who are not experienced in working with Windows (or OS/2), Windows 98 application development may present something of a challenge, if only because of the differences between conventional DOS or Unix programming and the requirements (and facilities) of the Windows environment. The topics and explanations in this book, however, are designed to present a clear introduction to event-driven programming as well as to the demands and capabilities of the Windows API functions and the MFC (Microsoft Foundation Classes) libraries. Please realize, however, that some familiarity with C/C++ programming is assumed.

Programmers who have previously worked with Windows 3.x will find both similarities and differences in developing applications for 32-bit Windows 98. This book explains the differences between earlier 16-bit API calls and the 32-bit system API calls and includes suggestions for converting programs from Windows 3.x to Windows 98.

Those who have worked with OS/2 programming should be familiar with basic principles of event-driven programming and programming with API function calls. This familiarity will be both an advantage and, in some respects, a disadvantage. The advantage lies in the similarities between the processes and handling in the two environments. The disadvantage is that you will need to learn new names for the messages and API functions as well as the different types and structures Windows uses as parameters.

What This Book Contains

This book demonstrates the principal elements of Windows 98 programming, including Windows application resources, using the Microsoft Visual C++ language. All of the topics discussed are illustrated with working examples. The complete listings for all examples are included on the CD accompanying this book.

This book is organized in five parts:

- Introduction to Windows 98 Programming

- Windows 98 Application Resources

- Advanced Application Designs

- Windows 98 Graphics

- Exchanging Information between Applications

These parts are followed by an appendix, which offers suggestions and procedures for porting existing applications from the 16-bit Windows 3.*x* environment to the 32-bit Windows 98 environment.

Part 1: Introduction to Windows 98 Programming

Before you can begin developing Windows 98 applications, the first step is to know how the new operating system works and what your tools and options will be. Therefore, this book begins with an overview of the Windows 98 environment, including the requirements for working with the operating system.

Chapter 2 presents a simple program designed to illustrate the basics of application development for Windows 98, as well as a Template.I include file, which is used in some of the demo programs.

In Chapter 3, we look at messages, message handling, and the MFC. We also cover how the application source code is created, as well as the structures, types, and classes.

The next three chapters deal with the basics of keyboard and mouse messages and windows controls. Chapter 4 includes a simple editor program to demonstrate how virtual-key codes are generated and interpreted. Chapter 5 looks at mouse-event messages and cursors. Chapter 6 concludes this part with a discussion of child window controls and control buttons.

Part 2: Windows 98 Application Resources

Instead of relying on program instructions to create dialog boxes, menus, and window controls such as buttons and scrollbars, the simpler method is to use a resource editor to draw the desired resource elements for you. Other, less visual, resource elements include keyboard accelerators and strings. Also, elements such as bitmaps, icons, and custom cursors can be created easily with a resource editor.

Resource elements do not appear in the application source code. Instead, they are created by separate editors and stored, before the application is compiled, as ASCII resource scripts (.RC files). Image resources are stored as .BMP, .ICO, or .CUR binary files, which are referenced with the resource script. Alternatively, all of these resource elements can also be stored in a compiled form as a .RES resource file.

Part 2 introduces application resources and resource editors. Chapter 7 provides an overview of resource types. Chapters 8 through 11 discuss bitmap, dialog box, menu, accelerator key, and string resources. Chapter 12 describes a demo program that combines all of these resource elements in a single application.

Part 3: Advanced Application Designs

For those who want to move beyond the basics, Windows 98 offers a variety of tools for more advanced applications. Chapter 13 begins Part 3 with a selection of extended resource elements, including pop-up menus and tip windows.

Chapter 14 discusses multithreading programs for handling synchronous activities. Chapter 15 explains how to use processes and pipes for communications between threads. Chapter 16 looks at multithreading using the Common Object Model (COM).

Chapter 17 introduces the system registry and registry keys as mechanisms for maintaining applications' critical data as well as user preferences. In Chapter 18, we turn to using exception-handling mechanisms in applications to cope with exceptional conditions that disturb the normal flow of execution. In Chapter 19, we look at memory management and how processes can share blocks of memory by creating file-mapping objects.

The final three chapters in this section cover topics related to connecting to other systems through a network, beginning in Chapter 20 with security and cryptography functions. Next, Chapter 21 discusses including Internet support in your Windows 98 applications. Chapter 22 concludes the part with a discussion of building network applications.

Part 4: Windows 98 Graphics

Part 4 introduces Windows graphics operations, beginning in Chapter 23 with the Windows device context and mapping modes. Chapter 24 continues with a discussion of colors and palettes and an illustration of the principal mapping modes.

Chapter 25 describes the basic tools for drawing and filling shapes, including curves and polygons as well as pen styles. Chapter 26 covers more drawing tools, including bitmapped brushes, fill modes, predefined bitmap patterns, and device-independent bitmaps (DIBs).

Chapter 27 focuses on text displays, including font selection, text alignment, and typefaces, as well as how to modify the device context to control text displays. In Chapter 28, we look at methods for working with graphics files.

Chapter 29 covers other drawing and selection operations. Chapter 30 illustrates more advanced selection methods, including interactive images and complex images. Chapter 31 addresses the topic of graphics simulations.

The final chapter in this part, Chapter 32, deals with graphics printing operations and creating grayscales for outputting color graphics on black-and-white printers.

Part 5: Exchanging Information between Applications

Even in a single-tasking environment such as DOS, there are various ways to permit applications to exchange information among themselves. These range from the simplicity of common file formats to more esoteric attempts involving TSRs that paste information into the keyboard buffer for retrieval by the foreground application.

In a multitasking environment such as Windows, information exchange between applications is both practical and, quite often, integral to an application's purpose. Windows 98 includes features that both permit and encourage sharing information, data, or even operations among applications. These processes and mechanisms are covered in Part 5.

Chapter 33 explains how metafiles can be used to record operations in one application and to replay them in another application. Chapter 34 explains how your application can use clipboard services to transfer various types of information. Chapters 35 and 36 describe the powerful data-sharing tools of DDE and OLE and the Windows 98 support for these functions.

Chapter 37 concludes this book with an introduction to multimedia application development, showing how multimedia services are used as extensions to other applications.

Special Features

Throughout this book, you'll find some extra information, supplied in the forms of notes and sidebars. The notes come in tip, warning, and plain old note flavors, and they provide the types of information that their names imply. The sidebars deal with a wide range of topics, but are not far-flung from the subject at hand. For example, you'll see sidebars about how to handle potential bugs, sidebars that provide colorful background, and sidebars with tips on making operations run more quickly.

You'll also see "CD" icons throughout the book. Each of these icons marks the beginning of a discussion about a demo program that is included on the CD accompanying this book. Within the text, the name of the program is in italic print to let you know that you can find it on the CD.

About the Demos

The demo programs described in this book and included on the accompanying CD have been written using Microsoft Visual C++ (version 5.0). They include examples in both C and C++, as well as numerous examples using the MFC. With a few exceptions, these demo programs run under both Windows 98 (and 95) and Windows NT. Where there are exceptions, the reasons for the differences are documented and explained in the text. Most exceptions occur where certain network and security features supported by Windows NT are not supported by Windows 98.

References to API documentation in both the text and the source code refer to the online documentation commonly supplied on your compiler's source CD. The source CD should always be available—either on a local CD drive or on a shared network drive. The savings in development time realized by having the online documentation available are immeasurable. (And, if a brain-dead system manager is responsible for the absence of such reference material, the situation may be corrected by the appropriate application of poison, cement boots, a large bear trap, or various methods of direct nerve stimulation.)

About the CD

All of the demo applications discussed in this book—together with their resource files, headers, relevant source code, and project files—are included on the accompanying CD. Also, a few extra examples that are not discussed in the book or are mentioned only briefly have been included on the CD.

The source files are arranged in folders, identified by chapter number, where each appears within subfolders for each application. In some examples, ... \RES subfolders, which are generated by the MFC and AppWizard, contain application resource files. Also, in most cases, an .EXE file (or files) is included for each demo program.

Before attempting to compile any of these program examples, copy the application directory—including all application files and subfolders—to your own hard drive.

Because the CD is a read-only device, the file attributes for the CD files are set to read-only. Many file-management utilities, including the Windows 98 Explorer, do not reset the flags for files copied from a CD. Therefore, after copying files to your hard drive, you should reset the file attributes. If you do not change the attributes, your compiler/editor will not permit you to edit these files (unless you save them under a different filename) and, in some cases, may refuse to compile them.

A Note from the Author

Although this book covers all of the most important subjects related to creating applications for Windows 98, simple limitations on space and time prevent me from exploring each and every topic that might be of interest. You can consider this book as your starting point, from which you can continue in any directions that your own interests (and needs) lead.

I welcome your comments and suggestions. My e-mail address is ben@ezzell.org. Also, please visit my Web page at http://www.ezzell.org.

Until next time, I wish you the best in developing your applications. Keep on hacking and don't let the bosses get you down.

PART 1

Introduction to Windows 98 Programming

The 32-Bit Windows 98 Environment

- Hardware requirements for Windows 98 programming

- 16-bit and 32-bit disk file systems

- Windows 98 features

- Cross-platform programming

- Dual-boot system installation

If you're reading this book, the reasonable assumption is that you're interested in creating applications for Windows 98. Before you can design and implement applications, you need to understand the environment where your applications will operate and the requirements necessary to support that environment. Toward this objective, this chapter describes the environment created by the Windows 98 operating system.

As a Windows application developer, you probably would like your applications to run under several Windows platforms. This chapter also provides an overview of the differences between Windows 98 and Windows NT, as well as between Windows 98 and Windows 95, from a programmer's perspective.

If you are planning to run Windows 98 along with another operating system, such as Windows NT, you need to make some special provisions. The final section of this chapter explains how to install a dual-boot system.

The Hardware Environment

Although previous versions of both MS-DOS and Windows have tried to provide support for all earlier hardware systems, much of this backward compatibility has been achieved at the expense of limiting functional capabilities. The support for the owners of earlier computer models, including 808x and 80286 CPUs, has prevented programmers from making the best use of the potential capacities of newer machines and, of course, placed the end user—knowingly or otherwise—under similar restrictions.

At some future time and in a similar fashion, the restrictions inherent in the Windows 98 operating system will also be considered archaic, restrictive, and cumbersome. When that time comes, Windows 98 will, in turn, be replaced by a new operating system.

For now, we're programming for the 32-bit environment and need to meet its requirements. We'll start with the requirements for the computer system, RAM, and hard drive space.

Machine and RAM Requirements

First, and most important, Windows 98 will not operate on an 8080, 8086, or 80286 system. The operating system requires a minimum platform consisting of an 80386, an 80486, or a P-5 or equivalent, or an MIPS R4000.

In *theory*, you can run Windows 98 on an 80386 system. And, again in *theory*, you can run Windows 98 on as little as 4MB of RAM.

Okay, so much for theory. In the real world, you should not attempt to run Windows 98 on anything less than a 486 and with anything less than 16MB of RAM. In fact, with 16MB of RAM, you will be running an essentially crippled version of Windows 98, with lots and lots of disk swapping as the system uses the hard drive as an extension of the system memory. A Pentium and 32MB of RAM are better; 64MB of RAM is not unreasonable. Many of the new features, such as broadcast services and the Active Desktop, really do need 32MB to perform comfortably. Granted, if you ask Microsoft marketing people, they will tell you otherwise; but, if you believe them, I have a wonderful bargain on a used bridge I would like to discuss with you.

TIP

While the Intel folks would like to consider the PC desktop market as their personal monopoly, there are a number of fine alternatives to the Intel line of processors, including the AMD K-6, the Cyrix 6x86MX, and the IDT WinChip C6. All of these are fully Windows-compatible and offer performance equal (or even superior) to the Pentium Pro chip series. On the other hand, today memory is less expensive than it ever has been, providing a cheap investment with remarkable yields in both speed and performance. If it really becomes a trade-off, buy a cheaper CPU and add more memory—you'll appreciate the differences.

Hard Drive Space Requirements

A second requirement is hard drive space. As you should already be aware, Windows 98 does not install from floppy diskettes (well, I suppose you could use floppies, but why?) and wants space to install a multitude of drivers, help files, system files, fonts, and so on (I won't waste space with the entire list).

To give you an idea of the requirements, running a quick assessment on the files and subdirectories on my own system, I found a total of more than 356MB under the Windows 98 directory. Granted, that count includes DLLs (dynamic link libraries) and other files that were not part of the Windows 98 installation itself but were added by other applications, and it also includes a host of files of questionable origin (which means that I'm not sure where they came from or why). But the main point is that this adds up to a third of a gigabyte just in the Windows directory!

Multigigabyte drives are nothing unusual today, and they're even relatively inexpensive (of course, they need to be easy to find and afford, considering the general bloat both in operating systems and applications). So, plan accordingly and figure on allocating at least a 0.5GB drive or partition just for the Windows 98 system itself.

TIP   Don't rush to throw that old drive away just because you've bought a newer, higher-capacity drive. Most IDE drives can be ganged as master/slave pairs, even if they're from different manufacturers. SCSI drives are even easier to gang together, with as many as six drives supported by a single SCSI controller.

Remember, however, that the suggested 512MB is a minimum. If you install all of your applications to the system-suggested default drive, which will be the same drive where Windows 98 is located, a 0.5GB partition can be exhausted very quickly. If this happens to your system, you can use a utility (such as Power-Quest's Partition Magic) to resize your partitions and/or drives.

In a pinch, you may want to use a disk-compression utility to increase the capacity of your existing hard drive. Before installing any compression utility, however, check that it is not only compatible with Windows 98, but that it is also compatible with any other operating systems you may be running (if you are operating a multi-boot system).

The Evolution of a File System

Over the years, the FAT16 system has gone through many evolutionary changes.

Originally, all files were written to a single file list, what we now refer to as the root directory. This single directory format had many limitations including limiting the number of

Continued on next page

separate files that could be written on a disk. However, since hard drives were essentially unknown at the time and a 5¼-inch diskette held 100KB (that's *kilo*, not *mega*), there were far more serious limits than the number of files that could be written. And as limited as the capacity was, few people noticed or complained, since the alternative was recording on a cassette—yes, the kind you listen to music on (or did before the advent of CDs).

Later, as capacities rose (first was the 360KB diskette, then the 1.2MB, and finally the 1.4MB 3½-inch diskette), the need for a new format quickly became obvious. The concept of subdirectories was borrowed from the Unix world. The still-limited root directory entries are used to point to locations that are not on the root directory tracks, where additional directory data—called *subdirectories*—is written. These subdirectory structures are stored as what are essentially special types of files.

Finally, a further enhancement was introduced with Windows 95 to allow long filenames. The original 8.3 format filenames were kept, but an extension to the directory was used to store a long filename. Of course, both OS/2 and Windows NT allowed long filenames before Windows 95 was introduced, but these were supported by properties of the quite different HPFS and NTFS file systems, which are not DOS/FAT-compatible.

Even with all of these advances, however, the FAT file system remained firmly committed to a 16-bit addressing system, which imposed its own limitations. Now, in its latest incarnation, we have the FAT32 file system.

File Systems: FAT16 versus FAT32

While the venerable DOS FAT16 file system continues to be the *lingua franca* of the PC world—despite several attempts to relegate it to the dinosaur graveyard—Windows 98 introduces a new FAT32 file system with a number of important advantages.

Perhaps the biggest advantage of a FAT32 (32-bit) file system is how the disk drive allocates space. With the 16-bit addressing scheme used by the old FAT system (now called FAT16), there is a limit on the number of clusters that can be created on a single drive (or on a logical partition on a physical drive).

In brief, since the FAT16 can handle only 2^{16} addresses, hard drives larger than 512MB need to allocate file space in 16KB blocks. This means that any fraction of a file less than 16KB still occupies a full 16KB block. Larger files occupy multiple blocks but, on most systems, there tend to be a lot of small files, many less than

100 bytes and even more in the 1KB or 2KB range. For example, in my own Windows 98 directories, I can find hundreds of files that are smaller than 2KB. On a FAT16 system, each of these would occupy a full 16KB of space.

> **NOTE**   Before you decide that my setup is unusual and that this doesn't really apply to your system, take a few minutes to check the files on your own hard drive. If you have a convenient utility that lets you sort files by size, you should find a very large number of files, in virtually any directory, that are less than 100 bytes and an even larger number that are less than a kilobyte in size. Also, the chances are that you will find a number of files that are 0 bytes in size but still occupy complete clusters.

Of course, a 1GB drive is also limited to 65,536 clusters, where the cluster size becomes 64KB.

The problem with the FAT16 system and the 1GB drive is that any individual file must occupy some integral number of clusters; that is, a file has a minimum size of one cluster. This means that if you write a file that uses only 1KB on a 250MB drive, for example, that 1KB file is still occupying 16KB of space; it is wasting 93.75 percent of that space. But that is only a part of the problem, because that 4.3KB file is occupying 8KB of space on a 256MB drive. Here the waste is smaller—only 46.25 percent—but this is added to the rest of the lost space on your drive. On a 1GB drive, where the cluster sizes are larger, the problem becomes worse.

The upshot is that only very large files—and you have relatively few of these—actually use space efficiently. The odds are very good that the FAT16 file system wastes 20 to 30 percent or more of your drive space.

Switching to the FAT32 file system, which can handle 2^{32} addresses, means that cluster sizes can be as small as 1KB (although 4KB is much more common). This applies even to 1GB or larger drives, without partitioning. The result is that the amount of wasted drive space can easily fall as low as 2 percent or less.

The drawback, however, is that at present only Windows 98 recognizes the FAT32 file system (just as only Windows NT recognizes the NTFS file system). This means that drives or partitions using FAT32 are not accessible by other operating systems. The good news is that in the future, beginning with Windows NT 5.0, FAT32 should be recognized by more operating systems.

If you are planning to dual-boot Windows 98 and Windows NT 4, the difference in their file systems is a concern. See the "Dual-Boot Systems" section later in the chapter for more information.

TIP

There are several utilities on the market that allow you to convert from FAT16 to FAT32 without losing your existing files or requiring that you reformat the drives or partitions. My own preference for this task is PowerQuest's Partition Magic, which not only converts from FAT16 to FAT32 (or the reverse), but also allows you to change the cluster size and to resize, create, or delete partitions—all without wiping out the existing data. Other FAT16-to-FAT32 conversion packages offer similar services.

New Features in Windows 98

Although Windows 98 is not as dramatic a departure from Windows 95 as Windows 95 was from Windows 3.1, there are some new features worth mentioning. Although these features have merit, for now, the majority of them are relatively unimportant from the application developer's perspective.

Plug-and-Play Drivers

Windows 98 comes with an extensive library of Plug-and-Play drivers, so there should be relatively few problems with oddball hardware installations. However, this does not mean that Windows 98 will automatically recognize all peripherals and add-in cards. The situation has improved, but it is still far from perfect. The opprobrious revision "Plug-and-Pray" is not likely to vanish from the common vocabulary in the near future.

NOTE

Most programmers can probably simply ignore Plug and Play as not immediately relevant to their current applications. However, there are valid reasons to suspect that Plug and Play will become important to the application developer in the not-too-distant future. In Chapter 18, we'll take a look at Plug-and-Play handling in Windows applications.

Support for New Technologies

One area that may prove to be of interest to application developers is support for the Universal Serial Bus (USB). This is a new standard designed to replace the present device dependence on a limited number of hardware interrupts. Existing systems have seen ever-increasing competition by peripherals— modems, mice, sound cards, and the like—for the limited resources represented by the 16 available hardware interrupts (a number of which were already reserved for the central system itself). The USB is designed to offer a virtually unlimited number of connections for existing and newer devices, while providing effective throughput speeds orders of magnitude higher than the speeds of existing channels.

Windows 98 claims to be USB-compatible (or USB claims to be Windows-compatible). At the time this book is being written, however, the USB standard is still too new to have exhibited any kind of track record, so whether this standard will be the universal panacea or not remains an open question. It is difficult to forecast or even imagine how the USB is going to affect application development. For now, you can consider the USB as an area worth watching.

In addition to the USB peripherals, Windows 98 includes support for AGP (Accelerated Graphics Port) video cards, MMX processors, and the still controversial DVD drive. Furthermore, you will also be able to connect multiple displays (multiple monitors using multiple display cards). Likewise, the new Multilink Channel Aggregation (MCA) technology allows you to boost bandwidth by combining two or more communication lines (although few ISPs currently permit the multiple logons necessary to support MCA connections).

New Utilities and Wizards

Windows 98 also provides a variety of new utilities and wizards, including the following:

Update Wizard   Connects to a Microsoft Web site to download the latest patches, drivers, and enhancements automatically.

Tune-Up Wizard   Schedules utilities to defragment drives and to delete unnecessary files.

System File Checker   Examines critical .DLL, .COM, .VXD, and other files, testing for corruption and/or modification. This utility will restore the original files if necessary.

Help Desk   Supports troubleshooting by linking to local and Internet help resources, such as Online Help, the Bug Reporting Tool, and Microsoft Knowledge Base.

Disk Defragmenter/Optimization Wizard   Creates a list and organizes the hard drive to make frequently accessed files readily available.

Accessibility Settings Wizard   Provides utilities and customization to adapt the Desktop for handicapped users, such as a screen magnifier for the visually impaired.

While none of the features have any immediate impact on how you design applications for Windows 98, they may offer opportunities and perhaps a few suggestions for the directions of your own development efforts.

Cross-System Application Development

Although this book is devoted to Windows 98 programming, you will probably want your applications to run on the other Windows platforms as well as on Windows 98. The likely candidates are Windows 95 and Windows NT 4.

I could simply assert that there are no real differences between Windows 98, Windows 95, and Windows NT 4, but that would be an oversimplification. In truth, there are worlds of differences. From a programming standpoint, however, most of the differences are invisible. Most applications written to run under Windows 98 will also execute under Windows NT and Windows 95, and vice versa. There are exceptions, but they are just that—exceptions.

I'll point out the exceptions in later chapters, whenever they apply to the subject at hand. For now, I'll just provide a general overview of some areas that may be of concern when you are designing cross-system applications.

TIP   If you are developing a cross-system application, the best approach is to periodically test your application on both operating systems. Then, if the application functions on one but not on the other, that's when the fun begins...and best of luck.

Windows NT Applications

Like Windows 95 and Windows 98, but unlike earlier versions of Windows, Windows NT is its own operating system and does not rely on the underlying presence of the 16-bit DOS operating system. Unlike Windows 95 and Windows 98, NT 3.1, 3.51, and now 4.0 are all true 32-bit operating systems. Windows 95 and Windows 98, unfortunately, are still hybrids relying on both 16-bit and 32-bit core code.

Sometimes, an application will perform on one system but not on the other because the developers have made use of some tricks that are possible under one operating system but not in the other. In many ways, Windows 98 is still a DOS-based operating system because, even though it is not visible on the surface, extensive support is still provided to ensure that the older DOS and Windows 3.x applications will function under Windows 98. Windows NT, however, avoids the limitations and problems inherent in this schizophrenic approach by simply not supporting the earlier system services.

In other cases, applications may not run on both systems because they have been written to depend on advanced operating system-specific features. For example Windows NT supports some features, such as networking APIs, that are not supported under other operating systems. (See Chapter 22 for information about adding network support to your applications.)

Another difference that can affect your applications is how security and access permissions are used in Windows NT. These permissions are not supported under Windows 98. (See Chapter 20 for details on the Win32 security and cryptography APIs.)

TIP   The Win32 driver model allows developers to create a single hardware driver that will function on both the Windows 98 and Windows NT (5.0) operating systems. Previously, developers were required to write separate and independent drivers for each operating system, making it difficult for both developers and users to upgrade hardware.

Windows 95 Applications

From a programming standpoint, there are no exceptionally striking differences between Windows 95 and Windows 98. This should not be particularly surprising to you, since Windows 98 is primarily an enhancement (and, in some cases, a patch) of the earlier operating system.

In subsequent chapters, I have noted some differences where performance has changed. However, none of these changes are significant enough to warrant much attention.

NOTE   For information about porting Windows 3.x applications to Windows 98, see Appendix A.

Dual-Boot Systems

If you are planning to run both Windows 98 and Windows NT on the same system, you will need to make sure your applications are installed properly to run on both platforms. Also, the incompatibilities between the FAT32 and NTFS file systems will affect your setup.

Application Installation

Often, the biggest conflict between Windows 98 and Windows NT is not an incompatibility issue but a simple misunderstanding. On a dual-boot system, an application installed under one operating system may be visible under the other (because all of its files are visible on the hard drive), but it will not run on the second operating system. This is usually not because of incompatibility but because the installation needs to be repeated on the second operating system.

Annoying? Yes, but there's a good reason for this annoyance. When an application is installed under either operating system, the installation program does more than simply create a directory and copy some files. Sometimes, the installation program also copies .DLL or other special files that are installed in the operating system's \SYSTEM directory. Each operating system has its own \SYSTEM directories, and the contents are not cross-compatible; they cannot be consolidated. Additionally, most application installation programs make entries to the operating system's registry. These entries are also separate and not cross-compatible.

NOTE   Some simple applications, which require no setup at all, can be executed on either operating system without installation. In such cases, the applications are usually self-contained and do not rely on DLLs or registry entries.

A dual-installation does not require duplicate directories and duplicate files, except for any files that are copied to each operating system's \SYSTEM directory. What is required is to make duplicate registry entries (and you don't want to try to do these by hand, because it just isn't worth the trouble).

Fortunately, the solution is relatively simple. If, for example, you are installing Microsoft Visual C++ and you wish to use it for both Windows 98 and Windows NT on a dual-boot system, follow these steps:

1. Boot either operating system.

2. Perform the installation normally.

3. Reboot the second operating system.

4. Repeat the installation to the same directory.

After installation, if the application fails to execute on one of the operating systems, check the application documentation to see if there are some special requirements or system incompatibilities. Then try the installation a second time.

File System Setup

If you are running a dual-boot system using Windows NT 4 and Window 98, you will need to maintain your C: drive as a FAT16 drive (or partition). This is necessary for the Ntldr (NT Loader) to function correctly.

Also, you must keep in mind that any FAT32 drives or partitions will be functionally invisible to your Windows NT 4 system, and any NTFS or HPFS drives or partitions will be functionally invisible to your Windows 98 system.

Now that you know about the environment you are designing your applications to run in, you are ready to start building those applications. In the next chapter, we'll begin by constructing two simple applications: a Windows version of the traditional 'Hello, World' demo program and a template application that can be used as the basis for other applications.

CHAPTER

TWO

2

Application Programming for Windows 98

- ■ "Hello World" in Windows

- ■ Message-mapping functions

- ■ A template for Windows application programs

- ■ Conventions used in Windows programming

For DOS programmers, writing applications for Windows 98 (or for Windows NT or Windows 95) constitutes a distinct and abrupt departure from familiar and accepted practices. In fact, this departure is sometimes so abrupt that many programmers find themselves wondering if they have changed languages as well as operating systems. They are surprised to discover distinctly Pascal-like elements appearing in their C code and to find that previously familiar shortcuts and procedures—such as main() or exit()—are either no longer valid or, in some cases, even fatal to the application or the operating system.

Others, particularly those who have worked with previous versions of Windows, or even with OS/2, may find that these new practices use familiar techniques, although they sometimes bear new names or have somewhat different syntax. Unfortunately, those who have programmed applications for Windows 3.*x* (either 3.0 or 3.1) may find themselves the most confused of all because many of the differences are slight; yet in many cases, these slight differences are also very critical.

So, even if you're an experienced Windows application programmer, you should take the time to study programming practices for Windows 98. Chapter 1 discussed mechanisms for compiling Windows 98 programs. Now it's time to look at the components of a Windows program, beginning, as the White King advised Alice, "at the beginning."

WinHello: An Introductory Windows Program

Traditionally, the introductory C program example has always been a "Hello, World" message, provided by about a half-dozen lines of code. For Windows 98, however, the equivalent introductory example will be a bit more complex, requiring some 130+ lines of code—roughly 20 times longer. This difference is not so much because Windows is that much more complex than DOS, but more a reflection of the fact that any Windows application, even a rudimentary example, operates in a more complex environment than its DOS counterpart. Accordingly, the Windows application requires some minimal provisions to match this environment.

NOTE   Because Windows applications generally include image (bitmapped) resources that their DOS counterparts lack, direct comparisons of .EXE files sizes are generally not valid. The real differences in size are more readily apparent in terms of source code sizes and development times.

Still, the flip side of this coin does not mean that all applications will be larger and more complex than their DOS counterparts. More commonly, larger Windows applications will become smaller than their DOS counterparts because many functions and services that are supplied by the application itself under DOS are called externally as system functions under Windows.

Theory aside, however, the *WinHello* source example is considerably larger than its DOS counterpart. Its actual size depends on how the application was created. For example, *WinHello*, a simple application program using no class definitions, consists of one source file; while *WinHello2*, an MFC (Microsoft Foundation Class library) application created using AppWizard, has 20 source files.

NOTE   The *WinHello* and *WinHello2* demos are included on the CD accompanying this book, in the Chapter 2 folder.

The Windows.H Header File

The Windows.H header file is the one essential include file required in all Windows source code. The reason for this is simple: Windows.H contains all of the definitions for Windows messages, constants, flag values, data structures, macros, and other mnemonics that permit the programmer to work without having to memorize thousands of hexadecimal values and their functions.

For earlier versions of Windows, the Windows.H file has been a single, massive text file (about 10,000 lines). With later versions, the Windows.H file has shrunk; it now consists principally of a list of other include files, the most important of which is the WinUser.H include file. This include file is the current counterpart of the older Windows.H file and, like its predecessor, is more than 8000 lines in length.

The following references to definitions provided by the Windows.H file may most likely be found in either the WinUser.H or WinDef.H files. Any of these references, however, may be located in other sources listed as include files in Windows.H.

If you are using MFC, the Windows.H header is included in the AppWizard-supplied STDAFX.H header as:

```
#define VC_EXTRALEAN        // Exclude rarely used stuff from Windows headers
#include <afxwin.h>         // MFC core and standard components
#include <afxext.h>         // MFC extensions
#ifndef _AFX_NO_AFXCMN_SUPPORT
#include <afxcmn.h>         // MFC support for Win98 common controls
#endif // _AFX_NO_AFXCMN_SUPPORT
```

The WinMain Procedure

Just as every DOS C program has a procedure titled main at its heart, every Windows program has a similar entry point with the title WinMain (and, yes, this title is case-sensitive). Also, just as a DOS C program may include provisions within the main procedure declaration to retrieve command-line parameters, the WinMain declaration includes a similar provision in the lpszCmdParam parameter, even though command-line parameters are rarely used under Windows.

TIP

When applications are created using the MFC foundation classes and the AppWizard, the WinMain procedure will not appear in the skeleton source files created for the various classes. However, the WinMain procedure has not vanished, it is now buried— out of sight and out of mind— inside the precompiled foundation class library. Although invisible, WinMain is still present and, if absolutely necessary, can be passed instructions to change the initial style and characteristics of the application.

In contrast to DOS programming, the declarations used for WinMain are not optional and must be declared in the exact order and form shown, regardless of whether each specific argument will be used or ignored. Remember, because the application's WinMain procedure is being called only indirectly by the user, with the actual calling format supplied by Windows, the calling format flexibility present in a DOS context is absent under Windows.

Also note that the reserved word PASCAL is used in all exported function declarations, indicating to the compiler that Pascal rather than C ordering is used for all *arguments* (values) pushed onto the stack. While C commonly uses inverted order, placing the least-significant bytes first on the stack, Windows uses Pascal ordering that, like Unix, places the most-significant bytes first.

There is another small but crucial difference. *Exported functions* are functions that will be called from outside the class or—in the case of a DLL— from other applications outside the unit (library). In a Windows application where subroutines are called from Windows itself or where a member function in one class is called from outside the class, even if both belong to the same application, the Pascal calling order is necessary.

On the other hand, all internal function declarations (functions and subprocedures called directly from other procedures within the application) will expect arguments to appear in standard C order and should not be declared using the PASCAL specification.

As far as how argument lists are declared in the procedure definitions, it makes absolutely no difference whether the Pascal or C calling conventions are used. These conventions affect only how the arguments are handled internally—that is, on the stack—and do not in any way affect how the programmer constructs the argument lists.

Of the four calling arguments shown below, the first two are of primary importance. The data type HANDLE refers to a 32-bit unsigned value; the hInstance and hPrevInstance arguments are unique identifiers supplied by the Windows 98 system. Unlike DOS where only one program (TSRs excepted) is active at a time, multitasking systems require unique identification, not only for each application, but also for each instance of an application that may be executing. Therefore, the hInstance and hPrevInstance parameters are assigned only when an application instance becomes active. They provide the equivalents of the task ID and process ID values common in other multitasking environments.

```
int PASCAL WinMain( HANDLE hInstance,
                    HANDLE hPrevInstance,
                    LPSTR  lpszCmdParam,
                    int    nCmdShow )
```

The data types used in these declarations may be unfamiliar to DOS programmers. See the introduction to Windows data types later in this chapter for more details. Windows programmers should note that the 16-bit **HANDLE** used in Windows 3.*x* is now a 32-bit unsigned value, which is a change that affects a number of aspects of Windows 98 programming.

The hPrevInstance (previous instance) identifier is the hInstance identifier previously assigned to the most recent instance of an application that is already executing. If there is no previous instance of the application currently running, which is frequently the case, this argument will be NULL (0). The reasons for this second process identifier will be demonstrated presently.

The third parameter, lpszCmdParam, is a long (FAR) pointer to a null-terminated (ASCIIZ) string containing any command-line parameters passed to the program instance. Although the command-line parameters are provided by Windows rather than by a conventional (DOS) command line, the user can specify these parameters through the Run dialog box invoked from the Start menu. In general, however, Windows applications rely on dialog boxes for specific input and on .INI entries for default values, rather than expecting command-line parameters.

The fourth calling parameter, nCmdShow, is simply an integer argument indicating whether the newly launched application will be displayed as a normal window, or initially displayed as an icon. Next, following the procedure declaration itself, a brief list of local variable declarations appears:

```
{
    static char szAppName[] = "WinHello";
    HWND        hwnd;
    MSG         msg;
    WNDCLASS    wc;
```

The HWND data type identifies a window handle; MSG identifies a message value; and WNDCLASS refers to a record structure used to pass a number of values relevant to the application's main window. We'll discuss these data types in more detail later in the chapter.

Registering a Window Class

The first task accomplished within the WinMain procedure depends on the hPrevInstance argument passed. If a previous instance of this application is already active, there is no need to register the window class a second time. It's more likely, of course, that this is the first instance of the application (hPrev-Instance is NULL) and, therefore, the window class definitions must be assigned and the window class registered.

The wc structure is defined in Windows.H (which must be included in all Windows applications). Of the WNDCLASS record fields, the second (lpfnWndProc) and last (lpszClassName) are the most important. The remainder of the fields can usually remain unchanged from one application to another. (See the section about Template.C at the end of this chapter for another example.)

The first field is the window-style specification. In this example, it is assigned two style flag values (combined by ORing bitwise). The CS_ flags are defined in Windows.H as 16-bit constants, each with one flag bit set. Here, the CS_HREDRAW and CS_VREDRAW flags indicate that the window should be redrawn completely anytime the horizontal or vertical size changes. Thus, for the *WinHello* demo, if the window size changes, the window display is completely redrawn, with the "Hello, World" message string recentered in the new display.

```
if( ! hPrevInstance )
{
    wc.style        = CS_HREDRAW | CS_VREDRAW;
    wc.lpfnWndProc  = WndProc;
```

The second field in the WNDCLASS structure, lpfnWndProc, is a pointer to the exported procedure—WndProc in this example—that will handle all windows messages for this application. The type prefix lpfn identifies this field as a "long pointer to function." But you should realize that these prefix conventions are provided for the benefit of the programmer. They are not absolutes, nor do these designations place any constraints on the compiler. However, predefined fields and identifiers can be considered an exception. Although you can change these, they are best left as defined, if only for the simple reason that redefinitions could easily result in a cascade of changes and confusion.

The next two record fields are integers, which are reserved to specify extra information about the class or window styles. Commonly, neither is required and, by default, both are initialized as zeros (0). (Incidentally, the cb_ prefix stands for "count of bytes.")

```
    wc.cbClsExtra   = 0;
    wc.cbWndExtra   = 0;
    wc.hInstance    = hInstance;
```

The next field, hInstance, is simply the recipient of the hInstance argument passed by Windows when the program is initially called. This field assignment is constant for all applications.

The next three data fields currently assign default values for the application's icon, cursor, and background color and pattern.

```
wc.hIcon        = LoadIcon( NULL, IDI_APPLICATION );
wc.hCursor      = LoadCursor( NULL, IDC_ARROW );
wc.hbrBackground = GetStockObject( WHITE_BRUSH );
```

The default IDI_APPLICATION specification for the icon assigns the predefined image of a white square with a black border. The IDC_ARROW cursor assigns the stock cursor graphic of a slanted arrow. In the third assignment, the hbrBackground field contains the background color and pattern used for the application's client region. (The hbr stands for "handle to brush," where *brush* refers to a pixel pattern used to fill or paint an area.)

Next, because this application does not have a menu assigned, the menu name is entered as a null value. The class name (lpszClassName) is assigned the null-terminated (ASCIIZ) string defined previously.

```
wc.lpszMenuName  = NULL;
wc.lpszClassName = szAppName;
RegisterClass( &wc );
}
```

And, last within this conditional subprocess, the RegisterClass function is called with the wc structure passed as a parameter (by address) to register this window class definition with the Windows 98 operating system. As mentioned previously, this registration is required only once. Thereafter, the registration and values assigned are available to any new instances of the application, as long as any instance of the application remains active. Once all instances of the application have been closed, the window class registration is discarded, and any future instance will need to execute the class registration process again.

Creating an Application Window

While the previous step, registering a window class, defined characteristics that are common to all instances of the application, the application window itself still must be created. Unlike the RegisterClass function call, which is called only once, the CreateWindow function must be called by every instance of the application to produce the actual window display.

The handle to the application window that is returned by the `CreateWindow` function will be used later as an argument in other function calls; it will be used as a unique identifier for the actual window belonging to the application instance. While many properties of the application class have already been defined, other properties specific to this instance of the application have not; they are passed now as parameters to the `CreateWindow` function.

```
hwnd = CreateWindow(
    szAppName,                    // window class name
    "Hello, World - Windows_98 Style",
                                  // window caption
```

The first two parameters passed are the application class name—the same ASCIIZ string that was used when the class was registered—and the application's initial window caption. Of course, the second of these is optional, and, if the window is defined without a caption bar or if no caption is desired, this parameter should be passed as NULL.

The third parameter defines the window style and, generically, is passed as WS_OVERLAPPEDWINDOW, a value that is a combination of individual flags defined in Windows.H.

```
    WS_OVERLAPPEDWINDOW,      // window style
    CW_USEDEFAULT,            // initial X position
    CW_USEDEFAULT,            // initial Y position
    CW_USEDEFAULT,            // initial X size
    CW_USEDEFAULT,            // initial Y size
```

The fourth through seventh parameters establish the application window's initial position and size. They can be passed as explicit values or, more often, as CW_USEDEFAULT. This parameter instructs Windows to use the default values for an overlapped window, positioning each successive overlapped window at a stepped horizontal and vertical offset from the upper-left corner of the screen.

The next parameter, the eighth, is passed as NULL for the simple reason that this application is not associated with a parent window. Alternatively, if this window were to be called as a child process belonging to another application, the parent's window handle would be passed as a parameter here.

```
    NULL,                     // parent window handle
    NULL,                     // window menu handle
```

The ninth parameter used in calling the `CreateWindow` function is also passed as NULL, directing the application to use the default system menu. Note, however, that the menu in question is the window frame's pull-down menu (upper-left icon on most window frames), not the menu bar (or toolbar), which is defined as an application resource and assigned during the application class registration.

The tenth calling parameter, which can never be passed as NULL, is the same instance handle originally supplied by the system.

```
hInstance,              // program instance handle
NULL );                 // creation parameters
```

The final parameter, again NULL in this example, may in other cases provide a pointer to additional data for use either by the application window or by some subsequent process. In most examples, however, this will be an empty (NULL) argument.

Showing the Window

Now, after CreateWindows has been called, the application window has been created internally in Windows 98's "world view" but does not yet appear on the actual screen display. Therefore, the next step is to call the ShowWindow function, passing as parameters the hwnd value returned by CreateWindow and the nCmd-Show argument supplied when WinMain was initially called.

```
ShowWindow( hwnd, nCmdShow );
UpdateWindow( hwnd );
```

The ShowWindow function, contrary to what you might assume, does only a portion of the task of creating (painting) the window display. It is principally responsible for creating the window frame, caption bar, menu bar, and minimize/maximize buttons. But this function does not create the client window area—the display area specific to the application itself. Therefore, one more function call is necessary before the window display is complete: a call to the UpdateWindow function with the hwnd window handle as an argument (this call actually posts a WM_PAINT message to the application instructing it to repaint its own window area—a process that will be discussed in a moment).

This completes the process of registering a window class, defining and creating the window itself, and updating the screen to show the window. But while more than a small task, this is only preparation for the application; the real task has not yet begun ... but will momentarily. One last, but very essential, portion of the WinMain function remains: the message-handling loop.

Handling Messages

Windows creates and manages a separate message queue for each active Windows program instance. Thus, when any keyboard or mouse event occurs, Windows translates this event into a message value. This value is placed in the application's message queue, where it waits until it is retrieved by the application instance, which is precisely the purpose of the message-handling loop.

TIP

An alternative to the message-handling loop, the use of CALLBACK procedures, is discussed and illustrated in Chapter 3.

The message-handling loop begins by calling the GetMessage function to retrieve messages from the application instance's message queue. As long as the message retrieved is not a WM_QUIT message (0x0012), GetMessage will return a TRUE (nonzero) result. The actual message value is returned in the msg structure, which was passed by address.

```
while( GetMessage( &msg, NULL, 0, 0 ) )
{
```

The syntax for the GetMessage function is defined as:

```
BOOL GetMessage( lpMsg, HWND, wMsgFilterMin, wMsgFilterMax )
```

In most cases, only the first parameter is actually used to return the message itself. The remaining three parameters are usually passed as NULL or zero.

The initial parameter is a pointer to a message structure to receive the message information retrieved and, subsequently, to pass this data on through to the TranslateMessage and DispatchMessage functions. Without this parameter, there would obviously be little point in calling the GetMessage function at all.

The second parameter is optional but can be used to identify a specific window (belonging to the calling application) and to restrict retrieval to messages that belong to that window. When passed as NULL, as in the present example, GetMessage retrieves all messages addressed to any window belonging to the application placing the call. The GetMessage function does not retrieve messages addressed to windows belonging to any other application.

The third and fourth parameters provide filter capabilities, restricting the message types returned. When both parameters are passed as 0, no filtering occurs. Alternatively, constants such as WM_KEYFIRST and WM_KEYLAST could be passed as filter values to restrict message retrieval to keyboard events or, by using WM_ MOUSEFIRST and WM_MOUSELAST, to retrieve only mouse-related messages.

Filters and window selection aside, the GetMessage function (together with the PeekMessage and WaitMessage functions) has another important characteristic.

Conventionally, loop statements monopolize the system until terminated, thus preempting or preventing other operations for the duration of the loop. And, in other circumstances—remember this as a *caution*—even under Windows, loop operations can tie up system resources.

The GetMessage function, however, has the ability to pre-empt the loop operation to yield control to other applications when no messages are available for the current application, or when WM_PAINT or WM_TIMER messages directed to other tasks are available. Thus, it can give other applications their share of CPU time to execute.

For the present, when the application receives an event message (other than WM_QUIT), the message value is passed. First, it goes to the Windows TranslateMessage function for any keystroke translation that may be specific to the application. Then it is passed to the DispatchMessage handler, where the message information is passed to the next appropriate message-handling procedure (back to Windows, either for immediate handling or, indirectly, for forwarding to the exported WndProc procedure).

```
        TranslateMessage( &msg );
        DispatchMessage( &msg );
    }
```

Finally, when the message-processing loop terminates, the wParam argument from the final message retrieved is, in turn, returned to the calling application—the system Desktop itself.

```
        return msg.wParam;
    }
```

Messages and Event-Driven Programming

In its simplest form, *message-driven* programming (also known as *event-driven* programming) is a process by which various subprocesses and/or applications communicate. In Windows, messages are the process used by Windows itself to manage a multitasking system and to share keyboard, mouse, and other resources by distributing information to applications, application instances, and processes within an application.

Thus, under Windows, instead of applications receiving information directly from the keyboard or the mouse driver, the operating system intercepts all input information, packaging this information using the MSG message structure (detailed in the following section) and then forwarding the prepared messages to the appropriate recipients. In turn, the recipient applications use `Translate-Message` for application-specific interpretation (particularly accelerator-key assignments) before calling `DispatchMessage` to forward individual traffic items to their appropriate handlers.

Furthermore, the process described is not limited to keyboard and mouse events. Instead, this includes all input devices (including ports), as well as messages generated by application child and subprocesses, Windows timers, or, quite frequently, by Windows itself.

NOTE   Abstract descriptions of message-driven programming provide only a theoretical outline without really illustrating how these processes function. Therefore, a fuller explanation will be left until subsequent examples in this book can provide both hands-on experience as well as practical illustrations (beginning, of course, with messages processed by the *WinHello* demo).

But before we get to how messages are transmitted, let's take a look at the message record structure and how messages are organized.

The Message Record Structure

The MSG (message structure) record type is defined in WinUser.H as:

```
typedef struct tagMSG
{   HWND    hwnd;
    UINT    message;
    WPARAM  wParam;
    LPARAM  lParam;
    DWORD   time;
    POINT   pt;         } MSG, *PMSG, NEAR *NPMSG, FAR *LPMSG;
```

NOTE   Both the NEAR and FAR types are essentially obsolete in 32-bit systems. Originally, NEAR meant an address within a 16KB block, and FAR indicated an address outside the "local" 16KB address space. Today, all addresses are NEAR without requiring the specification, and specifying FAR is obsolete. However, there are no penalties or conflicts arising for continuing to use FAR, and this term does continue to appear in many structure and function definitions, as in the MSG definition shown here.

The POINT data type is defined in WinDef.H as:

```
typedef struct tagPOINT
{  int  x;
   int  y; } POINT, *PPOINT, NEAR *NPPOINT, FAR *LPPOINT;
```

The message-event fields defined are used as:

hwnd The handle of the specific window to which the message is directed.

message A 16-bit value identifying the message. Constants corresponding to all message values are provided through Windows.H and begin with the WM_ (which stands for "window message") prefix. For example, a mouse-button event message might be identified by the constant WM_LBUTTON_DOWN (left button pressed).

wParam A 32-bit (double word) message parameter. The value format and meaning depend on the primary event message type. Variously, the wParam argument might convey a coordinate point pair, use the low-word value to identify a secondary message type, provide some other type of data, or be ignored entirely. In many cases, the wParam value will be treated as two separate word values with different functions.

lParam A 32-bit (long) message parameter. The value and meaning of this parameter depends on the primary event message type. Variously, the lParam argument might provide a pointer to a string or record structure; break down as a group of word, byte, or flag values; or, quite frequently, be completely unused.

time A double word value that identifies the time the message was placed in the message queue.

pt The mouse coordinates at the time the message was placed in the message queue (irrespective of the message event type or origin).

Note that these last two fields, `time` and `pt`, are not passed to the `WndProc` procedure. Instead, these two fields are used only by Windows, principally to resolve any conflict over the order of events and, of course, to determine where a specific event should be addressed.

NOTE   Each application is itself composed of a series of separate windows. These windows include the frame, the caption bar, the system menu, and minimize and maximize buttons, as well as the application's main display, which is referred to as the *client window* or, occasionally, the *display window*. Normally, only messages directed to the client window will be forwarded by the `DispatchMessage` procedure to the application's `WndProc` procedure. Messages directed to other application windows are generally handled indirectly (by Windows 98), even though this may result, in turn, in further messages being sent to the client window.

The WndProc Procedure

The `WndProc` procedure—by whatever name you prefer—is the point where each application actually begins to function. Remember, the `WndProc` procedure receives messages indirectly from the operating system but determines the application's response to the messages received.

Previously, when the application window class was registered, the address of the `WndProc` subroutine was passed to Windows as:

```
wc.lpfnWndProc = WndProc;
```

And, given this address, Windows calls `WndProc` directly, passing event messages in the form of four parameters, as:

```
long FAR PASCAL WndProc( HWND hwnd,    UINT msg,
                         UINT wParam, LONG lParam )
```

The four calling parameters received correspond to the first four fields of the `MSG` structure described in the previous section, beginning with the `hwnd` parameter identifying the window to which the message is directed. Because most applications have only one client window that will receive the message, this parameter may seem superfluous. This parameter will, however, frequently be needed as an argument for use by other processes.

At the present, it's the second calling parameter, msg, that is immediately crucial and identifies the window event message. The third and fourth parameters, wParam and lParam, provide amplifying information to accompany the window event message.

Typically, the WndProc procedure does relatively little or nothing outside the switch...case responding to the msg parameter. In the *WinHello* demo, local response is provided for only two event messages: the WM_PAINT and WM_DESTROY messages. All other event messages are handled by default (by the operating system).

The first of these two, WM_PAINT, is a message that is generally not issued directly. It will be issued indirectly anytime an application window is created, moved, resized, restored from an icon, or uncovered by a change in some other application window; it will also be issued indirectly when something occurs—in this or in some other application—to invalidate the client area of the present application.

The DOS equivalent of the *WinHello* program would consist principally of a print statement, possibly with an optional clear screen statement. For the Windows version, however, there are two main reasons for the differences:

- Because the response to the WM_PAINT message is not a one-time occurrence

- Because a bit more is accomplished than simply dumping the text to the screen

Before anything can be written to the client window, the first requirement is for the application to retrieve a handle (hdc) to the *device context* (the output device or, in this example, the screen). After the screen update is finished, this handle will be released by calling the EndPaint function.

```
switch( msg )
{
   case WM_PAINT:
       hdc = BeginPaint( hwnd, &ps );
       GetClientRect( hwnd, &rect );
```

After retrieving the device-context handle, the GetClientRect procedure is called to retrieve the rect structure with coordinates describing the client window. The rect structure consists of four fields, which report coordinates for the client window. However, the coordinates reported are relative to the client window itself. Therefore, the *left* and *top* fields are returned as zeros, and the *right* and *bottom* fields return the current width and height of the client window (reported in pixels).

Once the window coordinates have been retrieved, the rect structure can be used as an argument in the next step to specify the region where the actual message will be drawn.

```
DrawText( hdc, "Hello, World!", -1, &rect,
          DT_SINGLELINE | DT_CENTER | DT_VCENTER );
```

Since print statements, per se, cannot be used in Windows (because they are unsuited for a graphics display environment), the DrawText function is used instead. DrawText begins with the hdc argument providing access to the active display, followed by the string (text) to be drawn.

The third parameter, -1, indicates that the string argument is a null-terminated string. Alternatively, this parameter could be a value specifying the string length, with the second parameter an indirect reference to a character array.

The fourth argument is the address of the rect structure, identifying an area where the string will be drawn. The fifth argument is a combination of flags that set alignment and restrict the text drawn to a single display line. Other elements affecting the display, such as font, size, and color, use the system default settings (although these factors are subject to change, as you will see in future demos).

NOTE   The sprintf statement can still be used to format text to a buffer array, but direct screen print statements are not allowed.

Last, the EndPaint function is called, again with the client window handle and the paint structure (ps) as arguments. This function releases the device context and validates the now-restored client area, and incidentally, completes the response to the WM_PAINT message.

```
EndPaint( hwnd, &ps );
return( 0 );
```

The second application message requiring a local response is the WM_DESTROY message, which is issued when the application is ready to close. This message can be generated via several channels, as will be shown later, but for our example, it is issued only if or when the system menu Close option is selected.

```
case WM_DESTROY:
    PostQuitMessage(0);
    break;
```

The WM_DESTROY message is issued to give the application an opportunity to do any necessary cleanup before shutting down. Therefore, as circumstances demand, the application response at this point could include provisions for calling a dialog box to request confirmation, for closing or saving files, or for any other final tasks required for a smooth exit.

Finally (unless, of course, termination is to be aborted), the WM_DESTROY response is completed by calling the PostQuitMessage function that, in turn, places a WM_QUIT message in the application's message queue to terminate the message loop in WinMain.

Explicit handling has been provided for only two of the messages that might be sent to this application. As a default case, provisions are also required to return all messages that have not been explicitly handled here to Windows for processing.

```
    default:                        // if message unprocessed,
        return(                     // return to Windows
            DefWindowProc( hwnd, msg, wParam, lParam ) );
    }
    return( NULL );
}
```

This default provision returns the message—precisely as it was originally received—to Windows, and then it also returns the result from DefWindowProc to the Windows calling process. This final provision should be considered standard for all WndProc message-handler procedures.

Message Loop Alternatives

While a message loop is integral to all Windows applications, the message loop demonstrated in the *WinHello* application is only one format. MFC supports a second format employing message-mapping macros. In virtually all cases, the ClassWizard is used to create message-map entries which, in effect, link message commands to the message-handling functions.

Under conventional C/C++ programming, a similar process was possible using CALLBACK functions. However, MFC's message mapping offers advantages for many functions by customizing the parameter passed to the function handling the response. For example, when the OnDraw function is called in response to a WM_PAINT message, the OnDraw function is passed a pointer to the device context as an argument, making it unnecessary to call the BeginPaint()/EndPaint()

functions. Similarly, when the OnHScroll() function is called in response to a scroll-bar event, parameters are passed specifying the type of event and the thumbpad position. In conventional coding, this information would still be available but would require decoding before use.

Message-mapped functions appear in many of the demos discussed in this book, but, for a very brief example, a message map containing a ON_COMMAND macro might look something like this:

```
BEGIN_MESSAGE_MAP( CMyDoc, CDocument )
    //{{AFX_MSG_MAP( CMyDoc )
    ON_COMMAND( ID_MYCMD, OnMyCommand )
    ON_COMMAND( ID_FILE_OPEN, OnFileOpen )
    ON_WM_LBUTTONDOWN()
    ON_WM_MOUSEMOVE()
    ON_WM_LBUTTONUP()
    ON_WM_RBUTTONDOWN()
    ON_WM_RBUTTONUP()
    ON_WM_SIZE()
    // ... More entries to handle additional commands
    //}}AFX_MSG_MAP
END_MESSAGE_MAP( )
```

In this example, the ID_MYCMD event message is directed to the OnMyCommand() procedure, which will provide the response action. Other ON_COMMAND macro entries would be used to handle command messages generated by menus, buttons, and accelerator keys.

Likewise, the ID_FILE_OPEN event message is sent to the OnFileOpen procedure. The ON_WM_LBUTTONDOWN event and the following examples are other Windows event messages mapped to specific procedures that have been named and created—as skeletons—by the ClassWizard.

In each of these cases, the programmer must still provide the response to the message within the identified procedure. But the message maps generated by the ClassWizard are a convenient replacement for the conventional message-handling loops, which can often be quite cumbersome.

WARNING   Always use the ClassWizard to add, edit, or remove message-map entries. Manually editing the message map can quite easily cause your application to fail unceremoniously, offering little or no clue to the cause of the malfunction. Although you can edit the message map manually, you must do so in the full knowledge of what you are doing and why. And, of course, you must also check the results very carefully.

The .DEF (Define) File

For a Windows program, the .C source code is only a part of the story. In most cases, the application will also incorporate an .H header file and, almost always, a .RES resource file. These two elements will be discussed in later chapters. For the present, however, there is one more source file that all Windows application sources require, without exception.

When a program is compiled, the compiler processes each .C or .CPP source file (and any included .H header files) to produce an .OBJ (object) file bearing the same name. Subsequently, the linker combines .OBJ and .LIB (library) files to produce the executable program.

For DOS applications, this would be essentially all that's required. For Windows applications, however, the linker also expects a .DEF (definition) file.

TIP   Applications or DLLs produced using classes defined with the AFX_EXT_CLASS declaration may omit the .DEF definition files. The AFX_EXT_CLASS declaration marks the entire class as exported and, therefore, available for linking by other applications.

This definition file consists of simple ASCII text, but it contains an essential series of instructions for the linker.

```
;===================================;
;   WinHello module-definition file   ;
;   used by LINK.EXE                   ;
;===================================;

NAME          WinHello
DESCRIPTION   'Hello, World ... Win98 Style'
EXETYPE       WINDOWS
STUB          'WINSTUB.EXE'
CODE  PRELOAD MOVEABLE DISCARDABLE
DATA  PRELOAD MOVEABLE MULTIPLE
HEAPSIZE      1024
STACKSIZE     5120
```

From the top, the .DEF file begins with an application name and a brief description, both of which are optional and could be omitted (however, including a name and description is recommended for clarity and to alleviate future confusion). The third line, EXETYPE, is essentially a binary flag stating either that this is intended to be a Windows executable (WINDOWS) or a dynamic link library (DLL). Alternatively, if this code were being transported to OS/2 for compilation, the specification would be OS2 to identify that operating platform.

The fourth line, STUB, specifies the inclusion, during link, of the WINSTUB.EXE file. The stub program is simply a brief executable that, if the compiled application is called from DOS, displays a warning message stating that the application can be run only from Windows. Similarly, for the OS/2 system, 'OS2STUB.EXE' might be specified, or you might design your own stub program to be referenced as 'MYSTUB.EXE'.

The fifth and sixth lines provide flags identifying how the code and data segments should be treated during execution. Customarily, both the code and data are defined as PRELOAD (load immediately) and MOVEABLE (relocatable in memory). Also as a default, the code segment is normally defined as DISCARDABLE, permitting the memory used by the code segment to be overwritten when memory resources become limited. (Of course, discarding the code segment also means that the application will need to be reloaded from disk before execution can continue.) The MULTIPLE specification for the data segment permits separate data for each active instance of an application. Alternatively, using a SINGLE data specification forces data to be shared between multiple instances.

Next, the HEAPSIZE and STACKSIZE specifications provide default heap and stack memory requirements. The values shown are the suggested defaults and should serve most applications.

The preceding statements can be considered defaults suitable for virtually all applications, and they can be used as a template for future use. The final statements, however, are far more application-specific and, equally, far more important to the application compiling, linking, and executing correctly.

Last, but certainly important—and perhaps also the least familiar element in the .DEF file—is the EXPORTS statement, together with its subsequent list of export labels.

```
EXPORTS
    WndProc
```

Unlike DOS applications, where the application itself is responsible for all calls to internal procedures, Windows applications depend on exporting principal subprocedures and placing these entry points under the control of the operating system (such as Windows 98), where each will respond to control messages sent by the operating system. For this indirect control to function, the link process must ensure that the addresses of these procedures are known and available; ergo, each must be explicitly exported, which is accomplished by references in the .DEF file.

In this example, only one procedure is exported, WndProc, which provides the principal control structure for the application and forms the absolute minimum required by any Windows application (although the name used may be any valid label desired; it does not need to be named WndProc). However, it is not unusual for applications to have several, dozens, or in very complex situations, even hundreds of exported procedures.

The WinHello.DEF and WinHello.C files provide the minimum necessary to compile an executable Windows program.

TIP   Using MFC, the .DEF define files can be omitted entirely, as will be shown in later examples.

For future applications, this chapter provides a second program, which uses a slightly different approach. The next example is provided as a generic template for your own application development and also to demonstrate a second style for application development.

The Template Program: A Template for Application Development

The *Template* example, like *WinHello*, is a simple but functional Windows application. But unlike *WinHello*, *Template* has been designed specifically for use as a template for your own application development. The Template.I include file has also been used as the foundation for a number of the demo applications discussed in this book.

TIP   If you are using MFC and the AppWizard provided with the Developers Studio, you will not need nor want the **Template.I** include file, which is the core of the *Template* demo. The *Template* demo is included simply for those who, for various reasons, prefer to perform development without using the foundation class libraries.

Unlike familiar DOS programs, which generally have little, if any, source code in common—the `main` procedure aside—most Windows applications have a number of elements in common:

- The same `WinMain` procedure can be used by hundreds of programs, remaining unchanged except for a few string labels identifying the application by name.

- Essentially the same `WndProc` procedure can be used over and over. In this area, the sample provided by the *Template* demo will need to be expanded and altered to provide the specific needs of each separate application.

- Although the About dialog box used in the *Template* demo may not be satisfactory for all purposes, it does provide an example for use in constructing and programming generic dialog boxes.

NOTE   The *Template* demo, including the Template.C, Template.DEF, Template.H, Template.BAT, and Template.RC files, is on the CD accompanying this book, in the Chapter 2 folder.

The Template.C Source Code

The Template.C source code begins with two include statements referencing, the Windows.H and Template.H headers.

```
#include <windows.h>
#include "template.h"
```

Notice that the `template.h` include statement uses quotation marks rather than angle brackets (<>). This identifies the include file as one located locally, as part of the application source code, rather than a system file that is found in the Developer Studio include directory.

```
#define   APP_MENU    "TemplateMenu"
#define   APP_ICON    "Template"

HANDLE hInst;
char    szAppTitle[] = "Application Template";
char    szAppName[]  = "Template";
```

In the *WinHello* demo, only one string identifier was declared—in the `WinMain` procedure for the `szAppClass`—and all the other string references were entered directly as required.

For the *Template* demo, two strings and two defines are declared, both global to the entire program. This format was chosen for two reasons:

- Because the instructions referencing these strings are contained in an include file, not in the main source file

- Because this provides a convenient means to change these lines to match other applications without needing to search through the entire program for their occurrence

In some cases, the menu and icon names could also be declared as string variables. This format uses `#define` statements because there are circumstances where a `NULL` argument may be needed instead of strings (as you will see in Chapter 3).

In later examples, additional references will appear, similar to one of these two declaration styles and generally for the same reasons.

The balance of the Template.C source code is quite brief and contains only three functions: `WinMain`, `WndProc`, and `AboutProc`. The latter two are exported procedures and declared as such in Template.DEF.

The first of these, `WinMain`, is much briefer than its equivalent in the *WinHello* demo, even though both accomplish the same tasks. In *Template's* version of the `WinMain` procedure, however, the provisions required to initialize the application class and to initialize application instances have been transferred as independent subprocedures to the Template.I include file. The second procedure, `WndProc` in this example, provides a skeletal structure for application message handling. In this example, only a few message-response provisions are included: the `WM_COMMAND` and `IDM_ABOUT` subcommand messages, and the `WM_DESTROY` message.

The third procedure, `AboutProc`, parallels the `WndProc` procedure in many respects but provides message handling for the About dialog box.

The Template.I File

The Template.I include file contains the two subprocedures mentioned earlier. These are the `InitApplication` procedure, which initializes the application class (if this task has not already been accomplished), and the `InitInstance` procedure, which initializes each instance of the application. The operations and functions provided by both of the functions are essentially identical to the operations described earlier for the *WinHello* demo.

> **NOTE**
> This Template.I include file will be referenced by many of the examples discussed in this book.

The Template.H Header File

The *WinHello* demo did not require an .H header file, but the *Template* demo (and all further demos in this book) does require a header. In this case, this requirement is dictated by the need to define a new, application-specific message value. Remember, the Windows.H (or the WinDef.H) header supplies the stock definitions used, but values for any messages that are not already provided must be defined in the application's header file, where these definitions can be accessed by both the resource editor(s) and the C compiler.

```
//============================//
//   Template.H header file   //
//============================//

#define IDM_ABOUT 100
```

In this case, only one message value is required: IDM_ABOUT. However, in later examples, much longer lists of defines will be quite common. Also, in most cases, there is no need to worry about value conflicts between values defined in the application header and values defined in the Windows.H header because these will be used in different contexts. It may be useful, however, to avoid values less than 100. Using higher values will avoid confusion with some common standard button IDs and will help you to group values as much as practical for your own clarity.

Also, many programmers prefer to include forward function declarations in the application header, as shown in the following code. However, including these declarations is optional, and unless required by your own organization and function ordering, they may be omitted entirely.

```
//==========================================//
// forward function declarations (optional) //
//==========================================//

BOOL InitApplication( HANDLE );
BOOL InitInstance( HANDLE, int );
long FAR PASCAL WndProc( HWND, UINT, UINT, LONG );
BOOL FAR PASCAL AboutProc( HWND, UINT, UINT, LONG );
```

The Template.RC Script

The Template.RC script provides the basic elements required for the *Template* demo. We'll discuss application resources, resource files, and resource scripts in detail in later chapters.

The *Template* demo requires three resources: a menu bar (`TemplateMenu`), a dialog box (`AboutDlg`), and an icon image (`template.ico`). Notice also that the Template.RC script includes a reference to the Template.H header file.

NOTE   In the resource script shown here, note the Pascal-like elements—particularly the BEGIN and END statements—which were alluded to at the beginning of this chapter.

```
//================================//
//   Template.RC Resource Script  //
//================================//

#include "windows.h"
#include "template.h"

TemplateMenu MENU
BEGIN
   POPUP "&Help"
   BEGIN
      MENUITEM "&About Template...", IDM_ABOUT
   END
END
```

This section of the Template.RC script creates a simple menu bar with one pull-down menu titled Help (see Figure 2.1) with a single item, About Template...,
which returns the command message value defined by IDM_ABOUT. Of course,
most application menus are considerably more complex. We'll get to these complexities in later chapters.

The IDM_ABOUT command message returned from the menu calls a dialog box
that is also described in the resource script, as shown in the following lines:

```
AboutDlg DIALOG 22, 17, 144, 75
STYLE DS_MODALFRAME | WS_CAPTION | WS_SYSMENU
CAPTION "About Template"
BEGIN
    CONTROL "The Template application provides", -1,
            "STATIC",
            SS_CENTER | WS_CHILD | WS_VISIBLE | WS_GROUP,
            14,  7, 115, 8
    CONTROL "a generic template for designing", -1,
            "STATIC",
            SS_CENTER | WS_CHILD | WS_VISIBLE | WS_GROUP,
            14, 18, 115, 8
    CONTROL "Win98 applications.", -1, "STATIC",
            SS_CENTER | WS_CHILD | WS_VISIBLE | WS_GROUP,
            14, 29, 115, 8
    CONTROL "OK", IDOK, "BUTTON", WS_GROUP, 56, 50, 32, 14
END
```

The AboutDlg dialog box described also appears in Figure 2.1.

Last, the resource script includes a reference to an .ICO image file, which contains the application icon.

```
Template ICON "template.ico"
```

Because binary images are not readily adaptable to the present format (the
printed page), you will need to use an icon editor to create a sample icon image
with the Template.ICO filename or select an appropriate image from any of the
many available sources.

FIGURE 2.1:

The About Template
dialog box

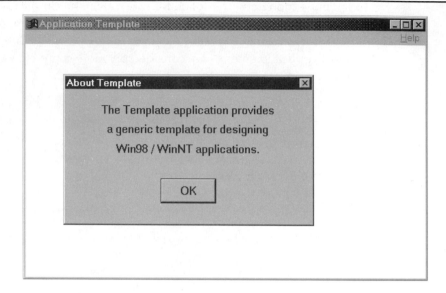

Windows Conventions and Data Types

The following sections describe some Windows 98 conventions for naming, as
well as some of the Windows data types, data structures, and handle identifiers.
You'll see these conventions used throughout this book.

Variable Names and Hungarian Notation

As programs have become more complex both in terms of size and of the proliferation of data types, many programmers have adopted a variable-naming convention, which is commonly referred to as *Hungarian notation* (apocryphally named
in honor of Microsoft programmer, Charles Simonyi).

NOTE   Over the past several years, several "standard" versions of Hungarian notation
have been proposed and/or published. The version given here is dictated in part by
personal preferences and in part by conventions established by Windows in naming constants, variable, and data structure definitions. Because all of these standards are intended to be mnemonic for your convenience, you may follow or alter
them as desired.

Using Hungarian notation, variable names begin with one or more lowercase letters that denote the variable type, thus providing an inherent identification. For example, the prefix h is used to identify a handle, as in hWnd or hDlg, referring to window and dialog box handles, respectively. In like fashion, the prefix lpsz identifies a long pointer to a null-terminated (ASCIIZ) string. Table 2.1 summarizes the Hungarian notation conventions.

TABLE 2.1:   Hungarian Notation Conventions

Prefix	Data type
b	Boolean
by	byte or unsigned char
c	Char
cx / cy	short used as size
dw	DWORD, double word or unsigned long
fn	Function
h	Handle
i	int (integer)
l	Long
n	short int
p	a pointer variable containing the address of a variable
s	string
sz	ASCIIZ null-terminated string
w	WORD unsigned int
x, y	short used as coordinates

Predefined Constants

Windows also uses an extensive list of predefined constants that are used as messages, flag values, and other operational parameters. These constant values are always full uppercase and most include a two- or three-letter prefix set off by an underscore. Here are some examples:

CS_HREDRAW	CS_VREDRAW	CW_USERDEFAULT
DT_CENTER	DT_SINGLELINE	DT_VCENTER
IDC_ARROW	IDI_APPLICATION	WM_DESTROY
WM_PAINT	WS_OVERLAPPEDWINDOW	

In the case of constant identifiers, the prefixes indicate the general category of the constant. Table 2.2 shows the meanings of the prefixes in the examples shown here.

TABLE 2.2: A Few Constant Prefixes

Prefix	Category
CS	Class style
CW	Create window
DT	Draw text
IDC	Cursor ID
IDI	Icon ID
WM	Window message
WS	Window style

Data Types

Windows also uses a wide variety of new data types and type identifiers, most of which are defined in either the WinDef.H or WinUser.H header files. Table 2.3 lists a few of the more common data types.

TABLE 2.3: A Few Windows Data Types

Data type	Meaning
FAR	Same as far. Identifies an address that originally used the segment:offset addressing schema. Now FAR simply identifies a (default) 32-bit address but may be omitted entirely in many cases.
PASCAL	Same as pascal. The pascal convention demanded by Windows defines the order in which arguments are found in the stack when passed as calling parameters.
WORD	Unsigned integer (16 bits)
UINT	Unsigned integer, same as WORD
DWORD	Double word, unsigned long int (32 bits)
LONG	Signed long integer (32 bits)
LPSTR	Long (far) pointer to character string
NEAR	Obsolete, previously identified an address value within a 16KB memory block.

Data Structures

Similarly, Windows adds a variety of new data structures. Again, most are defined in either WinDef.H or WinUser.H. The five examples shown in Table 2.4 appear in the *WinHello* demo.

TABLE 2.4: Five Windows Structures

Structure	Example	Meaning
MSG	msg	Message structure
PAINTSTRUCT	ps	Paint structure
PT	pt	Point structure (mouse position)
RECT	rect	Rectangle structure, two coordinate pairs
WNDCLASS	wc	Window class structure

Handle Identifiers

In like fashion, a variety of handles are defined for use with different Windows elements. Like constants, the handle types use all uppercase identifiers. Table 2.5 shows a few examples.

TABLE 2.5: Five Handle Identifiers

Handle type	Examples	Meaning
HANDLE	hnd or hd1	Generic handle
HWND	hwnd or hWnd	Window handle
HDC	hdc or hDC	Device-context handle (CRT)
HBRUSH	hbr or hBrush	Paint brush handle
HPEN	hpen or hPen	Drawing pen handle

This chapter has introduced many of the basic components of a Windows program, using the *WinHello* and *Template* demos as examples (these demos are on the CD that accompanies this book). Now, we will go into the details of Windows 98 application programming, beginning with message handling.

CHAPTER

THREE

3

Message Handlers and the Microsoft Foundation Classes

- Message-handling formats

- WM_PAINT message processing

- Windows font metrics and measurements

- Windowing text output

- Window resizing

In Chapter 2, we discussed the *WinHello* and *WinHello2* programs, which create a simple message in the center of the screen and then forget about it. That's all these programs are intended to do. They are provided with minimal capabilities because their real point is to demonstrate how a Windows program should be initialized and how to use a simple message-handling loop.

In this chapter, we will use another, slightly less simple, program to demonstrate several elements used in Windows applications. The *PainText* demo demonstrates writing a display larger than the application window, along with provisions for scrolling the display within the window. Also, unlike the WinHello demo, in which only one message is important, the *PainText* example responds to several event messages—a much more realistic eventuality. Another program discussed in this chapter is *PainText2*. This program handles the same tasks as *PainText*, but it uses the MFC classes.

Both programs also demonstrate an aspect of display handling that is necessary for Windows applications: re-creating the screen, in part or entirely, as required.

PainText versus PainText2: Conventional versus MFC Message Handling

For many programmers who began creating applications under DOS (or another early operating system, such as Unix or CP/M), the change to Window's event-message programming has required an adjustment in attitude and in their approach to programming. Creating a program as responses to event messages rather than a direct flow of actions is a very different milieu.

By now, after several generations and versions of both Windows and OS/2, event-driven programming is not only acceptable and convenient, but often it is the method of choice for triggering an action or activity, even when doing so requires defining and generating custom messages.

In a conventional Windows application, the message responses are normally handled in the WndProc procedure as a switch/case statement, where the various case statements may call subprocedures or may contain the code for the immediate response.

In an MFC-based application, however, the conventional WndProc procedure has been replaced by a message-map handler (see "Message Loop Alternatives" in Chapter 2), which directs the event messages to specific class methods that provide the responses. At the same time, the message mapping often also interprets the conventional message parameters in a more convenient format.

In the examples discussed in this chapter, using MFC for the *PainText2* demo introduces two principal changes from the *PainText* program:

- Instead of a message-handling loop, CALLBACK functions cause message events to connect directly to the event-response functions. There is still a message loop, but using MFC, it is effectively hidden from view.

- Rather than providing functions to handle scrolling as in *PainText*, the *PainText2* program uses the CScrollView class, allowing the MFC library to handle the scrolling for us. Functionally, the same tasks are performed but the handling is greatly simplified.

As a brief example, the switch/message handler for the *PainText* program (conventional version) is shown in Table 3.1, along with the equivalent MFC-class methods from the *PainText2* version and the CScrollView equivalents.

TABLE 3.1: Conventional versus MFC Message Handling

Conventional	MFC Equivalent	CScrollView Equivalent
switch(msg)		
{		
case WM_CREATE: …	OnCreate …	OnCreate … / OnUpdate …
case WM_SIZE: …	OnSize …	*Handled by CScrollView*
case WM_PAINT: …	OnDraw …	OnDraw …
case WM_VSCROLL: …	OnVScroll …	*Handled by CScrollView*
case WM_HSCROLL: …	OnHScroll …	*Handled by CScrollView*
case WM_DESTROY: …	*(Uses default handler)*	*Handled by CScrollView*
}		

While it is perfectly practical—and sometimes necessary—to incorporate an old-style `switch`/`case` statement in an MFC `OnCommand` function, the newer format is more convenient. Furthermore, by using the `CScrollView` class, most of the messages that the conventional application needed to handle are now handled automatically without requiring any provisions in the application.

The following sections discuss the conventional message-handling functions, referred to in the *PainText* application, while the MFC equivalents, from the *PainText2* version, are covered primarily where they differ from conventional message-handling functions or require special responses. At the end of the chapter, we will focus on the *PainText2* version and how MFC can simplify the same process by automating most of the operations required by the *PainText* demo.

NOTE   The *PainText* and *PainText2* demos are included on the CD accompanying this book, in the Chapter 3 folder.

Screen-Recovery Operations

Under DOS, once the screen is written, an application is pretty well free to forget about it and proceed with something else. Under Windows, however, even though an application is limited to its own client window, the display created is not inviolate, and the application must be prepared to re-create the display as required. And because the application does not "own" the display, it must be prepared for its display to be invalidated—by another window overlaying its display, by its display being resized or shrunk to an icon and restored, or by its application window simply being moved on the screen. The application itself may invalidate its display by overwriting some portion with a pull-down menu or a pop-up dialog box.

For a text-based display, pop-up dialog boxes and pull-down menus can provide their own screen recovery by saving a memory copy of the existing display and, when dismissed, can erase themselves by restoring the original display from memory. In text modes, this is relatively simple because less than 4KB are necessary to save an entire screen (80×25×2 bytes—character and attribute—per cell).

For a graphics display, however, a similar operation would require nearly 300KB, assuming a screen 640×480 with 16 colors. Of course, for SVGA and True

Color displays, memory requirements increase accordingly. Granted, data compression could reduce these requirements to some degree, but until super-fast terabyte memories become common, the saved image approach is not likely to be considered practical under general circumstances. Instead, Windows applications are expected to be able to re-create the screen as required.

NOTE

> There are circumstances in which Windows does save overwritten display areas, such as when the cursor overwrites the display or when an icon is dragged across a client area. Under these limited circumstances, no screen update is required. However, in all other cases, Windows notifies the application whose screen displays have been invalidated when it is appropriate to re-create the client window while Windows handles restoration of the application's frame.

The WM_PAINT Message

The WM_PAINT message is posted to an application as notification that the current screen display is invalid, requiring restoration. Thus, a WM_PAINT message is issued, notifying the application that it's time to repaint its display, under these conditions:

- When an application window has been hidden, partially or entirely

- When an application window has been resized (assuming the CS_HREDRAW and CS_VREDRAW flags were set in the style specification)

- When ScrollWindow is called to scroll the client area, horizontally or vertically

At the same time, there are circumstances under which the application may wish to issue its own WM_PAINT message. For example, during initialization, most applications call the UpdateWindow function, which instructs Windows to issue a WM_PAINT message addressed to the application's client window. Then, after the message loop begins processing, the WM_PAINT message is picked up and forwarded to the WndProc function, and finally, the initial window display is painted.

In other circumstances, the application may choose to use the InvalidateRect or InvalidateRgn functions, both of which explicitly generate WM_PAINT messages, along with information specifying the area requiring repainting. Applications written using MFC may simply call the Invalidate function for the same result.

At first, this may appear to be a rather roundabout means of accomplishing what, in other circumstances, would be a fairly straightforward task. After all, instructing Windows to send a message back to the application to request a repaint is a bit like riding 'round Robin Hood's barn.

NOTE   "Robin Hood's barn" refers to Sherwood Forest and is a common expression for a task carried out in the hardest possible manner.

The reasons, however, are far more than philosophical. For multiple applications to share a computer, as is the case under Windows, they must operate in a fashion permitting others to have access to the system resources. To accomplish this, applications are required to break their operations into a series of subtasks and, instead of initiating these tasks directly, to place *requests* (that is, messages) in a queue. Control of the system is passed back to Windows as each task is completed, and if necessary, Windows can then pass control to another application. The result is flexible time sharing, with Windows offering each application time and resources according to its needs.

The important item to remember is that applications must be prepared to re-create their display space *at any time.* They must be ready to write the screen on demand and to rewrite the screen on demand.

The PAINTSTRUCT Structure

Hand in glove with the WM_PAINT message is the PAINTSTRUCT information structure. A separate PAINTSTRUCT record is maintained by Windows for each application, with the structure defined as:

```
typedef struct tagPAINTSTRUCT
{ HDC   hdc;
  BOOL  fErase;
  RECT  rcPaint;
  BOOL  fRestore;
  BOOL  fIncUpdate;
  BYTE  rgbReserved[32];
} PAINTSTRUCT, *PPAINTSTRUCT, *NPPAINTSTRUCT,
  *LPPAINTSTRUCT;
```

The first three fields in PAINTSTRUCT—hdc, fErase, and rcPaint—are commonly used by applications. The latter three fields are used internally by Windows 98.

NOTE   If the rgbReserved field (the sixth field) is accessed directly when converting from Windows 3.x to Windows 98, be aware that the size of this field has changed from 16 to 32 bytes.

The first field, hdc, is simply a handle to the application's device context. Rather than accessing the hdc field from the PAINTSTRUCT field, however, applications should continue to depend on the value returned by the BeginPaint or GetDC functions called before any screen-update operations commence.

The second field, fErase, is a flag value with, confusingly, FALSE instructing Windows to erase the background of an invalidated rectangle, and TRUE indicating that the background has already been erased.

The third field, rcPaint, consists of a RECT structure defined as:

```
typedef struct tagRECT
{   LONG    left;
    LONG    top;
    LONG    right;
    LONG    bottom;
} RECT, *PRECT, NEAR *NPRECT, FAR *LPRECT;
```

The rcPaint field is used to keep track of the invalidated region within the application's client window. The four values in the rcPaint field define the sides of the smallest rectangle enclosing all invalidated areas.

When an application is finished responding to a WM_PAINT message (by calling EndPaint), the rcPaint field is reset, validating the entire client window. Subsequently, when some portion of the client window is overwritten by another application, pull-down menu, or pop-up dialog box, a new invalidated region is calculated. Likewise, when any application is moved, closed, or resized, Windows checks for other applications affected by these changes, resetting the invalidated areas as required and, as appropriate, posting WM_PAINT messages to instruct applications to restore their display areas.

NOTE   When you are using MFC and responding to the `OnDraw` method call—the MFC equivalent to a `WM_PAINT` message—the device context is supplied as a pointer, `pDC`, to the active device context. Also, under MFC, the `BeginPaint`/ `EndPaint` functions are not required. Applications using MFC do not have direct access to the `PAINTSTRUCT` structure.

The purpose of the invalidated rectangle is two-fold:

- Because paint operations are restricted to the area specified, an application overlapped by another application's window—or even by another of its own display elements—does not overwrite the higher-level display while restoring its own display area.

- This method restricts the area that requires repainting to the minimum actually necessary. While text-based displays can afford less-than-optimum screen updates without being visually apparent, graphics displays, requiring more processing, lack this luxury. To present a smooth, visually seamless display, they must use the optimum approach of executing the update in the shortest possible time, which also means within the smallest possible area.

Applications may also need to set their own update areas. This task is accomplished by calling the `InvalidateRect` function:

```
InvalidateRect( hwnd, NULL, TRUE );
```

The first parameter, `hwnd`, is the window handle. The second parameter specifies the region to be invalidated. Specifying the region as `NULL`, as in this example, is the equivalent of specifying the entire client area. Alternatively, you could use an `HRGN` argument to pass a handle to a data structure containing the precise region coordinates. If the third argument is passed as `TRUE`, it erases the background for the set region; if it's `FALSE`, it leaves the current background unchanged.

Painting Operations

While Windows is responsible for issuing the majority of the `WM_PAINT` messages, the application is responsible for responding to these messages and for creating or re-creating the application display as necessary. However, before the application can draw anything—even a single pixel—the application must begin by obtaining the device-context handle (commonly abbreviated hdc).

In the *WinHello* demo (discussed in Chapter 2), the device-context handle is returned by calling the BeginPaint function as:

```
hdc = BeginPaint( hwnd, &ps );
```

In this fashion, the application has not only obtained a handle to the device context but also, at the same time, retrieved the PAINTSTRUCT record (ps) by passing the address of a local variable of the appropriate type. The form shown is commonly used in response to WM_PAINT messages and is always matched, when the current operations are finished, with a corresponding EndPaint function call:

```
EndPaint( hwnd, &ps );
```

If you are using MFC, however, the painting operations are encapsulated in the OnDraw method instead of the BeginPaint and EndPaint instructions. Within the OnDraw method, the device context is supplied as an argument, but painting operations proceed in the same fashion as in response to the WM_PAINT message (see the parallel examples in later chapters).

In other circumstances, a second method of accessing the device context is:

```
hdc = GetDC( hwnd );
```

Or, using MFC, the CWnd::GetDC method is invoked to return a pointer to the device context:

```
CDC*  pDC;
pDC = GetDC();
```

The GetDC function is commonly used in any situation where immediate client window operations cannot wait to respond to a WM_PAINT message. For example, a Clock program, responding to a timer event, needs to update its image immediately and cannot simply wait for a WM_PAINT message to appear in the queue.

NOTE　The GetDC function is not restricted to paint operations; it is also used when an application requires information from a device context. For an example, refer to the font and text metrics example in Chapter 27.

Like the `BeginPaint` function, the `GetDC` function has its own closing statement:

```
ReleaseDC( hwnd, hdc );
```

Using MFC, instead of requiring a window handle, the `CWnd::ReleaseDC` method is called:

```
ReleaseDC( pDC );
```

WARNING `BeginPaint` must always end with `EndPaint`. `GetDC` is always closed with a `ReleaseDC` function call. Mixing these functions incorrectly will not produce a compiler error but will have serious, or possibly fatal, effects on an application's execution.

Okay, why two formats? Because each format has a different purpose, and each operates in a different fashion.

The `BeginPaint`/`EndPaint` process, as mentioned previously, returns and resets the invalidate region data, but it also restricts drawing operations to the region specified.

The `GetDC`/`ReleaseDC` process returns a clipping rectangle, which is equal to the entire client window, imposing no restrictions on drawing operations (aside from the inherent limitation to the application's window). At the same time, while `EndPaint` resets the invalidated region, `ReleaseDC` does not change existing settings and, therefore, does not clear information that might be needed later to restore an invalidated area.

NOTE While `GetDC` permits drawing operations over the entire client window area, Windows itself prevents these operations from overwriting an overlying application's window area, and restricts screen operations to the visible or physical portion of the display.

The `GetDC` and `ReleaseDC` functions are frequently used when only information about a device context—whether the display, a printer, or some other device—is required. You'll see this use demonstrated in the next section.

Controlling Graphics Text Displays

Within the Windows environment, four primary factors govern how text is drawn:

Position The row/column absolute screen positions used in a text environment are replaced, in Windows, with window-relative pixel coordinates. Positioning must also take into account *font metrics* (text sizing), alignment options, and *scroll positioning* (vertical and horizontal), as well as variable window sizing.

Text size and alignment In DOS text mode, characters are a fixed size and positioned automatically by the cursor position or by explicit row/column directions. In Windows, as with other graphics environments, text sizes, styles, and fonts can be mixed, and with the exception of a few fixed-width fonts, individual characters vary in size. Regardless of font, characters and/or strings are positioned by pixel coordinates, not by row and column.

Scrolling DOS text mode displays, conventionally, are limited to unidirectional vertical scrolling. When horizontal scrolling is permitted, movement is based on character columns. In Windows, both vertical and horizontal scrolling can be adjusted in single-pixel steps or in any other increment the developer desires. Text displays must take into account offsets from origin points, providing their own vertical (line) calculations. Fortunately, in most cases, horizontal positioning can simply be handled as an offset, without complex calculations.

Window limits DOS text displays can depend on autowrap to prevent too-long strings from extending beyond the physical display. In Windows, the virtual and physical displays do not share the same limits; therefore, applications must provide their own length calculations and line breaks. In some applications, text is sized to a phantom, virtual screen's limits, requiring scrolling to view various portions of the virtual window. In other cases, applications may reformat text to accommodate changes in window size.

In the Windows environment, these four elements are not entirely separate considerations. Instead, they tend to be interrelated or even synergistic in their effects. And while these relationships present their own problems, Windows shields you from many of the other problems that otherwise would be part and parcel of the process of sharing a variable-sized display in a multiple-application environment.

There are advantages as well. For one, because operations are always relative to the window, applications can be moved around the screen without the application requiring special provisions for repositioning. For another, the application itself does not need to recognize the hardware, screen size, and other display constraints and adjust its behavior

Continued on next page

accordingly. Also, though less commonly a consideration, Windows itself provides a variety of display fonts as well as offering accessibility to additional third-party fonts.

Of course, the real point is simply that Windows applications must take a different approach to writing any type of screen display than a similar application operating in the DOS environment.

Windows Font Metrics and Measurements

The *WinHello* demo (discussed in Chapter 2) uses the simplest possible text output, employing the DrawText function to write a single line centered in the application's client window. However, while the demo is suitable for brief text in a very simple context, most applications will require displays with more than one line of text and/or more sophisticated positioning.

For displays with multiple lines of text, two pieces of data are essential: vertical line spacing and horizontal line length (assuming a horizontal orientation). But neither of these characteristics is fixed; they both depend on font selection and, without knowing the relevant text metrics, cannot be arbitrarily assumed.

Also, even for system fonts, you cannot assume that font characteristics will be the same for all systems because, during installation, Windows matches fonts to the video-display capabilities. At the same time, video board manufacturers and third parties design and distribute their own system fonts as well as specialty fonts.

Thus, regardless of font selection, applications must treat the font metrics as variables and request the current font information through the GetTextMetrics function:

```
TEXTMETRICS    tm;

hdc = GetDC( hwnd );
GetTextMetrics( hdc, &tm );
ReleaseDC( hwnd, hdc );
```

This also provides an example of using the GetDC function in place of the BeginPaint function. Since no screen-painting operations are executed, there's no need for invalidated region information or for PAINTSTRUCT data. Thus, for a simple information retrieval, only the GetDC operation is necessary.

The TEXTMETRIC structure is defined as:

```
typedef struct tagTEXTMETRIC
{  LONG   tmHeight;
   LONG   tmAscent;             LONG   tmDescent;
   LONG   tmInternalLeading;    LONG   tmExternalLeading;
   LONG   tmAveCharWidth;       LONG   tmMaxCharWidth;
   LONG   tmWeight;             LONG   tmOverhang;
   LONG   tmDigitizedAspectX;   LONG   tmDigitizedAspectY;
   BYTE   tmFirstChar;          BYTE   tmLastChar;
   BYTE   tmDefaultChar;        BYTE   tmBreakChar;
   BYTE   tmItalic;             BYTE   tmUnderlined;
   BYTE   tmStruckOut;          BYTE   tmPitchAndFamily;
   BYTE   tmCharSet;          } TEXTMETRIC;
```

Of these twenty fields, the seven that control text spacing are illustrated in Figure 3.1.

FIGURE 3.1:

Windows font metrics

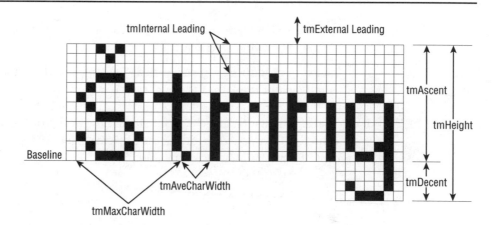

Figure 3.1 shows the following TEXTMETRIC fields:

tmInternalLeading Provides space for accent marks above characters as illustrated by the *S*-umlaut combination shown in Figure 3.1. Although accents are not commonly used in English, many other languages depend heavily on interlinear accent marks. In some cases, international character sets provide for these; in other cases, such as Thai, algorithms are employed to correctly combine characters, tone accents, and vowel marks. In all cases, this spacing should be the absolute minimum between lines.

tmExternalLeading Provides the font designer's suggested interlinear spacing. Although it's optional, white space between text lines increases the readability of the display.

tmAscent Specifies the height of an uppercase character, including the tmInternalLeading space.

tmDescent Provides space for character descenders, as in the characters *g*, *j*, *p*, *q*, and *y*.

tmHeight Identifies the overall height of the font, including the tmAscent and tmDescent values, but not the tmExternalLeading value.

In the *PainText* demo, the vertical line spacing used, cyChr, is calculated as:

```
cyChr = tm.tmHeight + tm.tmExternalLeading;
```

The length of a text string is not calculated as simply, however. TEXTMETRIC supplies two values for character widths:

tmAveCharWidth Specifies width calculated as the weighted average of the lowercase character widths.

tmMaxCharWidth Specifies width as the single widest character in the font, usually either the *W* or the *M* character.

If calculating the width of a character string is critical, you can approximate a third value for the average width of the uppercase letters for most fonts as 150 percent of the tmAveCharWidth value.

Text Sizing

Since font information will remain unchanged during program execution (unless a new font is selected, of course), the simplest method of calculating text spacing is to retrieve the text metrics information when the application is initiated; that is, in response to the WM_CREATE message, the first message WndProc receives.

Text sizing is accomplished in the *PainText* demo as:

```
case WM_CREATE:
    hdc = GetDC( hwnd );
    GetTextMetrics( hdc, &tm );
    ReleaseDC( hwnd, hdc );
    cxChr = tm.tmAveCharWidth;
    cxCap = (int)( cxChr * 3 / 2 );
    cyChr = tm.tmHeight + tm.tmExternalLeading;
    break;
```

This provides three basic values for positioning text using the current font: the average lowercase character width, the average uppercase character width, and the vertical line spacing (although only the cxChr and cyChr values are needed in the *PainText* demo).

In the MFC version of the *PainText* demo, *PainText2,* the Create method might appear to be the appropriate location for the corresponding code. However, attempting to call the GetDC function from the Create method will fail because the appropriate CWnd class has not yet been initialized. Instead, you could use the OnCreate method, which is the equivalent to the WM_CREATE message response. Alternatively, as in the *PainText2* demo, the OnShowWindow method serves nicely:

```
void CPainText2View::OnShowWindow(BOOL bShow, UINT nStatus)
{
    CScrollView::OnShowWindow(bShow, nStatus);

    if( bShow )
    {
        TEXTMETRIC   tm;
        CDC          *pDC;

        pDC = GetDC();
        pDC->GetTextMetrics( &tm );
        m_cyChr = tm.tmHeight + tm.tmExternalLeading;
        m_cxChr = tm.tmMaxCharWidth;
    }
}
```

Here, the bShow argument is tested to determine if the window is being shown or hidden, although the fact that the OnShowWindow method is being called at all should be sufficient assurance that we do have a window and, therefore, can call the GetDC method to retrieve a device context.

Notice, however, that unlike in the *PainText* demo, there is no instruction to call the ReleaseDC method because this is done automatically when the CDC class goes out of context. Also, we will use the retrieved information in a slightly different way, as you will see later in the chapter.

Window Coordinates and Limits

In DOS text mode, the row/column coordinate system is based on an origin point at the upper-left corner of the screen, beginning at 1,1. Under Windows, the default coordinate system used is nominally the same, with three provisions:

- The coordinates are relative to the window.

- The coordinates are in pixel, not row/column, units.

- The origin point is numbered 0,0, not 1,1.

Windows provides several mapping modes, each employing different scalar units and different coordinate origins. Mapping modes will be covered in detail in Chapter 23. For text displays, only the default text mapping mode is required.

Because Windows applications do not write directly to the screen—only indirectly through Windows API functions—applications do not need to know where their client windows lie in relationship to the physical screen. Instead, Windows applications simply write to their own virtual screens, using virtual (window-relative) coordinates, and they leave the mapping from the virtual to the physical to Windows.

When relevant, applications may limit operations to the present width and height of their client window. Alternatively, they may write to an assumed screen of optimum width and/or height (even if this is larger than the active window dimensions) and rely on scrollbar operations to position the *viewport* (the visible window) over the virtual display, as demonstrated by the *PainText* demo.

Outputting Text to a Window

After retrieving the TEXTMETRIC information and deriving the height and width information for the system font, the next obvious step is to write text to the client window (the application's screen display). In the *WinHello* demo (discussed in Chapter 2), the DrawText function is sufficient. However, in *PainText*, a more sophisticated display is provided by using the TextOut function.

Like the *WinHello* demo, the *PainText* demo follows the standard response pattern of painting the application screen in response to a WM_PAINT message. However, because the text displayed will be larger than the application window, the client window also has vertical and horizontal scrollbars to position the viewport over a larger virtual window.

The text metrics information has already been retrieved when the WM_CREATE message is received, but at this time, there is additional information that the application requires. Part of this information can be derived from the ps paint structure.

```
case WM_PAINT:
    hdc = BeginPaint( hwnd, &ps );
    nFirst = max( 0,           cyPos + ps.rcPaint.top / cyChr );
    nLast  = min( NUM_LINES, cyPos + ps.rcPaint.bottom / cyChr );
```

NOTE   cyPos is calculated in lines of text, not in pixels. In like fashion, the cxPos (horizontal) is measured in average character widths.

The cyPos variable contains the present vertical scrollbar settings (initially set to zero); cyChr is the vertical line spacing. The ps.rcPaint.top and ps.rcPaint.bottom arguments identify the top and bottom, respectively, of the window's invalidated rectangle area (these values are relative to the client window, of course).

In the MFC version (*PainText2*), we use a CRect instance to retrieve the client window coordinates (window size) and to calculate the beginning and ending lines for our display, because the ps structure is not available in the OnDraw method.

```
GetClientRect( cRect );
nFirst = max( 0, m_cyPos );
nLast  = min( NUM_LINES, m_cyPos + cRect.Height() / m_cyChr );
```

Another difference is the variable designation m_cyPos instead of simply cyPos. m_cyPos indicates a member variable; that is, a variable belonging to the class rather than to a local function. Member variables are globally available to all class methods. Local variables are not available outside of the method where they are declared.

Given this information, the calculated nFirst and nLast values will provide line numbers identifying text that needs to be repainted, as shown in Figure 3.2.

FIGURE 3.2:

Displaying multiple text lines

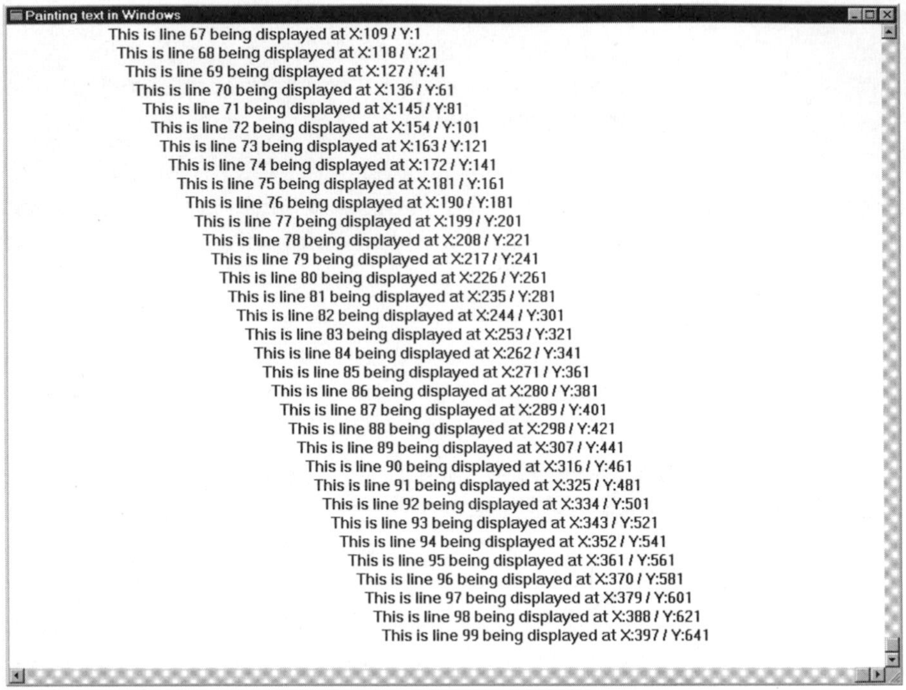

```
Painting text in Windows                                    
              This is line 67 being displayed at X:109 / Y:1
              This is line 68 being displayed at X:118 / Y:21
              This is line 69 being displayed at X:127 / Y:41
              This is line 70 being displayed at X:136 / Y:61
              This is line 71 being displayed at X:145 / Y:81
             This is line 72 being displayed at X:154 / Y:101
             This is line 73 being displayed at X:163 / Y:121
             This is line 74 being displayed at X:172 / Y:141
             This is line 75 being displayed at X:181 / Y:161
             This is line 76 being displayed at X:190 / Y:181
             This is line 77 being displayed at X:199 / Y:201
             This is line 78 being displayed at X:208 / Y:221
             This is line 79 being displayed at X:217 / Y:241
             This is line 80 being displayed at X:226 / Y:261
             This is line 81 being displayed at X:235 / Y:281
             This is line 82 being displayed at X:244 / Y:301
             This is line 83 being displayed at X:253 / Y:321
             This is line 84 being displayed at X:262 / Y:341
             This is line 85 being displayed at X:271 / Y:361
             This is line 86 being displayed at X:280 / Y:381
             This is line 87 being displayed at X:289 / Y:401
             This is line 88 being displayed at X:298 / Y:421
             This is line 89 being displayed at X:307 / Y:441
             This is line 90 being displayed at X:316 / Y:461
             This is line 91 being displayed at X:325 / Y:481
             This is line 92 being displayed at X:334 / Y:501
             This is line 93 being displayed at X:343 / Y:521
             This is line 94 being displayed at X:352 / Y:541
             This is line 95 being displayed at X:361 / Y:561
             This is line 96 being displayed at X:370 / Y:581
             This is line 97 being displayed at X:379 / Y:601
             This is line 98 being displayed at X:388 / Y:621
             This is line 99 being displayed at X:397 / Y:641
```

The two macros `min` and `max` are employed simply as a safeguard against errors in calculation. They are used to ensure that `nFirst` is never less than 0 and that `nLast` cannot be greater than `NUM_LINES`—the maximum number of lines that will be written.

Text Alignment

After the beginning and ending points have been determined, the next step is to set the appropriate text alignment before writing anything to the screen. Under DOS, text alignment is fixed, but in almost any graphics context, a choice of alignments is permitted. In this case, the TA_LEFT and TA_TOP settings provide that the text string will be written with the top and left extents aligned with the output coordinates:

```
SetTextAlign( hdc, TA_LEFT | TA_TOP );
for( i = nFirst; i <= nLast; i++ )
{
   x = 1 + cxChr * ( i - cxPos );
   y = 1 + cyChr * ( i - cyPos );
```

Here, the MFC version is virtually identical. The only real difference is in how the SetTextAlign function is called.

```
pDC->SetTextAlign( TA_LEFT | TA_TOP );
for( i = nFirst; i <= nLast; i++ )
{
    x = 1 + m_cxChr * ( i - m_cxPos );
    y = 1 + m_cyChr * ( i - m_cyPos );
```

New x-axis and y-axis screen positions (within the client window) are calculated for each line written, together with an x-axis offset to indent successive lines. Normally, the x-axis position used would be one character width (inset from the client window frame). In this case, a progressive offset is used to produce a display that is wider than any normal display terminal can handle and, thus, demonstrates horizontal scrolling.

Also, remember that the positions calculated take into account the scrollbar offsets. Therefore, either or both values may be negative integers, indicating that the current line begins outside the active client window. This is not an error—screen-painting operations may originate at coordinates outside the window, either in the negative or positive directions. When this happens, or when drawing operations extend outside the client window, Windows simply truncates the actual painting operation to the visible region, without requiring the application to make elaborate and complex accommodations.

The alternative, attempting to calculate where a string should be truncated in order to fit the active window and present the appropriate alignment, is not only cumbersome but, in practical terms, effectively impossible when a variable-width font is used.

On the other hand, asking the application to begin by writing several hundred lines of text above the visible screen (and hundreds more below), simply to include the visible portion of the display, would be both slow and unnecessarily cumbersome. Ergo, the simplest approach is to allow the application to execute its operations in a virtual space that is as large as necessary horizontally, with Windows providing clipping, but at the same time, provide reasonable beginning and ending points vertically. This approach is demonstrated in the *PainText* demo.

Formatted Text Output

In conventional programs, formatted text output is provided directly using the `printf` function (or an equivalent):

```
gotoxy( x, y );
printf( "This is line %d being displayed"
        " at X:%d / Y:%d", i, x, y );
```

In Windows, a somewhat different approach is required:

```
TextOut( hdc, x, y, szBuffer,
        wsprintf( szBuffer,
                "This is line %d being displayed"
                " at X:%d / Y:%d", i, x, y ) );
```

The `TextOut` function expects five parameters:

- The device-context handle (hdc)

- Two screen coordinates (x and y)

- A long pointer (LPSTR) to an ASCIIZ string to be written

NOTE   The term *ASCIIZ* is shorthand for a null-terminated ASCII string.

- The length of the string (in characters)

These parameters could be provided in a series of separate steps. For example, you could use the `sprintf` function to format the string to a buffer (an array of char), and then pass the buffer, together with its length, to the `TextOut` function. However, because the `wsprintf` function returns the string length directly while writing the text to a buffer, multiple separate instructions can be reduced to a single longer instruction. (Arguments are always evaluated from left to right; that is, in the same order listed.)

In the MFC version, instead of using a char array, a `CString` object is used to create the string. We do not need to supply a string length as a separate argument because the length is included in the `CString` object.

```
csText.Format( "This is line %d being displayed at"
                " X:%d / Y:%d", i, x, y );
pDC->TextOut( x, y, csText );
```

Notice that in all three cases—whether the `printf`, `wsprintf`, or `CString::Format` function is used—the arguments and format instructions are the same.

To sum up, it's a case of sixes and half-dozens, with little to choose among the three except personal preferences.

Scrollbar Operations

Scrollbars are a popular control feature normally associated with screen displays for adjusting the horizontal and vertical positioning (although scrollbars are seeing increasing use for other scalar adjustments). Perhaps the only drawback to scrollbars is that they frequently cannot be used without a mouse (many applications implement the arrow and page keys as alternative controls). However, since few (if any) Windows users lack a mouse, there is certainly no reason not to use scrollbars and every reason, including familiarity and programming convenience, to employ them.

Of course, there is always at least one fly in the ointment. For scrollbars, the fly is that the scrollbar operations are not automatic; applications require a few provisions before they can respond to scrollbar messages.

Scrollbar Messages

Figure 3.3 illustrates two scrollbars (vertical and horizontal), with labels showing the Windows messages posted when you click each scrollbar region with the mouse or release the mouse.

Each scrollbar has five active regions (unless it is created in too small a size): the two end arrows (endpads), the thumbpad, and the scrollbar body on each side of the thumbpad. When the mouse is clicked or released on any of these areas, each generates a different set of event messages, as shown in Figure 3.3.

Both scrollbars return `SB_LINEUP` messages when the mouse is clicked (button down) on the top or left endpad; they return `SB_LINEDOWN` messages when the mouse is clicked on the bottom or right endpad. Alternatively, if the mouse button is held down on any of the endpads, a continuous series of `SB_LINEUP` or `SB_LINEDOWN` messages is generated, providing continuous scrolling in the appropriate direction.

FIGURE 3.3:

Scrollbar messages

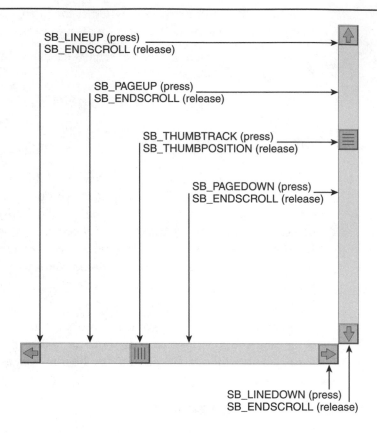

The body of the scrollbar—the area between either endpad and the thumbpad—is also an active control. If the mouse hit is above or to left of the thumbpad, an SB_PAGEUP message is generated. When the mouse hit is to the right of or below the thumbpad, an SB_PAGEDOWN message is generated. When the mouse button is released anywhere except on the thumbpad, an SB_ENDSCROLL message is returned.

The thumbpad itself generates a different type of message. It returns a series of SB_THUMBTRACK messages as long as the mouse button is down. When the mouse button is released, the thumbpad returns a single SB_THUMBPOSITION message, as long as the mouse cursor is still on the scrollbar. If the mouse cursor has moved off the scrollbar, no release message is posted.

Also, even if the SB_THUMBTRACK messages are ignored (by the application), as long as the mouse button is held down and the mouse remains on the scrollbar, Windows generates a thumbpad outline following the mouse position.

Scrollbar Ranges and Thumbpad Positions

In order for scrollbars to report and function correctly, each scrollbar must have both the range and thumbpad positions assigned.

For a standard Windows application, the SetScrollRange function is called with the application window's handle, an integer constant identifying the scrollbar type (horizontal or vertical), two integer arguments setting the minimum and maximum range values, and a Boolean flag directing the scrollbar to be redrawn (if TRUE).

```
SetScrollRange( hwnd, SB_VERT,
                nRangeMin, nRangeMax, FALSE );
SetScrollPos( hwnd, SB_VERT, nScrollPos, TRUE );
```

After setting or resetting the scrollbar range, the scrollbar's thumbpad position still must be set. Again, SetScrollPos is called with the application window's handle and a constant identifying the scrollbar type—a horizontal or a vertical scrollbar—followed by the new position and a flag directing the scrollbar to be redrawn, or if FALSE, to be left as is.

The actual scrollbar range adjustment is handled in response to the WM_SIZE message (discussed a bit later in the chapter, in the "Windows Sizing and Resizing" section). The scrollbar thumbpad position is updated regularly in response to WM_VSCROLL or WM_HSCROLL messages.

For an MFC-based application, the process is essentially the same, except that the SetScrollRange and SetScrollPos functions are CWnd class methods and do not require the window handle. On the other hand, both the SetScrollRange and SetScrollPos functions are internal when using the CScrollView class, so the SetScrollSizes function is used to set the scrollbar ranges as well as the scrollbar page and line step sizes.

Scrollbar Message Handling

Because the SB_*xxxxxx* messages posted by scrollbar events are secondary messages, a standard Windows application begins by looking for either a WM_VSCROLL or WM_HSCROLL message, indicating that the mouse event occurred in the vertical or horizontal scrollbar, respectively. The secondary event message is found in the wParam value.

For an MFC-based application, the equivalent is to use the ClassWizard to create two methods: OnHScroll and OnVScroll in the CPainText2View class. Here, however, instead of wParam and lParam values, three arguments are supplied. Two of these arguments are derived from the standard wParam and lParam arguments, identifying the type of scroll message and the thumbpad position on the scrollbar. The third argument is a pointer to the CScrollBar class instance originating the message.

Because the horizontal and vertical scrollbar responses are quite similar (in the *PainText* demo), the WM_VSCROLL message handling is used here to illustrate both cases, beginning as:

```
case WM_VSCROLL:
    switch( LOWORD( wParam ) )
    {
```

Under earlier Windows versions, the wParam argument was commonly accessed as switch(wParam) without requiring the LOWORD macro. In Windows 98, however, the wParam argument has changed from a 16-bit to a 32-bit argument. Despite this change, the secondary message value accompanying a WM_COMMAND, WM_VSCROLL, or WM_HSCROLL message (among others) is still a 16-bit value but is now passed as the low word in wParam. In many cases, because the high-word value will be NULL or zero, switch/case handling will function without including the LOWORD reference. But you can't depend on this. Ergo, the LOWORD macro should always be used to explicitly extract the 16-bit secondary message from the 32-bit argument.

In an MFC version, if you were handling the scrollbar events directly, they would already be identified in the nSBCode parameter and handled as:

```
switch( nSBCode )
{
```

NOTE   Remember, the *PainText2* application uses the CScrollView class and, therefore, in this demo, these functions are handled internally and do not appear in the source code.

Because the order in which the scrollbar events are handled is not important, the first two handled here will be the endpad messages: SB_LINEUP and SB_LINEDOWN.

```
case SB_LINEUP:
    cyStep = -1;
    break;

case SB_LINEDOWN:
    cyStep =  1;
    break;
```

Both vertical and horizontal scrollbar cases provide essentially the same response, using a set step value for vertical movement of one line up or down; for the horizontal scrollbar, the equivalent would be a character movement left or right. And, yes, for the present, the graphics text is being treated very much like a row/column text display.

Alternatively, the scrollbar positions themselves could be incremented or decremented at this point. But, for the moment, it's simplest to set a variable at this point and then later adjust the display and scrollbar positions appropriately.

The next two events are the SB_PAGEUP and SB_PAGEDOWN messages:

```
case SB_PAGEUP:
    cyStep = min( -1, -cyWin / cyChr );
    break;

case SB_PAGEDOWN:
    cyStep = max(  1,  cyWin / cyChr );
    break;
```

In these two instances, the movement range is calculated from the size of the client window (cyWin) and the vertical line spacing (cyChr), with a simple range check to return a minimum line adjustment of 1 (or –1).

The line and page scroll messages are relatively simple, but the SB_THUMBTRACK message requires a different provision. For this event, instead of an incremental adjustment, the scroll step size is the differential between the stored scrollbar position (cyPos) and the new position reported in the low word of the lParam argument.

```
case SB_THUMBPOSITION:
    cyStep = LOWORD( lParam ) - cyPos;
    break;
```

Remember, each scrollbar has already been assigned a range for full-scale movement. Windows, in the low word of `lParam`, is simply reporting the relative position on the assigned scale. At this point, the application is calculating the differential, so presently another calculation can be made to move the thumbpad to the same position that was reported. Slightly inefficient, isn't it?

Fortunately, execution efficiency isn't important in this particular series of routines. What is important—a smooth, seamless response to dragging the thumbpad—is being accomplished efficiently with a minimum of source code. As always, it's a choice of trade-offs.

If you've realized that no provisions have been made to track the thumbpad— the `SB_THUMBPOSITION` event repositions the thumbpad after the mouse button is released and not while it's being dragged—this is a good time to explain that these two forms are generally treated as alternatives, not complements.

Continuously tracking the thumbpad position has one major flaw: It tends to be sluggish, particularly if responding to a change in position requires much calculation or screen activity. Therefore, many applications prefer to use the `SB_THUMB-POSITION` message and ignore the `SB_THUMBTRACK` messages. However, if you wish, the following fragment can be implemented to provide thumbpad tracking:

```
case SB_THUMBTRACK:
    cyStep = LOWORD( lParam ) - cyPos;
    break;
```

For a comparison, try holding the button down on the scrollbar track, generating a series of `SB_PAGEDOWN` or `SB_PAGEUP` messages. Then execute a similar scroll using the `SB_THUMBTRACK` response. Of course, the vertical length of the display is also a factor, but overall, the differences are distinct.

Last, a default case is provided purely as a precaution to reset the step value:

```
default:
    cyStep = 0;
    break;
```

Before you decide that the default case is redundant, consider for a moment the results if, for example, a `SB_PAGEDOWN` event is followed by a series of unrecognized `SB_THUMBTRACK` messages, without resetting `cyStep`.

Cautionary tales aside, the rest of the story is found after the `switch`/`case` statement finishes.

```
if( cyStep = max( -cyPos, min( cyStep, cyMax - cyPos ) ) )
{
    cyPos += cyStep;
```

The first provision is simply a range check, after which the scrollbar position variable is incremented according to the `cyStep` value (which may be a negative or positive integer).

Having reset the `cyPos` variable, the next requirements are to adjust the window position to match and then update the position of the scrollbar's thumbpad.

```
ScrollWindow( hwnd, 0, -cyChr * cyStep, NULL, NULL );
SetScrollPos( hwnd, SB_VERT, cyPos, TRUE );
UpdateWindow( hwnd );
}
```

And, last, the `UpdateWindow` function is called to ensure that the client window is repainted. This results in a `WM_PAINT` message being posted and requires its own response.

In responding to the `ScrollWindow` function, Windows has set the invalidate rectangle coordinates to cover the area revealed by the scroll operation. Therefore, the subsequent `WM_PAINT` operation is required to paint only a portion of the screen, which is faster than repainting the entire client window.

Window Sizing and Resizing

While the *PainText* demo is deliberately designed to create a display larger than the actual client window, thus necessitating the use of scrollbars, further provisions are also required to respond to changes in the size of the client window.

Any time the client window changes size—vertically or horizontally, larger or smaller—a `WM_SIZE` message is posted to the application. Also, when the application was first created, a `WM_SIZE` message preceded the initial `WM_PAINT` message.

In the *WinHello* demo (discussed in Chapter 2), the `WM_SIZE` message is left for default handling by Windows instead of being handled by the application itself. The *PainText* application, however, is intended to be a bit more sophisticated in its response, and for this purpose, several operations are necessary.

Size Message Handling

In response to a WM_SIZE message, the first requirement is to retrieve the new cyWin and cxWin values that accompany the WM_SIZE message as the high-word and low-word values in the lParam argument, thus:

```
case WM_SIZE:
    cyWin = HIWORD( lParam );
    cxWin = LOWORD( lParam );
```

In the MFC version, the OnSize function, which is the response to a WM_SIZE message, is called with three parameters: the nType argument, which reports the type of sizing operation but which will be ignored here, and the cx and cy arguments, which report the new client window size.

```
void CPainText_View::OnSize( UINT nType,
                                int cx, int cy)
{
   CView::OnSize(nType, cx, cy);
                    // TODO: Add your message handler code here
   if( m_cxChr > 0 && m_cyChr > 0 )
   {                // don't do anything unless have text sizes
      m_cyWin = cy;
      m_cxWin = cx;
```

NOTE   Again, in the *PainText2* demo, the OnSize method is internal to the CScrollView class and no direct handling is required.

Before responding to the size-change message, the first step is to determine if you have vertical and horizontal character sizes. Using the MFC classes, the sequence of size messages is not quite as clean as it is in a conventional application. A size event will be reported before the system text metrics have been retrieved—depending, of course, on which version is used to test the text metrics. However, to prevent a runtime error caused by a divide-by-zero operation, a simple test is provided.

Also, in the MFC version, the size information is stored in member variables for the CPainText_View class rather than in global variables. The effect is the same, but the mechanism is slightly different.

Scrollbar Adjustments

Once you know the new window size, set the vertical and horizontal scrollbars to match. Begin by calculating a new value for cyMax and take into account the number of lines that can be displayed in the resized window.

```
cyMax = max( 0, NUM_LINES + 2 - cyWin / cyChr );
cyPos = min( cyPos, cyMax );
```

In like fashion, the scrollbar thumbpad position is also recalculated before next resetting the scrollbar range and thumbpad position.

```
SetScrollRange( hwnd, SB_VERT, 0, cyMax, FALSE);
SetScrollPos(   hwnd, SB_VERT,    cyPos, TRUE );
```

The MFC version follows essentially the same pattern.

And last, a similar treatment is accorded the horizontal scrollbar. In theory, and according to various documentation, the scrollbar ranges should only require adjusting when the application window is created or resized. Experience, however, has suggested that better results are achieved if the scrollbar range is reset immediately before adjusting the thumbpad position.

In later examples in this book, the text metrics operations demonstrated by the *PainText* program will be used in a variety of other applications, as will the scrollbar-handling provisions and the text-handling and positioning routines.

Simplified Operations with MFC

The *PainText2* demo shows a much simplified method of presenting information in a scrollable format by using the CScrollView class as the basis for the display window. In the *PainText2* demo, instead of the application writing only the information that will fit in the display window, a virtual space is supplied where the entire document can be written. Then, after the document is written, the CScrollView supplies all of the scroll operations.

This does not mean that a monstrous copy of the entire document is kept in memory as an image. As I'm writing this chapter, more than 40 pages of text are actively available, but only approximately a half-page is visible in the display window. In other cases, I may be working on a document containing several hundred pages, again with only a half-page or so visible.

And, remember, because that half-page—at my display resolution— requires roughly 2MB of memory to display, the entire document could demand 80MB to 90MB of memory (as an image).

Instead, the CScrollView class simply controls which part of the drawing operation is actually sent to the display context for viewing, but it allows the drawing operation to act as if it were writing everything. Furthermore, the CScrollView class manages the scrollbars for the view window, intercepts and interprets the scrollbar messages, and invisibly handles most of the operations demonstrated in the *PainText* demo.

Setup for CScrollView

Using the CScrollView class does, however, have its own requirements. First, because the information used for the display is artificially structured, you need to retrieve some information about the text metrics (the font size characteristics). For the *PainText2* demo, this retrieval was shown earlier in the OnShowWindow method (see "Text Sizing").

Once you have retrieved the font information, you use the OnUpdate method to provide four important pieces of information to the CScrollView class.

The first and obligatory piece of information is the mapping mode to be used in the CScrollView window. This argument may be any of the Windows mapping modes except MM_ISOTROPIC or MM_ANISOTROPIC. To use an unconstrained mapping mode, you should call SetScaleToFitSize instead of SetScrollSizes.

The second and the one really essential piece of data is the x/y size of the virtual window where you want to write your information. This pair of size coordinates does not restrict what you write (or draw), but it does place limits on how you can scroll across the virtual window. If the specifications are too small, you will simply not be able to view all of the contents. If the specifications are too large, the view will be able to scroll beyond the displayed data.

The third and fourth pieces of data are optional arguments and set the x/y scroll sizes for page and line steps, respectively. If not supplied, they will default to predefined step sizes.

The following code fragment, from the *PainText2* demo, shows one implementation.

```
void CPainText2View::OnUpdate( CView* pSender, LPARAM lHint,
                               CObject* pHint)
{
    if( m_cxChr > 0 && m_cyChr > 0 )
        SetScrollSizes( MM_TEXT,
                        CSize( m_cxChr*100, m_cyChr*100 ),
                        CSize( m_cxChr*10, m_cyChr*10 ),
                        CSize( m_cxChr, m_cyChr ) );
    else
        SetScrollSizes( MM_TEXT, CSize( 1300, 2000 ),
                        CSize( 130, 200 ), CSize( 13, 20 ) );
}
```

Here, two different provisions are offered. The first depends on font information to calculate the CScrollView window size and scroll step sizes; the second uses predefined sizes if the font information is not available.

In other circumstances—for example, when you wish to show a document—you may be less concerned with font information and more interested in document-size information. For this purpose, when implementing your custom document class, you would include a function to return a CSize response giving the size of the document, such as GetDocSize().

The OnDraw Method

Having set up the CScrollView class instance, the remaining task is painting the actual window display. In the *PainText2* demo, this is similar to the original *PainText* demo, but not identical The *PainText2* version use the OnDraw method, as shown here:

```
void CPainText2View::OnDraw(CDC* pDC)
{
    CPainText2Doc* pDoc = GetDocument();
    ASSERT_VALID(pDoc);

    CString    csText;
    int        i, x, y;
    TEXTMETRIC tm;

    pDC->GetTextMetrics( &tm );
    m_cyChr = tm.tmHeight;
    m_cxChr = tm.tmAveCharWidth;
    pDC->SetTextAlign( TA_LEFT | TA_TOP );
    for( i=0; i<=NUM_LINES; i++ )
```

```
    {
        x = 1 + m_cxChr * i;
        y = 1 + m_cyChr * i;
        csText.Format(
            "This is line %d being displayed at X:%d / Y:%d",
            i, x, y );
        pDC->TextOut( x, y, csText );
    }
}
```

Notice that the OnDraw method in *PainText2*, unlike the WM_PAINT response in *PainText*, does not calculate a beginning or ending line number and that no scrollbar positions are used to calculate offsets. Instead, the entire display is being written just as if the window were actually large enough to display all of the information. In turn, the CScrollView window provides the view and offsets into the virtual space.

Differences in the Demos

To summarize, you should note the following differences between the *PainText* and *PainText2* (MFC) examples:

- In the CScrollView-derived window, no efforts are made to track the scroll-bar positions or to offset the drawing information accordingly.

- No limits are placed on where and what information can be drawn.

- Window size information is required.

Also, if you compare Figure 3.4 with Figure 3.2, you should see the differences in the line offsets.

In Figure 3.2, the line offsets shown are relative to the window. In Figure 3.4, the line offsets are relative to the document (the offsets shown are relative to a much larger space than the space shown in the visible CScrollView window). By itself, this factor is a powerful argument for using the CScrollView class. By drawing in a virtual space of whatever size desired rather than trying to draw portions of an image to fit within a view window, the task of constructing a complex image or document is greatly simplified.

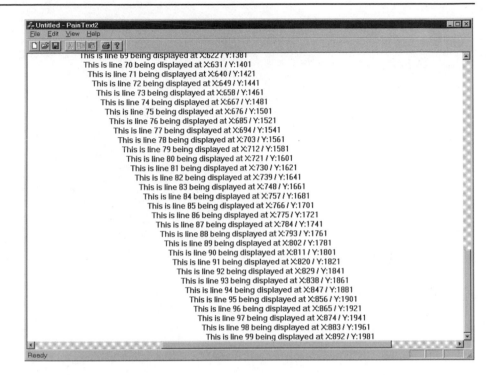

Multiple text lines in PainText2

This chapter described how to implement several provisions required by most Windows applications: writing a display larger than the application window, scrolling the display within the window, and responding to several event messages. We showed how these operations are done with conventional programming, in the *PainText* demo, and how they are simplified by using MFC, in the *PainText2* demo.

In the next chapter, we will address another requirement for Windows applications: responding to keyboard events.

CHAPTER

FOUR

4

Keyboards, Carets, and Characters

■ Keyboard-event message components

■ Virtual key codes and handling

■ Keyboard message responses and handling

■ Text caret (cursor) handling

■ Event message generation

The standard 89-key and the enhanced 101–102-key keyboards, as well as the newer one-handed key encoders, are the input devices of choice for today's computer user. And even though all types of applications—not just Windows 98 programs—are becoming increasingly mouse-interactive, until such time as either mechanical telepathy or direct neural interfaces become common and reliable, the keyboard will remain the primary system input device. Yes, I know that pen-based computers are out there. But can we really take them seriously? Not with my handwriting!

Because the keyboard is so important, knowing how Windows 98 handles keyboard events is critical. The different languages and character sets used around the world also require different programming considerations. This chapter will show you how to manage keyboard-events in Windows applications.

The Evolution of Keyboard Character Sets and International Language Support

Originally, PCs recognized a single character set with the character values 0x20 through 0x7E devoted to the English alphabet, the Roman number set, and assorted punctuation. The remaining 128 character values—0x80 through 0xFF—were devoted to the extended ASCII characters, providing a selection of Greek and mathematical symbols and a primitive series of box-drawing characters.

On the whole, this character set was strictly English-chauvinistic. For non-English writers, it provided an exercise in frustration, as they attempted to render their native languages via a restrictive display channel. And, while various approaches attempted to circumvent these limitations, these often innovative experiments have become, principally, a matter of historical interest only.

Today, since computers are international in both nature and recognition, a variety of keyboard drivers (with corresponding video and printer character sets) provide support for most, if not all, of the principal languages. In some cases, such as the Japanese Kanji alphabet, this support may involve special keyboard layouts. In other cases, such as the Thai alphabet, the familiar keyboard can be adapted (with only a change of key caps for Thai characters); only special support for the display format is required, along with an appropriate driver, of course.

Earlier versions of Windows provide international alphabets, but the 256 characters supported by an 8-bit character code, such as the familiar ANSI ASCII standard, are not adequate for true international support. For this reason, a new standard, called *Unicode,* has been defined. In Unicode, characters use a 16-bit char (or wide char) code to support a total of 65,536 characters—quite sufficient to encode all of the world's contemporary alphabets.

Of course, this does not mean that every keyboard will be required to support the entire Unicode char set. Instead, keyboard drivers access subsets of the Unicode standard for specific languages. Win32 (Windows 98) applications have the options of supporting either Unicode or the conventional ASCII character set or providing mixed support for both.

Although you don't need to worry about Unicode in most cases, sometimes it is important for international support, even on an introductory level. The *KeyCodes* and *Editor* demos, which are discussed in this chapter, demonstrate this support.

ANSI versus MBCS versus Unicode

The conventional ANSI character set consists of an 8-bit font (255 characters) and is limited to the Roman alphabet together with some European variations and an assortment of symbols. The shortcoming of the ANSI character set is that it limits displays to languages using the Roman alphabet—which also means that a large part of the world's population is not able to view computer displays in their native language(s).

Although multibyte characters (MBCS) have been used for a number of international languages, the multibyte approach has never been standardized; it often requires specific firmware and software while still leaving the operating system itself limited to an English (or Roman-alphabet) display. One example of the MBCS approach is in the Japanese Kanji script.

In contrast, Unicode characters—a.k.a. "wide characters"—use 16-bit character descriptors (for 65,535 characters) and include character sets for every language used in the modern world, including Kanji, as well as technical symbols and special publishing characters.

Admittedly, wide characters do take more space in memory than multibyte characters but they are processed faster. Another disadvantage to multibyte characters is that only one locale can be implemented at a time when using multibyte encoding, but Unicode representation encompasses all (terrestrial) character sets.

Continued on next page

Both MFC and the runtime library support Unicode or MBCS. (The MFC framework is Unicode-enabled throughout, except for the database classes; ODBC is not presently Unicode-enabled.)

Both Unicode and MBCS are enabled by means of portable data types in MFC function parameter lists and return types. These types are conditionally defined in the appropriate ways, depending on whether your build defines the symbol _UNICODE or the symbol _MBCS (which means *DBCS* or double-byte character set). Different variants of the MFC libraries are automatically linked with your application, depending on which of these two symbols your build defines.

Class library code uses portable runtime functions and other means to ensure correct Unicode or MBCS behavior.

Most traditional C and C++ code makes assumptions about character and string manipulation that do not work well for international applications; however, the application must still handle certain kinds of internationalization tasks in the application code. To simplify internationalization, always:

- Use the same portable runtime functions that make MFC portable under either environment.

- Make literal strings and characters portable under either environment using the _T macro.

- Follow precautions for MBCS strings during parsing; these precautions are not required under Unicode.

- Mix both ANSI (8-bit) and Unicode (16-bit) strings in an application if needed, but do not mix them in the same string.

- Never hard-code strings in any application. Instead, strings should always be STRINGTABLE resources in the application's .RC file. This allows an application to be localized without changing the source code and recompiling.

You can find more extensive information on Unicode versus ANSI character sets in the online documentation included with your compiler.

Handling Keyboard Events

One of the principal strengths of the Windows environment is its international adaptability. During installation, or via the International dialog box in the Control

Panel, you can select a variety of keyboard drivers, along with fonts and .DLL libraries that support various international keyboard configurations and character sets.

If you are reading this in English, most likely the keyboard drivers available with your version of Windows 98 are principally those suited to the Germanic/Romance languages. If you are reading a translated version of this book, your version of Windows 98 probably supplies a different selection of supported keyboards and alphabets.

No matter which keyboard driver you're using, Windows takes control of your keyboard and actively traps all keyboard events, long before they could be received and interpreted by an application. Routines supplied by Windows decode these key events, storing the results as keyboard-event messages in the application's message queue; Windows decides which message queue the keyboard input is intended for.

Then, the target application needs to retrieve the keyboard-event messages that Windows has stored in its message queue. When control returns to the target application, the `GetMessage` function (refer to the `WinMain` routine discussed in Chapter 2) retrieves the keyboard-event message from the queue. After it is retrieved, the application treats the event message as characters received directly from the keyboard, in a fashion similar to how the event message is handled under DOS.

However, you need to be careful because *similar* does not mean *identical*. The principal difference between a DOS application receiving keyboard-event messages and a Windows application retrieving keyboard-event messages from the application's message queue is primarily the amount of information that is reported.

Early computers, with their slow CPUs and limited memory, couldn't handle complex information from the keyboard without sacrificing what little speed of execution they were capable of. (Some very early machines did not even recognize, except via special provisions, a difference between uppercase and lowercase characters and handled only 6-bit char codes.) For these systems, the wealth of information available through a modern keyboard would be overwhelming.

Under DOS, the keyboard-event message is essentially the scan and char codes returned by the keyboard buffer. When the user presses the *a* key, a DOS keyboard buffer is fed only the single character *a* returned as the char code. The scan code, which identifies the physical key and some aspects of the Shift+Ctrl+Alt flag states, has already been discarded as unnecessary. (For details, see DOS interrupts 16h and 21h.)

But Windows 98 and, to a lesser degree, earlier versions of Windows are designed for operation on less limited and less time-constrained CPUs. Under Windows, the same physical event of pressing the *a* key begins by reporting three separate event messages:

- A WM_KEYDOWN event reporting that a key is being pressed

- A WM_CHAR event reporting the character code generated (in the wParam argument)

- A WM_KEYUP event reporting the subsequent key release (unless, of course, the key is held down for auto-repeat)

Each of these three messages is accompanied by wParam and lParam arguments. The WM_CHAR event comprises six separate information fields. Ergo, a total of eight data elements are reported for each message received, resulting in a grand total of twenty-four pieces of data generated by one keystroke!

Fortunately, applications are not required to use all of the information or even to recognize its existence, so you may feel free to wipe the worried sweat away from your brow and cease considering the keyboard as a potential instrument for hari kari. All of the information is there when needed, but it is not obligatory.

Types of Keyboard-Event Messages

Each keyboard event begins by generating a window message indicating that the event is one of two things: an *application message* or a *system keystroke message*. Application messages are WM_KEYDOWN, WM_KEYUP, WM_CHAR, and WM_DEADCHAR. System keystroke messages are WM_SYSKEYDOWN, WM_SYSKEYUP, WM_SYSCHAR, or WM_SYSDEADCHAR.

System keystroke messages, identified as WM_SYS*xxxxx*, are generally events that are more important to Windows than to the application. Normally, they are simply passed by default to DefWindowProc for handling. However, the *KeyCodes* demo described in this chapter traps and displays almost all keyboard-event messages, both system and application, together with all of the information accompanying each.

TIP

Because the system interprets the event message as requiring special actions, Windows, in some cases, takes control after the first part of the key event is processed. Thus, a few keyboard events are only partially trapped by this program. The reasons for such event instances should be readily apparent to any programmer even partially familiar with the Windows 98 interface. But, if you are not familiar with the interface, the discontinuity occurs simply because this program loses the input—and, therefore, the subsequent key events—whenever a hotkey combination redirects operations to another application or utility.

System-key event messages include Alt-key combinations, such as the Alt+Tab or Alt+Esc combinations, which are used to switch the active window or the system menu accelerators. (Alt-key combinations are discussed in detail in Chapter 11.) In some cases, these event messages may be used directly by applications, but they are normally left for Windows to recognize and handle.

In like fashion, the application ignores both the application and system *xxx*DEADCHAR messages. In general, these are used by non-US keyboards that include special keys for adding accents or diacritics to other letters. They can also provide other special functions or, in Unicode applications, produce other special selections. Because these messages do not, of themselves, generate characters, they are called "dead" and, for most applications, they can be safely ignored.

Similarly, the WM_KEYUP, WM_SYSKEYUP, WM_KEYDOWN, and WM_SYSKEYDOWN messages can generally be ignored by the application. If circumstances demand, however, the information held in these messages is available.

NOTE

Sometimes, such as when the Shift key is used to allow multiple selections, it's more important to know when a key has been released than which key was pressed. Or, under other circumstances such as a game, you might be interested in reaction times and want to know how long a key was held down by checking both the key down and key up events and the time stamps for each. If you have special requirements, this information is available even if it isn't normally used by most applications.

After all of these exclusions, the WM_CHAR message remains. This event provides the single keyboard message that applications normally process because it contains the actual character code identifying the key event.

Elements of Keyboard Messages

In DOS, in addition to the character and scan codes, keyboard shift-state information is also available, and this information can be retrieved separately from the keyboard event itself. The DOS keyboard shift-state information contains the current status of the right and left Shift keys, the right and left (assuming an enhanced keyboard) Ctrl and Alt keys, the CapsLock and NumLock keys, and the Scroll Lock and Insert keys (which are usually ignored). Under DOS, however, key-press and key-release events are not normally reported as separate events.

In Windows, the wParam and lParam arguments accompanying each keyboard-event message carry the event character code, the scan code, all of the shift-state information just mentioned and, in addition, an 8-bit key repeat count. Figure 4.1 illustrates the components of the the wParam and lParam arguments for WM_CHAR.

FIGURE 4.1:

WM_CHAR's wParam and lParam arguments

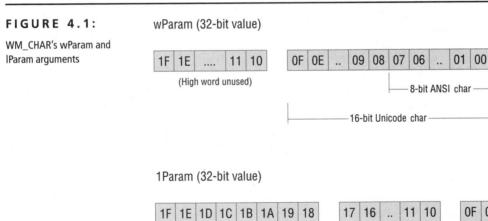

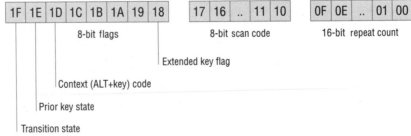

The wParam Argument

In previous versions of Windows, the character code was found in the low byte of the wParam argument.

Under Windows 98, the wParam argument has grown to 32 bits, and the character code can be either the low byte of the low word (for 8-bit ANSI ASCII values) or, for 16-bit Unicode char values, the low word itself. Which type of character code is expected is determined by compiler switch settings or by direct references to Unicode/ANSI API functions.

The high-word value in the wParam argument currently remains unused.

The lParam Argument

The lParam argument contains a variety of information, as explained in the following sections.

Repeat Count This 16-bit value reports the number of keystrokes represented by the event message and, normally, has a value of 1. However, if a key is held down and the application cannot process the keyboard messages quickly enough (for any reason), Windows will combine multiple WM_KEYDOWN, WM_SYSKEYDOWN, WM_CHAR, and WM_SYSCHAR messages into a single message, incrementing the repeat count appropriately. For WM_KEYUP or WM_SYSKEYUP messages the repeat count is always 1, of course.

One reason that the repeat count value may be higher than 1 is as a response to a *typematic* overrun. For example, you may observe typematic overruns while executing the *KeyCodes* demo, even on fast machines, simply because of the time required to write a full-line screen message for each key event. You might also generate typematic overruns by selecting a high repeat rate from the Control Panel. In neither case, however, should you take this as an indication that typematic overruns are likely in conventional applications.

In addition, the Page Up, Page Down, and up and down arrow keys are sometimes sources for typematic overruns, simply because the time required to respond to one instruction may be long enough for additional keystrokes to accumulate and, as a result, often cause applications to overscroll in response. For this reason, many applications prefer to ignore the repeat count value, particularly for specific keys. Experiment to determine whether individual applications should use or ignore the repeat count.

Scan Code The keyboard scan code is a value generated by the keyboard firmware to identify the actual physical key pressed or released. While the same char code may be generated by different keys—for example, the numeral *1* character can be returned either from the number key at the top of the main keyboard or from the key pad—the scan code is specific to the physical key.

Likewise, right and left Alt and Ctrl keys return separate scan codes, even though neither generates a char code. However, some physical keys may return different scan codes according to the Alt, Ctrl, or Shift states.

Extended Key Flag This flag is set to 1 if the present keystroke was generated by one of the keys specific to the enhanced keyboard. These keys include the nonkeypad cursor and page keys, as well as the Insert and Delete keys, the keypad slash key (/), the keypad Enter key, and the NumLock key.

Context Code Flag This flag is set to 1 if the Alt key is down during the present keystroke or if the current message is WM_SYSKEYUP or WM_SYSKEYDOWN. The context code flag is cleared (set to 0) for all WM_KEYUP and WM_KEYDOWN messages with two exceptions:

- Some non-English keyboards use combinations of the Shift, Ctrl, and Alt keys together with conventional keys to generate special characters. These may have the context code flag set but will not be reported as system keystrokes.

- If the active window is an icon, it does not receive the input focus, and, therefore, all keystrokes will generate WM_SYSKEYUP and WM_SYSKEYDOWN messages to prevent the active window (as an icon) from attempting to process these events. In these cases, the context code flag is set only if the Alt key is down.

Prior Key State Flag For WM_CHAR, WM_CHARDOWN, WM_SYSCHAR, and WM_SYSCHARDOWN messages, the prior key state flag is set to 1 if the same key was previously down, or it is cleared (set to 0) if the same key was previously up.

For WM_KEYUP and WM_SYSKEYUP messages, the prior key state flag is always set. Obviously, the key must have been down before it could be released.

Transition State Flag This flag provides redundant information. It is cleared (0) if a key is being pressed, as in a WM_KEYDOWN or WM_SYSKEYDOWN message. If the key is being released, as in a WM_KEYUP or WM_SYSKEYUP message, the flag is set to 1. For the WM_CHAR and WM_SYSCHAR messages, the transition flag is cleared (but it's also irrelevant).

The KeyCodes Demo: Deciphering Keyboard-Event Messages

The *KeyCodes* and *KeyCodes2* demos provide a window in which to examine keyboard-event messages in a degree and detail that are not available through conventional handling. Figure 4.2 illustrates a series of key-event messages captured by the *KeyCodes2* demo.

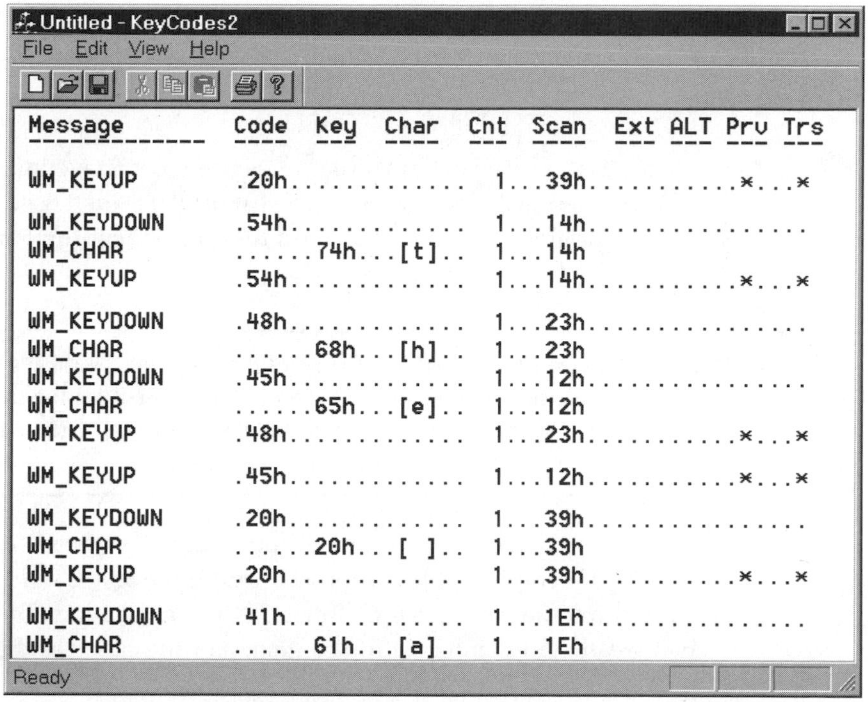

FIGURE 4.2:

Keyboard-event messages deciphered through the *KeyCodes2* program

```
Untitled - KeyCodes2                                    _ □ ✕
File   Edit   View   Help

[ D 🖙 🖬  🖾 🖻 🖺  🖶 ? ]

Message         Code  Key  Char  Cnt  Scan  Ext ALT Prv Trs
------------    ----  ---  ----  ---  ----  --- --- --- ---

WM_KEYUP        .20h............   1...39h...........*...*

WM_KEYDOWN      .54h............   1...14h...............
WM_CHAR         ......74h...[t]..  1...14h
WM_KEYUP        .54h............   1...14h...........*...*

WM_KEYDOWN      .48h............   1...23h...............
WM_CHAR         ......68h...[h]..  1...23h
WM_KEYDOWN      .45h............   1...12h...............
WM_CHAR         ......65h...[e]..  1...12h
WM_KEYUP        .48h............   1...23h...........*...*

WM_KEYUP        .45h............   1...12h...........*...*

WM_KEYDOWN      .20h............   1...39h...............
WM_CHAR         ......20h...[ ]..  1...39h
WM_KEYUP        .20h............   1...39h...........*...*

WM_KEYDOWN      .41h............   1...1Eh...............
WM_CHAR         ......61h...[a]..  1...1Eh

Ready                                    [     |     |     ]
```

The *KeyCodes* demo uses eight `case` statements to respond to the keyboard WM_*xxxxx* messages. The ShowKey subprocedure provides the mechanism to decipher and expand the keyboard-event messages. Let's look at a few provisions in this example that deserve some explanation.

NOTE

The *KeyCodes* and *KeyCodes2* demos are included on the CD accompanying this book, in the Chapter 4 folder.

Retrieving Text Metric Information

The first provision of interest is in the WndProc procedure. In response to the WM_CREATE message, the following code fragment is used to retrieve text metric information for the system fixed (monospace) font:

```
case WM_CREATE:
        hdc = GetDC( hwnd );
        SelectObject( hdc, GetStockObject( SYSTEM_FIXED_FONT ) );
        GetTextMetrics( hdc, &tm );
        cxChr = tm.tmAveCharWidth;
        cyChr = tm.tmHeight + tm.tmExternalLeading;
        ReleaseDC( hwnd, hdc );
        rect.top = 2 * cyChr;
```

The tm (text metric) data structure is used to retrieve information about the system fixed font. The character size (in pixels) is then used to set the cxChr and cyChr variables, which will be used to control the format and spacing of the actual display.

NOTE   SYSTEM_FIXED_FONT is only one of the many fonts available under Windows 98 (fonts will be discussed in Chapter 27). I choose it for the demo because it provides a simple, monospace font that is available on all (English/US) systems (and probably on most others as well).

The second, parallel provision is found in the response to the WM_PAINT message and in the ShowKeys subprocedure. Before text is written, the same Select-Object and GetStockObject functions are called again. But this time, instead of being called in an information context, they are called as the display font.

```
        InvalidateRect( hwnd, NULL, TRUE );
        hdc = BeginPaint( hwnd, &ps );
        SelectObject( hdc, GetStockObject( SYSTEM_FIXED_FONT ) );
        ...
        EndPaint( hwnd, &ps );
```

TIP   Remember, if you arrange spacing to fit a specific font, you also need to be sure that the same font is used for the actual display (unless you aren't particularly concerned about the results).

Responding to Keyboard Messages

Another part of the *Keycodes* demo that deserves some explanation is the switch-(msg)... tree, which provides eight case responses for the eight keyboard-event messages tracked:

```
switch( msg )
{
    ...
    case WM_KEYDOWN:
        ShowKey( hwnd, 0, FALSE, "WM_KEYDOWN",     wParam, lParam );
        break;

    case WM_KEYUP:
        ShowKey( hwnd, 0, TRUE,  "WM_KEYUP",        wParam, lParam );
        break;

    case WM_CHAR:
        ShowKey( hwnd, 1, FALSE, "WM_CHAR",         wParam, lParam );
        break;

    case WM_DEADCHAR:
        ShowKey( hwnd, 1, FALSE, "WM_DEADCHAR",     wParam, lParam );
        break;

    case WM_SYSKEYDOWN:
        ShowKey( hwnd, 0, FALSE, "WM_SYSKEYDOWN",   wParam, lParam );
        break;

    case WM_SYSKEYUP:
        ShowKey( hwnd, 0, TRUE,  "WM_SYSKEYUP",     wParam, lParam );
        break;

    case WM_SYSCHAR:
        ShowKey( hwnd, 1, FALSE, "WM_SYSCHAR",      wParam, lParam );
        break;

    case WM_SYSDEADCHAR:
        ShowKey( hwnd, 1, FALSE, "WM_SYSDEADCHAR", wParam, lParam );
        break;
    ...
}
```

In each case, the response is to call the ShowKey subprocedure with the appropriate data for the display, as shown in Figure 4.2.

NOTE   The demo provides a degree of grouping by including an extra half-line space after each WM_KEYUP or WM_SYSKEYUP event. However, as you may observe, the _KEYDOWN, _CHAR, and _KEYUP messages for a specific key do not always appear in strict sequential order.

Formatting the Text

In the demo, the remaining provisions for string handling and formatting the text display are fairly straightforward C code, with the possible exception of the TextOut function call. This function appears in text as:

```
TextOut( hdc, cxChr, cyWin - step, szBuff,
        wsprintf( szBuff, szFormat[iType],
          (LPSTR) szMsg, ...
```

In the ShowKey subprocedure, the wsprintf function is called with an explicit typecasting instruction (LPSTR) preceding the szMsg reference. LPSTR is defined as a far pointer to a string and is necessary because, in this instance, szMsg has already been passed as a local pointer reference from the WndProc procedure. For clarity—and to prevent a compiler warning message—the explicit redefinition is made from a local to a far pointer.

The remaining parameters, such as the two string references szBuff and szFormat[], are already passed to wsprintf as the expected far pointer references and do not require explicit typecasting. However, when in doubt, including explicit typecasting does no harm, but its omission might.

Ignoring Keyboard Messages

The _KeyCodes_ demo demonstrates intercepting and reporting keyboard-event messages, but it also shows the potential hazards in attempting to process every message received. As mentioned earlier, if an application (or system) is not fast enough to process every keyboard message generated, Windows will combine duplicate messages, incrementing the repeat count appropriately. This approach may seem useful, but keep in mind that processing all—or even most—keyboard messages is neither necessary nor desirable. The reasons for this are threefold:

- The WM_SYS*xxxx* messages are intended for Windows, not the application, to handle. Except under special circumstances, they can safely be left for processing via the DefMessageProc call.

- The WM_KEYDOWN and WM_KEYUP messages are essentially duplicates, and again, except under special circumstances, either or both can be ignored entirely. If, however, they are actually needed, most applications will confine themselves to responding to WM_KEYDOWN events while ignoring WM_KEYUP events.

- Even when WM_KEYDOWN messages are recognized, they are generally confined to cursor and special key events, not to retrieving conventional character key events. For this latter purpose, only the WM_CHAR message should be expected.

In the *KeyCodes* demo, all of the keyboard-event messages are given equal weight—a treatment that most applications will not indulge in. In the *Editor* demo discussed a bit later in this chapter, for example, only the WM_KEYDOWN and WM_CHAR messages are trapped, leaving the remaining six keyboard-event messages for default handling.

TIP   Windows applications should not depend on special key combinations, which may not be supported by many keyboard drivers and/or physical keyboards (especially non-English versions). Granted, this prohibition does eliminate a number of favorite "tricks," but there are alternatives to using special key combinations. Also, your application will benefit by not relying on deciphering complex key combinations, because the time required for processing keyboard messages can be greatly reduced.

Translating Character-Event Messages

Applications dealing with text input depend on WM_CHAR keyboard-event messages to provide character input (as shown in the *Editor* demo). However, the WM_CHAR messages may or may not correspond to the familiar ASCII codes. So, how do you ensure that your application receives the appropriate char code when a key is pressed?

Actually, in this respect, there is very little problem. To match the keyboard drivers generating these messages, Windows 98 also provides translation services that have been incorporated in all of the programming examples. As you may recall, the message loop in the `WinMain` procedure appears like this:

```
while( GetMessage( &msg, NULL, 0, 0 ) )
{
    TranslateMessage( &msg );
    DispatchMessage( &msg );
}
```

The `TranslateMessage` function provides the mechanism to convert keystroke-event messages into character messages. These messages are recognized and used by the application because the keyboard, per se, generates only keystroke information. Before this new keystroke information can be used, the keyboard driver must translate it into WM_*xxx*KEYDOWN and WM_*xxx*KEYUP messages.

This translation process derives the WM_CHAR and WM_DEADCHAR messages from WM_KEYDOWN events, and the WM_SYSCHAR and WM_SYSDEADCHAR messages from WM_SYSKEYDOWN events. The translation service also processes shift-status flags to generate uppercase and lowercase characters.

The important point to remember is that the WM_CHAR message, via the `TranslateMessage` function, provides character information. The VK_*xxxxx* message parameters provide all function, cursor, and special key data. (VK_*xxxxx* message parameters will be covered presently in the "Virtual Key Codes" section of this chapter.) Both of these methods are demonstrated by the *Editor* demo on the CD accompanying this book.

While the `TranslateMessage` function is an inherent part of all Windows application programs, this function is hidden in MFC-based applications, where you use another provision to examine keyboard events.

Using MFC to Handle Keyboard Messages

If you are using MFC and creating an application using the AppWizard, the conventional message loop is effectively hidden and unavailable. This does not mean, however, that you cannot trap all these message events in the fashion shown in the *KeyCodes* demo; it just means that a slightly different approach is required for interception.

The *Keycodes* application shows how to trap the keyboard events using the `Pre-TranslateMessage` member function in the `CKeycodesView` class. The keyboard-event message is received as an MSG structure, which is defined as:

```
typedef struct tagMSG
{
    HWND    hwnd;
    UINT    message;
    WPARAM  wParam;
    LPARAM  lParam;
    DWORD   time;
    POINT   pt;
}   MSG;
```

The MSG fields are defined as follows:

hwnd Identifies the handle of the window whose window procedure receives the message.

message Provides the message number or identifier.

wParam Provides additional information about the message. The exact meaning depends on the value of the `message` member.

lParam Provides additional information about the message. The exact meaning depends on the value of the `message` member.

time Provides the time when the message was posted.

pt Provides the cursor position, in absolute screen coordinates, at the time the message was posted.

The original *KeyCodes* demo program is only concerned with the `message`, `wParam`, and `lParam` fields in the MSG structure and ignores the `hwnd`, `time`, and `pt` fields. The `pt` field would be useful if you were intercepting mouse messages, but it really isn't relevant in this example, which demonstrates handling events generated from the keyboard.

In the *Keycodes2* demo's `PreTranslateMessage` handler, the `pMsg` structure is handled in the same fashion as the message events are handled in the original *KeyCodes* program (the non-MFC version). In this case, the exception is that the `pMsg` structure is provided in place of separate parameters and, therefore, must be decoded before passing the arguments needed to the ShowKey function for display.

```
BOOL CKeycodesView::PreTranslateMessage(MSG* pMsg)
{
    switch( pMsg->message )
    {
      case WM_KEYDOWN:
          ShowKey( 0, 0, "WM_KEYDOWN",     pMsg->wParam, pMsg->lParam );
          break;

      case WM_KEYUP:
          ShowKey( 0, 1, "WM_KEYUP",       pMsg->wParam, pMsg->lParam );
          break;

      case WM_CHAR:
          ShowKey( 1, 0, "WM_CHAR",        pMsg->wParam, pMsg->lParam );
          break;

      case WM_DEADCHAR:
          ShowKey( 1, 0, "WM_DEADCHAR",    pMsg->wParam, pMsg->lParam );
          break;

      case WM_SYSKEYDOWN:
          ShowKey( 0, 0, "WM_SYSKEYDOWN",  pMsg->wParam, pMsg->lParam );
          break;

      case WM_SYSKEYUP:
          ShowKey( 0, 1, "WM_SYSKEYUP",    pMsg->wParam, pMsg->lParam );
          break;

      case WM_SYSCHAR:
          ShowKey( 1, 0, "WM_SYSCHAR",     pMsg->wParam, pMsg->lParam );
          break;

      case WM_SYSDEADCHAR:
          ShowKey( 1, 0, "WM_SYSDEADCHAR", pMsg->wParam, pMsg->lParam );
          break;
    }
    return CView::PreTranslateMessage(pMsg);
}
```

Notice also that all of the events are returned for default handling by the parent class's PreTranslateMessage function. If we had not defined a custom PreTranslateMessage handler here, this would have been the default handling provided by MFC.

NOTE

Chances are that you will not need to provide this type of handling for any of your own applications. For most key events, MFC provides alternatives that do not need this level of interrogation. Nevertheless, you are still able to intercept keyboard (and other event) messages at the lowest possible level.

Handling Virtual Keys

Under DOS, many applications, particularly TSRs, spend a portion of their time filtering keyboard char codes while waiting for a specific keyboard event to trigger some action. This can be as complex as looking for a Ctrl+Alt+K combination or as common as waiting for an arrow or page key. Hotkey assignments under Windows 98 are not handled in the same fashion as DOS TSRs, nor should they be. In some ways, Windows can be thought of as a giant TSR parceling out keyboard-event information to applications requesting that information.

NOTE

DOS-based TSRs commonly install vectors to intercept all keyboard inputs. After checking each keystroke, the TSR returns the data to the original location so that it can be sampled by the next TSR and, finally, sent to the principal application.

Virtual-key handling is one area where applications moving from DOS to Windows may experience the greatest change, as they shift from filtering characters to simply responding to virtual-key messages. This practice is demonstrated in the *Editor* demo discussed in this chapter.

Required Key Codes

Customarily, the WM_KEYDOWN message is trapped while looking for virtual key messages, each of which is identified by a constant with the format VK_*xxxxx*, defined in WinUser.H.

Table 4.1 lists the virtual-key codes you'll encounter when programming for Windows keyboard events.

TABLE 4.1: Virtual Key Codes Defined in WinUser.H

Constant	Hex	Dec	Req	Keyboard	Comments
VK_LBUTTON	01h	1			Mouse emulation
VK_R1BUTTON	02h	2			Mouse emulation
VK_CANCEL	03h	3	✔	Ctrl+Break	Same as Ctrl+C
VK_MBUTTON	04h	4			Mouse emulation
	05 .. 07h				Not assigned
VK_BACK	08h	8	✔	Backspace	
VK_TAB	09h	9	✔	Tab key	
	0Ah .. 0Bh				Not assigned
VK_CLEAR	0Ch	12		Keypad 5	NumLock off
VK_RETURN	0Dh	13	✔	Enter	
	0Eh .. 0Fh				Not assigned
VK_SHIFT	10h	16	✔	Shift	Right or left
VK_CONTROL	11h	17	✔	Ctrl	Right or left
VK_MENU	12h	18	✔	Alt	Right or left
VK_PAUSE	13h	19		Pause	
VK_CAPITAL	14h	20	✔	Caps Lock	
	15h .. 19h				Reserved for Kanji system
	1Ah				Not assigned
VK_ESCAPE	1Bh	27	✔	Esc	
	1Ch .. 1Fh				Reserved for Kanji system

Continued on next page

TABLE 4.1 (CONTINUED): Virtual Key Codes Defined in WinUser.H

Constant	Hex	Dec	Req	Keyboard	Comments
VK_SPACE	20h	32	✔	Spacebar	
VK_PRIOR	21h	33	✔	Page Up	
VK_NEXT	22h	34	✔	Page Down	
VK_END	23h	35		End	
VK_HOME	24h	36	✔	Home	
VK_LEFT	25h	37	✔	Left Arrow	
VK_UP	26h	38	✔	Up Arrow	
VK_RIGHT	27h	39	✔	Right Arrow	
VK_DOWN	28h	40	✔	Down Arrow	
VK_SELECT	29h	41		Select	OEM specific
VK_PRINT	2Ah	42		Print	OEM specific
VK_EXECUTE	2Bh	43		Execute	OEM specific
VK_SNAPSHOT	2Ch	44		Print Screen	Win3 or later
VK_INSERT	2Dh	45	✔	Insert	
VK_DELETE	2Eh	46	✔	Delete	
VK_HELP	2Fh	47		Help	OEM specific
VK_0 .. VK_9	30h .. 39h	48 57	✔ ✔ ✔	0 through 9 keys	Same as ASCII 0 through 9 on main keyboard
	3Ah .. 40h				Not assigned
VK_A .. VK_Z	41h .. 5Ah	65 .. 90	✔ ✔ ✔	A..Z, a..z keys	Main keyboard

In Tables 4.1, 4.2 and 4.3, the column labeled Req (for "Required") indicates by checks (✔) the keys that are required for all Windows implementations and thus will always be available. Also, some of the notations in the Comments column of these tables require a bit of explanation:

- Three values with VK_xxxxx constants are identified as "mouse emulation." This is not because they will be returned by the mouse as keyboard-event messages, but because these codes are sometimes used to emulate mouse-button events.

- Values that do not have VK_xxxxx constants defined are noted as "not assigned." These are not used and/or supported by any keyboard variations, nor are these assigned for any emulation purposes.

- Two groups in Table 4.1 are noted as "reserved for Kanji system." These values are used with keyboards supporting the Japanese Kanji alphabet.

- Values noted as "OEM specific" may be supported by some keyboard variations but are not standard and should not be relied on except in special circumstances.

The virtual-key definitions do not include punctuation and symbols, and they do not distinguish between uppercase and lowercase. Also, applications should not attempt to use virtual-key definitions for text input.

New Windows Keys

The newer "Windows keyboards" include either two or three new keys. These may include two Windows keys, right and left, which call the Start menu, and a single Aps key. The function of the Aps key differs according to the active application, but, in general, it calls a pop-up menu in the same fashion as clicking the right mouse button does. These three new keys are defined in Table 4.2.

TABLE 4.2:   Virtual Key Codes for New Windows Keys

Constant	Hex	Dec	Req	Keyboard	Comments
VK_LWIN	5Bh	91		Left Windows key	Not on all keyboards
VK_RWIN	5Ch	92		Right Windows key	Omitted on some portables
VK_APS	5Dh	93		Aps key	Not on all keyboards

NOTE Because of space limitations, many portable computers provide only the left or right Windows key, not both.

Function Key and Other Special Key Codes

The function keys, keypad, arrow, Alt, Ctrl, and other special keys common to all keyboards are defined as shown in Table 4.3. In this table, along with some of the notations in the Comments column explained in the "Required Key Codes" section, those noted as "enhanced" are supported only by enhanced 101–102 keyboards.

Note that the left and right Shift, Ctrl, and Alt virtual keys are used only as parameters to the `GetAsyncKeyState` and `GetKeyState` functions. No other API functions or messages distinguish between the left and right keys in this fashion.

TABLE 4.3:   Virtual Key Codes for Function Keys and Other Special Keys

Constant	Hex	Dec	Req	Keyboard	Comments
	5Eh .. 5Fh				Not assigned
VK_NUMPAD0 .. VK_NUMPAD9*	60h .. 69h	96 .. 105		Keypad 0 .. Keypad 9	NumLock on
VK_MULTIPLY	6Ah	106		Keypad *	Enhanced
VK_ADD	6Bh	107		Keypad +	Enhanced
VK_SEPARATOR	6Ch	108			OEM specific
VK_SUBTRACT	6Dh	109		Keypad -	Enhanced
VK_DECIMAL	6Eh	110		Keypad .	Enhanced
VK_DIVIDE	6Fh	111		Keypad /	Enhanced
VK_F1 .. VK_F10	70h .. 79h	112 .. 121	✔ ✔ ✔	Function key F1 .. Function key F10	Standard

Continued on next page

TABLE 4.3 (CONTINUED): Virtual Key Codes for Function Keys and Other Special Keys

Constant	Hex	Dec	Req	Keyboard	Comments
VK_F11	7Ah	122		Function key F11	Enhanced
VK_F12	7Bh	123		Function key F12	Enhanced
VK_F13 .. VK_F24	7Ch.. .. 87h	124 .. 135		Function key F13 .. Function key F24	OEM specific
	88h .. 8Fh				Not assigned
VK_NUMLOCK	90h	144	✔	NumLock	
VK_SCROLL	91h	145	✔	Scroll Lock	
	92h .. 9Fh				Not assigned
VK_LSHIFT	A0h	160		Left Shift key	Enhanced
VK_RSHIFT	A1h	161		Right Shift key	Enhanced
VK_LCONTROL	A2h	162		Left Ctrl key	Enhanced
VK_RCONTROL	A3h	163		Right Ctrl key	Enhanced
VK_LMENU	A4h	164		Left Alt key	Enhanced
VK_RMENU	A5h	165		Right Alt key	Enhanced
	A6h .. E4h				Not assigned
VK_PROCESSKEY**	E5h	229			OEM specific
	E6h .. F5h				Not assigned
VK_ATTN**	F6h	246			OEM specific
VK_CRSEL**	F7h	247			OEM specific
VK_EXSEL**	F8h	248			OEM specific

Continued on next page

TABLE 4.3 (CONTINUED):   Virtual Key Codes for Function Keys and Other Special Keys

Constant	Hex	Dec	Req	Keyboard	Comments
VK_EREOF**	F9h	249			OEM specific
VK_PLAY**	FAh	250			OEM specific
VK_ZOOM**	FBh	251			OEM specific
VK_NONAME**	FCh	252			OEM specific
VK_PA1**	FDh	253			OEM specific
VK_OEM_CLEAR**	FEh	254			OEM specific
VK_KANA***	15h	21			Used for Kanji

*Because the keypad 5 key does not have a 'keypad' function, or at least not one that is commonly supported, the keypad 5 returns two different scan codes depending on whether the NumLock is set or cleared. See VK_CLEAR (0x0C).

**These VK_*xxxx* definitions are found in the WinUser.H header file, but many of these are duplicated in the WinRes.H header.

***VK_KANA is defined in AfxVer.H.

The Editor Demo: Basic Keyboard Handling

The *Editor* demo demonstrates basic keyboard-event handling, including responses to keyboard messages and text-input handling. As you'll see, as word processors go, the *Editor* demo is both a wimp and an idiot. It includes provisions for nothing except the simplest operations for input, control, and for display. As it stands, *Editor* does not even toggle between insert and overwrite modes, normally a feature of even the dumbest editor.

Although it's severely lacking, the *Editor* program does accomplish its objective—not to build a word processor, but to show how keyboard-event messages are handled and to demonstrate the basic caret (text cursor) functions (discussed later in this chapter). For now, we will focus on how the *Editor* demo handles virtual-key code trapping.

NOTE   MFC-based applications may prefer to use the CEdit or <SPAN class=op>CEdit-View classes to implement simple text-editor controls or windows without the labor of creating a full-featured editor.

In the following fragment from the *Editor* demo, the Home, End, Page Up and Page Down (VK_PRIOR and VK_NEXT), and arrow keys are trapped as virtual-key codes in the low word of the wParam argument that accompanies the WM_KEYDOWN message. Each key code exercises the appropriate control over the cursor position:

```
case WM_KEYDOWN:
   switch( LOWORD( wParam ) )
   {
      case VK_HOME:
         xCaret = 0;
         break;

      case VK_END:
         xCaret = cxBuff - 1;
         break;

      case VK_PRIOR:
         yCaret = 0;
         break;

      case VK_NEXT:
         yCaret = cyBuff - 1;
         break;

      ...

      case VK_DOWN:
         yCaret = min( yCaret+1, cyBuff-1 );
         break;
```

Since the *Editor* demo does not scroll and is limited to the client window display, the Page Up (VK_PRIOR) and Page Down (VK_NEXT) keys move the cursor to the top and bottom text positions within the window, respectively.

In other applications, almost any key that can be used to control, select, or activate can be found in the virtual-key list and trapped in a fashion similar to the one shown in the preceding example.

NOTE   The *Editor* demo is included on the CD that accompanies this book, in the Chapter 4 folder.

Getting Shift-State Data for Virtual Keys

The wParam and lParam arguments accompanying key-event messages carry a considerable amount of information, but they do not provide specific shift-key data other than for alphabetical characters (uppercase or lowercase) and other dual-character keys. To query the current shift states of the Shift, Ctrl, and Alt keys as well as the toggled shift keys, CapsLock and NumLock, you can use the GetKeyState function.

Realize, however, that the shift states reported by this function are the shift states associated with specific keyboard-event messages in the application's message queue—not the physical interrupt level state at the instant the inquiry is made. Thus, if the string "This is A TEST" were in the application's message buffer and the next char message to be read was a capital letter (assuming the right or left Shift key was used rather than the CapsLock key), the API function call GetKeyState(VK_SHIFT) would report the Shift key as down, regardless of the actual physical state of either Shift key at that instant. In like fashion, if the next char message were lowercase, the same inquiry would report both Shift keys were released.

For immediate information about the shift state of any of the shift keys—Shift, Ctrl, or Alt—use the GetAsyncKeyState function with the VK_SHIFT, VK_CONTROL, or VK_MENU parameter, respectively. Or, for even more specific information, you could use the VK_L*xxxxx* or VK_R*xxxxx* parameter to distinguish between the right and left Shift, Ctrl, or Alt key.

NOTE   You can also use the VK_LBUTTON, VK_RBUTTON, and VK_MBUTTON parameters with the GetKeyState function to query the mouse-button status. This is generally unnecessary, however, because the mouse-event messages already contain all the relevant information. See Chapter 5 for more information about mouse-event messages.

Handling Text Input

You already know how important the keyboard is as an input device. What is even more important is the ability of an application to cleanly receive and display text—anything from a few lines to full screens of structured or unstructured text.

And, in any case, there are a few basics that apply to all types of text input. Of course, with Windows, there are a few differences as well. As the Walrus said, "the time has come to speak of many things ...," but specifically, to speak of things governing Windows 98's ability to display text and to accept inputs.

The Caret versus the Cursor

In Windows, the word *cursor* has been reserved for the mouse cursor. The familiar DOS cursor (from the text-mode display) is now renamed the *caret*. Technically, this term more properly refers to the curious little hat-shaped character (^) , which C/C++ commonly recognizes as the bitwise XOR operator, and which other human European languages use as an accent (as in *â*, for example).

Of course, the caret displayed has no more resemblance to the caret character (thus far, no applications have appeared using a literal caret), than the cursor (mouse) resembles the DOS text cursor. In both cases, the displayed symbol for either the cursor or caret pointer device is a graphic and therefore flexible. Ergo, applications are free to modify both devices, although some standards and conventions do apply.

One standard that does not apply in Windows, however, is the DOS cursor standard of a blinking underbar cursor (caret). This is because Windows supports both flexible font sizes and proportionally spaced fonts, so no fixed character width applies, and the underline caret simply does not serve as an accurate position indicator. Instead, a blinking vertical line, the same height as either the font or the interline spacing, has replaced the blinking underbar in a wide variety of applications. Conventionally, the blinking line is positioned at the point where the next character will begin (or at the first or leftmost extent of an existing character).

For languages written from right to left, such as Hebrew, other conventions apply. For a vertical script, such as ancient Chinese ideograms, the solution might be a blinking horizontal bar. Of course, if a "bostriphon" (literally, as the ox plows) script remains in use anywhere in the world, the alternating right-to-left and left-to-right text would demand its own standards. In fact, this might be a situation where, curiously enough, the caret character positioned below the line, might serve nicely—certainly much better than a plain underbar.

Changing the Caret Type and Position

Because the caret (text cursor) is a system resource, individual applications are not free to create or destroy the caret any more than they are free to create and destroy the mouse cursor. Applications may, however, borrow the system caret—as long as the application holds the system (input) focus. During this time, an application can change the caret type, as well as control the caret position.

Caret Focus Messages

The first step, before the caret can be positioned or modified, is for the application to know when it gains or loses the system focus. Two Windows messages are devoted to precisely this function:

- WM_SETFOCUS notifies an application that it is receiving the system focus.

- WM_KILLFOCUS notifies an application that it is losing the system focus.

The two focus messages are always issued in pairs; that is, a WM_SETFOCUS will always be followed at some point by a WM_KILLFOCUS message, while the latter message will never be issued except when preceded by the former.

NOTE   WM_SETFOCUS and WM_KILLFOCUS are totally independent of the WM_PAINT, WM_SIZE, and other messages that instruct applications to update or adjust their displays. Applications can accomplish these and other appropriate tasks without receiving the system focus or coming to the front of the screen.

At the same time, receipt of a WM_SETFOCUS or WM_KILLFOCUS message does not indicate or suggest that an application is being created or destroyed. It just indicates that the focus is being shifted to or from the present application.

Conversely, a WM_CREATE message is always preceded by a WM_SETFOCUS message. In parallel fashion, a WM_KILLFOCUS message follows a WM_DESTROY message, providing opportunities to create and destroy application carets. Depending on your application's needs, you may provide responses to these event messages or simply ignore them as irrelevant.

Caret Shape and Position Functions

When an application receives the system focus, as notified by a WM_SETFOCUS message, the immediate response, if applicable, is usually to call the CreateCaret function to assign the desired caret shape, followed by SetCaretPos to position the caret and ShowCaret to make the caret visible:

```
case WM_SETFOCUS:
    CreateCaret( hwnd, (HBITMAP) 1, cxChr, cyChr );
    SetCaretPos( xCaret * cxChr, yCaret * cyChr );
    ShowCaret( hwnd );
    break;
```

The CreateCaret function is called with four parameters: a handle identifying the application window owning the caret and a bitmap handle providing the caret shape, and the width and height of the caret. The bitmap handle may have two default values: NULL to create a solid caret or one (1) to create a gray caret. In both cases, the caret will be a block (or line) with the dimensions specified by the third and fourth arguments. In the *Editor* demo, the caret is a gray block that is the height and width of a single character.

Because any call to CreateCaret destroys any previous caret shape, applications must be prepared to re-create their caret shape anytime the system focus is received. If this is not done, the caret displayed will be whatever shape was set by the last application holding the system focus and defining a caret format.

In addition to creating a caret (text cursor), functions are also provided to set the caret position, find the caret position, and make the caret visible.

The SetCaretPos function is called with the x-axis and y-axis coordinates for the caret position, nominally the position of the upper-left corner of the caret bitmap. If, however, the window was created using the CS_OWNDC class style, these coordinates are mapped to the mapping mode associated with the window, and the caret position—and appearance—are affected accordingly. (Mapping modes will be discussed and illustrated in Chapter 23.) The caret position is set regardless of whether the caret is visible.

The complementary function, GetCaretPos, is called with a long pointer to a POINT structure. It returns the caret's current position in client window coordinates or returns FALSE on failure.

The ShowCaret function is called to make the caret visible and has only one parameter: the handle identifying the window owning the caret. If the caret has been hidden two or more times in succession, the ShowCaret function must be called an equal number of times before the caret will become visible. Also, if the handle passed is NULL, the SetCaret function will work only if the caret is owned by a window in the current task (it is, however, very bad form for one application to try to show another application's caret).

The flip side of the WM_SETFOCUS message is the WM_KILLFOCUS message, which includes the HideCaret function.

```
case WM_KILLFOCUS:
    HideCaret( hwnd );
    DestroyCaret();
    break;
```

The HideCaret function, like its counterpart ShowCaret, is called with a single parameter identifying the application window owning the caret. Hiding the caret does not destroy the caret shape, which can be restored using the ShowCaret function. Multiple successive calls to the ShowCaret function must be matched by multiple calls to the HideCaret function before the caret will be hidden.

Also, if desired, the SetCaretBlinkTime function sets the caret blink rate as elapsed milliseconds between flashes. The function is called with a single argument (UINT), specifying both the delay between flashes and the flash duration.

The GetCaretBlinkTime function requires no parameters and returns a UINT value, specifying the blink time in milliseconds.

Caret (Cursor) Positioning for a Fixed-Width Font

The *Editor* demo uses a gray-block caret (see Figure 4.3) sized to fit the SYSTEM_FIXED_FONT. Because this is a fixed-width font, cursor positioning is quite simple.

With the caret initially located at the upper-left corner of the client window, the caret positioning provisions begin by watching for a WM_KEYDOWN message, such as:

```
case WM_KEYDOWN:
    switch( LOWORD( wParam ) )
    {
```

FIGURE 4.3:

A simple text-only editor program with a gray-block caret

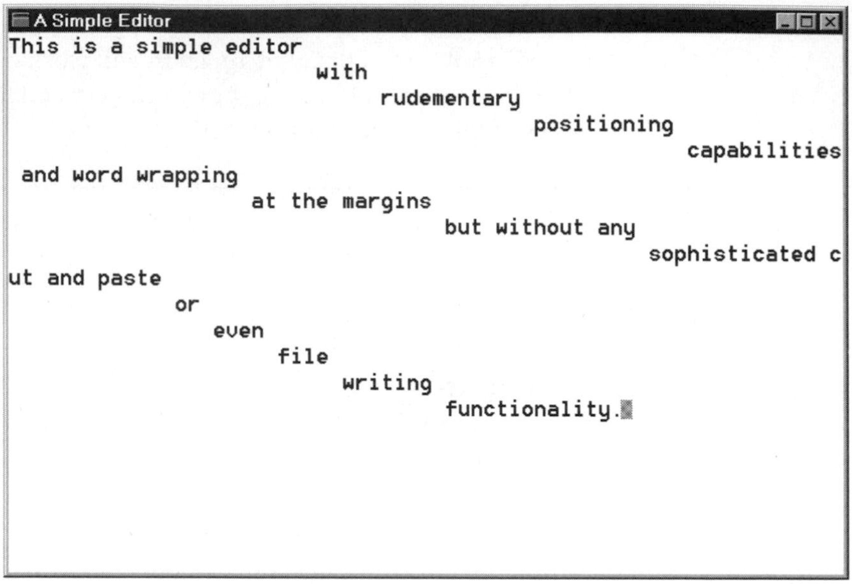

```
A Simple Editor                                                    _ □ ✕
This is a simple editor
                            with
                                    rudementary
                                              positioning
                                                        capabilities
 and word wrapping
                    at the margins
                                    but without any
                                                  sophisticated c
ut and paste
            or
                  even
                        file
                              writing
                                    functionality.▓
```

Most of the WM_KEYDOWN messages received will be ignored; a response will be generated only when the wParam argument identifies one of the cursor or page keys (identified by the appropriate VK_*xxxx* virtual key messages, as explained earlier in the chapter). Because this is a fixed-width font, the appropriate response is simply to increment or decrement the cursor in character (row/column) positions.

```
case VK_HOME:
   xCaret = 0;
   break;

case VK_END:
   xCaret = cxBuff - 1;
   break;

case VK_PRIOR:
   yCaret = 0;
   break;

case VK_NEXT:
   yCaret = cyBuff - 1;
   break;
```

```
case VK_LEFT:
    xCaret = max( xCaret-1, 0 );
    break;

case VK_RIGHT:
    xCaret = min( xCaret+1, cxBuff-1 );
    break;

case VK_UP:
    yCaret = max( yCaret-1, 0 );
    break;

case VK_DOWN:
    yCaret = min( yCaret+1, cyBuff-1 );
    break;
```

NOTE   For a variable-width font, such as the default font used for a WYSIWYG ("What You See Is What You Get") editor, the immediate response in most cases would be essentially the same. The application would keep track of the cursor position in terms of line and character positions and only convert these row/column equivalents to an actual screen position matching the string display position immediately before calling the `SetCaretPos` function.

Deleting the Character at the Caret Position

The page and arrow keys are only a few of the VK_*xxxxx* messages to which the *Editor* demo could respond. In this example, there's only one additional virtual key provided for: the VK_DELETE event, which is handled as:

```
case VK_DELETE:
    for( x = xCaret; x < cxBuff - 1; x++ )
        Buffer( x, yCaret ) = Buffer( x+1, yCaret );
    Buffer( cxBuff-1, yCaret ) = ' ';
```

Here, the response is a bit more elaborate than simply changing the cursor position. In this instance, the program deletes the character at the cursor position by shifting the remainder of the line left one character position and appending a blank at the end of the line. (The space ensures that the character previously following is overwritten with a blank.)

Updating the text buffer is only a part of the necessary response. The display also needs to be updated, which could be done in a couple of ways. For one, the application could simply invalidate the appropriate region, allowing a repaint to repair the screen. Or, as done in this case, an immediate screen update could be executed.

```
HideCaret( hwnd );
hdc = GetDC( hwnd );
SelectObject( hdc,
                GetStockObject( SYSTEM_FIXED_FONT ) );
TextOut( hdc, xCaret * cxChr, yCaret * cyChr,
          &Buffer( xCaret, yCaret ), cxBuff-xCaret );
ShowCaret( hwnd );
ReleaseDC( hwnd, hdc );
```

Notice that before updating the screen, the HideCaret function is called to remove the caret from the display, and after updating, ShowCaret restores the text cursor with the position unchanged. Removing the caret is a necessary operation anytime the screen is repainted, simply to ensure that the caret doesn't interfere with the paint operation (similar precautions are generally used when the mouse cursor is active). Feel free to experiment by commenting out both the HideCaret and ShowCaret API calls and observing the results directly.

For a VK_BACK (backspace) message, essentially the same response could be used, except that the program would also need to decrement the caret position. An alternative is to handle this through a WM_CHAR message, as explained shortly, in the "Handling WM_CHAR Messages" section.

Other possible VK_*xxxxx* messages might require quite different responses. For example, suppose provisions were made for the VK_INSERT message to toggle between insert and overwrite modes. Should the cursor shape, size, or format change to reflect the current mode?

Still, whatever operations are provided, the last provision within the VK_KEY- DOWN response is to update the caret position, even though many of the options may not have affected this position at all.

```
SetCaretPos( xCaret * cxChr, yCaret * cyChr );
break;
```

Calculating the position is simple using a fixed-width font; it requires nothing more than multiplying the row and column position by the character width and line spacing, respectively.

A different approach is required for a variable-width font. There are several possibilities, but perhaps the best approach might lie in the *current position* or cp, a Windows feature described in the next section.

Handling Carets for Variable-Width Fonts

The cp is an internal POINT structure that can be used by Windows to track drawing operations, with a separate cp for each device context. In some cases, cp is ignored and not updated during drawing operations.

For example, the TextOut function used to write (draw) the text display in the *Editor* demo does not normally keep track of the cp. However, this is subject to change. By calling the SetTextAlign function with the fmode argument, TA_UPDATECP will enable current position tracking.

When current position tracking is enabled, the GetCurrentPositionEx function can be called to retrieve the cp coordinates after writing a string or a portion of a string. For example, assume that the string displayed reads, "This is a positioning text," and the caret should be positioned immediately after the *a*. With a proportionally spaced font, the capital *T* will be wider than average, and the two *i*'s will be narrower. Obviously, attempting to estimate character positions from the tmAveCharWidth spacing is not going to produce accurate results. If, however, only a part of the string is drawn ("This is a"), and cp is retrieved before completing the sentence, the retrieved cp will provide the positioning for the caret.

The bad news is that it's not quite as simple as this illustration suggests. You will need to refer to the SetTextAlign, GetCurrentPositionEx, and TextOut functions for details on how to use each appropriately for the task. And, of course, you will need to do a bit of experimenting.

Handling WM_CHAR Messages

Like WM_KEYDOWN messages, WM_CHAR messages are also subject to a wide variety of processing. Most of the special provisions discussed here can also be handled by virtual-key responses in the WM_KEYDOWN message handling. In fact, they would be handled that way in most cases. But the WM_CHAR message-handling methods are alternatives that you may want to consider.

For an exercise in keycodes and functions, convert as much as is practical of the WM_CHAR message handling to WM_KEYDOWN handling. Just be sure to test your results carefully.

Repeat Characters

The first step, because the WM_CHAR message may well include a repeat count, is a loop controlled by the low word in the lParam argument:

```
case WM_CHAR:
    for( i = 0; i < (int)LOWORD(lParam); i++ )
    {
```

Within the loop, even though the high word of wParam should be simply a NULL, the LOWORD macro is used to discard any potentially conflicting data:

```
switch( LOWORD( wParam ) )
{
```

Backspace

The first char value trapped is the backspace character (\b).

```
case '\b':           // backspace
    if( xCaret > 0 )
    {   xCaret-;
        SendMessage( hwnd, WM_KEYDOWN, VK_DELETE, 1L );
    }
    break;
```

The Backspace key is easily handled by simply decrementing the caret position and then issuing a key down/delete key message. Alternatively, this could be handled as a virtual key (VK_BACK) in the preceding WM_KEYDOWN handler. In this case, the handling might well be almost exactly the same as shown here.

Tab

The tab char is easily provided for using a do .. while loop to insert spaces repeatedly until the desired character position is reached.

```
case '\t':           // tab
    do
        SendMessage( hwnd, WM_CHAR, ' ', 1L);
    while( xCaret % 8 != 0 );
    break;
```

Like the Backspace key, the Tab key can also be trapped by the preceding WM_KEYDOWN handler.

Carriage Return and Line Feed

The next two char events are handled as a pair. The first character watched for is the carriage return (\r or ASCII 0x0D), which resets the horizontal position to the beginning of the line. It is then allowed to fall through to the second case, the line feed, for further response.

```
case '\r':           // carriage return
    xCaret = 0;      // falls through to '\n'

case '\n':           // line feed
    if( ++yCaret == cyBuff )
        yCaret = 0;
    break;
```

The line feed character (\n or ASCII 0x0A), by convention, does not reset the horizontal position; instead, it is treated as the equivalent of the down arrow. In this example, both of these responses could as easily have been written as:

```
case '\r':
    SendMessage( hwnd, WM_KEYDOWN, VK_HOME, 1L );

case '\n':
    SendMessage( hwnd, WM_KEYDOWN, VK_DOWN, 1L );
    break;
```

Notice that the carriage return response is still allowed to fall through to the subsequent line feed response.

While the practice of responding to one keyboard-event message by issuing other keyboard-event messages may, at first, seem slightly redundant, the overall result is an economy of effort both for the programmer and for the program. After all, instead of duplicating essentially the same response (both as code and as executable), this approach allows code and executable to do double duty. In addition, this approach can be (and often is) applied to features other than keyboard responses.

Escape (Esc)

The Escape key (ASCII 0x1B) is another popular *hotkey*. In this example, it resets the text buffer and then issues a query for confirmation:

```
case '\x1B':        // escape
    if( MessageBox( hwnd, "Reset text buffer?",
        "Editor Query",
        MB_ICONEXCLAMATION | MB_OKCANCEL |
        MB_DEFBUTTON2 ) == IDOK )
```

The `MessageBox` API call presents a stock dialog box with the caption "Editor Query," the message "Reset test buffer?" and the OK and Cancel buttons. If the OK button is clicked, the function returns TRUE; if the Cancel button is selected, it returns FALSE. This value dictates whether or not the following provisions will be executed.

If the decision is to proceed, then a double loop overwrites the text buffer with blanks, the caret position is reset to the first character position at the upper-left, and last, the `InvalidateRect` function is called to clear the existing display by issuing a `WM_PAINT` message.

```
{
    for( y = 0; y < cyBuff; y++ )
        for( x = 0; x < cxBuff; x++ )
            Buffer( x, y ) = ' ';
    xCaret = 0;
    yCaret = 0;
    InvalidateRect( hwnd, NULL, FALSE );
}
break;
```

Other Character Events

As a final response to `WM_CHAR` messages, the default provision handles all other character events, which are assumed to be conventional alphabetic, numeric, or punctuation characters:

```
default:            // all other chars
    Buffer( xCaret, yCaret ) = (char) LOWORD( wParam );
    HideCaret( hwnd );
    hdc = GetDC( hwnd );
    SelectObject( hdc,
            GetStockObject( SYSTEM_FIXED_FONT ));
```

```
TextOut( hdc, xCaret * cxChr, yCaret * cyChr,
         &Buffer( xCaret, yCaret ), 1 );
ShowCaret( hwnd );
ReleaseDC( hwnd, hdc );
if( ++xCaret == cxBuff )
{
   xCaret = 0;
   if( ++yCaret == cyBuff ) yCaret = 0;
}
break;
      }   }
```

The handling used is essentially the same as shown earlier for the VK_DELETE message. However, in view of earlier remarks about sharing responses, couldn't the present duplication of code and executable be similarly avoided?

Finally, because some of the preceding responses have affected the caret position, the same closing provision is required here as in the WM_KEYDOWN response.

```
SetCaretPos( xCaret * cxChr, yCaret * cyChr );
break;
```

Generating Event Messages

The flip side of processing keyboard messages (or any other event messages) is being able to generate your own messages to request specific actions. You've seen several brief examples of message generation in the preceding code fragments.

Sending Messages to Applications

The SendMessage function is called with the same four parameters that are passed to the WndProc procedure:

```
SendMessage( HWND  hwnd,    UINT msg,
             DWORD wParam, LONG lParam );
```

SendMessage passes its arguments to Windows, which then places the message in the message queue for the application identified by the hwnd argument. In this fashion, the destination could be the same application window that originated the message, another window belonging to the same application, or even a window belonging to another application entirely.

PostMessage versus *SendMessage*

Two functions are provided for passing messages within an application: **SendMessage** and **PostMessage**. These work essentially the same way except for how they dispatch messages.

PostMessage places the message in the messaging queue and then returns immediately—without waiting for the message to be delivered. Using **PostMessage**, the posting procedure can continue operating and the called procedure—the message recipient—does not act until the message queue delivers.

In contrast, **SendMessage** places a message in the queue but does not return until the message has been processed and delivered to the recipient. In effect, **SendMessage** transfers operational control to another routine—the message recipient—and waits for the recipient to finish its task and return control. For sending messages to other applications, **SendMessage** is not the most efficient method. There are simpler ways to exchange information and instructions between applications, as explained in Part 5 of this book.

Scrolling with Arrow Keys

The *PainText* demo (discussed in Chapter 3) demonstrates how scrollbars are used to respond to mouse-event messages. Even though it is rare to find a computer without a mouse (at least, one that is running Windows), there may be times when using the keyboard for scrolling is more convenient.

To further demonstrate the **SendMessage** function, here is a patch for the *PainText* program, which allows the arrow keys to simulate mouse operations:

```
switch( msg )
{
  ...
  case WM_KEYDOWN:
    switch( LOWORD( wParam ) )
    {
      case VK_LEFT:
        SendMessage( hwnd, WM_HSCROLL, SB_LINEUP, OL );
        break;

      case VK_RIGHT:
        SendMessage( hwnd, WM_HSCROLL, SB_LINEDOWN, OL );
        break;
```

```
        case VK_UP:
            SendMessage( hwnd, WM_VSCROLL, SB_LINEUP, OL );
            break;

        case VK_DOWN:
            SendMessage( hwnd, WM_VSCROLL, SB_LINEDOWN, OL );
            break;
        ...
    }
        break;
    ...
}
    break;
    ...
```

In this fashion, the four arrow keys use the `SendMessage` function to generate scrollbar messages equivalent to clicking on the arrow keys at the ends of the scrollbars. Alternatively, for faster scroll operations, the Page Up (VK_PRIOR), Page Down (VK_NEXT), Home (VK_HOME), and End (VK_END) keys can be used to send the appropriate SB_PAGEUP and SB_PAGEDOWN messages to each scrollbar.

The `SendMessage` function can be used to generate any valid Windows messages, not just those shown here. Furthermore, this can be initiated in response to any appropriate circumstance, not just a keyboard (or mouse) event.

In Windows programming, messages are generated in response to a wide variety of circumstances and for a wide variety of purposes. In many senses, the message functions and operations are the heart of Windows applications (actually, life's blood might be a better metaphor).

In this chapter, we covered handling keyboard-event messages. In the next chapter, you will learn about handling mouse-event messages.

CHAPTER
FIVE

Mouse Operations

■ Mouse-event messages

■ Mouse-movement tracking

■ Mouse cursor shapes

■ Mouse-hit testing

If you have read the book up to this point or have had time to work on a Windows system (and who hasn't?), it should be quite obvious that Windows is totally mouse-oriented. Granted, there are keyboard options to permit switching between windows and applications without using the mouse but in reality, without a mouse, using Windows is almost impossible. At the same time, it is possible that your application could be designed in such a fashion that a mouse was not required—possible, but unlikely.

Besides, is there any real reason—short of some mechao-myomorphicphobia—for seeking to avoid these ubiquitous little pseudo-rodents? (Obviously, the question demands a negative response.)

NOTE   If you will pardon the bad Greek/Latin, *mechao-myomorphicphobia* is a fear of mechanical mice.

In any case, hypothetical phobias aside, at least a minimal knowledge of mouse operations is essential to any application. Furthermore, knowing how the mouse works may even suggest uses and possibilities relevant to your application design.

The Evolution of the Genus MusMechano

Originally, mouse devices were single-button (left-button equivalent) pointing devices—a primitive form that is still found today on Apple/Macintosh systems but that is virtually obsolete on contemporary DOS, Windows, and OS/2 systems (despite the fact that some sources continue to suggest that a single-button mouse should be considered a minimal standard).

For Windows 98, two standard mouse configurations are supported: the two-button variety typified by the standard Microsoft Mouse and the three-button variety represented by the Logitech Mouse. Support is also provided for some variant forms, such as mouse-emulation by joy sticks and lightpens, which are treated as single-button mice. A variety of less common devices—such as those for use by disabled persons or special-purpose variations ("un-mouse" pads, touch pads, joy-stick pointers, and so on)—attempt to make their interfaces indistinguishable from one of the standard interfaces.

Some mouse varieties ("mutations," if you prefer) have appeared, sporting dozens of "keys." These keys are usually used for numerical data operations, but in theory, they provide mini-keyboards on a mouse. These varieties require special drivers before any Windows 98 interface is possible, and for now, they can simply be ignored. Virtual devices, such as control gloves that sense spatial motion, are still experimental, and they also can be ignored for now.

Also, the newest "mouse" from Microsoft (and others) includes a wheel between the two buttons. The wheel is designed as an add-in for scrolling through Web pages but—at present— should not be considered a "standard" requiring support. For the moment, only the two "standard" mouse types require consideration. Even though the middle button on three-button mice can be extremely useful, this chapter concentrates on the minimalist standard of two mouse buttons: left and right.

Common usage emphasizes the left mouse button, regardless of the actual number of buttons available, as the equivalent of the Enter key. The right button is often used as the equivalent of the Escape key (south-paws can reverse this by going to the Control Panel, selecting the Mouse icon, and swapping the left and right buttons). When available, the middle button triggers optional short-cuts. If you are using a Logitech or equivalent mouse—one with a third button— the third button is still active, even if none of your applications respond to the middle-button-down (WM_MBUTTONDOWN) messages.

Is There a Mouse in the House?

Although it is usually safe to assume that a mouse is present, for critical applications, it is possible to query the system to ensure that a mouse is present. This task is accomplished using the GetSystemMetrics function, as:

```
if( GetSystemMetrics( SM_MOUSEPRESENT ) ) ...
```

If a mouse is present (and working), GetSystemMetrics will return TRUE; if no mouse is available, GetSystemMetrics will report FALSE. If the result is FALSE, mouse-critical applications can report accordingly.

How an application should respond to the absence of a mouse depends entirely on the application and the importance of mouse support. One possibility is to abort the program execution, as demonstrated in the *Mouse3* demo discussed later in this chapter.

Mouse Actions and Events

Three principal types of mouse actions are possible:

Clicking   Pressing and releasing a mouse button

Double-clicking   Clicking a mouse button twice rapidly

Dragging   Moving the mouse while holding down a mouse button

Other mouse actions may be implemented by an application; these are generally more a feature of the application than a standard mouse activity. For example, instead of dragging an object such as an icon to move it, some applications permit you to simply click once to select it and click again to release it in its new position, without holding down the mouse button. This form (and variations) are popular with many drawing programs and help to reduce mouse-wrist injuries (muscle/tendon strains caused by holding and dragging the mouse in applications requiring fine control for positioning).

Mouse events in Windows are different from mouse events under DOS in several respects:

- In the Windows environment, mouse-button events are not always paired because the environment is shared. For example, a button-down event can occur in one window while the release event is not reported until the mouse has entered another window. In this fashion, the application receives only one of these event messages, and if it depends on receiving both, may malfunction. For an example, see the discussion of the *Mouse2* demo later in this chapter.

- An application in Windows can hold the mouse focus, even after relinquishing the system focus. The application can also continue to receive all mouse messages, even though the mouse is outside the client window area.

- If a system-modal message or dialog box is active in a Windows application, no other application window can receive any mouse messages. System modal messages and dialog boxes prohibit switching to any other window or application until they are exited.

Special circumstances aside, however, there are normally no restrictions or special provisions required for handling mouse-event messages in Windows.

Mouse-Event Messages

A total of 22 mouse-event messages are defined in WinUser.H. Two of these have values duplicating other mouse messages and are apparently intended for internal use (or, perhaps, simply for variety). Of the remaining 20, these messages occur in pairs: one for client window events (mouse events occurring within the application's client window) and a corresponding event message for mouse actions that occur outside the client window. Table 5.1 lists these mouse-event messages and their values.

TABLE 5.1:   Mouse-Event Messages and Values

Client Window Events	Value	Nonclient Window Events	Value
WM_MOUSEMOVE[*]	0x0200	WM_NCMOUSEMOVE	0x00A0
WM_LBUTTONDOWN	0x0201	WM_NCLBUTTONDOWN	0x00A1
WM_LBUTTONUP	0x0202	WM_NCLBUTTONUP	0x00A2
WM_LBUTTONDBLCLK	0x0203	WM_NCLBUTTONDBLCLK	0x00A3
WM_RBUTTONDOWN	0x0204	WM_NCRBUTTONDOWN	0x00A4
WM_RBUTTONUP	0x0205	WM_NCRBUTTONUP	0x00A5
WM_RBUTTONDBLCLK	0x0206	WM_NCRBUTTONDBLCLK	0x00A6
WM_MBUTTONDOWN	0x0207	WM_NCMBUTTONDOWN	0x00A7
WM_MBUTTONUP	0x0208	WM_NCMBUTTONUP	0x00A8
WM_MBUTTONDBLCLK[**]	0x0209	WM_NCMBUTTONDBLCLK	0x00A9

[*]WM_MOUSEFIRST duplicates WM_MOUSEMOVE.

[**]WM_MOUSELAST duplicates WM_MBUTTONDBLCLK.

Normally, mouse-movement and mouse-button messages are reported only while the mouse remains within the application's client window. In these cases, the nonclient window mouse events are not issued to the application. However, there are circumstances where an application will request and track mouse events outside its own immediate jurisdiction; for example, a screen-capture application needs this information.

NOTE Because nonclient mouse messages are relevant only under special circumstances, they are not demonstrated in the examples in this chapter. They will be demonstrated in later chapters dealing with graphics, in Part 4 of this book.

The most important mouse-event messages for most applications are the nine client window mouse-button messages listed in Table 5.2.

TABLE 5.2: Mouse-Button Messages

Button	Pressed	Released	Double-Clicked
Left	WM_LBUTTONDOWN	WM_LBUTTONUP	WM_LBUTTONDBLCLK
Right	WM_RBUTTONDOWN	WM_RBUTTONUP	WM_RBUTTONDBLCLK
Middle	WM_MBUTTONDOWN	WM_MBUTTONUP	WM_MBUTTONDBLCLK

WM_xBUTTONDOWN and WM_xBUTTONUP messages are issued only once—when a mouse button is pressed or released. A WM_xBUTTONDBLCLK message is issued only when a mouse button is rapidly double-clicked (press+release+press). Unlike keyboard events, repeating mouse-button messages are not issued by holding down a mouse button, even though WM_MOUSEMOVE messages are issued for all mouse movements regardless of the button states.

The status of both (or all three) mouse buttons may, however, be retrieved from the information accompanying the WM_MOUSEMOVE message, as explained in the "Mouse Messages Information" section, coming up soon.

Double-Click Messages

Because not all applications require (or desire) double-click event messages, provisions are included in Windows 98 to control whether or not double-click events are reported. These provisions are controlled by the client window's (or child window's) style definition. WM_xxxxDBLCLK messages are generated only if the class style includes the CS_DBLCLKS flag, as in:

```
wc.style = CS_HREDRAW | CS_VREDRAW | CS_DBLCLKS;
```

If the CS_DBLCLKS flag is not set, a double-click is simply received as four separate events: WM_xBUTTONDOWN, WM_xBUTTONUP, WM_xBUTTONDOWN, and WM_xBUTTONUP. However, when CS_DBLCLKS is enabled, a double-click is received as WM_xBUTTONDOWN, WM_xBUTTONUP, WM_xBUTTONDBLCLK, and WM_xBUTTONUP, with the double-click message replacing the second-button-pressed message.

In general, responses to a double-click message are designed as continuations or expansions of single-click responses; before the double-click event is registered, the application has already received a button-pressed/button-released event message pair.

Also, if single- and double-click events are intended to perform quite different tasks, the response processing could become quite complex because the single-click event message will always be received before the double-click event. On the other hand, you can make this work for you.

For example, consider the Windows File Manager's handling of a single-click and a double-click on a subdirectory listing. A single-click changes the active directory; a double-click calls a new directory window displaying the selected directory. The result is that accidental entries perform in very much the same fashion, if not precisely the same, as the intended result.

NOTE   Under Windows 98 (and 95), File Manager is still available; it's in the Windows directory under the filename WinFile.EXE. Windows Explorer works in a quite different fashion than the File Manager example cited here.

Mouse-Movement Messages

Although many applications require only mouse-button event messages, the WM_MOUSEMOVE message is issued every time the mouse moves physically. However, this does not necessarily mean that the mouse has moved on the screen because movement is reported not per screen pixel but per unit of mouse motion.

Rapid mouse movement may cause WM_MOUSEMOVE messages to be reported irregularly. The *Mouse1* demo, discussed later in this chapter, may demonstrate this effect. This effect is produced partially by the accelerator settings, which multiply distances for rapid mouse movements, and partially by the inability of the system to respond to rapid movement events.

With slower mouse movement, the WM_MOUSEMOVE messages will most likely overlap, resulting in more than one message with the same screen coordinates. Overlapping mouse coordinates, however, ensure a solid series of painted screen coordinates.

NOTE   Mouse movement is reported in *mickeys*. (You already know that all programmers are punsters.) A high-resolution mouse reports 200 to 300 mickeys per inch (without acceleration). The speed of movement is reported as mickeys per second. Given the predilection of programmers for puns, it seems a wonder that this API was not named `MouseTrap()`.

Miscellaneous Mouse Messages

Three additional mouse messages are possible, but normally, they are not the direct concern of the application itself and are left to Windows for appropriate handling.

WM_MOUSEACTIVATE   Occurs when the cursor is in an inactive window and any mouse button is pressed.

WM_MOUSEENTER   Occurs when the mouse enters any window.

WM_MOUSELEAVE   Occurs when the mouse leaves any window.

Information in Mouse Messages

Each mouse-event message contains, in addition to the event itself, complete mouse button and Shift- and Ctrl-key status data in the wParam argument (as flag information), and mouse coordinate information in the lParam argument. The status data can be tested as:

```
if( wParam & MK_LBUTTON )...    // left button down
if( wParam & MK_RBUTTON )...    // right button down
if( wParam & MK_MBUTTON )...    // middle button down
if( wParam & MK_CONTROL )...    // Ctrl key pressed
if( wParam & MK_SHIFT )...    // Shift key pressed
```

The mouse coordinate information is in client-window pixel coordinates relative to the upper-left corner. As mentioned previously, this information is found in the lParam argument, with the x-coordinate in the low-order word and the y-coordinate in the high-order word. You can use the MAKEPOINTW macro to convert the lParam argument to a POINTW structure.

The Mouse1 Demo: Tracking the Mouse

The *Mouse1* demo demonstrates how WM_MOUSEMOVE messages are tracked. It plots a single pixel at the coordinates reported with each message received. Plotting is toggled on and off by the left mouse button. Plotting begins with one WM_LBUTTONDOWN message and ends with the next WM_LBUTTONDOWN message. For this example, only the WM_MOUSEMOVE and WM_LBUTTONDOWN messages are provided with responses.

The WM_LBUTTONDOWN message is used to toggle the fPaint variable by XORing fPaint and 1, flipping the value from TRUE to FALSE and vice versa. The value of fPaint was initialized as zero (0).

```
case WM_LBUTTONDOWN:
    fPaint ^= 1;
    MessageBeep(0);
    break;
```

As a minor bonus, the MessageBeep function is called to provide audio feedback. You can call MessageBeep with a zero argument, although this argument is simply the equivalent of MB_OK and produces the system default sound. Other options are listed in Table 5.3.

TABLE 5.3: MessageBeep Arguments

Argument	Sound
0xFFFFFFFF	Standard beep using the computer speaker
MB_ICONASTERISK	SystemAsterisk
MB_ICONEXCLAMATION	SystemExclamation
MB_ICONHAND	SystemHand
MB_ICONQUESTION	SystemQuestion
MB_OK	SystemDefault

The second response to the WM_MOUSEMOVE message depends on the current value in fPaint (TRUE or FALSE). It extracts the mouse's window coordinates from lParam and paints a single black pixel.

```
case WM_MOUSEMOVE:
    if( fPaint )
    {
        hdc = GetDC( hwnd );
        SetPixel( hdc, LOWORD( lParam ), HIWORD( lParam ), OL );
        ReleaseDC( hwnd, hdc );
    }
    break;
```

For tracking mouse movements, this method is sufficient. However, pay particular attention to how different rates of movement affect the dot spacing.

NOTE   The *Mouse1* demo is included on the CD accompanying this book, in the Chapter 5 folder.

The Mouse Cursor

Chapter 4 explained how the text pointer is now known as the *caret*, and the term *cursor* is now the property of the mouse pointer. And, while the mouse pointer points at a single pixel rather than a character cell position, the cursor proper is a bitmapped image that is tracked across the display while preserving the background image. One pixel location within this cursor image is known as the *hot spot*, which is the actual pointer location tracked.

Windows 98 provides 14 predefined cursor images, which are listed in Table 5.4. By default, Windows uses the slanted arrow (IDC_ARROW). Individual applications are free to define any of these standard cursors as their own default cursor. (Most of the applications discussed in this book follow Windows 98 in using the slanted arrow default.)

TABLE 5.4:   Windows Predefined Cursor Shapes

Cursor	Description
IDC_APPSTARTING	A standard arrow and small hourglass combination; used to show that an application is opening
IDC_ARROW	An arrow pointing diagonally up and left; the familiar default cursor
IDC_CROSS	A simple horizontal/vertical cross
IDC_IBEAM	An I-beam cursor; commonly used for word processing
IDC_ICON	An empty shape that can be used to hide the cursor; i.e., no cursor image (*obsolete*)
IDC_NO	An international negative; i.e., a circle with a diagonal slash
IDC_SIZE	*Obsolete,* see IDC_SIZEALL
IDC_SIZEALL	Four arrows, pointing in the four cardinal directions (up, down, left, and right)
IDC_SIZENESW	A tilted double-arrow, pointing diagonally up to the right (NE) and down to the left (SW)
IDC_SIZENS	A double-arrow, pointing up and down
IDC_SIZENWSE	A tilted double-arrow, pointing diagonally up to the left (NW) and down to the right (SE)
IDC_SIZEWE	A double-arrow pointing left and right
IDC_UPARROW	Similar to the default cursor, an arrow pointing directly up
IDC_WAIT	An hourglass, or wait, symbol

WARNING   While both the IDC_SIZE and IDC_SIZEALL cursors are documented as producing the identical four-pointed arrow, the IDC_SIZE cursor is now obsolete. For reliability, use IDC_SIZEALL instead.

Regardless of what the default cursor is, applications are free to change cursors at any time, as appropriate to specific tasks or to window areas. They also may define their own custom cursors. The predefined cursor shapes (see Table 5.4) are illustrated in the *Mouse2* demo.

The Mouse2 Demo: Mouse Cursor Shapes

As shown in Figure 5.1, the *Mouse2* demo subdivides the application client window into child windows, each appearing as a simple outline with a white background. These child windows are secondary to the principal purposes of the example, which are to demonstrate the predefined mouse cursor shapes supplied by Windows 98 and show how the mouse cursor is changed by the application. However, you must create and manage these child windows for the example, as described here. (See Chapter 6 for more details about child windows and control elements.)

FIGURE 5.1:

The Mouse2 demo shows multiple cursor shapes

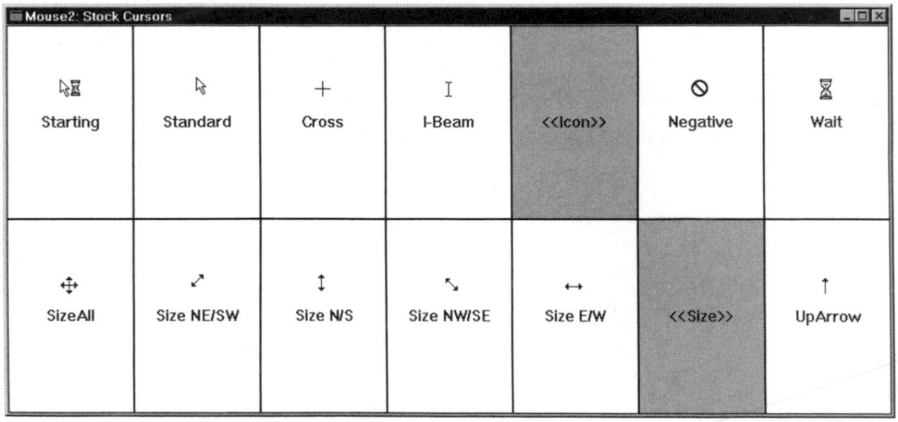

Mouse2: Stock Cursors						_ □ ×
Starting	Standard	Cross	I-Beam	«Icon»	Negative	Wait
SizeAll	Size NE/SW	Size N/S	Size NW/SE	Size E/W	«Size»	UpArrow

---

NOTE The *Mouse2* demo is included on the CD accompanying this book, in the Chapter 5 folder.

Creating the Child Windows

To create the child windows for *Mouse2*, the first step occurs in the WinMain procedure. After registering the window class in WinMain, the InitApplication subprocedure is called from the Template.I include file. This subprocedure is then used to make another local set of wc assignments to register the child classes.

```
if( ! hPrevInstance )
{
   if( ! InitApplication( hInstance ) )
      return( FALSE );
   //*** also register child window class ***//
   wc.style         = CS_HREDRAW | CS_VREDRAW;
   wc.cbClsExtra    = 0;
   wc.cbWndExtra    = 0;
   wc.hInstance     = hInstance;
   wc.hbrBackground = GetStockObject( LTGRAY_BRUSH );
   wc.lpszMenuName  = NULL;
   wc.lpfnWndProc   = ChildWndProc;
   wc.hIcon         = NULL;
   wc.hCursor       = NULL;            // essential!!! //
   wc.lpszClassName = szChildClass;
   RegisterClass( &wc );
}
```

This code includes the three critical wc assignments:

- The pointer to the ChildWndProc

- The assignment of the hCursor field as NULL

- The class name, which is a string defined at the beginning of the source code, following the fashion used for the main window class

After you have registered the child class, the main window is created, as usual, by calling the InitInstance subprocedure and then entering the message loop. Remember, however, that at this point, only the main window instance has been created; the child window class has been registered, but no instances of this class yet exist.

The actual child windows are created in the WndProc procedure, where an array of handles are defined as:

```
static HWND hwndChild[7][2];
```

These child window handles are defined as a static array of handles because the values assigned must remain, even when the application exits from this local procedure. Any nonstatic data may be overwritten between messages. This is fine for temporary variables, but the child window handles, once assigned by the Create-Window function call, must be preserved.

The WM_CREATE message is only issued once—when the application is first created. Therefore, 14 child window instances are created at this time, each returning a handle, which is stored in the hwndChild array.

```
case WM_CREATE:
    for( x=0; x<7; x++ )
        for( y=0; y<2; y++ )
            hwndChild[x][y] =
                CreateWindow( szChildClass,
                    NULL, WS_CHILDWINDOW | WS_VISIBLE,
                    0, 0, 0, 0, hwnd,
            (HMENU)  ( x | ( y << 8 ) ),
            (HANDLE) GetWindowLong( hwnd, GWL_HINSTANCE ),
            (LPVOID) NULL );
```

Here, there are three principal differences between the operation for the child window and the corresponding operation for the parent (application) window:

- Each child window is created using the hwnd handle identifying the parent window. For the parent, the corresponding argument was NULL.

- Each child window requires an ID value that must be unique within this application. In this case, the ID is generated as a word value ($x | y << 8$) and is typecast using the HMENU data type. Although HMENU is not the data type you might expect for a window ID, the CreateWindow function is also used to create menus, and this is the type definition expected in the function declaration. The equivalent HWND type will also work, but it will result in a warning message from the Microsoft C++ compiler. The corresponding ID values will be needed in ChildWndProc to identify specific child windows.

- The child window instance parameter is supplied by calling the GetWindow-Long function with the GWL_HINSTANCE argument. When the application's client window was initialized, Windows had supplied this argument as the hInstance parameter passed to the WinMain procedure. But now, 12 separate and unique instance handles are needed, and they must be supplied by Windows, indirectly or directly.

NOTE   In Windows 3.1, the child window instance parameter is supplied by calling the GetWindowWord function with the GWW_HINSTANCE argument.

There are other differences as well, such as the absence of window titles (identified as NULL) and the differences in the style flag, but these will vary depending on the style and type of child windows desired.

Also, these windows have all been created with both size and position set at zero. While the same was done for the main client window, the main window is sized automatically. The child windows, however, will not be defined as a style that will receive WM_SIZE messages. Therefore, to size and space these dozen children, a provision is required to accomplish this anytime the main client window's size changes.

Ergo, in response to the WM_SIZE message, the WndProc procedure begins by using the current window size in the high and low words in lParam:

```
case WM_SIZE:
    cxWin = LOWORD( lParam ) / 5;
    cyWin = HIWORD( lParam ) / 2;
    for( x=0; x<7; x++ )
        for( y=0; y<2; y++ )
            MoveWindow( hwndChild[x][y], x * cxWin, y * cyWin,
                        cxWin, cyWin, TRUE );
    break;
```

Once cxWin and cyWin hold the appropriate size and spacing for each child window, a double loop calls the MoveWindow function using the handles in the hwndChild array and sizes and positions each.

Operating the Cursor in the Child Windows

As the mouse moves from one child window to another in the *Mouse2* demo, the mouse cursor image changes for each window. To accomplish this, however, a bit of subterfuge is required. Initially, when the child window style was registered, the cursor was declared NULL, affecting all instances of the child class.

Now, as the mouse moves, each WM_MOUSEMOVE message is directed to whichever child window the mouse happens to occupy, and the response sets the mouse cursor shape appropriate to that child window. However, there is only one ChildWnd-Proc to handle responses for all of the child windows. To assign the appropriate cursor, the WM_MOUSEMOVE response requires one additional piece of information—which child window is currently being handled.

The WM_MOUSEMOVE response begins with an inquiry to retrieve the child window ID, as:

```
case WM_MOUSEMOVE:
    switch( GetWindowLong( hwnd, GWL_ID ) )
    {
```

Once the child window ID is known, the switch/case statement can branch to the appropriate response, as:

```
case 0x0000:
    SetCursor( LoadCursor( NULL, IDC_APPSTARTING ) );
    break;
...
case 0x0106:
    SetCursor( LoadCursor( NULL, IDC_WAIT ) );
    break;
```

Remember, the child window IDs were assigned using the formula $(x\,|\,(y<<8))$, but here it's simpler to just assign the appropriate constants, especially because formulas are not permitted as case statement IDs. Alternatively, a series of mnemonics could have been declared, but this is simple enough for demo purposes.

In the *Mouse2* demo, anytime you press the left (or primary) mouse button, the cursor will shift to the default arrow cursor. Likewise, anytime you press the right (or secondary) mouse button, the mouse cursor will be hidden until the button is released.

Also, the changing cursors are assigned (loaded) only in response to a mouse movement. Once the selected cursor has been replaced by the default cursor, the selected cursor is reloaded only when another mouse-movement message is received. To avoid this type of interruption, the mouse-button messages also need to be handled to ensure that the desired mouse cursor is shown.

Hiding the mouse cursor might be the simplest task of all. It requires only the ShowCursor function and an argument specifying whether the cursor is to be hidden or visible.

In Chapter 4, the ShowCaret and HideCaret functions were used in a similar fashion to hide and reveal the text caret. In that discussion, I mentioned that you could encounter a problem with multiple show or hide calls because they require equal occurrences of their counterparts before any action occurs.

The same holds true for the ShowCursor function, except that instead of a corresponding HideCursor function, ShowCursor accepts a TRUE or FALSE argument. However, if the ShowCursor(FALSE) function is called and the mouse is then moved to another child window before a ShowCursor(TRUE) call is made, a different problem may occur: The mouse cursor may not be visible again—at least not until you leave the application window entirely.

To prevent either problem from occurring, a Boolean variable, Visible, has been declared. This variable holds the current state of the mouse cursor, and ShowCursor(FALSE) is only permitted if Visible is TRUE and vice versa. A similar solution, if needed, can be applied to the ShowCaret/HideCaret functions.

There's also a second solution. The ShowCursor function returns the new display count resulting from the operation, and the cursor is hidden any time the count is negative and shown whenever the count is zero or higher; therefore, the following code lines will increment or decrement the show count until the appropriate value is reached:

```
while( ShowCursor(FALSE) >= 0 );      // hides cursor
while( ShowCursor(TRUE)  <  0 );      // reveals cursor
```

> **NOTE** As an alternative to using predefined cursors, you can include custom cursors in your application. See Chapter 8 for details.

The Mouse3 Demo: Hit Testing

 The *Mouse3* demo demonstrates how mouse-click events are registered. It uses a simple cruciform game field, which responds to both the left and right mouse buttons by displaying, respectively, an X or O. Figure 5.2 illustrates the game field.

> **NOTE** The "game" using this board was originally devised by a young lady of ten. She came up with a rather complex set of rules that, you may be properly relieved to know, are not implemented here.

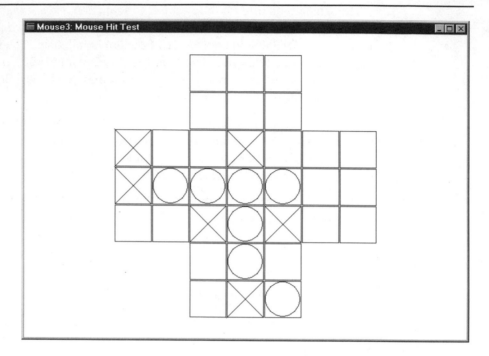

The actual grid is a 7×7 array, with four elements from each corner flagged as invalid and, therefore, not included in the paint operations. Each remaining grid element has a corresponding integer flag, which is set to 0 initially.

To demonstrate mouse-hit testing, the location of each WM_LBUTTONDOWN and WM_RBUTTONDOWN message is tested against the grid coordinates and then shifted according to the original state and the button clicked before invalidating the specific grid. Conversely, any mouse clicks that fall outside the grid area or on an array element flagged as invalid produce a warning beep.

As for playing the game, feel free to invent your own rules.

NOTE   The *Mouse3* demo is included on the CD accompanying this book, in the Chapter 5 folder.

In addition to handling mouse-event messages, the three programs discussed in this chapter demonstrate all the principal mouse operations within the client-window area: tracking the mouse, changing the mouse cursor, and testing mouse hits. Because mouse operations are integral to any Windows application, they will continue to be discussed in later chapter. But for now, we'll leave that topic and turn to some other basic elements of Windows applications, which we touched on briefly in this chapter: child windows and control elements.

Child Windows and Control Elements

- Types of window controls

- Control button styles

- Control button grouping

- Button event messages

You've already seen examples using child windows. In Chapter 5, two of the programs we discussed included child windows: one to demonstrate different system cursors, and another to respond to mouse-button events by displaying either crosses or circles in child windows.

Generically, child window controls are windows that process mouse and keyboard messages. They handle their own responses appropriately and notify the parent window in some suitable fashion as necessary when a control changes the child window's state (for example, a different radio button has been chosen or a scrollbar has been adjusted).

As you will be reassured to know, you can normally accomplish these tasks without the need for the elaborate provisions shown in the ChildWndProc procedures in the demo programs in Chapter 5. Instead, the usual child windows are predefined window classes, several of which will be demonstrated in this chapter and all of which will be demonstrated in future chapters.

Before moving on to Part 2, where you'll learn about an easier way of using window control elements, you need to understand how child windows are handled using direct, rather than indirect, interactions, which is the topic of this chapter.

The Programmer and Child Window Controls

The real use of child windows is in the form of child window controls, although they are not usually referred to as such. Instead, child window controls are commonly referred to by their functions: as buttons, checkboxes, radio buttons, edit boxes, list boxes, scrollbars, and so on.

NOTE   We've talked about scrollbars in earlier chapters, but only in one of their many possible forms. As you will see later, scrollbars can be used for a variety of purposes other than scrolling windows.

If you are familiar with Windows, you've already encountered a wide variety of Windows control elements and know how convenient they are for the user.

Equally important is just how convenient these control elements are for the programmer. The program (and, therefore, the programmer) does not need to be concerned with the mouse driver and mouse-button logic or with any of the other myriad details involved in using these controls, such as making control buttons change state or adjusting scrollbars when they are dragged. Instead, as the programmer, you are free to use them "as is," as the end user does.

As a programmer, the extent of your involvement is simple. You just define the control elements needed and the appropriate responses—and then wait. When a control is activated, a `WM_COMMAND` message is returned, together with additional information identifying which control and, if appropriate, specifics about the state of the control.

For example, in the *Mouse2* demo (discussed in Chapter 5), a child window class is defined and registered (in this case, in the `WinMain` procedure). Then, in the `WndProc` procedure, this child window class is initiated, as individual instances, using the `CreateWindow` function before positioning and sizing each using the `MoveWindow` function.

The *Button1* and *Button2* demos described in this chapter use a similar process, calling the `CreateWindow` function to create instances of predefined classes before positioning and sizing each using the `MoveWindow` function. For the predefined window classes, such as buttons and scrollbars, the process becomes much simpler. For these window controls, the classes and their responses are already defined, programmed, and compiled, and they are available simply as library functions.

The third demo described in this chapter, *Button3*, duplicates the codes returned by the child window controls, but uses MFC to create a dialog box–based application and introduces a wider variety of button styles.

Control Button Types

Windows provides three principal types of control buttons: pushbuttons, checkboxes, and radio buttons. Figure 6.1 shows several examples of each of these three types.

FIGURE 6.1:

Standard button
control styles

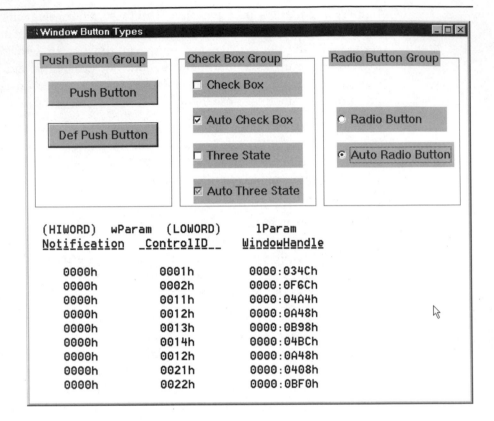

Another child window type also appears in Figure 6.1. A *group box* contains each
of the sets of examples. However, group boxes do not respond to mouse events or
issue WM_COMMAND messages. They are used only to visually group other control
elements (with or without group labels).

Because these child window buttons are "drawn" on a regular white window
background, rather than on the half-tone gray background common to dialog
boxes, here the controls appear unfinished. Because the purpose is to demonstrate messages from child windows, the incomplete appearance shouldn't
detract from the buttons' functions. (For a more polished version, see the discussion of the *Button3* demo, later in the chapter.)

Pushbutton Styles

Generic pushbutton controls are rectangular boxes that have a centered text label and an outline simulating a raised button (3-D shading). When activated, such as by a mouse click, the outline changes to simulate a button that has been physically depressed. This type of control button is commonly used to initiate immediate actions, without retaining or displaying any continuing status information.

For control buttons, the entire active area is enclosed by the button image, although the control button may be any size desired. Two types of pushbutton controls are predefined:

BS_PUSHBUTTON A control button displaying an optional text label. The pushbutton posts a message to the parent window when activated, while briefly changing state to simulate being physically pressed.

BS_DEFPUSHBUTTON A control button similar to the BS_PUSHBUTTON control, but with a heavy border. This button represents the default response and normally accepts the Enter key as equivalent to being pressed. (The heavy border represents the control that currently has the focus.)

NOTE   Another Windows button type, BS_PUSHBOX, was defined previously in Windows 3.x. The BS_PUSHBOX style appeared initially as only a text label without a button outline. When selected, the button outline appeared (as per BS_PUSHBUTTON) and the label was highlighted; it remained so until another pushbutton or control was selected and the input focus was lost.

Checkbox Styles

Checkboxes are small squares with text labels appearing to the right by default (but you can change them to the left with BS_LEFTTEXT, as explained in the "Special

Controls and Modifiers" section). The checked state is shown by a checkmark (or by an *X* in MFC) in the box.

Although the box element of the checkbox is fixed in size, the active area, including the optional label, can be any size desired (within practical limits). To select the button, the user can click the mouse anywhere within the checkbox window, not just on the checkbox proper, whether or not the region is visibly delineated.

Four checkbox styles are defined:

BS_CHECKBOX A checkbox that displays a bold border when the button is checked. The button state must be set by the owner (application) and is not displayed automatically.

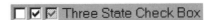

BS_AUTOCHECKBOX The same as BS_CHECKBOX, except that the button state is automatically toggled when selected or deselected.

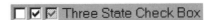

BS_3STATE The same as BS_CHECKBOX, except that three states can be selected: clear, checked, or grayed. The button state must be set by the owner (application) and is not displayed automatically.

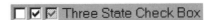

NOTE The grayed state is typically used to show that a checkbox has been disabled.

BS_AUTO3STATE The same as BS_3STATE, except that the checkbox automatically steps through the three states in clear, checked, gray-checked order (unless otherwise explicitly set by the application). In the third state, the checked state appears as a dark gray checkmark (or, using MFC, an *X*) against a lighter gray square.

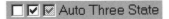

The state (setting) of any of these checkbox controls can be queried or set directly using the mouse.

Radio Button Styles

Radio buttons are small, circular buttons with optional text labels that appear to the immediate right by default (like checkbox labels, radio button labels can also be displayed on the left using BS_LEFTTEXT, as explained in the next section).

By custom and intention, radio button controls are used as groups representing mutually exclusive choices. Only one button in a group can be selected at any time. A set radio button is shown with a solid center. Selecting a radio button a second time (once it has been chosen) does not change the button status. Normally, a default or initial choice is selected when the group is initially displayed.

TIP   MFC also offers the option of creating radio buttons without mutual exclusivity—the equivalent of placing each radio button in its own group.

Two styles of radio buttons include:

BS_RADIOBUTTON A radio button that displays a bold outline when clicked, but does not display a set condition or clear set condition until explicitly directed by the owner (application).

Radio Button

BS_AUTORADIOBUTTON The same as BS_RADIOBUTTON, except when a button in a group is selected, a BM_CLICKED message notifies the application, the selected button is set automatically, and all other auto radio buttons in the group are cleared automatically. Any non-auto radio buttons within the group will not be affected without explicit instructions from the application.

Auto Radio Button

The state (setting) of either type of radio button control can be queried directly by the application or can be explicitly set as required.

Special Controls and Modifiers

Three additional BS_*xxxx* button types are defined for special purposes:

BS_OWNERDRAW This designates an owner-drawn button, but it does not provide any type of image or response. Instead, the parent window is notified when the button is clicked and is expected to supply provisions to paint, invert, and/or disable the button using application-supplied bitmap images.

BS_GROUPBOX This designates a rectangle used to visually group other buttons with or without an optional label that will be displayed in the rectangle's upper-left corner. The position and size for the group box must be specified appropriately to enclose the controls or area desired. The group box does not respond to mouse events or return any WM_COMMAND messages. (Figure 6.1, shown earlier, includes three group boxes.)

BS_LEFTTEXT This designates a flag used in combination with the BS_CHECKBOX, BS_RADIOBUTTON, or BS_3STATE style to shift the label to the left of the checkbox or button. This flag is not valid with pushbuttons.

Radio #4 ⊙

The Button1 and Button2 Demos: Button Operations

The button operations demonstrated in the *Button1* and *Button2* demos are less flexible than the usual standards typified by dialog-box button operations, because the only provisions included for these child window operations are to respond to the mouse. No provisions have been made to permit control selections using the Tab or cursor keys, nor do any of these, including the default pushbutton, respond to the Enter key.

Likewise, except for the BS_AUTOCHECKBOX, BS_AUTO3STATE, and BS_AUTORADIO-BUTTON styles, none of the controls demonstrated display any change of state beyond the immediate selection "flash" when clicked with the mouse.

Although this is not obvious in either demo, the child window controls demonstrated can obtain the input focus when selected with the mouse. However, they do not subsequently release the input focus to the parent window.

When selected, any of the buttons demonstrated send a WM_COMMAND message to the parent window. In the *Button1* demo, this message is displayed in a table below the buttons as a breakdown of the wParam and lParam arguments. (You can see this in Figure 6.1, shown earlier in the chapter.) The table shows (from left to right):

- The notification value (high word in wParam)
- The child window (control) ID (low word in wParam)
- The child window handle value (lParam)

You will learn all about notification values in the section "Button Control Communications: A Two-Way Channel," later in this chapter.

The *Button1* and *Button2* demos are included on the CD that accompanies this book, in the Chapter 6 folder.

Using CreateWindow for Buttons

The individual control buttons are generated using the same CreateWindow function that we have used to create an application's client window and, in Chapter 5, to create a series of child windows. This time, however, the CreateWindow function is going to be used in a somewhat unusual fashion—to create sets of buttons grouped together by a BM_GROUPBOX child window.

The parameters used in calling CreateWindow for this purpose are defined as:

lpszClassName ASCIIZ character string identifying the window class. This class may be a predefined window class or a registered custom class. Note that an error in this field does not cause a compiler error but will not allow an erroneous class object to be displayed.

lpszWindowText Pointer to an ASCIIZ character string, providing a label for the button or control.

dwStyle Double-word style identifier, which uses the predefined window and control styles.

x Integer specifying the initial x-axis position of the button class (relative to the parent window origin).

y Integer specifying the initial y-axis position of the button class (relative to the parent window origin).

nWidth Integer value specifying the control button width (in device units).

nHeight Integer value specifying the control button height (in device units).

hWndParent Parameter that identifies the parent window (owner) of the window or control being created.

hMenu Unique value identifying the child window (in other circumstances this value may identify a menu belonging to the window; the meaning depends on the style definition). Notice that the values used for this field are always cast as HMENU types, regardless of their intended function. This cast is necessary to prevent a compiler warning but does not affect the actual operation.

hInstance Parameter that identifies the instance creating the window or control.

lpParam Pointer used to address extra parameters or, in the *Button1* demo, to chain a series of window controls. The chain is terminated by passing the final lpParam argument as NULL.

The actual code is rather unwieldy, making the chain structure of these grouped controls difficult to follow. Therefore, the following list omits most of the parameter arguments in favor of illustrating the links in the declarations.

```
hwndGroup =
  CreateWindow
    ( ... , ... , ... , ... , ... ,
      ... , ... , hwnd, ... , ... ,
    CreateWindow
      ( ... , ... , ... , ... , ... ,
        ... , ... , hwnd, ... , ... ,
```

```
                    CreateWindow
                    (  ... , ... , ... , ... , ... ,
                       ... , ... , hwnd, ... , ... ,
                       CreateWindow
                       (  ... , ... , ... , ... , ... ,
                          ... , ... , hwnd, ... , ... ,
                          CreateWindow
                          (  ... , ... , ... , ... , ... ,
                             ... , ... , hwnd, ... , ... ,
                             NULL
    )  )  )  )  )
```

In this diagrammatic example, the `hwndGroup` contains five control window elements that are chained together in the declaration. The topmost element in this group is the declaration for the group box itself (though this is not an iron-clad requirement), while the first control button appears as the eleventh parameter in the group-box declaration, and so forth.

While there are no firm limits—memory and system limits aside—on such recursive declarations, this programming style is awkward. It may appear to produce a result that is not actually accomplished; contrary to what the structure seems to suggest, these control buttons are not grouped by the group box except visually, both on screen and in the program.

Grouping Controls

Grouping is not accomplished by the declaration tree (nor by the screen appearance). Instead, a group is declared by first calling `CreateWindow` to create the group box window and then by using the group-box handle (`hwndGroup`) as the owner of the group members when these are declared.

In the tree shown previously, all the elements in the declaration tree used the same parent window handle—that of the client window—by necessity.

In contrast, the *Button2* demo actually does create groups with member controls that are declared and created in the appropriate fashion, even if this is less elaborate.

Here is the *Button2* code in skeleton format:

```
hwndPB[0] =
    CreateWindow
    ( ... , ... , BS_GROUPBOX, ... ,
      ... , ... , ... , hwnd,
      ... , ... , NULL );
for( i=1; i<4; i++ )
    hwndPB[i] =
        CreateWindow
        ( ... , ... , BS_xxcontrolxx, ... ,
          ... , ... , ... , hwndPB[0],
          ... , ... , NULL );
```

Here, the first step returns a handle to the group box control, which has the application's client window as a parent/owner. This handle is then used, in the second step within the loop, to provide the parent/owner for the individual control instances. This format creates four child window controls. These controls belong to the group box and, therefore, are isolated from other controls—a necessary requirement for auto radio buttons, for example.

However, there's still a fly in the ointment! Why? Because this format, while satisfactory for the present demo purposes, is still not practical for general applications.

While the parent window, hwndPB[0], is a group box and does receive messages from the child window processes, it has no provisions to act on these messages and cannot forward them to any other process for action. Ergo, the only actions and responses in the *Button2* demo are those inherent in the button classes themselves.

The real solution is also quite simple and is used, in part, in the *Mouse2* and *Mouse3* demos (discussed in Chapter 5), when child window processes were first introduced. If you recall, in addition to creating the child windows used in the programs (refer particularly to *Mouse3*), a subprocess was also created with provisions to respond to messages from the child window. Thus, to use button controls in the fashion illustrated, the group box—whether it's visible or invisible—or another child window process serving as a parent to the controls would be created in similar fashion, complete with the appropriate responses to handle messages from the child window controls (the buttons).

Now, having been lead through this maze of complexity, you can proceed to forget about it—at least for the present—because your applications, and the examples discussed in later chapters, will use a quite different process to create these and other control elements. For the most part, you will create control elements by using dialog boxes and dialog box editors, not directly within the application code. Be assured, this is a much simpler, as well as a much more practical, route.

Before leaving this topic altogether, there are other aspects of child window controls that will be relevant, regardless of how the controls are created.

Controlling Button Communications: A Two-Way Channel

Although auto checkboxes and auto radio buttons change their state automatically when clicked, you need to be able to set initial states for checkboxes and radio buttons—for both the normal and automatic versions. At the same time, you need to be able to accept notifications from these (and other) controls and to query the status of these controls. These tasks are handled by sending messages to controls and recognizing messages generated by controls, as well as by setting initial states for the controls.

The *Button1* demo demonstrates how event messages are received from the button control elements as WM_COMMAND messages with amplifying data in the lParam and wParam arguments. The lParam argument, which will generally be ignored, contains the window identifier for the child window control. More immediately important is the wParam argument, which, in the low-order word, reports the control ID assigned by the application when the control was created.

The notification code in the high-order word of wParam informs the parent process precisely what event occurred. This notification code consists of one of the six values shown in Table 6.1.

TABLE 6.1:   User Button Notification Codes

Code Constant	Value
BN_CLICKED	0
BN_PAINT	1
BN_HILITE	2
BN_UNHILITE	3
BN_DISABLE	4
BN_DOUBLECLICKED	5

The *Button1* demo returns only two event types: 0 or 5. The second of these, BN_DOUBLECLICKED is only returned by the BS_RADIOBUTTON style control (but not by the BS_AUTORADIOBUTTON style control). Control notifications 1 through 4 are returned only by custom control buttons (not illustrated in this chapter) to prompt the parent application to take the appropriate action (if any) to update the control's image.

Sending Messages to Controls

The *Button2* demo demonstrates four group boxes containing groups of child button controls. Unlike in the *Button1* demo, these group boxes are actually parents to the controls enclosed. Because of this, setting an auto radio button in one group will not affect settings in another group, but it will reset other buttons in the same group, as you will see.

The *Button2* demo also demonstrates other aspects involving messages sent from the application to the control buttons. Five button-specific messages are defined in WinUser.H, each beginning with the prefix BM_ (for "button message"), as listed in Table 6.2.

TABLE 6.2: Button Control Messages

Code Constant	Value
BM_GETCHECK	00F0h
BM_SETCHECK	00F1h
BM_GETSTATE	00F2h
BM_SETSTATE	00F3h
BM_SETSTYLE	00F4h

NOTE   In Windows 3.*x*, the corresponding message values were defined as WM_USER+0 through WM_USER+4. However, if the defined message constants are used, no conversion will be required to move applications from Windows 3.*x* to Windows 98.

The BM_SETCHECK and BM_GETCHECK messages are sent by the parent window to a child window control button to, respectively, retrieve or set the check state of checkboxes and radio buttons (use with normal, auto, and three-state versions). In *Button2,* the BM_SETCHECK message sets three of the checkboxes in the Check-Boxes group, three of the auto radio buttons in the RadioButtons 1 group, and one of the radio buttons in the RadioButtons 2 group. Figure 6.2 shows the *Button2* display.

FIGURE 6.2:

Grouped control buttons

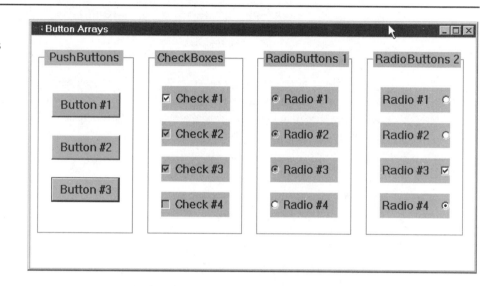

The display in the RadioButtons 1 group, with three auto radio buttons checked, is definitely anomalous and can only occur (short of bad programming) because of the explicit settings made by the application. Clicking any of the buttons in this group will correct the situation shown. The BM_SETCHECK message was sent as:

```
SendMessage( hwnd...., BM_SETCHECK, TRUE, 0L );
```

Conversely, to clear the check state of a button, another message would be sent as:

```
SendMessage( hwnd...., BM_SETCHECK, FALSE, 0L );
```

The first parameter is the child window (control button) handle, followed by the message identifier with the third parameter setting or clearing the flag state. The fourth parameter is unused and is passed as zero.

The BM_SETSTATE message is used to simulate the button flash that occurs when a button is clicked with the mouse or otherwise activated. In Figure 6.2, three of the checkboxes (shown with heavy outlines) have received BM_SETSTATE messages, which were sent in the same fashion as the BM_SETCHECK messages.

The third "set" message provides a means of changing the control button style during execution. *Button2* demonstrates this with two examples.

First, the BM_SETSTYLE message is used to change the style of the third (bottom) pushbutton from BS_PUSHBUTTON to BS_DEFPUSHBUTTON as:

```
SendMessage( hwndPB[3], BM_SETSTYLE,
             BStyle | BS_DEFPUSHBUTTON, 1L );
```

Unlike the earlier set messages, the BM_SETSTYLE message does use the fourth parameter, passing a nonzero argument to request that the control be redrawn immediately, using the new style settings. A zero argument leaves the control unchanged until some other circumstance causes the control to be redrawn.

Second, one more BM_SETSTYLE message is sent to change the style of the third radio button in the RadioButtons 2 group to a checkbox, but, at the same time, the message does not incorporate the BS_LEFTTEXT flag originally used with all controls in this group. As a result, the newly styled control button behaves precisely like any other checkbox but remains a member of the RadioButtons 2 group.

Querying Control States

The BM_GETCHECK and BM_GETSTATE messages are sent as information requests directed to specific button controls. They return the check or state status as TRUE if the button is checked or depressed (that is, the state flag is set) or FALSE if the appropriate flag is clear. As an example, the following instruction retrieves the check status:

```
fStatus = SendMessage( hwnd..., BM_GETCHECK, 0, 0L );
```

In this inquiry, only two parameters are relevant: the handle identifying the control element and the BM_GETCHECK message.

On the other hand, if the only requirement is to flip the state of a button or checkbox, you can combine the BM_GETCHECK and BM_SETCHECK instructions as:

```
SendMessage( hwnd..., BM_SETCHECK,
         (WORD)SendMessage( hwnd...,
                            BM_GETCHECK, 0, 0L), 0L );
```

However, this latter form is generally not required because the BM_AUTO*xxxxx* styles obviate the need for the application to handle the button state directly.

Changing Button (Window) Labels

One item that applications may wish to change on buttons and controls of all types—whether to present a different series of selections or to update other information types—are the button labels. This also applies to window captions and the window text for any window type. The `SetWindowText` function is written as:

```
SetWindowText( hwnd, lpszString );
```

The `hwnd` parameter identifies the window, and the string argument is passed as a long or far pointer to an ASCIIZ string. Button labels are constrained to a single line of text and line wrapping is not allowed.

TIP

You can create a multiline button using a static text field for the button text and omitting text entirely from the button. The disadvantage of this approach, of course, would be that the user would need to click the button itself—clicking the text would not set the button. This is true unless the application included additional code to recognize a hit on the separate label and to issue a button message in response.

At the same time, you can retrieve the current text label from any window type using the `GetWindowText` function, as:

```
nLen = GetWindowText( hwnd, &Buff, sizeof( Buff ) );
```

Obviously, the buffer must be large enough to hold the string information returned. The third parameter places a limit on the length copied. The value returned directly to `nLen` is the actual length copied.

If the length is unknown, the `GetWindowTextLength` function can be called as:

```
nLen = GetWindowTextLength( hwnd );
```

A More Elaborate Version: Button3

Figure 6.3 shows the *Button3* demo, which, like *Button1*, reports the event messages produced when the various buttons are pressed. Unlike the earlier version, however, this variation uses a dialog box–based application window, where the various buttons appear against the appropriate background.

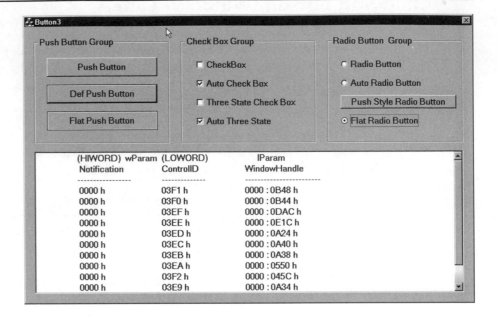

In addition to providing a more complete demo, *Button3* also demonstrates three additional button styles:

- The flat pushbutton
- The push-style radio button
- The flat radio button

These styles are provided by MFC; they are not included in the standard defined button styles.

NOTE The *Button3* demo is included on the CD that accompanies this book, in the Chapter 6 folder.

Now that you've finished this chapter, you may be tempted to simply forget almost all of it since these tasks can be accomplished in a simpler fashion. However, whether you use these forms directly or not, a clear understanding of how applications use child window controls is still, if not essential, certainly very valuable. After all, it isn't what you don't know that hurts half as much as what you think you know but actually don't.

In Part 1, you've seen the mechanisms from the inside; in Part 2, you will look at these same mechanisms (and others) from a higher (and easier to implement) level.

PART 2

Windows 98 Application Resources

CHAPTER

SEVEN

7

An Introduction to Application Resources

- Types of application resources

- Types of resource files

- Resource manager functions

Resources in Windows applications appear as a variety of elements. These elements range from text-based menus, to dialog box displays combining graphic and text elements, to purely graphic elements that include bitmaps, cursors, and icons. Each individual application may use many or all of these elements. For example, an application might include multiple menus and dialog boxes, dozens of bitmaps, and assortments of cursors representing different operations or modes.

In theory, resource elements can be created as part of an application's conventional executable code. Under DOS, this was essentially what was required. Windows, however, provides a different structural approach for executables. The approach used by Windows permits resources to be appended to an application's executable without being embedded within the operational portion of the program.

This chapter provides an overview of the application resources offered by Windows 98. These topics are then discussed in detail in the following chapters. In Chapter 12, we'll finish up by discussing two versions of an application that uses all the techniques covered in Part 2: the *FileView1* and *FileView2* demos.

Advantages of the Windows Structural Approach

When an application is loaded for execution, the resource elements are not loaded. Instead, resources, such as dialog boxes and menus, are loaded only on demand, as required. When a resource is no longer needed, it is discarded. The advantage of loading resources on demand is simple: Memory is expended only for currently operating elements. Memory is not used for storage of elements that may or may not be needed.

For example, one version of a solitaire program (Sol.EXE) contains 74 bitmaps (52 for the card faces alone), one menu, five dialog boxes, one accelerator table, one icon, and one custom resource type—a fairly small load as resource elements go.

In contrast, another application might contain only one resource and the application's icon, and then use a series of .DLL files. These .DLL files might contain hundreds of bitmap images, dozens of menus and dialog boxes, multiple accelerator key sets (for different circumstances), a hundred separate cursors, dozens of additional icons, and a huge string table.

In both cases, if these massive assortments of resources needed to be loaded into memory immediately on execution of the application, your system memory would quickly become overloaded. And only a small portion of these resources might actually be used at any time. Instead, under Windows, because the system loads resources only on demand (when they are needed), memory remains free for other uses.

Another advantage to the Windows approach is that you can edit application resources without needing to recompile the files. While the usual practice is for programmers to edit their own resource files before compiling and linking, they can now edit executable program resources.

NOTE   When executables are opened for resource editing, the original resource names do not appear. Instead, all resources are labeled by their identifier values.

Keep in mind, however, that application resources define only the appearance and organization of the resources, not their functional characteristics. By using a resource editor to edit a dialog box, for example, you can change the arrangement or appearance of that dialog box, but you cannot alter how the application responds to the dialog box controls. This means that you can make only cosmetic changes by editing resource elements. If you need to make functional changes, you must revise the application's source code and then recompile it.

Types of Resources

For your Windows 98 applications, the following resources are available:

Images   Three types of image resources are supported as bitmaps (.BMP), cursors (.CUR), and icons (.ICO). Each of these are bit images, but different rules and organizations are applied to create each one. You can edit image resources with a bitmap editor. The three bit-image resource types are discussed in Chapter 8.

On the Use of Resources

Because my tech reviewer has raised a few important questions concerning limitations on resources (there really aren't any), I'm repeating the questions here with approximate answers.

Q: How much free memory can be used for resources?

A: All of it. In theory, the only limitation—under any 32-bit version of Windows—is the 4GB limit on addressable memory. Remember, that the operating system uses roughly 12MB of RAM, *but* the swap file acts as an extension to system RAM. Therefore, on a 16MB system, somewhere in the neighborhood of 20MB–30MB of

RAM are available for resources. How much you use is entirely up to your application design. (And, yes, you could use a 2GB or 3GB hard drive as a dedicated swap file—why not, they're cheap now and relatively fast if you really need that much space.)

Q: List everything that is considered a *resource*.

A: List everything that isn't provided directly by your C/C++ source code. A resource—in addition to bitmaps, icons, toolbars, dialog templates, hotkey accelerators, string tables, and custom cursors—may include data objects, such as a database template, custom controls, default registry data, sound files (but these are usually external), or anything else you desire to include as a custom resource.

Q: How time-consuming is it to load and unload resources?

A: In actual fact, it isn't. Resources are part of the application's .EXE file (or .DLL library) and are loaded at the same time the executable runs. If there is insufficient free memory, some part of the executable or DLL is transferred to the swap file. This task is handled by Windows on a demand basis such that currently unneeded elements are off-loaded to a disk image of RAM and are recalled (moved back into active memory) when needed. In effect, there is no real way to say what the time constraints are except to observe that fast hard drives are more responsive than slow ones.

Q: Besides memory, what are the limitations on how many resources can be loaded at one time?

A: For all practical purposes, memory aside, there are none.

Toolbars   These resources are specialized bitmap images consisting of one or more individual button images. By default, each button is 16x15 pixels, but you can size buttons as desired. (While toolbars are bitmap images, most resource editors provide a toolbar editor for greater convenience.) Toolbar resources are discussed in Chapter 8.

Dialog boxes   These resources are generally message or input windows, but they may also be child windows used to organize a display. A dialog box editor provides an interactive means of constructing dialog boxes and showing the elements (list boxes, buttons, edit boxes, scrollbars, and so on) exactly as these will appear on screen. Dialog boxes are discussed in Chapter 9.

Menus   These resources provide lists of program options. The options may immediately execute commands, display submenus, or display dialog boxes for other operations. A menu editor allows you to define and test main and pull-down menus. You can also create menu resources using any plain-text editor (Windows Notepad, for example). Menus are discussed in Chapter 10.

Accelerators   These are keyboard resources. An accelerator resource is a key or key combination provided as an alternative to an individual menu item to invoke a command. One common example is pressing the Shift+Ins or Ctrl+V combinations as an alternative to pulling down the Edit menu to select the Paste option. You can define these hotkey shortcuts for menus with an accelerator editor or a plain-text editor. Accelerator resources are discussed in Chapter 11.

Strings   These resources are text strings that are displayed by an application in its menus or dialog boxes, for error messages or other information. By defining text strings as resources, rather than embedding them in the source code, you can conserve memory. Also, keeping all message strings in a single location makes it easier to standardize message formats and to maintain consistency. Another advantage of this approach is that it allows you to edit strings for language changes without recompiling. You can create string tables using any plain-text editor or a string table editor. String resources are discussed in Chapter 11.

Version   This resource contains information about the application, such as its version number, its intended operating system, and its original filename. It is intended for use with the File Installation library functions. Version resources are discussed in Chapter 11.

While application resources are, nominally, contained in the .RES resource script file during development, binary resource objects—such as bitmaps, cursors, and icons among others—are stored separately as individual files. Also, several custom file types can be used to store individual resource objects separate from the resource script.

Files and File Types

Most resource editors can create, import, export, or edit most resource files used by Windows, including executable files containing resources. A full list of standard resource types appears in Table 7.1.

TABLE 7.1:   Standard (Predefined) Resource File Types

File Extension	Type	Description
.EXE	Executable	Executable program code containing application resources and compiled program code
.RES	Resource	Compiled (binary) resource file
.DLL	Executable	Executable (dynamic link library) module, which may contain either executable code, application resources, or both
.H	Source code	Header file containing symbolic names for defined resources
.ICO	Resource	Individual icon-image resource file
.CUR	Resource	Individual cursor-image resource file
.BMP	Resource	Individual bitmap-image file
.DLG	Resource script	Individual dialog box resource script containing a single dialog box in ASCII text format
.RC	Resource script	ASCII resource script containing one or more resource elements, which may include image resources in hexadecimal format
.DRV	Device driver	Compiled device driver, which may contain resource elements, dialog boxes, and so on
.FON	Font library	File containing one or more fonts belonging to a single typeface (not commonly used as a resource element)

Continued on next page

TABLE 7.1 CONTINUED: Standard (Predefined) Resource File Types

File Extension	Type	Description
.FNT	Font typeface	File containing a single typeface font
.DAT	Resource	Raw data resource, which is used for custom resource types (can be copied, renamed, or deleted but cannot be edited, browsed, or created using a resource editor)

Linking Resources

Normally, the resources are compiled directly to an .RES (binary) file, permitting the Linker to link the compiled resources with the compiled .EXE executable. However, when editing an existing .EXE or .DLL source, no .RES file is created. Instead, the resources are written directly to the runtime program.

Using the Microsoft command-line compiler, NMake scripts (.MAK) contain instructions to compile .RC resource scripts before linking the resulting .RES compiled resources.

Note that both resource editors (and most other systems) create an .RC resource script file—a text file—that contains all of the nonimage resources. Image resources, such as bitmaps, icons, cursors, and toolbars, are normally stored as separate image files referenced by the .RC resource script.

Dynamic Link Libraries

A *dynamic link library* (DLL, sometimes pronounced "dill") is an executable module that may contain both application executables (compiled source code) and application resources. A DLL is similar in construction to a runtime library, except that it is not linked to the application during the compile process. Instead, DLLs are dynamically linked during execution when library resources—either executable routines or resources—are required.

DLLs have two important strengths:

- A single DLL can be accessed by more than one application without being duplicated within each application.

- Routines in DLLs can be revised and recompiled without modifying the programs using the called routines (assuming, of course, that the call-and-response format remains unchanged).

NOTE Just as .EXE resources can be modified without recompilation, .DLL resources may also be edited, extracted, or updated without recompilation. Unfortunately, the current Visual C/C++ compiler does not support opening resources from .EXE or .DLL sources, although other compilers have managed this task without difficulty.

Header Files

All application resources must be identified by numeric values. But, for humans, numeric identifiers are awkward and difficult to remember. Therefore, just as Windows 98 supplies mnemonic constants (see the Windows.H and included header files), programmers can also define .H header definition files to provide mnemonics for application resources (or use predefined mnemonics).

When creating resources using the Microsoft C++ integrated development compiler, the resource identifiers are created automatically and are found in the Resource.H header. The bulk of the resources appear as scripts in the .RC resource file. All image resources—bitmaps, cursors, and icons—appear as separate .BMP, .CUR, and .ICO files, which are referenced within the .RC script.

Using a Resource Editor

Although some resource types, such as dialog boxes, can be designed (however laboriously) by editing script files, image-based resource types are difficult to create without using some type of resource editor. In this part, we'll use the resource editor integrated into the Microsoft Developer Studio for our examples. If you prefer, you can select from a variety of other resource editors, all of which produce compatible application resources—both image-based and other types.

Figure 7.1 shows the Microsoft Developer Studio's main screen and primary menu together with the FileType dialog box open in the editor (the resource list appears to the left in the Developer Studio window).

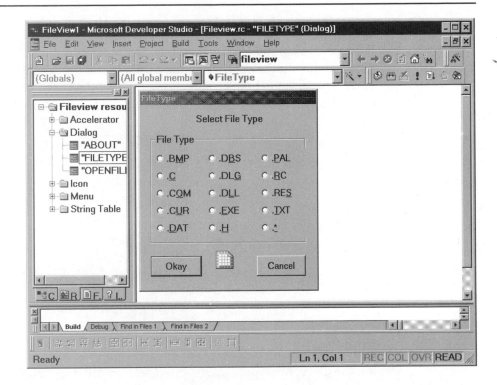

Like most Windows applications, the Developer Studio is designed principally for mouse operation. You can activate features by clicking menu options, buttons, or other controls. However, the Developer Studio also provides hotkey options that allow you to select items by pressing the key corresponding to the underscored letters. Thus, from the menu, Alt+F selects File, N selects New Project, and a pop-up dialog box or a submenu appears, offering a selection of preferences for creating a new file, a new project, and so on. Similar hotkeys are available in most dialog boxes and menus.

As with many other Windows applications, you can also use the Tab key to cycle through the buttons and/or fields. To select the highlighted option, press the Enter key or spacebar.

Opening Project and Resource Files

Because you can create and store resource elements separately from a project (but most commonly, they will be within a project), the Developer Studio makes provisions for opening both project and individual resource files. The Developer Studio's File menu has two "open" provisions: Open and Open Workspace:

You can use the Open option to open any type of file, including a project file. But the Open Workspace option provides a shortcut specifically for opening projects. Likewise, the Close Workspace option closes an open workspace and all associated files. When you reopen the workspace, all the files that were previously open are reopened.

On the other hand, if you want to work on an individual resource file or create a new resource file, without opening a project, simply click New to open the New dialog box, shown in Figure 7.2, and select the file type.

FIGURE 7.2:

Creating a new file or
resource

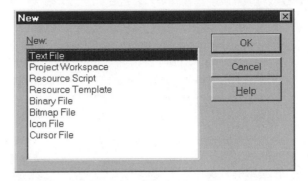

Notice here that there are individual options for bitmap, cursor, and icon files
but not for dialog boxes, menus, accelerator keys, and other resources. Instead, all
resource types except image resources are covered by the Resource Script option.

If you wish to open an individual resource file, select the Open option to see the
dialog box shown in Figure 7.3. Then you can select the type of resource (or other
file) from the Files of Type pull-down list.

FIGURE 7.3:

Opening a file outside a
project

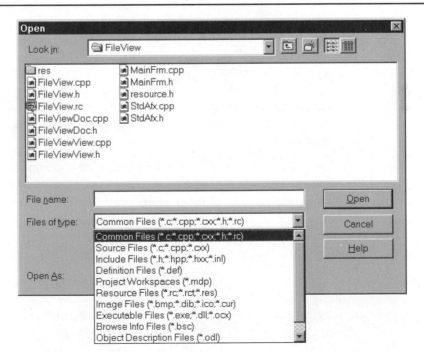

Adding and Editing Resource Elements

Normally, you will be working with a project, and you will want to create your resources as a part of the project rather than as individual resource files. For this purpose, instead of opening a new file, select Insert from the main menu, select Resource, and then choose the type of resource to create from the Insert Resource dialog box (by double-clicking the resource, or highlighting it and clicking OK), as shown in Figure 7.4.

FIGURE 7.4:

Adding a resource to a project

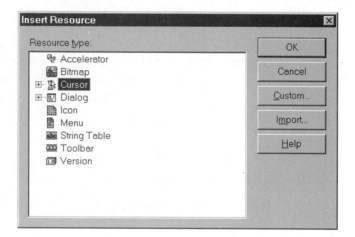

After you select the resource type, a new resource element is added to the resource list (on the left side of your screen) using a default type name, such as IDC_CURSOR1. At the same time, the appropriate editor is called to create the new resource element.

To create a custom resource element, select the Custom button from the Insert Resource dialog box, and then enter a name for the custom resource type. You must create custom resources independently, by whatever means are appropriate. The options here only permit you to include a custom resource and custom resource type within a project. You must handle all other provisions yourself, and they must conform to a response code within the application or an associated DLL.

You can change default element type names at any time by right-clicking the appropriate element in the resource list (on the left side of your screen) to call the pop-up menu. From the menu, select Properties to display the Properties dialog box, shown in Figure 7.5. Then simply enter a new resource name. A corresponding entry will be made in the Resource.H header automatically. This provides a convenient way to replace the default labels supplied when resource elements are generated with new mnemonic resource names.

FIGURE 7.5:

Entering a new resource name in the Properties dialog box

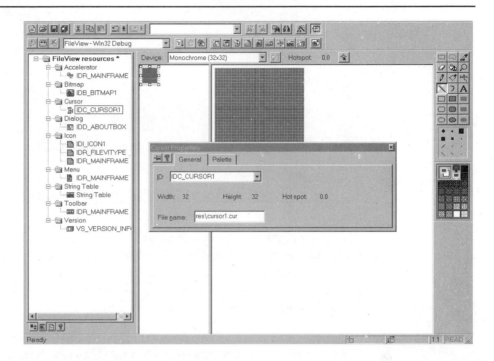

You can edit an existing resource element simply by double-clicking it (or highlighting it and pressing Enter) in the project's resource list. Doing this brings up the appropriate editor and loads the resource element.

Viewing and Changing Resource Identifiers

To view resource identifiers, select Resource Symbols from the View menu. The Resource Symbols dialog box appears, as shown in Figure 7.6. Here the resource identifiers are listed in alphabetical (not numerical) order.

FIGURE 7.6:

Viewing resource identifiers

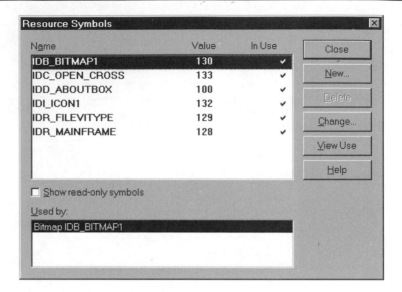

A checkmark in the In Use column on the right side of the dialog box indicates that an identifier is in use. The Used By box, at the bottom of the dialog box, shows where the highlighted identifier is used. When an identifier is used by more than one resource, multiple items appear in the Used By list. To view the use of an identifier, click the View Use button.

WARNING   Obsolete or unused identifiers may remain in the Resource.H header but will not be checked. You can delete or change them; however, you should be aware that unchecked identifiers may be mnemonic constants created for special messages. The lack of a checkmark simply means that the constant is not used by any resource element.

To change an identifier, click the Change button. If the selected identifier is in use, you will not be able to change that identifier through this dialog box. You can only change an identifier that is in use by changing the properties for the resource element. If the selected identifier is in use, the Delete button will be disabled. You can delete only identifiers that are not in use.

To edit the properties for most resources, right-click the resource item in the tree display, and then select Properties from the pop-up menu. You can then change the resource properties and identifier in the Properties dialog box. For string table entries, you can change the resource identifiers directly in the string table.

Copying Resource Elements

To duplicate a resource—for example, to use as the basis for creating a different version of the resource—select the resource to duplicate, and then use the Copy and Paste options on the Edit menu. A new resource identifier will be created for the duplicated resource.

The Insert menu also has a Resource Copy option; however, this option creates a copy of a resource element that is used only when a special condition is defined, or it creates a copy in a second language.

Managing Project Resources in the Borland C++ Builder

The Borland C++ Builder has adopted a quite different development approach from previous versions of the compiler (and other compilers), treating projects as containers for one or more applications (presumably associated), while treating applications as constructs largely built from standard components. This approach is similar to Delphi and Visual Basic application design.

The File menu offers options for creating or opening applications, application element files, and projects. Once a project is opened (or created), instead of a resource script, you will find yourself working with "forms," where each form is associated with a separate source file.

Borland's C++ Builder also offers a resource editor, but it is difficult to use with conventional C++ or MFC-based C++ application designs. This is because of the development approach taken by the C++ Builder, with its form-centric design and almost total dependence on predefined Borland classes and component-based programming.

As you learned in this chapter, application resources and resource editors can simplify your application development work. The individual resource types and editors are discussed in the following chapters. You'll also find explanations of how each type is used to create the resources for the *FileView1* and *FileView2* demos discussed in Chapter 12.

Bitmaps, Toolbars, Icons, and Cursors

■ The four types of image resources

■ Toolbar editing

■ Icon design

■ Cursor elements

Bitmap and toolbar images, icons, and mouse cursors are image resources, which you can manipulate with an image editor. This chapter describes the differences between these types of image resources and how to work with them.

Types of Image Resources

Although the four types of image resources are bit images, different rules and organizations apply for their creation.

Bitmap Images

The simplest bit-image type is the bitmap image, which is a pixel image using 2, 16, or 256 colors. Individually, bitmaps may be as large as the full screen (or larger) or as small as a few dozen pixels for a checkbox control or radio button; of course, they may also be medium-sized, as in the Solitaire card images. Bitmap images, however, are limited in that they consist only of a foreground image and cannot contain transparent areas.

Bitmap images can be created by any paint program and do not differ in any respect from conventional bitmaps. This means that you can import bitmap images from external sources. Furthermore, bitmap images can use palettes supporting 2, 16, or 256 colors with no limitations, aside from memory, of course.

Within applications, you can use bitmap images for decorative or informative purposes. You can also incorporate them as graphic controls.

Toolbar Images

Toolbars are a specialized bitmap-image format in which a long narrow image is subdivided into individual button images. The bitmap itself is a single continuous image, and the division into individual buttons is strictly an artifact of how the bitmap is presented.

To create a toolbar bitmap, the image editor begins with a blank bitmap the size of a single button. As one button image is created (edited or drawn), the editor adds a new blank to the end of the bitmap image. These blank button images do not appear on the actual bitmap but can be selected to create a new button image.

By default, toolbar buttons are 16×15 pixels. You can specify a new button size in the button properties, but keep in mind that changing the size of any of the buttons on a toolbar affects all of the toolbar buttons. All buttons on a toolbar must be the same size, both vertically and horizontally.

Icon Images

The icon image type is commonly used to represent an application within a Program Manager group or on the Desktop display. You can also include icons as bitmap images within dialog boxes or, with special handling, as menu elements.

Icon images are similar to bitmap images, but they have size limitations supporting only VGA resolution 32×32 (normal) or 64×64 bit image sizes. Like bitmaps, icon palettes can support 2, 16, or 256 colors. Unlike bitmap images, however, icons can include transparent areas or areas that interact with the Desktop or other underlying images by inverting the background pixels.

Cursor Images

The fourth bit-image type is the cursor, which, unlike the bitmap, toolbar, and icon types, always interacts with the background image.

A cursor bit image consists of two 32×32 bit images: a mask that interacts with the cursor background and the cursor pattern itself, which overlays the mask/background combination. Cursors are restricted to a default palette consisting of only four colors: black, white, transparent, and inverted.

Also, unlike other images, a cursor contains a *hotspot*, which is a pixel location within the image that defines the cursor's position. For example, the familiar arrow cursor's hotspot is located at the tip of the arrowhead.

Unfortunately, animated cursors (.ANI) are not supported by present resource editors—even though Windows 98 ships with a set of sample animated cursors—and require specialized facilities to create. Animated cursors are discussed in more detail later in the chapter.

Custom Fonts

At one time, custom fonts represented a fourth type of bitmapped resource. Application fonts, however, were limited to bitmapped font images. These custom fonts are no longer supported as resource elements.

Today, with a few exceptions, bitmapped fonts have been replaced by vectored (a.k.a. True Type) character fonts. These fonts have several advantages: They are resizable, adaptable to different screen resolutions, and generally cleaner and easier to read, as well as more attractive.

Vectored fonts, however, are not application resources; that is, they are not included as an integral part of the application. Instead, vectored fonts are used as system resources, available to all applications. These types of fonts are not intended to be application-specific.

To create custom fonts, consider using any of the numerous font editors available on the market (such as Fontographer or Adobe Font Manager). However, requiring a custom font or fonts for your application is not a recommended practice and should be done only under special circumstances.

A Bitmap Editor

Only the icon and cursor image types require the specialized formats provided by an image editor. You can also create bitmaps using a wide variety of other paint utilities (many of which are better suited for general illustration than either of these resource editors).

Microsoft's image editor, which is part of the Microsoft Developer Studio, supports bitmap, cursor, icon, and toolbar images. The image editor is shown in Figure 8.1, where the Setup.BMP image (from the D:\Win98 directory) is in a split-window display with a zoom view on the left.

The palette bar appears (in the lower-right in Figure 8.1) with 16 basic colors. The foreground and background colors are shown at the upper left of the palette bar. Click (with the primary mouse button) to select a foreground color; right-click (with the secondary mouse button) to select a background color. To change any palette entry, double-click that entry to bring up the Windows common dialog box for color selection.

FIGURE 8.1:

The Microsoft Developer Studio image editor has a split-window display, with independent zoom capabilities.

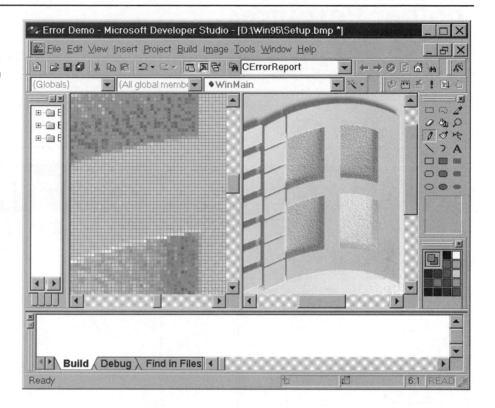

The toolbar appears as a vertical, three-column bar (in the upper-right in Figure 8.1), with 21 tools. When you select a brush, pen, airbrush, or similar tool, the rectangle below the tool buttons offers a choice of weights or tool shapes for the selection.

The drawing operations are essentially the same as in other familiar paint programs, such as the Paint program distributed with Windows.

For more complex bitmap images, a wide variety of paint programs are available, and any .BMP or .DIB image can be imported as an application resource.

TIP

The tools in Microsoft's image editor should be familiar to anyone who has used a paint program. For explanations about how the individual tools function, use the editor's Help menu options.

Toolbar Resources

Toolbar images are stored as simple .BMP image files, but they have some additional information in the bitmap header to specify the number and width of the buttons and other organizational details. When a resource editor opens a toolbar bitmap, the strip image is displayed as buttons, with separators where appropriate, as shown in Figure 8.2.

FIGURE 8.2:

A toolbar image

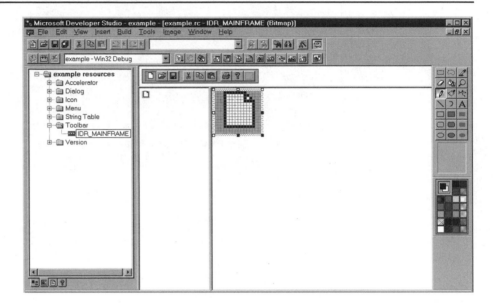

The toolbar also shows two views of a selected button: one (on the left) in actual size and the second (on the right) enlarged for editing. Drawing operations for a toolbar button are essentially the same as for any bitmap image.

Unlike some bitmaps, you can enlarge toolbar images (to add new buttons) by selecting the blank button at the end of the toolbar image and then drawing in the button image. A new, blank button will be added to the toolbar strip automatically. Note, however, that the blank button is not stored as part of the toolbar bitmap and does not appear during use.

You create the separations between buttons by selecting a button on the button strip and dragging it to the right. When you release the button, a separator space appears in the button order. To remove a separator, simply reverse the process.

By dragging on any of the three black handles in a toolbar button (bottom-center, bottom-right, or right-center), you can resize the button using the mouse. When you change the size of existing toolbar buttons, the existing images are repositioned (and resized as necessary) to fit the new button size. In other words, if you enlarge the buttons, the existing images are repositioned (centered) within the new button area. If you reduce the buttons in size, the images may be truncated from the sides. (As buttons are reduced, the editor attempts to keep the images for each by trimming pixels.)

You can summon the Toolbar Button Properties dialog box for an individual button by double-clicking the button in the toolbar image (at the top of the editor window). Figure 8.3 shows the Toolbar Button Properties dialog box. Using this dialog box, you can edit the button ID (a default button ID is assigned when the button is created), change the width and height for the button, and enter the prompt strings for the button.

FIGURE 8.3:

The Toolbar Button Properties dialog box

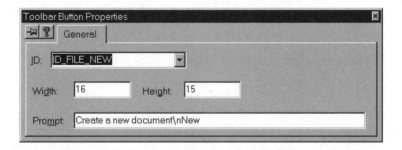

The Prompt field consists of two strings separated by a *newline* (\n) character. The first string is the prompt that appears on the application's status bar (normally at the bottom of the application window). The second string entry provides the pop-up tip (normally brief) that appears when the cursor is positioned on the button.

TIP

Although there are no technical limits on the number of buttons a toolbar can have, you should remember that application window sizes might be limited by the size and resolution of the end users' display monitors. Instead of creating exceptionally long toolbars, it may be a better idea to break a long toolbar (more than a dozen buttons) into two smaller toolbars.

Icon Resources

Icon resources are used to represent applications, system resources, subsystems, or controls within an application. Icons are commonly used to represent available programs or minimized programs. Some applications, such as the Clock program distributed with Windows 98, create their own dynamic icons. Aside from such custom icons, conventional icons are simply small bitmaps of a symbol representing the application.

Designing an icon is largely a matter of personal taste. Icons can be as colorful and gaudy or as starkly plain as you choose. However, there are a few points you should keep in mind when designing icons:

- Your application is not going to stand or fall on the quality of your icon (unless you have a very unusual application).

- There is always a temptation to put a great deal of detail into an icon, or to reproduce a company logo, or to execute some concept that sounds fantastic in conversation. But remember, an icon is small, and much of the detail is simply going to be lost as clutter. In general, a simple icon is best. Its only real purpose is to be recognizable, so that the user can easily locate and select the icon to launch the application it represents.

- Although you can design icons using fine color details, if they are executed on a simple VGA system (or on many laptops), they will be mapped to the nearest available colors in the palette. The result is that all of your careful work, and quite likely the image as well, is lost. On a monochrome system, the results can be even worse when the colors are dithered down to black and white.

The best rule is simple: as in "keep it simple." If you need contrast, you can always use inverted pixels to ensure that at least some of the icon will be visible regardless of the background.

Cursor Resources

Cursor resources (mouse pointers) are a specialized form of bitmap. Unlike other bitmap images, the bitmap images used for cursors do not replace the underlying background images. Instead, cursor images are intended to interact with the background but leave the underlying image unchanged after the cursor moves.

For maximum visibility, cursor images are normally created as outlines using the inverted pixels for contrast or highlighting. The transparent pixels are simply used for areas where the background is allowed to show through.

As with previous Windows versions, only black-and-white cursor images are supported, and cursor pixels are composed of four colors: black, white, transparent, and inverted. (Animated cursors—which do permit color—are not a standard cursor image.)

Cursor Elements

Cursors provide three principal elements:

Pointer image   The cursor image shows the mouse location and also frequently indicates the general function currently being executed.

Screen image   The screen image is a mask governing the interaction between the cursor (pointer) image and the underlying screen image. This image is generated automatically to fit the pointer image.

Hotspot   The hotspot is a location within the cursor image that corresponds to the mouse's absolute screen position and is assigned by the cursor's designer.

Figure 8.4 shows a simple hand cursor with a pointing finger. The hand is drawn in black, then outlined in white, and finally, filled using *inverted* pixels. All these elements were designed to maximize the appearance of the image against any background—light, dark, or mixed. The hotspot is located at the tip of the extended finger.

FIGURE 8.4:

A sample cursor image

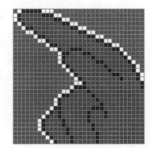

TIP
A simpler version of the cursor shown in Figure 8.4 could be drawn by using only inverted pixels for the image and leaving the rest of the field transparent. Alternatively, you could draw the image in black and use an inverted outline.

Animated Cursors

Animated cursors are a specialized format using the .ANI extension. They consist of a series of images that provide simple visual animation. A few interesting examples are distributed with Windows 98, including sand pouring though a small hourglass (AppStart.ANI), a spinning globe (Globe.ANI), and a large, animated hourglass (Hourglas.ANI). Animated cursors may also include color, unlike static cursor images.

The Microsoft C++ compiler suite does not provide support for creating or editing animated cursors, nor can animated cursors be readily imported as application resources. There are, however, third-party utilities available for animated cursor creation, if you are so inclined. Alternatively, you might create your own animation by using a separate thread to load a series of cursor images, which is essentially what an animated cursor does.

Two Icons for FileView

The *FileView* demo, which is described in detail in Chapter 12, uses two icon images, as illustrated in Figure 8.5. The primary application icon appears at the right; the icon on the left is used in one of the dialog boxes.

FIGURE 8.5:

Two resources for the FileView demo

Both icon images were designed to stand out against any background, beginning with a field drawn using the inverse brush. The letters are drawn using the screen (transparent) brush, and then they are outlined in light cyan.

NOTE   The *FileView* demo (both a *FileView1* and a *FileView2* version) is included on the CD that accompanies this book, in the Chapter 12 folder. Additional resources used by the *FileView* demo are discussed in the following chapters.

In this chapter, you learned about the various types of image resources: bitmap, toolbar, icons, and cursor. These are easy to produce and edit using image editors. In the next chapter, we'll talk about dialog box resources.

Dialog Box Resources

- ■ Dialog box editor features

- ■ Dialog box properties

- ■ Dialog box controls

- ■ Dialog box alignment, positioning, and sizing

Dialog boxes are integral to Windows applications. Because many applications use dozens of—or even more—dialog boxes, the total number of dialog box resources easily exceeds all other resource elements.

Although you can use ASCII scripts to define dialog boxes, dialog box editors provide a much more convenient method. In this chapter, we'll cover the use of a dialog box editor and describe the various types of dialog box controls.

A Dialog Box Editor

Microsoft's dialog box editor, part of the Microsoft Developer Studio, provides interactive dialog box design. This editor offers tools to create and arrange all standard dialog box resource elements, including control buttons, checkboxes, edit boxes, list boxes, and radio buttons. The use of the dialog box editor is largely intuitive; in many respects, it operates much like a paint program, using drag-and-drop tools to position and size resource elements selected from a toolbar.

NOTE   Borland's C++ Builder editor takes a different approach to constructing dialog boxes, using a format reminiscent of Visual Basic's "form-centric" theme. This is in contrast to Visual C++'s application-centric theme. C++ Builder even uses the term *form* rather than *dialog box*. However, even though they're called forms, the elements and construction are essentially the same as for building dialog boxes with Microsoft's Developer Studio or Borland's earlier Resource Workshop.

The main screen of the Microsoft Developer Studio dialog box editor is shown in Figure 9.1. Here you see a blank dialog box that contains only two buttons, the Controls toolbar (far right), and the status bar (bottom) with additional operator options and alignment tools.

The dialog box editor's Controls toolbar offers 22 tools: one represents the control cursor, 20 represent the standard dialog box element types, and the last (bottom-right) provides for custom dialog box resource types. These resource controls are discussed in more detail later in the chapter, in the section "Dialog Box Control Elements" (and illustrated later in Figure 9.7).

FIGURE 9.1:

The Microsoft Developer
Studio dialog box editor

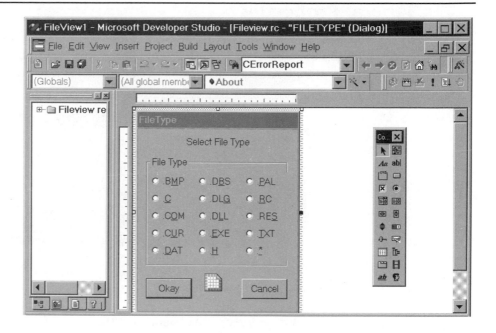

The Layout menu offers alignment and layout options, which are also available from the bottom toolbar. However, the menu also offers options for guide settings and tab-order arrangements, which are not found on the toolbar.

NOTE

The examples in this book were created using the Microsoft Developer Studio and Visual C++. However, the principles and designs are compatible with other compilers and tool sets, and in most cases, can be used with other languages as well.

Dialog Box Properties

With a dialog box editor, you can create a variety of dialog box types and styles. To set the properties for a dialog box with Microsoft's dialog box editor, select Properties from the Edit menu, or right-click on the dialog box in the editor. This brings up the Dialog Properties dialog box, which has General, Styles, More Styles, and Extended Styles tabs.

General Properties

The General tab of the Dialog Properties dialog box, shown in Figure 9.2, includes the dialog box ID and caption, along with font information, position information, the dialog menu, and an associated class name.

FIGURE 9.2:

The General tab of the Developer Studio Dialog Properties dialog box

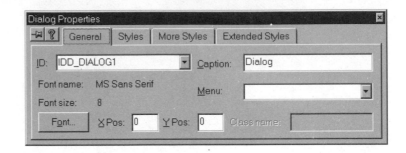

The General tab includes these fields:

ID   A mnemonic symbol defined in the header file. This may be a symbol (the customary default), an integer, or a quoted string.

Caption   Text appearing as the dialog box label. Change the default dialog box name supplied by the resource editor to a label identifying the purpose or function of the dialog box.

Menu   An optional resource identifier for a menu to be used in the dialog box.

Font Name   The typeface of the font used in all the controls in the dialog box. The bold version of the typeface is always used.

Font Size   The point size for the font used in all the controls in the dialog box.

X Pos and Y Pos   The x- and y- coordinates, in dialog box units (*DLUs*, a.k.a. dialog logic units), for the upper-left corner of the dialog box.

Class Name   The registered dialog class (a Windows operating-system window class, not a C++ class). Provided to support C programming, this element is disabled when using MFC library support.

The General tab also contains a Font button, which calls the Select Dialog Font dialog box, as shown in Figure 9.3. Here, you can change the default typeface or point size used with your dialog box. A sample of the selected typeface and size is shown at the bottom of the Select Dialog Font dialog box.

Choosing a default font for
your dialog box

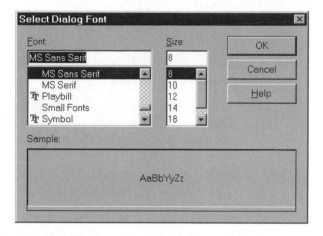

> **NOTE**   For applications written using Microsoft Visual C++, you may select only one font, which will be applied to all controls and text elements in the dialog box.

Dialog Box Styles

The Styles tab of the Dialog Properties dialog box offers controls for the overall appearance and behavior of the dialog box. Figure 9.4 shows this tab.

FIGURE 9.4:

The Styles tab of the
Developer Studio Dialog
Properties dialog box

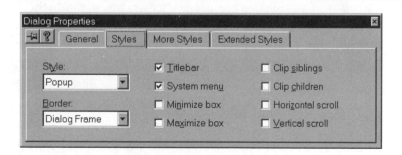

Dialog box styles may have the following values:

Style   You can choose from the following operation styles:

- Overlapped, which is always a top-level window and should have a caption and a border. Overlapped windows are pop-up windows that can be overlapped by other dialog box windows. Normally, only the main window in an application is defined as Overlapped.

- Popup, which is the default. Pop-up dialog boxes appear only when called by an application in response to a menu selection or some other program instruction.

- Child, which creates a dialog box defined as a child window belonging to another window. Child dialog boxes are generally used when several tiled windows are desired within an application, and they are displayed at all times (unless, of course, they are covered by another window or application). Child windows belonging to an application are not allowed to overlap.

Border   You can choose from four frame (border) styles, which determine the appearance of the dialog box frame and the presence or absence of a caption bar:

- None, which displays neither a border nor a caption bar.

- Thin, which displays a thin, single border without a caption bar.

- Resizing, which displays a double border without a caption bar.

- Dialog Frame, the default, which displays a double border with a caption bar.

Titlebar   If checked (the default), the dialog box appears with a title bar.

System Menu   If checked (the default), the dialog box appears with a system menu at the upper-left corner of the frame. The system menu appears only on captioned dialog boxes.

Minimize Box   If checked (unchecked is the default), the dialog box appears with a Minimize box at the upper-right corner of the frame. The Minimize box appears only on captioned dialog boxes.

Maximize Box   If checked (unchecked is the default), the dialog box appears with a Maximize box at the upper-right corner of the frame. Like the system menu and the Minimize box, the Maximize box appears only on captioned dialog boxes.

Clip Siblings   If checked (unchecked is the default), child windows are clipped relative to each other. Thus, when a particular child window is repainted, all other top-level child windows are clipped from the region of the child window to be updated. If cleared and child windows over-lap, drawing in the client area of a child window may draw in the client area of a neighboring child window. This option is for use with child windows only.

Clip Children If checked (unchecked is the default), this excludes the area occupied by child windows when drawing within the parent window. This option is used only when creating a parent window. Do not use this style if the dialog box contains a group box.

Horizontal Scroll If checked (unchecked is the default), the dialog box contains a horizontal scrollbar.

Vertical Scroll If checked (unchecked is the default), the dialog box contains a vertical scrollbar.

WARNING When a dialog box using the default Border style (Dialog Frame) contains scroll-bars, the scrollbars are drawn overlapping the borders of the dialog box rather than inside the frame, and the contents of the dialog box may be clipped incor-rectly. This is standard Windows behavior. Therefore, to use scrollbars with a dia-log box frame, select None, Thin, or Resizing for the Border style. This does not apply to scrollbar controls within the dialog box—only to scrollbars used to scroll the dialog box itself.

More Dialog Box Style Options

The More Styles tab of the Dialog Properties dialog box offers even more appearance and behavioral controls for the dialog box. Figure 9.5 shows this tab.

FIGURE 9.5:

The More Styles tab of the Developer Studio Dialog Properties dialog box

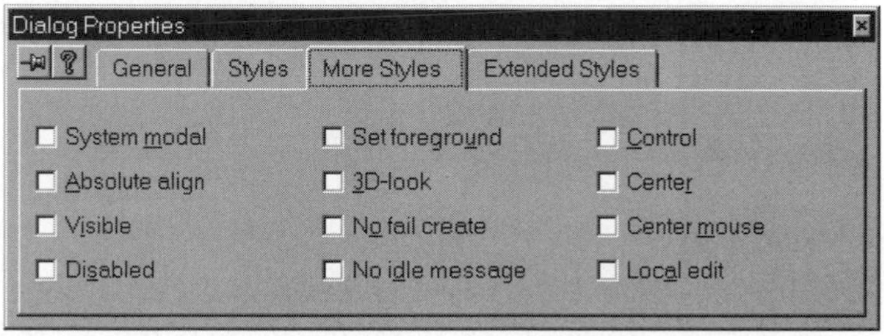

This tab offers the following selections, which are all unchecked by default:

System Modal   Makes the dialog box system-modal, which prohibits switching to another window or program while the dialog box is active. This option is used for warnings, queries, and other urgent or immediate messages.

Absolute Align   Aligns the dialog box relative to the upper-left corner of the screen. (By default, the dialog box is aligned relative to its parent window.)

Visible   Makes the dialog box visible when first displayed. This option is applicable to overlapping and pop-up windows. Do not check this option for form views and dialog-box template resources.

Disabled   Disables the dialog box when it first appears.

Set Foreground   Brings the dialog box to the foreground by internally calling the SetForegroundWindow function for the dialog box.

3D-look   Makes the dialog box appear with a nonbold font and draws three-dimensional borders around control windows in the dialog box.

No Fail Create   Creates the dialog box even if errors occur. For example, if a child window cannot be created or if the system cannot create a special data segment for an edit control, the dialog box will still be created.

No Idle Message   Suppresses the WM_ENTERIDLE message ordinarily sent to a dialog box's owner when no more messages are waiting in its message queue. This option is valid only for modal dialog boxes.

Control   Creates a dialog box that works well as a child window of another dialog box, similar to a page in a property sheet. This option permits the user to tab among the control windows of a child dialog box, use its accelerator keys, and so on.

Center   Centers the dialog box in the working area; that is, the area not obscured by the toolbar.

Center Mouse   Centers the mouse cursor in the dialog box on opening.

Local Edit   Specifies that edit-box controls in the dialog box will use memory in the application's data segment. Normally, all edit-box controls in dialog boxes use memory outside the application's data segment. This option should always be used if the application will be using the EM_SETHANDLE or EM_GETHANDLE messages.

Extended Dialog Box Style Options

The Extended Styles tab of the Dialog Properties dialog box offers additional appearance and behavioral controls for the dialog box. Figure 9.6 shows this tab.

FIGURE 9.6:

The Extended Styles tab of the Developer Studio Dialog Properties dialog box

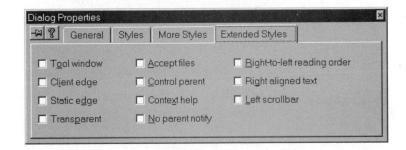

This tab offers the following selections, which are all unchecked by default:

Tool Window   Creates a tool window intended to be used as a floating toolbar. Tool windows have a shorter-than-normal title bar, and the title is drawn using a smaller font.

Client Edge   Creates a border with a sunken edge around the dialog box.

Static Edge   Creates a border around the dialog box.

Transparent   Creates a dialog box with a transparent window, so any windows beneath the dialog window are not obscured. The dialog window receives WM_PAINT messages only after all sibling windows beneath it have been updated. This option is useful for overlay drawing, but it does not function well for overlaying live video.

Accept Files   Allows the dialog box to accept drag-drop files. When a file is dropped on a dialog box, a WM_DROPFILES message is sent to the control.

Control Parent   Allows the user to navigate among the dialog child windows using the Tab key. (Navigation using the mouse also remains in effect.)

Context Help   Includes the Help question mark icon in the dialog box's title bar. When the user clicks the question mark, the cursor changes to a question mark with a pointer. Then, when he or she clicks a child window, the child receives a WM_HELP message. The WM_HELP message should be passed to the parent window procedure, which should call the `WinHelp` function using the HELP_WM_HELP command, so that the Help application can display a pop-up window with help information for the child window.

No Parent Notify   Stops the child window from sending the `WM_PARENT-NOTIFY` message to its parent window.

Right-to-Left Reading Order   Displays the dialog box text using right-to-left reading order properties.

Right Aligned Text   Right-aligns text within the dialog box.

Left Scrollbar   Displays the vertical scrollbar (if present) to the left of the client area.

Dialog Box Control Elements

Dialog boxes may contain a wide variety of controls, including buttons, scrollbars, list boxes, edit fields, images, spin buttons, and more. New control varieties are introduced regularly. While it would be literally impossible to describe every type of control, I will attempt to cover most of the standard types here, even though "new" standard types appear almost as often as new custom types.

The dialog box controls are on the dialog box editor's Controls toolbar. Figure 9.7 shows the Microsoft Developer Studio Controls toolbar, labeled with the names of the toolbar buttons. To select these control types, click the appropriate button, and then position the control in the dialog box outline.

Button Types

Buttons are used to define controls that permit user interactions. Three types of dialog box buttons are provided: pushbuttons, checkboxes, and radio buttons.

Pushbuttons

Pushbuttons are the simplest form of dialog box control. They execute an immediate response when you click them with the mouse, but normally do not maintain any status information. Pushbuttons usually contain a text label (caption) identifying their purpose.

When you choose the Button button on the Controls toolbar, you'll see the dialog box shown in Figure 9.8.

FIGURE 9.7:

Use the Controls toolbar in the Microsoft Developer Studio dialog box editor to add dialog box controls.

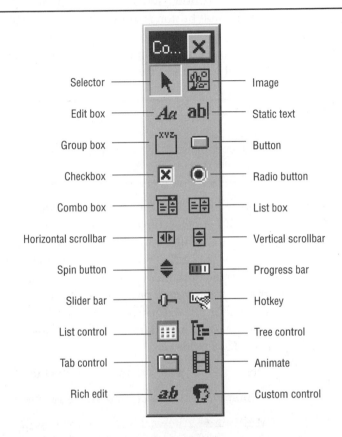

Co...
Selector
Image
Edit box
Static text
Group box
Button
Checkbox
Radio button
Combo box
List box
Horizontal scrollbar
Vertical scrollbar
Spin button
Progress bar
Slider bar
Hotkey
List control
Tree control
Tab control
Animate
Rich edit
Custom control

FIGURE 9.8:

Choosing pushbutton styles

Push Button Properties
General
Styles
Extended Styles
Default button
Owner draw
Icon
Bitmap
Multi-line
Notify
Flat
Horizontal alignment:
Default
Vertical alignment:
Default

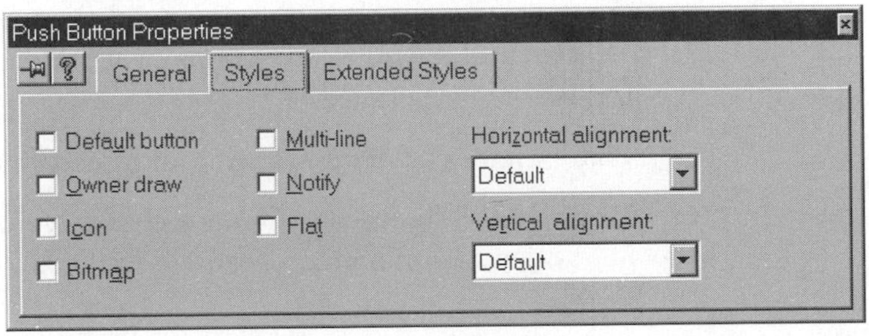

The Push Button Properties dialog box offers the following styles:

Default Button   Makes the control the default button in the dialog box. The default button is drawn with a heavy black border when the dialog box first appears, and it is executed if the user presses Enter without choosing another command in the dialog box. Windows allows only one default button in a dialog box.

WARNING   Unfortunately, the Developer Studio does not prevent you from creating more than one button with the Default Button style. The result of having multiple default buttons in a dialog box is generally failure of any of the buttons to respond to the Enter key.

Owner Draw   Used when an application needs to customize the appearance of a control. When you select this style, Windows does not handle the button appearance. Instead, when the button is activated, the parent window is notified with a request to paint, invert, or disable the button. The application must provide its own OnDrawItem message handler in the owner-window procedure (either the dialog box procedure or class derived from MFC class CDialog or CFormView). Owner-draw classes may also be derived from CButton using an override for the CButton::DrawItem method.

Icon   Displays an icon image for the button.

Bitmap   Displays a bitmap image for the button.

Multi-line   Allows the button text to wrap to multiple lines if it is too long to fit on a single line within the button rectangle.

Notify   Sends a notification to the parent window (the dialog box) when the pushbutton is clicked or double-clicked. By default, this option is not selected and the button functions by generating a message—using the button ID—when selected.

Flat   Creates a flat button without three-dimensional shading.

Horizontal Alignment   Offers a choice of how the control's caption text is positioned horizontally. Options are Default (centered), Left, Center, or Right.

Vertical Alignment Offers a choice of how the control's caption text is positioned vertically. Options are Default (centered), Top, Center, or Bottom.

Radio Buttons

Radio buttons and auto radio buttons are used to make a selection from a list of mutually exclusive options. Usually, when radio buttons are toggled on, dots appear inside the button. Labels adjacent to the buttons identify the option or selection. By convention, you can only select one button at a time in any group; all other buttons in the same group should be cleared.

Regular radio buttons require provisions within the application to send a set/clear message back to the button to initiate a change of state. Auto radio buttons, which look just like regular radio buttons, automatically reset their own state and, when selected, also clear any other radio buttons belonging to the same group. Whether or not radio buttons or auto radio buttons are used, the application is responsible for setting the initial, default selection in each group when the dialog box is initiated.

When you choose the Radio Button button on the Controls toolbar, you'll see the dialog box shown in Figure 9.9.

FIGURE 9.9:

Choosing radio button styles

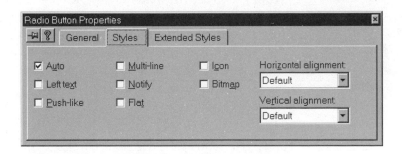

The Radio Button Properties dialog box offers the following styles:

Auto Displays the checked state automatically when the user selects the radio button. At the same time, any other radio buttons in the group are cleared (deselected). When a group of radio buttons is used with the Dialog Data Exchange (DDE), the Auto property must be set. This style is checked by default.

The Dialog Data Exchange (DDE) is an MFC-based mechanism that provides the exchange of data between dialog box elements and corresponding member variables within the `CDialog`-derived class. Using the DDE, instead of explicitly generating messages to read or write the state, text, or other values from and to dialog box elements, calling the `UpdateData` function with a `FALSE` argument causes all the elements to be updated with the values from their corresponding class members. Calling `UpdateData` with a `TRUE` argument retrieves the current values from all dialog box elements, storing (and validating when appropriate) these values in the member variables.

Left Text   Places the radio button's caption text on the left of the button rather than the right.

Push-like   Gives the radio button the appearance of a conventional push-button while still retaining the performance and characteristics of a radio button. A push-like radio button appears raised when unchecked and sunken when checked (pushed).

Multi-line   Allows the radio button text to wrap to multiple lines if it is too long to fit on a single line within the button rectangle.

Notify   Notifies the parent window when the radio button is clicked or double-clicked. Notification is used only when the parent is expected to take immediate action in response to a change rather than waiting to query the button status when the dialog box session concludes.

Because radio buttons are customarily used to establish settings or selections that will only become relevant after the dialog box closes—when the application returns to its primary tasks—the normal expectation is that the status of a radio button is queried only after the dialog box closes. This is not, however, a hard and fast rule; it's merely a generality. When an immediate response to a change in state is required, select the Notify option.

Flat   Creates a flat radio button without three-dimensional shading.

Icon   Displays an icon image for the radio button.

Bitmap   Displays a bitmap image for the radio button.

Horizontal Alignment   Offers a choice of how the control's caption text is positioned horizontally. Options are Default (text to the right of the button), Left, Center, or Right.

Vertical Alignment   Offers a choice of how the control's caption text is positioned. Options are Default (centered), Top, Center, or Bottom.

Checkboxes

Like radio buttons, checkboxes are usually identified by text labels set to the right or left of the checkbox image. Unlike radio buttons, checkboxes permit selection of none, one, or multiple items. Each checkbox resets its own image by displaying a checkmark when selected. A second mouse click on a checkbox cancels selection, resetting the image.

Checkboxes may be grouped, but they do not interact with others in a group. Each checkbox selection is assumed to be made independently of any other selections.

When you choose the Checkbox button on the Controls toolbar, you'll see the dialog box shown in Figure 9.10.

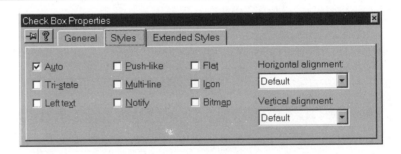

The Check Box Properties dialog box offers the following styles:

Auto   Toggles between the checked and unchecked states automatically when the user selects the checkbox. When checkboxes are used with the DDE, this property must be set to TRUE. This style is checked by default.

Tri-state   Allows the checkbox to display three states: checked, cleared, or grayed. A grayed checkbox indicates that the state represented by the control is undetermined or, alternately, the state of the checkbox selection is irrelevant (disabled).

Left Text   Places the checkbox's caption text on the left of the checkbox rather than the right.

Push-like Gives the checkbox the appearance of a conventional push-button while still retaining the performance and characteristics of a check-box. A push-like checkbox appears raised when unchecked and sunken when checked (pushed). For a tri-state push-like checkbox, the third state is depressed but grayed.

Multi-line Allows the button text to wrap to multiple lines if it is too long to fit on a single line within the button rectangle.

Notify Notifies the parent window when a checkbox is clicked or double-clicked. Notification is used only when the parent is expected to take immediate action in response to a change rather than waiting to query the button status when the dialog box session concludes.

Flat Creates a flat checkbox without three-dimensional shading.

Icon Displays an icon image for the checkbox.

Bitmap Displays a bitmap image for the checkbox.

Horizontal Alignment Offers a choice of how the control's caption text is positioned. Options are Default (left), Left, Center, or Right.

Vertical Alignment Offers a choice of how the control's caption text is positioned. Options are Default (centered), Top, Center, or Bottom.

General Properties for Other Controls

The General tab of the Properties dialog boxes for the text-oriented fields, range and adjustment controls, and other controls is similar for each type. Figure 9.11 shows the General tab of the Text Properties dialog box.

FIGURE 9.11:

The General tab of the Text Properties dialog box

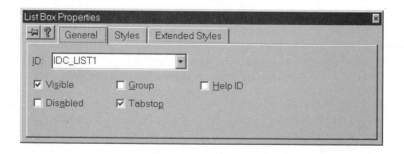

The text-oriented, range and adjustment, and other controls have the following general properties in common:

ID   Indicates the default resource ID for the control. You may retain the supplied ID or change to a mnemonic ID by entering the desired identifier. When you supply a new ID, a value is assigned automatically, and an entry is placed in the Resource.H header. The resource ID may be a symbol, integer, or quoted string.

Visible   Makes the control visible when the application is first run. This option is checked by default.

Disabled   Displays the resource as disabled when the dialog box is created (not relevant to static text controls).

Group   Makes the control the first control of a group of controls, where users can move from one control to the next by using the arrow keys. All controls in the tab order after the first control belong to the same group if the Group property is set to FALSE (unchecked). The next control in the tab order that has Group set to TRUE (checked) ends the first group of controls and starts the next group. For static text fields, this option is checked by default.

Tabstop   Allows the user to move to this control with the Tab key. This option is checked by default for all text-oriented controls except static text fields. It is also the default for sliders, hotkeys, and animated controls.

Help ID   Assigns a help ID to the control based on the resource ID (not relevant to static text).

Text-Oriented Fields

Six text-field types are provided: static text fields, edit boxes, list boxes, combo boxes, list control boxes, and tree controls.

Static Text Fields

Static text fields display labels and other information that cannot be entered or changed by the user. They may show information, ask questions, provide explanations, or simply provide labels for other controls or for edit boxes. Static text fields may be formatted as left-justified, right-justified, or centered.

When a static text field is created, a default identifier, IDC_STATIC, is assigned and the default caption *Static* is supplied. If an application needs to change the contents for a static text display, an individual resource ID should be assigned.

TIP   Static text fields may be assigned unique identifiers if there is any reason to have the displayed text change during execution of the application. After assigning a unique ID, the SetDlgItemText function can be used to assign new text to the static text field.

Along with the properties listed in the previous section, the General tab of the Text Properties dialog box contains a Caption property for the text string that appears in the static text field. If you want to change the default caption *Static*, this is where you would enter the new caption.

In addition to setting the options on the General tab for a static text field, you can also set the control's appearance using the Styles tab, shown in Figure 9.12.

FIGURE 9.12:

Setting static text field styles

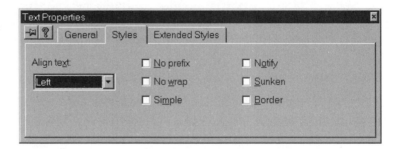

WARNING   Static text fields are limited to 255 characters. Multiple static text fields may overlap and conceal portions of other fields.

The Styles tab of the Text Properties dialog box offers the following options:

Align Text   Controls how text is aligned in the static text control: Left (the default), Center, or Right. This should be set to Left when No Wrap is selected.

No Prefix   Prevents ampersands (&) in the control's text from being interpreted as the mnemonic character. Normally, a string containing an ampersand is displayed with the ampersand removed and the next character in the string underlined. The No Prefix style is most often used when filenames or other strings that may contain an ampersand need to be displayed.

No Wrap   Displays text left-aligned; tabs are expanded but text is not wrapped, and any text extending beyond the end of a line is clipped.

Simple   Disables both the No Wrap and Align Text options; text does not wrap and is not clipped. Furthermore, overriding WM_CTLCOLOR in the parent window has no effect on the control.

Notify   Notifies the parent window if the control is clicked or double-clicked (not applicable to static text).

Sunken   Creates a border with a sunken edge around the static text control.

Border   Creates a border around the text control.

Edit Boxes

Edit boxes are used for entries and responses, but they may also display information or selections without allowing the user to change the entry. Usually, edit boxes permit the user to enter new text information or to edit existing text information. Although only one type of edit box is listed in the resource editor, these controls can be defined as single-line or multiline edit fields and may include vertical and/or horizontal scrolling and scrollbars.

When you create an edit box, the resource editor supplies a default ID value: IDC_EDITn. You can enter a new ID or select one from a list of defined IDs in the General tab of the Edit Properties dialog box. See the section "General Properties for Other Controls" earlier in the chapter for a description of the other properties on the General tab.

In addition to setting the properties on the General tab, you can also set the control's appearance using the Styles tab, as shown in Figure 9.13.

FIGURE 9.13:

Setting edit box styles

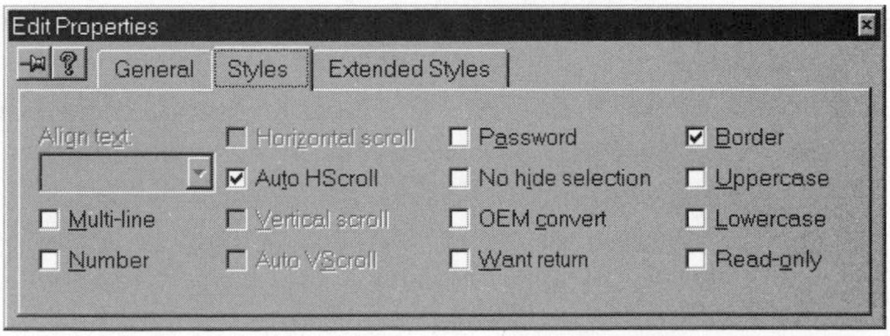

The Styles tab of the Edit Properties dialog box has the following options:

Align Text Offers a choice of Left (the default), Centered, or Right-aligned text (when the Multi-line option is selected).

Multi-line Creates a multiline edit-box control. When a multiline edit box is in a dialog box, pressing the Enter key selects the default button. Multiline edit boxes may have scrollbars and process their own scrollbar messages. They may also process scrollbar messages sent by the parent window. See also Horizontal Scroll, Auto HScroll, Vertical Scroll, and Want Return.

Number Restricts input to numeric characters and associated symbols; prevents any nonnumeric characters from being typed.

Horizontal Scroll Adds a horizontal scrollbar to a multiline control. This option is not available unless the Multi-line option has been selected.

Auto HScroll Scrolls text right automatically when a character is typed at the right end of the box. This option is checked by default. When Auto HScroll is selected, text automatically scrolls horizontally whenever the caret (text cursor) passes the right edge of a multiline edit box. The user must press the Enter key to start a new line. If Auto HScroll is not selected, the control automatically wraps words to the beginning of the next line when necessary.

Vertical Scroll Adds a vertical scrollbar to a multiline edit-box control. This option is not available unless the Multi-line option has been selected.

Auto VScroll In a multiline edit box, automatically scrolls text up one line when the user presses Enter on the last line. This option is not available unless the Multi-line option has been selected.

Password Displays all characters typed as asterisks (*). This property is not available for multiline edit boxes.

No Hide Selection Controls how text is displayed when an edit box loses and regains the focus. If set, text remains selected even when the edit box loses the focus.

OEM Convert Converts text typed in the edit box from the Windows character set to the OEM character set and then back to the Windows set. Selecting this option ensures proper character conversion when the application calls the `AnsiToOem` function to convert a Windows string in the edit box to OEM characters. This property is most useful for edit-box controls containing filenames.

OEM stands for original equipment manufacturer, but it refers to any kind of third-party addition, including special character sets for international use.

Want Return   Inserts a carriage return when the user presses the Enter key while typing text in a multiline edit box. If Want Return is not set, pressing the Enter key is the same as pressing the dialog box's default pushbutton. Want Return has no effect on single-line edit boxes.

Border   Draws a border around the edit box. This option is checked by default.

Uppercase   Converts all characters typed to uppercase.

Lowercase   Converts all characters typed to lowercase.

Read-Only   Prevents users from changing the contents of the edit box.

List Boxes

List boxes display text (or icon) lists, allowing the user to select one (or more) items. List box entries are supplied by the application. For example, a list box might contain a list of filenames. When the list is too long for the allocated space, a scrollbar appears for vertical scrolling.

Custom list boxes can also be defined as owner-drawn list boxes. Custom controls may include graphic as well as text entries, but they require provisions within the application to handle the display material. To create a custom list box, select either the Owner Draw Fixed or Owner Draw Variable option on the Styles tab of the List Box Properties dialog box. The Owner Draw Fixed style requires that all items in the list box have the same height; the Owner Draw Variable style permits the mixing of items of varying heights.

For more information about custom controls using the owner-drawn styles, refer to the Microsoft SDK.

When you create a list box, the resource editor supplies a default ID value: IDC_LIST*n*. You can enter a new ID or select one from a list of defined IDs in the General tab of the List Box Properties dialog box (see Figure 9.11, shown earlier). This dialog box contains the properties listed earlier in the section titled "General Properties for Other Controls."

The Styles tab of the List Box Properties dialog box contains options for setting the Control's appearance. Figure 9.14 shows this tab.

FIGURE 9.14:

Setting list box styles

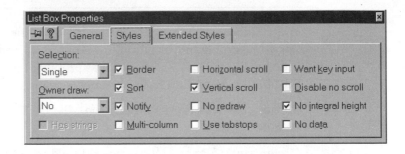

The Styles tab contains the following properties for list boxes:

Selection   Determines how items in a list box can be selected. Possible values are as follows:

- Single, which allows only one item in a list box to be selected at a time. This is the default selection method.

- Multiple, which allows more than one list-box item to be selected at a time. Clicking or double-clicking any unselected item selects it. Clicking or double-clicking any selected item deselects it. The Shift and Ctrl keys have no effect.

- Extended, which allows the Shift and Ctrl keys to be used together with the mouse to select and deselect list box items, select groups of items, and select nonadjacent items.

Owner Draw   Sets the owner-draw characteristics for the list box using one of the following values:

- No, which turns off the owner-draw style, limiting the list box contents to strings. This is the default setting.

- Fixed, which makes the owner of the list box responsible for drawing the contents of the list box. All items in the list box must be the same height. CWnd::OnMeasureItem is called when the list box is created, and CWnd::OnDrawItem is called when a visual aspect of the list box has changed.

- Variable, which makes the owner of the list box responsible for drawing the contents of the list box; however, items in the list box may be of varying heights. `CWnd::OnMeasureItem` is called for each item in the list when the list box is created, and `CWnd::OnDrawItem` is called when a visual aspect of the list box has changed.

Has Strings Specifies that an owner-drawn list box contains string items. The list box maintains the memory and pointers for the strings, allowing the application to use the `LB_GETTEXT` message to retrieve the text for a particular item. This option is available only if the Owner Draw option is set to either Fixed or Variable. If Owner Draw is set to No, the list box contains strings by default.

Border Creates a border around the list box. This option is checked by default.

Sort Sorts the contents of the list box alphabetically. This option is checked by default.

Notify Sends a notification to the parent window when the user clicks or double-clicks a list box item. This option is checked by default.

Multi-column Creates a multiple-column list box. In a multicolumn list box, the user scrolls horizontally. Use the `LB_SETCOLUMNWIDTH` message to set the width of the columns.

Horizontal Scroll Creates a horizontal scrollbar for the list box.

Vertical Scroll Creates a vertical scrollbar for the list box. This option is checked by default.

No Redraw Specifies that a list box's appearance is not updated when changes are made. You can change the No Redraw style via a `WM_SET-REDRAW` message or by calling `CWnd::SetRedraw`.

Use Tabstops Allows a list box to recognize and expand tab characters when drawing its strings. The default tab positions are 32 dialog box units (DLUs).

Want Key Input Sends the list box owner `WM_VKEYTOITEM` messages when the Has Strings style is used or `WM_CHARTOITEM` messages whenever a key is pressed and the list box has the input focus. The Want Key Input option allows an application to perform special processing on the keyboard input.

Disable No Scroll Displays a disabled vertical scrollbar in the list box when there are not enough items to scroll. By default, a scrollbar does not appear until the list box contains enough items to scroll.

No Integral Height   Specifies that the size of the list box is exactly the size specified by the application when the list box was created. Normally, the list box is sized so partial items are not displayed. This option is checked by default.

No Data   Prevents the list box from storing item data.

Combo Boxes

Combo boxes combine the features of edit boxes and list boxes. They permit the user to either select from a list or type an entry directly in the edit box.

Three styles of combo boxes are supported: simple, drop-down, and drop-down-list combo boxes (use the Styles tab of the Combo Box Properties dialog box to select these options). Custom combo boxes are defined using the Owner-Draw option on the Styles tab as well. These options will be covered in more depth in a moment.

As with the other resource types, the resource editor supplies a default ID value, IDC_COMBO*n*, when you create the combo box, but you can enter or select a new ID in the General tab of the Combo Box Properties dialog box. This dialog box contains the properties listed earlier in the section titled "General Properties for Other Controls."

The Data tab of the Combo Box Properties dialog offers one additional property, as shown in Figure 9.15. The Enter Listbox Items property is available only in resource files using MFC library support. This property allows you to enter the initial selections that will appear in the list portion of the combo box when the dialog box is created. To add entries, press Ctrl+Enter (line feed) at the end of each item to move to the next line.

FIGURE 9.15:

Setting the list box contents for combo boxes

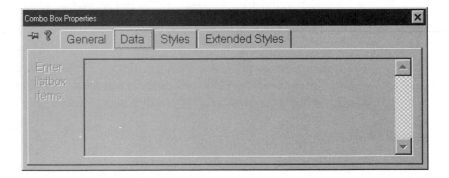

WARNING   A bug in Developer Studio 97 (Visual C++ version 5.0) causes the list box entry field in the Data tab to be permanently disabled. Earlier versions of VC++ offered this same functionality in a slightly different format without problems. At the time of this writing, there is no known patch to fix this problem, but you can edit the resource script directly—as ASCII text—to enter a default string list. Of course, irrespective of the resource script, an application can always add string entries at runtime.

The Styles tab of the Combo Box Properties dialog box allows you to set properties that affect the combo box's appearance. Figure 9.16 shows this tab.

FIGURE 9.16:

Setting combo box styles

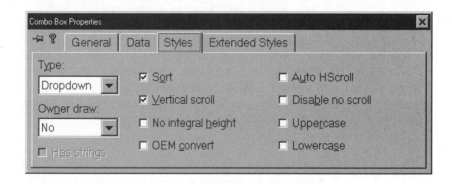

The Styles tab contains the following properties for combo boxes:

Type   Specifies the combo box as one of the following types:

- Simple, which creates a simple combo box combining an edit-box control for user input with a list-box control. The list is visible at all times, with the current selection from the list displayed in the edit-box control.

- Dropdown, which creates a drop-down combo box. A drop-down combo box is the same as a simple combo box, except the list is displayed only when the user selects the drop-down arrow at the right of the edit-box control portion. Because the lists appears only on demand, the area used can also be occupied by other controls. This is the default type.

- Drop List, which creates a drop-down-list combo box. A drop-down-list combo box is similar to the drop-down combo box except that the edit-box control is replaced by a static-text item displaying the current list selection. It does not accept user input; edit field entries must correspond to items already in the list.

Owner Draw   Sets the owner-draw characteristics for the combo box using one of the following values:

- No, which turns off the owner-draw style, limiting the list box contents to strings. This is the default setting.

- Fixed, which makes the owner of the combo box responsible for drawing the contents of the list box. All items in the list box must be the same height. `CWnd::OnMeasureItem` is called when the list box is created, and `CWnd::OnDrawItem` is called when a visual aspect of the list box has changed.

- Variable, which makes the owner of the combo box responsible for drawing the contents of the list box; however, list box items may be of varying height. `CWnd::OnMeasureItem` is called for each item in the list when the list box is created, and `CWnd::OnDrawItem` is called when a visual aspect of the list box has changed.

Has Strings   Specifies that an owner-drawn combo box contains string items. The list box maintains the memory and pointers for the strings, allowing the application to use the `LB_GETTEXT` message to retrieve the text for a particular item. This option is available only if the Owner Draw option is set to either Fixed or Variable. If Owner Draw is set to No, the list box contains strings by default.

Sort   Sorts the contents of the combo box alphabetically. This option is checked by default.

Vertical Scroll   Creates a vertical scrollbar for the list box. This option is checked by default.

No Integral Height   Specifies that the size of the combo box is exactly the size specified by the application when the combo box was created. Normally, the combo box is sized so partial items are not displayed.

OEM Convert   Converts text typed in the combo-box control from the Windows character set to the OEM character set and then back to the Windows set. This option ensures proper character conversion when the application calls the AnsiToOem function to convert a Windows string in the combo box to OEM characters. OEM Convert is most useful for combo boxes that contain filenames.

Auto HScroll   Scrolls text right automatically when the user types a character at the right end of the box.

Disable No Scroll   Displays a disabled vertical scrollbar in the list box when there are not enough items to scroll. By default, a scrollbar does not appear until the list box contains enough items to scroll.

Uppercase   Converts all characters typed to uppercase.

Lowercase   Converts all characters typed to lowercase.

List Control Boxes

List control boxes are an extension of the list-box type, with the additional capabilities of displaying either large or small icons, a multicolumn list with icons, or in a report format, columnar lists with a header. The four styles of list control boxes are illustrated in Figure 9.17.

FIGURE 9.17:

Four list control box styles

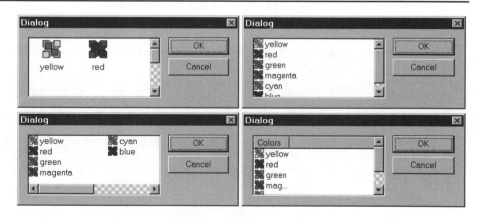

When a list control box is created, the default ID value IDC_LIST*n* (which follows the same format as a list box) is supplied. You can enter a new ID or select from a list of defined IDs in the General tab of the List Control Properties dialog box. This dialog box contains the properties listed in the earlier section titled "General Properties for Other Controls."

You set the appearance of the list control box using the Styles tab of the List Control Properties dialog box, shown in Figure 9.18.

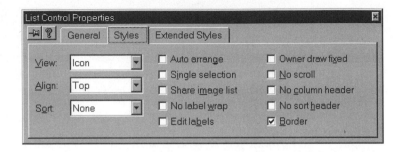

The Styles tab contains the following properties for list control boxes:

View Sets the display view for the list control box as one of the following:

- Icon, which sets the large icon view with the icons in a multicolumn arrangement. This is the default view.

- Small Icon, which sets the small icon view with the icons in a multi-column arrangement.

- List, which sets a list view as a single-column display with small icons (optional) along the left.

- Report, which sets a report view for a multicolumn text display with a column header.

Align Sets the alignment of icons in the list as one of the following:

- Top, which aligns icons at the top of the view. This is the default alignment.

- Left, which aligns icons at the left of the view.

Sort Sets the sort order for icons in the list as one of the following:

- None, which means no sort is applied. This is the default setting.

- Ascending, which sorts items in ascending order based on item text.

- Descending, which sorts items in descending order based on item text.

Auto Arrange   Automatically keeps icons arranged in both the Icon and Small Icon views.

Single Selection   Specifies that a user can select only one item at a time. By default, a user can select multiple items.

Share Image List   Specifies that the list control box does not assume ownership of the image lists assigned to it; that is, the image lists are not destroyed when the list control box is destroyed. This allows the same image list to be used with multiple list-control-box view controls.

No Label Wrap   Displays item text on a single line in Icon view. By default, item text may wrap in Icon view.

Edit Labels   Allows item labels to be edited in place. To support this, the parent window must process the LVN_ENDLABELEDIT notification message.

Owner Draw Fixed   Allows the owner window to paint items in the Report view. The list-control-box view control sends a WM_DRAWITEM message to paint each item but does not send separate messages for each subitem. The itemData member of the DRAWITEMSTRUCT structure contains the item data for the specified list-control-box view item.

No Scroll   Disables scrolling; all items must appear within the client area.

No Column Header   Specifies that no column header is displayed in the Report view.

No Sort Header   Prevents column headers from acting like buttons. Commonly, clicking a column head sorts the list by the column entries, but clicking may be implemented for some other action. If no action is provided as a response to a column-header click, setting this option will prevent a screen response.

Border   Creates a border around the list-control-box view control. This option is selected by default.

Tree Control Boxes

Tree control boxes are used to display hierarchical information in a tree format, where branches can be collapsed or expanded. The branches in the tree control may be displayed as a simple indented list or complete with node buttons and lines. Two styles of tree control boxes are illustrated in Figure 9.19.

FIGURE 9.19:

Two formats for tree controls

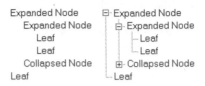

When a tree control box is created, the default ID value IDC_TREEn is supplied. You can enter a new ID or select one from a list of defined IDs in the General tab of the Tree Control Properties dialog box. This dialog box contains the properties listed in the earlier section titled "General Properties for Other Controls."

In addition to the General properties for the tree control box, the Styles properties allow you to set the control's appearance. Figure 9.20 shows this tab.

FIGURE 9.20:

Setting tree control box styles

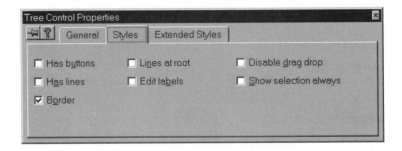

The Styles tab contains the following properties for tree control boxes:

Has Buttons   Displays plus (+) and minus (−) buttons next to parent items in the tree. These can be used to expand or collapse a parent item's list of child items. To include buttons with items at the root of the tree view, the Lines at Root option must be selected.

Has Lines   Uses lines to show the hierarchy for tree items.

Border   Creates a border around the tree control box.

Lines at Root   Uses lines to link items at the root of the tree control. The Lines at Root option is ignored if the Has Lines option is not selected.

Edit Labels   Allows the user to edit the labels of tree control items.

Disable Drag Drop   Prevents the tree control from sending TVN_BEGIN-DRAG notification messages.

Show Selection Always   Uses the system highlight colors to draw the selected item.

Range and Adjustment Controls

Standard dialog box features include horizontal and vertical scrollbars. Rather than being used to scroll the display within a window, dialog box scrollbars are often used as range slider controls or sometimes as range meters. For example, the Control Panel's Colors dialog box uses scrollbars to adjust the RGB intensities for custom colors. In like fashion, scrollbars might be used in a MIDI control application to set tone, voice, fade, and reverb.

More modern control versions adapted from scrollbars include slider and spin controls. In addition, the progress control, while not directly adapted from a scrollbar, shares some of the same characteristics. Figure 9.21 shows some examples of dialog box scrollbars and other range and adjustment controls.

FIGURE 9.21:

Scroll bars, sliders, and spin controls

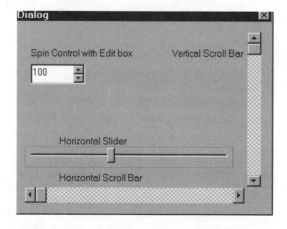

TIP

Remember, edit boxes, list boxes, and combo boxes supply their own scrollbars. They do not require separate provisions.

Horizontal and Vertical Scrollbars

Even though horizontal and vertical scrollbars are represented by different buttons on the dialog box editor's toolbar, these buttons are essentially a single tool differing only in their orientation. Both versions return the same event messages and respond to the same instructions (as do, incidentally, the slider and spin controls). The only real difference between the two forms of scrollbars is whether the SB_HORZ or SB_VERT argument is used when the scrollbar is generated.

When a scrollbar is created, a default ID value is supplied: IDC_SCROLLBAR*n*. You can enter a new ID or select one from a list of defined IDs in the General tab of the Scrollbar Properties dialog box, as shown in Figure 9.22.

FIGURE 9.22:

The General tab of the Scrollbar Properties dialog box

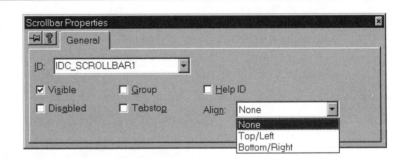

This dialog box contains the properties listed in the earlier section titled "General Properties for Other Controls," along with one additional property, Align. The options for the Align property include the following:

None   No special sizing or alignment is performed. The size of the scrollbar is the size specified in the resource script. This alignment is the default.

Top/Left   The scrollbar is set to a standard width (thickness) and aligned with the upper-left corner of the scrollbar window specified in the resource script. The scrollbar length is not changed.

Bottom/Right   The scrollbar is set to a standard width (thickness) and aligned with the lower-right corner of the scrollbar window specified in the resource script. The scrollbar length is not changed.

Selecting either Top/Left or Bottom/Right alignment sets the thickness of the scrollbar to match the width of the scrollbar's endpads and thumbpad.

Sliders

A slider control (also called a *trackbar)* is a scrollbar where the endpads of the conventional scrollbar are lost and the thumbpad is replaced by a choice of slider tabs. Slider controls may also include tick marks along their length, have slider tabs pointed to one side or the other, and be vertically or horizontally oriented.

The default resource ID for a new slider control is IDC_SLIDER*n*. You can change this ID and set the other general properties for the slider control through the Slider Properties dialog box. The General tab of this dialog box lists the same properties described earlier in "General Properties for Other Controls."

The Styles tab of the Slider Properties dialog box allows you to set orientation, tick marks, and other options. This tab is shown in Figure 9.23.

FIGURE 9.23:

Setting slider control styles

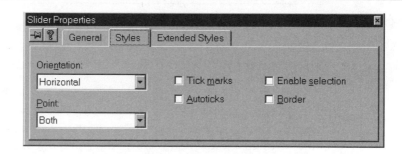

The Styles tab contains the following properties for slider controls:

Orientation   Displays the slider (trackbar) with a Horizontal (default) or Vertical orientation.

Point   Displays tick marks (if the Tick Marks property is enabled) on either or both sides of the slider and alters the slider knob. The tick marks and knob have the following orientations:

- Both, which displays tick marks on both sides of the slider. The slider knob is rectangular. This is the default setting.

- Top/Left, which displays tick marks on the top of a horizontal slider or on the left of a vertical slider. The slider knob changes to point to the selected side.

- Bottom/Right, which displays tick marks on the bottom of a horizontal slider or on the right of a vertical slider. The slider knob changes to point to the selected side.

Tick Marks   Enables the display of tick marks on a slider.

Autoticks   Sets a tick mark at each increment in the slider's range of values. Tick marks are created automatically by sending the TBM_SETRANGE message.

Enable Selection   Changes the narrow slider (seen earlier in Figure 9.21) to an open bar that can display a selection range with triangles and a highlighted area.

NOTE   Selection limits are not created during dialog box design but may be set during execution. This means that the triangles and highlight area will not appear during testing with the dialog box editor.

Border   Creates a border around the slider control.

Spin Controls

A spin control is a second variation of the scrollbar. In this adaptation, only the endpads remain in the form of two buttons; the body of the scrollbar and the thumbpad have vanished. The default form of a spin control is vertically oriented, with up and down arrows on the buttons. The alternative is a horizontal control, with the arrow buttons pointing right and left.

The spin control has a set range (established by the application). It may wrap values when the limits are reached or simply stop when the limits are encountered.

While you can use a spin control by itself, the spin button is commonly linked to an edit box (buddy window), as illustrated earlier in Figure 9.21, or to a static text field. In these cases, the spin control operations are automatically reflected in the buddy window.

NOTE   When an edit box is used as the buddy window and the `CSpinButton` class is used, changes in the edit box value are automatically reflected in the spin control's value.

Spin controls have the same General tab properties as the other types of controls (see the section "General Properties for Other Controls," earlier in the chapter). The default resource ID for a new spin button control is IDC_SPIN*n*.

On the Styles tab of the Spin Properties dialog box, you can specify the control's orientation, alignment, and other options. Figure 9.24 shows this tab.

FIGURE 9.24:

Setting spin button styles

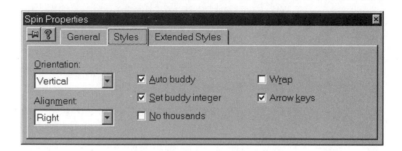

The Styles tab contains the following properties for spin controls:

Orientation   Sets the spin control display as Vertical (up/down, the default) or Horizontal (right/left).

Alignment   Sets the position where the spin control appears (on execution) relative to the buddy window. If no buddy window is established, alignment is irrelevant. The alignment value can be one of the following:

- Unattached, so that the spin control is not associated with any other control. This is the default setting.

- Left, so that on execution, the spin control is positioned next to the left edge of the buddy window. At the same time, the buddy window is moved right and the width adjusted to accommodate the width of the spin control.

- Right, so that on execution, the spin control is positioned next to the right edge of the buddy window. At the same time, the buddy window is moved left and the width adjusted to accommodate the width of the spin control.

TIP

Selecting Left or Right alignment does not change the layout of the controls during resource editing. The selected alignment appears only during execution.

Auto Buddy   Selects the previous window in the Z order (tab order) automatically as the spin control's buddy window. In turn, the buddy window displays the values (as text) set by the spin control. Normally, the buddy window will be an edit box or a static text field.

Set Buddy Integer   Sets the text of the buddy window using the WM_ SETTEXT message when the up or down buttons of the spin control are clicked. The text may have the setting value formatted as a decimal or hexadecimal string.

No Thousands   Prevents the buddy window from inserting a thousands separator between every three digits in decimal format.

Wrap   Wraps the spin-control value when it is incremented or decremented beyond the ending or beginning of the range.

Arrow Keys   Increments or decrements the value of the spin control automatically when the up or down arrow keys are pressed. This option is checked by default.

NOTE

In theory, a spin control could be "buddied" with any other type of control. For example, the label on a button might display the spin-control value, or a spin control might serve as a fine control for a slider or scrollbar. In practice, however, you will probably need to write your own provisions to make a spin control interact appropriately with anything except a numeric edit box or static text field.

Progress Bars

The progress bar is not a scrollbar derivative per se, even though it does have a similar appearance and, in the past, scrollbars were sometimes used to provide progress bar displays. The progress bar control is not a control in the usual sense. It does not react to user input, nor send messages to the application; its function is to show the progress of a task. For example, progress bars are commonly used when installing new software products. Figure 9.25 shows an example of a progress bar.

FIGURE 9.25:

A progress bar

The general properties for a progress bar are the same as those on the General tab of the other controls' Properties dialog boxes (see "General Properties of Other Controls," earlier in the chapter). There is one addition, however: the Border property, which creates a border around the trackbar control. The Border option is checked by default.

Other Control Types

The remaining control features are used to customize the appearance of a dialog box. You can add icons or bitmaps, provide visual grouping, and use shading to enhance the appearance of the dialog box. These controls include the following:

- Group boxes
- Hotkey controls
- Tab controls
- Pictures (bitmaps and icons)
- Animated controls
- Custom controls

With the exception of custom controls, each of these is illustrated in Figure 9.26.

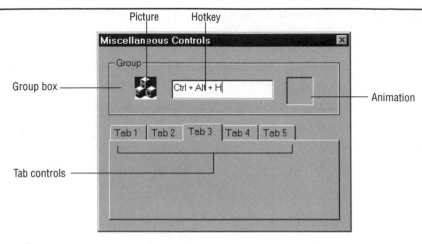

Group Boxes

Group boxes are simply outline boxes used to visually group controls by enclosing one or more controls in an outline with an optional group title.

The general properties for a group box are the same as for the other types of controls (see "General Properties for Other Controls," earlier in the chapter). However, group boxes also have a Caption property, which provides a label that appears in the upper-left corner of the group box frame.

The default resource ID for a group box is IDC_STATIC. This is the same ID used for a static text field—and for the same reason: A group box normally is not selectable and is not expected to receive or return messages.

Through the Styles tab of the Group Box Properties dialog box, you can set the horizontal alignment, add an icon or a bitmap, and set other properties. Figure 9.27 shows this tab.

The Styles tab contains the following properties for group boxes:

Horizontal Alignment   Sets the position of the group box's caption text to the Center, Right, or Default (left) position. »

Icon   Indicates that the group box title displays an icon. The Caption field in the General tab identifies the icon to display.

Bitmap   Indicates that the group box title displays a bitmap. The Caption field in the General tab identifies the bitmap to display.

Notify   Notifies the parent window when the user clicks or double-clicks a group box.

Flat   Gives the group box a flat appearance, without three-dimensional shading.

Pictures

The picture control is a static control element that does not respond to mouse selection and, by default, does not return any event messages. Instead, picture controls are customarily used simply to insert a graphic of some form into a dialog box.

Figure 9.28 shows the General tab of the Picture Properties dialog box. This tab has the same general properties as the other types of controls (see "General Properties of Other Controls"), plus a few extra properties.

FIGURE 9.28:

The General tab of the Pictures Properties dialog box

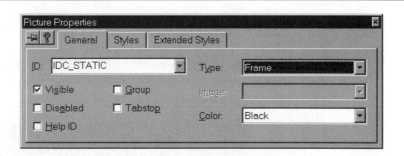

The following general properties are specific to pictures:

ID   Sets the ID for a picture control. The default resource ID for a picture control is IDC_STATIC*n*, the same as for a static text field or group box. If you want the picture to function as an active control—for example, as a button—the control type should be icon, bitmap, or metafile, and you should replace the default ID with a unique identifier. The new resource ID may be a symbol, integer, or a quoted string.

Type Sets the type of static graphic to display as one of the following:

- Frame, which displays a empty rectangle in the color specified in the Color property. Like a group box, a frame may be used to visually group controls. This is the default type.

- Rectangle, which displays a filled rectangle in the color specified in the Color property.

- Icon, which displays an icon in the dialog box. The identifier of the icon is specified in the Image property.

- Bitmap, which displays a bitmap in the dialog box. The identifier of the bitmap is specified in the Image property.

- Enhanced Metafile, which displays an enhanced metafile in the dialog box. The application must provide the means of identifying and executing the metafile.

NOTE   A *metafile* is a graphic image recorded as a series of instructions for its creation. Metafiles are discussed in Chapter 33.

Image Provides the identifier for the icon or bitmap to display.

Color Sets the color of a frame or rectangle to Black (the default), White, Gray, or Etched (which provides a three-dimensional appearance).

Figure 9.29 shows the Styles tab of the Picture Properties dialog box, which has properties for controlling the appearance of the picture.

FIGURE 9.29:

Setting picture styles

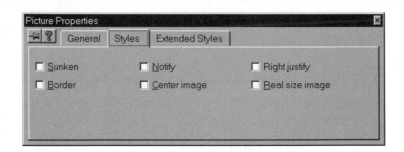

The Styles tab contains the following properties for pictures:

Sunken   Creates a border with a sunken edge around the picture control.

Border   Creates a border around the picture. This option is selected by default.

Notify   Allows the picture to notify the parent window when it's clicked or double-clicked.

TIP   Setting the Notify property allows an icon or bitmap image to respond as if it were a button. When setting the Notify property, however, you should change the default ID to a unique identifier to ensure proper handling and recognition of the message.

Center Image   Fills the rest of the client area with the color of the pixel in the top-left corner of the bitmap or icon if the bitmap or icon is smaller than the client area of the picture control.

Right Justify   Sets the lower-right corner of a picture control to remain fixed when the control is resized; only the top and left sides are adjusted to accommodate.

Real Size Image   Specifies that a static icon or bitmap control will not be resized as it is loaded or drawn. If the image is larger than the destination area, the image is clipped.

Hotkeys

A hotkey control is a simple input box in which a user can select a hotkey combination to assign to a particular task. When the hotkey control is selected, any key combination pressed is displayed as a hotkey combination. Figure 9.26, shown earlier, illustrates an example where pressing the *H* key while holding down the Ctrl and Alt keys is recognized as Ctrl+Alt+H.

The Ctrl, Alt, and Shift keys may be combined with any of the following:

Alphanumeric keys	Insert	Right	PgUp
Function keys	Delete	Left	PgDn
Number pad keys	Home	Up	CapsLock
Scroll Lock	End	Down	NumLock

Keys or combinations that cannot be used include:

Ctrl+Alt+Delete	Escape	Backspace	Tab
Windows key	System key	Enter	/ on number pad

WARNING   The hotkey control does apply minimum validation and will refuse some key combinations when entered. However, this control does not provide complete validation and, except for certain system hotkey codes, does not check the hotkey assignments against other conflicting assignments. Be sure to avoid assigning the same hotkey twice in a dialog box.

The default resource ID for a group box is IDC_HOTKEYn. The general properties for a hotkey control are the same as for the other controls (see "General Properties for Other Controls," earlier in the chapter), with the addition of a Border property. When the Border property is checked (the default), an outline appears around the hotkey control.

Animation Controls

An animation control is used to play back an animated sequence. This could be a simple sequence of images or a more elaborate video sequence. (But keep in mind that AVI sequences require a lot of storage space.)

The default resource ID for a group box is IDC_ANIMATEn. The general properties for an animation control are the same as for other controls, with these additions:

Center   Centers the animation in the animation control window.

Transparent   Draws the animation using a transparent background rather than the background color specified in the animation clip.

Auto-play   Sets the animation to begin playing as soon as the animation clip is opened.

Border   Creates an outline around the animation control. This option is checked by default.

Tab Controls

A tab control (see Figure 9.26, shown earlier) offers a method of arranging groups of controls in a dialog box as a sequence of tabs, with each tab containing a separate set of controls. The tab control may fill the dialog box or may use only a part of the space, leaving the remainder of the space for controls common to all tabs.

The number of tabs in a tab control and the labels for the tabs are set by the application, and a dialog box can contain several rows of tabs. The contents of the tabs are created as separate dialog boxes without title bars, system menus, and so on, and are then assigned to tabs by the application.

The general properties for a tab control are the same as for the other controls. The default resource ID for a tab control is IDC_TAB*n*.

On the Styles tab of the Tab Control Properties dialog box, shown in Figure 9.30, you can set the alignment, focus, and other features of the tab control.

FIGURE 9.30:

Setting tab control styles

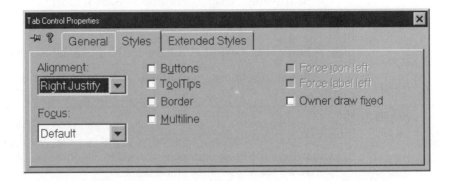

The Styles tab contains the following properties for tab controls:

Alignment   Sets the tab control alignment as one of the following:

- Right Justify, which adjusts the width of each tab so each row of tabs fills the entire width of the tab control. This is the default alignment.

- Fixed Width, which sizes all tabs to the width of the widest label.

- Ragged Right, which is used with multiline tabs; tab widths are not adjusted to fill the rows.

Focus   Determines how tabs are selected; choose from one of the following:

- Default, so keyboard selection may be used to select a tab or a tab may be selected by clicking with the mouse. (And of course, Default is the default setting.)

- On Button Down, so tabs receive the input focus (come to the front) when the tab is clicked.

- Never, so tabs do not receive the input focus when clicked. Instead, tabs must be selected by the application.

Buttons   Makes the tabs in the control resemble buttons. When tabs are displayed in button format, they should perform the same function as button controls; clicking a tab should carry out a task rather than display a tab page.

ToolTips   Creates a tooltip for each tab in the tab control.

Multi-line   Displays multiple rows of tabs.

Border   Creates an outline around the tab control.

Force Icon Left   Left-aligns the icon; the label remains centered.

Force Label Left   Left-aligns both the icon and the label.

WARNING   The reference to icons in the Force Icon Left and Force Label Left options is something of a mystery since selecting either option expands the tabs—a feature that is not mentioned—and the icons referred to are unknown. You can experiment for yourself to see how these properties work.

Owner Draw Fixed   Makes the parent window responsible for drawing tabs in the control.

Custom Controls

The custom control is undefined but provides a placeholder—a dark gray rectangle—representing a custom-control element. It is the responsibility of the application (or a custom library) to handle the appropriate screen display, to issue and respond to messages, and to handle any other required interactions. The General tab of the Custom Control Properties dialog box is shown in Figure 9.31.

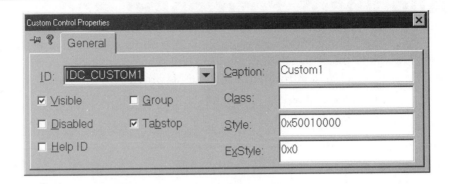

The default resource ID for a custom control is IDC_CUSTOM*n*. The general properties for a custom control are the same as for the other types of controls, with the following additional properties:

Caption   Sets a string entry that appears as a label for the custom control. To make one of the letters in the caption a mnemonic key (hotkey), place an ampersand (&) directly before the letter. A default caption name is supplied in the format "Caption *n*" (*n* represents a number matching the resource identifier).

Class   Sets the name of the control's Windows class. The named class must be registered before the dialog box containing the control is created. (During execution, the class must be registered before calling the dialog box.)

Style   Sets a 32-bit hexadecimal value specifying the control's style. This is primarily used to edit the lower 16 bits making up a user control's substyle.

ExStyle   Sets a 32-bit hexadecimal value specifying the control's extended style.

NOTE   The Style and ExStyle properties are undefined until a custom control is created. How or if these properties are used depends on the design and functionality of the custom control.

Alignment, Positioning, and Sizing Tools

You can position and size dialog box controls by using the mouse or, in some cases, by entering position and size information directly, but the easiest way to align controls is to use the tools provided by the resource editors.

Most of the Microsoft Developer Studio tools are accessible from its toolbar. Figure 9.32 shows this toolbar, with labels to identify the buttons.

FIGURE 9.32:

The Microsoft Developer Studio toolbar

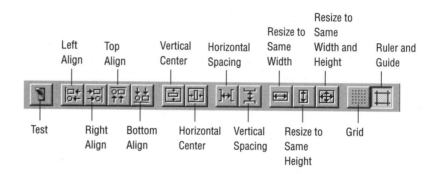

The toolbar buttons work as follows:

Test button   Allows you to test a dialog box during development, before the dialog box becomes part of an application.

Alignment buttons   Provide left, right, top, and bottom alignment. To align a group of controls, hold down the Shift key while clicking each control. The last control selected will become the reference control, and all other selected controls will be aligned to the position of that control.

Centering buttons   Provide vertical and horizontal centering. These can be used to center one or more controls relative to the dialog box itself. If you select more than one control, the selected controls are centered as a group but retain their positions relative to each other.

Spacing buttons   Provide horizontal or vertical spacing. These buttons give you the ability to select two (or more) controls and then space them equally across or down. If you are spacing controls horizontally, the leftmost and rightmost extremes are taken as the limits, and all controls selected are spaced equally between these two limits, without affecting individual vertical positioning. For vertical spacing, the highest and lowest extremes are taken as limits, and horizontal spacing remains unaffected.

Sizing buttons   Allow you to resize controls. Again, you must select more than one control, and the last control you select (identified by the dark handles on the outline) serves as the size reference. Multiple controls may be resized to the same width, to the same height, or with both height and width adjusted at the same time.

Grid button   Provides a background grid of fine dots, which can help you align controls. When the grid is enabled, the ruler and guides are disabled. Then, when you move a control, its position is snapped to the grid. Likewise, when you resize a control, the size is snapped to the grid.

Ruler and Guide button   Provides vertical and horizontal rulers in dialog box units, plus a guide that appears as a faint blue border or margin around the dialog box. When the guide is enabled, controls moved toward the guides tend to snap to the guide if they are close enough. From the Layout menu, select the Guide Settings option to change the guide settings and adjust grid spacing.

To adjust the tab ordering for dialog box controls, select Tab Order from the Developer Studio's Layout menu. When you select this option, all of the dialog box controls are labeled with a tab order number, as shown in Figure 9.33. To change the tab order, click the first control and then continue clicking controls in the order desired. The tab order numbers will change to reflect the new order. To stop setting the tab order, simply click anywhere except on a control.

FIGURE 9.33:

Selecting the Tab Order option from the Developer Studio's Layout menu shows your dialog box with tab order numbers.

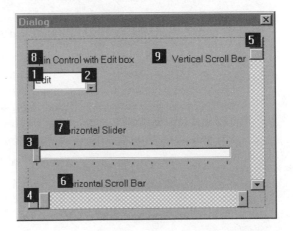

Dialog Box Testing Tips

When testing a dialog box during development, a few items to check in particular include the following:

- **Tab order for controls.** Use the Tab key to move between controls and make sure that the required groups, tab stops, and ordering are appropriate.

- **Radio button groups.** Be sure that radio button groups function correctly and that buttons reset appropriately. If there is a problem, check the tab order.

- **Overlapping elements.** Check particularly for static text elements that may be larger than the text they contain and may overlap (and conceal) other elements.

Three Dialog Boxes for FileView1

 The *FileView1* demo requires three dialog boxes: About, File Type, and Open File. These three dialog boxes are described in the following sections and are included in the FileView1.RC resource script on the CD accompanying this book. However, even though you do not need to re-create these dialog boxes using a dialog box editor, they illustrate some important features of dialog box construction.

> **NOTE**
>
> The *FileView2* demo uses the common dialog File Open facility, so it includes only one dialog box resource: the About dialog box. The script for this resource is included on the CD accompanying this book and needs no explanation.

The About Dialog Box

The About dialog box, shown in Figure 9.34, consists of a captioned dialog box without a system menu. The title bar bears the text "About FileView." Three dialog box elements appear as a centered text line, an icon box, and a single button.

FIGURE 9.34:

A simple About dialog box
with an icon

The single button returns a value, IDOK (0x01), which is defined in
Windows.H.

The File Type Dialog Box

The File Type dialog box, shown in Figure 9.35, again uses a captioned dialog box
with a static text instruction supplementing the caption. In this example, two control buttons appear at the bottom on either side of the File Type icon. The Okay
button, as the heavy outline illustrates, is the default.

FIGURE 9.35:

The File Type dialog box

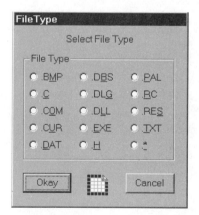

Inside the group box, 15 auto radio buttons offer a choice of file extensions.
When the dialog box is initialized by the *FileView* demo, the **.*** button will be
set as the default extension, but this is a provision of the program code, not the
dialog box.

Also, even though the auto radio buttons are enclosed by a group box outline, this is for visual purposes only; the group box here does not control the grouping. Instead, the grouping is assigned by setting the Group property for the first item in the group and setting the tab order for all of the buttons.

NOTE   The resources and dialog boxes created for the *FileView1* demo may be edited with either the Microsoft or Borland resource editor. The *FileView2* application files, however, are not compatible with the Borland compiler or resource editors.

The File Selection Dialog Box

In some respects, the File Selection dialog box used by the *FileView* demo is the most complicated and the most important. This dialog box, shown in Figure 9.36, offers two edit boxes, plus a list box where files matching the file specification will be displayed (together, of course, with directory and drive IDs). In addition to the customary Okay and Cancel buttons, a third button, File Type, is provided to call the File Type dialog box.

FIGURE 9.36:

The File Selection dialog box

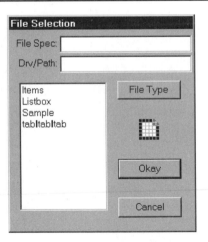

Beginning at the top, the File Spec edit box has been provided with a default test string, "*.*". This text string, however, is superfluous; when the dialog box is initialized, the application will provide its own string both here and in the Drv/Path edit box below the File Spec edit box.

Next, when the dialog box is initialized, the list box will be filled with file, directory, and drive information using the application-assigned, default file specification and the current (active) drive/path settings.

Last, the File Type button returns an IDM_TYPE message, which is used to instruct the application to load the File Type dialog box.

This completes our discussion of working with dialog box resources. We've covered all types of dialog box controls. Custom dialog box controls have been mentioned only briefly, as alternatives to the standard controls. Fortunately, the majority of applications will not require custom control designs.

Also, as you may have noticed, no mention has been made of adding menus to dialog boxes. This is not because menus are not supported, but because the dialog box editor is not the appropriate mechanism for constructing menus. We'll cover menu editors and menu construction in the next chapter.

CHAPTER
TEN

Menu Resources

- Menu editor features

- Menu item properties

- Menus in dialog boxes

- Menu scripts

For many Windows applications, the primary entry point is a menu bar that offers initial options and access to principal features. In other cases, dialog boxes may use menus to present further choices or applications may present different primary menus depending on the current operation.

In this chapter, we'll look at how menus are constructed and some of the possible arrangements for menus and submenus.

A Menu Editor

Menu resources are easy to create, and, in keeping with their text nature, require little more than ASCII scripts for their design. However, menu editors provide an easier way to construct and test menus. Menu editors can generate either an .RC menu script or a compiled .RES resource.

In the Microsoft Developer Studio menu editor, the menu is presented in a single window, and menu item properties are displayed in the pop-up Properties dialog box. Figure 10.1 shows a menu under construction in this menu editor.

Here you should notice two blank rectangles: one at the end of the primary menu bar and one at the bottom of the pull-down File menu. Neither of these items actually appears in the menu; they are simply placeholders, ready for your new entries.

To add a menu item, simply double-click the blank rectangle on the primary menu bar or on the pull-down menu, This brings up the Menu Item Properties dialog box for the item, as shown in Figure 10.2.

In the Menu Item Properties dialog box, enter an ID and caption (if appropriate) or select an option for the entry. A new blank item will appear as soon as you have entered the new caption or selected the Separator option. See the "Menu Item Properties" section later in the chapter for details on setting properties for your menu items.

To move a menu item to a different position in the menu, simply click and drag the entry to the position desired.

To remove a menu item, highlight the item and press the Delete key.

FIGURE 10.1:

The Microsoft Developer
Studio menu editor

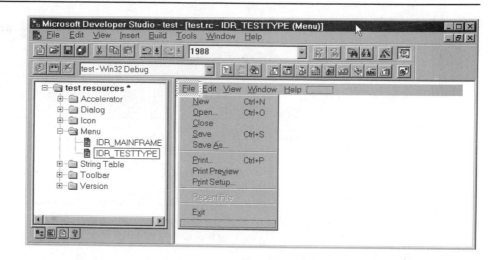

FIGURE 10.2:

The Developer Studio's Menu
Item Properties dialog box

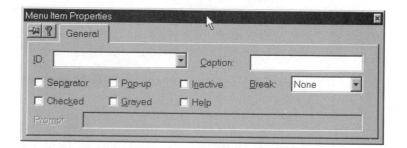

Menu Size Limitations

Theoretically, you can create a menu of virtually any size. But in practical terms, too large a menu probably means that you need to rethink your menu's organization.

As an unwieldy example, Figure 10.3 shows a primary menu bar with a total of 31 entries, requiring five lines to display on a screen 420 pixels wide.

Obviously, there must be some actual limits on the number of menu elements and the number of levels supported, although these limits have nothing to do with the resource compiler or Windows 98. To set practical limits, consider how much is too much. At what point does a menu bar become too complex to be comfortable to use? When does it become a liability instead of an asset?

FIGURE 10.3:

An unwieldy primary menu

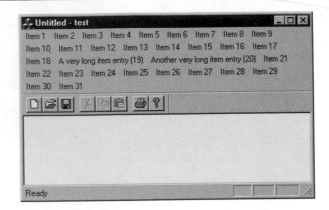

> **NOTE**   If you reduce the width of the window, the menu bar will be rearranged automatically to use as many lines as necessary. (This automatic rearrangement does not happen for toolbars, however.)

These questions apply not only to the number of primary entries but also to the number of levels and pop-up (pull-down) submenus.

As a general rule of thumb, the primary menu should not exceed one line (in a normal-size window), and the number of pop-up submenu levels should probably not go further than two or three. If your application needs more items than a simple menu structure can supply, consider creating a very simple primary menu, with the menu selections calling a series of dialog boxes to offer the more complex options.

> **TIP**   For an alternative to overloaded menus, consider using pop-up menus. See Chapter 13 for details.

Text for Menu Entries

Individual menu entries can be as simple as a single word, a brief phrase, or some combination of these. They may or may not include hotkey assignments or accelerator keys.

The text for a menu entry is one of its properties (the Caption property). In the Microsoft Developer Studio menu editor, enter the text in the Caption field of the Menu Item Properties dialog box. (You will read more about setting menu properties in the "Menu Item Properties" section later in the chapter.)

Note that you cannot enter a tab character directly by pressing the Tab key while typing in the menu item text. The C convention \t is recognized as a tab instruction and is commonly used to identify accelerator keys by setting them flush-right in the menu entry. (Accelerator keys are covered briefly in the next section and in detail in Chapter 11.) The \a instruction also causes the text following it to be right-justified.

Also note that no provisions are made for multiline menu entries, and carriage returns and line-feeds are not supported. Thus, even though the menu editor can accept entries up to 255 characters, this does not mean that the menu can display strings of that length (but certainly you should feel free to experiment).

Menu Hotkeys

The primary menu hotkeys, which are identified in the menus by the underscore character and in the script by the ampersand character (&), are automatic assignments generated when the menu script is compiled. By custom, most menu entries use the first letter in each entry as the hotkey; however, the hotkey does not need to be the first character. Also, Windows does not underscore the entry unless it is specifically instructed to do so.

For example, to select the O in Open… as the hotkey for that menu entry, type the text as &Open…. This entry will then appear in the menu as Open….

Within any menu or submenu, you cannot use the same hotkey twice at the same level. Thus Cut, Copy, and Close Clipboard—items that are all on the same level—use three different hotkeys (T, C, and L). However, if you added a Search entry that called a pop-up menu that had a Stop entry, the S hotkey could be used again because these items are on different levels.

TIP   If more than one ampersand appears in a menu item, only the last ampersand entry is recognized. If you want to include an actual ampersand in the menu entry text, enter a double ampersand (&&). For example, to create the menu item Search & Replace, enter `Search && Replace`. The ampersand will appear in the item as a single & character and will not be treated as a hotkey identifier.

In many cases, menu entries have secondary hotkeys identified as Shift+*key* or Ctrl+*key*. Another convention uses a simple syntax to identify hotkeys, with the caret character (^) indicating the Ctrl key. Both conventions are acceptable; however, simply identifying a secondary hotkey in the menu definition does not assign the key definition as a functional hotkey. These hotkey assignments are handled as accelerator keys.

Accelerator hotkeys, which are global, cannot be duplicated within a dialog box or application window, although the same accelerator key combination can be used for different purposes in different menus or in different dialog boxes. The use of accelerators is covered in the next chapter.

Menu Item Properties

To set menu item properties in the Microsoft Developer Studio menu editor, double-click a menu item to bring up the Menu Item Properties dialog box (see Figure 10.2, earlier in the chapter).

The following menu item properties generally apply to menu items created with menu editors, although they may be labeled with different names (for example, the identifier property is named ID in the Microsoft Developer Studio menu editor and Name in the Borland C++ Builder menu editor).

ID   Acts as an identifier; it is commonly a mnemonic symbol, defined in the header file. Unlike other resources, new menu resources do not get a default ID. However, the prefix IDM_ is commonly used to identify menu item messages. Pop-up menu items, which are handled internally, do not have ID values and do not return messages when selected. Similarly, menu separators, which cannot be selected, do not require ID values.

Caption   Sets the menu item text (see the "Text for Menu Entries" section earlier in the chapter).

Separator   Specifies that the menu item is a separator. Separator items do not have captions or IDs and cannot be selected.

Checked   Specifies that the menu item is initially checked when the menu opens.

Grayed   Sets the menu item as initially inactive and grayed and also sets the Inactive property. Before you can select an inactive (grayed) menu item, it must be enabled by the application (see CMenu::EnableMenuItem).

Prompt   Supplies text to appear in the status bar when this menu item is selected. The prompt entry is added to the resource string table using the same ID as the menu item.

NOTE   Unlike toolbar buttons, menu items do not support tooltips. Do not add a tip entry to the prompt string entry.

Pop-up   Sets the menu item as a pop-up item; that is, the primary item for a pop-up submenu. This is the default setting for top-level menu items.

Inactive   Sets the menu item as initially inactive, but *not* grayed. Before you can select an inactive menu item, it must be enabled by the application (see `CMenu::EnableMenuItem`).

Help   Right-justifies the item on the menu bar at runtime, but not during editing.

Break   Sets the break style as one of the following:

- None, for no break (the default).

- Column, for a static menu-bar item that you want to place on a new line. For a pop-up menu, the item is placed in a new column with no dividing line between columns. Setting the Column property affects the menu only at runtime, not during editing.

- Bar, for a static menu-bar item that you want to place on a new line. For a pop-up menu, the item is placed in a new column with a vertical dividing line between columns. Setting the Bar property affects the menu only at runtime, not during editing.

Adding Menus to Dialog Boxes

Menu resources can also be attached to dialog boxes quite easily. To add a menu to a dialog box, first create the menu as a resource.

Then, open the Dialog Properties dialog box for the dialog box resource and select the menu to attach from the Menu pull-down list. In Figure 10.4, the menu resource is identified by name (`"FILETYPE"`), but menu resources may also use mnemonic identifiers (such as `ID_FILETYPE_MENU`).

FIGURE 10.4:

Using the Dialog Properties dialog box to attach a menu to a dialog box

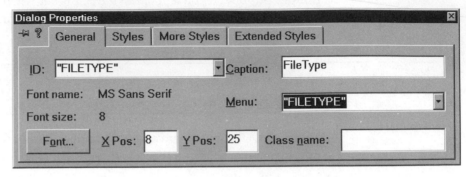

For an example of a menu in a dialog box, see the File Type dialog box in the *File-View1* demo (included on the CD accompanying this book, in the Chapter 12 folder).

Menu Scripts

A menu editor is a convenient tool, but it is not the only way to create menus. As an alternative, you can use any plain text editor, such as the Windows Notepad, to create a menu script. As an example, let's see how to create a script for a simple menu with four primary entries and an assortment of pull-down menus and further submenus.

The menu script begins with a name, IDM_MENU1, followed by the resource type identifier, MENU. On the next line, the keyword BEGIN identifies the start of the menu definition.

```
IDM_MENU1 MENU
BEGIN
```

TIP   You may see opening and closing brackets rather than BEGIN and END statements in scripts. Both formats are correct, although the Borland and Microsoft compilers may each complain about the other's syntax when moving a resource file from one compiler to the other.

The first menu item is identified by the keyword POPUP and followed by the text for this item. Because the pop-up entry will then be followed by at least one subentry, another BEGIN/END block is initiated on the next line.

```
POPUP "&Edit"
BEGIN
```

The next few lines define menu entries for the Edit submenu, each beginning with the keyword MENUITEM, followed by the entry text, the entry ID, and, optionally, one or more flag arguments controlling how the menu entry is initially displayed.

```
MENUITEM "C&ut\t^U",    201, CHECKED
MENUITEM "&Copy\t^C",   202
MENUITEM "&Paste\t^P",  203, INACTIVE, MENUBARBREAK
```

In this fragment, the first item on this submenu is presented with a checkmark (CHECKED). The third item uses the INACTIVE keyword to make the entry unselectable and the MENUBARBREAK keyword to cause a column break with a vertical separator bar.

Next, a new submenu entry is defined as an entry in the Edit submenu. The Search submenu has two entries, without any special features, but it does require a BEGIN/END pair to set off the submenu block.

```
POPUP "&Search\t^S"
BEGIN
    MENUITEM "&Find\t^F",    204
    MENUITEM "&Replace\t^R", 205
END
```

Following the Search submenu, a final entry is made in the Edit submenu but, this time, is disabled using the GRAYED keyword. The MENUBREAK keyword produces a column break but does not produce a vertical separator. The Clear clipboard menu entry is followed by an END statement to close the Edit submenu.

```
    MENUITEM "C&lear clipboard\t^L", 206, GRAYED, MENUBREAK
END
```

The remaining primary menu level entries are the next MENUITEMS. The Help menu item uses the keyword HELP to set this entry flush-right on the main menu bar. The script terminates with a closing END statement.

```
MENUITEM "&Print", 101
MENUITEM "&File",  102
MENUITEM "&Help",  103, HELP
END
```

Now that you've seen the fragments and explanations, the entire Menu_1 script follows, showing the overall structure and indentations (these indentations are for the programmer's benefit only and have no effect on how the menu script compiles).

```
IDM_MENU1 MENU
BEGIN
    POPUP "&Edit"
    BEGIN
        MENUITEM "C&ut\t^U",      201, CHECKED
        MENUITEM "&Copy\t^C",     202
        MENUITEM "&Paste\t^P",    203, INACTIVE, MENUBARBREAK
        POPUP "&Search\t^S"
        BEGIN
            MENUITEM "&Find\t^F",     204
            MENUITEM "&Replace\t^R", 205
        END
        MENUITEM "C&lear clipboard\t^L", 206, GRAYED, MENUBREAK
    END
    MENUITEM "&Print", 101
    MENUITEM "&File",  102
    MENUITEM "&Help",  103, HELP
END
```

Two Menus for FileView

The one menu script command that does not appear in the preceding example is the horizontal menu separator, SEPARATOR. This command is used in the following script, which is the script for the *FileView1* demo's menu (the *FileView1* and *FileView2* demos are discussed in Chapter 12 and included on the CD accompanying this book).

```
FILEVIEW MENU DISCARDABLE
BEGIN
    POPUP "&File"
    BEGIN
        MENUITEM "&Open...\t^O", IDM_OPEN    // = 103
        MENUITEM "&Type...\t^T", IDM_TYPE    // = 104
        MENUITEM SEPARATOR
```

```
        MENUITEM "&About",          IDM_ABOUT    // = 102
        MENUITEM "E&xit\t^X",       IDM_QUIT     // = 101
    END
END
```

The *FileView2* demo's menu script, shown here, is slightly different.

```
IDR_MAINFRAME MENU PRELOAD DISCARDABLE
BEGIN
    POPUP "&File"
    BEGIN
        MENUITEM "&Open...\tCtrl+O",             ID_FILE_OPEN
        MENUITEM SEPARATOR
        MENUITEM "E&xit",                        ID_APP_EXIT
    END
    POPUP "&View"
    BEGIN
        MENUITEM "&Toolbar",                     ID_VIEW_TOOLBAR
        MENUITEM "&Status Bar",                  ID_VIEW_STATUS_BAR
    END
    POPUP "&Help"
    BEGIN
        MENUITEM "&About FileView2...",          ID_APP_ABOUT
    END
END
```

Notice that both the *FileView1* and *FileView2* menu scripts are written using mnemonic identifiers rather than actual values. The constants are defined in the FileView.H header file.

As you learned in this chapter, menu editors provide a convenient way to create, define, and test application menus. If you prefer, you can also create menus as scripts, using any plain-text editor, such as the Windows Notepad.

CHAPTER
ELEVEN

11

Accelerators, Strings, Header Files, and Version Information

- Accelerators and accelerator editors

- String tables and string table editors

- Header files for resource IDs

- Version information

In addition to the more obvious resource types we've discussed so far—images, dialog boxes, and menus—you should know about two other resources: accelerator keys and string resources. Although these are less graphic and less impressive than other resources, they are just as important for the programmer.

Another type of programmer resource is the header definition file, which is also discussed in this chapter. When used properly, header files can prevent a great many errors that would otherwise be difficult to identify.

And finally, there are version resources. Even though these are very simple, they provide a convenient location to record version, copyright, and source notes within the application.

Accelerator Key Resources

Accelerator keys offer a fast shortcut—in the form of keyboard hotkey combinations—for issuing application commands. Although conventional (DOS) programs have often provided similar services, frequently employing TSR utilities to translate individual keystrokes or key combinations into command sequences, accelerator keys take a rather different form.

One of the most important differences is that, unlike DOS-based TSRs, accelerator keys do not depend on interrupt processing by an outside application. Instead, accelerator key processing is handled internally by Windows and is part and parcel of the Windows messaging system.

As explained in Chapter 4, Windows does not send keystroke information directly to the applications. Instead, all Windows applications rely on Windows to intercept the hardware keyboard events, translate these as necessary, and then forward them in the form of keyboard messages to the appropriate application. This approach allows you to add provisions for special key combinations to generate custom messages in place of key-event messages; in Windows, this is only a minor change. More important, each application can define its own accelerator key combinations and the messages to be generated by each.

Still, no matter how convenient or how smooth this translation may be, it remains the programmer's responsibility to define these accelerator hotkey combinations and to prepare this information in a form acceptable to the resource compiler for inclusion in the application's resources.

Accelerator Key Combinations

An accelerator key definition consists of two parts:

- A keyboard key or key combination
- A message value to be sent to the application when the key combination is entered

In general, single keystrokes are not used as accelerator keys simply because these key events have other purposes that take precedence. An accelerator key is commonly defined as a key combination requiring one conventional key plus one or more of the Ctrl, Alt, or Shift keys. For example, common shortcuts for Edit menu commands are Ctrl+C for Copy, Ctrl+X for Cut, and Ctrl+V for Paste. The conventional key can be defined as either an ASCII key or as a virtual key.

Virtual versus ASCII Keys

Virtually (the pun is unavoidable) all of the keys on the keyboard—whether a standard or an enhanced keyboard—can be defined as accelerator keys using the virtual key definitions provided in the WinUser.H header file.

Not all keys, however, have ASCII equivalents, and a few ASCII keys do not have virtual key equivalents, such as the exclamation point (!). Furthermore, some virtual key definitions do not correspond to anything found on the contemporary keyboard, such as the VK_ZOOM or VK_NONAME virtual keys; some refer to a non-keyboard device, such as the VK_MBUTTON virtual key. Table 11.1 lists the key codes that you don't want to use as accelerator keys.

TABLE 11.1: Key Codes Not Recommended for Use as Accelerator Keys

Key codes*	Comments
0Ch, 5Bh..5Dh, 60h..69h	Special requirements and functions
6Ah..6Bh, 6Dh..7Bh, A0h..A5h	Enhanced keyboards only
29h..2Fh, 2Ah..2Bh, 2Fh, 6Ch, 7Ch..87h, E5h, F6h..FEh	OEM-specific keys
05..07h, 0Ah..0Bh, 0Eh..0Fh, 1Ah, 3Ah..40h, 5Eh..5Fh, 88h..8Fh, 92h..9Fh, A6h..E4h, E6h..F5h	Not assigned
15h..19h, 1Ch..1Fh	Reserved for Kanji system

NOTE   Refer to Chapter 4 for more details on key codes and virtual key identifiers.

In general, however, an ASCII key refers to any of the alphanumeric keys that produce displayable characters on the screen. These include the punctuation keys and the spacebar.

Virtual key definitions (all of which begin with the prefix VK_) refer principally to the function, arrow, and keypad keys. Thus, the F1 key is defined as VK_F1, the PgDn key as VK_NEXT, the down-arrow key as VK_DOWN, and the left Shift key on an enhanced keyboard as VK_LSHIFT. The standard alphanumeric keys, however, are not excluded; they are identified as VK_A through VK_Z and VK_0 through VK_9.

NOTE   Keep in mind that uppercase and lowercase keys are not differentiated either as virtual keys or when used as accelerator keys employing an ASCII key definition.

Accelerator Key Scripts

Accelerator keys can be defined, in script form, using any plain-text editor, such as the Windows Notepad. Here is a sample script for the *FileView1* demo's keyboard accelerators (the *FileView* demo is discussed in the next chapter):

```
FILEVIEW ACCELERATORS
BEGIN
    "X", IDM_QUIT, ASCII, CONTROL    // = 101
    "O", IDM_OPEN, ASCII, CONTROL    // = 103
    "T", IDM_TYPE, ASCII, CONTROL    // = 104
END
```

In this example, the three accelerator keys are Ctrl+X, Ctrl+O, and Ctrl+T, returning the values IDM_QUIT, IDM_OPEN, and IDM_TYPE, respectively.

In the following example, the preceding accelerator keys are repeated in a different format, together with five new accelerator keys showing various Ctrl, Alt, and Shift key modifiers.

```
ACCLDEMO ACCELERATORS
BEGIN
    VK_X,   IDM_QUIT, VIRTKEY, CONTROL    // = 101
    VK_O,   IDM_OPEN, VIRTKEY, CONTROL    // = 103
    VK_T,   IDM_TYPE, VIRTKEY, CONTROL    // = 104
```

```
        VK_F1,  105,      VIRTKEY
        VK_F4,  106,      VIRTKEY
        VK_F6,  107,      VIRTKEY,          SHIFT
        "s",    108,      ASCII,    ALT,    SHIFT
        "G",    109,      ASCII,    CONTROL, SHIFT
    END
```

NOTE   The spacing is irrelevant to the resource compiler and has been added only to make the various elements of each definition easier to read. Also notice that it does not matter whether the ASCII key definition is entered as uppercase or lowercase, and the CapsLock status does not affect recognition of the accelerator key combination.

For non-ASCII keys, this virtual-key definition format is almost essential. However, a more convenient entry method is provided by an accelerator editor.

An Accelerator Editor

The Microsoft Developer Studio offers an accelerator editor, which includes the Accel Properties dialog box for entering or editing an accelerator table item. Figure 11.1 shows the accelerator editor and the Accel Properties dialog box.

FIGURE 11.1:

The Microsoft Developer Studio accelerator editor

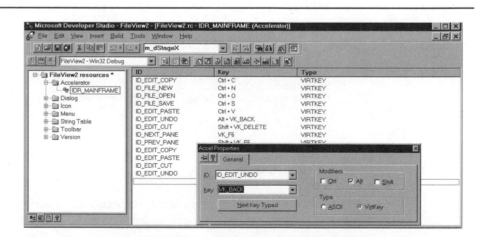

The editor offers the following properties for accelerators:

ID   Sets the resource ID, which is normally a mnemonic symbol defined in the header file, but it may also be an integer value or a quoted string.

Modifiers   Indicate whether the accelerator key is a combination formed with the Ctrl, Alt, or Shift keys. If the key value is an ASCII value, the Alt and Shift key combinations are not accepted. Instead, the defaults are True for Ctrl, but False for Alt and Shift. The Alt and Shift combinations can be used only with VK_xxxx (virtual key) combinations such as the Backspace (VK_BACK) or Delete (VK_DELETE) keys

Key   Specifies the accelerator key. It can be one of the following:

- Integer, in the range 0 to 255. Integers are interpreted as ASCII or virtual-key values, depending on the Type property.

NOTE   Any single digit is interpreted as a key value. To enter an ASCII value from 0 to 9, precede the number with two zeros (for example, 006). In like fashion, two digit codes may be preceded with a single zero, although this is not a firm requirement.

- Character, for a character value. Optionally, the character value may be preceded by a caret (^) to signify a control character.

- Virtual-key identifier, for any virtual-key identifier. Select the desired VK_xxxx value from the drop-down list.

Type   Identifies a key value as an ASCII value or a virtual key (VirtKey) value.

Next Key Typed   Accepts the next key combination typed as the accelerator key. The Key and Modifiers values are changed to match. If possible, the key selected is always interpreted as a virtual key. The choice between entering an accelerator key definition directly or using the Next Key Typed option is purely a matter of personal preference.

String Resources

Treating strings as resources instead of scattering the strings throughout the program code is a distinct departure from conventional programming practices. Most compilers gather such static data together, usually positioning this data toward the end of the .EXE code, along with other static-data elements.

Defining strings as resources has three advantages:

- Like other resources, strings are loaded into memory only when and as they are needed.

- Strings in a string table can be modified more conveniently than strings scattered throughout the source code.

- Multiple string tables can be defined. Each table can provide different language versions and be loaded according to the user's preference.

- Standardization of error message syntax is more easily controlled when all strings are grouped in one location rather than scattered through multiple source files or even scattered within a single source file.

As with menu and accelerator key resources, string tables can be created using a plain-text editor, such as the Windows Notepad, Write, or Unipad (for non-English languages). Alternatively, you can create string tables using a resource editor.

String Resource Definition

String resources may consist of any type of string data and may be used for any of the same purposes as conventional string data, including window captions, messages, labels, or even brief explanations. (String table entries are generally not used for button and control captions or menus because these text strings can be handled through an image or menu editor.)

TIP   Previously, in 16-bit systems, string table entries were limited to a length of 255 characters. Today, in 32-bit systems, this limitation has been raised to a generous (and useful) 32KB. This means that you can put far more than simple messages in string tables—anything from .RTF and .HTML texts to custom-formatted messages. For examples of how string table entries can be put to new and expanded uses, see *Windows Error Messages*, also written by Ben Ezzell (published by O'Reilly & Associates).

Individually, each string definition follows C conventions and is enclosed in double quotation marks. Strings also accept C's special embedded characters, such as \n for a line feed, \r for a carriage return, \t for a tab character, \\ for a single backslash, and \" for an embedded double-quotation mark.

String Table Construction

A typical (if brief) string table might look something like the following (this is excerpted from the FileView1.RC resource script):

```
STRING TABLE
BEGIN
```

```
    IDS_NAME,   "FileView"
    IDS_ERROR1, "File size indeterminate"
    IDS_ERROR2, "File too large for present example"
END
```

Each string in a string table is identified by a short integer value, placing an upper limit of 65,535 strings in the string table. In this example, the string IDs are provided by constants defined in the FileView.H header.

In the second version of this string table, the actual values are substituted for the mnemonic constants, and there are a few additional strings.

```
STRING TABLE
BEGIN
     1, "FileView"
     2, "File size indeterminate"
     3, "File too large for present example"
    16, "this string belongs to another group"
    17, "together with this second string"
    32, "and a third group"
END

STRING TABLE
BEGIN
    44, "this string is defined in a second string table"
    45, "as is this second string"
    46, "and this third string"
END
```

In this second example, two string table segments have been defined, but notice that there is nothing in the labels to identify these as separate segments.

More immediately important, strings are loaded in groups of 16, with all strings in a group loaded when any one of the strings is required. Groups are identified by their ID number, with numbers 0 through 15 forming the first group, 16 through 31 forming a second group, and so on. Thus, in the examples, strings 1, 2, and 3 form one group, strings 16 and 17 form a second group, string 32 is in a group by itself, and strings 44, 45 and 46 form a final group.

The programmer's objective is to group strings so strings that are needed will be loaded together, without loading unnecessary resources at the same time.

A String Table Editor

The Microsoft Developer Studio offers a separate string table editor, as shown in Figure 11.2.

FIGURE 11.2:

The Developer Studio string table editor

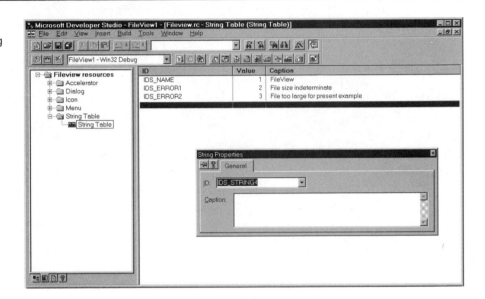

You can work in the Developer Studio string editor as follows:

- Add a string table entry by clicking the blank entry and entering a new ID and Caption in the Properties dialog box.

- Delete an individual string by selecting the string and pressing the Delete key.

- Move a string from one segment to another by changing the ID values.

- Move strings from one resource script (.RC) file to another by using the Cut and Paste options.

- Change a string or its identifier by editing the entry.

- Add formatting or special characters to a string.

Of course, you can accomplish the same tasks with a plain-text editor; the Developer Studio simply offers a more convenient tool for working with strings.

TIP   In the Developer Studio string editor, click the right mouse button to display a pop-up menu of resource-specific commands.

The string editor does not permit the creation of empty string tables. If you create a string table with no entries, it will be deleted automatically when you exit the Developer Studio.

Header File Resources

Header files provide a convenient place to define mnemonic constants used as links between resource files and application source code. It's far easier to remember that a radio button labeled IDD_RES, if selected, identifies a request for .RES source files than to remember that this button has a numeric identifier of 213.

Of course, once the .RC resource script has been compiled and linked with the application's executable code, the defined constants will all be replaced, but because the computer does lack a few of the programmer's more human shortcomings, this isn't the point. After all, the header file and the mnemonics are for the programmer's benefit, not the computer's.

Like the other application resources discussed in this chapter, you can create header files using a plain-text editor. However, you can also use a resource editor's facilities for maintaining ID constants.

An Editor for Headers

To create headers using the Microsoft Developer Studio editor, choose Resource Symbols from the View menu to see the dialog box shown in Figure 11.3.

FIGURE 11.3:

The Developer Studio
Resource Symbols
dialog box

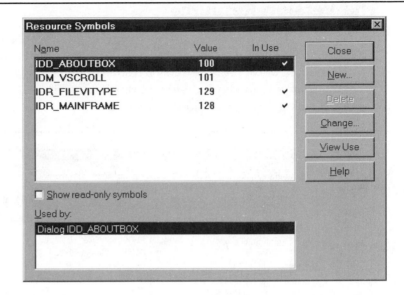

The Resource Symbols dialog box displays identifiers specific to the current project. It shows the value of the identifier, whether the identifier is used in the application (unchecked items are often orphaned IDs that you could remove), and where the selected ID is being used. If the ID is being used in more than one location, which is common, all of the uses will be listed.

When you select a use location and click the View Use button, the Developer Studio takes you directly to the appropriate source file.

The weakness of the Resource Symbols dialog box is that it does not function well with some non-MFC application source files. For example, the dialog box fails completely using the *FileView1* project, where the identifiers are all in the FileView.H header and not in a Resource.H header. However, in most circumstances, the Resource Symbols dialog box is a valuable tool.

TIP   If you need to search for an identifier that is defined in one of the multitude of associated library headers, use the Find in Files button (or menu option) in the Developer Studio.

The Version Resource

The Version resource is a structured text block that contains company and product identification, a product release (version) number, and copyright and trademark notifications. The Version resource editor allows you to add or delete string blocks or to modify individual string values. Figure 11.4 shows the Microsoft Developer Studio version resource editor.

FIGURE 11.4:

The version resource editor in the Developer Studio

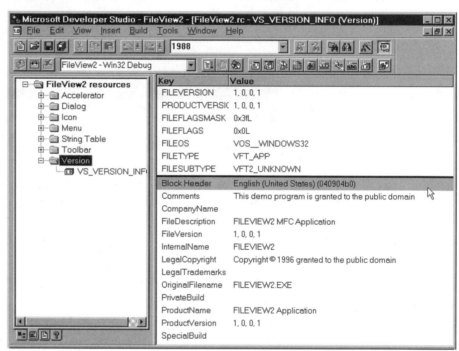

The Windows standard is for an application to contain only one version resource under the name VS_VERSION_INFO.

To use version information within an application, the GetFileVersionInfo and VerQueryValue functions offer access to the file. While this version information is not required by any application, it is a convenient location to collect information identifying the application and version.

A Header File for FileView1

The following is the FileView.H header file, which is shown in text format, for the *FileView* demo (discussed in Chapter 12).

```
#define   IDS_NAME      1
#define   IDS_ERROR1    2
#define   IDS_ERROR2    3

#define   IDD_FNAME    16
#define   IDD_FPATH    17
#define   IDD_FLIST    18

#define   IDM_QUIT    101
#define   IDM_ABOUT   102
#define   IDM_OPEN    103
#define   IDM_TYPE    104

#define   IDD_BMP     201
#define   IDD_C       202
#define   IDD_COM     203
#define   IDD_CUR     204
#define   IDD_DAT     205
#define   IDD_DBS     206
#define   IDD_DLG     207
#define   IDD_DLL     208
#define   IDD_EXE     209
#define   IDD_H       210
#define   IDD_PAL     211
#define   IDD_RC      212
#define   IDD_RES     213
#define   IDD_TXT     214
#define   IDD_ANY     215
```

This chapter completes our discussion of individual application resources. In the next chapter, we will look at the *FileView1* and *FileView2* demos, of which you've seen only fragments so far.

CHAPTER
TWELVE

Application Resources Working Together

- Global application resources

- Three dialog box resources for the *FileView* application

- A common dialog box resource for Windows 98 applications

So far, we've discussed each of the individual application resources. You've seen fragments of the *FileView1* and *FileView2* demos as examples. In this chapter, we will focus on how all of the application resources work together in these two demos.

The FileView1 Demo: Using Application Resources

The *FileView1* demo is a relatively simple application designed to open a file of any type and display the contents in a columnar, hexadecimal format. It shows the file offset addresses at the right and the corresponding ASCII characters at the left. Figure 12.1 shows a composite of the application with its three dialog boxes.

FIGURE 12.1:

The completed
FileView1 demo

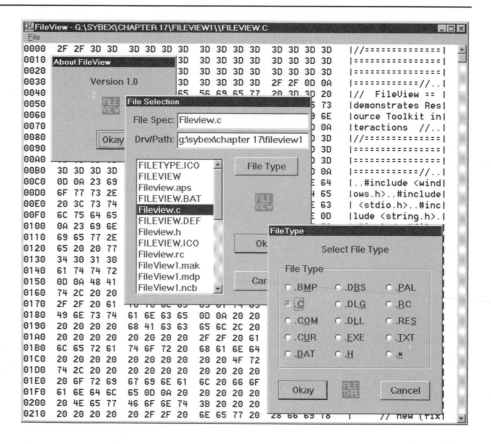

NOTE   The *FileView1* demo is included on the CD accompanying this book, in the Chapter 12 folder.

WinMain Operations

As you know, Windows loads application resources only when and as they are required and discards them when they are no longer needed. However, in the *FileView1* demo, one resource is required during initialization of the first instance of *FileView*: the application title. This title is contained in the string table, not in the source code. Thus, if no previous instance of *FileView1* is active, the Load-String function is called during the instance initialization to retrieve the appropriate entry from the string table:

```
if( !hPrevInstance ) // if no prev instance, t'is first
{
    LoadString( hInstance, IDS_NAME, (LPSTR) szAppName, 10 );
    wc.lpszClassName = szAppName;
```

Because the application title is global in this case, this string resource will be retained in memory without being discarded. In similar fashion, the application's cursor, icon, and menu are loaded as global resources:

```
wc.hCursor       = LoadCursor( NULL, IDC_ARROW );
wc.hIcon         = LoadIcon( hInstance, szAppName );
wc.lpszMenuName  = (LPSTR) szAppName;
```

This case is not unique to the *FileView1* application; a similar set of assignments appears in all Windows 98 applications. However, when using an MFC-based application, most of these operations are concealed from the programmer, as you may observe (or not observe) by checking the *FileView2* version.

NOTE   If for some reason you do not have the CD that comes with this book, in addition to entering the source code you will need to supply the two .ICO files as binary format files. You can create these using an image editor. See Chapter 8 for details.

Variable Initialization

Immediately following the instance initialization, provisions are also included to set default values for several global data variables:

```
iFileType = IDD_ANY - IDD_BMP;      // initial file type
lstrcpy( szFileExt, szFileType[iFileType] );
```

The iFileType variable is initialized using two symbolic constants, which are defined in the FileView.H header and which are used in the application resources. Once this is done, the szFileExt variable is initialized to match. Notice, however, that only global variables are being initialized, and this does not affect the initial settings of the dialog boxes.

Keyboard Accelerator Loading

Later, but still in the WinMain procedure, another set of resources is required, because these, too, are global to the application and cannot be discarded until *FileView1* terminates. This resource is the accelerator resource set, which is loaded immediately after the application has been initialized, as:

```
hAccel = LoadAccelerators( hInst, "FILEVIEW" );
while( GetMessage( &msg, NULL, 0, 0 ) )
{
    if( !TranslateAccelerator( hWndMain, hAccel, &msg ) )
    {
        TranslateMessage( &msg );
        DispatchMessage( &msg );
}   }
```

The LoadAccelerators function returns a handle to the accelerator resource table. However, because this handle is a global variable, the handle could be assigned to a different accelerator table elsewhere in the program as required, but it would still be used in the TranslateAccelerator call in the WinMain message loop.

The TranslateAccelerator function filters all of the keyboard-event messages directed to the application, permitting the majority of these to simply pass through without interference. However, when a key combination—or, more accurately, a key event accompanied by the appropriate shift-state flags—matches one of the resource accelerator-key events, this keyboard message is trapped or diverted. A new message—the action message defined for the accelerator event—is issued in its place.

Even applications that do not use accelerator keys will still call the message loop, but without the `TranslateAccelerator` invocation, as in:

```
while( GetMessage( &msg, NULL, 0, 0 ) )
{
    TranslateMessage( &msg );
    DispatchMessage( &msg );
}
```

Long Filenames

The *FileView1* demo can display complete long filenames. It is not limited to the older DOS-style 8.3 filename format, even though it uses only the standard Windows API functions.

For example, in the File Selection dialog box shown in Figure 12.1, you can see the long directory names chapter 17 and fileview1 in the Drv/Path edit box, and three filenames with more than eight characters appear in the file list.

If you browse around your hard drive using the *FileView1* demo, you should notice that all of your long filenames and long directory names—no matter how long they are—appear without any conversions to the archaic 8.3 format.

And, considering that this is accomplished without any special provisions in the code, you may wonder why so many applications that purport to be Windows NT/95/98 compatible or even "Designed for Windows NT/95/98" remain incapable of displaying anything except the old and obsolete 8.3 filename formats.

A certain amount of ire is a natural response as you go searching through a series of 30 or 40 subdirectories, each rendered as CHAP~nn, trying to find out where your Chapter 17 directory actually is. And, finally, if you are lucky and persevere, you may discover that Chapter 17 has been hashed to appear as CHAP~11— not exactly how you expected to find it.

Is this the product of a conspiracy of recalcitrant programmers who have banded together to attempt to preserve the old format in the same fashion that *Le Academy Francais* is attempting to preserve seventeenth-century French? Or is there some special stupidity at work here? It is definitely a mystery! (The solution appears later in this chapter.)

Dialog Box Handling

As discussed in Chapter 9, the *FileView1* demo uses three dialog boxes: About FileView, File Selection, and File Type. The three dialog boxes in the *FileView1* application were created as dialog box resources and are handled by procedures declared in FileView.DEF as exported.

NOTE   Exported procedures are simply procedures that need to be visible (accessible) from outside their immediate scope; that is, from outside the source file or class where they are declared. Procedures that are used only locally do not require export declarations. As a general rule, all functions that are used only within an EXE application are purely local. Functions within a DLL that are only called (used) by other functions and procedures belonging to the DLL are also local. This is true even for member functions—in either EXE applications or DLLs—belonging to one class that will be used by another class; as long as both classes exist in the same application; even if they are in multiple source files, they are still local functions. However, all functions within a DLL that will be called by applications using the DLL must be "exported" to make them accessible.

Once a dialog box has been invoked, the dialog box procedure exists as an effectively independent subprogram. The exported procedure receives its own messages from Windows, not directly from the parent application. Thus, declaring a procedure as exported makes the procedure's address available to the Windows kernel so messages can be passed to the dialog box.

The three dialog box procedures are invoked from instructions in the `WndProc` procedure, with very minimal invocations, as:

```
case IDM_ABOUT:
    DialogBox( hInst, "ABOUT", hwnd, About );
    break;

case IDM_TYPE:
    DialogBox( hInst, "FILETYPE", hwnd, FileType );
    break;
```

Under Windows 3.1, this dialog box invocation would be somewhat more complex and would look something like this:

```
case IDM_ABOUT:
    lpProc = MakeProcInstance( About, hInst );
    DialogBox( hInst, "ABOUT", hwnd, lpProc );
    FreeProcInstance( lpProc );
    break;
```

In fact, this format is still acceptable under Windows 98, but it is unnecessary. The MakeProcInstance procedure from Windows 3.1 is now defined as a macro that simply returns the first argument, with nothing required to create an instance of the procedure. And, because there is no requirement to create a procedure instance, the FreeProcInstance has also been redefined as a macro; this macro does absolutely nothing (aside from preventing the compiler from returning an error message because of an unrecognized term).

When the IDM_OPEN message is received, a slightly different response is used. It begins by initializing a directory path string and a file specification, passing these as arguments to the local CallFileOpen procedure, as:

```
case IDM_OPEN:        // set initial search path
    lstrcpy( szTmpFileSpec, szTmpFilePath );
    lstrcat( szTmpFileSpec, "*" );
    lstrcat( szTmpFileSpec, szFileType[iFileType] );
    if( CallFileOpen( hInst, hwnd,
            szTmpFileSpec, szFileType[iFileType],
            szTmpFilePath, szTmpFileName ) )
    {
```

The CallFileOpen procedure performs a few minor tasks of its own before using the same DialogBox API function, as was used to call the preceding two dialog boxes.

The About dialog procedure does very little except wait for the user to click the Okay button, after which it returns. There is no return value—or, at least, no response to a returned value—because nothing is decided in this dialog box.

The FileType and FileOpen dialog box procedures, however, are not as simple. Even though they return Boolean values, the major part of their work involves setting global string variables. This type of information cannot be conveniently treated as a returned value, even under Windows 98. However, the Boolean value returned by the exported FileOpen procedure to the Call-FileOpen procedure and then to the WndProc procedure is used because there is no reason to attempt to open a file if the user hasn't selected one; that is, if the Cancel button was selected instead of the Okay button.

Before either of these procedures can return anything, the dialog box procedures themselves still have several tasks to perform, including initializing the dialog boxes before they are displayed.

Dialog Box Initialization

The FileType and FileOpen dialog box procedures handle a number of operations, but at the moment, their responses to the WM_INITDIALOG messages are the important topic.

The FileType dialog box procedure has only two important tasks. The first of these tasks is setting the check state of the radio button to match the iFileType variable, thus:

```
case WM_INITDIALOG:
    CheckRadioButton( hDlg, IDD_BMP, IDD_ANY,
                      IDD_BMP + iFileType );
    iInitType = iFileType;
    return( TRUE );
```

However, because the radio buttons used for the 15 file extensions were defined as auto radio buttons belonging to a single group, you are not required to reset the remaining 14; this part of the task is handled automatically.

This leaves the second task: setting the local variable iInitType so it's equal to the global iFileType. Once this is done, the File Type dialog box is ready for display and awaits the user's selection.

On the other hand, the File Selection dialog box is a bit more complicated to initialize. First, the FileOpen dialog box procedure retrieves the current or active drive and directory path and then sends the filename list box an initialization instruction setting the length of each entry to a generous 80 characters (just in case we want the long filenames supported by the NTFS file system or by the Windows 98 extended filename format).

```
case WM_INITDIALOG:
    GetCurrentDirectory( sizeof(OrgPath), OrgPath );
    SendDlgItemMessage( hDlg, IDD_FNAME, EM_LIMITTEXT, 80, OL );
    DlgDirList( hDlg, szFileSpec, IDD_FLIST, IDD_FPATH,
                wFileAttr );
```

After initializing the list box, the next task is to fill it with entries from the current directory. The DlgDirList API function makes this task almost automatic. After all, aside from a handle to the dialog box (hDlg), the application is required only to provide a file specification (szFileSpec), a destination (a list box identified as IDD_FLIST), a directory path specification (IDD_FPATH), and the desired file-attribute flags (wFileAttr).

In other circumstances, you might want to use two list boxes: one for filenames and the other for drive and directory information. This format is a convenient one used by many Windows applications. For this purpose, the wFileAttr flags would specify files for one list. For the other list, a wDirAttr flag variable would request directory information.

Finally, as a last step, the current file specification is added to the edit text box above the list box, as:

```
SetDlgItemText( hDlg, IDD_FNAME, szFileSpec );
return( TRUE );
```

Long Filenames: The Solution

The solution to limiting filenames and directory names to the obsolete 8.3 format is actually quite simple. By specifying a 12-character limit—8 for the filename, 1 for the dot, and 3 for the extension—in the SendDlgItemMessage EM_LIMITTEXT instruction, the system is forced to report only the old-style filename whenever a longer format filename is encountered.

```
case WM_INITDIALOG:
    GetCurrentDirectory( sizeof(OrgPath), OrgPath );
    SendDlgItemMessage( hDlg, IDD_FNAME, EM_LIMITTEXT, 12, 0L );
    DlgDirList( hDlg, szFileSpec,
                IDD_FLIST, IDD_FPATH, wFileAttr );
```

This limitation is definitely a stupid one and does not excuse programmers from recognizing (or failing to recognize) new realities.

The guilty parties—and you know who you are—are sentenced to 50 lashes with a wet data stream...and no excuses.

Conversely, by specifying a larger entry size—such as the 80 character size used in the FileOpen procedure—the system is allowed to report the new, long filename format.

Of course, in all fairness, if any of you are using filenames longer than 80 characters, the *FileView1* demo will truncate your filenames. But, somehow, I can't find it in my heart to worry unduly about this possibility.

Dialog Box Information Retrieval

In addition to setting initial information in the two dialog boxes, provisions are also required to retrieve information from them. And, as mentioned previously, each of these dialog box procedures is essentially an independent subprogram.

The FileType Procedure

In the FileType dialog box procedure, the important task is tracking the array of radio buttons; fortunately, this task is easily accomplished. Within the File-Type dialog box procedure, button selections are tracked using the local variable, iInitType, leaving the global variable, iFileType, unaffected. In this fashion, when the user clicks any of the radio buttons, the array of buttons automatically resets because these were defined as auto radio buttons belonging to a single group. The selected button, however, sends an event message, which is intercepted, to the FileType dialog box procedure:

```
case WM_COMMAND:
    switch( LOWORD( wParam ) )
    {
        case IDD_BMP:    case IDD_C:
        case IDD_COM:    case IDD_CUR:
        case IDD_DAT:    case IDD_DBS:
        case IDD_DLG:    case IDD_DLL:
        case IDD_EXE:    case IDD_H:
        case IDD_PAL:    case IDD_RC:
        case IDD_RES:    case IDD_TXT:
        case IDD_ANY:
            iFileType = LOWORD( wParam ) - IDD_BMP;
            lstrcpy( szFileExt, szFileType[iFileType] );
            return( TRUE );
```

Remember, the wParam argument contains the button identifier, which is a value that will be in the range of 201 to 215. The array of file-type extensions, however, has indexes from 0 to 14. Therefore, the constant IDD_BMP is subtracted from the low word in wParam to provide a usable index value.

Last, if the user clicks the Okay button, the global variable iFileType can be reset. If the user clicks the Cancel button instead, the global variable is left unchanged, despite any local selections.

The FileOpen Procedure

In the FileOpen dialog box procedure, the responses are not quite as simple. First, in addition to the Okay and Cancel buttons, a third button, labeled File Type, returns the command message IDM_TYPE if selected. This offers an alternative method of calling the FileType dialog box procedure from within the FileOpen dialog box procedure. The response provided is very similar to the provisions in the WndProc procedure, as:

```
case IDM_TYPE:
    if( DialogBox( hInst, "FILETYPE",
                   hDlg,  FileType ) )
```

If FileType returns TRUE, meaning that a new file type was selected, the file specification is reset, and the DlgDirList function is called to update the directory list box, much the same as when the dialog box was initialized.

The list box, identified as IDD_FLIST, handles most of its own operations automatically, including scrolling, displaying text, and highlighting selections. There are, however, two messages that require handling within the dialog box procedure: the LBN_SELCHANGE and LBN_DBLCLK arguments accompanying an IDD_FLIST command message. These arguments are passed as high-word values in the wParam argument and must be tested using the HIWORD macro, as:

```
case IDD_FLIST:
    switch( HIWORD( wParam ) )
    {
        case LBN_SELCHANGE:
```

The LBN_SELCHANGE message simply states that a new item in the list box was selected and, in response, the edit file (IDD_FNAME) should be updated accordingly. As an alternative, if the dialog box had used a combo list box (combining a list box and edit box in a single feature), this task would be handled automatically, without involving the dialog box procedure.

The second IDD_FLIST argument, LBN_DBLCLK, states that an item in the list box has been double-clicked, indicating an immediate selection. In response, the first step is to call the DlgDirSelectEx API function to check if the selected entry is a directory or a file:

```
case LBN_DBLCLK:
    if( DlgDirSelectEx( hDlg, szFileName,
            sizeof(szFileName), IDD_FLIST ) )
    {
```

```
                    lstrcat( szFileName, szFileSpec );
                    DlgDirList( hDlg, szFileName,
                                IDD_FLIST, IDD_FPATH,
                                wFileAttr );
                    SetDlgItemText( hDlg, IDD_FNAME,
                                    szFileSpec );
            }
```

If DlgDirSelectEx reports TRUE, meaning the selected entry is a new directory, the DlgDirList function is called to update the list box and the edit box, and the process proceeds as before.

On the other hand, if a FALSE result is reported, the selection must be a filename rather than a directory and, therefore, the edit box is updated before sending an IDOK message to complete the selection process.

```
            else
            {
                SetDlgItemText( hDlg, IDD_FNAME,
                                szFileName );
                SendMessage( hDlg, WM_COMMAND,
                             IDOK, OL );
            }
            return( TRUE );
```

Because the edit box offers the user a chance to type in an entry directly, the IDD_FNAME message is also checked for the EN_CHANGE argument in the high-word value of the wParam argument.

Two final provisions are responses for the IDOK and IDCANCEL command messages. In the case of an IDOK message, the response required is simply to check the edit box and retrieve the current entry before saving this as the selected filename.

```
            case IDOK:
                GetDlgItemText( hDlg, IDD_FNAME, szFileName, 80 );
                ...
                EndDialog( hDlg, TRUE );
                return( TRUE );
```

The provisions for parsing the filename and the path/directory information are omitted here. The dialog box then closes with a return message TRUE to indicate to the calling procedure that a filename has been selected.

For the IDCANCEL message, the response is simple. After restoring the original drive/directory, the dialog box closes with a return message of FALSE to report that no selection has been made.

```
case IDCANCEL:
    SetCurrentDirectory( OrgPath );
    EndDialog( hDlg, FALSE );
    return( TRUE );
```

The FileView2 Demo:
Using a Common Dialog Box

The *FileView2* demo performs essentially the same task as *FileView1*, but instead of the File Type and File Selection dialog boxes, it uses the common File Open dialog box. Its main purpose is to demonstrate how an application can be revised to take advantage of the MFC libraries and of supplied resources.

The *FileView2* version has only one resource dialog box, the About dialog box, because the File Open dialog box is a common dialog box resource supplied by Windows 98, not by the application. Also, where the *FileView1* demo employed a File Type dialog box, the *FileView2* version omits this resource by loading the list of file types and associated extensions in the File Open dialog box, where they appear in the Files of Type pull-down list. Figure 12.2 shows the *FileView* demo with its two dialog boxes.

NOTE   The *FileView2* demo is included on the CD accompanying this book, in the Chapter 12 folder.

FIGURE 12.2:

The completed
FileView2 demo

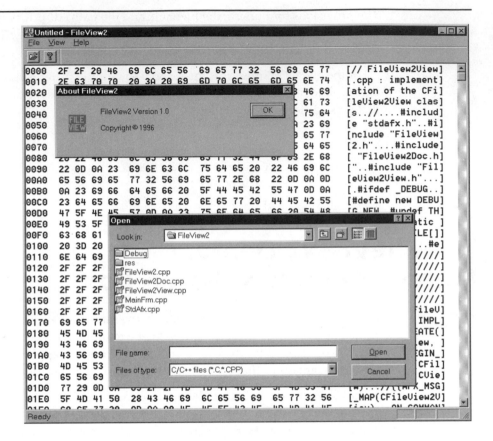

A Pointer to the CFileDialog Class

The main reason for discussing this second version is to show how the File Type and File Selection dialog boxes were replaced by the common File Open dialog box. The heart of this part of the operation occurs in the OnFileOpen method in the CFileView2View class, where we begin by defining a pointer to the CFile-Dialog class.

```
void CFileView2View::OnFileOpen()
{
    // TODO: Add your command handler code here
    CFileDialog*    pFileDlg;
    CString         csFilter;
```

The CFileDialog class encapsulates the Windows common File dialog box, which implements both the File Open and File Save As (or File Save) dialog boxes.

TIP   The File Open and File Save As dialog boxes can also serve for any other file-selection functions. Refer to the CFileDialog class documentation for details.

The Filter List

Defining a pointer to the class rather than an instance of the class provides a handle that will, in a moment, point to an instance of the class. Before creating an instance of the class, however, you must prepare.

```
csFilter =
    "Bitmaps (*.bmp)|*.bmp|"
    "C/C++ files (*.C,*.CPP)|*.c;*.cpp|"
    "Com files (*.com)|*.com|"
    "Cursors (*.cur)|*.cur|"
    "Data (*.dat)|*.dat|"
    "DBase files (*.dbs)|*.dbs|"
    "Dialogs (*.dlg)|*.dlg|"
    "Dynamic link libraries (*.dll)|*.dll|"
    "Executables (*.exe)|*.exe|"
    "Headers (*.h,*.hpp)|*.h;*.hpp|"
    "Palettes (*.pal)|*.pal|"
    "Resource scripts (*.rc)|*.rc|"
    "Resource files (*.res)|*.res|"
    "Text files (*.txt)|*.txt|"
    "All files (*.*)|*.*||";
```

The csFilter variable is an instance of the class CString and now contains a complete list of the file types and the file extensions for each type, with the | character used as a separator. Note also the doubled | |, which terminates the string. When the csFilter string is passed to the CFileDialog instance, the | characters are interpreted as 0x00—null characters that serve as delimiters.

Notice that each entry consists of two substrings. The first is the descriptive string, which will be displayed for selection. The second substring contains the file mask. In two cases—C/C++ and header files—two separate file masks are included by separating them with a semicolon (;).

There are no limits on the length of the prompt strings or file masks. Also, because a CString instance is not limited in length, there are no limitations on how many prompts and file masks can be included.

The only real stipulation that you need to observe is that the list provided will be presented in the exact same order; that is, the list of prompts and file masks will not be sorted.

The CFileDialog Instance

Now, once we have the filter list, the CFileDialog instance can be created thus:

```
pFileDlg = new CFileDialog( TRUE, NULL, NULL,
                            OFN_HIDEREADONLY | OFN_OVERWRITEPROMPT,
                            csFilter );
```

The calling parameters for CFileDialog are defined as:

```
CFileDialog( BOOL bOpenFileDialog, LPCTSTR lpszDefExt = NULL,
             LPCTSTR lpszFileName = NULL,
             DWORD dwFlags = OFN_HIDEREADONLY | OFN_OVERWRITEPROMPT,
             LPCTSTR lpszFilter = NULL, CWnd* pParentWnd = NULL );
```

The parameters used are defined as follows:

bOpenFileDialog   Set to TRUE to construct a File Open dialog box or to FALSE to construct a File Save As dialog box.

lpszDefExt   A default filename extension. If the filename edit box entry does not include an extension when the File Open dialog box returns, the lpszDefExt extension will be appended to the filename automatically. If this parameter is NULL, no filename extension is appended.

lpszFileName   A default filename that will appear in the filename edit box. If NULL, no initial filename appears.

dwFlags   Flags that are used to customize the dialog box. For a complete list of flags and options, refer to the OPENFILENAME structure in the Win32 SDK documentation.

lpszFilter   A sequence of string pairs that specify the filters that may be applied to the files. If no filter is supplied, all files are accepted, unless the user supplies a file mask.

pParentWnd   A pointer to the parent or owner window. If no parent or owner is specified, the Desktop becomes the parent.

Having provided the appropriate parameters, the CFileDialog instance is called using the DoModal method.

```
if( pFileDlg->DoModal() == IDOK )
{
```

Assuming that DoModal returns TRUE—meaning the user has selected the Open (IDOK) button rather than the Cancel button—the GetPathName method is called to retrieve the selected filename and the complete path/directory specification.

Note that this information is available after the dialog box returns but only as long as the CFileDialog instance has not closed. And, once you have this information, the OpenFile method is called.

```
m_csFilePath = pFileDlg->GetPathName();
OpenFile();
}
```

You can call the OpenFile method, which is a member of the CFileView2View class, without passing any arguments because the file information is contained in another member variable. This is the CString member m_csFilePath, which is directly available to the OpenFile method.

Last, call the delete operator to close the CFileDialog instance:

```
delete pFileDlg;
}
```

At this point, even though you're not finished with the file information (the file access and display is handled by other procedures), you are finished with the CFileDialog instance. Now you need to clean up to avoid a memory leak, which may be minor but can cause problems. In any case, all class instances should be closed when they are no longer needed.

WARNING Memory leaks are very easy to cause and very, very hard to identify later when they begin causing major debugging headaches and other problems. This is an area where the proverbial ounce of prevention is worth far more than many pounds of cure.

The remainder of the *FileView2* demo provisions are quite similar to the ones in the *FileView1* demo. Its differences are the obvious changes appropriate to using an MFC-based application and some other changes to make appropriate use of object classes, such as `CStrings`, to replace more conventional variable types. If you are interested, take a look at the `OpenFile`, `FormatLine`, and `PaintFile` methods in the `CFileView2View` class.

TIP

Because the main point of *FileView2* is to demonstrate a few interactions between the program code and the application resources, this chapter has not explained all of that program's operations. Feel free to experiment with the source code listing (on the CD that accompanies this book), where you will find annotations to identify other areas of interest.

In Part 2 of this book, we've gone though the main types of application resources under Windows and illustrated how they can be put together in your applications. In a sense, all of these elements are simply background—the nuts and bolts used for Windows applications. But, without the basic foundation, there's no point in trying to build more complete systems.

In Part 3, we'll look at more advanced topics. We'll focus on creating tools and building simple applications to illustrate how the tools function. In Chapter 13, we'll begin with the useful tools of pop-up windows and pop-up menus.

PART 3

Advanced Application Designs

## 13

Pop-Ups:
Tip Windows and Menus

◼ Pop-up windows for tips and messages

◼ Pop-up (floating) menus

◼ Pop-ups in dialog boxes

One of the problems that every programmer faces eventually is the need to present information to the user or to offer the user a series of choices. The obvious solution to these two problems—in a Windows environment—has always been to create a dialog box that either offers a series of controls or displays a message.

The advantage of using a message box (a message box is a specialized type of dialog box) is simplicity. Using the MFC classes, all you need to supply is the message string. Everything else is done for you. But there are some disadvantages to using a message box. One problem is that the message box display is modal, so it won't go away automatically. Another problem is that this display usually takes up more space on the screen than is needed to show the information.

Of course, you could use a conventional dialog box to display a message, but this approach also has some shortcomings. The conventional dialog box must be designed in advance and, like a message box, must be explicitly dismissed by the user. Granted, this first objection is not completely correct because you can create a dialog box and populate it with controls at runtime rather than depend solely on a predesigned dialog box, but the problems inherent in calculated layout and spacing make this approach generally impractical.

In this chapter, we will look at some alternatives to using conventional dialog boxes and message boxes: pop-up tip windows and pop-up menus.

Pop-Up Tip Windows

Pop-up tip windows have several advantages over dialog boxes and message boxes:

- They can present brief messages in a minimal amount of space.

- They do not require a user response; they can vanish automatically if desired.

- They can be positioned anywhere on the screen.

Common examples of pop-up tip windows are the tooltips that appear when the mouse is positioned over a toolbar control. These tip windows, however, are a function of the CToolbar class and depend on tip messages that were defined when the toolbar resource was defined (see Chapter 8 for more information about toolbar resources). Therefore, tooltips are limited in that they are connected to toolbar controls.

An alternative way to create pop-up tip windows is by using a CTipWnd class, which will let you display a pop-up message anywhere on the screen. Like a toolbar tip window, the pop-up tip window will occupy a minimum amount of screen real estate and will vanish automatically. This will be demonstrated shortly, when we discuss the *Popups* demo.

Pop-Up (Floating) Menus

Pop-up menus are useful for offering a selection "on the fly." They can provide a limited number of choices in a simple menu format. Pop-up menus have the following advantages:

- They can be created on the fly, in response to runtime conditions.

- They can be displayed as a pop-up anywhere on the screen without being attached to a frame window.

- They can be dismissed automatically if the user wishes to ignore them.

An example of a pop-up menu that is created in response to runtime conditions is the one displayed by Microsoft Word's on-the-fly spell checker. When you type a word that it does not recognize, the spell checker presents a menu with several options, along with some alternate spellings for the word. In this case, Word creates the list of alternate spellings at runtime in response to the unrecognized word and inserts them in the pop-up menu.

Anytime that you can define a list of options—actions, items to select from, alternative suggestions, or any other kinds of choices—you can instruct the application to create a menu showing these options. Once you have defined the menu, it can be displayed as a pop-up (floating) menu positioned anywhere on the screen. The *Popups* demo, discussed in the next section, demonstrates how to create pop-up menus.

The Popups Demo: Displaying Pop-Up Windows and Menus

 The *Popups* demo is a simple MFC-based application that uses a single document interface. This demo has provisions for displaying pop-up tip windows and pop-up (floating) menus.

NOTE   Although you could implement pop-up windows and menus using standard C/C++ programming and conventional Windows APIs, they are much easier to create using the MFC classes as a basis. For this reason, the *Popups* demo is offered only as an MFC-based application. If you desire, you can find parallel, non-MFC APIs for all of the important functions (commonly with the same names as the MFC class functions).

The *Popups* demo displays only one pop-up tip at a time. However, for illustration purposes, Figure 13.1 shows a composite with four pop-up messages displayed.

FIGURE 13.1:

A selection of pop-up messages

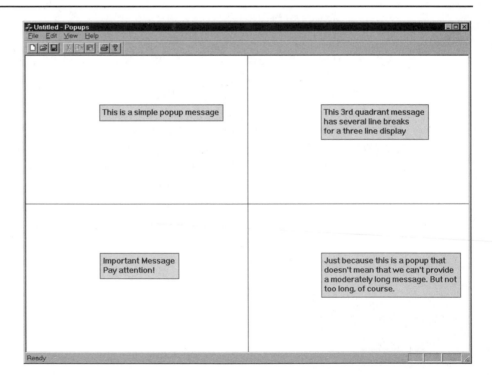

The pop-up messages in the demo program are displayed in response to a left mouse click in any of the four quadrants. In your own applications, you will have other reasons and the appropriate algorithms to determine which message you want to display and where within the application (or even outside it) you want the pop-up window to appear. Likewise, your applications are certainly free to display more than one pop-up window at a time.

The pop-up windows disappear immediately whenever a mouse button is clicked or any key is pressed on the keyboard. This satisfies the objective of making the pop-up window vanish without demanding a response from the user.

Similar to Figure 13.1, Figure 13.2 shows a composite with four pop-up menus from the *Popups* demo. The pop-up menus are displayed in response to a right mouse click in any of the four quadrants, summoning the menu for that quadrant. Also, partially to demonstrate how you can control as well as create menus on the fly, one element in each menu, which arbitrarily corresponds to the quadrant, has been disabled.

FIGURE 13.2:

A selection of pop-up menus

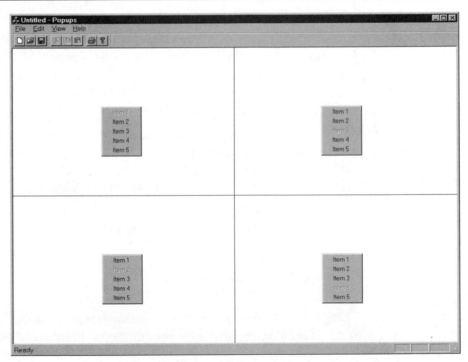

The *Popups* demo also includes provisions for displaying pop-up messages and a pop-up menu in a dialog box. As you will see, pop-ups in dialog boxes must be summoned by some condition other than a mouse click. We'll talk about how to activate pop-up message windows by conditions within the application in the "Pop-ups in Dialog Boxes" section later in the chapter.

NOTE   The *Popups* demo is included on the CD that accompanies this book, in the Chapter 13 folder.

Setting Up the Application Window

Once the application executes, the view window (via the `CPopupsView::OnDraw` function) is divided horizontally and vertically into four quadrants.

Also, using the Microsoft Developer Studio's ClassWizard, message-handling functions are established for four event messages: `OnInitialUpdate()`, `OnSize()`, `OnLButtonDown()`, and `OnRButtonDown()`.

The `OnInitialUpdate()` and `OnSize()` functions both serve similar purposes; in the examples that follow each has one line of code (in bold) added to the Class-Wizard–supplied handling. In each case, the object is to retrieve the size of the client window (the view window) and to store this information in a member variable (`m_cRect`), where the information will be available later.

The `OnInitialUpdate()` event occurs only once, after the window is created. This is, however, the earliest opportunity for the application to query the window size. In other applications, you might use this event as your cue to obtain other types of information that are available only after the application window has been created.

```
void CPopupsView::OnInitialUpdate()
{
    CView::OnInitialUpdate();
    GetClientRect( m_cRect );
}
```

The `OnSize()` function performs the same task as the `OnInitialUpdate()`function but is called anytime the size of the application's view window is changed.

```
void CPopupsView::OnSize( UINT nType, int cx, int cy )
{
    CView::OnSize(nType, cx, cy);
    GetClientRect( m_cRect );
}
```

The two remaining message-handling functions, OnLButtonDown() and OnR-ButtonDown(), provide responses to the left (or primary) and right (or secondary) mouse buttons. As mentioned, these events are used to display either a pop-up message (a tip window) or a pop-up menu, respectively.

<table>
<tr><td>NOTE</td><td>Although the Windows interface allows the left and right mouse buttons to be swapped or, with a three-button mouse, the buttons to be reassigned in any order, OnLButtonxxxx events always refer to the button selected by the user as the primary button, just as OnRButtonxxxx events always refer to the secondary button regardless of the user's preferences. Optionally, for a three-button mouse, the OnMButtonxxxx events reference the third mouse button. However, you should not rely on this message because the third mouse button is not standard. Refer to Chapter 5 for details on mouse messages under Windows.</td></tr>
</table>

In both the OnLButtonDown(...) and OnRButtonDown(...) event functions, the mouse position is checked to determine which of the four quadrants the user clicked in.

```
void CPopupsView::OnLButtonDown( UINT nFlags, CPoint point )
{
    if( point.x > ( m_cRect.Width() / 2 ) )
        m_nQuad = 2;  else  m_nQuad = 0;
    if( point.y > ( m_cRect.Height() / 2 ) )
        m_nQuad ++;
    PopupTips( m_nQuad );
//  CView::OnLButtonDown(nFlags, point);
}

void CPopupsView::OnRButtonDown( UINT nFlags, CPoint point )
{
    if( point.x > ( m_cRect.Width() / 2 ) )
        m_nQuad = 2;  else  m_nQuad = 0;
    if( point.y > ( m_cRect.Height() / 2 ) )
        m_nQuad ++;
    PopupMenu( m_nQuad );
//  CView::OnRButtonDown(nFlags, point);
}
```

Notice that the default provisions calling the parent CView class functions have been commented out. As long as the mouse clicks have occurred within the client window, which is the only time these messages will be received within the CPopupsView class, there is no need for any default response. These two lines of code could be restored, however, without affecting the application's operation.

Setting Up the Pop-Up Tips

The PopupTips(...) function in the CPopupsView class demonstrates how to provide a selection of different messages and to position each one in a different quadrant of the application view window.

In order to present several different responses according to the quadrant where the event has occurred, the PopupTips function is called with a quadrant argument that was calculated in the OnLButtonDown or OnRButtonDown functions according to the event position.

```
void CPopupsView::PopupTips( int nQuad )
{
    CPoint    cPoint;
    CString   csTip;
    CTipWnd * pTip;

    cPoint = CPoint( m_cRect.Width()/6, m_cRect.Height()/6 );
    switch( nQuad )
    {
        case 0:
            csTip = "This is a simple popup message";
            break;

        case 1:
            cPoint.y += m_cRect.Height()/2;
            csTip = "Important Message\r\nPay attention!";
            break;

        case 2:
            cPoint.x += m_cRect.Width()/2;
            csTip = "This 3rd quadrant message\r\n"
                    "has several line breaks\r\n"
                    "for a three line display";
            break;
```

```
        case 3:
            cPoint.y += m_cRect.Height()/2;
            cPoint.x += m_cRect.Width()/2;
            csTip = "Just because this is a popup that\r\n"
                    "doesn't mean that we can't provide\r\n"
                    "a moderately long message. But not\r\n"
                    "too long, of course.";
            break;
    }
    ClientToScreen( &cPoint );
```

NOTE
In your own applications, of course, you will want to use some more relevant criteria for deciding what kind of message to display. See the "Pop-ups in Dialog Boxes" section later in the chapter for an example of using conditions to trigger a message.

Rather than arbitrarily breaking a long line, there is a provision that will handle the embedded \r\n (CRLF) characters to provide a multiline display, as you will see in a moment. If you prefer, however, you could create algorithms to provide line breaks and simply pass an unformatted string, allowing the CTipWnd class to decide where breaks should occur for the best effect.

After selecting a message and position, we call an instance of the CTipWnd class to display the pop-up window, passing the message and position as arguments to the CTipWnd::Create(...) method.

```
        pTip = new CTipWnd();
        pTip->Create( csTip, cPoint );
    }
```

Creating the CTipWnd Class

To create the CTipWnd class, we use the Developer Studio's ClassWizard and base the new class on the CWnd class. In the generated TipWnd.H header, ClassWizard has defined a Create(...) method for the new class as:

```
// Overrides
    // ClassWizard generated virtual function overrides
    //{{AFX_VIRTUAL(CTipWnd)
    public:
    virtual BOOL Create( LPCTSTR lpszClassName, LPCTSTR lpszWindowName,
                DWORD dwStyle, const RECT& rect, CWnd* pParentWnd,
                UINT nID, CCreateContext* pContext = NULL );
    //}}AFX_VIRTUAL
```

Normally, when creating a new child class, you would simply accept the generated Create(...) method. However, for a tip window, we are not interested in supplying a wealth of unneeded information. Instead, we replace the supplied Create(...) method with a much simpler Create(...) method defined as:

```
// Overrides
    // ClassWizard generated virtual function overrides
    //{{AFX_VIRTUAL(CTipWnd)
    public:
    virtual BOOL Create( CString csMessage, CPoint cPoint );
    //}}AFX_VIRTUAL
```

Here, only two arguments are passed to the Create(...) method: the message string and position (in absolute screen coordinates) where we want the pop-up window to appear.

Are we cheating by not supplying the arguments that the original Create(...) method expected? In one sense, yes, but also no. In a moment, you'll see that the missing arguments are still being supplied to the parent CWnd::CreateEx(...) method. The difference is that some of these arguments will be calculated within the CTipWnd::Create(...) method, while others are simply treated as constants rather than being supplied as calling arguments.

But first we have a few other tasks to take care of. Because the CTipWnd::Create(...) method is called only once, when the instance is instantiated, the csMessage argument needs to be stored in a local member variable so that this one critical piece of information will be available later when needed.

Also, once the string value has been copied to the member variable, the Calc-WndSize() method is called to determine what size to make the pop-up window for the message. The CalcWndSize() method is discussed momentarily, but, in brief, it parses the supplied string and uses default font information to calculate a width and height for the pop-up window. At the same time, the cPoint argument will position the window, but this argument and the returned cSize argument do not need to be retained for future use.

```
BOOL CTipWnd::Create( CString csMessage, CPoint  cPoint )
{
    CBrush   cBrush;
    UINT     nResult;
    CSize    cSize;

    m_csMessage = csMessage;
    cSize = CalcWndSize();
```

A CBrush instance is created to supply a window background. Like the size and position arguments, the background brush is needed only once, when the window class is registered. The CBrush instance becomes part of the pop-up window instance but does not require separate maintenance.

```
cBrush.CreateSolidBrush( DWCOLOR );
LPCTSTR lpszTipClass =
    AfxRegisterWndClass( CS_HREDRAW | CS_VREDRAW,
                         ::LoadCursor( NULL, IDC_ARROW ),
                         HBRUSH( cBrush ), NULL );
nResult = CWnd::CreateEx(
              WS_EX_NOPARENTNOTIFY | WS_EX_TOPMOST | WS_EX_WINDOWEDGE,
              lpszTipClass, csMessage, WS_POPUPWINDOW | WS_VISIBLE,
              cPoint.x, cPoint.y, cSize.cx, cSize.cy,
              GetSafeHwnd(), 0 );
```

Now, when we call the parent class CWnd::CreateEx(...) method, the arguments that would have been passed in the original CTipWnd::Create(...) method are supplied as constants or as calculated values. Notice that we've passed the original message argument as the window title, even though this window instance will not have a title (or a frame, system menu, and so on).

Also notice that the original return value, a call to the CWnd::Create(...) method, which was supplied by ClassWizard, has been commented out because it was replaced by the CreateEx(...) function. Instead, the value reported by the call is returned to the CreateEx(...) function.

Before exiting the CTipWnd::Create(...) method, we have one more task to handle: calling SetCapture() to capture the mouse input. The reasons for this action will be discussed presently in the "Capturing the Mouse and Keyboard" section.

```
    SetCapture();
    return nResult;
//  return CWnd::Create(lpszClassName, lpszWindowName, dwStyle, rect,
pParentWnd, nID, pContext);
    }
```

Once we have created the pop-up window, the OnPaint() method, which was supplied in skeletal form by the ClassWizard, provides a forum for actually displaying the intended message.

First, because we did not store the window size as a member variable, we will call GetClientRect(...) to find the client window rectangle. Then, since the window was deliberately created slightly larger than the message required in the CalcWndSize() method, we call the CRect::DeflateRect(...) method to reduce the rectangle size (and position) and to supply a margin around the displayed message. Without this, the message would be positioned full left and full top within the window. This provision is not simply cosmetic; it also makes the information easier to read.

```
void CTipWnd::OnPaint()
{
    CRect      cRect;
    CPaintDC dc(this);          // device context for painting
    GetClientRect( cRect );
    cRect.DeflateRect( 5, 5, 5, 5 );
    dc.SetBkColor( DWCOLOR );
    dc.DrawText( m_csMessage, &cRect, DT_LEFT | DT_WORDBREAK );
    // Do not call CWnd::OnPaint() for painting messages
}
```

Similarly, the SetBkColor(...) function ensures that the text background and the window background match. By default, the text background color is white. However, in this example, a yellow background was used for the window, so we need to set the same background color before writing the message.

And last, we will use the DrawText(...) method to write the actual message within the reduced rectangle. Note that the DT_LEFT and DT_WORDBREAK flags are necessary to permit the embedded \n\r (CRLF) codes to be recognized as formatting instructions.

Capturing the Mouse and Keyboard

In this application, the pop-up window automatically closes whenever the user clicks either mouse button anywhere on the Desktop or presses any key on the keyboard.

To accomplish the mouse-click response, six message-mapped functions are included:

```
void CTipWnd::OnLButtonDown(UINT nFlags, CPoint point)
{
    ShutDown();
    CWnd::OnLButtonDown(nFlags, point);
}

void CTipWnd::OnNcLButtonDown(...
void CTipWnd::OnMButtonDown(...
void CTipWnd::OnNcMButtonDown(...
void CTipWnd::OnRButtonDown(...
void CTipWnd::OnNcRButtonDown(...
```

In each case, the response calls the ShutDown() method before passing the mouse event to the default CWnd::On... method for further handling.

Because we also want the pop-up window to vanish whenever a key is pressed, we supply two additional message-mapped methods for the key and system key events:

```
void CTipWnd::OnKeyDown(UINT nChar, UINT nRepCnt, UINT nFlags)
{
    ShutDown();
    CWnd::OnKeyDown(nChar, nRepCnt, nFlags);
}

void CTipWnd::OnSysKeyDown(UINT nChar, UINT nRepCnt, UINT nFlags)
{
    ShutDown();
    CWnd::OnSysKeyDown(nChar, nRepCnt, nFlags);
}
```

Again, the only special provision is to call the ShutDown() method before passing the event along for default handling.

TIP

You could also supply a time delay to make the pop-up close without any action of any kind. If you like, you can experiment with adding this provision.

Calculating the Window Size

Calculating the window size is not particularly difficult, but it does seem a bit surprising that there is no default function for this purpose (for example, a function that calculates a size from a string while taking into consideration line breaks within the string). However surprising or not, the shortcoming is real enough because the only available functions—the CDC::GetTextExtent() methods—simply report sizes for unbroken strings.

Before you can calculate the size of the string in terms of the display space required, you need to know several other factors, such as the video resolution and the default font and the font size. To get this type of information, you need to start with a device context. (Determining system capabilities will be covered in more detail in Chapter 23.)

```
CSize CTipWnd::CalcWndSize()
{
    CDC      cDC;
    CSize    cSize, cSizeFinal;
    CString  csTemp;
    int      nLen, nLenTrim, nLines;

    cDC.CreateIC( _T("DISPLAY"), NULL, NULL, NULL );
```

In this case, because we are not actually drawing anything, we will use the CDC::CreateIC(...) method instead of an active device context to create an information context, using the _T("DISPLAY") argument to identify the display device.

Having created an information context, the remainder of the task is relatively simple. The message string that we intend to display is scanned for \r\n character pairs to identify carriage returns and new line breaks, and then substrings are copied to a local CString variable.

Once each substring has been copied, we can obtain the display length—not the character length— of the substring by using the GetTextExtent(...) function.

```
    nLines = 0;
    nLenTrim = 0;
    cSizeFinal.cx = 0;
    cSizeFinal.cy = 0;
    csTemp = m_csMessage;
    do
    {
```

```
nLen = csTemp.Find( "\r\n" );
if( nLen > 0 )
{
    csTemp = csTemp.Left( nLen );
    nLenTrim += ( nLen + 2 );
    nLines++;
    cSize = cDC.GetTextExtent( csTemp );
    csTemp = m_csMessage.Right( m_csMessage.GetLength() -
                               nLenTrim );
}
else
{
    nLines++;
    cSize = cDC.GetTextExtent( csTemp );
}
cSizeFinal.cy = cSize.cy;
cSizeFinal.cx = max( cSizeFinal.cx, cSize.cx );
```

For the horizontal size of the pop-up window, we're interested in finding the longest individual line. For the vertical size, we can simply assume that all lines are the same height and keep the height of any of the lines. We do, however, need to count the number of lines.

```
    }
    while( nLen >= 0 );
```

Once the message string has been parsed, we'll add a margin for borders to the maximum width, calculate the height as the height of an individual line multiplied by the number of lines, and then add a border margin to the height.

```
    cSizeFinal.cx += 15;    // add margin for borders
    cSizeFinal.cy *= nLines;
    cSizeFinal.cy += 15;    // add margin for borders
    return cSizeFinal;
}
```

The return value— returned as a CSize argument—contains the dimensions necessary to display the message with multiple lines and completes the handling for the pop-up message windows.

Setting Up the Pop-Up Menus

The provision for pop-up (floating) menus in the *Popups* demo is somewhat simpler than the provision for pop-up windows. Because the MFC CMenu class already has all of the important provisions to handle pop-up menus, we do not need to create a custom class for this purpose. However, for your own applications, you might consider creating a custom class to simplify some elements.

For the demo, we begin by determining a position according to the quadrant where the mouse click occurs. This position is a purely arbitrary one used for demonstration purposes, and it places each pop-up menu roughly in the center of the selected quadrant (see Figure 13.2, shown earlier in the chapter).

```
void CPopupsView::PopupMenu( int nQuad )
{
    CPoint      cPoint;
    CMenu     * pMenu;

    cPoint = CPoint( m_cRect.Width()/5, m_cRect.Height()/5 );
    switch( nQuad )
    {
        case 0:                                          break;
        case 1:     cPoint.y += m_cRect.Height()/2;      break;
        case 2:     cPoint.x += m_cRect.Width()/2;       break;
        case 3:     cPoint.y += m_cRect.Height()/2;
                    cPoint.x += m_cRect.Width()/2;       break;
    }
    ClientToScreen( &cPoint );
```

> **NOTE**   The PopupMenu(...) method in CPopupsView.CPP is written simply as a demonstration. In your own applications, you will want to use other methods for positioning the pop-up menus (and, of course, for populating the menu with selections). For example, you might pass the mouse-event position as an argument and use the event position to position the pop-up menu.

Creating the Menu

Once we've determined a position, the next step is to create a CMenu instance, call the CreatePopupMenu() method, and then add items to the menu.

```
pMenu = new CMenu();
pMenu->CreatePopupMenu();
pMenu->AppendMenu( MF_STRING, ID_POPUP_MENU1, "Item 1" );
pMenu->AppendMenu( MF_STRING, ID_POPUP_MENU2, "Item 2" );
pMenu->AppendMenu( MF_STRING, ID_POPUP_MENU3, "Item 3" );
pMenu->AppendMenu( MF_STRING, ID_POPUP_MENU4, "Item 4" );
pMenu->AppendMenu( MF_STRING, ID_POPUP_MENU5, "Item 5" );
```

The CreatePopupMenu() method supplies a blank menu where you can use the AppendMenu(...) and InsertMenu(...) functions to add entries (items) to the menu. The AppendMenu(...) adds items to the end of the menu list. The InsertMenu(...) function permits an item to be placed anywhere in the list, which is especially useful when adding entries to an existing menu.

In this example, we use a series of predefined constants to identify the menu selections. However, for your own on-the-fly menus, you will probably not have the luxury of having a series of identifiers. Instead, you will need to use a series of numerical values that are also generated on the fly. But as long as you can identify the selection by the value returned and match the value to something, such as an entry in a linked list of any kind of element, it really doesn't matter whether the value is supplied by a defined mnemonic or not.

Enabling and Disabling Menu Items

Once we have created the menu, we can use the EnableMenuItem(...) function to enable or disable individual menu entries.

```
pMenu->EnableMenuItem( ID_POPUP_MENU1 + nQuad,
                       MF_GRAYED | MF_BYCOMMAND | MF_DISABLED );
```

The ability to disable a menu item and show it as grayed is very useful to application developers. You can use it to indicate options that may be invalid under certain circumstances or that you may not want users to select at various times.

TIP   Menu items can also be checked, unchecked, enabled, or disabled at anytime, either when the menu is created or while the menu is in use. The CheckMenuItem(...) and CheckMenuRadioItem(...) functions place a checkmark or a bullet next to a menu item.

Displaying a Floating Window

After we have finished working with the individual menu items, enabling or disabling them as needed, we call the `TrackPopupMenu(...)` function to display the menu as a floating window.

```
pMenu->TrackPopupMenu( TPM_LEFTALIGN | TPM_RIGHTBUTTON,
                       cPoint.x, cPoint.y, this );
}
```

The `TrackPopupMenu(...)` function supports three flag values controlling the horizontal position of the pop-up menu. The supported alignment flags are as follows:

TPM_LEFTALIGN Aligns the menu with the left side at the x-coordinate.

TPM_CENTERALIGN Centers the menu horizontally on the x-coordinate.

TPM_RIGHTALIGN Aligns the menu with the right side at the x-coordinate.

The top of the pop-up menu is always aligned on the specified y-coordinate.

Two additional flags cause the menu to track the position of either a left or right mouse-button click:

TPM_LEFTBUTTON Sets the pop-up menu to track hits from the left mouse button.

TPM_RIGHTBUTTON Sets the pop-up menu to track hits from the right mouse button.

The next two arguments shown in the example specify the x-axis and y-axis coordinates relative to the screen where the pop-up menu will appear.

The last argument shown is a pointer identifying the window owning the pop-up menu. In the example, the `this` argument identifies the current window instance.

A final argument—optional and omitted in the current example—is an `lpRect` or `CRect` argument identifying a rectangular area where a mouse click will not dismiss the pop-up menu. If this parameter is `NULL` or is omitted, the menu vanishes automatically anytime the mouse is clicked outside the menu window.

Pop-Ups in Dialog Boxes

The previous sections discussed how to show pop-up messages and pop-up menus overlying an application window. You can also display both types of pop-ups in dialog boxes, but there are some constraints regarding how they are summoned.

Figure 13.3 shows a composite (from the *Popups* demo) of a half-dozen different pop-up messages displayed in a simple dialog box. Each message is triggered by a different set of conditions.

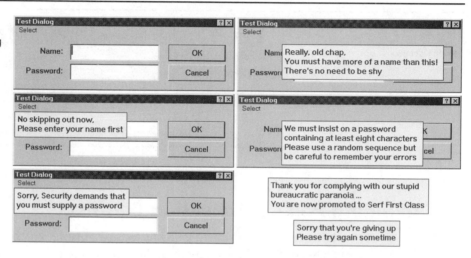

At the top left in Figure 13.3, there is a dialog box without a pop-up message. Below that, the center-left illustration shows the message that appears when the user has not entered a name, and the bottom-left illustration shows the message that appears when the user fails to supply a password.

On the right in Figure 13.3, the first (top) illustration shows the message that is triggered when the name entered is too short. In the center-right dialog box, the message indicates that the password entered is not long enough. The two bottom-right messages, which are generated from the dialog class, appear when the dialog box closes: The first message appears after the OK button is clicked if the edit boxes are both filled in correctly, and the second message appears when the Cancel button is selected.

NOTE   If you are interested in deciphering the details of the conditions summoning each message, see the code in the *Popup* demo (on the CD that accompanies this book).

A few elements have been used in the handling that make some tests for summoning the pop-up messages mutually exclusive (as discussed presently). Therefore, the Select menu in the dialog box, shown in Figure 13.4, allows you to choose which fields are tested.

FIGURE 13.4:

Selecting test options

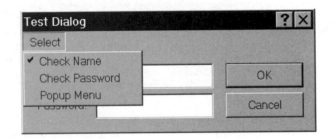

Avoiding Pop-Up Activation Conflicts

The dialog box's Select menu also has a third option, which is for a pop-up menu. This option is provided to demonstrate one of the hazards you can encounter with pop-ups in dialog boxes. If you select the Popup Menu option from the Select menu and then click the right mouse button in the dialog box window, you will see a pop-up menu—but only if the mouse click occurs outside one of the dialog box controls.

The problem is simply a matter of a mouse-click handling conflict. The dialog box controls have their own right-mouse-button handling functions, and when a mouse event occurs on a control, the event message does not reach the parent dialog class.

This does not mean that you cannot use a pop-up menu in a dialog box; it just shows that the pop-up menu must be activated by some condition other than the mouse click—in the same way that the demo's pop-up message windows are activated by conditions within the application.

Setting Up Mutually Exclusive Conditions

In the dialog box example in the *Popups* demo, an OnKillfocusxxxxx message map has been created for the Name and Password edit boxes. These functions are called whenever the edit box loses the focus (when the focus is shifted to another control, such as another edit box or one of the buttons). By calling UpdateData() when the focus is lost, the contents of the field can be checked immediately.

As you can see in the following fragments, the pop-up tip window is opened when the conditions of the test are not met.

```
void CTestDlg::OnKillfocusUserName()
{
    if( m_bCheckName )
    {
        GetClientRect( &m_cRect );
        m_cPoint.y = m_cRect.left;
        m_cPoint.x = m_cRect.top;
        UpdateData();
        if( m_csUserName.IsEmpty() )
        {
            m_csTip = "No skipping out now,\r\n"
                        "Please enter your name first";
            ClientToScreen( &m_cPoint );
            m_pTip = new CTipWnd();
            m_pTip->Create( m_csTip, m_cPoint );
            GetDlgItem( IDC_USER_NAME )->SetFocus();
} } }

void CTestDlg::OnKillfocusUserPassword()
{
    if( m_bCheckPassword )
    {
        GetClientRect( &m_cRect );
        m_cPoint.y = m_cRect.left;
        m_cPoint.x = m_cRect.top;
        UpdateData();
        if( m_csPassword.IsEmpty() )
        {
            m_csTip = "Sorry, Security demands that\r\n"
                        "you must supply a password";
            ClientToScreen( &m_cPoint );
            m_pTip = new CTipWnd();
            m_pTip->Create( m_csTip, m_cPoint );
            GetDlgItem( IDC_USER_PASSWORD )->SetFocus();
} } }
```

Notice that if the test fails, the focus is returned to the tested control using the SetFocus() function. The conditional flags allow only one of the tests to be implemented, so only one control is allowed to reclaim the focus.

If both tests were implemented at the same time, this would cause a conflict. When the focus moved from one edit box to the other, both of the edit boxes would be trying to regain the focus, producing a cascade of pop-up tip windows.

An alternative way to avoid such a conflict would be to allow the control(s) to lose the focus, displaying a message if the entries were not acceptable but not trying to reclaim the focus. Feel free to experiment with this and other alternatives, and find your own conflicts.

Pop-up menus and pop-up tips may not solve all of your programming problems, but they do provide a pair of very useful tools, allowing you to impart information to users and offer them choices. Such elements are greatly appreciated by the people who use your application. (Remember, how the end user sees your program is far more important than how you as a programmer see the application.)

In the next chapter, we will look at an application feature that is not obvious to your application users but nonetheless useful to them (and you). Chapter 14 explains how using threads allows programs to perform multiple tasks synchronously and, on the increasingly popular multiple-CPU systems, share tasks across multiple processors.

14

Multiple Threading Applications

■ How threads work

■ Commands for creating and modifying threads

■ Mutexes, events, semaphores, and critical sections for synchronizing threads

■ A demonstration of threads in action

A program of any complexity at all is a maze of instructions that loop and branch and are full of forks, jumps, and returns. The processor makes decisions as the program runs, and each decision leads through a different set of instructions. Each time the program executes, the processor follows a different path from start to finish. When Theseus fought the Minotaur, he marked his way through the labyrinth by unwinding a thread behind him. When a program wants to do several things at once, it creates objects called *threads*, and each thread winds its own way through the program's code.

Another way to look at it is to say that threads let a program be in two places at once. The system keeps a list of all the threads and cycles through them, giving each a slice of time on the processor. When a time slice ends, the system records the current CPU register values in the thread object, including a pointer to whatever instruction the thread was about to execute. The system then selects another thread, restores *its* CPU registers, and resumes execution wherever the thread last left off. A thread marks a location in the program, and by marking several locations with different threads, the program effectively clones itself and seems to execute in many places at the same time.

This is how threads work in a single-CPU system, which is what most of us are still relying on today. However, the wave of the future is multiple-CPU systems—desktop systems with as many as four CPUs and a multiprocessor environment. Here is where threads really shine. With multiple processors to handle tasking, the system is able to allocate different threads to different processors; it spreads the load across several CPUs. Each CPU can execute separate tasks simultaneously for different threads.

One area where this will be particularly advantageous is 3-D modeling and image processing, where different threads can share aspects of creating an image among two or more CPUs. Another area is in Windows itself, which must handle a variety of tasks of its own in addition to the tasks of the applications it is supporting. Again, a workload shared among several processors makes faster progress than sharing time-slices on a single processor.

This chapter begins with a conceptual introduction to threads, then surveys the commands for using threads, and finishes with a sample program demonstrating threads. By the end of this chapter, you will understand when and how to create threads in your programs, how to manage them while they run, and how to synchronize them so they don't interfere with each other. Mutexes, semaphores, events, and critical sections will hold no more mysteries for you.

Thread Concepts

Threads are closely related to *processes*. A process is a program loaded into memory, complete with all the resources assigned to the program, but a process is static and does nothing by itself.

A thread executes program commands, following a path through the code. Every process possesses one initial thread. Optionally, the initial thread (also called the *primary thread*) may create other threads. All the threads belonging to one process share the assets of that process. They all follow instructions from the same code image, refer to the same global variables, write to the same private address space, and have access to the same objects. Think of a process as being house that is inhabited by threads.

Life without Threads

While an operation without threads does accomplish similar tasks, the process of doing so is less versatile. For a single-threaded application, initiating a subprocess (or child process) requires temporarily tabling the main process and only resuming when the subprocess is completed. In earlier versions of Windows, all applications were single-threaded of necessity, even though Windows itself performed something like a multithreaded process—sharing processor time among multiple applications so each had its own chance to execute.

At the same time, background processes—such as spell-checking, image-rendering, or file maintenance—are often relegated to low priority while GUI processes, which are immediately visible to the user, take precedence. Without threads, the allocation of resources often results in a slow response from the GUI elements when tasks of this nature do become active. Threads, while not in themselves a cure-all, do permit a smoother time-share in such circumstances.

When to Create Threads and Processes

You should consider creating new threads any time your program handles asynchronous activity. Programs with multiple windows, for example, generally benefit from creating a thread for each window. Most MDI (Multi-Document Interface) applications create threads for the child windows. A program that interacts with several asynchronous devices creates threads for responding to each device.

A desktop publisher, for example, might assign responsibility for the main window to a single thread of high priority. When the user initiates a lengthy operation, such as pouring text into an empty layout, the program creates a new thread to do the formatting in the background. Meanwhile, the first thread continues to manage the main window and responds quickly to new commands from the user. If the user then asks to cancel the formatting, the input thread can interrupt the formatting thread by terminating it. Threads can also be useful for performing slow disk operations in the background or for communicating with other processes. One thread sends messages, and another waits to receive them.

NOTE

Each window that a program creates belongs to the thread that creates it. When a thread creates a window, the system gives it a message queue, and the thread must enter a message loop to read from its queue. If a single thread creates all of a program's windows, the program needs only a single message loop. Conversely, any thread that wants to receive messages must create a window for itself, even if the window remains hidden. Only threads that create windows get message queues.

One example of synchronous activity that is familiar to many users would be using a contemporary word processor with the automatic spell-checker enabled. Here one (or probably more) threads are responsible for responding to the keyboard activity, updating the text on the screen, and managing a regular update of the backup version of the working file. At the same time, another thread is busy checking what has been written against the selected dictionary or dictionaries and, when a word is not recognized, sending a message to tell the display thread to highlight the unknown word. As long as the word processor is working smoothly, all of these tasks are occurring synchronously even though at different rates.

Any thread can create other threads. Any thread can also create new processes. When a program needs to do several things at once, it must decide whether to create threads or processes to share the work. Choose threads whenever you can because the system creates them quickly and they interact with each other easily. Creating a process takes longer because the system must load a new executable file image from the disk. However, a new process has the advantage of receiving its own private address space. You might also choose processes over threads as a way of preventing them from interfering, even accidentally, with each other's resources. (For more details about processes, refer to Chapter 15.)

Thread Objects

At the system level, a thread is an object created by the Object Manager. Like all system objects, a thread contains attributes (or data) and methods (or functions). Figure 14.1 represents a thread object schematically, listing its attributes and methods.

STANDARD OBJECT HEADER	
Thread Attributes	**Thread Methods**
Client ID	Create thread
Context	Open thread
Dynamic priority	Query thread information
Base priority	Set thread information
Processor affinity	Current thread
Exicutiontime	Terminate thread
Alert Status	Get context
Suspension count	Set context
Impersonation token	Suspend
Termination port	Resume
Exit status	Alert
	Test alert
	Register termination port

Most of the thread methods have corresponding Win32 functions. When you call SuspendThread, for example, the Win32 subsystem responds by calling the thread's Suspend method. In other words, the Win32 API *exposes* the Suspend method to Win32 applications.

NOTE   The Win32 API is a library (or libraries) of methods that are called directly or indirectly by applications to request services performed by the operating system. For a simple example, asking for a list of files or directories is accomplished though an API call. Under DOS, a similar task would be accomplished by calling a DOS interrupt function. Under Windows, the principal remains the same; an API call invokes a system-supplied function to perform a task.

The thread context attribute is the data structure for saving the machine state whenever the thread stops executing. You'll learn about other thread attributes later in the chapter.

Objects and Handles

Windows has always protected some internal structures, such as windows and brushes, from direct manipulation; programs that run at the system's user level (as opposed to the more privileged kernel level) may not directly examine or modify the inside of a system object. Only by calling Win32 API routines can you do anything at all with an object. Windows gives you a handle to identify the object, and you pass the handle to functions that need it. Threads, too, have handles, as do processes, semaphores, files, and many other objects. Only the Object Manager touches the inside of an object.

The function that creates a thread returns a handle to the new object. With the handle, you can do the following:

- Raise or lower the thread's scheduling priority.

- Make the thread pause and resume.

- Terminate the thread.

- Find out what value the thread returned when it ended.

Under 16-bit Windows, an object has only one handle. The handle may be copied into several variables, but it is still one handle. And when the object is destroyed, all the copies of the handle become invalid. Starting with Windows 95, however, some new objects in Win32 began to work differently. Several threads or processes may have different handles to the same object. Brushes, windows, and device contexts still support only one handle; but a single thread, process, or mutex may have many different handles. As each finishes with the object, it calls `CloseHandle`. When the last handle closes, the system destroys the object.

NOTE   Although the total number of handles in the system is limited only by available memory, no single process may possess more than 65,536 open handles.

Scheduling and Synchronizing Threads

Working with threads requires more than just starting and stopping them. You also need to make threads work together, and effective interaction requires control over timing. Timing control takes two forms: priority and synchronization. Priority controls how often a thread gets processor time. Synchronization regulates threads when they compete for shared resources and imposes a sequence when several threads must accomplish tasks in a certain order.

Process, Base, and Dynamic Priority

When the system scheduler preempts one thread and looks for another to run next, it gives preference to threads of high priority. Some activities, such as responding to an unexpected power loss, always execute at a very high priority. System interrupt handlers have a higher priority than user processes. Every process has a priority rating, and threads derive their base scheduling priority from the process that owns them.

As shown earlier in Figure 14.1, a thread object's attributes include a base priority and a dynamic priority. When you call commands to change a thread's priority, you change the base priority. You cannot push a thread's priority more than two steps above or below the priority of its process. In other words, threads can't grow up to be very much more important than their parent.

Although a process cannot promote its threads very far, the system can. The system grants a sort of field promotion—dynamic priority—to threads that undertake important missions. When the user gives input to a window, for example, the system always elevates all the threads in the process that owns the window. When a thread waiting for data from a disk drive finally receives it, the system promotes that thread, too. These temporary boosts, added to the thread's current base priority, form the dynamic priority. The scheduler chooses threads to execute based on their dynamic priority. Process, base, and dynamic priorities are distinguished in Figure 14.2.

Dynamic priority boosts begin to degrade immediately. A thread's dynamic priority slips back one level each time the thread receives another time slice and finally stabilizes at the thread's base priority.

FIGURE 14.2:

How the range of a thread's priority derives from the priority of the process

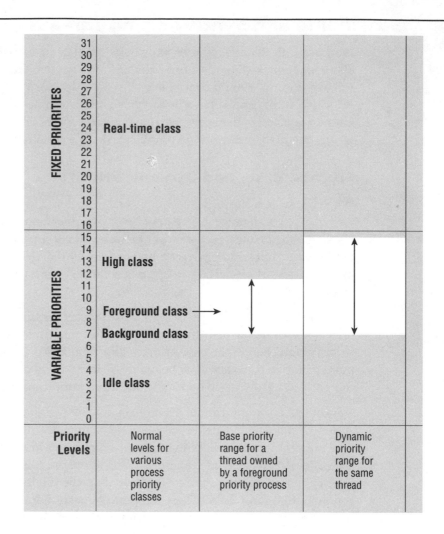

Priority Levels	Normal levels for various process priority classes	Base priority range for a thread owned by a foreground priority process	Dynamic priority range for the same thread

How Scheduling Happens

To select the next thread, the scheduler begins at the highest priority queue, executes the threads there, and then works its way down the rest of the list. But the dispatcher ready queue may not contain all the threads in the system. Some may be suspended or blocked. At any moment, a thread may be in one of six states:

Ready   Queued, waiting to execute

Standby   Ready to run next (in the batter's box)

Running   Executing, interacting with the CPU

Waiting   Not executing, waiting for a signal to resume

Transition   About to execute when the system loads its context

Terminated   Finished executing, but the object is not deleted

When the scheduler selects a ready thread from the queue, it loads a *context* for the thread. The context includes a set of values for the machine registers, the kernel stack, a thread environment block, and a user stack in the address space of the thread's process. (If part of the context has been paged to disk, the thread enters the transition state while the system gathers the pieces.)

Changing threads means saving all the pieces of one context and loading all the pieces of the next one into the processor. The newly loaded thread runs for one time slice, which is likely to be on the order of 20 milliseconds. The system maintains a counter measuring the current time slice. On each clock tick, the system decrements the counter; when it reaches zero, the scheduler performs a context switch and sets a new thread running.

For those familiar with how multiple executables function under, for example, Windows 3.1, executing threads is very much like executing separate applications. The real difference is simply that single applications are now able to separate tasks for parallel execution instead of executing in serial fashion.

How Synchronization Happens

To run at all, threads must be scheduled; to run well, they often need to be synchronized. Suppose one thread creates a brush and then creates several threads that share the brush and draw with it. The first thread must not destroy the brush until the other threads finish drawing. Or suppose one thread accepts input from the user and writes it to a file, while another thread reads from the file and processes the text. The reading thread must not read while the writing thread is writing. Both situations require a means of coordinating the sequence of actions in several threads.

One solution would be to create a global Boolean variable that one thread uses to signal another. The writing thread might set bDone to TRUE, and the reading thread might loop until it sees the flag change. That would work, but the looping thread wastes a lot of processor time. Instead, Win32 supports a set of synchronization objects:

- A *mutex* object works like a narrow gate for one thread to pass through at a time.

- A *semaphore* object works like a multiple-lane toll gate that a limited number of threads can pass through together.

- An *event* object broadcasts a public signal for any listening thread to hear.

- A *critical section* object works just like a mutex but only within a single process.

All are system objects created by the Object Manager. Although each synchronization object coordinates different interactions, they all work in a similar way. A thread that wants to perform some coordinated action waits for a response from one of these objects and proceeds only after receiving it. The scheduler removes waiting objects from the dispatch queue so they do not consume processor time. When the signal arrives, the scheduler allows the thread to resume.

How and when the signal arrives depends on the object. For example, the one essential characteristic of a mutex is that only one thread can own it. A mutex doesn't do anything apart from letting itself be owned by one thread at a time (*mutex* stands for *mut*ual *ex*clusion). If several threads need to work with a single file, you might create a mutex to protect the file. Whenever any thread begins a file operation, it first asks for the mutex. If no one else has the mutex, the thread proceeds. If, on the other hand, another thread has just grabbed the mutex for itself, the request fails and the thread *blocks,* becoming suspended while it waits for ownership. When one thread finishes writing, it releases the mutex, and the waiting thread revives, receives the mutex, and performs its own file operations.

The mutex does not actively protect anything. It only works because the threads that use it agree not to write to the file without owning the mutex first. Nothing actually prevents all the threads from trying to write at once. The mutex is just a signal, much like the Boolean bDone in our looping example. You might create a mutex to protect global variables, a hardware port, a handle to a pipe, or a window's client area. Whenever several threads share any system resource, you should consider whether to synchronize their use of it.

Mutexes, semaphores, and events can coordinate threads in different processes, but critical sections are visible only to threads in a single process. When one process creates a child process, the child often inherits handles to existing synchronization objects. Critical section objects cannot be inherited.

Fundamentally a synchronization object, like other system objects, is simply a data structure. Synchronization objects have two states: signaled and not signaled. Threads interact with synchronization objects by changing the signal or waiting for the signal. A waiting thread is blocked and does not execute. When the signal occurs, the waiting thread receives the object, turns the signal off, performs some synchronized task, and turns the signal back on when it relinquishes the object.

Threads can wait for other objects besides mutexes, semaphores, events, and critical objects. Sometimes it makes sense to wait for a process, a thread, a timer, or a file. These objects serve other purposes as well, but like the synchronization objects, they also possess a signal state. Processes and threads signal when they terminate. Timer objects signal when a certain interval passes. Files signal when a read or write operation finishes. Threads can wait for any of these signals.

Bad synchronization causes bugs. For example, a deadlock bug occurs when two threads wait for each other. Neither will end unless the other ends first. A race condition occurs when a program fails to synchronize its threads. Suppose one thread writes to a file and another thread reads the new contents. Whether the program works depends on which thread wins the race to its I/O operation. If the writing thread wins, the program works. If the reading thread tries to read first, the program fails.

Thread-Related Commands

As an introduction to the features of multithreaded programming, the following sections survey the parts of the Win32 API that relate to threads. First, we will look at commands for creating and modifying threads, and then we will examine commands for synchronizing threads.

Making and Modifying Threads

The life cycle of a thread begins when you call CreateThread. Other functions let you examine the thread, suspend or resume it, change its priority, and terminate it.

Creating Threads

Any thread can create another thread by calling CreateThread. The arguments to CreateThread specify the properties a thread needs to begin life: primarily security privileges and a starting function. The starting function is to a thread what main or WinMain is to a full program. The thread's life coincides with the life of its main function. When the function returns, the thread ends. A thread can start at any function that receives a single 32-bit parameter and returns a 32-bit value.

The parameter and return value are for your convenience. You need to declare them, but you don't need to use them. CreateThread lets you pass a DWORD into the starting function. If several threads execute the same function, you might pass each one a different argument. Each might receive a pointer to a different filename, for example, or a different object handle to wait for.

CreateThread takes six parameters:

```
// prototype for the CreateThread function
HANDLE CreateThread(
    LPSECURITY_ATTRIBUTES  lpThreadAttributes,  // access privileges
    DWORD                  dwStackSize,         // say 0 for default
    LPTHREAD_START_ROUTINE lpStartAddress,      // pointer to function
    LPVOID                 lpParameter,         // value passed to function
    DWORD                  dwCreationFlags,     // active or suspended
    LPDWORD                lpThreadId );        // system returns ID here
```

The first parameter points to a SECURITY_ATTRIBUTES structure that determines who may share the object and whether other processes may modify it. The structure contains a security descriptor that assigns access privileges for various system users and groups of users. Most programs simply accept the default descriptor that comes with the current process. The security structure also contains an inheritance flag. If you set the flag to TRUE, any child processes you create will automatically inherit a handle to this object.

```
    typedef struct _SECURITY_ATTRIBUTES        /* sa */
    {
        DWORD  nLength;                 // size of(SECURITY_ATTRIBUTES)
        LPVOID lpSecurityDescriptor;    // NULL to accept process's descriptor
        BOOL   bInheritHandle;          // TRUE if children may inherit object
    } SECURITY_ATTRIBUTES, *LPSECURITY_ATTRIBUTES;
```

You don't need to create a SECURITY_ATTRIBUTES structure unless you want the thread to be inherited. If you pass NULL as the first parameter to Create-Thread, the new thread receives the default descriptor and will not be inherited. If you do want to create a handle with limited access rights to its object, investigate the four SetSecurityDescriptor functions.

The next three parameters give the new thread material to work with. By default, each thread receives a stack the same size as that of the primary thread. You can change the size with the second parameter. If the stack later needs more room, the system expands it automatically. The third parameter points to the function where the thread will start, and the value in the fourth parameter becomes the argument passed to the starting function.

WARNING   Beware of using a local variable to pass a value to a new thread. The local variable will be destroyed when its procedure ends, and the thread may not have used it yet. Use global variables, allocate memory dynamically, or make the first thread wait for the new thread to terminate before it returns.

The dwCreationFlags parameter may be one of two values: either 0 or CREATE_SUSPENDED. A suspended thread does not actually begin to run until you give it a push with ResumeThread. A program that creates a number of threads might suspend them, accumulate their handles, and, when ready, start them all off at once. That's what the sample program later in the chapter does.

The last parameter points to an empty DWORD where CreateThread places a number to identify the thread uniquely in the system. A few functions require you to identify threads by their ID number instead of by their handles.

CreateThread returns a handle to the new thread. If the thread could not be created, the handle will be NULL. Be aware that the system will create the thread even if the lpStartAddress or lpParameter values are invalid or point to inaccessible data. In those cases, CreateThread returns a valid handle, but the new thread terminates immediately and returns an error code. You can test a thread's viability with GetExitCodeThread, which returns STILL_ACTIVE if the thread has not ended.

Unless you give CreateThread an explicit security descriptor, the new handle comes with full access rights to the new object. In the case of threads, full access means that with this handle you can suspend, resume, terminate, or change the priority of the thread. The handle remains valid even after the thread terminates.

To destroy the thread object, close its handle by calling `CloseHandle`. If more than one handle exists, the thread will not be destroyed until the last handle is closed. If you forget to close the handle, the system will do it automatically when your process ends.

Creating Threads Using MFC

An alternative method of creating threads using MFC is to create a class based on the `CWinThread` class. A skeletal example of the process follows:

```
// CThreadExample

IMPLEMENT_DYNCREATE(CThreadExample, CWinThread)

CThreadExample::CThreadExample()
{
    ...    // class member variables are initialized
}

CThreadExample::~CThreadExample()
{
}

BOOL CThreadExample::InitInstance()
{
    // TODO:  perform any per-thread initialization here
    ...
    // this is the point where non-variable initializations,
    // such as creating instances of other class objects, are
    // handled
    return TRUE;
}

int CThreadExample::ExitInstance()
{
    // TODO:  perform any per-thread cleanup here
    ...
    return CWinThread::ExitInstance();
}

BEGIN_MESSAGE_MAP(CThreadExample, CWinThread)
    //{{AFX_MSG_MAP(CThreadExample)
    // NOTE - ClassWizard will add/remove mapping macros here.
    //}}AFX_MSG_MAP
END_MESSAGE_MAP()
```

A CWinThread object represents an execution thread within an application. Where the application's main thread of execution is normally provided by a CWinApp-derived object, the CWinApp class itself is derived from CWinThread. Additional CWinThread objects, as shown in the example, allow multiple threads within the application.

MFC-based applications must use CWinThread-derived classes to ensure that the application is thread-safe. Under MFC, the framework uses thread local data to maintain thread-specific information for CWinThread-managed objects.

Furthermore, any thread created by the runtime function _beginthreadex cannot use any MFC APIs.

MFC Thread Types

Two general types of threads are supported: *working threads* and *user-interface* threads. Working threads do not require a message handler. For example, a thread performing background calculations in a spreadsheet functions without any interaction with the user and does not need to respond to messages.

In contrast, user-interface threads must process messages received from the system (from the user) and require a message handler. User-interface threads can be derived from CWinApp or directly from the CWinThread class.

A CWinThread object commonly exists for the duration of the thread, but the behavior of the object may be modified by setting the m_bAutoDelete member to FALSE.

How to Create an MFC Thread

Threads are created by calling AfxBeginThread. For a user-interface thread, you call AfxBeginThread with a pointer to the CRuntimeClass of the CWinThread-derived class. For a working thread, you call AfxBeginThread with a pointer to the controlling function and the parameter for the controlling function.

For both working and user-interface threads, you may specify additional parameters to modify the priority, stack size, creation flags, and security attributes for the thread. AfxBeginThread returns a pointer to the new CWinThread object.

Alternatively, you can construct and then create a CWinThread-derived object by calling the CreateThread function for the class. Using this format permits the CWinThread-derived object to be reused between successively creating and terminating thread executions.

Changing a Thread's Priority

High-priority threads get more time on the processor, finish their work more quickly, and are more responsive to the user. But making all of your threads high priority entirely defeats the purpose of priorities. If a number of threads have the same priority—whether their priority is high or low—the scheduler must give them equal processor time. One thread can be more responsive only if the others are less responsive. The same rule applies equally to processes. Restrict your threads and processes as much as possible to low or average priority levels, and stay at high levels only as long as you must.

These functions retrieve or modify any thread's base priority:

```
BOOL SetThreadPriority(
    HANDLE hThread                  // a thread to modify
    int    iPriority );             // its new priority level

int GetThreadPriority( HANDLE hThread );
```

SetThreadPriority returns TRUE or FALSE for success or failure. GetThread-Priority returns the thread's current priority. To name the possible priority values for both functions, use the following set of constants:

THREAD_PRIORITY_LOWEST	Two levels below process
THREAD_PRIORITY_BELOW_NORMAL	One level below process
THREAD_PRIORITY_NORMAL	Same level as process
THREAD_PRIORITY_ABOVE_NORMAL	One level above process
THREAD_PRIORITY_HIGHEST	Two levels above process
THREAD_PRIORITY_TIME_CRITICAL	Fifteen (in normal user processes)
THREAD_PRIORITY_IDLE	One (in normal user processes)

The first five values adjust the thread's base-priority level with respect to the level of its parent process, as shown earlier in Figure 14.2. The last two, for critical and idle priority, express absolute priority levels at the upper and lower extremes of the parent's priority class. (The extremes for real-time priority codes are 16 and 31.) The idle priority level works well for screensavers because they should not execute unless nothing else is happening. Use the time critical level with extreme caution and only for short periods because it will starve lower-priority threads of processor time.

Suspending and Resuming a Thread's Execution

A suspended thread stops running and will not be scheduled for processor time. It remains in this state until some other thread makes it resume. Suspending a thread might be useful if, for example, the user interrupts a task. You could suspend the thread while waiting for the user to confirm the cancellation. If the user chooses to continue, the interrupted thread can resume where it left off. The *Threads* demo, discussed later in this chapter, suspends several drawing threads whenever the user resizes the window. Then when the window is repainted, the threads continue drawing.

A thread calls these functions to make another thread pause and resume:

```
DWORD SuspendThread( HANDLE hThread );
DWORD ResumeThread( HANDLE hThread );
```

A single thread may be suspended several times in succession without any intervening resume commands, but every SuspendThread command must eventually be matched with a ResumeThread command. The system counts the number of pending suspension commands for each thread (the thread suspension count attribute). SuspendThread increments the counter, and ResumeThread decrements it. Both functions return the previous value of the counter in a DWORD. Only when the counter returns to 0 does the thread resume execution.

A thread can suspend itself but cannot resume itself. However, a thread can put itself to sleep for a set amount of time. The Sleep command delays execution, removing the thread from the scheduler's queue until some interval passes. Interactive threads that write or draw information for the user often take short naps to give the user time to see the output. Sleep is better than an empty loop because it doesn't use processor time.

A thread calls these functions to pause for a set time:

```
VOID Sleep( DWORD dwMilliseconds );

DWORD SleepEx(
    DWORD dwMilliseconds,  // duration of pause
    BOOL bAlertable );     // TRUE to resume if I/O operation finishes
```

The extended SleepEx function typically works in conjunction with background I/O functions and can be used to initiate a read or write operation without waiting for the operation to finish. The operation continues in the background. When it finishes, the system notifies the user by invoking a callback procedure from the program. Background I/O (also called *overlapping I/O*) is particularly helpful in interactive programs that must remain responsive to the user while working with relatively slow devices, such as tape drives and network disks.

The Boolean parameter in SleepEx lets the system wake the thread prematurely if an overlapping I/O operation finishes before the sleep interval expires. If Sleep-Ex is interrupted, it returns WAIT_IO_COMPLETION. If the interval passes without interruption, SleepEx returns 0.

Getting Information about Existing Threads

A thread can easily retrieve the two pieces of its own identity: a handle and an identifier.

These functions return information identifying the current thread:

```
DWORD GetCurrentThreadID( VOID );
HANDLE GetCurrentThread( VOID );
```

The return value from GetCurrentThreadID matches the value in lpIDThread after a CreateThread command. It is the value that uniquely identifies the thread to the system. Although few of the Win32 API commands require you to know a thread's ID, it can be useful for monitoring threads system-wide without needing to keep handles open for each one. Open handles prevent threads from being destroyed.

The handle that GetCurrentThread returns serves the same purpose as the handle returned from CreateThread. Although it works in the same manner as other handles, it is actually a *pseudohandle*. A pseudohandle is a special constant that the system always interprets a certain way, much as a single dot (.) in DOS always refers to the current directory and this in C++ always points to the current object. The pseudohandle constant returned from GetCurrentThread always refers to the current thread. Unlike real handles, a pseudohandle does not work when passed to other threads. Here's what a thread must do to acquire a real, transferrable handle to itself:

```
HANDLE hThread;

hThread = DuplicateHandle(
    GetCurrentProcess(),        // source process
    GetCurrentThread(),         // original handle
    GetCurrentProcess(),        // destination process
    &hThread,                   // new duplicate handle
    0,                          // access rights (overridden by last parameter)
    FALSE,                      // children do not inherit the handle
    DUPLICATE_SAME_ACCESS );    // copy access rights from original handle
```

While CloseHandle has no effect on a pseudohandle, the handle Duplicate-Handle creates is real and must eventually be closed. Using pseudohandles lets GetCurrentThread work more quickly, because it assumes a thread should have full access to itself and returns its result without bothering about any security considerations.

Terminating the Execution of a Thread

Just as a Windows program ends when it comes to the end of WinMain, a thread normally meets its demise when it comes to the end of the function where it began. When a thread comes to the end of its starting function, the system automatically calls ExitThread, as:

```
VOID ExitThread( DWORD dwExitCode );
```

Although the system calls ExitThread automatically, you may call it directly if some condition forces a thread to an untimely end:

```
DWORD ThreadFunction( LPDWORD lpdwParam )
{
    HANDLE hThread = CreateThread( <parameters> );

        // initialization chores happen here
        // test to see if there was a problem

    if( <error condition> )
    {
        ExitThread( ERROR_CODE );    // cancel the thread
    }
        //
        // no error, work continues
        //
    return( SUCCESS_CODE );          // this line causes the system
}                                    // to call ExitThread
```

ERROR_CODE and SUCCESS_CODE are whatever you define them to be. In this simple example, you could just as easily have canceled with a return command:

```
    if( <error condition> )
    {
        return( ERROR_CODE );            // cancel the thread
    }
```

This `return` command has exactly the same effect as `ExitThread`; in fact, it even results in a call to `ExitThread`. The `ExitThread` command is genuinely useful for canceling from within any subroutines `ThreadFunction` calls.

When a thread ends at a `return` statement, the 32-bit return value becomes the exit code passed automatically to `ExitThread`. After a thread terminates, its exit code is available through this function:

```
// one thread calls this to find out how another ended
BOOL GetExitCodeThread( HANDLE hThread, LPDWORD lpdwExitCode );
```

`GetExitCodeThread` returns FALSE if an error prevents it from determining the return value.

`ExitThread`, whether called explicitly or implicitly as a consequence of `return`, permanently removes a thread from the dispatch queue and destroys the thread's stack. It does not, however, destroy the thread object. That's why you can still ask about the thread's exit status even after the thread stops running. When possible, you should close thread handles explicitly (call `CloseHandle`) to avoid wasting space in memory. The system destroys a thread when its last handle is closed. The system will not destroy a running thread, even if all its handles are closed. (In that case, the thread is destroyed when it stops running.) If a process leaves handles open when it terminates, the system closes them automatically and removes orphaned objects no longer held by any process.

With `ExitThread`, a thread stops itself gracefully at a place of its own choosing. Another function allows one thread to stop another abruptly and arbitrarily:

```
// one thread calls this to stop another
BOOL TerminateThread( HANDLE hThread, DWORD dwExitCode );
```

A thread cannot protect itself from termination. Anyone with a handle to the thread can force the thread to stop immediately, regardless of its current state (providing, of course, that the handle allows full access to the thread). Using the default security attributes in `CreateThread` produces a handle with full access privileges.

`TerminateThread` does not destroy the thread's stack, but it does provide an exit code. Both `ExitThread` and `TerminateThread` set the thread object to its signaled state, so any other threads waiting for this one to end may proceed. After either command, the thread object lingers lifelessly until all its handles have been closed.

Using C Runtime Functions

Several C runtime library commands duplicate some of the Win32 thread commands:

```
unsigned long _beginthread(
    void( *start_address )( void * ), // starting function
    unsigned stack_size,              // initial stack size
    void *arglist );                  // parameter for starting function

void _endthread( void );
void _sleep( unsigned long ulMilliseconds );
```

_beginthread performs some of the internal initialization for a new thread that other C runtime functions, such as signal, depend on. The rule is consistency: If your program manipulates threads with C runtime functions, then use only C runtime functions wherever you have a choice. If your program uses Win32 functions with its threads, then stick to CreateThread and ExitThread. Also, if the thread calls C runtime functions, then create it with the C functions rather than the Win32 API. A few C routines require the initialization that _beginthread performs.

Synchronizing Threads

To work with threads, you must be able to coordinate their actions. Sometimes coordination requires ensuring that certain actions happen in a specific order. Besides the functions to create threads and modify their scheduling priority, the Win32 API contains functions to make threads wait for signals from objects, such as files and processes. It also supports special synchronization objects, such as mutexes and semaphores.

The functions that wait for an object to reach its signaled state best illustrate how synchronization objects are used. With a single set of generic waiting commands, you can wait for processes, threads, mutexes, semaphores, events, and a few other objects to reach their signaled states. This command waits for one object to turn on its signal:

```
DWORD WaitForSingleObject( HANDLE hObject,        // object to wait for
                           DWORD dwMilliseconds ); // maximum wait time
```

WaitForSingleObject allows a thread to suspend itself until a specific object gives its signal. In this command, a thread also states how long it is willing to wait for the object. To wait indefinitely, set the interval to INFINITE. If the object is already available or if it reaches its signal state within the designated time, WaitForSingleObject returns 0 and execution resumes. If the interval passes and the object is still not signaled, the function returns WAIT_TIMEOUT.

WARNING   Beware when setting the interval to INFINITE. If for any reason the object never reaches a signaled state, the thread will never resume. Also, if two threads establish a reciprocal infinite wait, they will deadlock.

To make a thread wait for several objects at once, call WaitForMultiple-Objects. You can make this function return as soon as any one of the objects becomes available, or you can make it wait until all the requested objects finally reach their signaled states. An event-driven program might set up an array of objects that interest it and respond when any of them signals.

```
DWORD WaitForMultipleObjects(
    DWORD    dwNumObjects,      // number of objects to wait for
    LPHANDLE lpHandles,         // array of object handles
    BOOL     bWaitAll,          // TRUE, wait for all; FALSE, wait for any
    DWORD    dwMilliseconds );  // maximum waiting period
```

Again, a return value of WAIT_TIMEOUT indicates that the interval passed and no objects were signaled. If bWaitAll is FALSE, a successful return value, which has a flag from any one element, indicates which element of the lpHandles array has become signaled. (The first element is 0, the second is 1, and so on.) If bWaitAll is TRUE, the function does not respond until all flags (all threads) have completed.

Two extended versions of the wait functions add an alert status allowing a thread to resume if an asynchronous read or write command happens to end during the wait. In effect, these functions say, "Wake me up if the object becomes available, if a certain time passes, or if a background I/O operation runs to completion."

```
DWORD WaitForSingleObjectEx(
    HANDLE hObject,            // object to wait for
    DWORD  dwMilliseconds,     // maximum time to wait
    BOOL   bAlertable );       // TRUE to end wait if I/O completes

DWORD WaitForMultipleObjectsEx(
    DWORD    dwNumObjects,      // number of objects to wait for
    LPHANDLE lpHandles,         // array of object handles
```

```
BOOL     bWaitAll,        // TRUE to wait for all; FALSE to wait for any
DWORD    dwMilliseconds,  // maximum waiting period
BOOL     bAlertable );    // TRUE to end wait if I/O completes
```

Successful wait commands usually modify the awaited object in some way. For example, when a thread waits for and acquires a mutex, the wait function restores the mutex to its unsignaled state so other threads will know it is in use. Wait commands also decrease the counter in a semaphore and reset some kinds of events.

Wait commands do not modify the state of the specified object until all objects are simultaneously signaled. For example, a mutex can be signaled, but the thread does not receive ownership immediately because it is required to wait until the other objects are also signaled; therefore, the wait function cannot modify the object. In addition, the mutex may come under the ownership of another thread while waiting, which will further delay the completion of the wait condition.

Of course, you must create an object before you can wait for it. Start with mutexes and semaphores because they have parallel API commands to create the objects, acquire or release them, get handles to them, and destroy them.

Creating Mutexes and Semaphores

The creation functions for mutexes and semaphores need to be told what access privileges you want, some initial conditions for the object, and an optional name for the object.

```
HANDLE CreateMutex(
    LPSECURITY_ATTRIBUTES lpsa,   // optional security attributes
    BOOL bInitialOwner            // TRUE if creator wants ownership
    LPTSTR lpszMutexName )        // object's name

HANDLE CreateSemaphore(
    LPSECURITY_ATTRIBUTES lpsa,   // optional security attributes
    LONG lInitialCount,           // initial count (usually 0)
    LONG lMaxCount,               // maximum count (limits # of threads)
    LPTSTR lpszSemName );         // name of the semaphore (may be NULL)
```

If the security descriptor is NULL, the returned handle will possess all access privileges and will not be inherited by child processes. The names are optional; they are useful for identification purposes when several different processes want handles to the same object.

By setting the bInitialOwner flag to TRUE, a thread both creates and acquires a mutex at once. The new mutex remains unsignaled until the thread releases it.

While only one thread at a time may acquire a mutex, a semaphore remains signaled until its acquisition count reaches iMaxCount. If any more threads try to wait for the semaphore, they will be suspended until some other thread decreases the acquisition count.

Acquiring and Releasing Mutexes and Semaphores

Once a semaphore or a mutex exists, threads interact with it by acquiring and releasing it. To acquire either object, a thread calls WaitForSingleObject (or one of its variants). When a thread finishes whatever task the object synchronizes, it releases the object with one of these functions:

```
BOOL ReleaseMutex( HANDLE hMutex );

BOOL ReleaseSemaphore(
    HANDLE hSemaphore,
    LONG lRelease,          // amount to increment counter on release
                            // (usually 1)
    LPLONG lplPrevious );   // variable to receive the previous count
```

Releasing a mutex or a semaphore increments its counter. Whenever the counter rises above 0, the object assumes its signaled state, and the system checks to see whether any other threads are waiting for it.

Only a thread that already owns a mutex—in other words, a thread that has already waited for the mutex—can release it. Any thread, however, can call ReleaseSemaphore to adjust the acquisition counter by any amount up to its maximum value. Changing the counter by arbitrary amounts lets you vary the number of threads that may own a semaphore as your program runs. You may have noticed that CreateSemaphore allows you to set the counter for a new semaphore to something other than its maximum value. You might, for example, create it with an initial count of 0 to block all threads while your program initializes and then raise the counter with ReleaseSemaphore.

WARNING   Remember to release synchronization objects. If you forget to release a mutex, any threads that wait for it without specifying a maximum interval will deadlock; they will not be released.

A thread may wait for the same object more than once without blocking, but each wait must be matched with a release. This is true of mutexes, semaphores, and critical sections.

Working with Events

An *event* is the object a program creates when it requires a mechanism for alerting threads if some action occurs. In its simplest form—a manual reset event—the event object turns its signal on and off in response to the two commands SetEvent (signal on) and ResetEvent (signal off). When the signal is on, all threads that wait for the event will receive it. When the signal is off, all threads that wait for the event become blocked. Unlike mutexes and semaphores, manual reset events change their state only when some thread explicitly sets or resets them.

You might use a manual reset event to allow certain threads to execute only when the program is not painting its window or only after the user enters certain information. Here are the basic commands for working with events:

```
HANDLE CreateEvent(
    LPSECURITY_ATTRIBUTES lpsa,   // security privileges (default = NULL)
    BOOL bManualReset,            // TRUE if event must be reset manually
    BOOL bInitialState,           // TRUE to create event in signaled state
    LPTSTR lpszEventName );        // name of event (may be NULL)

BOOL SetEvent( HANDLE hEvent );

BOOL ResetEvent( HANDLE hEvent );
```

Using the bInitialState parameter, CreateEvent allows the new event to arrive in the world already signaled. The SetEvent and ResetEvent functions return TRUE or FALSE to indicate success or failure.

With the bManualReset parameter, CreateEvent lets you create an automatic reset event instead of a manual reset event. An automatic reset event returns to its unsignaled state immediately after a SetEvent command. ResetEvent is redundant for an automatic reset event. Furthermore, an automatic reset event always releases only a single thread on each signal before resetting. An automatic reset event might be useful for a program where one master thread prepares data for other working threads. Whenever a new set of data is ready, the master sets the event and a single working thread is released. The other workers continue to wait in line for more assignments.

Besides setting and resetting events, you can pulse events.

```
BOOL PulseEvent( hEvent );
```

A pulse turns the signal on for a very short time and then turns it back off. Pulsing a manual event allows all waiting threads to pass and then resets the event. Pulsing an automatic event lets one waiting thread pass and then resets the event. If no threads are waiting, none will pass. Setting an automatic event, on the other hand, causes the event to leave its signal on until some thread waits for it. As soon as one thread passes, the event resets itself.

NOTE   The *NamedPipe* demo, discussed in Chapter 15, demonstrates the use of automatic and manual reset events.

Sharing and Destroying Mutexes, Semaphores, and Events

Processes—even unrelated ones—can share mutexes, semaphores, and events. By sharing objects, processes can coordinate their activities, just as threads do. There are three mechanisms for sharing. One is inheritance, where one process creates another and the new process receives copies of the parent's handles. Only those handles marked for inheritance when they were created will be passed on.

The other methods involve calling functions to create a second handle to an existing object. Which function you call depends on what information you already have. If you have handles to both the source and destination processes, call DuplicateHandle. If you have only the name of the object, call one of the Open functions. Two programs might agree in advance on the name of the object they share, or one might pass the name to the other through shared memory, DDEML (DDE Management Library), or a pipe.

```
BOOL DuplicateHandle(
    HANDLE  hSourceProcess, // process that owns the original object
    HANDLE  hSource,        // handle to the original object
    HANDLE  hTargetProcess, // process that wants a copy of the handle
    LPHANDLE lphTarget,     // place to store duplicated handle
    DWORD   fdwAccess,      // requested access privileges
    BOOL    bInherit,       // may the duplicate handle be inherited?
    DWORD   fdwOptions );   // optional actions, e.g., close source handle
```

```
HANDLE OpenMutex(
    DWORD fdwAccess,          // requested access privileges
    BOOL bInherit,            // TRUE if children may inherit this handle
    LPTSTR lpszName );        // name of the mutex

HANDLE OpenSemaphore(
    DWORD fdwAccess,          // requested access privileges
    BOOL bInherit,            // TRUE if children may inherit this handle
    LPTSTR lpszName );        // name of the semaphore

HANDLE OpenEvent(
    DWORD fdwAccess,          // requested access privileges
    BOOL bInherit,            // TRUE if children may inherit this handle
    LPTSTR lpszName );        // name of the event
```

NOTE   By the way, those **LPTSTR** variable types are not a misprint. It's a generic text type that compiles differently depending on whether an application uses Unicode or ASCII strings.

Mutexes, semaphores, and events persist in memory until all the processes that own them end or until all the object's handles have been closed with `CloseHandle`.

```
BOOL CloseHandle( hObject );
```

Working with Critical Sections

A critical section object performs exactly the same function as a mutex except that critical sections may not be shared. They are visible only within a single process. Critical sections and mutexes both allow only one thread to own them at a time, but critical sections work more quickly and involve less overhead.

The functions for working with critical sections do not use the same terminology as the functions for working with mutexes, but they do roughly the same things. Instead of creating a critical section, you *initialize* it. Instead of waiting for it, you *enter* it. Instead of releasing it, you *leave* it. Instead of closing its handle, you *delete* the object.

```
VOID InitializeCriticalSection( LPCRITICAL_SECTION lpcs );
VOID EnterCriticalSection( LPCRITICAL_SECTION lpcs );
VOID LeaveCriticalSection( LPCRITICAL_SECTION lpcs );
VOID DeleteCriticalSection( LPCRITICAL_SECTION lpcs );
```

The variable type LPCRITICAL_SECTION names a pointer (not a handle) to a critical section object. InitializeCriticalSection expects to receive a pointer to an empty object, &cs , which you can allocate like this:

```
CRITICAL_SECTION cs;
```

The Threads Demo:
Multiple Threads at Work

The *Threads* demo, shown in Figure 14.3, puts into code some of the ideas explained in this chapter. It creates four secondary threads, each of which draws randomly shaped and colored rectangles in a child window until the program ends. The top of the window contains a list box showing information about all four threads. By selecting a thread and choosing a menu command, you can suspend, resume, and change the priority of any thread. From the Options menu, you can also activate a mutex so only one thread draws at a time.

FIGURE 14.3:

The Threads demo

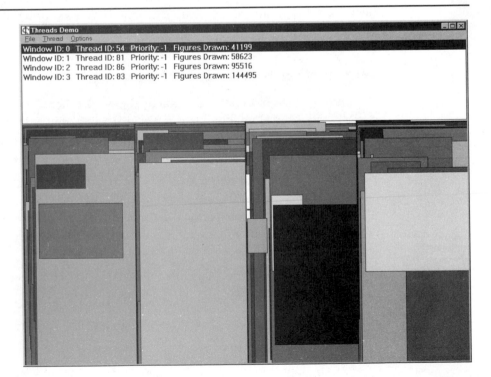

NOTE	The *Threads* demo is included on the CD accompanying this book, in the Chapter 14 folder.

Initialization Procedures

The initialization procedures register two window classes, one for the main over-lapping window and one for the child windows where the threads draw. They also create a timer. At five-second intervals, the list box updates the information about each thread. The `CreateWindows` function creates and positions all the windows, including the list box that shows information about each thread. The four threads are created during the WM_CREATE message handler.

```
/*----------------------------------------------------------------
   WIN MAIN
       Calls initializing procedures and runs the message loop
   -------------------------------------------------------------

int WINAPI WinMain(  HINSTANCE hinstThis, HINSTANCE hinstPrev,
                  LPSTR lpszCmdLine,   int iCmdShow  )
{
   MSG msg;

   hInst = hinstThis;          // store in global variable
   if( ! InitializeApp( ) )
   {
      // if the application was not initialized, exit here
      return( 0 );
   }
   ShowWindow( hwndParent, iCmdShow );
   UpdateWindow( hwndParent );
        // receive and forward messages from our queue
   while( GetMessage( &msg, NULL, 0, 0 ) )
   {
      TranslateMessage( &msg );
      DispatchMessage( &msg );
   }
   return( msg.wParam );
}
```

NOTE
Note the absence of a `PeekMessage` loop in `WinMain`. That's a clear sign that you have entered the world of preemptive multitasking. (In *preemptive multitasking*, the system interrupts executing threads to permit other threads access to the CPU; in *permissive multitasking* the system waits for a thread to relinquish control of the CPU.) The threads can draw continuously without monopolizing the processor. Other programs can still run at the same time.

In addition to registering the application class and following the usual setup procedures, the `InitializeApp` procedure sets the thread priority and starts each thread in a suspended state.

```
/*_____

    INITIALIZE APP
        Register two window classes and then create the windows
    _____*/

BOOL InitializeApp ( void )
{
    ...
        // mark the initial state of each thread as SUSPENDED
        // that is how they will be created
    for( iCount = 0; iCount < 4; iCount++ )
    {
        iState[iCount] = SUSPENDED;
    }
        // make the primary thread more important to facilitate user i/o
    SetThreadPriority( GetCurrentThread(), THREAD_PRIORITY_ABOVE_NORMAL );
        // create all the windows
    return( CreateWindows( ) );
}
```

The call to `SetThreadPriority` increases the priority of the primary thread. If all the secondary threads were busy working at the same priority as the main thread, the menus would respond sluggishly. You can test this yourself by raising the priority of the secondary threads as the program runs.

The `CreateWindows` function creates not only the main window but also a list box and a series of child windows for the threads.

```
/*--------------------------------------------------------------
   CREATE WINDOWS
      Create the parent window, the list box window, and the four
      child windows.
   ----------------------------------------------------------*/
BOOL CreateWindows ( void )
{
   char   szAppName[MAX_BUFFER];
   char   szTitle[MAX_BUFFER];
   char   szThread[MAX_BUFFER];
   HMENU  hMenu;
   int    iCount;

      // load the relevant strings
   LoadString( hInst, IDS_APPNAME, szAppName,  sizeof(szAppName));
   LoadString( hInst, IDS_TITLE,   szTitle,    sizeof(szTitle));
   LoadString( hInst, IDS_THREAD,  szThread,   sizeof(szThread));

      // create the parent window
   hMenu = LoadMenu( hInst, MAKEINTRESOURCE(MENU_MAIN) );
   hwndParent = CreateWindow( szAppName, szTitle,
                              WS_OVERLAPPEDWINDOW | WS_CLIPCHILDREN,
                              CW_USEDEFAULT, CW_USEDEFAULT,
                              CW_USEDEFAULT, CW_USEDEFAULT,
                              NULL, hMenu, hInst, NULL );
   if( ! hwndParent )
   {
      return( FALSE );
   }
      // create the list box
   hwndList = CreateWindow( "LISTBOX", NULL,
                            WS_BORDER | WS_CHILD | WS_VISIBLE |
                            LBS_STANDARD | LBS_NOINTEGRALHEIGHT,
                            0, 0, 0, 0, hwndParent, (HMENU)1,
                            hInst, NULL );
   if( ! hwndList )
   {
      return( FALSE );
   }
      // create the four child windows
   for( iCount = 0; iCount < 4; iCount++ )
   {
      hwndChild[iCount] = CreateWindow( "ThreadClass", NULL,
                                        WS_BORDER | WS_CHILD |
```

```
                                        WS_VISIBLE | WS_CLIPCHILDREN,
                                        0, 0, 0, 0, hwndParent, NULL,
                                        hInst, NULL );
        if( ! hwndChild ) return( FALSE );
    }
    return( TRUE );
}
```

Message-Handling Procedures

Most of the message-handling functions are simple. `Main_OnTimer` calls a procedure to clear the list box, generate four new strings of information, and display them. The `Main_OnSize` function suspends all the secondary threads while the program repositions the child windows to accommodate the new size. Otherwise, the busy threads would slow down the display operation. In addition to creating threads, `Main_OnCreate` creates a mutex.

```
/*-----------------------------------------------------------------
    MAIN_WNDPROC
        All messages for the main window are processed here.
  ---------------------------------------------------------------*/
LRESULT WINAPI Main_WndProc( HWND hWnd,          // message address
                             UINT uMessage,       // message type
                             WPARAM wParam,        // message contents
                             LPARAM lParam )       // more contents
{
    switch( uMessage )
    {
        HANDLE_MSG( hWnd, WM_CREATE, Main_OnCreate );
            // create the window and the threads
        HANDLE_MSG( hWnd, WM_SIZE, Main_OnSize );
            // reposition the child windows when the main window changes
        HANDLE_MSG( hWnd, WM_TIMER, Main_OnTimer );
            // update the list box every five seconds
        HANDLE_MSG( hWnd, WM_INITMENU, Main_OnInitMenu );
            // put a check by the Use Mutex menu item if bUseMutex is TRUE
        HANDLE_MSG( hWnd, WM_COMMAND, Main_OnCommand );
            // process menu commands
        HANDLE_MSG( hWnd, WM_DESTROY, Main_OnDestroy );
            // clean up and quit
```

```
        default:
            return( DefWindowProc(hWnd, uMessage, wParam, lParam) );
    }
    return( 0L );
}
```

The *Threads* demo uses the message-cracker macro, HANDLE_MSG. As a result, the compiler may produce a series of warnings saying, "unreferenced formal parameter" for the message handlers. To avoid these, include the argsused *pragma* following:

```
#ifdef __BORLANDC__
#pragma argsused
#endif
```

The Main_OnCreate function completes the process of initializing the several threads and setting up the mutex synchronization.

```
/*-------------------------------------------------------------
   MAIN_ONCREATE
      create the four threads and set the timer.
   ----------------------------------------------------------*/
BOOL Main_OnCreate( HWND hWnd, LPCREATESTRUCT lpCreateStruct )
{
   UINT uRet;
   int  iCount;

   // create the four threads, initially suspended
   for( iCount = 0; iCount < 4; iCount++ )
   {
      iRectCount[iCount] = 0;
      dwThreadData[iCount] = iCount;
      hThread[iCount] = CreateThread( NULL, 0,
            (LPTHREAD_START_ROUTINE) StartThread,
                        (LPVOID) ( & ( dwThreadData[iCount] ) ),
                                CREATE_SUSPENDED,
                        (LPDWORD) ( & ( dwThreadID[iCount] ) ) );
      if( ! hThread[iCount] )      // was the thread created?
      {
         return( FALSE );
      }
   }
      // create a timer with a five-second period
```

```
        // the timer is used to update the list box
    uRet = SetTimer( hWnd, TIMER, 5000, NULL );
    if( ! uRet )
    {                                    // unable to create the timer
        return( FALSE );
    }

        // create a mutex synchronization object
    hDrawMutex = CreateMutex( NULL, FALSE, NULL );
    if( ! hDrawMutex )
    {                                    // unable to create mutex
        KillTimer( hWnd, TIMER );   // stop the timer
        return( FALSE );
    }
        // start the threads with a priority below normal
    for( iCount = 0; iCount < 4; iCount++ )
    {
        SetThreadPriority( hThread[iCount], THREAD_PRIORITY_BELOW_NORMAL );
        iState[iCount] = ACTIVE;
        ResumeThread( hThread[iCount] );
    }
            // Now all four threads are running!
    return( TRUE );
}
```

The `Main_OnSize` function not only needs to resize the application window, but it also needs to resize—and move—all of the child windows at the same time; this is because we have multiple child windows and because the main application window is resizable.

```
/*—————————————————————————————————————————————————————————————————

    MAIN_ONSIZE
        Position the list box and the four child windows.
    —————————————————————————————————————————————————————————————————*/
void Main_OnSize( HWND hWnd, UINT uState, int cxClient, int cyClient )
{
    char* szText = "No Thread Data";
    int   iCount;

        // Suspend all active threads while the windows
        // resize and repaint themselves. This pause
        // enables the screen to update more quickly.
    for( iCount = 0; iCount < 4; iCount++ )
```

```
{
   if( iState[iCount] == ACTIVE )
      SuspendThread( hThread[iCount] );
}
   // Place the list box across the top 1/4 of the window.
MoveWindow( hwndList, 0, 0, cxClient, cyClient / 4, TRUE );
   // Spread the 4 child windows across the bottom 3/4 of the
   // window. (The left border of the first one should be 0.)
MoveWindow( hwndChild[0], 0, cyClient / 4 - 1, cxClient / 4 + 1,
            cyClient, TRUE );
for( iCount = 1; iCount < 4; iCount++ )
{
   MoveWindow( hwndChild[iCount], (iCount * cxClient) / 4,
               cyClient / 4 - 1,  cxClient / 4 + 1, cyClient, TRUE );
}
   // Add the default strings to the list box, and initialize
   // the number of figures drawn to zero.
for( iCount = 0; iCount < 4; iCount++ )
{
   iRectCount[iCount] = 0;
   ListBox_AddString( hwndList, szText );
}
ListBox_SetCurSel(hwndList, 0);
   // Reactivate the threads that were suspended while redrawing.
for( iCount = 0; iCount < 4; iCount++ )
{
   if( iState[iCount] == ACTIVE )
   {
      ResumeThread( hThread[iCount] );
   }
}
   return;
}
```

A timer message may not be the optimum choice for updating the list box. Ideally, the operations responsible for causing a change that should be reported would direct this event. In this case, however, a timer is a simple provision accomplishing the task.

```
/*-------------------------------------------------------------
    MAIN_ONTIMER
        Process the timer message by updating the list box.
-------------------------------------------------------------*/

void Main_OnTimer( HWND hWnd, UINT uTimerID )
{
        // update the data shown in the list box
    UpdateListBox();
    return;
}
```

The `Main_OnInitMenu` function is simply used to check (or uncheck) the Use Mutex menu command.

```
/*-------------------------------------------------------------
    MAIN_ONINITMENU
        Check or uncheck the Use Mutex menu item based on the
        value of bUseMutex.
-------------------------------------------------------------*/

void Main_OnInitMenu( HWND hWnd, HMENU hMenu )
{
    CheckMenuItem( hMenu, IDM_USEMUTEX, MF_BYCOMMAND |
            (UINT)( bUseMutex ? MF_CHECKED : MF_UNCHECKED ) );
    return;
}
```

The `Main_OnCommand` function is provided to parcel out all messages that have not already been handled by message crackers. (The message crackers are found in `Main_WndProc`, where the HANDLE_MSG macros are used to redirect messages to the appropriate functions.)

```
/*-------------------------------------------------------------
    MAIN_ONCOMMAND
        Respond to commands from the user.
-------------------------------------------------------------*/

void Main_OnCommand( HWND hWnd, int iCmd, HWND hwndCtl, UINT uCode )
{
    switch( iCmd )
    {
        case IDM_ABOUT:      // display the About box
            MakeAbout( hWnd );
            break;

        case IDM_EXIT:       // exit this program
```

```
        DestroyWindow( hWnd );
        break;

    case IDM_SUSPEND:    // modify the priority or state of a thread
    case IDM_RESUME:
    case IDM_INCREASE:
    case IDM_DECREASE:
        DoThread( iCmd );             // adjust a thread
        break;

    case IDM_USEMUTEX:   // toggle the use of the mutex
        ClearChildWindows( );         // make all thread windows white
        bUseMutex = !bUseMutex;       // toggle mutex setting
        break;

    default:
        break;
    }
    return;
}
```

Modification Procedures

The DoThread procedure responds to menu commands by modifying whichever thread is currently selected in the list box. DoThread can raise or lower a thread's priority, and suspend or resume threads. The iState array records the current state, either active or suspended, of each thread. The hThreads array holds handles to each of the four secondary threads.

```
/*-------------------------------------------------------------------
    DO THREAD
        Modify a thread's priority or change its state in response
        to commands from the menu.
    -----------------------------------------------------------------*/
void DoThread( int iCmd )
{
    int iThread;
    int iPriority;

        // determine which thread to modify
    iThread = ListBox_GetCurSel( hwndList );
    switch( iCmd )
    {
```

```
case IDM_SUSPEND:
    // if the thread is not suspended, then suspend it
    if( iState[iThread] != SUSPENDED )
    {
        SuspendThread( hThread[iThread] );
        iState[iThread] = SUSPENDED;
    }
    break;

case IDM_RESUME:
    // if the thread is not active, then activate it
    if( iState[iThread] != ACTIVE )
    {
        ResumeThread( hThread[iThread] );
        iState[iThread] = ACTIVE;
    }
    break;

case IDM_INCREASE:
    // increase the thread's priority (unless it is
    // already at the highest level)
    iPriority = GetThreadPriority( hThread[iThread] );

    switch( iPriority )
    {
        case THREAD_PRIORITY_LOWEST:
            SetThreadPriority( hThread[iThread],
                                THREAD_PRIORITY_BELOW_NORMAL );
            break;

        case THREAD_PRIORITY_BELOW_NORMAL:
            SetThreadPriority( hThread[iThread],
                                THREAD_PRIORITY_NORMAL );
            break;

        case THREAD_PRIORITY_NORMAL:
            SetThreadPriority( hThread[iThread],
                                THREAD_PRIORITY_ABOVE_NORMAL );
            break;

        case THREAD_PRIORITY_ABOVE_NORMAL:
            SetThreadPriority( hThread[iThread],
                                THREAD_PRIORITY_HIGHEST );
            break;
```

```
            default:        break;
        }                   break;

    case IDM_DECREASE:
        // decrease the thread's priority (unless it is
        // already at the lowest level)
        iPriority = GetThreadPriority( hThread[iThread] );
        switch( iPriority )
        {
            case THREAD_PRIORITY_BELOW_NORMAL:
                SetThreadPriority( hThread[iThread],
                                   THREAD_PRIORITY_LOWEST );
                break;

            case THREAD_PRIORITY_NORMAL:
                SetThreadPriority( hThread[iThread],
                                   THREAD_PRIORITY_BELOW_NORMAL );
                break;

            case THREAD_PRIORITY_ABOVE_NORMAL:
                SetThreadPriority( hThread[iThread],
                                   THREAD_PRIORITY_NORMAL );
                break;

            case THREAD_PRIORITY_HIGHEST:
                SetThreadPriority( hThread[iThread],
                                   THREAD_PRIORITY_ABOVE_NORMAL );
                break;

            default:        break;
        }                   break;
    default:                break;
    }
    return;
}
```

Thread Procedures

When Main_OnCreate constructs the secondary threads, it passes a pointer to the StartThread function in each call to CreateThread. StartThread becomes the main procedure for all the threads. They begin and end executing here.

If bUseMutex is TRUE, then the threads will wait to acquire the mutex before they draw, and only one thread will draw at a time.

```
/*----------------------------------------------------------------------
    START THREAD
        This is called when each thread begins execution.
    ------------------------------------------------------------------*/
LONG StartThread ( LPVOID lpThreadData )
{
    DWORD *pdwThreadID;      // pointer to a DWORD for storing thread's ID
    DWORD dwWait;            // return value from WaitSingleObject

        // retrieve the thread's ID
    pdwThreadID = lpThreadData;

        // draw continuously until bTerminate becomes TRUE
    while( ! bTerminate )
    {
        if (bUseMutex)        // are we using the mutex?
        {
            // draw when this thread gets the mutex
            dwWait = WaitForSingleObject( hDrawMutex, INFINITE );
            if( dwWait == 0 )
            {
                DrawProc( *pdwThreadID );   // draw rectangles
                ReleaseMutex( hDrawMutex ); // let someone else draw
            }
        }
        else
        {
            // not using mutex; let the thread draw
            DrawProc( *pdwThreadID );
        }
    }
        // this return statement implicitly calls ExitThread
    return( 0L );
}
```

DrawProc draws a batch of rectangles. However, GDI (Graphics Device Interface) calls do not always occur immediately to avoid the overhead of many small messages passing between a program and the Win32 subsystem. For this reason, graphics commands are held in a queue and periodically flushed. These delays somewhat exaggerate the effect of changing priorities in the *Threads* demo.

```
/*———————————————————————————————————————————————————————————————————
   DRAW PROC
      Draw five random rectangles or ellipses.
   ——————————————————————————————————————————————————————————————————*/
void DrawProc ( DWORD dwID )
{
   ...
   if (bUseMutex)
   {
      iTotal = 50;     // if only one thread draws at a time,
   }                   // let it draw more shapes at once
   else
   {
      iTotal = 1;
   }
      // reseed the random generator
   srand( iRandSeed++ );
      // get the window's dimensions
   bError = GetClientRect( hwndChild[dwID], &rcClient );
   if( ! bError ) return;
   cxClient = rcClient.right - rcClient.left;
   cyClient = rcClient.bottom - rcClient.top;
      // do not draw if the window does not have any dimensions
   if( ( ! cxClient ) || ( ! cyClient ) )
   {
      return;
   }
      // get a device context for drawing
   hDC = GetDC( hwndChild[dwID] );
   if( hDC )
   {
         // draw the five random figures
      for( iCount = 0; iCount < iTotal; iCount++ )
      {
         iRectCount[dwID]++;
            // set the coordinates
         xStart = (int)( rand() % cxClient );
         xStop  = (int)( rand() % cxClient );
         yStart = (int)( rand() % cyClient );
         yStop  = (int)( rand() % cyClient );
```

```
        // set the color
    iRed   = rand() & 255;
    iGreen = rand() & 255;
    iBlue  = rand() & 255;
        // create the solid brush
    hBrush = CreateSolidBrush(                    // avoid dithered colors
            GetNearestColor( hDC, RGB( iRed, iGreen, iBlue ) ) );
    hbrOld = SelectBrush( hDC, hBrush );
        // draw a rectangle
    Rectangle( hDC, min( xStart, xStop ), max( xStart, xStop ),
                    min( yStart, yStop ), max( yStart, yStop ) );
        // delete the brush
    DeleteBrush( SelectBrush(hDC, hbrOld) );
    }
        // If only one thread is drawing at a time, clear
        // the child window before the next thread draws
    if( bUseMutex )
    {
        SelectBrush( hDC, GetStockBrush(WHITE_BRUSH) );
        PatBlt( hDC, (int)rcClient.left,  (int)rcClient.top,
                    (int)rcClient.right, (int)rcClient.bottom,
                PATCOPY );
    }
        // release the HDC
    ReleaseDC( hwndChild[dwID], hDC );
    }
    return;
}
```

After you have run the *Threads* demo and experimented with priorities, turned the mutex on and off, and suspended and resumed a few threads, you might want to try running the Process Viewer that comes with the Win32 SDK. In Figure 14.4, you can see what the Process Viewer says about Threads. Note that it shows five threads for the program because it includes the primary thread as well. Browsing with Process Viewer gives you a better sense of how Windows 98 works.

FIGURE 14.4:

Examining threads using the Win32 SDK Process Viewer

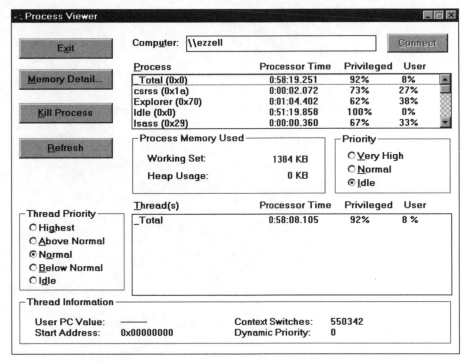

This chapter has explored the use of multiple threads. The *Threads* demo gives a practical example of threads in action. In this discussion, I've mentioned processes and interprocess communication through pipes and shared memory. In Chapter 15, you'll learn how to create and manage processes.

CHAPTER
FIFTEEN

15

Processes and Pipes

- Child and parent processes

- Pipes for communication between processes

- Commands for creating and modifying processes and pipes

- Anonymous and named pipes

In Chapter 14, you saw how one process can create many threads. A program that needs to do several things at once usually creates threads rather than whole new processes. Threads are generally preferable to processes because they are created more quickly with less overhead, they share resources such as handles and variables, and they are easy to synchronize. This chapter shows what happens when you decide to divide a task among several distinct processes, each with its own threads and its own private address space.

Processes and pipes are closely related topics. Processes often pass pipe handles to new processes they create in order to establish a channel for exchanging information. Along with the threads and synchronization objects you read about in Chapter 14, pipes and processes form the basic core of tools for multitasking in Windows 98. In this chapter, you'll learn how to launch a new child process, pass it handles, connect the parent to the child with a pipe, and send information through the pipe.

Process Concepts: Division of Labor

The multitasking capabilities of Windows 98 depend on the system's handling of processes and threads. Both terms designate ways of dividing labor in the operating system. The term *process* refers to an executable program and all of the program's resources as it runs in the system:

- Its virtual address space

- The access token that assigns it a privilege level

- The resource quotas determined by the user's privilege level

- One or more execution threads

- Other objects as they are assigned dynamically, such as an open file or a shared memory block

Every process has at least one thread of execution—one path the processor follows through its code. A process can also choose to divide its work into several tasks and create separate threads for each one. Multitasking happens when one machine runs several programs at once; multithreading happens when one program runs several threads at once. The Process Manager creates and destroys processes and their threads. It also suspends threads and resumes them.

Preemptive versus Permissive Multitasking

The simple difference between Windows 98 and Windows NT is that Windows NT—like OS/2— uses a preemptive multitasking system while Windows 98 exercises permissive multitasking.

- In a preemptive multitasking system (Windows NT or OS/2), the operating system summarily suspends executing threads to allow other threads an appropriate time slice for operation.

- In a permissive multitasking system (Windows 98), the operating system depends on the applications to regularly relinquish control of the operating system so other applications have the opportunity to gain their time slices.

Obviously, a preemptive multitasking system has the ability to provide much smoother execution of multiple tasks and threads. This type of system does not need to depend on the good graces of each program (or the skills of the respective programmers) in surrendering control of the CPU.

For permissive multitasking, all applications and all threads within an application must be well behaved and regularly relinquish control to permit other applications and other threads access to the CPU.

Inheritance

The documentation often refers to processes as *parents*, *children*, and *siblings*. A process that creates other processes is called the parent, and the new processes are its children. All the children of a single parent are siblings. Once a parent creates a child, the child no longer depends on the parent. If the parent terminates, the child may continue. The Win32 subsystem does not enforce any strong hierarchical dependence between parents and children.

The familial metaphor extends to one other action: inheritance. A new process *inherits* some attributes from its parent. Inherited attributes include the following:

- An environment block with environment variables

- A current working directory

- Standard input and output handles

- Any other handles the parent may want its children to have

A child of a console process—that is, of a parent that uses the console API instead of the Windows GUI for drawing on the screen—also inherits its parent's console window. A child may inherit handles to processes, threads, mutexes, events, semaphores, pipes, and file-mapping objects. It may also inherit handles created with `CreateFile`, including files, console input buffers, console screen buffers, serial communication devices, and mailslots.

NOTE   Consoles simulate character-based display. The Windows 98 command shells, for example, run in a console window.

When a child inherits a handle, both the parent and the child end up with handles to the same object. Whatever one does to the object affects the other. If a child's thread waits for and acquires a shared mutex, any parent threads that wait for the same object will be blocked. If a parent writes to a file, a child using the same handle will find its file position marker has moved forward, too.

When a child inherits a handle, it really only inherits access to the object. It does not inherit handle variables. When creating a child, the parent must both arrange for inheritance and pass the handles explicitly. The handles may be passed in several ways: on the command line, through a file, or through a pipe.

An easier but less intuitive option involves the standard I/O channels. Recall that character-based C programs frequently direct their I/O through three standard channels called `stdin`, `stdout`, and `stderr`. Win32 processes automatically possess the same three channels, although they do not have the same predefined names. The standard I/O channels are generally useless to a GUI application because they are not actually connected to any device. (A GUI application may, however, open a console window and use its standard I/O devices there.) Normally, a child inherits the same standard I/O devices its parent uses, but when creating the child, the parent may specify a different set of handles for the child to receive. The child retrieves its inherited handles with `SetStdHandle`. The parent may also change one or more of its own devices before creating the child. The child inherits the changes.

Children do not inherit all kinds of objects. Memory handles and pseudo-handles are excluded from inheritance, for example. Each process has its own address space, so it cannot inherit memory objects from another process. Pseudo-handles, such as the value returned by `GetCurrentThread`, are by definition valid only in the place where they originate. Nor do children inherit DLL module handles, GDI handles, or USER handles, including `HBRUSH` and `HWND` objects. Similarly, children do not inherit their parent's priority class. By default a child's priority will be `NORMAL_PRIORITY_CLASS`. There is one exception: the `IDLE_PRIORITY_CLASS` is inheritable. By default, low-priority parents create low-priority children; the poor stay poor. Parents of any other priority create children of normal priority.

Life Cycle of a Process

Process resources include an access token, a virtual address space description, and a handle table. Every process has a primary thread, which is the one that begins execution at `WinMain`, and may create other threads as it runs.

All the threads in one process share a single image of the executable file, but each new process requires the system to map the executable file into a new address space. The command for creating a process asks for the name of an .EXE file. An application that creates child processes to perform part of its work needs to be written and compiled as several distinct programs.

All Win32 processes begin life when some other process invokes them with `CreateProcess`. The Win32 subsystem starts up all its clients with that command. During `CreateProcess`, the system sets up a virtual address space, loads an executable file image, and creates a primary thread. `CreateProcess` returns a handle to the new process and a handle to its primary thread. The parent may close the handles, relinquishing control over its child. Or the parent may keep them to change the child's priority class, terminate the child, or read the exit code when the child ends by itself. Like threads, even after they've finished executing, processes remain in memory until all handles to the process have been closed.

A process remains active until its primary thread reaches the end of its starting procedure and stops executing or until any of its threads call `ExitProcess`. `ExitProcess` causes the system to notify all supporting DLLs that this module has stopped. It also causes any other threads in the same process to terminate immediately.

Pipe Concepts: Communication between Processes

Sometimes, the processes the user runs have nothing to do with each other, but the ability to exchange information among processes sometimes produces a synergistic effect when their cooperation makes it possible to perform tasks neither program could manage alone. For example, a phone dialer and a paint program probably have little in common but, if we wanted the paint program to dial a remote connection to transfer information, a link to a phone dialer would make perfect sense. Windows 98 allows many channels of communication, including the clipboard, DDE, OLE, and other channels. In Chapter 19, for example, you'll see how processes can share memory by opening views onto the same memory-mapped file.

Pipes are an easy mechanism for different programs to exchange information. Unlike some other channels, pipes have no formal standards or protocols to govern how information is passed. That makes pipes easier to use and more flexible than, say, DDE conversations, but it also limits them to programs that recognize each other and know how to parse the information they agree to exchange.

TIP

The use of pipes was originally introduced under Windows NT and later supported by Windows 95, then Windows 98 in the form of anonymous pipes. However, only Windows NT supports the use of named pipes; these are not supported by Windows 98.

A *pipe* is a section of shared memory where processes leave messages for each other. A pipe resembles a file where one program writes and another reads. Because a pipe is dedicated to interprocess communication, the Win32 API can provide a range of commands to facilitate the exchange of information. Conceptually, a pipe is a cross between a computer file and a post office mailslot. One process writes something in the file, and another process looks to see what was left behind.

The Life Cycle of a Pipe

A pipe appears when one program decides to create it. The program that creates a pipe is called the pipe's *server*. Other processes, called *clients,* may connect to the pipe's other end. The server assumes responsibility for the life of the pipe. Any process may be a server or a client, or both at once on different pipes.

After the pipe is created and another process connects to it, either the client or the server, or sometimes both the client and the server, write into its end. Anything written at one end is read from the other. Reading and writing operations rely on the same commands you use to work with any file: `ReadFile` and `WriteFile`. Typically, a process that expects to receive a series of messages creates a new thread to wait for them. The thread repeatedly calls `ReadFile` and blocks, remaining suspended until each new message arrives.

Eventually, the server decides that the conversation has ended and breaks the connection. To destroy the pipe, the server calls `CloseHandle`. (The pipe will not actually be destroyed until all handles to it, both the server's and the client's, have been closed.) Alternatively, the server may decide to connect the old pipe with a new client.

Varieties of Pipes

Pipes come in several varieties:

- Inbound, outbound, or duplex
- Byte or message
- Blocking or nonblocking
- Named or anonymous

Most of these attributes are determined when the pipe is created.

Inbound, Outbound, and Duplex Pipes

The first set of terms—inbound, outbound, and duplex—distinguishes the direction in which information flows through the pipe. *Inbound* and *outbound* describe one-directional pipes, where one side only writes and the other side only reads. An inbound pipe lets the client send and the server receive. An outbound pipe lets the server send and the client receive. A *duplex* pipe allows both sides to send and receive.

Byte and Message Pipes

What the participants write determines whether the pipe should have a reading mode of type *byte* or type *message*. The reading mode helps the system decide when a read operation should stop. With a byte-mode pipe, a read operation stops when it either reaches the last byte of data in the pipe or else fills its reading buffer. With a message-mode pipe, however, a read operation stops when it reaches the end of a single message.

Internally, the system marks messages in a message-mode pipe by prefacing each newly written segment with a header stating its length. The programs on either end of the pipe never see the message headers, but `ReadFile` commands on a message-mode pipe automatically stop when they reach the end of a segment.

Blocking and Nonblocking Pipes

Pipes may also be either *blocking* or *nonblocking*. This attribute affects read, write, and connect commands. When any of these commands fail on a nonblocking pipe, the command returns immediately with an error result. On a pipe that allows blocking, the commands do not return until they succeed or an error occurs. Table 15.1 summarizes the ways in which blocking and nonblocking modes affect three operations.

TABLE 15.1:   The Effects of Blocking and Nonblocking Modes

Operation	Blocking Mode	Nonblocking Mode
ConnectNamedPipe	Blocks until a client connects to the other end.	Returns FALSE immediately.
ReadFile	If the pipe is empty, blocks until a message arrives.	If the pipe is empty, returns an error immediately.
WriteFile	If the pipe is nearly full, blocks until another process reads from the other end.	If the pipe is nearly full, returns immediately. For a byte-mode pipe, `WriteFile` will first write as much as it can. For a message-mode pipe, `WriteFile` returns TRUE and writes no bytes.

Named and Anonymous Pipes

A pipe may be *named*, in which case the creator has endowed it with an identifying name string, or it may be *anonymous*, meaning it has no name string. Like synchronization objects, such as mutexes and semaphores, a pipe may be given a name to help other processes identify it. Windows 98 does not support named pipes; it currently supports only anonymous pipes.

Anonymous pipes require less overhead but perform only a limited subset of the services named pipes can perform. They pass messages in only one direction: either server to client or client to server, but not both. Also, anonymous pipes do not work over networks. The server and client must inhabit the same machine.

Named pipes, which are supported by Windows NT, can do several things that anonymous pipes cannot. They can pass information in both directions through one pipe, connect across a network to a process on a remote machine, exist in multiple instances, and use more pipe modes. The ability to exist in multiple instances permits a named pipe to connect one server with many clients. Each instance is an independent channel of communication. Messages in one instance do not interfere with messages in another instance. Multiple instances of a single pipe result when one or more servers pass the same identifying name to `CreateNamedPipe`.

Named Pipes in Windows 98 versus Windows NT

Under Windows 98, you cannot compile an application to use named pipes. Or, more accurately, you can compile the application without any errors, but any calls to the `CreateNamedPipe` API, which are integral to using named pipes, will simply fail.

The curious side of this is that you can compile the application under Windows NT and, once it has been compiled, it will run under Windows 98.

Rather unhelpfully, if you debug the *NamedPipe* demo (also discussed later in this chapter) under Windows 98, the `ShowErrorMsg` function will display a system error message reporting, "This function is only valid in Win32 mode."

Process-Related Commands

In many ways, the commands for creating and managing processes resemble the commands for creating and managing threads, which you saw in Chapter 14. To create a process, you specify security attributes and receive a handle. With the handle, you can manage the process; for example, you can change the priority of the process or terminate it. Even after a process stops running, it continues to exist as long as any handles to it remain open. To destroy a process, close all of its handles.

The following sections describes the Win32 API commands for creating processes. The *AnonPipe* and *NamedPipe* demos, described later in this chapter, demonstrate most of the commands explained here.

Making and Modifying Processes

Under Windows 98, the `CreateProcess` command starts every new process. The old `WinExec` and `LoadModule` commands still exist for backward compatibility, but internally both now call `CreateProcess`.

```
BOOL CreateProcess(
    LPCTSTR lpszImageName,             // image file (.EXE) name
    LPCTSTR lpszCmdLine,               // command line for new process
    LPSECURITY_ATTRIBUTES lpsaProcess, // how process will be shared
    LPSECURITY_ATTRIBUTES lpsaThread,  // how new thread will be shared
    BOOL bInheritHandles,              // TRUE to inherit handles
    DWORD fdwCreate,                   // creation flags
    LPVOID lpvEnvironment,             // new environment (default = NULL)
    LPTSTR lpszCurrentDir,             // name of new current directory
    LPSTARTUPINFO lpStartupInfo,       // gives info about new process
    LPPROCESS_INFORMATION lpProcInfo ) // receives info about new process
```

CreateProcess Parameters

The `CreateProcess` function's parameters permit control over the new process's starting conditions. First, every process requires code to execute. Together, the first two parameters create a complete command line naming a program file and passing it arguments.

The first parameter, `lpszImageName`, must point only to the name of the executable file (for example, `Child`). Do not include any arguments. In locating a file named in this parameter; the system does not search the PATH directories. The program must be in the current directory, or the string must contain a full path name.

The second parameter, `lpszCmdLine`, may be NULL if you have no arguments to pass. If you do pass arguments, the first item in the `lpszCmdLine` string must be what C programmers call the `argv[0]` value.

The first item is typically, but not necessarily, the name of the program, even if you have already given it in `lpszImageName`. You can omit the path and extension if they appear in the `lpszImageName`, but some item must precede the first argument.

To make `CreateProcess` search along the environment PATH for the file, leave the first parameter blank and pass the complete command line in the second parameter. Table 15.2 lists some examples of using the first and second `Create-Process` parameters.

TABLE 15.2:   Using CreateProcess Parameters

First Parameter	Second Parameter	Result
`d:\dev\bin\qgrep`	NULL	Runs **qgrep** without arguments only if **qgrep** is found in the `\dev\bin` directory.
`qgrep.exe`	`qgrep -L-y "ERROR_" *.h`	Runs **qgrep** with arguments only if **qgrep** is in the current directory.
NULL	`qgrep -L-y "ERROR_" *.h`	Runs **qgrep** with arguments if it can be found anywhere on the path.

Security Attributes   The next two parameters in `CreateProcess` provide security attributes for both the new process and its primary thread. (Every process receives an initial thread; otherwise, nothing would ever execute.) You saw the same SECURITY_ATTRIBUTES structure in the discussion of creating new threads in Chapter 14, and you will see it often in commands that create new objects. The information in this structure controls what another process may do with the object if it opens a duplicate handle. It also controls whether child processes may inherit a handle to the new object. By default, other processes receive full access to the new object and children do not inherit it.

WARNING   Under Windows 98, the security attributes do not apply and are simply ignored. If your application is intended only for Windows 98 and not for the Windows NT environment or if no security is needed, this argument may be passed as NULL.

Blocking Inheritance   The bInheritHandles parameter of CreateProcess gives you a second chance to prevent a child from inheriting other handles you have already created. If bInheritHandles is FALSE, the new process inherits no handles, even if they were marked inheritable when they were created. Blocking inheritance is useful because many objects, including threads and processes, persist in memory until all the handles to them are closed. If every new child inherits a full set of handles from its parent, many objects will stay in memory until all the child processes exit and their handles are destroyed. Children should be allowed to inherit only the handles they actually need.

Process Type and Priority   The creation flags in the fdwCreate parameter govern the type and priority of the new process. The new process may be initially suspended; it may have a console or a GUI window; it may receive debugging information from its child; and it may receive a particular priority class. Here are some of the values that can be combined in the creation flag parameter:

> DEBUG_PROCESS   The parent receives debugging information about the child and any of its children.
>
> DEBUG_ONLY_THIS_PROCESS   The parent receives debugging information about the child but not about any of the child's children.
>
> CREATE_SUSPENDED   The primary thread of the new process is initially suspended.
>
> DETACHED_PROCESS   The new process does not use a console window.
>
> CREATE_NEW_CONSOLE   The new process receives its own new console window.
>
> IDLE_PRIORITY_CLASS   The process runs only when the system is idle.
>
> NORMAL_PRIORITY_CLASS   The process has no special scheduling needs.

HIGH_PRIORITY_CLASS The process preempts all threads of lower priority in order to respond quickly to some critical situation.

REALTIME_PRIORITY_CLASS The process preempts even important system tasks.

Environment and Directory Settings Each process has its own set of environment variables and its own current directory setting. If the lpszEnvironment and lpszCurrentDir parameters are NULL, the new process copies the block of environment variables and the directory setting from its parent. Environment variables are those defined with the SET command at the command prompt, typically in an Autoexec file. Programmers usually define variables, such as BIN, LIB, and INCLUDE, to tell the compiler and linker where to find particular kinds of files.

More generally, environment variables are a convenient way to customize programs by putting information where it is always available. A parent can send information to its children by defining environment variables. To give the child an entirely new environment, the parent should create a buffer and fill it with null-terminated strings of the form *<variable>=<setting>*.

TIP

You should be careful to ensure that no spaces appear next to the equal sign. For example, the form *<variable>* = *<setting>* is invalid and will not be accepted.

The last string must be followed by two null characters. To give the child a slightly modified version of the parent's existing environment, the parent can temporarily modify its own settings with GetEnvironmentVariable and SetEnvironmentVariable, create the child, and then restore the old settings.

Process Information Structures The last two parameters of CreateProcess point to structures. The parent fills out the STARTUPINFO structure before calling CreateProcess and receives information about the new process in the PROCESS_INFORMATION structure.

```
// You fill this out to describe a new process in advance
typedef struct _STARTUPINFO  /* si */
{
    DWORD    cb;                    // size of(STARTUPINFO)
    LPTSTR   lpReserved;           // should be NULL
    LPTSTR   lpDesktop;            // name of desktop object to run in
    LPSTR    lpTitle;              // caption for console title bar
    DWORD    dwX;                  // upper-left corner for new window
    DWORD    dwY;
    DWORD    dwXSize;              // width of new window
    DWORD    dwYSize;              // height of new window
    DWORD    dwXCountChars;        // width of new console window
    DWORD    dwYCountChars;        // height of new console window
    DWORD    dwFillAttribute;      // text/background colors for console
    DWORD    dwFlags;              // activates fields in this structure
    WORD     wShowWindow;          // iCmdShow parameter value
    WORD     cbReserved2;          // zero
    LPBYTE   lpReserved2;          // NULL
    HANDLE   hStdInput;            // handles for the
    HANDLE   hStdOutput;           //    child's standard
    HANDLE   hStdError;            //    I/O devices
} STARTUPINFO, *LPSTARTUPINFO;
```

You must fill in the first field of the STARTUPINFO structure, but you can initialize all the rest to 0 or NULL to accept default values.

The lpDesktop field is ignored under Windows 98. If you want your programs to also run under Windows NT, however, lpDesktop points to a zero-terminated string specifying either the name of the Desktop only or the name of both the window station and Desktop for this process. The Desktop is the background window on which a user's programs run. The current system allows only two Desktops: one for logging on and one for the current user. A backslash in the string pointed to by lpDesktop indicates that the string includes both Desktop and window-station names. Otherwise, the lpDesktop string is interpreted as a Desktop name. If lpDesktop is NULL, the new process inherits the window station and Desktop of its parent process.

The lpTitle field is used only for console purposes to supply a title in the title bar when a new console window is created. If lpTitle is NULL, the name of the executable is used instead. For GUI or console processes, which do not create a new console window, this parameter should be NULL.

Many of the other fields in a STARTUPINFO structure matter only for nongraphics processes that will run in console windows instead of regular GUI windows. Most of the fields are ignored unless the values in dwFlags alert the system to use them. dwFlags may contain the values listed in Table 15.3, each value activating a different field or set of fields from the STARTUPINFO structure. You do not need to initialize any of these fields unless you activate them with a flag in dwFlags.

TABLE 15.3:   dwFlag Values in CreateProcess

Flag	Field(s) Activated
STARTF_USESHOWWINDOW	wShowWindow
STARTF_USESIZE	dwXSize, dwYSize
STARTF_USEPOSITION	dwX, dwY
STARTF_USECOUNTCHARS	dwXCountChars, dwYCountChars
STARTF_USEFILLATTRIBUTE	dwFillAttribute
STARTF_USESTDHANDLES	hStdInput, hStdOutput, hStdError

Additional values for dwFlags do not activate specific fields. The STARTF_FORCEONFEEDBACK and STARTF_FORCEOFFFEEDBACK values force the system to display or omit the waiting cursor that gives the user feedback as an application starts up.

I/O Handles   The last three fields allow you to specify standard I/O handles for the child that differ from those of the parent. Normally, the child inherits whatever I/O devices the parent has. The I/O handles provide an easy way to pass the child any handles it needs to receive, such as one end of a pipe. If you use any of the fields, you should set values in all of them. The child receives an invalid handle for any device you leave NULL. Call GetStdHandle to copy any of the parent's standard device handles into these fields.

NOTE   A process created with the DETACHED_PROCESS flag cannot inherit its parent's standard I/O devices. The console program initialization procedures do not correctly receive the devices when the process has no console. Microsoft identified this limitation in an early release of Windows NT and added the handle fields as a work-around. They work for any child but are necessary for detached children.

CreateProcess Return Values

CreateProcess returns TRUE if it succeeds in creating the new object and FALSE if an error occurs. If CreateProcess returns TRUE, it also returns information about the new process and its primary thread in the final parameter, the PROCESS_ INFORMATION structure.

```
// CreateProcess fills this out to tell you what it created
typedef struct _PROCESS_INFORMATION  /* pi */
{
    HANDLE hProcess;          // handle to the new process
    HANDLE hThread;           // handle to its primary thread
    DWORD  dwProcessId;       // number identifying new process
    DWORD  dwThreadId;        // number identifying new thread
} PROCESS_INFORMATION;
```

If your program does not make use of the handles for the new process and its primary thread, you should close both right away. Otherwise, even if the PROCESS_INFORMATION structure is a local variable and goes out of scope, abandoning whatever it contained, the two object entries remain in your process's object table and the system counts them as open handles.

Because the size of physical system memory limits the total number of processes that can be created, be sure to check for error returns. As an example, one of the early beta versions of Windows NT allowed a 16MB machine to create about 40 processes before failing for lack of memory. This limit will vary from version to version and machine to machine, but it is finite. Memory shortage can also cause CreateThread to fail, though threads consume significantly fewer resources than processes.

C Runtime Equivalents

The spawn and exec functions in the C runtime library also create new processes. Internally, however, they map to the same Win32 CreateProcess call. Through its parameters, CreateProcess offers more ways to customize the new process than do the C functions. The C runtime functions _getenv and _putenv, which work with a process's environment variables, also duplicate the Win32 API functions, GetEnvironmentVariable and PutEnvironmentVariable.

Getting Information about a Process

Once a process starts up, it can call several commands to find out about itself.

Getting the Handle and ID

Like threads, processes are identified by a handle and an ID number. The parent receives both from the CreateProcess call; the child receives them by calling GetCurrentProcess and GetCurrentProcessId. Like the GetCurrentThread call, GetCurrentProcess returns a pseudohandle valid only in the current process. Pseudohandles may not be passed to other processes. To convert a pseudohandle to a real handle, use DuplicateHandle.

```
HANDLE GetCurrentProcess( void );
DWORD GetCurrentProcessId( void );
```

NOTE   The C runtime function _getpid duplicates GetCurrentProcessId.

Getting the Environment Settings

The next function retrieves the environment settings inherited from the parent.

```
DWORD GetEnvironmentVariable(
    LPTSTR lpszName,      // name of environment variable
    LPTSTR lpszValue,     // address of buffer for variable value
    DWORD  dwValue );     // size of the lpszValue buffer in characters
```

You fill out the lpszName buffer with a variable name, such as PATH. The function looks up the corresponding value and copies it into lpszValue. The DWORD return value tells how many characters it copied into the lpszValue buffer. It is 0 if the variable was not found.

Getting the Command Line

Another function retrieves a pointer to the command line, but the same information is usually available by other means as well. Console programs written in C can read the command line using argc and argv; GUI programs can retrieve it through the lpszCmdLine parameter of WinMain.

```
LPTSTR GetCommandLine( void );
```

Changing Process Priority

With the reation flags in `CreateProcess`, the parent can assign one of four base priority classes to a new process:

- `IDLE_PRIORITY_CLASS`

- `NORMAL_PRIORITY_CLASS`

- `HIGH_PRIORITY_CLASS`

- `REALTIME_PRIORITY_CLASS`

The default priority class is `NORMAL_PRIORITY_CLASS`. Do not use `HIGH_PRIORITY_CLASS`, and especially not `REALTIME_PRIORITY_CLASS`, unless you must. Both levels impair the performance of lower-priority processes. Programs that do run at higher priorities should do so only for short periods of time.

Here are the functions to find out and modify a process's priority class:

```
DWORD GetPriorityClass( HANDLE hProcess );

BOOL SetPriorityClass(
    HANDLE hProcess,            // process to modify
    DWORD fdwPriority );        // new priority class
```

The `DWORD` values in both functions should be one of the four `PRIORITY_CLASS` flags just listed. The priority class of a process becomes the base priority for all its threads. Refer to the discussion of thread priorities in Chapter 14 to see how the base priority influences a thread's dynamic priority.

Synchronizing Processes

Chapter 14 also explained how threads coordinate their separate tasks by waiting for signals from synchronization objects. Besides the four standard synchronization objects—mutexes, semaphores, events, and critical sections—threads can wait for other threads and for files, timers, and processes. Waiting for a thread or a process means waiting for it to stop execution. A thread waits for a process by passing the process handle to `WaitForSingleObject` or `WaitForMultipleObjects`. When the process terminates, it enters its signaled state and all threads waiting for it resume execution.

One other synchronization command works only when waiting for processes. Instead of waiting for the process to terminate, you can wait for it to be idle. For this purpose, a process is considered idle when it has finished initializing and no user input is waiting to reach it.

```
DWORD WaitForInputIdle(
    HANDLE hProcess,        // process to wait for
    DWORD  dwTimeout );     // time-out time in milliseconds
```

Parents frequently call `WaitForInputIdle` immediately after creating a new process to allow the child time to establish itself. When the new process initializes and reaches its idle state, the parent can try to communicate with it.

What `WaitForInputIdle` returns depends on how it ends. It returns 0 for a successful wait when the process becomes idle. If the time-out period elapses before the process idles, `WaitForInputIdle` returns `WAIT_TIMEOUT`. To indicate an error, it returns (HANDLE) 0xFFFFFFFF (-1, a.k.a. INVALID_HANDLE_VALUE).

NOTE   `WaitForInputIdle` tests the child's message queue for pending messages. It is intended only for GUI applications. Character-based console applications, lacking a message queue, are *always* idle by this definition.

Sharing Handles

Like handles to threads and synchronization objects, handles to processes can be shared. Several different processes might possess handles to any one process. As usual, you can't simply pass a handle directly from one process to another. You must instead rely on one of several transfer mechanisms to perform the conversion that makes a handle valid in a new address space.

One mechanism is inheritance. If you tell `CreateProcess` to let the child inherit handles, the child receives copies of all the inheritable handles in its own object table. Children cannot use the handles there directly—they must still receive the handle on their command line or through a pipe—but inheritance makes the handle valid when it reaches the child process. If you pass a child a handle it has not already inherited, the handle will not work.

Making a Handle Copy

Inheritance helps in passing handles only between related processes. To create a handle that can be passed to any other process, related or unrelated, call `Duplicate-Handle`. You saw that function in Chapter 14. Given the original handle and a source and destination process, `DuplicateHandle` creates a new handle valid in the destination process. `DuplicateHandle` also allows you to modify the attributes of a handle you want to keep. If, for example, you want only one of several children to inherit a particular handle, you create the first child, allowing inheritance, and then call `DuplicateHandle` to make a noninheritable copy. Close the original inheritable handle and keep only the copy. Subsequent children will not inherit it.

NOTE   The *AnonPipe* demo program, discussed later in this chapter, uses `Duplicate-Handle` to control inheritance. Look for the `StartProcess` procedure in the demo, which is included on the CD accompanying this book.

Opening a Process

Another command allows any process to open a handle to any other process.

```
HANDLE OpenProcess(
    DWORD fdwAccess,        // desired access privileges
    BOOL  bInherit,         // TRUE for children to inherit the handle
    DWORD dwProcessId );    // number identifying the process
```

NOTE   Under Windows NT, you can open a process only if the security descriptor of your own process endows you with sufficient clearance. Security privileges do not apply under Windows 98.

`OpenProcess` requires you to identify the process by its ID number. Normally, you know the number only if you created the process or if the process itself, or one of its relatives, passes you the number (through a pipe or a DDE conversation, for example).

It is possible to generate a list of ID numbers for all the currently running processes, but the task is not trivial. It involves enumerating information stored in the system registry under the HKEY_PERFORMANCE_DATA key (see Chapter 17 for more information about the registry). The online help file contains sample code showing how to search the registry with `RegEnumKey`, `RegEnumValue`, and `Reg-QueryInfoKey`. The structure of the HKEY_PERFORMANCE_DATA key is documented in Winperf.H. The SDK comes with the source code for its Process Viewer utility (see Figure 14.4 in Chapter 14); it enumerates threads and processes.

Ending a Process

Normally, you do not do anything special to end a process, just as you do not do anything to end a thread. When a thread reaches the `return` instruction at the end of its startup procedure, the system calls ExitThread and the thread termi-nates, leaving an exit code behind. When the primary thread in a process comes to the end of its starting procedure (usually WinMain), the system implicitly calls ExitProcess instead of ExitThread. ExitProcess forces all the threads in a process to end, no matter what they may be doing at the time. Any thread, however, may call ExitProcess explicitly to end its process at any time.

```
void ExitProcess( UINT fuExitCode );
```

You define the exit code to be whatever you like. Like threads, processes remain in memory even after they terminate, only dying when all the handles to them are closed. To determine a process's exit code, keep its handle and call GetExit-CodeProcess.

```
BOOL GetExitCodeProcess(
    HANDLE  hProcess,           // handle to the process
    LPDWORD lpdwExitCode );     // buffer to receive exit code
```

If the process has not ended, GetExitCodeProcess reports the exit code as STILL_ACTIVE.

Normally, a process ends when its primary thread ends. The primary thread may, however, choose to quit without ending the process. If the primary thread ends with an explicit call to ExitThread, the system does not call ExitProcess. Other threads in the process continue to execute, and the process runs until any thread calls ExitProcess directly or until the last thread ends.

A number of things happen when a process ends:

- All of the process's handles are closed; all of its file handles, thread handles, event handles, and any other handles are destroyed. The objects they point to will also be destroyed, but only if no other processes also possess handles to them.

- Any DLLs the process has called receive notification when the process ter-minates, giving them a chance to clean up and exit.

- The terminating process acquires an exit code. More specifically, the Exit Status attribute of the process object changes from STILL_ACTIVE to what-ever value ExitProcess assigns.

- The process object enters its signaled state, and any threads waiting for it to end resume execution.

Note that when a parent process dies, it does not take its children with it. The children, if there are any, continue to run independently.

Forcing a Process to Exit

Another command, TerminateProcess, also forces a process to exit. Actually this command brings the process to an abrupt and crashing halt, preventing some of the usual cleanup from happening. DLLs, for example, are not notified when TerminateProcess kills one of their clients. Like TerminateThread, Terminate-Process is abrupt, messy, and best avoided whenever possible.

```
BOOL TerminateProcess(
    HANDLE hProcess,              // handle to the process
    UINT fuExitCode );            // exit code for the process
```

Pipe-Related Commands

As explained earlier in the chapter, pipes allow two processes to communicate with each other. A pipe is a memory buffer where the system preserves data between the time one process writes it and another process reads it. The API commands ask you to think of the buffer as a pipe, or conduit, through which information flows from one place to another. A pipe has two ends. A one-way pipe allows writing only at one end and reading only at the other; all the information flows from one process to the other. A two-way pipe allows both processes to read and write, so the information flows both ways at once. When you create a pipe, you also decide whether it will be anonymous or named. Anonymous pipes are simpler, and the only type supported by Windows 98, so we'll start with them.

Creating Anonymous Pipes

An anonymous pipe passes information in only one direction, and both ends of the pipe must be on the same machine. The process that creates an anonymous pipe receives two handles: one for reading and one for writing. To communicate with another process, the server must pass one of the handles to the other process.

```
BOOL CreatePipe(
    PHANDLE phRead,                  // variable for read handle (inbound)
    PHANDLE phWrite,                 // variable for write handle (outbound)
    LPSECURITY_ATTRIBUTES lpsa,      // access privileges
    DWORD   dwPipeSize );            // size of pipe buffer (0=default)
```

The size of the pipe buffer determines how much information the pipe can hold before it overflows. No one can deposit messages in a full pipe until someone makes room by reading the old information from the other end.

If all goes well, `CreatePipe` returns TRUE and deposits two new valid handles in the variables indicated by the PHANDLE parameters. Next, the creating process usually needs to pass one of the handles to another process. Which handle you give away depends on whether you want the other process to send (write) or receive (read) information through the pipe. You can pass the handle to a child process on its command line or through its standard I/O handles. An unrelated process would need to receive the handle by other means, such as through a DDE conversation or a shared file. Connections through anonymous pipes are easier to arrange when the processes are related.

Creating Named Pipes

Many Windows NT system objects may be assigned name strings to identify them. While the named pipe operations can be created (compiled) only under Windows NT, applications using named pipes can be run under Windows 98, where they perform essentially the same as anonymous pipe objects. The advantage to using named pipe objects is that names allow other processes to locate objects more easily. Unnamed objects are known only by their handles, and handles are valid only in the process where they originate. Any process that knows the name of an object, however, can ask the system to search its object name hierarchy. Given a name, the system can find any object on any connected machine.

If a pipe has a name, the client program does not need to wait for the server to pass it a handle. Instead, the client can acquire a handle by calling `CreateFile` or `CallNamedPipe`. In either case, the client needs to know only the pipe's name string. A parent might pass the string to a child process on the command line, or any process might pass it to any other through a shared file or a DDE conversation. Most often, however, two processes sharing a named pipe have been written by the same developer, so they simply agree on a name string in advance.

The following commands work only with named pipes. Do not create an anonymous pipe if you need the functions these commands provide.

`CallNamedPipe`	`GetNamedPipeInfo`
`ConnectNamedPipe`	`ImpersonateNamedPipeClient`
`CreateFile`	`RevertToSelf`
`CreateNamedPipe`	`SetNamedPipeHandleState`
`DisconnectNamedPipe`	`TransactNamedPipe`
`GetNamedPipeHandleState`	`WaitNamedPipe`

To create named pipes, you use the `CreateNamedPipe` command:

```
HANDLE CreateNamedPipe(
    LPTSTR  lpszPipeName,            // string naming new pipe object
    DWORD   fdwOpenMode,            // access, overlap, and write-through
    DWORD   fdwPipeMode,            // type, read, and wait modes
    DWORD   dwMaxInstances,         // maximum number of instances
    DWORD   dwOutBuf,               // outbound buffer size in bytes
    DWORD   dwInBuf,                // inbound buffer size in bytes
    DWORD   dwTimeout,              // time-out interval in milliseconds
    LPSECURITY_ATTRIBUTES lpsa );   // access privileges
```

CreateNamedPipe Parameters

Because named pipes have more features, `CreateNamedPipe` takes more parameters.

The first parameter points to the string you provide to name the new object. The system stores this name in its hierarchical tree of system object names. Pipe name strings should follow this form:

`\\.\pipe\<pipename>`

The first backslash designates the root node of the system's object name hierarchy. The other three backslashes separate the names of subsequent nodes. The dot (.) stands for the local machine. Although pipes can connect with clients on other network servers, a new pipe object always appears on the local server where it was created.

Under the server name is a node called `pipe`, holding the names of all the pipe objects on the local machine. Within the name string, the substring *<pipename>* is the only section the programmer chooses. This substring may be as long as 256 characters and is not case-sensitive because object names are not sensitive to case.

Servers and clients both use the dot (.) to represent the local server, but a client wishing to open a pipe on a remote server must know the server's name. One way to learn remote server names is to enumerate them with the `WNetOpenEnum`, `WNetEnumResource`, and `WNetCloseEnum` functions, but enumeration is slow.

TIP   To find out about a better method for enumerating remote server names, see "Distinguishing Pipes from Mailslots" later in this chapter.

The `CreateNamedPipe`, `CreateFile`, `WaitNamedPipe`, and `CallNamedPipe` functions require a pipe's name string as a parameter.

Access, Write-through, and Overlapping The next parameter after the name string, `fdwOpenMode`, combines flags to set several pipe attributes. The most important attribute is the access mode, which determines the direction information flows through the pipe. `fdwOpenMode` must include one of the following three access flags:

PIPE_ACCESS_OUTBOUND The server only writes, and the client only reads.

PIPE_ACCESS_INBOUND The server only reads, and the client only writes.

PIPE_ACCESS_DUPLEX Both the server and client may read and write.

The other two flags in this parameter are optional:

FILE_FLAG_WRITE_THROUGH Disables buffering over a network.

FILE_FLAG_OVERLAPPED Enables asynchronous read and write operations.

For efficiency, when a pipe extends to a remote machine, the system normally does not send every message immediately. Instead, it tries to accumulate several short messages in a buffer and send them across the pipe in a single operation. If too much time passes and the buffer remains only partly full, the system sends the buffer anyway. The FILE_FLAG_WRITE_THROUGH flag prevents the system from buffering; each new message is sent immediately, and write commands do not return until their output has been transmitted. Turn off the buffering if you expect to send messages only infrequently.

Because they involve physical devices, read and write operations are usually slow. The second optional flag, FILE_FLAG_OVERLAPPED, allows read and write commands to return immediately while the action they initiate continues in the background.

When a Windows NT program reads from a file, for example, it may choose simply to start the read process, name a procedure to be called when the read operation ends, and then continue executing while the system reads in the background. When the read operation finally ends, the system schedules an asynchronous procedure call and invokes the callback function named in the read command. The callback function then processes the newly retrieved information. Making the system do your reading and writing in the background is called *asynchronous I/O* or *overlapping I/O*. Pipes also support overlapping I/O. Overlapping

I/O is more difficult to program because you need to write a callback function, but it's also more efficient.

Type, Read, and Wait   The fdwPipeMode parameter combines flags to designate another set of pipe features: the read mode, the type, and the wait flag. The type and the read mode are closely related; they might be better named the write mode and the read mode. Together, they control how information in the pipe is organized and interpreted. Both offer a choice between byte and message modes.

The pipe type (write mode) flags are PIPE_TYPE_BYTE and PIPE_TYPE_MESSAGE. The read mode flags are PIPE_READMODE_BYTE and PIPE_READMODE_MESSAGE

The information in a byte-mode pipe is read and written in the normal binary manner and understood as being nothing more than a series of bytes.

Sometimes, however, it is more convenient to divide the information in a pipe into discrete messages, where the output from each separate write command constitutes a new message. A message-mode pipe automatically and transparently prefaces each new message with an invisible header specifying the length of the message. The header enables a read command to stop automatically when it reaches the end of one message. The recipient recovers messages one at a time, exactly as they were written.

If one program sends to another a long series of integers, for example, it would probably use a byte-mode pipe, because the receiver does not care how many integers were written at a time. Everything it retrieves is simply another integer. But if a program were sending commands written in a script language, the receiver would need to retrieve the commands one at a time, exactly as written, in order to parse them. Because each command might be a different length, the two programs would use a message-mode pipe.

The write mode and read mode are designated independently, but not all combinations make sense. Specifically, you cannot combine PIPE_TYPE_BYTE and PIPE_READMODE_MESSAGE. A byte-type pipe writes bytes without message headers, so the receiver cannot recover message units. On the other hand, you can combine PIPE_TYPE_MESSAGE with PIPE_READMODE_BYTE. In this case, the sender includes message headers but the receiver chooses to ignore them, retrieving the data as a series of undifferentiated bytes. (The receiver still does not see the invisible message headers.)

Besides the flags to set the type and read mode for a pipe, the fdwPipeMode parameter accepts one other flag for the wait mode. The wait mode determines what happens when some condition temporarily prevents a pipe command from completing. For example, if you try to read from an empty pipe, some programs might want to forget about reading and move onto the next instruction, but other programs might need to wait for a new message before proceeding.

By default, pipes cause reading threads to block and wait, but you can prevent blocking by adding the PIPE_NOWAIT flag to fdwPipeMode. (The default flag is PIPE_WAIT.) The wait mode affects write commands as well as read commands. A program that tries to write when the pipe buffer is full normally blocks until another program makes room by reading from the other end. The wait mode also affects a server trying to connect with a client. If the ConnectNamedPipe command finds no ready clients, the wait mode determines whether the command waits for a client to connect or returns immediately.

Pipe Instances A server program may wish to open pipes for more than one client, but it may not know in advance how many clients it will have. It would be inconvenient to invent a new pipe name for each new client. How would all the clients know in advance what name to use when they open their end of the pipe? To circumvent this problem, Win32 permits the server to create the same pipe over and over.

Each time you call CreateNamedPipe with the same name, you get a new instance of the same pipe. Each new instance provides an independent communication channel for another client. The server might begin by creating the same pipe four times. It would receive four different handles, and it could wait for a different client to connect to each one. All the clients would use the same pipe name to request their own handles, but each would receive a handle to a different instance. If a fifth client tried to connect, it would block until the server disconnected one of the first four instances.

The dwMaxInstances parameter of the CreateNamedPipe command sets an upper limit on the number of instances one pipe will support before Create-NamedPipe returns an error. The PIPE_UNLIMITED_INSTANCES flag indicates no upper limit. In that case, the maximum number of instances is limited only by system resources. The value of dwMaxInstances may not exceed the value of PIPE_UNLIMITED_INSTANCES. (Winbase.H defines the value of dwMaxInstances as 255.)

Buffer Sizes   The dwOutBuf and dwInBuf parameters set the initial size of the buffers that store anything written to the pipe from either end. For an outbound pipe (PIPE_ACCESS_OUTBOUND), only the output buffer matters; for an inbound pipe, only the input buffer size is significant.

The limits set by the buffer size parameters are flexible. Internally, every read or write operation on a pipe causes the system to allocate buffer space from the kernel's pool of system memory. The buffer size value is interpreted as a quota limiting these allocations. When the system allocates buffer space for a write operation, it charges the space consumed to the write buffer quota. If the new buffer size fits within the quota, all is well. If it does not, the system allocates the space anyway and charges it to the *process's* resource quota. To avoid excessive charges to the process quota, every WriteFile operation that causes the buffer to exceed its quota blocks. The writing thread suspends operation until the receiving thread reduces the buffer by reading from it.

In estimating buffer sizes, you'll need to take into account the fact that each buffer allocation is slightly larger than you expect because it includes an internal data structure of about 28 bytes in addition to the message contents. The exact size is undocumented and may vary from version to version.

To summarize, the system allocates buffer space dynamically as needed, but threads that frequently exceed their buffer size may block excessively. The *Anon-Pipe* and *NamedPipe* demos, discussed later in this chapter, leave the buffer size at 0 and suffer no apparent harm. Programs that send frequent messages or that expect the buffers to back up occasionally will benefit from increased buffer sizes.

Time-out Period   The dwTimeout value matters only when a client calls Wait-NamedPipe to make a connection, and it matters then only if the client accepts the default time-out period. The default period is the number the server sets in the dwTimeout parameter of CreateNamedPipe, but the client may set a different period in WaitNamedPipe.

Security Attributes   The final parameter, a pointer to a SECURITY_ATTRIBUTES structure, should look very familiar by now. The values in it determine which operations the new handle allows you to perform on its object, and they also determine whether child processes may inherit the new handle. As usual, if you leave the field NULL, the resulting handle has full access privileges and cannot be inherited.

NOTE
Anonymous pipes always have the characteristics that are the default state for named pipes: PIPE_TYPE_BYTE, PIPE_READMODE_BYTE, PIPE_WAIT, no overlapping I/O, and network buffering enabled.

CreateNamedPipe Return Values

CreateNamedPipe returns a valid handle if it succeeds. If an error occurs, it returns the value (HANDLE)0xFFFFFFFF (a.k.a., INVALID_HANDLE_VALUE).

WARNING
Applications that are compiled under Windows 98 and use CreateNamedPipe will always return failure (INVALID_HANDLE_VALUE).

Catching Errors

You may have noticed that many of the functions we've described seem to have rudimentary error returns. CreateThread, CreateMutex, CreateProcess, CreatePipe, and CreateNamedPipe, for example, all might fail for a variety of reasons. The system might be low on memory, or a particular mutex might already exist, or a network connection might fail, or a parameter might be invalid. Yet all of these creation functions indicate errors only by returning either FALSE or an invalid handle.

Better diagnostics are available. The system keeps a large set of error messages in a single collective message table and identifies each message with a different number. Whenever a command fails, it stores an error message number for the active thread. Immediately after a function fails call GetLastError to retrieve the message number. To translate the number into an explanatory string suitable for showing in a message box, call FormatMessage.

Even functions from the Windows 3.1 API sometimes set error codes under Win32. Microsoft's online help file regularly identifies error-setting commands in the descriptions of their return values: "To get extended error information, use the GetLastError function." The *AnonPipe* and *NamedPipe* demos, described later in this chapter, construct a procedure for displaying the appropriate message after any error. Look for ShowErrorMsg in the listings.

Connecting to an Existing Pipe

After a server opens a named pipe, it must wait for a client to open the other end. A client may open its end in any of several ways, but the most common is the CreateFile function. This is the same function you use to open disk files. It also works with named pipes, communications devices, and the I/O buffers of a character-based console window. The ReadFile and WriteFile commands also work with the same set of objects. Using a single unified API for several different objects makes programming easier.

```
HANDLE CreateFile(
    LPCTSTR lpszName,              // name of the pipe (or file)
    DWORD fdwAccess,               // read/write access (must match the pipe)
    DWORD fdwShareMode,            // usually 0 (no share) for pipes
    LPSECURITY_ATTRIBUTES lpsa,    // access privileges
    DWORD fdwCreate,               // must be OPEN_EXISTING for pipes
    DWORD fdwAttrsAndFlags,        // write-through and overlapping modes
    HANDLE hTemplateFile );        // ignored with OPEN_EXISTING
```

The pipe name must match the string the server passed to CreateNamedPipe. If the server and client programs are connecting over a network, the string must name the network server machine instead of using a dot (.).

The fdwAccess parameter tells whether you want to read or write to the pipe. If the pipe was created with the PIPE_ACCESS_OUTBOUND flag, you should specify GENERIC_READ in CreateFile. For an inbound pipe, the client needs GENERIC_WRITE privileges. For a duplex pipe, the client needs GENERIC_READ | GENERIC_WRITE privileges.

The fdwShareMode should generally be 0 to prohibit sharing the pipe with other processes. Occasionally, however, a client might use the share mode to duplicate the pipe handle for another client. In that case, both clients have handles to the same instance of the same pipe, and you might need to worry about synchronizing their read and write operations.

The security attributes in the lpsa parameter should be familiar to you by now. The fdwCreate flag must be set to OPEN_EXISTING because CreateFile will not create a new pipe; it simply opens existing pipes. Other flags allow CreateFile to create new file objects where none existed before, but those flags produce errors when lpszName designates a pipe object.

The last two parameters normally govern file attributes, such as hidden, read-only, and archive settings, but CreateFile uses the attributes only to create new files. When you open an existing object (with OPEN_EXIST), the object keeps whatever attributes it already has. However, there are two exceptions; two flags in the `fdwAttrsAndFlags` parameters do work when opening an existing named pipe: `FILE_FLAG_WRITE_THROUGH` and `FILE_FLAG_OVERLAPPED`. The client may set flags that differ from the server, enabling or disabling network buffering and asynchronous I/O to suit its own preferences.

Modifying an Existing Pipe

Two ends of the same pipe may have different read or wait modes, but `Create-File` always copies the original attributes when it opens a handle for a client. Any process, however, can modify its pipe handle with `SetNamedPipeHandleState`.

```
BOOL SetNamedPipeHandleState(
    HANDLE  hNamedPipe,                    // handle of a named pipe
    LPDWORD lpdwModes,                     // read and wait mode flags
    LPDWORD lpdwMaxCollect,                // transmission buffer size
    LPDWORD lpdwCollectDataTimeout );      // max time before transmission
```

The first parameter is a handle returned by `CreateNamedPipe` or `CreateFile`.

The second parameter, like the `fdwPipeMode` parameter of `CreateNamedPipe`, combines flags to set several attributes at once. The `lpdwModes` parameter controls whether read operations use the byte or message mode and whether certain commands will block while they wait for the pipe to become available. The read mode may be `PIPE_READMODE_BYTE` or `PIPE_READMODE_MESSAGE`. (Specifying the message read mode for a pipe that was created with `PIPE_TYPE_BYTE` causes an error.) The read-mode pipe may be combined with either `PIPE_WAIT` or `PIPE_NOWAIT`.

The last two parameters matter only for pipes that connect with a remote machine. They control how the system buffers network transmissions. (They have no effect on pipes with the `PIPE_FLAG_WRITE_THROUGH` attribute, which disables network buffering.) Buffering allows the system to combine several messages into a single transmission. It holds outgoing messages in a buffer until either the buffer fills or a set time period elapses. `lpdwMaxCollect` sets the size of the collection buffer, and `lpdwCollectDataTimeout` sets the time period in milliseconds.

Getting Information about an Existing Pipe

Three functions retrieve information about a pipe without changing any of its attributes.

Getting State Information

The first information command is the counterpart of SetNamedPipeHandleState, but it retrieves more information than its partner sets:

```
BOOL GetNamedPipeHandleState(
    HANDLE  hNamedPipe,              // handle of named pipe
    LPDWORD lpdwModes,              // read and wait modes
    LPDWORD lpdwCurInstances,       // number of current pipe instances
    LPDWORD lpcbMaxCollect,         // max bytes before remote transmission
    LPDWORD lpdwCollectTimeout,     // max time before remote transmission
    LPTSTR  lpszUserName,           // user name of client process
    DWORD   dwMaxUserNameBuff );    // size in chars of user name buffer
```

The lpdwModes parameter may contain the PIPE_READMODE_MESSAGE and PIPE_NOWAIT flags. To indicate the byte mode or wait mode, which are the default states, no flags are set.

lpdwCurInstances counts the number of instances that currently exist for a pipe. In other words, it tells how many times the server has called CreateNamed-Pipe with the same name string.

The collect and time-out parameters retrieve the same network buffering information that SetNamedPipeHandleState controls.

The last two parameters help a server learn about its client. They return the null-terminated string naming the user who is running the client application. Usernames are the names users give to log in. They are associated with particular configuration and security privileges. The server might want the name for a log or a report, but probably this parameter exists for compatibility with OS/2, which also makes the username available. The lpszUserName parameter must be NULL if hNamedPipe belongs to a client; in other words, if it was created with CreateFile rather than CreateNamedPipe.

Any of the pointer parameters may be set to NULL to ignore the value normally returned in that place.

Getting Fixed Attributes

Another function that returns additional information about a pipe is GetNamed-PipeInfo. This function returns attributes that may not be changed. (GetNamed-PipeHandleState returns attributes that may change during the life of a pipe.)

```
BOOL GetNamedPipeInfo(
    HANDLE  hNamedPipe,          // handle of named pipe
    LPDWORD lpdwType,            // type and server flags
    LPDWORD lpdwOutBuf,          // size in bytes of pipe's output buffer
    LPDWORD lpdwInBuf,           // size in bytes of pipe's input buffer
    LPDWORD lpdwMaxInstances );  // maximum number of pipe instances
```

The lpdwType parameter may contain either or both of two flags: PIPE_TYPE_MESSAGE and PIPE_SERVER_END. If no flags are set, the handle connects to the client end of a pipe that writes in bytes. The input and output buffer sizes are set in CreateNamedPipe.

The lpdwMaxInstances parameter returns the value set by CreateNamedPipe as an upper limit for the number of simultaneous instances allowed to exist for one pipe.

Retrieving a Message

Normally, when you read from a pipe, the read operation removes from the buffer the message it retrieves. With PeekNamedPipe, however, it is possible to retrieve a message without clearing it from the buffer.

TIP   The ineptly named PeekNamedPipe command works with both named and anonymous pipes.

```
BOOL PeekNamedPipe(
    HANDLE  hPipe,               // handle of named or anonymous pipe
    LPVOID  lpvBuffer,           // address of buffer to receive data
    DWORD   dwBufferSize,        // size in bytes of data buffer
    LPDWORD lpdwBytesRead,       // returns number of bytes read
    LPDWORD lpdwAvailable,       // returns total number of bytes available
    LPDWORD lpdwMessage );       // returns unread bytes in this message
```

The lpvBuffer parameter points to a place where the command can store whatever information it copies from the pipe. Keep in mind that PeekNamedPipe cannot retrieve more than dwBufferSize bytes, even if more information remains in the pipe.

lpdwBytesRead returns the number of bytes the function actually did read, and lpdwMessage returns the number of bytes remaining in the current message, if any. lpdwMessage is ignored if the pipe's read mode is PIPE_READMODE_BYTE. In that case, there are no message units to measure. (All anonymous pipes use the byte read mode.)

The total number of available bytes returned in `lpdwAvailable` includes all bytes in all messages. If the buffer currently holds several messages, `*lpdwAvailable` may be greater than the sum of `*lpdwBytesRead` and `*lpdwMessage`.

It is legal to retrieve only a partial information set by leaving some parameters NULL. If all you want to know is how many bytes are waiting in the buffer, you may, for example, set everything to 0 or NULL except the handle and `lpdwAvailable`.

When reading from a pipe set to the message read mode, `PeekNamedPipe` always stops after reading the first message—even if the data buffer has room to hold several messages. Also, `PeekNamedPipe` never blocks an empty pipe the way `ReadFile` does if PIPE_WAIT is set. The wait mode has no effect on `PeekNamed-Pipe`, which always returns immediately.

Reading and Writing through a Pipe

All the choices you make to create a pipe—named or anonymous, byte or message, blocking or nonblocking—prepare for the moment when you actually send a message through the pipe. One program writes to its handle, and the other program reads from its handle. This most basic transaction typically involves two functions: `WriteFile` and `ReadFile`.

```
BOOL WriteFile(
    HANDLE hFile,                   // place to write (pipe or file)
    CONST VOID *lpBuffer,           // points to data to put in file
    DWORD dwBytesToWrite,           // number of bytes to write
    LPDWORD lpdwBytesWritten,       // returns number of bytes written
    LPOVERLAPPED lpOverlapped );    // needed for asynchronous I/O

BOOL ReadFile(
    HANDLE hFile;                   // source for reading (pipe or file)
    LPVOID lpBuffer;                // buffer to hold data retrieved
    DWORD dwBytesToRead;            // number of bytes to read
    LPDWORD lpdwBytesRead;          // returns number of bytes read
    LPOVERLAPPED lpOverlapped );    // needed for asynchronous I/O
```

Bytes to Read or Write

The number of bytes to read or write need not be as large as—but should not be larger than—the size of the buffer. If you call `ReadFile` on a message-mode pipe, however, and give `dwBytesToRead` a value smaller than the size of the next message, ReadFile reads only part of the message and returns FALSE. A subsequent call to GetLastError discovers an error code of ERROR_MORE_DATA. Call ReadFile again or PeekNamedPipe to read the rest of the message. When WriteFile writes to a nonblocking byte-mode pipe and finds the buffer nearly full, it still returns TRUE, but the value of *lpdwBytesWritten will be less than dwBytesToWrite.

Blocking

Depending on the pipe's wait mode, both WriteFile and ReadFile may block. WriteFile might need to wait for a full pipe to empty out from the other end; an empty pipe causes ReadFile to block waiting for a new message.

Asynchronous I/O

The final parameter of both commands points to an OVERLAPPED structure that provides extra information for performing asynchronous or overlapping I/O. Asynchronous I/O allows the command to return immediately, even before the read or write operation is finished. Asynchronous commands do not automatically modify the position of the file pointer, so the OVERLAPPED structure includes an offset pointing to the place in the file where the operation should begin.

The structure also contains a handle to an event object. A thread in the reading program can wait for the event's signal before examining what ReadFile placed in the retrieval buffer. You must supply an OVERLAPPED structure when using file handles that were created with the FILE_FLAG_OVERLAPPED attribute.

Another method of performing asynchronous I/O involves the ReadFileEx and WriteFileEx commands. Instead of signaling completion with an event, these commands invoke a procedure you provide to be called at the end of each operation.

With respect to pipes, overlapping I/O is a useful strategy for dealing with multiple clients connected to different instances of a single pipe. Synchronous I/O is easier to program, but slow read and write commands might hold up other waiting clients. A server can create a separate thread for each client, but that involves more overhead than the situation actually requires.

A single thread can read and write simultaneously to different pipe instances with asynchronous I/O because each command always returns immediately, leaving the thread free while the system finishes in the background. With WaitForMultipleObjects, a thread can arrange to block until any pending operation is completed. The efficiency of asynchronous I/O can make a big difference over slow network connections. Also, it is easier to protect program resources when you have fewer threads to synchronize.

Synchronizing Connections

At any time, a client may call CreateFile to open its end of a named pipe. Two problems, however, may arise:

- The server often needs to know when a client has connected to a pipe. Writing to an unconnected pipe serves little purpose, and CreateFile does not tell the server when a connection occurs.

- If all the instances of a pipe are busy, CreateFile always immediately returns INVALID_HANDLE_VALUE without establishing a connection. The client may prefer to wait for a pipe instance to become available when another client finishes.

In short, both server and client must be able to block while waiting for conditions that permit a connection to occur. To do so, the server calls ConnectNamedPipe and the client calls WaitNamedPipe.

```
BOOL ConnectNamedPipe(
    HANDLE hNamedPipe,              // handle of an available named pipe
    LPOVERLAPPED lpOverlapped );   // info for asynchronous operation

BOOL WaitNamedPipe(
    LPTSTR lpszPipeName,           // points to string naming pipe object
    DWORD dwTimeout );             // maximum wait time in milliseconds
```

> **NOTE** These coordinating functions work only with named pipes because a client cannot create its own handle to an anonymous pipe; it must receive a handle directly from the server, and in that case, the connection is already made.

Signaling a Connection

Like ReadFile and WriteFile, ConnectNamedPipe can respond asynchronously. The lpOverlapped parameter contains an event handle, and the event object signals when a client connects.

How ConnectNamedPipe behaves depends on whether the pipe was created with, or subsequently modified to include, the FILE_FLAG_OVERLAPPING flag and the PIPE_WAIT mode. Its operation is most intuitive on pipes that allow waiting.

The unintuitive use of TRUE and FALSE returns results from the fact that Connect-NamedPipe returns TRUE only if the pipe begins in a listening state and a client connects after the connect command begins and before it returns. If the pipe is already connected and the command responds asynchronously (returns without waiting) or is called for a pipe that does not allow waiting, the command generally returns FALSE.

Client Waiting

The client's wait command, WaitNamedPipe, does not actually create a connection. It returns TRUE when a pipe is or becomes available, but it does not return a handle to the available pipe.

It is common for a client to repeat the wait-then-create cycle until it acquires a valid handle. Normally, WaitNamedPipe considers a pipe available only when the server calls ConnectNamedPipe to wait for a link. The two commands work together to synchronize server and client. If, however, the server creates a new pipe and has never connected to any client, WaitNamedPipe returns TRUE even without a matching ConnectNamedPipe.

The purpose behind the apparent inconsistency is to guarantee that Wait-NamedPipe connects only at times when the server knows its pipe is available. If a client breaks a connection, the server may not realize it right away; and if another client connected immediately, the server could not know it had a new partner. By recognizing only new pipes and pipes made available through ConnectNamedPipe, WaitNamedPipe prevents clients from sneaking in on the middle of a running conversation.

NOTE   WaitForSingleObject does not work with pipes because pipes do not have signal states.

Closing a Connection

A client breaks its connection by calling CloseHandle. A server may do the same, but sometimes it may prefer to disconnect without destroying the pipe, saving it for later reuse. By calling DisconnectNamedPipe, the server forces the conversation to end and invalidates the client's handle.

```
BOOL DisconnectNamedPipe( HANDLE hNamedPipe );
```

If the client tries to read or write with its handle after the server disconnects, the client receives an error result. The client must still call CloseHandle.

Any data lingering unread in the pipe is lost when the connection ends. A friendly server can protect the last messages by calling FlushFileBuffers first.

```
BOOL FlushFileBuffers( HANDLE hFile );
```

When FlushFileBuffers receives a handle to a named pipe, it blocks until the pipe's buffers are empty.

Disconnecting a pipe from its client does not destroy the pipe object. After breaking a connection, the server should call ConnectNamedPipe to await a new connection on the freed pipe or else call CloseHandle to destroy that instance. Clients blocked on WaitNamedPipe do not unblock when a client closes its pipe handle. The server must disconnect its end and call ConnectNamedPipe to listen for a new client.

Making Transactions

There are two more commands that facilitate conversations through duplex pipes: TransactNamedPipe and CallNamedPipe combine read and a write operations into single transactions. Transactions are particularly efficient over networks because they minimize the number of transmissions.

To support reciprocal transactions, a pipe must have the following characteristics:

- Set up as a named pipe
- Set to use the PIPE_ACCESS_DUPLEX flag
- Set as the message type
- Set to message-read mode

The server sets all those attributes with CreateNamedPipe. The client can adjust the attributes, if necessary, with SetNamedPipeHandleState. The blocking mode has no effect on transaction commands.

Sending a Request

The first command, TransactNamedPipe, sends a request and waits for a response. Clients and servers both may use the command, although clients tend to find it more useful.

```
BOOL TransactNamedPipe(
    HANDLE hNamedPipe,              // handle of named pipe
    LPVOID lpvWriteBuf,            // buffer holding information to send
    DWORD dwWriteBufSize,         // size of the write buffer in bytes
    LPVOID lpvReadBuf,            // buffer for information received
    DWORD dwReadBufSize,         // size of the read buffer in bytes
    LPDWORD lpdwBytesRead,        // bytes actually read (value returned)
    LPOVERLAPPED lpOverlapped );  // info for asynchronous I/O
```

In spite of its many parameters, the function is straightforward. It writes the contents of lpvWriteBuf into the pipe, waits for the next response, and copies the message it receives into the lpvReadBuf buffer.

The function fails if the pipe has the wrong attributes or if the read buffer is too small to accommodate the entire message. In that case, GetLastError returns ERROR_MORE_DATA, and you should finish reading with ReadFile or PeekNamedPipe.

TransactNamedPipe handles one exchange through a pipe. After establishing a connection, a program might call TransactNamedPipe many times before disconnecting.

Using a Pipe for a Single Transaction

Another command, CallNamedPipe, works for clients that need a pipe for only a single transaction. CallNamedPipe connects to, reads from, writes to, and closes the pipe handle.

```
BOOL CallNamedPipe(
    LPTSTR lpszPipeName,    // points to string naming a pipe object
    LPVOID lpvWriteBuf,     // buffer holding information to send
    DWORD dwWriteBuf,       // size of the write buffer in bytes
    LPVOID lpvReadBuf,      // buffer for information received
    DWORD dwReadBuf,        // size of the read buffer in bytes
    LPDWORD lpdwRead,       // bytes actually read (value returned)
    DWORD dwTimeout );      // maximum wait time in milliseconds
```

For its first parameter, CallNamedPipe expects the name of a pipe that already exists. Only clients call this function. Most of the other parameters supply the buffers needed to perform both halves of a transaction.

CallNamedPipe condenses into a single call a whole series of commands: WaitNamedPipe, CreateFile, WriteFile, ReadFile, and CloseHandle. The final parameter, dwTimeout, sets the maximum waiting period for the WaitNamedPipe part of this transaction.

If the read buffer is too small to hold an entire message, the command reads what it can and returns FALSE. GetLastError reports ERROR_MORE_DATA, but because the pipe has already been closed, the extra data is lost.

Disguising the Server

Often, a client sends commands or requests through a pipe for the server to perform some action on its behalf. The client might, for example, ask the server to retrieve information from a file. Because the client and the server are different processes, they may also have different security clearances. A server might want to refuse to perform commands for which the client lacks adequate clearance. The server may temporarily assume the client's security attributes before complying with a request and then restore its own attributes after responding, using these commands:

```
BOOL ImpersonateNamedPipeClient( HANDLE hNamedPipe );

BOOL RevertToSelf( void );
```

The impersonation command fails on anonymous pipes, and it will not allow the server to impersonate the client on remote machines. The command temporarily modifies the security context of the thread that calls it.

> **NOTE**
> A similar function, DdeImpersonateClient, allows servers conversing with DDE (Dynamic Data Exchange) clients to modify their own security context, too. DDE is discussed in Chapter 35.

The RevertToSelf command ends the masquerade and restores the original security context.

Destroying a Pipe

Like most of the objects we've discussed so far, a pipe object remains in memory until all the handles to it are closed. Whenever any process finishes with its end of a pipe, it should call CloseHandle. If you forget, the ExitProcess command closes all your remaining handles for you.

Distinguishing Pipes and Mailslots

Pipes are similar to another object called a *mailslot*. Like a pipe, a mailslot is a buffer where processes leave messages for each other. Mailslots, however, always work in only one direction, and many applications may open the receiving end of the same mailslot.

A program that opens a handle to receive messages in a mailslot is a *mailslot server*. A program that opens a handle to broadcast messages through a mailslot is the *mailslot client*. When a client writes to a mailslot, copies of the message are posted to every server that has a handle to the same mailslot.

A pipe takes information from one end and delivers it to the other end. A mailslot takes information from one end and delivers it to many other ends.

Mailslots have string names just as named pipes do. The commands for mailslot operations resemble the pipe API functions:

- To create a server's read-only mailslot handle, call `CreateMailslot`.

- To retrieve or modify its attributes, call `GetMailslotInfo` and `SetMailslotInfo`.

- To create the client's write-only mailslot handle, call `CreateFile`.

- To send and receive mailslot messages, call `WriteFile` and `ReadFile`.

- To destroy a mailslot, close its handles with `CloseHandle`.

Besides the advantage of broadcasting a message to multiple recipients, mailslots make it easier to connect with processes over a network. For a pipe client to connect with a remote server, the client must first ascertain the name of the server's machine, which may require a slow enumeration of network servers and repeated attempts to connect with each until the pipe is found. But in naming a mailslot for `CreateFile`, the mailslot client may use an asterisk (*) to represent the current network domain. (A *domain* is any group of linked workstations and network servers to which an administrator has assigned a common name. One network system may contain a single all-inclusive domain, or it may be divided into several associated domains.)

```
\\*\mailslot\<mailslotname>
```

Using a name of that form, the handle the client receives broadcasts messages to all processes in the current domain that have opened a mailslot using the *<mailslotname>* string. This ability to broadcast across a domain suggests one of the ways mailslots might

Continued on next page

be used. Processes that want to connect through a remote pipe link may prefer to find each other through a mailslot first, using this procedure:

1. Both processes open a mailslot with the same name.

2. The client broadcasts the name of its pipe, including in the name string the name of its own network server.

3. The recipient uses the broadcast string to connect with the pipe and avoids laboriously enumerating all the available servers.

4. The client and server find each other through a one-way mailslot, and then establish a private two-way pipe to continue the conversation.

Processes Communicating through a Pipe

The *AnonPipe* and *NamedPipe* demos demonstrate the use of processes and pipes. In both versions, a parent process creates a child process and communicates with it through a pipe. As their names suggest, *AnonPipe* uses an anonymous pipe, and *NamedPipe* uses a named pipe.

In each demo, a command on the parent's menu lets you launch the child process. Once both are running, you can select shapes, colors, and sizes from the parent program's menu. The parent sends the command information through a pipe, and the client draws the requested shape. In the *NamedPipe* demo, you can launch several children, and the parent creates multiple instances of its pipe.

The *AnonPipe* Demo: One-Way Communication

An anonymous pipe is the easiest way to establish single-instance one-way communication between related processes on the same machine. (With two anonymous pipes you can communicate in both directions.)

The parent and child program windows of the *AnonPipe* demo appear in Figure 15.1. In this example, the user has selected a small red triangle from the parent's menu, and the resulting shape appears in the child's window.

NOTE   The *AnonPipe* demo is included on the CD accompanying this book, in the Chapter 15 folder.

Caveat on Testing the AnonPipe Demo

To test the *AnonPipe* demo, you will want to begin by compiling both the Parent and Child executables. Once these are compiled, you can execute the Parent program (in the Debug directory) and use the Parent program to launch the Child process. However, if you attempt to execute the Parent program from the Developer's Workshop (as for debugging), you will receive a message stating: "The system cannot find the file specified."

However, if you first copy the compiled Child.EXE program from the /Debug subdirectory to the /AnonPipe directory, the Parent.EXE application will again be able to find the Child.EXE program and launch it.

The problem—if you are not already ahead of me—is that under the debugger, the Parent.EXE application is not looking in the directory where it is located but in the immediate root directory (where the source files are found).

On the other hand, when the Parent application is executed directly, it looks in the current directory to find the Child.EXE for launch.

For alternatives, refer to the "CreateProcess Parameters" section earlier in this chapter, and feel free to modify the AnonPipe Parent.C source to experiment with different arrangements.

The Parent Process

The parent process files are Parent.H, Parent.RC, and Parent.C. The child process files are Child.H, Child.RC, and Child.C. The two programs together share an additional header, Global.H, which defines structures and values both processes use to communicate with each other.

When the parent puts command information into the pipe, it uses a descriptive structure called FIGURE. A FIGURE variable holds values that represent commands from the parent's menu. The commands determine the shape, size, and color of the figure the child should draw.

FIGURE 15.1:

Parent and child windows of the *AnonPipe* demo

Initializing The global variables at the top of Parent.C include a handle for the child process, a handle for the pipe, and a FIGURE variable. These three pieces of information are what the parent needs to communicate with its child. WinMain initializes figure to describe a small red rectangle.

```
/*-------------------------------------------------------------------

   PARENT.C   [anonymous pipe version]

   Contains the parent process for the PROCESS demo program.
   In this version, the two processes communicate through
   an anonymous pipe.
   -----------------------------------------------------------------*/
```

```
int WINAPI WinMain( HINSTANCE hinstThis, HINSTANCE hinstPrev,
                    LPSTR lpszCmdLine,   int iCmdShow )
{
    ...
        // This global FIGURE structure records whatever choices
        // the user makes to choose the shape, size, and color
        // of the figure drawn in the client's window. Here
        // we initialize it to the program's startup defaults.

    figure.iShape = IDM_RECTANGLE;      // draw a rectangle
    figure.iSize  = IDM_SMALL;          // don't fill the whole window
    figure.iColor = IDM_RED;            // make the rectangle red
    ...
}
```

Responding to System Messages   The window procedure looks for only three messages. When the user begins to make a choice from a menu, the parent program intercepts WM_INITMENU to update the appearance of the menu. If the child process does not exist, the parent disables the commands that work only with the child present, including Terminate and all the shape options. Figure 15.2 shows two images of the Parent application's Options menu.

FIGURE 15.2:

Two views of the
Options menu

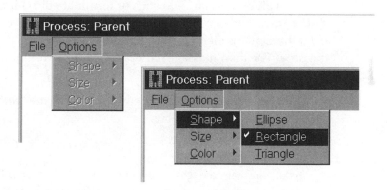

In the first instance (upper-left), no child process has been created and, therefore, all of the selections under Options are disabled. In the second instance (lower-right), after the child process is active, the menu options are enabled and, on the Shape submenu, the current selection is indicated by a checkmark.

The first message handler, WM_INITMENU, also places checkmarks by all the options currently selected.

```
/*------------------------------------------------------------------
    PARENT_WNDPROC
    This is where the messages for the main window are processed.
    ------------------------------------------------------------------*/

LRESULT WINAPI Parent_WndProc(
    HWND    hWnd,                   // message address
    UINT    uMessage,              // message type
    WPARAM  wParam,                // message contents
    LPARAM  lParam )               // more contents
{
    switch (uMessage)
    {
        HANDLE_MSG( hWnd, WM_INITMENU, Parent_OnInitMenu );
        HANDLE_MSG( hWnd, WM_COMMAND, Parent_OnCommand );
        HANDLE_MSG( hWnd, WM_DESTROY, Parent_OnDestroy );
        default:
            return( DefWindowProc( hWnd, uMessage, wParam, lParam ) );
    }
    return( 0L );
}
```

The second message handler responds to WM_COMMAND messages from the menu.
The user gives commands to start or terminate the child, to modify the shape the
child draws, and to close the Parent program. If the user makes any selection
from the Options menu, SendCommand writes the updated figure variable into
the pipe. The third message handler ends the Parent program in response to
WM_DESTROY.

The Parent_OnInitMenu procedure provides the handling to check and
uncheck several menu options.

```
/*------------------------------------------------------------------
    PARENT_ONINITMENU
    Check whether the child process exists and enable or
    disable the Start, Terminate, and Options commands
    accordingly. Also put checkmarks on the option commands
    that reflect the user's most recent choices.
    ------------------------------------------------------------------*/

void Parent_OnInitMenu( HWND hWnd, HMENU hMenu )
{
    // While the child process does not exist, some of the
    // menu commands make no sense and should be disabled.
    // These include the Terminate command and the figure
    // options commands.
```

```
    // get a handle to the options popup menu
HMENU hmenuOptions = GetSubMenu( hMenu, 1 );

if( hProcess )
{   // child process exists; enable Terminate and shape options
    EnableMenuItem( hMenu, IDM_START, MF_GRAYED );
    EnableMenuItem( hMenu, IDM_TERMINATE, MF_ENABLED );
    EnableMenuItem( hmenuOptions, 0, MF_ENABLED | MF_BYPOSITION );
    EnableMenuItem( hmenuOptions, 1, MF_ENABLED | MF_BYPOSITION );
    EnableMenuItem( hmenuOptions, 2, MF_ENABLED | MF_BYPOSITION );
}
else
{   // child process does not exist; disable Terminate and shape options
    EnableMenuItem( hMenu, IDM_START, MF_ENABLED );
    EnableMenuItem( hMenu, IDM_TERMINATE, MF_GRAYED );
    EnableMenuItem( hmenuOptions, 0, MF_GRAYED | MF_BYPOSITION );
    EnableMenuItem( hmenuOptions, 1, MF_GRAYED | MF_BYPOSITION );
    EnableMenuItem( hmenuOptions, 2, MF_GRAYED | MF_BYPOSITION );
}

    // set a checkmark on one of the three shape commands
CheckMenuItem( hMenu, IDM_ELLIPSE,
    ( ( figure.iShape == IDM_ELLIPSE) ? (int)MF_CHECKED :
                                        (int)MF_UNCHECKED ) );
CheckMenuItem( hMenu, IDM_RECTANGLE,
    ( ( figure.iShape == IDM_RECTANGLE) ? (int)MF_CHECKED :
                                          (int)MF_UNCHECKED ) );
CheckMenuItem( hMenu, IDM_TRIANGLE,
    ( ( figure.iShape == IDM_TRIANGLE) ? (int)MF_CHECKED :
                                         (int)MF_UNCHECKED ) );

    // set a checkmark on one of the two size commands
CheckMenuItem( hMenu, IDM_SMALL,
    ( ( figure.iSize == IDM_SMALL) ? (int)MF_CHECKED :
                                     (int)MF_UNCHECKED ) );
CheckMenuItem( hMenu, IDM_LARGE,
    ( ( figure.iSize == IDM_LARGE) ? (int)MF_CHECKED :
                                     (int)MF_UNCHECKED ) );

    // set a checkmark on one of the three color commands
CheckMenuItem( hMenu, IDM_RED,
    ( ( figure.iColor == IDM_RED ) ? (int)MF_CHECKED :
                                     (int)MF_UNCHECKED ) );
```

```
CheckMenuItem( hMenu, IDM_GREEN,
    ( ( figure.iColor == IDM_GREEN ) ? (int)MF_CHECKED :
                                        (int)MF_UNCHECKED ) );
CheckMenuItem( hMenu, IDM_BLUE,
    ( ( figure.iColor == IDM_BLUE ) ? (int)MF_CHECKED :
                                        (int)MF_UNCHECKED ) );

return;
UNREFERENCED_PARAMETER( hWnd );
}
```

Creating the Pipe and the Child   When you choose Start from the File menu, the program calls its StartProcess procedure to create the pipe, launch the child, and send the child its first command. Some complications arise in arranging for the child to inherit one end of the pipe.

The CreatePipe command must not simply accept the default security attributes because, by default, the new handles cannot be inherited. StartProcess begins by filling out a SECURITY_ATTRIBUTES structure to set the bInherit-Handle field to TRUE. If the next command were CreateProcess, the new child would automatically inherit copies of both handles—the reading end and the writing end of the pipe.

Unfortunately, that's still not quite what we want to happen. The child needs only one handle. Anonymous pipes work only one way, and our child needs only to read from the pipe. It should not inherit hPipeWrite. The next command, Duplicate-Handle, modifies the handle by changing its inheritance attribute. Because the parameter for the copied handle is NULL, the command does not actually make a copy; instead, it modifies the original. Now we have a reading handle that can be inherited and a writing handle that cannot.

Generally, the child should not inherit handles it does not need. Most objects stay open as long as any process holds an open handle to them. If a child inherits an assortment of extraneous handles, many objects may be forced to linger in memory even after the parent ends. Furthermore, in this particular case, if the child owned handles for both ends of the pipe, it would not know when the parent destroyed its end of the pipe. From the child's point of view, the pipe would remain open because someone (itself) still had a handle to the other end.

When one process closes its end of a pipe, the other process normally notices because of error results from the read or write commands. That's why we went to the trouble of making sure the child inherits only one of the two pipe handles.

StartProcess checks for errors after almost every command. If any
fails, StartProcess closes all the handles created to that point. The Show.
Msg procedure, which comes at the end of Parent.C, displays a message bo.
describing the last error that occurred.

```
/*------------------------------------------------------------------
    START PROCESS
        In response to the IDM_START command, launch the child
        process and create the pipe for talking to it.
    ----------------------------------------------------------------*/

void StartProcess ( void )
{
    char szProcess[MAX_BUFFER];      // name of child process image
    SECURITY_ATTRIBUTES sa;          // security privileges for handles
    STARTUPINFO sui;                 // info for starting a process
    PROCESS_INFORMATION pi;          // info returned about a process
    int iLen;                        // return value
    BOOL bTest;                      // return value
    HANDLE hPipeRead;                // inbound end of pipe (for client)

        // load name of process image file from resources
    iLen = LoadString( hInst, IDS_PROCESS, szProcess, sizeof(szProcess) );
    if( ! iLen )
    {
        return;
    }

        // fill out a SECURITY_ATTRIBUTES struct so handles are inherited
    sa.nLength = sizeof(SECURITY_ATTRIBUTES);   // structure size
    sa.lpSecurityDescriptor = NULL;             // default descriptor
    sa.bInheritHandle = TRUE;                   // inheritable

        // create the pipe
    bTest = CreatePipe( &hPipeRead,      // reading handle
                        &hPipeWrite,     // writing handle
                        &sa,             // lets handles be inherited
                        0 );             // default buffer size

    if( ! bTest )                        // error during pipe creation
    {
        ShowErrorMsg( );
        return;
    }
```

Inheriting a handle is not enough, however
still needs to receive the handle explicitly from
its only the *right* to use the handle, not the hand
an entry in its object table but no handle to the e
a way to pass the handle to the new process. The
object table entry to be an open handle even thoug
to it. The handle that the parent later passes directly
inherited object table entry and does not count as a s

Rather than passing a handle on the command line,
standard I/O device channels. The STARTUPINFO proce
Process contains three standard I/O handles. Two are t
by GetStdHandle, but the third is the pipe handle. The ch.
devices. (It will use only the pipe handle, but it's best to pa
through STARTUPINFO.)

To review, the StartProcess procedure performs these st

1. Loads the string that names the child program's executal

2. Creates the pipe with inheritable handles.

3. Modifies the write-only handle with DuplicateHandle so it
    inherited.

4. Puts the read-only handle in a STARTUPINFO variable.

5. Creates the child process, which both inherits the read-only han
    receives a copy of the handle as its own stdin device. (The child
    other handles from this parent.)

6. Closes the parent's read-only handle to the pipe. The child has its o
    now, and the parent doesn't need it.

The STARTUPINFO structure allows the parent to decide how and where the
child's window will appear. Many of the fields, however, apply only to charac
based console windows. The Child program uses a graphics window, not a cha
acter window. Furthermore, because we have set only one activation flag in the
dwFlags field, CreateProcess will ignore most of the values anyway. At a minimum, however, you should initialize the cb field, the lpDesktop field, the
dwFlags field, and the three reserved fields.

```
                // make an uninheritable duplicate of the outbound (write) handle
      bTest = DuplicateHandle( GetCurrentProcess( ),
                               hPipeWrite,          // original handle
                               GetCurrentProcess( ),
                               NULL,                // don't create new handle
                               0,
                               FALSE,               // not inheritable
                               DUPLICATE_SAME_ACCESS );

      if( ! bTest )                                 // duplication failed
      {
         ShowErrorMsg( );
         CloseHandle( hPipeRead );
         CloseHandle( hPipeWrite );
         return;
      }

                // fill in the process's startup information
      memset( &sui, 0, sizeof(STARTUPINFO) );
      sui.cb          = sizeof(STARTUPINFO);
      sui.dwFlags     = STARTF_USESTDHANDLES;
      sui.hStdInput   = hPipeRead;
      sui.hStdOutput  = GetStdHandle( STD_OUTPUT_HANDLE );
      sui.hStdError   = GetStdHandle( STD_ERROR_HANDLE );

                // create the drawing process
      bTest = CreateProcess( szProcess,       // .EXE image
                             NULL,            // command line
                             NULL,            // process security
                             NULL,            // thread security
                             TRUE,            // inherit handles-yes
                             0,               // creation flags
                             NULL,            // environment block
                             NULL,            // current directory
                             &sui,            // startup info
                             &pi );           // process info (returned)
                // did we succeed in launching the process?
      if( ! bTest )
      {
         ShowErrorMsg( );                     // creation failed
         CloseHandle( hPipeWrite );
      }
      else                                    // creation succeeded
```

```
    {
        hProcess = pi.hProcess;          // save new process handle
        CloseHandle( pi.hThread );       // discard new thread handle
        figure.iShape = IDM_RECTANGLE;   // reset to default shape
        SendCommand( );                  // tell child what to draw
    }
    CloseHandle( hPipeRead );            // discard receiving end of pipe
    return;
}
```

If the `CreateProcess` command succeeds, `StartProcess` performs several final actions. First, it looks at the two handles returned in the `PROCESS_INFORMATION` structure. It moves the new process's handle to a global variable. The `pi` variable also holds a handle to the primary thread of the new child process. Having no use for that handle, the program closes it immediately. Then it closes the handle to the child's end of the pipe and calls `SendCommand` to tell the child what to draw first.

Resetting the `figure` variable before `SendCommand` is very important. The parent process can open and close a child many times in one session. To close the child, the parent puts `IDM_TERMINATE` in the `figure` variable and writes that to the pipe. The line that resets `figure.iShape` to `IDM_RECTANGLE` ensures that the child will not receive a leftover `IDM_TERMINATE` command as its first message.

Writing to the Pipe The Parent program sends the Child program a message immediately after launching the child when you choose a new shape attribute and when you choose Terminate from the Process menu. At each point, the program calls SendCommand to put information in the pipe.

```
/*─────────────────────────────────────────────────────────────────
    SEND COMMAND
        Tell the child program what to draw. Write the current
        contents of the global FIGURE variable into the pipe.

    Return
        TRUE indicates the write operation succeeded. FALSE means
        an error occurred and you have lost contact with the child.
────────────────────────────────────────────────────────────────*/

BOOL SendCommand()
{
    BOOL bTest;                  // return value
    DWORD dwWritten;             // number of bytes written to pipe
```

```
        // pass the choices to the child through the pipe
bTest = WriteFile( hPipeWrite,      // anonymous pipe (outbound handle)
                   &figure,          // buffer to write
                   sizeof(FIGURE),   // size of buffer
                   &dwWritten,       // bytes written
                   NULL );           // overlapping i/o structure
if( ! bTest )                        // did writing succeed?
{
    // If the write operation failed because the user has
    // already closed the child program, then tell the user
    // the connection was broken. If some less predictable
    // error caused the failure, call ShowErrorMsg as usual
    // to display the system's error message.

    DWORD dwResult = GetLastError();

    if( ( dwResult == ERROR_BROKEN_PIPE ) ||  // pipe has been ended
        ( dwResult == ERROR_NO_DAT ) )        // pipe close in progress
    {
        // presumably the user closed the child
       MessageBox( hwndMain, "Connection with child already broken.",
                   "Parent Message", MB_ICONEXCLAMATION | MB_OK );
    }
    else    // an unpredictable error occurred
       ShowErrorMsg();
}
    // If a write error occurred, or if we just sent an IDM_TERMINATE
    // command to make the child quit, then in either case we break
    // off communication with the child process.
if( ( ! bTest ) || ( figure.iShape == IDM_TERMINATE ) )
{
    CloseHandle( hProcess );         // forget about the child
    hProcess = NULL;
    CloseHandle( hPipeWrite );       // destroy the pipe
}
   return( bTest );
}
```

The WriteFile command may fail for any of several reasons. One likely problem arises if the user closes the Child program from the child's menu. The parent does not know the child is gone until it tries to write to the pipe and receives an error. In that case, the GetLastError function, which returns a number identifying what error last occurred in a given thread, indicates either ERROR_BROKEN_ PIPE or ERROR_NO_DATA.

Instead of handling these results like any other error, SendCommand raises a message box explaining that the connection has been broken. If the pipe fails for any reason at all, however, the parent makes no effort to reestablish contact. It closes the pipe handle and the child process handle. The program also resets the process handle to NULL, which CloseHandle does not do. The Parent_OnInit-Menu message handler relies on the value of hProcess to determine whether the child still exists.

A separate ShowErrorMsg procedure uses the FormatMessage function to present error messages.

```
/*─────────────────────────────────────────────────────────────
   SHOW ERROR MESSAGE
──────────────────────────────────────────────────────────────*/

void ShowErrorMsg ( void )
{
   LPVOID lpvMessage;                          // temporary message buffer

      // retrieve a message from the system message table
   FormatMessage( FORMAT_MESSAGE_ALLOCATE_BUFFER |
                  FORMAT_MESSAGE_FROM_SYSTEM,
                  NULL, GetLastError(),
                  MAKELANGID(LANG_ENGLISH, SUBLANG_ENGLISH_US),
                  (LPTSTR) &lpvMessage, 0, NULL );
      // display the message in a message box
   MessageBox( hwndMain, lpvMessage, "Parent Message",
                  MB_ICONEXCLAMATION | MB_OK );
      // release the buffer FormatMessage allocated
   LocalFree( lpvMessage );
   return;
}
```

ShowErrorMsg is built around the FormatMessage command, which chooses a message from the system's internal message table to describe the most recent error. (The most recent error value is maintained separately for each thread.) Given the flags we've set in its first parameter, FormatMessage dynamically allocates a message buffer and puts the address in the lpvMessage variable. Note that FormatMessage wants to receive the *address* of the buffer pointer, not the pointer itself.

The Child

The CreateProcess command in the parent's StartProcess procedure launches a program called Child. The parent stores the string *child.exe* in its table of string resources.

Inheriting a Pipe Handle and Creating a Thread   The *AnonPipe* version of Child dedicates a secondary thread to the task of waiting for data to arrive through the pipe. The primary thread processes system messages for the program's window. When the secondary thread receives a new command from the parent, it updates the global variables iShape, iSize, and iColor, and then invalidates the window. The primary thread receives a WM_PAINT message and redraws the display using the new shape values. The secondary thread runs in a loop that ends when it reads an IDM_TERMINATE command from the pipe.

The first part of the Child.C listing includes WinMain, the initialization procedures, and the message handlers. The child performs its most important initialization tasks in response to the WM_CREATE message.

Child_OnCreate recovers the pipe handle inherited from the parent and creates a new thread to read from the pipe. If either action fails, the procedure returns FALSE and the process ends.

```
/*------------------------------------------------------------
    CHILD_ONCREATE
        On startup open the pipe and start the thread that will
        read from it.
    ------------------------------------------------------------*/
BOOL Child_OnCreate( HWND hWnd, LPCREATESTRUCT lpCreateStruct )
{
    // open the pipe for reading
    hPipeRead = GetStdHandle( STD_INPUT_HANDLE );
    if( hPipeRead == INVALID_HANDLE_VALUE )
    {
        ShowErrorMsg();
        return( FALSE );
    }
    // Create the thread that will read from the pipe. It is created
```

```
                       // suspended so its priority can be lowered before it starts.
              hThread = CreateThread( NULL,                    // security attributes
                                      0,                       // initial stack size
                                      (LPTHREAD_START_ROUTINE) PipeThread,
                                      NULL,                    // argument
                                      CREATE_SUSPENDED,        // creation flag
                                      &dwThreadID );           // new thread's ID
              if( ! hThread )
              {
                 ShowErrorMsg();
                 return( FALSE );
              }
                       // lower the thread's priority and let it run
              SetThreadPriority( hThread, THREAD_PRIORITY_BELOW_NORMAL );
              ResumeThread( hThread );
              return( TRUE );
              UNREFERENCED_PARAMETER(hWnd);
              UNREFERENCED_PARAMETER(lpCreateStruct);
           }
```

To retrieve the pipe handle, the child calls GetStdHandle. This command finds
the handle that the parent told CreateProcess to deposit in the child's stdin
device slot. The child creates its secondary pipe-reading thread in a suspended
state to adjust the thread's priority. Because the primary thread responds to user
input, we set the secondary thread to a lower priority. This difference ensures that
the child will respond quickly to keyboard and menu input.

The paint procedure (not shown here) is long but straightforward. It simply
reads the current values of iShape, iSize, and iColor; creates the pens and
brushes it needs; and draws an ellipse, a rectangle, or a triangle.

Reading from the Pipe   Child_OnCreate designates PipeThread as the
main procedure for the secondary thread. The new thread immediately enters a
while loop that ends when the global bTerminate flag becomes TRUE. The flag
changes when you choose Exit from the child's menu, when the parent sends
an IDM_TERMINATE command, or if the child encounters an error reading from
the pipe. When the while loop finally does end, the thread posts a WM_DESTROY
message to the program window. The secondary thread exits, the primary
thread receives the destroy command, and the program ends.

```
/*----------------------------------------------------------------
    PIPE THREAD
        The WM_CREATE handler starts a thread with this procedure
        to manage the pipe connection. This thread waits for
        messages to arrive through the pipe and acts on them.
    ------------------------------------------------------------*/

LONG PipeThread( LPVOID lpThreadData )
{
    while( ! bTerminate )         // read from pipe until terminate flag = true
        DoRead();
        // when bTerminate is TRUE, time to end program
    FORWARD_WM_DESTROY( hwndMain, PostMessage );
    return( 0L );                 // implicit ExitThread()
    UNREFERENCED_PARAMETER(lpThreadData);
}
```

The DoRead procedure is responsible for reading from the pipe and for making three decisions. The first is to determine if the read is successful or, if not, to report an error. Second, assuming a successful read, the IDM_TERMINATE command is checked to determine if the thread should terminate. And, third, if the read is successful and it is not a terminate message, the shape, color, and size variables are read from the piped message and the child window is updated so a new shape will be drawn.

```
/*----------------------------------------------------------------
    DO READ
        Read from the pipe and set the figure to be drawn.
    ------------------------------------------------------------*/

void DoRead( void )
{
    FIGURE figure;
    DWORD dwRead;
    BOOL bTest;

        // read from the pipe
    bTest = ReadFile( hPipeRead,         // place to read from
                      &figure,           // buffer to store input
                      sizeof(figure),    // bytes to read
                      &dwRead,           // bytes read
                      NULL );
```

```
    if( bTest )
    {                                     // the read command succeeded
        if( figure.iShape == IDM_TERMINATE ) // is new command Terminate?
            bTerminate = TRUE;            // set flag to end this thread
        else
        {                                 // thread continues; draw new shape
            // copy the new shape attributes to global variables
            iShape = figure.iShape;
            iColor = figure.iColor;
            iSize  = figure.iSize;
            // force the parent window to repaint itself
            InvalidateRect( hwndMain, NULL, TRUE );
            UpdateWindow( hwndMain );
        }
    }
    else                                  // the read command failed
    {
        ShowErrorMsg( );                  // tell user what happened
        bTerminate = TRUE;                // let the child end
    }
    return;
}
```

The while loop in the secondary thread does one thing: It calls DoRead over and over. The DoRead procedure performs one ReadFile command, interprets the message, and ends. Each call to DoRead retrieves one more message. Because all anonymous pipes use the waiting mode, the thread blocks on each call to Read-File until data arrives. ReadFile may return immediately if the pipe is full or if an error occurs. For example, it will return immediately if the Parent program has already exited and the pipe handle has become invalid.

If the read command succeeds, the child must determine whether it has received a command to terminate or to draw a new shape. If the command fails, the child notifies the user by displaying the system's error message. The child also assumes the connection has been broken and exits.

Although this pipe, like all anonymous pipes, writes and reads in byte mode, the Child program still manages to always retrieve one message at a time, even if several messages are waiting. Because the parent always writes exactly `sizeof(FIGURE)` bytes into the pipe, the child knows where one message ends and the next begins.

The Child program's `About_DlgProc` and `ShowErrorMsg` procedures duplicate the corresponding procedures in the Parent program almost exactly.

The NamedPipe Demo: Multiple Communication Channels

An anonymous pipe serves the needs of the *AnonPipe* demo's Parent and Child programs perfectly well. They communicate in only one direction, use only one instance of the pipe at a time, and both run on the same machine. The *NamedPipe* version, however, allows the parent to create any number of children and communicate with several of them at once. Rather than creating a new anonymous pipe for each client, this version creates two instances of a single named pipe.

WARNING   Although the *NamedPipe* version of the program works fine under Windows NT, it will not compile correctly under Windows 98.

If you launch many child processes, only the first two will connect with the parent. The others will block, waiting for one of the existing connections to break.

Choosing Terminate from the parent's menu causes all the currently connected children to quit. When the link with one child breaks, that instance of the pipe becomes available for one of the waiting children. In Figure 15.3, the parent process has launched three children. Two are connected and have drawn the currently selected shape, while the third is waiting for an available pipe instance.

NOTE   The *NamedPipe* demo is included on the CD that accompanies this book, in the Chapter 15 folder.

FIGURE 15.3:

Parent process with three children, only two of which are connected to instances of the named pipe

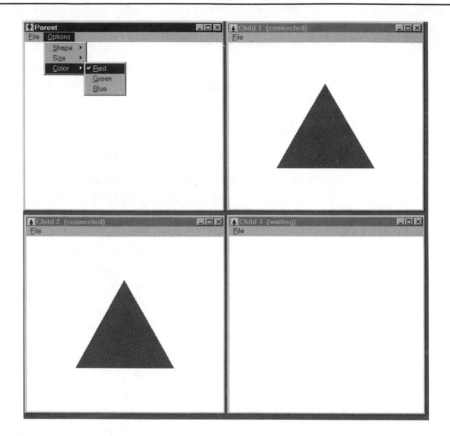

The Parent Process

To use a named pipe, both processes must agree on a name string for the pipe they will share. The name string belongs in the string table of both the parent and the child. We've set the string in a shared resource file, Global.STR, and modified both resource scripts to include it. The shared header file, Global.H, adds a new constant to identify the common string resource. Notice that the name string in Global.STR contains double the expected number of backslashes:

```
/*————————————————————————————————————————————————————
    GLOBAL.STR

        Contains a string that should be included in the string
        tables of both the parent and child halves of the
        PROCESS demo program.
    ————————————————————————————————————————————————————*/
```

```
    IDS_PIPE,  "\\\\.\\pipe\\procdemo"      // name of pipe object
```

The resource compiler uses the backslash character to signal the beginning of an ASCII code sequence. Each pair of backslashes inserts a single literal backslash in the resource string.

The new Parent.H header defines the constant NUM_PIPE_INSTANCES, giving it the value of 2. To have the parent create more instances of its pipe and connect with more children simultaneously, modify the definition.

TIP

Figure 15.3 shows three child instances where only two have connected—due to the specified NUM_PIPE_INSTANCES limit. When the parent is instructed to close the child processes, the unconnected child will remain open and will assume one of the freed connections.

Creating the Named Pipe   The anonymous pipe parent destroys its pipe each time the child process terminates. If you launch a new child, the parent creates a new pipe. A named pipe, however, often lives through several connections with different clients. The named pipe parent creates its pipe instances only once, during initialization. The parent calls its MakePipeInstance procedure twice. Each successive call produces a handle to the program's pipe object and a new thread to support the new instance.

Parent_OnCreate also produces two other important objects, both events. Each event object broadcasts a signal to as many threads as happen to be listening.

```
/*------------------------------------------------------------------------

    PARENT_ONCREATE
        Create all the pipe instances and the two event objects used
        to synchronize the program's threads
    ------------------------------------------------------------------------*/

BOOL Parent_OnCreate( HWND hWnd, LPCREATESTRUCT lpcs )
{
    int i;
    int iNumInstances = 0;                  // counts instances created

        // Create all the instances of the named pipe. The
        // MakePipeInstance command also starts up a new
        // thread to service each pipe instance.

    for( i = 1; i <= NUM_PIPE_INSTANCES; i++ )
        if( MakePipeInstance() )            // make one instance
            iNumInstances++;                // if successful, increment counter
```

```
if( iNumInstances != NUM_PIPE_INSTANCES )   // did we make all of them?
{
   char szBuffer[128];
   wsprintf( szBuffer, "Created only %i instances\n\r", iNumInstances );
   MessageBox( hwndMain, szBuffer, "Parent Message",
             MB_ICONEXCLAMATION | MB_OK );
   return( FALSE );                  // creation failed
}
   // Create the event object used for signaling the pipe
   // instance threads when the user makes a command.
hCmdEvent = CreateEvent( NULL,      // default security attributes
                         TRUE,      // manual reset event
                         FALSE,     // initially not signaled
                         NULL );    // no name
if( hCmdEvent == NULL )
{
   ShowErrorMsg();                  // event creation failed
   return( FALSE );
}
   // Create the event that coordinates the pipe threads when
   // the program terminates all linked children. The threads
   // block on this event until all the clients have received
   // the IDM_TERMINATE message.
hNotTerminatingEvent = CreateEvent( NULL,     // default security attributes
                                    TRUE,     // manual reset event
                                    TRUE,     // initially signaled
                                    NULL );   // no name
if( hNotTerminatingEvent == NULL )
{
   ShowErrorMsg( );                 // event creation failed
   return( FALSE );
}
return( TRUE );
UNREFERENCED_PARAMETER(hWnd);
UNREFERENCED_PARAMETER(lpcs);
}
```

The Parent program uses one event to notify its pipe threads whenever the user makes a new choice from the menu. In response, the pipe threads send the new command to their clients. This is a manual reset event, so all listening pipes will unblock when the signal arrives. (Automatic reset events unblock only one thread on each signal.)

The other event coordinates the threads while they are sending termination commands to multiple clients. It, too, is a manual reset event. This one, however, begins life already in its signaled state. You'll see why in the code for the pipe instance threads.

Because no other processes have any reason to use either event object, the events do not need names.

Creating a New Named Pipe Instance To create a new instance of a named pipe, use the MakePipeInstance procedure. It begins by loading the resource string that names the pipe object. The subsequent call to CreateNamedPipe sets the pipe's attributes.

```c
/*-----------------------------------------------------------------
    MAKE PIPE INSTANCE
        Create a new instance of the named pipe.
    Return    TRUE if the procedure creates a new instance;
              FALSE if an error prevents creation.
    ------------------------------------------------------------*/

BOOL MakePipeInstance ( void )
{
    char    szPipe[MAX_BUFFER];     // name of pipe
    int     iLen;                   // return value
    HANDLE  hPipe;                  // handle to new pipe
    HANDLE  hThread;                // handle to new thread
    DWORD   dwThreadID;             // ID of new thread

        // get name to use for sharing pipe
    if( ! LoadString( hInst, IDS_PIPE, szPipe, sizeof(szPipe) ) )
        return( FALSE );
        // Create a new instance of the named pipe. This command will
        // fail if two instances already exist
    hPipe = CreateNamedPipe( szPipe,                   // name
                    PIPE_ACCESS_OUTBOUND, // open mode
                    PIPE_TYPE_BYTE | PIPE_READMODE_BYTE |
                    PIPE_WAIT,
                    NUM_PIPE_INSTANCES,   // max instances
                    0,                    // out buffer size
                    0,                    // in buffer size
                    0,                    // time-out value
                    NULL );               // security attributes
```

```
    if (hPipe == INVALID_HANDLE_VALUE)
    {
       ShowErrorMsg( );                              // creation failed
       return( FALSE );
    }
    hThread = CreateThread( NULL,          // security attributes
                            0,             // initial stack size
    (LPTHREAD_START_ROUTINE) PipeInstanceThread,
                (LPVOID) hPipe,            // argument for thread proc
                         CREATE_SUSPENDED,     // creation flag
                         &dwThreadID );        // new thread's ID

    if( ! hThread )
    {
       ShowErrorMsg( );
       CloseHandle( hPipe );
       return( FALSE );                       // thread creation failed
    }
       // lower the thread's priority and let it run
    SetThreadPriority( hThread, THREAD_PRIORITY_BELOW_NORMAL );
    ResumeThread( hThread );
       // let go of the handle, for which we have no further use
    CloseHandle( hThread );
    return( TRUE );
}
```

Because the parent and child send information in only one direction, the program uses a one-way outbound pipe. For clarity, specify all three mode flags even though the pipe's particular characteristics—byte mode and wait mode—are the default values. We do not need the message mode because the parent's messages are always the same length. NUM_PIPE_INSTANCES prevents CreateNamedPipe from producing more than two handles to this pipe.

The first call to CreateNamedPipe sets the pipe's maximum number of instances, and subsequent creation commands will fail if they specify a different number. The zero values for the buffer sizes instruct the system to allocate message space dynamically as needed.

For each pipe handle, MakePipeInstance also creates a new thread. The pipe instance thread waits for the user to choose commands from the parent menu and writes the new command into its pipe. We might equally well have stored the pipe handles in an array and created a single thread to write to all the instances on each new command. Again, as with the anonymous pipe child, the program sets secondary threads to a lower priority, reserving normal priority for only the primary thread—the one thread that responds directly to the user.

This time, pass a parameter to the thread's starting function. A thread function always receives a 32-bit parameter when it starts up, but until now the programs have not used it. Each instance thread, however, requires a different pipe handle, so hPipe becomes the fourth parameter of CreateThread.

Launching the Child When you choose the Start command from the parent's File menu, the program calls StartProcess. In this version, the Start command is always enabled, permitting you to launch any number of children.

As an exercise in using the command line, the parent passes to each child an identifying number. The first child is 1, the second is 2, and so on. To pass arguments to a child on its command line, ignore the first parameter of Create-Process and pass the entire command line, including the program name, in the second parameter. The command-line parameter string looks like this:

```
child.exe 1
```

Use the first parameter, lpszImage, when you have no arguments to pass or do not want the system to search for the child's .EXE file along the system PATH.

Because children can acquire their own pipe handles with CreateFile, there is no need to arrange for inheritance. Even if the Parent program had created inheritable handles, the children would not inherit any of them because we pass FALSE as the fifth parameter to CreateProcess.

```
/*-------------------------------------------------------------------
    START PROCESS
        In response to the IDM_START command, create a new
        child process. The user may create any number of children.
-------------------------------------------------------------------*/
void StartProcess()
{
    STARTUPINFO         sui;        // info for starting a process
    PROCESS_INFORMATION pi;         // info returned about a process
    static int iChildNum = 1;       // counts child processes
    char szProcess[MAX_BUFFER];     // name of child process image
    char szCmdLine[MAX_BUFFER];     // child's command line
    BOOL bTest;                     // return value
        // load name of process image file from resources
```

```
if( ! LoadString( hInst, IDS_PROCESS, szProcess, sizeof(szProcess) ) )
    return;                      // loading string failed
    // fill in the process's startup information
sui.cb                = sizeof(STARTUPINFO);
sui.lpReserved        = NULL;        // must be NULL
sui.lpDesktop         = NULL;        // starting desktop
sui.lpTitle           = NULL;        // title for new console window
sui.dwX               = 0;           // window starting offsets
sui.dwY               = 0;
sui.dwXSize           = 0;           // window starting size
sui.dwYSize           = 0;
sui.dwXCountChars     = 0;           // console screen buffer size
sui.dwYCountChars     = 0;
sui.dwFillAttribute   = 0;           // console text colors
sui.dwFlags           = 0;           // flags to activate startup fields
sui.wShowWindow       = 0;           // iCmdShow parameter
sui.cbReserved2       = 0;
sui.lpReserved2       = NULL;

    // prepare child's command-line argument, a window caption string
wsprintf( szCmdLine, "%s %i", (LPSTR)szProcess, iChildNum++ );
    // create the drawing process
bTest = CreateProcess( NULL,            // .EXE image
                       szCmdLine,       // command line
                       NULL,            // process security
                       NULL,            // thread security
                       FALSE,           // inherit handles
                       0,               // creation flags
                       NULL,            // environment block
                       NULL,            // current directory
                       &sui,            // startup info
                       &pi );           // process info (returned)
if( ! bTest )
{
   ShowErrorMsg();                      // creation failed
   return;
}
WaitForInputIdle( pi.hProcess, 5000 );  // wait for child to start up
CloseHandle( pi.hProcess );             // we don't need the handles
CloseHandle( pi.hThread );
return;
}
```

Synchronizing the Threads Whenever you change the shape options by choosing a new figure, size, or color, the program must write new commands in all its pipes. The primary thread receives and processes your command. It needs a way to make all the pipe instance threads transmit the new information. One of the event objects created during initialization serves this purpose.

When you pick a new option, the procedures that store the command also pulse the event. The `PulseEvent` command combines the `SetEvent` and `ResetEvent` commands into one operation. The event remains signaled just long enough to unblock all waiting threads and then immediately returns to its unsignaled state.

The `ChangeShape` procedure incorporates one other modification. When it receives the IDM_TERMINATE command, it saves the old shape value in a global variable, `iPrevShape`. After all the connected children quit, the parent restores the `iPrevShape` value to the `figure.iShape` field. If children are waiting, they will connect immediately to the newly released pipes; if `figure.iShape` still held IDM_TERMINATE, the children's first command would shut them down. The `iPrevShape` variable allows newly connected children to draw immediately whatever shape was last selected.

```
/*---------------------------------------------------------------
    CHANGE SHAPE
        Record a shape command from the user. If the user has chosen
        a new shape, send the updated FIGURE structure to the child.
    ----------------------------------------------------------------*/

void ChangeShape ( int iCmd )
{
    if( iCmd != figure.iShape )         // new shape?
    {
        // After sending a terminate command, you need to
        // restore the last shape drawn so that newly
        // connected clients can still draw whatever the
        // user last chose.

        if( iCmd == IDM_TERMINATE )
            iPrevShape = figure.iShape; // save old shape command
        figure.iShape = iCmd;           // record new shape command
        PulseEvent( hCmdEvent );        // tell threads shape has changed
    }
    return;
}
```

The ChangeSize procedure doesn't have much to do except for recording the new size and then, like the ChangeShape procedure, calling the PulseEvent function to tell the thread that a change has occurred.

```
/*----------------------------------------------------------------
    CHANGE SIZE
        Record a size command from the user. If the user has chosen
        a new size, send the updated FIGURE structure to the child.
    ----------------------------------------------------------------*/

void ChangeSize( int iCmd )
{
    if( iCmd != figure.iSize )          // new size?
    {
        figure.iSize = iCmd;            // record it
        PulseEvent( hCmdEvent );        // tell threads shape has changed
    }
    return;
}
```

Again, the ChangeColor procedure simply records the new color, and then calls the PulseEvent function to tell the thread that a change has occurred.

```
/*----------------------------------------------------------------
    CHANGE COLOR
        Record a color command from the user. If the user has chosen
        a new color, send the updated FIGURE structure to the child.
    ----------------------------------------------------------------*/

void ChangeColor ( int iCmd )
{
    if( iCmd != figure.iColor )         // new color?
    {
        figure.iColor = iCmd;           // record it
        PulseEvent( hCmdEvent );        // tell threads shape has changed
    }
    return;
}
```

Connecting with Clients The threads that run each pipe instance begin life at the PipeInstanceThread procedure. Each new thread enters an endless loop waiting for clients to connect with its instance of the pipe. When a client does connect, a smaller nested loop begins.

While the connection lasts, the thread waits for command signals from the event object. Each time the event pulses, the thread unblocks, copies the current contents of the global figure variable into its pipe, and resumes its wait for a new command.

If the write operation fails for any reason, the thread assumes its client process has terminated. The thread calls DisconnectNamedPipe, returns to the top of its outer loop, and issues ConnectNamedPipe to wait for a new client. The loop also maintains a connection count in the global variable iNumConnections. Each time a thread succeeds in connecting, it increments the counter. When the connection breaks, it decrements the counter. The Parent_OnInitMenu procedure reads the counter to decide which menu options should be enabled. If the parent has no listening clients, all the shape option commands are disabled.

The outer loop of PipeInstanceThread begins with a while (TRUE) command, so the loop can never break. The pipe threads stop running when the primary thread reaches the end of WinMain and the system calls ExitProcess. At the customary W4 warning level, using a constant for a conditional expression causes the compiler to complain. The #pragma commands surrounding the procedure suppress the warning.

```
// Tell the compiler not to complain about the "while (TRUE)" loop
#pragma warning (disable :4127)
```

Adding to the complexity of this procedure is the task of coordinating the threads when they all disconnect their clients in response to a Terminate command from the user. Several potential problems arise along the way. First, the parent should not write its IDM_TERMINATE command to the pipe and then disconnect immediately because DisconnectNamedPipe destroys any data still lingering in the pipe's buffer. The command could be lost before the child had a chance to read it. When passed a pipe handle, FlushFileBuffers blocks until the receiving program clears the pipe by reading all its contents. Only a program with write access to its pipe may call FlushFileBuffers. The command fails when passed a read-only handle.

As each thread disconnects from its terminated client, it returns to the top of the loop and waits for a new connection. As soon as it connects, it sends the client an initial message to make it draw something right away. But if other threads are still terminating their clients, the global figure variable still contains the IDM_TERMINATE command. The thread will terminate its newly connected client by mistake. We need a way to prevent any thread from sending that initial message to a new client until after all the old clients have been disconnected. The hNotTerminatingEvent object solves the problem.

Near the top of the outer loop you'll find a `WaitForSingleObject` command that every thread passes before writing its first message to a new client. Most of the time, the event remains signaled and all threads pass by quickly. As soon as one thread sends a termination command, however, it calls `ResetEvent` to turn off the signal, indicating that a termination sequence has started. Now when any thread finds a new client, it will block before sending the first message. The last thread to terminate its client resets the `figure.iShape` command to `iPrevShape`, the value it last held before the termination began. The last thread also calls `SetEvent` to restore the event signal and unblock the other waiting threads. A thread knows when it is the last to terminate its client because the `iNumConnections` counter reaches 0.

```
LONG PipeInstanceThread ( HANDLE hPipe )
{
    BOOL bConnected;     // true when a client connects to the pipe

        // This loop runs endlessly. When a client disappears, the
        // loop simply waits for a new client to connect. This thread is
        // terminated automatically when the program's primary thread exits.
    while( TRUE )
    {
          // wait for a connection with some client
        ConnectNamedPipe( hPipe, NULL );
```

If other threads are terminating their clients, then `figure.iShape` still holds the `IDM_TERMINATE` command. The thread blocks here until the last client is terminated. The last terminating thread resets `figure.iShape` to its previous value.

```
    WaitForSingleObject( hNotTerminatingEvent, INFINITE );
        // now the connection is made and a command message is ready
    iNumConnections++;                      // update global variable
    SendCommand( hPipe );                   // give client its first command
        // send another message each time the Command event signals
    bConnected = TRUE;
    while( bConnected )
    {
        WaitForSingleObject( hCmdEvent, INFINITE ); // wait for signal
        if( ! SendCommand( hPipe ) )        // send new shape command
            bConnected = FALSE;
            // The connection failed - probably we just sent IDM_TERMINATE or
            // the user exited from the client. Show no error message.
    }
    FlushFileBuffers( hPipe );     // wait for child to read message
    DisconnectNamedPipe( hPipe ); // break connection
    iNumConnections-;               // update global variable
```

The following if condition coordinates threads when they are all terminating their clients. When a thread discovers it has just sent the IDM_TERMINATE command, it sets the hNotTerminatingEvent object to the nonsignaled state. Other threads will block until the last thread to disconnect restores the signal. The last thread also replaces the IDM_TERMINATE command with IDM_RECTANGLE so all the threads will have a useful command to send in the first message to their new clients.

```
    if( figure.iShape == IDM_TERMINATE ) // did we just terminate?
    {                                     // have all connections
        if( iNumConnections > 0 )         // been terminated?
        {                                 // NO; block other threads
            // while terminating proceeds
            ResetEvent( hNotTerminatingEvent );
        }
        else                              // YES
        {
            figure.iShape = iPrevShape;   // restore previous command
            SetEvent( hNotTerminatingEvent );   // unblock threads
        }
    }
  }
  return( 0L );
}
```

Last, the conditional expression warning is reenabled.

```
// allow the "conditional expression constant" warning again
#pragma warning (default :4127)
```

Writing to the Pipe   Within the PipeInstanceThread loops, the program repeatedly calls SendCommand to write the current values from figure into the pipe. If the connection with the client breaks, the procedure returns FALSE. The connection may break in either of two ways, and each has different consequences for the program's behavior.

The program disconnects most gracefully when the user chooses Terminate and the parent breaks the links itself. In that case, SendCommand returns FALSE immediately after sending the message, and the program seeks new replacement clients immediately. But if a client closes its handle to the pipe's other end, the server does not know. If the user chooses Exit from the menu of a connected child process, the parent discovers the break only when it later tries to send a new message and

WriteFile returns an error value. Furthermore, the broken pipe remains technically connected until the server calls DisconnectNamedPipe. As a consequence,
if you end one of the connected child programs while a third child is blocked
on WaitNamedPipe, the waiting child remains blocked until you issue another
command.

Using a two-way duplex pipe would smooth this transition because the client
could send the server a termination message before it exits and the server could
disconnect immediately. To accommodate that arrangement, the server would
probably dedicate two threads to each pipe instance: one to send and one to
receive, or perhaps one thread to do all the writing for all instances and another
to do the reading.

```
/*-------------------------------------------------------------
    SEND COMMAND
        Tell the child program what to draw. Write the current
        contents of the global FIGURE variable into the pipe.

    Return
        TRUE indicates the write operation succeeded. FALSE means
        an error occurred and we have lost contact with the child.
    -----------------------------------------------------------*/

BOOL SendCommand ( HANDLE hPipe )
{
    BOOL bTest;                        // return value
    DWORD dwWritten;                   // number of bytes written to pipe

    // pass the choices to the child through the pipe
    bTest = WriteFile( hPipe,          // named pipe (outbound handle)
                       &figure,        // buffer to write
                       sizeof(FIGURE), // size of buffer
                       &dwWritten,     // bytes written
                       NULL );         // overlapping i/o structure

    if( ! bTest )                      // did writing succeed?
    {
```

If the write operation failed because the user has already closed the child program, then we don't need to do anything special about the error. If, however,
some less predictable error caused the failure, call ShowErrorMsg as usual to display the system's error message.

```
        DWORD dwResult = GetLastError();

        if( ( dwResult != ERROR_BROKEN_PIPE ) && // pipe has been ended
            ( dwResult != ERROR_NO_DATA ) )       // pipe close in progress
        {
            ShowErrorMsg();                        // unpredictable error
        }
    }
```

SendCommand returns FALSE on errors to indicate that the connection has failed; SendCommand also returns FALSE after it tells a child to quit because that also makes a connection fail.

```
        return( ( bTest ) && ( figure.iShape != IDM_TERMINATE ) );
    }
```

The Child Process

The child process requires fewer changes. One change is visible in Figure 15.3 (shown earlier). Because the parent now creates multiple children, we distinguish each with a different number in its window caption. The parent passes each child its own number through the command-line parameter of Create-Process. The child's window caption also states whether the child is connected to a pipe or waiting for a connection.

```
    BOOL CreateMainWindow ( void )
    {
        char szAppName[MAX_BUFFER];
        char szBuffer[MAX_BUFFER];
        char *pToken;

            // load the relevant strings
        LoadString( hInst, IDS_APPNAME, szAppName,  sizeof(szAppName) );
```

You use the command-line string from the parent to create the window's caption. The basic caption has the form, Child 1 %s. The identifying number comes from the parent through the command line. We use wsprintf to insert the phrase *waiting* or *connected* into the title as appropriate.

```
        strcpy( szTitle, "Child " );        // begin with "Child "
        strtok( GetCommandLine(), " " );    // move past first word
        pToken = strtok( NULL, " " );       // get first argument
        if( pToken )                        // is there one?
```

```
    {
        strcat( szTitle, pToken );        // append it
    }
    strcat( szTitle, " %s" );             // append a wsprintf format mark
```

During initialization, each child retrieves its assigned number with GetCommand-Line. This command returns a pointer to a string containing all the command-line arguments separated by spaces. The first item on the command line should be the name of the program (Child.EXE), so calling strtok twice extracts the child's sequence number, the second item on the command line. The program constructs a base string of the form "Child 1 %s" and calls wsprintf to replace the %s marker with a string describing the program's current status, which is initially "waiting" but may change to "connected."

```
        // The global szTitle now contains the base caption.
        // Insert a current status marker in it.
    wsprintf( szBuffer, szTitle, (LPSTR)" (waiting)" );
        // create the parent window
    hwndMain = CreateWindow( szAppName, szBuffer,
                             WS_OVERLAPPEDWINDOW | WS_CLIPCHILDREN,
                             CW_USEDEFAULT, CW_USEDEFAULT,
                             CW_USEDEFAULT, CW_USEDEFAULT,
                             NULL, NULL, hInst, NULL );
        // return FALSE for an error
    return( hwndMain != NULL );
}
```

Creating a Thread and Connecting to the Pipe Because CreateMainWindow has already set the window caption, the new Child_OnCreate procedure no longer loads a caption from the resource string table. Because the child has not inherited a pipe handle, this version also omits the original call to GetStdHandle. Instead, the new thread function, PipeThread, now coordinates all the pipe actions.

PipeThread first loads the pipe name string both programs share in the Global.STR file, and then it passes the name to CreateFile. The system searches its object name tree and finds the pipe with this name. If an instance of the pipe is available, CreateFile returns a handle to it. Because the original pipe was created with the PIPE_ACCESS_OUTBOUND flag, the client must request GENERIC_READ access rights.

```
LONG PipeThread ( LPVOID lpThreadData )
{
    char    szBuffer[MAX_BUFFER];    // used for pipe name and window caption
    BOOL    bConnected;              // TRUE when we have a pipe handle
    HANDLE  hPipeRead;               // receiving handle to 1-way pipe
```

```
        // load the string that contains the name of the named pipe
   if( ! LoadString( hInst, IDS_PIPE, szBuffer, sizeof(szBuffer) ) )
      return( FALSE );
        // This while loop continues until an instance of the named
        // pipe becomes available. bConnected is a global variable,
        // and while it is FALSE the primary thread paints "Waiting..."
        // in the window's client area.
        // If an unpredictable error occurs, the loop sets the bTerminate
        // flag, this procedure ends quickly, and it kills the program
        // on its way out.
   bConnected = FALSE;
```

PipeThread embeds the CreateFile command in a while loop that runs until CreateFile returns a valid handle. The loop begins with a WaitNamedPipe command, causing the thread to block waiting for an available instance. WaitNamed-Pipe does not, however, initiate the connection; CreateFile does that.

```
      while( ! bConnected && ! bTerminate )
      {
            // wait for a pipe instance to become available
         WaitNamedPipe( szBuffer, NMPWAIT_WAIT_FOREVER );
```

Between the execution of the WaitNamedPipe command and the execution of CreateFile, the system can schedule another thread that grabs the pipe for itself. If that happens, CreateFile will fail even though WaitNamedPipe returned TRUE. If CreateFile fails during PipeThread, the while loop notices the error and tries again. If CreateFile produces an error message indicating any problem other than busy pipes, the loop sets the bTerminate flag, and the process ends a few lines later.

```
        // open the named pipe for reading
   hPipeRead = CreateFile( szBuffer,        // name of pipe
                     GENERIC_READ,    // access mode
                     0,               // share mode
                     NULL,            // security descriptor
                     OPEN_EXISTING,   // don't create new object
                     FILE_ATTRIBUTE_NORMAL, // file attributes
                     NULL );                 // file from which
                                             // to copy attributes
        // check that the pipe's handle is valid
   if( hPipeRead == INVALID_HANDLE_VALUE )
   {
```

```
        // If CreateFile failed simply because other waiting threads
        // grabbed pipe, don't bother user with error message.
    if( GetLastError() != ERROR_PIPE_BUSY )
    {
            // an unpredictable error occurred; show message
        ShowErrorMsg();
        bTerminate = TRUE;              // break loop; end program
    }
}
else
    bConnected = TRUE;                  // succeeded in connecting
}
```

When the client child successfully links to the server parent, the procedure updates the window caption and enters another loop to wait for messages to arrive through the pipe. The receiving loop ends when the user chooses Exit from the child's menu or when the child receives an IDM_TERMINATE command from the parent.

```
    // change window caption to show this window is connected
wsprintf( szBuffer, szTitle, (LPSTR)" (connected)" );
SetWindowText( hwndMain, szBuffer );
```

To read messages from the parent, the DoRead procedure calls ReadFile. It needs no revisions to work with a named pipe.

```
    // read messages from the pipe until we receive a terminate command
while( ! bTerminate )
    DoRead( hPipeRead );
    // when bTerminate is TRUE, end the program
FORWARD_WM_DESTROY( hwndMain, PostMessage );
return( 0L );                                   // implicit ExitThread()
UNREFERENCED_PARAMETER( lpThreadData );
}
```

This chapter described how parent and child processes interact and how pipes allow processes to communicate. The demos discussed here also introduced the GetLastError and FormatMessage functions for signaling to the user when something goes wrong. Later in this part (in Chapter 18), you'll learn about structured exception handling, a more advanced mechanism for dealing with unexpected failures.

In the next chapter, we'll look at another aspect of threads, where ATL COM objects are used for multithreading. We'll also examine how to use ActiveX components.

CHAPTER

SIXTEEN

16

ATL COM Objects and ActiveX Controls

- Common Object Model (COM) basics

- Active Template Library (ATL) support for COM objects

- ActiveX component basics

- Developer Studio's ATL COM AppWizard

- ActiveX (OCX) control development

The Common Object Model (COM), Active Template Library (ATL), and ActiveX are three separate but interrelated topics of interest to application developers. Unfortunately, a single chapter—or even an entire book—cannot provide a truly comprehensive view of these subjects.

Having made this disclaimer, I will try to provide a useful overview of all three of these topics, together with an example of developing an ActiveX control using ATL and COM. You can use the information presented in this chapter as guidelines and suggestions for your own development projects.

An Overview of COM

COM is the "object model" used as the basis for ActiveX and OLE objects. COM permits an object to expose its functionality to other components and to host applications. It defines both how the object exposes itself and how the exposure works—across processes and across networks. In addition, COM defines the life cycle of the object.

COM is a standard, not an object-oriented language. As such, COM does not impose specifications on how an application should be structured, leaving the details of language and implementation to the programmer. COM specifies an object model and programming requirements that enable COM objects (a.k.a., *OLE components* or simply *objects*) to interact with other objects.

Interacting objects may exist within a single process, may be in different processes, or may even be on different machines and have been written in different languages. Thus, COM is referred to as a binary standard—a standard that applies after a program has been translated to binary machine code.

COM Requirements

The single language requirement for COM is that the code must be generated using a language that supports pointer structures and—explicitly or implicitly—can call functions through pointers. This includes object-oriented languages that provide programming mechanisms, such as C++ and Smalltalk, which simplify the implementation of COM objects, as well as non-object-oriented languages, such as Ada, BASIC, C, Java, and Pascal.

In general, a software object consists of a set of data and functions that manipulate the data. A COM object is simply one in which access to the data elements is achieved exclusively through one or more sets of related functions (*methods*), known as *interfaces*. Also, COM requires that the methods belonging to an interface must be accessible only through a pointer to the interface.

In addition to imposing the basic binary object standard, COM also defines a set of basic interfaces providing functions common to all COM objects as well as a small number of APIs required by all components. Furthermore, COM defines how objects interact over a distributed environment and includes security features to ensure system and component integrity.

COM Concepts and Terminology

Before learning how to create COM objects, you should understand some of the concepts and terms used for COM objects.

Interfaces

Interfaces are the mechanisms exposing the functionality of a COM object to the outside applications. In COM, an interface is a table of pointers (similar to a C++ vtable) to functions implemented by the object. An object may expose multiple interfaces, offering different sets of properties for different purposes.

Each object interface is based on the fundamental COM interface, IUnknown, where the IUnknown methods allow navigation to other interfaces exposed by the object. (IUnknown is described next.)

Each interface receives a unique interface ID (IID), making it easy to support new interface versions. The COM, OLE, and ActiveX interfaces each have predefined IIDs.

IUnknown

IUnknown provides the base interface for all COM functions, including those made public through the Interfaces member. IUnknown defines three methods: QueryInterface, AddRef, and Release. QueryInterface allows an interface user to ask the object for a pointer to another one of its interfaces. The AddRef and Release functions implement reference counting on the interface. The following sections describe querying for an interface and reference counting.

Querying for an Interface

QueryInterface is the method used to query an object for a specific interface (request a pointer to a specific interface). Although there are mechanisms by which an object can express the functionality it provides statically (before it is instantiated), the fundamental COM mechanism is to use the IUnknown Query-Interface method.

Since all interfaces are derived from IUnknown, every interface has an implementation of QueryInterface that queries an object, using the IID of the interface, to retrieve a pointer to the interface. If the requested interface is supported, QueryInterface returns a pointer while also calling the AddRef method. If the requested interface is not supported, QueryInterface returns the E_NOINTERFACE error code.

Reference Counting

Reference counting allows an object (or, more accurately, the interface) to determine when it is no longer being used and, therefore, when it is free to remove (close) itself from memory.

An object is not automatically removed from memory by COM when COM believes that the object is no longer being used. Instead, the application calling the object is responsible for calling the IUnknown AddRef and Release methods to maintain the reference interface count for an object. Here's how this works:

- When a client receives an interface pointer to a COM object, the client is responsible for calling the AddRef member to increment the reference count.

- When the client is finished with the COM object, the client is expected to call the Release method to decrement the reference count.

- When the reference count reaches zero, the interface is no longer used by anyone and, finally, is free to remove itself from memory.

Reference counting may also be implemented to count each reference to an object rather than references to an individual interface. In this usage, each AddRef and Release call is delegated to a central implementation of the object, and a call to Release frees the entire object when the reference count reaches zero.

Marshaling

Marshaling is the mechanism that permits objects to be used across threads, across processes, and across boundaries—permitting location independence. Marshaling allows interfaces that have been exposed by an object in one process to be used by another process. In marshaling, COM provides code (or uses code from the interface developer) to package a method's parameters in a format that can be shared across processes (or across machines) and to unpack those parameters for the remote process.

Marshaling is not required when an object interface is used in the same process as the object. However, marshaling may be required between threads.

Containment and Aggregation

Aggregation is the mechanism that allows one object to make use of another object. For example, an object's developer might wish to have an object take advantage of services provided by another, prebuilt object and, of course, want that object to appear as a natural part of the prebuilt one. COM provides these services through containment and aggregation.

By using containment and aggregation, the containing (outer) object creates the contained (inner) object as a part of its own creation process. When this is done, the contained object's interfaces are exposed by the containing object.

Any object may be aggregatable or not but, if an object is aggregatable, the object must follow the rules for aggregation before it will work properly. Also, all `IUnknown` method calls to the contained object must be delegated to the containing object.

An Overview of the ATL

The ATL (Active Template Library) is a set of template-based C++ classes with which you can easily create small, fast COM objects. It has special support for key COM features, including the following:

- Stock implementations of `IUnknown`, `IClassFactory`, `IClassFactory2`, and `IDispatch`
- Dual interfaces

- Standard COM enumerator interfaces
- Connection points
- Tear-off interfaces
- ActiveX controls

Also, ATL code can be used for single-threaded objects, apartment-model objects, and free-threaded objects.

The ATL is supplied as source code that is included in an application. A DLL (ATL.DLL), which contains code that can be shared across components, is also available. However, the ATL.DLL is optional and is not required for ATL-produced components.

Template Libraries versus Standard C++ Libraries

A template is similar to a macro and, like a macro, when a template is invoked, it expands—with parameter substitution—to provide the initial code for an application or a set of classes. However, unlike macros, templates also permit the creation of new classes—based on types passed as parameters—that implement type-safe methods of performing operations expressed in the template code.

The ATL differs from traditional C++ class libraries in the following ways:

- The ATL is supplied only as source code or with minimal supporting run-time code.
- The ATL is not inherently hierarchical in nature.
- With ATL, a descendant class is not derived from an existing class to inherit existing functionality. With ATL templates, a new class is instantiated, and this class does not depend on previous class libraries.

ATL versus MFC

When you are developing components and applications, you have a choice between using MFC or using ATL.

The advantage of ATL is that it is a fast, easy method of creating a COM component in C++ while maintaining a small footprint. The ATL should be used when you do not need the extensive functionality provided by MFC.

On the other hand, MFC provides full support for applications, ActiveX controls, and active documents. If a control has already been created using MFC, you should continue its development with MFC.

An Overview of ActiveX Components

ActiveX is an open platform used principally to develop application components for use on the Internet or on internal company (*intranet*) networks. Types of ActiveX components include the following:

- ActiveX controls (previously called OLE controls) are objects that can be included in Web pages or in other ActiveX control containers. ActiveX controls include everything from buttons to graphic charts to stock and news tickers.

- ActiveX documents are documents that can be displayed by Web browsers and other ActiveX document viewers. Previously, embedded document objects were limited to a single page and were shown embedded within the host document. In contrast, ActiveX documents may be displayed full-frame within the entire client area window and do not have size restrictions.

- ActiveX Server frameworks permit extending Web servers to provide customized Web pages displaying content from databases or other sources. The MFC ISAPI classes offer the basis for writing custom server extensions and filters.

- Internet Data Download Services can be used to download data using HTTP, FTP, and Gopher protocols. Use the MFC `WinInet` classes to abstract the TCP/IP and Winsock protocols, to perform downloads without blocking, and to render large objects asynchronously.

- Active Scripts, created with VBScript or other scripting languages, permit you to connect controls and add interactive functionality to Web pages. The advantage is that scripting moves the processing from the server to the client system. For example, form entries can be validated on the client side before being returned to the server.

As you can see from this list, ActiveX controls offer a wide variety of possible uses.

Using the ATL COM AppWizard

With Visual C++/Developer Studio, you can create an ActiveX component by using the ATL COM AppWizard. As an introduction to the basics of ActiveX component development, we will build a custom control. The first step is to start a new project. Then we will create and implement the ActiveX control.

Building a Project with the ATL COM AppWizard

To use the ATL COM AppWizard, follow these steps:

1. Open the Developer Studio, select File ➢ New, and click the Projects tab. The ATL COM AppWizard appears in the list of projects, as shown in Figure 16.1.

FIGURE 16.1:

Creating an ATL COM AppWizard project

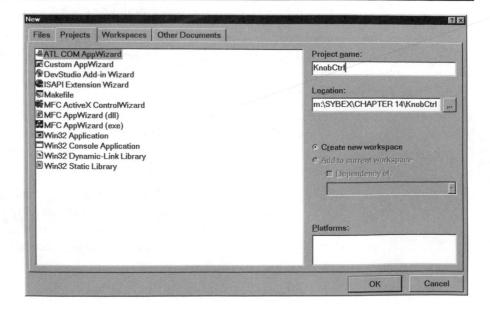

2. In the Project Name box, enter the name **KnobCtrl** for this example. In the Location box, select the location (drive/directory) where you want to store the project. Then click OK. The ATL COM AppWizard displays a dialog box showing options that apply to your ATL project, as shown in Figure 16.2. Options include three server types:

    -   Dynamic Link Library (DLL), for an in-process server

    -   Executable (EXE), for a local, out-of-process server

    -   Service (EXE), a Windows NT service executed in the background when NT is started

FIGURE 16.2:

Choosing ATL project options

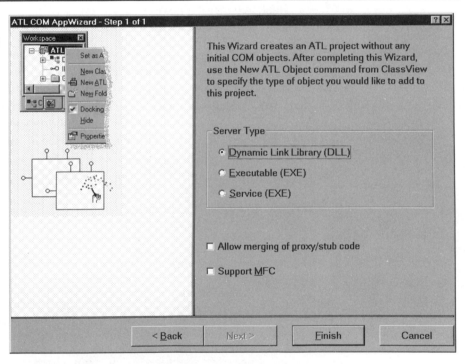

3. Because we are designing a control, choose DLL as the server type. A control must always be an in-process server. Controls are not intended to act alone; as an in-process server, the control is able to communicate with the application using it. The ATL COM AppWizard offers two other options that are useful in particular situations:

    -   If you need marshaling of interfaces, you might want to select the Allow Merging of Proxy/Stub Code option. When you select this option, the MIDL-generated proxy and stub code is included in the same DLL as the server. We won't use marshaling in our example.

- If you expect to need MFC functionality, such as the `CString` class, select the Support MFC option. For this example, to keep a minimal footprint, we'll forego MFC support.

4. Click Finish to generate the project. The AppWizard will create the project and display information about it.

5. When the project is built, in addition to release and debug configuration choices, you also have the option of generating a MinSize or MinDependency configuration. The MinSize option generates a smaller component using shared code from the ATL.DLL library, but this requires distributing ATL.DLL with your component. The MinDependency option generates a larger component, because all the necessary code is linked in the component, but the ATL.DLL library is not required. For this example, choose Min-Dependency.

The ATL COM AppWizard generates a number of files for a project. These files and their contents are listed in Table 16.1.

TABLE 16.1: Files Generated by the ATL COM AppWizard

File	Description
KnobCtrl.CPP	Implementation file; contains implementation code for `DllMain`, `DllCan-UnloadNow`, `DllGetClassObject`, `DllRegisterServer`, and `DllUnregister-Server`, as well as the object map (a list of the ATL objects in the project). The object map is initially blank (because no objects have been created yet).
KnobCtrl.DEF	Standard Windows module definition file for the DLL.
KnobCtrl.DSW	Project workspace file.
KnobCtrl.DSP	Project settings file.

Continued on next page

TABLE 16.1 (CONTINUED): Files Generated by the ATL COM AppWizard

File	Description
KnobCtrl.IDL	Interface Definition Language (IDL) file; describes the interfaces specific to objects.
KnobCtrl.RC	Resource file; initially contains version information and a string containing the project name.
Resource.H	Header for resource file.
KnobCtrlps.MK	Make file to build a proxy/stub DLL (not needed).
KnobCtrlps.DEF	Module definition file for proxy/stub DLL (not needed).
StdAfx.CPP	File with #include statements for ATL implementation files.
StdAfx.H	File with #include statements for ATL header files.

At this point, the KnobCtrl ActiveX object is simply a skeleton, with no functionality beyond the bare minimum necessary to compile and link. Our next step is to start the ATL Object Wizard to add an object or a control to the project.

Adding Objects and Controls

You can start the ATL Object Wizard in several ways:

- With an ATL project open, select Insert ➢ New ATL Object from the menu.

- Select the Class View tab from the project workspace, right-click the topmost classes folder, and select New ATL Object from the pop-up menu.

- With the WizardBar visible, click the Actions drop-down list and select New ATL Object.

- Click the New ATL Object button on the ATL toolbar.

Any of these methods brings up the ATL Object Wizard window, as shown in Figure 16.3.

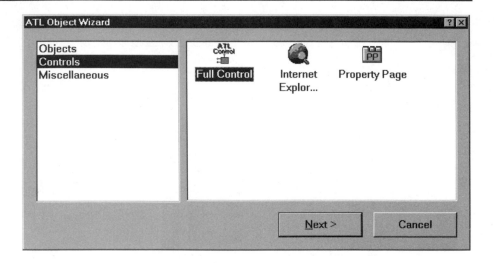

On the left side of the window, the ATL Object Wizard offers three object categories: Objects, Controls, and Miscellaneous. On the right side of the window, the Wizard displays icons for the objects in the selected category. Table 16.2 lists the objects in each category.

TABLE 16.2: ATL Objects in the ATL Object Wizard

Object	Description
Objects Category	
Simple object	A minimal COM object.
Internet Explorer object	An object supporting the interfaces needed by Internet Explorer, but without user-interface support.
Add-in object	A COM object that extends the Developer Studio shell with custom toolbar buttons and event handling. (This is the same functionality available with the Developer Studio Add-in Wizard on the Developer Studio File ➤ New Projects tab.)
ActiveX Server component	An object used by the Active Server Pages feature of an Internet Information Server (IIS).

Continued on next page

TABLE 16.2 (CONTINUED): ATL Objects in the ATL Object Wizard

Object	Description
Objects Category (continued)	
Microsoft Transaction Server component	A component that includes header files needed by the Transaction Server and defines an object as non-aggregatable.
Component Registrar object*	An object that implements the `IComponentRegistrar` interface and can be used to register any objects in an in-process server that declare the `DECLARE_OBJECT_DESCRIPTION` macro.
Controls Category	
Full control	An object that supports the interfaces for all containers.
Internet Explorer control	An object that supports the interfaces needed by Internet Explorer. This object includes user-interface support.
Property page	An object that implements a property page.
Miscellaneous Category	
Dialog	An object that implements a dialog box.

*This object is used to register or unregister objects individually (in contrast to `DllRegisterServer` and `DllUnregisterServer`, which register and unregister all objects in the server). A list of objects in the server and descriptions are available through the `IComponent-Registrar::GetComponents` method.

You can add multiple COM objects to a project and, for each object, the ATL Object Wizard will generate .CPP and .H files, as well as an .RGS file for script-based registry support. (The .RGS file contains information to be used to register the COM object on the system where it will be used.)

To add an object or a control using the ATL Object Wizard, double-click the control or object you want to insert. The ATL Object Wizard will display a dialog box showing options that apply to the selected object or control.

For this example, select a Full Control object. You will see the ATL Object Wizard Properties dialog box, as shown in Figure 16.4.

FIGURE 16.4:

The Names tab of the ATL
Object Wizard Properties
dialog box

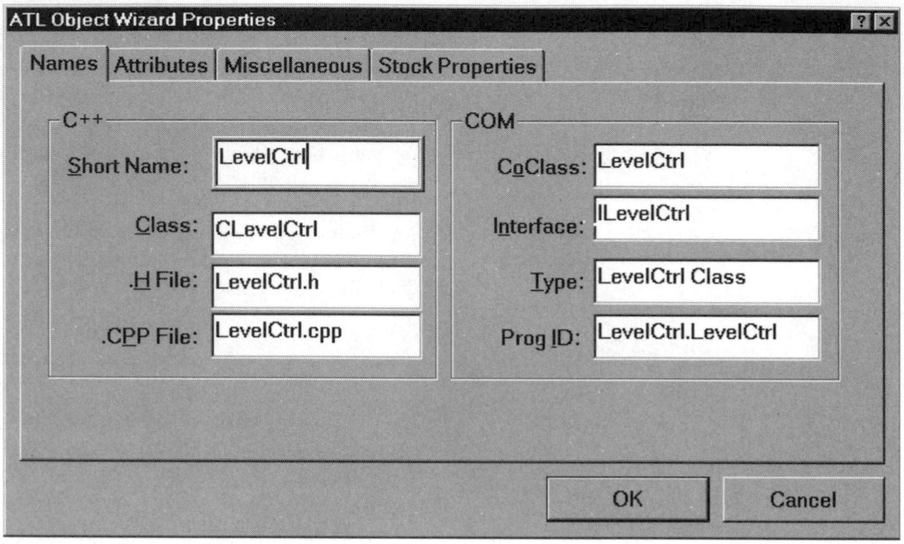

Setting Object Properties

In the Properties dialog box, you specify object names, attributes, and other properties for the COM object. The tabs and options in the dialog box vary depending on the type of object or control you selected.

Specifying Names   Use the Names tab to specify object and class names and enter description strings. This tab (shown in Figure 16.4) has the following options:

> **Short Name**   By default, the short name becomes the root for all of the other names entered on the Names tab. For this example, enter the short name **LevelCtrl**. If the automatically generated entries are not satisfactory, you can supply custom class, file, and COM names for the object.
>
> **Class**   The name of the class implementing the COM object.
>
> **.H File**   The header file for the object class implementation.
>
> **.CPP File**   The source file for the object class implementation.
>
> **CoClass**   The component class containing the list of interfaces supported by the object.

Interface   The name for the interface for this object. The interface will contain custom methods for this object class. For most objects and components, the Wizard creates an interface with the name specified. For Property Page objects, no custom interface is created, and the Wizard assigns IUnknown as the object interface. Dialog objects do not create an interface.

Type   A description string for the object, which is placed in the registry.

ProgID   An alternate name for containers to use in place of the object's CLSID (CLaSsID).

Setting Attributes   The Attributes tab of the ATL Object Wizard Properties dialog box contains options for the object's threading model, interface type, and aggregation support, as shown in Figure 16.5.

FIGURE 16.5:

The Attributes tab of the ATL Object Wizard Properties dialog box

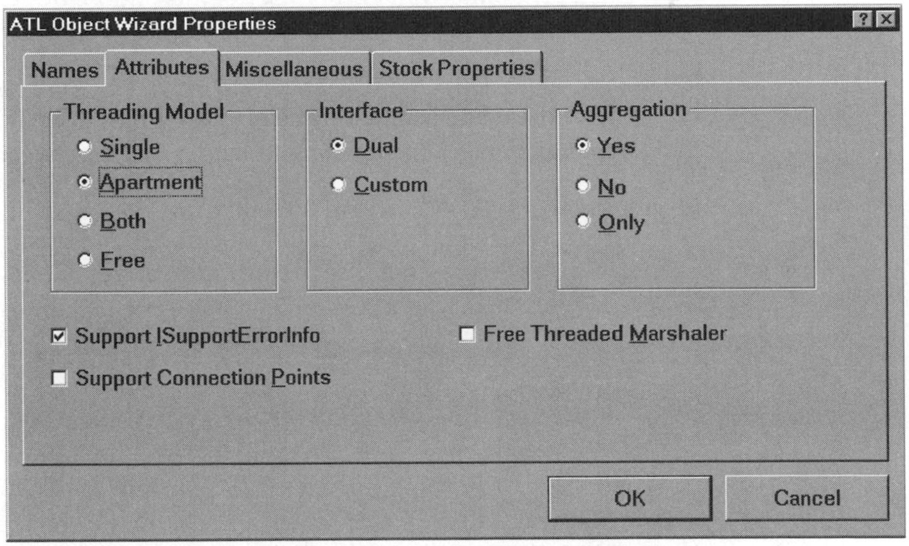

This tab contains the following choices:

Threading Model   Choose from the supported threading models: Single, Apartment (the default), and Free Threaded. You can also use a combination of the Single and Apartment models by selecting the Both option.

Interface   The Dual option (the default) allows the object's interfaces to be derived from both IDispatch and from custom methods (the vtable has both custom-interface functions and late-binding IDispatch methods), which permits both COM clients and Automation controllers to access the object. The Custom option derives the object's interfaces from IUnknown (the vtable has custom-interface functions but no IDispatch methods). The advantage of a custom interface is faster operation, especially across process boundaries.

Aggregation   Select Yes for normal instantiation or Only if the object should be instantiated only when being aggregated. Select No if you do not wish interfaces from the inner object to be exposed as if they were interfaces of the outer objects.

Support | SupportErrorInfo   Select this option to have the object implement the ISupportErrorInfo interface for error reporting.

Support Connection Points   Select this option to add connection point support. The object class will be automatically derived from IConnection-PointContainerImpl.

Free Threaded Marshaler   Select this option to create a free-threaded marshaler object to marshal interface pointers between threads in the same process.

Setting Appearance and Execution Attributes   The Miscellaneous tab, shown in Figure 16.6, provides several options for the appearance and execution of the object.

This tab contains the following options:

View Status   The Opaque option makes the control completely opaque; none of the container is visible behind the control object. This setting allows the container to draw the control faster. The Solid Background option, which is relevant only if the Opaque option is selected, sets the control background to a solid color rather than a pattern.

Misc Status   The Invisible option makes the control invisible at runtime. Invisible controls can be used to perform operations in the background, such as firing events at timed intervals. The Acts Like Button option enables the control to act like a button—specifically, to display itself as the default button based on the ambient property DisplayAsDefault. The Acts Like Label option enables the control to replace the container's native label.

FIGURE 16.6:

The Miscellaneous tab of the ATL Object Wizard Properties dialog box

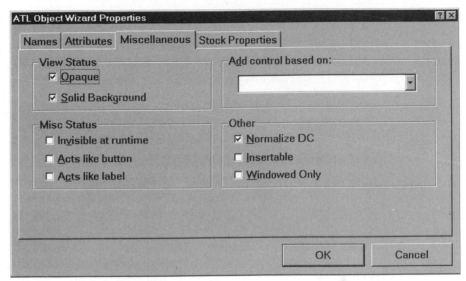

Add Control Based On   Use this option to superclass one of the standard window classes. The drop-down list contains window class names defined by Windows. When you select one of these, the ATL Object Wizard adds a CContainedWindow member variable to the control's class. CContained-Window::Create will superclass the window class specified.

Other   The Normalize DC option creates a normalized device context when called to draw itself. This standardizes the control's appearance but is less efficient. The Insertable option has the control appear in the application's Insert Object dialog box (in applications that support embedded objects, such as Microsoft Word and Microsoft Excel), allowing the object to be inserted through that dialog box. The Windowed Only option forces the control to be windowed, even in containers that support windowless objects. If this option is not selected, the control will automatically be windowless in containers that support windowless objects, and automatically be windowed in containers that do not support windowless objects.

Setting Stock Properties   In the Stock Properties tab, shown in Figure 16.7, select the stock properties you want the object to support, such as Caption or Border Color. You can select all the stock properties at once by clicking the >> button.

FIGURE 16.7:

The Stock Properties tab of the ATL Object Wizard Properties dialog box

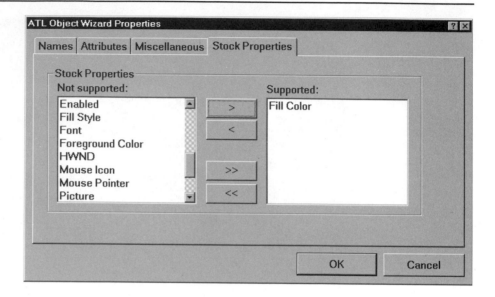

For the LevelCtrl object, select only the Fill Color property. This property will be used to change the fill color while drawing the control. All other drawing properties required for this control are supported without explicit selection.

Entering Strings for Property Page Objects   The ATL Object Wizard Properties dialog box for Property Page objects includes a Strings tab. In this tab, you enter names for the Property Page object, as follows:

Title   The text that appears on the property page's tab.

Doc String   The text string that describes the page. The property frame may use this description in a status line or tooltip (currently, the standard property frame does not use this string).

Helpfile   The name of the associated help file. This entry should be the simple name without a path. When Help is selected, the frame opens the help file in the directory named in the HelpDir key in the property page registry entries under the object's CLSID.

Selecting Add-in Object Features For Add-in objects, the dialog box includes an Add-in tab. On this tab, you can select the following features for the Add-in object:

> **Provide Toolbar** Use this option to create a toolbar button to carry out a command added by the Add-in object.
>
> **Command Name** The name of the command added to Developer Studio by the Add-in object. This name appears in the list on the Add-ins and Macro Files tab on the Tools menu's Customize option.
>
> **Method Name** The name of the method implementing the command.
>
> **Toolbar Text** The text to appear on the toolbar button.
>
> **Status Bar Text** The status bar prompt that appears when the Add-in command is executed.
>
> **Tool Tips Text** The text to appear in the tooltip message for the toolbar button.
>
> **Application Events** Choose this option to allow the Add-in object to catch application events.
>
> **Debugger Events** Choose this option to allow the Add-in object to catch debugger events.

Selecting ActiveX Server Object Features The ATL Object Wizard Properties dialog box for ActiveX Servers includes an ASP tab. This tab contains the OnStartPage/OnEndPage option, which is selected by default, to add the OnStartPage and OnEndPage methods to the object. You can choose which intrinsic objects will be available as member pointers in the object's class. By default, each intrinsic object is selected.

Selecting Transaction Server Component Features For Microsoft Transaction Server components, the MTX tab includes options for the interface implementation (Dual or Custom) and support for connection points. These options are the same as the ones in the Attributes tab for other kinds of objects. In addition, the MTX tab has two unique options:

> **Support IObjectControl** This option provides access to the three IObjectControl methods: Activate, CanBePooled, and Deactivate.

CanBePooled   Select this option to tell the Transaction Server runtime environment that the object should be returned to an instance pool after deactivation, rather than destroyed. This option cannot be selected unless the Support IObjectControl option is selected.

Reviewing the Source and Header Files

At this point, we have exhausted the ATL Object Wizard property options. Now we're ready to proceed by creating the LevelCtrl object using the KnobCtrl and LevelCtrl source and header files that the AppWizard and the ATL Object Wizard have created for us.

For the sample LevelCtrl and KnobCtrl objects, the AppWizard has created four new source files:

LevelCtrl.H	Header (and implementation) for the `CLevelCtrl` class
LevelCtrl.CPP	Skeleton source code for the `CLevelCtrl` class
LevelCtrl.RGS	Text file containing a registry script to register the control
LevelCtrl.HTM	HTML file containing the source for a Web page that contains a reference to the newly created control, used for testing the control in Netscape or Internet Explorer

The ATL Object Wizard made several changes to the code in existing source files:

- An `#include` was added to the StdAfx.H and StdAfx.CPP files to include the ATL files necessary for controls.

- The registry script LevelCtrl.RGS was added to the project resource.

- KnobCtrl.IDL was changed to include details of the new control.

- The new control was added to the object map in KnobCtrl.CPP.

Since we really haven't done anything to customize the control yet, we can reliably expect the application to compile without errors. However, we still need to test the results.

NOTE   Two versions of the *LevelCtrl* ActiveX control are included on the CD accompanying this book. The differences between the *LevelCtrl* and *LevelCtrl2* versions are in how the control draws the pointer and markers but, functionally, the two are the same.

Testing an ActiveX (OLE) Control

Unlike with conventional applications, you cannot simply click the Execute or Debug button in Developer Studio and watch your ActiveX control pop open and run. Instead, you have two options:

- You can use the .HTM page prepared by the AppWizard together with Netscape or Internet Explorer to view the compiled control.

- You can call the ActiveX Control Test Container (accessed from the Tools menu).

The ActiveX Control Test Container is not elaborate, but it does provide a convenient platform for testing a control. Select Tools ➤ ActiveX Control Test Container and click the Insert button (leftmost button on the toolbar) to display the Insert OLE Control dialog box. This dialog box lists the registered objects, as shown in Figure 16.8.

FIGURE 16.8:

The Insert OLE Control dialog box in the ActiveX Control Test Container

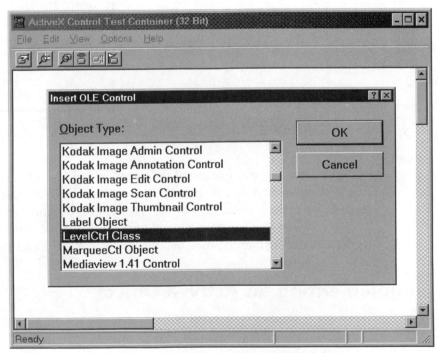

The LevelCtrl object was registered automatically when the project was compiled. To test it, simply scroll down the list, highlight the control, and click the OK button. In response, the LevelCtrl control is activated and appears in the ActiveX Control Test Container window, as shown in Figure 16.9.

FIGURE 16.9:

A first version of the LevelCtrl ActiveX control

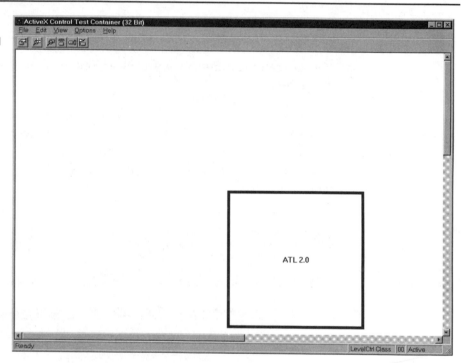

As you can see, this first cut of the LevelCtrl object is not much to look at. But, remember, we have not yet provided any type of drawing instructions or control actions. What you see in Figure 16.9 is simply the default control provided by the ATL Object Wizard. And while it isn't much, it is enough to demonstrate the default handling and to prove that we have compiled a working ActiveX control.

Implementing an ActiveX Object

Now we're ready to go in and write some real code of our own and make the LevelCtrl object do something for us. First, of course, we need to have some idea of what we intend this control to do. Here, the purpose selected for the LevelCtrl object is to emulate an old-fashioned volume control knob—the kind that might be found on an old radio or stereo—and to return a level setting, in the range 0 to 19.

We could implement this control in several fashions. For one, we could have the pointer track the mouse as long as the mouse button is down. Or, for another, we could require clicking the pointer and then dragging it around to set the level.

But, for now, let's keep it simple: A mouse click on the right of the control to increment; a click on the left to decrement. Not to leave well enough alone, clicking the secondary mouse button functions in the exact opposite fashion, but that's a minor provision.

Implementing the object requires three main steps:

- Add a property to the control (for our example, a level that can be incremented and decremented).

- Add drawing code to show what the control is doing.

- Add events to respond to the mouse so that the user can operate the control.

Adding a Property

The first provision, before we can set a level, is to add a property to the object to contain the level. To add a property, right-click the ILevelCtrl class under the KnobCtrl classes list to bring up the pop-up actions menu, as shown here:

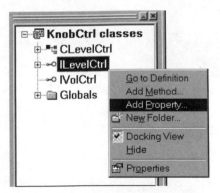

From the menu, select the Add Property option to display the Add Property to Interface dialog box, as shown in Figure 16.10. In the dialog box, the Return Type setting has defaulted to HRESULT and is not a selectable item. The Property Type setting shows short as the return value for this control, although you can choose another type from the drop-down list. The Property Name setting shows the member variable designation as m_nLevel. Normally, these defaults should remain unchanged since they are established by the object itself.

In the Function Type group, both the Get Function and Put Function options should be selected, providing methods to retrieve the value set and to pass an initial value. The Implementation box shows the provisional implementation for the Get and Put functions. Also in this group, as a default, the PropPut option is selected. This function returns a copy of the object, which is the most common method of making the property writable. The alternative, PropPutRef, returns a reference to the object rather than the object itself. This option is useful for objects that have significant initialization overhead, such as structures and arrays.

Having selected these provisions, the next step is to click the Attributes button to display the Edit Attributes dialog box, shown in Figure 16.11.

FIGURE 16.11:

The Edit Attributes dialog box

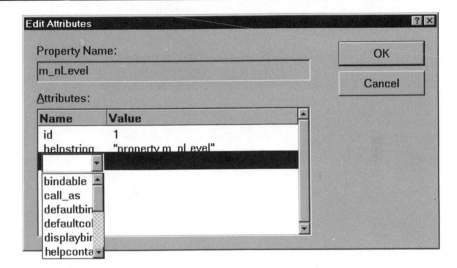

In the Edit Attributes dialog box, the Attributes list box shows the property id and helpstring entries, which were generated automatically when the property (member variable) was created. From the Edit Attributes dialog box, you can expand on these defaults or change them, as well as add other attributes. To add an attribute, choose one from the drop-down list (shown in Figure 16.11), and enter a value for the attribute, if necessary.

Modifying the Code: First Changes By creating a property member for the ActiveX control, MIDL (the program that compiles IDL files) defines a Get method to retrieve the new property and a Put method to set the property. When MIDL compiles the file, these two methods are automatically defined in the interface by prepending put_ and get_ to the property name; in this case, creating the put_m_nLevel and get_m_nLevel functions.

These two functions appear in the LevelCtrl.IDL file as:

```
[propget, id(1), helpstring("property m_nLevel")]
    HRESULT m_nLevel([out, retval] short *pVal);
[propput, id(1), helpstring("property m_nLevel")]
    HRESULT m_nLevel([in] short newVal);
```

They appear in the LevelCtrl.H header as:

```
STDMETHOD(get_m_nLevel)(/*[out, retval]*/ short *pVal);
STDMETHOD(put_m_nLevel)(/*[in]*/ short newVal);
```

They appear in the LevelCtrl.CPP source as:

```
STDMETHODIMP CLevelCtrl::get_m_nLevel(short * pVal)
{
    return S_OK;
}

STDMETHODIMP CLevelCtrl::put_m_nLevel(short newVal)
{
    return S_OK;
}
```

Notice that the implementations of the two functions are empty shells. They do nothing until you provide some functionality.

Before you can do any kind of set or retrieve operation, you need to specify a place to store the value. In the LevelCtrl.H header, add a member variable as:

```
short m_nLevel;
```

Then you can implement the get_m_nLevel and put_m_nLevel methods as follows:

```
STDMETHODIMP CLevelCtrl::get_m_nLevel(short * pVal)
{
    *pVal = m_nLevel;
    return S_OK;
}
```

The get_m_nLevel function simply returns the m_nLevel member via the pVal pointer.

The put_m_nLevel method imposes a limit test, insisting on a value greater than or equal to zero and less than or equal to INCREMENTS. (The INCREMENTS constant is defined in LevelCtrl.CPP with a value of 20.)

```
STDMETHODIMP CLevelCtrl::put_m_nLevel(short newVal)
{
    if( newVal < 0 || newVal >= INCREMENTS )
        return Error( _T("Value must be in the range 0..19") );
    m_nLevel = newVal;
    return S_OK;
}
```

You need to impose this test because, even though this function accepts only a value, it is possible to call this function—through the interface—and enter a value directly. And, actually, if you put this control to use, you might very well expect exactly that to happen—before displaying the control, an application would expect to be able to set (display) an existing level.

When an invalid value is passed, the ATL Error function places an error message in the IErrorInfo interface. This error is not displayed to the user but is available if the container wishes to report more about the error than the returned HRESULT.

NOTE   Instead of reporting an error, an alternative is to simply provide code to limit the value supplied if it is out of range. This is what we'll do when we implement the control, a bit later in the chapter.

We now have a property, m_nLevel, and methods to set and retrieve the property. The next step is to do something with it.

Drawing the Control

The drawing code initially provided by the AppWizard isn't exactly exciting. As illustrated earlier in Figure 16.9, the drawn control is simply a rectangle with a caption in the center. The default code is:

```
HRESULT CLevelCtrl::OnDraw( ATL_DRAWINFO& di )
{
    RECT& rc = *(RECT*)di.prcBounds;
    Rectangle(di.hdcDraw, rc.left, rc.top, rc.right, rc.bottom);
    DrawText(di.hdcDraw, _T("ATL 2.0"), -1, &rc, DT_CENTER |
            DT_VCENTER | DT_SINGLELINE);
    return S_OK;
}
```

You can remedy this with the following steps:

- Remove the DrawText instruction, because there is no point in keeping this label.

- Add instructions for what you actually want to draw. For the knob control, we'll draw a series of small circles in a ring to show the detent positions (the positions where the knob would stop if this were a mechanical stepped control) and a knob pointing at the detent corresponding to the level value. Also, just to make the control a little more interesting visually, we will shade the detent indicators above the level differently from those at and below the level value.

- To clarify the use of the control, we'll add a plus sign (+) on the right side of the control and a minus (–) on the left. At the bottom, we will show the setting as a numerical value.

Here is the code to accomplish this:

```
HRESULT CLevelCtrl::OnDraw( ATL_DRAWINFO& di )
{
    RECT      &rc = *(RECT*) di.prcBounds;
    HDC       hDC = di.hdcDraw;
    COLORREF  colorPointer;
    HBRUSH    hOldBrush, hBrush;
    HPEN      hOldPen,   hPen;
    POINT     ptCenter;
    double    dxRadius, dyRadius, dAngle, dDiff;
    char      szStr;
    long      x, y;

    OleTranslateColor( m_clrFillColor, NULL, &colorPointer );
    hPen = (HPEN)GetStockObject( BLACK_PEN );
    hOldPen = (HPEN)SelectObject( hDC, hPen );
    hBrush = (HBRUSH) GetStockObject( WHITE_BRUSH );
    hOldBrush = (HBRUSH) SelectObject( hDC, hBrush );
    Rectangle( hDC, rc.left, rc.top, rc.right, rc.bottom );
```

We begin by setting up a color—using OleTranslateColor to make sure this will be acceptable to the system where it appears—and create a new pen and a new brush before drawing an outline for the control.

```
    rc.left  += 10;   rc.right  -= 10;
    rc.top   += 10;   rc.bottom -= 10;
```

After drawing the outline, we decrement the rectangle (the area) so that subsequent operations leave a margin on all sides. Since we are not using MFC, all of these operations require a few more instructions than the corresponding MFC code, but this is a small trade-off against the overhead of supporting MFC.

Then, in the reduced space, we position three labels:

```
_itoa( m_nLevel, &szStr, 10 );
DrawText( hDC, &szStr, -1, &rc, DT_RIGHT | DT_BOTTOM | DT_SINGLELINE);
DrawText( hDC, _T("+ "), -1, &rc, DT_RIGHT | DT_TOP | DT_SINGLELINE);
DrawText( hDC, _T(" -"), -1, &rc, DT_LEFT| DT_TOP | DT_SINGLELINE);
```

The next step is to set two member rectangles equal to the entire area (less the margins) and then reduce each of these so that one covers the left side of the area and the other covers the right side.

```
m_rectLeft = m_rectRight = rc;
m_rectLeft.right = m_rectRight.left = rc.left + ( ( rc.right - rc.left ) / 2 );
```

These two rectangles will be used later in response to mouse events to decide which side of the control was clicked.

More immediately, we need to derive a radius and determine a center.

```
dxRadius = ( rc.right - rc.left ) / 2;
dyRadius = ( rc.bottom - rc.top ) / 2;
ptCenter.x = ( rc.left + rc.right ) / 2;
ptCenter.y = ( rc.top + rc.bottom ) / 2;
```

Then we divide the circle into INCREMENT sections to prepare for placing detent (step) indicators in a circle around the control.

```
dAngle    = ( 3 * PI / 2 );
dDiff   = PI / INCREMENTS;
hBrush = (HBRUSH) GetStockObject( BLACK_BRUSH );
for( short i=0; i<INCREMENTS; i++ )
{
    x = (long)( dxRadius * cos( dAngle ) + ptCenter.x + 0.5 ) - 5;
    y = (long)( dyRadius * sin( dAngle ) + ptCenter.y + 0.5 ) - 5;
    Ellipse( hDC, x, y, x+10, y+10 );
    dAngle += 2 * dDiff;
    if( i == m_nLevel )
        SelectObject( hDC, hBrush );
}
```

Notice that, after drawing the detent indicator for the current level, we have changed brushes to complete operations.

The next step is to calculate a set of points that will be used to draw the actual knob and to point it at the appropriate angle.

```
dAngle     = ( 3 * PI / 2 ) + ( ( 2 * PI / INCREMENTS ) * m_nLevel );
m_arrPoint[0].x = (long)( dxRadius * cos( dAngle ) + ptCenter.x + 0.5 );
m_arrPoint[0].y = (long)( dyRadius * sin( dAngle ) + ptCenter.y + 0.5 );
dAngle     += ( PI - dDiff );
m_arrPoint[1].x = (long)( dxRadius * cos( dAngle ) + ptCenter.x + 0.5 );
m_arrPoint[1].y = (long)( dyRadius * sin( dAngle ) + ptCenter.y + 0.5 );
dAngle     += dDiff;
m_arrPoint[2].x = (long)( 3*dxRadius/4 * cos( dAngle ) + ptCenter.x + 0.5 );
m_arrPoint[2].y = (long)( 3*dyRadius/4 * sin( dAngle ) + ptCenter.y + 0.5 );
dAngle     += dDiff;
m_arrPoint[3].x = (long)( dxRadius * cos( dAngle ) + ptCenter.x + 0.5 );
m_arrPoint[3].y = (long)( dyRadius * sin( dAngle ) + ptCenter.y + 0.5 );
```

After calculating the points for the knob, we create a brush and call `Polygon` to draw the shape.

```
hBrush = CreateSolidBrush( colorPointer );
SelectObject( hDC, hBrush );
Polygon( hDC, m_arrPoint, 4 );
```

Last, we do a little cleanup by restoring the original pen and brush and then return S_OK to confirm to the container application that the drawing operation has completed successfully.

```
SelectObject( hDC, hOldPen );
SelectObject( hDC, hOldBrush );
DeleteObject( hBrush );
return S_OK;
}
```

Also, since member variables have been added, as always, it's a good idea to modify the class constructor to ensure that these variables are appropriately initialized. In this case, the constructor method is found in the .H header, not in the .CPP source file.

```
public:
  CLevelCtrl()
  {
    m_nLevel = 0;    // initial setting for level
    m_clrFillColor = RGB( 0, 0xFF, 0 );
  }
```

And that's it. Now we have an ActiveX CLevelCtrl that actually draws a display. The fact that this is all that it does is irrelevant. We'll add mouse-event functionality in a moment.

Note for Release Builds Only

When the ATL COM AppWizard generates the default project, the macro _ATL_MIN_CRT is defined so that the C runtime library does not need to be brought into the ActiveX application if it is not required.

Since the KnobCtrl control needs the C runtime library startup code to initialize the floating-point functions, you will need to remove the _ATL_MIN_CRT macro before building a release version.

To remove the macro, follow these steps:

1. Select Project ➤ Settings. From the Settings For drop-down list, select Multiple Configurations.

2. In the Select Project Configuration(s) to Modify dialog box, click the checkboxes for all four release versions, then click OK.

3. On the Project Settings C/C++ tab, select the General category and remove _ATL_MIN_CRT from the Preprocessor Definitions edit box.

4. On the Link tab, select the Output category to remove DllMain from the Entry-Point Symbol edit box.

Testing the Drawing Operations Now let's see how the control looks after adding the drawing functions and do some more testing. Open the ActiveX Control Test Container (Select Tools ➤ ActiveX Control Test Container) and insert the control. This time, you should see a pointed knob in the control, a ring of small circles, and three text elements, as shown in Figure 16.12.

FIGURE 16.12:

The revised LevelCtrl Object

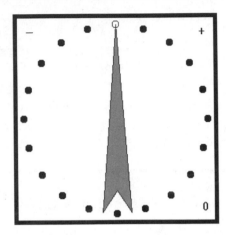

Because we have not yet added any event functionality to the control, we need to use the Invoke Methods option to test it. In the ActiveX Control Test Container, select Edit ➢ Invoke Methods to display the Invoke Control Method dialog box, as shown in Figure 16.13.

FIGURE 16.13:

The Invoke Control Method dialog box

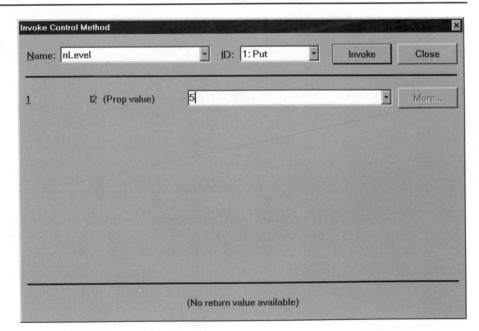

In the Invoke Control Method dialog box, from the Name drop-down list, select the nLevel property. Then, from the ID drop-down list (operations), select the Put method. Next, enter a value (from 0 to 19) in the Prop Value edit box and click the Invoke button.

At this point, the control should not change. Although you have changed the m_nLevel property, you still have not yet supplied any instructions to have the control repaint to display the changed condition.

If you would like to test this yourself, simply iconize the ActiveX Control Test Container and then restore it. Now you should see the pointer in a new position.

To make the control update automatically, you need to add a call to the FireViewChange function.

NOTE   In conventional applications, you're accustomed to calling the Invalidate or InvalidateRect function to cause a redraw operation. However, here you're operating under a different set of strictures, and the FireViewChange is the appropriate means of requesting an update. The FireViewChange function invokes the InvalidateRect API directly.

Rather than modifying the put_m_nLevel function by adding the FireView-Change instruction, we're going to take a more flexible approach. We will create a ChangeLevel function that is called with the new value and invoke the ChangeLevel function from the put_m_nLevel function.

```
.STDMETHODIMP CLevelCtrl::put_m_nLevel(short newVal)
{
    if( newVal < 0 || newVal >= INCREMENTS )
        return Error( _T("Value must be in the range 0..19") );
    ChangeLevel( newVal );
    return S_OK;
}
```

Next, we need to create the ChangeLevel function where, being provident, we will include a test to ensure that the value assigned cannot fall outside the range 0..INCREMENTS-1. Here, we invoke the FireViewChange function to ensure that the control is updated whenever the m_nLevel value changes.

```
void CLevelCtrl::ChangeLevel( short newLevel )
{
    m_nLevel = min( INCREMENTS - 1, max( 0, newLevel ) );
    FireViewChange();
}
```

Now that these changes have been implemented, rebuild the ActiveX Knob-Ctrl control and test it again (using the procedure described at the beginning of this section). This time, when you change the nLevel value, the control should be redrawn immediately.

Still, having to use the Invoke Control Method dialog box to change a value is not exactly what we have in mind for the control. Next, we will add an event to the control.

Adding an Event to a Control

Because we want the ActiveX control to respond to mouse events, we need a method for recognizing the mouse clicks. The COleControl class defines the base event Fire_Click, which is triggered when a mouse event occurs over an ActiveX control. However, our version will be the ClickUp and ClickDn (and the Fire_ClickUp and Fire_ClickDn) methods, which will report an increment or decrement event, respectively, depending on which mouse button is clicked on which side of the control.

Specifying an Event Interface   The first requirement for firing events is to specify an event interface in the library section in the KnobCtrl.IDL file. Unfortunately, there is no wizard to provide this service. You need to make the changes shown below in bold print.

```
library KNOBCTRLLib
{
    importlib("stdole32.tlb");
    importlib("stdole2.tlb");

    [
        uuid(8B946F76-0A74-11D1-85FB-50914CC10000),
        helpstring("Event interface for LevelCtrl")
    ]
    dispinterface _LevelEvents
    {
        properties:
        methods:
            [id(1)] void ClickUp( [in] long x, [in] long y );
            [id(2)] void ClickDn( [in] long x, [in] long y );
```

```
};
[
    uuid(8B946F75-0A74-11D1-85FB-50914CC10000),
    helpstring("LevelCtrl Class")
]
```

WARNING   Pay particular attention to the GUIDs (the *uuid* identifiers) here. When you create your own ActiveX control, the GUIDs will be different and will need to be changed accordingly. In this example, the new GUID (added in bold print) is taken from the GUID immediately following, incrementing the first part of the GUID by 1. The existing GUID begins **8B946F75**-0A74-11D1-85FB-50914CC10000; the new GUID is entered as: **8B946F76**-0A74-11D1-85FB-50914CC10000.

Be careful not to duplicate GUIDs and, most important, do not alter or overwrite the existing GUID. The first GUID also appears elsewhere in the source files (in KnobCtrl.H, KnobCtrl.IDL, KnobCtrl_I.C, KnobCtrl.HTM, and KnobCtrl.RGS) and was entered in the registry when the application was initially compiled.

After recompiling, the new GUID will also appear in multiple files. If you change it in one place, you will also need to find and change all other occurrences of that GUID.

The IDs for the methods, on the other hand, have no special restrictions beyond being unique within the class. In this example, they are simply numbered consecutively.

NOTE   The interface name, **_LevelEvents**, must begin with an underscore. This is a convention indicating that the interface is internal and will not be displayed to the users by programs that permit browsing COM objects.

After you've entered the `ClickUp` and `ClickDn` methods in the interface definition, add another entry (shown in bold print below) to indicate that this is the default source interface.

```
coclass LevelCtrl
{
    [default] interface ILevelCtrl;
    [default, source] dispinterface _LevelEvents;
};
```

```
[
    uuid(8B946F79-0A74-11D1-85FB-50914CC10000),
    helpstring("LevelProp Class")
]
coclass LevelProp
{
    interface IUnknown;
};
};
```

The source attributes indicate that the control is the source for notifications and that this is the interface that the container will call.

After declaring the interface, the next step is to implement a connection point interface and a connection point container interface for the control. You can accomplish this task by using the ATL Proxy Generator to create an interface wrapper.

COM and Connection Points

In COM, events are implemented through connection point mechanisms. To receive an event from a COM object, a container creates an advisory connection to the connection point implemented by the COM object.

Because a COM object may have multiple connection points, COM also implements a connection point container interface that allows the container to determine which connection points are supported. The interface implementing a connection point is called IConnectionPoint; the interface implementing a connection point container is called IConnectionPointContainer.

The ATL provides a proxy generator that generates the IConnectionPoint interface by reading the type library and implementing a function for each event that can be fired.

Creating an Interface Wrapper To simplify programming our ActiveX component, follow these steps to use the ATL Proxy Generator:

1.   Select Project ➤ Add to Project ➤ Components and Controls to display the Components and Controls Gallery dialog box, as shown in Figure 16.14.

FIGURE 16.14:

The Components and Controls Gallery dialog box

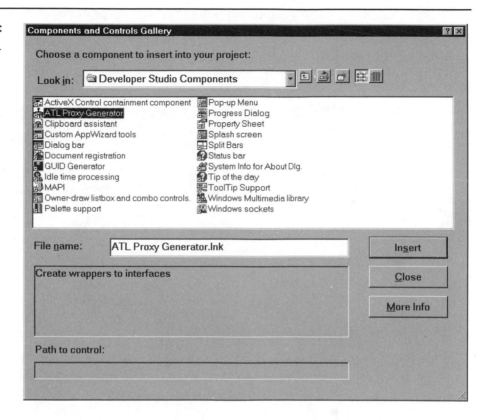

NOTE

You must compile and link (build) the project at least once to create the type library (.TLB) file before you can access the ATL Proxy Generator. Another way to create the TLB file is to right-click the IDL file in the FileView and then select Compile KnobCtrl.IDL from the pop-up menu.

2. In the Look-in drop-down list box, choose Developer Studio Components (the full path is DevStudio/Shared IDE/Gallery/Developer Studio Components) and then select the ATL Proxy Generator.

3. In the ATL Proxy Generator window, click on the button at the right of the TypeLibrary name edit box to display a directory list. By default, the directory list shows TypeLib (.TLB) files in the current project directory. Select the .TLB file for the current project. You will see a list of properties in the Not Selected list box on the right.

4. Choose the property—the _LevelEvents property in this example— and click on the > button to transfer it to the Selected list box on the left, as shown in Figure 16.15. Note that the Connection Point option is selected as the Proxy Type by default.

FIGURE 16.15:

The ATL Proxy Generator window

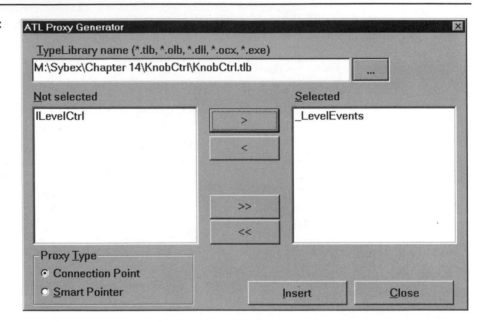

5. Click the Insert button.

Now the CPKnobCtrl.H header file appears in the Files list under External Dependencies. This header file provides an interface wrapper that includes the Fire_ClickUp and Fire_ClickDn methods used for mouse-button events.

Editing the LevelCtrl Files   Next, you need to make some changes to the LevelCtrl.H header file. First, enter an #include statement in the LevelCtrl.H file:

```
#include <math.h>
#include "resource.h"        // main symbols
#include "CPKnobCtrl.h"
```

Now add the CProxy_LevelEvents class to the CLevelCtrl class inheritance list in the LevelCtrl.H file to implement IConnectionPointContainer. ATL supplies an implementation of this interface in the class `IConnectionPointContainerImpl`. Therefore, add these two lines to the `CPolyCtl` class inheritance list in PolyCtl.H:

```
public CProxy_LevelEvents<CLevelCtrl>,
public IConnectionPointContainerImpl<CLevelCtrl>
```

You also want to make the interface `_LevelEvents` the default outgoing interface. To do this, rewrite the exiting `IProvideClassInfo2Impl` declaration in the `CLevelCtrl` class inheritance list in LevelCtrl.H to replace the second parameter, which is initially `NULL`, with `&DIID__LevelEvents`.

Once these changes are accomplished, the `CLevelCtrl` class declaration should look something like this (the changes are shown in bold print):

```
/////////////////////////////////////////////////////////////////////////////
// CLevelCtrl
class ATL_NO_VTABLE CLevelCtrl :
    public CComObjectRootEx<CComSingleThreadModel>,
    public CComCoClass<CLevelCtrl, &CLSID_LevelCtrl>,
    public CComControl<CLevelCtrl>,
    public CStockPropImpl<CLevelCtrl, ILevelCtrl, &IID_ILevelCtrl,
        &LIBID_KNOBCTRLLib>,
    public IProvideClassInfo2Impl<&CLSID_LevelCtrl, &DIID__LevelEvents,
        &LIBID_KNOBCTRLLib>,
    public IPersistStreamInitImpl<CLevelCtrl>,
    public IPersistStorageImpl<CLevelCtrl>,
    public IQuickActivateImpl<CLevelCtrl>,
    public IOleControlImpl<CLevelCtrl>,
    public IOleObjectImpl<CLevelCtrl>,
    public IOleInPlaceActiveObjectImpl<CLevelCtrl>,
    public IViewObjectExImpl<CLevelCtrl>,
    public IOleInPlaceObjectWindowlessImpl<CLevelCtrl>,
    public IDataObjectImpl<CLevelCtrl>,
    public ISupportErrorInfo,
    public ISpecifyPropertyPagesImpl<CLevelCtrl>,
//=== add ===
    public CProxy_LevelEvents<CLevelCtrl>,
    public IConnectionPointContainerImpl<CLevelCtrl>
```

To expose `IConnectionPointContainer` through the `QueryInterface` function, you need to make an entry to the application's COM map. (You do not need to expose `IConnectionPoint` because the client will obtain this interface through

IConnectionPointContainer.) In LevelCtrl.H, add one entry to the end of the
COM map (the changed entry is in bold print):

```
BEGIN_COM_MAP(CLevelCtrl)
    COM_INTERFACE_ENTRY(ILevelCtrl)
    COM_INTERFACE_ENTRY(IDispatch)
    COM_INTERFACE_ENTRY_IMPL(IViewObjectEx)
    COM_INTERFACE_ENTRY_IMPL_IID(IID_IViewObject2, IViewObjectEx)
    COM_INTERFACE_ENTRY_IMPL_IID(IID_IViewObject, IViewObjectEx)
    COM_INTERFACE_ENTRY_IMPL(IOleInPlaceObjectWindowless)
    COM_INTERFACE_ENTRY_IMPL_IID(IID_IOleInPlaceObject,
                                 IOleInPlaceObjectWindowless)
    COM_INTERFACE_ENTRY_IMPL_IID(IID_IOleWindow, IOleInPlaceObjectWindowless)
    COM_INTERFACE_ENTRY_IMPL(IOleInPlaceActiveObject)
    COM_INTERFACE_ENTRY_IMPL(IOleControl)
    COM_INTERFACE_ENTRY_IMPL(IOleObject)
    COM_INTERFACE_ENTRY_IMPL(IQuickActivate)
    COM_INTERFACE_ENTRY_IMPL(IPersistStorage)
    COM_INTERFACE_ENTRY_IMPL(IPersistStreamInit)
    COM_INTERFACE_ENTRY_IMPL(ISpecifyPropertyPages)
    COM_INTERFACE_ENTRY_IMPL(IDataObject)
    COM_INTERFACE_ENTRY(IProvideClassInfo)
    COM_INTERFACE_ENTRY(IProvideClassInfo2)
    COM_INTERFACE_ENTRY(ISupportErrorInfo)
    COM_INTERFACE_ENTRY_IMPL(IConnectionPointContainer)
END_COM_MAP()
```

One more task is required: You need to inform the ATL implementation of
IConnectionPointContainer which connection points are available. To do this,
add a connection point map following the COM map that you just modified. (A
connection point map is a list of the interface identifiers for each supported connection point.)

```
BEGIN_CONNECTION_POINT_MAP(CLevelCtrl)
    CONNECTION_POINT_ENTRY(DIID__LevelEvents)
END_CONNECTION_POINT_MAP()
```

NOTE   Notice that the identifier name for the interface contains two underscore characters. Because MIDL prepends DIID_ to the original interface name, which begins
with an underscore, the result is a double underscore.

Modifying the Message Map

Now that you have finished implementing code to support events, it's time to add code to recognize mouse clicks in the control and to fire the events at the appropriate time. In this example, we're going to fire either a ClickUp or ClickDn event. The ClickUp event will be fired when the left (primary) mouse button is clicked on the right side of the control or when the right (secondary) mouse button is clicked on the left side. The ClickDn event will report a left mouse button on the left or a right mouse button on the right.

To trigger these events, you need to add handlers for WM_LBUTTONDOWN and WM_RBUTTONDOWN messages. In LevelCtrl.H, add the two lines shown below in bold print to the message map:

```
BEGIN_MSG_MAP(CLevelCtrl)
    MESSAGE_HANDLER(WM_PAINT, OnPaint)
    MESSAGE_HANDLER(WM_SETFOCUS, OnSetFocus)
    MESSAGE_HANDLER(WM_KILLFOCUS, OnKillFocus)
//=== add map entries ===
    MESSAGE_HANDLER(WM_LBUTTONDOWN, OnLButtonDown)
    MESSAGE_HANDLER(WM_RBUTTONDOWN, OnRButtonDown)
END_MSG_MAP()
```

NOTE   If you are accustomed to using MFC, then the odds are that you are also accustomed to using the ClassWizard to make message-map entries. For your ActiveX project, however, the ClassWizard isn't ready to recognize the project classes, so you need to make this change directly in the header file.

Next, you need to supply an implementation for these two message functions. In LevelCtrl.CPP, add the following:

```
LRESULT CLevelCtrl::OnLButtonDown( UINT uMsg,     WPARAM wParam,
                                   LPARAM lParam, BOOL &bHandled )
{
    POINT    pt;

    pt.x = LOWORD(lParam);
    pt.y = HIWORD(lParam);
    if( PtInRect( &m_rectLeft, pt ) )
    {
        Fire_ClickDn( pt.x, pt.y );
        ChangeLevel( -m_nLevel );
```

```
        }
        else
        if( PtInRect( &m_rectRight, pt ) )
        {
            Fire_ClickUp( pt.x, pt.y );
            ChangeLevel( ++m_nLevel );
        }
        return FALSE;
    }
```

When the mouse event occurs, the mouse x/y coordinates are found in the high and low words in the lParam argument. If this were an MFC-based `CWnd::OnL-ButtonDown`-derived procedure, two arguments would be supplied: a `flags` argument containing the button status flags and a `POINT` argument with the x/y coordinates. However, since we are not using MFC for this example, you need to convert the lParam argument to a `POINT` structure.

NOTE

Alternatively, you could convert the **lParam** argument to individual x/y variables. However, the **POINT** structure is more convenient because you can use it directly for the **PtInRect** test to determine if the event has occurred in the right or left rectangle. (Remember, these rectangles were calculated earlier in the **CLevelCtrl::OnDraw** function.)

Then, depending on which side the mouse click hit, you call `Fire_ClickUp`, including the mouse coordinates as arguments, and then call `ChangeLevel`, with an argument to decrement or increment the `m_nLevel` member.

Now you can see the benefit of creating the `ChangeLevel` function rather than simply calling `FireViewChange` directly. You have three calls to the `ChangeLevel` function, which performs the limit test and update instructions, rather than needing to perform these tasks in three different locations.

Now add the implementation for the `OnRButtonDown` function. `OnRButtonDown` performs the same task as `OnLButtonDown`, except that the increment and decrement instructions are reversed.

```
LRESULT CLevelCtrl::OnRButtonDown( UINT uMsg,      WPARAM wParam,
                                   LPARAM lParam, BOOL &bHandled )
{
    POINT    pt;

    pt.x = LOWORD(lParam);
```

```
        pt.y = HIWORD(lParam);
        if( PtInRect( &m_rectLeft, pt ) )
        {
            Fire_ClickUp( pt.x, pt.y );
            ChangeLevel( ++m_nLevel );
        }
        else
        if( PtInRect( &m_rectRight, pt ) )
        {
            Fire_ClickDn( pt.x, pt.y );
            ChangeLevel( -m_nLevel );
        }
        return FALSE;
}
```

And, finally, you have a fully functional ActiveX control. Simply compile and execute it, either by using the supplied .HTML page or the ActiveX Control Test Container. Then test the finished control, which should look similar to the one shown in Figure 16.16.

FIGURE 16.16:

The working ActiveX KnobCtrl control

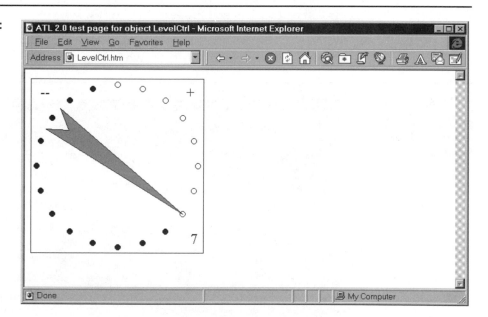

However, even though you have a working ActiveX control, you still aren't quite finished. As a final touch, let's add a property page to the control. A property page is a dialog box used to display configuration information to the user and to enable the user to modify the information. (One or more property pages constitute a property sheet.)

Adding a Property Page to a Control

In ActiveX objects, property pages are implemented as separate COM objects. This allows property pages to be shared if necessary.

Creating a Property Page Object

To add a Property Page object to the KnobCtrl project, follow these steps:

1. Return to the ATL Object Wizard using any of the methods described earlier in the chapter (see "Adding Objects and Controls").

2. From the ATL Object Wizard window (see Figure 16.3), select Controls from the list on the right and Property Page as the type of control to create.

3. In the ATL Object Wizard Properties dialog box, enter the name **LevelProp** in the Short Name edit box, as shown in Figure 16.17.

FIGURE 16.17:

ATL Object Wizard Properties dialog box for a Property Page control

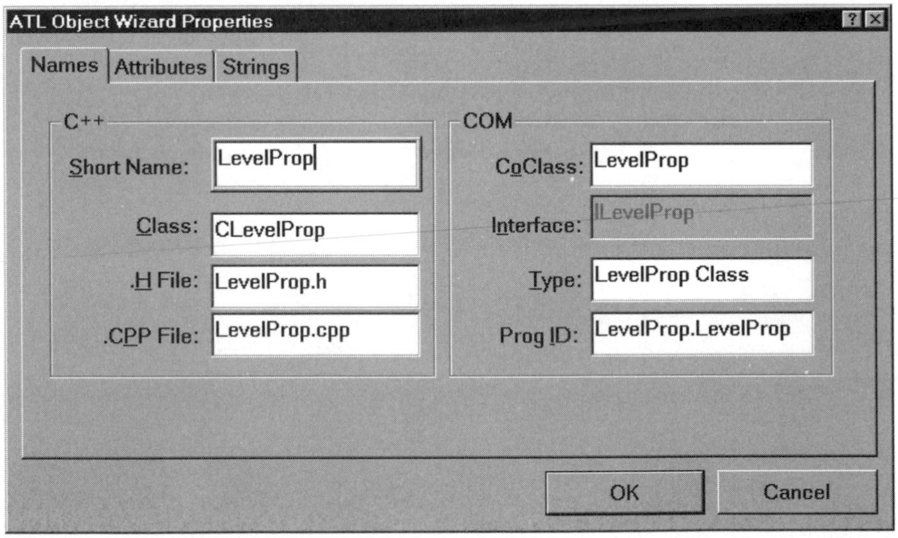

NOTE   Notice that the Interface edit box is disabled (grayed out). This is because a property page does not require nor support a custom interface.

4. Click the Strings tab. In the Title edit box, enter the string that you want to appear in the tab for that page (**Level Control** in this example). The Doc String entry is a brief description, which a property frame can place in a status line or tooltip. (At present, the standard property frame does not use the Doc String entry.) Leave the Helpfile entry blank; we do not plan to generate a help file for this example. Figure 16.18 shows this tab.

FIGURE 16.18:

The Strings tab for a Property control

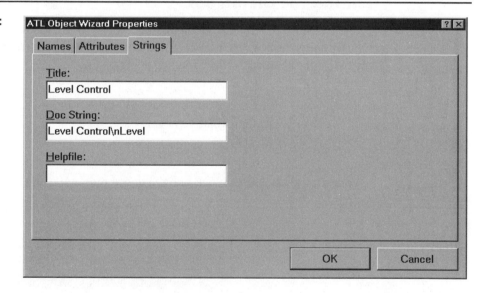

5. Click OK to create the Property Page object.

For the Property Page object, the ATL Object Wizard generates three source files:

LevelProp.H	Header file that contains CLevelProp class implementing the property page
LevelProp.CPP	File that includes the LevelProp.h file
LevelProp.RGS	Registry script to register the Property Page object

Also, the following changes are made to existing application source files:

- The new property page is added to the object entry map in KnobCtrl.CPP.
- The LevelProp class is added to the KnobCtrl.IDL file.
- A second registry script, LevelProp.RGS, is added to the project resources.
- A dialog box template for the property page is added to the project resources.
- The two property strings specified are included in the resource string table.

Editing the Dialog Box

The next step is to edit the dialog box IDD_LEVELPROP (using the dialog box editor). Initially, the dialog box is empty except for a label instructing you to enter property page controls. Make the following changes:

- Deleting the existing label.
- Add a new static text label: **Level**.
- Add an edit box identified as IDC_LEVEL.

Your dialog box should look like the one shown in Figure 16.19.

FIGURE 16.19:

The Level Properties dialog box

As you can see, this is a very simple dialog box. It does not have a caption, a system menu, a frame or frame controls, or OK and Cancel buttons. It just has the label and the edit box. We need only the bare functionality here, because this dialog box will not be used in the usual fashion. Instead, we will use this dialog box fragment as a tab in the Property Page dialog box for this control, and that dialog box will supply an Apply button as well as the usual frame, title bar, and OK and Cancel buttons. You'll see how this works shortly, but first we need to make some changes in the source files to finish the property page.

Editing the LevelProp Files

Next, you need to include KnobCtrl.H in the LevelProp.H header:

```
#include "KnobCtrl.h"              // definition of ILevelCtrl
```

You also need to enable the CLevelProp class to set the level when the Apply button is clicked. Initially, the Apply function should look something like this:

```
STDMETHOD(Apply)(void)
{
    USES_CONVERSION;
    ATLTRACE(_T("CLevelProp::Apply\n"));
    for( UINT i = 0; i < m_nObjects; i++ )
    {
        // Do something interesting here
        ICircCtl* pCirc;
        m_ppUnk[i]->QueryInterface(IID_ICircCtl, (void**)&pCirc);
        pCirc->put_Caption(CComBSTR("something special"));
        pCirc->Release();
    }
    m_bDirty = FALSE;
    return S_OK;
}
```

The minimal instructions in the supplied code are simply a place-holder. You need to replace the body of the loop with some real instructions, as follows (changes are shown in bold print):

```
STDMETHOD(Apply)(void)
{
    USES_CONVERSION;
    ATLTRACE(_T("CLevelProp::Apply\n"));
    for( UINT i = 0; i < m_nObjects; i++ )
    {
        CComQIPtr<ILevelCtrl, &IID_ILevelCtrl> pLevel(m_ppUnk[i]);
        short nLevel = (short)GetDlgItemInt(IDC_LEVEL);
        if FAILED( pLevel->put_m_nLevel( nLevel ) )
        {
            CComPtr<IErrorInfo> pError;
            CComBSTR            strError;

            GetErrorInfo( 0, &pError );
            pError->GetDescription(&strError);
```

```
                MessageBox( OLE2T(strError), _T("Error"),
MB_ICONEXCLAMATION );
                return E_FAIL;
            }
        }
        m_bDirty = FALSE;
        return S_OK;
    }
```

Because a property page may have more than one client attached at any time, the Apply function loops to call the put_m_nLevel function for each client, using the value retrieved from the edit box. Here, we are using the CComQIPtr class, which performs the QueryInterface for each object to obtain the ILevelCtrl interface from the IUnknown member (stored in the m_ppUnk array).

Also, the loop contains a check to determine whether the Level property functioned. In the case of failure, the loop displays a message with error details supplied by the IErrorInfo interface.

Ideally, a container class would begin by requesting the ISupportErrorInfo interface from an object and then checking InterfaceSupportsErrorInfo to decide whether the object supports setting error information. However, because you already know that error information is supported, this check is not necessary.

There are several other conveniences supplied as well:

- Because CComPtr automatically handles the reference count, you do not need to call Release for this interface.

- Because CComBSTR performs the BSTR processing, there is no need to call a final SysFreeString.

- Because the USES_CONVERSION macro was set at the start of this function, the various string-conversion classes can also be invoked to convert the BSTR value if necessary.

Next, by setting the property page's dirty flag—setting m_bDirty to FALSE—the Apply button can be enabled when the value in the Level edit box is changed. This does require, however, an addition to the LevelProp.H message map, as shown below (the addition is in bold print):

```
BEGIN_MSG_MAP(CLevelProp)
    COMMAND_HANDLER( IDC_LEVEL, EN_CHANGE, OnLevelChange )
```

```
        CHAIN_MSG_MAP(IPropertyPageImpl<CLevelProp>)
END_MSG_MAP()
```

And, last, add the OnLevelChange function following the Apply function:

```
        LRESULT OnLevelChange( WORD wNotify, WORD wID, HWND hWnd, BOOL
&bHandled )
        {
            SetDirty(TRUE);
            return FALSE;
        }
```

Now OnLevelChange will be called when a WM_COMMAND message is sent with the EN_CHANGE notification for the IDC_LEVEL control. In turn, OnLevelChange then calls SetDirty, passing TRUE to indicate the property page is dirty and the Apply button should be enabled.

As a final task, you need to add the property page to the control. The ATL Object Wizard does not do this automatically because there may be multiple controls in a project. Modify the property map in LevelCtrl.H by adding the LEVEL_ENTRY line, as shown below (in bold print):

```
BEGIN_PROPERTY_MAP(CLevelCtrl)
    // Examples of entries
    // PROP_ENTRY("Property Description", dispid, clsid)
    PROP_ENTRY( "Level", 1, CLSID_LevelProp )
    PROP_PAGE( CLSID_StockColorPage )
END_PROPERTY_MAP()
```

NOTE   An alternative is to add a PROP_PAGE macro with the CLSID of the property page—as appears for the CSLID_StockColorPage—but the PROP_ENTRY macro has the advantage of saving the Level property value when the control is saved.

The three parameters to the PROP_ENTRY macro are the property description, the DSPID of the property, and the CSLID of the property page containing the property. This is useful, for example, if the control is used in Visual Basic and the value is set at design time. By using the PROP_ENTRY macro, the value is saved with the Visual Basic project and is restored when the Visual Basic project is reloaded.

Testing the Property Page

To test the property page, rebuild the control, open the ActiveX Control Test Container and insert the control. Then select Edit ➢ Embedded Object Functions ➢ Properties. When the property page appears, the Apply button will be disabled, as shown in Figure 16.20.

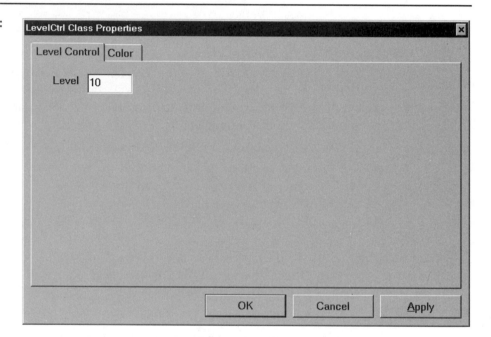

As you can see, the Level tab contains only the label and edit box that you created for the Level Properties dialog box. On the other hand, the Color tab displays stock properties in a dialog box that you did not create. This dialog box is automatically enabled because the control contains a color member.

Entering a value in the Label edit box or selecting the Color tab and changing the color selection will enable the Apply button. Clicking the Apply button causes an immediate change in the control, after which the Apply button is again disabled.

Try entering an invalid value in the Label edit box and clicking Apply. In response, you will see an error message cautioning you that the value supplied is not allowed. Also note that the Apply button remains enabled.

Adding an ActiveX Control to a Web Page

Now that the ActiveX control is ready for operation, it's time to add the control to a Web page and see how it operates in the real world. If you recall, when you created the control using the ATL Object Wizard, it also created an HTML file, KnobCtrl.HTM, for the control.

The provided HTML file needs only a couple of minor modifications in the form of a VB Script before the LevelCtrl ActiveX control can actually run on a Web page. Here is the HTML file with the VB Script addition (in bold print):

```
<HTML>
<HEAD>
<TITLE>ATL 2.0 test page for object LevelCtrl</TITLE>
</HEAD>
<BODY>
<OBJECT ID="LevelCtrl" <
 CLASSID="CLSID:8B946F75-0A74-11D1-85FB-50914CC10000">
>
</OBJECT>
<SCRIPT LANGUAGE="VBScript">
<!-
Sub LevelCtrl_ClickUp(x, y)
    LevelCtrl.Level = LevelCtrl.Level + 1
End Sub
Sub LevelCtrl_ClickDn(x, y)
    LevelCtrl.Level = LevelCtrl.Level - 1
End Sub
->
</SCRIPT>
</BODY>
</HTML>
```

With these additions, you can now start Internet Explorer and open the Level-Ctrl.HTM file.

ActiveX Control Testing Precautions

Microsoft offers a few notes of caution about testing ActiveX controls: In Internet Explorer, make sure your Security settings are set to Medium (select View ➤ Options, select the Security tab and click Safety Level to get to the Security settings). Now open LevelCtrl.HTM. A Safety Violation dialog box may inform you that Internet Explorer does not know if the control is safe to script.

What does this mean? Suppose that you had a control that, for example, displayed a file but also had a Delete method that deleted a file. The control would be safe if you just viewed it on a page, but wouldn't be safe to script, because someone could call the Delete method. This message is Internet Explorer's way of saying that it doesn't know if someone could do damage with this control, so it is asking the user.

Perhaps because development and testing for this book has been done under beta versions of Windows 98 together with Internet Explorer 4.0, no safety violations or warnings were observed. Instead, when clicking on the control, I did receive intermittent reports that the VB Script functions being called were not supported. However, despite these warnings, the LevelCtrl control functioned normally. By the time the release version of Windows 98 appears, these warnings may no longer appear.

If you do receive these warnings, adding an implementation of the `IObjectSafetyImpl` to the list of inherited classes and an entry in the COM map is enough to prevent security warnings.

First, add a new last line to the list of inherited classes, remembering to add a comma to the end of the preceding line, as:

```
public IObjectSafetyImpl<CLevelCtrl>
```

Then add the following entry to the COM map, also in LevelCtrl.H:

```
COM_INTERFACE_ENTRY_IMPL(IObjectSafety)
```

Now rebuild the LevelCtrl control and open the LevelCtrl.HTM page in Internet Explorer. If you saw the Safety Violation dialog box previously, it should not appear after you've made the revisions outlined here. If you have received the "not supported" warnings, these may appear again.

Second (and Third) Thoughts on ActiveX Controls

ActiveX controls are a nice idea, but they have definite limitations ... and, very likely, some serious security problems as well. For example, I just mentioned the possibility of an ActiveX control having the ability to delete a file, and then suggested using the `IObjectSafetyImpl` class as a method of circumventing some security checks.

Being paranoid (but justifiably so), you can envision ActiveX controls functioning as viruses—or worse. After all, if `IObjectSafetyImpl` can assure the container that the control is safe ... well, you can fill in the blanks yourself.

> **WARNING**   There is some reason to suspect that the cautions and the safety measures are no longer relevant with version 4 of Internet Explorer. This does not, however, mean that ActiveX controls are safe beyond question. Unfortunately, there are too many malign crackers out there who are probably exploring this question right now. Ergo, caution is suggested before allowing ActiveX controls access to your system.

Questions of safety aside, ActiveX components do not work on all Internet browsers (and, no matter how much Microsoft might like to be the producer of the preeminent browser in the entire Internet, it is not nor is it likely to become so).

Until such time as ActiveX controls are supported universally and all questions of malign action are reasonably settled by preventive measures within the browsers, their value as Web tools may be considered questionable. Of course, this question also applies to the value of devoting extensive effort to the development of ActiveX controls.

If ActiveX controls are of somewhat questionable value, our next topics—the registry and registry keys—are not only undeniably valuable but are also virtually essential for many types of Windows applications. In brief, the system registry offers an appropriate and opportune location for keeping application-specific data, and it can also be the source of data relevant to the system configuration and to other installed components.

CHAPTER
SEVENTEEN

Registry Operations

- ■ The Registry Editor

- ■ The structure of the Windows 98 registry

- ■ Registry entries and data types

- ■ Registry API functions

- ■ Registry operations

The registry is a relatively new phenomenon. Under Windows 3.*x* and DOS, applications commonly create initialization files to store configuration parameters, user preferences, status flags, and various other application settings. For example, the Win.INI file holds system configuration data, the Reg.DAT file stores file associations and object linking and embedding, and the System.INI file records the hardware configuration. Other individual .INI files contain settings for specific applications.

All of these initialization files are in ASCII format, easily accessible with any text editor. Of course, Windows and application designers did not intend for users to access or edit the initialization files. Ideally, these files would be altered only by the applications themselves and would not be subject to tampering by the uninformed—neither Joe Public nor Jane Engineer.

But, ideally, Lil' Abner's schmoo laid both eggs and bottles of grade A milk, tasted better than anything you could imagine, and dropped dead at a hungry glance.

The reality is a very different animal. Not only are these initialization files untrustworthy and subject to damage, but they are also easily misplaced or erased, often with disastrous consequences. In short, initialization files are a pain.

With the introduction of Windows NT (version 3.1), the system registry appeared as a replacement for a scattered multitude of individual initialization files, including the System.INI, Win.INI, Protocol.INI, Config.SYS, and Autoexec.BAT files. Like Windows NT, Windows 95 and now Windows 98 use the registry to store system settings.

NOTE   Even today, a few applications still use .INI files to contain application parameters. Many of these .INI settings are read into the registry on startup and, thus, become enshrined in two formats. Hence, a registry change may simply be undone on reboot unless the offending .INI file is located and also changed.

The reality of the registry is that it is also a pain, just not quite as bad as the initialization files… in some ways. As an application developer, you will need to know how to work with the registry. In this chapter, we will look at methods for creating registry keys, writing data to the registry and, perhaps most important, retrieving information from the registry.

Welcome to the System Registry

The Windows system registry is a structured database containing all of the settings, paths, variables, and application parameters that were previously parceled among a host of individual initialization files.

TIP   The bulk of the registry is contained in the User.DAT and System.DAT files in the Win98 directory. Backup copies of the System.DAT and User.DAT files are contained in the System.DA0 and User.DA0 files and can be used to recover from registry corruption.

The database format offers several advantages. The registry entries are protected from both casual tampering and accidental erasure. Also, because all of the information is in a single place, you can access the information you need without searching through a multitude of sources to find specific data.

The Registry Editor

The registry data is not directly accessible; that is, you cannot view or edit it in the same fashion as a .INI file. To view or edit the registry, you use the Windows 98 Registry Editor (the RegEdit.EXE or RegEd32.EXE utility). Figure 17.1 shows the Registry Editor window.

FIGURE 17.1:

Using the Registry Editor to examine the registry

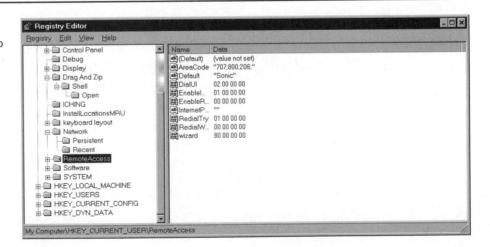

Windows does not install the RegEdit or RegEd32 utility in a program group or program menu for ready access. This is not an oversight on the part of the designers at Microsoft; it's a deliberate choice to keep the Registry Editor from being discovered by inexperienced users, because this utility is not intended for casual use. Used incorrectly, the Registry Editor has the ability to literally trash your system.

Before changing registry information using the Registry Editor, *always* make a backup copy of the registry. From the Registry Editor, select Registry ➤ Export Registry File to write the entire registry to a backup file. Pick a convenient location, such as the root directory, and a recognizable name, such as Registry.REG. Do not change the .REG extension or you may have difficulty restoring the saved data. Note that the saved file will be in ASCII format and may easily occupy 4MB or 5MB of space.

Then, if your changes result in any serious problems, you can restore the original registry, either by using the Registry Editor to import the saved version or by simply double-clicking on the file you exported. In the case of a severe error, you can use that backup copy to replace the damaged registry files (System.DAT and User.DAT) and restore your previous configuration.

NOTE Under Windows NT, the system automatically creates backup copies of the System.DAT and User.DAT files as System.DA0 and User.DA0, which can be used to restore the last known good configuration. Unfortunately, this service is not supported by Windows 98.

Cautions aside, there may still be occasions when you need to access the registry directly, even if only for information. As you might guess, simply looking for an entry by scrolling though the tree would be a rather frustrating task. The only practical method of finding a particular entry (unless you're fairly certain of the location) is to use the Edit ➤ Find and Find Next functions to search for a string or another known value.

NOTE As an example, you might want to view information about OLE applications using the Registry Editor. See Chapter 36 for details on OLE application development and the OLE information recorded in the registry.

From a developer's standpoint, more important than editing the registry is how your own applications can use the registry to contain important information by creating and writing registry entries and by later retrieving the information from the registry. For this purpose, you must first understand the structure of the registry.

The Registry Structure

The registry is structured as keys and subkeys. For convenience, it's easy to visualize the registry structure as a directory tree where the keys and subkeys are directories and subdirectories (and in the Registry Editor, this is exactly how the registry database is presented). At any level, a key may contain one or more pieces of data—just as a directory may contain one or more files—or it may simply contain links to subkeys.

The Windows 98 registry structure begins with the six top-level keys listed in Table 17.1. These top-level keys are predefined system keys, and you can use them for access to subkeys within the registry. For example, the demo discussed in this chapter, *Reg_Ops*, uses the HKEY_CURRENT_USER key for user-specific information and the HKEY_LOCAL_MACHINE key for system-specific data.

TABLE 17.1: Top-level Registry Keys

Key	Contents
HKEY_CLASSES_ROOT	Information about registered classes, application extensions, etc. This key is actually a link to the HKEY_LOCAL_MACHINE\SOFTWARE\ Classes subkey.
HKEY_CURRENT_USER	Information about the current user's configuration, Desktop layout, preferences, network and dial-up settings, etc. This key is actually a link to the HKEY_USERS subkey for the current user.
HKEY_LOCAL_MACHINE	Information about the system (hardware) configuration, including global application settings, supported services, device maps, etc.
HKEY_USERS	Information sets for all users registered on the local system (see HKEY_CURRENT_USER).
HKEY_CURRENT_CONFIG	This key is actually a link to the HKEY_LOCAL_MACHINE\ Config\xxxxxx subkey where xxxxxx is the numeric value of the hardware configuration currently used.
HKEY_DYN_DATA	Dynamic data for Plug-and-Play devices and VdX virtual device drivers.

NOTE

For complete and comprehensive details on the Windows registry, I highly recommend Ron Petrusha's *Inside the Windows 95 Registry*. Although the title refers specifically to Windows 95, the contents are comprehensive and apply to the Windows 98 registry (and the Windows NT registry) as well.

Registry entries, named fields, can hold various types of data, as shown in Table 17.2. Of these, the REG_DWORD and REG_SZ formats are most commonly used. However, which data format is used makes little difference in reading or writing to the registry (because of the handling format of the RegQueryValueEx and RegSetValueEx APIs, described in the next section).

TABLE 17.2: Registry Data Types

Value	Meaning
REG_BINARY	Binary data in any format.
REG_DWORD	DWORD (32-bit) value.
REG_DWORD_LITTLE_ENDIAN	DWORD (32-bit) value using the little-endian format where the most significant word is in the high-order byte. This is the same as REG_DWORD and is standard for Windows 98/95/NT systems.
REG_DWORD_BIG_ENDIAN	DWORD (32-bit) value using big-endian format where the most significant value byte appears in the low-order (low-word, low-byte) byte.
REG_EXPAND_SZ	Null-terminated string containing unexpanded references to variables (i.e., "%PATH%"). May be either Unicode or ANSI, depending on whether Unicode or ANSI functions are being used.
REG_LINK	Unicode symbolic link.
REG_MULTI_SZ	An array of null-terminated (ASCIIZ/UnicodeZ) strings. The array is terminated by two null characters.
REG_NONE	No value type defined.
REG_RESOURCE_LIST	Device-driver resource list.
REG_SZ	Null-terminated (ASCIIZ/UnicodeZ) string. May be either Unicode or ANSI, depending on whether Unicode or ANSI functions are being used.

As an example of the structure of registry keys and entries, take a look at Figure 17.2. This figure illustrates the data used for the *Reg_Ops* demo, where five subkeys have been created and each subkey has two named fields: Password and Status. The Password field contains a string entry, which is a string-validation check for a password, not the actual password. The Status field contains a DWORD value, shown here in hex format.

FIGURE 17.2:

The structure of registry entries

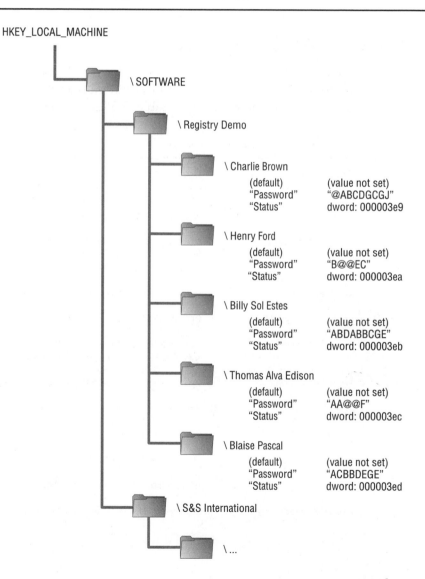

HKEY_LOCAL_MACHINE

\ SOFTWARE

\ Registry Demo

\ Charlie Brown
(default)	(value not set)
"Password"	"@ABCDGCGJ"
"Status"	dword: 000003e9

\ Henry Ford
(default)	(value not set)
"Password"	"B@@EC"
"Status"	dword: 000003ea

\ Billy Sol Estes
(default)	(value not set)
"Password"	"ABDABBCGE"
"Status"	dword: 000003eb

\ Thomas Alva Edison
(default)	(value not set)
"Password"	"AA@@F"
"Status"	dword: 000003ec

\ Blaise Pascal
(default)	(value not set)
"Password"	"ACBBDEGE"
"Status"	dword: 000003ed

\ S&S International

\ ...

NOTE   The (default) field, showing *(value not set)* in Figure 17.2, is a holdover from Windows 3.*x*, where key fields could contain only one unnamed value and additional subkeys were required to hold further values. While the default field can still be accessed using Windows 3.*x* functions, this is not recommended. Instead, all registry entries should rely on named fields to hold values.

Registry Access Methods

Windows supplies 26 registry API functions (or 21, excluding the 5 functions provided for Windows 3.*x* compatibility), but most applications are likely to use only three or four of these functions. Table 17.3 lists all the registry API functions.

TABLE 17.3:   Registry API Functions

Registry API	Use
RegCloseKey	Closes (releases) the handle of a specified key but does not update the registry. (See also **RegFlushKey**.) (*all versions*)
RegConnectRegistry	Establishes a connection to a predefined registry handle on another (remote or network) computer. Not required for local registry operations. (*all versions*)
RegCreateKey*	Creates a specified key or, if the key exists, opens the key. (*Win3.x*)
RegCreateKeyEx**	Creates a specified key or, if the key exists, opens the key. (*Win98/95/NT*)
RegDeleteKey	Deletes a specified key and all its descendent keys. (*Win98/95*) Deletes a specified key but does not delete descendent keys. (*WinNT*)
RegDeleteValue	Removes a named value from a specified registry key. (*all versions*)
RegEnumKey*	Enumerates subkeys of a specified open key. (*Win3.x*)
RegEnumKeyEx	Enumerates subkeys of s specified open key. (*Win98/95/NT*)
RegEnumValue	Enumerates the values contained in an open key. (*Win98/95/NT*)
RegFlushKey	Writes all attributes of the specified key to the registry. (*all versions*)
RegGetKeySecurity	Retrieves the security descriptor for a specified open key. (*WinNT*)

Continued on next page

TABLE 17.3 (CONTINUED): Registry API Functions

Registry API	Use
RegLoadKey	Creates a subkey, under **HKEY_USER** or **HKEY_LOCAL_MACHINE**, before copying registry information from a specified file to the subkey. (*all versions*)
RegNotifyChangeKeyValue	Notifies caller when the attributes or contents of an open key have changed. Does not notify if a key is deleted. (*all versions*)
RegOpenKey*	Opens a specified key but does not create the key if it does not exist. (*Win3.x*)
RegOpenKeyEx	Opens a specified key but does not create the key if it does not exist. (*Win98/95/NT*)
RegQueryInfoKey**	Retrieves subkey information, including size, number, class, security, etc., about an open key. (*Win98/95/NT*)
RegQueryMultipleValues	Retrieves type and data for a list of value names associated with an open key. (*all versions*)
RegQueryValue*	Retrieves a value associated with an unnamed value in a specified open key. (*Win3.x*)
RegQueryValueEx**	Retrieves type and data for a specified value name in an open key. (*Win98/95/NT*)
RegReplaceKey	Replaces the file backing a key and subkeys with a new file; when the system is restarted, the key and subkeys will assume the values stored in the new file. (*Win98/95/NT*)
RegRestoreKey	Reads registry information from a specified file, copying it to a specified key and subkeys. (*all versions*)
RegSaveKey	Saves a specified key, subkeys, and values to a file. (*all versions*)
RegSetKeySecurity	Sets the security of an open key. (*WinNT only*)
RegSetValue*	Associates an unnamed value (text) with a key. (*Win3.x*)
RegSetValueEx**	Stores data in the value field of an open key, and may set additional value and type information for a key. (*Win98/95/NT*)
RegUnLoadKey	Unloads (removes) the specified key, subkeys, and values from the registry. (*Win98/95/NT*)

*Function provided for Windows 3.1x compatibility.

**A commonly used function.

The RegSetKeySecurity and RegGetKeySecurity APIs, and the security fields in several other functions, are relevant only under Windows NT. Windows 98 (and Windows 95) does not support registry security; security settings are simply ignored or returned as null.

In many ways, these API functions seem rather archaic, because they are not MFC-based and do not support or recognize MFC classes. For example, they do not support the CString data type, so string information can be supplied or retrieved only as an array of char.

The Regs_Ops Demo: Demonstrating Registry Operations

The *Reg_Ops* demo demonstrates how the registry operates. As you can see in Figure 17.3, the dialog-box-based application shows a combo list box and a series of status buttons.

The *Reg_Ops* demo is included on the CD accompanying this book, in the Chapter 17 folder.

FIGURE 17.3:

The Reg_Ops demo demonstrates registry operations.

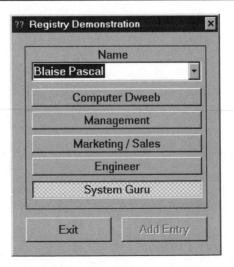

You can select an existing name from the drop-down list (you will be prompted for a password), or you can enter a new name in the edit box, assign a status, and enter a password for the entry. The name will become a new subkey in the registry, with the status and password validation code as named value fields.

Preparing for the Reg_Ops Demo

Before you run the *Reg_Ops* demo, open the *Special.REG* file included on the CD accompanying this book (in the Chapter 17 folder), using Windows Explorer, File Manager, or the file browser of your choice. When you double-click Special.REG, the RegEdit utility will be invoked to write several entries to your system registry under the heading HKEY_LOCAL_MACHINE\SOFTWARE\. The following are the plain-text contents of the Special.REG file:

```
REGEDIT4

[HKEY_LOCAL_MACHINE\SOFTWARE\Registry Demo]

[HKEY_LOCAL_MACHINE\SOFTWARE\Registry Demo\Charlie Brown]
"Password"="@ABCDGCGJ"
"Status"=dword:000003e9

[HKEY_LOCAL_MACHINE\SOFTWARE\Registry Demo\Henry Ford]
"Password"="B@@EC"
"Status"=dword:000003ea

[HKEY_LOCAL_MACHINE\SOFTWARE\Registry Demo\Billy Sol Estes]
"Password"="ABDABBCGE"
"Status"=dword:000003eb

[HKEY_LOCAL_MACHINE\SOFTWARE\Registry Demo\Thomas Alva Edison]
"Password"="AA@@F"
"Status"=dword:000003ec

[HKEY_LOCAL_MACHINE\SOFTWARE\Registry Demo\Blaise Pascal]
"Password"="ACBBDEGE"
"Status"=dword:000003ed

[HKEY_LOCAL_MACHINE\SOFTWARE\Not Very Secret]
"Secret Key"="Rumplestiltskin"
```

The *Reg_Ops* demo uses these registry entries to provide preliminary data for illustrating operations.

Opening a Key

The *Reg_Ops* demo begins in OnInitDialog, when the application opens, by calling RegCreateKey to open a handle to the application's private key under the HKEY_LOCAL_MACHINE root key.

```
BOOL CReg_OpsDlg::OnInitDialog()
{
    CDialog::OnInitDialog();

    ...
        // begin by opening keys to your registry entries
    RegCreateKey( HKEY_LOCAL_MACHINE, "SOFTWARE\\Registry Demo",
                &m_hRegKey );
    ResetButtons();
        // then initialize the combo list box
    InitializeListBox();
    return TRUE;  // return TRUE unless you set the focus to a control
}
```

> **NOTE** Calling this a "private" key is something of a misnomer—privacy does not apply to registry keys. All keys are accessible to all applications if the application knows that the key exists or goes to the trouble of finding it. Still, since there is no reason for any other application to want to use this key, it is private in the sense that it has meaning only within the *Reg_Ops* application.

Because this is a list of user names, status flags, and password validation keys, the demo stores this information under HKEY_LOCAL_MACHINE rather than under HKEY_USER. If you were registering information about a specific user's preferences, you would place this information under HKEY_CURRENT_USER, so that the user's settings would be immediately available when he or she logged on to the system. This way, you would not need to query to find out who the user is but simply assume that he or she is the same person who logged on.

The RegCreateKey function opens the key if it already exists or, if not, creates the key, returning a handle to the key in m_hRegKey. By using a member variable (type HKEY), m_hRegKey is available to other functions in the application. When you expect multiple accesses or frequent access to a key, it's convenient to open a handle to the key once and then to use this handle to access subkeys later. In other cases, when you need only occasional access to a key, you can wait and open it if and when needed.

Reading Registry Keys

Next, the demo uses m_hRegKey to initialize the contents of a combo list box by reading entries from subkeys in the registry (see Reg_OpsDlg.CPP).

```
BOOL CReg_OpsDlg::InitializeListBox()
{
    DWORD     dwName, dwSubkeys, dwIndex = 0;
    long      lResult;
    TCHAR     szBuff[MAX_PATH+1];
    CString   csBuff;

    EnableButtons( FALSE );
    lResult = RegQueryInfoKey( m_hRegKey, NULL, NULL, NULL, &dwSubkeys,
                               NULL, NULL, NULL, NULL, NULL, NULL, NULL );
    if( lResult == ERROR_SUCCESS )
        dwIndex = dwSubkeys;
    else ReportError( lResult );
```

In this case, before reading the subkeys, we're using the RegQueryInfoKey API to find out how many subkeys HKEY_LOCAL_MACHINE\SOFTWARE\Registry Demo contains. The RegQueryInfoKey contains a number of arguments to return different values, but you may also simply set any undesired arguments to NULL, as done here. This way, you can query a single value and not worry about items that you don't need to know.

The RegQueryInfoKey is defined as:

```
LONG RegQueryInfoKey
(   HKEY      hKey,                    // handle of key to query
    LPTSTR    lpClass,                 // class string
    LPDWORD   lpcbClass,               // size of class string buffer
    LPDWORD   lpReserved,              // reserved
    LPDWORD   lpcSubKeys,              // number of subkeys
    LPDWORD   lpcbMaxSubKeyLen,        // longest subkey name length
    LPDWORD   lpcbMaxClassLen,         // longest class string length
    LPDWORD   lpcValues,               // number of value entries
    LPDWORD   lpcbMaxValueNameLen,     // longest value name length
    LPDWORD   lpcbMaxValueLen,         // longest value data length
    LPDWORD   lpcbSecurityDescriptor,  // security descriptor length
    PFILETIME lpftLastWriteTime        // last write time
);
```

Table 17.4 describes the `RegQueryInfoKey` arguments. The only argument that is absolutely required is `hKey`, which specifies the registry key that you want information about.

TABLE 17.4:   RegQueryInfoKey Arguments

Data Type	Argument	Description
HKEY	hKey	Handle of key being queried (required)
LPTSTR	lpClass	Class string; description of class associated with key
LPDWORD	lpcbClass	Size of class string buffer, must be supplied with lpClass
LPDWORD	lpReserved	Reserved; always NULL
LPDWORD	lpcSubKeys	Number of subkeys belonging to the reference key
LPDWORD	lpcbMaxSubKeyLen	Longest name length for subkeys
LPDWORD	lpcbMaxClassLen	Longest class string length for classes associated with subkeys
LPDWORD	lpcValues	Number of value entries in reference key
LPDWORD	lpcbMaxValueNameLen	Longest value name length in reference key
LPDWORD	lpcbMaxValueLen	Longest value data length in reference key
LPDWORD	lpcbSecurityDescriptor	Security descriptor length (*WinNT only*)
PFILETIME	lpftLastWriteTime	Last write time (*WinNT only*)

Assuming that you have used Special.REG to initialize the registry with the sample data (see "Preparing for the Reg_Ops Demo" earlier in the chapter), `RegQueryInfoKey` should report five subkeys.

Now that we know how many subkeys our selected key has, the next step is to set `dwName` to the size of the `szBuff` array. Since the size of `szBuff` is not going to change, we can get away with doing this once and leaving it at that.

```
dwName = sizeof( szBuff );
do
{
    lResult = RegEnumKey( m_hRegKey, -dwIndex, (LPTSTR)szBuff, dwName );
```

Since the subkey entries are zero-indexed, before we use dwIndex, the value needs to be decremented; that is, for five subentries, we ask for index numbers 4, 3, 2, 1, and 0.

> **NOTE**
>
> Rather than asking for index numbers, we could have initialized **dwIndex** as zero and then incremented it after each call. We don't really need to know how many subkeys we're going to query because we have other means of discovering when the list of subkeys is exhausted. However, we do need an index value for the retrieval.

Using RegEnumKey, we are able to execute a cyclic query to discover the names of the subkeys. RegEnumKey is defined as:

```
LONG RegEnumKey( HKEY    hKey,      // handle of key to query
                 DWORD   dwIndex,   // index of subkey to query
                 LPTSTR  lpName,    // address of buffer for subkey name
                 DWORD   cbName );  // size of subkey name buffer
```

Each time we call RegEnumKey with a different index value (dwIndex), the lpName argument returns with the name of another substring. If the substrings are exhausted, RegEnumKey returns an error value, ERROR_NO_MORE_ITEMS, telling us that we have no more items to find.

The order in which these items are retrieved really doesn't matter. Until we pass an index that does not correspond to a subkey entry, we can expect to return ERROR_SUCCESS and to find a new subkey name in the lpName array. If we receive any return value other than ERROR_SUCCESS or ERROR_NO_MORE_ITEMS, then we want to report the error.

```
if( lResult != ERROR_SUCCESS && lResult != ERROR_NO_MORE_ITEMS )
    ReportError( lResult );
```

We'll cover the ReportError procedure, as well as turning system error messages into intelligence, later in "Interpreting System Error Messages." For the moment, we still need to use the subkey name returned by RegEnumKey.

```
else
if( lResult == ERROR_SUCCESS )
{
    HKEY    hKeyItem;
    ULONG   ulSize, ulType;
    int     nIndex;

    m_csNameEntry = szBuff;
```

Assuming the result was ERROR_SUCCESS, we want to transfer the string from szBuff to a CString member, m_csNameEntry. We'll reuse szBuff in a moment, but we don't want to lose the information returned a moment before.

Next, we call RegCreateKey again. This time, we use the m_hRegKey handle as the root key and the string value in szBuff to identify the subkey to open, and we'll get a new handle, hKeyItem, identifying the subkey.

```
RegCreateKey( m_hRegKey, szBuff, &hKeyItem );
```

Since we already know the key exists—RegEnumKey assured us of that—we simply assume that RegCreateKey has opened the key returning a handle, and now we can use this handle to query the values in the key. Notice, however, that we supply the size of the member receiving the data as part of the request.

```
ulSize = sizeof( m_dwNameStatus );
lResult = RegQueryValueEx( hKeyItem, "Status", NULL, &ulType,
                           (LPBYTE) &m_dwNameStatus, &ulSize );
```

In this call to RegQueryValueEx, we're asking for the value contained in a named field, "Status". Along with the value, the data type is also returned in the ulType member as an unsigned long. The size of the data is returned in the ulSize member. Regardless of what kind of data you are requesting—whether it is a DWORD value, a string, a binary array, or any other type—the address of the variable to receive the data is always cast as a pointer to byte. If you made a mistake, such as using a DWORD variable to retrieve a string, you would simply get back the first four bytes of the string, because that is all the space specified.

Next, we again check the lResult returned to be sure that the function performed correctly; if not, we'll report the error.

```
if( lResult != ERROR_SUCCESS ) ReportError( lResult );
```

At this point, we've retrieved the status member from the subkey and we've retrieved a name from the key itself. Before the loop continues for the next subkey, we need to use these values. We do this by placing them in the ComboList-box member as a string entry and as an associated value.

```
            nIndex = m_cbNamesList.AddString( m_csNameEntry );
            m_cbNamesList.SetItemData( nIndex, m_dwNameStatus );
        }
```

Then, until we reach the end of the subkeys, we allow the loop to continue for the next subkey.

```
    }
    while( lResult != ERROR_NO_MORE_ITEMS );
    return TRUE;
}
```

TIP

Using the same basic techniques, you could be reading much more complex data and even recording the data as structures rather than individual keys. For example, I know of an application that uses the registry to record default operating parameters for a dozen different types of motorized microscope stages, along with specific parameters for a each installation plus operator preferences. Altogether, these comprised several hundred settings, some in binary and others as string values. This may sound like a lot, but compared to the array of parameters governing how Windows 98 performs in your custom configuration, these several hundred elements were a very small entry.

The ConfirmPassword subroutine demonstrates reading a registry as a string value. In this subroutine, a name entry retrieved from the combo list box is used to open a handle to a key and then to retrieve the password-verification entry.

```
BOOL CReg_OpsDlg::ConfirmPassword()
{
    HKEY    hKeyItem;
    ULONG   ulSize, ulType;
    long    lResult;
    TCHAR   szBuff[MAX_PATH+1];
    CString csBuff, csPassword;

    RegCreateKey( m_hRegKey, m_csNameEntry, &hKeyItem );
    ulSize = sizeof( szBuff );
    lResult = RegQueryValueEx( hKeyItem, "Password", NULL, &ulType,
                               (LPBYTE) szBuff, &ulSize );
    if( lResult != ERROR_SUCCESS )
    {
        ReportError( lResult );
        return FALSE;
    }

    CEnterPassword *pDlg = new CEnterPassword();
    if( pDlg->DoModal() == IDOK )
```

```
        csPassword = theApp.Encrypt( pDlg->m_csPassword );
    else
        return FALSE;
    return( csPassword == szBuff );
}
```

Again, the demo includes verification for error results. Then the password returned from the CEnterPassword dialog box is passed to the Encrypt routine, in CReg_OpsApp, before comparing the password entries for verification.

Writing Registry Keys

In some ways, writing a registry key is even simpler than reading one. We begin, as before, by using RegCreateKey to open (or create) a key.

NOTE   If you want to ensure that you are not overwriting an existing key, you can begin by using RegOpenKey as a test. If the key already exists, you can then abort the operation. However, in the demo, we really don't care whether there is an existing key or not. If a key exists, we're prepared to write new information; if not, we'll create it.

After opening or creating the appropriate registry key, we call RegSetValueEx to write the registry information. RegSetValueEx is defined as:

```
LONG RegSetValueEx( HKEY      hKey          // handle of key to set value for
                    LPCTSTR   lpValueName,  // address of value to set
                    DWORD     Reserved,     // reserved
                    DWORD     dwType,       // flag for value type
              CONST BYTE * lpData,          // address of value data
                    DWORD     cbData );     // size of value data
```

The RegSetValueEx parameters are used as follows:

hKey Identifies a currently open key or any of the following predefined reserved handle values: HKEY_CLASSES_ROOT, HKEY_CURRENT_USER, HKEY_LOCAL_MACHINE, HKEY_USERS.

lpValueName Points to a string containing the name of the value to set. If the named value is not already present, it is added to the key. If this parameter is

NULL or a pointer to an empty string and dwType is REG_SZ type, the value is set to the (default) unnamed value (per RegSetValue for Windows 3.*x*).

Reserved Reserved, must be NULL (zero).

dwType Identifies the information type to be stored. The type identifiers are those listed in Table 17.2.

lpData Points to a buffer containing the data to be stored.

cbData Identifies the size in bytes of the information pointed to by lpData. If the type is REG_SZ, REG_EXPAND_SZ, or REG_MULTI_SZ, cbData must allow for the terminating null character.

The size of a value is limited by available memory. To improve performance, values larger than 2KB should be stored as external files (store the filename in the registry). Likewise, elements such as icons, bitmaps, and executables should also be stored as files and not included in the registry.

Also, the opened registry key must be opened using KEY_SET_VALUE access using RegCreateKeyEx or RegOpenKeyEx. (KEY_SET_VALUE is assumed automatically using RegCreateKeyEx.)

The AddToRegistry procedure offers two examples using RegSetValueEx to write registry data. In the first RegSetValueEx operation, we write a string using the REG_SZ specification:

```
BOOL CReg_OpsDlg::AddToRegistry()
{
    HKEY    hKeyNew;

    RegCreateKey( m_hRegKey, m_csNameEntry, &hKeyNew );
    RegSetValueEx( hKeyNew, "Password", NULL, REG_SZ,
                    (LPBYTE)( (LPCTSTR)m_csPassword,
                            m_csPassword.GetLength()+1 ) );
```

Because we are using the REG_SZ specification, we need to include one extra character in the final size argument to allow for the terminating null character, which the GetLength function does not include.

Earlier, I mentioned that the registry functions do not recognize MFC classes such as CString, but here we used two CString references as arguments. Notice, however, that we have typecast the first use as LPCTSTR, making it appear to be an array of char, and the second instance uses an integer value returned by a member function.

In the second `RegSetValueEx` operation, we write a DWORD value:

```
RegSetValueEx( hKeyNew, "Status", NULL, REG_DWORD,
               (LPBYTE)&m_dwNameStatus, sizeof( m_dwNameStatus) );
    return TRUE;
}
```

This operation is just as simple as the first `RegSetValueEx` operation, except that we specify REG_DWORD as the data type. Again, the value to be written is passed by address and followed with the size of the data (in bytes).

Notice also that the two `RegSetValueEx` operations each typecast the data argument as LPBYTE, a pointer to byte, and the data must always be passed by address.

And that's about it for writing data to the registry. All in all, it's really very simple.

Interpreting System Error Messages

Earlier, we discussed using the `ReportError` procedure to translate error results returned by the `RegQueryInfoKey`, `RegEnumKey`, and `RegQueryValueEx` functions. The `ReportError` procedure is called with the error value returned by any of the registry functions. This procedure uses the `FormatMessage` function with the FORMAT_MESSAGE_FROM_SYSTEM flag to retrieve an explanatory string from the system.

The FORMAT_MESSAGE_ALLOCATE_BUFFER flag allows you to use a void pointer to a buffer without actually allocating the buffer. Instead, the `FormatMessage` function handles the memory allocation according to the size of the message it finds. If you use this flag, you must call the `LocalFree` function to free the memory allocated when you're finished with it.

```
void CReg_OpsDlg::ReportError( long lError )
{
#ifdef _DEBUG
    LPVOID lpMsgBuf;

    FormatMessage( FORMAT_MESSAGE_ALLOCATE_BUFFER | FORMAT_MESSAGE_FROM_SYSTEM,
                   NULL, lError,
                   MAKELANGID(LANG_NEUTRAL, SUBLANG_DEFAULT), // default language
                   (LPTSTR) &lpMsgBuf, 0, NULL );
    MessageBox( (char *)lpMsgBuf );
    LocalFree( lpMsgBuf );
#endif
}
```

If you substitute the GetLastError() function for the lError argument, this routine can be used to report other errors where an error value has not already been explicitly returned.

This error-report function is not intended for release applications. The error messages returned are not very informative to users; they are strictly suitable for programmers during debugging—hence the #ifdef _DEBUG / #endif provisions. You should make other provisions for error reports in your finished applications.

TIP

For more on error messages and how to report errors in a manner acceptable to the users, you can refer to my book: *Windows Error Messages* (published by O'Reilly & Associates, 1997). Granted, this is a shameless plug, but the real shame is in the error messages common in most applications today.

Running the Reg_Ops Demo

The real topics of interest in the *Reg_Ops* demo are not in the presentation but inside the code. Still, simply for amusement, each of the status buttons (except for Computer Dweeb) requires a small test. Also, the System Guru button demands that you exhibit a small bit of knowledge about the registry (it really isn't that hard) before you can be granted this status.

TIP

To help you achieve System Guru status, there are a few hints within this chapter, as well as in the registry and on the CD.

The password encryption accepts a string and produces a validation code, which can be used subsequently to compare with a new password entry without actually storing the password. The mechanism used is a very simple one and not particularly foolproof, but it is sufficient for the purpose of this demo. If you are interested, you can look at the function to see how it works, but keep in mind that there are much better processes for encrypting passwords for real security.

The following are the sample names, supplied by the Special.REG file, and the passwords for each (these are not matched, but you shouldn't find it too hard to figure out which password goes with which name):

Charlie Brown	Countess
Henry Ford	Menlo
Billy Sol Estes	fefifofum
Thomas Alva Edison	edsel
Blaise Pascal	anhydrous

In this chapter, you may have learned more than it's really safe to know about the registry. For the average user, we would certainly not suggest any access to the registry. Of course, as a professional, you're expected to understand how to handle such potentially dangerous territory. But, in any case, do be careful because casual changes to the registry can have far-reaching consequences.

Next, in Chapter 18, we'll look at how to deal with consequences—which we hope will be unrelated to registry errors—by trapping and handling exceptions during application execution.

Exception Handling

- Exception-handling basics

- Structured exception handling

- Exception-handling functions, classes, and macros

As a program runs, various conditions may disturb its normal flow of execution. The CPU may complain of an improper memory address; the user may interrupt by pressing Ctrl+C; a debugger may halt and resume a program arbitrarily; or an unexpected value may produce an overflow or underflow in a floating-point calculation. Exceptional conditions such as these may arise in user mode or kernel mode, or on a RISC or an Intel chip; either the hardware or the software may signal their occurrence. Furthermore, each programming language must find a way to cope with exceptional conditions. To unify the processing required for all these different situations, Windows 98 builds structured exception-handling mechanisms into the system at a low level.

Exceptions closely resemble interrupts. Both signals cause the CPU to transfer control to some other part of the system; however interrupts and exceptions are not the same. An interrupt occurs asynchronously, often as a result of some hardware event such as a keypress or serial-port input. A program has no control over such interruptions, and they may occur at any time. An exception, on the other hand, arises synchronously, as a direct result of executing a particular program instruction.

Often, exceptions indicate error conditions, and usually they can be reproduced by running the same code again within the same context. These generalizations are useful guidelines, but in practice the distinction between errors and exceptions is not quite as firm as it might at first appear. The decision to signal some API failures with error returns and others by raising exceptions must sometimes be arbitrary. This chapter explains exception handling and illustrates some examples of using exception-handling routines.

Traps and the Trap Handler

Besides switching from thread to thread, the kernel must respond to *interrupts* and *exceptions.* These are signals that arise within the system and interrupt the processor to handle some new condition. When the kernel detects an interrupt or an exception, it preempts the current thread and diverts control to a different part of the system—which part depends on what condition the signal indicates. The *trap handler* is the part of the kernel invoked to answer interrupts and exceptions. It interprets the signal and transfers control to some procedure previously designated to handle the indicated condition.

Interrupts versus Exceptions

Although the system's handling of interrupts will sound familiar to DOS programmers, there are two important differences. First, DOS uses only interrupts, not exceptions. Interrupts are asynchronous, meaning they may occur at any time, and their causes have nothing to do with any code the processor may be executing. Hardware devices, such as a mouse, a keyboard, and a network card, often generate interrupts to feed their input into the processor. Sometimes, software generates interrupts, too. The kernel, for example, initiates a context switch by causing an interrupt.

Exceptions, on the other hand, are synchronous, meaning they arise within a sequence of code as the result of executing a particular instruction. Often, exceptions arise when some piece of code encounters an error it cannot handle. Divide-by-zero errors and memory-access violations, for example, cause the system to raise an exception. But not all exceptions are errors. Windows 98 also raises an exception when it encounters a call for a system service. In handling the exception, the kernel yields control to the part of the system that provides the requested service.

When it receives an interruption signal, the trap handler first records the machine's current state so it can be restored after the signal is processed. Then it determines whether the signal is an interrupt, a service call, or an exception and passes the signal accordingly to the interrupt dispatcher, the system service dispatcher, or the exception dispatcher. These subsidiary dispatchers locate the appropriate handler routine and transfer control there.

Interrupt Priority Levels

In addition to the trapping of exceptions as well as interrupts, Windows 98 differs from DOS in assigning priority levels for each interrupt. The priority assigned to an interrupt is called its *interrupt request level* (IRQL). Do not confuse this with a thread's dynamic priority, which is assigned to a sequence of code; IRQLs are assigned to interrupt sources. The mouse has an IRQL, and its input is processed at one level of priority. The system clock also generates interrupts, and its input is assigned another IRQL.

The CPU also has an IRQL, which changes as the system runs. Changing the CPU's IRQL allows the system to block out interrupts of lower priority. Only kernel-mode services, such as the trap handler, can alter the processor's IRQL.

User-mode threads do not have that privilege. Blocked interrupts do not receive attention until some thread explicitly lowers the CPU's level. When the processor runs at the lowest IRQL, normal thread execution proceeds and all interrupts are permitted to occur. When the trap handler calls an *interrupt service routine* (ISR), it first sets the CPU to that interrupt's IRQL. Traps of a lower level are masked while the ISR runs in order to prevent relatively unimportant events, such as device-input signals, from interfering with critical operations, such as the power-loss routines. When the processor's IRQL level drops, any interrupts that were masked are drawn from their queue and duly processed. Eventually, the processor returns to the lowest IRQL and the interrupted thread resumes.

Interrupt Handlers

To process any interrupt, the trap handler must first locate an appropriate handler routine somewhere in the system. It keeps track of interrupt handlers in the *interrupt dispatch table* (IDT). The IDT has 32 entries, one for each IRQ level. Each entry points to a handler, or possibly to a chain of handlers if several devices happen to use the same IRQL.

When new device drivers are loaded into the system, they immediately add their own handlers to the appropriate IDT entry. They do this by creating and connecting an *interrupt object*, a structure containing all the information the kernel needs to augment the IDT. By using an interrupt object, drivers are able to register their interrupt handlers without knowing anything about the interrupt hardware or the structure of the interrupt dispatch table.

Structured Exception Handling

Any exception that arises must be handled, if not by the program, then by the system itself. Some code somewhere must respond and clear it. Exception handling, then, means providing blocks of code to respond if an exception occurs. A program is likely to have many small handler blocks guarding different portions of code against different exceptions.

In searching for a block of code prepared to deal with a particular condition, the system looks first in the current procedure, then backward through the stack to other active pending procedures in the same process, and finally to the system's own exception handlers. If the offending process happens to be under the scrutiny of a debugger, then the debugging program also gets a chance to handle the exception.

Provisions for Error Handling

The provisions for handling errors differ with the subsystem and the programming language. The WOW subsystem, for example, must handle all exceptions directly because its Win16 clients have no way to do it themselves. Also, different languages may choose to expose exception handling through different syntax. But the name *structured exception handling* implies that the language itself must include some control structure for dealing with exceptions.

Microsoft's C/C++ Exception Handling

Microsoft's C/C++ compilers supply the keywords try and catch, each introducing a new block of code. A try block marks code that might raise exceptions. A catch block contains code to run if an exception occurs. From the programmer's perspective, these syntax structures conveniently separate code that handles exceptional conditions from code that handles normal tasks.

MFC Exception Handling

MFC uses an exception-handling scheme that is modeled on, but not identical, to the system proposed by the ANSI standards committee for C++. Following either the proposed standard or the MFC version requires an exception handler to be initiated before calling a function that may encounter an abnormal situation. If the function encounters an abnormal condition, an exception is thrown and control is passed to the exception handler.

Visual C++ Exception Handling

In Visual C++, exception handling is supported by several mechanisms:

- Exception-handling functions, which structure exception handling

- Exception-handling classes, which provide responses to specific exception types

- Exception macros, which structure application exception handlers

- Exception-throwing functions, which generate exceptions of specific types

All of these mechanisms are designed to throw exceptions or specialized exceptions and to terminate programs if necessary.

The basic exception-handling statements in Visual C++ are `try` and `catch`. The `try/catch` structure separates the code for exceptional situations from the code for normal situations.

```
try                              // beginning of try block
{
    <guarded code statements>  // code that may produce exceptions
}
catch( <filter> )              // beginning of exception handling block
{
    <exception handling code>  // code to execute if an exception occurs
}
```

DOS Exception Handling

Under DOS, the `try` keyword becomes `__try`, `catch` becomes `__except` and a third keyword, `__finally`, is also supported. The `__finally` block contains code to run when a `__try` block ends, even if the `__try` block fails or is interrupted.

For those interested in the DOS exception handling, several DOS-based examples are included on the CD accompanying this book. Look in the Chapter 18 folder for the Errors, Jumps, Nest, and Unwind subfolders, which contain DOS examples (originally published in *Mastering Windows NT Programming*, by Brian Myers and Eric Hamer). These examples have been revised for compatibility with Visual C/C++, and they will appear in a DOS window when compiled and executed. In addition, some notes have been added to explain current performance.

For more information about DOS exception handling, see the *NT 4/Windows 95 Developer's Handbook*, by Ben Ezzell with Jim Blaney (published by Sybex).

Filtering Exceptions

In any implementation, structured exception handling associates a block of code for handling exceptions with a block of code it is said to guard. If an exception occurs while the guarded block executes, control transfers to the filter expression.

Usually, the filter expression asks what the exception is and decides how to proceed. Exceptions that pass through the filter reach the exception-handling code. If the filter blocks an exception, then the handler is not invoked. The system continues to search elsewhere for a handler that will take the exception.

The filter expression may be complex. It may even call a separate function. Sometimes the filter does the real work of responding to an exception, leaving the catch block empty. In many cases, CException and CException-derived MFC classes may be used to handle exception events.

What Is Exceptional?

Programmers new to structured exception handling sometimes have the false impression that they no longer need to check for error returns after executing each command. An error, however, is not the same thing as an exception. A function can fail without raising an exception. For example, consider these lines of code:

```
hBrush = CreateSolidBrush( RGB(255, 0, 0) );
hOldBrush = SelectObject( hDC, hBrush );
Rectangle( hDC, 0, 0, 100, 100 );
```

If the first command fails and returns NULL for the brush, then SelectObject fails, too. The third command still draws a rectangle but does not color it correctly. No exceptions are raised. The only way to protect against those failures is to check the return values. Here's another example:

```
HANDLE hMemory;
char *pData;

hMemory = GlobalAlloc( GHND, 1000 );
pData = (char *)GlobalLock( hMemory );
```

If the allocation fails, then hMemory becomes NULL, GlobalLock fails, and pData becomes NULL, too. Neither failure, however, produces an exception. But the next line does produce an exception when it tries to write to an invalid address:

```
pData[0] = 'a';              // raises exception if pData = NULL
```

In the *Exceptions* demo, to create an exception, a similar process is used:

```
void CExceptionsView::ForceException()
{
    int    *p = 0x00000000;    // void pointer

    *p = 999;                  // invalid memory access
}
```

Here, assigning a void pointer is perfectly valid, but attempting to assign a value to the void pointer is not. This latter action is guaranteed to produce an exception, which is exactly what we want to do to test the exception-handler mechanisms.

NOTE   Using a memory-access violation to generate an exception is something of an extreme case; none of the **CException** classes provide explicit handling for this type of error. But, as you will see later in this chapter when we discuss the *Exception* demo routines, there is still a way to handle it!

An exception is a kind of error that a command cannot process. If GlobalAlloc cannot find enough room, it simply returns NULL. But if the assignment operator has no valid destination to place a value, it can do nothing, not even return an error. It must raise an exception, and if the process cannot handle the exception, the system must close down the process.

The line between exceptions and errors is sometimes difficult to draw. The difference between an error and an exception is sometimes a matter of implementation. Recognizing commands that might raise exceptions takes a little practice. You should learn which exceptions can arise and then imagine which operations might cause them. For example, a faulty assignment statement causes an *access-violation* exception. The list of possible exceptions varies on different machines, but here are some exceptions that the Windows 98 kernel defines:

- Data-type misalignment
- Debugger breakpoint
- Debugger single-step
- Floating-point divide by zero
- Floating-point overflow and underflow
- Floating-point reserved operand
- Guard-page violation

- Illegal instruction
- Integer divide by zero
- Integer overflow
- Memory-access violation
- Page-read error
- Paging file quota exceeded
- Privileged instruction

Frame-Based Exception Handling

The exception-handling mechanisms in Visual C++ are *frame-based*, meaning that each catch block is associated with, or framed in, the procedure that contains it. The term *frame* describes a layer in the program stack. Each time a program calls a procedure, the program pushes a new set of information on the stack. The information includes, for example, parameters passed to the new procedure and an address showing where to return when the called procedure ends. If the second procedure calls a third and the third a fourth, each successive call pushes a new frame onto the stack, as you see in Figure 18.1.

FIGURE 18.1:

Frames in a program stack

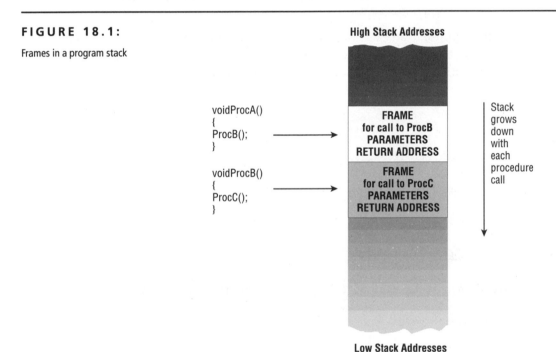

Each frame represents an activated procedure waiting for its subroutines to finish before resuming. At any point, it is possible to trace back through the stack frames to discover which procedures have been called. When an exception occurs, the system traces back, looking for exception handlers in each pending procedure.

The internal mechanisms that support exception handling vary from system to system. An MIPS machine, for example, implements handlers through tables, not stacks.

Order of Execution

When an exception arises, the system first saves the machine context of the interrupted thread, just as it does when it performs a context switch for normal multitasking. Depending on how the exception is eventually handled, the system may later use the saved context to resume execution at the beginning of the line where the exception occurred.

In response to an exception, the system generally tries to execute the exception filter first, and then the exception handler. However, you can provide for a variety of exceptions by stacking catch blocks, as illustrated by the following fragment:

```
try
{
    ...             // something that might cause an exception
}
catch( CMemoryException *e )        // out of memory exception
{
    // yadda, yadda, yadda
}
catch( CFileException *e )          // file exception
{
    // yadda, yadda, yadda
}
catch( CArchiveException *e )       // Archive/Serialization exception
{
    // yadda, yadda, yadda
}
catch( CNotSupportedException *e )  // response to request for
{                                   // unsupported service
    // yadda, yadda, yadda
}
catch( CResourceException *e )      // resource allocation exception
{
    // yadda, yadda, yadda
}
catch( CDaoException *e )           // database exceptions (DAO classes)
```

```
{
    // yadda, yadda, yadda
}
catch( CDBException *e )            // database exceptions (ODBC classes)
{
    // yadda, yadda, yadda
}
catch( COleException *e )          // OLE exceptions
{
    // yadda, yadda, yadda
}
catch( COleDispatchException *e )  // dispatch (automation) exceptions
{
    // yadda, yadda, yadda
}
catch( CUserException *e )         // user exception
{
    // yadda, yadda, yadda
}
catch( CException *e )             // must follow all derived classes or
{                                  // compiler will flag error
    // yadda, yadda, yadda
}
catch(...)                         // catch everything!!!
{
    // yadda, yadda, yadda
}
```

Here, all of the CException-derived classes are included in catch statements. An example that follows this structure is included in the *Exceptions* demo. However, in practice, you will probably not need to use such a through exception-handler routine. There are two items to note here:

- The catch(CException *e) block must follow all of the catch blocks using derived classes. If this ordering is not followed, the compiler will post an error warning that the derived blocks following catch(CException *e) will not be recognized because the CException block will have already trapped the exception.

- The catch(...) block follows everything else because this block catches exceptions that are not handled by the CException and CException-derived blocks.

Exception Handling and Debuggers

The task of finding a handler becomes more involved when a process is being debugged, because the system transfers control to the debugger *before* seeking the program's own exception handlers. Typically, the debugger uses this early alert to handle single-step and breakpoint exceptions, allowing the user to inspect the context before resuming.

If the debugger decides *not* to handle an exception during the early alert, the system returns to the process in search of a handler. If the process also refuses the exception, the system gives the debugger a second chance to handle what has now become a more serious situation. If the debugger refuses a second time, then the system finally gives up and settles for providing its own default response, which is usually to terminate the process.

Exception-Handling Macros

As an alternative to using the `try`/`catch` functions directly, you can structure your code with exception-handling macros. When using the macro approach, you'll begin with the TRY macro, which sets up a TRY block identifying a block of code that might throw exceptions.

Exceptions raised in the TRY block are handled in the following CATCH and AND_CATCH blocks. Also, recursion is allowed; exceptions may be passed to an outer TRY block, either by ignoring them or by using the THROW_LAST macro.

All CATCH blocks end with an END_CATCH or END_CATCH_ALL macro. If no CATCH block is supplied, the TRY block must include the END_CATCH or END_CATCH_ALL macro.

The THROW and THROW_LAST macros throw the specified exception, interrupting program execution and passing control to the program's associated CATCH block. If a CATCH block is not provided, control is passed to an MFC library module, which displays an error message and then exits. The THROW_LAST macro throws the exception back to the next outer CATCH block.

Nested exception handling is discussed in the following section.

Exception Classes

MFC provides a group of exception-handler classes, based on the CException class, for handling specific types of exceptions. Table 18.1 lists the derived classes.

TABLE 18.1: CException-derived Classes

Class	Description
CMemoryException	Out-of-memory exception
CNotSupportedException	Request for an unsupported operation
CArchiveException	Archive-specific exception
CFileException	File-specific exception
CResourceException	Windows resource not found or cannot be created
COleException	OLE exception
CDBException	Database exception; i.e., exception conditions arising for MFC database classes based on ODBC (Open Database Connectivity)
COleDispatchException	OLE dispatch (automation) exception
CUserException	Exception that indicates that a resource could not be found
CDaoException	Data access object exception; i.e., exception conditions arising for DAO classes
CInternetException	Internet exception; i.e., exception conditions arising for Internet classes

These exceptions are intended to be used with the try/catch block functions or the TRY, CATCH, AND_CATCH, THROW, THROW_LAST, and END_CATCH macros.

Customarily, you use a derived class to catch a specific exception type, but you may also use CException to trap all exception types before calling CObject::IsKind-Of to differentiate between the derived classes. Remember, however, that

`CObject::IsKindOf` applies only to classes declared using the IMPLEMENT_DYNAMIC macro, taking advantage of dynamic type checking. Any CException-derived class that you create should use the IMPLEMENT_DYNAMIC macro, too.

You can use the `GetErrorMessage` and `ReportError` member functions with any of the CException-derived classes to report details about exceptions.

If an exception is caught by one of the macros, the CException object is deleted automatically; do not delete it yourself. If an exception is caught by using a catch keyword, it is not automatically deleted, so you do need to delete it yourself.

> **NOTE**
> For more information about exception macros, refer to the Exception Processing or the Exceptions article in the online Visual C++ Programmer's Guide.

Because CException is an abstract base class, you cannot create CException-derived classes; you must create custom classes from derived classes. If you need to create your own CException type, use one of the derived classes listed as a model. Also, ensure that the derived class uses the IMPLEMENT_DYNAMIC macro to support dynamic type checking.

Catching Everything

In addition to using explicit CException-derived classes for catch clauses, you can also supply an ellipsis as the argument: catch (...). When you use an ellipsis as the exception declaration statement, the catch clause handles all types of exceptions, including C exceptions as well as system-generated and application-generated exceptions. These include exceptions such as memory protection, divide-by-zero, and floating-point violations.

> **NOTE**
> Remember, just as the CException handler must follow any CException-derived handler, an ellipsis catch handler must always be the last handler for its try block.

Plug-and-Play Event Messages

Plug-and-Play messages are not precisely the same as exception messages, but they do serve a similar purpose. They warn an application that something that could potentially affect operations has occurred. Note particularly the word *potentially*—the report is not that an error event has occurred, but simply that a normal and permitted event is taking place; the notification is provided as a courtesy.

More specifically, a Plug-and-Play event message is a hardware-level event issued as notification that some element of the system hardware is being added or removed. Whether this occurrence may affect operations or not is up to the application to determine and then handle if necessary.

At present, Plug-and-Play events are most relevant to laptop machines, with or without docking stations. However, as portable systems are coming to supplant conventional desktop systems and with the introduction of the Universal Serial Bus (which allows system components to be removed and added without powering down the main computer), Plug-and-Play events are becoming increasingly important to every application.

In brief, the current Plug-and-Play standards under Windows make provisions for generating WM_COMMAND/WM_DEVICECHANGE messages to report event codes describing the type of change and, in general, the device whose availability is changing. Plug-and-Play messages can provide notification of a variety of events, including the following:

- A request to dock or undock from a station, which may result in availability of new resources such as a docking station drive or network drive, or loss of resources currently in use

- A request to insert or disconnect a removable drive or other device such as a modem card, network card, or SCSI controller

The ability to recognize such events allows you to have an application adapt its operations to accommodate such changes or to warn the user that a change has affected the available resources.

A Plug-and-Play message is received as a WM_COMMAND event message where the event identifier WM_DEVICECHANGE is found in the low-word value in the wParam argument. Accompanying this in the high-word value is an identifier for the type of the event. The event types are as follows:

Value	Meaning
DBT_QUERYCHANGECONFIG	Permission is requested to change the current configuration (dock or undock).

Continued on next page

Value	Meaning
DBT_CONFIGCHANGED	The current configuration has changed due to a dock or undock.
DBT_CONFIGCHANGECANCELED	A request to change the current configuration (dock or undock) has been canceled.
DBT_DEVICEARRIVAL	A device has been inserted and is now available.
DBT_DEVICEQUERYREMOVE	Permission is requested to remove a device. Any application can deny this request and cancel the removal.
DBT_DEVICEQUERYREMOVEFAILED	A request to remove a device has been canceled.
DBT_DEVICEREMOVEPENDING	A device is about to be removed. This request cannot be denied.
DBT_DEVICEREMOVECOMPLETE	A device has been removed.
DBT_DEVICETYPESPECIFIC	A device-specific event has occurred. This is a generic interface allowing for media-specific information to be obtained from a hardware device.
DBT_USERDEFINED	The meaning of this message is user-defined.

In the same message, the lParam argument provides a pointer to a PDEV_BROADCAST_HDR structure, where the **dbch_devicetype** field identifies the type of device as:

```
((PDEV_BROADCAST_HDR) lParam )->dbch_devicetype
```

The device types are as follows:

Value	Meaning
DBT_DEVTYP_OEM	OEM-defined device type.
DBT_DEVTYP_DEVNODE	Device node number (*Win95/Win98 specific, not valid in WinNT*).
DBT_DEVTYP_VOLUME	Logical volume (a drive; may be either local or remote).

Continued on next page

Value	Meaning
DBT_DEVTYP_PORT	Serial or parallel port.
DBT_DEVTYP_NET	Network resource (UNC).

The following are additional DBT_* event codes:

DBT_DEVNODES_CHANGED	DBT_SHELLLOGGEDON
DBT_CONFIGMGAPI32	DBT_VOLLOCK_*
DBT_CONFIGMGPRIVATE	DTB_NO_DISK_SPACE

Paralleling Plug-and-Play events are two other event messages that deserve note here: **WM_DISPLAYCHANGE** and **WM_POWERBROADCAST**. **WM_DISPLAYCHANGE** allows applications to recognize a change in the display resolution (mode). **WM_POWERBROADCAST** allows applications to recognize situations where automatic power-down provisions have changed system behavior. Although this is usually applied to the monitor, many laptops also perform other types of shutdown to conserve battery power, including suspending drive and CPU operations even though they have not been turned off. This message is a feature of the Advanced Power Management (APM) system introduced by Windows 95.

Whether or not you incorporate any of these provisions in your application depends on the nature and needs of your program, of course. Recognizing such events, however, is a trivial exercise.

The Exceptions Demo: Exception-Handling Examples

The *Exceptions* demo provides examples of several types of exception handling. From the program's menu, select the example to run:

Simple Handler   Demonstrates a simple try/catch exception-handling structure.

Nested Handler   Demonstrates a nested try/catch exception-handling structure.

Failed Catch   Fails to catch a memory-access error; may require reboot.

Resource Exception   Fails to load a nonexistent resource.

User Exception   Throws a user exception.

For convenience, each of the examples displays a series of text messages in the application window, tracing the execution of the exception handling. Ideally, you should compile the example in debug mode, place breakpoints in the source code, and watch the execution directly, but the displayed messages offer an overview of the execution.

NOTE   The *Exceptions* demo is included on the CD accompanying this book, in the Chapter 18 folder.

A Simple Exception Handler

Beginning with the simplest example in the demo, a `try/catch` block is interrupted when the `ForceException` procedure is called to create a memory-access exception. The `ForceException` procedure was discussed briefly earlier in this chapter, in the "What Is Exceptional?" section. Figure 18.2 shows the display, where the messages trace the execution of the procedure.

FIGURE 18.2:

Displaying actions in a simple exception handler

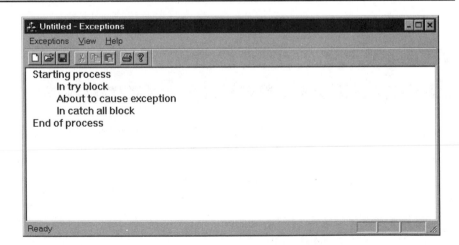

NOTE   Perhaps this is overly simple and too obvious to mention, but the message display would not be part of a conventional application. These messages are used here only to demonstrate the flow of events.

In this case, the exception has been trapped in the catch(...) block and has not produced a system fault.

```
void CExceptionsView::OnExceptionsSimplehandler()
{
    CDC     *pDC = GetDC();
    CSize   cSize = pDC->GetTextExtent( "A", 1 );    // get vertical size for text
    int     vSize = cSize.cy,
            iLine = 0;
    CString csText;
```

Each of the subroutines begins by getting a device context and then using the GetTextExtent function to determine the vertical size of a line of text so that we can use this value for spacing when displaying the messages. Also, the Invalidate and OnPaint calls are used to erase any text that we may have been left behind from a previous example.

```
    Invalidate();    OnPaint();                      // erase anything previous
    csText = "Starting process";
    pDC->TextOut( 10, vSize*iLine++, csText );
    try
    {
        csText = "In try block";
        pDC->TextOut( 50, vSize*iLine++, csText );
        csText = "About to cause exception";
        pDC->TextOut( 50, vSize*iLine++, csText );
        ForceException();                // shown previously
```

Even though the exception occurs in a separate subroutine, execution of the try block is suspended and passed to the catch(...) block. Therefore, the next line of text will not be displayed in the view window (see Figure 18.2). Instead, execution resumes in the catch block, where a different message is presented.

```
    csText = "This line will not display because execution has passed "
             "to the catch block";
    pDC->TextOut( 50, vSize*iLine++, csText );
}
catch(...)          // catch everything!!!
```

```
    {
        csText = "In catch all block";
        pDC->TextOut( 50, vSize*iLine++, csText );
    }
    csText = "End of process";
    pDC->TextOut( 10, vSize*iLine++, csText );
}
```

In a real application, the catch block might have any number of provisions, ranging from warning the user about the problem to executing some specific recovery operations. What exactly should occur, of course, depends on the exception and what operations were attempted.

A Nested Exception Handler

The second example in the demo, using nested exception handling, places one try/catch block inside an outer try block. Also, the inner catch block has a series of catch statements, illustrating how the various CException-derived classes might be employed. Last, a throw statement in the inner catch block throws the trapped exception to the outer catch block.

```
void CExceptionsView::OnExceptionsNestedhandlers()
{
    CDC     *pDC = GetDC();
    CSize   cSize = pDC->GetTextExtent( "A", 1 );
    int     vSize = cSize.cy, iLine = 0, *p = 0x00000000;
    CString csText;

    Invalidate();    OnPaint();                    // erase anything previous
    csText = "Starting process";
    pDC->TextOut( 10, vSize*iLine++, csText );
    try
    {
        csText = "In outer try block";
        pDC->TextOut( 50, vSize*iLine++, csText );
        try
        {
            csText = "In inner try block";
            pDC->TextOut( 90, vSize*iLine++, csText );
            csText = "About to cause exception ...";
            pDC->TextOut( 90, vSize*iLine++, csText );

            ForceException();
```

At this point, we're in the inner `try` block, and `ForceException` is about to produce an exception event, throwing execution to the inner `catch` block and preventing the next instructions from executing.

```
        csText = "This line will not display because execution "
                 "has passed to the catch block";
        pDC->TextOut( 50, vSize*iLine++, csText );
    }
```

Next, we have a series of `catch` blocks, each one explicitly trying to catch a particular type of exception defined by one of the `CException`-derived classes. However, this particular exception—a memory-access error—is not covered by any of these; therefore, the actual `catch` will not occur until a suitable handler is reached.

Because the body of each of these `catch` statements is essentially the same except for the display string, these have been truncated to save space.

```
catch( CMemoryException *e )            // out of memory
{
    TCHAR     szCause[255];

    csText = "CMemoryException cause: ";
    e->GetErrorMessage( szCause, 255 );
    csText += szCause;
    pDC->TextOut( 90, vSize*iLine++, csText );
}
catch( CFileException *e )              // file exception
{
    ...
}
 catch( CArchiveException *e )          // Archive/Serialization exception
{
    ...
}
 catch( CNotSupportedException *e )     // response to request for
{                                       // unsupported service
    ...
}
 catch( CResourceException *e )         // resource allocation exception
{
    ...
}
```

Because the demo application was not created using database support, the CDaoException and CDBException classes are not recognized and are commented out.

```
/*
                // no database support; ergo, CDaoException and
                // CDBException are not recognized in this example
    catch( CDaoException *e )           // database exceptions (DAO classes)
    {
        ...
    }
    catch( CDBException *e )            // database exceptions (ODBC classes)
    {
        ...
    }
*/
    catch( COleException *e )           // OLE exceptions
    {
        ...
    }
    catch( COleDispatchException *e )   // dispatch (automation) exceptions
    {
        ...
    }
    catch( CUserException *e )          // exception alerts the user with message
    {                                   // box, then throws a generic CException
        ...
    }
```

Finally, the CException catch appears after the derived classes. Otherwise, as mentioned earlier, the compiler would flag the derived catch blocks as errors.

```
    catch( CException *e )             // must follow all derived classes or
    {                                 // compiler will flag error
        TCHAR    szCause[255];

        csText = "CException cause: ";
        e->GetErrorMessage( szCause, 255 );
        csText += szCause;
        pDC->TextOut( 90, vSize*iLine++, csText );
    }
```

And, last, since we know that none of these CException classes will actually handle this particular exception, we include the catch(...)block, which catches everything but is not very informative about what has happened.

```
catch(...)                              // catch everything!!!
      {
          csText = "In inner catch all block: ";
          pDC->TextOut( 90, vSize*iLine++, csText );
          csText = "Throwing exception to outer catch block: ";
          pDC->TextOut( 90, vSize*iLine++, csText );
          throw;          // will throw exception to outer catch block below
      }
```

TIP

While using the catch(...)block is valid for preventing a program fault, it's better to try the CException classes first. You want to use only those classes that are relevant to the exception(s) you actually want to trap so that you can identify the exception and take appropriate recovery actions.

The exception occurred in the inner try block, was captured in the inner catch block, and is now being thrown to the outer catch block. The throw statement is simply a way to prevent the code following the try/catch blocks from being executed. This is essentially the same handling that occurred automatically in the inner try block when the original exception occurred. The only difference is that here, because of the exception entering the inner catch block, we have decided that we do not want the outer try block to continue either. In brief, this is simply an option to provide additional control over how the application executes and allows us to prevent the following program instructions from operating.

```
          csText = "This line will not display because execution has "
                  "been thrown to the outer catch block";
          pDC->TextOut( 50, vSize*iLine++, csText );
      }
      catch(...)                              // catch everything!!!
      {
          csText = "In outer catch all block, catching thrown exception";
          pDC->TextOut( 50, vSize*iLine++, csText );
      }
      csText = "End of process";
      pDC->TextOut( 10, vSize*iLine++, csText );
  }
```

Figure 18.3 shows the flow report generated by the Nested Exception example. The report explains how the exception has been caught and redirected to the outer `catch` block.

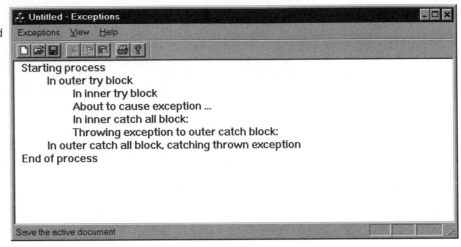

```
Untitled - Exceptions                                      _ □ ×
 Exceptions   View   Help

 □ ☞ 🖫   🖺 🖻 🖻   🖨 ?

 Starting process
        In outer try block
                In inner try block
                About to cause exception ...
                In inner catch all block:
                Throwing exception to outer catch block:
        In outer catch all block, catching thrown exception
 End of process




 Save the active document
```

NOTE   Perhaps some of you remember using GOTO and LABEL instructions for similar purposes. In one sense, the **throw** function is less flexible; in other respects, it is simply more rigorous in its structuring. But however you view it, the **throw** statement does provide a means of bypassing a block of instructions in response to a failed circumstance. In many circumstances, this may be exactly what you need to prevent further or more serious malfunctions.

A Failed Catch Example

The failed catch example illustrates what happens when a `try/catch` combination attempts to guard execution of an area of code but fails to correctly trap an exception; that is, the program encounters an exception that is not trapped.

The code for this example is essentially the same as the code for the simple exception handler.

```
void CExceptionsView::OnExceptionsFailedcatch()
{
    CDC     *pDC = GetDC();
    CSize   cSize = pDC->GetTextExtent( "A", 1 );
    int     vSize = cSize.cy, iLine = 0, *p = 0x00000000;
    CString csText;

    Invalidate();    OnPaint();                    // erase anything previous
    csText = "Starting process";
    pDC->TextOut( 10, vSize*iLine++, csText );
    try
    {
        csText = "In try block";
        pDC->TextOut( 50, vSize*iLine++, csText );
        csText = "About to cause exception ...";
        pDC->TextOut( 90, vSize*iLine++, csText );
```

In addition to the text display, the routine also displays a modal dialog message with a warning, as shown in Figure 18.4, because this routine is intended to fail.

```
        MessageBox( "WARNING!\r\nThis exception may require a reboot\r\n"
                    "for full recovery!" );
        *p = 999;
    }
    catch( CException *e )                         // CException will not catch the
    {                                              // memory access error ...
        TCHAR   szCause[255];

        csText = "In catch block";
        pDC->TextOut( 50, vSize*iLine++, csText );
        csText = _T("CException cause: ");
        e->GetErrorMessage( szCause, 255 );
        csText += szCause;


    }
```

FIGURE 18.4:

The warning for the failed catch example

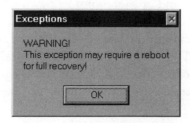

NOTE The failed catch example may either terminate the demo application or corrupt system memory to the point of requiring a reboot to recover. We cannot be sure which of these events will occur because Windows 98 does not protect memory as rigorously as does Windows NT; but in either case, you are appropriately warned.

The `catch(...)`handler is commented out because this is the only handler that can catch the memory-access fault, and the point of this example is what happens when the exception is not handled. You could enable the `catch(...)` block to prevent the failure.

```
/*            // enabling the catch(...) block will
              // prevent the system from trapping the error
    catch(...)                                // catch everything ... including
    {                                         // the memory access error!
        csText = "In catch all block";
        pDC->TextOut( 50, vSize*iLine++, csText );
    }
*/
    csText = "End of process";
    pDC->TextOut( 10, vSize*iLine++, csText );
}
```

A Resource Exception Example

Not all exceptions are automatically generated by the system. In many cases, you will want to raise an exception because you have detected a malfunction or error and need to branch execution or to avoid executing subsequent instructions. This task is best accomplished by throwing an exception to a `catch` block, for reporting or for alternative handling.

For example, you might be translating a lengthy string table for internationalization and one (or more) strings might be lost in the process (accidents do happen). As long as the resource identifier was not lost, the code will still compile, even though there are instructions to retrieve a string table entry that does not exist. This mishap does not in itself raise an exception. Instead, the `LoadString` instruction simply returns a zero length reporting that the item was not found. In most cases, you will not have even bothered to check the return value. However, the resource exception example in the demo does check and uses the error to raise an exception.

The resource exception example begins with both an inner and outer `try` block, to illustrate the `throw` operation again. In the inner `try` block, it attempts to load a string resource.

```
void CExceptionsView::OnExceptionsResourceexception()
{
    CDC      *pDC = GetDC();
    CSize    cSize = pDC->GetTextExtent( "A", 1 );
    int      vSize = cSize.cy, iLine = 0;
    CString  csText, csMsg;

    Invalidate();    OnPaint();                    // erase anything previous
    csText = "Starting process";
    pDC->TextOut( 10, vSize*iLine++, csText );
    try
    {
        csText = "In outer try block";
        pDC->TextOut( 50, vSize*iLine++, csText );
        try
        {
            csText = "In inner try block";
            pDC->TextOut( 90, vSize*iLine++, csText );
            csText = "About to cause exception ...";
            pDC->TextOut( 90, vSize*iLine++, csText );
            if( ! csText.LoadString( IDS_NON_STRING ) )
                AfxThrowResourceException();
            pDC->TextOut( 90, vSize*iLine++, csText );
        }
```

If the `LoadString` operation succeeded, the application would have proceeded by displaying the string. However, there is no corresponding string table entry, even though the Resource.H file has a definition for the resource identifier. Therefore, `AfxThrowResourceException` is called and throws an exception, forcing execution into the following `catch` blocks.

```
    catch( CResourceException *e )           // resource allocation exception
    {
        TCHAR    szCause[255];

        csText = "CResourceException cause: ";
        e->GetErrorMessage( szCause, 255 );
```

```
        csText += szCause;
        pDC->TextOut( 90, vSize*iLine++, csText );
    }
```

Here, the CResourceException class does catch the exception and reports the cause of the exception as "A required resource was unavailable," as you can see in Figure 18.5.

```
catch( CException *e )                  // must follow all derived classes or
{                                       // compiler will flag error
    TCHAR    szCause[255];

    csText = "CException cause: ";
    e->GetErrorMessage( szCause, 255 );
    csText += szCause;
    pDC->TextOut( 90, vSize*iLine++, csText );
}
catch(...)                              // catch everything!!!
{
    csText = "In inner catch all block: ";
    pDC->TextOut( 90, vSize*iLine++, csText );
    csText = "Throwing exception to outer catch block: ";
    pDC->TextOut( 90, vSize*iLine++, csText );
    throw;         // will throw exception to outer catch block below
}
```

FIGURE 18.5:

Raising a resource exception

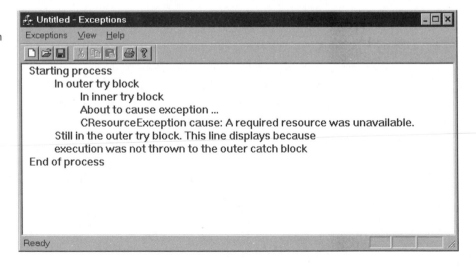

Notice that while the catch(...) handler does have a throw instruction, the CResourceException handler did not. Since the exception has trapped (handled) in the CResourceException handler, the throw instruction is not executed. Therefore, the outer try block continues execution and displays the following message.

```
        csText = "Still in the outer try block. This line displays because";
        pDC->TextOut( 50, vSize*iLine++, csText );
        csText = "execution was not thrown to the outer catch block";
        pDC->TextOut( 50, vSize*iLine++, csText );
    }
    catch(...)                                      // catch everything!!!
    {
        csText = "In outer catch all block, catching thrown exception";
        pDC->TextOut( 50, vSize*iLine++, csText );
    }
    csText = "End of process";
    pDC->TextOut( 10, vSize*iLine++, csText );
}
```

By using different exception handlers, depending on the exception, the application can respond in different fashions. And, always remember, the catch handlers may contain a variety of different responses to the exception, as appropriate.

TIP

This example uses a string resource, but any type of missing resource could be justification for raising a resource exception. You might consider experimenting with other types, such as dialog boxes or custom resource types.

A User Exception Example

Like a resource exception, a user exception must almost always be raised explicitly. The system does not have any way of recognizing a user error because these errors occur within the application's context. It is up to you to define the user exception. Raising a user exception is not particularly different from raising a resource exception.

In most cases, when a user error occurs, you should simply have provisions in place to recognize them, to alert the user, and to suggest corrective actions. Raising an exception should not be the automatic response. Still, there may be circumstances where the only practical way to avoid more serious problems as a result of a user mistake is to raise an exception and to throw execution to a `catch` handler for resolution.

Because the exception does not necessarily need to occur in the same procedure as the `try/catch` blocks, the demo uses a subprocedure to illustrate this fact.

```
BOOL CExceptionsView::UserException()
{        // assume something has gone wrong
    AfxMessageBox( "Drat! The XDR Veng operation failed!" );
    AfxThrowUserException();
    return TRUE;
}
```

Here, the `UserException` procedure displays a message box reporting a failure, as shown in Figure 18.6, and then uses `AfxThrowUserException` to raise an exception.

FIGURE 18.6:

Raising a user exception

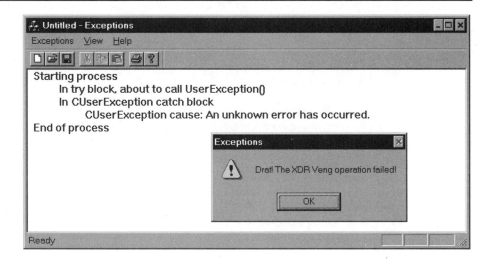

The `UserException` procedure is called from the following process, where the `try/catch` blocks appear:

```
void CExceptionsView::OnExceptionsUserexception()
{
    CDC        *pDC = GetDC();
    CSize    cSize = pDC->GetTextExtent( "A", 1 );
```

```
int        vSize = cSize.cy, iLine = 0, *p = 0x00000000;
CString    csText, csMsg;

Invalidate();    OnPaint();                    // erase anything previous
csText = "Starting process";
pDC->TextOut( 10, vSize*iLine++, csText );
try
{
    csText = "In try block, about to call UserException()";
    pDC->TextOut( 50, vSize*iLine++, csText );
    if( UserException() )
    {
        csText = "In try block, the XDR Veng operation succeeded (impossible)";
        pDC->TextOut( 50, vSize*iLine++, csText );
    }
    csText = "Continuing try block";
    pDC->TextOut( 50, vSize*iLine++, csText );
}
```

Since we expect UserException to throw an exception, the message reporting the operation as successful will never be executed. If you trace this process, you will not see a return value from the UserException subprocedure, because execution has been thrown directly to the catch handlers.

```
catch( CUserException *e )
{
    TCHAR    szCause[255];

    csText = "In CUserException catch block";
    pDC->TextOut( 50, vSize*iLine++, csText );
    csText = "CUserException cause: ";
    e->GetErrorMessage( szCause, 255 );
    csText += szCause;
    pDC->TextOut( 90, vSize*iLine++, csText );
}
```

In the CUserException handler, the cause for the exception is reported as "unknown." After all, the CUserException class has no way to know why the exception was raised. However, by using a custom, derived class, you could provide explanations and include mechanisms for identifying different types of exceptions.

```
catch( CException *e )
{
    TCHAR    szCause[255];

    csText = "In CException catch block (unexpected)";
    pDC->TextOut( 50, vSize*iLine++, csText );
    csText = "CException cause: ";
    e->GetErrorMessage( szCause, 255 );
    csText += szCause;
    pDC->TextOut( 90, vSize*iLine++, csText );
}
csText = "End of process";
pDC->TextOut( 10, vSize*iLine++, csText );
return;    // no exception thrown
}
```

This concludes our introduction to exception handling. Exceptions are a useful tool and, in addition to the *Exceptions* demo, a number of other examples are included on the CD accompanying this book. Additional information is also available in the online documentation that is included on your Visual C++ CD.

Also note that although this chapter did not demonstrate the use of the TRY and CATCH macros (in favor of using the clearer try/catch block instructions), these macros are still worth consideration.

In the next chapter, we move to another aspect of Windows 98 application development: memory management.

CHAPTER

NINETEEN

19

Memory Management

- How the Virtual Memory Manager handles memory

- Virtual memory commands

- Heap management

- File-mapping objects for sharing memory

Besides the flashy interface and the multitasking, one of Windows' great attractions has always been memory management. From the 8086 target machine of version 1 all the way up through the 80486, 16-bit Windows has always helped programs make full use of whatever resources the system offers. But MS-DOS, the underlying trellis on which Windows grew, was inherently a 1MB system, and much of the potential of a 32-bit processor remained untapped.

The first crack in the 1MB barrier came with the protected addressing mode of the 80286 processor, which offered access to more memory but was incompatible with the DOS real mode. The result was a flurry of proposed memory-management standards and DOS-extender programs blazing new routes into the frontiers. The methods were ingenious. Temporarily unneeded blocks of code or data were swung up like a Murphy bed into higher memory, and clever programmers insinuated their code into the lowest levels of the system software to hijack allocation requests and smuggle goods across the 1MB border. The original 80286 was never designed for one program to run in two modes. When switching from one to the other, the CPU ground to a halt and reset itself. Like Janus, the two-faced god of doorways, the DOS extender must stand with one leg on each side of the abyss. And 16-bit Windows never entirely freed itself from this schizophrenic existence; it just became better adjusted to its inherent neuroses.

Beginning with Windows NT and continuing with Windows 95 and 98, Windows has finally transcended the restrictions of DOS. Windows NT is a true protected-mode system, where attempts to address illegal memory space result in the errant application being terminated. Unfortunately, Windows 98 is not so fully protected, and errant applications are more likely to crash the system than to be terminated by the system.

This chapter begins by summarizing the hardware mechanisms and system policies that underlie the memory management of Windows 98, and explaining the translation from virtual to physical memory and the paging scheme that supports the protected address spaces. A new set of virtual memory API routines gives you control over individual memory pages. The Win32 API also adds improved heap management while still preserving the old global and local memory functions from the Win16 API. After discussing these memory-management commands, we'll see how processes in protected address spaces can share blocks of memory by creating file-mapping objects.

Memory-Management Concepts

The Windows 98 memory management API, working with an imagined logical address space of 2GB, is supported internally by the Virtual Memory Manager (VMM), which in turn bases its services on the features of advanced 32-bit processors. Windows 98 requires its hardware to use 32-bit memory addresses, to map virtual to physical addresses, and to perform memory paging. From these basic capabilities, the VMM constructs its own mechanisms and policies for managing virtual memory.

NOTE   Windows NT memory management differs from Windows 98 memory management in one way: Windows NT works with an imagined logical address space of 4GB, while Windows 98 is limited to a mere 2GB. Currently, both of these limits are well in excess of anything we expect to see physically installed in any system (in the near future, at least). No doubt, when RAM in excess of 1GB becomes a common feature, some extension will be introduced to allow addressing spaces well in excess of either limit. Functionally, this single issue aside, the memory management APIs perform essentially the same for both systems.

The Virtual Memory Manager (VMM)

Like virtual reality, virtual memory isn't the real thing but does a good job of pretending to be. The 2GB of memory addresses that every program commands is a virtual space. The system does not contain 2GB of physical memory, yet somehow a program is able to use any address in the full range. Obviously, a translator somewhere in the background must silently convert each memory reference into an existing physical address. From this silent conversion, the VMM draws much of its power.

The VMM is the part of the Windows system responsible for mapping references to a program's virtual address space into physical memory. It decides where to put each memory object and which memory pages should be written to disk. It also isolates each process in a separate address space by refusing to translate virtual addresses from one process into the physical memory used by another process. It supports the illusion of an idealized, logical space of 2GB, just as the GDI supports the illusion that every program draws to idealized logical display coordinates. The system translates logical addresses or coordinates into physical locations and prevents programs from colliding with each other by trying to use the same resource at the same time.

Pointers and Movable Memory

MS-DOS programmers customarily work with pointers to memory objects. If the object moves to another location, the pointer becomes invalid. On a machine that runs only one program at a time, pointers work fine. But multitasking systems need to manage system memory more actively, loading and discarding pieces on demand and moving pieces to make more room.

The first versions of Windows got around the problem by substituting handles for pointers wherever possible. A handle points to an entry in an object table, and the table remembers where each object actually is at any given moment. When the system moves an object, it updates the table. The handles pointing to the table remain valid even when the object moves because they point to the place where the real pointer is kept, and the system keeps the real pointer current.

Selectors and Offsets

Processors running in a protected mode provide a similar layering mechanism for all memory addresses. Instead of working with pointers containing segments and offsets, Intel CPUs work with *selectors* and offsets. A selector is to memory what a handle is to Windows—a pointer to a pointer.

To give a simplified account, the selector, with its offset, refers to a system table that keeps track of memory addresses. In a sense, protected mode has built-in memory handles. The difference is that selectors live at a much lower level in the system than handles do. The hardware knows what a selector is— the CPU can decode them—but only Windows knows what a handle is. Windows can have handles only where Windows itself creates them. You must make an effort to use handles instead of pointers, but protected mode gives you selectors whether you want them or not.

Even when you lock down memory, the system lets you see only the selector, not the physical address. Your program doesn't care. The code that worked with pointers works just as well with selectors, only now it doesn't matter if the system moves what your selector "points" to. The operating system can move objects through memory with impunity as long as it remembers to update the corresponding memory table entry. The entry may change, but the selector does not. The selector always points to the same place in the table, and the table is guaranteed to point to your memory object. As a consequence, you can safely use and preserve a pointer without impeding any other program.

Conversion to Physical Addresses

The conversion from a selector and its offset to a physical address involves two stages: a trivial conversion from a logical to a virtual address and a complex conversion from a linear address to a physical address.

The first conversion, from a logical segmented address to a virtual linear address, simply adds an offset to a base address. Win32 makes this conversion trivial by keeping the base address set always to 0. If the segment is constant, only the offset matters. The 32-bit offset may range from 0 to 2GB, exactly the range of the system's flat linear addresses. Under Win32, a 32-bit selector addresses all of virtual memory in much the same way that small-model programs address their entire segment with a single near pointer. But a linear address is still not a physical address.

In the second and more complex conversion, the VMM parses the linear address into indices for the process's paging tables, which contain physical addresses.

Paging

The use of virtual addresses confers many benefits, among them the illusion of working in a very large space. Win32 allows the virtual addresses to range from 0 to 2GB, regardless of the physical memory actually installed on the current system. Obviously, a problem arises if all the running programs try to allocate all the virtual memory that they think they see at once. Like a bank, the system goes suddenly broke if all its customers cash in at the same time. Physical memory always imposes some kind of upper limit, but a paging system raises the limit considerably by setting off part of a hard disk to act as additional memory.

Pages and Page Frames

The CPUs on which Windows runs have built-in memory-paging capabilities. Small blocks of memory called *pages* can be saved to the disk when not in use to make more room. A page interrupt occurs whenever a program tries to read a part of memory that has been moved to the disk. The program doesn't ever know the memory is gone; the CPU generates an error, the operating system reloads the missing page, and the program resumes. If blocks of memory can be saved and restored as needed, nothing prevents the system from over-committing memory. If you have a thousand pages of memory, you could have two thousand pages' worth of code. It can't all be in memory at once, but any block can always be loaded when needed. Of course, disks are slower than RAM and virtual memory always works best if your hard drive is large, fast, and partially empty.

Much of the VMM's energy goes into moving and recovering pages of memory. Windows can work with pages of up to 64KB, but the Intel CPU enforces a size of 4KB. A 4KB block of memory aligned on a 4KB boundary is called a *page frame*. The term *page* refers to the data a program stores in a page frame. There are usually more pages than page frames; some of the pages have been saved in the paging file. Although the contents of a page remain the same, those contents may appear in different page frames at different times as the VMM adjusts to the demands of all the current programs.

Page Databases, Tables, and Directories

In order to satisfy requests for memory, the VMM maintains several data structures. It must be able, for example, to traverse a list of page frames to see which are free and which are full and also to determine which process currently owns any given page. (Obviously, this also requires each process to occupy some integral number of pages regardless of their actual requirements.)

The structure that holds this set of information is the *page frame database*. Through the database, the VMM, given any page, can find the process that owns it. Another data structure, called a *page table*, works in the other direction. Every process has at least one page table; given any process, the VMM can find all the pages it owns.

When the VMM assigns physical memory to a process, it updates the database and also adds an entry to a page table. Whenever a process refers to a virtual address, the VMM looks up the address in a page table to find the associated memory. Besides a virtual address and its corresponding physical address, the page table entry records other information about each page, including whether the page is protected (read-only, for example) and whether it is in memory or swapped to the disk. A swapped page is marked invalid in the page table (*invalid* meaning that it resides in the swap file rather than in memory).

For the convenience of the hardware, a single page table takes up exactly 4KB. One 4KB page table has room for 1024 different entries. Each entry points to a single page. If one page table can point to 1024 pages and each page is 4KB, then one page table can address 4MB of memory (1024 × 4096). A process that uses more memory receives more page tables.

Each process has a single master table, called a *page directory*, pointing to all its page tables. A page directory also holds up to 1024 entries. With 1024 page tables, each addressing 4MB, a process can reach up to 4GB (4MB × 1024). Because each page directory and page table occupies exactly 4KB, or one page frame, the system can easily swap the directory and tables in and out of memory along with all the other pages as needed.

The diagram shown in Figure 19.1 should help clarify how page directories point to page tables that point to pages, and at the same time the page frame database keeps a separate list of each page's current status. Most memory operations occur more rapidly than this elaborate indexing scheme seems to allow, because the CPU caches frequently used virtual address translations in a fast hardware buffer called the translation look-aside buffer (TLB).

FIGURE 19.1:

How the system finds a process's physical memory through the page directory and page tables

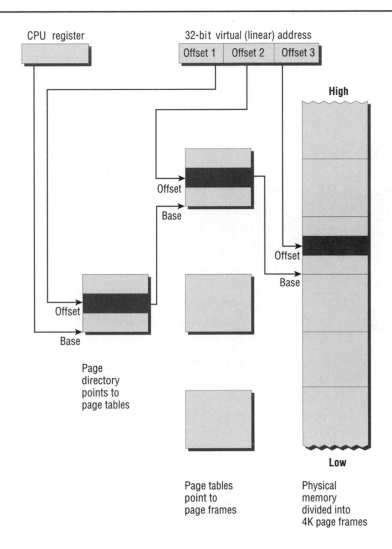

CPU register

32-bit virtual (linear) address

| Offset 1 | Offset 2 | Offset 3 |

High

Offset

Base

Offset

Base

Offset

Base

Page directory points to page tables

Page tables point to page frames

Physical memory divided into 4K page frames

Low

Page Frame States

The page frame database records the current state of each page frame. A page frame is always in one of six states (or has one of six status markers):

Valid   A frame that contains a page that some process is using. A page table entry points to it.

Standby   A frame that contains a page that was in use, but the VMM has decided to free it for some process. A standby page has been removed from the process's working set.

Modified   A frame that contains a page that the VMM wants to discard, but because the process has modified the page, it must first be saved to disk.

Free   A frame that is no longer owned by any process. Anything it contained has been saved to disk.

Zeroed   A frame belonging to no one and full of nothing but zeros. Only zeroed pages may be given to any process. When a frame is zeroed, the information it held is moved to virtual memory (a disk swap file) and must be reloaded.

Bad   A frame that generated a parity error or other hardware error and cannot be used.

Within the page frame database, all the page entries with the same status marker are linked to each other. The VMM can follow a different series of links to find all the zeroed pages, all the free pages, all the standby pages, and so on.

Releasing a page frame involves several steps, and the status marker reflects how far along the process the VMM has come. When it needs to make room, the VMM looks for frames that haven't been used recently and marks them for later disposal. If the page has not been changed by its process, it is marked standby. If the process has written to the page so that it needs to be saved to the disk, it is marked modified. Both markers indicate that the page is ready to be released but has not yet been released. If the owning process tries to use the page while it is still marked standby or modified, the system responds quickly to the resulting page fault because it does not need to read the page back from the disk. It simply changes the status back to valid.

WARNING   One of the more obvious ways for a page fault to occur is for an application to attempt to perform its own memory operations and to write to an invalid address (an address that the application or process does not own). Under Windows NT, where operations are very tightly controlled, the usual result is that the process will be terminated by the system. Under Windows 98, memory addressing is not so thoroughly policed and improper addressing may trash the system itself.

For security reasons, any page frame assigned to a process must be zeroed first. No process may receive memory that still contains information left behind by another program. When the list of available zeroed pages runs low, the memory manager reads through the page frame database following all the links to free pages and zeroes them. If memory is still low, the VMM wakes one of its threads to find modified pages and save them, slowly and one by one in the background, so as not to interfere with system performance.

Policies and Working Sets

It should be clear by now that the VMM keeps a constant watch over the status of all the system pages. If one process uses more physical memory than allowed in its security quota, the VMM steps in and invalidates some of its pages by marking them standby or modified, and eventually their page frames may be released. The group of page frames currently in use by one process is the process's *working set*. Like an embezzler, the VMM sneaks through the system and steals frames out from under processes as they run, hoping no one will notice. When a process begins to complain with a flurry of page faults, the VMM placates it by enlarging its working set. Busy programs end up with bigger sets.

The VMM follows defined policies in deciding when to retrieve swapped pages, where to place restored pages in memory, and what to swap out first when the system needs more room. This retrieval policy is called demand paging with clustering. *Demand paging* means that the VMM loads pages only when a program asks for them, rather than trying to minimize delays by anticipating what a program will need. The system does try to anticipate to some extent by *clustering*; thus, in response to each demand, the system actually loads several adjacent pages, figuring that memory operations often center on a single region, so nearby pages may be needed soon.

The placement policy determines where reloaded pages are stored. The VMM tries to put them on the first zeroed page frames it finds in the page frame database. When it runs out of zeroed frames, it begins searching the lists of frames in other states.

When deciding on pages to swap out, the VMM follows a local FIFO replacement policy. *Local* in this context means that the system makes room for one page in a process by dropping another page from the same process. By keeping the working set for each process to a roughly constant size, the system prevents one program from monopolizing resources. *FIFO* means "first in first out." Within one process's working set, the pages that have been in memory longest are the first to go. Pages a program touches often may be marked invalid but the process will probably recover them from their transitional standby or modified state before the VMM actually saves the contents and zeroes the frame.

Commitments and Reservations

Now that you know the VMM is sneaky because it steals pages and that it's lazy because it often invalidates them without bothering to discard them, perhaps you won't be surprised to learn that it sometimes only pretends to allocate the memory you request.

To allocate memory, the VMM must construct page tables and search the page frame database for suitable zeroed areas. It may even need to find other invalidated pages and prepare them for use, possibly readjusting the working sets of other programs. If a program allocates a large virtual space but ends up using only parts of it, the VMM's efforts will have been largely wasted. Instead of allocating physical memory, the VMM often simply marks part of the process's virtual address space as being in use without securing physical memory to back it up. It *reserves* memory without *committing* it.

Reserving memory is like paying with a promissory note. When a program later tries to use some of the reserved memory, cashing in its IOU, the hardware notices because it can't find a page table entry for the given virtual address. It issues a page fault. The VMM steps in and finally pays its debt, committing physical pages to fulfill an allocation. Of course, even as it commits new page frames for one request, it may be invalidating other pages to make room. The entire sequence of reserving addresses, receiving a page fault, and committing new memory is intended to be invisible to the process.

Virtual Address Descriptors

To support the illusion of a vast address space, the VMM requires yet another data structure. A tree of virtual address descriptors (VADs) records each allocation and suballocation that the process makes in its range of virtual addresses. Whenever a program allocates memory, the VMM creates a VAD and adds it to the tree, as shown in Figure 19.2. A VAD records the range of addresses an allocation claims, the protection status for all pages in the range, and whether child processes may inherit the object contained in the range. If a thread uses an address that falls outside the range of any of its VADs, the VMM knows the address was never reserved and recognizes an access violation.

FIGURE 19.2:

Tree of virtual address descriptors (VADs)

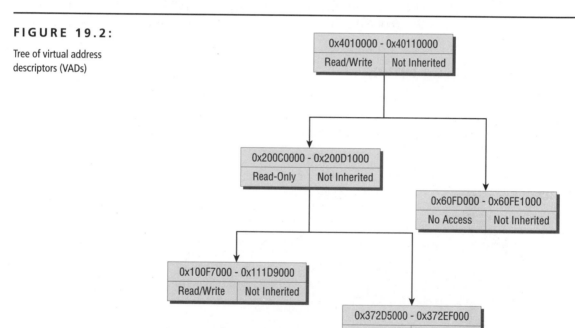

Constructing a VAD is much simpler than constructing a page table and filling it with valid page frame addresses. Furthermore, the size of the allocation has no effect on the speed of the response. Reserving 2KB is no faster than reserving 2MB; each request produces a single VAD. When a thread actually uses the reserved memory, the VMM commits page frames by copying information from the descriptor into new page table entries.

Virtual Memory APIs

Often, programs have no need to concern themselves with the differences between reserved and committed memory. Usually it's enough to know that memory will be available when you expect it to be. Among its new features, however, Win32 boasts a set of virtual memory APIs that give you precise control over reserving, committing, and protecting pages of memory. By using these APIs, you can allocate a very large memory object, fill it only partially, and not waste any memory. The usual example is a spreadsheet because most of its cells are likely to be empty, with data clustering together in a few areas. If you reserve a large range of addresses to represent the entire spreadsheet as an array, the VMM commits physical memory only for the areas actually in use, and it still allows convenient access to any part of the array through a full range of continuous addresses.

The Address Space

Most of what you've read about so far goes on behind the scenes. From the perspective of a running program, what matters most is not the page tables and working sets but the 2GB of virtual address space. Figure 19.3 shows how the system organizes the space.

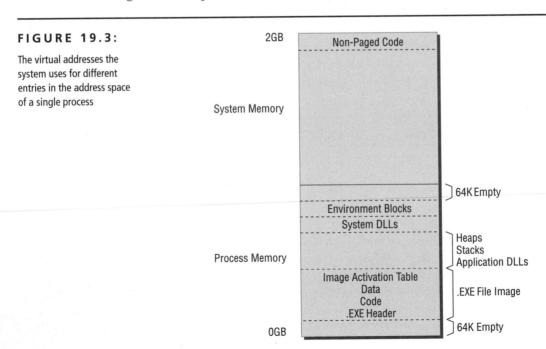

FIGURE 19.3:

The virtual addresses the system uses for different entries in the address space of a single process

Although a process does indeed run in a 2GB address space, the process gets to use only 1GB of those addresses. The system reserves the upper half of the addresses for itself. The high half of the address space is the same for every application, but only kernel-mode threads may use it. In other words, it is accessible only to the operating system. At the very highest addresses, the system keeps critical system code that cannot be paged out of memory; for example, the part of the VMM that performs paging operations is stored at the high addresses.

All the pieces of memory over which you have control are mapped into the lower 1GB of the address space. That's where the code and data for a process reside, along with a stack for each thread, at least one default heap, and the program's own DLLs. The system always loads a process's code near the bottom of the address space at the 64KB mark. The 64KB at the top of a process's 1GB space also remain permanently empty. The no-man's land at either end helps the system identify invalid pointers. For example, 0 is never a valid address.

At the lowest available address is an image of the process's .EXE file, including its header, code, data, and an *image activation table.* The activation table aids in dynamic linking. When the linker finds a `CreateWindow` command in your code, for example, it cannot know in advance where in memory to find the `CreateWindow` code. For all such unresolved dynamic links, the linker creates an entry in the image activation table. When the system loads an executable file, it searches for all the DLL entry points listed in the activation table, locates the appropriate DLL, and fixes the table to include the current entry addresses. The linker speeds loading by guessing where the DLLs will be and providing tentative addresses. The Win32 subsystem always tries to map its system DLLs to the same addresses near the top of the 1GB space. If, on loading a program, the system discovers that the DLLs are indeed in the expected place, then the activation table does not need fixing. (You can specify a preferred loading address for your own DLLs, too.)

The loader may not actually copy an entire .EXE file into memory. It is more likely to reserve virtual addresses for the .EXE file and let the VMM commit physical pages later if the code refers to those addresses. The Win32 subsystem DLLs have been structured to cluster related commands in adjacent addresses. As a result, common calling sequences usually require a minimum of new pages to be loaded.

An application's own DLLs, heaps, and stacks may be allocated anywhere in the address space between the .EXE file image and the system DLLs. Normally, the first allocation begins at 0×00010000, or 64KB.

Memory-Mapped Files

Alert readers may already have wondered what happens when a user initiates several instances of a single program. Given that every process has its own secure address space, must the system load a new copy of the .EXE file for each new instance? If not, how do two processes share the block of memory that contains the file image? The situation calls for a new strategy and one widely useful in many other situations as well.

Normally, the VMM protects programs from each other by ensuring that a virtual address from one process never translates to a page frame in use by another process. Because the VMM always translates every virtual address into a physical address, no program reaches memory directly, and the VMM easily routes every memory access to a safe location. The scheme also allows for the VMM to make a single page frame visible in the virtual addresses of different processes. At the operating-system level, a block of shared memory is called a *section object*.

The Win32 subsystem exposes the functionality of section objects to its clients in the form of *memory-mapped files*. Two programs cannot share memory directly, but they can share the same disk file. Of course, most of what the process perceives as physical memory is already in a disk-swapping file. In effect, the VMM lets you retrieve information from the swap file by reading from particular memory addresses. In fact, you can access any disk file the same way, using memory addresses, by creating a memory-mapped file. As an extension of this memory I/O capability, two processes may open the same block of memory as though it were a file, read from it, and write to it. To share memory without creating a new disk file, the programs link the shared object to the system's normal page-swapping file.

When the user launches multiple instances of a program, the system creates a mapped-file object to enable all instances to share a single copy of the .EXE file image.

Memory-Management Commands

The Win32 memory management commands fall into three main categories: virtual memory functions, heap functions, and the familiar global and local allocation functions. Each set includes commands to allocate and free blocks of memory, but each set manages memory a little differently. We'll survey each group, look briefly at a few related commands, and finish this section with the API for memory-mapped files.

Virtual Memory Commands

The virtual memory commands, which have names like `VirtualAlloc` and `VirtualFree`, expose some of the VMM's operations that the other two command sets hide. With the virtual memory commands, you can imitate the VMM by reserving addresses without committing memory to support them and by protecting ranges of memory with read-only, read/write, or no-access flags. You can also lock pages in memory to prevent them from being swapped to disk. The other command sets are built on top of the virtual memory commands; these are the basic operations from which the Win32 API builds its other memory services.

Allocating Memory

The `VirtualAlloc` command is the starting point for managing your own virtual address space. Its parameters tell how much memory to allocate, where in the address space to situate the new block, whether to commit physical memory, and what kind of protection to set.

```
LPVOID VirtualAlloc
(
    LPVOID  lpvAddress,          // desired address for new block
    DWORD   dwSize,              // size of new memory block
    DWORD   fdwAllocationType,   // reserve addresses or commit memory
    DWORD   fdwProtect           // no access, read-only, or read/write
);
```

`VirtualAlloc` tries first to find a range of free addresses marking a block of `dwSize` bytes beginning at `lpvAddress`. To do this, it searches the process's tree of VADs. If the requested range is free, the function returns `lpvAddress`. If some part of it is in use, the function searches the entire address space looking for any sufficiently large free block. If it finds one, it returns the starting address. Otherwise it returns NULL.

Most often, programs set the first parameter to NULL and allow `VirtualAlloc` to place the block anywhere. Controlling the placement of a block may occasionally be useful if, for example, you are debugging a DLL that usually loads at a particular address. By using `VirtualAlloc` to reserve that address before the DLL loads, you can force it to another location.

The `fdwAllocationType` parameter may be MEM_RESERVE, MEM_COMMIT, or both. To reserve a range of addresses, `VirtualAlloc` simply makes a new VAD marking an area in use. It does not, however, allocate any physical memory, so the reserved addresses cannot yet be used for anything. Attempts to read or write reserved pages produce access-violation exceptions. On the other hand, no other allocation command may use previously reserved addresses either. `GlobalAlloc` and `malloc`, for example, cannot place new objects in a range that overlaps with reserved space. If you call `VirtualAlloc` to reserve your entire 1GB of address space, all subsequent allocations will fail, even though `VirtualAlloc` has not yet taken up any physical memory.

Reserving addresses has no effect on the system's physical memory. The VMM makes no guarantee that physical pages will be available when you begin to commit a reserved area. Only when you commit memory does the VMM find pages to support it. As a consequence, the system does not charge reserved memory against a process's system resource quotas. Only memory actually in use counts against the quota.

WARNING   A problem arises when you try to write to pages that have been reserved but never committed. The system generates an access-violation exception. You might choose to call `VirtualQuery` before every read or write to be sure the page is committed, but that takes time. The usual practice, demonstrated in the *List* demo (discussed later in this chapter), is to let the exception arise and provide an exception handler to deal with it. The handler calls `VirtualAlloc` to commit the required page and lets the program continue.

Memory cannot be committed without being reserved. By combining the MEM_RESERVE and MEM_COMMIT flags, you can reserve and commit at the same time. More often, programs call `VirtualAlloc` once—using MEM_RESERVE—to reserve a large area, and then many times subsequently—using MEM_COMMIT—to commit parts of the area piece by piece.

The `fdwProtect` flag determines how a page or range of pages may be used. For memory that is only reserved, the flag must be PAGE_NOACCESS. When committing memory, you can optionally change the protection to PAGE_READONLY or PAGE_READWRITE. No other programs can read memory in your address space anyway, so read-only protection guards against bugs in your own program that might accidentally corrupt some important part of your data. Protection levels apply to individual pages. The pages in a single range of memory may have different protection flags. You can, for example, apply PAGE_READONLY to an entire block and temporarily change single pages to allow write access as needed. You cannot write-protect just part of a page. The protection flags apply to entire pages.

`VirtualAlloc` cannot reserve more than 1GB because a process has control over only the bottom half of its 2GB address space. In fact, the actual limit is slightly smaller because of the 64KB free area at either end of a process's 1GB space (see Figure 19.3, earlier in the chapter). Also, `VirtualAlloc` reserves memory in blocks of 64KB and commits memory in blocks of one page. When reserving memory, `VirtualAlloc` rounds `lpvAddress` down to the nearest multiple of 64KB. When committing memory, if `lpvAddress` is NULL, `VirtualAlloc` rounds `dwSize` up to the nearest page size boundary. If `lpvAddress` is not NULL, `VirtualAlloc` commits every page containing any bytes in the range `lpvAddress` to `lpvAddress + dwSize`. A 2-byte allocation, if it crosses a page boundary, would require the commitment of two entire pages. On most Windows 98 systems, a page is 4KB, but if you need to know the size, call `GetSystemInfo`.

Uses for Reserved Memory

The ability to reserve memory without committing it is useful for dynamically allocated structures and sparse arrays. A thread that expands some structure, perhaps a list, as the program runs can reserve room to prevent other threads from using up addresses the structure may need as it expands.

The reserved area does set an upper limit on the size of the structure because there is no such command as "VirtualReAlloc" to expand a reserved area. Resizing requires allocating a second block, copying the first block into it, and freeing the original. On the other hand, given a 1GB range of possible addresses, you can reasonably set the upper size limit of the original allocation quite high.

Reserved memory also makes it easy to create a sparse array (a large array) with only a few elements filled. For example, a spreadsheet is a sparse array of empty cells with only a few positions occupied, and those positions are usually clustered in adjacent areas. With the virtual memory commands, you can reserve a large address space for all the possible cells and commit memory only for the areas in use. Although there are other ways for spreadsheet programs to minimize their allocations, the virtual memory solution to sparse arrays is particularly convenient because you can still address the array as a range of contiguous addresses.

Freeing Memory

When a process ends, the system automatically releases any memory that was still in use. To free memory sooner, call `VirtualFree`.

```
BOOL VirtualFree
(
    LPVOID lpvAddress,      // address of memory to free
    DWORD  dwSize,          // size of memory block
    DWORD  fdwFreeType      // decommit or release
);
```

VirtualFree can decommit a set of committed pages leaving their addresses still reserved, or it can release a range of reserved addresses, or it can do both at once. Decommitting can release small blocks, and the blocks may include a mix of both reserved and committed pages.

When you are releasing reserved addresses, you must free the entire range of addresses as originally allocated, and all the pages in the range must be in the same state—either all reserved or all committed. lpvAddress must contain the base address previously returned by VirtualAlloc, and the value of dwSize is ignored because the whole range is freed at once. dwSize matters only when decommitting sections of a range.

Before decommitting a page, be sure no part of it is still in use. The *List* demo, discussed later in the chapter, fits four list items on each 4KB page. Deleting one item does not make it safe to delete a page, because the other three items might still be in use.

Programs that use the virtual memory commands usually need some kind of garbage-collection mechanism to decommit pages when they become empty. The mechanism could be a low-priority thread that occasionally cycles through an allocated area looking for entirely empty pages.

Protecting Memory

After reserving address space, you call VirtualAlloc again to commit individual pages and VirtualFree to decommit or release them. When committing pages, VirtualAlloc also changes the protection state from no-access to read-only or read/write. To change the protection for a page already committed, call VirtualProtect.

```
BOOL VirtualProtect
(
    LPVOID lpvAddress,          // address of memory to protect
    DWORD  dwSize,              // size of area to protect
    DWORD  fdwNewProtect,       // new protection flags
    PDWORD pfdwOldProtect       // variable to receive old flags
);
```

lpvAddress and dwSize indicate the range of addresses to protect. The two flag parameters each contain one of the familiar protection flags: PAGE_NOACCESS, PAGE_READONLY, or PAGE_READWRITE. Flags apply to whole pages. Any page even partially included in the given range will be changed. The pfdwOldProtect parameter returns the previous state of the first page in the range.

VirtualProtect works only with pages already committed. If any page in the range is not committed, the function fails. The pages in the range do not, however, need to have identical protection flags.

The primary advantage of protection is in guarding against your own program bugs. For an example, refer to the revised AddItem and DeleteItem procedures used in the *List* demo described later in this chapter.

Querying Memory Information

Sometimes you need to get information about a block of memory. Before writing to a page, for example, you might want to find out whether the page has been committed. VirtualQuery fills a structure variable with information about a given block of memory:

```
DWORD VirtualQuery(
    LPVOID lpvAddress,                          // address of area to be described
    PMEMORY_BASIC_INFORMATION pmbiBuffer,       // address of description buffer
    DWORD dwLength );                           // size of description buffer

typedef struct _MEMORY_BASIC_INFORMATION  /* mbi */
{
    PVOID BaseAddress;          // base address of page group
    PVOID AllocationBase;       // address of larger allocation unit
    DWORD AllocationProtect;    // allocation's initial access protection
    DWORD RegionSize;           // size, in bytes, of page group
    DWORD State;                // committed, reserved, free
    DWORD Protect;              // group's access protection
    DWORD Type;                 // type of pages (always private)
} MEMORY_BASIC_INFORMATION;

typedef MEMORY_BASIC_INFORMATION *PMEMORY_BASIC_INFORMATION;
```

The lpvAddress parameter of VirtualQuery points to an arbitrary address. Any given location in memory may be part of two different allocation units. It may be part of a large block of reserved pages, and it may also be part of a smaller region of pages subsequently committed, decommitted, or protected together. A region consists of all contiguous pages with the same attributes.

In the BaseAddress field, VirtualQuery returns the address of the first page in the smaller region that contains lpvAddress. The AllocationBase field returns the address of the larger allocation that first reserved lpvAddress. AllocationBase matches the value returned previously by `VirtualAlloc`. Whatever protection flags the original `VirtualAlloc` applied to the range are returned in `Allocation-Protect` (MEM_NOACCESS, MEM_READONLY, or MEM_READWRITE).

The other fields describe the smaller subgroup of like pages, giving its size, current status, and protection flag. The last field always returns MEM_PRIVATE, indicating that other processes cannot share this memory. The existence of this field suggests that Microsoft may later consider adding other mechanisms for processes to share memory.

Although they are not part of the virtual memory command set, two other commands also retrieve information about memory. `GlobalMemoryStatus` returns the total size and remaining space for physical memory, the page file, and the current address space. `GetSystemInfo` returns, among other things, the system's physical page size and the lowest and highest virtual addresses accessible to processes and DLLs. (Generally these values are 4KB, 0×00010000, and 0×7FFEFFFF.)

Locking and Unlocking Pages

Two other virtual memory commands lock and unlock pages. A locked page cannot be swapped to disk while your program executes. When your program is not currently executing, however, all of its pages, including locked pages, may be swapped to disk. In effect, locking a page guarantees that it will become a permanent part of the program's working page set. In a busy system, the working set manager may reduce the number of pages a process may lock. The maximum for any process is approximately 30 to 40 pages. The exact value varies slightly with the size of system memory and the application's working set.

Locking memory is discouraged because it constrains the VMM and makes organizing physical memory more difficult. For the most part, only device drivers and other system-level components lock any of their pages. A program that must respond very rapidly to system signals might lock some pages to ensure that unexpected disk reads don't delay the response.

```
BOOL VirtualLock(
    LPVOID lpvAddress,          // beginning of area to lock
    DWORD  dwSize );            // size of area to lock

BOOL VirtualUnlock(
    LPVOID lpvAddress,          // beginning of area to unlock
    DWORD  dwSize );            // size of area to unlock
```

There is no lock count on virtual memory. `VirtualLock` commands do not always require a matching `VirtualUnlock`. You can, for example, lock three contiguous pages with three different commands and then unlock them all with a single command. All the pages must already be locked, but the range does not need to correspond exactly with the range given in any previous lock command.

Before being locked, memory must be committed. When a process ends, the system automatically unlocks any remaining locked pages. `VirtualFree` releases pages even if they are locked.

> **NOTE**
>
> Be aware that `GlobalLock` and `VirtualLock` do very different things. `Global-Lock` simply translates handles into pointers. It locks an allocated object into a virtual address but has no effect at all on physical memory. `VirtualLock`, on the other hand, is more severe. It locks pages, not objects, and the locked pages are forced into physical memory whenever the program runs.

Heap Functions

A *heap* is a block of memory from which a program allocates smaller pieces as needed. A 16-bit Windows program draws memory from both a global heap and a local heap. The local heap is faster but limited to 64KB.

For Windows 98 (as well as Windows 95 and NT), a flat address space abolishes the difference between *global* and *local* and between *near* and *far*, making the entire address space a single, undifferentiated heap.

Even with such a large, contiguous memory space, working from a smaller heap sometimes still makes sense. Reserving and committing virtual memory has obvious advantages for large dynamic or sparse structures. But what about algorithms that call for many small allocations? The heap memory commands allow you to create one or more private heaps in your address space and suballocate smaller blocks from them.

The heap commands conveniently group allocations together in a small section of the address space. Clustering allocations serves several purposes:

- It can separate and protect related allocations. A program that makes many small allocations that are all the same size can pack memory most efficiently by making them contiguous. A heap allows that.

- If all your linked-list nodes come from one heap and your binary-tree nodes come from another, a mistake in one algorithm is less likely to interfere with the other.

- Memory objects used in conjunction with each other should be grouped together to minimize page swapping. If several addresses happen to reside on the same memory page, a single disk operation retrieves all of them.

Creating a Heap

The memory you get from a heap is just like the memory you get any other way. In fact, you can write your own heap implementation using the virtual memory commands; that's exactly what the Windows subsystem does. Heap commands make internal calls to the virtual memory API. To create a heap, you give a starting size and an upper limit:

```
HANDLE HeapCreate(
    DWORD dwOptions,            // heap allocation flag
    DWORD dwInitialSize,        // initial heap size
    DWORD dwMaximumSize );      // maximum heap size
```

Behind the scenes, the Win32 subsystem responds by reserving a block of the maximum size and committing pages to support the initial size. Subsequent allocations make the heap grow from the bottom to the top. If any allocation calls for new pages, the heap commands automatically commit them. Once committed, they remain committed until the program destroys the heap or the program ends.

The system does not manage the inside of a private heap. It does not compact the heap or move objects within it. Therefore, a heap may become fragmented if you allocate and free many small objects. If allocations fill the heap to its maximum size, subsequent allocations fail. If dwMaximumSize is 0, however, the heap size is limited only by available memory.

The dwOptions parameter allows a single flag to be set: HEAP_NO_SERIALIZE. By default, without this flag (the argument is passed as 0), the heap prevents threads that share memory handles from interfering with each other. A serialized heap disallows simultaneous operations on a single handle. One thread blocks until another finishes. Serialization slows performance slightly. A program's heap does not need to be serialized if the program has only one thread, if only one of its threads uses the heap, or if the program itself protects the heap, perhaps by creating a mutex or a critical section object (see Chapter 14 for more information about threads, mutexes, and critical section objects).

Allocating from a Heap

HeapAlloc, HeapReAlloc, and HeapFree—like the Win16 commands their names recall—allocate, reallocate, and free blocks of memory from a heap. All of them take as one parameter a handle returned from HeapCreate.

```
LPSTR HeapAlloc(
    HANDLE hHeap,              // handle of a private heap
    DWORD  dwFlags,            // control flags
    DWORD  dwBytes );          // number of bytes to allocate
```

HeapAlloc returns a pointer to a block of the requested size. It may include two control flags:

> **HEAP_GENERATE_EXCEPTIONS** This flag influences how the command handles errors. Without the flag, HeapAlloc indicates failure by returning NULL. With the flag, it raises exceptions instead for all error conditions.

> **HEAP_ZERO_MEMORY** This flag causes HeapAlloc to initialize the newly allocated block with zeros. If the function succeeds, it allocates at least as much memory as requested and may allocate slightly more to reach a convenient boundary.

To discover the exact size of any block, call HeapSize. Besides the bytes in the block itself, each allocation consumes a few extra bytes for an internal supporting structure. The exact size varies but is near 16 bytes. You need to know this only because it may prevent you from squeezing as many allocations out of one heap as you expect. If you create a 2MB heap and attempt two 1MB allocations, the second one is likely to fail.

To change the size of a memory block after it has been allocated, call HeapReAlloc.

```
LPSTR HeapReAlloc(
    HANDLE hHeap,              // handle of a private heap
    DWORD  dwFlags,            // flags to influence reallocation
    LPSTR  lpMem,              // address of memory block to reallocate
    DWORD  dwBytes );          // new size for the memory block
```

Besides the two flags HeapAlloc uses to zero memory and to generate exceptions, the dwFlags parameter of HeapReAlloc accepts one other flag: HEAP_REALLOC_IN_PLACE_ONLY. (To the best of our knowledge, five words is a record for Microsoft's manifest constants.) This flag prevents HeapReAlloc from moving the memory block to a more spacious area. If other nearby allocations prevent the block from expanding in place, this flag makes HeapReAlloc fail rather than relocate. (HEAP_REALLOC_IN_PLACE_ONLY would normally be used with one of the other flags.)

Destroying a Heap

When you have no more use for an allocated block, release it with `HeapFree`. When you have no more use for the heap itself, release it with `HeapDestroy`.

```
BOOL HeapFree(
    HANDLE hHeap,               // handle of a private heap
    DWORD  dwFlags,             // unused (must be zero)
    LPSTR  lpMem );             // address of a memory block to free


BOOL HeapDestroy( HANDLE hHeap );
```

Freeing a memory block does not decommit the page it occupied, but it does make the space available for subsequent allocations in the same heap. `Heap-Destroy` decommits and releases all the pages in the heap whether or not the heap still contains allocated blocks. After `HeapDestroy`, the `hHeap` handle is invalid (undefined).

Global and Local Memory Commands

In making the transition from a 16-bit to 32-bit system, many of the earlier system and memory API commands have been dropped. Most of the obsolete memory commands, such as `AllocSelector`, refer to low-level features specific to Win16 or to Intel CPUs. For backward compatibility, many of the more familiar memory commands are retained:

GlobalAlloc	GlobalFree	GlobalMemoryStatus
LocalAlloc	LocalFree	*No local equivalent*
GlobalDiscard	GlobalHandle	GlobalReAlloc
LocalDiscard	LocalHandle	LocalReAlloc
GlobalFlags	GlobalLock	GlobalSize
LocalFlags	LocalLock	LocalSize
		GlobalUnlock
		LocalUnlock

The Win32 environment forces a few semantic changes. Most important, both sets of commands, global and local, now work with the same heap. On loading, every process receives a default heap, and the old API commands work from that.

It is now legal (though confusing) to mix global and local commands in a single transaction. For example, you could, just to be perverse, allocate an object with GlobalAlloc and release it with LocalFree. Also, the 32-bit pointer LocalLock now returns is indistinguishable from the 32-bit pointer GlobalLock returns.

The default heap expands as needed, limited only by physical memory. Even the humble LocalAlloc can allocate megabytes. The default heap automatically serializes operations to prevent different threads from corrupting the heap by using the same handle at the same time.

Pages allocated by GlobalAlloc or LocalAlloc are committed and marked for read/write access. Unlike HeapFree, GlobalFree checks for empty pages and releases them back to the system. The allocation commands still recognize the flags that make memory fixed or movable, but with Windows 98's paging and virtual addressing, even "fixed" memory moves. The only practical use for GMEM_FIXED is to make GlobalAlloc return a pointer instead of a handle.

A few of the other flags are now ignored, including LOWER, NOCOMPACT, NODISCARD, NOT_BANKED, and NOTIFY. More significant than the loss of these minor flags is the loss of GMEM_DDESHARE. Like other Win32 object handles, handles to allocated memory refer to the object table of a specific process. A handle passed from one program to another becomes invalid in the new address space. DuplicateHandle makes it possible for processes to share some handles, but it fails on memory handles. The GMEM_DDESHARE flag still exists (is still defined) because Microsoft apparently plans for it to signal some optimization appropriate for DDE conversations, but the old method of sharing memory handles is simply not supported. Sharing a block of memory now requires a memory-mapped file.

The Win32 global and local memory commands differ from the heap commands in creating movable and discardable objects. Objects created by HeapAlloc do not change their virtual address (though their physical address may change). The local and global functions, at the expense of more memory management overhead, do move objects to minimize fragmentation. With a memory manager as flexible as the VMM, discardable memory is less important than it used to be.

The primary advantage of the old API functions is the obvious one: They are portable. To write source code that ports easily from 16 bits to 32 bits, limit yourself to the Win16 memory commands. In Win32, the global and local sets are interchangeable, but you should pick the set that would make the most sense in a Win16 program. For small, fast allocations, use the local functions. For large allocations, use the global functions. Under Windows 98 both sets perform alike, but since their advantage is portability, you should use them in a portable fashion.

The heap and virtual memory command sets are faster and more efficient than the older commands. You can allocate from the default heap with less overhead by doing this:

```
HeapAlloc( GetProcessHeap(), 0, dwSize );
```

GetProcessHeap returns a handle to the default heap.

WARNING   Do not pass the handle returned by GetProcessHeap to HeapDestroy.

System Limits

Because 32-bit Windows does not use the descriptor tables that limited 16-bit Windows to a system-wide total of 8192 handles, the new system supports many more allocations. Nevertheless some limits remain:

- VirtualAlloc never reserves an area smaller than 64KB, so allocating 16,383 blocks fills up the 1GB user address space.

- VirtualAlloc cannot create more than 32,767 (32K) handles in one process. (HeapAlloc has no such limit; Microsoft says it has created over a million handles on a single heap in tests.)

- GlobalAlloc and LocalAlloc combined cannot create more than 65,535 (64K) handles. The limit applies only to movable objects, however.

NOTE   Memory objects allocated using the GMEM_FIXED or LMEM_FIXED flags do not return handles. Instead, they return direct pointers to the memory allocated.

Validation Commands

Another set of commands tests the validity of pointers. Each receives a virtual address and returns TRUE if the process does not have a particular access privilege. Call these to make your programs more robust by testing values before using them. The validation commands are listed in Table 19.1.

TABLE 19.1: Validation Commands

Function	Argument	Validation Test
IsBadCodePtr	Pointer to a function	Tests for read access to the beginning of the function
IsBadReadPtr	Pointer to a memory block	Tests for read access to a range of addresses
IsBadStringPtr	Pointer to a string	Tests for read access to all bytes up to the end of the string
IsBadWritePtr	Pointer to a memory block	Tests for write access to a range of addresses

NOTE Be aware that other threads, and even other processes (such as debuggers), could conceivably change the contents or protection of a memory page between the time an IsBad function confirms validity and the time you try to touch the address yourself.

C Runtime Equivalents

Under Windows, the malloc family of C runtime functions calls system heap routines internally. The C routines work perfectly well in Windows 98, although they do not perform the same suballocations they do in the 16-bit versions.

The runtime memory buffer commands such as memset now have competition from four new Win32 routines: CopyMemory, FillMemory, MoveMemory, and ZeroMemory. However, these commands link dynamically to the system DLLs only on an MIPS machine. Obviously, they provide no special benefits for Windows 98 applications at all. Instead, on an x86 machine, all four map back to the standard C runtime functions: memcopy, memmove, and memset.

The List Demo: Reserving and Committing Memory

The *List* demo, shown in Figure 19.4, creates a list by reserving virtual memory and committing it as the user enters new items. A list box filling the window's client area displays the entire list. The List menu allows you to add and delete items.

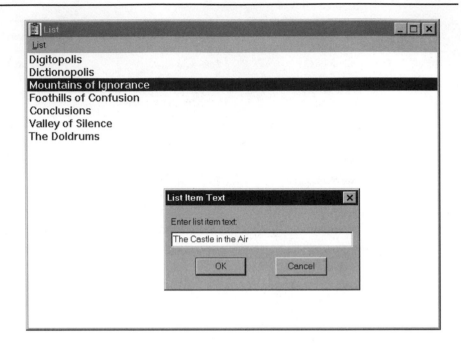

FIGURE 19.4:

The List demo accepting
a new item entry

To create a dynamic list of identically sized nodes in 16-bit Windows you would probably create a structure of linked nodes. Each new entry would require an allocation, using `GlobalAlloc` (or `malloc` with MSC 7.0). An array would be easier to program but much more wasteful since it would allocate more memory than it ever used. Under Windows 98, however, the virtual memory commands make a large dynamically allocated array quite practical, and that is how *List* implements its data structure.

Writing a virtual memory program calls for a decision about how to deal with uncommitted pages. The *List* demo uses exception handling to commit pages on demand as page faults occur. A second approach would be to have procedures to query the state of each page before writing and to keep all pages write-protected except when actually writing new data to specific pages.

NOTE   The `List` demo is included on the CD that accompanies this book, in the Chapter 19 folder.

Setting the List's Size and Structure

The header file defines two constants governing the size and structure of the list. Each array element has room for 1024 characters. Because the system's page size (4KB) is a multiple of the element size (1KB), no list item will cross a page boundary; therefore, retrieving an item never requires reading more than a single page from the disk. The *List* demo sets the array's maximum size to a mere 500, figuring that filling even that small number will challenge the patience of most readers. Setting the limit to 20,000 would still tie up less than 1 percent of the 1GB user address space.

Among the program's global variables are two arrays: iListLookup and bInUse.

```
int  iListLookup[MAX_ITEMS];  // matches list box index to array position
BOOL bInUse[MAX_ITEMS];       // marks array positions that are in use
```

The lookup array links lines in the list box to elements in the dynamic array. If iListLookup[4] is 7, then string 5 in the list box is stored in element 7 of the array. (The list box and the array both begin numbering at 0.)

The second array contains a Boolean value for each element in the dynamic array. Whenever the program adds or deletes a string, it changes the corresponding element of bInUse to TRUE for an occupied position and FALSE for an empty position. To add a new string, the program searches bInUse for an empty array element. To delete the currently selected string, the program locates the array element by referring to iListLookup.

Initializing Data Structures

When the program starts, the CreateList function is called to reserve memory and initialize the supporting data structures. VirtualAlloc reserves a 1MB range of addresses. Like all reserved pages, these must be marked PAGE_NOACCESS until they are committed.

```
BOOL CreateList ( void )
{
   int i;
     // reserve one meg of memory address space
   pBase = VirtualAlloc( NULL,                 // starting address (anywhere)
                      MAX_ITEMS * ITEM_SIZE,  // one megabyte
                      MEM_RESERVE,            // reserve; don't commit
                      PAGE_NOACCESS );        // can't be touched
```

```
if( pBase == NULL )
{
   ShowErrorMsg( __LINE__ );
   return( FALSE );
}
   // initialize the status variables
for( i = 0; i < MAX_ITEMS; i++ )
{
   bInUse[i] = FALSE;                    // show no entries in use
   iListLookup[i] = 0;
}
bListEmpty = TRUE;                       // update global flags
bListFull = FALSE;
return( TRUE );
}
```

Adding an Item

When you choose Add Item from the *List* demo's menu, the AddItem procedure performs the following steps:

1. Locate the first empty slot in the array (iIndex).

2. Ask the user to enter the new string in a dialog box.

3. Copy the new string into the memory allocated during CreateList.

4. Update the list box and several global variables.

The first unused position in the array may happen to occupy an uncommitted memory page. In that case, the lstrcpy command that tries to put a string there generates an exception. The exception handler around lstrcpy looks for the EXCEPTION_ACCESS_VIOLATION signal and responds by calling VirtualAlloc to commit a single page from the previously reserved range.

```
void AddItem ( void )
{
   char szText[ITEM_SIZE];              // text for one item
   int  iLen;                           // string length
   int  iIndex;                         // position in array
   int  iPos;                           // position in list box
   int  iCount;                         // count of entries in list box
   BOOL bDone;                          // TRUE when free array entry found
```

```
      // determine the location of the first free entry
   bDone = FALSE;
   iIndex = 0;
   while( ( ! bDone ) && ( iIndex < MAX_ITEMS ) )
   {
      if( ! bInUse[iIndex] )           // is entry in use?
         bDone = TRUE;                 // found an empty entry
      else
         iIndex++;                     // advance to next entry
   }

      // ask user for new text string
   iLen = GetItemText(szText);
   if( ! iLen ) return;
```

The `try` block copies the new text to an empty place in the item array. If that memory page is uncommitted, `lstrcpy` raises an exception. The exception filter commits the page and the command continues.

```
   try
   {      // put text in the item
      lstrcpy( &( pBase[iIndex * ITEM_SIZE] ), szText );
   }
   except( CommitMemFilter( GetExceptionCode(), iIndex ) )
   {
         // the filter does all the work
   }
      // mark this entry as in use
   bInUse[iIndex] = TRUE;
   bListEmpty = FALSE;
```

Next, the program adds the new text to the list box. The string is inserted at `iPos`, and `iListLookup[iPos]` is updated to indicate where in the item array the new entry was stored (`iIndex`).

```
   iCount = ListBox_GetCount( hwndList );
   iPos = ListBox_InsertString( hwndList, iCount, szText );
   iCount++;
   ListBox_SetCurSel( hwndList, iPos );
   iListLookup[iPos] = iIndex;
   if (iCount == MAX_ITEMS)               // did we fill the last place?
   {
      bListFull = TRUE;
   }
   return;
}
```

The CommitMemFilter function provides an exception-handling filter for the AddItem function. If a page fault occurs, CommitMemFilter attempts to commit the page and, on success, returns to lstrcopy and proceeds. If CommitMemFilter fails, the search for an appropriate exception handler continues.

```
LONG CommitMemFilter(
    DWORD dwExceptCode,        // code identifying the exception
    int iIndex )               // array element where fault occurred
{
    LPVOID lpvResult;
        // If the exception was not a page fault, then refuse
        // to handle it.  Make the system keep looking for
        // an exception handler.
    if( dwExceptCode != EXCEPTION_ACCESS_VIOLATION )
    {
        return( EXCEPTION_CONTINUE_SEARCH );
    }
        // Try to commit the missing page.
    lpvResult = VirtualAlloc(
        &( pBase[iIndex * ITEM_SIZE] ), // bottom of area to commit
        ITEM_SIZE,                      // size of area to commit
        MEM_COMMIT,                     // new status flag
        PAGE_READWRITE );               // protection status
    if( ! lpvResult )                   // did allocation fail?
    {
        // if we can't commit the page, then we can't handle the exception
        return( EXCEPTION_CONTINUE_SEARCH );
    }
        // The missing page is now in place.  Tell the
        // system to go back and try again.
    return( EXCEPTION_CONTINUE_EXECUTION );
}
```

Deleting an Item

When DeleteItem removes an element from the virtual array, it also checks to see whether any other entries remain on the same memory page. If all four entries are empty, it decommits the page, releasing 4KB to the system. The virtual addresses that pointed to the page remain reserved. Whether or not it frees a page, DeleteItem then removes the string from the list box and updates the global status variables.

Two other procedures help with these tasks. GetBasePageEntry receives an array index and returns the index of the first element on the same page frame. In other words, it rounds down to the nearest multiple of four. AdjustLookupTable removes the entry it held for a newly deleted list box string and slides up all the following elements to fill in the gap.

```
void DeleteItem ( void )
{
    int  iCurSel;    // position of current selection in list box
    int  iPlace;     // position of current selection in item array
    int  iStart;     // first position on same memory page as selection
    int  i;          // loop variable
    BOOL bFree;      // TRUE if all 4 entries on one page are unused
    BOOL bTest;      // for testing return results

        // retrieve the memory offset of the currently selected entry
    iCurSel = ListBox_GetCurSel( hwndList );
    iPlace = iListLookup[iCurSel];
        // zero out the deleted entry
    FillMemory( &(pBase[iPlace * ITEM_SIZE]), ITEM_SIZE, 0 );
        // mark this entry as free
    bInUse[iPlace] = FALSE;
```

Next, we figure out which entry number is first on the current page. If all four entries on the page are empty, we'll uncommit the page to release memory.

```
    iStart = GetPageBaseEntry( iPlace );
    bFree = TRUE;
    for( i = 0; i < 4; i++ )                    // check four entries
    {
        if( bInUse[i + iStart] )                // in use?
        {
            bFree = FALSE;                      // page is not free
        }
    }
```

If a whole memory page is now unused, free it.

```
    if( bFree )                                 // is page free?
    {                                           // YES; release it
        bTest = VirtualFree( &( pBase[iStart * ITEM_SIZE] ),
                        ITEM_SIZE, MEM_DECOMMIT );
```

```
    if( ! bTest )
    {
        ShowErrorMsg( __LINE__ );
        ExitProcess( (UINT)GetLastError() );
    }
}
```

Last, we update the list box display and the lookup table array, then check to see if any entries remain in the list.

```
ListBox_DeleteString( hwndList, iCurSel );
AdjustLookupTable( iCurSel );
bListEmpty = TRUE;
i = 0;
while( ( i < MAX_ITEMS ) && ( bListEmpty ) )
{
    // if the item is in use, then the list is not empty
    bListEmpty = !bInUse[i++];
}
    // reposition the selection marker in the list box
if( ! bListEmpty )
{
    if( iCurSel )                   // did we delete the first item?
    {                               // no; select item above deletion
        ListBox_SetCurSel( hwndList, iCurSel-1 );
    }
    else                            // deleted item was at top
    {                               // select new top entry
        ListBox_SetCurSel( hwndList, iCurSel );
    }
}
return;
}
```

The DeleteList function is called when the program ends to delete all the entries in the list and free the memory the entries occupied.

```
void DeleteList()
{
    // decommit the memory and then release the address space
    // Note: we must supply a size for the MEM_DECOMMIT operation
    if( ! VirtualFree( (void*)pBase, MAX_ITEMS*ITEM_SIZE, MEM_DECOMMIT ) )
        ShowErrorMsg( __LINE__ );
```

```
        // now release the memory from the base address - no size required
    if( ! VirtualFree( (void*)pBase, 0, MEM_RELEASE ) )
        ShowErrorMsg( __LINE__ );

    return;
}
```

Given an index into the list, GetPageBaseEntry figures out which entry is first on the same page by finding the first integer divisible by four and less than or equal to iPlace.

```
int GetPageBaseEntry ( int iPlace )
{
    while( iPlace % 4 )
        iPlace-;
    return( iPlace );
}
```

When a list box entry is deleted, the array that matches the list box entries and the memory offsets must be updated. The iStart parameter gives the position in the list box from which a string was just deleted.

```
void AdjustLookupTable ( int iStart )
{
    int i;

        // This loop starts at the position where an entry
        // was just deleted and works down the list, scooting
        // lower items up one space to fill in the gap.

    for( i = iStart; i < MAX_ITEMS - 1; i++ )
        iListLookup[i] = iListLookup[i + 1];

    iListLookup[MAX_ITEMS - 1] = 0;
    return;
}
```

NOTE   The remaining procedures in the *List* demo run the dialog box where the user enters text, display the About box, and show error messages when something goes wrong. They appear in the complete listing on the CD.

Procedures for Write-Protecting List Pages

Instead of waiting for page faults and scurrying for last-minute commitments, an alternative version of the *List* demo could invest a little overhead and manage its array in a more deliberate fashion. Here are versions of AddItem and DeleteItem that call VirtualProtect before and after each modification to ensure that every page is committed in advance and write-protected afterward.

```
void AddItem( void )
{
    MEMORY_BASIC_INFORMATION MemInfo;   // info about a memory block
    char szText[ITEM_SIZE];             // text for one item
    DWORD dwOldState;                   // memory status flags
    int iLen;                           // string length
    int iIndex;                         // position in array
    int iPos;                           // position in list box
    int iCount;                         // count of entries in list box
    BOOL bDone;                         // TRUE when free array entry found
    BOOL bTest;                         // for testing return values

        // determine the location of the first free entry
    bDone = FALSE;
    iIndex = 0;
    while( ( ! bDone ) && ( iIndex < MAX_ITEMS ) )
    {
        if( bInUse[iIndex] == 0 )       // is entry in use?
            bDone = TRUE;               // found an empty entry
        else
            iIndex++;                   // advance to next entry
    }
        // retrieve the text
    iLen = GetItemText(szText);
    if( ! iLen )
        return;
```

Next, we retrieve information about this entry's memory page.

```
        // fill out a MEMORY_BASIC_INFORMATION structure
    VirtualQuery( &( pBase[ITEM_SIZE * iIndex] ),
                  &MemInfo, sizeof(MemInfo) );
    if( MemInfo.State == MEM_COMMIT )
    {
```

If the memory is committed, we remove the access protection to allow reading and writing.

```
    bTest = VirtualProtect(
        &( pBase[ITEM_SIZE * iIndex] ),    // bottom of area to protect
        ITEM_SIZE,                         // size of area to protect
        PAGE_READWRITE,                    // new protection status
        &dwOldState );                     // old protection status
    if( ! bTest )
        ShowErrorMsg( __LINE__ );          // protection failed
}
else                              // this page is not yet committed
{
```

If the memory has been not committed yet, we call `VirtualAlloc` to commit a block at the bottom of the previous memory block.

```
    LPVOID lpvResult;

    lpvResult = VirtualAlloc(
        &( pBase[iIndex * ITEM_SIZE] ),    // bottom of area to commit
        ITEM_SIZE,                         // size of area to commit
        MEM_COMMIT,                        // new status flag
        PAGE_READWRITE );                  // protection status
    if( ! lpvResult )
    {
        ShowErrorMsg( __LINE__ );
        return;                            // allocation failed
    }
}
    // put text in the item
lstrcpy( &(pBase[iIndex * ITEM_SIZE]), szText );
    // restore the protection state of this page to read-only
bTest = VirtualProtect(
    &( pBase[iIndex * ITEM_SIZE] ),        // bottom of area to protect
    ITEM_SIZE,                             // size of area to protect
    PAGE_READONLY,                         // new protection status
    &dwOldState );                         // previous protection status
if( ! bTest )
    ShowErrorMsg( __LINE__ );
    // mark this entry as in use
bInUse[iIndex] = 1;
bListEmpty = FALSE;
```

Next, we add the new text to the list box, inserting the string at iPos, then update iListLookup[iPos] to indicate where in the item array the new entry was stored (iIndex).

```
iCount = ListBox_GetCount( hwndList );
iPos = ListBox_InsertString( hwndList, iCount, szText );
iCount++;
ListBox_SetCurSel( hwndList, iPos );
iListLookup[iPos] = iIndex;
if( iCount == MAX_ITEMS )              // did we fill the last place?
   bListFull = TRUE;
return;
}
```

The DeleteItem function removes an item from the list, zeroing the memory previously used and, when a page is emptied, releasing the memory for reuse.

```
void DeleteItem ( void )
{
   int iCurSel;        // position of current selection in list box
   int iPlace;         // position of current selection in item array
   DWORD dwOldState;   // previous memory-protection flags
   int iStart;         // first position on same memory page as selection
   int i;              // loop variable
   BOOL bFree;         // TRUE if all 4 entries on one page are unused
   BOOL bTest;         // for testing return results

      // retrieve the memory offset of the currently selected entry
   iCurSel = ListBox_GetCurSel( hwndList );
   iPlace = iListLookup[iCurSel];
      // set the protection to read/write and zero out the entry
   bTest = VirtualProtect(
      &( pBase[ITEM_SIZE * iPlace] ),   // bottom of area to protect
      ITEM_SIZE,                        // size of area to protect
      PAGE_READWRITE,                   // new protection status
      &dwOldState );                    // previous protection status
   if( ! bTest )
   {
      ShowErrorMsg( __LINE__ );
      return;
   }
   FillMemory( &( pBase[iPlace * ITEM_SIZE] ), ITEM_SIZE, 0 );
      // mark this entry as free
   bInUse[iPlace] = 0;
```

Then we figure out which entry number is first on the current page. If all four entries on the page are empty, we'll uncommit the page to release memory.

```
iStart = GetPageBaseEntry( iPlace );
   bFree = TRUE;
   for( i = 0; i < 4; i++ )                // check four entries
   {
      if( bInUse[i + iStart] )             // in use?
         bFree = FALSE;                     // page is not free
   }
```

If a whole memory page is now unused, free it. If not, restore its read-only protection.

```
   if (bFree)                              // is page free?
   {                                       // YES; release it
      bTest = VirtualFree( &( pBase[iStart * ITEM_SIZE] ),
                     ITEM_SIZE, MEM_DECOMMIT );
   }
   else
   {                                       // NO; protect it
      bTest = VirtualProtect( &( pBase[ITEM_SIZE * iPlace] ),
                     ITEM_SIZE, PAGE_READONLY, &dwOldState );
   }
   if( ! bTest )
      ShowErrorMsg( __LINE__ );
```

Last, the list box display is updated along with the lookup table array, then a check is made to see if any entries remain in the list before repositioning the selection marker.

```
   ListBox_DeleteString( hwndList, iCurSel );
   AdjustLookupTable( iCurSel );
   bListEmpty = TRUE;
   i = 0;
   while( ( i < MAX_ITEMS ) && ( bListEmpty ) )
   {
         // if the item is in use then the list is not empty
      bListEmpty = !bInUse[i++];
   }
      // reposition the selection marker in the list box
   if( ! bListEmpty )
   {
      if( iCurSel )                        // did we delete the first item?
```

```
      {                                // no; select item above deletion
         ListBox_SetCurSel( hwndList, iCurSel - 1 );
      }
      else                             // deleted item was at top
      {                                // select new top entry
         ListBox_SetCurSel( hwndList, iCurSel );
      }
   }
   return;
}
```

NOTE   The procedures for write-protecting list pages presented in this section are not on the CD accompanying this book. You can experiment with developing this (and your own) alternative version of the *List* demo on the CD.

File-Mapping Objects

For two processes to share a block of memory, they must create a file-mapping object. Such objects have two purposes: They facilitate file I/O, and they create a memory buffer that processes can share. To explain sharing memory, we need to begin with files.

Mapped Files

After opening a disk file, a program may optionally create an associated file-mapping object in order to treat the file as a block of memory. The system reserves a range of addresses from the process's space and maps them to the file instead of to physical memory. The process reads and writes to these addresses as it would to any other memory address, using functions like lstrcpy and FillMemory. You can even type-cast the base address to make an array pointer and retrieve file records by indexing the array. The VMM responds to page faults in a file-mapping object by swapping pages from the disk file rather than the system's paging file.

This ingenious file I/O technique also allows processes to share memory. If two programs can open handles to the same file, what difference does it make if the file happens to be in memory? If the cooperating programs want to share memory but don't need to create a disk file, they can link their shared file-mapping object to the system's paging file. Then the memory in the mapped file is paged exactly the same way all other memory is paged.

Setting up a new mapped file requires three commands:

CreateFile   Opens a disk file.

CreateFileMapping   Returns a handle to a file-mapping object.

MapViewOfFile   Links a region in the file to a range of virtual addresses and returns a pointer.

CreateFile should be familiar from Chapter 15, where we talked about its use for opening existing named pipes, as well as from Chapter 12, where we talked about its use for opening conventional files.

CreateFileMapping creates a new system object, adds an entry to the process's object table, and returns a handle. The new object creates the potential for parts of the file to be held in memory, but you cannot actually read the file until you also create a view into it.

A *view* is a small section of a larger object—a window into a section of the file. MapViewOfFile creates a view by associating positions in the file with positions in the address space. Operations on that range of addresses become operations on the file.

You can create a view big enough to contain the entire file, but in theory, a file can be much larger than your entire address space, so an alternative is necessary. The alternative is to create a smaller view and move it when you need to reach new parts of the file. After creating a file-mapping object, you can map, unmap, and remap your view of it over and over. You can even map several simultaneous views of a single file. Figure 19.5 diagrams the relationship between a file and its view.

Creating a File-Mapping Object

CreateFileMapping requires a file handle to associate with the new object. Normally you receive the handle from CreateFile. To share memory without creating a separate file, you may instead pass the file handle as (HANDLE)0xFFFFFFFF. The system then maps from the system paging file.

```
HANDLE CreateFileMapping(
    HANDLE hFile,                     // handle of file to map
    LPSECURITY_ATTRIBUTES lpsa,       // optional security attributes
    DWORD fdwProtect,                 // protection for mapping object
    DWORD dwMaxSizeHigh,              // high-order 32 bits of object size
    DWORD dwMaxSizeLow,               // low-order 32 bits of object size
    LPTSTR lpszMapName );             // name of file-mapping object
```

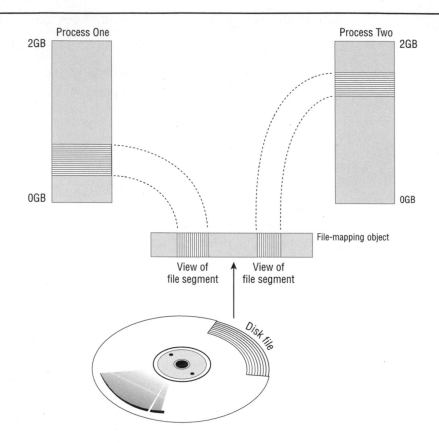

The fdwProtect parameter sets the protection flag for all the memory pages the mapped file uses. It may be PAGE_READONLY, PAGE_READWRITE, or PAGE_WRITECOPY. The first two you know, but PAGE_WRITECOPY is new. We'll talk more about it in a moment when we discuss coherent views.

The next two parameters of CreateFileMapping, both DWORDs, together tell the size of the file-mapping object. If the file-mapping object is smaller than the file it maps, not all of the file is accessible through it. The last part of the file is excluded from sharing. The system interprets dwMaxSizeHigh and dwMaxSizeLow as the high and low halves of a single value. The size is an 8-byte quantity to allow for the possibility that disk files may exceed the value of ULONG_MAX (2GB). Programs that work only with files of subastronomical sizes always set dwMaxSizeHigh to 0. Setting both parameters to 0 instructs the system to set the maximum size from the file's current size. If hFile is passed as (HANDLE)0xFFFFFFFF however, the size may not be 0; that is, you must set an explicit size in order to work from the system swap file.

The final parameter, lpszMapName, gives the new object a name. lpszMap
Name is not the name of a disk file; if there is a disk file, its name is passed to
CreateFile. lpszMapName assigns a name to the new file-mapping object for
the convenience of other processes. Processes use the name to share the object,
just as they use pipe names to share pipes. Other processes open their handles
to the same object by passing the name string to OpenFileMapping. The name
of a file-mapping object may not exceed MAX_PATH characters (currently 260)
and may not contain backslashes. (MAX_PATH is defined in WinDef.H.)

NOTE   The rule against backslashes in mapped filenames contrasts with the requirements
for naming pipes. Pipe names always begin with the sequence \\.\pipe\ but
may contain additional backslashes indicating other subnodes. The rules for naming are different because pipes are implemented as a file system, and mapped files
belong to the heap-management system.

CreateFileMapping returns a valid handle if it succeeds and NULL if it fails. If
the name string in lpszMapName designates a mapping object that already exists,
and if the requested protection attributes match, CreateFileMapping returns a
valid handle to the existing object. That may not be what you want.

A program trying to create a new mapping object may be surprised if another
program happens to have used the same name for its own object. To detect whether
your new handle belongs to an old object, call GetLastError even after Create-
FileMapping *succeeds* and test for ERROR_ALREADY_EXISTS.

Mapping a View

MapViewOfFile connects a section of memory with a section of the file. It makes
part of the file visible in memory. A mapped file is "mapped" because of what
this function does: It associates every byte of the memory range with a corresponding byte in the file.

```
LPVOID MapViewOfFile(
    HANDLE hMapObject,          // mapped file to view
    DWORD fdwAccess,            // access mode
    DWORD dwOffsetHigh,         // high-order 32 bits of file offset
    DWORD dwOffsetLow,          // low-order 32 bits of file offset
    DWORD dwViewSize );         // size of view in bytes
```

The hMapObject handle must be created with CreateFileMapping or Open-
FileMapping. The second parameter requests access privileges for the pages
within the view. The privileges requested here must not conflict with those

already set in the original `CreateFileMapping` command. For example, a file-mapping object created with the PAGE_READONLY flag will not support a view with FILE_MAP_WRITE access. Many processes may open views to a single file-mapping object. The following are the view-access flags:

FILE_MAP_WRITE   Grants write access. Requires PAGE_READWRITE.

FILE_MAP_READ   Grants read-only access. Requires PAGE_READONLY or PAGE_READWRITE.

FILE_MAP_ALL_ACCESS   Synonym for FILE_MAP_WRITE. Requires PAGE_READWRITE.

FILE_MAP_COPY   Grants copy-on-write access. Requires PAGE_WRITECOPY.

When you finish with one view and want to inspect another region of the file, unmap the first view and call `MapViewOfFile` again.

```
BOOL UnmapViewOfFile( LPVOID lpvBaseAddress );
```

`lpvBaseAddress` is the same value received earlier from `MapViewOfFile`. `UnmapViewOfFile` writes any modified pages in the view back to the disk and releases the virtual address space reserved for the mapping. (The `FlushViewOf-File` command also forces modifications to be saved.)

File-Mapped Object Sharing

In order for two processes to share a file-mapping object, both must acquire a handle. Child processes may inherit file-mapping handles from their parents. If the second process is not a child, and if the name string is not coded into both programs, one process must pass the file-mapping object to the other process through a pipe, a mailslot, a DDE conversation, or by some other arrangement. `OpenFileMapping` converts a name string into a handle for an existing object.

```
HANDLE OpenFileMapping(
    DWORD   dwAccess,       // access mode
    BOOL    bInheritHandle, // TRUE for children to inherit the handle
    LPTSTR  lpszName );     // points to name of file-mapping object
```

After receiving its handle, the second process also calls `MapViewOfFile` to see what the file contains.

Preserving Coherence

If several processes open views on a shared file-mapping object, any changes one makes will be visible to the others. All their view pointers will point to different places in the same coherent object. The file-mapping object coordinates modifications from all its open views. The file may become incoherent, however, if the views derive from two different concurrent file-mapping objects linked to a single file. If the viewers write their changes to different file-mapping objects, they create conflicting versions of the file.

Figure 19.6 shows how two file-mapping objects may contain different versions of the disk file and fall out of sync. Any modifications the first two processes make will be deposited in the first file-mapping object; any modifications made by the third process will be put in the second file-mapping object. If all processes unmap their views and write their changes to the disk, only one set of changes is saved, because one set writes over the other on the disk. When file views become incoherent, he who saves last saves best.

FIGURE 19.6:

How deriving views from different file-mapping objects produces incoherence

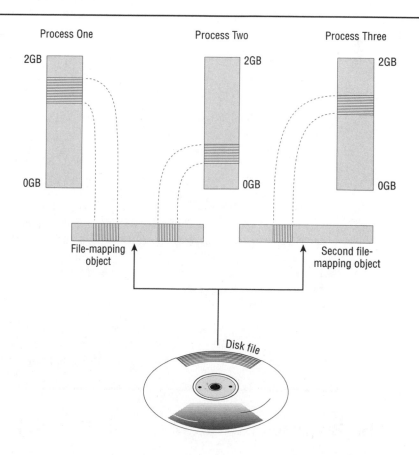

To enforce coherence, Microsoft recommends that the first program to open the file should specify exclusive access (set 0 in the share-mode parameter). Then no other program can open the file to create a second mapping object.

Three other situations can also produce incoherence:

- Normal I/O performed on a disk file that other processes are viewing as a mapped object causes incoherence. The changes will be lost when the file-mapping object saves its version of the file.

- Processes on different machines may share mapped files, but since they cannot share the same block of physical memory across a network, their views remain coherent only as long as neither process writes to its view.

- If two processes modify a copy-on-write mapped file, they are not writing to the same pages. The modified pages are no longer shared, and the views are not coherent.

Uses of Copy-on-Write Protection

Copy-on-write protection means that when a process tries to write on a page, the system copies the page and writes only to the copy. The original page cannot be modified. In other words, the process has read-only access to the original and gets automatic copies of any parts it decides to change.

Copy-on-write protection can be useful for preserving a buffer's original state until all the changes are final. A half-edited spreadsheet, for example, with all its formulas linking cells, might be useless in its unfinished state. Simply saving changed areas back to the original file could cause problems because the changes in one edited place might invalidate the data in another unedited place. Copy-on-write protection leaves the original buffer and its file intact while editing proceeds. Of course, the problem doesn't arise with unmapped files. In that case, you would need to keep an extra copy of the entire spreadsheet, not just the modified pieces.

As another example, debuggers use copy-on-write protection when altering code to add a breakpoint. If another instance of the process is running outside the debugger, both instances still share all of the source code image except for the altered page.

The Browser Demo: Mapping Memory

Each instance of the *Browser* demo opens a handle to the same file-mapping object and maps a view of it. The object represents a small buffer of only 6KB and is backed by the system's paging file.

A multiline edit box in the program window shows the contents of the shared buffer. A set of six radio buttons permits the user to inspect different sections of the shared buffer. When the user selects a new section, the program copies part of the shared buffer into the edit box, where it can be examined and modified. In Figure 19.7, two instances of *Browser* have written information to different parts of the same buffer.

FIGURE 19.7:

Two instances of the Mapped File Browser program sharing views of the same mapped file

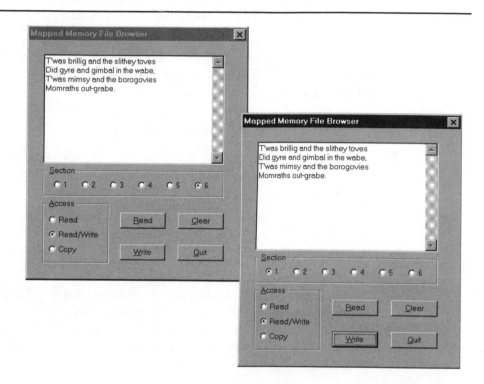

Pushbuttons issue commands to write from the screen back to the buffer, read from the buffer to refresh the screen, clear text from the edit window, and quit the program. Three more radio buttons set the page protection for the current page to read, read/write, or copy-on-write. If the user clicks the Write button while viewing a read-only page, the program traps the resulting exception.

NOTE   The *Browser* demo is included on the CD that accompanies this book, in the Chapter 19 folder.

Creating and Using the Mapped File

Two constants in the header file direct the program in creating and using the mapped file. The program's window has room for six radio buttons across its width, so we want to divide the buffer into six sections. Each section should roughly fill the buffer, so that as the user switches from section to section, new contents come into view. SECTION_SIZE tells how big one section is (1KB), and NUM_SECTIONS tells how many sections there are (6).

The resource script includes a string to name the file-mapping object. Because all instances use the same name string, all receive handles to the same object. Also in the resources is a dialog template describing the program's main window, which is a dialog box.

Initializing the Mapped File

Browser keeps information about its file-mapping object in two global variables: hMapFile is a handle to the object, and lpView points to a mapped view of the object.

Because the program's main window is a dialog box, WinMain omits the usual message loop. Instead, it simply calls an initialization procedure and invokes a modal dialog box. When the dialog box quits, WinMain releases its objects and ends.

InitApp creates the file-mapping object and maps a view of it. Because the instances of Browser want only to share memory, not to create a disk file, the CreateFileMapping command passes (HANDLE)0xFFFFFFFF as the file handle. The buffer will be mapped from the system's paging file. If we wanted to create a new disk file for the *Browser* instances to share, we would need to call Create-File first:

```
    // create the file to be mapped
hFile = CreateFile( szFileName,           // filename string
    GENERIC_READ | GENERIC_WRITE,         // access rights
    0,                                    // don't share files being mapped
    (LPSECURITY_ATTRIBUTES)NULL,          // default attributes
    CREATE_ALWAYS,                        // if file doesn't exist create it
    FILE_ATTRIBUTE_NORMAL,                // no special attributes
    NULL );                               // no special attributes
```

The file-mapping object allows read/write access, but individual views may request different protection flags. PAGE_READWRITE is compatible with all the possible view access flags.

After creating the file-mapping object, InitApp next maps a view of it. Initially, the view allows the user both read and write privileges by specifying FILE_MAP_ALL_ACCESS. The next two zeros make the beginning of the mapped view begin with the first byte of the file, and the final zero parameter causes the view to extend to the end of the file.

CreateFileMapping sets the file's size to NUM_SECTIONS * SECTION_SIZE, which happens to be 6KB. The size and starting point of the view never change in this program. The starting point can't change because it must be a multiple of 64KB. For a 6KB file, the view must begin at byte 0. To show different sections of the 6KB shared buffer, *Browser* uses lpView to treat the buffer as an array of characters.

All instances of *Browser* initialize in the same way. If the program mapped its buffer to an independent disk file, the first instance would need to initialize differently. Only the first instance would call CreateFile, and subsequent instances could be made to call OpenFileMapping rather than repeating the original CreateFileMapping command.

```
    // get a handle for an existing file-mapping object
hMapFile = OpenFileMapping( FILE_MAP_ALL_ACCESS,  // access privileges
                            FALSE,                // inheritable?
                            szMapFile );          // name of object
if( ! hMapFile )
{
    ShowErrorMsg( __LINE__ );                     // initialization failed
    return( FALSE );
}
```

Because Windows 98 always passes NULL to WinMain for the hPrevInstance parameter, *Browser* requires another mechanism to check for other instances. FindWindow works for overlapping windows, but standard dialog windows don't have a documented class name. (The class for standard dialog windows seems to be #32770, as you can verify with Microsoft's Spy utility, but undocumented features may change in future releases.) Successive instances of *Browser* could also identify their precedence if the first instance created a named pipe or added a string to the global atom table. Each instance could determine whether it has a predecessor by checking for the existence of the signal object.

Running the Dialog Box

The next procedures receive and respond to messages for the dialog box. The *Browser* dialog box initializes its controls when it receives WM_INITDIALOG. Among other things, Browser_DoInitDialog sets a limit on the number of characters the user may enter in the edit box. The limit prevents the user from entering more text than the current section of the mapped file can hold. Browser_DoCommand calls other procedures to manipulate the mapped file view in response to input from the user.

```
void Browser_DoCommand( HWND hDlg,
                        UINT uCmd )  // control ID of the button pressed
{
    static int iCurSection = 0;
```

The static variable iCurSection records the user's most recent selection from the Section radio buttons.

```
        switch( uCmd )
        {
          case IDD_WRITE:
             DoWrite( hDlg, iCurSection );
             break;

          case IDD_READ:
             DoRead( hDlg, iCurSection );
             break;

          case IDD_CLEAR:
             DoClear( hDlg );
             break;

          case IDD_SECTION1:
          case IDD_SECTION2:
          case IDD_SECTION3:
          case IDD_SECTION4:
          case IDD_SECTION5:
          case IDD_SECTION6:
             iCurSection = uCmd - IDD_SECTION1;  // save current choice
             DoClear( hDlg );                    // clear edit box
             DoRead( hDlg, iCurSection );         // show new file section
             break;

          case IDD_READ_ACCESS:
          case IDD_READWRITE_ACCESS:
          case IDD_WRITECOPY_ACCESS:
             ChangeAccess( uCmd );
             break;
```

```
            case IDCANCEL:
            case IDD_QUIT:
                EndDialog( hDlg, TRUE );
                break;
        }
        return;
    }
```

Modifying the Shared Object

When the user clicks the Write, Read, or Clear button, the program calls DoWrite, DoRead, or DoClear. In response to commands from the Access radio buttons, the program calls ChangeAccess.

DoWrite and DoRead send WM_GETTEXT and WM_SETTEXT messages to the edit control. DoWrite copies the contents of the edit buffer to a section of the mapped file, and DoRead copies a section of the mapped file to the edit control. In both procedures, this expression points to the beginning of the current section of the mapped view:

```
&( lpView[ iSection * SECTION_SIZE ] )
```

lpView is type LPSTR, so it points to an array of characters. iSection tells which radio button is currently checked. The first button is 0, so the result of iSection*SECTION_SIZE is the number of the first byte in the given file section. lpView[] evaluates to a character, and &(lpView[])gives the address of the character.

```
void DoWrite( HWND hDlg, int iSection )
{
        // get the edit control handle
    HWND hwndEdit = GetDlgItem( hDlg, IDD_EDIT );

    if( hwndEdit )
    {
        try
        {
            // copy the text from the edit buffer to the mapped file
            Edit_GetText( hwndEdit,          // edit control
                    &( lpView[iSection*SECTION_SIZE] ),
                                            // pointer into the view
                    SECTION_SIZE );    // bytes in section
    }
```

The exception handler in `DoWrite` is designed to catch the error when the user write-protects the mapped view and then tries to use the Write button. We could disable the button, but allowing the error to occur seemed more instructive and a better demonstration of what write protection does.

```
except( EXCEPTION_ACCESS_VIOLATION )
{
    // assume the exception was due to read-only access
    MessageBox( hDlg, "Memory is read only.\n\rNo data was written.",
                "Browser Message", MB_OK | MB_ICONEXCLAMATION );
}
}
return;
}
```

The `DoRead` function reads text from the mapped file, copying the retrieved text to the edit control buffer.

```
void DoRead( HWND hDlg, int iSection )
{
    HWND hwndEdit;

    // get the edit control handle
    hwndEdit = GetDlgItem( hDlg, IDD_EDIT );
    if( hwndEdit )
    {
        // retrieve the text from memory and display it
        Edit_SetText( hwndEdit,
                    &( lpView[iSection*SECTION_SIZE] ) );
                                                // pointer in view
    }
    return;
}
```

On the other hand, the `DoClear` procedure does nothing to the mapped file but does clear the text in the edit buffer.

```
void DoClear( HWND hWnd )
{
    HWND hwndEdit;
    char *szText = "\0";

    // empty the edit buffer by filling it with a null string
    hwndEdit = GetDlgItem( hWnd, IDD_EDIT );
```

```
        if( hwndEdit )
        {
            Edit_SetText( hwndEdit, szText );
        }
        return;
    }
```

Last, `ChangeAccess` unmaps the current view of the file-mapping object in order to remap it with a different access privilege. Every instance of the program may choose different access flags because each has its own independent view of the object. An instance that uses `FILE_MAP_COPY` remains synchronized with the other instances' views until it writes to the buffer. At that moment, the system intervenes and creates a copy of the protected page for the program to modify. From then on, the program never sees the original unmodified page again, even though the other instances do.

```
void ChangeAccess( int iNewAccess )          // requested access rights
{
    DWORD fdwAccess;                         // new access flag

    // close the previous mapping
    UnmapViewOfFile( lpView );
    // choose new access flag
    switch( iNewAccess )
    {
        case IDD_READWRITE_ACCESS:
            fdwAccess = FILE_MAP_ALL_ACCESS;
            break;

        case IDD_READ_ACCESS:
            fdwAccess = FILE_MAP_READ;
            break;

        default: // IDD_WRITECOPY_ACCESS
            fdwAccess = FILE_MAP_COPY;
            break;
    }
    // remap the view using the requested access and view number
    lpView = MapViewOfFile( hMapFile,  // handle to mapping object
                            fdwAccess, // access privileges
                            0, 0,      // starting offset in file
                                       // (low order 32-bits, high order 32-bits)
```

```
                          0 );        // size of view area (all of file)
   if( lpView == NULL )                // error?
   {
      ShowErrorMsg( __LINE__ );        // yes; tell user
   }
   return;
}
```

Since *Browser* shows the buffer in 1KB sections, four sections fill one page frame. If one instance writes to the first section with copy-on-write protection, it loses synchronization in the first four sections (one page frame). Its view of sections 5 and 6, however, will continue to reflect changes made by other instances. Also, changes the first program makes to its copy-on-write buffer will never be visible to other instances. The copied pages are private.

In this chapter, you've seen some of the new powers of the Windows 98 VMM. The virtual memory API passes on to you some of these powers, especially the ability to reserve a range of addresses without immediately committing physical memory to support them. The ability to guarantee that a range of contiguous addresses will be available as an object grows, or as an array slowly fills in, makes working with sparse memory structures easy.

Given the VMM's effectiveness in isolating each process from memory used by any other process, sharing blocks of memory becomes problematic. Programs have moved apart into private address spaces. Gone are the neighborly days of passing memory handles from program to program. In their place are the high-tech miracles of memory-mapped files, and with them come all the modern concerns for protection, coherence, and point of view. The *Browser* demo discussed in this chapter demonstrates how to address some of these concerns.

In the next chapter, we'll discuss another concern of modern applications: security.

CHAPTER
TWENTY

20

Security and Cryptography

- ■ Differences in security in Windows 98, Windows 95, and Windows NT

- ■ The Win32 security API

- ■ An overview of encryption

- ■ The crypto API

Security has become an important topic for application developers, as more programs are required to function across networks of all types, including the Internet and company intranets. In this chapter, we will begin by discussing the level of security provided by Windows 98 and how it differs from Windows NT security. Then we will take a look at the Win32 security API, which is only fully supported by Windows NT. Even if you are developing software to run only under Windows 98, you should familiarize yourself with the security API. By understanding how Windows NT implements security for itself and makes s ecurity available for server applications, you will be aware of the issues that you need to consider when developing client applications that need to access secure data.

Next, we will look at an area of security that is available under both Windows 98 and Windows NT: data encryption and authentication, provided by the cryptography API (crypto API). Data authentication and confidentiality, online financial transactions, and protection from rogue software are reasons to enlist the help of cryptography. The crypto API provides a standard way to access encryption, hashing, signing, and authenticating algorithms from a variety of different security vendors.

Finally, we'll wrap up the chapter by looking at some other security-related considerations, which will help you avoid potential pitfalls in designing secure applications.

Windows 98 Security versus NT Security

Although Windows 98 does not implement built-in security anywhere near the level found in Windows NT, a number of security-related features have been added and/or improved upon from Windows 95. These changes, in a nutshell, are as follows:

- Support for secure channels
- Support for smart cards
- Built-in crypto API support
- Built-in Authenticode support
- Built-in Microsoft Wallet support

Secure channels support includes Point to Point Tunneling Protocol (PPTP), which enables users to connect securely to a remote network, even over an intervening insecure network if necessary. This is accomplished by means of encrypted encapsulated packets and enables one protocol to be nested inside another. Thus, a user can connect, for example, to the Internet via TCP/IP, then establish a secure IPX connection to his or her office network. Support for Secure Socket Layer (SSL) has been upgraded to SSL 3.0, which increases the level of encryption that can be applied to Internet and intranet data exchanges.

Smart card support consists of a two-layer driver model designed to encompass smart card reader hardware, together with the APIs used to authenticate, write to, and retrieve data from smart cards. These cards have at least three important uses: as user authentication in place of (or in addition to) logon sequences, for transacting financial business over the Internet and elsewhere, and as portable data repositories for storing bits of information such as one's drug allergies or dental history.

Crypto API, Authenticode, and Microsoft Wallet support first appeared as part of Internet Explorer (IE), and they are still being included with the various platform versions of IE.

Table 20.1 summarizes the security features of Windows 95, Windows 98, and Windows NT.

TABLE 20.1: Security Features in Windows 95, 98, and NT

Technology	Windows 95	Windows 98	Windows NT
Authenticode	Add-on (IE4)	Yes	Yes
PPTP client	Add-on	Yes	Yes
PPTP server	No	Yes	Yes
Smart cards	Add-on	Yes	Yes
Crypto API	Add-on (IE4)	Yes	Yes
Microsoft Wallet	Add-on (IE4)	Yes	Yes
Group-level security	Partial	Partial	Yes
File-level security	No	No	Yes
Object rights and privileges	No	No	Yes

As you can see from the Table 20.1, Windows NT and Windows 98 share many of the same security technologies, particularly the Internet-related security technologies. The chief way that they differ is in Windows NT's absolute, "from the ground up" internal security features, which incorporate myriad low-level security checks at every point where objects can be accessed within the operating system.

A good example of the different levels of security in Windows NT and Windows 98 is in file access. In Windows 98 (and Windows 95), security is only on a folder and drive level; you cannot set individual access rights at the file level. In part, this is because there are many different means of getting at a file in Windows 98—through various DOS interrupts, BIOS functions, Windows APIs, and various language (Pascal, C++, and so on) file-access APIs. With these various file-access methods come many resulting security loopholes, which would require extensive patching to fix and would likely break many existing applications in the process. (Keep in mind that much of this code was "adapted" from good old 16-bit code.) Also, there is the overhead such checks would add to file access.

Such compromises were understandably deemed undesirable for an operating system that is marketed more to home users than to business users, who have a greater need for security. As the Internet keeps growing to subsume more of our daily affairs, such security will become increasingly necessary even for the home users, who have been flocking enthusiastically to the Internet.

In short, these differences between Windows 98 and Windows NT center primarily around the thorough way that Windows NT internally checks access rights and in the security hooks exposed at the programming level, which allow programmers to build the same level of robust security into their own applications. This security technology is exposed by what is referred to as the security API. Although this API is considered part of the Win32 API (or of late, the Win Base API), it is fully implemented only in Windows NT.

What these differences mean to programmers is that truly secure applications require Windows NT. This should come as no surprise to you—one of the main advantages Windows NT has over Windows 98 is its extensive built-in security.

Therefore, despite this being a book about programming Windows 98 applications, in this chapter we'll devote some space to a discussion of the workings of Windows NT's security. Even if you have no interest in incorporating security in your own applications, knowledge of the security API is important for the following reasons:

- References to security parameters and options keep showing up in many other Win32 API functions, which you will undoubtedly find occasion to use.

- There is the danger of inadvertently creating security loopholes, particularly in server applications, when your applications neglect to make use of security API functions properly (or at all).

- Armed with this knowledge, you can choose whether and to what degree to implement client-type security in your Windows 98 applications.

Although Windows 98 provides minimal support for the security API, there is good news regarding Windows 98's support for encryption. This means that you can use encryption with Windows 98 applications to provide an effective level of access control in certain instances. Currently, every function of the crypto API (except those few functions that deal with data in Unicode format) works the same on both Windows 98 and Windows NT platforms.

Windows 98 and Security API Functions

You will probably not be surprised to learn that only very few of the security API functions are implemented in Windows 98. Your application may call any one of these functions while running on a Windows 98 station, but it had then better be prepared to check the error-return code, note that the function failed, and take appropriate action.

The only correct way to use the Windows NT security API functions is in the context of a server application. While it is possible to design a server application to run on a Windows 98 station, it is not possible to do this where the server application needs to implement Windows NT-level security (using the Win32 security API at any rate). And this would seem to be the case for most, if not all, server applications. The better and simpler approach is to require the application to be run on Windows NT, and simply issue a complaint message and exit if someone tries to run the application on a Windows 98 station.

Having said that, let me also suggest that you may not want to simply perform an operating system version check and then exit if the version number doesn't match. I have seen some older Windows applications that, when run on the latest versions of Windows NT, get confused and complain that they require a newer version of the operating system. So assumptions about what is or isn't an appropriate operating system to run an application, based solely on getting the operating system version number, are prone to errors in certain cases. A better approach is to look at those categories of functionality needed by your application that are not currently supported by a subset of the operating systems that are otherwise capable of running your application. Then, when your application loads, have it perform checks for any missing functionality, and either exit or else modify its behavior or functionality accordingly.

Security Concepts

Currently, there are approximately 80 API functions pertaining to security in Windows NT (excluding the crypto API functions), and only a handful of these are fully or partially supported under Windows 98. Of course, as is standard in other areas of the Win32 API, any Windows NT security functions not supported by Windows 98 will at least have function stubs located in an appropriate DLL, so your Windows NT application can load on a Windows 98 system without linking errors. Therefore, when you are designing an application to make use of Windows NT security, it is your responsibility to determine what functionality this application should provide when running under Windows 98—if indeed it should even be permitted to run at all.

Planning Security for Your Applications

What sorts of applications really need to be concerned with Windows NT security? Simply put, anything intended to run on a *server* is a strong candidate for needing to implement security. Additionally, at the client-level, any applications that need to access their own secured objects (shared memory, files, semaphores, the registry, and so on) and most applications that will run as a *service* will need to make use of at least some Windows NT security functions.

When thinking about Windows NT's security, one important point you should keep in mind is the distinction between automatically protected objects in NT and those objects you create yourself and must protect by implementing your own security checks. An example of automatic security would be the security checking that takes place within the kernel whenever access attempts occur on files or directories that are located on an NTFS partition.

On the other hand, "manual" or "do-it-yourself" security would be called for if you needed to prevent, for example, unauthorized access to only certain types of functionality within an application or to certain parts of a database file. In these cases, you can plan the security as follows:

- Create a list of all data objects and/or types of functionality that cannot be open to all users indiscriminately.

- Develop a logical plan of specific rights or privileges that can be assigned or restricted to the various individuals and/or groups using your system.

- Add security checks to *every* point in your software where the protected objects or functionality can be accessed.

- If the protected objects can possibly be accessed in any way from outside your software (by standard file access, for example), restrict access there also. This usually can be done by specifying Administrator-only access on the object, and then have your application run using Administrator privileges so it can access the object itself.

The Per-User Security Model

An important concept to understand about Windows NT security is that it is based on a per-*user* security model. Everything that a user does after logging in to Windows NT—from starting applications, to accessing printers and drives, to opening and saving files—is allowed or not allowed based on what rights and privileges are granted that user.

Windows NT's security API also provides system-level and application-level *event-logging* features. These features allow you to later determine who had access to what, and when that access occurred.

Figure 20.1 shows a simplified representation of how Windows NT's security system keeps track of users versus *objects*. Whenever a user successfully logs on to a trusted server, that user is identified internally by an *access token*. That access token sticks with the user as long as that user is logged in, wherever he or she goes within the NT network. Each system object, on the other hand, is represented by a *security descriptor* (SD), which holds a number of pieces of security-related information (discussed a bit later in the chapter). Whenever a user attempts to access an object, NT's security compares the access token against the permissions in the security descriptor.

Security for Objects

A Windows NT system *object*, in the context we are using in this chapter, does not mean a C++ object, an OLE object, or a COM object. Here, it refers to any "object" created and managed by one of the three main Windows NT subsystems: Kernel, User, and GDI.

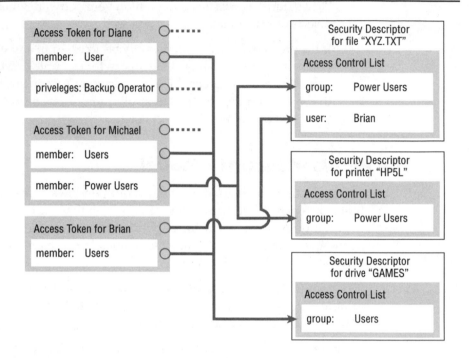

FIGURE 20.1:

Each user logged in to Windows NT is represented internally by an access token. Each system object (or user object) is identified by a security descriptor.

For various reasons, NT's built-in security is only implemented on Kernel objects. Thus, you are not required (via the API) to worry about security when creating objects such as bitmaps, cursors, pens, brushes, icons, metafiles, or window handles. But you do need to provide at least a security descriptor parameter (or a NULL value) when creating or managing Kernel objects, such as files, folders, storage devices, pipes, mailslots, serial ports, registry keys, console devices, and printer queues.

In addition to system objects, there are also user- or application-defined objects. These are any objects that your application defines, creates, and recognizes. These types of objects can include anything from particular functionality in your application, to NT objects from the User and GDI subsystems (if you need to protect a bitmap, for instance), to subdivided areas of files. This category also encompasses anything else your application must interact with and control access to—a piece of data, a menu command, a particular view of a dataset, or whatever else you might come up with.

NOTE Sometimes, a further distinction is made between Windows NT objects created by NT and NT objects created by end users, via their use of the system or various applications. This distinction becomes important in understanding the difference between SACLs and DACLs, as we'll discuss later at the chapter.

Built-in versus Application Security

Windows NT internally and automatically handles the storage and checking of security settings only on its own Kernel system objects; any other objects you define and create are not protected automatically. If you need to enforce security on your objects, you must implement this security yourself.

To add access restrictions (security) for anything not covered by NT's built-in/automatic security, you need to specify the desired permissions and then check those permissions every time an attempt is made to access your object. NT's security API gives you some help in accomplishing this; its set of functions are identical to the functions used by NT's own internal security. Therefore, the process you go through to secure your own objects has much in common with what NT does to provide security for its objects.

The distinction between NT's built-in security and application security is not absolute. If you're creating some object that, in turn, makes use of one or more system objects, NT may automatically provide *some* level of security for these system objects. If you store your object in a file, for example, that file will be subject to NT's built-in file security just like any other file (if it's located on an NTFS partition, that is).

This overlap of NT's system security with additional security that you may implement is not only welcome, but is essential to the proper implementation of security in your application. For example, NT itself knows how to restrict access to files, subdirectories, and drives. But, as an example, it doesn't know anything about the fact that part of your database file contains data that should be available to only certain users, while other parts may be appropriate for general access. In this particular case, you would need to protect your database file in two ways. First, you would use NTFS's file security to permit direct file access only by system (or database) administrators. Second, you would need to write your database server application to take all the incoming data requests from various users and provide the additional level of security based on permissions that you have previously defined at the user or group levels. This server application, by the way, would itself be able to access the database file directly, because it would run using the Administrator (or other appropriate) access rights.

WARNING   When implementing security on any object that might be accessed from outside your application, always restrict any and all *direct* access (file, communications, and so on) to this object by also using Windows NT's built-in security attributes, wherever applicable. Typically, this means setting Administrator-only access on all "outside" approaches to your object, then having your server application internally make further decisions about granting or denying access on a case-by-case basis.

As you may surmise, it is generally foolhardy to attempt to implement security from within your application when either the application or its data files will end up being stored on a FAT (or other non-NTFS) partition. You could get around this partially by using encryption on your data files, as discussed later in this chapter. However, even with encryption, there are likely to be security loopholes if users are able to directly access your application's data in any way.

Security Is for Servers

When planning your security implementation, always design using the *client/ server* model! In other words, do not use the security API just anywhere in your Win32 applications; these functions belong only in software that will be run on a server.

Split the project into a client application, which individual users will use, and a server application, which runs on a server and handles all incoming requests for secured objects. Why insist on this extra work? There are several reasons:

- The software running on the client side might end up being run under Windows 98 or another operating system that doesn't support security, such as a Web browser.

- This provides a clear division between a server application, which handles all security and therefore "clears" all your secured-object requests, and the client application, which makes use of the objects. The client/server model centralizes the security issues on one machine, rather than several or many, leaving that many fewer potential security loopholes.

- Separating the client and server functions provides you with much greater flexibility down the road, in terms of adding new types of client applications or extending the size of your LAN. You eliminate the need to change your server implementation, which would thereby reopen a can of security worms.

WARNING   Always use the client/server model when designing systems that need Windows NT's security services. The security checking should always (and only!) be performed by an application functioning on a server or in a server capacity. A client application, running on the user's system, should use any of the standard network communications means to request access to the secured objects from the server application. This technique allows you to combine secure access with the ability to access the objects via workstations that do not internally support NT security—for example, from Windows 98, a Java applet running in a Web browser, or a Unix or Macintosh machine.

So how is the client application supposed to communicate with the server application? There is more than one right answer to this; however, the method you choose must be a secure one. Typically, any of the following means of communicating between client and server applications can be used:

- Named pipes
- Remote procedure calls
- Distributed COM (DCOM)
- Secure sockets (and supporting Web server)

These are not the only means you could use, of course. However, in most cases, any one or a combination of those listed here are excellent choices.

Security Attributes

You cannot do much programming in the Win32 API without running into the many Kernel object-manipulation functions, which always take a pointer to a

SECURITY_ATTRIBUTES structure. Take CreateFile, for instance, which is defined as follows:

```
HANDLE CreateFile(
    LPCTSTR        lpFileName,             // pointer to name of file
    DWORD          dwDesiredAccess,        // access (read-write) mode
    DWORD          dwShareMode,            // share mode
    LPSECURITY_ATTRIBUTES  lpSecurityAttributes,// (see below)
    DWORD          dwCreationDistribution, // create mode
    DWORD          dwFlagsAndAttributes,   // open, delete, close attributes
    HANDLE         hTemplateFile );        // optional source for attributes
```

What! All this just to create a file? You may take one look at this and decide to go back to using their favorite "normal" means of opening files: fopen, OpenFile, or Delphi's Reset, for example.

But CreateFile has far more uses than its name implies. In a Win32 application, it is the primary means of opening all sorts of objects in addition to files; it opens pipes, mailslots, communications sessions, disk devices, and so on. CreateFile is not only used for creating these objects, but can also be used for opening, closing, and even deleting them, given the right combinations of flags. As you learned in Chapter 15, CreateFile is also capable of doing both synchronous and asynchronous (overlapped) I/O operations.

Performing any of these CreateFile operations on a secured object causes NT's built-in security checking to go to work. NT compares access rights contained in your lpSecurityAttributes structure with any permissions or restrictions that have been placed on the object and causes your function to succeed or fail, as appropriate.

Typically, you would most often use CreateFile by simply filling in a NULL value for the lpSecurityAttributes. This is fine for routine object access, because when you specify the NULL value, the default set of SECURITY_ATTRIBUTES for the current process is used, which in most cases is exactly appropriate. This is also, by the way, exactly what happens when you open files using fopen, OpenFile, or any other means of file access under NT. As you might guess, all these functions behave similarly because they trace right back to the same code (and security checking) as used by CreateFile itself.

If you want anything more sophisticated than the default security behavior provided by using a NULL value for your SECURITY_ATTRIBUTES structure, you need to supply an actual SECURITY_ATTRIBUTES structure. Roll up your sleeves and prepare to do some rather strenuous mental exertion.

The SECURITY_ATTRIBUTES Structure

The SECURITY_ATTRIBUTES structure looks benign and simplistic at first glance:

```
typedef struct _SECURITY_ATTRIBUTES {
    DWORD  nLength; // set this to sizeof( SECURITY_ATTRIBUTES );
    LPVOID lpSecurityDescriptor; // "complex" structure.
    BOOL   bInheritHandle; // whether child process inherits handle.
} SECURITY_ATTRIBUTES; , *LPSECURITY_ATTRIBUTES;
```

Setting the nLength field is simple (and important!). Setting the bInherithandle flag is straightforward enough—it's a Boolean value. However, that middle field, which is actually a pointer to a SECURITY_DESCRIPTOR, is where the rubber really hits the road, in a security sense.

The security descriptor (SD) is one of the four major data structures used by NT's security API. (The SECURITY_ATTRIBUTES doesn't count as "major," because it's only a wrapper for supplying the SD to NT.) As mentioned earlier, the SD represents an object or a group of objects to NT's security system. It makes sense that the various Win32 API functions dealing with securable objects each takes a SECURITY_DESCRIPTOR by encapsulation in the SECURITY_ATTRIBUTES structure.

Let's take a look at each of the four main types of security structures, including the SECURITY_DESCRIPTOR, so that you will better understand how Windows NT handles security.

The Four Major Security Structures

Although these are not the only security-related information structures, the following four structures are certainly the "heavy-hitter" structures used for keeping track of Windows NT security-related information:

- Access tokens
- Security descriptors (SDs)
- Security identifiers (SIDs)
- Access Control Lists (ACLs, also known as SACLs and DACLs)

Although these are structures, you're required to consider them as *opaque*, meaning initializing them and setting their values must be accomplished by means of the supplied appropriate API functions. We'll discuss exactly which functions should be used for manipulating each structure after we examine the structures themselves.

Access Tokens

Each user logged on to an NT system is assigned an access token. This token is
checked against SDs of any objects that the user is trying to access. The access
token contains user privileges; security descriptors contain access rights.

Security Descriptors (SDs)

Inside the SD are the collected pieces of information that together exactly specify
the owner, permitted users and groups, and permissions granted (or denied) to
particular users or groups of users of that object.

Subelements of the SD include the owner and group security identifiers (SIDs),
as well as two Access Control Lists (ACLs).

NOTE Again, the security API provides an entire array of functions for querying and
manipulating the various security structures. Because these are *structures*, rather
than OOP (object-oriented programming) objects, the way you interact with them
is by using appropriate API functions, which expect as a parameter a pointer to a
particular type of security structure.

SIDs An SID is a structure of variable length that uniquely refers to a user
or group of users. Internally, an SID contains (among other things) a 48-bit
authority value, which is a unique value comprised of a revision level, an
identifier-authority value, and a subauthority value.

Once an SID is created, an NT system will not permit it to ever be reused, even
if the SID is deleted. The SD of each object contains two SIDs:

Owner SID   Identifies the current owner of the object.

Primary group SID   Identifies that group of users that has specific access
rights or restrictions for the given object.

Note that SIDs are used in several other areas of NT security. Every access token, for example, contains an SID that identifies the groups that user is a member of. Also, each Access Control Entry (ACE) in an ACL has its own SID that specifies the individual or group being granted or denied a set of permissions or rights.

ACLs   An ACL is a list of rights or restrictions placed on a user or group for a given object (or group of objects). Each SD can contain two types of ACLs:

> **System ACL (SACL)**   Keeps track of permissions that are set on an object at the system level. Only users who have system-level access can change the SACL.

> **User or discretionary ACL (DACL)**   Keeps track of permissions that are set by the owner of the object. The DACL can be changed by whoever is currently specified as the object's owner ("currently" because one of the rights that can be set on an object is the ability to change who the current owner is).

These ACLs are identical in form. Both types can contain zero or one or more Access Control Entries (ACEs). Each ACE contains three parts: users or groups this ACE pertains to, which rights are affected, and whether the rights are being granted or revoked.

An ACL can be in one of three states:

- It can be empty. In an ACL's initial state, it is empty, which is in effect the same as saying no access rights have been given for this object, so no users will have access to it.

- It can be NULL. An ACL that is explicitly set to NULL means *no* security has been assigned to the object and therefore *all access* is granted.

- It can contain one or more ACEs. Once you add a single ACE to a previously NULL ACL, the object loses its "general access" (or lack of security) and is available only to those users or groups specified by the ACE.

WARNING Do not confuse a NULL DACL with an empty DACL! They are actually opposites in their effect. An empty DACL (the initial state in a new SD) means no *access* has been granted. A NULL DACL means no *restrictions* exist for the object, so it is accessible to all users. A DACL only becomes NULL by being set that way explicitly.

So, you should now understand, at least in theory, how an object's access is specified for any condition: complete access, no access, access granted to some, and access restricted to some.

Self-Relative versus Absolute SDs SDs can be represented in either absolute or self-relative format. Figure 20.2 illustrates how these two formats differ.

SDs contain fields (the ACLs) that hold a variable number of entries (ACEs), and each field could be either NULL or empty. Therefore, it is much easier to update (add and remove) entries and settings in an SD if the SD itself is stored in memory as a structure of pointers (to structures with other pointers, usually). Otherwise, each time anything changed, a larger chunk of memory would need to be allocated, and the entire structure would need to be copied to the new area along with the new changes. This "update-friendly" format that makes use of pointers is called (somewhat confusingly) *absolute* format.

On the other hand, because pointers point to RAM, and RAM is generally only accessible by the computer owning it, it would not work very well to send an SD across the network (or save it to disk) because you would be sending (or writing) only a set of pointers, instead of the various structures themselves. Therefore, the SD can be stored in a second format where the entire structure, including all its current fields, is stored in one contiguous block of memory. This more "transfer-friendly" format is called *self-relative* format. As you might surmise, this is the format in which SDs are returned to you when you request them from the system. You can look at (read) the SD in this format, but when you need to change (write to) the SD, you must first convert the SD into absolute format.

Fortunately, there are two API functions you can use to do this conversion: `Make-AbsoluteSD` and `MakeSelfRelativeSD`. Unfortunately, you will need to use them each and every time you get or put an SD and also need to make changes to the SD.

FIGURE 20.2:

SDs come in two flavors: the absolute, which is useful for updating the SD's fields, and the self-relative, which is better suited for *transfer-ring* the SD to a file, a different process, or across the network.

SECURITY DESCRIPTORS

Absolute [used for *Setting/Changing* security settings]

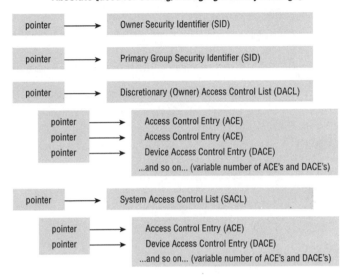

Self-Relative [used for *transferring* the SD (e.g. to a file or across the network)]

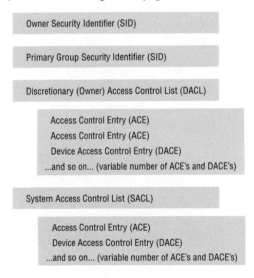

Client Impersonation

The procedure whereby a server application checks that a connected client actually has access rights to a requested object is called *client impersonation*. In this process, when the client application makes an object request of the server application, it passes along its access token. The server application uses this access token to log on as the client (impersonate the client), attempting to access the desired object in the same manner that the client is asking for it.

NOTE It is true that the server application could instead look up the security information for the client, and then get the security information for the asked-for object, and see whether the client has the desired permissions that way. However, impersonation is the simpler and more foolproof method of doing this.

Here are the steps a server application might typically make to use client impersonation in implementing server-side security:

1. The client application establishes a connection with the server application.

2. The client application asks the server application for access to a particular object.

3. The server application uses `ImpersonateLoggedOnUser` to obtain an impersonated access token, which it then uses to attempt access in the same manner as the client application.

4. The server application reverts to its own access level, by making a call to `RevertToSelf`, so that it can be available to handle other clients' requests.

5. If the server application's access attempt succeeded, it passes back to the client either an actual handle to the requested object or to some other prearranged proxy token by which the client application can refer to the requested object in future requests to the server application.

6. Each time the client application wants access (again) to a secured object, the server application should call `ImpersonateLoggedOnUser` again before accessing the object to ensure that the client's access rights haven't changed during the interim. When the request is handled, the server application again calls `RevertToSelf`.

7. When the client disconnects from the server, the server application can delete the impersonated access token.

For private objects, the server and client must establish some consistent means of referring to desired objects. This could be done by using either a handle or token type, which the server assigns and keeps track of. Alternatively, it may be a string or whatever other protocol the server and client applications implement to refer to server-application managed objects.

For private objects whose security is being handled by the server application (as opposed to some other server application running on the same or another machine), it is still important to use ImpersonateLoggedOnUser, since in the course of handling the client's request, the server may need to open or access objects for which Windows NT does have some level of built-in security assigned. By using impersonation through the entire request-handling section, the server application ensures that it won't inadvertently do something on the client's behalf that is explicitly restricted from that user.

Individual server threads (or processes) can each have a different impersonation access token assigned. This is necessary for permitting simultaneous services to multiple clients.

Checking Access Rights

Whenever an attempt is being made to access a Windows NT-secured object, NT internally calls a function called AccessCheck, which compares the user's access token with the access rights contained in the requested object's SD. This either succeeds or fails. In the case of failure, the function that made the access request returns an ERROR_ACCESS_DENIED error (traditionally called an error #5, but always use the constant).

In the same way, server applications need to call AccessCheck whenever and wherever access to a server-application–protected object is being attempted. If you leave even one place in your code where the server can access an object on behalf of a client without calling AccessCheck (and heeding the results!), your server application's security can be compromised, so be careful. It greatly simplifies your implementation if you can make all access to a server-application–protected object occur in the same (one) place in your code.

A similar function, called PrivilegeCheck, is useful for checking for required privileges. Also, before calling the checking functions, you may need to create a rights mask containing the appropriate bits set for the requested access rights.

Adding New Rights

In addition to the built-in, or predefined system rights that appear in Windows NT's User Manager (or User Manager for Domains), you can create new rights of various types if your application requires them. Rights are stored in a bit field, so individual rights are checked using bit masks and constants.

There are three types of rights:

Standard rights   Those where the assigned bit means the same, or approximately the same thing, across any objects that use them.

Specific rights   Those that could use the same bit values in different objects, but mean different things for different objects. These are the type you would use to define some completely new right that does not have much in common with already existing (predefined) rights.

Generic rights   Rights with very broad meanings, which can be interpreted somewhat differently by different applications. Generic rights can be mapped to specific and standard rights, where there is some similarity of meaning between the name of the general right and the functionality being mapped to it.

Security-Related Commands

The security functions are one of the more complex areas of Windows NT programming, particularly due to the nonobject-orientedness of the implementation. Just creating one of the needed structures is usually a multiple-step process. However, security is an important area, and it should not be implemented less often simply because it's more trouble to do so.

> **NOTE**   Remember, only a few of the security API functions are fully or partially supported under Windows 98. Although your applications can call one of these functions while running under Windows 98, most likely that function will fail.

A good strategy for dealing with these security functions is to learn how they work, then either cut and paste from existing working code, or wrap up the relative complexity in a tidy object wrapper. You may find that writing an object wrapper for these functions is much easier than trying to handle allocating and deallocating, initializing, recursing, changing, converting back and forth, and updating these structures.

Tables 20.2 through 20.13 list the security functions by categories:

Access token functions	Access-checking functions
Impersonation functions	Privileges functions
SD functions	Window station functions
SID functions	Local Service Authority functions
ACL functions	Security information functions
ACE functions	Auditing functions

TIP

For information about each function's prototype (parameters), see the online help included with your compiler. The online help provides a comprehensive, alphabetized list of all these functions (however, they are not grouped in categories, as in this chapter). Click on a function to see its prototypes.

TABLE 20.2: Access Token Functions

Function	Description
AdjustTokenGroups	Adjusts the groups in an access token.
AdjustTokenPrivileges	Adjusts privileges for an access token.
DuplicateToken	Creates a new access token identical to one supplied.
GetTokenInformation	Returns user, group, privileges, and other information about a token.
SetThreadToken	Assigns an impersonation token to a given thread.
SetTokenInformation	Modifies user, group, privileges, or other information within a given access token.
OpenProcessToken	Retrieves the access token for a given process.
OpenThreadToken	Retrieves the access token for a given thread.

TABLE 20.3: Impersonation Functions

Function	Description
CreateProcessAsUser	Identical to CreateProcess, but creates the process for a given access token.
DdeImpersonateClient	Allows a DDE server to impersonate a DDE client application, to make system accesses using the client's security.
ImpersonateLoggedOnUser	Lets a calling thread impersonate a given user (takes an access token).
ImpersonateNamedPipeClient	Allows the server end of a named pipe to impersonate the pipe client.
ImpersonateSelf	Returns an access token impersonating that of the calling process (often used for changing access at a thread level).
LogonUser	Allows a server application to acquire an access token for a given user, to use in impersonated access.
RevertToSelf	Terminates the impersonation of a client application.

NOTE LogonUser isn't included in the online alphabetical list of security functions, but I think it belongs here. You can frequently use it in your server applications to ensure that requests you're fulfilling on the requesting user's behalf match the security settings assigned to that user.

TABLE 20.4: Security Descriptor (SD) Functions

Function	Description
MakeAbsoluteSD	Creates an SD in absolute format, given one in relative format.
MakeSelfRelativeSD	Creates a SD in self-relative format, given one in absolute format.
InitializeSecurityDescriptor	Initializes a new SD for use. This defaults to no rights granted of any kind.
IsValidSecurityDescriptor	Validates an SD by checking the revision level of each part of the SD.

Continued on next page

TABLE 20.4 CONTINUED: Security Descriptor (SD) Functions

Function	Description
GetSecurityDescriptorControl	Retrieves an SD's control and revision information.
GetSecurityDescriptorLength	Returns the size in bytes for a given SD.
GetSecurityDescriptorDacl	Returns a pointer to the DACL for a given SD.
GetSecurityDescriptorGroup	Returns a pointer to the primary group SID for a given SD.
GetSecurityDescriptorOwner	Returns a pointer to the owner SID for a given SD.
GetSecurityDescriptorSacl	Returns a pointer to the SACL for a given SD.
SetSecurityDescriptorDacl	Updates a given SD's DACL with new settings.
SetSecurityDescriptorGroup	Updates a given SD's group SID with new settings.
SetSecurityDescriptorOwner	Updates a given SD's owner SID with new settings.
SetSecurityDescriptorSacl	Updates a given SD's SACL with new settings.

TABLE 20.5: Security Identifier (SID) Functions

Function	Description
AllocateAndInitializeSid	Allocates and initializes an SID with up to eight subauthorities (groups or users).
AllocateLocallyUniqueId	Allocates a locally unique identifier.
InitializeSid	Initializes an SID structure with given number of subauthorities.
CopySid	Returns copy of a SID to a buffer.
EqualPrefixSid	Boolean test of two SIDs' prefix values for equality.
EqualSid	Boolean test of two SIDs' prefix values for equality.
FreeSid	Boolean test of two SIDs' exact equality.
GetSidIdentifierAuthority	Returns a pointer to a SID's top-level authority (in SID_IDENTIFIER_AUTHORITY).
GetSidLengthRequired	Returns the length needed in bytes, to store an SID with a given number of subauthorities.

Continued on next page

TABLE 20.5 (CONTINUED): Security Identifier (SID) Functions

Function	Description
GetSidSubAuthority	Returns a pointer to the nth subauthority for a given SID.
GetSidSubAuthorityCount	Returns the number of subauthorities in a given SID.
GetLengthSid	Returns the length, in bytes, of a given SID.
IsValidSid	Validates a given SID by verifying that the revision number is within a known range and that the number of subauthorities is below the maximum.
LookupAccountSid	Returns the account name and first domain found for a given SID.

NOTE   With SIDs, you can allocate and initialize using a single function call. As with SDs, a newly allocated SID needs to be initialized before you can use it.

TABLE 20.6: Access Control List (ACL, DACL, and SACL) Functions

Function	Description
InitializeAcl	Creates a new ACL structure.
GetAclInformation	Retrieves information (such as the revision number, size, and ACE count) for a given ACL.
IsValidAcl	Validates a given ACL by checking that its version number is correct and that the number of ACEs matches the ACE count.
SetAclInformation	Sets information about an ACL.

TABLE 20.7: Access Control Entry (ACE) Functions

Function	Description
AddAce	Adds one or more ACEs to a given ACL, at specified index position.
AddAccessAllowedAce	Adds an access-allowed ACE to an ACL, thereby granting access for a particular SID.

Continued on next page

TABLE 20.7 CONTINUED: Access Control Entry (ACE) Functions

Function	Description
AddAccessDeniedAce	Adds an access-denied ACE to an ACL, thereby denying access for a particular SID.
AddAuditAccessAce	Adds a system-audit ACE to a SACL.
DeleteAce	Deletes the nth ACE from a given ACL.
FindFirstFreeAce	Returns a pointer to the first free position in an ACL.
GetAce	Returns a pointer to the nth ACE for a given ACL.

WARNING   When calling **AddAce** or **DeleteAce,** you must supply an index parameter—the ordering of ACEs in an ACL *matters*.

TABLE 20.8:   Access-Checking Functions

Function	Description
AccessCheck	Used by a server application to check whether a client has access to an object.
AccessCheckAndAuditAlarm	Performs **AccessCheck** and generates corresponding audit messages.
AreAllAccessesGranted	Compares granted with desired rights to see whether all specified access rights have been granted.
AreAnyAccessesGranted	Compares granted with desired rights to see whether any specified access rights have been granted.
PrivilegeCheck	Tests whether the given access token contains the desired privilege(s).
PrivilegedServiceAuditAlarm	Does **PrivilegeCheck** and generates corresponding audit messages.
MapGenericMask	Maps generic access rights to specific and standard access rights.

WARNING Keep in mind that overhead (extra time) attaches to each object access while auditing of that object is enabled. How much overhead this incurs depends primarily on how often you will need to access the object. For infrequent access, the auditing overhead isn't a problem, but when you're performing very frequent operations on an object, the overhead required for auditing can noticeably impact performance. The best approach is to test your application with and without auditing enabled to ensure that with the auditing overhead, performance is still within an acceptable range.

TABLE 20.9: Privileges Functions

Function	Description
MapGenericMask	Maps generic access rights of a given mask to specific and standard access rights.
PrivilegeCheck	Tests whether a given access token has the specified privilege(s).
LookupPrivilegeDisplayName	Retrieves the displayable name associated with a particular privilege.
LookupPrivilegeName	Returns the privilege name associated with the given local unique identifier (LUID).
LookupPrivilegeValue	Returns the LUID associated with a given privilege on a given system.
ObjectPrivilegeAuditAlarm	Generates audit messages when the given user (access token) attempts to perform privileged operations on a particular object.
PrivilegedServiceAuditAlarm	Generates audit messages when the given user (access token) attempts to perform privileged operations.

TABLE 20.10: Window Station Functions

Function	Description
GetProcessWindowStation	Returns a handle to the window station associated with the calling process.
SetProcessWindowStation	Assigns a given window station to the calling process.

TABLE 20.11:   Local Service Authority (LSA) Functions

Function	Description
InitLsaString	Creates a LSA_UNICODE_STRING for the given privilege name.
LsaOpenPolicy	Opens (or creates) a given policy on target machine.
LsaLookupNames	Returns an account name (and SID) for given access token.
LsaRemoveAccountRights	Revokes privileges for the specified user(s).
LsaAddAccountRights	Grants privileges to the specified user(s).
LsaClose	Closes a given policy.
LsaEnumerateAccountRights	Enumerates rights or privileges that are currently granted to a given account.
LsaEnumerateAccountsWithUserRight	Enumerates all accounts on a given system that have been granted a given privilege.

TABLE 20.12:   Security Information Functions

Function	Description
GetFileSecurity	Obtains the SD for a particular file or directory.
GetKernelObjectSecurity	Obtains the SD for a specified Kernel object.
GetPrivateObjectSecurity	Obtains the SD for a specified private object.
GetUserObjectSecurity	Obtains the SD for a specified user object.
SetFileSecurity	Updates a file or directory's security using the supplied SD.
SetKernelObjectSecurity	Updates a Kernel object's security using the supplied SD.
SetPrivateObjectSecurity	Updates a private object's security using the supplied SD.
SetUserObjectSecurity	Updates a user object's security using the supplied SD.
CreatePrivateObjectSecurity	Allocates and initializes a self-relative SD to be used with a new private object.
DestroyPrivateObjectSecurity	Deletes the given private object's SD.

NOTE

A *window station* is a set of one or more desktops. NT's default window station is WinSta0. Each window station can contain one or more Desktops. A *Desktop* in this context can be thought of as a set of visible windows. The default WinSta0 window station, for example, has three Desktops: logon, screen saver, and application. The SwitchDesktop API function allows you to make a different Desktop visible.

TABLE 20.13: Auditing Functions

Function	Description
ObjectOpenAuditAlarm	Generates audit messages to log when a user attempts to gain access to an existing object or create a new one.
ObjectCloseAuditAlarm	Generates audit messages when the handle of an object is closed.
ObjectDeleteAuditAlarm	Generates audit messages when the handle of an object is deleted.
ObjectPrivilegeAuditAlarm	Generates audit messages when the given user (access token) attempts to perform privileged operations on a particular object.
PrivilegedServiceAuditAlarm	Generates audit messages when the given user (access token) attempts to perform privileged operations.
AccessCheckAndAuditAlarm	Performs AccessCheck and generates corresponding audit messages.

The FileUser Demo: Checking and Updating SDs

The *FileUser* demo shows how (on Windows NT only) to get a file's current SD, and then update it by adding either an AccessAllowed ACE or an AccessDenied ACE for a given user. To keep this example simple, we're using a command-line, Win32 console application. The program expects a filename, a username, and a + (plus sign, specifying access allowed) or – (minus sign, specifying access denied) to be passed from the command line.

NOTE
The *FileUser* demo is included on the CD accompanying this book, in the Chapter 20 folder. This demo makes use of advanced security features that are currently supported only on Windows NT. Windows 98 will simply return a failure status on most functions used by this program.

This example should give you some understanding of how Windows NT's object-level security is set or modified for an object. You can experiment and modify this sample program to allow no access rights or all access rights, or to change ownership of the file. By changing the DACL type, you can also use this code to modify the security on other types of objects.

The *FileUser* demo, along with the information presented in the preceding sections, should give you a clear idea of how data objects (or functionality) can be secured on a Windows NT server application by using the security functions built into NT. Now we will look at another, complementary approach to securing information, which both Windows 98 and NT support fully: encryption.

Encryption Technology Concepts

Individual packets of data that traverse a network can be intercepted or monitored by anyone who can access the packets at any point along their path from sender to receiver. This means that if you want to exchange data securely over an insecure network, you need to use some form of encryption.

Cryptography is possible without a computer, but most often the information to be encrypted originates or at least ends up at some point in machine-readable form—a word processing document, ASCII, EBCDIC, or some other standard computer format. Thus, computers have given rise to the means by which information is most often encrypted, and have also provided a huge and growing population of potential users of encryption.

Do You Need Encryption?

There are certain costs involved in implementing and using encryption—in terms of development time, the degree to which data throughput is affected, increased complexity for users, and so on. Therefore, the decision of whether or not to use encryption isn't necessarily a "no-brainer."

Here are some pertinent questions you may wish to use as starting points in evaluating whether to use encryption:

- Is this data really worth encrypting?

- How many people need to have access to this information?

- How quickly will the information become outdated (and therefore less sensitive)?

- What do you consider an acceptable level of risk (of information compromise)?

- If the data needs to be exchanged across a network, how secure is the network itself?

- What are the possible repercussions of your secured data falling into the wrong hands (what's the worst that could happen)?

- How valuable (in terms of time, money, or other values) is this information to you?

- How valuable could this information be to someone else?

- What costs are involved, both in implementing and in using the desired encryption technology?

These are your considerations for the present. As software development tools progress, encryption objects will make built-in support for encryption become almost trivial. End users will find encryption becoming easier to use and more integrated into their software.

Remaining issues regarding encryption costs will probably center more around the degree to which encryption impairs data throughput over networks. With current technology, the degree to which throughput is affected varies from little or negligible impact to extremely significant (factors of a thousand or more times slower than without in some cases!), with the primary determinant being the complexity (and presumably the effectiveness) of the algorithm being used. It will be interesting to see whether using faster computers solves this problem or just elevates it to another level. (I would bet on the latter, since faster computers means faster ways to attack the algorithms as well.)

Encryption Methods

In recent years, many advances have been made in cryptographic technology and various approaches have been taken. The different approaches achieve varying levels of strength against cracking.

Public-Key Encryption

One type of encryption that is quite popular because of its strength and other features is *public-key* encryption.

Public-key encryption involves each party having two keys: one that is kept private to everyone but the owner and another that can be made very public. This other key can be placed on Web pages, sent in an e-mail message, given out on floppy disks, and so on. Messages (or data) are then encrypted using the private key of the sender plus the public key of the intended recipient. On the other end, the data can only be successfully decrypted using the opposite pair of the sender's public key combined with the recipient's private key.

This type of encryption achieves its high level of security at the expense of speed. It takes several orders of magnitude longer to encrypt and decrypt using public-key technology than using certain other forms of encryption algorithms. This is because public-key encryption usually involves much more bit-crunching to encrypt a given amount of plain text, as compared to symmetric-key encryption, for example.

Digital Signatures and Authentication

The public-key approach provides a second, built-in feature, which is arguably just as important as encryption itself: the ability to "sign" encrypted data in such a way that the recipient can be certain that the decrypted message actually came from the individual whose public key was used in decrypting.

Because two keys are always used, it would be necessary for someone to steal one or the other private key before the thief could "forge" a public-key encrypted message that decrypts successfully using the recipient's private key. Moreover, it is also possible to use the same encryption techniques to get the signature or "verified sender" benefit without needing to encrypt the information. This becomes useful in situations where neither party cares whether the information conveyed is made public. They are only interested in whether the message originated from whom it claims to, and whether the message was altered (accidentally or intentionally) while in transit.

Symmetric-Key Encryption

Another popular form of encryption, called *symmetric-key* encryption, requires using the same key for both encrypting and decrypting. Obviously, this works only if the key used remains undisclosed to anyone but the sender and recipient.

This technique, while not as secure as public-key encryption, is significantly faster in operation—as much as a thousand or more times faster—than using the public-key technology. A disadvantage of the symmetric-key approach is that it requires that the key also be conveyed somehow from sender to recipient.

Combining Public- and Symmetric-Key Encryption

Because public-key algorithms provide extreme security (plus signatures) at the expense of speed, and symmetric algorithms provide speed at the expense of somewhat weaker security, another common approach is to use a combination of both techniques.

A symmetric encryption algorithm is used to encrypt the main body of plain text (or data), and then the symmetric key is encrypted using the stronger but slower public-key encryption. This public-key encrypted symmetric key can then be safely included along with the body of encrypted text (*ciphertext*), and allows the symmetric key to be retrieved by the recipient (or recipients) whose public keys were used to encrypt the sender's symmetric key. This combines the benefits of faster encryption for the bulk of the information, with stronger encryption to safeguard the enclosed symmetric key, and also provides the benefit of a digital signature.

In order to safely include a key along with encrypted data, the key itself must encrypted. The crypto API permits doing this by built-in functionality that can export the encrypted key for you. This encrypted key is called a *key blob*.

Encryption Algorithm Operations

Certain encryption algorithms are designed to operate on streams of data. They take the data a character at a time, and output encrypted data at the same rate. *Block-encryption* algorithms, on the other hand, are designed to encrypt chunks or blocks of data all together. Generally, block encryption is viewed as being somewhat more secure. When this type of algorithm is used, the final block of data will rarely fill the entire block, so padding bytes are usually added to the final block.

Many encryption algorithms generate a residual, or *hash*, value that is continually combined with the current data, producing a new hash, which is again combined with the current hash. A hash value of a certain number of bits is generated by applying some encryption-like algorithm to the data, so that the resulting hash value will be different if even one bit of the source data is lost or tampered with. Obviously, the longer the hash value, the lower the odds are of a hash value equaling another hash value produced from a tampered-with file.

Hashing can be used either by itself or along with encryption. In either case, it provides a value that can be used for digital signing and for error- and tamper-proofing a chunk of data.

NOTE Virus checkers frequently use a form of hashing on executable files, to determine whether the file has been tampered with. Java code, ActiveX controls, and other software downloaded from the Internet may be subject to similar verification techniques.

Hashing is also used to help ensure that repetitious data does not result in an encryption process producing identical blocks of encrypted data. You do *not* want repetition to show up in the encrypted data, because this can provide enough information to a hacker to completely recover your encryption key. In fact, because of this, some algorithms also allow you to "seed" the hash algorithm periodically by supplying additional random bits, which are incorporated into the encryption algorithm to further scramble the output. *Salt* values, or *salt bits*, as they are called, can be thought of as additional key information, which, like a key, must also be available for successful decrypting.

The Crypto API and Cryptographic Service Providers

In recent years, many companies, individuals, and government institutions have devised their own algorithms based on variations of the public-key and symmetric-key approaches. At least for now, the stronger candidates among these methods are quite secure indeed. One remaining problem of using encryption generally has been a lack of standards. Not only are the algorithms used very different, but even with the same published algorithm, software implementations done by different people can result in incompatible encrypted output.

Initiatives such as Microsoft's crypto API are exciting in their potential, because their modular design addresses the problem of encryption standards. With the crypto API, users can install any third-party cryptographic algorithms as simply as they install a new printer driver. Programmers are free to concentrate on building applications that can make use of whichever algorithms are chosen by the users (subject to certain restrictions, such as the applicability of the algorithm to encryption of streaming versus blocks of data, or key-only types of encryption algorithms).

A *cryptographic service provider* (CSP) is any agency that offers an algorithm, or a set of algorithms, that corresponds to the crypto API interface. Through this interface, application software is able to make use of encryption algorithms by selecting them at runtime.

The Crypto API Functions

The Microsoft RSA Base Provider (which comes with the crypto API and provides a default CSP set of functionality) consists of a software implementation of the PROV_RSA_FULL provider type. The RSA public-key cipher is used for both key exchange and digital signatures, with a key length of 512 bits. The RC2 and RC4 encryption algorithms are implemented with a key length of 40 bits. The MD2, MD5, and SHA hashing algorithms are also provided.

NOTE   RSA is a public-key encryption algorithm that is based on the difficulty of factoring large prime numbers. It was invented in 1977 and gets its name from the first letter in the last names of each of its three inventors: Ron Rivest, Adi Shamir, and Leonard Adleman.

The following sections describe the crypto API functions, grouped in four categories:

- CSP (cryptographic service provider) functions
- Key functions
- Encryption functions
- Hashing functions

NOTE   More detailed information about each function's parameters and usage is available in the crypto API documentation file, which ships with the crypto API SDK.

CSP Functions

Table 20.14 lists the CSP functions. You can consider `CryptAcquireContext` and `CryptReleaseContext` as two bookend functions that need to go at the start and end, respectively, of the code in your applications that uses any of the crypto API functions. Note that `CryptAcquireContext` can be called with a NULL value for the CSP, which results in the default CSP for the current user being used.

TABLE 20.14: Cryptographic Service Provider (CSP) Functions

Function	Description
CryptAcquireContext	Acquires a handle to the current user's key container within a particular CSP.
CryptGetProvParam	Retrieves attributes of a CSP.
CryptReleaseContext	Releases the handle acquired by `CryptAcquireContext`.
CryptSetProvider	Specifies the user default CSP for a particular CSP type.
CryptSetProvParam	Specifies attributes of a CSP.

Key Functions

Table 20.15 lists the crypto API key functions. `CryptGenRandom` is very useful for coming up with keys to be used with symmetric-key algorithms. Remember that you need to save your generated keys somewhere; saving is not done for you automatically. The proper way to save a key is to create an exportable version of it using `CryptExportKey`, then use `CryptImportKey` when you need to read it back from disk.

TABLE 20.15: Key Functions

Function	Description
CryptDestroyKey	Destroys a given key.
CryptExportKey	Converts a key from the CSP into a key blob that can be safely shared or saved to disk.
CryptGenRandom	Generates some random data. (Used for salt bits.)
CryptGetKeyParam	Retrieves the parameters for a given key.
CryptGetUserKey	Retrieves a handle to an exchange key or a signature key.
CryptImportKey	Converts a key blob into a key usable by a CSP.
CryptSetKeyParam	Sets the parameters for a key.

Encryption Functions

Table 20.16 lists the two encryption functions. These two functions are the crypto API star players. They perform encryption or decryption using the specified algorithm on a data block or stream.

TABLE 20.16: Encryption Functions

Function	Description
CryptEncrypt	Encrypts a block or stream of data using the specified encryption key.
CryptDecryp	Decrypts a block or stream of data using the specified encryption key.

Hashing Functions

Table 20.17 lists the hashing functions. Hashing can be used for verifying both that received data is from an authentic source, and that it hasn't been tampered with. The odds of two different chunks of data randomly happening to have the same hash value is so small as to be almost impossible.

The CryptHashSessionKey and CryptHashData functions are useful for creating hashes of keys or data, respectively. CryptSignHash and CryptVerifySignature can be used on either end to add a signature to the hash, or to verify that a signature "squares" with a hash value.

TABLE 20.17: Hashing Functions

Function	Description
CryptCreateHash	Creates an empty hash object.
CryptDestroyHash	Destroys a hash object.
CryptGetHashParam	Retrieves a parameter from a hash object.
CryptHashData	Hashes a block of data and includes the result in a specified hash object.
CryptHashSessionKey	Hashes a session key and includes the result in a specified hash object.
CryptSetHashParam	Sets a parameter of a given hash object.
CryptSignHash	Signs the specified hash object.
CryptVerifySignature	Verifies the digital signature from a signed hash object.

Adding Encryption Support to Applications

By using the crypto API, you can easily add support for encryption to your applications. However, before you can try out the crypto API functions, you need to make sure that your system is properly configured to use these functions.

Getting Started

If you happen to have an older compiler, you may need to download the crypto API from Microsoft's Web site. Older, non-Microsoft compilers may require you to generate an import library. Windows 98 includes the crypto runtime, however if you intend to deploy software on Windows 95 stations, you may need to add the crypto runtime to each station. Finally, before software that uses the crypto runtime will run correctly the first time, you must generate a default CSP and default keys. The following sections describe each of these procedures.

Obtaining the Crypto API SDK

You can get the crypto API SDK either by free download from the Internet (at Microsoft's developer pages) or from the latest MSDN (Microsoft Developer Network) CD-ROM.

NOTE   If you have a recent compiler, it probably already includes the WinCrypt.H header file, help files, and library files, so you will not need to download the crypto API SDK.

Obtaining Import Libraries

If you're using a non-Microsoft compiler, you may also need to come up with import libraries (or import units, if you're using Delphi) for the crypto API functions. If you're lucky, your compiler vendor will have made a set of import libraries/units available on its BBS or Web site.

For Microsoft compilers, the import library will be available as part of the crypto API SDK. Also, Borland C++ 5.0 and later and C++ Builder already include the crypto API header and library.

For older Borland C/C++ compilers, it's a simple matter to create import libraries using Implib.EXE. (Simply run `implib dllname`).

If you're using Borland Pascal or Delphi (prior to version 3.0), you'll need to create an import unit, which is simply a Pascal unit that has function prototypes specified (in Pascal), along with an implementation section that specifies which DLL each function is exported from. If you need an example of an import library, see the Delphi Windows import units, which show how this is done.

Installing the Crypto API Runtime Support

Although Windows 98 stations will already have the crypto runtime installed, older Windows 95 stations may not. To install the crypto API runtime support, you have two options:

- Install Microsoft's Internet Explorer (version 3.0 or later), which makes use of, and therefore installs, the crypto API.

- Run the Setup applet that comes with the crypto API SDK.

Creating a Default CSP

Even if the crypto runtime is already installed on your system, chances are that you will also need to create a default CSP and a set of default keys as well, before you can make use of the crypto API functions. Fortunately, the crypto API SDK comes with a sample applet which, when run, installs these for you. Look for a file called Inituser.C. Simply compile and run this once to complete the initialization process.

At this point, you should be ready to begin using the crypto API. The *Encrypt* and *Decrypt* demos, discussed next, should get you started.

The Encrypt Demo: Encrypting a File

The *Encrypt* demo shows how to encrypt a file (passed on the command line) using the RC2 block-type encryption (which is one of the algorithms supplied with the crypto API runtime). It demonstrates getting the default user's exchange key, generating an encrypted key, making an exportable key blob, and writing this to disk. Finally, the data from an input file is encrypted and written to an output file.

NOTE The *Encrypt* demo is included on the CD that accompanies this book, in the Chapter 20 folder. However, the actual software routines that perform the encryption and decryption in the *Encrypt* (and *Decrypt*) demo are not included on the CD. These routines must be installed, either as built-in support (for Windows 98 and Windows NT systems and newer compilers) or manually, as explained in the preceding sections. Also note that if you are using a special version of Windows 98 that does not support encryption (such as the French version), you will not be able to run the *Encrypt* and *Decrypt* demos.

Let's begin with the #define and #include statements.

```
#include <windows.h>
#include <wincrypt.h>
#include <stdio.h>
```

Since we'll be using the encryption API, note that you'll need to include the WinCrypt.H header file.

Next, we define the constants we'll use to allocate the two buffers for raw and encrypted data.

```
const IN_BUFFER_SIZE    = 2048;
const OUT_BUFFER_SIZE   = IN_BUFFER_SIZE + 64; // extra padding
```

Note that the OUT_BUFFER_SIZE is slightly larger than the input buffer. This is necessary because the encrypted data could end up being, at most, one encryption block size larger than the data supplied by the input buffer.

Next, we have the main program declaration, followed by the set of variables.

```
int __cdecl main(int argc, char * argv[])
{
    HANDLE      hInFile, hOutFile;
    BYTE        pbBuffer[OUT_BUFFER_SIZE];
```

Note that because CryptEncrypt actually encrypts the data in place, we need only a single buffer (pbBuffer), which we can use both for reading the data in and for encrypting.

Here are the rest of our declared variables.

```
        BOOL            finished;
        HCRYPTPROV      hProvider = 0;
        HCRYPTKEY       hKey = 0, hExchangeKey = 0;
        DWORD           dwByteCount, dwBytesWritten;
```

We'll need a handle to a CSP (HCRYPTPROV) and one or more handles to crypto keys (HCRYPTKEY).

In this example, we'll need two keys: an exchange key and an exportable key. The encryption function, plus `ReadFile` and `WriteFile`, will make use of the `dwByteCount` and `dwBytesWritten` variables.

Next, if the user hasn't supplied the correct number of parameters, we show a usage message and exit.

```
if (argc != 3) {
    printf("Usage: ENCRYPT infile outfile\n");
    exit(0);
}
```

Now, we're ready to begin the actual steps of the file encryption. The first thing we need to do is retrieve a handle to the default CSP. Specifying NULL rather than an explicit CSP causes the current user's default CSP to be used.

```
// Get handle for the default provider (use RSA encryption).
CryptAcquireContext(&hProvider, NULL, NULL, PROV_RSA_FULL, 0);
```

Our next step is to open both the input and output files.

```
// Open infile and create outfile.
HInFile = CreateFile(argv[1], GENERIC_READ, FILE_SHARE_READ,
    NULL, OPEN_EXISTING, FILE_ATTRIBUTE_NORMAL, NULL);
hOutFile = CreateFile(argv[2], GENERIC_WRITE, FILE_SHARE_READ,
    NULL, CREATE_ALWAYS, FILE_ATTRIBUTE_NORMAL, NULL);
```

We now need to retrieve the exchange key and generate a random, exportable key. The exchange key will be used to encrypt our random key into a blob, which is then saved to include in our encrypted output file.

```
// Generate a random key (in "simple blob" format).
CryptGetUserKey(hProvider, AT_KEYEXCHANGE, &hExchangeKey);
CryptGenKey(hProvider, CALG_RC2, CRYPT_EXPORTABLE, &hKey);
```

Next, we create an exportable key blob with a call to `CryptExportKey`. Note that calling this function with a NULL for the fifth parameter causes the function to simply calculate and return the number of bytes needed for our buffer to hold the exportable key.

```
// The first call to ExportKey with NULL gets the key size.
dwByteCount=0;
```

```
CryptExportKey(hKey, hExchangeKey, SIMPLEBLOB, 0, NULL,
            &dwByteCount);
CryptExportKey(hKey, hExchangeKey, SIMPLEBLOB, 0, pbBuffer,
            &dwByteCount);
```

We now have an encrypted version of our encryption key, in "simple blob" format. This is safe to write to the output file. We first write the size of this blob, so the decryption program knows how much data to expect when loading the key blob. Then, we write out the blob itself. The data that immediately follows this blob will be the encrypted data, which we will write out next.

```
// Write size of key blob, then key blob itself, to output file.
WriteFile(hOutFile, &dwByteCount, sizeof(dwByteCount),
        &dwBytesWritten, NULL);
WriteFile(hOutFile, pbBuffer, dwByteCount, &dwBytesWritten, NULL);
```

Now, we read in a block of data, encrypt it using CryptEncrypt, and write it out to the output file, repeating this until we reach the end of the input data. Note the third parameter to CryptEncrypt needs to be a Boolean value that tells Crypt-Encrypt when we're passing it the last block of data to encrypt.

```
// Now, read data in, encrypt it, and write encrypted data to output.
do
{
    ReadFile(hInFile, pbBuffer, IN_BUFFER_SIZE, &dwByteCount,NULL);
    finished = (dwByteCount < IN_BUFFER_SIZE);
    CryptEncrypt(hKey, 0, finished, 0, pbBuffer, &dwByteCount,
            OUT_BUFFER_SIZE);
    WriteFile(hOutFile, pbBuffer, dwByteCount, &dwBytesWritten,
            NULL);
} while (!finished);
```

And we're finished—almost. All we need to do now is clean up. We're finished with both keys at this point, so let's delete them.

```
// Clean up: release handles, close files.
CryptDestroyKey(hKey);
CryptDestroyKey(hExchangeKey);
```

We're finished using the CSP handle, so we must release it. We close the input and output files, and we're finished.

```
CryptReleaseContext(hProvider, 0);
CloseHandle(hInFile);
CloseHandle(hOutFile);

return(0);
}
```

NOTE For clarity in the code, error checking in the *Encrypt* and *Decrypt* demos is nonexistent. The only thing that is likely to go wrong is that you don't have the default CSP or keys installed. Fortunately, these crypto API functions also return Boolean success/failure results, so you could surround the first few functions with a **Check** function if you need some help with debugging your crypto installation.

The Decrypt Demo: Decrypting a File

Much of the code in the *Decrypt* demo is identical to the code in the *Encrypt* demo. The #define and #include statements are the same as for *Encrypt*; however, we need only a single buffer size for decrypting. The size of the buffer needs to be a multiple of the encryption block size. Since both RC2 and RC4 encryption (the two block encryption algorithms supplied by the Microsoft base CSP), use 40-bit and 64-bit block sizes, respectively, the *Decrypt* demo uses a buffer size that is an even multiple of both. This way, you can change the encryption type in both programs without needing to worry about changing the buffer size.

```
#include <windows.h>
#include <wincrypt.h>
#include <stdio.h>

// note: the IN_BUFFER_SIZE used here is purposely an even multiple of the
// various possible encryption block sizes, namely 1, 8, and 64 bytes.
const BUFFER_SIZE    = 64 * 100; // needs to be multiple of block size.
```

NOTE The *Decrypt* demo is included on the CD that accompanies this book, in the Chapter 20 folder. As noted earlier, the software that does the actual work is not in this demo's code; it is installed as part of the crypto API.

The variables are also almost identical to those in the *Encrypt* demo, except that the buffer being allocated is a different size.

```
int __cdecl main(int argc, char * argv[])
{
    HANDLE     hInFile, hOutFile;
    BYTE       pbBuffer[BUFFER_SIZE];
    BOOL       finished;
    HCRYPTPROV hProvider = 0;
```

```
HCRYPTKEY    hKey = 0;
DWORD        dwByteCount, dwBytesWritten;

if (argc != 3)
{
   printf("Usage: DECRYPT infile outfile\n");
   exit(0);
}
```

As in the *Encrypt* demo, we first need to get a handle to the default CSP.

```
// Get handle for the default provider (use RSA encryption).
CryptAcquireContext(&hProvider, NULL, NULL, PROV_RSA_FULL, 0);

// Open infile and create outfile.
hInFile = CreateFile(argv[1], GENERIC_READ, FILE_SHARE_READ,
      NULL, OPEN_EXISTING, FILE_ATTRIBUTE_NORMAL, NULL);
hOutFile = CreateFile(argv[2], GENERIC_WRITE, FILE_SHARE_READ,
      NULL, CREATE_ALWAYS, FILE_ATTRIBUTE_NORMAL, NULL);
```

We now read in, in the same order as they were written, the key blob size and then the key blob itself.

```
// Read in key blob size, then key blob itself from input file.
ReadFile(hInFile,&dwByteCount,sizeof(dwByteCount),
      &dwBytesWritten,NULL);
ReadFile(hInFile, pbBuffer, dwByteCount, &dwBytesWritten, NULL);
```

Now, we convert the key blob back into a key (internally to the CSP), with the call to CryptImportKey.

```
// Import Key blob into "CSP"
   CryptImportKey(hProvider, pbBuffer, dwByteCount, 0, 0, &hKey);
```

Next, we read encrypted data in, decrypt it using CryptDecrypt, and write the decrypted data to our output file. Like the CryptEncrypt function, Crypt-Decrypt takes a "finished" Boolean flag to tell it when we're sending it the last buffer to decrypt.

```
// Read data in, encrypt it, and write encrypted data to output file.
do
{
    ReadFile(hInFile, pbBuffer, IN_BUFFER_SIZE, &dwByteCount,NULL);
    finished = (dwByteCount < IN_BUFFER_SIZE);
    CryptDecrypt(hKey, 0, finished, 0, pbBuffer, &dwByteCount);
    WriteFile(hOutFile, pbBuffer,dwByteCount,&dwBytesWritten,NULL);
} while (!finished);
```

We're finished, so we now delete our key, release the CSP handle, and close the input and output files.

```
// Clean up: release handles, close files.
CryptDestroyKey(hKey);
CryptReleaseContext(hProvider, 0);
CloseHandle(hInFile);
CloseHandle(hOutFile);

return(0);
}
```

Other Security Considerations

The effectiveness of security and encryption is in large part determined by the care with which it is used. Some of the most elaborate data-protecting schemes can be more easily compromised than simpler ones, just because people get lazy and take it for granted or are insufficiently aware of the weaker points that, of necessity, exist in every design. Here, we'll take a look at some potential pitfalls to be aware of when designing a secure information system.

Exclusive ORing Techniques

One of the simpler encryption techniques is based on exclusive-ORing (XORing) the plain-text data with a key value. If you do this on a file that has lots of blank space or repeated strings of the same character, it's very possible to determine the encryption key. By simply re-XORing the repeated areas with their own value, the plain-text values cancel out, leaving the key.

You might think that with such a weakness, XORing against a key value wouldn't continue to be used. But one advantage of XORing is its extreme speed; XOR is one of the most fundamental computer operations performed.

There are several ways to strengthen an XOR algorithm:

- Use a longer, or ideally, an *extremely* long key value.

- Combine additional information, such as the offset position of the character in the file, or the value of the preceding character(s), with the plain-text character before encrypting.

- Use XOR as only one level of a multilevel encryption scheme.

Using Random Keys and Combining Techniques

The discussion of XORing brings up two important points. The first is that, surprisingly, even an operation as simple as XOR can be used to create the strongest type of encryption known, provided that the key used is completely random and is equal (or longer) in length to the data stream to be encrypted. How you come up with completely random numbers is another matter entirely—whole books can, and have been, written on that subject.

The second point is that combining two or more techniques can result in a much stronger resulting algorithm. Taking this point up at a different level, consider how a system that assigns memorable but unpredictable passwords (or keys) has a significant edge over a system that assigns very difficult to remember passwords. In the latter case, it is human nature that a certain number of people will inevitably write down their password on a slip of paper and perhaps even tape it to their monitor!

As a different example on the same theme, consider the advantage one type of encrypted e-mail has over another type. One was written using couched phrases or only implicitly conveys a message. The other states its content in plain language. The first one stands a good chance of remaining confidential even if the encryption is broken, whereas the second message is cracked at the same time its encryption is breached. This illustrates again how multiple levels, particularly different types of levels, can combine synergistically to achieve a more secure result.

Protecting Against Brute Force

Most efforts to break encryption eventually come down to "brute force" approaches—simply trying every possible key value until one fits. Encryption's effectiveness usually depends on the huge range of possible keys values to make the chore of guessing take so long as to be impractical.

Many strong encryption algorithms are much stronger in theory than they turn out to be when implemented in software, because the programmer slips up and introduces less randomness in a key value by using pseudo-random (more predictable) computer-generated sources for key values or parts of key values. Such mistakes result in less work required to crack the resulting encryption, because the possible range of key values has been reduced.

Another somewhat more sophisticated version of "brute force" attack uses educated guesses to attempt to narrow down the key value. For example, someone could begin guessing a password by using a person's first and last names, then spouse's name, then pet's name, and continuing with other common sources for passwords. In the case of encrypted e-mail, eliminating predictable headers (for example, "Dear Sue,"), and footers ("later, Joe") and compressing blank space (and perhaps also removing the carriage-returns and line feeds!) goes a long way toward tightening up the plain text and making it harder for such attacks to gain an easy foothold.

Remember, too, that any encryption scheme is only as strong as its weakest link. It does no good to have an extremely fancy encryption scheme when the decryption keys, for example, are not safeguarded. When saving a key value along with encrypted data, how do you encrypt the key itself? It doesn't hurt to use even stronger encryption for the key value and to store the key at a random location in the file, or even vary the length of the key used.

Finally, keep in mind that, as the saying goes, there is more than one way to skin a cat. If attackers cannot get in through the front door, they may resort to the back door, side door, or window, or even rip themselves a hole in your system. Consider the case of a sophisticated encryption algorithm that is snugly packed away in a nice DLL, ActiveX control, or some other dynamic (or even static) code library. If a function in this library takes passwords or key values, or stores them by calling another function, couldn't someone simply replace the code library with his own, or (less likely in Windows NT) even intercept or "hook" a function that gets called? The moral is that you should be very, very careful at each stage of the designing and implementation process. Make sure that you haven't inadvertently left a gaping hole.

If all this talk about security and encryption sounds too paranoid for you, then perhaps your system really doesn't have a need for security. But I'll bet even then you would agree on this point: Security is one area where, if you need it at all, it only makes sense to do it right. The demos discussed in this chapter—*FileUser*, *Encrypt*, and *Decrypt*—will give you a good start on designing your own secure applications.

In the next chapter, we'll talk about a subject of interest to nearly every modern application developer: Internet support for your applications. This is certainly an area where you may need to use security for your applications.

CHAPTER
TWENTY-ONE

21

Internet Support

■ An overview of Microsoft's Internet support

■ The Winsock API functions

■ The Internet API functions

■ The ActiveX Web controls

■ Active Channels and Active Server Pages

Developing Internet-aware software that runs on Windows poses many challenges for any software developer. These challenges involve keeping informed, making sure your applications remain compatible, and simply in leveraging all the technology that is currently available and applicable. On the other hand, the opportunities are richer, and the tools and SDKs currently available are both more powerful and more usable than ever before. They enable the development of many ingenious new solutions for business, commerce, and home applications.

In this chapter, we'll begin with a survey of the Internet-related technologies Microsoft has been promoting over the last two years. Next, we'll take a look at some Internet-related concepts of concern to those developing Internet software. Then we will focus on the three chief toolkits or APIs for writing Windows Internet software: Winsock 2.0, the Internet API, and the ActiveX Web controls. You can think of these as the low-level, the medium-level, and the high-level Windows Internet toolkits.

We'll also look at what Active Channels are and discuss how to convert a normal Web site to use an Active Channel. Finally, we'll finish up with a brief discussion of Active Server Pages.

Two Years' Worth of Progress (at Microsoft)

At the time Windows 95 was introduced, Internet support in Microsoft operating systems was limited to dial-up and Ethernet TCP/IP support, plus a handful of Unix-style command-line utilities, such as ftp, ping, tracert, and the like. Actually, this was not a bad start, since by using the built-in TCP/IP stack and the FTP client a user could download a Web browser and other Internet software and be set to access the Internet.

In the course of two years, Microsoft has done an amazing turnabout and embraced Internet technologies on a scale unprecedented even by Microsoft's own previous efforts in other areas. If this sounds even the least bit overdramatic to you, take a look at the software tools and applications listed in Tables 21.1 through 21.6. Microsoft has either adopted or introduced these since its "embrace the Internet" announcement made in January 1996.

TABLE 21.1: Improved Internet Connectivity in Operating Systems

Feature	Description
Multi-channel modem binding	Allows two or more modems (or other devices) to be treated as a single network connection—doubling or tripling (or more!) the throughput available to all Internet and/or other network-aware software.
Improved WINS (Windows Internet Name Service) and DHCP (Dynamic Host Control Protocol)	Allows WINS and DHCP to be administered more easily and to work seamlessly with other clients (such as Macintosh clients).
PPTP (Point-to-Point Tunneling Protocol)	Provides a secure way to transparently interconnect wide-area networks across insecure networks such as the Internet by encapsulating network packets inside a secure packet "envelope."
Windows ISDN	Brings integrated support for internal and external ISDN modems to Windows 98 and NT. Includes support for multiple-channel binding.

TABLE 21.2: Tools for Web Page Design and Management

Tool	Description
Microsoft FrontPage	Supports HTML page authoring and Web site management.
Microsoft GIF Animator	Supports creation of GIF and animated GIF files for use with Web pages.
Microsoft Image Composer	Simplifies creating and manipulating images for placement on Web pages.

TABLE 21.3: Internet Servers

Server	Description
Internet Information Server (IIS)	Provides a high-performance Web server with support for WSAPI .DLL extensions, secure Web pages, performance monitoring, and flexible FrontPage Server extensions.
Peer Web Servers	Provides built-in peer Web, Gopher, and FTP servers.

Continued on next page

TABLE 21.3 CONTINUED: Internet Servers

Server	Description
Microsoft (Catapult) Proxy Server	Allows multiple PCs to connect to the Internet via a single server connection, even using other protocols (instead of TCP/IP). Also fetches and caches most-often used Web pages for all users.
Internet News Server	Gives companies (or individuals) their own self-managed newsgroups.
Chat Server	Keeps a running round-table dialog, displayed via Web pages.
White Pages Indexing/Locator Server	Automatically indexes an entire Web site, providing keyword searches.
Content Replication Server	Assists in porting and/or mirroring part or all of a Web site's content from one server to another.
Server Personalization System	Provides Web content customized for each connected user, as an addition to IIS.
Mail Server	Provides sites with POP and SMTP server support (plus MS Mail support).
Merchant Server	Supports "store-front" shopping via Web pages.

TABLE 21.4: Internet-Related Programmer's Tools

Tool	Description
Visual J++ 1.0, 1.1	Provides a Visual Java environment, including Java compiler, debugger, and Windows SDK class libraries.
Jscript	Allows embedding Java script applets in HTML pages (supported in IE).
Visual Basic 5.0	Allows development of ActiveX Controls, component packaging for Internet downloading, and native code support.
VBScript	Provides a Visual Basic scripting language for embedding in HTML pages (supported in IE).
Visual C++ 4.2 and 5.0	Provides enhanced support for various Internet APIs, DCOM, ActiveX, etc.

NOTE   Although we do not cover Java, Jscript, or VBScript here, these are significant application-development technologies. These tools have entire books devoted to them (Java in particular!).

TABLE 21.5: Internet-Related SDKs and APIs

SDK or API	Description
Winsock 2.0	Provides expanded support for socket-style Internet programming, including AppleTalk, IPX, and other networking protocols in addition to TCP/IP. Also supports encrypted socket communications using PCT and SSL.
Internet API	Simplifies adding TCP/IP support to applications, encapsulating and abstracting Winsock-style functionality.
ActiveX Web Control Pack	Simplifies adding Internet support to applications, via drop-in ActiveX objects. Includes Web browser, FTP, e-mail, and news client objects.
Windows SDK for Java	Provides class libraries for Java applets to access Windows-specific functionality.
Game SDK	Includes support for multiplayer gaming over the Internet.
Crypto API	Provides public and private key encryption and decryption, code and message signing and authentication.
Uploading API	Provides a set of functions to simplify the job of uploading or moving Web pages to and from a Web site.
Ratings API	Provides functions to set content restrictions and query content ratings tags from HTML pages.
URL Security Zoning	Divides URL name spaces into zones that can have different levels of trust assigned to them (supported in IE 4 and accessed either via Control Panel or browser settings).
Secure Sockets Layer (SSL) for Winsock	Provides encrypted socket-style communications as an extension to Winsock 2.0.
Active Channels	Allows Web sites to support Web-casting of content to channel-viewing software such as IE 4 or the Active Desktop of Windows 98.

Continued on next page

TABLE 21.5 CONTINUED: Internet-Related SDKs and APIs

SDK or API	Description
Cascading Style Sheets	Provides a (non-Microsoft) standard that adds some 70 new style properties, extending control over the layout and presentation of Web pages (supported in IE 4).
Dynamic HTML	Enables Web authors to dynamically change the rendering and content of a document (without necessarily reloading the page).
Design-time Control SDK	Allows creation of controls that can simplify designing Web page content.
NetMeeting SDK	Allows integration of real-time Internet multimedia conferencing via software or embedded in Web pages.
WebWizard SDK	Allows creation of wizards that can automate the creation of specialized Web pages.
Active Server Pages	Provides pages that contain scripting or ActiveX controls that are executed on the Web server.
Personal Information Exchange (PFX)	Provides protocols for securely transferring personal identity information, private keys, personal certificates, and other miscellaneous "secrets" over the Internet.
Web Content Management	Provides a Microsoft initiative to reduce the complexity of managing larger Web sites (currently, primarily by using features of Visual SourceSafe).
Cabinet (CAB) SDK	Simplifies compression, packaging, and online distribution of Java classes and other software.
Common Internet File System (CIFS)	Provides a standard remote file-system-access protocol for enabling groups of users to work together and share documents across the Internet or within their corporate intranets.
HTMLHelp API	Modeled on the WinHelp function, allows easier porting of Windows help files to the new HTML Help format.
Web Publishing API	Provides functions to simplify the process of uploading Web pages to a Web site.

NOTE Although we won't go into detail about all of the APIs, you should be aware of their suitability for more specialized uses. The Game SDK includes much more than support for multiplayer game communications over the Internet. DirectPlay, Direct-Sound, DirectVideo, Direct3D, and related technologies provide speedy access to a wide variety of video, sound, and control hardware. The SSL API is an extension to Winsock 2, providing encrypted data flow through the normal socket architecture. The Ratings API provides access to functions useful for setting, checking, and managing access to classes of information that have been assigned particular ratings, such as for violence and profanity. The crypto API, which is already being used by Microsoft's Internet Explorer, is covered in detail in Chapter 20.

TABLE 21.6: Other Internet-Related Technologies

Item	Description
Internet Explorer	A Web browser that now supports Netscape plug-ins, ActiveX controls, VBScript, Jscript, SSL, code signing and certificates, pop-up menu controls, auto-installation of ActiveX controls, and content ratings system.
Internet Assistants	Programs that export data from Access, Excel, Power-Point, Word, and Schedule+ to formatted HTML pages.
Data Viewers for Word, PowerPoint, and Excel	Viewers that display Word, PowerPoint, and Excel files on stations not equipped with Word, PowerPoint, or Excel.
NetMeeting	A multiuser collaboration tool that supports text and voice chatting, white boarding, and file transfers.
ISAPI and FrontPage Server Extensions	Support for CGI-like server extensions, with less overhead than an interpreter or loading and unloading standard binary executable files.
DCOM (Distributed Component Object Model)	Support for remote-object access and execution using TCP/IP (as well as other protocols).
Authenticode	Support for code-signing and authentication using certificates.
CAB Files	Files initially used for installing Microsoft software, now expanded for simplified downloading of Java source files.

In addition to offering the tools and applications listed in these tables, Microsoft has been rushing to include Internet hooks and functionality into *all* of its software applications. Furthermore, it has switched Microsoft Network (MSN) to be Internet-based rather than proprietary, and has moved all of its public (and beta) support forums from CompuServe over to the Internet. Each individual Microsoft product has its own Web page, and there are currently more than 325 public Internet newsgroups run by Microsoft alone, not including many independent newsgroups, which focus, for example, on various elements of Win32 programming.

This explosive usage of the Internet has benefited both software end users and software developers. On the Internet, you can find more accessible (and timely) documentation, significant peer support, software upgrades, bug fixes, and enhancements.

And this survey covers recent developments at only one (admittedly rather huge) company. We could also review (were enough space available) all the Internet work being done by Netscape, Sun, IBM, Symantec, Apple, and literally thousands of other companies. Much of their work also has some bearing on Windows Internet software development.

Internet-Related Concepts

Those who are interested in designing Internet software need to be aware of the many Internet-related concepts and terms. Here, we will briefly cover IP addressing, Internet protocols, and sockets.

IP Addresses

Most new Internet users quickly become familiar with the fact that they have an e-mail address and an IP address. Setting up a computer for TCP/IP networking (using a TCP/IP protocol stack, as it is sometimes called), typically involves specifying IP addresses for a Domain Name server and network gateway, and entering POP and SMTP server names. IP addresses are typed in using dotted, or dotted-quad notation, where each byte of the 4-byte address is displayed in decimal and separated from the next byte value with a period. As you probably know, this dotted notation is simply to allow easier reading by human users. Computers and other hardware on the Internet always use the 4-byte (32-bit) values directly.

Because every computer on the Internet has its own IP address (at least while it's connected) and because the number of computers joining the Internet has been and continues to increase rapidly, work is being done to devise a new address scheme using wider network addresses. There are still some issues remaining to be hashed out though, so for the near future, we can continue programming using the 32-bit Internet (IP) addresses.

Internet Protocols

TCP/IP is actually a whole suite of related protocols, some higher level than others. At the lower levels, for example, are the two main packet protocols that transport data in either sequenced, two-way "conversations" or connectionless "radio-style" (one-way) transmissions: TCP and UDP.

IP (Internet Protocol) is the Internet "delivery system" protocol, which underlies the other Internet protocols. IP itself uses connectionless datagrams, thus IP packets are often called IP datagrams.

TCP (Transmission Control Protocol) provides a sequenced, two-way connection-based protocol using byte streams. It is considered "reliable" because it takes responsibility for check-summing each received packet and re-requesting any dropped or damaged packets.

UDP (User Datagram Protocol), on the other hand, is termed "unreliable," in the sense that it provides connectionless transport of data packets, and therefore cannot support built-in error checking. Instead, it acts analogously to a radio signal—you can be certain that it was transmitted but cannot verify that it was received.

These two approaches are complementary. Connectionless transport is faster, because it does not have the overhead associated with verification of accurate reception and transmission. TCP, with its greater overhead, ensures that data correctly reaches its destination, and thereby makes up for a multitude of potential failure points within the underlying networking hardware (cabling, switching mechanisms, and so on).

At a higher level is a set of protocols with more specialized purposes. These higher-level protocols are the various service-related protocols, which are used to transfer e-mail, files, Web documents, and so on. They include the following:

SMTP (Simple Mail Transfer Protocol)   Commonly used for sending e-mail to a server.

POP3 (Post Office Protocol 3)   Commonly used for retrieving e-mail from a server.

> **FTP (File Transfer Protocol)** Widely used for uploading and downloading files.
>
> **HTTP (Hypertext Transfer Protocol)** Used as the standard World Wide Web protocol.
>
> **Telnet (Remote Terminal Access)** Used for remote login and interactive access to remote servers.

Whereas the lower-level transport protocols package their routing information and data using rather complex structures and packet arrangements, the higher-level protocols use techniques that human programmers generally find friendlier to implement. These higher-level service protocols have the following common properties:

- They start with recognizable four-character command strings.

- They assume a client and a server conversation, established via a bi-directional socket.

- They use a numerical scheme for response codes.

TIP

Later in this chapter, we will look at a program that implements SMTP to send an e-mail message to a mail server. You may find it interesting to experiment directly with these protocols by using your Windows 98 or NT Telnet client to send properly formatted protocol strings to an FTP, SMTP, POP3, or HTTP server, and view the incoming replies generated by the server.

Sockets and Winsock

Most Internet programming has traditionally been done using the "sockets" paradigm. In the early days, when TCP/IP became integrated with the Unix operating system, a set of functions, which came to be called the Berkeley sockets standard, was originated. These functions let you create a socket, listen for incoming connections (in the case of a server), connect the socket to a given host computer and port number (as a client), and send and receive data via the socket.

A socket is analogous to a file handle, and on some versions of Unix, can be used directly with the file I/O functions. There are two types of sockets, corresponding to the connected and connectionless protocols:

- *TCP sockets* require that a connection be established between a socket and a host computer.

- *UDP sockets* only require that you specify where the data should end up (a specific port number at a specific IP address).

Several years ago, a consortium of individuals and companies got together and came up with a version of socket functions for Windows. Winsock, as it is called, is somewhat different from Berkeley sockets. Because earlier versions of Windows, unlike Unix, were not a true multitasking operating system, certain provisions had to be made. These provisions generally took two approaches. First, functions that might take a while to receive a response or otherwise complete execution could be "blocking," or simply not return until they were finished. Although this works under Windows, it understandably isn't considered good programming practice. Using lots of blocking functions in an application can cause the application to become sluggish at best, or completely unresponsive (or crash!) at worst.

Therefore, Winsock also provides a set of asynchronous functions, which can notify a Windows application when they have finished executing by sending a special message to a specified window. The application then simply needs to call the function, continue other processing, and check for a function return message in the message queue. This worked about as well as could be expected, considering that 16-bit Windows cannot do preemptive multitasking of Windows applications.

Windows 95, 98, and NT on the other hand, have no problem with multitasking (although to retain backward compatibility, the 32-bit Winsock functions remain almost unchanged). With these versions of Windows, an application can use blocking functions in the Unix style of spawning a separate thread, to allow continued execution of the application while the function completes. Certain functions that block for the sake of ease of use in Windows 3.1 don't need to block in Windows 98. Also, by and large, GUI-based Win32 applications (which have a window to receive notification messages) often use the asynchronous Windows versions of the socket functions, although console applications and some multithreaded applications go with the more "traditional" synchronous socket functions.

The Winsock 2 API Functions

Winsock 2 is important for several reasons:

- It supports various protocols.

- It's the best way to produce fast, close-to-the-hardware, transport code.

- It's the only way to go when writing servers or when speed and efficiency of throughput are essential (more important than development time, for example).

- It provides more cross-platform support.

In its current version, Winsock 2 maintains most functions of previous Winsock releases and adds a few functions that improve multiprotocol support. Although Winsock is probably most often used for TCP/IP, it also supports socket connections over several other protocols, including IPX, SPX, Banyan VINES, and Apple-Talk. In this chapter, we will be looking at Winsock in its TCP/IP capacity, but keep in mind that socket applications can often be "ported" to use other protocols with little additional work.

Within the Winsock set of functions, there are both synchronous and asynchronous socket functions. Additionally, there are some data-conversion functions and database-lookup functions.

Socket Functions

Table 21.7 lists the Winsock socket functions. These are the traditional set of synchronous functions.

TABLE 21.7: Winsock Socket Functions

Function	Description
accept	Accepts a connection on given socket.
AcceptEx	Accepts a new connection, returns local and remote addresses, plus the first block of data sent by the client.
bind	Associates a local address with a socket.
closesocket	Closes a socket.
connect	Connects a socket with given peer.

Continued on next page

TABLE 21.7 CONTINUED: Winsock Socket Functions

Function	Description
GetAcceptExSockaddrs	Parses data from AcceptEx and passes the local and remote addresses, along with the first block of data received upon connection.
ioctlsocket	Gets or sets socket mode parameters.
listen	Places a given socket in listen mode.
recv	Retrieves data from a given socket.
recvfrom	Retrieves a datagram along with source address.
select	Determines the status of one or more sockets.
send	Sends data on a given (connected) socket.
sendto	Sends data to a given destination.
Setsockopt	Sets a socket option.
shutdown	Disables sending and/or receiving on a specified socket.
socket	Creates a socket bound to a given transport service provider.

Data-Conversion Functions

Another set of Winsock functions deals with converting data between *network byte order* and *host byte order*. It is recommended that these functions be used even where it is known that the order is the same on both machines, as this makes for more consistent code, which is more easily portable. Table 21.8 lists the data-conversion functions.

TABLE 21.8: Winsock Data-Conversion Functions

Function	Description
htonl	Converts a 32-bit value from host to TCP/IP network byte order.
htons	Converts a 16-bit value from host to TCP/IP network byte order.
inet_addr	Converts a dotted IP address string to an unsigned long value.
inet_ntoa	Converts a network address as unsigned long into a dotted IP address string.
ntohl	Converts a 32-bit value from TCP/IP network byte order to host byte order.
ntohs	Converts a 16-bit value from TCP/IP network byte order to host byte order.

Database-Lookup Functions

Another, smaller set of Winsock functions are called the *database-lookup* functions. These functions, which are listed in Table 21.9, have the duty of looking up correct IP addresses, domain names, service IDs, and protocol port numbers. The database functions behave much like their Unix counterparts. The services information and (usually) a small number of domain names and IP addresses are typically stored in two text files on each host computer: the HOSTS and SERVICES files. The socket functions make use of these as their first source of information for addresses or service numbers during address or service resolution.

TABLE 21.9: Winsock Data-Lookup Functions

Function	Description
gethostbyaddr	Gets host information for a given address.
gethostbyname	Gets host information for a given host name.
gethostname	Gets the standard host name for local machine.
getpeername	Gets the address of the peer connected to a given socket.
getprotobyname	Gets protocol information for a given protocol (name).
getprotobynumber	Gets protocol information.
getservbyname	Gets service information for a given service name and protocol.
getservbyport	Gets service information for given port number and protocol.
getsockname	Gets the local name for a given socket.
getsockopt	Gets the current value for a specified socket option.

HOSTS and SERVICES Files

Whether on a Windows 98, Windows NT, or Unix computer, the HOSTS files contains pairs of addresses and host names, and the SERVICES file contains information about "well-known" services, along with their port numbers, the low-level protocol used, and one or more optional alias names. On Windows 98, these files are located in the \WINDOWS directory. (On Windows NT, the SERVICES and HOSTS file can be found in the \WINNT\SYSTEM\DRIVERS\ETC directory.)

The following is part of a typical SERVICES file, taken from a Windows 98 station. (Similar files exist on Windows 95 and NT stations.) Note how each entry matches up a service name with a port and protocol type, and one or more optional service name aliases.

```
# Copyright (c) 1993-1995 Microsoft Corp.
#
# This file contains port numbers for well-known services as defined by
# RFC 1060 (Assigned Numbers).
#
# Format:
#
# <service name>  <port number>/<protocol>  [aliases...]    [#<comment>]
#

echo            7/tcp
echo            7/udp
discard         9/tcp     sink null
discard         9/udp     sink null
systat          11/tcp
systat          11/tcp    users
daytime         13/tcp
daytime         13/udp
netstat         15/tcp
qotd            17/tcp    quote
qotd            17/udp    quote
chargen         19/tcp    ttytst source
chargen         19/udp    ttytst source
ftp-data        20/tcp
ftp             21/tcp
telnet          23/tcp
smtp            25/tcp    mail
time            37/tcp    timserver
time            37/udp    timserver
rlp             39/udp    resource      # resource location
name            42/tcp    nameserver
name            42/udp    nameserver
whois           43/tcp    nicname       # usually to sri-nic
domain          53/tcp    nameserver    # name-domain server
domain          53/udp    nameserver
nameserver      53/tcp    domain        # name-domain server
nameserver      53/udp    domain
```

```
mtp              57/tcp                    # deprecated
bootp            67/udp                    # boot program server
tftp             69/udp
rje              77/tcp     netrjs
finger           79/tcp
link             87/tcp     ttylink
supdup           95/tcp
hostnames        101/tcp    hostname       # usually from sri-nic
iso-tsap         102/tcp
dictionary       103/tcp    webster
x400             103/tcp                   # ISO Mail
x400-snd         104/tcp
csnet-ns         105/tcp
pop              109/tcp    postoffice
pop2             109/tcp                   # Post Office
pop3             110/tcp    postoffice
```

The following shows a typical HOSTS file. This file is usually kept quite small, with most names being resolved via a DNS (Domain Name Service) server.

```
# HOSTS file used by Microsoft TCP/IP

102.54.94.97     rhino.acme.com      # source server
38.25.63.10      x.acme.com          # x client host
127.0.0.1        localhost
```

In this file, each IP address is matched with a host name. Note the standard address of 127.0.0.1, which is mapped to the local host. By convention, 127.0.0.1 is always a reference to the local host itself. Pinging 127.0.0.1 is sometimes used as a test of one's own IP address.

NOTE

On Windows 98 (and also Windows NT), there is also typically a file similar to the HOSTS file, called LMHOSTS. This performs a similar function, however, the host names are NetBIOS names, and certain extensions are allowed (such as #DOM: to handle Windows NT domains).

Most often, an address lookup will not be resolved by finding a corresponding entry in the HOSTS file. Instead, the lookup request is passed along to the DNS server, which either fills the lookup request, or passes along the request to a first-level DNS server. These IP address and name servers contain many, but by no means all, names and corresponding IP addresses, as registered by InterNIC

(InterNIC is responsible, in the United States, for maintaining the DNS entries for all top-level domains, except for the *mil* or military domain). If a match is not found on a first-level server, the request is passed down to the next DNS server in the hierarchy, and so on. This continues until either a match is found or no entry is found (in which case, you may see an error message).

The *FindAddr* demo, discussed a little later in this chapter, is an example of using host name-to-IP address resolution (as well as IP address-to-host name reverse resolution).

Asynchronous Versions of the Winsock Functions

To do asynchronous Windows socket programming, you use the WSA version of a socket function, which typically takes a window handle as a parameter and posts a status or completion message to that window's message queue when the function completes or needs to communicate information to the application. Because Windows 98 supports multithreading, you can also use the synchronous functions by spawning off a separate thread, thus freeing the main application to continue with other processing while waiting for a function to finish executing. Table 21.10 lists the asynchronous functions.

TABLE 21.10: Asynchronous Winsock 2 Functions

Function	Description
WSAAsyncGetHostByAddr	Gets host information for a given address.
WSAAsyncGetHostByName	Gets host information for a given host name.
WSAAsyncGetProtoByName	Gets protocol information for a given protocol name.
WSAAsyncGetProtoByNumber	Gets protocol information for a given protocol number.
WSAAsyncGetServByName	Gets service information for given service name and protocol.
WSAAsyncGetServByPort	Gets service information for given port number and protocol.
WSAAsyncSelect	Requests Windows message-based notification of network events occurring on specified socket.
WSACancelAsyncRequest	Cancels an (incomplete) asynchronous socket operation.
WSAAccept	Conditionally accepts a connection based on the return value of an (optional) condition function, creating or joining a socket group.

Continued on next page

TABLE 21.10 CONTINUED: Asynchronous Winsock 2 Functions

Function	Description
WSAAddressToString	Converts all addresses in a **SOCKADDR** structure into human-readable string representations.
WSACleanup	Terminates use of Winsock.DLL.
WSACloseEvent	Closes an event object handle.
WSAConnect	Connects to a peer, exchanges connect data, and specifies needed quality of service based on supplied flow specification.
WSACreateEvent	Creates a new event object.
WSADuplicateSocket	Returns a **WSAPROTOCOL_INFO** structure, which can be used to create a new socket descriptor for a shared socket.
WSAEnumNameSpaceProviders	Retrieves information about the available name space providers.
WSAEnumNetworkEvents	Retrieves information about which network events have occurred on a given socket.
WSAEnumProtocols	Retrieves information about available transport protocols.
WSAEventSelect	Specifies an event object to be associated with given FD_*xxx* network events.
WSAGetAddressByName	Resolves an address by name and returns the first available result.
WSAGetLastError	Returns the error status for the last failed Winsock operation.
WSAGetOverlappedResult	Returns the results of an overlapped operation on the given socket.
WSAGetQOSByName	Initializes a QoS (Quality of Service) structure based on a named template.
WSAGetServiceClassInfo	Retrieves the class information for a service class from a specified name space provider.
WSAGetServiceClassNameByClassId	Returns the generic service name for a given service type.
WSAHtonl	Converts an unsigned long from host byte order to network byte order.
WSAHtons	Converts an unsigned short from host byte order to network byte order.
WSAInstallServiceClass	Registers a service class schema within a name space.

Continued on next page

TABLE 21.10 CONTINUED: Asynchronous Winsock 2 Functions

Function	Description
WSAIoctl	Sets the mode of a given socket and also configures sockets for secure communications using SSL or PCT.
WSAJoinLeaf	Joins a leaf node into a multipoint session, exchanges connection data, and specifies needed QoS based on supplied flow specification.
WSALookupServiceBegin	Returns a handle that can be used in further client queries to search for specified service information.
WSALookupServiceEnd	Frees a query handle created by WSALookupServiceBegin.
WSALookupServiceNext	Retrieves the next set of service information using given query handle.
WSANtohl	Converts an unsigned long from network byte order to host byte order.
WSANtohs	Converts an unsigned short from network byte order to host byte order.
WSARecv	Receives data from a given socket.
WSARecvDisconnect	Terminates reception on a given socket, retrieving disconnect data if applicable.
WSARecvFrom	Retrieves a datagram and the source address.
WSARemoveServiceClass	Permanently unregisters a service class schema.
WSAResetEvent	Resets the state of a specified event object to be "nonsignaled."
WSASend	Sends data on a connected socket and permits asynchronous, or overlapped, I/O.
WSASendDisconnect	Initiates termination of a given socket connection and sends disconnect data.
WSASendTo	Sends data to a given destination, using overlapped I/O where applicable.
WSASetEvent	Sets the state of the specified event object to be "signaled."
WSASetLastError	Sets the error code which is returned by subsequent calls to WSASetLastError.
WSASetService	Registers or unregisters a service instance within one or more name spaces.

Continued on next page

TABLE 21.10 CONTINUED: Asynchronous Winsock 2 Functions

Function	Description
WSASocket	Creates a socket that is bound to a specific transport service provider, optionally creating or joining a socket group.
WSAStartup	Initiates use of Winsock.DLL by a process.
WSAStringToAddress	Converts a human-readable address string to a socket address structure.
WSAWaitForMultipleEvents	Returns one or all of the specified event objects are in the signaled state, or when the time-out expires.

The FindAddr Demo: An IP Address Lookup Example

The *FindAddr* demo performs an IP address lookup using a given host name. If this lookup is successful, the program then attempts to use the newly acquired IP address to, in turn, look up the host name. This latter procedure is called a *reverse lookup*.

> **NOTE**   The *FindAddr* demo is included on the CD that accompanies this book, in the Chapter 21 folder.

The program starts out by defining WIN32_LEAN_AND_MEAN to trim excess fat from the executable, then includes the Stdlib.H , Stdio.H, and Winsock2.H header files. Following this, we define version constants that are used to specify the minimum desired Winsock version in the call to WSAStartup.

```
// Insist on at least Winsock version 1.1 (you may use 2.0)
const      VERSION_MAJOR  =  1;
const      VERSION_MINOR  =  1;
```

Although you could set the VERSION_MAJOR to 2 and the VERSION_MINOR to 0, for example, to specify Winsock 2.0, it is best not to do this unless your program specifically needs version 2.0. Rather, your application should request the minimum Winsock version needed to run successfully.

Next, the ShowUsage function is defined, which simply displays the command-line syntax expected, and exits the application.

```
void ShowUsage(void)
{
    printf("usage: FINDADDR some.address.com\n");
    exit(0);
}
```

We next have the start of the `main` application function, followed by four variable declarations:

```
// Takes string IP address and attempts to look up numeric IP address.
int main(int argc, char *argv[])
{
    WSADATA     WSData;
    LPHOSTENT   lpHostEntry;
    DWORD       dwIPAddress;
    LPSTR       szIPAddress;
```

The data type `WSADATA` is actually a Winsock data structure that is used by `WSAStartup` to return Winsock information such as the Winsock version number found, the maximum number of sockets that can be opened by the application, the maximum size, in bytes, for a UDP, and other vendor-specific information.

An `LPHOSTENT` is a long pointer to a `HOSTENT` (Host Entry) structure, which is returned by the `gethostbyname` function. This program uses `szIPAddress` to store the mail server's dotted IP address (in string format), which it gets by doing a DNS lookup on the mail server name. The dotted-address string is converted to a 32-bit value by `inet_addr`, which is then stored in `dwIPAddress`.

After the variables section, we check for the expected number of command-line arguments, and if necessary, call `ShowUsage`.

```
    // Check for valid # of command-line arguments.
    if ( argc != 2 ) ShowUsage();
```

Next, we want to initialize Winsock, which we do with a call to `WSAStartup`. `WSAStartup` returns 0 if successful, and fills `WSData` with information.

```
    // Attempt to initialize Winsock (1.1 or later).
    if ( WSAStartup(MAKEWORD(VERSION_MAJOR, VERSION_MINOR), &WSData) )
    {
        printf("Cannot find Winsock (v%d.%d or later)!\n",
          VERSION_MAJOR, VERSION_MINOR);
        return(1);
    }
```

Next, we use `gethostbyname` to look up the mail server's IP address. This causes a DNS lookup to be performed, and the resulting address is returned as a field inside the `lpHostEntry` structure.

```
lpHostEntry = gethostbyname( argv[1] );
```

Provided the lookup was successful in retrieving an IP address, we next convert the retrieved 32-bit IP address into a more readable dotted-address string so it can be displayed.

```
if ( lpHostEntry == NULL )
   printf("Unable to find %s!\n", argv[1]);
else {
   // Success. Convert address into dotted-notation (string).
   szIPAddress = inet_ntoa( *(LPIN_ADDR) *(lpHostEntry->h_addr_list) );

   // Display resolved address.
   printf("Found! IP address is %s\n", szIPAddress );
```

That done, we next attempt a reverse lookup, using the retrieved IP address to look up the corresponding name. To do this, we first need to convert the szIPAddress back into a 32-bit value, which is done via a call to `inet_addr`. It's true there's already a copy of this 32-bit value still stored inside the `lpHostEntry` structure, but the *FindAddr* demo uses `inet_addr` to demonstrate how it works.

```
// Now, let's try reverse lookup.
dwIPAddress = inet_addr( szIPAddress ); // Convert to 32-bits.
```

NOTE   Reverse lookups are used in some TCP/IP server programs, such as e-mail and Web servers, to verify that a given client address is authentic. Web servers usually let you disable this reverse-lookup feature, since performing the lookup will add extra wait time to each incoming client connection.

The reverse lookup is performed via a call to `gethostbyaddrr`, which takes a pointer to our 32-bit IP address value, an address size parameter (specified in bytes), and the AF_INET constant, which specifies the TCP/IP protocol family (since Winsock could be used for IPX or other protocols that have different-sized network addresses).

```
lpHostEntry = gethostbyaddr( (LPSTR) &dwIPAddress, sizeof(
dwIPAddress), AF_INET);
```

In this example, the `gethostbyaddr` function will usually succeed, since we have already successfully retrieved the IP address using a name. There are some instances, however, where reverse lookup would return a name that is different than the one that was used to look up the IP address. This can happen if the DNS mapping does not contain a reverse-lookup entry, such as is often the case with dynamically assigned IP addresses.

```
// Display reverse-resolved address (or error message).
if ( lpHostEntry == NULL )
    printf("Hm... Unable to reverse lookup %s\n", szIPAddress);
else
    printf("Successful reverse lookup of %s yields %s\n",
        szIPAddress, lpHostEntry->h_name );
}
```

The final step in using the Winsock functions is to call `WSACleanup`, to allow Winsock to release any resources allocated for this application, and decrement the usage count on the Winsock DLL.

```
// Clean up Winsock resources and terminate.
WSACleanup();
return(0);
}
```

Note that in addition to address and domain-name lookup functions, Winsock also has a port lookup function, which returns the port number used for a given TCP/IP protocol or service, which then is used to bind a socket to the desired port. There's an example of this in the *SendMail* demo, discussed next.

The SendMail Demo: Sending E-Mail

Our second Winsock example uses not only the TCP stream-oriented protocol, but also the higher-level SMTP to send e-mail. It takes four command-line parameters: mail server-address, from- and to- e-mail addresses, and the name of a text file. The program connects to the specified mail server, and e-mails the text file to the specified "to" address. As a bonus, this program actually has some practical uses! You can write a batch file, for instance, which generates a report file and then e-mails it using *SendMail*. You could also redirect some program's output to a file, and then e-mail that output file to an e-mail account.

The *SendMail* demo is included on the CD that accompanies this book, in the Chapter 21 folder.

Here's another handy example: Let's say you have a Windows 98 workstation or server that runs FTP or Web services and connects to the Internet via a dial-up connection. Most often, this means that the IP address will be dynamically assigned. In this case, you'll have no way of connecting to that station remotely unless you first get someone to go to the station, see what the currently assigned IP address is, and read it to you. Then, you need to repeat this procedure anytime the connection breaks. You can solve this problem by writing a batch file that looks like this:

```
rasdial MyConnection username password
netstat -r > current-ip
sendmail mailserver me@mydomain.com me@mydomain.com current-ip
```

The net effect (pun intended) of this script is to connect to the Internet, output the currently assigned IP address to a file, and e-mail this file to some account that you have access to. You can use a program scheduler to cause this script to be run at a certain time of day (or week), so that either at connect time or at specified time intervals, you can find out the station's current IP address by simply checking your latest e-mail. You could even add multiple `sendmail` lines if you want to notify other users of the IP address change. (Of course you'll get people's permission first, as over time this could generate a number of, probably unwanted, e-mail messages.)

TIP You could write a program similar to *SendMail* that looks for incoming mail from *SendMail* and retrieves it from your mail server. A program that reads e-mail would look similar to *SendMail*, except it would typically use the POP3 protocol to retrieve the e-mail.

The *SendMail* demo includes a few more header files than the *FindAddr* demo:

```
#define WIN32_LEAN_AND_MEAN
#include <stdio.h>
#include <stdlib.h>
#include <fstream.h>
#include <iostream.h>
#include <windows.h>
#include <winsock2.h>
```

In particular, we've added the Fstream.H and Iostream.H header files. We implement the text file I/O in this example using a file stream, hence the Fstream.H inclusion. Then, since the program was already using one stream, it made sense to use the C++ standard I/O streams as well. This makes for a bit of variety as well.

As in the *FindAddr* demo, we want to ensure the user is at least running Winsock version 1.1.

```
// Insist on at least Winsock v1.1, can be changed to 2.0
const    VERSION_MAJOR  = 1;
const    VERSION_MINOR  = 1;
```

For clarity, CRLF is defined so we can use it for adding carriage return/line feeds to the SMTP strings and to each line of the outgoing e-mail message.

```
#define  CRLF  "\r\n"   // carriage-return/line-feed pair.
```

As usual, we have a ShowUsage function, but this time, it uses the standard stream I/O to output the usage strings.

```
void ShowUsage(void)
{
    cout << "Usage: SENDMAIL mailserv to_addr from_addr messagefile";
    cout << endl;
    cout << "Example: SENDMAIL smtp.myisp.com rcvr@elsewhere.com ";
    cout << "my_id@mydomain.com message.txt" << endl;
    exit(1);
}
```

Next, there is a short error-checking function. It is designed to be used only with the send and recv socket functions, because it checks for SOCKET_ERROR return codes.

```
// Basic error checking for send() and recv() functions.
void Check( int iStatus, char *szFunction )
{
    if (iStatus != SOCKET_ERROR && iStatus != 0) return;

    cerr << "Error during call to " << szFunction << ": ";
    cerr << iStatus << " - " << GetLastError() << endl;
}
```

Now, we start the main program declaration, and declare needed variables.

```
int main(int argc, char *argv[])
{
    WSADATA          WSData;
    LPHOSTENT        lpHostEntry;
    LPSERVENT        lpServEntry;
    SOCKADDR_IN      SockAddr;
    SOCKET           hServer;
    int              iProtocolPort;
    char             szSmtpServerName[64], szToAddr[64], szFromAddr[64];
    char             szBuffer[4096], szLine[255], szMsgLine[255];
```

Note that the first three variables are identical to those used in the *FindAddr* demo. A socket address (input) or SOCKADDR_IN is necessary for binding the socket to the mail port. The iProtocolPort variable stores the mail port number, and hServer is the socket we will create to communicate with the mail server.

The next three string variables hold copies of the mail server name, and the e-mail "from" and "to" addresses. The szBuffer variable is used to hold incoming socket data, szLine is what we read each line of the text file into, and szMsgLine is used to format each line of the outgoing e-mail message.

After a standard check for the proper number of command-line parameters, the first three parameters are copied to easier-to-read string variables.

```
// Check for four command-line args.
if (argc != 5) ShowUsage();

// Load command-line args (for clarity).
lstrcpy( szSmtpServerName, argv[1]);
lstrcpy( szToAddr,         argv[2]);
lstrcpy( szFromAddr,       argv[3]);
```

Next, the text file that will supply the body of our e-mail message is initialized as a file-input stream. Note that we use argv[4] here directly, since it is used immediately.

```
// Create input stream for reading email message file.
ifstream MsgFile( argv[4] );
```

As in *FindAddr*, we next prepare to use Winsock by calling the WSAStartup initialization function. If we needed to, we could look at the information returned in the WSData structure, but in this case, we don't need to know, for instance, the maximum number of sockets we can open, since we'll need only one.

```
// Attempt to initialize Winsock (1.1 or later).
if ( WSAStartup(MAKEWORD(VERSION_MAJOR, VERSION_MINOR), &WSData) )
{
    cout << "Cannot find Winsock v";
    cout << VERSION_MAJOR << "." << VERSION_MINOR;
    cout << " or later!" << endl;
    return(1);
}
```

If you've studied the *FindAddr* demo, this next step should look familiar as well. We again use `gethostbyname` to look up the host IP address for the e-mail server.

```
// Lookup email server's IP address.
lpHostEntry = gethostbyname( szSmtpServerName );
if (lpHostEntry == NULL)
{
    cout << "Cannot find SMTP mail server ";
    cout << szSmtpServerName << endl;
    return(1);
}
```

Now, we need to create a socket. The first parameter specifies that this socket will be used in a TCP/IP context (as opposed to some other network protocol). Next, we want to specify a stream-type socket, because we will be using SMTP, which uses TCP, which is a stream protocol. And, since we don't need a specific protocol type at this point to create the socket, we can specify a zero as the third parameter.

```
// Create a TCP/IP socket, no specific protocol.
hServer = socket( PF_INET, SOCK_STREAM, 0);
if (hServer == INVALID_SOCKET)
{
    cout << "Cannot open mail server socket\n";
    return(1);
}
```

The next function finds the port number that has been assigned to the "mail" service, if one exists.

```
// Get the mail service port.
lpServEntry = getservbyname( "mail", 0);
```

If there isn't a specific entry for the mail service, we'll use the default port number for SMTP.

```
// Use the SMTP default port if no other port is specified.
if (lpServEntry == NULL)
    iProtocolPort = htons(IPPORT_SMTP);
else
    iProtocolPort = lpServEntry->s_port;
```

We next need to fill in the family, port, and address fields of the input socket address structure, which will be used to connect to our just-created socket. The socket family is type AF_INET (for TCP/IP), the port number is the mail service port that we've just determined, and the address filled in should be that of the mail server, which we retrieved above in our call to gethostbyname.

```
// Setup a Socket Address structure.
SockAddr.sin_family = AF_INET;
SockAddr.sin_port = iProtocolPort;
SockAddr.sin_addr = *((LPIN_ADDR)*lpHostEntry->h_addr_list);
```

Now, we connect our stream socket to the mail server, at the mail service port. Note that connect returns zero if successful. Also, the third parameter must specify the size of the socket address structure, since the connect function can be used to connect other socket types, and must therefore know what socket-address type it's dealing with. If all goes well, when this function returns, we will have established a "live" socket connection.

```
// Connect the socket.
if (connect( hServer, (PSOCKADDR) &SockAddr, sizeof(SockAddr)))
{
    cout << "Error connecting to Server socket.\n";
    return (1);
}
```

Typically, a server will generate some initial response to the client upon connecting. This is always the case with the simple mail protocol, so we must next read this initial response from our socket connection. If you wish to see what this response looks like, you can send szBuffer to cout or else connect to the mail server using Telnet, and use it to send each string as we do here.

```
// Receive initial response from SMTP server.
Check( recv( hServer, szBuffer, sizeof(szBuffer), 0),
            "recv() Reply");
```

Our next step, according to the simple mail protocol, is literally to say "hello," which is done by sending HELO followed by a space, and the client's host name. Terminating every line in this protocol is a carriage-return/line-feed pair.

Note that in this example we are assuming the mail server host name and the client's gateway host name are identical. However, frequently you will have a scenario where you'll want to distinguish these and simply specify the client host name.

```
// Send HELO server.com
sprintf( szMsgLine, "HELO %s%s", szSmtpServerName, CRLF);
Check( send( hServer, szMsgLine, strlen(szMsgLine), 0), "send() HELO");
Check( recv( hServer, szBuffer, sizeof(szBuffer), 0), "recv() HELO");
```

NOTE   It's important to be aware that in the SMTP, every time you send, you need to receive back an acknowledgment. As you'll see shortly, there is one exception to this rule: When you're sending the body of the message, all lines of the message body are sent before reading back any acknowledgment from the mail server.

Note that we aren't doing anything with the data received from the server. We *could* look at it, and in a robust commercial application, particularly when using protocols that are not as lock-step (not as reliant on expected command/reply pairs) as SMTP, we would want to look at and parse the result code from each response. This would allow the application to more gracefully recover from particular error conditions. However, in the case of SMTP, once we are connected, it is very unlikely we will get an unexpected reply. And in the case of a connection error, the Check function will at least give us an indication that we have a problem.

Having sent the HELO to (and received a response from) the server, the next step is to tell the server we have a mail message and indicate the return e-mail address. This is done by sending MAIL FROM: , followed by a space, and the reply-to address in angle brackets. Again, a CRLF pair always terminates each response in SMTP, and after sending, we must read back the server's reply before sending again.

```
// Send MAIL FROM: <sender@mydomain.com>
sprintf( szMsgLine, "MAIL FROM:<%s>%s", szFromAddr, CRLF);
Check( send( hServer, szMsgLine, strlen(szMsgLine), 0), "send() MAIL FROM");
Check( recv( hServer, szBuffer, sizeof(szBuffer), 0), "recv() MAIL FROM");
```

Next, we send one (or more, if desired) destination e-mail address, using the form RCPT TO:, followed by a space, and the to-address enclosed in angle brackets.

```
// Send RCPT TO: <receiver@domain.com>
sprintf( szMsgLine, "RCPT TO:<%s>%s", szToAddr, CRLF);
Check( send( hServer, szMsgLine, strlen(szMsgLine), 0), "send() RCPT TO");
Check( recv( hServer, szBuffer, sizeof(szBuffer), 0), "recv() RCPT TO");
```

You may send mail to as many recipients as you like this way, but remember to read the server reply after sending each recipient string. Also, if you're attempting to send to many recipients, it is possible to reach the mail server's maximum recipient count. If this happens, the server would return an error result (which you could detect by checking the result returned each time by recv).

When we're finished sending the message header information, we signal this to the server by sending DATA (again, followed by a CRLF pair).

```
// Send DATA.
sprintf( szMsgLine, "DATA%s", CRLF);
Check( send( hServer, szMsgLine, strlen(szMsgLine), 0), "send() DATA");
Check( recv( hServer, szBuffer, sizeof(szBuffer), 0), "recv() DATA");
```

Note that we could add more optional lines to our header, but the sender and the recipient e-mail addresses are the only parts essential to getting the message delivered.

Now, it's time to send each line of the message body text. Since we're sending the contents of a text file, we'll want to read each line and send it in turn. Note that we do not attempt to read back a reply from the server until we have completed sending all the lines in the message body.

```
// Send all lines of message body (using supplied text file.)
MsgFile.getline( szLine, sizeof(szLine)); // get first line.
do // for each line of message text...
{
sprintf( szMsgLine, "%s%s", szLine, CRLF);
Check( send( hServer, szMsgLine, strlen(szMsgLine), 0), "send() message-line");
MsgFile.getline( szLine, sizeof(szLine)); // get next line.
} while ( MsgFile.good() );
```

To signal the server that we're finished sending the body text, we must send a single period on a line by itself. Then, the server issues an acknowledgment reply, which we need to read.

```
// Send blank line and a period.
sprintf( szMsgLine, "%s.%s", CRLF, CRLF);
Check( send( hServer, szMsgLine, strlen(szMsgLine), 0), "send() end-message");
Check( recv( hServer, szBuffer, sizeof(szBuffer), 0), "recv() end-message");
```

At this point, we could either send another e-mail message or quit. Since we don't have anything else to send, we will indicate to the server that we wish to quit. This is done by sending a QUIT string.

```
// Send QUIT.
sprintf( szMsgLine, "QUIT%s", CRLF);
Check( send( hServer, szMsgLine, strlen(szMsgLine), 0), "send() QUIT");
Check( recv( hServer, szBuffer, sizeof(szBuffer), 0), "recv() QUIT");
```

Locally, we want to indicate to our user that the message has been sent.

```
// Report message has been sent.
cout << "Sent " << argv[4] << " as email message to " << szToAddr << endl;
```

And, since we're finished using our server socket, we need to close it.

```
// Close server socket and prepare to exit.
closesocket( hServer );
```

Finally, since we've completed using the Winsock functions, we need to call WSACleanup, which allows Winsock to deallocate any resources it was maintaining for our application. After calling WSACleanup, our application can go ahead and exit.

```
WSACleanup();

return(0);
}
```

Winsock Applications

The demos discussed in the previous sections should give you a good idea of what is required to write a simple Winsock application. Moreover, it should also give you a basic understanding of how the higher-level TCP/IP protocols communicate information between client and server. POP3, FTP, and HTTP are quite similar in this respect, although in the case of FTP and HTTP, the order in which commands and replies occur is more loosely structured. With SMTP, you can implement sending an e-mail message by means of a very predictable series of send/receive pairs, executing in "see-saw" or lock-step fashion. An HTTP or FTP server, on the other hand, requires a more flexible approach, and would be better implemented using a state-table or an event-driven program structure.

You may find it interesting to experiment directly with these protocols by using your Windows 98 or NT Telnet client to send properly formatted protocol strings to an FTP, SMTP, POP3, or HTTP server and view the incoming replies generated by the server. To do this, you will need to locate and download the appropriate protocol specification from the Internet to learn what the command strings and response codes are for a particular protocol. In the Telnet Connect dialog box, enter the corresponding protocol into the Port combo box (yes, many of the protocols are not listed in the combo box, but you can type in whatever you want).

Although the socket paradigm is reasonably straightforward and eases the task of communicating via TCP and UDP, it can still be quite tedious to implement the various higher-level protocols in your applications. These protocols vary in their sets of possible states, their message tokens, and behavior. Furthermore, once you have written and debugged your application, you may still need to revisit it periodically to add support for new server implementations, new additions, or changes to the protocol specification. With FTP, for example, although the message tokens are standard, the formats used by various FTP servers to return requested directory listings can vary to some degree. The recently introduced set of Win32 functions called the Internet API address these problems. We will look at these functions next.

The Internet API Functions

If you need to write FTP, Gopher, or HTTP client applications, the Internet API may be ideal for your purposes. This set of functions eliminates the need for dealing with TCP/IP implementation details or for using Winsock-related structures and functions. It encapsulates the FTP, HTTP, and Gopher protocols at the task level. Rather than requiring you to open and close sockets, and listen for and accept socket connections, this API lets you manage tasks, such as uploading or downloading files, using a single function call. Moreover, the Internet API encapsulates (hides) the differences in file-listing formats used by different FTP servers, so you can search for files and directories without worrying about which type of FTP server you're connected to.

All the Internet API functions are fully-reentrant and thread-safe, so you can use them in multithreaded applications without any problems. Another benefit to using the Internet API is that protocol-specific behavior, which is subject to change, can be isolated from application code and replaced by updating your copy of the Wininet.DLL file (which is the DLL that supplies Internet API functionality).

One drawback to using the Internet API is that it is intended only for Internet *client* applications. Microsoft documentation states clearly that these functions do not provide the appropriate level of control at the protocol or I/O levels to be usable in server implementations. Also, because of the protocol encapsulation and the abstraction of various differences in server behavior, there is likely to be at least a small performance hit as well. But if you need to quickly develop an FTP, Gopher, or HTTP client application, the Internet API will let you get your application up and running in a hurry.

The Internet API functions are listed in the following sections, grouped in seven categories:

- Connect and disconnect functions
- File finding, reading, and writing functions
- FTP-, Gopher-, and HTTP-specific functions
- Cookie functions
- URL-related functions
- Time and date functions
- Error and status functions

NOTE   The Internet API automatically caches Internet URLs and recently transferred data. Thus, some functions may return repeat data faster than you might normally expect, because the information does not need to be retrieved again; it is transparently copied from a buffer.

Connect and Disconnect Functions

You interact with the various Internet API functions by using a special Internet handle, called HINTERNET. Unlike the Winsock socket handles or Win32 handles created using CreateFile, the HINTERNET handles are completely unusable with the normal Win32 handle I/O functions, such as ReadFile or CloseHandle. Instead, you use the Internet API functions, such as InternetReadFile or InternetCloseHandle, to read from an opened resource or to close an opened handle.

HINTERNET handles are created in a hierarchy, or tree. A top-level handle is returned by the InternetOpen function, which you must call before using almost any of the other Internet API functions. Next, you open a connection handle to a particular site by using InternetConnect. Finally, you open one or more FTP, Gopher, or HTTP file or search handles, which can then be used in calls to InternetReadFile, InternetFindNextFile, and similar functions.

InternetCloseHandle is used to close HINTERNET handles of any type, including Internet session, connection, search, and resource handles. Also, because these handles are hierarchical, any lower-level handles will be closed automatically when you close a parent handle. Thus, you could, with a single call to InternetCloseHandle (passing the handle returned from your InternetOpen call), close all other handles in your application that were opened using the Internet API functions. For consistency (and good programming practice), however, you may prefer to keep to the habit of closing each handle specifically when you're finished with it.

Table 21.11 lists the Internet API connect and disconnect functions.

TABLE 21.11: Internet API Connect and Disconnect Functions

Function	Description
InternetAttemptConnect	Attempts to connect to the Internet. Typically, this should be called prior to using the other Internet functions. It returns ERROR_SUCCESS if connection is made; otherwise, it returns a Win32 error condition.
InternetOpen	Internet API initialization function. This must be called prior to using the Internet API functions. (Use InternetCloseHandle when finished.)
InternetConnect	Connects to the specified FTP, Gopher, or HTTP server, and returns a handle. (Use InternetCloseHandle when finished.)
InternetCloseHandle	Closes handles (and subhandles) created by InternetOpen, InternetConnect, FtpOpenFile, GopherOpenFile, and HttpSendRequest.

File Locating, Reading, and Writing Functions

Table 21.12 lists the Internet API commands for finding, reading, and writing files.

TABLE 21.12: Internet API File-Handling Functions

Function	Description
`InternetFindNextFile`	Continues a search started with `FtpFindFirstFile` or `GopherFindFirstFile` and accepts a search handle created by either of these functions.
`InternetQueryDataAvailable`	Queries the amount of data available from an HTTP, a Gopher, or an FTP resource.
`InternetReadFile`	Reads data from a handle opened by `InternetOpenUrl`, `FtpOpenFile`, `GopherOpenFile`, or `HttpOpenRequest`. (See also `FtpGetFile` and `FtpPutFile`.)
`InternetWriteFile`	Writes data to an open file.
`InternetSetFilePointer`	Sets the file position for the next `InternetReadFile` call. It returns the current file position if successful; otherwise, it returns a −1. Note that some servers and URL types do not support random access.

FTP-, Gopher-, and HTTP-Specific Functions

Finding an FTP or Gopher file on a given host connection is very similar to finding a file on a local or network drive using the `FindFirst` and `FindNext` functions. Start searching an FTP or Gopher directory with a call to `FtpFindFirstFile` or `GopherFindFirstFile`, followed by repeated calls to `InternetFindNextFile`, recursing as necessary until you locate the file (or exhaust the available search directories). Remember to close the search handles returned by each `FtpFindFirst` or `GopherFindFirst` call.

Table 21.13 lists the Internet API FTP-, Gopher-, and HTTP-related functions.

TABLE 21.13: Internet API FTP, Gopher, and HTTP Functions

Function	Description
FtpFindFirstFile	Starts file enumeration or searching in the current server directory. Use this with **InternetFindNextFile** and **InternetCloseHandle**.
FtpGetFile	Retrieves an entire file from the server.
FtpPutFile	Writes an entire file to the server.
FtpDeleteFile	Deletes a file on the server.
FtpRenameFile	Renames a file on the server.
FtpOpenFile	Opens a file on the server for reading or writing. (Use with **Internet-QueryDataAvailable**, **InternetReadFile**, **InternetWriteFile**, and **InternetCloseHandle**.)
FtpCreateDirectory	Creates a new directory on the server.
FtpRemoveDirectory	Deletes a directory on the server.
FtpSetCurrentDirectory	Changes the connection's current directory on the server.
FtpGetCurrentDirectory	Returns the connection's current directory on the server.
GopherFindFirstFile	Starts enumerating a Gopher directory listing. (Use with **Internet-FindNextFile** and **InternetCloseHandle**.)
GopherOpenFile	Opens a Gopher object on the server for retrieval. (Use with **Internet-QueryDataAvailable**, **InternetReadFile**, **InternetWriteFile**, and **InternetCloseHandle**.)
GopherCreateLocator	Forms a Gopher locator for use in other Gopher function calls.
GopherGetAttribute	Retrieves attribute information on the Gopher object.
HttpOpenRequest	Opens an HTTP request and returns a request handle. (Use **Internet-CloseHandle** to close.)
HttpAddRequestHeaders	Adds HTTP request headers to the HTTP request handle.
HttpSendRequest	Sends the specified request to the HTTP server. (Use with **Internet-QueryDataAvailable** and **InternetReadFile**.)
HttpQueryInfo	Retrieves information about an HTTP request.

Cookie Functions

The two functions listed in Table 21.14 deal with setting and retrieving cookie values. At first glance, this might seem to imply that the Internet API is being expanded to support writing server applications; however, these cookie functions deal only with the cookie database that is located on the client station. You could use these to set or retrieve cookie values that are in memory or have been saved to disk. However, for now, you cannot use them to access cookie data stored on a host or peer station.

NOTE   *Cookies* are handy strings of information stored by Web browsers on a user's local hard drive (or at least in RAM), whose values are set and then later retrieved by specific Web sites. This permits persistent storage of information between visits to that Web site. The term *cookie database* refers to the file(s), initially used by Web browsers (but now also by the Internet API) to save cookie values to disk between sessions. Netscape (and other browsers) use their own techniques and file(s) for saving cookie values. Netscape currently stores its cookies in a file called Cookies.TXT. Internet Explorer and the Internet API currently store their cookies as separate files, in a directory called \Windows\Cookies.

TABLE 21.14: Internet API Cookie Functions

Function	Description
InternetGetCookie	Fills supplied buffer with the cookie data for the specified URL and all its parent URLs. Intended for interacting with local cookie database.
InternetSetCookie	Sets cookie data for a given cookie name at a specified URL. Intended for interacting with local cookie database.

URL-Related Functions

The URL-related functions are useful for creating, splitting, and combining URLs. These functions are handy for converting between a URL and its component pieces or for converting between relative and absolute URLs. Table 21.15 lists the Internet API functions associated with URLs.

TABLE 21.15: Internet API URL-Related Functions

Function	Description
InternetCrackUrl	Parses a URL string into components.
InternetCreateUrl	Creates a URL string from components.
InternetCanonicalizeUrl	Converts a URL to canonical form. This is used to convert a URL into a server-safe URL, because it converts to escape sequences any spaces or other characters that could be misinterpreted by specific servers.
InternetCombineUrl	Combines base and relative URLs.
InternetOpenUrl	Begins retrieving an FTP, a Gopher, or an HTTP URL.

Time/Date Conversion Functions

The Internet API also supplies functions for converting back and forth between (local) system time and HTTP Internet time strings. HTTP time/date strings are used, for example, in the "Expires:" optional header setting embedded in some HTML documents. The two time/date conversion commands are listed in Table 21.16.

TABLE 21.16: Internet API Time/Date Conversion Functions

Function	Description
InternetTimeFromSystemTime	Converts a Win32 SYSTEMTIME structure into a string, formatted according to the HTTP RFC 1.0 time/date string format.
InternetTimeToSystemTime	Converts an HTTP time/date string to a SYSTEMTIME structure.

Error and Status Functions

You can perform error checking by first checking the Boolean return value for each function, and then using the standard GetLastError Win32 API function to return a specific error code. More specific information can be retrieved by calling

InternetGetLastResponseInfo, although in some cases, this tends to return more information than you need. You can also display Internet-specific information using the InternetErrorDlg function. To control protocol-specific settings, use InternetQueryOption and InternetSetOption.

Table 21.17 lists the Internet API error and status functions.

TABLE 21.17: Internet API Error and Status Functions

Function	Description
InternetSetStatusCallback	Assigns a callback function to be called with status information. This is useful for monitoring functions that take some time to complete.
InternetErrorDlg	Displays predefined dialog boxes for common Internet error conditions.
InternetConfirmZoneCrossing	Detects when your application is moving either from a secure to an insecure URL, or vice versa.
InternetQueryOption	Queries the current setting of a given Internet option.
InternetSetOption	Sets an Internet option.
InternetGetLastResponseInfo	Returns buffer containing data from the last reply; typically used to retrieve more detailed or specialized status or error information.

The FtpGet Demo: Simple FTP Transfer

The *FtpGet* demo uses the Internet API to perform a simple FTP transfer. As you'll see, in comparison to implementing the FTP protocol directly in your application using Winsock calls, the Internet API is really a breeze to use.

The *FtpGet* demo downloads a given FTP file using the Internet API functions. It starts by calling InternetOpen to open an Internet session, then connects to the desired FTP server using InternetConnect. If a path has been prepended to the specified filename, this directory is made the current directory on the FTP server, and then the file is downloaded to the client computer using FtpGetFile.

NOTE   The *FtpGet* demo is included on the CD that accompanies this book, in the Chapter 21 folder.

To start off, we need to include the necessary header files, including Wininet.H, the Internet API header file.

```
#include <windows.h>
#include <iostream.h>
#include <stdio.h>
#include <wininet.h>
```

NOTE   If your compiler does not yet include the Wininet.H header file and import library, you will need to either download these or otherwise obtain them from Microsoft or your compiler vendor. Currently, you can get the necessary files by downloading the Internet ActiveX SDK—all 10MB of it. It's this size because it includes the Wininet.DLL, .LIB, and .H files, along with other files, including a few sample programs.

Next, we declare two variables to hold the username and password that will be used to log in to the FTP server. For servers permitting anonymous login, the preset values are satisfactory, although you may want to set the password to your own e-mail address, as is customary. For nonanonymous logins, you will definitely need to change both of these values, as appropriate.

```
// Customize login info as appropriate.
char    szUsername[64]    = "anonymous";
char    szPassword[64]    = "user@domain.com";
```

This program uses two other global variables. The first, szAppName, is used to hold the name that is passed to the InternetConnect function. The dwBinary variable is a flag that will be needed by the FtpGetFile function. Unless you are definitely transferring a text (ASCII) file, be sure to use FTP_TRANSFER_TYPE_ BINARY to perform a binary file transfer; otherwise, your file will almost certainly fail to transfer the file correctly.

```
// General Globals
char    szAppName[20]    = "FtpGet";
DWORD   dwBinary         = FTP_TRANSFER_TYPE_BINARY;
```

In case this app gets called from a batch file, I've defined a set of exit codes for various error conditions that could occur.

```
// Application exit codes.
const int    ERR_SUCCESS            = 0;
const int    ERR_USAGE              = 1;
const int    ERR_CONNECTING_INTERNET = 2;
const int    ERR_CONNECTING_HOST    = 3;
const int    ERR_BAD_DIRECTORY      = 4;
const int    ERR_FTP_TRANSFER       = 5;
```

The `LastErrorMsg` function returns a string containing the error message or status information returned from the last Internet API function call. This information is retrieved by making a call to `InternetGetLastResponseInfo` and passing it a pointer to the error code, a buffer to fill, and the length of the message buffer. In the event `InternetGetLastResponse` fails (as would happen if there is no Wininet.DLL, for instance), the Win32 `GetLastError` function is called to retrieve whatever Win32 error code might be available.

```
char *LastErrorMsg(void)
{
    static char szErrorMsg[4096];
    ULONG       dwErrorNum, dwLength;

    dwLength = sizeof( szErrorMsg );
    if (!InternetGetLastResponseInfo( &dwErrorNum, (LPSTR) szErrorMsg, &dwLength))
    {
        sprintf( szErrorMsg, "Unable to get error information, Error# = %d ",
        GetLastError() );
    }
    return( szErrorMsg );
}
```

The main program section starts by declaring the variables that will be used. First listed are two `HINTERNET` handles. These are "opaque" Internet API handle types, which are allocated by Internet API functions and are the only handle types suitable for use with the Internet API functions that take a handle as a parameter. (They are "opaque" in that there is no useful information directly accessible inside these handles, and they can only be used with Internet API functions.) Note that `HINTERNET` handles actually include four types: an "Internet" handle, a session handle, a search handle, and a URL/file handle. The `szHost` will refer to the FTP server address, and `szPath` and `szFile` will contain the path and file, once these have been split apart from the input path/filename supplied to the program.

```
int main( int argc, char *argv[] )
{
    HINTERNET   hInternet, hHost; // handles.
    int         i;
    char        szHost[128];
    char        szPath[MAX_PATH];
    char        szFile[MAX_PATH];
```

Next comes the standard usage check, which displays usage information if fewer than two parameters were supplied (remember, zero is always the application name).

```
if (argc < 3)
{
    cout << "Usage: FtpGet ftp.domain.com \\path\\filename\n";
    return ERR_USAGE;
}
```

Next, we copy the two supplied command-line parameters to szHost and szFile.

```
lstrcpy( szHost, argv[1] );
lstrcpy( szFile, argv[2] );
```

The path default is set to a single slash. We then start at the end of the path/filename, searching for a forward slash or a backslash. If either is found, we know where to split the filename and path; otherwise, we'll assume the entire string is a filename.

```
lstrcpy(szPath, "/"); // Use root as default path.
// Get the path, if prepended to filename.
for (i=strlen(szFile); i>0; --i)
{
    if (szFile[i]=='/' || szFile[i]=='\\')
    {
        strncpy(szPath, szFile, ++i);
        szPath[i]= 0; // terminate.
        lstrcpy(szFile, szFile+i);
        break;
    }
}
```

Note that we do not need to worry about converting forward slashes to back-slashes (or vice versa). This is because the Internet API functions that take file-names know how to convert the slashes and backslashes to the form expected by the server.

Now, we initialize the Internet API for this application by calling `Internet-Open`. The second parameter tells Wininet that we will need a proxy server to connect. If the handle returned is zero, an error occurred and we display an error message and exit.

```
hInternet = InternetOpen( szAppName, LOCAL_INTERNET_ACCESS , NULL, 0, 0 );
if (!hInternet)
{
    cerr << "Error opening Internet: " << LastErrorMsg();
    InternetCloseHandle( hInternet );
    return ERR_CONNECTING_INTERNET;
}
```

NOTE   A *proxy server* is software that permits networked computers to access the Inter-net via a trusted server. The proxy server usually works with some level of firewall functionality and sometimes even using network protocols other than TCP/IP, with the appropriate proxy client software.

Having called `InternetOpen`, we are now ready to begin using the other Inter-net API functions. We first make a call to `InternetConnect`, which establishes a connection to the specified FTP host, using our supplied username and pass-word. If an error occurs at this point, we display an error message and exit.

```
hHost = InternetConnect( hInternet, szHost,
                    INTERNET_INVALID_PORT_NUMBER, szUsername, szPassword,
                    INTERNET_SERVICE_FTP, INTERNET_FLAG_PASSIVE , 0);
if (!hHost)
{
    cerr << "Error connecting to " << szHost << ": " << LastErrorMsg();
    InternetCloseHandle( hInternet );
    return ERR_CONNECTING_HOST;
}
```

Next, we set the current directory on the remote server to point to the directory containing the file we're going to download.

```
if (!FtpSetCurrentDirectory( hHost, szPath ))
{
    cerr << "Unable to find remote directory : " << szPath << endl;
    cerr << LastErrorMsg() << endl;
    InternetCloseHandle( hInternet );
    return ERR_BAD_DIRECTORY;
}
```

Now, we're ready to perform the download. This is accomplished in the Internet API via a single call to `FtpGetFile`. The second and third parameters specify the source and destination filenames, respectively. These can be the same, since we've already changed to the correct directory. However, `FtpGetFile` will allow you to include a path name on either (or both) the source and target filenames. If we didn't need to split the filename off for the destination directory, it would have been simpler just to let `FtpGetFile` handle the path name internally.

```
if (!FtpGetFile( hHost, szFile, szFile, FALSE,
                 INTERNET_FLAG_RELOAD, dwBinary, 0 ))
{
    cerr << "Unable to transfer file : " << szFile << endl;
    cerr << LastErrorMsg() << endl;
    InternetCloseHandle( hInternet );
    return ERR_FTP_TRANSFER;
}
```

At this point, we want to let our user know the file has finished transferring.

```
cout << "Transferred " << szFile << endl;
```

NOTE
It is possible to set a callback function using the `InternetSetStatusCallback` function, to be called periodically when Internet API functions that take an extended period of time are busy executing. This would be a nice addition if you need to transfer larger files.

We can now close the handle to the host (FTP server) connection, and the handle to our Internet connection, signaling the Internet API that we have finished using it in this application.

```
        // Finished, clean up and exit.
        InternetCloseHandle( hHost );
        InternetCloseHandle( hInternet );

        return ERR_SUCCESS;
    }
```

Internet Applications

As you can see from the *FtpGet* demo, performing an FTP download using the Internet API is straightforward and quite trivial to implement.

One nice feature you could add to the *FtpGet* demo is a searching feature, so that the user would not need to specify the file path on the remote server. This would not be difficult to add; you could use the `FtpFindFirst` and `InternetFindNext` functions to recursively search each directory for the desired file. Another handy use for these find-first and find-next functions would be to implement a utility that transfers an entire FTP (or Gopher or Web) site from one server to another, by recursing through all directories and copying all files at each level from the host to the client.

Also, note that while the demo makes use of the `FtpGetFile` function, you could instead, almost as easily, use the `FtpOpenFile` function, followed by repeated calls to `InternetReadFile`, to read successive blocks from the server. This requires slightly more code but gives you the opportunity to calculate and display a progress indicator as the data is transferring.

Alternatively, instead of `FtpOpenFile`, you could use `InternetOpenUrl`, which has the added benefit of being protocol-independent. `InternetOpenUrl` is able to parse different URL types and automatically determine the type of server connection to open. In this way, you can use the same code to open various types of URLs. The protocol-independent data transfer is then performed by making repeated calls to `InternetReadFile`.

The Internet API is a powerful yet easy-to-use API, and indications are that support for additional protocols is being planned for future versions. Perhaps by the time you read this, there will also be functions for sending and retrieving e-mail. The Internet API has all the earmarks of becoming a widely used Windows API.

If you prefer working with visual controls, you may be especially interested in the Internet Control Pack, which we'll take a look at next.

ActiveX Web Controls

The Microsoft Internet Web Control Pack is a set of ActiveX controls available via Microsoft's Web site (or FTP site). The Control Pack makes building an FTP client, Web browser, news, or e-mail client as easy as dropping the appropriate control onto your form and adding only a few lines of code. You can use these controls in Delphi, as well as in Visual Basic or even in Visual C++. Table 21.18 lists the ActiveX controls included in the Control Pack.

NOTE   ActiveX controls are not quite as transparent to use in Visual C++. In Chapter 16, you learned about using Visual C++/Developer Studio to create an ActiveX component by using the ATL COM AppWizard. Although Visual C++ is great for *writing* ActiveX controls, accessing them is not quite as clean and simple as it is in Delphi or Visual Basic (at least currently). Rather than simply referring to a property or method by name, for example, you must make function calls, which in turn set or retrieve information for each property.

TABLE 21.18: ActiveX Web Controls in the Internet Control Pack

Control	Description
FTP Control (client)	Adds support for searching and browsing file listings and downloading files using FTP.
HTML Control (client)	Adds support for (simple) Web browsing.
HTTP Control (client)	Adds support for HTTP to your application.
NNTP Control (client)	Adds news transport support to your application.
POP Control (client)	Adds support for POP to your application, to retrieve e-mail.
SMTP Control (client)	Adds support for sending e-mail. You can use it together with the POP control to easily add e-mail send and receive functionality to your application.
Winsock TCP and UDP Controls	Adds TCP/IP or datagram support to your applications. These comes in both client and server versions, and allow you to define your own specialized protocols.

In addition to the FTP, HTTP/HTML, news, and e-mail controls, there are also both client and server versions of TCP and UDP Winsock controls, which you can use to create your own specialized, higher-level Internet protocol or build your own Internet server or client.

Unlike the Internet API functions, the ActiveX controls encapsulate Winsock functionality in a way that simplifies Winsock programming, yet provides you with enough control over how connections are established to permit building Internet server applications. Again, due to the overhead involved in encapsulating the Winsock functionality inside an ActiveX control, you are not likely to achieve the same performance you would get using the Winsock API itself. On the other hand, the performance hit does not seem very noticeable, and whatever performance these controls sacrifice is well-compensated for by their extreme ease of use.

One Control and One Line of Code

After you install the ActiveX controls, programming is a cinch. For example, it literally requires only placing the HTML control on your application's form and writing a single line of code to initially browse a Web page! For example, this line is all it takes to cause the Web browser to display Microsoft's home page.

```
Html1.RequestDoc('http://www.microsoft.com');
```

Running the application produces a window the size of your HTML control, which establishes a connection to www.microsoft.com. After a few seconds, you should see the resulting HTML page in the control window!

Although you can pass the desired URL through to your application (or recompile each time), a much better approach is to add a combo box to your application, which can be tied to the HTML control and used to supply it with a desired URL. This provides a URL-entry area similar to that found in any Web browser.

Installing Microsoft's Internet ActiveX Controls in Delphi

For any Delphi users out there, these controls are really a treat. The quick compile time combined with extremely simple visual configuration of the Internet Web Controls will allow you to crank out Internet applications in no time! My first attempts in installing the controls into Delphi led me to believe that Delphi just wasn't compatible with these

Continued on next page

controls. However, I figured it out and am passing these instructions on to other Delphi users, so you can avoid my mistakes. Here are the steps:

1. Download and install the MS Internet Control Pack.

2. Start Delphi.

3. From the main menu, select Component/Install.

4. Click the OCX button.

5. Scroll through the Registered Controls list, until you come to (for example) the Microsoft FTP Client Control. Highlight it.

6. Go down to the Unit File Name field and change the filename to something descriptive but unique. For example, for FTP use MSFTP.PAS; for NNTP, use MSNNTP.PAS; and for HTTP, use MSHTTP.PAS.

7. Go to Class Names. Where it says TFTP Control, delete the second word *Control*, plus any blank characters. Be careful not to add any spaces or a carriage return. You will get an "Invalid class name" error message if there are any characters beyond the single-word class name.

8. Click OK.

Repeat steps 5 through 8 for each OCX control you wish to add. When you're finished installing controls, click OK again. Reply to the message box which asks "Save changes to project?" (most likely you will choose No). At this point, Delphi will rebuild the component library. Depending on how fast your machine is and the total number of controls installed, it may take anywhere from seconds to minutes to rebuild your component library. After it finishes, you should be able to click the OCX tab of your component toolbar and see icons for the new Internet controls you've added.

You can find online help files for each control in your \WINDOWS\SYSTEM directory (for Windows 98) or \WINNT\SYSTEM32\ directory (for Windows NT).

The Internet controls are now available for use in Delphi. Have fun!

The WebView Demo: A Simple Web Browser

The *WebView* demo makes use of the HTML control to create a simple but functional Web browser.

NOTE The example assumes you are using Delphi. If you are using Visual Basic, the online help for the HTML control has a good Visual Basic sample program that you can use instead of *WebView*.

Creating Web Browser with Delphi

Here are the steps to follow to make a very simple Web browser in Delphi 2.0:

1. Start a new application by selecting File ➤ New Application.

2. Click the OCX tab in your tools palette, and then click the HTML tool icon.

3. Click your application form to place a copy of the HTML control on the form.

4. In the Object Inspector window, change the name of this control to **Html**.

5. Select the Events tab, and double-click the entry-area of the `OnBegin-Retrieval` event.

6. Place the following code under the `HTMLBeginRetrieval` procedure declaration:

```
var  i: integer;  found: boolean;
begin
  found:= FALSE;
  for i:= 0 to UrlBox.Items.Count -1 do
    if (UrlBox.Items[i] = Html.Url) then begin
      found:= TRUE;
      break;
    end;
  if (not found) then
    UrlBox.Items.Add( Html.Url );
  UrlBox.Text:= Html.Url;
end;
```

7. Place a combo-box control on your form. This can be positioned just above the HTML control.

8. In the Object Inspector window, change the name of this control to **UrlBox**.

9. Select the Events tab, and double-click the entry-area for the `OnClick` event.

10. Place the following line inside the `UrlBoxClick` procedure:

    ```
    Html.RequestDoc( UrlBox.Text );
    ```

11. Back in the Object Inspector window, select the UrlBox's Events tab, and double-click the entry-area for the `OnKeyDown` event. Place the following line of code inside the `UrlBoxKeyDown` procedure:

    ```
    Html.RequestDoc( Default_Page );
    ```

12. Double-click a blank area of your form, and enter the following line into the `FormCreate` procedure:

    ```
    Html.RequestDoc( Default_Page );
    ```

13. In the Object Inspector window (and with the main form selected), double-click the `OnResize` event, and enter the following into the `FormResize` procedure:

    ```
    UrlBox.width:= ClientWidth;
    Html.width:= ClientWidth;
    Html.height:= ClientHeight - UrlBox.Height;
    ```

14. Below the `implementation` line, and just above your first procedure declaration, enter the following constant declaration. (Feel free to change to your favorite URL.)

    ```
    CONST
    DEFAULT_PAGE = 'www.webcrawler.com';
    ```

15. Save your unit1.pas file as **mainwin.pas**, and your project as **webview.pas**. If you like, also rename the main form to **frmmainwin**. (This last step is not really necessary.)

At this point, you should have an approximately 71-line Delphi program, which looks very similar to the listing for the *WebView* demo (on the CD accompanying this book). Try compiling the project. If you have any problems, double-check for syntax errors caused by typos or other mistakes. (To save time, you may want to load the file from the CD, or at least compare your source code with it.)

NOTE The *WebView* demo is included on the CD that accompanies this book, in the Chapter 21 folder.

If the project compiles, try running it. You will need to have an active connection to the Internet (or your intranet) for this application to work. If you have auto-dialing enabled, a connection may be established automatically. Assuming you have a "live" TCP/IP connection to the Internet, your default URL should appear in the browser window within several seconds. To go to a new URL, enter it into the URL area (combo box), and press Enter. To return to a previous URL, select it from the combo-box list.

How WebView Works

As you've probably noticed, the function used to make the HTML control go to a URL and display it is `RequestDoc( SomeURL )`. The `UrlBox` combo box watches each keypress. When it detects a carriage return (`VK_RETURN`), it feeds its current text into `RequestDoc`. The current URL is added conditionally to `UrlBox` at the start of each page load, when the `BeginRetrieval` event is triggered. The code checks to see if the URL is already in the `UrlBox` list, and if not, it adds it; otherwise, it simply redisplays it.

ActiveX Web Control Applications

As you may have already noticed, the HTML control has several other properties, events, and methods. By using more of these and adding more of your own code, you could create a Web browser that is functionally quite similar to Internet Explorer. You can add Next and Previous buttons, for example, and a menu with configuration options (such as default home page, background color, and link colors). You can add Delphi toolbar buttons to easily change the font size(s), and add bookmarks. Because there are events that are triggered during and at the end of each page load, you could even add a progress indicator, such as a bitmap animation or a progress bar.

Keep in mind that the HTML control can be used for purposes other than displaying pages. You might also use it to retrieve and parse HTML pages to look for certain search words and follow links—creating a little search "bot," which can search for pages for you and perhaps log each pertinent URL it visits.

Also, don't forget that you can combine different Internet controls or have many of the same Internet controls in your application. You could retrieve mail from one account via a POP control and forward it to another account using an SMTP control. Also, these controls let you easily Internet-enable other applications that you have already written. For example, you could add an SMTP control, and your application would be able to send you an e-mail message when it's finished processing. Better yet, add an FTP control, and your report application can transfer a copy of that report to any FTP server it has access to.

The UDP and TCP controls can be used for datagram and streaming communications, either as servers or clients (or both). You could even define your own protocol, perhaps modeled after FTP or SMTP, to accomplish some special purpose (such as reading the temperature or remotely controlling a PC). Then you could easily implement it using one of these socket controls (probably a TCP control).

Active Channels

One much-heralded innovation included in Windows 98 is its support for Active Channels. An Active Channel is a content stream provided by any Web site that supports sending "webcast" style content to channel-receiving browsers, such as Internet Explorer 4 or Windows 98's Active Desktop. Typically, this is done by providing a Channel Definition File (CDF). The CDF file provides an index of content and resources supplied by the channel, along with a recommended schedule for when the information and resources should be updated on the user's computer. At the user's request, particular channels may be selected as the active screen-saver or be placed somewhere on the Desktop as an Active Desktop item.

NOTE   The Active Desktop is what Microsoft has chosen to refer to the browser-as-Desktop feature introduced with Windows 98. Active Channels can appear on your Active Desktop (or inside your browser). Active Server Pages, discussed in the next section, are one of the ways that fancier Web pages can be created on certain types of Web servers.

There are two primary differences between an Active Channel and a normal Web site:

- Channel content is sent to the user automatically, rather than requiring the user to come to it.

- Channel content can be sent to users on a schedule that ensures that they receive the latest version on either a regular basis or whenever the page content changes.

Active Channel Design

The following are typical types of information included in a Active Channel:

- Brand icons or logos to represent the channel in the channel bar.

- A site map detailing the content made available by the Active Channel.

- One or more Web pages, which may contain images, ActiveX controls, and scripting.

What types of Web pages are good candidates for becoming Active Channels? You might consider any pages that will frequently change and provide either general-purpose type of information or specialized information that users may repeatedly consult. Essentially, Active Channels save the user from needing to visit your site. Instead, the site (or at least portions of it) are delivered to the user.

Active Channels can be hosted on any Web server that supports the content types used by your channel Web pages. If you used streaming RealAudio, for instance, you still need the services of a RealAudio server. Similarly, if you mixed Active Server Pages (described next) into your channel content, you would need an Active Server Page-compatible Web server to host these pages.

TIP   Before designing your own Active Channel, you should check the latest information concerning the CDF file and then submit your channel to the Microsoft channel guide. Currently, you can find this information at http://www.microsoft.com/sbnmember/channels/channels.asp#logo.

Web Site-to-Active Channel Conversion

Here are the steps for converting an existing Web site into an Active Channel:

1. Create logo images that will be used in the Desktop and Explorer channel bars.

2. Create a CDF file, which lists the resources (logo files, descriptions, and Web pages) to be included in the channel. (There is a new Microsoft "Add Channel" logo and script that you can add to your page.)

3. Create a channel preview page for users to browse prior to subscribing to your channel.

4. Post the CDF file on your Web server and place a visible link to this CDF file on your page. When users click this link, your channel will be added to their channel selection bar and they will be prompted for a subscription option.

TIP   You can also submit your channel to the Microsoft Active Channel Guide Web page for inclusion in that online list of available channels. The URL for the English channels guide is currently http://www.iechannelguide.com/guide/en/en_us.asp.

Active Server Pages

Not to be confused with Active Channels or the Active Desktop, Active Server Pages are simply pages residing on a server. These pages have an .ASP extension (rather than .HTM or .HTML) and contain scripting and/or ActiveX controls that are executed *on the server*. Although somewhat similar to the idea of using CGI scripts, Active Server Pages allow code to be run as a service of the Web server and are optimized for multiple threads and multiple users.

One disadvantage to using Active Server Pages is that very few Web servers currently support it (Microsoft's IIS is one of the few). If it is not yet practical to set up your own Active Server Page-compatible Web server, you might want to use a Web-hosting service. A number of Internet service providers are currently providing Active Server Page Web hosting as a premium service (typically for an additional monthly fee).

For what it's worth, Active Server Pages currently seem to be Microsoft's preferred means of offering server-modified content. These days, ISAPI DLLs (if you remember them) have taken a backseat to the server scripting and ActiveX controls supported by Active Server Page technology.

Despite the dynamic activity and resulting state of flux with all things Internet-related, the topics covered here should whet your Internet programming appetite. As you can see, the Internet API and the ActiveX controls make many common Internet tasks practically child's play to implement. And for down-to-the-wire or high-performance-type applications (or for designing more portable Internet software), Winsock 2 provides all the functionality you need, with both synchronous and asynchronous sets of socket functions. With the introduction of Active Channels, the Active Desktop, and Active Server Pages comes more ways to tailor Web page content and delivery.

CHAPTER

TWENTY-TWO

Network Programming

- NetBIOS support implementation

- WNet API functions

- LANMan functions

- Winsock 2 for networking applications

- Named pipes and mailslots for networking

- An introduction to RPC and DCOM

As Windows has grown up, it has taken a variety of approaches toward network solutions. The good news is that much progress has been made. The not-so-good news is that it is not always obvious which APIs or technologies are best suited for a particular purpose.

Another unfortunate aspect to Windows network programming is that many of the APIs are not fully supported by Windows 98; full functionality is supported only on Windows NT (Workstation and Server versions). This applies in particular to the LANMan functions and to some degree to RPC (Remote Procedure Calls), pipes, and mailslots. Mailslots, for example, ignore security attributes under Windows 98; named pipes work only on the client side in Windows 98; and RPC is supported on Windows 98, however with fewer underlying protocol choices than are available on Windows NT. If you need networking support, and your application must run on Windows 98 (or earlier), your best bet is to use the Winsock API or DCOM/ActiveX controls. However, you may find that for certain networking projects, you will be better served by using Windows NT (excuse the weak pun).

In this chapter, we'll look at the various networking APIs and their relative merits. Then we'll go over some examples of using the Winsock API, pipes and mailslots, and RPC. The final sections provide an overview of DCOM and other networking technologies.

The NetBIOS Functions

NetBIOS has the distinction of being the only networking API function that was built into DOS. For programmers faced with porting old applications, which made use of NetBIOS DOS interrupt calls, to Win32, the `Netbios` API function can simplify the conversion process. Instead of calling the NetBIOS interrupt, you fill a Network Control Block (NCB) structure and pass a pointer to it in your call to the `Netbios` API.

However, except for the porting scenario, it is unlikely that you will want to use `Netbios` itself in your applications, since a richer set of functions is available via named pipes, RPC, WNet functions, or Winsock, all of which are explained in this chapter. For applications that will never need anything but NetBIOS support, and for programmers already very familiar with it, the `Netbios` API provides an efficient way to implement NetBIOS support.

Here's how the Netbios function is defined:

```
UCHAR Netbios
(
    PNCB   pncb      // address of network control block
);
```

The NCB structure is defined as follows:

```
typedef struct _NCB { // ncb
    UCHAR  ncb_command;
    UCHAR  ncb_retcode;
    UCHAR  ncb_lsn;
    UCHAR  ncb_num;
    PUCHAR ncb_buffer;
    WORD   ncb_length;
    UCHAR  ncb_callname[NCBNAMSZ];
    UCHAR  ncb_name[NCBNAMSZ];
    UCHAR  ncb_rto;
    UCHAR  ncb_sto;
    void (*ncb_post) (struct _NCB *);
    UCHAR  ncb_lana_num;
    UCHAR  ncb_cmd_cplt;
    UCHAR  ncb_reserve[10];
    HANDLE ncb_event;
} NCB;
```

The ncb_command field must always be set to one of the Netbios function values, which are listed in Table 22.1. ncb_length must always be set to the size of the NCB structure, and certain other fields must be set as appropriate for each function. Upon completion, Netbios returns the status code in ncb_retcode.

TABLE 22.1: NetBIOS Functions

Command	Description
NCBACTION	Enables extensions to the transport interface.
NCBADDGRNAME	Adds a group name to the local name table.
NCBADDNAME	Adds a unique name to the local name table.
NCBASTAT	Retrieves the status of the adapter.
NCBCALL	Opens a session with another name.

Continued on next page

TABLE 22.1 CONTINUED: NetBIOS Functions

Command	Description
NCBCANCEL	Cancels a previous command.
NCBCHAINSEND	Sends the contents of two data buffers to the specified session partner.
NCBCHAINSENDNA	Sends the contents of two data buffers to the specified session partner without waiting for acknowledgment.
NCBDELNAME	Deletes a name from the local name table.
NCBDGRECV	Receives a datagram from any name.
NCBDGRECVBC	Receives a broadcast datagram from any host.
NCBDGSEND	Sends a datagram to a specified name.
NCBDGSENDBC	Sends a broadcast datagram to every host on the LAN.
NCBENUM	Enumerates LAN adapter (LANA) numbers.
NCBFINDNAME	Determines the location of a name on the network.
NCBHANGUP	Closes a specified session.
NCBLANSTALERT	Notifies the user of LAN failures that last for more than one minute.
NCBLISTEN	Enables a session to be opened with another name.
NCBRECV	Receives data from the specified session partner.
NCBRECVANY	Receives data from any session corresponding to a specified name.
NCBRESET	Resets a LANA adapter.
NCBSEND	Sends data to the specified session partner.
NCBSENDNA	Sends data to specified session partner and does not wait for an acknowledgment.
NCBSSTAT	Retrieves the status of the session.
NCBTRACE	Activates or deactivates NCB tracing. Support for this command is optional and system-specific.
NCBUNLINK	Unlinks the adapter.

A few additions and enhancements have been made to the Netbios function for better integration into Windows programs. Functions can be executed asynchronously either by posting (using ncb_post) or by using signal-completion events (using ncb_event).

In the posting approach, the function specified in ncb_post takes only a single parameter, which (like Netbios) is a pointer to an NCB. This makes your implementation much more consistent and portable across different versions (or platforms) of Windows.

In the events approach, the ncb_event is set to the nonsignaled state when an asynchronous NetBIOS command is requested and is set to the signaled state when the command has completed.

The WNet API

The WNet functions, listed in Table 22.2, first appeared in Windows for Workgroups, primarily as a higher-level API. Occasionally, these functions, like the LANMan functions, provide an easier API for performing protocol-independent simple networking tasks. However, most (if not all) the functionality is duplicated (or expanded) in the other Win32 network APIs.

TABLE 22.2: WNet Functions

Function	Description
WNetAddConnection	Connects a local device to a network resource. This creates a persistent connection if successful. This command has been updated to WNetAddConnection2 and WNetAddConnection3.
WNetAddConnection2	More recent version that replaces WNetAddConnection.
WNetAddConnection3	Similar to WNetAddConnection2, but it also takes a handle to a window that the network provider can use as an owner window for dialog boxes.
WNetCancelConnection	Breaks an existing network connection. This command has been updated to WNetCancelConnection2.
WNetCancelConnection2	Replaces WNetCancelConnection. It removes persistent network connections that are not currently connected.

Continued on next page

TABLE 22.2 CONTINUED: WNet Functions

Function	Description
WNetCloseEnum	Ends a network-resource enumeration started by the **WNet-OpenEnum** function.
WNetConnectionDialog	Starts a general browsing dialog box for connecting to network resources.
WNetDisconnectDialog	Starts a general browsing dialog box for disconnecting from network resources.
WNetEnumResource	Continues a network-resource enumeration started by the **WNetOpenEnum** function.
WNetGetConnection	Retrieves the name of the network resource associated with a local device.
WNetGetLastError	Retrieves the most recent extended error code set by a Windows network function.
WNetGetUniversalName	Takes a drive-based path for a network resource and obtains a data structure that contains a more universal form of the name.
WNetGetUser	Retrieves the current default username or the username used to establish a network connection.
WNetOpenEnum	Starts an enumeration of network resources or existing connections.

WNet and Network Resources

In the WNet way of doing things, any network resource is represented by means
of a NETRESOURCE structure, which is defined as follows:

```
typedef struct _NETRESOURCE {
    DWORD   dwScope;
    DWORD   dwType;
    DWORD   dwDisplayType;
    DWORD   dwUsage;
    LPTSTR  lpLocalName;
    LPTSTR  lpRemoteName;
    LPTSTR  lpComment;
    LPTSTR  lpProvider;
} NETRESOURCE;
```

In its original form, the WNet API provided for displaying network dialog boxes that the user could use to browse network resources and connect or disconnect by using the mouse. Although the dialog boxes are still supported in Windows 98 (and Windows 95/NT), the functions that display them seem to have been phased out. The Win32 SDK documentation discourages using them, and new functions have been added to replace them and provide a similar yet expanded functionality. Win32 programs should make use of the WNetAdd-Connection2 API function, as shown in this sample program, discussed in a bit. However, you can still display browsable network connect and disconnect dialog boxes, using the WNetConnectionDialog and WNetDisconnectDialog functions, respectively.

The WNetDemo Demo: Mapping a Drive

The *WNet* demo is a simple Delphi program that uses the newer WNetAdd-Connection2 function to map a user-specified network drive to a specified local name.

> **NOTE**   The *WNet* demo is included on the CD accompanying this book, in the Chapter 22 folder. If you're building this example from scratch, just open a new project in Delphi 2, place a couple of edit fields onto your form, add a button, and then add the source code into your button's **buttonclick** method.

In the program, we begin by defining nr as a TNetResource (or NETRESOURCE in C/C++), followed by three string variables that will be used to hold any error message, plus the local and network resource names, as zero- (NULL) terminated strings.

```
var  nr: TNetResource;
     szErrorMessage, szLocalName, szRemoteName: ShortString;
```

Next, we set the hourglass cursor, and start by copying/converting the local and remote resource names (as entered by the end user), from the edit controls to the null-terminated string variables.

```
begin
  // Clear NetResource structure, load local and remote names.
  Cursor:= crHourGlass;
  Button1.Cursor:= Cursor;
  fillchar(nr, sizeof(nr), #0);
  strpcopy(@szLocalName, Edit2.Text);
  strpcopy(@szRemoteName, Edit1.Text);
```

Then, we fill in the NETRESOURCE fields, as required for a call to WNetAddConnect2. First, dwType is set to specify that we want to attach to a disk-type network device. The local and remote resource names are filled in, and the display type is set to "generic."

```
// Now, fill NetResource fields.
with nr do
begin
  dwType:= RESOURCETYPE_DISK;
  lpLocalName:= @szLocalName;
  lpRemoteName:= @szRemoteName;
end;
```

NOTE In Delphi, the @ symbol is equivalent to the address-of & symbol in C and C++.

Now the call to WNetAddConnection2 can be made. Note that parameters two and three could specify another username and password. This example simply uses NIL, which defaults to using the current user's password and name.

```
// Call WNetAddConnection2, using default username and password.
if (WNetAddConnection2( nr, NIL, NIL, 0) <> NO_ERROR) then
```

As with some of the C++ examples, if an error occurs, we use FormatMessage to retrieve the Win32 system error message corresponding to the return code provided by GetLastError. ShowMessage displays this message in a dialog box.

```
begin
// If any error occurred, retrieve system error text and display it.
FormatMessage( FORMAT_MESSAGE_FROM_SYSTEM, NIL, GetLastError,
  LANG_SYSTEM_DEFAULT, @szErrorMessage, sizeof(szErrorMessage), NIL);
ShowMessage('Error attempting connection: '+strpas(@szErrorMessage));
end
else
ShowMessage(Edit1.Text
 +' has been successfully connected and mapped to '+Edit2.Text);
```

Finally, we restore the hourglass cursor to the normal or default cursor. Note that because each object on the form can have its own cursor setting, we set both the form's cursor and the button's cursor, to make sure the user sees the cursor change when clicking the button.

```
Cursor:= crDefault;
Button1.Cursor:= Cursor;
```

That's it! These WNet functions are quite easy to use. You simply set and/or retrieve fields in a NETRESOURCE structure and let the function (or your end user!) make the desired connection.

The LANMan Functions

The LAN Manager API has been around since Microsoft's LAN Manager, predating Windows NT. The function set has been modified and expanded with each consecutive version of Windows NT. For the most part, these functions are duplicated in various other Win32 API functions, which often include additional features and parameters. For example, if you read the section on the security API in Chapter 20, you may have noticed that the user and group security functions provided in the LANMan function set are simpler to use, but leave out important aspects of Windows NT security. There are no parameters, for instance, which take the ACCESS_TOKEN or allow you to impersonate a user. On the other hand, if you do not need these aspects of security, you may want to take advantage of the LANMan functions' ease of use.

NOTE   You may be wondering (because of the functionality overlap with other parts of the API) whether the LANMan functions are on the way out. In fact, this does not appear to be the case. There is no mention in the SDK documentation of these functions being phased out. Moreover, a couple functions were even added in the Windows NT 4.0 release.

You might want to use these functions where convenient in smaller applications. But before you do, check if there is a better alternative provided elsewhere in the Win32 API; this will often be the case. Additionally, when you're implementing security, some things can only be done using the security API. For consistency, it is probably better to avoid mixing calls to both types of security functions in the same program.

If you decide to use the LANMan functions (which require Windows NT), keep in mind that, at least currently in Windows NT 4.0, the functions that use strings always use Unicode-style strings. You'll need to convert strings back and forth using the MultiByteToWideChar and related string-conversion functions.

The LANMan functions are not supported by Windows 98. In some cases, the function names are exported, but with empty functions which only return an error code. Other functions are simply not callable unless you're running the application on a Windows NT station. If you want more information about the LANMan functions, they're easy to find in the Win32 online help. Just look for functions beginning with "Net."

Winsock 2.0 for Network Programming

We discussed the Winsock 2.0 functions in Chapter 21, which covered Internet support. Here, we will look at this API from a network application point of view.

Although Winsock started life as a means of unifying different vendors' implementations of TCP/IP for the Windows platforms, one of the stated goals of the Winsock consortium was to make Winsock be protocol-independent. With Winsock 2.0, this has largely been accomplished. I say "largely" only because there are certain protocol-specific details you must still be aware of, although admittedly, these have to do with things such as dealing with different network address sizes, which differ among the different network protocols. Also, areas of functionality that are unique to certain protocols are supported by using Winsock's protocol-dependent constants and structures, typically defined in an extra protocol-specific header file.

In reality, Winsock 2.0 is probably as network-independent as you can get; that is, without taking some form of lowest-common-denominator approach. In each protocol, you communicate by sending and receiving data using the sockets model. Initializing and querying of protocol-specific information is done via common functions, but by making use of protocol-specific structures and settings. Additional protocol-specific functionality is accessed by using the `set-sockopt` "set socket option" function (as demonstrated in the *MacSock* demo).

TIP
Winsock version 1.1 shipped with Windows 95 and earlier versions of Windows NT. Winsock 2 ships with Windows 98 and NT 4.0, and is automatically upgraded in older Windows 95 installations by installation of the Windows 95 Service Pack or certain other upgrade files that are available for download via Microsoft's Web site (www.microsoft.com).

New Features of Winsock 2

New features of Winsock 2 include the following:

- Faster performance using overlapped I/O

- Protocol-independent multipoint/multicase support

- Quality of service (QoS)

- Simultaneous support for multiple network protocols

- Encrypted socket traffic via SSL (Secure Socket Layer) and PCT (Private Communication Technology)

Just as `CreateFile`, `ReadFile,` and `WriteFile` can be used to do overlapped (or asynchronous and concurrent) file or pipe I/O, Winsock sockets can also be read from and written to asynchronously, with (if you wish) multiple sockets transferring data simultaneously. This permits each socket to transfer data at its own rate of speed, unencumbered by any throughput problems on other network protocols or hardware connections.

The built-in protocols supported by Winsock 2 currently include TCP, UDP, NetWare IPX and SPX, NetBEUI (using NetBIOS), AppleTalk, and TP4. Support for additional protocols can be added by other vendors, who conform to Winsock's SPI (Service Provider's Interface) specification.

The transport protocol annex of Winsock 2 handles the area of additional protocol-specific functionality. The SPI allows network service providers to supply their own name space resolution code and supports simultaneous network communications via multiple protocols.

QoS is another 2.0 feature that allows applications to adjust for throughput speeds and connection quality, and to request changes in connection quality (such as by opening another ISDN channel when necessary).

During this last year, Winsock has also gained support for secure data transmission via encryption using protocols such as SSL and PCT. This means you can have your Internet application negotiate a secure connection to an SSL supporting Web server, and then retrieve data over a secure socket. In practice, SSL and PCT support in Winsock make heavy use of the `WSAIOCtrl` API function, and once the desired socket has been configured in this way and the secure connection has been established, encrypted data can be sent and received transparently by means of the various Winsock functions.

The MacSock Demo: Winsock 2 and AppleTalk

Chapter 21 included a couple of examples of using Winsock for TCP programming. Here, we'll go though a simple example of using the Winsock API to do AppleTalk programming. This example demonstrates how Winsock handles other protocols gracefully.

The *MacSock* demo is included on the CD that accompanies this book, in the Chapter 22 folder. You will need the AppleTalk protocol installed on a Windows NT system, plus one or more Macintosh computers on your network, in order to actually run the *MacSock* demo. If you don't have a Mac or an NT system, you can still follow along with the example to see how it works.

The demo simply creates an NBP (Name Binding Protocol) AppleTalk datagram socket, binds it to an AppleTalk address, then registers a network name on a specific AppleTalk zone.

As with some of the other examples, we use stream I/O to output program information to stdout. Thus, Iostream.H is included, as well as Winsock2.H (which replaces the older Winsock.H header file). Since this application uses the AppleTalk protocol, we also need to include the Atalkwsh.H header file, which defines AppleTalk-specific structures and constants.

```
#include <iostream.h>
#include <winsock2.h>
#include <atalkwsh.h> // Appletalk-specific definitions
```

This demo will insist on at least version 2.0 of Winsock. (At the time of this writing, the latest Winsock specification is actually version 2.2.)

```
const VERSION_MAJOR  =  2;  // Winsock version 2.0 required by this app.
const VERSION_MINOR  =  0;
```

Inside the main application function, we define the five variables that will be used:

iStatus The result (or error) status codes from the various Winsock functions.

SOCKET The AppleTalk socket that is created.

WSData A standard Winsock initialization structure.

SockAddr An AppleTalk-specific socket address structure.

RegName An AppleTalk-specific structure that is used for registering a name in a given zone on the network.

```
main (int argc, char *argv[])
{
    int        iStatus;   // Error result
    SOCKET     hSocket;   // the socket that is opened
    WSADATA    WSData;    // WinSock initialization structure

    SOCKADDR_AT          SockAddr; // AppleTalk address structure
    WSH_REGISTER_NAME    RegName;  // name registration structure
```

The WSAStartup call initializes Winsock and checks to be sure the Winsock version is 2.0 or later.

```
// Initialize Winsock API (require version 2.0 or later!)
if ( WSAStartup(MAKEWORD(VERSION_MAJOR, VERSION_MINOR), &WSData) )
{
    cout << "Cannot find Winsock version ";
    cout << VERSION_MAJOR << "." << VERSION_MINOR << " or later!\n";
    return(1);
}
```

Next, we attempt to open an AppleTalk NBP datagram socket. Note that the protocol family specifier is set to PF_APPLETALK. We flush the output stream after each section to ensure that the status is visible at each point in the program; otherwise, all the text written to stdout would be buffered until the end of the program.

```
cout << "Attempting to open AppleTalk socket: ";

// Open an AppleTalk NBP datagram socket.
hSocket = socket(PF_APPLETALK, SOCK_DGRAM, DDPPROTO_NBP);
if ( iStatus == SOCKET_ERROR )
{
    cout << "Failed - " << WSAGetLastError() << endl;
    goto Cleanup;
}
else
    cout << "Success!\n";
cout << flush;
```

NOTE   Er... is that a *label* I used, in the event of an error? Yes, indeed it is. I've come to the conclusion this actually makes the code easier to read, in this particular case. My philosophy on using labels has mutated slightly over the years. I used to go to great lengths never to use a single label, but I now find on rare occasions that a single label can sometimes simplify code that needs to perform cleanup duties that are performed within the same function.

Assuming that we've successfully opened a socket, the next step is to prepare a SockAddr structure (remember, this is an AppleTalk-specific socket address structure). If you're testing this application on a large AppleTalk network, you may need to set the network and node numbers to something more specific than zero.

```
// Prepare SockAddr strucure to bind to the socket.
SockAddr.sat_family = PF_APPLETALK;   // AppleTalk family
SockAddr.sat_net    = 0;              // network number–SET THIS!
SockAddr.sat_node   = 0;              // the node number
SockAddr.sat_socket = hSocket;        // the AppleTalk socket
```

Next, we need to bind the socket to the address specified in our SockAddr structure. Note that the third parameter to bind specifies the size of SockAddr, which in this case will be different than a "normal" TCP address structure. In a similar way, if you were binding to an IPX socket, you would use a different-sized address structure that is unique to IPX.

```
cout << "Attempting to bind address to socket: ";

// Attempt to bind address to socket.
iStatus = bind( hSocket, (LPSOCKADDR)&SockAddr, sizeof(SockAddr));
if ( iStatus == SOCKET_ERROR )
{
   cout << "Failed - " << WSAGetLastError() << endl;
   goto Cleanup;
}
else
   cout << "Success!\n";
cout << flush;
```

Now the RegName structure is filled with an object name, type name, and zone name. The object name and type can be what you want, but you will need to set the zone name to a valid zone on your AppleTalk network if you are actually running this application. Each corresponding string-length field also must be set accordingly.

```
// Prepare RegName structure for registering our name on the network.

// Set name strings.
strcpy(RegName.ObjectName, "MacSock Server"); // name on network
strcpy(RegName.TypeName,   "Winsock2 Type");  // name type
strcpy(RegName.ZoneName,   "Granny Smith");   // zone name
```

```
// Set corresponding string lengths in RegName structure.
RegName.ObjectNameLen   = strlen(RegName.ObjectName);
RegName.TypeNameLen     = strlen(RegName.TypeName);
RegName.ZoneNameLen     = strlen(RegName.ZoneName);
```

At this point, we use the Winsock `setsockopt` call to register our name on the specified AppleTalk zone. The second parameter specifies that the option we're requesting is part of the "AppleTalk level," and the third parameter specifies that we want the "register name" option. Parameter four is a pointer to our option structure. The fifth parameter specifies the size of this structure.

Incidentally, this function call may take as long as ten seconds (or perhaps even longer) to execute, so be patient!

```
cout << "Attempting to register name: " << flush;

// Attempt to register name.
iStatus = setsockopt(
    hSocket,                     // Appletalk socket
    SOL_APPLETALK,               // option level
    SO_REGISTER_NAME,            // option value requested
    (char *)&RegName,            // pointer to option buffer
    sizeof(WSH_REGISTER_NAME)    // size of option request buffer
);
if ( iStatus == SOCKET_ERROR )
    cout << "Failed - " << WSAGetLastError() << endl;
else
    cout << "Success!\n";
cout << flush;
```

At this point, we can close the socket and call `WSACleanup` to tell Winsock we're finished.

```
Cleanup:

    closesocket( hSocket );
    WSACleanup();

    return 0;
}
```

That's it, as far as this example goes. In "real life," you would obviously proceed to do something on the network—as either a client or a server (or perhaps both). You should get a successful return code when registering the name, but instead of exiting immediately, you would go onto do something else, then eventually deregister your name when finished, and finally exit.

Because Winsock 2 not only supports other protocols, but also supports using multiple protocols in the same application simultaneously, you could create a server application that serves Apple, NetWare, and TCP/IP clients, perhaps using some new user-level protocol you've devised. Or, you could use Winsock to build a software router, reading stream or datagram data from one network type, and forwarding it over a second protocol. Depending on the combination of protocols used, however, this could mean needing to convert different-sized data packets that would require using an intermediate packet-repackaging strategy.

Named Pipes and Mailslots for Network Programming

Named pipes, and their cousins the mailslots, initially made their appearance in OS/2, and they continue to be an excellent high-level means of passing data and messages between Windows NT stations connected on a network. Mailslots and named pipes are similar in the way that they are created, read from, and written to. They differ in the respect that mailslots are one-way and connectionless; named pipes can be two-way and require that a connection be established on each end prior to use. If you're familiar with TCP/IP, mailslots are analogous to UDP—both are used for connectionless, datagram transfers. Named pipes are analogous to TCP—both of these are used for connection-oriented messages or stream I/O.

One drawback to using named pipes is that currently Windows 98 (and Windows 95 and Windows for Workgroups) supports only client-side pipes. This means that any server applications you write that use named pipes must run on a Windows NT workstation or server. Windows 98 does support mailslots; however, the security descriptor parameter is ignored unless your software is run on a Windows NT station.

Another drawback is that pipe and mailslot communications are only as dependable as the network protocol that is being used to support them. In most cases, this should not be a problem, but for transferring very large amounts of data completely error-free, the Win32 file-system functions, for example, would provide better data integrity.

On the other hand, there are several benefits to using pipes and mailslots: They are easy to implement, protocol-independent, and can transfer data asynchronously using overlapped I/O. Because they are implemented as devices in the operating system, they can also be used to redirect I/O to or from other devices, either locally or across a network.

> **NOTE**
>
> There are also unnamed (or anonymous) pipes, which work very much like named pipes and can be used for interprocess and interapplication communication on the same workstation. Anonymous pipes are supported by Windows 98. They differ from named pipes in that they can only be read from and written to locally on the station that creates them. Use the `CreatePipe` function to create an anonymous pipe. See Chapter 15 for details.

Pipes and mailslots are discussed in Chapter 15, and the functions that are pertinent to creating and using pipes are listed in that chapter. Table 22.3 lists the Win32 API functions related to mailslots and I/O functions supporting pipes and mailslots.

TABLE 22.3: Mailslot-Specific Functions and I/O Functions Supporting Pipes and Mailslots

Function	Description
CreateMailslot	Creates and returns a handle to a mailslot with the specified name.
GetMailslotInfo	Retrieves information about the specified mailslot.
SetMailslotInfo	Sets the time-out value used for read operations on the specified mailslot.
CreateFile	Creates a pipe or mailslot.
ReadFile	Reads from a pipe or mailslot.
WriteFile	Writes to a pipe or mailslot.
ReadFileEx	Allows overlapped (asynchronous) reading from a pipe or mailslot.
WriteFileEx	Allows overlapped (asynchronous) writing to a pipe or mailslot.
CloseHandle	Closes a handle to a pipe or mailslot.

Remote Procedure Calls

Remote Procedure Calls (RPC) provides a mechanism that makes it possible for programs or code located on one computer to call functions and procedures located on another computer, and to do so in a way that makes the calling syntax exactly like calling procedures located in a standard DLL on the local station.

With the debut of DCOM in Windows NT 4.0 and now also in Windows 98, RPC is taking on significance not only in its own right, but also because it is the means used by Microsoft to make the Windows implementation of COM (Component Object Model) work remotely across networks (called DCOM). In other words, it is worth your while to learn RPC, not only to be able to make remote procedure calls, but also to be able to make and access remote *objects*.

The RPC "glue" implemented in Windows 98 conforms to the Open Software Foundation (OSF) specifications. This means that conforming to RPC (or DCOM) in your application ensures that functions you call can be located on a remote computer running a completely different operating system or, conversely, that procedures or object methods you've implemented on Windows 98 (or Windows 95 or NT) can be accessed by applications running on other operating systems—even using different bit-size hardware or a different byte-ordering scheme.

Along with these benefits, as you might guess, comes a measure of added complexity. Although implementing RPC and DCOM has gotten somewhat easier with recent compiler tools, understanding how these technologies work is still more difficult than perhaps it should be. In any case, we will see how RPC and DCOM work, and show you how to get started with implementing these technologies into your applications.

As mentioned earlier in this chapter, certain aspects of the networking APIs are not as fully implemented in Windows 98. As with other forms of networking communications, this affects RPC in the sense that although you can create RPC clients and servers for Windows 98, you cannot add the same level of security to RPC servers as you could when the servers are running on Windows NT. Additionally, there are certain network-transport mechanisms that are fine for RPC use but are only supported client-side for Windows 98 (named pipes are an example).

Thus, although it is possible to write an application that functions as an RPC server and have it run on Windows 98, the lesser security and fewer number of server-transport choices available may make you think twice about the utility of doing so.

RPC Concepts

Before going into the details of what you'll need to use RPC, you should understand some RPC-related concepts and terms. These include UUID, GUID, interface class, and marshaling. We touched on these topics in Chapter 16, in a brief overview of the COM. Here, we will go into a bit more detail relating to how these concepts apply to networking applications.

UUIDs and GUIDs

A UUID is a *universally unique identifier*, also known as a *globally unique identifier*, or GUID. In Window systems, a UUID or GUID is used to ensure that RPC *interfaces* and COM *classes* are absolutely, positively guaranteed to have a unique identifier entry in the system registry. (The system registry, among other things, maintains settings information for each interface and class that is registered with the system.)

UUIDs or GUIDs are guaranteed to be unique, provided all RPC and (D)COM programmers abide by two simple rules:

- Every interface and class must be assigned a separate and unique UUID. This UUID is always a 128-bit (16 byte) value, which you can produce either by running a program such as UUIDGEN or GUIDGEN, or by submitting a request to Microsoft for a "block of UUIDs." (Microsoft usually responds to such a request quickly, and you typically get a block of 100 UUIDs via e-mail or floppy.)

- Anytime you change an interface definition (or a COM or DCOM class), you must leave the old interface intact and define a new interface with a new UUID.

Provided every programmer follows these rules, UUIDs or GUIDs are extremely unlikely to conflict in the registry. This is good, because the Windows system registry would become very confused if two or more interfaces (or classes) tried to refer to themselves using the same identifier.

NOTE In case you're wondering, the UUIDs are generated via an algorithm that mixes together the address of your Ethernet network adapter (which for other reasons, is also supposed to be completely unique; every network card manufacturer is assigned a different range of such addresses to draw from), plus system information. This algorithm produces a number that is extremely unlikely to ever occur twice on either the same or different machines.

Interface Classes

An RPC/COM interface is a group of one or more related functions. RPC applications usually have only a single interface, although they could have more. COM classes also have at least one interface, and they most frequently have at least two or three. Again, each interface is one group of one or more related functions.

Each interface can have a string name as well as the UUID. The string name you assign an interface is not nearly as important as the unique UUID that you give it. However, to keep things simple, you should try to assign descriptive string names for your interfaces as well as unique UUIDs.

For example, if you needed to implement an RPC server that could execute a set of mathematical functions and also some string-manipulation functions, you might implement a `mymath` interface and a `mystring` interface. In this case, the client RPC application would then use either the `mymath` interface to access your math functions or the `mystring` interface to access your string functions. An application can certainly use both interfaces, but each interface can only be used to access functions that are part of that particular interface.

Marshaling Code

The way RPC differs from local procedure calling is primarily in the extra steps that are required to package (and unpack) the function parameters so they can be shipped across the network each time a function is called. At runtime, these parameter-handling steps are performed by a set of functions that have been linked into your client (or server) application. These functions know all about the function prototypes being called and how to pack and unpack the parameters correctly. This process of packaging and unpackaging function parameters for transport across the network is called *marshaling*. As you'll see, much of the work involved in implementing RPC has to do with the steps required to create the marshaling code stubs that are linked into your application.

Marshaling includes taking care of pointer and string parameters so that they work as expected on both ends. If you think about it, passing a pointer to a string across a network means that the string itself needs to be sent across the network. A new chunk of RAM must be allocated for the string on the other computer, the string contents need to be copied into this new RAM, and a new pointer variable must be created. This pointer variable has the same data type as the original pointer, but points to this new string copy. If this pointer-to-a-string parameter is defined in our IDL files as an `[in, out]` parameter (as described , shortly), then the string-copy process needs to happen a second time, to send the (presumably) modified string back to the original client program. Finally, marshalling code on the client side needs to copy this version of the pointed-to string back into the original string pointed to by the client's string pointer.

As you can see, RPC (and for the same reason, COM and DCOM) completely changes the normal perception of pointers as a very efficient way to pass parameters. When sent remotely, pointers are actually very inefficient! But the bit of time and network traffic eaten up by passing this parameter (and copying it) are the price for the flexibility and power that remote procedure calling (and DCOM) provide.

TIP It is still best to take more than the normal care when designing functions that will be called over RPC. Engineer them for efficient parameter passing across the network. In addition to decreasing the amount of data passed in parameters, you should also look for opportunities to reduce the number of times individual functions are called. This may mean packing several function calls together into one function, perhaps passing an array or structure of parameters, rather than using more function calls using fewer parameters.

The RPC Network Connection

The actual network connection required for making RPC calls is determined by either making an explicit choice of a networking protocol in your software (which must be consistent on both the client and server sides), or else by allowing the computer to search the network namespace for the required server and protocol, and connecting accordingly. There are several things to note here:

- Because the name space is not maintained by Windows 98 stations, if you wish to go this route, you will either need to run the server side of your application on a Windows NT machine or else at least to configure the Windows 98 station to use a Windows NT station for its name space server.

- Although RPC servers can be run on Windows 98, you must take care not to specify a protocol that requires Windows NT in order to function in a server capacity. For example, creating a server-side named pipe requires Windows NT (although a Windows 98 system can connect to and communicate with such a server-side pipe as a client).

One benefit to using the name-space approach is that locations (and protocols) do not need to be hard-coded into your program, and thus both client and server RPC software can more easily be moved from one machine to another. Disadvantages of using the name-space approach are its somewhat greater complexity, that the search itself is initiated somewhat differently between Windows NT and Windows 98, and that under certain conditions you may need to specify which domain to search in. Also, the search itself can take time, causing an irritating delay as your program attempts to connect. This is especially true when you do not specify particular protocols and the connection process proceeds to cycle through all the installed protocols.

Compiler Preparations for RPC and DCOM

If you do not currently have tools configured in your compiler/editor environment for generating UUIDs, compiling IDL files, and registering .REG files, you may find the going a bit easier if you following the procedures presented here to add these tools to your Tools menu. These specific procedures are the steps needed for adding the tool entries to Visual C++ version 4.x.

If you're using a different vendor's compiler that also supports adding custom tool entries, you should not have any trouble adapting these steps to what works for your IDE. For Borland C++ 4.x or 5.0 users, we first go over the general steps required to add a tool.

Adding a Tool in Borland C++

Here are the basic steps for adding a custom tool to the Borland compiler's Tools menu:

1. From the main IDE menu, select Options.

2. Select Tools to bring up a Tools dialog box.

3. Click the New button.

4. Enter the path, program name, and command-line arguments in the corresponding fields.

5. Enter a descriptive name for the tool in the Menu Text field.

6. When you're finished, click the OK button. This should add the new tool to your Tools menu.

Adding a "Generate UUID" Tool in VC++

Here are the steps for adding a tool for generating UUIDs in Visual C++:

1. From the main menu, select Tools.

2. Select Customize to bring up a Customize dialog box.

3. Click the Tools tab.

4. Click the Add button.

5. When it asks for the command, enter **UUIDGEN**.

NOTE If you have Borland's tools, you may prefer to use the GUIDGEN tool, which has a graphical interface. If so, just make sure GUIDGEN.EXE is in your path, and then enter it as the command. Then click the OK button.

---

6. For UUIDGEN (or GUIDGEN), no command-line arguments are needed. Otherwise, you would enter these in the Arguments field.

7. In the Menu Text field, enter **Generate UUID**.

8. If you are using UUIDGEN, place a check in the checkbox labeled Redirect to Output Window. (If using GUIDGEN, this option should not be available.)

9. The new tool should now be installed. Leave the Tools dialog box open, so you can add the other two tools, as described next.

Adding a Compile IDL File Tool in VC++

Assuming you've just added the UUID tool, you should still have the Customize/ Tools tabbed dialog box open. If not, follow steps 1 through 3 in the previous section. Then continue as follows:

1. Click the Add button.

2. Enter **MIDL** as the command. If you don't have a path to it, add the complete path. A typical installation directory you may find it in would be C:\MSDEV\BIN\.

NOTE The MIDL.EXE program is Microsoft's IDL compiler. It is called a compiler, although it would probably be more accurately called a translator, since it outputs an .H and two .C files.

---

3. In the Arguments field, enter:

   ```
   -ms_ext -char unsigned  -env win32 -c_ext $(FileName)$(FileExt)
   ```

4. In the Initial Directory field, enter:

   ```
   $(FileDir)
   ```

5. For Menu Text, enter:

   ```
   Compile IDL file
   ```

6. Place a check in the checkbox labeled Redirect to Output Window.

Adding a Register .REG File Tool in VC++

You should still have the Customize/Tools tabbed dialog box opened. If not, repeat steps 1 through 3 in the section titled "Adding a Generate UUID Tool in VC++." Then continue as follows:

1. Click the Add button.

2. Enter **REGEDIT** as the command. Note that you should not need to add a path to this, because it should be located in your \WINDOWS directory (or in \WINNT for Windows NT).

3. In the Arguments field, enter the following:

   ```
   -s $(FileName)$(FileExt)
   ```

4. In the Initial Directory field, enter:

   ```
   $(FileDir)
   ```

5. For Menu Text, enter:

   ```
   Register .REG File
   ```

6. Click the Close button at the bottom of the Customize dialog box.

At this point, all three tools should be added and should be visible from your Tools menu. These will come in handy when you are writing RPC, COM, ActiveX, or DCOM applications.

NOTE

For the sample RPC program, the registry tool is not used. You may decide to postpone installing it, although it will still be useful in other projects.

The next sections describe how to create each of the files needed to build the RPC client and server applications.

Mathlib.CPP: A Function Library

Before you can write an application that uses RPC, you need to come up with the set of functions that will be called remotely. These do not need to be in a separate file, but it is very wise to set them up that way. This lets you test and debug the functions in a "normal" program, before you begin implementing the RPC portions of your client and server programs.

The *RPC* demo applications discussed a little later in this chapter use a very simplistic set of math functions. These are placed in a separate source file, which is named Mathlib.CPP.

> **NOTE**
>
> Obviously, the small amount of work these simple math functions do wouldn't justify the overhead of using RPC. But in choosing the functions for this demo, my goal was to keep them as simple as possible, yet still include both passing and receiving of integer values, and sending and receiving of strings.

The first thing to note about the math library is that it includes the Rpc.H header file. Initially when debugging your functions, you may want to comment this out, because you'll presumably be statically linking the functions to your test program.

The Mathlib.H header file bears mention also. Initially, you will want this to be a normal function prototype header file, which you can easily make just as you would any other normal header file. (By simply copying the function header from your source file and placing semicolons at the end of each.) Once you've verified that each function works correctly, you will want to rename this header file to get it out of the way, since one of the steps to building an RPC application results in generating a new header file for this set of functions. However, it's a good idea to save your "normal" header file, in case you need to do further debugging down the road.

```
#include <iostream.h>
#include <rpc.h>
#include "mathlib.h"
```

The first of the functions declared simply prints to standard output the client name that is passed to it. Remember that eventually these functions will execute on the RPC server, so the client will call SendClientName, passing a string, and the server will actually execute the call.

```
void SendClientName( char *pszClientName )
{
    cout << endl << "Client: " << pszClientName << endl;
    cout << flush;
}
```

As with previous applications, the output stream is flushed here, because otherwise you would not see the display update immediately as each function is called.

The next function returns a string back to the calling program. Again, this will be the RPC client application, although the function will actually execute on the server.

```
char *GetMathServerName( void  )
{
    static char szServerName[64];

    strcpy( szServerName, "Name of Server" );

    return szServerName;
}
```

Next, we have the four math functions, which each take two long integers, perform a simple calculation with them, and return a long result value back to the calling program. These examples are simple, but you can make your RPC functions perform as much complex number crunching (or other processing) as you wish. Perhaps the server machine will have a coprocessor, or multiple CPUs, or MMX support, which the client machine can take advantage of by offloading to it the most CPU-intensive functions.

```
long Add(long lNum1, long lNum2)
{
    cout << "Call to Add(" << lNum1 << ", " << lNum2 << ")\n";
    cout << flush;

    return( lNum1 + lNum2 );
}
```

```
long Subtract(long lNum1, long lNum2)
{
    cout << "Call to Subtract(" << lNum1 << ", " << lNum2 << ")\n";
    cout << flush;

    return( lNum1 - lNum2 );
}

long Multiply(long lNum1, long lNum2)
{
    cout << "Call to Multiply(" << lNum1 << ", " << lNum2 << ")\n";
    cout << flush;

    return( lNum1 * lNum2 );
}

long Divide(long lNum1, long lNum2)
{
    cout << "Call to Divide(" << lNum1 << ", " << lNum2 << ")\n";
    cout << flush;

    return( lNum1 / lNum2 );
}
```

Incidentally, another thing this demo does that you may want to avoid in a real application is update the display in each function call. In real applications, at least when your functions are likely to get called many times, it might make sense to move any function-related display updating to a different thread (or eliminate it altogether). Anything that can be done to increase the speed of your function execution will allow the function result to be returned back to the calling program that much sooner.

This completes the file that defines the functions that will ultimately get called via RPC. Again, for testing and debugging, execution profiling, and other maintenance, you will usually find it much easier to prepare a normal header file and call these functions directly, without further complicating things by using RPC. Once your functions are working to your satisfaction, you can switch back to using RPC quite easily. In fact, you may want to use your RPC client application as the test program that calls your functions statically in "test" mode, and via RPC in "deployment" mode.

Mathlib.IDL: The IDL Function Interface Definition

In order to create the code that will "know" how to properly pack and unpack the function parameters (which then get sent over the network), it is necessary to create an IDL file. The IDL file gets its name from the abbreviation for the Interface Definition Language, which it is written in. Why do these functions need to be declared using IDL rather than C or C++? Well, one answer is, that's what the OSF stipulates in its distributed-computing specifications. Another answer is that perhaps a bit more information is needed to be known about each function than C or C++ normally provides. In fact, if you look at an IDL file, it rather closely resembles C function prototypes, but with the addition of zero, one, or more attributes enclosed inside square brackets, which precede various function parameters and return values. These attributes most frequently simply identify whether the parameter is an input and/or output parameter:

- An input parameter is signified by [in].

- An output parameter is signified [out].

- A parameter that is passed in and is modified is signified by [in, out].

The attribute information might also include additional data-typing information, as we'll see with the string parameters in our example.

Furthermore, starting out the IDL file is a header that includes a UUID. In the case of our Mathlib example, the corresponding IDL file starts with a header that looks like this:

```
[
uuid (E1CA13A0-388B-11d0-B0C6-0000C0FBDC5A),
version(1.0),
pointer_default(unique)
]
```

The blank space (and blank lines) between the various parts enclosed between the square brackets is optional, but typically is used to make the header more human-readable.

At this point, if your compiler IDL tool is configured as described in the previous sections (and if you have a network adapter installed), you should be able to go to your Tools menu, select the Generate GUID option, and have a new GUID appear. Each time you do this, note that a somewhat different identifier appears. This is how you generate new interface and class GUIDs.

NOTE The number in brackets after the uuid was created by my copy of GUIDGEN, running on my computer. So if you compile the *RPC* demo programs here and change anything, go ahead and generate a new GUID and replace mine with yours each place it appears in all the files discussed in this section. Don't worry—it doesn't appear in too many places, although references to it are used more often.

The second part of the Mathlib.IDL file is the interface definition. Again, this looks very much like a C++ class definition, except that you'll notice there are square brackets containing *attribute* information, preceding certain parameters or variables. The [unique, string], for example, makes it clear that the Get-MathServerName function returns a string type, and that the string value is to be treated as a unique value (not copied into a string-duplicates table that replaces identical strings with duplicate references, for example). The [in, string] makes it clear that the parameter being passed to SendClientName is a string and can be ignored after the function executes. If it included the out attribute, additional code would be generated that would copy the string back again after the function executed, and then send that string value back to the client. (If you're wondering *who* is generating *what* code, we'll get to that shortly.)

```
interface mathlib
{
    [unique, string] char *GetMathServerName ( void );
    void   SendClientName ( [in, string] char *string );
    long   Add            ( long lNum1, long lNum2 );
    long   Subtract       ( long lNum1, long lNum2 );
    long   Multiply       ( long lNum1, long lNum2 );
    long   Divide         ( long lNum1, long lNum2 );
}
```

The MIDL compiler will use the Mathlib.IDL file to create Mathlib.H and a marshaling stub file for the RPC server and client applications. But before we can use Mathlib.IDL, we need to also create a file called Mathlib.ACF, which is what we'll do next.

Mathlib.ACF: The Marshaling Interface Handle File

The next thing we need to do is create a marshaling interface handle file. For our example, we'll use an automatic interface handle. You could define your own interface handle, but this would require that you write your own marshaling code as well. Since we are using "standard" data types, we can use automatic marshaling for this project, and our .ACF file should contain the following interface handle declaration:

```
[auto_handle]
interface mathlib
{
}
```

If we were planning to support multiple RPC interfaces in our project, we would need to add multiple interface declarations, rather than just the mathlib one we've declared in this file.

Mathlib.H, Mathlib_c.C, and Mathlib_s.C

Armed with the Mathlib.IDL and Mathlib.ACF, plus our MIDL Tool entry, we are now ready to "compile" the mathlib interface definition to produce an RPC header file and client and server proxy stubs.

Assuming there are no typos in either the Mathlib.IDL or Mathlib.ACF file, you should be able to do this easily. Open the Mathlib.IDL file in your C++ IDE and, make sure it's the selected window. Then choose the Compile IDL File from the Tools menu. If all goes well, you should get three new files:

> **Mathlib.H**   An "RPC-icized" header file that the RPC client and server applications will need to include
>
> **Mathlib_c.C**   The client proxy stub that needs to be added to the RPC client application
>
> **Mathlib_s.C**   The server proxy stub that needs to be included in the RPC server project

The Mathlib_c.C and Mathlib_s.C files contain the code that makes the RPC mechanism properly handle the parameters being sent out and received back in each function call. When the client and server applications link with these files, they think the function is being linked locally, but in reality, hooks to the RPC mechanism are set up to be invoked to process each function call at runtime. Note that outside of adding __RPC_x entries to type the arguments and return values in some of the functions, the header file looks pretty much like a normal header file would.

The client and server proxy stubs are lengthier. You can look at those listings (included on the CD that accompanies this book) or generate the code with the MIDL compiler to see the proxy stub code. Fortunately, it's not necessary to understand this code in order to compile and link it into your client and server application projects.

> **NOTE**   The *RPC* demos are included on the CD that accompanies this book, in the Chapter 22 folder. The RPC client application will run on Windows 98. However, the RPC server, should be run on Windows NT because it uses named pipes for communicating.

The RPClient Demo: A Client Application

The next step in putting together this RPC project is to write the RPC client application. This is reasonably straightforward, although there are a few items for you to note.

> **NOTE**   The *RPClient* demo is included on the CD that accompanies this book in the Chapter 22 folder.

First, we include the Mathlib.H file, which was generated by compiling the .IDL file. The project file does *not* include the Mathlib.CPP file but does need to include the Mathlib_c.C file (which essentially fools the compiler into thinking we're linking to these functions locally).

```
#include <iostream.h>
#include <rpc.h>
#include "..\mathlib.h"
```

Another thing we need to do in both the client and server applications is define a pair of memory allocation and freeing functions, which will be called at runtime by the RPC mechanism when it needs to create local storage for parameters. This is how the RAM pointed to by the RPC pointer copies can have valid addresses inside the client (or server) processes. It actually *is* allocated by the process whenever RPC makes the allocation or deallocation calls.

```
void __RPC_FAR *__RPC_API midl_user_allocate( size_t len )
{
    return( malloc(len) );
}

void __RPC_API midl_user_free( void __RPC_FAR *ptr )
{
    free( ptr );
}
```

The __RPC_API, __RPC_FAR, and _CRTAPI1 should be included just as they are here, although, oddly when you look these up in the Rpc.H header file, it appears that they are defined to nothing. Nevertheless, the use of these in the SDK examples suggests that it is wise to follow their lead for future and/or backward compatibility.

```
void _CRTAPI1 main(void)
{
    int a = 100;
    int b =  25;
```

Inside the main function, the a and b variables are defined and initialized. These will be the two integer parameters in calls to the RPC server Mathlib functions.

Next, we have what looks like the start of exception-handling code, except we use RpcTryExcept. This is exception handling, but done RPC style.

WARNING   Exception handling is optional in standard C++ Win32 programs, but it is *mandatory* in RPC client programs. Leave out RpcTryExcept, and you won't have a working RPC application.

RpcTryExcept

```
SendClientName( "Client's name" );
cout << "Connected to Math Server " << GetMathServerName() << ".\n";

cout << a << " plus       " << b << " = " << Add(a, b) << endl;
cout << a << " minus      " << b << " = " << Subtract(a, b) << "\n";
cout << a << " times      " << b << " = " << Multiply(a, b) << "\n";
cout << a << " divided by " << b << " = " << Divide(a, b) << "\n";
```

After the `RpcTryExcept`, the client application tries out each of the `mathlib` interface's functions, displaying the results of each call. If any RPC runtime exceptions occur, they will be handled by the code after `RpcExcept`, which simply displays an error message in this example.

```
RpcExcept(1)

    cout << "RPC Runtime error occurred.\n";

RpcEndExcept
}
```

Finally, `RpcEndExcept` ends the exception handling, and the client RPC program terminates.

TIP   For debugging purposes, you may want to make a DebugRpc.H header file, which defines the RPC exception handling as empty macros. If you then add the Mathlib.CPP source into the client project and temporarily remove the Mathlib_c.C file from the project, the resulting application will let you run, test, and debug the functions locally.

The RPCServ Demo: A Server Application

 The last source file that must be written is the RPC server. This program may strike you as rather odd, in that apparently, nowhere are any of the Mathlib functions being called.

NOTE   The *RPCServ* demo is included on the CD that accompanies this book in the Chapter 22 folder.

Actually, the server application's primary duties are to register its existence with the RPC mechanism, specify what network protocol(s) it will use to listen on, and then wait around for clients to connect and make RPC calls. The actual calls are then intercepted via the RPC mechanism, which causes the Mathlib functions exported by the server application to be called.

```
#include <iostream.h>
#include <rpc.h>
#include "..\mathlib.h"
```

```
void _CRTAPI1 main(int argc, char *argv[])
{
   RPC_STATUS            status;
   RPC_BINDING_VECTOR    *pBindingVector;
```

As with the client application, we include Iostream.H and Rpc.H header files, plus the Mathlib.H header file, which was generated via the MIDL compiler. The RPC_BINDING_VECTOR can be thought of as a table of function pointers to all the functions defined in the `mathlib` interface. However `pBindingVector` will not be initialized until several steps into our program.

```
UCHAR *pszProtocolSequence = (UCHAR *) "ncacn_np";
WORD   wMinCalls           = 1;
WORD   wMaxCalls           = 30;
UCHAR *pszEndPoint         = (UCHAR *) "\\pipe\\auto";
WORD   fWaitFlag           = FALSE;
UCHAR *pszEntryName        = (UCHAR *) "/.:/Autohandle_mathlib";
```

The `pszProtocolSequence` variable specifies that named pipes are the method this RPC server will use to accept RPC client calls. The `wMinCalls` and `wMaxCalls` specify the minimum and maximum simultaneous calls this server will handle. The `pszEndPoint` variable specifies the name of the pipe used to listen for client calls, which uses the named pipe of `auto` for automatic marshaling.

The `fWaitFlag` will be used to tell RPC not to let this server terminate, but to wait, listening for client calls. The `pszEntryName` variable contains the name server entry which the `mathlib` interface will be registered as, so that it can be located by name.

The first RPC function is a call to `RpcServerUseProtseqEp`, which in unabbreviated form means "use specified protocol sequence and endpoint" for incoming RPC calls. So in this case, we're specifying that we want a named pipe for clients to connect through.

```
status = RpcServerUseProtseqEp(
        pszProtocolSequence,    // protocol sequence
        wMaxCalls,              // maximum concurrent calls
        pszEndPoint,            // end point (using pipe)
        NULL );                 // security (default used)

if (status)
{
   cout << "error "<< status << " setting endpoint!\n";
   exit;
}
```

Next, we need to register the `mathlib` interface via a call to `RpcServer-RegisterIf`. The first parameter is the interface ID defined by the MIDL compiler. The `NULL` second parameter specifies to use a nil-type manager UUID. This and the `NULL` third parameter sets the server to use the default manager and entry-point vector as generated by our MIDL-compiled proxy stub.

```
status = RpcServerRegisterIf(
   mathlib_v1_0_s_ifspec,   // Interface
   NULL,                    // Default/nil MgrTypeUUID
   NULL );                  // MIDL-generated Entry-point vector

if (status)
{
   cout << "error "<< status << " registering server!\n";
   exit;
}
```

Then we request a pointer to the binding handles (vector table), through which RPC calls can be received.

```
status = RpcServerInqBindings( &pBindingVector );

if (status)
{
   cout << "error "<< status << " retrieving bindings!\n";
   exit;
}
```

The final preparatory function we need to call is `RpcNsBindingExport`, which establishes an entry in the name-service database that includes the binding handles we've just retrieved in the previous call.

```
status = RpcNsBindingExport(
      RPC_C_NS_SYNTAX_DEFAULT,   // name syntax type
      pszEntryName,              // Name Service name
      mathlib_v1_0_s_ifspec,     // interface handle
      pBindingVector,            // binding vector (we received)
      NULL );                    // UUID object vectors (none)

if (status)
{
   cout << "error "<< status << " Exporting bindings!\n";
   exit;
}
```

Having registered and advertised our RPC interface "service," we now only need to tell the RPC runtime library to listen for incoming RPC calls.

```
cout << "Listening for RPC calls..." << endl << flush;

status = RpcServerListen(
    1,                          // minimum calls
    30,                         // maximum calls
    FALSE );                    // wait value (FALSE = DO wait)

if (status)
{
    cout << "error "<< status << " during listen!\n";
    exit;
}
```

If we call `RpcServerListen` and tell it to return immediately, then the following code needs to execute instead, to prevent this server application from exiting before RPC calls arrive. With the last parameter set to FALSE, however, the following section of code can be ignored.

```
if ( fWaitFlag )
    {
        status = RpcMgmtWaitServerListen();

        if (status)
        {
            cout << "error "<< status << " during listen!\n";
            exit;
        }
    }
}
```

The final code in the server is again a pair of memory allocation and freeing functions, identical to those defined in the RPC client. The RPC runtime code calls these functions when it needs to allocate local memory for copying buffers, arrays, strings, and pointers.

```
// These get called by MIDL

void __RPC_FAR *__RPC_API midl_user_allocate( size_t len )
{
    return( malloc(len) );
}
```

```
void __RPC_API midl_user_free( void __RPC_FAR *ptr )
{
    free( ptr );
}
```

This concludes the server source file. After compiling both the server and client applications, we can test them.

RPC Client and Server Testing

Assuming the compiling went as planned, testing these two programs should be very easy. Just start up the *RPCServ* application in one prompt window, and start *RPClient* in another. The client should locate the server, display the results of each function call, and terminate. Figure 22.1 shows an example of the client screen output. The server should display each RPC call coming in, then wait for more calls. Figure 22.2 shows an example of an RPC server screen.

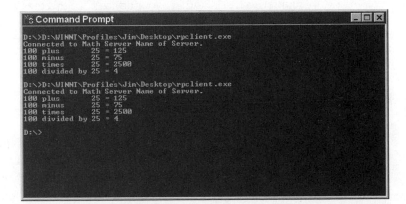

FIGURE 22.1:

An RPC client screen

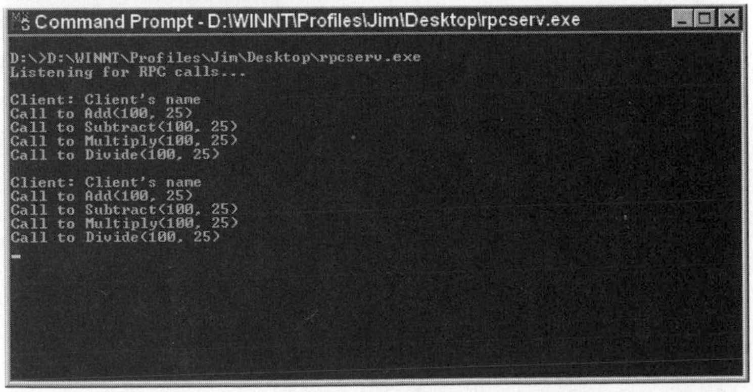

FIGURE 22.2:

An RPC server screen

If the test works correctly, then once you remove the default security restrictions on named pipes, you should be able to run the client and server programs on different workstations. There are three ways to do this:

- Make an entry in the registry file corresponding to the `auto` named pipe, and then allow access to this pipe via the Windows NT User Manager (or Windows User Manager for Domains).

- On a Windows NT domain, you could test by using the identical login account on both systems.

- Apply the information in Chapter 20 concerning creating a NULL DACL (Device Access Control List), attach this to an SD, and then use this SD rather than NULL in the security parameter for the `auto` named pipe.

NOTE   As explained in Chapter 20, security is enabled by default, and it takes explicit removal of restrictions before a device can be accessible to some (or all) users. If you attach a NULL DACL to your device's SD, this tells Windows NT to permit access by all users.

An Introduction to DCOM

The good news is that if you understand how to write client and server applications using RPC, then you already understand the *D* in DCOM. On the other hand, understanding how the *COM* (Component Object Model) part of DCOM works truly requires an entire book in itself. Here, we'll just outline the basic concepts required for writing and using DCOM objects.

Just as RPC is defined by the OSF to be a cross-platform means of interprocess and interapplication procedure calling, COM (and DCOM) is defined by OSF to be a cross-platform object model. In a nutshell, DCOM provides the ability to do remote, cross-platform, object-oriented programming. As more and more DCOM objects come online (literally!), it will probably become commonplace to have various parts of an application spread out across a network, over even the Internet, executing on a motley assortment of different operating systems and computer hardware. This is the goal for DCOM, as stated by Microsoft.

DCOM made its debut with the release of Windows NT 4.0. Then, Microsoft made DCOM for Windows 95 available as a download from the Internet. Currently, DCOM ships as part of Windows 98, and it is still available as an add-on for Windows 95. Versions of DCOM for several flavors of Unix are rumored to be in the works, including a reference version (with source code!) for Linux. By the time you are reading this, there may also be a version of DCOM available for the Apple operating system.

COM, OLE, and OCX Controls

COM, as it is implemented by Microsoft, is very similar to OLE (object linking and embedding). OLE was originally built on a set of COM classes, and the many built-in OLE interfaces were defined in terms of COM interfaces. If you've read the previous section on RPC, then you need only to understand the technology underlying OLE to know almost everything necessary to write a DCOM component or to use one from a DCOM client application.

As you explore the underpinnings of the Windows 98 interface, you will discover that most of the user interface has been implemented as a set of OCXs. The OCX controls, which now are called ActiveX controls, also derive their "objectness" from COM technology. In fact, with the growing use of ActiveX controls on the Internet, Microsoft has permitted ActiveX to return more to its COM roots; you no longer need to include a number of OLE interfaces to build a valid ActiveX component. Moreover, there is now a newly formed quasi-independent ActiveX standards body, which purportedly will assist in making DCOM more platform- and vendor-independent. (See Chapter 16 for details on ActiveX components.)

Remote Servers

Before the advent of DCOM, COM could be either an *in-process* or *out-of-process* server. In-process servers had their proxy code implemented in a DLL, which when loaded by a calling application, resulted in the COM objects being created within the client process's address space. Out-of-process servers, on the other hand, implemented the proxy code in a separate executable file, which meant that the COM objects were created in a separate address space from the client application. With the arrival of distributed COM, the former out-of-process servers are referred to as *local servers*. Servers implementing DCOM, and therefore running on remote stations, are called *remote servers*. So we now have three types of servers: in-process, local, and remote.

Because DCOM is really an incremental technology that leverages COM through the technology of RPC, it is possible to reverse-implement DCOM on already existing COM objects (also called COM components) without making any changes to the original binary COM object. This means that OLE server applications, out-of-process COM servers, OCX controls, and ActiveX controls, all benefit in the same way: They can have their methods be accessed across the network! All that is needed to make any of these available for remote calling is to create the required registry entry that tells the client which server should be used to access instances of that object.

COM Objects, Classes, and Interfaces

COM objects are also referred to as COM *classes*. More often, a COM class refers to an uninstantiated class, which is made available by a COM server. Each COM class has a GUID, just as each RPC interface does. Unlike RPC interfaces, which don't need to be registered in the system registry, COM classes are registered in the system registry. Their GUID ensures that they have a unique registry entry and can be located via that GUID and by any client program that desires to create an instance of the object.

Although it's not a requirement, COM classes can also have a string identifier (name), which allows them to be referred to by name rather than GUID. COM objects also have a registry entry which contains the module name and complete path location for an in-process and/or local server that knows how to create this class of COM object. With the arrival of DCOM, a third registry entry is supported, to allow the module name and path to be specified for a remote server. The path can specify the remote server via UNC, through an IP address, or even by an Internet-style domain name.

Class Factories

Servers that know how to create COM objects of a certain class are referred to as *class factories*. A COM server is a class factory for each class it knows how to instantiate. Client applications seeking to create instances of a given COM object follow this procedure:

- The application makes a COM or OLE call that performs a registry (and/or network namespace) lookup first to determine where the class factory "lives."

- Assuming the calling application has sufficient security rights to access this object, the appropriate class factory module is loaded (if it is not already running).

- One or more classes are instantiated.

COM Interfaces

COM objects always possess at least one, and usually more, COM interfaces. An abstract definition of an interface (RPC or COM) is a collection of related functions. A lower-level explanation is that each interface is a vector table, or *vtable*, of pointers to functions. One entry exists in an interface's vtable for each function contained in that interface. In RPC, the vtable is usually created "behind the scenes," by the RPC runtime library and the proxy stub code that is generated by the IDL compiler, and linked into the application. Calls to functions in a particular interface are simply made in the calling program with the same syntax as calling "normal" functions. Again, behind the scenes, each call is traced to the corresponding interface's vtable, and the correct function is called.

With COM objects, the process is similar, but instead of the vtable being completely hidden from the programmer, it is made available as a C++ style collection of class methods. In other words, each COM interface is made available to the calling client as if it were a C++ object (or a C++ class, which is the same thing). In fact, the vtable that is used in COM (and indirectly by RPC) exactly matches the virtual method table used by C++ compilers to implement C++ classes, or objects.

COM Functions

Because each COM interface in a COM class is actually implemented for all practical purposes as a C++ class, you might think that making use of a particular COM interface would be quite easy. Unfortunately, it isn't quite that simple. The complications arise because, when COM was designed, the designers decided it also needed to be capable of supporting multiple platforms, different byte orders, and different programming languages (not just C or C++, for instance). Furthermore, it had to help applications be robust—something that it wouldn't do if programmers could simply call into the internal guts of any object without verifying they had the correct interface class or function prototype, for example.

The price for COM's flexibility and robustness, in most folk's assessment, is obtuseness and difficulty of implementation. COM is an interesting approach to addressing a variety of important issues regarding software reuse, extensibility, and inheritance. It also tackles the cross-platform issues—at least in theory.

The way robustness of the interfaces is implemented—or put another way, the means used to enforce interface-type checking prior to all interface function access—is through an intermediate step whereby a calling program asks for a desired interface specifically, before attempting to call functions of that particular interface.

By calling a function called `QueryInterface` and specifying the desired interface GUID, the client application can receive an "officially approved" interface pointer, which can then be used as a normal pointer to a C++ class instance to access any function that really is part of that interface.

The complication here is that `QueryInterface` itself is a method of an interface; specifically, it is a function (or method) of the `IClassFactory` interface. So, in order to call `QueryInterface` on an object, you must first call `CoCreateInstance` to create an instance of the COM class, which contains the `ClassFactory` method appropriate for creating the COM class you're interested in. If this succeeds, you can then call `QueryInterface` to retrieve the `IClassFactory` interface pointer. You can then use this pointer in a call to `CreateInstance`, whereby you specify the interface GUID you want to be able to use, which should (if all goes well) finally return an interface pointer to the desired interface of the desired object. You can now use this interface pointer to make function calls to the various functions within that interface. But if you need to access other functions in other interfaces of that object, then you must call `QueryInterface` again and retrieve an interface pointer to the new interface.

Fortunately, a recent function addition, `CoCreateInstanceEx`, permits several of these steps to be packaged together into one function call. With this function, an array of structures containing pointers to multiple interface classes can be returned in one fell swoop.

After you're finished with a COM object, you must release the object. Releasing the object decrements the object's reference counter so that it can be safely automatically unloaded from the server as soon as all users have released it and the usage counter or reference counter reaches zero.

OOP, COM Style

One key aspect of COM objects is they actually support the key object-oriented attributes of extensibility, inheritance, and polymorphism. Extensibility arises from the fact you can take a COM object and add one or more new interfaces to it. Inheritance (even multiple inheritance) arises from the fact that you can define a new COM object that uses COM interfaces from multiple other COM objects. Polymorphism comes from the fact that the same interface can be implemented in many different COM objects.

TIP

To learn more about COM programming, pick up a copy of the classic *Inside OLE*, by Kraig Brockschmidt (Microsoft Press) and digest that material. Then go over the few examples that are provided in the Microsoft SDK.

Current Trends in DCOM Programming

During this last year, Microsoft and other companies have been working to make DCOM technology more accessible to programmers by upgrading their programming tools to include more integrated support of DCOM. Borland's most recent offerings—Delphi 3 and C++ Intrabuilder—both include classes to build DCOM clients and servers, which make this task practically as easy as building standard objects. Visual C++ 5.0 and Visual Basic 5 have similar provisions.

Aside from limited MFC support for OLE and DCOM, Microsoft now also provides C++ templates, called the Active Template Library (or ATL), which encapsulate much of the boilerplate DCOM code and can greatly simplify the generation of classes which support DCOM (in the process, reducing many of the possibilities for typos and bugs to creep in to the code). Using the ATL is covered in Chapter 16.

DCOM is not always called DCOM in usage, because ActiveX controls (which possess the minimal COM interface classes) can be made to communicate in a distributed environment (that is, over a network), simply by creating appropriate registry entries and then pointing the client side to the right endpoint (using the server's IP address or other locating information). On the other hand, not every ActiveX control on a Web page (for example) is using DCOM. In many cases, there is no need for this; the control simply interacts with the script code in the browser for instance. But as time progresses, we are definitely going to see a greater usage of distributed ActiveX controls (although end users might not even be aware that they are using a distributed control, unless the connection with the server is down or behaves inconsistently).

Other Network Programming Approaches

In addition to DCOM, RPC, and the various built-in Win32 networking APIs, there are also other, vendor-specific networking APIs. As a programmer, you may sometimes need to go beyond the common-level functionality provided by the approaches described in this chapter.

If you're primarily interested in network communications, your best bet is to first look at using Winsock. Winsock 2 provides efficient access to protocol-specific features for several protocols now, including Banyan VINES, Apple-Talk, DEC, and NetWare IPX and SPX. Unless you need to do really esoteric stuff, Winsock 2 provides just the right mix of fast, close-to-the-wire control with higher-level, protocol-independent socket programming.

If you need more than this, you should contact individual network vendors (Banyan, Novell, or Apple, for instance) for information about any networking toolkits that they might provide or recommend.

Windows 98 (and Windows 95 and NT) includes a rather limited NetWare API. These functions are found in the NWAPI32.DLL file, located in the \WINDOWS\ SYSTEM directory (or \WINNT\SYSTEM32 directory for Windows NT). In Windows 95 and versions of Windows NT prior to version 4.0, this DLL contained only about 25 functions. The newer versions now include approximately 115 functions, although many seem to be duplicate or triplicate versions of the same behavior. Novell's NetWare client for NT includes NCPWIN32.DLL, which exports hundreds of NCP (NetWare Core Protocol) functions.

TIP

If you need to write low-level NetWare client software for Windows 98 (or Windows 95 or NT) that makes use of the NCP functions, check out Sven Schreiber's November 1996 article in *Dr. Dobb's Journal*, "Undocumented Windows NT and the NetWare Core Protocol." In this article, Mr. Schreiber explains how you can use the undocumented `NwlibMakeNcp` function (included in both Windows 98 and NT), to implement your own NCP function library.

In addition to all the network-related APIs, you may need to devise other methods, based on combinations of these techniques or involving your own approaches. A combination approach would work well, for instance, in an RPC client application that needs to locate all available RPC servers on a network. Although RPC itself provides a mechanism for working with different protocols, you might find it easier to locate these available servers using `WNetEnumResource` or initially establishing communications using named pipes or mailslots.

You might also choose to take advantage of the fact that the Windows 98 (and Windows 95 and NT) I/O functions themselves are endowed with networking abilities. In fact, because it's so simple, you might easily overlook the fact that file I/O functions can be used in a completely platform- and protocol-independent way to convey information. Your application could, for example, open a dozen files using `CreateFile`, with each file existing on a different host computer, which is running a different operating system and using different networking protocols. As long as you specify the file's location, your application can access these files as easily as if they were located on a local drive.

Network communications using files have the advantages of being fast, simple to implement, easy to debug, and network protocol-independent. In fact, not only is this approach *completely* network-independent, it is even operating system-independent (except for byte-ordering); it does not even require any changes to be made to either the client or server programs in order to add support for new platforms or network protocols. Simply define your communications file structure, devise a means of identifying "completed" message files, and you're set to begin implementing. If you need to deal with different byte-ordering schemes, it is not difficult to create a set of conversion functions (similar in fact to those used in Winsock programming).

Another variation on this approach is to use databases to communicate between running processes or applications. Again, this has the advantages of being network-independent plus at least partially platform-independent. It requires only that all communicating stations be able to access the same database file. This approach works best in asynchronous, message-based communication, such as logging, broadcasting, or the queuing of job requests.

This chapter has covered a relatively large amount of technology in a relatively short space. The main goal was to give you an idea of what network programming options are out there for you as a Windows application developer to use to extend the capabilities of your software.

This concludes our discussion of advanced application designs. In the next chapter, we will begin Part 4 with an introduction to Windows graphics systems.

PART 4

Windows 98 Graphics

The Windows Graphics Device Interface

- Device-context access

- Information-context access

- Device capability information

- Windows mapping modes

- The viewport versus the window

This chapter provides an introduction to the Windows Graphics Device Interface (GDI). It begins with the topic of the device context (DC), which is the heart of the GDI. Then it covers the device-context information that can be retrieved. Finally, you'll learn about the Windows mapping modes, as well as the viewport versus window coordinates and sizes.

The Device Context

Unlike in DOS, where applications simply own the entire display, printer, or other device, under Windows, the output device is a shared resource. The *device context* is a method of permitting peaceful coexistence between applications sharing the resource.

Device-Context Handles

Before a Windows application can draw anything to the screen, the application must begin by gaining access to the GDI, which means obtaining a handle to the device context. Asking Windows for a handle to a device context (hDC or hdc) is the equivalent of asking permission to share the output resource. And, in like fashion, including the handle in subsequent calls to GDI output functions not only tells Windows which output device is being addressed, but also assures the GDI that permission has been granted to access the shared device.

The hdc is not only a handle to the device context, but also to a virtual device that has been allocated to the application. The virtual device provides a private space for the application's own display operations. Furthermore, the device-context handle is not only a pointer to a virtual space, but is also a pointer to a data structure detailing device (graphic) settings.

> **NOTE**   After the contents of the virtual display are mapped by the GDI to the physical display, the virtual display can be discarded, at least until further screen operations are needed.

For example, when a call is made to the TextOut function, font and color information are not included in the call because attributes have already been set for the device context (default settings are provided if no other selections are made). Thus, TextOut requires only string data and coordinates as parameters for each output operation. In like fashion, other device contexts used by other applications have their own attribute settings, which are independent of the current device context.

Device-Context Handles in MFC

Using MFC-based programming, you usually handle screen updates and drawing operations only in response to calls to the OnPaint function (even when you generate these calls indirectly using an Invalidate instruction). You usually expect the MFC shell to pass a handle to the device context to you. Or, more accurately, it passes a pointer to a CDC class instance, which you subsequently pass on to your specialized painting or drawing routines.

However, don't become too complacent about expecting this level of service and let yourself lapse into not attempting any graphics operations except when you have been passed a pointer to the device-context class. Remember that whether you use a handle to the device context or an instance of the CDC class, the device context is available at any point. You are not required to "wait" for permission to draw! You can, instead, demand permission.

Why Query a Device Context?

The attribute settings for a device context can include color palettes, mapping modes, alignment settings, and so on. These settings can be queried or changed by calling other API functions, called with the appropriate hdc parameter to identify the proper device context.

By querying a device context, you can get various information, such as the following:

- Information about supported palettes (colors)
- Font-sizing information (what fonts are available for display and in which sizes)
- Available printer fonts
- Printer resolutions (for optimizing bitmapped images)
- The presence or absence of special hardware capabilities

Device Context Access

To access the device context, you use either the BeginPaint or GetDC functions to retrieve the hdc. It's important to emphasize that no application should attempt to hold onto a device context beyond the immediate operation. Under Windows, device-context handles are a limited resource and must be shared among executing applications. Use the EndPaint or ReleaseDC functions when you're finished with the device-context handle.

NOTE   In like fashion, if you're using an instance of the **CDC** class rather than the **BeginPaint** or **GetDC** function to access a device handle, you should also conclude by closing the instance when finished. However, when you're using a class instance, the device context is released automatically by the class destructor when the class goes out of scope. By all means, use the convenience inherent in the class, but keep in mind what is happening behind the scenes.

A device context should always be released or deleted as soon as the immediate output operation is completed. Of course, once the device-context handle is released, the device context itself is no longer valid.

The PAINTSTRUCT Structure

To obtain a handle to the device context, the BeginPaint function is called with two parameters, and when finished, the EndPaint function accepts the same pair.

```
hdc = BeginPaint( hwnd, &ps );
    ...
    EndPaint( hwnd, &ps );
```

Here, two calling parameters are included:

- The hwnd argument identifying the application accessing the device context

- A pointer to the ps structure, a structured variable of type PAINTSTRUCT, which contains information specifying which portion of the screen should be repainted (rcPaint), whether the background (existing image) should be erased (fErase), and so on.

The PAINTSTRUCT structure is defined in WinUser.H as:

```
typedef struct tagPAINTSTRUCT
{    HDC     hdc;
     BOOL    fErase;
     RECT    rcPaint;
     BOOL    fRestore;
     BOOL    fIncUpdate;
     BYTE    rgbReserved[32];
} PAINTSTRUCT, *PPAINTSTRUCT, *NPPAINTSTRUCT, *LPPAINTSTRUCT;
```

The BeginPaint and EndPaint functions are commonly used in response to WM_PAINT messages when only a portion of a screen should be updated (which is faster than repainting an entire screen).

In similar fashion, the GetDC and ReleaseDC functions are used when operations are required over the entire client window area.

Other Device-Context Access Methods

There are several other methods of accessing the device context:

GetWindowDC   Unlike GetDC, provides access to the entire window, including the window frame, caption, and menu bar. Access is restricted, however, to the current application's window.

CreateDC   Obtains a device context that allows operations outside an application's client window area, such as for a screen-capture utility.

CreateIC   Obtains a handle to an information context as opposed to a device context. An information context, unlike a device context, does not provide a handle for output operations. Instead, the handle returned can be used to obtain information about an output device without actually outputting anything. The use of CreateIC is described in the next section.

The Information (Device) Context

In most cases, when access to a device such as the video display is required, the GetDC function in invoked to return a handle (hDC) to the device context. In the *DC* demo described in this chapter, however, two device-context handles are declared: hDC and hDCInfo. Since either handle could be used for either purpose, this is slightly redundant. On the other hand, using two handles makes it clear that two quite different device contexts are being used: a conventional *hardware* device context and an *information* device context.

The difference between these two contexts is simple. Unlike the conventional device context, which is used for output, the information context, provided by CreateIC, allows you to access information about the context but does not provide any output capabilities. The information context requires less overhead and is sufficient for retrieving information.

The first requirement in using the CreateIC function is to determine the device for which you are requesting information. For the video display, the video device is accessed using the default specification "DISPLAY".

```
hdc = CreateIC( "DISPLAY", NULL, NULL, NULL );
```

TIP   For Windows 98 (and Windows 95) Win32-based applications, you can call CreateIC or CreateDC by identifying the driver using the the null-terminated string "DISPLAY" and entering the remaining arguments as NULL. For Windows NT only, you may also specify a device context for a printer using the string "WINSPOOL".

Under Windows 3.*x*, the Win.INI file, normally found in the Windows directory, contains printer device information that can be extracted with the GetProfileString function and used to create an information device context. As explained in Chapter 17, under Windows 98 (and 95 and NT) most of the information previously stored in the Win.INI file has been moved to the registry, a less readily readable storage format. Therefore, the printer device context is no longer available in this fashion and must be accessed via a different route.

The string information needed to describe the printer can be returned by calling the EnumPrinterDrivers and EnumPrinters procedures. With this information, the CreateIC function and subsequent processes are carried out in the same fashion as demonstrated for the display device in the *DC* demo.

NOTE   The *DC* demo is included on the CD that accompanies this book, in the Chapter 23 folder. It is discussed in more detail later in the chapter.

The *DC* demo includes a simple routine to query the system and return a list of printer devices. Figure 23.1 shows an example of the Printer Selection dialog box displayed by the *DC* demo.

FIGURE 23.1:

The Printer Selection
dialog box displayed in
the DC demo

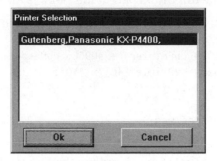

NOTE

Examples of the EnumPrinterDrivers and EnumPrinters procedures can be found in the EnumPrt.C program (part of the Printer.C demo) distributed with the Visual C++ toolkit, located in the x:\DEVSTUDIO\VC\SAMPLES\SDK\WIN32\ PRINTER directory.

The Printer Selection dialog box is called in a fashion slightly different than that used for most dialog boxes. In the WndProc procedure, under the msg/WM_COMMAND response, you'll find the following:

```
case IDM_PRINTER:
    CheckMenuItem( hMenu, IDM_DISPLAY, MF_UNCHECKED );
    CheckMenuItem( hMenu, IDM_PRINTER, MF_CHECKED );
```

The first two provisions are simple. They show which type of device is being selected by making sure that the Display menu option is unchecked and that the Printer menu option is checked.

The third provision creates the dialog box and passes a reference to the Printer-Proc procedure, which contains the handler and the provisions to query the available printers. If the DialogBox procedure returns TRUE (meaning that a selection has been made), then the program invalidates the client window so that it will be redrawn with new information.

```
if( DialogBox( hInst, "PRINTER", hwnd, PrinterProc ) )
    InvalidateRect( hwnd, NULL, TRUE );
break;
```

The important part at this point is the `PrinterProc` procedure.

```
BOOL APIENTRY PrinterProc( HWND hDlg, UINT msg, UINT wParam, LONG lParam )
{
    DWORD cbPrinters = 4096L, cbNeeded, cReturned;
    char  szPrinter[40] = "\0";
    int   i, j;

    switch( msg )
    {
```

The first step in handling the query is to initialize the dialog box, beginning by allocating a buffer to hold the information we're about to request.

```
    case WM_INITDIALOG:
        if( ! ( gpPrinters = (PPRINTER_INFO_1)
            LocalAlloc( LMEM_FIXED | LMEM_ZEROINIT, cbPrinters ) ) )
        {
            ErrorMsg( "gpPrinters local alloc failed." );
            return( FALSE );
        }
```

After allocating the buffer, and assuming success, we proceed by issuing a query requesting that the system printers be enumerated.

```
        if( ! EnumPrinters( PRINTER_ENUM_LOCAL, NULL, 1,
                (LPBYTE) gpPrinters, cbPrinters, &cbNeeded,
                &cReturned ) )
        {
```

Note that we have also anticipated the failure of this query, giving full consideration to the possibility that the buffer provided will not be large enough.

```
            if( GetLastError() == ERROR_INSUFFICIENT_BUFFER )
            {
```

However, if the buffer isn't big enough, the response is simple: Free the allocated buffer and then allocate a new buffer using the size requirement reported by the original query.

```
                LocalFree( (LOCALHANDLE) gpPrinters );
                gpPrinters = (PPRINTER_INFO_1)
                    LocalAlloc( LMEM_FIXED | LMEM_ZEROINIT, cbNeeded );
                cbPrinters = cbNeeded;
```

After reallocating the buffer using the new information, we query the printer list a second time.

```
    if( ! EnumPrinters( PRINTER_ENUM_LOCAL, NULL, 1,
                (LPBYTE) gpPrinters, cbPrinters, &cbNeeded, &cReturned ) )
    {
        ErrorMsg( "Can't enumerate printers" );
        return( FALSE );
    }
}
else
{
    ErrorMsg( "Can't enumerate printers" );
    return( FALSE );
}
}
```

The second (and first) queries conclude with report provisions to cover complete failure—just in case.

Assuming that one of our queries has been successful, we check the cReturned count. If cReturned is zero, we simply report that there are no printers installed and then return.

```
        if( ! cReturned )
        {
            ErrorMsg( "No printers installed" );
            EndDialog( hDlg, FALSE );
            return( FALSE );
        }
```

Otherwise, since at least one printer has been reported, we copy the reported printers to the dialog box's list box and then set the current selection to the first item (with the zero index).

```
        for( i=0; i<(INT)cReturned; i++ )
            SendDlgItemMessage( hDlg, IDM_PRINTLIST, LB_ADDSTRING, 0,
                        (LPARAM) gpPrinters[i].pDescription );
        SendDlgItemMessage( hDlg, IDM_PRINTLIST, LB_SETCURSEL, 0, 0 );
        return( TRUE );
```

The final provision occurs when the Ok button is clicked. (No provisions have been included to handle a double-click on a selection.)

```
case WM_COMMAND:
    switch( LOWORD( wParam ) )
    {
        case IDOK:
                // LB_GETCURSEL message retrieves the index of currently
                // selected item, if any, in a single-selection list box
            i = SendDlgItemMessage( hDlg, IDM_PRINTLIST, LB_GETCURSEL, 0, 0 );
                // LB_GETTEXT message retrieves a string from a list box
            SendDlgItemMessage( hDlg, IDM_PRINTLIST, LB_GETTEXT, (WPARAM) i,
                                (LPARAM)(LPCTSTR) szPrinter );
                // Parse the string into device, driver and port names
            j = 0;
            i = -1;
            while( szPrinter[++i] != ',' )
                gszDeviceName[i] = szPrinter[i];
            gszDeviceName[i] = '\0';
            while( szPrinter[++i] != ',' )
                gszDriverName[j++] = szPrinter[i];
            gszDriverName[j] = '\0';
            j = 0;
            while( szPrinter[++i] != '\0')
                gszPort[j++] = szPrinter[i];
            gszPort[j] = '\0';
            EndDialog( hDlg, TRUE );
            return( TRUE );
```

Clicking the Ok button simply copies the selection information to the local buffers for further use before closing the dialog box. If the user does not make a selection, and provisions are included for a default selection, the dialog box will refuse to close.

Alternatively, if the Cancel button is clicked, the dialog box simply closes without supplying a printer specification.

```
                case IDCANCEL:
                    EndDialog( hDlg, FALSE );
                    return( FALSE );
            }
            break;
    }
    return 0;
}
```

Once you have retrieved a device specification, you have a wealth of information available—probably more than you're likely to want at any one time.

As a general rule, access to a printer-specific information context shouldn't be necessary. One of the strengths of Windows (any version) is being able to let the system handle device-specific details, such as the resolution and capabilities of a printer.

Device-Context Information

Device-context information describes the resolution and capacities of hardware output devices, such as the video display, a printer or plotter, a camera device, or even a metafile (a file of GDI function calls in binary format).

GDI Identifier Constants

The device context contains a variety of information that can be requested via the identifier constants defined in WinGDI.H. Many of these inquiries return integer values; others return word values composed of bit flags that can be broken down, again using flag constants defined in WinGDI.H. Most of these constants are demonstrated in the *DC* demo, which is discussed in the next section. Table 23.1 summarizes the GDI information indexes and flag constants.

TABLE 23.1: GDI Information Indexes and Flag Constants

GDI Information Index and Flags	Description
Driver Version and Device Types	
DRIVERVERSION	Device driver version
TECHNOLOGY	Device classification
DT_PLOTTER	Vector plotter
DT_RASDISPLAY	Raster display
DT_RASPRINTER	Raster printer

Continued on next page

TABLE 23.1 CONTINUED: GDI Information Indexes and Flag Constants

GDI Information Index and Flags	Description
Driver Version and Device Types	
DT_RASCAMERA	Raster camera
DT_CHARSTREAM	Character-stream, PLP
DT_METAFILE	Metafile, VDM
DT_DISPFILE	Display file
Device Dimensions	
HORZSIZE	Horizontal size (millimeters)
VERTSIZE	Vertical size (millimeters)
HORZRES	Horizontal width (pixels)
VERTRES	Vertical width (pixels)
ASPECTX	Pixel width
ASPECTY	Pixel height
ASPECTXY	Pixel hypotenuse
LOGPIXELSX	Pixels/logical inch (width)
LOGPIXELSY	Pixels/logical inch (height)
Device Color Capabilities	
BITSPIXEL	Bits per pixel (color)
PLANES	Color planes
NUMBRUSHES	Device-specific brushes
Device Color Capabilities	
NUMPENS	Device-specific pens
NUMMARKERS	Device-specific markers
NUMFONTS	Device-specific fonts
NUMCOLORS	Device-specific colors

Continued on next page

TABLE 23.1 CONTINUED: GDI Information Indexes and Flag Constants

GDI Information Index and Flags	Description
Device Color Capabilities	
SIZEPALETTE	Entries in physical palette
NUMRESERVED	Reserved entries in palette
COLORRES	Actual color resolution
Miscellaneous	
PDEVICESIZE	Device descriptor size required
Printer-Related Device Capabilities*	
PHYSICALWIDTH	Width (device units)
PHYSICALHEIGHT	Height (device units)
PHYSICALOFFSETX	x-margin, printable area
PHYSICALOFFSETY	y-margin, printable area
SCALINGFACTORX	x-axis scaling factor
SCALINGFACTORY	y-axis scaling factor
Graphics, Image, and Font-Handling Capabilities	
CURVECAPS	Curve capabilities
CC_NONE	Curves not supported
CC_CIRCLES	Circles
CC_PIE	Pie wedges
CC_CHORD	Chord arcs
CC_ELLIPSES	Ellipses
CC_WIDE	Wide lines
CC_STYLED	Styled lines
CC_WIDESTYLED	Wide styled lines

* These replace the appropriate Escapes from earlier versions.

Continued on next page

TABLE 23.1 CONTINUED: GDI Information Indexes and Flag Constants

GDI Information Index and Flags	Description
Graphics, Image, and Font-Handling Capabilities	
CC_INTERIORS	Interiors
CC_ROUNDRECT	Rounded rectangles
LINECAPS	Line capabilities
LC_NONE	Lines not supported
LC_POLYLINE	Polylines
LC_MARKER	Markers
LC_POLYMARKER	Polymarkers
LC_WIDE	Wide lines
LC_STYLED	Styled lines
LC_WIDESTYLED	Wide styled lines
LC_INTERIORS	Interiors
POLYGONALCAPS	Polygonal capabilities
PC_NONE	Polygonals not supported
PC_POLYGON	Polygons
PC_RECTANGLE	Rectangles
PC_WINDPOLYGON	Winding polygons
PC_TRAPEZOID	Trapezoids
PC_SCANLINE	Scan lines
PC_WIDE	Wide borders
PC_STYLED	Styled borders
PC_WIDESTYLED	Wide styled borders
PC_INTERIORS	Interiors
TEXTCAPS	Text capabilities
TC_OP_CHARACTER	Character output precision

Continued on next page

TABLE 23.1 CONTINUED: GDI Information Indexes and Flag Constants

GDI Information Index and Flags	Description
Graphics, Image, and Font-Handling Capabilities	
TC_OP_STROKE	Stroke output precision
TC_CP_STROKE	Stroke clip precision
TC_CR_90	Character rotation, 90 degree
TC_CR_ANY	Character rotation, any angle
TC_SF_X_YINDEP	x/y independent scaling
TC_SA_DOUBLE	Double scaling
TC_SA_INTEGER	Integer scaling
TC_SA_CONTIN	Continuous scaling
TC_EA_DOUBLE	Embolden (double weight)
TC_IA_ABLE	Italics
TC_UA_ABLE	Underline
TC_SO_ABLE	Strikeout
TC_RA_ABLE	Raster fonts
TC_VA_ABLE	Vector fonts
TC_RESERVED	Reserved
CLIPCAPS	Clipping capabilities
CP_NONE	Output clipping not supported
CP_RECTANGLE	Output clipped to rectangle
CP_REGION	Output clipped to region
RASTERCAPS	Raster/`BitBlt` capabilities
RC_NONE**	Raster capabilities not supported
RC_BITBLT	Standard `Blt`
RC_BANDING	Banding support required

** If RC_NONE is not defined in WinGDI.H, do not attempt to use this constant (it really isn't necessary anyway).

Continued on next page

TABLE 23.1 CONTINUED: GDI Information Indexes and Flag Constants

GDI Information Index and Flags	Description
Graphics, Image, and Font-Handling Capabilities	
RC_SCALING	Scaling support required
RC_BITMAP64	Bitmap up to 64KB support
RC_GDI20_OUTPUT	Has 2.0 output calls
RC_GDI20_STATE	Function not documented
RC_SAVEBITMAP	Function not documented
RC_DI_BITMAP	DIB to memory support
RC_PALETTE	Palette support
RC_DIBTODEV	DIBitsToDevice support
RC_BIGFONT	Font up to 64KB support
RC_STRETCHBLT	StretchBlt support
RC_FLOODFILL	FloodFill support
RC_STRETCHDIB	StretchDIBits support
RC_OP_DX_OUTPUT	Function not documented
RC_DEVBITS	Function not documented

The DC Demo: Reporting Device Capabilities

The *DC* (for Device Capacity) demo demonstrates how device (hardware) information can be retrieved for the Windows device drivers. This demo uses a single function, GetDeviceCaps, to retrieve a list of integer values describing specific device capabilities. In many cases, the information returned is an integer value, such as the supported vertical or horizontal pixel size. In other cases, the value returned is a flag value that must be deciphered, as individual bits, to identify the presence or absence of specific capabilities.

The *DC* demo is included on the CD accompanying this book, in the Chapter 23 folder. In the *DC* demo, you will find that the information available has been grouped in related categories, principally for display convenience. Conventionally, these values would not be displayed at all; they would only be requested as needed for use by an application. Or, far more often, this information would not be requested at all, except by the GDI to determine how to best map an application's display (or other output) to the available device. In general, neither the programmer nor the application should be concerned with any aspect of the physical device, leaving these to be handled by Windows' GDI.

GetDeviceCaps is called with two parameters: a device-context handle (hDC), which identifies a specific device such as a video display or printer, and an integer argument, which specifies the information requested.

In most cases, the capabilities reported by the GetDeviceCaps function are provided by graphics coprocessor devices incorporated in the output devices themselves. In a video display, this would be a coprocessor found on the video card. In hard-copy devices, the presence or absence of a graphics coprocessor depends partially on the age of the device and partially on the sophistication (and price) of the model. For example, older laser printers, though still capable of excellent print quality, often predate the development of graphics coprocessors. Other, more modern devices, such as ink-jet printers, may lack not only coprocessors but also sufficient memory for full-page graphics and, therefore, may require banding (downloading page images in bands) support provided by Windows.

Device Palette (Color) Capabilities

The basic capabilities reported for the video display are shown in Figure 23.2. Figure 23.3 shows the capabilities reported for a printer device.

In general, when speaking of device-palette capabilities, the first thought that comes to mind is of video-display capabilities. And, in most cases, this is accurate. However, hard-copy devices that support palettes with more than two colors (black and white) are becoming increasing popular. Therefore, even if we tend to speak of palettes as if we were referring only to the video device, remember that the video display is not the only color device available. It is, however, generally the most sophisticated device.

FIGURE 23.2:

An example of CRT device information (SVGA)

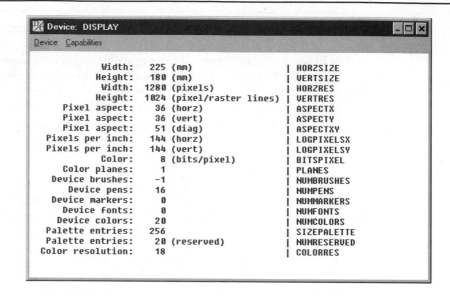

```
Device: DISPLAY
Device  Capabilities

            Width:   225 (mm)                      | HORZSIZE
           Height:   180 (mm)                      | VERTSIZE
            Width:  1280 (pixels)                  | HORZRES
           Height:  1024 (pixel/raster lines)      | VERTRES
     Pixel aspect:    36 (horz)                    | ASPECTX
     Pixel aspect:    36 (vert)                    | ASPECTY
     Pixel aspect:    51 (diag)                    | ASPECTXY
   Pixels per inch:  144 (horz)                    | LOGPIXELSX
   Pixels per inch:  144 (vert)                    | LOGPIXELSY
            Color:     8 (bits/pixel)              | BITSPIXEL
     Color planes:     1                           | PLANES
    Device brushes:   -1                           | NUMBRUSHES
       Device pens:   16                           | NUMPENS
    Device markers:    0                           | NUMMARKERS
      Device fonts:    0                           | NUMFONTS
     Device colors:   20                           | NUMCOLORS
   Palette entries:  256                           | SIZEPALETTE
   Palette entries:   20 (reserved)                | NUMRESERVED
 Color resolution:   18                            | COLORRES
```

FIGURE 23.3:

An example of printer device information

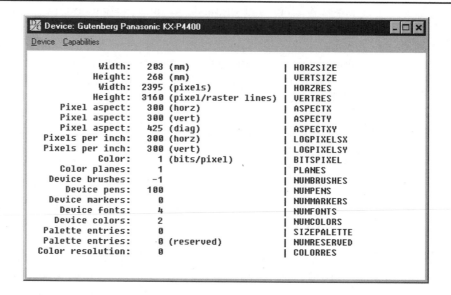

```
Device: Gutenberg Panasonic KX-P4400
Device  Capabilities

            Width:   203 (mm)                      | HORZSIZE
           Height:   268 (mm)                      | VERTSIZE
            Width:  2395 (pixels)                  | HORZRES
           Height:  3160 (pixel/raster lines)      | VERTRES
     Pixel aspect:   300 (horz)                    | ASPECTX
     Pixel aspect:   300 (vert)                    | ASPECTY
     Pixel aspect:   425 (diag)                    | ASPECTXY
   Pixels per inch:  300 (horz)                    | LOGPIXELSX
   Pixels per inch:  300 (vert)                    | LOGPIXELSY
            Color:     1 (bits/pixel)              | BITSPIXEL
     Color planes:     1                           | PLANES
    Device brushes:   -1                           | NUMBRUSHES
       Device pens:  100                           | NUMPENS
    Device markers:    0                           | NUMMARKERS
      Device fonts:    4                           | NUMFONTS
     Device colors:    2                           | NUMCOLORS
   Palette entries:    0                           | SIZEPALETTE
   Palette entries:    0 (reserved)                | NUMRESERVED
 Color resolution:    0                            | COLORRES
```

As a general rule, the DC demo reports video palettes in bits per pixel (BITSPIXEL) and color planes (PLANES). In most cases, one of these two elements will be reported as value 1, and only the remaining element is relevant in determining the device's supported color range. This limitation (or context, if you prefer) is mostly a matter of how the hardware's device driver is written and not a matter of how the actual physical device operates.

The *DC* demo also reports device colors (NUMCOLORS), which can be useful information. Figure 23.2 shows the device capabilities reported by the *DC* demo for a Matrox Pulsar video device which (deliberately, because of requirements set by other system uses) is restricted to a 256-color palette. Table 23.2 shows how the reported results vary according to equipment capabilities for different types of devices.

TABLE 23.2: Comparing Device Color Capabilities

Device Type	Color Planes	Bits/Pixel	Calculated Palette Size	Reported Palette Size	Possible Colors
EGA/VGA	4	1	16	16	256
SVGA	1	8	256	20	16,777,216
Printer	1	1	2	2	2
Plotter	1	1	2	8	N/A

You may notice a few discrepancies in the table, such as the fact that the SVGA palette size is calculated as 256 colors while the reported palette size is only 20. No, this is not an error; the reported palette size is the number of palette entries that are predefined, not the number of possible (calculated) palette entries. Thus, for an SVGA system, the palette size is 256 color entries, of which 20 have been reserved by the system (Windows) for standard palette colors. The remaining 236 palette entries are undefined and must be defined either by the application or, in some cases, by the user.

Another discrepancy appears in the entries for the plotter device, where a calculated palette size of 2 is at odds with the reported palette size of 8. This discrepancy occurs because the plotter reported in this table is a pen-carousel plotter, which has eight color pens but still has only one color plane and one bit per pixel. For the plotter, a specific instruction is required to select a color pen, and all subsequent instructions until another pen is selected are essentially monochromatic.

Incidentally, you may also be wondering where the count of possible colors (rightmost column) is determined since this last piece of information is not inherent in the reported device capabilities. The details of color ranges are covered in Chapter 24. Just note now that the raw data is essentially correct.

NOTE
When you are reviewing device information, keep in mind that the information reported by the system for a specific device can be useful, but you must understand how these facts are derived and reported.

Version and Device Types

The DRIVERVERSION and TECHNOLOGY index arguments request the device driver version number and the device type. Driver version numbers are reported as word values in hexadecimal format. For example, a version number reported as 0x0103 identifies version 1, revision 3.

Seven device types are defined: vector plotter, raster display (CRT), raster printer (laser-jet or ink-jet), raster camera, character stream, metafile, and display file. Normally, of course, the video device will be a raster display. Depending on the equipment and configuration, however, the reported hard-copy device could be a vector plotter, raster printer, raster camera, or even a metafile or display device.

Size and Resolution

Device size and resolution cover a variety of elements, including physical size, pixel or dot resolutions, colors and palettes, and pixel or dot aspect ratios—in effect, all salient information about a device's reproduction capabilities. Table 23.3 shows size and resolution data for four devices.

Notice that the numbers shown do not always tell the entire story. For example, the PaintJet printer reports 1 color bit per pixel, 1 color plane, and 8 device colors; but, finally and correctly, it reports a 16-color palette.

TIP
What the PaintJet report does not tell you is that these 16 palette colors can be assigned from a much wider range using RGB specifications. See Chapter 24 for details.

TABLE 23.3: Comparing Basic Device Resolutions

Data	Video 57P card / ViewSonic PT770 Monitor*	Panasonic KX-P4400	HP LaserJet IID Printer	HP PaintJet XL Printer (standard)
Width (mm)	225	203	203	203
Width (pixels/dots)	1280	2395	2400	1440
Height (mm)	180	268	266	260
Height (pixel/raster lines/dots)	1024	3160	3150	1846
Horizontal (pixel/ dot aspect)	36	300	300	180
Vertical (pixel/dot aspect)	36	300	300	180
Diagonal (pixel/dot aspect)	51	425	425	255
Pixels per inch/dots per inch (horizontal)	144	300	300	180
Pixels per inch/dots per inch (vertical)	144	300	300	180
Color (bits per pixel)	8	1	1	1
Color (planes)	1	1	1	1
Device brushes	-1	-1	-1	-1
Device pens	16	100	10	40
Device fonts	0	0	0	0
Device markers	0	4	0	0
Device colors	20	2	2	8
Palette entries	256	0	2	16
Palette entries (reserved)	20	0	2	16
Color resolution (bits per pixel)	18	0	0	0

*Some of these values depend on the monitor rather than the video card used.

Raster Capabilities

Because most output devices are raster devices (yes, this includes laser printers), RASTERCAPS reports on general device capabilities, such as banding (device memory dependent), bitmap handling, fill operations, scaling, and device palettes. Table 23.4 shows raster capabilities for some different devices.

TABLE 23.4:   Comparing Raster Capabilities

RASTERCAPS	Video 57P Video Card	Panasonic KX-P4400	HP LaserJet IID Printer	HP PaintJet XL Printer (standard)
Banding support required		✓		
Bitmap transfer	✓	✓	✓	✓
Bitmaps up to 64KB	✓	✓	✓	✓
SetDIBits and GetDIBits	✓	✓		
SetDIBitsToDevice	✓	✓		
Floodfill				
Windows 2.0 features	✓	✓		
Palettes	✓			
Scaling				
Fonts up to 64KB	✓	✓		
StretchBlt	✓	✓	✓	✓
StretchDIBits	✓	✓	✓	✓

Raster capabilities typically receive more sophisticated support from video devices than from printers. For either type of device, support may be partially determined by the amount of memory available, on the video card or in the printer. Because all of the printers used for the example have more than adequate memory for full-page graphics, no banding support is required for any of these. In like fashion, the video card represented has 2MB of RAM and supports large bitmaps as well as large fonts, even though, in general, large fonts are not sent directly to display devices (normally, bitmapped images of text are transferred instead).

NOTE   The choice between downloading a font versus sending a bitmapped text image is determined by the printer type and, of course, the printer driver. Happily, in normal circumstances, this decision does not need to be made by the programmer. If you are designing printer drivers, however, some experimentation may be necessary to decide when and where the trade-offs occur.

Bitmap Operations

In the `GetDeviceCaps` function, bitmap operations are reported as capabilities under the heading of raster capabilities. From a graphics operation standpoint, however, these operations are also probably the most important device capabilities. Bitmaps inherently require more than a little handling to write to the screen or to move, superimpose, or manipulate in any other fashion.

Characters, whether bitmapped or stroked, are commonly written to the screen as foreground images only and, therefore, generally leave the greater portion of the screen unaffected. A rough estimate suggests that 20 percent or less of the screen pixels are actually written during text operations. Because of this, character operations are inherently faster than bitmapped image operations, which require writing all pixels within the image area.

To offset this speed discrepancy, sophisticated graphics coprocessors include special hardware functions that are devoted to fast bitmap transfers, handling of bitmaps larger than 64KB, and bitmap-scaling operations. If any of these capabilities are supported, most common graphics operations are executed at much higher speeds than they can be with video equipment (or printers) that does not support these functions.

Clip Capabilities

Clipping capabilities, which are reported by the CLIPCAPS request, define the ability of a device to clip drawing instructions to a specified region. Most devices have rectangular clipping capabilities. Region-clipping capabilities, permitting a more complex area definition, are also possible. Table 23.5 shows clipping capabilities for several devices.

TABLE 23.5:   Comparing Clip Capabilities

CLIPCAPS	Video 57P Video Card	Panasonic KX-P4400	HP LaserJet IID Printer	HP PaintJet XL Printer (standard)
No output clipping support				
Output clipped to rectangle	✓	✓	✓	✓
Output clipped to region				

Curve Capabilities

The curve capability flags (CURVECAPS) report the capabilities of the output device to handle its own curve definitions. These may include circles, arcs, pie wedges, and ellipses as well as special borders. Table 23.6 shows the curve capabilities of several devices.

TABLE 23.6:   Comparing Curve Capabilities

CURVECAPS	Video 57P Video Card	Panasonic KX-P4400	HP LaserJet IID Printer	HP PaintJet XL Printer (standard)
Curves not supported		✓		
Circles	✓		✓	✓
Pie wedges			✓	✓
Chord arcs			✓	✓
Ellipses	✓		✓	✓
Wide borders			✓	✓
Styled borders			✓	✓
Wide and styled borders			✓	✓
Interiors	✓		✓	✓
Rounded rectangles	✓			

Line Capabilities

Line-capability flags (LINECAPS) report on line-style support and some interior-fill operations. As with curve capabilities, line capabilities are widely (if not universally) supported. Although line capabilities are less calculation-intensive than curve operations, providing external support for line-drawing calculations still increases throughput for both display and hard-copy devices. Table 23.7 shows the line capabilities of some devices.

TABLE 23.7: Comparing Line Capabilities

LINECAPS	Video 57P Video Card	Panasonic KX-P4400	HP LaserJet IID Printer	HP PaintJet XL Printer (standard)
Lines not supported				
Polylines	✓	✓	✓	✓
Markers			✓	✓
Polymarkers			✓	✓
Wide lines			✓	✓
Styled lines	✓	✓	✓	✓
Wide and styled lines			✓	✓
Interiors			✓	✓

Polygon Capabilities

Polygon capability flags (POLYGONALCAPS) report on device capabilities for executing alternate and winding fill operations on polygon figures, as well as plain and styled borders and interiors.

NOTE A winding fill operation is slower than an alternate fill but also fills enclosed areas that might otherwise be omitted. The difference between alternate and winding fill operations is explained in more detail in Chapter 25 and illustrated in the *Pen-Draw3* demo, discussed in that chapter.

As with curve and line capabilities, polygon support is common but not universal. In terms of the calculations required, support for polygon capabilities probably falls somewhere between those for curves and lines, although the fill algorithms may run a close second to curves in terms of the CPU's workload. Again, external support for these tasks does increase throughput and display or output speed.

Table 23.8 shows the polygon capabilities of some devices.

TABLE 23.8: Comparing Polygonal Capabilities

POLYGONALCAPS	Video 57P Video Card	Panasonic KX-P4400	HP LaserJet IID Printer	HP PaintJet XL Printer (standard)
Polygonals not supported				
Alternate fill polygon	✓		✓	✓
Rectangles			✓	✓
Winding fill polygon			✓	✓
Scan lines	✓	✓	✓	✓
Wide borders			✓	✓
Styled borders	✓		✓	✓
Wide and styled borders			✓	✓
Interiors	✓		✓	✓

Text Capabilities

Text capability flags (TEXTCAPS) report device capabilities for character output, including stroked output, character rotation and scaling, and clipping precision, as well as italic, boldface, underlining, and strikeout. Also reported are the handling capabilities for both raster and vector fonts.

In general, printers provide more sophisticated text capabilities than video cards. For either type of device, the text source may be more important than the device itself. A WYSIWYG editor, such as Microsoft Word or CorelDraw, may provide character rotation regardless of the display or printer support. If such support is provided by the output device, the result is simply faster output operation, not new or different capabilities.

Table 23.9 shows text capabilities for some devices.

Note that these are device capabilities, not font characteristics. For font characteristics, refer to the **LOGFONT** structure for a specific font. Chapter 27 discusses fonts in more detail.

TABLE 23.9: Comparing Text Capabilities

TEXTCAPS	Video 57P Video Card	Panasonic KX-P4400	HP LaserJet IID Printer	HP PaintJet XL Printer (standard)
Character output precision			✓	✓
Stroke output precision			✓	✓
Stroke clip precision	✓		✓	✓
90° character rotation				
Any character rotation				
Independent x/y scaling				
Doubled character scaling				
Integer multiple scaling				
Any multiple scaling				
Double-weight characters				✓
Italic				
Underlining			✓	✓
Strikeout			✓	✓
Raster fonts		✓		
Vector fonts			✓	✓

Mapping Modes

Under DOS, all graphics operations (with some rare exceptions) use a single mapping mode in which the logical unit is the screen pixel. The screen origin —the 0,0 point—is located in the upper-left corner, which is a convention established by and held over from text display and video memory-mapping conventions. Although applications might create both text and graphics windows, the use of this same mapping-mode convention was almost as inevitable as the sun rising in the east. Things have changed under Windows.

Windows Mapping Modes

Windows supports eight separate mapping modes, each providing a different set of conventions appropriate for different circumstances. Another difference from the mapping mode used by DOS is that the modes (with the exception of MM_TEXT, which corresponds to the DOS standard) use the lower-left corner—not the upper-left—as the default screen origin, when they do not use a variable origin point.

The eight mapping modes under Windows are listed in Table 23.10.

TABLE 23.10: Windows Mapping Modes

| | | | Default | Origins |
Mapping Mode	Value	Logical Units	x-Axis	y-Axis
MM_TEXT	1	Pixel	Left	Top
MM_LOMETRIC	2	0.1 mm	Left	Bottom
MM_HIMETRIC	3	0.01 mm	Left	Bottom
MM_LOENGLISH	4	0.01 inch	Left	Bottom
MM_HIENGLISH	5	0.001 inch	Left	Bottom
MM_TWIPS	6	$\frac{1}{1440}$ inch	Left	Bottom
MM_ISOTROPIC	7	Variable ($x=y$)	Variable	Variable
MM_ANISOTROPIC	8	Variable ($x!=y$)	Variable	Variable

The Default Text Mode

Beginning with the familiar, the MM_TEXT mode (default) corresponds to the DOS graphics mode, allowing the application to operate in terms of pixel positions (virtual or physical device pixels). In the MM_TEXT mode, the default origin lies at the upper-left corner of the screen with the x- and y-axis coordinates increasing to the right and down. Figure 23.4 illustrates the MM_TEXT mode.

FIGURE 23.4:

The MM_TEXT mode

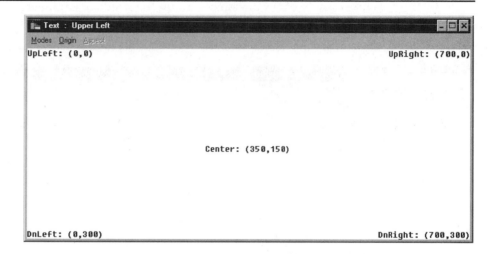

The MM_TEXT mode is used by default if no other mapping mode has been selected. As its name suggests, this mode is optimized for text displays—that is, for text displays following European/American conventions with the text flowing from left to right and top to bottom. Your applications are not required to change modes to perform their specific tasks. This means that any operation can be accomplished in MM_TEXT mode, if you are willing to perform the necessary coordinate conversions yourself, just not always as conveniently. Convenience is no small consideration and is the real reason for providing such a variety of mapping modes.

The Cartesian Coordinate Modes

The MM_HIENGLISH, MM_HIMETRIC, MM_LOENGLISH, MM_LOMETRIC, and MM_TWIPS modes follow the familiar Cartesian coordinate system, with coordinate values increasing up and to the right of the origin point. These five modes differ in their logical units. They provide measurements appropriate to applications that need to draw in physically meaningful units: English, metric, or typesetting units.

The MM_HIMETRIC and MM_LOMETRIC modes use logical units of 0.01 and 0.1 millimeter, respectively, to provide high- and low-resolution imaging. Figure 23.5 shows an example of the MM_LOMETRIC mode. Similarly, the MM_HIENGLISH and MM_LOENGLISH mapping modes use units of 0.01 and 0.001 inch, again providing high and low resolution. Together, these four modes adequately provide for a wide variety of circumstances to suit the needs of engineers, scientists, and artists. (Scaling, of course, can be applied as necessary.)

FIGURE 23.5:

The MM_LOMETRIC mode

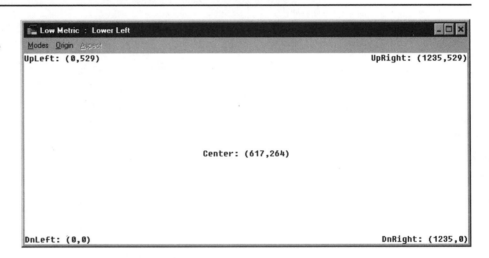

The fifth mapping mode, MM_TWIPS, requires a bit more explanation. The logical units are $\frac{1}{144}$ inch which, while unfamiliar to an engineer or scientist, just happens to be one-twentieth of a printer's point (72 points = 1 inch). Using MM_TWIPS mode, a 10-point typeface can be drawn 200 logical units in height, providing sufficient detail to render even the most complex typeface, regardless of whether the actual display device can support a similar resolution.

The Isotropic and Anistotropic Modes

The MM_ISOTROPIC and MM_ANISOTROPIC modes provide both variable logical units and variable origin points. They can be adapted to provide any scale or arrangements that might arise and that are not covered by one of the standard modes.

For example, using the MM_ANISOTROPIC mode, where the x- and y-axes can be assigned different scales, the vertical direction might be mapped in thousands of dollars (or the numerical equivalent) and the horizontal direction could represent dates to create a business graph. Equally practical, the MM_ISOTROPIC mode could be used with measurements defined as astronomical units with the 0,0 origin at the center to plot the orbital path of a comet on its passage through the solar system. In both cases, the GDI would provide conversion from the internal modal units to the actual physical display but would not require these conversions to be handled by the application.

Remember, however, that the MM_ISOTROPIC mode has the same logical units assigned to both the x- and y-axes. This mode is useful when preserving the exact shape of an image is important. Figure 23.6 shows an example of the MM_ISOTROPIC mode. The MM_ANISOTROPIC mode may have each axis scaled differently. Furthermore, both modes may have the origin point located anywhere within the application window or even somewhere outside the application window entirely.

FIGURE 23.6:

The MM_ISOTROPIC mode

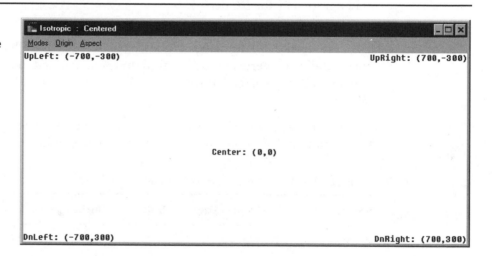

Getting and Setting Mapping Modes

The SetMapMode and GetMapMode functions are provided to set or retrieve the eight defined mapping modes.

```
SetMapMode( hdc, nMapMode );
nMapMode = GetMapMode( hdc );
```

The nMapMode argument used to call SetMapMode would, normally, be one of the predefined constants, but it could be simply an integer argument in the corresponding range. The value returned by SetMapMode reports the previous (existing) mapping mode.

As with SetMapMode, the value returned by GetMapMode will correspond to one of the defined mapping modes, or if there is an error, will return as zero. Until a different mapping mode is explicitly selected, the initial (default) mode will always be MM_TEXT, mapped in pixels with the 0,0 origin at the upper-left corner of the application window, just as in DOS.

After a different mapping mode is selected, the values returned by SetMapMode and GetMapMode will correspond to that mode. For example, after MM_LOMETRIC is selected, the origin point is at the lower-left corner of the application window, with coordinates increasing up and right. At the same time, instead of specifying coordinates in pixels, coordinates are specified in 0.1 millimeter increments, which on the average SVGA monitor provides a full-screen vertical resolution of 1560 units and 2080 units horizontally (assuming the 208-by-156 millimeter display reported by the *DC* demo).

Remember, however, that the actual physical display mode, assuming standard SVGA resolution, is only 640 pixels wide and 480 pixels high. This means that, horizontally and vertically, 3.25 logical units are mapped to each physical unit, or in overall terms, a total of 10.56 (3.25^2) logical pixels are mapped to each physical pixel.

Table 23.11 shows the logical size and corresponding inches and millimeters for several output devices and modes, arranged in descending order of magnitude.

TABLE 23.11: Device and Mode Resolutions

Device	Logical Size	Unit	Inches	Millimeters
EGA video (H/V)	640 / 350	Pixels	0.012795 / 0.017547	0.3250 / 0.4457*
VGA video (H/V)	640 / 480	Pixels	0.012795	0.3250
MM_LOENGLISH	0.01	Inches	0.010000	0.2540
SVGA video (H/V)	1024 / 768	Pixels	0.079960	0.2031
MM_LOMETRIC	0.1	MM	0.003940	0.1000
LaserJet printer	300	DPI	0.003333	0.0846
MM_HIENGLISH	0.001	Inches	0.001000	0.0254

Continued on next page

TABLE 23.11 CONTINUED: Device and Mode Resolutions

Device	Logical Size	Unit	Inches	Millimeters
High-resolution SVGA	1280 / 1024	Pixels	0.008515	0.0191
MM_TWIPS	$^1/_{20}$	Points	0.000694	0.0176
Typesetter	2000	DPI	0.000500	0.0127
MM_HIMETRIC	0.01	MM	0.000394	0.0100

*The physical measurements (inches and millimeters) for video modes are based on standard monitor screens sizes as specified by the manufacturers with a display area approximately 10.9 inches wide and 7.9 inches high (a nominal 14-inch monitor). Because actual physical units may vary, depending both on monitor adjustments and on larger physical screen sizes, the values shown are for comparative resolutions only.

Coordinate Translations: Viewport versus Window

Mapping the logical, virtual display to the physical display is not the application's concern because all relevant operations are handled by the GDI. What is the application's concern—or, more properly, the programmer's concern—is selecting the mapping mode appropriate to the task's requirements, and then setting the origins, window, and viewport extents accordingly.

Under Windows, each application is contending with two separate coordinate systems which, combined, form the client window display. These two reference systems have been given the titles *viewport* and *window*—a nomenclature that is responsible for more than a little confusion.

The term *window* is used to refer to the application's client window, meaning the area of the screen where the application's display actually appears. And, for an even longer time, the term *viewport* has been used, particularly in non-Windows contexts, to refer to a clipping region or a boundary restricting graphics operations.

Under Windows, and specifically when referring to mapping modes, the term *viewport* does, indeed, refer to the screen display where the physical device coordinates must and do apply. When referring to *viewport* coordinates on the screen, the reference is in terms of pixels, and the origin is always at the upper-left corner (just like under DOS).

The term *window*, however, refers to the virtual space where the application is executing its drawing operations. The window coordinates are expressed in logical coordinates. Furthermore, all GDI functions accept coordinates as logical, not physical, units.

The mapping modes are simply a description of how Windows (the system) translates coordinates from the window, which is using logical coordinates, to the viewport, which uses device (hardware) coordinates. The conversion from window coordinates (xWindow, yWindow) to viewport (screen) coordinates (x Viewport, y Viewport) uses two formulas:

$$xViewport = xViewOrg + ((xWindow - xWinOrg) * \frac{xViewExt}{xWinExt})$$

$$yViewport = yViewOrg + ((yWindow - yWinOrg) * \frac{yViewExt}{yWinExt})$$

The additional parameters used in these formulas are the variables describing the selected mapping mode:

x_ViewOrg/y_ViewOrg   Describe the viewport origin in device or screen coordinates.

x_WinOrg/y_WinOrg   Describe the window origin in local, logical coordinates.

x_ViewExt/y_ViewExt and x_WinExt/y_WinExt   Define a conversion ratio between "size" in virtual units of the window and an equally fictional "size" for the viewport expressed in device units.

If both the viewport and window were using the same scalar coordinate systems (pixel units) and origin points (0,0 at upper left), these formulas could be greatly simplified as:

```
xViewport = xViewOrg + xWindow

yViewport = yViewOrg + yWindow
```

However, such a simplification would destroy the very flexibility that Windows has introduced by using mapping modes (although, essentially, this relationship is found in the default MM_TEXT mode).

Also, when an application does require conversion from the application's logical coordinate context to the physical device context (or vice versa), Windows provides two functions: DPtoLP and LPtoDP.

The DPtoLP function converts device points to logical points.

```
DPtoLP( hdc, &Points, 1 );
```

The Points argument is an array of POINT structures to be converted. The hdc argument specifies the device context, and the third parameter indicates how many points should be converted.

The reverse process, from logical points to device points, is accomplished by calling the LPtoDP function, which has the same arguments:

```
LPtoDP( hdc, &Points, 1 );
```

As another example, assume that an application needs to convert the client window rectangle to device coordinates. This would be accomplished as:

```
GetClientRect( hwnd, &rect );
LPtoDP( hdc, (LPPOINT) &rect, sizeof(rect) / sizeof(POINT) );
```

TIP   Remember that most of the time, Windows will provide all the translation required between the viewport and window coordinate systems without application provisions. But if you need to handle these, these functions are available.

Setting Window and Viewpoint Origins

Under Windows, all mapping modes have variable origin points, even though six of these modes conventionally use the default origins indicated in Table 23.10 (earlier in the chapter). These defaults can be changed by using the SetViewportOrgEx and SetWindowOrgEx functions.

The SetViewportOrgEx function sets the viewport (device context) origin and is invoked as:

```
SetViewportOrgEx( hdc, xPos, yPos, &Point );
```

The xPos and yPos arguments are in device-context units (pixels for the video device). Point is returned reporting the previous origin coordinates, with the y-coordinate in the high-order word and the x-coordinate in the low-order word. Optionally, this fourth parameter can be passed as NULL if no return value is desired.

The SetWindowOrgEx function provides a similar flexibility within the virtual context and is invoked as:

```
SetWindowOrgEx( hdc, xPos, yPos, &Point );
```

With this function, xPos and yPos are expressed in logical units appropriate to the mapping mode selected. Again, an optional Point returns the previous origin coordinates.

NOTE In Windows 3.x, similar services are supplied by the SetViewportOrg and SetWindowOrg functions. However, these have different calling parameters and return values.

Remember that changing the viewport or window origins has no effect on the position of the client window on the screen. Each is, in effect, a fiction providing an adjustable offset that affects how and which portion of an application's display is mapped from the virtual to the physical display. (To change the window position on the screen, use the SetWindowPos function.) Also, in general, only one of these two functions is used at any time, since they perform what are, in essence, redundant functions.

Setting the Window and Viewport Extents

The SetWindowExtEx and SetViewportExtEx functions are used to set the window and viewport extents. They set the scale and offset sizes, which provide the mapping ratios (see the formulas shown earlier). These ratios determine how an application's client window image is mapped to the physical (device) viewport context. These two functions are valid only when the mapping mode is set to MM_ISOTROPIC or MM_ANISOTROPIC; they are ignored if any other mapping mode is in effect.

The SetWindowExtEx function specifies the window size in logical units and is called as:

```
SetWindowExtEx( hdc, xSize, ySize, &OldSize );
```

The xSize and ySize parameters specify the window extent (size) in logical units. The fourth parameter (OldSize) is returned with the previous window extent. If the original settings are not needed, this argument can be passed as NULL, and nothing will be returned.

The SetViewportExtEx function is called in similar fashion to specify the viewport extent in device units.

```
SetViewportExtEx( hdc, xSize, ySize, &OldSize );
```

Two constraints apply when the MM_ISOTROPIC mapping mode is in effect:

- SetWindowExtEx must be called before calling SetViewportExtEx.

- The ySize parameter is ignored by both functions in favor of the xSize setting, keeping the aspect ratio constant.

In MM_ANISOTROPIC mode, the xSize and ySize parameters can be specified independently, setting different scales along each axis.

The ratios between the x- and y-viewport extents and the x- and y-window extents define how much the GDI should stretch or compress units in the logical coordinate system to fit units in the device (physical) coordinate system. In isotropic mode, the x- and y-axes always maintain the same ratios; in anisotropic mode, these ratios can be determined independently.

As an example, consider an application window using the anisotropic mode with the window x-extent set to 200 and the viewport x-extent at 400. In this situation, the GDI would map two logical units (along the x-axis) to four device units. Continuing with the assumption that the window y-extent is also set at 200 and the viewport y-extent at 100, the GDI would map two logical units to one device unit along the y-axis.

However, since no provision has been made to alter this, the y-axis in the window increases from bottom to top; the same y-axis in the viewport increases from top to bottom. The result is that the image mapped is, in effect, inverted. Of course, if this is not desired, either the viewport or window y-axis can be assigned a negative value, thus inverting the inversion. On the other hand, if both are negative, the situation remains unchanged.

The Modes Demo: Mapping Mode Effects

The *Modes* demo demonstrates how the mapping modes affect the window's size (in logical units) as well the window's origin point. Figure 23.7 shows the *Modes* main screen.

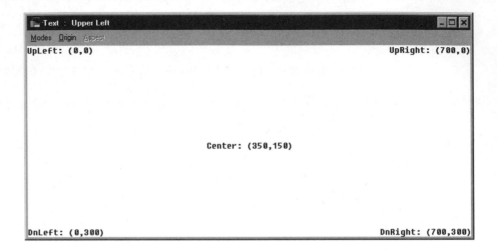

NOTE   The *Modes* demo is included on the CD accompanying this book, in the Chapter 23 folder.

The main menu offers three selections:

Modes   This option displays a submenu listing the eight mapping modes.

Origin   This mode offers the origin choices of upper-left, center, or lower-left.

Aspect   When the isotropic or anisotropic mode has been selected, this option displays the dialog box shown in Figure 23.8, which allows you to change the horizontal and vertical viewport and window extents. With other modes, this option is grayed.

The *Modes* demo demonstrates two menu-handling procedures that you may find useful. The first checks and unchecks menu items according to selection; the second changes the grayed state of the Aspects menu item, enabling this selection only when the isotropic or anisotropic mapping modes are selected.

FIGURE 23.8:

The Viewport/Windows Aspects dialog box in the Modes demo

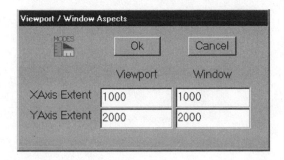

The demos described in this chapter, *DC* and *Modes*, provide an introduction to the GDI. Because the *DC* demo is intended simply to show how device capabilities can be queried, this program is provided only in a conventional Windows C-code format; no MFC/C++ equivalent is provided. Although actual applications might query specific device capabilities for the purpose of setting some internal handling, they would not normally report these capabilities to the user.

The next chapters continue to demonstrate aspects of the GDI.

CHAPTER

TWENTY-FOUR

Colors and Color Palettes

- The Windows standard palette

- How dithering works

- Custom color palettes

- Windows color drawing modes

- Color-to-gray-scale conversions

The procedures for handling colors under Windows are distinctly different from the color procedures under DOS. In part, this causes some additional complexity for the programmer, but overall, it provides greater flexibility. The application programmer no longer needs to make separate provisions for various hardware capabilities. Rather, you are free to devote your time to the application's principal objectives instead of writing code for a multitude of display systems.

For the application developer, one of the most important reasons to use color is to provide information in forms more readily recognizable than a simple monochrome display. Even for such simple tasks as spreadsheets or editing program code, the addition of color to highlight various elements provides additional, easily recognized information that could be lost on a simple black-and-white (or black-and-amber or black-and-green) display. With color, when an accountant says that a company is in the red, he can be speaking quite literally, without needing to reach for a red pen to make an entry in a ledger sheet.

In part, the use of color (or shades of gray) simply presents a display with the appearance of greater depth and detail than a monochrome display. And, even though first impressions are hardly an appropriate basis for judging an application's design and usefulness, they are still important. Your current and prospective clients will take that first look, and decide how much consideration to give to your application and how much effort they will expend in discovering the real strengths of your design.

Of course, there's also a flip side to this coin. Excessively elaborate graphics or absurdly garish color choices may have precisely the opposite of the desired effect: a bad first impression or, worse, general confusion while operating an application. Thus, restraint is also appropriate.

This is not, however, a lecture on the aesthetics of design (regardless of how relevant the topic might be). Instead, the present topic is how colors *can* be used. How you choose to use them remains up to you.

Windows Palettes

The earliest video cards provided video RAM (VRAM) on the order of 32KB to 64KB, enough for simple displays with limited colors. Today, even an inexpensive video card is expected to provide at least 1MB of RAM—enough for a 1024×768 display with a 256 color palette. And many video cards include twice this amount of RAM or more.

Color Definitions

Video uses an RGB color scheme to create colors. When painting a screen with light, combinations of red, green, and blue lights are sufficient to create an entire range of colors; black is the absence of any colored light, and white is a balanced combination of the three primary colors.

Using DOS, the video palette was defined in a relatively restrictive fashion with a fixed palette of 16 colors. These colors were defined using the RGBI flag system, where the flag bits controlled the red, green, and blue color guns together with a single intensity flag.

With the introduction of the EGA/VGA video boards, the palette expanded to 64 colors by exchanging the single intensity bit for three separate intensity bits: one each for the red, green, and blue color guns.

Today, both of these color specification systems have been supplanted by the Windows 32-bit color specification, where each color value is defined as a DWORD value in the format 0x00BBGGRR. In this format, the least-significant byte (eight bits) holds the value for red, the second byte is green, and the third byte is blue. The fourth, most-significant byte remains zero.

You may wonder why this is a 32-bit color specification when we've been talking about 24-bit color. The remaining eight bits in the DWORD value are used for a different purpose, which we'll discuss later in the chapter.

Table 24.1 shows the CGA, EGA/VGA, and Windows equivalents for a 16-color palette.

TABLE 24.1: System Color Definitions

Color names	CGA Colors		EGA/VGA Colors		Windows Equivalents*
	binary	iRGB	binary	rgbRGB	0x .. BB GG RR
Black	0000	----	000000	......	0x00 00 00 00
Dark Blue	0001	...B	000001	.....B	0x00 77 00 00

Continued on next page

TABLE 24.1 (CONTINUED): System Color Definitions

Color names	CGA Colors		EGA/VGA Colors		Windows Equivalents*
	binary	iRGB	binary	rgbRGB	0x .. BB GG RR
Dark Green	0010	..G.	000010	....G.	0x00 00 77 00
Dark Cyan	0011	..GB	000011	....GB	0x00 77 77 00
Dark Red	0100	.R..	000100	...R..	0x00 00 00 77
Dark Magenta	0101	.R.B	000101	...R.B	0x00 77 00 77
Brown	0110	.RG.	000110	...RG.	0x00 00 77 77
Light Gray	0111	.RGB	000111	...RGB	0x00 77 77 77
Dark Gray	1000	i...	111000	rgb...	0x00 3F 3F 3F
Light Blue	1001	i..B	111001	rgb..B	0x00 FF 00 00
Light Green	1010	i.G.	111010	rgb.G.	0x00 00 FF 00
Light Cyan	1011	i.GB	111011	rgb.GB	0x00 FF FF 00
Light Red	1100	iR..	111100	rgbR..	0x00 00 00 FF
Light Magenta	1101	iR.B	111101	rgbR.B	0x00 FF 00 FF
Yellow	1110	iRG.	111110	rgbRG.	0x00 00 FF FF
White	1111	iRGB	111111	rgbRGB	0x00 FF FF FF

*In a Windows color specification, the most-significant byte is used, in other circumstances, as a flag value indicating the type of color reference.

In the Windows color specification system, each primary color (red, green, or blue) has a possible range of 0 to 255, and individual colors are identified by 24-bit combinations of the RGB components, yielding a total of 16,777,216 possible hues.

However, because video boards (with the exception of the newest 24-bit video board) cannot support individual pixel color specifications, these 24-bit values are written to a color palette. The pixels in the image map itself consist of 8-bit index references to the color palette.

Thus, while an SVGA video card can support 24-bit color specifications, it can only do so as a palette containing 256 entries. Furthermore, partially in support of earlier 16-color standards, Windows reserves 20 of these palette entries, leaving 236 colors for custom use.

From the 16-Color to the True-Color Palette

Earlier EGA/VGA devices were limited to16 colors, which were pixel colors defined by four color planes, each holding one bit per pixel. For the EGA/VGA drivers, the four color planes consisted of red (R), green (G), blue (B), and intensity (i). The intensity plane (or bit) shifted between green and light green, blue and light blue, and so forth. Thus, the 16 colors in the standard palette were determined by the available combinations of the three primary colors and the intensity of the color combination. White consisted of RGB and i, light gray was produced by RGB without the intensity bit, and dark gray was set by the intensity bit alone; that is, by very low levels of RGB combined.

For a VGA system, despite limitations inherited from the EGA color schema, there were actually six color planes consisting of both a high- and a low-intensity red (R and r), a high- and low-intensity green (G and g), and a high- and low-intensity blue (B and b). Thus, the VGA video card actually supported 64 (2^6) individual colors.

For the SVGA system, today's de facto standard, the color definition shifts from four or six color planes with one bit per pixel to one color plane holding eight bits per pixel, yielding a palette with 256 color entries (20 of which are reserved by the system for predefined hues).

Each of these palette entries is defined by three eight-bit values (RGB), giving each pure color a total of 256 levels (from black to full intensity) and a total of 16,777,216 possible colors (combining all possible RGB level combinations). Remember, however, that only 256 of these 16 million possible colors can be defined in the device palette, and the device—the video card—has only one palette.

For most purposes, a palette of 256 colors is adequate. Even my wallpaper and screen savers (which include paintings by Rousseu, wildlife and landscape photographs, and undersea images) are excellent when displayed in a 256-color palette. Of course, they are even more colorful when rendered using 24 bits per pixel color.

Generically titled *true color*, today's high-resolution video cards do not use palettes at all. Instead, they provide a full 24 bits of color information for each and every pixel in the display: eight bits each for the red, green, and blue components of every pixel.

Continued on next page

To provide this capability, the memory requirements rise drastically. For a 1024×768 display using 24-bit color, more than 2MB of VRAM is required. And, for a 1280×1024 display, the requirements jump to 4MB of VRAM.

But the VRAM requirements are only a part of the story. These upper-end video cards (as well as most of today's less expensive cards) use sophisticated graphics coprocessors, such as the Tseng ET-4000 or the newest S3 graphics coprocessors, because the amount of information required to render the screen display requires sophisticated processing as well as adequate storage. Without these coprocessors, rendering the screen display can slow the CPU to a crawl.

Ideally, true-color video boards provide enough memory to hold a full 24 bits of color. As a trade-off, however, some otherwise sophisticated video cards save memory by displaying only 16 bits per pixel rather than 24, using 5 bits each for the red, green, and blue components and using the sixteenth bit as an intensity flag applied equally to these components.

Because the human eye cannot distinguish between the 16- and 24-bit results—we simply cannot distinguish 16 million plus hues—the real requirements for high-resolution 24-bit color become somewhat problematic. Still, as memory costs fall and monitor sizes and resolutions rise, the overkill of full 24-bit color is the sunrise on the horizon.

But, even when every system sold is a true-color video system, there will still be a use for color palettes. The 256-color palette will be with us for a long time to come.

The Standard Palette

In DOS, the standard palette consisted of the 16 colors originally defined by EGA video cards or their VGA/SVGA equivalents.

Windows defines a standard palette of 20 static colors (the default palette). On an EGA or VGA system, where only 16 of the 20 colors are actually available, Windows emulates the remaining 4 colors by dithering (a process which will be demonstrated in a moment). On contemporary SVGA systems, where the hardware supports a device palette of 256 colors, the 20 default entries appear as individual hues without adjustments. Table 24.2 shows the RGB color values for each of the standard palette's 20 colors.

TABLE 24.2: The Windows Default Palette Values

Index	Color	R	G	B	Index	Color	R	G	B
0	Black	0	0	0	10	Off-white	266	251	240
1	Dark Red	128	0	0	11	Med. Gray	160	160	164
2	Dark Green	0	128	0	12	Dark Gray	128	128	128
3	Gold	128	128	0	13	Red	255	0	0
4	Dark Blue	0	0	128	14	Green	0	255	0
5	Violet	128	0	128	15	Yellow	255	255	0
6	Dark Cyan	0	128	128	16	Blue	0	0	255
7	Light Gray	192	192	192	17	Magenta	255	0	255
8	Pale Green	192	220	192	18	Light Cyan	0	255	255
9	Pale Blue	166	202	240	19	White	255	255	255

Technically, these 20 standard colors belonging to the stock system palette are inviolable and cannot be altered by an application, even when the application defines its own color values for corresponding palette entries. Because color priority is given to the foreground application, however, and the application's palette takes priority over the standard palette, background displays may be remapped.

Background displays may appear in whichever application colors provide the closest match to the standard colors, even when this results in a distinct change in the screen appearance. In some cases, the color difference may be quite striking, such as when a 256-color bitmap is used as wallpaper and an application has defined its own 256-color palette. But once the new image is displayed, the background colors should return to their original palette colors. Similar effects can be observed using a paint program (such as PhotoShop Pro) when multiple images are loaded or while switching between images when a few moments are required to change between two quite different palettes.

NOTE The *ViewPCX* demo, discussed in Chapter 28, provides a striking example of the effect of changing background display colors. As *ViewPCX* is loading an image from a file (having already defined a new palette), the background image is displayed using the *ViewPCX* palette.

The Color1 Demo: Painting with the Standard Palette

The *Color1* demo was created to demonstrate the Windows standard color palette. As you can see in Figure 24.1, except for an optional icon, *Color1* has no menu, dialog boxes, or other resources. Execution occurs entirely within the exported WndProc procedure, with a minimum of operations.

FIGURE 24.1:

The Colors1 display of the Windows standard palette

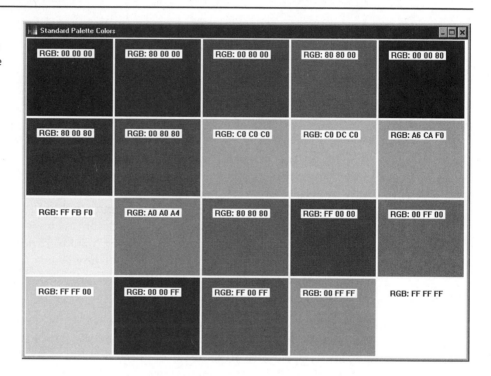

Because all that we intend to accomplish in the *Color1* demo is to paint squares using the default (stock) palette entries, we divide the client window into four rows of five squares each, defining these dimensions as XSTEPS and YSTEPS.

Within the WndProc procedure, in response to the WM_SIZE message, when we receive the client window size in the lParam argument, the x and y sizes for the individual rectangles are calculated.

```
case WM_SIZE:
        xSize = ( LOWORD( lParam ) ) / XSTEPS;
        ySize = ( HIWORD( lParam ) ) / YSTEPS;
```

```
            InvalidateRect( hwnd, NULL, TRUE );
            break;
```

Then, in response to the WM_PAINT message, we set up two loops:

```
case WM_PAINT:
    hdc = BeginPaint( hwnd, &ps );
    for( j=0; j<YSTEPS; j++ )
        for( i=0; i<XSTEPS; i++ )
        {
```

Within the loops, the first step is to use the PALETTEINDEX macro to convert the i and j values into a rectangle number and then, in the COLORREF crColor variable, into a palette index in the form 0x010000*xx*. PALETTEINDEX sets the high byte of the high word to 0x01, indicating that this COLORREF value is a palette-entry specification rather than an absolute RGB color value (see the next section, "Types of RGB Color Specifications").

```
            crColor = PALETTEINDEX( i + ( j * xSteps ) );
            hPen = CreatePen( PS_SOLID, 1, crColor );
            hOldPen = SelectObject( hdc, hPen );
            hBrush = CreateSolidBrush( crColor );
            hOldBrush = SelectObject( hdc, hBrush );
```

Next, we need to create a pen and a brush using the crColor specification and then select the new pen and brush, making them the active drawing pen/brush for the next operations. Notice that we keep handles to the old pen and brush, supplied when SelectObject is called, so that we can reselect the original objects before deleting the two we created.

Once we have both a pen and brush in the desired color, we call the Rectangle function to draw a solid rectangle. The active (selected) pen is used to outline the rectangle and the active brush to fill it, but because both of these are the same color, we simply see a solid rectangle with no outline except the white background of the underlying window.

```
        Rectangle( hdc, i * xSize + 2, j * ySize + 2,
                   ( i + 1 ) * xSize - 2,
                   ( j + 1 ) * ySize - 2 );
        SelectObject( hdc, hOldPen );    // restore original pen
        SelectObject( hdc, hOldBrush );  // and brush then delete
        DeleteObject( hPen );            // discards so we don't
        DeleteObject( hBrush );          // run out of handles
```

Finally, as mentioned, we reselect the original pen and brush and then delete the new pen and brush. If we did not do this, we could run out of available handles.

TIP

To experiment, comment out the closing `SelectObject` and `DeleteObject` statements, then recompile and execute the demo. Then drag or resize the window—either of which results in redrawing the window. You should see the squares come up as white with a black outline once the custom brush and pen handles are exhausted. (The stock black pen and white brush remain available and are used by default when new handles are no longer available.)

Next, we call the `GetNearestColor` function, using the `crColor` palette-index specification, to get the actual RGB color values for the index entry. We report these, now using the default black pen and white brush, on top of the colored rectangles. The results are visible in Figure 24.1 (shown earlier).

```
                // report palette entries as RGB values
         crRGB = GetNearestColor( hdc, crColor );
         wsprintf( szColor, " RGB: %02X %02X %02X ",
                 GetRValue( crRGB ), GetGValue( crRGB ),
                 GetBValue( crRGB ) );
         TextOut( hdc, i * xSize + 20, j * ySize + 20,
                 szColor, strlen(szColor) );
      }
   EndPaint( hwnd, &ps );
```

This is a fairly simple process, but it does demonstrate the standard palette colors. It also leads to an explanation of three types of RGB color specifications.

NOTE

The complete listing for the *Color1* demo is included on the CD accompanying this book, in the Chapter 24 folder.

Types of RGB Color Specifications

Three types of RGB color specifications are demonstrated in the *Color1* program: absolute, palette-index, and palette-relative values.

Absolute RGB COLORREF Values

Both the CreatePen and CreateBrush functions are called with a color reference parameter. Conventionally, this parameter is an RGB long integer (DWORD) following the form 0x00BBGGRR, as shown in Table 24.1. Thus, for a white brush, the color value would be specified as 0x00FFFFFF; for black brush, the value would be 0x00000000.

In all cases, the most-significant byte is 0; the red, green, and blue values are each specified by byte (8-bit) values in the range 0 to 255. If necessary for display, the system will map the specified color to the nearest available color in the active palette.

Palette-Index RGB COLORREF Values

In the *Color1* demo, instead of using absolute RGB values, a second COLORREF format is used. In this format, the color parameter is a palette index identifying an existing palette value. For palette-index entries, the COLORREF value takes the form 0x0100*xxxx*. with the low word (16 bits) providing an index to a logical palette or, in this case, the system palette.

Palette-Relative RGB COLORREF Values

Windows 98 also supports a third format for specifying COLORREF values: the palette-relative RGB value. For this format, the high-order byte value is 2 and the COLORREF value takes the format 0x02BBGGRR. This format is used for output devices that support logical palettes, allowing Windows to match a palette-relative RGB value to the nearest actual color supported by the output device.

Alternatively, if the output device doesn't support a logical palette (probably because it is a video card supporting 24-bit true-color), Windows treats the palette-relative value as if it were an absolute RGB value; that is, instead of palette mapping, Windows attempts to handle the RGB value directly.

Dithered Colors

Although individual palette colors can be assigned to any of the 16 million possible hues, this does not guarantee that the physical device is capable of displaying such a wide range of colors. As explained previously, this limitation is imposed by the graphics video card's limits more than by the video monitor's limits. Most monitors are capable of near-infinite color resolution.

Limitations imposed by the graphics hardware can be circumvented through a process known as *dithering*. The Sunday newspaper comic pages and comic books don't use the same precise techniques but the end results are very similar. In the comics and in colored ads, a fairly wide range of colors is produced by combining three or four primary colors to create what the eye perceives as many gradations of color.

The computer (or TV) screen creates colors by combining red, green, and blue light against a black background. Printed materials use a white background (the paper) and combine light-absorbing inks consisting of cyan, magenta, yellow, and black (CMYK). In this fashion, a strong brown, for example, is produced by placing dots of black or magenta and cyan over a nearly solid yellow background; a softer brown consists of a halftone of yellow with fewer blacks. Similarly, pinks and certain flesh tones combine yellow and magenta with the white paper showing through; dark colors use greater or lesser degrees of black.

On the computer screen, the same principle applies, except that the lights—the pixels—in primary colors are used rather than their complements as inks.

The Color2 Demo: A Dithering Demonstration

The *Color2* demo demonstrates this principle on an SVGA graphics system by setting the background color to a specific color configuration. Because the requested color is not provided as a palette color, Windows attempts to render the requested color by dithering entries from the default 20-color entries.

As shown in Figure 24.2, three scrollbars are used to select color settings for a single colored area, which displays dithered colors created from the standard palette.

FIGURE 24.2:

Creating dithered colors

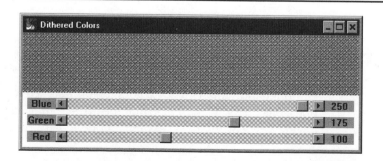

NOTE The complete listing for the *Color2* demo is included on the CD accompanying this book, in the Chapter 24 folder. If your system is set for 24-bit color (true-color) or for anything greater than a 256-color palette, the *Color2* demo will render solid hues rather than dithered mixes. To execute the *Color2* demo, you must select a 256-color palette system.

Figure 24.3 shows a series of dithered color samples (unfortunately, rendered here in black and white).

FIGURE 24.3:

Dithered samples

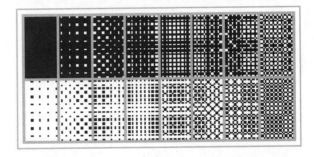

Characteristics of Dithered Colors

Although dithered color patterns are a feature provided by Windows and do not require nor demand your attention, you should note the following characteristics:

- Dithered colors are always an 8×8 pattern, spreading the simulated color over a minimum area of 64 pixels.

- Dithering cannot be used for lines that are always drawn using a primary hue supported by the display device.

- Even though 20 (or more) individual hues are available, dithered colors are composed of 4 individual colors. (These are not, of course, the same 4 shades in all cases.)

- Although dithered colors will fill irregular outlines, individual pixels in the fill may combine (visually) with outlines or borders, creating some appearances of irregularity.

Dithering is not limited to color systems. It is also applied to monochrome and gray-scale displays, as will be discussed presently.

Custom Colors

In many cases, whether the resulting color specification appears as a solid hue or as a dithered pattern is irrelevant and makes no difference to your application. In other cases, however, precise color control can be a very important element. When this is the case, dithered colors just aren't in the running; it's either precise color control or nothing!

When exact colors are required, the solution is to reset one or more palette entries to produce the desired hues. Although this sounds simple enough, in practice, there are a few requirements and limitations.

The primary limitation is physical. Windows, no matter how sophisticated, cannot change the physical characteristics of the system video card. If the physical device supports a palette of only 16 colors, then only 16 custom colors can be displayed and all remaining palette entries will be mapped to the 16 supported physical colors. In like fashion, on an SVGA system, a physical palette limitation of 256 colors may be imposed by the system hardware.

Of course, if you are using one of the new true-color video cards that supports 24 bits of color information per pixel instead of palettes, all of this becomes moot, and you're free to write any information desired to the screen. This particular freedom, however, applies to very few programmers. Therefore, we'll assume that your programs are still bound by hardware limitations.

The Color3 Demo: A Custom Color Palette

The *Color3* demo creates a new palette using custom color settings, which can be adjusted using the same scrollbar controls illustrated in *Color2*. Figure 24.4 shows the *Color3* display.

> **NOTE**   For demonstration purposes, the custom palette used in this example is limited to eight entries. This is a range supported by all graphics cards. It's also large enough to compare several color samples but still small enough to present a clean display.

FIGURE 24.4:

The Color3 display of a custom color palette

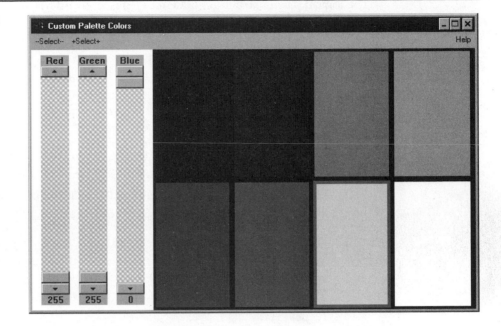

In the *Color3* demo, the three scrollbars control the red, green, and blue color specifications and also show the present levels for the selected color sample. The –Select– and +Select+ menu items step through the eight palette entries, identifying the active selection with a gray outline.

The first step in creating a custom palette requires a few declarations:

```
long APIENTRY WndProc( ... )
{
    static LPLOGPALETTE  lPal;
    ...
    HPALETTE        NewPal;
    HBRUSH          NewBrush, OldBrush;
    HPEN            NewPen,   OldPen;
    ...
```

The lPal variable is a static pointer to a logical palette structure. The remaining variables provide handles (pointers) to two palettes, two brushes, and two pens, all of which will be used presently. Also defined, but not shown here, is an array of eight RGB color values that is used to initialize the color palette and to track changes in the color palette settings.

The logical palette structure (LOGPALETTE) referenced by lPal is defined in WinGDI.H as:

```
typedef struct tagLOGPALETTE
{
    WORD          palVersion;          // Windows version (0x0300)
    WORD          palNumEntries;       // size of array
    PALETTEENTRY  palPalEntry[1];      // array of palette entries
} LOGPALETTE;
```

The version number is always 0x0300 (version 3.0), regardless of the version of Windows (3.1, 3.11, 95, 98, or NT) being used.

The palPalEntry field specifies an array of PALETTEENTRY data structures defining the actual color entries. The PALETTEENTRY structure is defined as:

```
typedef struct tagPALETTEENTRY
{
    BYTE peRed;
    BYTE peGreen;
    BYTE peBlue;
    BYTE peFlags;
} PALETTEENTRY;
```

The three color bytes accept values in the range 0 to 255. The peFlags field accepts a flag value identifying how the palette entry will be used, or it may be NULL. The following are the valid flag values:

PC_EXPLICIT Identifies the palette entry as a hardware palette index, allowing the application to use the display driver's palette. The RGB color specification will be used to find the nearest matching device palette entry.

PC_NOCOLLAPSE Specifies that the color will be placed in an unused entry in the system palette rather than being matched to an existing palette entry. If no unused entries are available, the color is matched normally. Once a new color entry has been made, further palette entries can be matched to this entry.

PC_RESERVED Indicates that the logical palette entry will be used for animation and, therefore, is changeable. As such, other palette entries should not be matched to this entry. If no unused palette entries are available for this color specification, the color specification is not matched to any other existing entries and is not available for animation.

If the peFlags field is NULL, the palette entry is added to the palette if space is available. If not, the entry is matched to the nearest system palette entry.

Much of the processing in *Color3* should be familiar to you from earlier examples in this and preceding chapters. The principal elements here are found in the WndProc procedure's message-handling provisions.

The initial color-processing provision is found in the response to the WM_CREATE message. Here, memory allocation is performed for the lPal palette structure and two initial values are assigned: the palette version and the number of palette entries.

```
switch( msg )
{
    case WM_CREATE:      // initialize the logical palette
        lPal = (LPLOGPALETTE)
        LocalAlloc( LMEM_FIXED | LMEM_ZEROINIT,
                    sizeof(LOGPALETTE) + sizeof(PALETTEENTRY) * 8 );
        lPal->palVersion = 0x300;
        lPal->palNumEntries = 8;
        break;
```

Next, in response to the WM_COMMAND message, the IDM_PLUS (+Select+) and IDM_MINUS (–Select–) instructions step through the palette entries. As they step through the entries, they update the positions of the three scrollbars and the text displays for each to correspond to the current (active) palette settings.

```
case WM_COMMAND:
    switch( LOWORD( wParam ) )
    {
        case IDM_PLUS:
            nPal++;
            if( nPal >= 8 ) nPal = 0;
            for( i=0; i<3; i++ )
            {
                SetScrollPos( hwndScrl[i], SB_CTL, CVal[i][nPal], TRUE );
                SetWindowText( hwndVal[i], itoa( CVal[i][nPal], szBuff, 10 ) );
            }
            InvalidateRect( hwnd, 0L, TRUE );
            break;

        case IDM_MINUS:
            nPal-;
            if( nPal < 0 ) nPal = 7;
```

```
                    for( i=0; i<3; i++ )
                    {
                        SetScrollPos( hwndScrl[i], SB_CTL, CVal[i][nPal], TRUE );
                        SetWindowText( hwndVal[i], itoa( CVal[i][nPal], szBuff, 10 ) );
                    }
                    InvalidateRect( hwnd, OL, TRUE );
                    break;

                case IDM_HELP: ...
            }
        break;
```

The scrollbars used for controls in both the *Color2* and *Color3* demos are the
Windows analog of a vernier or sliding potentiometer control and should be
familiar to you from many Windows applications. Their use here demonstrates
how scrollbars can be used in any context where a variable control is needed.

TIP   Normally, to select a color specification, instead of placing scrollbars (or slider or
other types of controls) in the main application or in a resource dialog box, the
common dialog class **CColorDialog** is used.

Handling for the three scrollbars is found in three separate locations: one in
the WinMain procedure, where the scrollbars are created, and two in the message
responses in the WndProc procedure.

The first provision in the WinMain procedure, occurring at the same time the
three scrollbars are created, is to assign a range to each scrollbar, consisting of
a minimum and a maximum value. In each of the scrollbars used, the range
assigned is 0 to 255, which is the range of the RGB color values. Initial values, or
thumbpad positions, are also assigned at this time.

```
for( i=0; i<=2; i++ )
{
    hwndScrl[i] = CreateWindow( "scrollbar", OL, CHILD_STYLE | WS_TABSTOP | SBS_HORZ,
                               0, 0, 0, 0, hwnd, (HMENU) i, hInst, OL );
    hwndTag[i]  = CreateWindow( "static", szColorLabel[i], CHILD_STYLE | SS_CENTER,
                               0, 0, 0, 0, hwnd, (HMENU)(i+4), hInst, OL );
    hwndVal[i]  = CreateWindow( "static", itoa( CVal[i], szBuff, 10 ),
                                CHILD_STYLE | SS_CENTER,
                               0, 0, 0, 0, hwnd, (HMENU)(i+7), hInst, OL );
    SetScrollRange( hwndScrl[i], SB_CTL, 0, 255, 0 );
    SetScrollPos( hwndScrl[i], SB_CTL, CVal[i], 0 );
}
```

Next, in the response to the WM_SIZE message, the scrollbars are positioned within the application window and sized to fit appropriately.

```
case WM_SIZE:
    cxWnd = LOWORD( lParam );
    cyWnd = HIWORD( lParam );

    hdc = GetDC( hwnd );
    GetTextMetrics( hdc, &tm );
    cyChr = tm.tmHeight;
    cxChr = tm.tmAveCharWidth;
    ReleaseDC( hwnd, hdc );
    xOffset = cxChr * 26;

    xSize = ( cxWnd - xOffset ) / xSteps;
    ySize =  cyWnd / ySteps;
    MoveWindow( hwndRect, 0, 0, cxChr * 26, cyWnd, TRUE );
    for( i=0; i<=2; i++ )
    {
        MoveWindow( hwndTag[i], cxChr * ( ( i * 8 ) + 2 ),
                    (INT)(cyChr * 0.5), cxChr * 6, cyChr, TRUE );
        MoveWindow( hwndVal[i], cxChr * ( ( i * 8 ) + 2 ),
                    cyWnd - (INT)( cyChr * 1.5 ),
                    cxChr * 6,   cyChr, TRUE );
        MoveWindow( hwndScrl[i], cxChr * ( ( i * 8 ) + 2 ),
                    (INT)(cyChr * 1.5), cxChr * 6,
                    cyWnd - ( 3 * cyChr ), TRUE );
    }
    SetFocus( hwnd );
    break;
```

Last, in the response to the WM_HSCROLL message in the *Color2* demo (with horizontal scrollbars) or the WM_VSCROLL message in the *Color3* demo (with vertical scrollbars), the position of each scrollbar's thumbpad is adjusted according to where the scrollbar was clicked or where the thumbpad was dragged.

```
case WM_VSCROLL:
    i = GetWindowLong( (HWND) lParam, GWL_ID );
    switch( LOWORD( wParam ) )
    {
        case SB_PAGEDOWN:    CVal[i][nPal] += 15;                 // no break!
        case SB_LINEDOWN:    CVal[i][nPal]  = MIN( CVal[i][nPal] );   break;
        case SB_PAGEUP:      CVal[i][nPal] -= 15;                 // no break!
        case SB_LINEUP:      CVal[i][nPal]  = MAX( CVal[i][nPal] );   break;
```

```
    case SB_TOP:        CVal[i][nPal]  =   0;                break;
    case SB_BOTTOM:     CVal[i][nPal]  = 255;                break;
    case SB_THUMBPOSITION:
    case SB_THUMBTRACK:  CVal[i][nPal] = HIWORD( wParam );    break;
}
SetScrollPos( hwndScrl[i], SB_CTL, CVal[i][nPal], TRUE );
SetWindowText( hwndVal[i], itoa( CVal[i][nPal], szBuff, 10 ) );
InvalidateRect( hwnd, OL, TRUE );
break;
```

The CVal variable array consists of a 3x8 array of byte values containing the RGB color values for the eight palette entries used.

The real work of displaying the palette begins in response to the WM_PAINT message. It starts, as usual, with a BeginPaint instruction. However, before painting anything, a loop is used to read the present values from the CVal array into the palette entries indicated by lPal.

```
    case WM_PAINT:
        hdc = BeginPaint( hwnd, &ps );
        for( i=0; i<8; i++ )
        {
            lPal->palPalEntry[i].peRed   = CVal[0][i];
            lPal->palPalEntry[i].peGreen = CVal[1][i];
            lPal->palPalEntry[i].peBlue  = CVal[2][i];
            lPal->palPalEntry[i].peFlags = PC_RESERVED;
        }
        NewPal = CreatePalette( lPal );
        SelectPalette( hdc, NewPal, FALSE );
        RealizePalette( hdc );
```

After initializing the palette values in memory, the CreatePalette function creates a new logical palette before SelectPalette makes NewPal the current (active) palette. Optionally, SelectPalette returns a handle to the old (default) palette.

Last, RealizePalette is called to activate the newly selected palette; that is, to make this the current drawing palette within the present device-context handle (hdc).

At this point, the device-context handle is ready for drawing using the new palette. The next segment of code consists of provisions to draw the eight rectangles composing the palette display.

```
for( i=0; i<8; i++ )
{
    j = i % 4;
    k = (int) i / 4;
    if( i == nPal )
        NewPen = CreatePen( PS_SOLID, 5, 0x007F7F7F );
    else
        NewPen = CreatePen( PS_SOLID, 1, PALETTEINDEX(i) );
    OldPen = SelectObject( hdc, NewPen );

    NewBrush = CreateSolidBrush( PALETTEINDEX(i) );
    OldBrush = SelectObject( hdc, NewBrush );

    Rectangle( hdc, xOffset + j * xSize, k * ySize,
                    xOffset + ( j + 1 ) * xSize - 1,
                    ( k + 1 ) * ySize - 1 );
```

Notice that within the loop, a parallel to the CreatePalette/SelectPalette provisions occurs as the CreatePen/CreateSolidBrush and SelectObject instructions create and select a pen and brush to draw each rectangle. The original (default) pen and brush have been saved as the OldPen and OldBrush handles.

```
SelectObject( hdc, OldBrush );
DeleteObject( NewBrush );
SelectObject( hdc, OldPen );
DeleteObject( NewPen );
```

After each pen and brush is used, the original pen and brush are reselected and the new pen and brush deleted.

Once the paint operation is completed, the new palette is deleted.

```
}
EndPaint( hwnd, &ps );
DeleteObject( NewPal );
break;
```

Each of these closing provisions is every bit as important as creating the palette, pens, and brushes in the first place. As stressed in Chapter 23, Windows can support only a finite number of handles to logical devices, so you must release handles when you no longer need them.

As a final provision, the new palette is deleted before the WM_PAINT message response concludes. The memory allocated for the palette structure and the pointer lPal is not released, however, and remains available for further use. This memory will be needed the next time the window is updated. All that has been lost is a temporary palette, a temporary pen, and a temporary brush. The originals have been restored, leaving the Windows system in the proper condition for other applications or for other actions by the present application.

WARNING
Remember, restoring the original condition is not just good manners—it's essential! If these handles are not released when they are no longer needed—immediately after use—and the originals restored, not only can the current application fail suddenly, but Windows itself can be left in a very hazardous state. If you wish to experiment, simply comment out the restoration provisions (but be sure to save your work before trying this).

There is one more element of cleanup required. This last bit is only necessary when the application exits and is handled in response to the WM_DESTROY message:

```
case WM_DESTROY:
    LocalFree( lPal );
    PostQuitMessage(0);
    break;
```

The WM_DESTROY message is an application's opportunity for a final cleanup before exiting. In previous examples, it has responded simply by posting a quit message to notify any child processes of an impending exit (a standard default provision even when there are no child processes). In this case, however, this is the appropriate point in time to release the memory allocated for the palette structure, as shown above, before notifying WinMain's message loop to exit, completing the shutdown.

All special brushes and pens and the logical palette have already been taken care of within the paint procedure, and this concludes cleanup for the application.

NOTE
The complete listing for the *Color3* demo is included on the CD accompanying this book, in the Chapter 24 folder.

Custom Brushes and Color Messages

In the *Color2* demo, a custom color was demonstrated by changing the background color. Then, in the *Color3* demo, custom colors were demonstrated by creating solid color brushes.

In both the *Color2* and *Color3* demos, an interesting addition would be to color the three scrollbars using the individual red, green, and blue settings. This is something you can try on your own. However, to facilitate the experiment, a few comments and suggestions follow.

In Windows 3.1, when a window control was to be redrawn, the parent window was sent a WM_CTLCOLOR message with the high word in the lParam argument containing the control type and the low word containing the control element's ID value. Both values, of course, were 16 bits.

Under Windows 98, where control elements are now 32-bit rather than 16-bit, the WM_CTLCOLOR message has been replaced by a series of seven WM_CTL-COLOR*xxxxx* messages, which explicitly identify the control element type, as shown in Table 24.3.

TABLE 24.3: CTLCOLOR Messages

Message Constant	Control Type
WM_CTLCOLORMSGBOX	Message box
WM_CTLCOLOREDIT	Edit control
WM_CTLCOLORLISTBOX	List box control
WM_CTLCOLORBTN	Button control
WM_CTLCOLORDLG	Dialog box
WM_CTLCOLORSCROLLBAR	Scrollbar control
WM_CTLCOLORSTATIC	Static control

Accompanying the WM_CTLCOLOR*xxxxxx* message, the wParam argument contains a handle to the display context for the child window (the control to be repainted). The lParam argument contains the 32-bit child window handle.

There are a few cautions involved with using these messages. First, when an application explicitly processes any of these messages, the application must return a handle to a brush to paint the control background. If this is not done, the application will probably crash. A fragmentary example follows:

```
case WM_CTLCOLORxxxxxx:
    hCtrlBrush = GetWindowLong( lParam, GWL_ID );
    DeleteObject( hCtrlBrush );
    RGBColor = RGB( rVal, gVal, bVal );
    hCtrlBrush = CreateSolidBrush( RGBColor );
    UnrealizeObject( hCtrlBrush );
    return( hCtrlBrush );                // return the handle to the GDI
```

Another, less critical precaution, is to make sure that the application aligns the brush origin with the upper-left corner of the child window. If you don't accomplish this, particularly when you're using patterned brushes, the control may not be painted properly.

The MFC OnCtlColor Method

In applications using MFC classes, the corresponding operation is the OnCtl-Color method, which is called when a child control is about to be drawn. Most controls send this message to their parent (usually a dialog box) to prepare the pDC for drawing the control using the correct colors.

In the OnCtlColor method, to change the text color used by a control, call the SetTextColor member function with the desired red, green, and blue values. To change the background color of a single-line edit control, the brush handle is set in both the CTLCOLOR_EDIT and CTLCOLOR_MSGBOX message codes. Also, in response to the CTLCOLOR_EDIT code, call the CDC::SetBkColor function.

Because the list box in a drop-down combo box is actually a child window belonging to the combo box but is not a child of the window, the OnCtlColor is not called for the list box. Thus, to change the color of the drop-down list box, create a custom CComboBox class that includes an override of OnCtlColor that checks for CTLCOLOR_LISTBOX in the nCtlColor parameter. In this handler, the SetBkColor member function must be used to set the background color for the text.

NOTE   The `OnCtlColor` member function is called by the framework to allow an application to handle a Windows message. The parameters passed to the function reflect the parameters received by the framework when the message was received. If the base-class implementation of this function is called, the implementation will use the parameters originally passed with the message and not any of the custom parameters supplied.

The UnrealizeObject Function

The `UnrealizeObject` function, called with a handle to an object, is used to reset the origin of the object. In the preceding example, the object was the handle to a brush that would be used to paint a control object's background. When you use `UnrealizeObject`, the GDI is directed to reset the origin of an object, such as a brush, when the object is next selected. The `UnrealizeObject` function is also used with logical palettes as an instruction to the GDI to remap the logical palette to the system palette.

The `UnrealizeObject` function should not be called while a drawing object, such as a brush or pen, is currently selected in a device context. However, when you use this function to remap a palette, the palette specified may be the currently selected palette in a device context.

The DeleteObject Function

During execution of the *Color2* demo, each time a WM_HSCROLL message is received, the existing background brush is deleted before a new brush (using the new color settings) is created. But before the application exits, a final call to the **DeleteObject** function is needed:

```
case WM_DESTROY:
    DeleteObject( (HGDIOBJ) GetClassLong( hwnd, GCL_HBRBACKGROUND ) );
    PostQuitMessage(0);
    break;
```

If we had included provisions to paint the scrollbars or other controls, these brushes would also need provisions to delete each object before exiting. In earlier examples, the only objects used were standard objects—brushes, pens, and the like—and so no special provisions for cleanup were needed. However, custom brushes, as well as other custom objects, require some memory. If you do not delete custom objects prior to exit, they will continue to occupy memory (at least, until the computer is rebooted).

NOTE
An advantage in using C++ object classes, such as the MFC classes, is that class objects are self-destroying and delete themselves when they go out of scope, thus relieving the programmer of some of the cleanup tasks.

Color Drawing Modes

Under DOS, only one graphics drawing mode is supported. In this mode, each pixel drawn (including pixels comprising lines and the like) simply overwrites or replaces the existing pixels using the current drawing color.

In contrast, Windows supports multiple drawing modes, in which the image is combined with the existing (background) image in a variety of fashions. These drawing modes are referred to variously *as bit-wise Boolean operations* or, in Windows, as *raster operations*.

Windows ROP2 Operations

Since the drawing-mode operations involve two pixel patterns—the object image and the screen image—they are also referred to as *ROP2 operations*. In WinGDI.H, they are identified by R2_*xxxx* constants. Sixteen ROP2 operations are defined, as shown in Table 24.4.

TABLE 24.4: Binary Raster Operations

Mode Constant	Operation	Resulting Image
R2_NOP	Screen	Screen not affected (no operation)
R2_NOT	~Screen	Existing screen inverted
R2_COPYPEN	Pen	Pen overwrites screen (default)
R2_NOTCOPYPEN	~Pen	Inverted pen overwrites screen

Continued on next page

TABLE 24.4 (CONTINUED): Binary Raster Operations

Mode Constant	Operation	Resulting Image
R2_MASKPEN	Pen & Screen	Pen ANDed with screen
R2_MASKNOTPEN	~Pen & Screen	Inverted pen ANDed with screen
R2_MASKPENNOT	Pen & ~Screen	Pen ANDed with inverted screen
R2_NOTMASKPEN	~(Pen & Screen)	Pen ANDed with screen, result inverted
R2_MERGEPEN	Pen | Screen	Pen ORed with screen
R2_MERGENOTPEN	~Pen | Screen	Inverted pen ORed with screen
R2_MERGEPENNOT	Pen | ~Screen	Pen ORed with inverted screen
R2_NOTMERGEPEN	~(Pen | Screen)	Pen ORed with screen, result inverted
R2_XORPEN	Pen ^ Screen	Pen XORed with screen
R2_NOTXORPEN	~(Pen ^ Screen)	Pen XORed with screen, result inverted
R2_BLACK	0	Black line (drawing color ignored)
R2_WHITE (R2_LAST)	1	White line (drawing color ignored)

The ROP2 constants listed are ordered according to function, not according to integer values. Thus, the first ROP2 mode listed, R2_NOP, has no effect on the screen image at all. However, it is still useful, since the current position (cp) is updated by LineTo or LineRel operations when using the R2_NOP mode.

The second ROP2 mode, R2_NOT, draws by inverting the existing image (for example, white becomes black) using bit-wise color inversion. This is useful for two reasons:

- It ensures absolute screen visibility (with the exception of screen areas that are approximately 50 percent gray).

- The original screen can be restored by executing a second, identical drawing operation.

The third ROP2 mode, R2_COPYPEN, is the default drawing mode, corresponding to the conventional DOS drawing mode discussed previously.

The next 11 ROP2 modes produce varying effects, which are more readily demonstrated by the *PenDraw1* demo than by description. The *PenDraw* demo is discussed in the next section.

The last two ROP2 modes, R2_BLACK and R2_WHITE, draw lines using complete black or white, respectively, regardless of the current drawing color.

The PenDraw1 Demo: Demonstrating Drawing Modes

The *PenDraw1* demo begins by writing labels along the right side of the screen before drawing a background. The background drawing starts at the left with five vertical gray bars, ranging from 0 percent black (white) to 100 percent black; then continues with six color bars in blue, green, cyan, red, magenta, and yellow.

> **NOTE** The labels at the right in *PenDraw1* are intended to extend into the color bars at the left, further demonstrating how the ROP2_*xxxx* operations interact with background images.

Against this background, 16 horizontal lines are drawn using the 16 drawing modes (in the functional order listed in Table 24.4, not in numerical order), each employing the active drawing color. A range of eight drawing colors can be selected from the menu. Figure 24.5 shows an example of the *PenDraw1* display.

FIGURE 24.5:

Binary raster operations

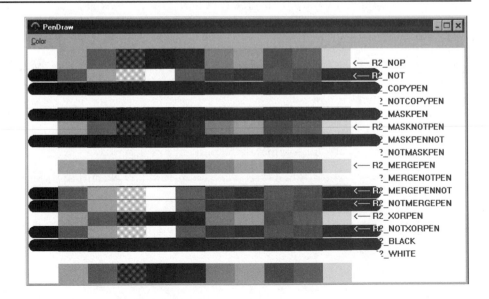

Notice in Figure 24.5 and when executing the *PenDraw1* demo that the default white background is not treated in the same fashion as a white background drawn by a brush or as background to the text display. This is easily observed by selecting the yellow drawing color and observing the effects where the lines overlap the labels: R2_NOT, R2_MASKPEN, and R2_NOTXORPEN. Because the lines drawn are slightly wider than the text labels, a thin section of background white appears above and below the labels.

NOTE   The *PenDraw1* demo is included on the CD accompanying this book, in the Chapter 24 folder.

Color to Gray-Scale

Windows has its own provisions for handling most gray-scale conversions for color programs executing on monochrome video systems. On some plasma and LCD screens (displays that are virtually an endangered species), even though the display is technically monochrome, the video system still accepts color-input information, translating the color data into 16, 32, or 64 gray levels.

In both of these situations, not only is the process of converting colors to gray-scale handled without the programmer's participation, but the programmer is effectively forbidden to intervene (except for offering palette choices that produce optimum contrast and clarity).

Even though most gray-scale conversions are handled by Windows, some circumstances do remain where programmers must supply their own conversions (for example, to show how a color image would appear on a monochrome printer, as explained in Chapter 32). How this is done depends on the circumstances, the equipment, and the desired results. There are no hard and fast rules, nor are there any absolutes.

Following are a few suggestions for producing color to gray-scale conversions. You can apply these techniques to hard-copy devices, such as printers, as well as to monitors.

Gray-Scale Palettes

One popular method of accomplishing gray-scale conversion is to create a palette of grays suitable for mapping the original color palette. For example, assume a palette of 16 colors (as per EGA/VGA) ranging from white to black. The obvious gray-scale for correspondence would be a 4×4 pixel (or dot) pattern, as shown in Figure 24.6.

FIGURE 24.6:

A 16-bit gray scale

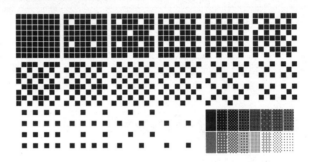

Here, the 16-bit patterns range from solid black to one-sixteenth black. (Reduced views of the same patterns appear at the lower right.) As an alternative, you could drop one of the intermittent patterns to adjust the gray-scale from solid black to solid white.

But remember, dithered colors use an 8×8 pattern. Applying similar patterns in black and white would offer a possible scale of 64 grays, providing a wider range of grays or a finer texture for hard-copy output.

> **WARNING** Adjacent elements in a 64-level, gray-scale palette can be very difficult to distinguish. Select carefully.

The gray-scale patterns suggested in Figure 24.6 form a uniform range that is about the best that can be accomplished with only 16 elements. Moving up to a 64-bit pattern presents the possibility of matching the gray-scale density to the intensity (or darkness) of the color being mapped.

To do so, the first step is to understand a few basic principles of color perception. The human eye does not perceive all colors equally, in terms of absolute intensity. Of the three primary colors—red, green, and blue—the eye perceives green almost twice as strongly as red. In turn, the eye's response to blue is approximately one-third the response to red. Thus, an approximate gray-scale formula reflecting the perception curve of the human eye is:

```
Intensity = Red * 0.30 + Green * 0.59 + Blue * 0.11
```

Thus, since Windows uses the RGB values in the range 0 to 255, the gray equivalent matching a 24-bit color specification becomes:

$$W = \left\lceil \frac{R * 0.30}{255} \right\rceil + \left\lceil \frac{G * 0.59}{255} \right\rceil + \left\lceil \frac{B * 0.11}{255} \right\rceil$$

Using this formula, if the R, G, and B are all at maximum (255), resulting in white on the screen, the formula yields a value of 100 percent white and 0 percent black.

On the other hand, for a soft blue with an RGB value of 43, 128, 210, here's the formula:

$$W = \left\lceil \frac{43 * 0.30}{255} \right\rceil + \left\lceil \frac{128 * 0.59}{255} \right\rceil + \left\lceil \frac{210 * 0.11}{255} \right\rceil$$

and the equivalent proportions of white to black become:

```
W = ( 0.050 ) + ( 0.296 ) + ( 0.090 ) = 43.6% white (or 56.4% black)
```

Calculating a gray-scale using an 8x8 pattern, the optimum gray would be 36 black pixels (or dots) to 28 white pixels.

The problem in converting colors to grays is that quite distinct colors can yield the same gray values simply because they have the same relative intensities. For this problem, there is no simple cure.

On the other hand, optimizing printing a color image by creating 8×8 blocks for each pixel in the image is a rather frustrating process, if only in the annoyances involved in creating the 64-dot patterns need. Instead, there is a simpler approach.

Rather than creating an elaborate system of dots, you can simply convert the color image to a gray image by mapping the color pixels to their gray-intensity equivalents. For this, you can use the original formula:

```
I = ( R * 0.30 ) + ( G * 0.59 ) + ( B * 0.11 )
```

Once I has been calculated, the equivalent gray palette entry would be created as:

```
RGB( I, I, I )
```

Or, even easier, begin by creating a palette with gray-scale entries as:

```
for( i=0; i<256; i++ )
{
    lPal->palPalEntry[i].peRed   = i;
    lPal->palPalEntry[i].peGreen = i;
    lPal->palPalEntry[i].peBlue  = i;
    lPal->palPalEntry[i].peFlags = PC_RESERVED;
}
NewPal = CreatePalette( lPal );
SelectPalette( hdc, NewPal, FALSE );
RealizePalette( hdc );
```

This code fragment would create and realize a palette with 256 shades of gray ranging from black to white. To convert a color image to gray, the only real requirement would be to calculate the intensity, using the perception-response formula, for each pixel and then assign the intensity as the pixel's palette index.

Once this is done, simply printing to any hard-copy device, which has its own routines to print gray equivalents, results in a black-and-white image that maintains the intensities of the original.

Gray-Scales and Plaiding

There is one hazard inherent in using gray-scale on black-and-white output devices: Plaiding can occur when the gray-scale pattern is not matched to the device resolution. Figure 24.7 shows an example of plaiding deliberately produced on the screen, showing that video devices are no more immune than printers to this problem. The illustration in Figure 24.7 is an excerpt from Figure 24.6, enlarged to show the mismatch between the image's dot pattern and the screen resolution.

As a simple rule of thumb, to prevent plaiding, make sure that the pixel dimension of the image (or dot dimension on a printer) after conversion to gray-scale is an even multiple of the dot resolution of the reproduction size.

FIGURE 24.7:

Plaiding in gray-scales

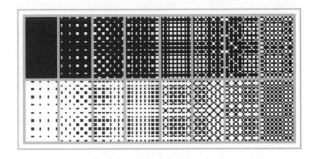

For example, assume a 200×150 pixel bitmap is converted to a 16-shade gray-scale. After conversion, the result is 800×600 pixels. To reproduce this image on a laser printer with a resolution of 300 dpi, without plaiding, the minimum size would be 2.666 inches wide by 2 inches high. Or, for a larger image, a print size of 8 inches wide by 6 inches high would also fit with the image scaled to 2400×1800 pixels.

Alternatively, if the image used a 64-shade gray-scale, the smallest acceptable image would be 5.333 inches by 4 inches.

How you employ gray-scaling is up to you and your requirements. Moreover, if you are content with the conversion capabilities provided by Windows and many output devices, you'll probably have little need for this facility. But if you do, you now know the basics of color-to-gray-scale conversion.

Gray-Scale to Color Conversions

A less common requirement than color to gray-scale is converting a gray-scale to color. This process is commonly referred to as *false-color conversion*. Normally, this is not an attempt to reproduce a color image from a monochrome source, since there simply is not enough information for that task to be accomplished automatically. The automatic gray-to-color (false-color) conversion is an attempt to render an image where the only information is gray to a form where colors are used to make differences in intensity stand out.

Exotic examples include radio-star maps rendered in full glorious false color, or topological or meteorological maps, where color enhances readability. In infrared images, false-color assignments make it possible to print thermographic maps where temperatures are easily recognized as ranges of color.

TIP

The false-color process can be applied to virtually any type of information. There is just one thing that you must remember: The color information applied is purely arbitrary and should be chosen only for ease of recognition, not for artistic whim. Producing an image in alternating shades of chartreuse and puce may get you into the Guggenheim, but it's not a good way to convey information (unless you're trying to tell the world that you're color blind).

Implementation of false coloration is simple. Just decide on a color range and what levels of intensity to depict, and then construct a palette where the intensity levels (as palette indexes) have the appropriate color values.

Regardless of the number of levels in the original, it is often a good idea to restrict the false-color palette to a reasonably small number of hues, such as 20 or 32, rather than implementing a large palette of 256 shades. You should experiment to find the base palette size.

This chapter has covered all you need to know about handling color in your Windows 98 applications. We have discussed color palettes, custom colors, and gray-scale conversions. In the next chapter, we'll talk about the Windows drawing tools.

CHAPTER

TWENTY-FIVE

25

Drawing Tools

- Line styles

- Hatch-fill styles

- Shape-drawing functions

- Business graphs: bar and pie charts

While folk wisdom maintains that a picture has value equal to a thousand words, this same adage has been most honored in dispute, disagreement, sarcastic rebuttal, and jest—not to mention outright subversion by pundits found everywhere from Madison Avenue to the halls of government. Still, the real truth might better be that, more often than not, a picture is preferred to a thousand words.

And, in like fashion, a graphic is often preferred to a thousand words. This preference, despite rumors concerning the literary acuity of CEOs and other board members, is not so much founded in any relative values but is based on the simple fact that a good graphic can convey information in a form more readily understood than many thousands of words or columns of figures.

One popular example of this principal is found in data-generated graphics in which images are created as visual analogs of numerical or scalar data, giving clarity to the relative relationships between elements at the expense of absolute magnitudes. Graphics of this type may be composed of simple shapes, such as those used in pie or bar graphs; may be less structured forms, such as with flow charts, schematics, or other diagrams; or may be composed of bitmapped images, as with the iconized buttons and controls found in any of a variety of Windows applications.

The topic of this chapter is creating graphics images using the drawing tools supplied by the Windows API functions. We will look at the various tools available, and then see how these tools work in applications.

Graphics Tools and Shapes

In Chapter 24, we discussed Windows color palettes and line-drawing modes. Those are the simplest of the tools supplied. Windows also offers a wide variety of other drawing features, including a selection of standard shapes, varying line styles, and a selection of fill styles for solid shapes.

Standard Shapes

Windows provides a series of functions to draw standard shapes, either as solids or outlines. Table 25.1 lists the functions and the shapes that they draw.

TABLE 25.1: Standard Shapes

Function	Shape
Arc	Open curve, either elliptical or circular
Chord	Arc with the endpoints connected by a chord
Ellipse	Closed curve, either elliptical or circular
Pie	Arc with endpoints connected to center
Polygon	Any multisided figure
Polypolygon	Multiple multisided figures
Rectangle	Rectangle with square corners
RoundRect	Rectangle with rounded corners

NOTE   The *PenDraw2* demo illustrates five of these eight shape functions, and the *Pen-Draw3* demo demonstrates two others. Both of these demos are discussed later in this chapter.

You'll see how to use these functions to create shapes presently. However, before these shapes can be drawn, a drawing pen is also required.

Logical Pens

Windows defines a selection of logical pens, each with a predefined pattern. The default pen if no other selection has been made is a solid, black line with a width of one logical unit. The defined pen (line) styles are listed in Table 25.2.

TABLE 25.2: Pen (Line) Styles

Style ID	Line Type
PS_SOLID	————————
PS_DASH	— — — — — —
PS_DOT	· · · · · · · · · · · ·

Continued on next page

TABLE 25.2 CONTINUED: Pen (Line) Styles

Style ID	Line Type
PS_DASHDOT	— · — · — · — · — ·
PS_DASH2DOT	— · · — · · — · · — · ·
PS_NULL	No line (blank)
PS_INSIDEFRAME	If the pen width is greater than one logical unit, ensures that the line is drawn inside the closed shape. Valid with all primitive shapes except polygons.

NOTE The PS_INSIDEFRAME style may be used in combination with any of the other line styles listed in Table 25.2. If the pen color does not match an available RGB palette color, the pen is drawn with a dithered (logical) color. If the pen width is one, PS_INSIDEFRAME is treated as PS_SOLID.

The initial step in selecting a new logical pen is to call the CreatePen function with specifications for the style, width, and drawing color.

```
hPen = CreatePen( nPenStyle, nPenWidth, RGBColor );
hOldPen = SelectObject( hdc, hPen );
```

After creating a new pen, the SelectObject function is called to associate the new pen with the device context, returning a handle to the previous pen.

Optionally, you could create a selection of pens—for example, as an array of handles—and then select each pen as needed (using SelectObject). But remember, each pen (or brush) you create consumes some memory. When the object is no longer needed, dispose of it via the DeleteObject function.

```
DeleteObject( hPen );
```

One caution: A created pen (or brush) should not be deleted while associated with a device context (unless, of course, the device context is about to be closed). Instead, before deleting a pen (or brush), the SelectObject function can be called to restore the original pen. For example, instead of simply calling Delete-Object with the handle of the pen to delete, use a compound statement:

```
DeleteObject( SelectObject( hdc, hOldPen ) );
```

Logical Brushes

Windows also defines a selection of logical brushes, each with a color specification and a predefined pattern. (Width, of course, does not apply.) Windows 98 provides a variety of hatched brushes (identifying constants are defined in Win-GDI.H), which correspond to hatch-fill patterns supported by Windows 3.*x*. The hatch-fill styles are listed in Table 25.3.

TABLE 25.3: Hatch-Fill Patterns

Hatch Fill Style	Pattern
HS_HORIZONTAL	Horizontal lines
HS_VERTICAL	Vertical lines
HS_FDIAGONAL	Forward diagonal (forward slash marks, approximately 45°)
HS_BDIAGONAL	Backward diagonal (backslash marks, approximately 45°)
HS_CROSS	Horizontal cross-hatch
HS_DIAGCROSS	Diagonal cross-hatch

A logical hatch-fill brush is created in the same fashion as a logical pen, as explained in the previous section, and is subject to the same restrictions.

```
hBrush = CreateBrush( nHatchStyle, RGBColor );
hOldBrush = SelectObject( hdc, hBrush );
```

As with any other object, when you no longer need the brush, you should dispose of it.

```
DeleteObject( SelectObject( hdc, hOldBrush ) );
```

Guarding Against Squandered Memory

Unfortunately, you are allowed to create a brush or a pen without the formalities of saving a handle to either the new brush or pen, or the old brush or pen; that is, without making any provisions to delete the new object or restore the original. The following code will function without reporting any errors or warnings:

```
SelectObject( hdc, CreatePen( nPen-IDM_SOLID, 1, cColor ) );
SelectObject( hdc, CreateHatchBrush( nHatch-IDM_HORIZ, cColor ) );
```

Continued on next page

Each `CreateHatchBrush` and `CreatePen` call allocates memory for the brush or pen, which is not disposed of until either Windows is exited or the system is rebooted. The bottom line is simple: There are no guards against this type of error except for your awareness and careful programming practices.

The PenDraw2 Demo: Drawing Shapes

The *PenDraw2* demo illustrates five of the eight shape-drawing functions: `Rectangle`, `Ellipse`, `Arc`, `Chord`, and `Pie`. This program permits you to select shape, line, and fill styles from a menu. The menu also offers a choice of colors, with a palette of eight shades predefined as RGB color values. Figure 25.1 shows an example of a shape drawn in *PenDraw2*.

FIGURE 25.1:

The PenDraw2 demo

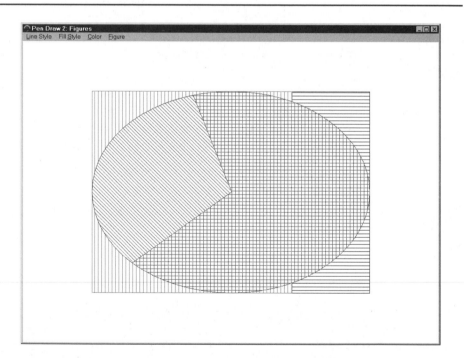

NOTE

The *PenDraw2* demo is included on the CD that accompanies this book, in the Chapter 25 folder.

Drawing Rectangles and Squares

The `Rectangle` function requires only four parameters to specify the coordinates (in device-context terms) for the upper-left and lower-right corners.

```
Rectangle( hdc, xUL, yUL, xLR, yLR );
```

A square is simply a special case of a rectangle and can be provided as:

```
Rectangle( hdc, xUL, yUL,
                xUL + min( xLR-xUL, yLR-yUL ),
                yUL + min( yLR-yUL, xLR-xUL ) );
```

The demo draws the rectangle or square using the current color, pen, line style, and fill style.

The `RoundRect` function (which is not demonstrated in *PenDraw2*) operates in the same fashion as the `Rectangle` function, except for the addition of two parameters specifying the x and y radii for the ellipsis forming the corners.

```
RoundRect( hdc, xUL, yUL, xLR, yLR, xRadius, yRadius );
```

In general, `xRadius` and `yRadius` are equal, making the corner arc circular, but this is not a fixed requirement; the corner ellipse can be elongated in either dimension. Figure 25.2 shows three corner examples: the left with `xRadius` > `yRadius`, the middle with `xRadius` = `yRadius`, and the right with `xRadius` < `yRadius`.

FIGURE 25.2:

Three corners using
RoundRect

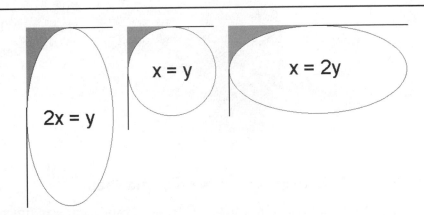

Drawing Ellipses

In Windows, an ellipse is defined in terms of a theoretical rectangle bounding the ellipse. Like the `Rectangle` function, the `Ellipse` function is called with four coordinates identifying the upper-left and lower-right corners of a bounding rectangle.

```
Ellipse( hdc, xUL, yUL, xLR, yLR );
```

> **NOTE**
>
> Mathematically and in more sophisticated applications, ellipses are described in terms of x and y radii and loci coordinates. In comparison, the C/C++ version of an ellipse is rather restricted in orientation.

Also, just as a square is a special case of a rectangle, a circle is simply a special case of an ellipse, in which the x and y radii are equal.

```
Ellipse( hdc, xUL, yUL,
            xUL + min( xLR - xUL, yLR - yUL ),
            yUL + min( yLR - yUL, xLR - xUL ) );
```

Figure 25.3 shows three elliptical shapes together with their bounding rectangles. (These bounding rectangles are not drawn by the Ellipse function but are provided simply as illustration.)

FIGURE 25.3:

Three ellipses

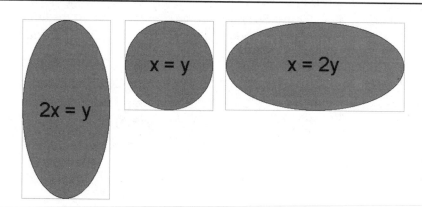

Drawing Arcs, Chords, and Pies

Like the Ellipse function, the Arc, Chord, and Pie functions also use coordinate parameters to define a bounding rectangle that determines the shape of the arc, chord, or pie. But in addition to the basic curve, each of these functions also requires two pairs of additional coordinate parameters to identify the beginning arc position (xp1,yp1) and the ending arc position (xp2,yp2). The three functions are called as:

```
Arc(   hdc, xUL, yUL, xLR, yLR, xStart, yStart, xEnd, yEnd );
Chord( hdc, xUL, yUL, xLR, yLR, xStart, yStart, xEnd, yEnd );
Pie(   hdc, xUL, yUL, xLR, yLR, xStart, yStart, xEnd, yEnd );
```

Figure 25.4 shows arc, chord, and pie shapes, together with the bounding rectangles and the radii determining the begin and end angles.

FIGURE 25.4:

Arc, chord, and pie shapes

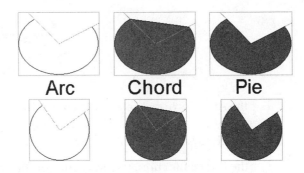

The beginning and endpoints of arcs are defined, not by angles, but by points defining radii intersecting the arc. As shown in Figure 25.5, the arc is drawn counter-clockwise, beginning at an angle defined by the xStart,yStart coordinates and ending at the angle defined by the xEnd,yEnd point.

The xStart,yStart point identifies a radius drawn from the center of the arc through the point specified and does not necessarily lie on the arc itself (though it may). The arc begins at the point where the radius and arc intersect. Or, if you prefer, the xStart,yStart point, together with the centerpoint, defines an angle for the arc starting point. In like fashion, the xEnd,yEnd point defines a radius setting the endpoint of the arc.

> **NOTE**   Under DOS, using C++ functions, an arc (or associated shape) is drawn by defining a center point, the radius (or x and y radii) and defining the beginning and endpoints as angles, with the 0° angle located horizontally to the right. In Windows, the shape of the arc segment, like the ellipse, is defined by a bounding rectangle.

FIGURE 25.5:

Defining arc angles

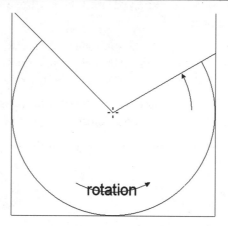

For the Arc function, the process ends with determining the starting point and endpoint of the arc. For an arc, the resulting shape is not closed and no fill brush is used, although the arc itself is drawn using the current line style and color.

For the Chord function, the endpoints of the arc are connected with a straight line to complete a closed figure, which is filled in the *PenDraw2* demo using the selected hatch brush.

For the Pie function, the endpoints of the arc are also connected, but instead of a line between the two arc ends, two lines connect the endpoints with the center-point of the arc to create a pie slice. Again, the closed figure is filled using the selected hatch brush.

> **NOTE**
>
> Remember, for the Chord and Pie functions, the points used are the endpoints of the arc, not the points passed as arguments to define the radii, which, in turn, determine the arc endpoints. Later, in the *PieChart* demo, we'll use conventional trigonometry to calculate points that do lie on the arc (which is easier than calculating points that do not). Just keep in mind that these determining points are not required to lie on the arc itself.

Creating Business Graphs

One useful application for the shape-drawing functions is to create business graphs, such as bar graphs and pie charts. Although business graphs may not be your favorite subjects for programming (and certainly aren't mine), business applications are often required to produce such graphs. So, setting aside personal preferences, I've developed the *BarGraph* and *PieGraph* demos to illustrate how the `Rectangle` and `Pie` functions can be used with data sets.

Both the *BarGraph* and *PieGraph* demos use data arrays that are declared as static information within the program source code. In actual applications, of course, business graphs would use data either read directly from an external source or data calculated from external sources. For demo purposes, defining a data format and creating external source files is unnecessary for the actual objective. Do note, however, that both demos use the same data sets.

The BarGraph Demo: Building a Bar Graph

The *BarGraph* demo displays four years' worth of data broken down into eight categories. Colors identify data by years, and the bars are grouped by category.

TIP   Optionally, you could also use varying fill patterns to identify category groups or to replace the year colors (for example, for monochrome displays).

In this application, there are advantages to using separate horizontal and vertical scale ranges and, therefore, it uses the `MM_ANISOTROPIC` mode. Another advantage of using anisotropic mapping is that it allows you to change the vertical scaling to accommodate variations in the maximum values that need to be graphed.

Once the mode is selected, the origin point is set near the lower-left corner of the window but slightly up and to the right, leaving room to accommodate labels below each group of bars. Also, after the client window is painted, the original (entry) mapping mode, which was saved when the `MM_ANISOTROPIC` mode was set, is restored, as are the original pen and brush sets. Figure 25.6 illustrates a sample bar graph.

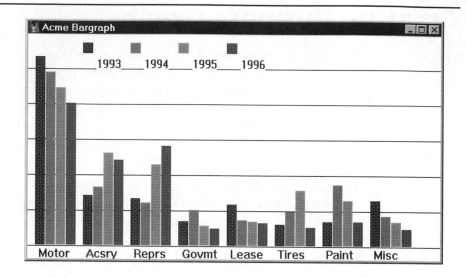

The principal elements specific to the *BarGraph* demo are found in the WM_PAINT response.

```
for( j=0; j<4; j++ )
{
    TextOut( hdc, ( j + 1 ) * 70 + 20, -2 * MaxVal - 20,
             szBuff, sprintf( szBuff, "%d", Years[j] ) );
    hPen = CreatePen( PS_SOLID, 1, lpColor[j+1] );
    SelectObject( hdc, hPen );
    hBrush = CreateSolidBrush( lpColor[j+1] );
    SelectObject( hdc, hBrush );
    Rectangle( hdc, (j+1)*70, 2*MaxVal+20, (j+1)*70+15, 2*MaxVal+5 );
```

The outer loop executes for the four years, writing a label to identify each year before creating a small block showing the color used for the year.

The next step executes a loop through the data elements for the year, creating a rectangle for each category using the brush and color created for the current year.

```
    for( i=0; i<8; i++ )
        Rectangle( hdc, j * 15 + 1 + i * 70, 0, ( j + 1 ) * 15 + i * 70,
                   2 * Accounts[j][i] );
    DeleteObject( hPen );
    DeleteObject( hBrush );
}
```

Last, the pen and brush objects are deleted because they are no longer necessary. However, compare the present usage to the methods suggested previously where the original pen and brush handles were saved and restored before the new pen and brush objects were deleted.

NOTE   The *BarGraph* demo is included on the CD that accompanies this book, in the Chapter 25 folder.

The PieGraph Demo: Building a Pie Graph

The *PieGraph* demo displays data for one year at a time in a pie-section format. Of course, pie graphs are generally expected to be round rather than elliptical. Instead of the MM_ANISOTROPIC mode, the *PieGraph* demo uses the MM_ISOTROPIC mode with the viewport origin in the center of the client window—a format selected for the convenience of the application.

Also, because C/C++ lack a predefined value for pi, PI2 is defined as a macro with the value 2.0 * 3.14159, providing a means to convert values to angles (in radians) before using the derived angles to calculate points on the circumference.

The data used for the pie graph is an array of individual values. To draw the pie graph, these values must be converted into proportions of a total (proportions of the total circumference) before they can be converted to angles. Therefore, a loop is used to determine the total for the year:

```
TotVal[0] = 0;
for( i=0; i<8; i++ )
    TotVal[i+1] = TotVal[i] + Accounts[Year][i];
```

Once this has been done, the array TotVal contains the values necessary to calculate an angle for each category (in radians).

Before each pie section is calculated, a new pen and colored brush are created.

```
for( i=0; i<8; i++ )
{
    ...
    hPen = CreatePen( PS_SOLID, 1, lpColor[i] );
    SelectObject( hdc, hPen );
    hBrush = CreateSolidBrush( lpColor[i] );
    SelectObject( hdc, hBrush );
    ...
```

```
Pie( hdc, -Radius, Radius, Radius, -Radius,
        (int) ( Radius * cos( PI2 * TotVal[i] / TotVal[8] ) ),
        (int) ( Radius * sin( PI2 * TotVal[i] / TotVal[8] ) ),
        (int) ( Radius * cos( PI2 * TotVal[i+1] / TotVal[8] ) ),
        (int) ( Radius * sin( PI2 * TotVal[i+1] / TotVal[8] ) ) );
```

Because the mapping mode is isotropic and the viewport origin is at the center of the window, the rectangle bounding the pie section (or, more accurately, bounding the circle from which the pie section will be cut) requires no more calculation than the simple coordinate point pairs: -Radius, Radius and Radius, -Radius. However, we do need to calculate the point coordinates for the starting and ending points for each pie section. For simplicity, these are calculated as points on the circumference of the pie.

And that's it. Each pie section is created as a fraction of the total circle using a different pen color for the outline and a brush with the corresponding color for the interior. The results are shown in Figure 25.7.

NOTE   The *PieGraph* demo is included on the CD that accompanies this book, in the Chapter 25 folder.

FIGURE 25.7:

A sample pie graph

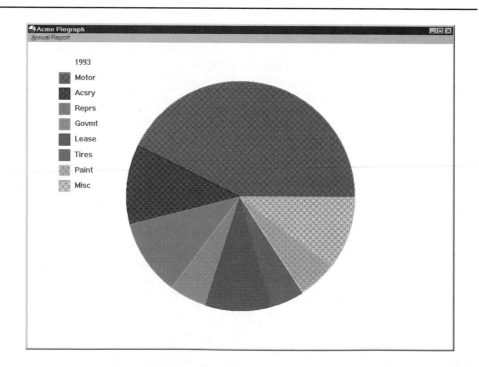

Drawing Polygon Figures

Like the `Rectangle`, `Ellipse`, and `Pie` functions, the `Polygon` and `PolyPolygon` functions draw bordered, closed, and filled shapes, but with a few differences. The first and principal difference is that the shapes can be more complex than a simple rectangle, although they are limited to straight lines; unlike the shapes drawn with the `Ellipse` or `Pie` function, the shapes drawn by either of the polygon functions cannot include curves.

The second difference is how you specify the data describing the shape. Where the `Rectangle` function expects a fixed set of coordinates, the `Polygon` function is more flexible and accepts a pointer to an array of coordinates (an array of POINT) with a further parameter specifying the number of points in the array.

```
Polygon( hdc, lpPoints, nPoints );
```

Each coordinate pair in the array of POINT identifies one vertex in a polygon. The `Polygon` function connects successive points with straight lines, finishing by connecting the last vertex to the first if necessary to close the shape. (For open shapes, use the `PolyLine` function.)

Similarly, the `PolyPolygon` function creates a series of closed polygons and is called as:

```
PolyPolygon( hdc, lpPoints, lpPolyCounts, nPolygons );
```

Again, the `lpPoints` parameter is a pointer to an array of POINT, identifying coordinates for each vertex in the polygon. The next parameter, `lpPolyCounts`, is a pointer to an array of integers, which defines the number of points in each polygon. The final argument, `nPolygons`, identifies the number of polygons (or, equally, the number of entries in `lpPolyCounts`).

Unlike the `Polygon` function, the `PolyPolygon` vertex arrays must be explicitly closed. The final vertex in each polygon must have the same coordinates as the first vertex, because `PolyPolygon` does not automatically close each figure. Also, using either function, individual polygons may overlap, but this is not required.

Polygon Fill Modes

The shapes we've used so far are simple, closed outlines with contiguous interiors, which did not require special handling to fill. However, the interior areas of polygon shapes may or may not be contiguous; if the area is not contiguous, it requires a different approach for filling.

For this reason, two different fill modes are supported (the names describe the algorithms used to determine which points lie inside the figure and which lie outside):

Alternate   This fill mode considers regions as interior only when they are reached by crossing an odd number of boundaries (1, 3, 5, and so on). Regions reached by crossing an even number of boundaries are not filled.

Winding   This fill mode, although slower to calculate, has the advantage of filling all interior (bounded) regions irrespective of the number of boundaries crossed.

The PenDraw3 Demo: Creating Polygons

The *PenDraw3* demo demonstrates the `Polygon` function by drawing two polygons: a five-pointed star and a seven-pointed star, as shown in Figure 25.8. In the figure, each shape has been filled using the alternate algorithm. The winding algorithm is available as a menu selection and will fill all interior spaces.

FIGURE 25.8:

Polygons and fill modes

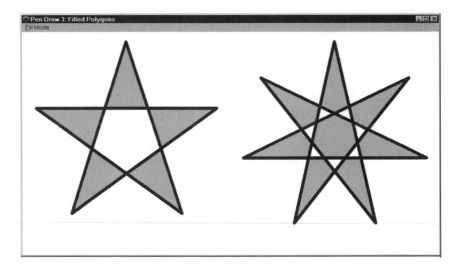

The demo draws the shapes after calculating the appropriate vertexes, using simple trigonometric functions similar to those employed in the *PieGraph* demo. For the five-pointed star, the vertex coordinates are calculated in the order 0, 2, 4, 1, 3, using the formula j=(j+2)%5. (If these points were calculated in successive order, the result would be a simple pentagon with a contiguous interior.)

```
for( i=j=0; i<5; i++, j=(j+2)%5 )        // 5 points
{
    pt[0][i].x = (int)( sin( j*PI2/5 ) * 100 ) - 110;
    pt[0][i].y = (int)( cos( j*PI2/5 ) * 100 );
}
```

For the seven-pointed star, the formula j=(j+3)%7 serves the same purpose, with the points calculated in the order 0, 3, 6, 2, 6, 1, 4.

```
for( i=j=0; i<7; i++, j=(j+3)%7 )        // 7 points
{
    pt[1][i].x = (int)( sin( j*PI2/7 ) * 100 ) + 110;
    pt[1][i].y = (int)( cos( j*PI2/7 ) * 100 );
}
```

The constants used—+110 and –110—offset each star to the right of center and the left of center.

Alternatively, to use the PolyPolygon function, instead of calculating the points for the two shapes, you could use a static array of points:

```
static POINT  pts[] =
    {  -110, 100,  -52, -80, -205,  30, -15,  30,
       -168, -80, -110, 100,  110, 100, 153, -90,
         32,  63,  207, -22,   13, -22, 188,  62,
         67, -90,  110, 100 );
static int poly[] = { 6, 8 };
```

The array pts provides the vertexes for the two shapes, and the array poly declares the number of points in each polygon. With this data available, the PolyPolygon function could be called as:

```
PolyPolygon( hdc, &pt, &poly,
             sizeof(poly) / sizeof(POINT) );
```

Remember, where the Polygon function for our example requires only five and seven vertex coordinate points, respectively, the PolyPolygon function requires six and eight vertex coordinate pairs. The final coordinate points in each set are the same as the first, thus closing each figure.

NOTE   The *PenDraw3* demo is included on the CD that accompanies this book, in the Chapter 25 folder.

We've covered four graphics elements in this chapter: pen styles, fill patterns, drawing functions for regular shapes, and drawing functions for irregular shapes. These are only a few of the graphics functions supported by Windows, and they are also the simplest. More sophisticated graphics functions are demonstrated in the following chapters, beginning in Chapter 26 with bitmap graphics operations.

26

Brushes and Bitmaps

- Data-array defined bitmaps

- Resource bitmaps

- Old-style bitmaps

- Device-independent bitmaps

In Chapter 25, you learned how to use a variety of solid and hatched (or patterned) brushes to fill shapes. In this chapter, you'll learn that any pattern (bitmap), within certain limitations, can be used as a brush pattern.

Of course, fill patterns are only one of many uses for bitmaps. Because bit-mapped brushes provide both a beginning point and one of the simplest uses, we'll start our coverage of bitmaps with this subject. Later chapters will cover more complex uses of bitmaps.

Bitmaps Defined as Arrays

While obvious to the point of being trite, the first step in creating a bitmapped brush is creating the bitmap itself. For a brush, this will be a (minimum) 8×8 bitmap image.

You could define a bitmap image within the source code as an array of BYTE, for example:

```
static BYTE wBricks[] = {  0xFF, 0x08, 0x08, 0x08, 0xFF, 0x80, 0x80, 0x80  };
```

This array defines an 8×8 bit pattern similar to the BRICKS image shown in Figure 26.1, which appears a bit later in the chapter, and could be used to produce a pattern brush similar to the one shown in Figure 26.4 (left half of pentagonal star), also presented later in the chapter. However, notice that the preceding statement has been qualified using the condition "similar." Even though the patterns are similar, the array wBricks describes a monochrome pattern, while the brush patterns used in the two illustrations are polychrome.

Array to Bitmap Conversion

In order to use wBricks as a brush pattern, the next step is to call the API function CreateBitmap to convert the value array into a (memory) bitmap image:

```
hBitmap = CreateBitmap( 8, 8, 1, 1, (LPSTR) wBricks );
```

The CreateBitmap function creates a device-dependent bitmap (in memory) for monochrome images. The parameters work as follows:

- The first two parameters (8, 8) are the width and height specifications.
- The third parameter (1) sets the number of color planes in the bitmap (each plane has nWidth * nHeight/nBitCount bits).

- The fourth parameter (1) sets the number of color bits per display pixel. (Remember that wBricks describes a monochrome image pattern, which is compatible with all video systems.)

- The final parameter is a pointer to the array of bytes, which defines the initial bitmap bits. If this argument is NULL, the bitmap will remain uninitialized.

After you create a device-dependent bitmap, the next step is to create a brush using the pattern.

A Brush with the Bitmap Pattern

To create a brush using the bitmap pattern, you use the bitmap handle with a call to CreatePatternBrush:

```
hBrush = CreatePatternBrush( hBitmap );
SelectObject( hdc, hBrush );
```

After calling SelectObject, the new pattern becomes the current brush object.

Don't forget that you should delete both the bitmap and the brush when they are no longer needed:

```
DeleteObject( hBrush );
DeleteObject( hBitmap );
```

Disadvantages of Bitmaps Defined as Arrays

Even though bitmaps can be defined as arrays of data within the program source code, this approach has three principal drawbacks:

- With the exception of monochrome images, the bitmaps created using CreateBitmap are device-dependent. Thus a bitmap defined for VGA, using four color planes with one color bit per pixel (per plane), will not be compatible with an SVGA system that uses a quite different arrangement.

- Although monochrome bitmaps can be written out as hex data, color bitmaps in the same format are a real pain to create.

- Static data arrays within the compiled application waste memory during execution—and do so quite unnecessarily. Granted, under Windows 98, this may be less of a problem than with previous Windows versions, but why bother when there are simpler ways?

Resource Bitmaps

Resource bitmaps offer an alternative to bitmaps defined as arrays, without the problems. This approach has the following advantages:

- Using a bitmap editor (or any other paint program) makes creating bitmaps convenient, regardless of whether they are monochrome or color.

- The bitmaps created are device-independent, whether in monochrome or color, and can be displayed on any video system. Windows supplies any necessary conversions.

- Since the bitmap data is contained in the resource section and loaded into active memory only as needed, the data does not waste memory when not required.

For our example of how to use resource bitmaps, we'll use four bitmap images. The first three are for the stripes, diamond, and bricks brushes, as shown in Figure 26.1. The fourth is the chains bitmap, shown in Figure 26.2.

FIGURE 26.1:

Three 8×8 bitmap patterns

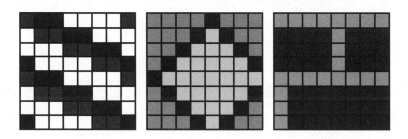

The three bitmaps in Figure 26.1 are acceptable for use as brushes under Windows 98 (as well as under Windows 95 and NT).However, under Windows 98 (or Windows 95 or Windows 3.1), if the bitmap pattern is larger than 8 pixels square, only the upper-left corner (8×8) of the image is used. Under Windows NT, there is no limit on bitmap brush size.

FIGURE 26.2:

A 24×24 bitmap pattern

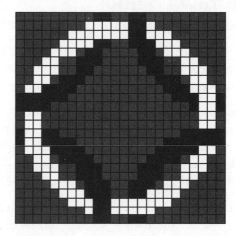

This discrepancy between Windows NT and Windows 98 can be seen in Figure 26.3, where the same bitmap (24×24) results in quite different brush patterns. When you execute the *PenDraw4* demo (discussed next) under Windows 98 and select the chains bitmap, the resulting brush fill pattern will look like the one shown on the left side of Figure 26.3. When the application is executed under Windows NT and the chains bitmap is selected, the resulting fill pattern uses the entire bitmap image, as shown on the right side in Figure 26.3.

FIGURE 26.3:

The chains bitmap under Windows 98 and NT

Image in Windows 98 ——————— 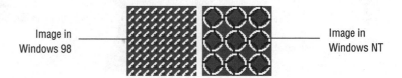 ——————— Image in Windows NT

After the bitmap images have been created, either as part of a .RES resource file or as external .BMP images referenced by a .RC resource script, the linker combines these with the rest of the resources as a part of the .EXE executable. Remember that the resource section of the application is not loaded on execution. Instead, elements from the resource section are loaded on demand as required and discarded when no longer required.

The PenDraw4 Demo:
Using Resource Bitmaps for Brushes

The *PenDraw4* demo uses four bitmaps to create four patterned brushes, which are selected from the menu. The brushes are used to draw the same five- and seven-pointed stars that the *PenDraw3* demo creates, as described in Chapter 25.

Besides the resource bitmaps used for the brushes, there is one other important difference between the *PenDraw3* and *PenDraw4* demos. In *PenDraw3*, the two figures are created from calculated data using the `Polygon` function. In *PenDraw4*, a single static array of coordinates is used together with the `PolyPolygon` function, which was discussed but not demonstrated in Chapter 25.

The *PenDraw4* demo uses only one brush at a time. However, for illustration purposes, Figure 26.4 shows a composite of the four bitmapped brushes.

FIGURE 26.4:

Four patterned brushes for the PenDraw4 program

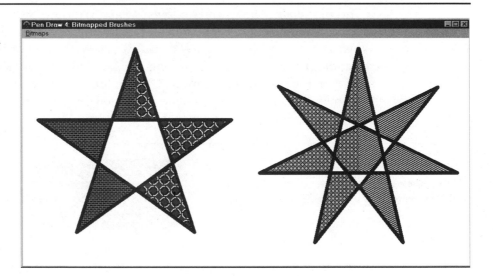

Loading the Bitmaps

Using these bitmaps as resources begins with a LoadBitmap instruction. In the
PenDraw4 demo, this is accomplished in the exported WndProc procedure in
response to a WM_CREATE message:

```
static HBITMAP hBitMap[4];
...
switch( msg )
{
    case WM_CREATE:
        hBitMap[0] = LoadBitmap( hInst, "BRICKS"  );
        hBitMap[1] = LoadBitmap( hInst, "CHAINS"  );
        hBitMap[2] = LoadBitmap( hInst, "DIAMOND" );
        hBitMap[3] = LoadBitmap( hInst, "STRIPES" );
        break;
```

The four bitmap images are loaded using a static array of handles (hBitMap[]).
The LoadBitmap function loads the bitmap resource specified (by the lpBitmap-
Name argument) from the resource section of the executable or, optionally, from
some other module specified by the hInst parameter.

TIP

Alternatively, you could load individual bitmaps as they are selected, load them
globally from the WinMain procedure, or, in another application, load them when
some subprocedure is initiated.

Creating and Selecting the Brush

After loading a bitmap, the next steps are to create the brush and select the brush
as the active object. In *PenDraw4*, these tasks are executed in response to the
WM_PAINT message.

```
hBrush = CreatePatternBrush( hBitMap[ nBitMap ] );
SelectObject( hdc, hBrush );
```

When the brush is no longer needed, DeleteObject is called to cancel the
brush handle.

```
DeleteObject( hBrush );
```

Note that `DeleteObject` is not called for the bitmaps themselves. This is because these bitmaps are resource elements, and they were not created using the `CreateBitmap` function.

Predefined Bitmaps

In addition to loading resource bitmaps, the `LoadBitmap` function can access the Windows predefined bitmaps. For this usage, the `hInst` parameter is specified as NULL, and the `lpBitmapName` parameter must be one of the values shown in Table 26.1.

TABLE 26.1: Predefined Windows Bitmaps

Win3.x, Win98/95 or WinNT		Win98/95 or WinNT*	pre-Win3.0**
OBM_CLOSE	OBM_BTNCORNERS		OBM_OLD_CLOSE
OBM_UPARROW	OBM_UPARROWD	OBM_UPARROWI	OBM_OLD_UPARROW
OBM_DNARROW	OBM_DNARROWD	OBM_DNARROWI	OBM_OLD_DNARROW
OBM_RGARROW	OBM_RGARROWD	OBM_RGARROWI	OBM_OLD_RGARROW
OBM_LFARROW	OBM_LFARROWD	OBM_LFARROWI	OBM_OLD_LFARROW
OBM_REDUCE	OBM_REDUCED		OBM_OLD_REDUCE
OBM_ZOOM	OBM_ZOOMD		OBM_OLD_ZOOM
OBM_RESTORE	OBM_RESTORED		OBM_OLD_RESTORE
OBM_MNARROW	OBM_COMBO		
OBM_BTSIZE	OBM_CHECK		
OBM_SIZE	OBM_CHECKBOXES		

*These four bitmaps are not supported by Windows 3.x.

**All bitmap names with the form OBM_OLD_xxxxx represent bitmaps used by Windows versions prior to version 3.0.

NOTE   For an application to use any of the **OBM_*xxxxxx*** constants, the constant **OEMRESOURCE** must be defined before including the Windows.H header.

Alternatively, you can use the MAKEINTRESOURCE macro to create a DWORD value with the bitmap ID as the low-order word and the high-order word NULL. Then you can use the resulting value in place of the lpBitmapName argument, serving the same purpose.

The predefined bitmaps listed are used in a variety of Windows resources. For example, the OBM_UPARROW bitmap should be familiar from Windows 3.*x*, where it appears in the upper-right corner of every application's frame as the Maximize button. For Windows 98 (and Windows 95 and NT 4.0), the OBM_ZOOM bitmap is the current equivalent. The OBM_CHECK bitmap, as its name might suggest, is a simple checkmark. The OBM_SIZE bitmap provides the diagonal marker that appears in the lower-right corner of a resizable window.

If you would like a simple way to experiment with these, modify the *PenDraw4* demo as follows:

```
case WM_CREATE:
    hBitMap[0] = LoadBitmap( NULL, MAKEINTRESOURCE( OBM_UPARROW ) );
    hBitMap[1] = LoadBitmap( NULL, MAKEINTRESOURCE( OBM_ZOOM ) );
    hBitMap[2] = LoadBitmap( NULL, MAKEINTRESOURCE( OBM_CHECK ) );
    hBitMap[3] = LoadBitmap( NULL, MAKEINTRESOURCE( OBM_SIZE ) );
    break;
```

Remember that the DeleteObject function must be called to delete each bitmap handle returned by the LoadBitmap function.

NOTE Because the *PenDraw4* demo uses these bitmap resources as brush patterns, under Windows 98, only the upper-left 8×8 pixels of the bitmap become the brush pattern. If you run the demo under Windows NT, the bitmap patterns will be fully visible.

Old-Style Bitmaps

The old-style bitmaps originated with Windows 1.0. These bitmaps have the principal drawback of being device-dependent, which means that old-style bitmaps are structured to match specific display formats and cannot be conveniently transported to other device contexts.

Functions for Old-Style Bitmaps

Windows provides four principal functions for creating old-style bitmaps:

```
hBitmap = CreateBitmap( cwWidth, cyHeight, nPlanes, nBitsPixel, lpBits );
hBitmap = CreateBitmapIndirect( &bitmap );
hBitmap = CreateCompatibleBitmap( hdc, cxWidth, cyHeight );
hBitmap = CreateDiscardableBitmap( hdc, cxWidth, cyHeight );
```

The cxWidth and cyHeight arguments define the width and height, in pixels, of the bitmap. As described earlier in the chapter, the CreateBitmap function accepts specifications for the number of color planes and number of bits per pixel, matching the image to the device-context requirements.

As alternatives, in the CreateCompatibleBitmap and CreateDiscardable-Bitmap functions, the device-context handle (hdc) permits Windows to access the number of color planes and the color bits per pixel directly. However, both of these functions create uninitialized bitmap images and require the SetBitmap-Bits function to include image information (see the following discussion of the SetBitmapBits and GetBitmapBits functions).

The CreateBitmapIndirect function uses the structure BITMAP to define the bitmap data, including size, colors, and image, in a fashion paralleling the original CreateBitmap function. The BITMAP structure is defined in WinGDI.H as:

```
typedef struct tagBITMAP
{   LONG    bmType;          // should be 0
    LONG    bmWidth;         // width in pixels
    LONG    bmHeight;        // height in pixels
    LONG    bmWidthBytes;    // width in bytes (must be even)
    WORD    bmPlanes;        // number of color planes
    WORD    bmBitsPixel;     // color bits per pixel
    LPVOID  bmBits;          // pointer to image data
} BITMAP, *PBITMAP, NEAR *NPBITMAP, FAR *LPBITMAP;
```

Bitmap Image Data

The SetBitmapBits function is used to copy a char (or byte) array into an existing bitmap, usually an unititialized bitmap.

```
SetBitmapBits( hBitmap, dwCount, lpBits );
```

As an alternative, the image data can be retrieved from an existing bitmap via the GetBitmapBits function.

```
        GetBitmapBits( hBitmap, dwCount, lpBits );
```

The GetBitmapBits function copies dwCount bits from hBitmap to the array addressed as lpBits. If the size information is not known, you can calculate dwCount by first calling the GetObject function to retrieve the bitmap structure data:

```
        GetObject( hBitmap, sizeof(BITMAP), (LPSTR) &bm );
```

And, once the data is available in bm, dwCount can be calculated as:

```
        dwCount = (DWORD)( bm.bmWidthBytes * bm.bmHeight * bm.bmPlanes );
```

Finally, because these bitmaps are GDI objects, you should use the Delete-Object function to cancel the object when it is no longer needed.

```
        DeleteObject( hBitmap );
```

Old-Style Monochrome Bitmaps

Earlier in the chapter, we discussed using the wBricks array to create an 8×8 monochrome brush from an array of byte values. For bitmaps not intended simply for use with brushes, the 8×8 limitation does not apply, even though each scan line of the bitmap must be an even number of bytes in width (some multiple of 16 bits with zeros used to right-pad the data).

For example, a simple monochrome bitmap consisting of a 9×9 square with two diagonals crossing in the center could be defined as:

```
    1 1 1 1 1 1 1 1   1 0 0 0 0 0 0 0   =   FFh 80h
    1 1 0 0 0 0 0 1   1 0 0 0 0 0 0 0   =   C1h 80h
    1 0 1 0 0 0 1 0   1 0 0 0 0 0 0 0   =   A2h 80h
    1 0 0 1 0 1 0 0   1 0 0 0 0 0 0 0   =   94h 80h
    1 0 0 0 1 0 0 0   1 0 0 0 0 0 0 0   =   88h 80h
    1 0 0 1 0 1 0 0   1 0 0 0 0 0 0 0   =   94h 80h
    1 0 1 0 0 0 1 0   1 0 0 0 0 0 0 0   =   A2h 80h
    1 1 0 0 0 0 0 1   1 0 0 0 0 0 0 0   =   C1h 80h
    1 1 1 1 1 1 1 1   1 0 0 0 0 0 0 0   =   FFh 80h
```

To make the bitmap 9×9, each scan line requires 7 pad bits (zeros), for a total width of 16 bits or 2 bytes.

To implement this particular image, the corresponding BITMAP structure could be defined as:

```
    static BITMAP bm = { 0, 9, 9, 2, 1, 1 };
```

The corresponding image data would be stored in an array of bytes as:

```
static BYTE CheckBox[] =
{  0xFF, 0x80, 0xC1, 0x80, 0xA2, 0x80, 0x94, 0x80, 0x88,
   0x80, 0x94, 0x80, 0xA2, 0x80, 0xC1, 0x80, 0xFF, 0x80  };
```

> **NOTE** For old-style bitmaps, the images are coded from the top down. In the new DIB format, images are coded from the bottom up. Of course, because the present example is symmetrical, direction becomes irrelevant.

The simplest method of creating a bitmap from the sample data is to use the `CreateBitmap` function.

```
hBitmap = CreateBitmap( 9, 9, 1, 1, CheckBox );
```

Alternatively, you could use the `CreateBitmapIndirect` function.

```
bm.bmBits = (LPSTR) CheckBox;
hBitmap = CreateBitmapIndirect( &bm );
```

However, there is a potential bug in this format. Because Windows expects to be able to move data around as necessary, the address returned for **CheckBox** may or may not remain valid after it has been assigned. This potential error can be avoided by first creating the bitmap and then transferring the bitmap image to the display (device) context.

```
hBitmap = CreateBitmapIndirect( &bm );
SetBitmapBits( hBitmap, (DWORD) sizeof(CheckBox), CheckBox );
```

Old-Style Color Bitmaps

For color bitmaps, using Windows old-style is both extremely device-dependent as well as quite a bit more complex than for monochrome bitmaps. To illustrate why, following is the 16-color equivalent of **CheckBox**, using only two colors: dark green and white (assuming a standard palette). The bitmap image is calculated as:

```
F F F F F F F F F 0 0 0   =   FFh FFh FFh FFh F0h 00h
F F 2 2 2 2 2 F F 0 0 0   =   FFh 22h 22h 2Fh F0h 00h
F 2 F 2 2 2 F 2 F 0 0 0   =   F2h F2h 22h F2h F0h 00h
F 2 2 F 2 F 2 2 F 0 0 0   =   F2h 2Fh 2Fh 22h F0h 00h
F 2 2 2 F 2 2 2 F 0 0 0   =   F2h 22h F2h 22h F0h 00h
F 2 2 F 2 F 2 2 F 0 0 0   =   F2h 2Fh 2Fh 22h F0h 00h
```

```
F 2 F 2 2 2 F 2 F 0 0 0  =  F2h F2h 22h F2h F0h 00h
F F 2 2 2 2 2 F F 0 0 0  =  FFh 22h 22h 2Fh F0h 00h
F F F F F F F F F 0 0 0  =  FFh FFh FFh FFh F0h 00h
```

Again, each scan line is padded to a WORD width by adding three zero (black) pixels at the end of each scan line.

For an EGA/VGA device, this bitmap can be interpreted as a marked checkbox in white against a dark-green background, with each four bits representing the color of one pixel. However, if the display device is, for example, an IBM8514/A, where 8 bits are interpreted as the color value for each pixel, not only will the colors be different, but the image will also be quite different. Or, what about the case where a true-color video is used as the display context and 24 bits of color data are expected for each pixel? The solution is found in the newer device-independent bitmap format described in the next section.

Device-Independent Bitmaps

The device-independent bitmap (DIB) format originally appeared as an extension of the OS/2 Presentation Manager bitmap format (and, perhaps, the only good element to come out of OS/2 version 1.1). This format presents an RGB color table defining all the colors used in the bitmap. Most (if not all) bitmap editors or paint programs automatically create DIB image files. However, because device-independent bitmaps have become so common, the .DIB extension is rarely used; files bearing the .BMP extension are almost always device-independent images, not device-dependent.

The DIB File Format

The DIB image file format consists of several sections: the DIB header, the BITMAP-INFOHEADER, the color table, and the image data. Each of these is described in the following sections.

The DIB File Header

The DIB bitmap file begins with a file header that provides information about the structure of the file itself. The DIB header (defined in WinGDI.H) consists of a 14-byte record, shown in Table 26.2.

TABLE 26.2:   DIB Header Format

Field	Size	Sample Data	Value	Description
bfType	WORD	42 4D	"BM"	Bitmap ID (constant, all DIBs)
bfSize	DWORD	96 00 00 00	96h	Total file size (example only)
reserved1	WORD	00 00	0h	Set to 0
reserved2	WORD	00 00	0h	Set to 0
bfOffBits	DWORD	76 00 00 00	76h	Offset to bitmap image from first of file (example only)

NOTE   Remember that all data is arranged in `lsb...msb` order. For example, the data bytes 96 00 00 00 represent the value 00000096h, not 96000000h. While this ordering may appear strange, it is simply a firmly entrenched artifact that originated in the early days of computing when the `lsb...msb` (least significant/most significant) order made it faster to process values by storing them in the stack in this fashion. This reverse order made it possible to extract values—one byte at a time as required by 8-bit CPUs—from the stack in the order in which they would be processed.

The BITMAPINFOHEADER Structure

The file header information is followed by a second data header defined by the BITMAPINFOHEADER structure. This data is shown in Table 26.3.

TABLE 26.3:   BITMAPINFOHEADER Data

Field	Size	Sample	Value	Description
BiSize	DWORD	28 00 00 00	28h	Size of BITMAPINFOHEADER
BiWidth	LONG	08 00 00 00	8h	Bitmap pixel width
BiHeight	LONG	08 00 00 00	8h	Bitmap pixel height
BiPlanes	WORD	01 00	1h	Color planes (always 1)
BiBitCount	WORD	04 00	4h	Color bits per pixel (1, 4, 8, 24)

Continued on next page

TABLE 26.3 (CONTINUED): BITMAPINFOHEADER Data

Field	Size	Sample	Value	Description
BiCompression	DWORD	00 00 00 00	0h	Compression scheme (0=none)
BiSizeImage	DWORD	20 00 00 00	20h	Bitmap image size (used only if compression is set)
BiXPelsPerMeter	LONG	00 00 00 00	0h	Horizontal resolution (pixels/meter)
BiYPelsPerMeter	LONG	00 00 00 00	0h	Vertical resolution (pixels/meter)
BiDlrUsed	DWORD	00 00 00 00	0h	Number of colors used in image
BiClrImportant	DWORD	00 00 00 00	0h	Number of important colors (archaic and rarely, if ever, used today)

The BITMAPINFOHEADER contains quite a bit of data about the DIB image. However, as you can see from the example, often several of these fields are left blank, particularly biXPelsPerMeter and biYPelsPerMeter (the horizontal and vertical resolution). The final two fields, biDlrUsed and biClrImportant (the number of colors used and the number of important colors), are often used for additional information about custom colors or multiple color palettes; zero values indicate defaults.

Notice also that color is represented only as multiple color bits per pixel, regardless of how a specific device might expect to handle color. Thus, color will be specified as one bit per pixel for monochrome, four for 16-color bitmaps, eight for 256-color bitmaps, or twenty-four for true-color images (16 million colors).

Also, if data compression is used, the data-compression scheme is identified together with the actual size of the uncompressed bitmap (in bytes), thus providing a redundancy check for use in decompressing the image. Four compression schemes are defined, as shown in Table 26.4.

TABLE 26.4: Compression Formats and Identifiers

Constant	Value	Comment
BI_RGB	0	No compression used
BI_RLE8	1	8-bit run-length encoding format
BI_RLE4	2	4-bit run-length encoding format
BI_TOPDOWN	4	

NOTE   Despite provisions for identifying compression formats, many bitmap editors (or paint programs) do not support (or recognize) compressed image data.

The DIB BITMAP Color Table

The DIB color table follows the BITMAPINFOHEADER. This table consists of a series of RGBQUAD structures. These are read, in order, with the first byte blue, the second green, the third red, and the fourth byte in each quad set to zero.

The biBitCount field identifies the number of RGBQUAD structures. For a monochrome image, this field is set as 1 color bit. Two RGBQUAD records are required to identify the foreground and background colors. If biBitCount is 4, 16 RGBQUAD color identifiers are needed. If biBitCount is 8, 256 RGBQUAD values are required.

If the biClrUsed field is nonzero, this value (instead of the biBitCount field) identifies the number of RGBQUAD structures in the color table.

Table 26.5 shows the default color values for a VGA 16-color palette expressed as RGBQUAD values.

TABLE 26.5:   A Sample Color Palette for a DIB Bitmap

Palette Entry	RGBQUAD Data	Color Value			Approximate Color
		R	G	B	
0	00 00 00 00	00	00	00	Black
1	00 00 80 00	80	00	00	Dark Red
2	00 80 00 00	00	80	00	Dark Green
3	00 80 80 00	80	80	00	Gold Green
4	80 00 00 00	00	00	80	Dark Blue
5	80 00 80 00	80	00	80	Purple
6	80 80 00 00	00	80	80	Blue Gray
7	80 80 80 00	80	80	80	Dark Gray
8	C0 C0 C0 00	C0	C0	C0	Light Gray

Continued on next page

TABLE 26.5 (CONTINUED):   A Sample Color Palette for a DIB Bitmap

Palette Entry	RGBQUAD Data	Color Value			Approximate Color
		R	G	B	
9	00 00 FF 00	FF	00	00	Light Red
10	00 FF 00 00	00	FF	00	Light Green
11	00 FF FF 00	FF	FF	00	Yellow
12	FF 00 00 00	FF	00	00	Light Blue
13	FF 00 FF 00	FF	00	FF	Magenta
14	FF FF 00 00	00	FF	FF	Cyan
15	FF FF FF 00	FF	FF	FF	White

The DIB BITMAP Image

The final section of the bitmap file is the bitmap image itself. The arrangement of this section partly depends on the number of colors (as reported by the biBit-Count field), but it is also affected by two other factors, which are constant for all bitmaps:

- Each row of the bitmap image must be a multiple of four bytes (a DWORD multiple). Each data row begins with the leftmost pixel of the scan line and is right-padded with zeros, as necessary.

- Unlike the original bitmap format (Windows 1.0 or 2.0), the bitmap format for DIBs begins with the bottom scan line in the image, not the top.

For a monochrome bitmap—one color bit per pixel—the bit image begins with the most-significant bit of the first byte in each row. If the bit value is zero (0), the first RGBQUAD color value is used (background). If the bit value is one (1), the second RGBQUAD value is used (foreground).

For a monochrome bitmap, the BRICKS bitmap data would be coded as:

```
80 80 80 FF 08 08 08 FF
```

This data would break down, as a pixel image, as:

```
1 1 1 1 1 1 1 1        // FFh
0 0 0 0 1 0 0 0        // 08h
0 0 0 0 1 0 0 0        // 08h
0 0 0 0 1 0 0 0        // 08h
1 1 1 1 1 1 1 1        // FFh
1 0 0 0 0 0 0 0        // 80h
1 0 0 0 0 0 0 0        // 80h
1 0 0 0 0 0 0 0        // 80h
```

Again, as a reminder, notice that the image data, from left to right, appears in the image from bottom to top, not top down.

For a 16-color bitmap, as used in the Bricks.BMP file with four bits per pixel, each pixel is represented by a four-bit value that serves as an index to the palette entries in the table (as shown in Table 26.5). The color bitmap image appears as:

```
81 11 11 11    81 11 11 11    81 11 11 11    88 88 88 88
11 11 81 11    11 11 81 11    11 11 81 11    88 88 88 88
```

The color image data is decoded as:

```
8 8 8 8 8 8 8 8        // 88h 88h 88h 88h
1 1 1 1 8 1 1 1        // 11h 11h 81h 11h
1 1 1 1 8 1 1 1        // 11h 11h 81h 11h
1 1 1 1 8 1 1 1        // 11h 11h 81h 11h
8 8 8 8 8 8 8 8        // 88h 88h 88h 88h
8 1 1 1 1 1 1 1        // 81h 11h 11h 11h
8 1 1 1 1 1 1 1        // 81h 11h 11h 11h
8 1 1 1 1 1 1 1        // 81h 11h 11h 11h
```

In a similar fashion, for a 256-color bitmap, each pixel is represented by a byte value indexing the 256 entries in the color table.

For a 24-bit-per-pixel color bitmap, with the biClrUsed field specified as zero, instead of a color table with 16 million entries (predicating a minimum file size of 64MB just for the color table), no color table is used. Each pixel is represented by a three-byte RGBColor value. If biClrUsed is not zero, a color table is included and pixels are indexed to the table.

OS/2 Bitmaps

OS/2 version 1.1 and later uses a bitmap structure that is very similar to Windows, with only two principal structure changes. First, instead of a BITMAPINFOHEADER structure, OS/2 uses a BITMAPCOREHEADER structure, which is defined in WinGDI.H as:

```
typedef struct tagBITMAPCOREHEADER
{   DWORD   bcSize;                    // offset to color table
    WORD    bcWidth;
    WORD    bcHeight;
    WORD    bcPlanes;
    WORD    bcBitCount;
} BITMAPCOREHEADER, FAR *LPBITMAPCOREHEADER,
  *PBITMAPCOREHEADER;
```

Second, instead of a color table consisting of RGBQUAD records, the OS/2 bitmaps use RGBTRIPLE records.

Perhaps the simplest method of identifying the two formats is to check the two byte values in the image file for the value BM, identifying Windows bitmap format. If these two bytes do not identify Windows format, the OS/2 structure can be confirmed by testing the first DWORD value in BITMAPIMAGEHEADER/BITMAPCOREHEADER structures to determine the structure size.

Bitmap Dimension Functions

Windows supplies two bitmap dimension functions: SetBitmapDimensionEx and GetBitmapDimensionEx. However, despite what the names might initially suggest, these two functions do not deal with the pixel dimensions of a bitmap because, once an image is created, the pixel size of the image cannot be changed. Instead, this function pair provides a means of setting or retrieving bitmap dimensions in logical units (the MM_LOMETRIC mode is assumed). These dimensions are not used by the GDI for screen display but may be used by other applications to scale bitmaps that have been exchanged using the clipboard, DDE, or other channels.

The SetBitmapDimensionEx and GetBitmapDimensionEx functions are called as:

```
SetBitmapDimensionEx( hBitmap, xUnits, yUnits, lpSize );
GetBitmapDimensionEx( hBitmap, lpSize );
```

The lpSize variable returns with the previous size data (when new dimensions are set) or the current size data (when the get function is called). The SIZE data structure is defined in WinDef.H as:

```
typedef struct tagSIZE
{   LONG  cx;
    LONG  cy;  } SIZE, *PSIZE, *LPSIZE;
```

NOTE   In general, the two bitmap size fields (biXPelsPerMeter and biYPelsPer-Meter) are set to zero except when needed by special circumstances, such as when you are providing additional rendering (sizing) information for hard-copy devices. These two values are rarely employed and may be overridden (or ignored) even when set.

Device-Independent Bitmap Creation

Ideally, it would be nice if Windows supplied a simple function to create (or load) and display a bitmap, requiring only a device context, bitmap name, and position. This function might look something like this:

```
DrawBitmap( hwnd, lpBitmapName, xPos, yPos );
```

However, even though bitmaps are both important and integral to Windows, no such basic display function is provided. Instead, Windows provides a series of bitmap primitives that can be used to construct a number of the missing high-level bitmap handlers, beginning with a function titled, appropriately, Draw-Bitmap.

The following sections describe the basic steps required to create and display a device-independent bitmap.

Step One: Providing a Global Instance Handle

Up to this point, all the program examples have included one provision which, thus far, has not been used, needed, explained, or (most likely) even noticed. The provision in reference, which does have more than a few uses, begins with the global handle declaration:

```
HANDLE  hInst;
```

In the `WinMain` procedure, the `hInst` variable is assigned as:

```
hInst = hInstance;
```

Without this provision in the *PenDraw4* demo, for example, the `LoadBitmap` instructions in response to the `WM_CREATE` message in `WndProc` would need to have been executed in the `WinMain` procedure using the `hInstance` handle.

Although there are other ways to retrieve an application's instance handle, the global instance handle costs a mere 16 bits of overhead memory, so why bother with false economies?

Once the global `hInst` instance handle is available, the `LoadBitmap` function can be implemented within our theoretical `DrawBitmap` function without invoking special provisions to retrieve the application's instance handle.

Step Two: Defining DrawBitmap

The basic form of `DrawBitmap` is called with four parameters: the window handle (hwnd), the bitmap name (lpName), and x and y coordinates to position the bitmap. And, as a result, `DrawBitmap` displays a bitmap at the coordinates specified. Ergo, the function declaration begins as:

```
BOOL DrawBitmap( HWND hwnd, LPSTR lpName,
                 int  xPos, int    yPos )
   {
```

> **NOTE** `DrawBitmap` is also provided with the capability to return a Boolean result, reporting success or failure. But as with most C functions, the returned value may be used or ignored, as desired.

A few local variables will be needed, and they are declared as:

```
HDC     hdc, hdcMem;
BITMAP  bm;
HBITMAP hBitmap;
```

Declarations finished, the function is now ready to load a bitmap from the resource segment of the .EXE program. Notice, however, that this is also the point where the global `hInst` handle becomes essential.

```
if( !( hBitmap = LoadBitmap( hInst, lpName ) ) )
    return( FALSE );
```

Of course, if the load operation fails, DrawBitmap will immediately terminate, returning FALSE. This is the only error check provided.

If successful, once the bitmap is loaded, the next step is to establish a suitable device context to display the bitmap.

Step Three: Creating the Device Context

Unlike in DOS, where once a graphics mode has been established anything can be written (drawn) on the screen, under Windows, a bitmap image cannot be drawn (or copied) directly to the display-device context. Instead, before the bitmap image can be drawn, a separate device context is created. This is created as a memory device context (with no immediate connection to an output device), using the hdc-Mem variable declared local to the DisplayBitmap function.

However, the application's actual output device context cannot simply be ignored. Therefore, the next order of business is to retrieve a handle to the application's device context.

```
hdc = GetDC( hwnd );
hdcMem = CreateCompatibleDC( hdc );
```

The trick here is that a reference device context (hdc) is needed before the CreateCompatibleDC function can be called to create the memory context (hdcMem). The memory device context is simply a block of memory that acts as an analog for the real display context. For a bitmap, the memory device context can be used to prepare an image in memory before transferring the image to the display context (to the screen or another output device).

When the memory device context is created, the GDI automatically assigns a "display surface" sized for a 1×1 monochrome image; that is, a one-pixel monochrome bitmap. But, while this is hardly sufficient space for any real operations, this deficiency can be corrected immediately by calling SelectObject to use the bitmap that was loaded a moment before as the active object for the device context:

```
SelectObject( hdcMem, hBitmap );

SetMapMode( hdcMem, GetMapMode( hdc ) );
```

After selecting the bitmap into the memory context, SetMapMode assigns the mapping mode used by the active device context (hdc) to the memory device context (hdcMem), thus making the memory image of the bitmap a suitable match for the output device.

At this point, the bitmap has become the active object for the memory device context, while the memory device has the same mapping mode as the actual device context. But the job isn't done yet; there is still quite a bit of information that needs to be transferred from the source bitmap (hBitmap) to the local bitmap record (bm).

Step Four: Transferring Bitmap Definition Data

The GetObject function can be used to transfer most of the information needed to fill the buffer (bm) to define the logical object (the selected bitmap). For a bitmap, GetObject returns the width, height, and color format information. This function is called as:

```
GetObject( hBitmap, sizeof( BITMAP ), (LPSTR) &bm );
```

But still, the actual image data has not been retrieved yet. This operation comes next.

Step Five: Retrieving Image Data

The BitBlt (short for bit-block-transfer and pronounced "bit-blit"), PutBlt, and StretchBlt functions compose Windows pixel-manipulation power operations. However, while each of these function names implies a block-transfer operation, there's more involved here than simply copying bits from one memory location to another. Instead, there is also a choice of raster operations, as will be explained in a moment.

While not the simplest of the three operations, the BitBlt operation is, for the present purpose, the operation of choice. It is used to complete the task of writing the bitmap image to the client window:

```
BitBlt( hdc, xPos, yPos, bm.bmWidth, bm.bmHeigth,
        hdcMem, 0, 0, SRCCOPY );
```

The BitBlt operation moves the bitmap image from the source device (hdcMem) to the destination device (hdc), with the xSrc and ySrc parameters (0,0 in the example) specifying the origin (in the source device context) of the bitmap to be transferred.

The xPos, yPos, bm.bmWidth, and bm.bmHeight parameters provide the origin and rectangle size (in the destination device context) to be filled by the bitmap image. Unlike many previous operations, instead of RECT rectangular coordinates, the origin point is specified in device-context coordinates. The width and height are passed as logical units, not as device coordinates. As demonstrated, these last two values are taken directly from the bitmap data. Optionally, you can assign the width and height values on some other basis.

The final parameter is a ternary raster-operation code specifying how the GDI will combine colors between a current brush (pattern), the source image, and any existing destination image. For the DrawBitmap operation, the SRCCOPY ROP copies the source bitmap image directly to the destination (hdc).

The 15 principal ternary raster operations are defined in WinGDI.H and listed in Table 26.6.

TABLE 26.6:   Raster Operation Codes (Ternary Raster Ops)

Constant	Operation	Description
SRCCOPY	Dest = Source	Source copied to destination
SRCPAINT	Dest = Source | Dest	Destination ORed with source
SRCAND	Dest = Source & Dest	Source ANDed with destination
SRCINVERT	Dest = Source ^ Dest	Source XORed with destination
SRCERASE	Dest = Source & !Dest	Destination inverted before ANDing with source
NOTSRCCOPY	Dest = !Source	Inverted source copied to destination
NOTSRCERASE	Dest = !Source & !Dest	Inverted destination ANDed with inverted source
MERGECOPY	Dest = Source & Patt	Source ANDed with pattern
MERGEPAINT	Dest = !Source | Dest	Destination ORed with inverted source
PATCOPY	Dest = Patt	Pattern copied to destination
PATPAINT	Dest = Patt | !Source | Dest	Pattern ORed with inverted source, result ORed with destination
PATINVERT	Dest = Patt ^ Dest	Pattern XORed with destination
DSTINVERT	Dest = !Dest	Destination inverted
BLACKNESS	Dest = Black (0)	Destination turned black
WHITENESS	Dest = White (1)	Destination turned white

Raster operations involving monochrome images are fairly straightforward: Bits will be either on or off according to the logical operations selected. For color bitmaps, however, the GDI executes separate operations for each color plane or for each set of color bits, depending on the device-context organization. The best way to understand these operations is to experiment, preferably with relatively simple bitmaps and patterns.

Step 6: Cleaning Up

Calling the BitBlt API completes the task of drawing the bitmap, but before DrawBitmap returns, some cleanup is still required. This is accomplished as:

```
ReleaseDC( hwnd, hdc );
DeleteDC( hdcMem );
DeleteObject( hBitmap );
return( TRUE );
```

Initially, three local memory allocations were made, returning three handles as hdc, hdcMem, and hBitmap. The first of these is simply released rather than being deleted; that is, the hdc handle is released, but the application device context is not deleted. The local memory device context, however, is deleted entirely, deallocating all memory involved, not just the memory handle. The locally allocated and loaded bitmap is treated in a similar fashion.

After this cleanup is completed, the DrawBitmap function is free to return, reporting success.

The DrawBitmap function is demonstrated in the *PenDraw5* demo, which is discussed after we cover one more bitmap operation.

Stretching Bitmaps

Drawing a bitmap using a one-for-one transfer is probably the most common operation. However, another bitmap operation you may find useful is provided by StretchBlt, which permits stretching or distorting a bitmap to fit any rectangular space desired. This function moves a bitmap from a source rectangle to a destination rectangle, stretching or compressing the bitmap as appropriate to fit the destination dimensions.

Calling the StretchBlt operation is similar to calling BitBlt, but with two differences:

```
   BitBlt( hdc,    xPos, yPos, xWidth,    yHeight,
           hdcMem, xOrg, yOrg, dwRasterOp );
StretchBlt( hdc,    xPos, yPos, xWidth,    yHeight,
            hdcMem, xOrg, yOrg, xWidthOut, yHeightOut, dwRasterOp );
```

The `StretchBlt` operation is called with two additional parameters specifying the destination width and height; for the `BitBlt` operation, source and destination width and height are the same. It is precisely this difference that instructs `Stretch-Blt` to stretch or compress the bitmap during transfer. Since `xWidth/xWidthOut` and `yWidth/yWidthOut` are independent, the bitmap could be stretched along one axis and compressed along another.

As with the `BitBlt` operation, the `dwRasterOp` specification controls how the source and destination (if any) bitmaps are combined during the `StretchBlt` operation.

`StretchBlt` operations are not necessarily limited to resizing images. You can also use `StretchBlt` to create a mirror image of a bitmap (laterally or vertically), by specifying different the signs for the source and destination width or the source and destination height. For example, if the destination width is negative and the source width is positive, `StretchBlt` creates a mirror image rotated about the vertical axis (swapping left for right). Likewise, for a difference in sign of the height parameters, the image is mirrored along the horizontal axis. If both pairs are opposite in sign, the image is simply rotated 180° but without mirror inversion.

Because the `StretchBlt` operation resizes a bitmap image, one additional factor controls how data is added or subtracted to create the new image: the `StretchBlt` mode. You set the active mode by calling the `SetStretchBltMode` function as:

```
SetStretchBltMode( hdc, nStretchMode );
```

Four `StretchBlt` modes are defined in WinGDI.H, as described in Table 26.7.

TABLE 26.7: StretchBlt Modes

Constant	Value	Description
BLACKONWHITE	1	Eliminated lines are ANDed with retained lines; preserves black pixels at expense of white
WHITEONBLACK	2	Eliminated lines are ORed with retained lines; preserves white pixels at expense of black
COLORONCOLOR	3	Eliminated lines are deleted without preserving information
HALFTONE	4	Color information in destination approximates source pixels, averaging information from source to destination

The BLACKONWHITE and WHITEONBLACK modes are typically used to preserve the background or foreground pixels in monochrome bitmaps, respectively. The COLORONCOLOR and HALFTONE modes are typically used to preserve color in color bitmaps, with the principal difference between the two being that the HALFTONE mode produces higher-image quality but does so at the expense of execution time.

The PenDraw5 Demo: Displaying Device-Independent Bitmaps

The *PenDraw5* demo demonstrates the DrawBitmap function described earlier, as well as the BitBlt and StretchBlt API functions. *PenDraw5* requires five bitmaps, four 16×16 images, and one 40×70 image, as illustrated in Figure 26.5.

FIGURE 26.5:

Five bitmap images used in the PenDraw5 demo

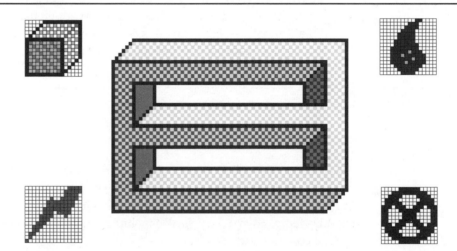

<hr>

TIP   You can use bitmaps other than the ones shown in Figure 26.5 if you prefer. Just be sure to make the appropriate changes in the source and resource codes to identify the desired bitmaps.

<hr>

Initially, the DrawBitmap function draws all five bitmaps, placing the four smaller bitmaps at the corners of the client window and the larger bitmap in the center. For each of these, the bitmap is drawn with the upper-left corner of the image at the coordinates specified. Several variations are also used in the demo:

- DrawCenBitmap centers each image (horizontally and vertically) on the coordinate points.

- LineGraph uses a brief array of data to position a series of smaller bitmaps in a form appropriate for a simple line graph.

- StretchBitmap uses the StretchBlt API to resize a bitmap to fit a specified rectangle.

- StretchBitmap2Client stretches a bitmap to fill the entire client window.

- MoveBitmap tracks mouse movement by repositioning a bitmap each time the left mouse button is pressed or, if the button is held down, by tracking the mouse cursor directly. (Bitmaps are not well-suited to this last operational format, MoveBitmap; this is intended more as a demonstration than as a serious example of practical programming.)

NOTE
The *PenDraw5* demo is included on the CD accompanying this book, in the Chapter 26 folder.

This chapter described two programs that demonstrate bitmap operations: The *PenDraw4* demo shows how to use resource bitmaps to create brushes, and the *PenDraw5* demo demonstrates how to work with device-independent bitmaps. Another demo, *SVGA_Win*, is also included on the CD to demonstrate several types of color palettes.

Bitmap operations are very powerful tools with a wide variety of uses, extending well beyond the few examples employed in this chapter. For example, bitmaps can be copied from the screen itself, generated or modified off-screen, saved as external files, or cut and pasted from one window to another.

# CHAPTER TWENTY-SEVEN

Typefaces and Styles

- Text-output features

- Windows' default fonts

- Logical font selection

- Font characteristics

- Font sizing and mapping modes

Windows 98 provides a selection of typefaces and the capabilities to vary these typefaces with considerable convenience and flexibility. You've seen examples of text operations in previous chapters. Now it's time to examine a few of the advanced text features, including font selection, font sizing, text justification, character weighting, and other stylistic changes.

Before we get to fonts and typefaces, we'll take a closer look at some of Windows' text-output features. There are a few that we haven't covered yet, and they deserve some introduction or further explanation.

Text-Output Features

Thus far in the book, most text-display examples have used one of these two general formats:

```
TextOut( hdc, xPos, yPos, lpStr, nCount );

TextOut( hdc, xPos, yPos, szBuff, wsprintf( szBuff, ... ) );
```

The second format employs the wsprintf function both to return the character count required by the TextOut API function and to create a formatted string. But, regardless of the format used, previous examples have, almost exclusively, used the default, flush-left text alignment.

Using the MFC classes, a third format for text display has appeared as:

```
pDC->TextOut( xPos, yPos, csBuff );
```

In this format, no handle to the device context is passed because the TextOut function is a member of the CDC class. Likewise, because the CString instance contains the string-length information, this value is also not required as an argument.

All of these text formats provide only the simplest form of text display, without alignment, font selection, or special formatting.

Text Alignment

The SetTextAlign function provides control not only over the horizontal text alignment, relative to the specified x- and y-coordinate specifications, but also over vertical alignment and current position updating. SetTextAlign is called as:

```
SetTextAlign( hdc, wFlags );
```

The SetTextAlign settings affect text displayed using both the TextOut and ExtTextOut functions. The wFlags argument consists of one or more text-alignment specifications combined using the OR operator. Eight alignment constants are defined in WinGDI.H. These are listed in Table 27.1.

The bounding rectangle is a rectangle surrounding the text string, passed as an argument to the TextOut or ExtTextOut functions.

TABLE 27.1: Horizontal Text Alignment Flags

Flag ID	Bit Flags	Value	Comments
Vertical Alignment at yPos			
TA_TOP *	0000 0000	0	Aligns with top of bounding rectangle
TA_BASELINE	0001 1000	24	Aligns with baseline of selected font
TA_BOTTOM	0000 1000	8	Aligns with bottom of bounding rectangle
Horizontal Alignment at xPos			
TA_LEFT *	0000 0000	0	Aligns with left side of bounding rectangle
TA_RIGHT	0000 0010	2	Aligns with right side of bounding rectangle
TA_CENTER	0000 0110	6	Aligns with horizontal center of bounding rectangle (current position is not affected)
Current Position Control			
TA_NOUPDATECP *	0000 0000	0	Does not update current position after TextOut or ExtTextOut calls
TA_UPDATECP	0000 0001	1	Updates current position after TextOut or ExtTextOut calls
Combined Flags			
TA_MASK	0001 1111	31	TA_BASELINE + TA_CENTER + TA_UPDATECP

* The default flags are TA_LEFT, TA_TOP, and TA_NOUPDATECP

Because not all fonts are written horizontally (for example, the Japanese Kanji font is written vertically), two additional flag values substitute for the TA_BASE-LINE and TA_CENTER flags. These are defined as shown in Table 27.2.

TABLE 27.2: Vertical Text Alignment Flags

Constant	Replaces	Comments
VTA_BASELINE	TA_BASELINE	Aligns reference point with baseline of text
VTA_CENTER	TA_CENTER	Aligns reference point vertically with center of bounding rectangle

The SetTextAlign function returns an unsigned integer specifying the previous text alignment, or if an error occurs, ERROR is returned.

Extended Text Output Options

The ExtTextOut function expands on the TextOut function. It adds a rectangle specification that can be used for clipping, opaquing, or both, as well as a pointer to an array of data to control character spacing. The ExtTextOut function is called as:

```
ExtTextOut( hdc, xPos, yPos, fOptions, lpRect,
            szString, nCount, lpDx );
```

The hdc, xPos, yPos, szString, and nCount parameters perform in precisely the same fashion as with the TextOut function. The differences are found in the fOptions, lpRect, and lpDx parameters.

fOptions This parameter may be NULL, or it may be either or both (ORed) of the following flag values:

- ETO_CLIPPED, which clips the text to fit the rectangle specification

- ETO_OPAQUE, which fills the rectangle using the current background color

lpRect This parameter points to a RECT structure specifying the enclosing rectangle, or it may be passed as NULL.

lpDx This parameter points to an array of integer values that specify the distance between adjacent character cells in logical units. For example, element lpDx[i] sets the spacing between the origins of the characters szString[i] and szString[i+1]. If lpDx is NULL, the default character spacing is used.

By default, the current position is not updated by calls to ExtTextOut. However, if the SetTextAlign function is called to set TA_UPDATECP, two changes occur. First, the initial call to ExtTextOut uses the xPos, yPos parameters, updating the current position after drawing the text parameter. Then, on the second and subsequent calls to ExtTextOut, the xPos and yPos parameters will be ignored and only the current position data will be used. The current position will continue to be updated with the results of each call.

Tabbed Text

Conventionally, graphics text functions have not included any tab provisions, an oversight which is now corrected by the TabbedTextOut function. This function permits an output string to be tabbed according to spacing arguments specified in an lpnTabStopPositions array. The TabbedTextOut function is called as:

```
TabbedTextOut( hdc, xPos, yPos, szString, nCount,
               nTabPositions, lpnTabStopPositions, nTabOrigin );
```

The first five parameters are the same as the equivalent parameters in the TextOut function. The difference is that tab characters can be included in the szString parameter as embedded \t (or 0x09) characters.

The other parameters are as follows:

nTabPositions This parameter is an integer argument specifying the number of tab stops to be set (the number of entries in the lpnTabStop-Positions array) or the number of tab stops to be used. Three variations may be used:

- If nTabPositions is zero (0) and lpnTabStopPositions is NULL, all tabs are expanded to eight times the average character width.

- If nTabPositions is one (1), all tabs are incremented by the first distance specified in the lpnTabStopPositions array.

- If lpnTabStopPositions contains multiple values, subsequent tabs are set according to these values up to the number specified by nTabPositions.

lpnTabStopPositions This parameter points to an array of tab stops (in increasing order) defined in device units, or it may be NULL.

nTabOrigin This parameter is an integer specification, in device units, specifying an initial offset from which the tab specifications are expanded. The nTabOrigin argument also allows an application to call TabbedTextOut two or more times for a single line, specifying a new offset each time.

Gray Text

The GrayString function draws text using a gray brush. It draws gray text by first writing the text in a memory context as a bitmap, graying the bitmap, and then copying the bitmap to the text display. The drawn text is grayed independently of any brush or background color active in the device context used for the display. The font used is the font currently selected in the device context specified by the hdc parameter.

The GrayString function is called as:

```
GrayString( hdc, hBrush, lpOutputFunct, lpData, xPos, yPos, nWidth, nHeight );
```

The parameters are as follows:

hdc This parameter specifies the device context where the grayed string will be displayed.

hBrush This parameter identifies the brush to be used to gray the text.

lpOutputFunct This parameter is an optional procedure instance address for an application-supplied function to be used to draw the string. If this is specified as NULL, the TextOut function will be used.

lpData This parameter may be a pointer to data to be passed to the lpOutputFunct function, or if lpOutputFunct is NULL, must be a pointer to the string to be displayed.

xPos/yPos These parameters specify, in device coordinates, the starting position of a rectangle bounding the string displayed.

nWidth/nHeight These parameters specify the width and height, in device units, for the rectangle enclosing the text display. If either parameter is zero (0) and lpData is a pointer to a string, GrayString calculates the width or height.

A FALSE result is returned if the GrayString function fails, if the lpOutputFunct returns failure, or if memory limitations prevent the bitmap from being created.

TIP   You can also draw grayed strings on any device that supports a solid-gray color, without using the `GrayString` function, by using the system color **COLOR_GRAYTEXT**. To do this, call `GetSystColor` to retrieve the color value for **COLOR_GRAYTEXT**. If the result is not zero (0), call `SetTextColor` to select this color before drawing the string directly. If the returned color value is zero, grayed text can only be drawn using the `GrayString` function.

Multiple Text Lines

The `DrawText` function displays formatted text within a specified rectangular area. Unlike the other functions, `DrawText` is specifically designed to display multiple lines, inserting line breaks as required to format the text within the indicated rectangle. The `DrawText` function is called as:

```
DrawText( hdc, szString, nCount, lpRect, wFormat );
```

The `hdc`, `szString` and `nCount` parameters are used to identify the device context, the string to be printed, and the number of characters in the string. The `lpRect` argument is a pointer to a RECT structure identifying a rectangle, in device coordinates, where the text will be drawn.

The fifth argument, `wFormat`, is an unsigned integer and consists of an ORed combination of the flags listed in Table 27.3.

TABLE 27.3: DrawText Format Flags

Constant	Comments
Horizontal Justification	
DT_LEFT	Aligns text flush-left
DT_CENTER	Centers text
DT_RIGHT	Aligns text flush-right
Vertical Justification	
DT_TOP	Top-justifies text (single line only)
DT_VCENTER	Centers text vertically (single line only)
DT_BOTTOM	Bottom-justifies text; must be combined with **DT_SINGLELINE**

Continued on next page

TABLE 27.3 (CONTINUED): DrawText Format Flags

Constant	Comments
Format and Spacing Instructions	
DT_EXTERNALLEADING*	Adds font external leading to line spacing
DT_NOCLIP*	Disables clipping to rectangle (operation is marginally faster)
DT_SINGLELINE	Sets single line only; carriage returns and line feeds do not produce line breaks
DT_WORDBREAK	Enables automatic line breaks at word boundaries as required to fit text to rectangle
DT_EXPANDTABS	Expands tab characters (default is 8 times average character width per tab)
DT_TABSTOP	Sets tab stops using bits 15-8 of the high byte of the low word in wFormat to specify the number of characters for each tab (if zeros, default spacing is used)
DT_NOPREFIX*	Turns off processing of prefix character
DT_INTERNAL*	Not documented
Automatic Rectangle Calculation	
DT_CALCRECT*	Enables automatic calculation of rectangle area but does not draw actual text

*Cannot be used with the DT_TABSTOP flag.

Here are a few additional notes about two of the flags listed in Table 27.3:

- The DT_NOPREFIX flag disables the use of the ampersand (&) character to underline the character immediately following. When DT_NOPREFIX is not set (characters following the ampersand will be underlined), an ampersand can be entered as &&, producing a single & as output.

- The DT_CALCRECT flag enables automatic calculation of the rectangle area. If there are multiple lines of text, DrawText uses the rectangle width specified by the lpRect parameter, extending the base of the rectangle to bound the last line of text. If there is only one line of text, DrawText modifies the width (right size) to bound the last character in the line. In both cases, DrawText returns the height of the formatted text but does not draw the actual text.

Device-Context Elements

Along with the text-output functions and their flags, the text display is also governed by the active device context. Elements specified by the device context include not only the foreground and background colors, but also how the text-display pixels are combined with the existing background image.

By default, when text is drawn, the text background (the area between and around characters) is also filled in using the background color. This drawing mode is the OPAQUE background mode, but it can be changed by calling the SetBkMode function.

```
SetBkMode( hdc, nMode )      // OPAQUE or TRANSPARENT
```

The foreground and background color functions have been used in previous examples in this book. In general, they are called as:

```
SetTextColor( hdc, rgbColor );
SetBkColor( hdc, rgbColor );
```

As with pen and brush colors, the rgbColor argument is converted to the nearest solid color supported by the active device. Dithered colors, which are permitted with brushes, are not supported for text or pen displays.

Rather than wondering what colors might be supported, however, the two preceding API calls can be rewritten to request colors that are known to be supported:

```
SetTextColor( hdc, GetSysColor( COLOR_WINDOWTEXT ));
SetBkColor( hdc, GetSysColor( COLOR_WINDOW ));
```

The default colors for the foreground and background are, respectively, black and white. If you want to change these colors, it is also useful to include a provision (in WndProc) to repaint the entire client window when the changes occur. Since no system color changes can be made without issuing a notification message to all applications, the simplest method is to include a WM_SYSCOLORCHANGE response:

```
case WM_SYSCOLORCHANGE:
    InvalidateRect( hwnd );
    break;
```

Fonts and Typefaces

An obvious prerequisite for a text display is one or more fonts with which to create the display. Under DOS (in conventional text mode), the system hardware—generally, the video card itself—supplied the display font in the form of a ROM-based, bitmapped character set tailored to the device's display capabilities. Thus, CGA video cards supplied one set of bitmaps, EGA video another, and VGA still a third.

Of course, all of this was quite transparent to the software. Applications had no need to ask or to know what the display characteristics consisted of, or even the display's capabilities. Applications simply wrote to the output, as ASCII character codes, and let the hardware take care of the rest. Earlier displays were limited to a single typeface and, essentially, a single type size.

Today, in a graphics environment, the old-style text displays are gone. Graphics displays can not only mix text, graphics, and colors, but they can use many different character fonts (typefaces), in many different sizes. Furthermore, they can vary typeface and size in a variety of styles, such as bold and italic, and in many cases, may also vary font widths, slants, and weights.

Programmers now have a wide range of flexibility in handling of graphics text displays. But, to make use of these opportunities, it may help to understand both the origins of type fonts and the characteristics which determine fonts.

Reminiscences of a Printer's Devil

In personal terms (primarily because of a long personal history in the newspaper business beginning long before electronic typesetting), the word *typeface* conjures images of large flat trays of small compartments filled with individual metal characters in an assortment of sizes and typeface designs.

Most of the typesetting, of course, was accomplished by a huge and intricate machine known as a linotype, operated by a highly skilled (and very well paid) individual who knew both the precision mechanics of the triple keyboard, as well as the massive armatures and injection molds that for many decades produced newspapers, books, and the bulk of all manner of printed material.

Continued on next page

Larger type sizes, such as those used for ads, headlines, and other features, were not supported by the linotype and its banks of molds. These fell to nimble fingers to choose, arrange, and align individual characters from the appropriate trays with a speed that might well have been envied by even expert typists.

Still, by the time I graduated from high school (and, at the same time, completed a 12-year apprenticeship in the mysteries of the newspaper business), it was clear that, soon—at least in technologically historical terms—both the gentle monster and the type trays would be little more than museum exhibits. It was not too many years later that both did, indeed, disappear. They were replaced, first, by electronic/optical/photographic processes and then, a scant decade after that, under my own supervision (as a visiting computer consultant), by purely electronic processes.

Today, of course, these are only the memories of a one-time printer's devil. But, even if the old order has passed, the type tray and linotype laid the foundations for the modern world. They are reflected not only in modern fonts and typestyles, but also in the terminology that defines font characteristics and in the methods that manipulate their appearance.

A Brief History of Typefaces

When computers were young, typefaces were an embellishment limited to high-end, hard-copy devices, such as daisywheel printers; even then, they were changed only by physically changing the print wheel. For computer monitors, type styles were quite simply firmware built into the system. In general, they consisted of 8×8 or 8×9 bitmapped (also called *raster*) characters for CGA video systems. These ranged up to 8×18 bitmapped characters for VGA systems.

Bitmapped Fonts

Figure 27.1 shows three bitmapped characters in an 8×12 format. Bitmapped fonts have some obvious advantages. Since each character's pixel image is already defined, the character can be transferred to the screen by simply copying the bit pattern directly to the video. This process is speedy and places minimal demands on system resources.

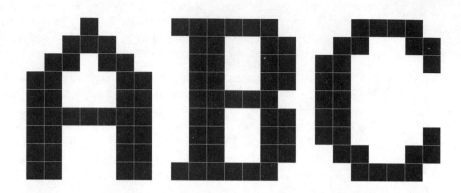

However, there are disadvantages to using bitmapped fonts. They can be resized only as simple multiples and cannot be created in any in-between sizes. When enlarged, the resulting characters tend to be jagged in appearance.

Also, while some systems did offer more than one font, the selection was generally limited to two or three sizes, such as font provisions for a 43- or 50-line display as alternatives to the standard 25 lines, but without offering any variations in style, pitch, or weight. Of course, on early computers, there was little or no demand for larger typefaces or even for varying typefaces. It remained for the advent (and popularity) of graphics display systems to demonstrate the advantages of sizable fonts.

Stroked Fonts

One early approach to creating fonts for a graphics environment involved creating libraries of bitmapped fonts in incremental sizes. As a solution, however, this was never popular for several reasons: because of the sheer mass of data required for the fonts, because of relatively slow response times, and because of the demands on the system memory.

Instead, a different way to define characters was devised (or, more accurately, borrowed from existing typesetting technologies already in use by printers in the newspaper and publishing industries). These are known as *stroked* or *vectored* fonts. In this system, the structure of each character is described by a series of vectors, not by an array of pixels.

There are some disadvantages to the stroked font approach. For small font sizes, the vectored data is, in general, larger than an equivalent bitmapped font and requires more processing to produce each display character. But the disadvantages are minor, placing only minimal demands on modern CPUs and contemporary video systems.

The advantages are tremendous. Stroked fonts can not only be resized, but they can also be reproportioned, weighted, slanted, rotated, inverted, or otherwise manipulated with minimal effort and maximal effect. And, most important, a single set of font data provides a variety of sizes and styles within a single typeface. Once a font is defined as stroked data, the resulting typeface is available in any size desired—as italics, boldface, or with sufficiently sophisticated processing, as outline, condensed, or extra-bold forms.

Figure 27.2 shows three characters created using a vectored font, sized for 48 points. The *A* shows the vectors defining the character as black lines. The *B* and *C* characters show the outlines after processing.

FIGURE 27.2:

A stroked, or vectored, font

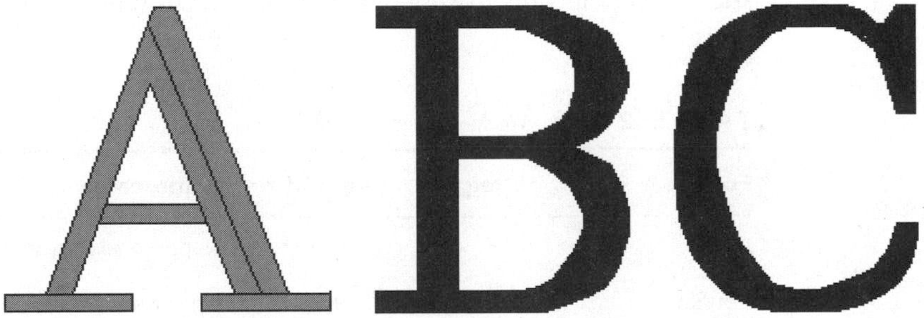

Under Windows 98 (and Windows 95 and NT), the older, bitmapped fonts have been largely (but not entirely) discarded in favor of stroked fonts.

Windows Default Fonts

Windows 98 supplies the 15 standard fonts shown in Figure 27.3. Each of these fonts appears in its default height, width, and weight.

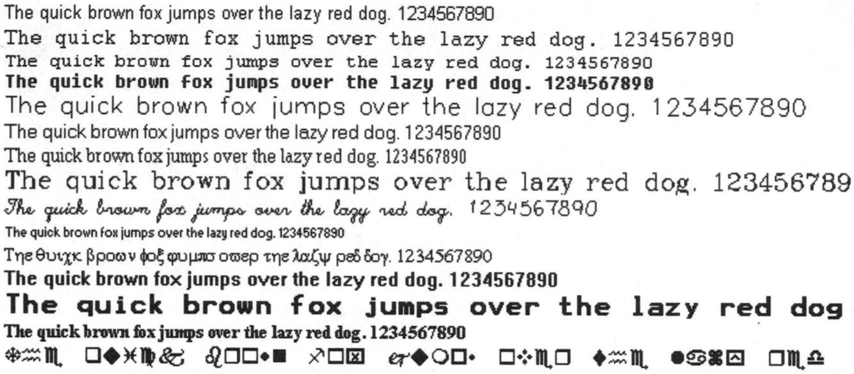

FIGURE 27.3:

Fifteen standard fonts

The quick brown fox jumps over the lazy red dog. 1234567890
The quick brown fox jumps over the lazy red dog. 1234567890
The quick brown fox jumps over the lazy red dog. 1234567890
The quick brown fox jumps over the lazy red dog. 1234567890
The quick brown fox jumps over the lazy red dog. 1234567890
The quick brown fox jumps over the lazy red dog. 1234567890
The quick brown fox jumps over the lazy red dog. 1234567890
The quick brown fox jumps over the lazy red dog. 123456789
The quick brown fox jumps over the lazy red dog. 1234567890
The quick brown fox jumps over the lazy red dog. 1234567890
Τηε θυιχκ βροων φοξ φυμπσ οπερ τηε λαζψ ρεδ δογ. 1234567890
The quick brown fox jumps over the lazy red dog. 1234567890
The quick brown fox jumps over the lazy red dog
The quick brown fox jumps over the lazy red dog. 1234567890

Table 27.4 lists the fonts illustrated, in their order of appearance in Figure 27.3, together with the default height and average width for each. The default weight for all fonts is 400, or normal weight. (See the discussion of the lfWeight field in the "Font Selection Using Logical Fonts" section for more information about font weights.)

TABLE 27.4: Windows Standard Fonts

Font	Height	Avg Width	Comments
Arial	16	6	Proportional sans-serif font; similar to Gothic
Courier	16	9	Typewriter or dot-matrix standard (with serifs)
Courier New	16	8	Same as Courier but slightly narrower
Fixedsys	15	8	Fixed-width OEM (system) font (sans-serif)
Modern	18	10	Proportional sans-serif stroked font
MS Sans Serif	16	7	Another sans-serif with narrower defaults
MS Serif	16	6	Proportional serif font; similar to Times-Roman
Roman	18	11	Serif equivalent of Modern; similar spacing

Continued on next page

TABLE 27.4 (CONTINUED): Windows Standard Fonts

Font	Height	Avg Width	Comments
Script	18	8	Font that resembles handwriting (appears small for point size)
Small Fonts	11	5	Small sans-serif font; good for readable fine print
Symbol	16	8	Greek, math, and other symbols
System	16	7	Proportional-width system font (sans-serif)
Terminal	16	13	A rather broad sans-serif font
Times New Roman	17	6	Popular proportional-width, general-purpose font
Wingdings	16	13	Useful symbols; also called Dingbats

The Courier, Fixedsys, MS Sans Serif, MS Serif, Small Fonts, System, and Terminal fonts are essentially bitmapped fonts.

Of the remaining eight fonts, the Modern, Roman, and Script fonts consist only of strokes. When they are drawn as enlarged characters (for example, at a height of 400 in text mode), they quite clearly show the strokes comprising each character in a fashion similar to the stroked *A* in Figure 27.1.

The other five fonts—Arial, Courier New, Symbol, Times New Roman, and Wingdings—are stroked outline (or True-Type) fonts. Stroked outline fonts are created as outline strokes with the interiors filled. When these are drawn in larger sizes, they remain fully solid, even though their outlines may begin to show a slight grain or irregularity.

NOTE The fonts distributed with the release version of Windows 98 may be different from those listed above, and individual fonts are being changed from stroked to full True-Type fonts. Also, since you may have fonts installed on your system from several different sources, the comments on specific fonts should be taken only as a general guideline.

Font Selection Using Logical Fonts

While you might think of font selection as simply being a matter of requesting a typeface and specifying a character size, for computers, this is a bit too simple. This is not because computers require complexity, but because a font—even a sizable font—still must match the display characteristics of the device, at least to a minimal degree.

Thus, instead of simply naming a typeface and size, an application makes a request identifying the font name, size, and other characteristics desired. For this purpose, the LOGFONT structure is defined in WinGDI.H as:

```
typedef struct tagLOGFONTA
{
    LONG lfHeight;
    LONG lfWidth;
    LONG lfEscapement;
    LONG lfOrientation;
    LONG lfWeight;
    BYTE lfItalic;
    BYTE lfUnderline;
    BYTE lfStrikeOut;
    BYTE lfCharSet;
    BYTE lfOutPrecision;
    BYTE lfClipPrecision;
    BYTE lfQuality;
    BYTE lfPitchAndFamily;
    char lfFaceName[LF_FACESIZE];
} LOGFONTA;
```

Two structure definitions are provided: LOGFONTA, for use with an ANSI environment, and LOGFONTW, for use with a wide, or Unicode, character set. However, since the choice of environment is controlled by a compiler directive, the only source code reference required is LOGFONT. Depending on the compiler directive, this will be mapped to either the ANSI or Unicode structure, as appropriate.

The following sections describe the fields in the LOGFONT structure.

Height and Width Fields

The lfHeight field specifies the desired height of the font in logical units. If the value is positive or negative, the absolute value is transformed to device units and matched against the cell heights of the available fonts.

A 0 (zero) height simply instructs the GDI to select a reasonable (default) height. This is normally the smallest size that will accommodate the strokes comprising the font characters.

In all cases, the font mapper looks for the largest font—the most detailed font (character) description—that does not exceed the requested size. If none match this requirement, the smallest available font is used.

The lfWidth field specifies the average width (in logical units) of the characters in the font. If lfWidth is 0, the device aspect ratio is matched against the digitization aspect ratio; that is, the width in units which the font will require for display. Selection is based on the closest match, or the smallest absolute difference between the two ratios. In general, a 0 value allows the character width to be matched against the character height.

In actual practice, bitmapped fonts, such as the Courier, Fixedsys, MS Sans Serif, MS Serif, Small Fonts, System, and Terminal fonts (illustrated in Figure 27.3 and listed in Table 27.4) are used, as long as the bitmap size matches the display context relatively well. If any of these are enlarged, however, Windows substitutes a default stroked font, usually Arial, which can be more readily sized. (You can see this in action in the *Fonts* demo, discussed later in the chapter.)

Weight Field

The lfWeight field specifies the desired weight of the font. This field accepts values in the range 0 to 1000. If lfWeight is 0, a default weight is used (normal). As you can see in Table 27.5, currently only two weights are actually employed: 400 for normal or 700 for bold. However, future versions (probably with higher-resolution displays) are expected to use a wider range of weights.

TABLE 27.5: Font Weights

Weight Constant	Value	Comments	Alternatives
FW_DONTCARE	0		
FW_THIN	100	Not supported	
FW_EXTRALIGHT	200	Not supported	FW_ULTRALIGHT
FW_LIGHT	300	Not supported	
FW_NORMAL	400	Default weight	FW_REGULAR

Continued on next page

TABLE 27.5 CONTINUED: Font Weights

Weight Constant	Value	Comments	Alternatives
FW_MEDIUM	500	Not supported	
FW_SEMIBOLD	600	Not supported	FW_DEMIBOLD
FW_BOLD	700	Boldface	
FW_EXTRABOLD	800	Not supported	FW_EXTRABOLD
FW_HEAVY	900	Not supported	FW_BLACK

Italic, Underline, and Strikeout Fields

The lfItalic field is simply a Boolean flag. If TRUE, the font is created as italics (if possible). The lfUnderline and lfStrikeOut fields operate in the same fashion.

Character Set Field

The lfCharSet field specifies the character set desired. Identifiers are predefined in WinGDI.H, as shown in Table 27.6.

TABLE 27.6: Character Set Constants

Character set	Value	Comments
ANSI_CHARSET	0	Default; ANSI characters
UNICODE_CHARSET	1	Unicode (32-bit) characters
SYMBOL_CHARSET	2	Symbols
SHIFTJIS_CHARSET	128	Japanese Kanji characters
HANGEUL_CHARSET	129	Non-Roman/Arabic characters
CHINESEBIG5_CHARSET	136	Chinese characters
OEM_CHARSET	255	Device-dependent characters
The following character sets are defined only for WinVer 0x0400 (Windows 95/98/NT) & later.		
JOHAB_CHARSET	130	
HEBREW_CHARSET	177	Hebrew (Judaic) characters

Continued on next page

TABLE 27.6 (CONTINUED): Character Set Constants

Character set	Value	Comments
The following character sets are defined only for WinVer 0x0400 (Windows 95/98/NT) & later.		
ARABIC_CHARSET	178	Arabic characters
GREEK_CHARSET	161	Greek characters
TURKISH_CHARSET	162	Turkish characters
VIETNAMESE_CHARSET	163	Vietnamese characters
THAI_CHARSET	222	Thai (Thailand) characters
EASTEUROPE_CHARSET	238	Eastern European characters
RUSSIAN_CHARSET	204	Russian characters
MAC_CHARSET	77	Macintosh characters
BALTIC_CHARSET	186	Baltic (region) characters
FS_LATIN1	0x00000001L	Latin characters
FS_LATIN2	0x00000002L	Latin characters
FS_CYRILLIC	0x00000004L	Russian characters
FS_GREEK	0x00000008L	Greek characters
FS_TURKISH	0x00000010L	Turkish characters
FS_HEBREW	0x00000020L	Hebrew (Judaic) characters
FS_ARABIC	0x00000040L	Arabic characters
FS_BALTIC	0x00000080L	Baltic (region) characters
FS_VIETNAMESE	0x00000100L	Vietnamese characters
FS_THAI	0x00010000L	Thai (Thailand) characters
FS_JISJAPAN	0x00020000L	Japanese characters
FS_CHINESESIMP	0x00040000L	Chinese characters
FS_WANSUNG	0x00080000L	Chinese characters
FS_CHINESETRAD	0x00100000L	Chinese characters
FS_JOHAB	0x00200000L	
FS_SYMBOL	0x80000000L	Symbol font

WARNING   Although fonts supporting character sets other than those defined may be present in a system, do not attempt to translate or interpret strings to be rendered with such fonts.

Escapement and Orientation Fields

Both the lfEscapement and lfOrientation fields are expressed in 1/10° increments. The lfEscapement value sets the string orientation with an angle of 0° for horizontal alignment, increasing in a counter-clockwise direction.

The lfOrientation value determines the angle of the character's baseline relative to horizontal. Thus, for a value of 0, a *T* or *L* remains vertical; for a value of 900 (90°), '*T*' will be drawn horizontally and the *L* will be lying on its back.

Table 27.7 summarizes both the text and character orientation at 90° intervals for lfEscapement and lfOrientation.

TABLE 27.7:   Text and Character Orientation

Value	Degrees	lfEscapement (String Orientation)	lfOrientation (Character Orientation)
0	0°	Left to right (default)	Normal (vertical, default)
900	90°	Vertical, rising	Rotated 90° counter-clockwise
1800	180°	Right to left	Inverted
2700	270°	Vertical, falling	Rotated 90° clockwise

Out-Precision, Clip-Precision, and Quality Fields

The lfOutPrecision, lfClipPrecision, and lfQuality fields are used to request specific matches between the fonts selected and the device-output capabilities.

lfOutPrecision defines how closely the actual output must match the requested font's characteristics, such as height, width, orientation, and pitch. Output precision values are defined as shown in Table 27.8.

TABLE 27.8:   Output Precision

Constant	Value	Comments
OUT_DEFAULT_PRECIS	0	
OUT_STRING_PRECIS	1	Maintain string precision
OUT_CHARACTER_PRECIS	2	Maintain character precision
OUT_STROKE_PRECIS	3	Maintain stroke precision
OUT_TT_PRECIS	4	New, not documented; support unknown
OUT_DEVICE_PRECIS	5	New, not documented; support unknown
OUT_RASTER_PRECIS	6	New, not documented; support unknown
OUT_TT_ONLY_PRECIS	7	New, not documented; support unknown
OUT_OUTLINE_PRECIS	8	Maintain outline precision

NOTE   Several of the flag values for the lfOutPrecision, lfClipPrecision, and lfQuality fields are new and may or may not be fully supported by present versions of Windows 98 and/or by present video and output device drivers. Before you rely on a specific precision flag, you should experiment with it. Unimplemented precision flags may be supported later or may be supported by specific device drivers.

The lfClipPrecision field specifies how characters that are partially outside the clipping region are clipped. Eight values are defined in WinGDI.H, as shown in Table 27.9.

TABLE 27.9:   Clipping Precision

Constant	Value	Comments
CLIP_DEFAULT_PRECIS	00h	
CLIP_CHARACTER_PRECIS	01h	Clip entire character
CLIP_STROKE_PRECIS	02h	Clip only strokes
CLIP_MASK	0Fh	New, not documented; support unknown

Continued on next page

TABLE 27.9 CONTINUED: Clipping Precision

Constant	Value	Comments
CLIP_LH_ANGLES	10h	New, not documented; support unknown
CLIP_TT_ALWAYS	20h	New, not documented; support unknown
CLIP_EMBEDDED	80h	New, not documented; support unknown

The lfQuality field specifies the desired output quality, which is how well the output (physical font) is matched to the requested logical font attributes. Three values are defined in WinGDI.H, as shown in Table 27.10.

TABLE 27.10: Output Quality

Constant	Value	Comments
DEFAULT_QUALITY	00h	Appearance not important
DRAFT_QUALITY	01h	Appearance of minimal importance; font scaling fully enabled for all GDI fonts; bold, italic, underline, and strikeout synthesized as necessary
PROOF_QUALITY	02h	Character quality more important than matching logical font attributes; GDI font scaling disabled; only closest font sizes chosen; bold, italic, underline, and strikeout synthesized as necessary

Pitch and Family Field

The lfPitchAndFamily field specifies both the pitch (spacing) and the font family. The two low-order bits specify the font spacing, using one of the three values defined in WinGDI.H, as shown in Table 27.11.

TABLE 27.11: Font Pitch

Pitch Constant	Value	Comments
DEFAULT_PITCH	00h	Don't care or don't know
FIXED_PITCH	01h	Fixed spacing (characters per inch)
VARIABLE_PITCH	02h	Variable spacing (proportional)

The high-order nibble of the lfPitchAndFamily byte specifies a family of fonts and can be any of the six values defined in WinGDI.H, as shown in Table 27.12.

TABLE 27.12: Font Family

Family Constant	Value	Comments
FF_DONTCARE	00h	Don't care or don't know
FF_ROMAN	10h	Serif, variable character width, such as Times Roman and Century Schoolbook
FF_SWISS	20h	Sans-serif, variable character width, such as Helvetica and Swiss
FF_MODERN	30h	Constant character width, serif or sans-serif, such as Pica, Elite, and Courier
FF_SCRIPT	40h	Cursive, for example
FF_DECORATIVE	50h	Old English, for example

Face Name Field

The lfFaceName field contains the address of a null-terminated string specifying the typeface name of the desired font. The string must not exceed 32 characters. If no font name is specified (the argument is NULL), the GDI uses a default typeface such as Arial.

> **NOTE** For typesetting purposes, WinVer 0x0400 (Windows 95/98/NT) and later also support a number of additional font specifications, including an extensive series of Panose definitions, which are not discussed here. The Panose font-classification values are contained in a **PANOSE** structure and describe the characteristics of a True Type font. For further information, refer to the online documentation.

The Fonts Demo: Demonstrating Logical Fonts

The *Fonts* demo provides a platform to demonstrate the three principal features of using logical fonts:

- Using the EnumFonts function to list available typefaces
- Setting font characteristics (height, width, and so on)

- Showing fonts under different mapping modes

Figure 27.4 shows the *Fonts* demo window.

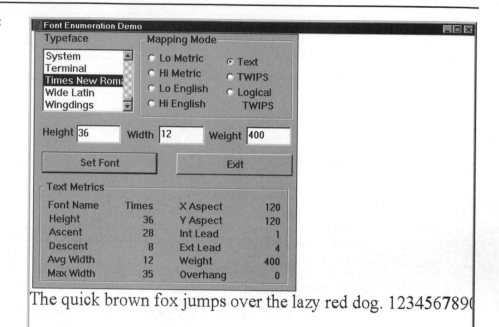

A standard font-selection dialog box is supplied through the MFC CFont-Dialog class as one of the Windows common dialog boxes. The advantage of using the standard Fonts dialog box is that you do not need to provide your own font-selection mechanisms. (For an example of the common font dialog box, refer to the FontView demo included with the Visual C++ compiler.)

NOTE   The *Fonts* demo is included on the CD that accompanies this book, in the Chapter 27 folder. This listing should provide you with the basic structure for designing your own font-manipulation facilities.

Font Selection

The first feature demonstrated in the *Fonts* demo is the use of the EnumFonts function to query the GDI and list all available typefaces, in this case, by loading the font names in a list box.

As a first step, we define the record type FONTLIST:

```
typedef struct tagFONTLIST
{
   GLOBALHANDLE   hGMem;
   int            nCount;
} FONTLIST;
```

A variable of type FONTLIST is used to record a list of fonts and the number of fonts located.

In most of the other demos discussed in this book, the WndProc procedure provides the heart of the application. In addition to message handling, this procedure is responsible for a greater or lesser portion of the application's task handling. In contrast, in the *Fonts* demo, the majority of the work is shifted away from the WndProc procedure to a modeless dialog box and to the DlgProc procedure-handling messages addressed to the dialog box. The few provisions necessary in WndProc for creatng DlgProc should, at this point, already be familiar to you from previous examples.

The exported DlgProc procedure begins by declaring two static variables. One of these is lpEnumProc, a pointer to the FontEnumFunc procedure, which will actually make the call to the API EnumProc function. The other is a FontList variable to point to the returned data (the typeface names). A third variable is declared as a long pointer to a string, lpFontName, providing a second handle to the font list.

```
BOOL APIENTRY DlgProc( HWND hDlg, UINT msg, UINT wParam, LONG lParam )
{
   static FARPROC  lpEnumProc;
   static FONTLIST FontList;
   LPSTR           lpFontName;
   HDC             hdc;
   int             i, nSel;
   char            szFont[LF_FACESIZE];
```

In response to the WM_INITDIALOG message, another call is made to the Make-ProcInstance macro to return a handle (lpEnumProc) to the FontEnumFunc procedure. This handle is used to tell the EnumFonts function where to find the FontEnumFunc callback function.

```
      switch( msg )
      {
         case WM_INITDIALOG:
            ...
            lpEnumProc = MakeProcInstance( FontEnumFunc, hInst );
```

```
          FontList.hGMem = GlobalAlloc( GMEM_MOVEABLE |
                                        GMEM_ZEROINIT, 1L );
          FontList.nCount = 0;
```

The FontList variable also requires initialization by allocating and zeroing one (1) byte, returning the memory pointer to the FontList.hGMem field. Additional memory will be allocated as required, but since the number of fonts is not presently known, it would be pointless to attempt to allocate memory for an unknown number of strings at this time. The FontList.nCount field is also initialized to 0 but will be used presently to track the number of typefaces found.

The next requirement is a device-context handle (hdc), which is obtained using GetParent(hDlg) to return a device context for the main application window rather than the dialog window. And, finally, the EnumFonts API function is called using the retrieved device-context handle, a pointer to the FontEnumProc function, and a pointer to the FontList variable.

```
          hdc = GetDC( GetParent( hDlg ) );
          EnumFonts( hdc, NULL, lpEnumProc, (LPVOID) &FontList );
```

The second parameter, passed as NULL in this example, could have been used as a long pointer to a string (LPSTR) to specify a particular typeface; in effect, to query if a specific typeface was available. By passing this specification as NULL, all available typefaces will be reported.

The FontEnumProc procedure, while not an exported procedure in the usual sense of receiving messages directly from Windows, is used as a callback function by the EnumFonts API function.

The FontEnumProc procedure is called from EnumFonts with four parameters: a pointer to a LOGFONT structure reporting the logical attributes of a font, a pointer to a TEXTMETRIC structure reporting the physical font attributes, a short integer indicating the font type (bit flags), and the same far pointer to FontList that was originally passed to EnumFonts.

```
int APIENTRY FontEnumFunc( LPLOGFONT       lf,
                           LPTEXTMETRIC    tm,
                           short           nFontType,
                           FONTLIST FAR *  FontList )
{
    LPSTR lpFontFace;
```

The first task accomplished in the FontEnumFunc procedure is a GlobalRe-Alloc to allocate enough additional memory for one more typeface name. If this is successful, GlobalLock is called to ensure that the memory allocated is not moved until the present task is finished.

```
          if( ! GlobalReAlloc( FontList->hGMem,
                               (DWORD) LF_FACESIZE * ( FontList->nCount + 1 ),
                               GMEM_MOVEABLE ) )
             return( FALSE );
          lpFontFace = GlobalLock( FontList->hGMem );
          lstrcpy( lpFontFace + ( ( FontList->nCount ) * LF_FACESIZE ),
                   (LPSTR) lf->lfFaceName );
          GlobalUnlock( FontList->hGMem );
          FontList->nCount++;
          return( TRUE );
       }
```

Once memory is allocated and locked, the font name (`lf->lfFaceName`) reported by EnumFonts is copied to the offset of the newly allocated memory, the memory is unlocked, and `FontList->nCount` is incremented.

NOTE   As you may have already realized, the bulk of the information passed by **Enum-Fonts** has been discarded; only the font name has been retained. But, in this case, the font name is all that we really need. Actually, there wasn't any choice about what information was passed to the **FontsEnumFunc** procedure from the **Enum-Fonts** API function. The only choice was to select which portion was actually wanted, discarding the excess. (We'll talk about another alternative in a bit.)

The next step is to copy the font list into the list box in the dialog box. And, again, this process begins by globally locking the memory where the data is stored.

```
          lpFontName = GlobalLock( FontList.hGMem );
          SendDlgItemMessage( hDlg, IDD_FONTLIST, WM_SETREDRAW,
                              (WPARAM) 1, (LPARAM) 0 );
          SendDlgItemMessage( hDlg, IDD_FONTLIST,
                              LB_RESETCONTENT, NULL, NULL );
```

Before copying the data, however, as a precaution, two initial messages are sent to the list box to instruct it to be redrawn. These ensure that the new data will be visible. Also, a reset message is sent to clear any contents that the list box might happen to contain.

Once this housekeeping is out of the way, a simple loop, using `FontList.nCount` as the limit, copies the string data. The names are copied one item at a time, using the same offset addresses as before, into the list box.

```
for( i=0; i<FontList.nCount; i++ )
    SendDlgItemMessage( hDlg, IDD_FONTLIST, LB_ADDSTRING, 0,
        (LPARAM)(LPSTR)( lpFontName + ( i * LF_FACESIZE ) ) );
GlobalUnlock( FontList.hGMem );
GlobalFree( FontList.hGMem );
FontList.hGMem = NULL;
FreeProcInstance( lpEnumProc );
ReleaseDC( GetParent( hDlg ), hdc );
```

After the data has been copied over to the list box, the allocated memory (hGMem) and the address variable for the FontEnumProc procedure are no longer required. Therefore, the allocated memory is unlocked and freed, the lpEnumProc function handle is freed, and to finish the housekeeping, the device context is released.

Finally, after calling the ShowMetrics function to update the dialog box display, the WM_INITDIALOG response, rather than returning on a break; statement, is allowed to fall through to the WM_SETFOCUS message response, setting the active focus to the dialog box.

```
ShowMetrics( hDlg );  // fall through to SetFocus

case WM_SETFOCUS:
    SetFocus( GetDlgItem( hDlg, IDD_HEIGHT ) );
    break;
```

At this point, the list box in the dialog box is primed with a list of available fonts, ready for the user to select the typeface desired. And, when this is done, the dialog box display will be updated to reflect the selection. The main application window will display the sample text string using the chosen typeface.

TIP

If the process of retrieving the font list seems rather roundabout, a portion could be simplified. For instance, what about rewriting the FontEnumFunc callback function to load the list box directly? This would simplify matters, wouldn't it? This is an experiment that you may want to try.

Font Characteristic Variations

In addition to allowing the user to select typefaces from the list box, the *Fonts* demo also provides three edit boxes for entry of height, width, and weight specifications. Values entered in these three edit boxes are used (when the Set Font button is clicked) in the tm (text metric) request that selects the new font (or new size).

The resulting text metrics information items reported at the bottom of the dialog box (look back at Figure 27.4) represent the best match found by the GDI and reflect the actual font displayed in the application's main window (immediately below the dialog box).

TIP   In the Font demo's current form, only four of the text metrics fields can be edited directly or indirectly; these are the height, width, weight, and typeface. The remaining fields are assigned default values. As another experiment, you could add control features for any or all of the other text metrics.

Font Sizing and Mapping Modes

The *Fonts* demo also includes a provision for selecting the different mapping modes. This part of the program demonstrates how different fonts appear when resized, how fonts can be changed proportionally by varying the width and height, and how the GDI selects fonts appropriate to the mapping mode and sizes requested. (For more information about mapping modes, see Chapter 23.)

Notice particularly that, when one of the bitmapped fonts is requested in a too-large size, the GDI replaces it with a stroked or outline font, which is more suitable for the purpose.

TIP   You may wish to change the defaults assigned to the `lfPitchAndFamily` specification and observe how this affects the GDI's choices. Last, for the adventurous or the dedicated, the `lfEscapement` and `lfOrientation` fields offer ample opportunities for departure from the straight and horizontal. Please feel free to explore the possibilities.

The real test of typeface flexibility lies in the applications using these facilities. Any shortcomings are more likely to lie in the application design than in the provided resources.

As you have seen, the basic tools permit virtually any degree of text elaboration desired. For those requiring additional typefaces, a variety of fonts are available from third-party sources. You can also find toolkits for designing custom fonts.

Now that we've covered the advanced text operations, we can return to graphics operations. The next chapter discusses images and image file formats.

CHAPTER

TWENTY-EIGHT

Graphics Utilities and File Operations

- ■ A screen-capture program for bitmap images

- ■ Bitmap compression techniques

- ■ Commands for handling graphics files

- ■ A PCX file viewer

- ■ Techniques for converting 24-bit color images

A variety of formats have been developed for saving, storing, and displaying graphics images. A number of popular formats predated Windows, including ZSoft's Paintbrush PCX, CompuServe's GIF and, for more demanding circumstances, TrueVision Inc.'s TARGA or TGA formats. Today, Windows has its own native BMP format.

All of these formats have one factor in common: Each is designed for a specific image type or system. TrueVision's TGA images, for example, are designed for video-camera images, generally incorporating 16, 24, or 32 bits of color per pixel. In contrast, ZSoft's PCX, CompuServe's GIF, and Windows BMP formats are palette-based, encoding images by first including palette-color information in the image file and then referencing the individual pixels as palette colors.

In this chapter, we'll take a look at how to handle graphics files. We'll begin by discussing a demo program that captures Windows bitmap images either to the clipboard or to a file. Then we'll cover commands for handling graphics files, treatments for file formats other than the native BMP files, and techniques for converting 24-bit color images.

A Screen-Capture Utility

Under Windows, where all displays are graphical in nature, a graphics screen-capture utility can be a basic tool for transferring graphics information among applications or for simply saving images for later use. Capturing a screen under Windows is greatly expedited and simplified by procedures inherent within Windows.

Principal among these methods is the Windows clipboard, a facility which provides both storage and information transfer among Windows applications. (Although the clipboard handles several types of information, each with its own format, only the graphics image or bitmap format is relevant to this discussion.)

Capturing a bitmap to the clipboard is a task well-supported by Windows API functions, making this task almost automatic. In contrast, a similar capture to a file format requires several steps. Procedures for both capturing to the clipboard and to a file are included in the *Capture* demo.

The Capture Demo: Capturing and Displaying Screen Images

The *Capture* demo is a screen-capture utility that stores and retrieves only information that is in bitmap format. Other types of information loaded to the clipboard—such as data, metafiles, or other formats—are ignored.

As an example of the use of the clipboard to store a bitmap, take a look at Figure 28.1. This figure was created using the *Capture* demo.

Figure 28.1 is neither a trick nor a composite. It's an actual screen display, which was created as follows:

1. Begin by loading two instances of the *Capture* demo. Initially, one image is reduced to an icon, and the second is used to capture the screen to the system clipboard. During the capture process, the second instance automatically reduces itself to an icon at the bottom of the screen; then it resumes normal size after the capture is completed.

2. After the first capture, both copies of *Capture* are restored to windows. Both show the clipboard image using the Fit to Window option.

FIGURE 28.1:

Recursively captured views

3. One copy of *Capture* is used to repeat the process of capturing the screen, including the image of the other copy of *Capture* and the previous clipboard image. Each new image is automatically written to the clipboard and then displayed by both copies of *Capture*.

4. Repeating this process yields the recursive image shown in Figure 28.1, where it becomes a tunnel effect.

5. Finally, call the last capture operation to capture the recursive image, but this time, rather than capturing the image to the clipboard for display, write the image directly to a .BMP file. The instance making the capture reduces itself to an icon during capture. Therefore, that instance loses the active focus, which reverts to the open window showing the previous clipboard image.

Because the final operation saves the image to a file rather than to the clipboard, the previously displayed image is not replaced. If a different utility were used to capture an image to the clipboard, both of the *Capture* windows would display that image.

Both capture options in the *Capture* demo—To Clipboard and To File—include a five-second time delay (audible beeps are sounded at one-second intervals during the wait time), during which the user may use the mouse or keyboard to shift the active focus, to select a different application window, to pull down menus, or to activate other features.

NOTE   The Capture demo is included on the CD that accompanies this book, in the Chapter 28 folder.

Screen-Capture Operations

Screen capture is based on rectangular coordinates that define the area to be copied. For the example, the *Capture* demo simply checks the size of the Desktop (the main screen), using the HWND_DESKTOP window handle, to capture the entire display. Other screen-capture applications could include provisions to select only the active application's display, to select only a specific window, or to use the mouse to select some other rectangular area.

In operation, because the Capture menu offers the To Clipboard and To File choices, two responses are provided for the WM_COMMAND/IDM_CLIP and WM_COM-MAND/IDM_FILE messages:

```
case WM_COMMAND:
   switch( LOWORD( wParam ) )
   {
      ...
      case IDM_CLIP:
         Action = TOCLIPBD;
         CloseWindow( hwnd );
         Clock = SetTimer( hwnd, 1, 1000, NULL );
         iSec = 0;
         break;

      case IDM_FILE:
         if( DialogBox( hInst, "GETNAME", hwnd,
                        FileNameDlgProc ) )
         {
            Action = TOFILE;
            CloseWindow( hwnd );
            Clock = SetTimer( hwnd, 1, 1000, NULL );
            iSec = 0;
         }
         break;
```

The two responses are essentially the same. The difference is that before an image can be saved to a file, the FileNameDlgProc is invoked, requesting a file-name and, optionally, a drive and path specification.

In both responses, the CloseWindow API is called to minimize the *Capture* application before initializing a timer for one-second intervals and setting the seconds counter (iSec) to zero.

Subsequently, as WM_TIMER messages are received, iSec is incremented. Until iSec reaches five seconds (or whatever interval is desired), the MessageBeep function is called to provide an audible timer signal.

```
case WM_TIMER:
   if( ++iSec == 5 )
      PostMessage( hwnd, WM_COMMAND, IDM_CAPTURE, 0 );
   else
      MessageBeep( MB_ICONEXCLAMATION );
   break;
```

The sound (waveform) associated with each **MB_ICON*xxxxx*** constant may be changed using the Sound Control Panel. These assignments, however, are under the control of the user, not the application.

The **MB_ICONEXCLAMATION** argument used here in calling the **MessageBeep** API function is probably more familiar as an argument in a **MessageBox** API call requesting inclusion of the exclamation icon. However, the **MB_ICONEXCLAMATION** constant, as well as the **MB_ICONASTERISK**, **MB_ICONHAND**, **MB_ICONQUESTION**, and **MB_OK** constants, can also be used as parameters to request a system sound that is defined as a .WAV waveform file and reproduced by a sound card, such as Sound Blaster. If no sound card is installed, the system speaker will provide the traditional default beep using the system's internal speaker.

Next, when the IDM_CAPTURE message is received, a final beep is issued and the timer process is halted (killed) before either the **SaveBitmap** function is called to create a bitmap file or the **CaptureBitmap** function is called to copy the image to the clipboard.

```
case IDM_CAPTURE:
    MessageBeep( MB_OK );
    KillTimer( hwnd, Clock );
    SetCursor( LoadCursor( NULL, IDC_WAIT ) );
    switch( Action )
    {
        case TOFILE:
            SaveBitmap();            break;
        case TOCLIPBD:
            CaptureBitmap( hwnd ); break;
    }
    SetCursor( LoadCursor( NULL, IDC_ARROW ) );
    OpenIcon( hwnd );
    break;
```

Once the appropriate process is completed, the **OpenIcon** API function is called to restore the application to its original window size and state. At this time, the application also regains the active focus.

The two capture processes—**CaptureBitmap** and **SaveBitmap**—use parallel operations but are not identical.

Clipboard-Capture Operations

The CaptureBitmap process begins by calling the GetDC API function but, instead of using the application's window handle (hwnd), we use the Desktop handle (HWND_DESKTOP).

```
int CaptureBitmap( HWND hwnd )
{
    HDC          hdc, hdcMem;
    HBITMAP      hBitmap;
    static int   i, j, CRes, LnWidth, LnPad = 0,
                 xSize, ySize;

    SetCursor( LoadCursor( NULL, IDC_WAIT ) );
    hdc = GetDC( HWND_DESKTOP );
    xSize = GetDeviceCaps( hdc, HORZRES );
    ySize = GetDeviceCaps( hdc, VERTRES );
```

Once we have retrieved a handle to the Desktop device context, we can use the GetDeviceCaps function to query the current display resolution. To capture only a specific application's window, the parallel process would be to simply use the application's handle; for example, use the GetFocus API function to retrieve a handle for the active application's window.

The next step is to create a memory context that is compatible with the selected device context, and then to create a compatible bitmap.

```
    hdcMem = CreateCompatibleDC( hdc );
    hBitmap = CreateCompatibleBitmap( hdc, xSize, ySize );
```

Notice that the compatible bitmap created here is not a display bitmap. Rather, hdcMem is a memory device-context handle that contains a copy of the display image. This way, we can manipulate the image data without affecting the actual display.

The next step includes a provisional test before proceeding to ensure that a valid bitmap handle was returned. If the call to CreateCompatibleBitmap is successful, hBitmap will be non-NULL, and the capture process can proceed by calling Select-Object to select the bitmap, hBitmap, into the logical context, hdcMem. However, it is the subsequent StretchBlt instruction that actually transfers the image from the screen to the memory device-context handle.

```
    if( hBitmap )
    {
        SelectObject( hdcMem, hBitmap );
        StretchBlt( hdcMem, 0, 0, xSize, ySize,
                    hdc,    0, 0, xSize, ySize, SRCCOPY );
```

Although both BitBlt and StretchBlt provide a means of copying information between display contexts (hdc and hdcMem in this example), StretchBlt optionally provides the additional capability of stretching (or shrinking) the image to fit the available display space. The BitBlt function simply executes an exact copy.

> **NOTE**
>
> Notice that even though StretchBlt is being used for the transfer, the source and destination rectangles are the same size. Thus, no distortion is imposed on the image being copied. The StretchBlt operation is necessary to copy the image pixels from the active device context to the memory context, where they become the bitmap referenced by the **hBitmap** handle.

The memory device context, however, is not the actual destination for this bitmap. Rather, hdcMem is used as an environment where the copy of the original image can be stretched or shrunk to fit the application's display context.

Copying to the Clipboard

We want to give the bitmap a more permanent storage location and make it accessible to other applications. Calling OpenClipboard opens the clipboard for examination. The next instruction, EmptyClipboard, gives the current application temporary ownership of the clipboard, dumping the current contents (if any) of the clipboard.

```
OpenClipboard( hwnd );
EmptyClipboard();
SetClipboardData( CF_BITMAP, hBitmap );
CloseClipboard();
```

Next, we call SetClipboard to transfer the new material—the bitmap image—to the clipboard, specifying the data type with the CF_BITMAP argument. Then we call CloseClipboard, releasing ownership of the clipboard.

> **NOTE**
>
> The preceding sequence is a fairly standard example of clipboard use, beginning with **OpenClipboard** and ending with **CloseClipboard**. Between the **Open...** and **Close...** commands, a variety of different actions can be executed. But, remember that control (ownership) of the clipboard is always temporary and should be relinquished as quickly as possible. See Chapter 34 for more information about clipboard operations.

Finally, as with any process, a degree of cleanup is required. It begins, still within the conditional process, by invalidating the application's window to ensure that the application will be repainted after it is restored:

```
        InvalidateRect( hwnd, NULL, TRUE );
    }
    DeleteDC( hdcMem );
    ReleaseDC( HWND_DESKTOP, hdc );
    return 0;
}
```

The remaining cleanup provisions are not conditional but consist simply of deleting the memory context and releasing the device context.

Painting from the Clipboard

In response to the WM_PAINT message, the *Capture* demo displays any bitmap image contained by the clipboard, regardless of the source of the image. Again, the first step (after initializing the customary device context) is to open the clipboard. This time, however, we do not call the EmptyClipboard function, and the application does not assume ownership, only access.

```
        case WM_PAINT:
            hdc = BeginPaint( hwnd, &ps );
            OpenClipboard( hwnd );
            if( hBitmap = GetClipboardData( CF_BITMAP ) )
            {
                SetCursor( LoadCursor( NULL, IDC_WAIT ) );
                hdcMem = CreateCompatibleDC( hdc );
                SelectObject( hdcMem, hBitmap );
                GetObject( hBitmap, sizeof( BITMAP ),
                           (LPSTR) &bm );
```

This time, we use the hBitmap handle to retrieve the bitmap from the clipboard. If there is no bitmap image, the process is aborted.

Two methods of displaying a retrieved image are used: either actual-size or sized-to-fit. In the first case, we use the BitBlt function to execute a direct copy to the window. In the second instance, we call the StretchBlt function to copy the bitmap to fit the application window.

```
            if( fExpand
            {
                SetStretchBltMode( hdc, iStrMode );
                StretchBlt( hdc, 0, 0, cxWnd, cyWnd,
                            hdcMem, 0, 0,
                            bm.bmWidth, bm.bmHeight,
                            SRCCOPY );
            }
            else
                BitBlt( hdc, 0, 0, cxWnd, cyWnd,
                        hdcMem, 0, 0, SRCCOPY );
            SetCursor( LoadCursor( NULL, IDC_ARROW ) );
            DeleteDC( hdcMem );
        }
```

Last, we must call the `CloseClipboard` function before the painting operation concludes:

```
        CloseClipboard();
        EndPaint( hwnd, &ps );
        break;
```

As you can see, the big advantage of using the clipboard is simplicity. The operations involved are brief and uncomplicated, and their execution is quite speedy. Unfortunately, the corresponding operations directed toward building a bitmap file are not quite so simple and execute more slowly, although only marginally so.

File-Capture Operations

Capturing a bitmap to the clipboard is a task well-supported by Windows API functions, making this task almost automatic. In contrast, a similar capture to a file format is less well supported, requiring several specific subtasks to create a .BMP file image.

NOTE The MFC `CBitmap` class does provide some further support. Unfortunately, this class implementation is woefully incomplete.

Creating the File Information Structures

A bitmap image file consists of three parts:

- A file header (BITMAPFILEHEADER)

- An information header (BITMAPINFOHEADER), which includes color-palette information

- The actual image information

Of these, the palette information and the image data vary in structure, depending on the type of color information and the encoding method (or lack thereof) used to store the image information.

Before any of these information structures can be created, however, the first step is to create a device context and to retrieve information about the device context and parameters, which will be used to describe the bitmap image. As with the process for capturing to the clipboard, this example begins by using the HWND_DESKTOP handle to retrieve a device-context handle. It then continues by querying the palette size and bits per pixel, as well as the horizontal and vertical device resolution.

```
int SaveBitmap()
{
   HDC       hdc, hdcMem;
   HANDLE    hBits, hFil;
   HBITMAP   hBitmap;
   HPALETTE  hPal;
   LPVOID    lpBits;
   RGBQUAD   RGBQuad;
   DWORD     ImgSize, plSize, dwWritten;
   int       i, CRes, Height, Width, LnWidth, LnPad;
   BITMAPFILEHEADER  bmFH;
   BITMAPINFO        bmInfo;
   LPLOGPALETTE      lp;

   SetCursor( LoadCursor( NULL, IDC_WAIT ) );
//=== open file for write ================================
   hFil = CreateFile( szFName, GENERIC_WRITE, 0,  NULL,
            CREATE_ALWAYS, FILE_ATTRIBUTE_NORMAL, NULL );
   if( hFil == NULL )
      return( ErrorMsg( "Can't open file" ) );
```

```
hdc = GetDC( HWND_DESKTOP );
CRes = GetDeviceCaps( hdc, SIZEPALETTE );
plSize = CRes * sizeof( RGBQUAD );        // palette size
bmInfo.bmiHeader.biBitCount =
   GetDeviceCaps( hdc, BITSPIXEL );
Height = GetDeviceCaps( hdc, VERTRES );
Width  = GetDeviceCaps( hdc, HORZRES );
if( GetDeviceCaps( hdc, BITSPIXEL ) == 8 )
   LnWidth = Width;
else
   LnWidth = Width / 2;
if( LnWidth % sizeof(DWORD) )
   LnPad = sizeof(DWORD) - ( LnWidth % sizeof(DWORD) );
ImgSize = (DWORD)( (DWORD)( LnWidth + LnPad ) * 480 );
```

As the necessary raw information is retrieved, several local data variables are also calculated, including the raw image size, palette size, and the width of the individual scan lines.

The File Header The bitmap file begins with a file header defined by the BITMAPFILEHEADER structure, which holds information about the type, size, and layout of a DIB (device-independent bitmap) file.

> **NOTE**
>
> The terms bitmap and device-independent bitmap, along with the file extensions .BMP and .DIB, were once quite different. The .BMP extension identified only bitmaps using a device-specific structure supported by Windows 2.*x*. Today, device-dependent bitmaps are effectively obsolete. Common usage has allowed the .DIB extension to fall into disuse. The .BMP extension is used for all bitmaps, and it's assumed that all bitmap images are device-independent. Despite this assumption, however, the BITMAPFILEHEADER structure is still used.

The BITMAPFILEHEADER is defined as:

```
typedef struct tagBITMAPFILEHEADER
{  WORD    bfType;
   DWORD   bfSize;
   WORD    bfReserved1;
   WORD    bfReserved2;
   WORD    bfOffBits;
} BITMAPFILEHEADER;
```

The BITMAPFILEHEADER fields are described in Table 28.1.

TABLE 28.1: BITMAPFILEHEADER Data Fields

Field	Description
bfType	Specifies the file type; must be BM
bfSize	Specifies the file size in DWORD units
bfReserved1	Reserved; must be zero
bfReserved2	Reserved; must be zero
bfOffBits	Offset in bytes from BITMAPFILEHEADER to the start of the actual bitmap in the file

The following code excerpt shows how these fields are set in the *Capture* demo:

```
bmFH.bfType      = 0x4D42;            // type is "BM"

bmFH.bfReserved1 = 0L;
bmFH.bfReserved2 = 0L;
bmFH.bfOffBits   = plSize +          // bitmap offset
                   sizeof( BITMAPINFO ) +
                   sizeof( BITMAPFILEHEADER );
bmFH.bfSize      = ImgSize +         // file size
                   bmFH.bfOffBits;
WriteFile( hFil, &bmFH, sizeof( bmFH ),
           &dwWritten, NULL );       // write file header
```

The bfOffBits field, which is the offset from the first of the image file to the beginning of the image data, is calculated as the palette size (plSize), plus the size of the BITMAPINFO structure, plus the size of BITMAPFILEHEADER. Once this file header is complete, this block of data is written directly to the file, using the WriteFile API function.

The Bitmap Information Structure Within the DIB file, the BITMAPFILE-HEADER structure is followed immediately by either a BITMAPINFO or BITMAP-COREINFO data structure. In the *Capture* demo, the BITMAPINFO structure defines the dimensions and color information for a DIB file. BITMAPINFO is defined as follows:

```
typedef struct tagBITMAPINFO
{
   BITMAPINFOHEADER  bmiHeader;
   RGBQUAD           bmiColors[1];
} BITMAPINFO;
```

The BITMAPINFO fields are described in Table 28.2.

TABLE 28.2:   BITMAPINFO Data Fields

Field	Description
bmiHeader	BITMAPINFOHEADER containing information about the dimensions and color format of a DIB
bmiColors	An array of RGBQUAD data structures defining the colors in the bitmap

The Bitmap Information Header Structure   The BITMAPINFOHEADER structure provides information about the size and organization of the bitmap image data and is defined as:

```
typedef struct tagBITMAPINFOHEADER
{
    DWORD    biSize;
    DWORD    biWidth;
    DWORD    biHeight;
    DWORD    biPlanes;
    DWORD    biBitCount;
    DWORD    biCompression;
    DWORD    biSizeImage;
    DWORD    biXPelsPerMeter;
    DWORD    biYPelsPerMeter;
    DWORD    biClrUsed;
    DWORD    biClrImportant;
} BITMAPINFOHEADER;
```

Table 28.3 describes the BITMAPINFOHEADER data fields.

TABLE 28.3:   BITMAPINFOHEADER Data Fields

Field	Description
biSize	Number of bytes required by the BITMAPINFOHEADER structure
biWidth	Width of the bitmap in pixels
biHeight	Height of the bitmap in pixels
biPlanes	Color planes for target device; must be 1

Continued on next page

TABLE 28.3 CONTINUED: BITMAPINFOHEADER Data Fields

Field	Description
biBitCount	Bits per pixel; must be 1, 4, 8, or 24 (see Table 28.4)
biCompression	Type of compression for a compressed bitmap (see Table 28.5)
biSizeImage	Image size in bytes
biXPelsPerMeter	Horizontal resolution in pixels per meter of the optimum target device (applications may use this value to select from a resource group a bitmap that best matches the characteristics of the current device)
biYPelsPerMeter	Vertical resolution in pixels per meter of the optimum target device (applications may use this value to select from a resource group a bitmap that best matches the characteristics of the current device)
biClrUsed	Number of color indexes in the color table used by the bitmap (see Table 28.6)
biClrImportant	Number of color indexes considered important for displaying the bitmap; if 0, all are important

The biBitCount field of the BITMAPINFOHEADER structure determines the number of bits defining each pixel, as well as the maximum number of colors in the bitmap. This biBitCount field may be set to any of the values shown in Table 28.4.

TABLE 28.4:   Bitmap Bit Count

Value	Description
1	Monochrome bitmap; bmiColors field must contain two entries and each bit in the bitmap array represents one pixel. If the bit is clear (0), the first color entry is used; if set (1), the second color entry is used.
4	Maximum 16 colors; bmiColors field must contain the maximum of 16 entries with each pixel in the bitmap represented by a 4-bit index to the color table.
8	Maximum 256 colors; bmiColors field contains a maximum of 256 entries with each pixel in the bitmap represented by a byte index to the color table.
24	Maximum 2^{24} colors; bmiColors field is NULL. Each pixel in the bitmap is represented by 3 bytes in the data array representing the relative pixel intensities of red, green, and blue.
32	Maximum 2^{32} colors; if bmiColors is BI_RGB, bmiColors field is NULL. Each pixel in the bitmap is represented by 3 bytes in the data array representing the relative pixel intensities of red, green, and blue. The high byte in each DWORD is ignored.

In Windows 98, when **biCompression** is BI_BITFIELDS, only one 32 bits per pixel color mask is supported as blue = 0x000000FF, green = 0x0000FF00, red = 0x00FF0000. (The result, of course, is WHITE). In Windows NT, when **biCompression** is BI_BITFIELDS, bits set in each **DWORD** mask must be contiguous and should not overlap the bits of another mask. You do not need to use all the bits in the pixel.

The **biCompression** field of the BITMAPINFOHEADER structure identifies the compression format used, as listed in Table 28.5. (Bitmap compression formats are discussed later in the chapter.)

TABLE 28.5: Compression Format Identifiers

Field	Description
BI_RGB	Bitmap is not compressed.
BI_RLE8	Run-length encoded format for bitmaps, with 8 bits per pixel; uses a 2-byte format consisting of a count byte followed by a color-index byte.
BI_RLE4	Run-length encoded format for bitmaps with 4 bits per pixel; uses a 2-byte format consisting of a count byte followed by a byte containing two color indexes (nibbles).
BI_BITFIELDS	Bitmap is not compressed; color table consists of three **DWORD** color masks, which specify the red, green, and blue components, respectively, of each pixel. Valid when used with 16- and 32-bit-per-pixel bitmaps.

The **biClrUsed** field specifies the number of color indexes in the color table that are actually used by the bitmap. If the **biClrUsed** field is set to 0, the bitmap uses the maximum number of colors corresponding to the value of the **biBitCount** field, as listed in Table 28.6.

TABLE 28.6: Values for biClrUsed

Value	Description
0	Bitmap uses the maximum number of colors specified in the **biBitCount** field.
1..15	**biClrUsed** specifies the actual number of colors accessed by the device driver or graphics image.
16..*nn*	**biClrUsed** specifies the size of the color table used to optimize performance for Windows color palettes. If **biBitCount** is 16 or 32, the optimal color palette starts immediately following the three **DWORD** color masks.

> **NOTE** If the bitmap is a packed bitmap—the bitmap array immediately follows the `BITMAPINFO` header and is referenced by a single pointer. The `biClrUsed` member must be either 0 or the actual size of the color table.

Colors in the `bmiColors` table should appear in order of importance, putting the highest frequency colors first. This way, if a bitmapped image is displayed on a device with a lower color resolution, the most important colors are mapped to the high-frequency colors in the palette.

In the *Capture* demo, the BITMAPINFOHEADER assignments are implemented as:

```
bmInfo.bmiHeader.biSize =
    (DWORD) sizeof( BITMAPINFOHEADER );
bmInfo.bmiHeader.biWidth         = Width;
bmInfo.bmiHeader.biHeight        = Height;
bmInfo.bmiHeader.biPlanes        = 1;
bmInfo.bmiHeader.biCompression   = BI_RGB;
bmInfo.bmiHeader.biSizeImage     = 0L;
bmInfo.bmiHeader.biXPelsPerMeter = 0L;
bmInfo.bmiHeader.biYPelsPerMeter = 0L;
bmInfo.bmiHeader.biClrUsed       = 0L;
bmInfo.bmiHeader.biClrImportant  = 0L;
WriteFile( hFil, &bmInfo.bmiHeader,
           sizeof( bmInfo.bmiHeader ),
           &dwWritten, NULL );       // write info header
```

Writing the Bitmap Palette

Thus far, only the header information has been written to the bitmap file. Both palette and image information remain to be written. The *Capture* demo is set for two types of bitmaps: those with either 16- or 256-color palettes. (For monochrome, 24- or 32-bit-per-pixel bitmaps, additional provisions are necessary, as described earlier in this chapter.)

> **NOTE** 32-bit-per-pixel color information is essentially the same as 24-bit-per-pixel data except for an 8-bit **NULL** in each entry used to pad the entry to a **DWORD** size.

Retrieving Palette Colors The following excerpt shows the handling for retrieving the palette color information and begins by allocating and locking sufficient memory space to contain the palette information:

```
                // note: GHND = GMEM_FIXED | GMEM_ZEROINIT
hPal = GlobalAlloc( GHND, sizeof(LOGPALETTE) +
                    ( CRes * sizeof(PALETTEENTRY) ) );
                    // allocate memory for palette
lp = (LPLOGPALETTE) GlobalLock( hPal );
                    // lock the memory allocated
lp->palNumEntries = CRes;
lp->palVersion    = 0x0300;
                    // fill in size and version (3.0)
GetSystemPaletteEntries( hdc, 0, CRes,
                    lp->palPalEntry );
                    // and get the palette information
```

After allocating space for the palette information, the palette size is initialized (CRes) and the version number is set. With this done, the last step is calling Get-SystemPaletteEntries to retrieve the actual palette color information and fill the lp->palPalEntry structure.

Converting Palette Colors Once we retrieve the palette information, but before the data is stored as part of the bitmap image, we must convert the PALETTEENTRY RGB order to the RGBQUAD format used by bitmap images.

The PALETTEENTRY structure is defined as:

```
typedef struct tagPALETTEENTRY
{
    BYTE   peRed;
    BYTE   peGreen;
    BYTE   peBlue;
    BYTE   peFlags;
} PALETTEENTRY;
```

In contrast, the RGBQUAD structure used by bitmap images is the same size— 4 bytes—but uses an entirely different ordering for the colors. The RGBQUAD structure is defined as:

```
typedef struct tagRGBQUAD
{
    BYTE   rgbBlue;
    BYTE   rgbGreen;
    BYTE   rgbRed;
```

```
      BYTE   rgbReserved;
   } RGBQUAD;
```

As you can see, the PALETTEENTRY structure uses red-green-blue color order; the RGBQUAD structure uses blue-green-red. Therefore, provisions are necessary to convert the RGB order of the retrieved palette information to the bitmap's GRB order, as shown here:

```
RGBQuad.rgbReserved = 0;
for( i=0; i<=CRes; i++ )
{
   RGBQuad.rgbRed   = lp->palPalEntry[i].peRed;
   RGBQuad.rgbGreen = lp->palPalEntry[i].peGreen;
   RGBQuad.rgbBlue  = lp->palPalEntry[i].peBlue;
   WriteFile( hFil, &RGBQuad, sizeof( RGBQuad ),
             &dwWritten, NULL );
}
```

As each palette entry is converted to RGBQUAD format, the converted entry is written to the bitmap file. Also, for each entry to the file, the `rgbReserved` field remains 0.

After looping though the palette information and creating the bitmap palette, the last step is to unlock and free the memory allocated to hold the palette.

```
GlobalUnlock( hPal );      // don't forget to unlock
GlobalFree( hPal );        // and release the memory
```

Still, the task is not finished. Thus far, the bitmap file and information header have been written, followed by the color palette data, but the image data has not been written yet.

Writing the Image Data

Earlier, I mentioned that various color resolutions use specific formats to encode the image data, even ignoring the data-compression formats entirely. As discussed, a 16-color image coded each pixel as a nibble of data (4 bits); a 256-color image requires a byte of data for each pixel; and a true-color (24-bit) image expects 3 bytes of data per pixel.

Rather than providing separate and different encoding methods for each color format, however, the CreateCompatibleBitmap function creates a memory device context that is compatible with the hardware device context (HWND_DESK-TOP in the *Capture* demo). Then, by copying the bitmap image to this memory context, the bitmap bits are automatically rendered in the format appropriate to be written to the file.

```
hdcMem = CreateCompatibleDC( hdc );
hBitmap = CreateCompatibleBitmap( hdc, Width, 1 );
hBits = GlobalAlloc( GHND, LnWidth );
lpBits = (LPVOID) GlobalLock( hBits );
SelectObject( hdcMem, hBitmap );
```

Because a large bitmap requires substantial space (increasing with higher color resolutions), we use a small trick here. Instead of allocating memory space to contain the entire image at once, we allocate only enough space to contain one scan line from the image. And, this done, we lock the allocated space and select the bitmap into the memory context—the buffer, in effect.

The `SelectObject` function is only a setup for the device context. Although the bitmap has been selected to the context, no image data has yet been assigned to this bitmap. Therefore, in the next loop, the screen is read one scan line at a time, beginning at the bottom and working up, into the memory context; that is, into the bitmap that was sized for a single scan line.

```
for( i = Height - 1; i >= 0; i-- )
{
    BitBlt( hdcMem, 0, 0, Width, 1,
            hdc,     0, i, SRCCOPY );
    GetBitmapBits( hBitmap, Width, lpBits );
    WriteFile( hFil, lpBits, LnWidth, &dwWritten, NULL );
}
```

The whole purpose of this exercise, however, is not to create a bitmap one pixel high, but rather to use the `GetBitmapBits` function to copy this segment of image—first from the bitmap to the `lpBits` array and then from the `lpBits` array to the image file. In this fashion, instead of providing conversions to fit various color resolutions, the `BitBlt` function provides automatic conversion by writing the data to a memory bitmap. This memory bitmap is sized to match the original image and, therefore, is exactly the right size to be written to the file.

NOTE   It may have occurred to you that instead of using a loop, all of this could have been done in a single step (even though more memory would be required). What you must remember, however, is that the bitmap file also requires the image to be written from the bottom up. Copying the entire image in a single step would produce an inverted (mirrored) result. By using a loop, in addition to saving memory, you also avoid the necessity of inverting the image before writing the file.

Now, once the image has been written, the usual cleanup is necessary to release the various memory allocations and context and handle assignments:

```
    GlobalUnlock( hBits );           // don't forget to unlock
    GlobalFree( hBits );             // and release the image,
    hBits = NULL;                    // optional but good form
    DeleteDC( hdcMem );              // delete and release the
    ReleaseDC( HWND_DESKTOP, hdc );  // device contexts
    CloseHandle( hFil );             // and close the file
    SetCursor( LoadCursor( NULL, IDC_ARROW ) );
    return( TRUE );
}
```

Finally, the CloseHandle API function is called to close the completed bitmap image file, and the wait cursor is replaced by the default arrow cursor.

Bitmap Compression Formats

Compression is used with most image formats to reduce both memory and disk storage requirements. Windows supports two compression formats for bitmaps: one for 16-color images with 4 bits per pixel and one for 256-color images with 8 bits per pixel. The bitmap compression format flags are listed back in Table 28.5, and the BI_RLE8 and BI_RLE4 formats are described in the following sections.

The BI_RLE8 Format

For 256-color images that use 8 bits per pixel to index pixels to the color palette, the BI_RLE8 format offers two compression modes: encoded or absolute. Both of these modes may occur in the same bitmap (and usually do).

Encoded Mode Encoded mode uses WORD values, where the first byte in each WORD value specifies some number of consecutive values (01h..FFh) to be drawn using the color index indicated by the second byte. As an exception, the first byte may be set to zero to indicate an escape sequence, with the second byte denoting the end of a scan line, the end of the bitmap, or a delta escape, as listed in Table 28.7.

TABLE 28.7:   Compression Escape Sequences

First byte	Second byte	Definition
0	0	End of scan line
0	1	End of bitmap
0	2	Delta; the WORD value following the escape sequence contains horizontal (first byte) and vertical (second byte) offsets (relative) to the next pixel position

Absolute Mode   Absolute mode is indicated by a WORD value, with the first byte set to zero and the second byte in the range 03h..FFh. The second byte represents the number of bytes following that contain absolute color indexes for a single pixel.

Since absolute mode also requires that each run be aligned on a WORD boundary, absolute runs are null-padded by byte as necessary to end each run on a WORD boundary.

BI_RLE8 Example   Following is an example of hexadecimal WORD values from an 8-bit compressed bitmap, together with the corresponding decompression sequences:

    0304 0506 0003 4556 6700 0278 0002 0501 0278 0000 091E 0001

Compressed Bytes	Decompressed Results / Pixel Values
03 04	04 04 04
05 06	06 06 06 06 06
00 03 45 56 67 00	45 56 67 (a single null byte is added for padding for this absolute mode run but is not included in the decompressed image)
02 78	78 78
00 02 05 01	Move 5 pixels right, 1 pixel down
02 78	78 78
00 00	End of scan line
09 1E	1E 1E 1E 1E 1E 1E 1E 1E 1E
00 01	End of RLE bitmap

The BI_RLE4 Format

For 4-bit-per-pixel images, the BI_RLE4 format is used. Like BI_RLE8, this format incorporates two modes: encoded or absolute. Both modes may occur anywhere within an individual bitmap (and usually do).

Encoded Mode   In the encoded mode, WORD values are used, and the first byte in each WORD value specifies some number of consecutive values (01h..FFh) to be drawn using the two color indexes contained in the second byte. Since the second byte contains two separate color indexes—one in the high-order nibble and one in the low-order nibble—the pixel sequence is drawn by alternating the two values indicated. With this sequence, the first pixel uses the first color index, the second pixel uses the second color index, the third pixel uses the first color index, and so on, until the indicated number of pixels have been written.

As an exception, the first byte may be set to zero to indicate an escape sequence with the second byte denoting the end of a scan line, the end of the bitmap, or a delta escape (see Table 28.7).

Absolute Mode   In absolute mode, the first byte contains zero, while the second byte specifies the number of absolute color indexes (as nibble values) following. Subsequent bytes contain pairs of color indexes in the high- and low-order nibbles, with four color indexes in each WORD value.

Since absolute mode also requires that each run be aligned on a WORD boundary, absolute runs are null-padded by nibble as necessary to end each run on a word boundary.

BI_RLE4 Example   Following is an example of hexadecimal WORD values from a 4-bit compressed bitmap, together with the corresponding decompressed sequences. (Single-digit values represent color indexes for single pixels.)

0540 0506 0005 4567 8000 0477 0002 0501 0478 0000 091E 0001

Compressed Bytes	Decompressed Results / Pixel Values
06 40	4 0 4 0 4 0
05 06	0 6 0 6 0
00 05 45 67 80 00	4 5 6 7 8 (three null nibbles are added for padding for this absolute mode run but are not included in the decompressed image)

Continued on next page

Compressed bytes	Decompressed Results / Pixel Values
04 77	7 7 7 7 7 7 7 7
00 02 05 01	Move 5 pixels right, 1 pixel down
04 78	7 8 7 8 7 8 7 8
00 00	End of scan line
09 1E	1 E 1 E 1 E 1 E 1
00 01	End of RLE bitmap

Windows 98 Graphics File Operations

Windows 3.*x* and earlier depended on the conventional C/C++ file operators to read and write files using, for example, the familiar fopen/fwrite/fclose functions. Windows 98 and Windows NT have replacements for these old standards in the form of API function calls, three of which are introduced here as direct replacements.

File-Open Operations

In any file operation, the first task is to open a file for either input or output. However, instead of the fopen function call familiar to C/C++ and Windows 3.1 programmers, you use the CreateFile API:

```
hFil = CreateFile( szFName, GENERIC_WRITE, 0, NULL,
                   CREATE_ALWAYS, FILE_ATTRIBUTE_NORMAL, NULL );
if( hFil == NULL )
    return( ErrorMsg( "Can't open file" ) );
```

Although the CreateFile function is equivalent to the fopen function, the calling format, as well as the options and capabilities supported, are different. The CreateFile function is defined as:

```
HANDLE CreateFile( LPCTSTR lpszName,
                   DWORD fdwAccess,
                   DWORD fdwShareMode,
```

```
    LPSECURITY_ATTRIBUTES lpsa,
                    DWORD fdwCreate,
                    DWORD fdwAttrsAndFlags,
                    HANDLE hTemplateFile  )
```

The CreateFile function creates, opens, or truncates a file, returning a handle to the file for subsequent access.

If successful, the CreateFile function returns an open handle to the specified file. If the operation fails, the returned value is -1 (0xFFFFFFFF), and you can use the GetLastError function to retrieve extended error information.

NOTE   You can use the CreateFile, WriteFile, and ReadFile functions with named pipes and mailslots (with Windows NT) and with communication resources, although you may need to observe some special features or restrictions. For further details, refer to Chapter 15 and to the online API function documentation on pipes.

The CreateFile Parameters

The calling parameters for the CreateFile API function are explained in the following sections.

lpszName   This is the filename argument passed as a pointer to a null-terminated string. The lpszName parameter specifies the name of a file, pipe, communications resource, or console to be created or opened.

fdwAccess   The fdwAccess parameter identifies the file-access type and may be either or both of the following flag values:

GENERIC_READ   Provides file read access; permits data to be read from the file and the file pointer to be moved.

GENERIC_WRITE   Provides file read/write access; permits data to be read from and written to the file and the file pointer to be moved.

fdwShareMode   The fdwShareMode parameter specifies if and how the file can be shared and must be some combination of the following flag values:

0   File cannot be shared.

FILE_SHARE_READ   File can be opened for read-only access by other applications; used to open the client end of a mailslot.

FILE_SHARE_WRITE   File can be opened for read/write access by other applications.

lpsa   The lpsa parameter is a pointer to a SECURITY_ATTRIBUTES data structure specifying file-security attributes. The file system, such as NTFS, must support security attributes before these have any effects.

NOTE

The FAT/FAT32 file systems under Windows 98 do not support security attributes. Also, Windows NT currently does not recognize FAT32 file systems.

---

fdwCreate   The fdwCreate parameter specifies the action taken when the named file already exists or when no file with this name exists. This parameter must have one of the following values.

CREATE_NEW   Creates a new file, failing if the specified filename already exists.

CREATE_ALWAYS   Creates a new file, overwriting any existing file.

OPEN_EXISTING   Opens an existing file but fails if no file exists.

OPEN_ALWAYS   Opens an existing file or creates a new file if none exists.

TRUNCATE_EXISTING   Opens an existing file, truncating the file to a zero size or failing if the named file does not exist. The file must be opened using GENERIC_WRITE access (see the fdwAccess parameter).

When CreateFile creates a new file, if the fdwAttrsAndFlags argument is not NULL, the file attributes and flags defined are ORed with the FILE_ATTRIBUTE_ ARCHIVE bit (see Table 28.8 in the next section). In like fashion, if an hTemplate-File parameter (discussed later) is specified, CreateFile copies the extended attributes associated with the specified template file to the newly created file. Otherwise, the security attributes assigned to the new file are specified by the lpSecurityAttributes parameter. Last, the newly created file's length is set to zero.

When CreateFile is used to open an existing file, the dwFlagsAndAttributes and hTemplateFile arguments are simply ignored, as is the lpSecurityDescriptor member of the lpSecurityAttributes argument. However, the remaining flag values in the SECURITY_ATTRIBUTES structure remain valid.

fdwAttrsAndFlags The `fdwAttrsAndFlags` argument specifies the file attributes and flags assigned to a file. Any combination of the flags and attributes listed in Table 28.8 is acceptable, except that all other flag attributes override the `FILE_ATTRIBUTE_NORMAL` flag.

TABLE 28.8:   File Attribute Flags

Attribute Flag	Meaning
FILE_ATTRIBUTE_ARCHIVE	Sets archive bit, marking the file for backup
FILE_ATTRIBUTE_HIDDEN	Marks the file as hidden; will not be included in an ordinary directory listing
FILE_ATTRIBUTE_NORMAL	Marks file with no other attribute bits set; valid only if used alone
FILE_ATTRIBUTE_READONLY	Marks file as read-only; cannot be written or deleted
FILE_ATTRIBUTE_SYSTEM	Marks file as part of or used exclusively by the operating system
FILE_ATTRIBUTE_TEMPORARY	Marks file as temporary; applications should write to this file only if absolutely necessary
FILE_ATTRIBUTE_ATOMIC_WRITE	Marks file as an atomic write file; applications should write to the file using atomic write semantics
FILE_ATTRIBUTE_XACTION_WRITE	Marks file as a transaction write file; applications should write to the file using transaction write semantics
FILE_FLAG_WRITE_THROUGH	Instructs system to always write through any intermediate cache and go directly to the file
FILE_FLAG_OVERLAPPED	Instructs system to initialize the file so that `ReadFile`, `WriteFile`, `ConnectNamedPipe`, and `TransactNamedPipe` operations, which take a significant time to process, will return `ERROR_IO_PENDING`; this return may be used to implement flow control
FILE_FLAG_NO_BUFFERING	Opens file without intermediate buffering or caching by the system; all reads and writes are executed on sector boundaries, which is useful for rapid reads/writes of large data images
FILE_FLAG_RANDOM_ACCESS	Accesses file randomly (used by Win32 API to optimize file caching)
FILE_FLAG_SEQUENTIAL_SCAN	Accesses file sequentially from beginning to end; applications should not reposition the file pointer (used by Win32 API to optimize file caching)

Continued on next page

TABLE 28.8 (CONTINUED):   File Attribute Flags

Attribute Flag	Meaning
FILE_FLAG_DELETE_ON_CLOSE	Instructs system to delete the file immediately after all file handles have been closed
FILE_FLAG_BACKUP_SEMANTICS	Marks file as being opened or created for a backup or restore operation
FILE_FLAG_POSIX_SEMANTICS	Accesses file according to POSIX rules; because POSIX rules allow multiple files with the same name, differing only in case, files created with this flag may not be accessible from DOS, Win16, or Win32 but may be accessed from WinNT

NOTE   When you use FILE_FLAG_OVERLAPPED, the system does not maintain the file pointer. Instead, the file position is passed as part of the OVERLAPPED structure argument to ReadFile and WriteFile calls. The ReadFile and WriteFile functions must also specify an OVERLAPPED structure. The FILE_FLAG_OVER-LAPPED specification and OVERLAPPED structure permit separate processes or threads to execute simultaneous operations on a single file. Using the OVER-LAPPED structure, each process is responsible for maintaining and updating its own file-position pointer.

hTemplateFile   The hTemplateFile parameter specifies a handle with GENERIC_READ access to a template file, which supplies extended attributes for the file being created. Attributes derived from a template file override any attributes supplied as explicit parameters (by the dwFlagsAndAttributes and lpSecurityAttributes arguments).

File-Write Operations

The WriteFile function is defined as:

```
BOOL WriteFile(  HANDLE hFile,
          CONST VOID *lpBuffer,
             DWORD nNumberOfBytesToWrite,
            LPWORD lpNumberOfBytesWritten,
       LPOVERLAPPED lpOverLapped   )
```

Like the `fwrite` function that `WriteFile` replaces, the purpose of the function is to write data to a file, beginning at the position indicated by the file pointer. After the write is completed, the file pointer is adjusted by the number of bytes actually written, except when the file is opened with FILE_FLAG_OVERLAPPED. If the file handle was created for overlapped I/O, the application must explicitly adjust the position of the file pointer after the write.

The `WriteFile` function has the following parameters:

hFile   Identifies the file to be written. The file handle must have been created with GENERIC_WRITE file access.

lpBuffer   Points to a buffer containing the data to be written to the file.

nNumberOfBytesToWrite   Specifies the number of bytes to be written to the file. A value of 0 is interpreted as a null write.

lpNumberofBytesWritten   Returns the number of bytes actually written to the file and is automatically zeroed before any work is done or any error checking is executed. This argument cannot be NULL and must be the address for a valid DWORD variable.

lpOverlapped   Points to an OVERLAPPED structure, which is required if the file was opened as FILE_FLAG_OVERLAPPED. Otherwise, this argument may simply be passed as NULL. (See the "Overlapped File Operations" section.)

The `WriteFile` function does support a few features not normally encountered or not relevant during DOS file operations, two of which are applicable to conventional disk file operations:

- The `WriteFile` function will fail if the target file is locked by another process and the attempted write overlaps the locked portion.

- If nNumberOfBytesToWrite is zero, `WriteFile` does not truncate or extend the file. Instead, the `SetEndOfFile` function can be used to truncate or extend the file.

NOTE   Truncating a file is usually done to reset a file size to zero before rewriting the file with new data but is occasionally used to discard portions of a record file. Extending a file is commonly employed to add space to a file before executing a direct write. In most cases, using conventional file-management techniques, neither of these operations are necessary.

File-Read Operations

The ReadFile function replaces the traditional and familiar fread function. The ReadFile function is defined as:

```
BOOL ReadFile(
        HANDLE    hFile,                  // file handle
        LPVOID    lpBuffer,               // address of input buffer
        DWORD     nNumberOfBytesToRead,   // bytes to read
        LPDWORD   lpNumberOfBytesRead,    // count of bytes read
   LPOVERLAPPED   lpOverlapped  )         // overlapped I/O structure
```

The ReadFile function reads data from a file, beginning at the position indicated by the file pointer. After the read is completed, the file pointer is adjusted by the number of bytes actually read, except when the file handle has been created with FILE_FLAG_OVERLAPPED. If the file handle was created for overlapped I/O, the application must adjust the position of the file handle after the read.

The following are the ReadFile function's calling parameters:

hFile   Identifies the file to be read. The file handle must have been created using GENERIC_READ or GENERIC_WRITE file access.

lpBuffer   Points to the buffer to receive data read from the file.

nNumberOfBytesToRead   Specifies the number of bytes to read from the file.

lpNumberOfBytesRead   Returns the number of bytes actually read and is automatically zeroed before any work is done or any error checking is executed. This argument cannot be NULL but must be a valid address for a DWORD variable.

lpOverlapped   Pointer to an OVERLAPPED structure, which is required if the file was opened with FILE_FLAG_OVERLAPPED. Otherwise, this argument may be passed simply as NULL. (See the "Overlapped File Operations" section.)

If the return value is TRUE but the number of bytes read is reported as zero, the file pointer was beyond the current end of the file at the time of the read.

The ReadFile function will fail (returning FALSE) if part of the file has been locked by another process and the read overlaps the locked portion.

Overlapped-File Operations

The OVERLAPPED structure, which remains an optional argument in ReadFile calls when file sharing is not enabled, can be used to set a custom file pointer—that is, a custom pointer to a location (offset) within a file.

The OVERLAPPED structure is defined as:

```
typedef struct _OVERLAPPED
{
   DWORD  Internal;
   DWORD  InternalHigh;
   DWORD  Offset;
   DWORD  OffsetHigh;
   HANDLE  hEvent;
} OVERLAPPED;

typedef OVERLAPPED *LPOVERLAPPED;
```

The structure's fields are defined as follows:

Internal   Reserved for system use; specifies a system-dependent status that is valid only when GetOverlappedResult returns without setting the extended error information to ERROR_IO_PENDING.

InternalHigh   Reserved for system use; specifies the length transferred; valid only when GetOverlappedResult returns TRUE.

Offset   DWORD value specifying the low-order 32-bits of the offset address for the transfer. The specification is a file position defined as a byte offset from the start of the file.

OffsetHigh   Optional DWORD value specifying the high-order 32 bits of the offset address for the transfer.

hEvent   Identifies an event to be set to the signaled state when the transfer is complete. The hEvent argument is optional; however, if an event is used, it must be identified here before calling the ReadFile, WriteFile, ConnectNamedPipe, or TransactNamedPipe API functions.

NOTE   Both the Offset and OffsetHigh fields are ignored when reading from and writing to named pipes and communications devices.

Most applications, when opening a file for read or write, will call CreateFile without using the FILE_FLAG_OVERLAPPED flag. In this case, both ReadFile and WriteFile calls can be made passing the lpOverlapped argument as NULL, initiating the read or write operation at the current file position. If, however, the lpOverlapped argument is provided, the read or write operation will be initiated at the file offset specified in the OVERLAPPED structure. In either case, neither ReadFile nor WriteFile will return until the file operation is completed.

Alternatively, if CreateFile was called using the FILE_FLAG_OVERLAPPED flag, the lpOverlapped argument is required to provide the current file position for both read and write operations. If this argument is not provided, both ReadFile and WriteFile will return FALSE, and GetLastError will report ERROR_INVALID_PARAMETER.

When a valid lpOverlapped argument is supplied, the read or write operation begins at the offset specified. However, either ReadFile or WriteFile may return before the operation is completed, returning a result of FALSE, and GetLastError reports ERROR_IO_PENDING. This provision allows the process calling ReadFile or WriteFile to continue with other tasks as the read or write operation continues independently.

File-Size Reports

The GetFileSize API function includes provisions to recognize and report on files that are larger than 4GB, even though such generous file sizes are currently unlikely.

```
DWORD GetFileSize
(
    HANDLE  hFile,              // handle of file to get size of
    LPDWORD lpFileSizeHigh
                    // address of high-order DWORD for file size
);
```

The GetFileSize function returns a DWORD value reporting the low-order 32 bits of the file size. The second argument, LPDWORD, is an optional pointer to a second DWORD value, which will receive the high-order 32 bits of the file size.

If an error occurs, the return value in the low-order 32 bits will be 0xFFFFFFFF. If the actual file size causes this same value to be returned, a call to the Get-LastError function will report NO_ERROR. However, in general, even though a maximum file size of 1.8×10^{19} bytes can be reported, most present applications can simply ignore the high-order 32-bit value (by using NULL as the calling argument) and assume that the actual file size is smaller than the 4GB still possible. For larger files, you would supply a pointer to a DWORD value to receive the high-order 32-bit value.

File-Close Operations

For file operations, the CloseHandle function replaces the familiar fclose function. The CloseHandle function requires only one argument: the file handle originally returned by the CreateFile function call.

CloseHandle invalidates the specified object handle, decrements the object's handle count, and performs object-retention checks. Once the last handle to an object is closed, the object is removed from the system. The CloseHandle function, however, does not close module objects.

> **NOTE** The CloseHandle function is not limited to closing files. It can also be used with handles for console input or output, events, file mapping, mutex, named pipes, processes, semaphores, and threads. See Chapters 14, 15, and 17 for examples.

Image File Formats

Along with the Window's native BMP image format, many other image formats exist. You may need to work with various formats when you are importing and exporting images between applications.

Here, we will cover three popular image file formats: .PCX, .GIF, .TIF, and .TGA. Other formats that you may encounter include the GEM/IMG format, used by Ventura Publisher among others; the PIC or MacPaint format, used by the Apple Macintosh; and PostScript (.EPS) image formats.

Paintbrush's PCX Format

For a long time, ZSoft's Paintbrush (.PCX) format provided the de facto standard for non-Windows (DOS) bitmapped images. Most graphics programs contain some provision for conversion from their native formats to .PCX formats. Also, the original PBRUSH.EXE paintbrush program distributed with Windows was written by ZSoft and included .PCX/.BMP conversion facilities.

As graphics devices have become increasingly sophisticated, the .PCX image format has kept pace. Instead of being a single format, the PCX standard comprises a series of formats including 8-, 16-, and 24-bit color formats, as well as true-gray and monochrome formats.

PCX File Structure

All PCX image files begin with a header defined as:

```
typedef struct tagPCXHEAD
{
    char   manufacturer;      // always 0xA0
    char   version;           // version number
    char   encoding;          // should be 1
    char   bits_per_pixel;    // color depth
    short  xmin, ymin;        // image origin
    short  xmax, ymax;        // image dimensions
    short  hres, yres;        // image resolution
    char   palette[48];       // color palette
    char   reserved;
    char   color_planes;      // color planes
    short  bytes_per_line;    // line buffer size
    short  palette_type;      // gray or color palette
    short  hscreensize;       // horizontal screen size
    short  vscreensize;       // vertical screen size
    char   filler[54];        // null filler
} PCXHEAD;
```

> **NOTE** For 16-bit Windows systems, the `xmin`, `xmax`, `ymin`, `ymax`, `hres`, `vres`, `bytes_per_line`, `palette_type`, `hscreensize`, and `vscreensize` fields have been commonly defined as `int`. For 32-bit Windows, because `int` is now defined as a 4-byte value, this definition has been changed to `short` to preserve the necessary 2-byte field length.

The header has the following fields:

manufacturer   A check identifying the file as a Paintbrush format image and should always be 0x0A.

version   Identifies the version of PC Paintbrush which created the image file. Valid values are 0 (no palette information; Paintbrush 2.5, the earliest incarnation), 2 (valid palette information), 3 (monochrome or the display's default palette), 4 (Paintbrush for Windows), or 5 (Paintbrush 3.0 or later, including 24-bit image files).

encoding   Should always be 1, indicating that PCX's run-length encoding (RLE) has been used. Note, however, that other values may indicate newer versions and newer encoding schemes.

bits_per_pixel   Reports the number of bits to represent each pixel (per color plane). Possible values are 1, 2, 4, 8, or 24.

xmin, ymin   Specify an offset position for the upper-left corner of the image relative to the upper-left corner of the screen (or window). In most cases, no offset is specified, and xmin and ymin will be 0. (Even when an offset is specified, it is still the prerogative of the application, or programmer, to accept or ignore this offset as desired.)

xmax, ymax   Specify the image dimensions. Note that the sizes indicated by xmax and ymax are off by 1, because the actual pixel count begins with zero. For example, for an image with a width of 480 pixels, the xmax value would be 479. The actual width and height of the image should always be calculated as:

```
width  = ( pcxHead.xmax - pcxHead.xmin ) + 1;
height = ( pcxHead.ymax - pcxHead.ymin ) + 1;
```

hres, vres   Provide the resolution of the device (or video mode) where the image was created; for most purposes, these values may be ignored.

palette   A buffer that contains the palette color information for images with 16 or fewer colors (3 bytes per palette entry or 48 bytes in length). For larger palettes (such as 256-color palettes), this information is appended at the end of the image data. The palette structure used in either case consists of a series of RGB triplets, with the first byte in each defining the red level, the second defining the green level, and the third byte defining the blue level.

color_planes   Defines the image's color planes. The value is 4 for EGA 16-bit color images or 1 for all other images, including monochrome.

bytes_per_line   Reports the number of bytes to allocate for a scan-line plane. This value must be an even number and cannot be calculated by subtracting xmin from xmax.

palette_type   Originates with the advent of VGA graphics systems with a value of 1 for gray-scale and a value of 2 for full color. This field is ignored in later versions of Paintbrush.

hscreensize, vscreensize   Report the horizontal and vertical screen size (of the original system) in pixels. These fields were defined for Paintbrush IV and Paintbrush IV+; for all other versions, these should be NULL.

filler   Pads out the header to 128 bytes and should be filled with nulls (zeros). (Future revisions may redefine the image header by using parts of the filler field for new purposes.)

The ViewPCX Demo: Reading a PCX Image

The *ViewPCX* demo demonstrates reading a 256-color PCX image and provides an example of a file lookup dialog box to select an image file. Note that no provisions are made for changing the filename extension or for displaying any format of PCX file except one with a 256-color palette.

Since all .PCX images use the same header structure, the first step for reading any .PCX file is to retrieve the header data. The *ViewPCX* demo uses the Windows **CreateFile** and **ReadFile** API functions. More important, *ViewPCX* makes use of the OVERLAPPED structure to maintain a custom file pointer while executing an asynchronous file read.

The first step is to open the file to read:

```
hFile = CreateFile( PCXFile, GENERIC_READ, 0, NULL,
                    OPEN_EXISTING, FILE_ATTRIBUTE_NORMAL, NULL );
```

Of course, there is always the need for a provision to report possible errors. If the CreateFile function fails, the return value (in hFile) will be INVALID_HANDLE_VALUE, which is handled in a relatively typical fashion:

```
if( hFile == INVALID_HANDLE_VALUE )
{
    wsprintf( szBuff, "Error: %d - unable to open %s!",
              GetLastError(), PCXFile );
    ErrorMsg( szBuff );
    return( FALSE );
}
```

Assuming the file is opened correctly, the image header is retrieved:

```
ReadFile( hFile, &pcxHd, sizeof(PCXHEAD), &fRes, NULL );
if( ( fRes != sizeof(PCXHEAD) ) ||
    ( pcxHd.manufacturer != 0x0A ) )
```

```
    {
        CloseHandle( hFile );
        ErrorMsg( "Not a valid .PCX file" );
        return( FALSE );
    }
```

The ReadFile operation is followed by two checks: The first check tests fRes (the byte count actually returned) against the expected (and requested) byte size, ensuring that a complete header structure was found and retrieved. The second check tests the identification byte to ensure that it is identified as a PaintBrush PCX format image.

At this point, the image has been identified as, presumably, a proper PCX format. However, there are several possible PaintBrush formats; any further progress depends on the image type and the palette information (if any).

NOTE It is easy to add decode and display provisions for black-and-white and 16-color palettes to the demo. For 24-bit color images, you will need to make slightly more elaborate provisions, beginning with a 24-bit video card and an appropriate driver. But, remember, no palette is included in 24-bit-per-pixel images because each pixel contains its own color information as a 3-byte RGB value.

Because 256-color palettes require 3 bytes per color, or a total of 728 bytes to define the palette, the .PCX file header lacks sufficient space to contain the palette information. Instead, the palette information is appended to the end of the PCX image file.

The logical first step, since we are assuming that this is a 256-color image, is to make sure that the image file is large enough to actually contain, at a minimum, the image header, plus a 768-byte palette, plus a 1-byte palette ID. This is easily accomplished:

```
    fSize = GetFileSize( hFile, NULL );
    if( fSize < ( 769 + sizeof(PCXHEAD) ) )
    {    // wrong format – too small for palette
        CloseHandle( hFile );
        ErrorMsg( "Not a 256 color image format" );
        return( FALSE );
    }
```

The next logical check is to test the header version number where a value of 5 indicates the presence of a palette. However, the mere presence of a palette of some size does not ensure that the image is a 256-color format. Therefore, the next step is to retrieve the palette information by using a seek to an offset from the end of the file.

Using conventional DOS file operations, this could have been done using the fseek function:

```
fseek, fp, -769L, SEEK_END );
```

However, using the ReadFile API function, a different approach is necessary to accomplish a similar task. In the *ViewPCX* demo, an initial offset value is assigned:

```
fPos.Offset = fSize - 769;      // seek palette start
fPos.OffsetHigh = 0L;
fPos.hEvent = NULL;
```

The assigned offset is the file size (fSize) minus 769, placing the file pointer one byte ahead of the expected palette. Since a file size greater than 4GB is not anticipated, the fPos.OffsetHigh field is set as zero and will be ignored. Last, the fPos.hEvent field is set as NULL, because no special reports or controls are needed.

After setting the offset, the ReadFile API is called to return a single byte that will be tested for the palette identifier. Then, after incrementing the offset to account for the byte just read, ReadFile is called a second time to retrieve the assumed palette information.

```
bResult = ReadFile( hFile, &chPal, 1, &fRes, &fPos ); // get palette ID
fPos.Offset++;                                         // advance pointer
bResult = ReadFile( hFile, &pcxPal, 768, &fRes, &fPos ); // get palette
```

A Problem for Your Attention

While I was writing this book, using the supposed final, feature-complete beta version of Windows 98, I experienced a problem with the operation used in the *ViewPCX* demo to find the palette offset within a .PCX image. In the following code block, the **ReadFile** operation will fail, even though the subsequent error test will report the operation as successfully completed.

Continued on next page

```
        fPos.Offset = fSize - 769;      // seek palette start
        fPos.OffsetHigh = 0L;
        fPos.hEvent = NULL;
            // get palette ID
        nResult = ReadFile( hFile, &chPal, 1, &fRes, &fPos );
        if( ! nResult )
        {
            CloseHandle( hFile );
            FormatMessage( FORMAT_MESSAGE_ALLOCATE_BUFFER |
                           FORMAT_MESSAGE_FROM_SYSTEM,
                           NULL, GetLastError(),
                           MAKELANGID( LANG_NEUTRAL,
                                       SUBLANG_DEFAULT ),
                           (LPTSTR) &lpMsgBuf, 0, NULL );
            ErrorMsg( lpMsgBuf );
            LocalFree( lpMsgBuf );
            bHaveImage = FALSE;
            return( FALSE );
        }
```

The offset operation works correctly in Windows 95 and in Windows NT but, in Windows 98, it returns an anomalous operation result and an incorrect error result. If we're lucky, this error won't occur in the final release of Windows 98. I mention the problem here simply so that you will be aware of a potentially serious flaw.

Last, the version number, palette ID, and returned palette size are tested. If any of these three tests fail, the file is closed, an error message reports that the image was not acceptable, and the process exits:

```
    if( ( pcxHd.version != 5 ) ||   // check version number
        ( chPal != 0x000C ) ||      // check palette ID
        ( fRes != 768 ) )           // check palette size
    {
        CloseHandle( hFile );
        ErrorMsg( "Not a 256 color image format" );
        return( FALSE );
    }
```

Assuming that everything else is acceptable, the retrieved palette information is decoded to a format acceptable to the device context, a logical palette structure.

```
SetCursor( LoadCursor( NULL, IDC_WAIT ) );
//========= create palette ===========================
hPCXPal = GlobalAlloc( GHND, sizeof(LOGPALETTE) +
                       256 * sizeof(PALETTEENTRY ) );
lPal = (LPLOGPALETTE) GlobalLock( hPCXPal );
lPal->palVersion = 0x0300;
lPal->palNumEntries = 256;
for( i=j=0; i<256; ++i )
{
   lPal->palPalEntry[i].peRed   = pcxPal[j++];
   lPal->palPalEntry[i].peGreen = pcxPal[j++];
   lPal->palPalEntry[i].peBlue  = pcxPal[j++];
   lPal->palPalEntry[i].peFlags = PC_NOCOLLAPSE;
   //  use PC_NOCOLLAPSE instead of PC_RESERVED -- //
   //  PC_RESERVED maps to nearest existing color //
   //  but no good matches exist for this purpose //
}
hPCXPal = CreatePalette( lPal );
hOldPal = SelectPalette( hdc, hPCXPal, FALSE );
RealizePalette( hdc );          // palette is now active
```

After retrieving the image palette information, the application needs to return the image data. Using the DOS file functions, this task would have been accomplished as:

```
fseek( fp, 128L, SEEK_SET );
```

However, using the ReadFile API, the process reverts to using the OVERLAPPED structure to set the offset:

```
fPos.Offset = 128;      // set file ptr to image data
```

Because the PCX header, regardless of the image type, is always 128 bytes in length, finding the beginning of the image data is easy. However, decoding the data does require a few provisions.

Also, to simplify the decoding process, the image data is read and decoded one scan line at a time. However, because the image is RLE, it's hardly practical to determine exactly how many bytes are in a single scan line before reading the data. Therefore, in order to continually update the fPos.Offset value, a new variable, Index, is used during the decode process to determine how many bytes of data have been used and, before the next scan line is read, to increment the offset.

A 256-color PCX image always uses RLE, much the same as in other image formats. Thus, while reading the data, if the two high bits are set (the byte value is greater than 0xC0), then the byte is read as byte count specifying the repeat count for the following byte. For example, the byte value 0xFE indicates that the next byte read will be repeated 0x3E or 62 times (0xFE – 0xC0 = 0x3E).

Now, as you may realize, this also means that individual pixels with palette values in the range 0xC0..0xFF, which make up 75 percent of the total palette, require two bytes, rather than appearing as a single byte. Therefore, a run of pixels with the palette values 0xDE, 0xDF, 0xDF, 0xEA, 0xE2, 0xE7 would be encoded as 0xC1, 0xDE, 0xC2, 0xDF, 0xC1, 0xEA, 0xC1, 0xE2, 0xC1, 0xE7, which is not precisely a savings. This does, however, illustrate the importance of building the palette with the high-frequency color entries appearing first. Still, shortcomings aside, RLE does generally reduce rather than increase file size.

There are still a few tricks involved in decoding an RLE image. For example, the decoding provision used in *ViewPCX* begins by initializing two values, i and j, before initiating a loop for the scan lines.

```
j = Index = 0;        // initialize position
while( j < depth )
{
    fPos.Offset += Index;
    i = Index = 0;
    ReadFile( hFile, &ImgArray, sizeof(ImgArray), &fRes, &fPos );
```

The offset field in fPos is incremented at the beginning of each cycle of the loop; the first time around, however, Index is already zero, so the offset remains at 128 bytes, which is the beginning of the image data. On subsequent cycles, after the offset is adjusted, Index is reset to zero in preparation for the following decode process. At this point, the ReadFile call has read a block of image data, beginning at the specified offset.

After reading the data, a new loop is initialized to handle decoding a single scan line from the image. Within this loop, the first step is a test to determine if the current byte is a repeat value:

```
do
{
    if( ( ImgArray[Index] & 0xC0 ) == 0xC0 )
    {
```

If the current byte is a repeat byte (greater than 0xC0), the count variable is derived, and a new for loop begins to paint the required number of pixels using the next byte in the data array as the palette index.

```
count = ImgArray[Index++] & 0x3F;
for( k=0; k<count; k++ )
{
    SetPixelV( hdc, i++, j,
               PALETTEINDEX( ImgArray[Index] ) );
    if( i >= pcxHd.bytes_per_line ) k = count;
}   // if line is too long just ignore any wraps
}
```

The SetPixelV API function is essentially the same as the customary SetPixel API call, with one difference: Where SetPixel returns the existing color index for the pixel written, SetPixelV is marginally faster because it does not handle a return value. But remember that the image data is not an RGB value but rather a palette-index entry. However, both SetPixel and SetPixelV expect a COLORREF value, supplied here by calling the PALETTEINDEX macro with the palette index as an argument.

Last, purely as a precaution against encoding errors (which are not entirely unknown), if the repeat count extends beyond the scan-line length, the variable k is reset to terminate the inner loop.

If the initial test shows that the byte value is not a repeat count, SetPixelV is called once:

```
else
    SetPixelV( hdc, i++, j,
               PALETTEINDEX( ImgArray[Index] ) );
```

In either case, the Index value is incremented once more to point to the next element in the data array:

```
        Index++;
    }
    while( i < pcxHd.bytes_per_line );
    j++;
    i = 0;
}
```

The loop continues until i reaches the length of the scan line, after which, the vertical position (j) is incremented and the horizontal position (i) is reset to the first of the line.

Remember, the variable Index is used both to track the current position within the data array and, after decoding each scan line, to reset the OVERLAPPED offset before reading the next data block.

The *ViewPCX* demo is included on the CD that accompanies this book, in the Chapter 28 folder.

Alternatives for Decoding PCX Images

Several alternatives are possible for decoding PCX images. The code shown in the *ViewPCX* demo is not the most efficient in terms of display; it was chosen to demonstrate using the OVERLAPPED structure.

One alternative is to use a different format to dynamically allocate an array large enough to hold all of the image data returned by a single ReadFile operation. With this method, a DWORD variable, such as Index, would keep track of the position within the data in the same fashion demonstrated within the loop in *ViewPCX*. The advantage, however, is that you need only one read operation, which would obviously accelerate operations.

A second alternative might be considered because the present method requires reading and decoding the image file every time a WM_PAINT message is received. You could change the handling, reading the image as a PCX file but creating a memory bitmap image from the result. This operation would be done only once, when the image file was selected rather than when the WM_PAINT message was received.

Then when a screen repaint is required, all that would be necessary would be to repaint the screen image using the BitBlt function, which is intrinsically faster than repeatedly reading and decoding the image file. Using the SetPixelV (or the SetPixel) function to paint a bitmap image is also intrinsically slow compared to using BitBlt (or StretchBlt) to simply transfer an image in bulk from a memory context to the screen context.

You can find the basics required for this second alternative in the Capture-Bitmap function in the *Capture* demo discussed earlier in this chapter (see the complete listing on the CD). Don't forget, however, to set the palette for the memory device as well as the active device context; otherwise, the resulting colors may be interesting but unexpected.

Implementing either of these alternatives, which you could also combine, is left as an exercise for the reader. However, the program listings (on the CD) include a code fragment showing how to create a bitmap from the PCX image data. As you will observe, the PCX image data must be decoded one line at a time before being transferred, using BitBlt, to build up the bitmap image.

24-Bit PCX Files

When you're working with 24-bit-per-pixel PCX images, remember that they do not contain any palette information. Instead, these images provide full 24-bit color information for each pixel in the image. Identified as version 5 or later, 24-bit PCX images store their data as 8 bits per color plane, in three planes. These are decoded in the same fashion as 16-color images, except that byte values (8 bits) are read as lines of red, green, and blue, in that order.

Therefore, to decode 24-bit PCX images, three scan lines are read as red, green, and blue image lines. After RLE decoding, these lines are treated by combining the first byte of each scan line as an RGB-triplet pixel value, rather than as a palette value. The second pixel uses the second byte from each scan line, and so forth.

Monochrome PCX Images

For monochrome PCX files, decoding is quite simple. First, if the two high bits of a byte are clear (ANDing with 0xC0), then the six least-significant bits are written to the image as a series of six pixels. (If a bit is set, the pixel is on; otherwise, the pixel is off.)

If the two high bits are set, an index count is created by ANDing the byte with 0x3F and using this count (0..63) to repeat the next byte *count* number of times, optionally up to a total of 504 pixels (the repeated byte defines an 8-pixel series).

Obviously, the PCX encoding scheme is heavily weighted for use with images containing large contiguous areas. This is not, however, particularly efficient for scanned images (but, then, scanners were quite uncommon when the PCX format was created).

16-Color PCX Images

Paintbrush PCX images may have 2, 4, 8, or 16 colors before jumping to 256 color images. But, for 16 or fewer colors, the handling remains essentially the same, because the image is treated as four interleaved monochrome images, which is consistent with the EGA video format.

Although this format may sound mysterious, the reason lies in the structure of EGA video cards that were the intended environment for 16-color images. On EGA cards, four 32KB memory pages were treated as layers: one each for red, green, blue, and intensity. (Admittedly, this is an oversimplification.) The point is that the 4 bits selecting a palette color are written 1 bit to each plane, if you're working in machine language and accessing these planes directly.

In this circumstance, however, the question is how to decode the image, not the mechanics of an EGA card. To decode a 16-color PCX image, four scan lines are read and, initially, treated as monochrome masks. To create color (palette) information, the first bit from each scan line is combined after decoding, by shifting the bit from the second scan line one place left, the third scan line two places left, and the fourth scan line three places left to produce a 4-bit nibble.

This sequence of nibbles creates a single scan line for the image and can be written to the screen (or converted to another format) as index values to the 16-color palette.

CompuServe's Graphics Interchange Format

Perhaps one of the most popular image formats in general use—in terms of images available on bulletin boards, disk libraries, and CD-ROMs—is the Graphics Interchange Format (GIF). This format was developed by CompuServe as a vehicle for graphics images which could be transferred between different computer systems. Although GIF is copyrighted by CompuServe, a blanket, nonexclusive, limited, royalty-free license has been granted to all developers, permitting free use of the GIF format in computer graphics applications.

The GIF format uses a very effective compression scheme, utilizing variable-length LZW compression (named for its developers: Lempel, Ziv, and Welsh). Although relatively complex to encode and decode, LZW compression has an important advantage over the simpler RLE compression schemes used by BMP and PCX images: reduced size. Images using LZW compression are virtually always considerably smaller than corresponding images created using RLE compression. LZW compression builds tables of patterns from the original, replacing repetitive patterns or pixel sequences with indexes to the table entries. LZW compression is also available in the public domain and is used in a variety of applications and forms, not just for image compression.

Other features supported by the GIF format include provisions for multiple images within a single file, local color tables including 256 colors, and interleaving scan lines (as used in PCX formats). The GIF format also has provisions for user-defined extensions.

GIF images are currently identified by two signatures, GIF87A and GIF89A, found in the first six bytes of the image and identifying, respectively, the original 1987 and 1989 revisions.

TIP

Current GIF standards and specifications (GIF89A) are readily available on Compu-Serve (GO GRAPHIC SUPPORT FORUM), as well as from a variety of other online services and private BBSs. A wide variety of GIF display programs, format conversion programs, source code examples, and GIF images are available through these same sources.

Tagged Image File Format

The Tagged Image File Format (TIFF) is perhaps the most complex of the popular formats. This format incorporates a variety of methods for describing images and, depending on the implementation, may provide several different means of data compression.

A second strength of the TIFF image format is that .TIF images, stored in uncompressed format, are capable of tremendous compression using standard file-compression utilities. Compressions of 97 to 99 percent are not uncommon.

This format is popular with typesetting and production graphics applications, partially because it was one of the earlier formats capable of supporting high-resolution images and partially because it provides several subformats optimized for different types of images. The following five classes of TIFF images are supported:

- Class B TIFF files consist of black-and-white images, coded as one bit per pixel and providing three compression formats: none, CCITT Group 3, and PackBits.

- Class G TIFF files are used for gray-scale images consisting of 4 or 8 bits per pixel (16 or 256 shades of gray) and are either uncompressed or use LZW compression.

- Class P TIFF files support color palettes using 1 to 8 bits per pixel and are either uncompressed or use LZW compression.

- Class R TIFF files are used for 24-bit-per-pixel images and, optionally, use LZW compression.

- Class F TIFF files are used for fax images.

TIFF formats can be used as demanded by circumstances. Remember, however, that these are provisions only of the TIFF specification. No actual implementation of the TIFF image software includes all possible formats or compression schemes. There are a number of other TIFF variations in use that do not follow any published standards. In general, these tend to consist of variant compression algorithms but may vary in other ways as well.

Typically, a TIFF encoder/decoder may run five to ten thousand lines of code.

TIP   The TIFF file specification and format instructions are available by request from either Aldus or Microsoft. Examples are available for a variety of systems.

Truevision's TARGA Format

The TARGA (TGA) file format, originally developed by Truevision, Inc., has been the predominate 24-bit image format used with frame-grabber boards. Truevision markets computer/camera interface boards that are used extensively on machine imaging, as well as for a variety of other applications. Using TARGA cards, or any of a variety of competing brands and models, images are captured directly from video cameras with pixel depths of 16, 24, or 32 bits.

Previously, a TARGA card (or equivalent) was required, usually along with a second, high-resolution monitor, to display TGA images. Today, you can use a single monitor and a wider variety of video cards that are capable of supporting 24-bit-per-pixel images, although these are not yet in widespread use.

All three of the image formats supported (16, 24, or 32 bits per pixel) can be considered true-color formats. And, speaking from personal experience in a color-critical application, I can report that the differences between images using these three formats are quite indistinguishable to the human eye, even tested in side-by-side displays of highly magnified gemstones.

Pixels in the 24-bit image format consist of three 8-bit color values in RGB order. The 32-bit format also contains three 8-bit color values, but also include a fourth 8-bit field, which is NULL and simply ignored, having no purpose except to pad the entry to a DWORD size for convenience in handling and alignment.

The third format, 16 bits per pixel, consists of three 5-bit color values with the sixteenth, high bit treated as an intensity bit. If the high bit is set, the three 5-bit image color values each correspond to the five most-significant bits in the corresponding 8-bit color values. If the high bit is cleared, the three 5-bit values are shifted right one 1 bit, decreasing color intensity.

TIP   TARGA image file specifications can be requested from Truevision, Inc, 7340 Shadeland Station, Indianapolis, IN 46256-3919. The phone numbers are 317-841-0332 (voice) and 317-576-7700 (fax).

Techniques for Converting 24-Bit Color Images

Although 24-bit true-color cards are becoming popular, they are still not common. For the present, SVGA (256-color) cards remain the high-resolution standard and are likely to continue so for at least the next few years. At the same time, the 24-bit video frame-capture systems are also popular but cannot be readily displayed on SVGA systems.

There is a solution: Convert 24-bit color images captured by video cameras to 256-color palette images, which can be displayed on most available systems. (Some graphics programs designed to manipulate 24-bit color images offer just such a palette-compression feature under the generic title Posterizing.)

Converting a potential palette of 16 million colors (2^{24} = 16,777,216) to a palette with a mere 256 colors does seem to be a considerable degradation in image quality, but it isn't really quite as bad as it sounds. While the potential palette size of a 24-bit image is over 16 million colors, the actual image (assuming 400×512 pixels) is a total of only 204,800 pixels. Assuming that no individual pixels share the same color, the reduction to a 256-color palette is only an 800-to-1 color reduction rather than 65536-to-1, an improvement of 82:1.

Commonly, however, a typical image will contain a much smaller range of actual colors—perhaps as many as 400 or 500 distinct shades, but usually fewer. And, even when the color variation is high, many shades that are technically different will still be relatively close in hue and can be represented by a single palette entry.

Several methods exist for converting 24-bit images to 256-color palette images. The simplest method, although not necessarily the best approach, is to begin by constructing a 256-color palette containing a range of hues that can be used for a variety of images. The drawback to this method is that the resulting palette does not match any image very well and the resulting displays have a rather cartoon-like quality about them. The following sections suggest some other methods.

A Frequency-Ordered Palette

A better method than constructing a simple 256-color palette is to begin by constructing a histogram of the colors represented in a specific image. This entails processing the entire image to construct a frequency record for each individual color in the image.

After this is completed, you can build a custom, frequency-ordered palette from the highest frequency colors with the remaining image pixels mapped to their nearest equivalents from the palette. (Hint: Reserve two of the 256 palette entries: one each for pure white and pure black.)

Next, after constructing a palette of the high-frequency colors, map the original palette values as indexes to their corresponding palette entries or, if no matching palette entries exist, to the closest available palette entry.

A Distributed Palette

Another conversion approach follows the same general pattern of creating a histogram of the actual colors; however, instead of simply taking the 256 (or 254) highest frequency colors to create the palette, you create a distributed palette.

In this format, after creating a binary tree of color frequencies, the color tree is scanned for the total number of entries and for the range of differences between colors. If fewer than 256 entries are found in the tree, the palette can be constructed directly, based on frequency.

If more than 256 entries are found in the tree, you need to apply a color-conversion algorithm to find the closest matches in the tree, reducing the branches of the tree by eliminating the lowest frequency entries that have close matches. When the tree is reduced to a suitable number of entries, the remaining entries are used to create the palette.

If the number of branches (total colors) is, arbitrarily, less than one and a half times the palette size, a distributed palette is probably not necessary. On the other hand, if the number of colors exceeds this arbitrary threshold, a distributed palette may provide a better color spread than a frequency-ordered palette.

There are two considerations in selecting entries for a distributed palette: the uniqueness of the palette entry and the frequency of the color.

Taking the second consideration first, it should be fairly obvious that there's little benefit in devoting a limited resource—a palette entry—to a color that is used by very few pixels in the image. Precisely where this cutoff should be established is arbitrary, but in an image composed of 200,000 pixels, a frequency of 20 pixels is 0.01 percent of the total or 0.25 percent of the average. This value is low enough to suggest that the color in question could be safely mapped to an existing palette entry.

The first consideration, uniqueness of a palette entry, is a different matter. This factor must be calculated carefully, taking all three of the color components (red, green, and blue) into account. The obvious method of comparing two color values is to sum the absolute difference of the red, green, and blue components:

$$dC = abs(\ R_1 - R_2\ ) + abs(\ G_1 - G_2\ ) + abs(\ B_1 - B_2\ )$$

The objective here, however, is to emphasize the difference between two colors and to find which colors in the image are the closest to each other and can, therefore, be represented by a single palette entry. The color difference (dC) can be better emphasized using a nonlinear formula:

$$dC = (\ R_1 - R_2\ )^2 + (\ G_1 - G_2\ )^2 + (\ B_1 - B_2\ )^2$$

This second formula shifts the weighting to emphasize differences in a single color component over difference distributed throughout the three color components.

For example, assume three colors, C1, C2, and C3, with RGB values 0x1F2C3B, 0x1F2A3B, and 0x1E2D3A, respectively. Using the first, unweighted formula, C1 and C2 have a color difference of 2 (in the green component); C1 and C3 have a color difference of 3 (1 each in the red, green, and blue values).

Using the second, weighted formula, however, the C1 and C2 entries have a weighted difference of 4 against the weighted difference of 3 for C1 and C3.

Still, as discussed previously when speaking of gray-scaled palettes and converting colors to true-grays, the human eye's response to colors is itself nonlinear. This weighting can be incorporated into a third formula, which calculates the difference between colors using the same weighting as the eye's response:

$$dC = abs(\ (\ R_1 - R_2\ ) * 0.30\ ) +$$
$$abs(\ (\ G_1 - G_2\ ) * 0.59\ ) +$$
$$abs(\ (\ B_1 - B_2\ ) * 0.11\ )$$

Using this third formula, the difference between the C1 and C2 color entries becomes 1.18 versus a difference between C1 and C3 of 1.00. This is a more appropriate result than the first formula yielded, but less distinctive than the second.

However, we can combine the second and third formulas:

$$dC = (\ (\ R_1 - R_2\ ) * 0.30\ )^2 + (\ (\ G_1 - G_2\ ) * 0.59\ )^2 + (\ (\ B_1 - B_2\ ) * 0.11\ )^2$$

The difference between C1 and C2 becomes 1.39 versus a difference between C1 and C3 of 0.45.

This final revision of the weighting formula offers a distinctive difference in results both by incorporating the nonlinear response of the human eye and by emphasizing the difference in one color component over differences spread across all color components.

TIP

A small difference in speed could be achieved in the calculations by converting the percentage weights to integer values (for example, changing 0.30 to 30), thus removing all floating-point operations in favor of integer calculations. In most cases, however, this is not likely to provide a notable change in calculation times.

Experimenting with Color Differences

If you are interested, you can experiment with the *Color3* demo discussed in Chapter 24 to compare color differences. Here are some points to look for:

- What is the minimum total difference in all color components that can be readily identified by the human eye?

- What is the minimum difference in any one color component that can be readily identified?

- How do differences in each of the three component fields (red, green, and blue) compare?

- How do differences in intensity compare at different absolute intensities (how do absolute differences appear in proportion to absolute intensities)?

Ignoring extreme variations (commonly referred to as color blindness), color perception still varies widely between individuals and may also be affected by age, health, and the use of corrective lenses.

This chapter explained how to capture bitmap images to the clipboard or to a file and how to work with various image file formats. We also took a look at the Windows graphics file operations and some techniques for converting 24-bit color images.

Next, in Chapter 29, we'll look at graphics selection operations and then, in Chapter 30, at creating interactive graphics.

Graphics Selection Operations

- Area-selection tool features

- Adjustable target overlays

- Custom cursors

- Mouse-hit testing

- Bitmap file access and display

One aspect of graphics operations that is not commonly mentioned is how to select a section within an image or to select a region of interest. This requirement comes up quite frequently when working with live-video applications but is also applicable to static bitmaps.

In this chapter, we will look at a method of creating a nondestructive target overlay on top of an image. The sample program described here, *Target*, contains provisions for moving the target, resizing the target, and changing cursors to indicate which operations are being performed.

The *Target* demo also demonstrates a different approach to accessing bitmap files. It uses MFC classes and methods in place of some of the API functions and conventional operations illustrated in previous chapters.

Area-Selection Tools

A common requirement in many graphics operations involves selecting an area from either a static bitmap or an active video image. For both types of images, a nondestructive overlay works well as an area-selection tool.

Static Bitmap Area Selection

For static bitmaps, selection usually involves creating a tool to select an area, with the selection shown as an outline. For example, the Windows Paint program provides two selection tools: a free-form area tool and a rectangular area tool. Using the rectangular tool, you can select any rectangular region in an image then, subsequently, "pick up" or drag the selection. The free-form selection tool functions in the same fashion, except that you are allowed to "draw" an irregular region for selection.

The first case, rectangular selection, is the more common and is the type of selection discussed here. Selecting an irregular region involves much the same process, except that you must keep a list of boundary points and transfer the selected region as a series of image row sections.

The simplest way to select an area and to provide visual feedback to the user is to draw a rectangle enclosing the area on top of the existing image. Using a conventional drawing operation, however, is destructive to the existing image. Simply drawing a rectangle on top of a bitmap would be fine if you wanted to add the rectangle to the image. But for selection, a different process is needed. You need to draw the rectangle using a method that allows the original image to be restored, without requiring redrawing the entire image.

The simplest method of drawing and then undrawing a figure is to use the ROP2 XOR operation, or R2_XORPEN, which is described in Chapter 25. Using the XOR drawing mode, the first time a shape is drawn, the drawing pen (and brush, if any) is XORed with the underlying image. This usually ensures that the drawn shape is optimally visible, regardless of the background image. More important, when the same shape is drawn a second time, the second drawing operation has the effect of canceling the first and, therefore, restoring the original background image, without needing to repaint the entire screen.

Aside from using the XOR drawing mode, the actual process of drawing the overlay is trivial. However, there is one caution: Whatever image or form is used for the overlay, it must be redrawn exactly to erase it before any changes occur in the position or size.

Active Video Image Selection

In the case of active video images, depending on the type of graphics capture card and processor, the selection process may involve capturing a static image first and then manipulating the static bitmap in much the same fashion demonstrated in the *Target* demo discussed in this chapter.

In other cases, where multiple video planes are supported, the selection process may be accomplished by drawing the area, or other targeting information, in a separate video plane and letting the system combine the targeting information with the active video for presentation. In the case of multiple video planes, drawing the overlay using the XOR mode still remains the fastest method of repeatedly drawing and removing targeting, selection, or region outline information.

> **WARNING** No matter how fast the system and the video card, restoring the entire image is still time-consuming and almost always unacceptable, especially when you're working with an active video image.

Area-Selection Tool Conventions

In many drawing applications, the current convention for area selection is to draw an overlay consisting of a dotted outline with rectangular handles at the corners and centers of the sides. By placing the mouse cursor anywhere within the outline and pressing the mouse button, the selected region can be dragged to another position. On the other hand, by clicking on one of the handles, the outline can be dragged to a new size.

In the case of irregular areas, depending on the application, small "handles" may appear at nodes representing the vertices of a polygon outline. These handles are treated in the same fashion as a rectangular outline, permitting a vertex to be relocated. In other cases, such as in the Windows Paint program, no methods are provided for adjusting a free-form outline.

In the *Target* demo, a different set of conventions is used. For selection, you use a set of crosshairs that extend to the window margins and a circle that approximates the target area or region of interest (ROI). Figure 29.1 shows an example of a screen in the *Target* demo, with a bitmap displayed behind the target-selection overlay.

FIGURE 29.1:

Targeting an area in a bitmap

This format is common in machine-vision applications, where the user is selecting an area for examination. Because the crosshairs extend to the margins of the window, they can be used to indicate a position on scales along the sides. The center of the crosshairs is left open, so that the specific target is not obscured. The circular target-area marker is used to select an area for closer examination or for action by other associated tools. As an alternative, an elliptical, rather than circular, shape could be used for the target-area marker.

In most applications, after a user selects a rectangular or irregular region, the selection is moved, copied, or otherwise processed. During this processing, the common convention is to show an outline surrounding the selection. While it would be possible to capture or process a circular or irregular area, the usual practice is to process a rectangular image. This simplification is commonly used to show the actual area being processed, as well as to facilitate drag operations.

In the *Target* demo, when the right mouse button is pressed to initiate a capture (though no actual capture is done in this example), the crosshairs and circular target are replaced by a rectangle bounding but outside the region of interest. Figure 29.2 shows an example of the selection rectangle.

FIGURE 29.2:

Indicating the selected region of interest

Whether you use these conventions or any of several others depends on the needs of your application. There is no single set of conventions that apply to all cases and cover all requirements.

The Target Demo: Selecting Parts of an Image

 The *Target* demo demonstrates using adjustable target overlays, testing for mouse hits with overlapping targets, and setting custom mouse cursors.

Bitmap File Operations

The *Target* demo provides an option to open a bitmap file for a background image. It uses essentially the same bitmap file and display operations demonstrated in Chapter 28. However, there are a few differences because the version presented here relies heavily on MFC-defined classes rather than the standard APIs and conventional programming methods. You can look in the CTarget-View::ReadBitmap procedure to see how these bitmap operations work.

Also worthy of your attention is the single TRY...CATCH exception handler used when opening a bitmap file:

```
TRY
{
    CFile cFile( csFName, CFile::modeRead | CFile::typeBinary );
    SetCursor( LoadCursor( NULL, IDC_WAIT ) );
    ...
    read the bitmap file here
    ...
}
CATCH( CFileException, e )
{
    #ifdef _DEBUG
```

```
            afxDump << "File access failed: " << e->m_cause << "\n";
        #endif
        return FALSE;
    }
    END_CATCH
```

The CFile constructor, which is used to open the file for reading, like any class constructor, does not return an error, regardless of what might go wrong. Therefore, to catch an error when opening a file in this fashion, the TRY...CATCH exception handling is required.

NOTE   C/C++ supports several forms of try...catch and TRY...CATCH exception handling. This latter form uses macros and is demonstrated in the *Target* demo. Refer to Chapter 18 for more information about exception handling.

Mouse Responses

In the *Target* demo, the selection overlay needs to be able to respond to the mouse in several different fashions, depending on where the mouse is clicked:

- If the mouse is clicked in the center of the target, the target can be dragged to a new position but without changing the size.

- If the mouse is clicked on the left or right side of the target, or on the top or the bottom of the target, the target can be resized horizontally or vertically (but not both) without changing the center position.

- If the mouse is clicked on a corner of the target—upper left, upper right, lower left, or lower right—the target can be resized both horizontally and vertically, again without changing the center position.

In each case, the circular target is the focus of these operations; the crosshairs simply follow the center position of the target. Also, the background image remains unaffected by any of these operations.

Changing the Cursor

The *Target* demo also includes provisions to change the cursor to reflect the type of operation about to occur when the left mouse button is pressed. Although the

Windows GDI offers a variety of standard cursors, these are not always readily visible against a complex background (see Chapter 8 for more information about Windows cursors). The original program from which *Target* was derived provides a set of custom cursors, which have been incorporated into the demo as well.

These five custom cursors appear in Figure 29.3:

- North-south cursor (NS_CURSOR)

- Northeast-southwest cursor (NESW_CURSOR)

- Hand cursor (HAND_CURSOR)

- Northwest-southeast cursor (NWSE_CURSOR)

- East-west cursor (EW_CURSOR)

FIGURE 29.3:

Five custom cursors

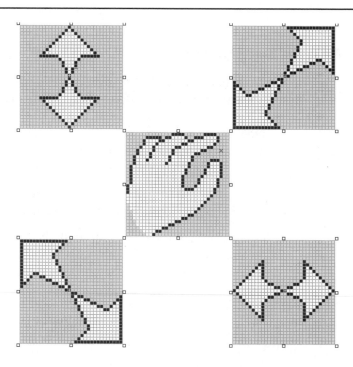

In each case, the cursor image consists of a white body with a reversed outline. A small mark has been added to each image to identify the position of the cursor's hotspot.

Determining the Hit Position

To manage dragging and resizing operations for the target overlay, the first step is to determine where the mouse hit occurs; that is, the mouse's position when the primary mouse button was pressed.

In the CTargetView class, the OnLButtonDown method is called whenever the left (or primary) mouse button is pressed and receives two parameters: nFlags and point. In this case (as in most), we ignore the nFlags argument, which contains status information, and rely on the point information, which tells us where the mouse was when the event occurred relative to the application client window.

NOTE
By default, the mouse handler causes an OnLButtonDown call when the left mouse button is pressed. However, if the Mouse utility in the Control Panel has been used to swap the mouse buttons, the OnLButtonDown call responds to the right mouse button being pressed. For programming purposes, the primary mouse button always identifies itself with a WM_LBUTTON*xxxxx* message, and the secondary button always reports as WM_RBUTTON*xxxxx*, regardless of which physical mouse button is pressed.

Before any tests are made, the m_nTrack member is initialized as NO_TARGET. Subsequently, if a hit is identified in any target region, m_nTrack is reassigned a value to identify the correct region.

Also, before any other operations, the SetCapture method is called to ensure that mouse messages from outside the current window will still be received. The mouse capture will be released when the mouse button is released.

```
void CTargetView::OnLButtonDown(UINT nFlags, CPoint point)
{
    m_nTrack = NO_TARGET;
    SetCapture();
```

Next, the m_xRadius and m_yRadius members contain the size of the target ellipse and the m_cPoint member contains the centerpoint. To limit the drag operation to the center of the target area, the first target rectangle is defined using two-thirds of the vertical and horizontal radii. After creating the rectangle, the NormalizeRect function is called, purely as a precaution, to ensure that the bottom coordinate of the rectangle is greater than the top and the right side is greater than the left.

```
CPoint   cPoint( m_cPoint );
CRect    cRect( cPoint.x - ( ( m_xRadius / 3 ) * 2 ),
                cPoint.y - ( ( m_yRadius / 3 ) * 2 ),
                cPoint.x + ( ( m_xRadius / 3 ) * 2 ),
                cPoint.y + ( ( m_yRadius / 3 ) * 2 ) );

cRect.NormalizeRect();
if( cRect.PtInRect( point ) )
```

The `PtInRect` method simply returns TRUE if the `point` argument lies within the rectangle, or FALSE if not. While such a test is not difficult to perform, the provided member function is more convenient than writing a separate operation for each check that is made here.

If `PtInRect` returns TRUE, the `m_nTrack` member is set to ALL, meaning that the entire target overlay will be dragged when the next mouse-movement message is received, and the hand cursor is loaded as the active cursor.

```
{
    m_nTrack = ALL;
    m_hCursor = SetCursor( LoadCursor( theApp.m_hInstance,
                           "HAND_CURSOR" ) );
}
```

If the `PtInRect` function returns FALSE, the `OnLButtonDown` method continues through a series of `else` statements, testing each target area in turn. If a hit is found, it sets the `m_nTrack` variable to the appropriate operation and loads the correct cursor.

The real key here is to ensure that the target rectangles are tested in the correct order. Figure 29.4 shows nine overlapping target rectangles, numbered in the order tested.

What Figure 29.4 does not show is that region 1 overlaps regions 2, 3, 4, and 5. However, if a hit is found in the first region, no other regions are tested, making the overlapped areas irrelevant.

In like fashion, area 6 is overlapped by areas 1, 2, and 4. But because this area is tested last, a hit will be identified for this area only if it occurs within the irregular region shown. The same holds true for the regions identified as 7, 8, and 9; each is overlapped by three other regions that are tested first.

FIGURE 29.4:

The mouse-hit target rectangles

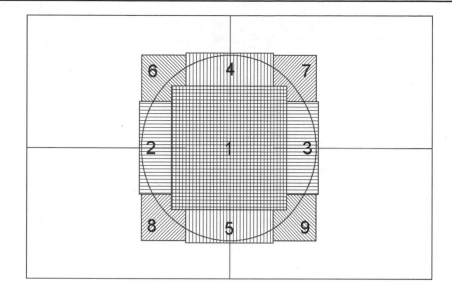

The point is that it's unnecessary to define complex hit areas when the same task can be accomplished by testing simpler regions in the proper order. On the other hand, when it is absolutely necessary to test complex regions, you can use other methods, such as those demonstrated in Chapter 30.

Last, the CView::OnLButtonDown method is called to provide default handling for the mouse messages.

```
        }
    m_bDrawOverlay = TRUE;
    CView::OnLButtonDown(nFlags, point);
}
```

Because we've already provided complete handling, calling the default method is optional, but it's still good practice.

Once we've decided where the mouse hit occurred, the next step is to wait for the OnMouseMove function to be called, indicating that the mouse has moved. The OnMouseMove method, like the OnLButtonDown method, is called with nFlags and point arguments, and again, the nFlags argument can simply be ignored as irrelevant.

Before doing anything based on the m_nTrack action flag, the next step is to decide if the mouse is still in the client window. If it is not—if the mouse has been moved outside the application window—then we will release the mouse capture and do nothing.

```
void CTargetView::OnMouseMove(UINT nFlags, CPoint point)
{
    CRect       cRect;

    if( m_bDrawOverlay )
    {
        GetClientRect( cRect );
        if( ! cRect.PtInRect( point ) )  // cursor outside of client area
        {
            m_nTrack = NO_TARGET;
            SetCursor( m_hCursor );
            ReleaseCapture();
            return;
        }
```

Next, assuming the mouse is still in the window, the response is to call the DrawOverlay method to erase the existing target overlay.

```
        DrawOverlay();                    // erase the overlay target
        switch( m_nTrack )
        {
            case NO_TARGET:           /* no action */
                break;
```

If the m_nTrack member indicates NO_TARGET, then we'll take no action. If m_nTrack is set to ALL, then the m_cPoint member needs to be updated as:

```
case ALL:
    m_cPoint.x = max( m_xRadius, min( point.x,
                                 ( cRect.right - m_xRadius - 2 ) ) );
    m_cPoint.y = max( m_yRadius, min( point.y,
                                 ( cRect.bottom - m_yRadius - 2 ) ) );
    break;
```

Alternatively, if m_nTrack is set to TOP, the vertical radius should be adjusted according to the mouse movement:

```
        case TOP:
            m_yRadius = max( 30, m_cPoint.y - point.y );
            break;
```

The remaining case statements allow adjustments according to the quadrant selected, and the switch statement is followed by a test to ensure that the target is not dragged outside the client window. The bulk of these provisions, however, are routine.

The one important provision remaining is to call `DrawOverlay` a second time to redraw the target overlay at the changed position or with the changed size.

```
    ...
    DrawOverlay();                      // redraw the overlay target
}
    CView::OnMouseMove(nFlags, point);
}
```

Finally, when the mouse button is released, the `OnLButtonUp` method is called. Here, the same arguments are supplied, but now both `nFlags` and `point` can be ignored. We don't really care where the mouse was released or what the flags were; our only interest is that the mouse button has been released. And the response to the mouse-button release is simple: Reset the member flags, restore the default cursor, and release the mouse-message capture.

```
void CTargetView::OnLButtonUp(UINT nFlags, CPoint point)
{
    m_bDrawOverlay = FALSE;
    m_nTrack = NO_TARGET;
    SetCursor( m_hCursor );
    ReleaseCapture();
    CView::OnLButtonUp(nFlags, point);
}
```

For the right mouse button, the provisions are even simpler: When the right mouse button is pressed, check and see if the event occurred in the target rectangle.

```
void CTargetView::OnRButtonDown(UINT nFlags, CPoint point)
{
/*
    //=== routine to show target areas ===//
    DrawOverlay();
    DrawTargets();
    DrawOverlay();
*/
    CRect cRect( m_cPoint.x - ( ( m_xRadius / 3 ) * 2 ),
                 m_cPoint.y - ( ( m_yRadius / 3 ) * 2 ),
                 m_cPoint.x + ( ( m_xRadius / 3 ) * 2 ),
                 m_cPoint.y + ( ( m_yRadius / 3 ) * 2 ) );

    if( cRect.PtInRect( point ) )            // is cursor in client area?
    {
```

If the mouse event is in the target, set the capture flag, call DrawOverlay to remove the target overlay, and then call DrawROITarget to create the ROI outline.

```
            m_bCapture = TRUE;
            DrawOverlay();
            SetCapture();
            DrawROITarget();
        }
        CView::OnRButtonDown(nFlags, point);
    }
```

If you were tracking mouse movement while the right mouse button is down, this would occur in the same OnMouseMove method used to track movement with the primary button down. The only difference would be that you would need to include some provisions, such as the m_bDrawOverlay and m_bCapture flags, to determine which type of event was being tracked. Or, more directly, the nFlags argument accompanying the mouse-movement message could be queried to find out which mouse button was pressed or if both buttons were pressed.

In this case, we really don't care about movement. All that we're waiting for is for the right mouse button to be released.

```
    void CTargetView::OnRButtonUp(UINT nFlags, CPoint point)
    {
        if( m_bCapture )
        {
            m_bCapture = ! m_bCapture;
            ReleaseCapture();
            Invalidate();
            DrawOverlay();
        }
        CView::OnRButtonUp(nFlags, point);
    }
```

Once the right mouse button is released, we reset our flag, call the Invalidate function to redraw everything in the window, and then call DrawOverlay to restore the target overlay. The DrawROITarget function does not use R2_XORPEN; therefore, there is no easier way to remove the ROI target rectangle.

A Note about Custom Cursors

Some of you may have noticed that the use of the SetCapture method in the *Target* demo appears rather redundant since, as soon as the mouse moves outside the client window,

Continued on next page

ReleaseCapture has been called. Why call SetCapture and then release it as soon as it becomes useful?

The reason is that by calling SetCapture, you ensure that the cursor you assign to the mouse remains the active cursor and is not replaced by the default cursor as soon as the mouse moves.

The explanation for this behavior is found in the notes for the SetCursor function (from the MFC online documentation):

"If your application must set the cursor while it is in a window, make sure the class cursor for the specified window's class is set to NULL. If the class cursor is not NULL, the system restores the class cursor each time the mouse is moved."

The trick is how to set the class cursor to NULL. SetCapture provides a convenient alternative in this instance. However, the proper way to set custom cursors for a window under MFC is to intercept the PreCreateWindow function and to modify the WNDCLASS member of the CREATSTRUCT argument, setting the hCursor member to NULL. The revised WNDCLASS structure, however, must be registered before use through the RegisterClass function.

The long and the short of this is that setting custom cursors is not conveniently accomplished.

Other Methods of Interest

A provision has also been included in the source code to draw the several target areas used to test for mouse hits. This provision is found in the DrawTargets methods and was used to create the illustration shown previously in Figure 29.4. This provision can be enabled in the OnRButtonDown method.

Also of interest are the OnFileOpen, ReadBitmap, and OnDraw methods used in the *Target* demo. These parallel earlier examples but offer new versions using MFC classes and methods in place of some of the API functions and conventional operations illustrated in previous chapters.

The complete target-drawing and mouse-hit recognition operations are found in the TargetView.H and .CPP files, which are part of the *Target* demo included on the CD accompanying this book.

This chapter explained how your application can support selecting areas within graphic images using a simple tool. In Chapter 30, we'll look at some more advanced techniques for working with complex bitmap images. We'll examine methods of creating interactive images, principally as maps but using techniques that could be adapted to other types of images.

CHAPTER

THIRTY

30

Interactive Images

- Events in complex regions

- Color-keying events

- Hidden color maps

- The drunkard's walk algorithm

- Recursive searches

In the previous chapter, we examined some methods for selecting sections, or regions of interest, within a bitmap image. The methods discussed there work well with simple bitmaps, but they are not suitable for bitmaps that contain more complex shapes. In this chapter, we'll look at several methods of mapping mouse events to complex bitmap regions.

Complex Regions in Interactive Images

A major element, and a major problem, in many graphics applications is identifying the location within an image where an event, such as a mouse click, has occurred. If you're interested in only the window coordinates where the event occurred, this information is supplied in the lParam argument accompanying a WM_*x*BUTTON*xxxx* message. Using MFC, the information is found in the point argument passed to the On*x*Button*xxxx* and OnMouseMove methods. However, determining where a mouse click has occurred in relation to a displayed bitmap or some other region defined on the screen is a more difficult matter, particularly when the region is not conveniently defined by a series of bounding coordinates.

For simple rectangular shapes, you can use the PtInRect method, as explained in Chapter 29. However, for any other shapes, this method fails, and a new approach is required.

For example, consider Figure 30.1, where three shapes are depicted representing possible screen areas:

- The first shape, or region, at the left, could be defined using a half-dozen coordinate pairs: one pair for each vertex. You could then identify a mouse event occurring within the bounded region by testing the area as two rectangular regions.

- The center region in Figure 30.1 is a simpler shape, with only four vertices. But it is also more complex, because the boundary lines are diagonal rather than rectilinear. In this case, a more complex test is required to calculate where the edges lie in relation to the mouse-click event.

- The third region, at the right, is the most complex of all. Following conventional processes, it requires a relatively large number of coordinates describing the convolutions followed by the area's outline.

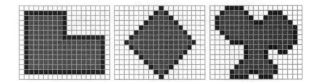

Methods for Identifying Regions and Enclosures

Although it's possible to create custom algorithms tailored for specific, individual types of images, for a generic mapping process, a different approach to identifying regions and enclosures is desirable. You can use a number of processes for this purpose, as explained in the following sections.

Identifying Regions by Color

One identification approach involves color keying. This approach is demonstrated in the *MapDemo* demo discussed in this chapter. The demo uses the USMAP01 bitmap.

Identification by color matching relies on the fact that each region (each state) in the United States map depicted by the USMAP01 bitmap possesses a unique color value. Figure 30.2 shows the USMAP01 bitmap image displaying the contiguous United States, with Alaska and Hawaii inserted at the lower left.

The *MapDemo* demo contains a lookup table that matches each state's color with the state's name; the color choices themselves are quite arbitrary.

This approach has a few obvious restrictions, including being limited to use on systems with capacities to display more than 16 colors and requiring that the image consist of areas of continuous color. Also, any two areas with the same color value will be identified as the same region. Overall, however, it is a practical and useful method of identifying a large number of irregular regions.

FIGURE 30.2:

The USMAP01 bitmap

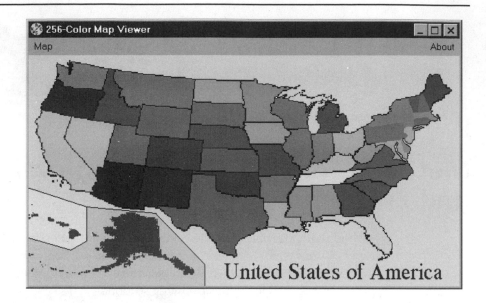

Using a Hidden Color Map

Another identification process involves using a memory-map color mask to determine where events have occurred in a bitmap that is not composed of contiguous color regions. This method uses a second color map that is not displayed; that is, it is created in a memory context, not a display context.

This second map contains the color-identification values for the primary bitmap that appears on the screen. Then, when the mouse is used to select a point on the displayed bitmap, you look for the pixel value in the hidden bitmap and match this color to the keys.

Using the Drunkard's Walk Algorithm

An algorithm that is particularly useful for identifying irregular regions is the drunkard's walk algorithm, titled thus because the search pattern follows a trace reminiscent of an inebriated and staggering pedestrian. (This type of motion is also known as Brownian motion, as exhibited by microscopic particles subject to thermal agitation.)

Where a drunkard—or a microscopic particle—simply continues indefinitely, the drunkard's walk algorithm executes a test after each staggering step (rather like a drunkard searching for any lamppost in reach) to determine if it has reached an identifiable point, and halts when such an encounter occurs. These target points are assigned locations within each enclosed region and are indexed to uniquely identify the region.

The drunkard's walk algorithm begins at a point indicated by the mouse click and proceeds in any arbitrary direction until one of these events occurs:

- A boundary is reached.

- A random instruction instigates a change in direction.

- The drunkard's search reaches a target coordinate identifying the enclosed region.

In the first case, reaching a boundary identified either by a change in color (or in the *MapDemo* demo, by a specific, preselected border color), the drunkard's path simply bounces or reverses. The drunkard then retraces its path until the second instance, a random change, forces a new direction or until, ultimately, the path intersects an identifiable point.

In the second case, a pseudo-random generator initiates a change in direction, on average every ten steps. Although in one chance out of eight, this chance is not a change at all, the overall effect is to trace paths with an average length of ten steps (or, in this case, pixels) between changes in direction.

The third case is illustrated in Figure 30.3. This figure shows the same three regions illustrated in Figure 30.1, but this time with a drunkard's walk trace, which ends by intersecting the desired target coordinates (shown as a small box outline).

FIGURE 30.3:

The drunkard's walk search

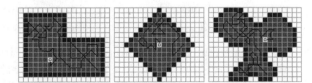

Using a Recursive Search

An alternative to the drunkard's walk algorithm is a recursive search algorithm. This algorithm begins, from the initial coordinates, by initiating a recursive search. For example, the recursive search might begin by searching to the immediate left, then down, then up, and finally to the right, with each point searched initiating a further recursive search in the same direction until a border is reached or the target is found.

For example, assume a recursive search beginning at point 100,100. The recursive process calls itself, first with the coordinates for the point to the immediate left (99,100). When this first search returns, assuming that the target point has not been found, the next search will be up (100,99), then down (100,101), and then right (101,100).

However, the first search at (99,100) initiates its own searches at (98,100), (99,99), (99,101), and (100,100), which is the same point where the search started. And each of these searches executes its own recursive search.

But since each search is looking for either a border, which terminates further recursion in that branch, or the target point, which also terminates recursion, this algorithm is not infinitely recursive. But, even with finite recursion, the number of active recursions does increase geometrically. Furthermore, each recursion requires its own register values to be pushed on to the stack, and this can very quickly lead to stack overflow. Even if the recursive procedure is very carefully designed, this can still be a problem.

An advantage of this approach is that a well-designed recursive search is absolutely certain to succeed. It will find the target location, even if it must check absolutely every location within a region. But a well-designed recursive search is not necessarily any faster than a drunkard's walk search, and it consumes considerably more of the system's resources. At its worst, the drunkard's walk algorithm is sometimes a bit slower but only rarely and randomly so. In general, the drunkard's walk algorithm tends to be faster, as well as more efficient in overall usage of system resources and, most important, of CPU time.

Finally, on the basis of simple aesthetics, the drunkard's walk algorithm is far more satisfying to the soul (the programmer's, at least, if not the machine's) than the stolidly pedestrian recursive search. After all, getting there is half the fun, isn't it?

The MapDemo Demo: Identifying Event Locations

As explained earlier in the chapter, the *MapDemo* demo uses the USMAP01 bitmap, which is a map of the United States. This program demonstrates the use of the color matching and drunkard's walk algorithm techniques for event identification.

The upper New England states (which appear relatively small in the USMAP01 bitmap) are displayed separately in the USMAP02 bitmap and are used to demonstrate the second area-identification algorithm. You can select the USMAP02 image either by clicking on the upper New England states in USMAP01 or through the Map menu.

NOTE   The *MapDemo* demo is included on the CD accompanying this book, in the Chapter 30 folder.

Color Matching

Within the *MapDemo* demo, while the USMAP01 bitmap is displayed, a WM_ LBUTTONDOWN message calls the ColorCheckMap function, which passes three parameters: the window handle (hwnd) and the two mouse-click coordinates derived from the lParam argument accompanying the mouse-button event message.

```
case WM_LBUTTONDOWN:
    ...
        CoordCheckMap( hwnd, LOWORD( lParam ),
                             HIWORD( lParam ) );
    break;
```

The mouse-click x-axis coordinate is reported in the low word of lParam, and the high word reports the y-axis coordinate.

The ColorCheckMap function appears to be a simple process, but it does require a bit of finesse to comply with Windows' requirements.

```
void ColorCheckMap( HWND hwnd, WORD xCoord, WORD yCoord )
{
    HDC     hdc;
    DWORD   RColor;
```

```
WORD      SColor;
int       i;

...
hdc = GetDC( hwnd );
RColor = GetPixel( hdc, xCoord, yCoord );
        // need RGB palette-relative color value
ReleaseDC( hwnd, hdc );
```

The GetPixel function returns a DWORD value containing the RGB color value for the selected pixel in the form 0x00rrggbb. However, while this is the color of the pixel itself, the data identifying the several states consists of the simpler palette-index values rather than their RGB equivalents. Ergo, the next task is to match the color returned to the bitmap's palette, retrieving the palette index.

To accomplish this, the first requirement is to lock the pointer to the global palette information (pGLP) and then lock a handle to the logical palette (hGPal) before calling the CreatePalette and RealizePalette functions to temporarily re-create and activate the bitmap palette.

```
LocalLock( hGLP );
LocalLock( hGPal );
        // lock and create palette for reference
hGPal = CreatePalette( pGLP );
if( hGPal == NULL ) ErrorMsg( "Palette not found!" );
        // make palette active for device context
RealizePalette( hdc );
        // get palette index for comparison
SColor = GetNearestPaletteIndex( hGPal, (COLORREF) RColor );
        // unlock everything but don't delete palette
LocalUnlock( hGLP );
LocalUnlock( hGPal );
```

Finally, after the palette is created (or re-created), the GetNearestPalette-Index function returns the palette-index value as SColor. Of course, before finishing, the two memory locks on the global and re-created palettes should be released. Neither, however, should be freed from memory since they may be needed again.

Once the palette index has been retrieved, a pair of simple loops is all that is required to identify the corresponding state or, in the case of the upper New England states, to display the USMAP02 bitmap30.

```
for( i=0; i<12; i++ )
   if( SColor == NewEngland[i] )
```

```
                    // if this is any New England state, switch maps
               PostMessage( hwnd, WM_COMMAND, IDM_MAP2, OL );
          for( i=0; i<=StateColors; i++ )
            if( SColor == CState[i].Color )
               LocationMsg( CState[i].State );
          MessageBeep( MB_ICONASTERISK );
       }
```

Once the state or area is identified, a variety of other responses can be implemented as elaborately or simply as desired. In this demo, a simple pop-up dialog box with a "Welcome to the great state of *xxxxxx*" message appears, identifying the state selected.

The data matching the states and colors is provided by a simple structure listing these by name and palette index. An abbreviated sample follows:

```
ColorState CState[StateColors] =
{  "Arizona",         2,      "New Mexico",      7,
   "Oklahoma",        9,      "Georgia",        11,
   "Oregon",         12,      "Colorado",       13,
   "Missouri",       15,      "South Carolina", 16,
   "Texas",          17,      "Hawaii",         18,
   ...
```

The Drunkard's Walk Search

Implementing the drunkard's walk search algorithm (CoordCheckMap) is a relatively simple task. As in the ColorCheckMap function, this search is called with three arguments: the window handle and the x- and y-axis coordinates reported by the mouse-click event message.

```
void CoordCheckMap( HWND hwnd, WORD xCoord, WORD yCoord )
{
   BOOL     Done = FALSE, Reverse;
   HDC      hdc;
   WORD     i;
   int      j, k, x, y;

   ...
   randomize();
   hdc = GetDC( hwnd );
   x = random(3)-1;
   y = random(3)-1;
```

Initially, `CoordMapCheck` retrieves the device-context handle for the window displaying the map and selects step directions (x,y) in the range –1 to 1. Since these are used to increment the `xCoord` and `yCoord` values, the result is a search track beginning in one of eight compass directions (N, NE, E, SE, S, SW, W, NW).

> **NOTE**
>
> There is also one chance in nine that the initial search step will be (0,0), which is no search at all. This will, however, correct itself automatically when the next random search direction is selected.

Before the search is initiated, the first step is to check the present coordinates against a loop testing all of the identified coordinate pairs. Also, rather than requiring a perfect hit on the target coordinates, the actual test accepts any point that is within ten pixels of the target (total offset on both axes). As in a game of horseshoes, close *does* count. An exact match is not required, simplifying the search.

```
do
{
   for( i=0; i<AllCoords; i++ )
   {
      if( ( abs( xCoord - Coord[i].xPos ) +
            abs( yCoord - Coord[i].yPos ) ) < 10 )
      {
         if( i < StateCoords )
            LocationMsg( Coord[i].State );
         else
            PostMessage( hwnd, WM_COMMAND, IDM_MAP1, 0L );
         Done = TRUE;
      } }
```

If the current coordinates are within a total of ten units of the target coordinates, a match is simply assumed. The hidden assumption here is that no target point is located within ten pixels of a border; otherwise, it could be misidentified by being detected from the wrong side of the border.

In other cases, a closer (or looser) match might be appropriate, so you would adjust the algorithm adjusted accordingly. For the present, a range of ten pixels is adequate for the purpose.

State coordinate pairs in the *MapDemo* demo are identified, together with the appropriate state names, as a simple structure table:

```
CoordState Coord[AllCoords] =
{  "Connecticut",   267, 208,   "Delaware",      202, 311,
   ...
   "Vermont",       238, 132,   "RETURN",         14, 337,
   "RETURN",        331, 290,   "RETURN",        122,  81  };
```

In addition to the state coordinates, the program provides three area coordinates that do not fall within a specific state: one below the upper New England states and two in the blank areas surrounding these states. Intersecting any of these three locations sends the application back to the USMAP01 display.

Alternatively, as long as a match is not found, the next test is to determine whether the bitmap borders have been reached:

```
Reverse = FALSE;
if( ( xCoord >= bmWidth-1  ) || ( xCoord <= 1 ) ||
    ( yCoord >= bmHeight-1 ) || ( yCoord <= 1 ) )
   Reverse = TRUE;
```

If the search is approaching the bitmap border, the Boolean `Reverse` flag is set and, subsequently, will reverse the search direction. Without this provision, the usual result under Windows will be a system application error, often trashing the system memory as well.

Next, as long as the search remains away from the bitmap border, a second loop executes a check of the immediate vicinity, searching for pixels identifying a border encounter and again reversing direction if a border is found.

```
else
   for( j=-1; j<2; j++ )
      for( k=-1; k<2; k++ )
         if( GetPixel( hdc, xCoord+j, yCoord+k ) == BORDER )
            Reverse = TRUE;
```

The program could have executed a simple, straight-ahead search, but this would have one fairly dangerous flaw: Narrow borders can leak through either single-pixel gaps or diagonal "pores," both of which are illustrated in Figure 30.4.

FIGURE 30.4

Leaky borders using the
drunkard's walk algorithm

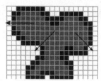

Here, a gap in the left border is one potential leak where a search trace could escape. Two other locations show pores where a diagonal search trace could escape. The remaining potential gaps in the original have been blocked in this version. Going through a bitmap looking for potential problems of this type is a tedious process and prone to error. Instead, the broad area-checking provisions in the preceding code accommodate a much less rigorous border condition.

Finally, if any of the preceding tests have set the `Reverse` flag, both the x and y increment variables are inverted by multiplying by –1.

```
if( Reverse )
{
    x *= -1;
    y *= -1;
}
else
if( ! random(10) )
{
    x = random(3)-1;
    y = random(3)-1;
}
```

Alternatively, if no reverse condition has been encountered, a simple random test is used to change the search direction on a one-in-ten chance. Like the original one, the new search direction is selected randomly.

NOTE

A provision has been included in *MapDemo* to render the search trace visible by drawing a white dot at each step. This is implemented quite simply as:

```
//=== option to trace random walk algorithm =========
        SetPixel( hdc, xCoord, yCoord, 0x00FFFFFF );
//===================================================
```

To disable this trace provision, simply comment out this line of code.

Last, the current x and y incremental values are added to the xCoord and yCoord values before the do...while loop continues.

```
    xCoord += x;
    yCoord += y;
}
while( ! Done );
...
return;
}
```

Figure 30.5 shows several drunkard's walk searches executed in various New England states. The illustration was created by having the search paint its own trail markers. After the screen image was captured, the fill colors for each state were replaced by white, and the target points, which appear as small red dots in the map image, were replaced by asterisks for easier identification.

FIGURE 30.5:

Drunkard's walk searches in
New England

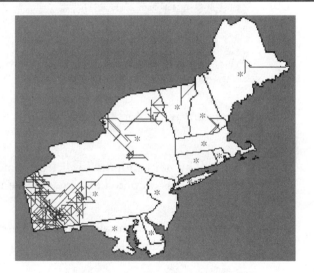

As you can readily see in the traces in Figure 30.5, the drunkard's walk algorithm is not the most efficient search method. Furthermore, as previously mentioned, there are times when this method is indeed ineffective.

For example, Figure 30.6 shows an enlargement of the search executed in Pennsylvania, with a circle added both to make the target region more visible and to show the nominal target radius. The search shown begins in the northeastern portion of the state, then passes relatively close to the target location, but not quite close enough to trigger a match, before executing a rather massive search of the western region and, finally, returning to the central region to find the target coordinates. On the other hand, since even a complex search like this executed in a matter of a less than a second, the inefficiency involved was relatively minor.

FIGURE 30.6:

Searching Pennsylvania

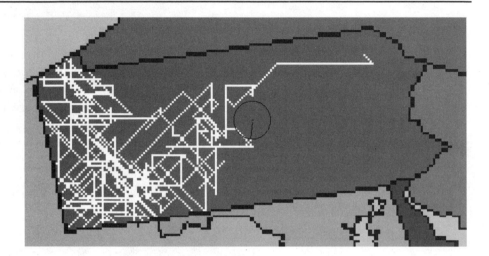

Also, there are two factors that tend to mask these potential inefficiencies in the algorithm:

- A natural human tendency to click on some point roughly near the center of any area (as compared to human perversity in selecting bottlenecked regions)

- The probability that the algorithm will tend to quickly execute an escape from such a bottlenecked region

A third guard can be provided by selecting extra coordinate points within such regions. For an example, see the provisions for New York and Long Island in the *MapDemo* demo. (On the map, the island of Long Island is separate from the remainder of the state and has its own target coordinates.)

> **NOTE**
>
> The drunkard's walk algorithm is not without an occasional shortcoming. Stuart Ozer, who was my technical reviewer for the Windows 3.1 version of an earlier volume, reported finding a starting point on Cape Cod from which the algorithm required ten minutes or more to identify Massachusetts. Such a flaw could be blamed on the geometry of the search versus the boundary configuration, or it could be simply bad luck in the pseudo-random number sequence directing the search.

Alternative Area-Identification Methods

Although it may appear odd or even inefficient, the drunkard's walk algorithm is, overall, a very fast technique for determining a regional location. There is, however, one alternative which, on first consideration, sometimes appears more efficient: Search the coordinate list for the coordinate pair closest to the starting point, then look for a border between the two points.

The reasons for this second step are simple but are best illustrated by an example. Consider the states of Pennsylvania and New Jersey and assume that the coordinate pairs for each are located at, approximately, Altoona (Pennsylvania) and East Brunswick (New Jersey), placing each location roughly at the center of the state.

A mouse click in the region of Philadelphia (Pennsylvania) would not, however, select the Altoona coordinates as nearest because the East Brunswick coordinates in New Jersey are considerably closer.

Of course, searching for a border between the initial point and the closest target would identify the problem and allow another search for the next closest coordinates (and so on) to proceed. But the search for a border is almost as time-consuming as a simple drunkard's walk and is more difficult to program reliably.

Now suppose that the located coordinate set is correct—that it lies in the same state or region as the mouse click—but that a straight line between the origin and the coordinate point must cross two borders. Sound unlikely? It isn't. For example, look back at Figure 30.5, where the state of Maryland (at the bottom of the map) is virtually split in two by the Chesapeake Bay. At the same time, Long Island and the mainland portion of the state of New York are technically all one region but, physically, are two separate areas on the map. In this instance, neither of the algorithms discussed—the drunkard's walk or the closest points with border-crossing tests—is adequate.

The solution for both the cases of discontinuous or extremely convoluted areas is to provide more than one coordinate point. In the *MapDemo* demo, the USMAP02 provides two coordinate points to identify New York: one on Long Island and one on the mainland.

For Maryland, a second point located across the Chesapeake Bay would simplify searching and would also prevent an error that is present in the current version: Selecting a point across Chesapeake Bay is very likely to locate Delaware, not Maryland.

It would also be possible to provide a larger number of coordinate point targets in each area and, granted, this should ensure very fast searches. The only drawback would be the effort of building tables of points and ensuring that there were no errors in the result. The trade-off in speed—which is minimal from the user's viewpoint—however hardly seems worth the effort.

Another consideration that may be applicable to your own applications is how to identify areas without having them visible on the displayed image. For example, in the case of the United States map, you might wish to display a topographic or meteorological map of the country without delineating the states, which would mean no borders. As mentioned earlier in the chapter, using a hidden color map—a second map image the same size as the first that does not appear on the screen—would allow you to still be able to identify the states. You would create this second map in a memory context. Then, when the user clicks to select a point on the displayed bitmap, the search would be executed from the corresponding point on the hidden bitmap.

In this chapter, we've looked at several methods for working with interactive, complex bitmaps. The *MapDemo* demo, including on the CD accompanying this book, demonstrates two methods for mapping mouse events to complex bitmap regions. You can experiment with these and the other methods mentioned here to see how they suit the needs of your applications.

In the next chapter, we will look how graphics simulations work and methods for developing your own simulation applications.

31

Graphics Simulations

- A synthetic cosmos for modeling physical interactions

- Variable timing for simulated events

- Choices for simplifying simulations

- Mechanical simulations

- Theoretical system simulations

Over the past two decades, computers have revolutionized more of our world than most people realize. Granted, the Internet is the current buzzword, and most people are aware that computers are used for special effects in movies and commercials on television. Some people are even familiar with using computers to study fluid dynamics, weather patterns, engineering structures, and other technical subjects. But these are only a few of the areas where computers have radically changed the traditional arts, crafts, and sciences. A complete list of affected areas would fill a large book, which would be out-of-date long before it could be published.

But this chapter is not about the computer revolution. It's about an area that did not even exist, with a few modest exceptions, prior to computers: the field of graphics simulations or, more accurately, the mathematical simulation of dynamic systems in general, including both physical and nonphysical systems.

Benefits of Graphics Simulations

Simulations do not necessarily require graphics and, in some cases, would be slowed down by graphics. We do, however, have a very human desire to see what is happening rather than reading about the results afterwards. As an example, the *Forest* demo discussed in this chapter displays a small universe of 10,000 acres, simulating the growth of trees.

The simulation begins with bare ground that is randomly seeded with 100 starting plots. As the simulation progresses, the various wooded areas grow, age, and propagate, spreading trees to new areas.

Of course, if this were the extent of the simulation, the mini-universe would simply fill with trees until there was no bare ground left. The result could be derived simply by calculating the average time necessary to fill the forest. This simulation, however, is not so limited.

Instead, as a defined area of tree population ages, the trees eventually die, rot, and leave a new plot of bare ground. At the same time, in emulation of the real world, the simulated forest is subject to fires. And, once a fire starts, it spreads. The older trees are easiest to ignite, and changing wind patterns affect the spread of the fire.

Overall, if the simulation's only output were a statistical report listing the forested acres for each year, we might learn almost as much. But almost as much is not the same as watching it happen; by watching the forest grow, burn, and reseed, we gain some small measure of understanding of two new and very important elements: the patterns of growth and death, and the way that changing the parameters affects not only the end results but the patterns themselves.

NOTE   If you have any doubts about the relative importance of simple statistical results versus patterns, consider the extreme examples of any fractal algorithm. In fractal calculations, such as the Henon Attractor or the Malthusian equation (another famous simulation), statistical results reveal almost nothing; the patterns, visible only when plotted graphically, reveal everything.

Some Background on Computer Simulations

In the ages B.C. (Before Computers), the sheer volume of calculations required for simulations ruled out modeling even the simplest systems unless some measurable physical analog could be employed. In some cases, there were alternatives. Physical erosion was relatively easy to study using a slant box of sand and a water source. Minimal route-mapping problems could be solved using soap films. And many ballistic and navigational problems were attacked using electronic (and some mechanical) analog systems.

As for more general simulations, however, the Life program was played out with paper and pencil, usually by students who might have better spent their time studying. This was roughly the practical limit for an unaided human. (For your amusement, the Life program in electronic form is included on the CD accompanying this book.)

In the Life program, the "world" consists of a grid which, for convenience, is finite but unbounded (see "The Toroidal Model" section in this chapter) and each grid location may initially be "alive" or "dead". Provisions are included in the demo to "seed" the grid randomly or to create an initial configuration known as a "launcher," which will generate two child "flyers," which will fly across the screen on a diagonal path.

At intervals of ½ second, a new generation of Life is calculated according to the current state of the "world" and three simple rules:

1. Any "alive" location that has more than three neighbors dies of overcrowding in the next generation.

Continued on next page

2. Any "alive" location that has less than two neighbors dies of loneliness in the next generation.

3. Any location—"alive" or "dead"—that has exactly three neighbors will be alive in the next generation.

Advancing beyond these three simple rules governing the Life program and expanding beyond what is, essentially, a very small universe, the complexity and volume of the calculations required for most simulations have simply overwhelmed both human patience and practical capacities. Some few individuals have accomplished prodigious feats of cogitation and calculation, such as the compilation of the Rudolphine Tables (Kepler) or calculation of the trigonometric functions (Napier), but these are exceptions as well as monumental endeavors. (The Aztec calendar might also qualify but was almost certainly a prolonged group effort.)

Thus, for the most part, simulations of any complexity have waited for the advent of our newest and most powerful tool: the computer. Using this tool, we are now able to study—through simulation—systems about which, previously, we could only theorize.

All of this says nothing about the accuracy of our simulations, but it does permit testing our theories against actual performance. Therefore, if your theory holds that playing to fill an inside straight is better than folding on the sixth card, you can create a simulation to test this theory faster and more accurately (as well as more cheaply) than testing the theory at Saturday night poker games. (Of course, this question can also be settled by probability theory without requiring simulations, but we won't go into that here.)

Dynamic (Memory) Cosmos Creation

The *Forest* demo demonstrates the creation of a synthetic cosmos. By intention, the forest exists only as a shadow, mimicking reality without requiring the complexity of rules (natural laws) that govern what we familiarly consider reality. Instead, the simulation uses simpler rules that can be manipulated, compressed, and studied. Thus, by analogy and experimentation, we are able to better understand the complexities of reality.

Rather than modeling the growth and complexity of individual trees (along with the weather patterns, soil composition, and myriad other factors) and repeating this for the thousands of acres of trees composing the forest, the forest is calculated as areas following a simple statistical growth pattern with a uniform composition within the area. In this fashion, we *can* see the forest for the trees; we are able to look at the forest as an entity while ignoring the trees themselves.

The Cosmos Size

Our simulated forest exists in a cosmos consisting of a scant 10,000 units (100 by 100), which for convenience only are referred to as acres. Because this is a simple simulation, the essential status for each unit is stored in an array of BYTE.

For convenience, two arrays are used, permitting the second array to be updated by reference to the first and to then replace the first array. In this fashion, the first array, which holds the prior status, is not affected by changes that would produce recursive effects.

As you know by now, although DOS and Windows 3.*x* impose limits on array sizes of a mere 64KB, Windows 98, using 32-bit addressing, has revoked this limitation in favor of a theoretical array size of 4GB. Of course, we still face physical limitations imposed by the amount of memory available; even on small systems, however, this is a considerable increase in freedom.

NOTE   If you need to use extremely large arrays, in sizes beyond available memory limits, you can use disk files as an extension of RAM. Unfortunately, this approach has the disadvantages of being relatively slow and somewhat cumbersome.

Rules of the Cosmos

Had I been present at the creation, I might have offered the creator much valuable advice.
— remark attributed to Alphonso the YYs.

The Forest cosmos is governed by a series of relatively simple rules, which appear as numerical algorithms within the program:

- The Forest cosmos begins as bare ground and is randomly seeded, initially, with 100 plantings.

- On subsequent cycles (years), the planting age is shown by changing colors.

- After a minimum of five cycles, the forest plots are developed well enough to propagate and, if adjacent plots are bare, may seed these areas, initiating new growth.

- Old-growth acres—arbitrarily those over 11 years old—are susceptible to natural death. A simple simulation provides for old age and other causes. As with natural forests, however, this is a minor element and affects approximately 1 percent of the forest.

- Fire is a major event in the Forest cosmos, just as it is in real-world forests. For simplicity, only one fire can start during any cycle. Minor fires are not simulated, but a fire may spread to adjacent acreage.

- Fires die out when their fuel is exhausted, but they are also affected by wind direction and speed.

- Fires can spread only to mature acreage; young plots are not affected (under the assumption that young trees are scattered and little deadwood is available to fuel a major burn).

Given these relatively simple rules, the Forest cosmos simulates the same patterns of growth and death exhibited by real forests. And a correspondence in patterns is the hallmark by which a simulation is tested.

Boundary Problems

Any simulation that re-creates or models a subset of a larger reality is subject to a boundary problem in one form or another. If you'll recall from Chapter 28, when we talked about image enhancements, a boundary problem came up when transform operations left a one-pixel border around the original image. Although this border data was used when calculating transformations for adjacent pixels, because these pixels did not themselves have a complete complement of neighbors, they were not included in the transformed image.

In the Forest cosmos, the boundary problem is avoided by the simple expedient of making the cosmos a closed, unbounded universe. What appears to be the left edge of the map actually adjoins the right edge; the top edge of the map joins and continues at the bottom. Topologically, this type of closure is the equivalent of a *toroidal* surface (a doughnut or inner tube provide physical examples of a toroidal surface). Although toroidal surfaces are not commonly encountered in our universe (at least, not on any macrocosmic scale), this is a popular method of avoiding boundary problems in simulations.

There are other, more complex methods for dealing with boundary problems. For example, a method popular in the study of the physical universe involves using a spherical surface. Another, even more complicated and computation-intensive approach involves using algorithms to simulate the effects of areas outside the actual simulation boundaries.

For most planar simulations, the toroidal universe provides the simplest approach and the fastest computational results. Furthermore, if your simulated cosmos is not planar but a volume, such as a fluid or gaseous volume, this same practice can be extended to create a hypertoroid in cybernetically four-dimensional space.

The Toroidal Model

The practice of creating or simulating a closed but unbounded cosmos in cyber-space is both simple and complex. On the simple side, because the data describing a simulation is stored in one or more arrays or matrixes, the primary consideration in using the toroidal surface model is to test all coordinate references (that is, refer-ences to array data) and to provide adjustments for references that fall outside the array limits, thus "wrapping" the index back into the array from "the other side."

On the complex side, although simple rectilinear offsets are easily converted, operations involving vectors, angles, or curves are not always easily handled. When operations of this or a similar type are necessary, the simplest approach is to use a separate matrix where the operation can be carried out without crossing a boundary. The results can be mapped, using whatever offsets and adjustments are necessary, into the simulation space.

In spatial terms, the most important element is to make sure that all operations that wrap across an array boundary are correctly adjusted for the wrap. Failure to do so can have strange and interesting results that are not always easy to identify or recognize.

Colors in Simulations

One principal characteristic of graphic simulations is the use of color to make information clear. In many cases, commonly referred to as *false-color mapping* or *false-color imaging*, color assignments are arbitrary and have no real-world relation to the source or the data.

For example, false-color imaging is often used in astronomy to "translate" radio-frequency images for visual presentation. The translation involved can take several different forms, including using color to represent intensities, radio frequencies, densities, or even gravitational gradations—none of which have any direct correspondence to the visual spectrum.

Another mapping format uses colors that are chosen to represent approximate analogs of the data. An example of this latter approach is used in the Forest simulation. Bare ground is represented by browns, various stages of forest growth by shades of green, fires and embers by reds, and ashy ground by grays.

You can also use a combination of both representational color and false-color coding. This approach generally involves switching between display formats, showing first one information set and then another. For example, you could create a switched display for the Forest program by adding provisions to show simulated rainfall patterns, temperature profiles, or soil-composition characteristics.

The Forest Demo:
Operating the Simulation

Deciding how to set up a simulation is the first step; coding the simulation is the second. Both steps require provisions for a variety of circumstances.

As an example, Figure 31.1 shows the Forest cosmos some 6703 years after seeding and 22 days into a major burn-off. The illustrated burn began somewhere in the northwest of the display but has not spread too widely, despite a current wind from the west at a strength of 4 (the maximum is 5). Allowing the simulation to continue, the fire revives as the winds change direction and finally burns itself out after 73 days.

All of these events, of course, exist only in the computer's memory and result from pseudo-random number sequences. Nonetheless, they provide a faithful emulation of patterns of growth and burn-off that have been observed in natural forests.

NOTE   The *Forest* demo is included on the CD accompanying this book, in the Chapter 31 folder.

FIGURE 31.1:

Here the forest is 6703 years old, 22 days into a burn condition with the wind from the west at a strength of 4.

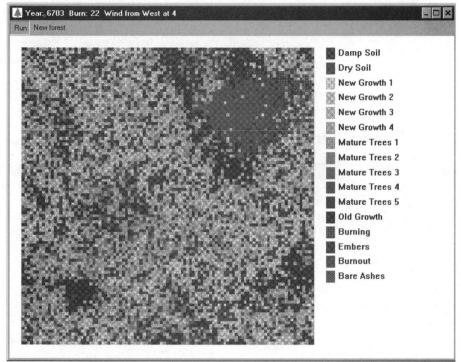

Color Palette Definition

In the *Forest* demo, a palette of 16 colors has been defined. Two of these represent bare ground (light brown and dark brown). Ten shades of green represent trees at various ages. Light and dark red represent fires and embers, respectively. A dark gray is used to represent freshly burnt, ashy ground. A third brown is used for ground left bare by a fire.

The palette colors are defined in Forest.H as RGB values, each with a corresponding integer constant as a convenient identifier. (These latter elements are for the programmer's convenience only—but, then, what is more important?)

However, although these RGB values are defined for each color, this palette is never activated for the device context. Instead, while the RGB colors are referenced as drawing colors, Windows is allowed to dither the existing default palette colors in drawing the simulation map.

NOTE The decision to permit dithering instead of activating the color palette is arbitrary, but this method does show, even on SVGA systems, how a similar display might appear on standard VGA systems. The alternative of activating the defined palette colors is left as an exercise for the reader (and is demonstrated numerous times in other sample programs accompanying this book).

Cosmos Initiation

Lacking the resources to initiate a primal fireball and to then wait for nature to evolve a life form from the first primordial globule, the first provision in the Forest simulation is to set the initial conditions for the simulation. This is accomplished in two steps; beginning in response to the WM_CREATE message.

```
case WM_CREATE:
    randomize();
    ActiveTimer = 0;
    wsprintf( szBuff, szCaption, nYears );
    SetWindowText( hwnd, szBuff );
    for( i=0; i<GRID; i++ )          // init world as
        for( j=0; j<GRID; j++ )      // bare ground
            Acres[i][j] = random(2);
    break;
```

The randomize function ensures that new initial conditions (that is, a new pseudo-random number sequence) are used each time the program is executed.

NOTE If you are using the Microsoft C/C++ compiler rather than the Borland C/C++ compiler, the randomize function is not available. The function can be provided other ways; for example, by using the system clock (seconds since January 1, 1980) to seed the pseudo-random generator.

The second provision, the double loops, sets the world to a random mixture of damp and dry soils shown by the two browns. Within the program, both are treated simply as fertile ground, without regard to their moisture content. In a more elaborate version, the two browns might be used as different conditions, representing wet and dry ground or high and low terrain. For the current version, two shades of brown are simply not as dull as a single uniform color.

The second stage of initialization occurs only when the New Forest option is selected from the menu. When this option is selected, the program resets the nYears variable to zero and seeds 100 random locations, setting the corresponding array elements as iNewGrowth.

```
case IDM_RESEED:
    randomize();
    nYears = 0;
    for( i=0; i<100; i++ )
    {
        xPos = random(GRID);
        yPos = random(GRID);
        Acres[xPos][yPos] = iNewGrowth;
    }
    EnableMenuItem( GetMenu(hwnd), IDM_STOPTIMER, MF_ENABLED );
    PostMessage( hwnd, WM_COMMAND, IDM_STARTGROWTH, 0L );
    InvalidateRect( hwnd, NULL, FALSE );
    break;
```

The pull-down Run menu has two options, Start and Stop, both of which are initially disabled. After the forest is seeded, the Stop option is enabled, and a message is posted to start the ID_GROWTH timer. Last, the InvalidateRect function is called to repaint the window.

Variable Timing for Events

After the initial conditions for a simulation are set (your cosmos is created), normally the next step is to initiate a sequence of events. In some simulations, such as for plotting fractal algorithms, it is the end result that is important. This type of process is normally carried out as quickly as possible.

More commonly, however, simulations are executed at some regular process rate. Ideally, this rate is fast enough to prevent boredom but slow enough to permit us to observe how the simulation is developing. Generally, for macro simulations such as those in our example, this is compressed time for the simple reason that no one is interested in waiting a year to watch a simulation complete a forest's growth cycle. Alternatively, if you were trying to simulate the first three minutes of the creation of the cosmos, you would probably want to expand time to permit the observation of events that happened too quickly for conventional observation.

In the *Forest* demo, two different compressed time rates are used, each rate controlled by a system timer: one for normal growth and another for forest fires.

Forest-Growth Simulation

Initially, forest growth is simulated at 1 year = 1 second, with a one-second timer stepping through the growth cycle. Thus, at one-second intervals, the ID_GROWTH timer sends a WM_TIMER message to the WndProc procedure. In response, a number of events are initialized.

```
case WM_TIMER:
    switch( LOWORD( wParam ) )
    {
        case ID_GROWTH:
            wsprintf( szBuff, szCaption, nYears++ );
            SetWindowText( hwnd, szBuff );
            AgeWorld();
            PropagateTrees();
```

The first response is to update the window caption, displaying the current year (the number of cycles since the initial seeding) before calling AgeWorld to cycle the forest through a year's growth.

The next step, PropagateTrees, calls a subprocedure to seed new areas from existing growth. In this simulation, three factors control the rate of the spread of the forest:

- The age of the existing growth (within each plot)

- Selection of a single plot within a range of three plots in any direction (quite arbitrarily)

- Whether the target plot is fertile ground (in this case, any bare soil)

All of these factors could be variables or could be changed arbitrarily to experiment with new environmental conditions. Still, the present settings serve as a good foundation for a forest simulation.

Growth and seeding operations are carried out by writing new values to a copy of the original data array, ensuring that the new conditions do not overwrite the existing conditions used to generate the new ones. However, because of this separation of present and future, the StepForest procedure is called to copy this future status back to the present array.

In the current simulation, the potential conflicts between the present and future states of the forest are minimal. The second array could be disposed of, and all operations could be carried out in a single array. In other simulations, however, duplicate arrays may be essential. Moreover, circumstances may require several arrays to store not only present and future, but also various data types, which may include constants (such as terrain) or contain factors affecting larger areas (such as rainfall).

Forest-Fire Simulation

After the current state of the forest is updated, the `InitBurns` procedure is called to simulate potential forest fires:

```
StepForest();
InitBurns( hwnd );
InvalidateRect( hwnd, NULL, FALSE );
break;
```

And, when the forest fires (if any) conclude, the display is updated to show the new conditions.

The `InitBurns` procedure begins by selecting an arbitrary location for a fire to start:

```
void InitBurns( HWND hwnd )
{
    int  x, y, NoChance = 20;

    x = random( GRID );
    y = random( GRID );
```

Here, a couple of quite arbitrary conditions have been established:

- Only one fire can be started in any year.

- Any fire that does start completely burns out the affected plot (no plots are partially burned).

- The constant, `NoChance`, is included to adjust the chances for a burn to start.

As with the growth-simulation conditions, all of these factors, including the algorithm, can be changed or may include variables to adjust for various ignition potentials.

To actually decide if a fire starts in the targeted area, a simple algorithm is applied:

```
if( random( iOldGrowth + NoChance ) <= (int) Acres[x][y] )
```

Here, a random value is generated and must be less than the growth state of the plot selected before a fire is initiated. In effect, the older the growth on the target plot, and therefore the more fuel available, the greater the chances of a fire starting.

Assuming that a fire is initiated, another simulation sequence is started, beginning by setting nDay to zero and selecting an initial wind direction:

```
    {
        nDays = 0;
        nWind = random(4);
        Acres[x][y] = iBurning;
        PostMessage( hwnd, WM_COMMAND, IDM_STOPGROWTH, OL );
        PostMessage( hwnd, WM_COMMAND, IDM_STARTBURNS, OL );
    }
}
```

Last, to initiate the actual burn-simulation sequence, the first timer (ID_GROWTH) is turned off and a second timer (ID_FIRES) is started.

NOTE Because two separate timers are involved in the simulation, and because the Start and Stop menu options are intended to operate either of these independently, a set of purely internal message procedures are used to trigger these options indirectly rather than directly.

After the ID_FIRES timer has been initiated, all subsequent WM_TIMER messages carry the ID_FIRES identifier and are used to control the new simulation sequence.

Because the burn events are an important departure from the normal growth pattern, the MessageBeep function is used to call attention to these changes. Also, the global nWind wind direction is allowed to change at random intervals before calling the TrackFire subprocedure:

```
    case ID_FIRES:
        MessageBeep( 0 );
        if( ! random(4) ) nWind = random(4);
        if( ! TrackFire() )
        {
            PostMessage( hwnd, WM_COMMAND, IDM_STOPBURNS, OL );
            PostMessage( hwnd, WM_COMMAND, IDM_STARTGROWTH, OL );
        }
        InvalidateRect( hwnd, NULL, FALSE );
```

```
        break;
    default:
        return( DefWindowProc( hwnd, msg, wParam, lParam ) );
    }
    break;
```

As long as fires continue to burn, the TrackFire procedure returns TRUE, and the ID_FIRES timer continues uninterrupted. When there are no remaining fires and a FALSE value is returned, the ID_FIRES timer is killed and the ID_GROWTH timer restarted.

The TrackFire subprocedure accomplishes two tasks:

- It ensures that fires do burn out to embers and then to ashy ground. This is governed by a fairly simple algorithm that allows fires to sustain a long burn initially but, after the fires have been burning, causes later burns to develop swiftly but last only briefly. In effect, after a forest fire is well developed, the fires burn hotter, ignite new areas easier, but burn out faster.

- It provides a means for fires to spread to new areas. This is affected by three factors. The first two—wind direction and wind speed—are relatively obvious. The third is simply a provision to ensure that young acreage does not catch fire and burn off.

Simulation Design

In the *Forest* demo, the processes involving the growth of a forest have been greatly simplified. For example, no provisions have been made to account for rainfall or, during burn phases, for rains that limit or even extinguish the fire's spread. No provisions have been made for seasonal variations, such as wet springs and dry summers or for longer-term climatic variations. Similarly, it includes only a single, generic species of trees, with no other plant life present and with no insect damage or disease damage simulated. Likewise, there are no prevailing winds, rainfall patterns, erosion, or soil fertility variations.

Even so, if all of these factors were included in the simulation, this would still be a very simplified cosmos. The point is that any simulation must be restricted to some degree, if only to allow the computer to handle it in a reasonable time and with reasonable memory requirements.

On the other hand, simplifying the simulation does not mean that the results must be simple. Since the object is to model reality, there is certainly every reason for the results of the simulation to mimic the complexities of reality.

Simplification Choices

The problem of simplification is threefold:

- To decide which elements of reality are essential to the simulation

- To develop algorithms that mathematically mimic reality

- To present the results of the computations in a format that will show what is happening

Because the *Forest* demo was designed solely to demonstrate a graphic simulation and to serve as an example, many elements reflecting reality that would also have increased the complexity of the program were omitted. Instead, two principal factors were selected for representation:

- Propagation rates and patterns for the development of the forest

- Fires to destroy older growth and make room for new additional growth

Given these two principal factors, the resulting simulation (in terms of burn-off and regrowth patterns) still mimics the patterns observed in natural forests quite accurately, which is exactly what is desired as an initial objective.

In addition to the propagation and burn patterns, one minor evolutionary provision was added: having older growth die off without burning. In the present simulation, the relatively minor decline of old growth by simple attrition is masked by the larger effect of fires, producing the natural pattern observed in dry-climate forests.

If, however, the burn frequency is decreased or stopped, the old-growth decline will become a major rather than a minor effect, producing a pattern typical of wetland forests, where large-scale fires are virtually unknown. And, as you may observe by varying the pattern, such a forest will tend toward a steady-state climax forest, which is quite typical of existing, older wetland forests where older growth dominates and younger growth is sparse.

Simulation Extensions

Once a basic simulation is operating with a satisfactory degree of validity—when the operations correspond somewhat faithfully to reality—you can add further extensions to simulate additional factors. The advantage of a simulation is that any of these additional factors (or any combination of additional factors) can be tested, varied, and tested again to observe how changes in various parameters affect the progress of the overall simulation.

Even the simple *Forest* demo could be expanded to include more factors and used to study the effects of various cutting patterns and the effect on the recovery and long-term management of sustained yield for a real forest. You might include factors such as elevation and erosion effects, rainfall, and leftover debris from cutting operations and its effects on the spread of fires. Other factors that might affect the overall health of a forest, such as insect infestation and disease, might simply be ignored as irrelevant during the tests. But then, if some validity is found for considering further factors—perhaps the cutting of debris provides a breeding ground for the insect population—then these factors should also be included in the model. Otherwise, the model may show effects that were not anticipated or fail to show effects that were.

How you extend a simulation depends on what you are trying to learn. The real value of a simulation is to reveal how processes occur, how elements interact, or where and how patterns appear within a system.

Mechanical System Simulations

Modeling of interactions among living systems is just one of the areas in which simulation is useful. Another fruitful area for simulation design lies in analyzing mechanical systems.

Although CAD systems are commonly thought of as design utilities, simulating how mechanical elements interact is an integral part of any mechanical design process. After all, if a set of gears is going to jam when two driven mechanical arms unexpectedly attempt to pass through the same volume of space, it's considerably cheaper to find the flaw in an electronic simulation than discovering this same surprise after tooling up to begin production or worse, after building a physical model.

You may be thinking that mechanical modeling certainly could be carried out without any accompanying visual elements. After all, it should be faster to calculate (for example) how two gears mesh than to draw the two gears on screen and to repeatedly redraw them as they turn, right? If the only consideration was the two gears, perhaps. But what about that movement arm driven by the gearing which, in another few seconds of arc, will attempt to pass through one of several mechanical support members? These supports are static and weren't included in the calculated motions—a small oversight, but one that the real universe is not likely to duplicate.

Instead of attempting to calculate the place where every point belonging to every element (both static and dynamic) may potentially interact with some other point, it is simpler to draw the various elements, redrawing each one as often as necessary. This allows the best processors of all, the human eye and brain, to spot the potential conflicts.

Mechanical simulations should not be limited to the interactions of cams, gears, and cogs. Instead, as currently implemented in some virtual reality simulations, the humans (or other creatures) using the machines being designed also become part of the simulation process.

WARNING   If you are interested or active in mechanical simulations involving human users, please remember that human beings, unlike machine parts, do not come in standard sizes. Not all men are 5 foot 11 inches tall and not all women are 5 foot 2 inches. Design for the taller and smaller people, too.

Speeding Up Floating-Point Calculations

One problem often encountered in simulations has been slow processing caused by repetitive floating-point calculations. In some cases, floating-point calculations simply cannot be avoided. In these cases, the only solution is a fast CPU with a good math coprocessor. In other cases, however, even when fractional interim values are desired or needed, these can be derived using integer rather than floating-point operations, by the simple expedient of limiting accuracy to what is actually required.

For example, suppose that an algorithm that is called repeatedly (several thousand times per simulation cycle) needs to calculate a radial distance using `pi`. Since the result of the calculation will be cast as an integer and used as an index to a data array, the calculation does not need to be carried out to ten or twelve decimal places, or even three or four

Continued on next page

places. Therefore, instead of using a floating-point value for π, such as 3.14159, the calculation can be carried out using integer operations (which are faster) using the value 402 (equals $\pi * 128$), and then dividing the result by simply shifting the value seven places to the right.

The bit-shift operation is considerably faster than any decimal division, and the entire process is markedly faster than floating-point operations, while (within limits) achieving the same result.

Theoretical System Simulations

Physical realities—whether they are living systems or mechanical constructs—offer their own physical appearances as a basis for graphic simulation. Other systems, however, which may be theoretical or nonphysical, do not offer quite the same convenience; instead these require imagination and artistry in deciding how to display the information generated by a simulation.

As an example, the operations of a computer chip are often simulated by a computer program, particularly during the design process for a new chip. During design, two quite different elements are taken into consideration: the physical and the electronic layouts for the chip.

Of these, the fabricated layout of the chip is relatively simple: How many circuits can be fabricated within a given area of silicon? The electronic layout, on the other hand, is not only more complex but is also directly affected by the physical layout. In this respect, considerations include the signal path between various elements and, therefore, the signal time between two components; how the components interact electronically; what leakage currents and capacitive effects must be accounted for; and, far from least, how the various components function cybernetically.

So, how is a system this complex simulated? And how is the simulation shown graphically?

First, no single simulation—graphic or otherwise—will suffice (except, possibly for a very simple chip), because of the level of physical complexity in contemporary monolithic integrated circuits. Instead (referring strictly to the physical layout), small portions of the chip might be simulated on the screen. Or, for an overview, color-coded areas might represent repetitive circuit areas or areas dedicated to some specific function.

The electronic functions, however, are not this easily coded. They would probably require several different simulations and displays to handle the various elements. For example, a histogram might be used to show signal-path times for different elements; remember, with today's high-speed chips, even the paths required for clock pulses can be critical, and more than one engineer has vainly expressed a wish for faster electricity. Still other elements are even less easily displayed. Thus, in many cases, instead of attempting to show the simulations directly, only the results of simulations are shown.

Computer chip and other electronic circuitry designs are only one area involving nonphysical simulations. There are other valid areas that have even less connection to traditional physical reality. Some are simply constructs of our own observations. For example, consider a simulation of the population growth patterns using the Malthusian equation:

$$P_{n+1} = R * P_n * (1 - P_n)$$

where R represents the growth rate for successive populations (P). Okay, population grows linearly, doesn't it? So, wouldn't a simple line graph be appropriate for this equation?

If the whole suggestion sounds like a loaded question, you're right—it is.

First, after a half-dozen initial steps, the equation given is anything but linear. And, second, this particular simulation will yield results unlike anything you might normally expect. In fact, the Malthusian equation is a member of a loose group of formulas referred to as *strange attractors* because of the curves generated over successive reiterations from what initially appear to be only scattered points. The equation produces an interesting simulation, and simulations can show interesting results that would not be visible simply by examining long columns of numbers.

TIP

To experiment with the Malthusian equation, one convenient method is to plot successive points (P_n and P_{n+1}) as x- and y-coordinate pairs. After a few thousand generations, the resulting plots will begin to show an interesting curve. Next, by varying the growth rate R (try the range from 2.3 to 3.8 in steps of 0.1 or smaller), a single curve becomes an interesting group of curves, complete with inflections and bifurcation points.

In other cases, such as plotting radiation-intensity patterns from a broadcast antenna or reception sensitivity for a receiver, the results are lobes. In other instances, the results are landscapes ranging from smoothly undulating hills and valleys to fields of jagged peaks and crevasses.

Regardless of the source of the data plotted or the algorithms used for a simulation, the visual presentation is not simply a gimmick to impress board members and visiting bigwigs but a very valuable tool to allow the use of our own most sensitive tools: color eyesight, superior image processing, and unequaled pattern recognition. Graphics can aid in the simulation of all types of dynamic systems, including both physical and nonphysical systems. The *Forest* demo discussed in this chapter and included on the CD that accompanies this book is a simple example. To learn more, expand the demo to experiment with various effects.

In the next chapter, we will conclude our discussion of graphics programming with a look at graphics printing operations.

# CHAPTER THIRTY-TWO

Graphics Printing Operations

■ Procedures for copying images from a display context to a printer context

■ Checks for a color or black-and-white printer

■ Gray-scale definition

■ Gray-scale printing enhancements

■ Considerations for color printing

Being able to print a graphic image is almost as important as (or perhaps more important than) creating the image in the first place. The tools demonstrated in this chapter provide the basis for such facilities using both black-and-white and gray-scale color conversion.

If and how you use these features depends entirely on the needs of your applications. Most likely, you will need to adapt these features and perhaps also add some controls specific to your application. Alternatively, if you require only an occasional screen capture, you might prefer to combine the printer-output procedures with one of the screen-capture processes described in Chapter 28.

Incidentally, if you have access to color-reproduction facilities, you might also consider adding provisions for printing color separations; that is, printing separate red, green, and blue images for use as color screens in conventional printing processes.

Printer Operations

In many ways, Windows has greatly facilitated graphics image handling, with capabilities that range from providing hardware-independent graphics display environments to translating between different image formats. Just as Windows provides support for a wide variety of displays, it also provides support for a wide variety of printers, ranging from dot-matrix printers to all types of laser printers.

Furthermore, provisions exist (using the `BitBlt` or `StretchBlt` function) for copying images from a display context to a printer context, and from there to the printer itself. On the whole, Windows includes almost everything you need for hard-copy output of graphics images.

Unfortunately, almost is not everything. One fly remains in the ointment: Although most monitors are color, color printers are still less common than black-and-white printers. Windows does not offer any automatic solutions for printing color images to a black-and-white printer. As a general rule, when you direct a color image to a monochrome printer without any provisions for shading, the printer will print all colors except white as a solid black, which is generally not a very useful result.

Still, if no automatic solution has been provided, a custom solution is not beyond the realm of the possible and practical, as will be shown momentarily. But before tackling the solution, the first step is to understand the problem.

Win.INI versus Up-to-Date Printer Information

During installation, Windows offers an option to select one or more printers. When you choose printers to install, Windows copies the appropriate printer drivers to the Windows directory and lists these drivers in the registry.

NOTE As explained in Chapter 17, the registry is a 32-bit Unicode data file, which you can access via the Registry Editor (RegEdit.EXE or RegEdit32.EXE).

Under Windows 3.1, the system stores the printer driver information in the Win.INI file, where a series of flag strings are used to locate and identify installed devices. The following is a fragment of a Win.INI file:

```
[windows]
...
device=HP LaserJet Series II,HPPCL,LPT1:
...
[devices]
HP LaserJet Series II=HPPCL,LPT1:
...
[HP LaserJet Series II,LPT1]
Paper Size=1
Number of Cartridges=1
...
[PrinterPorts]
HP LaserJet Series II=HPPCL,LPT1:,15,45
```

Under Windows 98, the old printer-control features continue to be implemented, even though the Win.INI file itself is obsolete. However, obsolete does not mean absent, and you probably have a Win.INI file in your Windows 98 directory. The problem is that any application that expects to find printer information in the Win.INI file may very well find that information, but the information may be completely out-of-date.

For example, in my own Windows 98 system, the Win.INI file identifies my system printer as an HP LaserJet, even though I installed a different printer after I switched to Windows 95, more than three years ago. On the other hand, the version of the Win.INI file in my Windows NT directory, which was not carried forward from an older Windows 3.x installation, does not contain any printer references.

The point is that applications written for Windows 98 should always use the new printer-selection mechanisms and not rely on the old handling methods. Older methods are highly likely to access outdated or incorrect information.

The good news is that you do not need to write a printer-selection process for your applications. Instead, you can use the default printer-selection mechanisms supplied by Windows.

> **TIP**
>
> All applications created using Visual C++ and the AppWizard are supplied with a default File menu that contains Print, Print Preview, and Page Setup options, as well as default provisions to connect to the appropriate handlers and dialog boxes. The advantage is that this is all default code, which does not need to be duplicated. A common dialog box is provided for printer selection, including capabilities to connect to network printers. Users do not need to decipher a new selection mechanism.

Printer Queries

The Windows system and the MFC classes handle the task of getting and listing the available printers for you. However, certain applications may need to get other information about printer capabilities and limitations.

The *DC* demo, discussed in Chapter 23, demonstrates how to query the system device drivers and obtain information about device capabilities and limitations. In the *DC* demo's demonstration, all of the information available about a device is shown. Displaying all of these data elements requires a relatively long list of information requests. In other cases, instead of asking for everything available, you can make a more moderate request, restricting queries to only the appropriate or needed data.

The GrayImage Demo: Sending a Bitmap to a Printer

The *GrayImage* demo demonstrates both simple printer access and the grayscaling of images. A number of the features in the GrayImgView.CPP section, such as selecting and displaying a bitmap image, should be familiar from demos discussed in earlier chapters, such as *Shades* and *ViewPCX*. The two processes of interest in *GrayImage* are for drawing an image to the printer context and for converting an image from black and white to a printed, half-tone gray. For now, we'll begin with the procedures for sending an image to a printer.

NOTE   The *GrayImage* demo is included on the CD accompanying this book, in the Chapter 32 folder.

The Printer Context

In previous examples, when a bitmap is presented in the client window, the bitmap image (file) is read, using the procedures demonstrated in those chapters. Then, when it's time to update (redraw) the client window, the bitmap palette is selected, a compatible memory device context is obtained, and the handle to the bitmap is used to copy the bitmap to the memory device context. The *GrayImage* demo uses essentially the same procedures to retrieve the bitmap:

```
void CGrayImageView::OnDraw(CDC* pDC)
{
    ...
    if( m_hBitmap )
    {
        if( m_pPal ) pOldPalette = pDC->SelectPalette( m_pPal, FALSE );
        nBitPxl = pDC->GetDeviceCaps( BITSPIXEL );
        nPlanes = pDC->GetDeviceCaps( PLANES );
        pDCMem = new CDC();
        pDCMem->CreateCompatibleDC( pDC );
        pDCMem->SelectObject( m_hBitmap );
```

In previous examples, once the bitmap is in the memory context, the `BitBlt` function is called to copy the image from the memory context to the display context—the client window.

```
        pDC->BitBlt( 0, 0, m_bmWidth, m_bmHeight, pDCMem, 0, 0, SRCCOPY );
```

And, after copying the image to the display, a little bit of cleanup is performed to take care of the palette and the memory device context.

```
        if( m_pPal )
        {
            pDC->SelectPalette( pOldPalette, FALSE );
            pDC->RealizePalette();
        }
        delete pDCMem;
    }
```

Under previous versions of Windows, a separate procedure would have been required to copy a bitmap to a printer device. This print function would need provisions to query the installed printers, find out what the printer capabilities were, select a printer, get a printer device context, and finally write the image (or other data) to the printer queue.

Now, however, this task is greatly simplified because, when you select the printer icon from the toolbar or select Print from the File menu (assuming the application is being created with the AppWizard or another development tool), the OnDraw method is called with a pointer to a device context for output. For a printer-output operation, the only change from refreshing the screen is that the device context is a pointer to a printer context instead of a screen context.

Beyond this provision, the OnDraw function is expected to write to the printer in essentially the same fashion as it writes to the video display. The difference is that some of the output methods preferred for the video display may not be compatible with the printer context, even when writing to a color printer.

A Check for a Color or Monochrome Printer

Given the current popularity of color printers, not anticipating the presence of a color printer could be a serious error. If you simply attempt to provide gray-scaled output for hard-copy and the default color provisions for the video display, the result will be a blank sheet of paper when a color printer is encountered.

To understand why this happens, we need to take another look at the default process to copy the image to the screen, shown in the previous code fragment as:

```
//=== copy the bitmap to the screen ==(NORMAL)============
pDCMem->SelectObject( m_hBitmap );
pDC->BitBlt( 0, 0, m_bmWidth, m_bmHeight, pDCMem, 0, 0, SRCCOPY );
```

Here, pDCMem is a memory context that is compatible with the device context supplied, pDC, when the OnDraw function is called by Windows. As long as pDC is a video context, pDCMem will be compatible with the HBITMAP object, m_hBitmap.

If pDC is a monochrome printer context, some degree of compatibility is still maintained. However, in most cases, if you use the SelectObject and BitBlt functions, the result will be that all colors (except white) are treated as black—not exactly the printout desired.

You can, however, persuade the monochrome printer to render approximate half-tones (gray-scale) by using the SetDIBitsToDevice function instead of the SelectObject and BitBlt functions. The only problem with this approach is that the gray-scale image produced will probably be rather coarse, which is the real reason for the gray-scale conversion routine discussed presently.

The next case occurs when the SelectObject and BitBlt functions attempt to print to a color context. The pDC context supplied by Windows for the printer drawing operation is normally a 32-bit per pixel scheme, which results in the pDCMem–> SelectObject function failing, simply because the pDCMem context (created to be compatible with pDC) and the bitmap are not compatible. The result is a blank sheet of paper.

However, by using the SetDIBitsToDevice function and a pointer to the bitmap bits instead of a handle to a bitmap, you can avoid these potential problems. SetDIBitsToDevice can produce a color image on the screen, a native gray-scale image on a monochrome printer, and a color image on a color printer (leaving only the question of producing a better gray-scale image for our special routine). These rendering options and devices are summarized in Table 32.1.

TABLE 32.1:   Color-Image Rendering Functions

Function/Device	SelectObject/BitBlt	SetDIBitsToDevice
Screen	Produces color image	Produces color image
Monochrome Printer	All colors except white treated as black	Colors rendered using native (printer) gray-scale
Color printer	Blank (no image)	Color image

So, why are we still using SelectObject and BitBlt? Simply because, when compatible with the desired operation, they are faster than the SetDIBitsToDevice function. Of course, for most video systems (printers are simply slower in any case) and in most cases, either route is sufficiently fast that the results will be indistinguishable, making the choice a moot point.

The revised OnDraw response begins, as before, by checking the bits-per-pixel and number of color planes to determine if you have a color or monochrome device.

```
if( ( nBitPxl * nPlanes ) > 1 )
{
    if( m_pPal )
```

```
{
    pOldPalette = pDC->SelectPalette( m_pPal, FALSE );
    pDC->RealizePalette();
}
```

If this is a color device (either the screen or a printer), you want to select the palette for the image and realize it (make it active).

The next step is the critical decision. Since you don't know, without awkward tests, whether this is a printer context or a video screen, you can simply attempt the SelectObject operation.

```
if( pDCMem->SelectObject( m_hBitmap ) )
```

If SelectObject succeeds, you know that you have a compatible context and assume that this is the video device. Because the context is compatible (the bitmap was selected correctly), calling BitBlt will copy the image to the device.

```
pDC->BitBlt( 0, 0, m_bmWidth, m_bmHeight, pDCMem, 0, 0, SRCCOPY );
```

The alternative is that SelectObject failed, which probably means that this is a printer device context but still one supporting color. In this case, you want to call SetDIBitsToDevice, supplying the device-context handle (hDC) from the supplied device context, specifying the image size and position information, and providing pointers to the bitmap bits and to the bitmap information structure.

```
else
    SetDIBitsToDevice( pDC->m_hDC, 0, 0, m_bmWidth, m_bmHeight,
                       0, 0, 0, m_bmHeight,
                       m_pBits, m_pBmInfo, DIB_RGB_COLORS );
```

The final specification, DIB_RGB_COLORS, simply says how the color data is to be treated; it says that the bitmap information contains RGB colors in the color table. The alternative is DIB_PAL_COLORS, suggesting that the device palette should be used, which normally would not be appropriate.

NOTE   In many cases, especially when printing a hard-copy of an image, you may want to be able to resize the image. To resize the image on screen, the StretchBlt function is the ideal choice. But for the printer context, just as SelectObject/BitBlt fails, SelectObject/StretchBlt will also fail. Instead, for a printer device context, the choice would be to use the StretchBlt function to copy the image between memory contexts, resizing the image while doing so. Then, after resizing the image, use the SetDIBitsToDevice function to copy the resized image to the printer.

Last, to clean up, `SelectPalette` is called again to restore the original palette.

```
    if( m_pPal )
    {
        pDC->SelectPalette( pOldPalette, FALSE );
        pDC->RealizePalette();
    }
}
else
    ... use gray-scale conversion to monochrome printer
```

Image Gray-Scaling

So what do you do when you need to output to a black-and-white printer but want something better than the relatively coarse default gray-scale supplied by most printer devices? The solution is to create a custom gray-scale by translating each color pixel in the original image to an array of black-and-white pixels. However, this also means that you must enlarge the original. If this is not convenient or practical, there remains the option of using the native gray-scaling.

Translating Colors to Gray Intensities

The first consideration in translating colors to grays is that, for the video display, colors are described by three digital values: red, green, and blue. Thus, using the `RGBTriplet` format, each of these color components has a value in the range 0 to 255 and the corresponding display ranges from black to full intensity. The result you see on the screen is a combination of the three primary colors. The relative intensities of each primary color, as well as the overall intensity, determine the "color" or hue perceived.

But the human eye is not linear. It responds differently to each of the three primary colors, with the strongest response (59 percent) to green. Our second strongest response is to red (30 percent), and our response to blue is the weakest (at 11 percent). Therefore, to translate red, green, and blue intensities into a gray scale, the absolute intensities of the three components must be weighted to match or, more accurately, the relative darkness of each component must be weighted to produce the appropriate portion of black ink on the page.

NOTE For more details about translating colors to grays and creating gray-scale palettes, see Chapter 23, which covers Windows color handling and color palettes.

Defining Gray-Scale Patterns

Before matching colors to gray equivalents, it will help to have a range of grays for the matches. Thus, before writing the matching algorithm, the first step is to create a gray-scale for the printer. For demonstration purposes, we use a simple 16-step (4×4) gray-scale. However, for your own applications, you could implement a 25-step (5×5), 36-step (6×6), 64-step (8×8), or even 256-step (16×16) gray-scale.

NOTE The choice of a square gray pattern is dictated by convenience but is not quite an absolute. Using grays that are not squares, however, would require quite different handling and mapping and would produce distortion in the output image.

Figure 32.1 shows 16 4×4 matrices, ranging from full black to complete white. A sample of the resulting gray-scale appears below each 4×4 matrix.

FIGURE 32.1:

A gray-scale as a matrix series

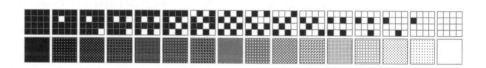

WORD hex values providing binary descriptions of each pattern are 0x0000, 0x0400, 0x0401, 0x0501, 0x0505, 0x0525, 0xA425, 0xA5A5, 0xA7A5, 0xE5B5, 0xF5B6, 0xF5F5, 0xF5FD, 0xF7FF, 0xFFFF. As you may notice, one possible permutation of blacks and whites—0xF7FD (nine black to seven white, distributed among the 16 squares)—has been omitted.

These 16 patterns were selected to provide an even distribution and to avoid as much as possible any undesired elements, such as lines, herringbone patterns, or other artifacts.

Calculating a Gray-Scale

As an alternative to creating a predefined gray-scale, you can create a less rigorous (and somewhat more versatile) gray-scale by calculation. In its simplest form, each color pixel is mapped to a square grid in the printer context, as described in the previous section. However, instead of mapping the color pixel as a predefined pattern, each point in the square for the pixel is assigned a black or a white value in proportion to the calculated gray balance and the size of the square. In place of a predetermined pattern, you use a pseudo-random generator (such as C's `random` function) to assign the appropriate percentage of black pixels and white pixels in an essentially random pattern.

In general, this approach works best with a relatively large matrix for each pixel (8×8 or larger) and does not require an exact match between the range of grays used and the size of the pattern matrix. Of course, there are also a few disadvantages, such as a slight loss of edge definition, a need to keep the range of grays used relatively close to the matrix size, and some increase in mapping times because of increased complexity. But overall, the advantages can outweigh the disadvantages when wider ranges of grays are required.

Mapping Color Images to Gray Patterns

The process of mapping color images to gray patterns begins with a requirement for several new variables in the declaration, starting with `hTargetBM`, which is declared as an `HBITMAP` and serves as a buffer for the gray-scaled image during conversion. `pDCMem` and `pDCSrc` are handles for device contexts used while the color image is converted to a gray-scale image.

```
CDC       *pDCMem, *pDCSrc;
UINT      i, j, m, n;
int       nBitPxl, nPlanes, nGrayWd, nGrayHt;
BYTE      rVal, gVal, bVal, Gray;
DWORD     Color;
HBITMAP   hTargetBM;
WORD      Mask,
          GrayPal[] =                   // gray-scale masks
              { 0x0000, 0x0400, 0x0401, 0x0501,
                0x0505, 0x0525, 0xA425, 0xA5A5,
                0xA7A5, 0xE5B5, 0xF5B6, 0xF5F5,
                0xF5FD, 0xF7FD, 0xF7FF, 0xFFFF  };
```

The GrayPal (gray-palette) array (shown earlier in Figure 32.1) is declared here as an array of WORD.

Next, after we have decided that the device context supplied is a monochrome device, the nGrayWd and nGrayHt values are calculated.

```
else
{       // if this is a monochrome device - i.e., a printer -
        //      get the max size supported by the device
    nGrayWd = min( (int)(4 * m_bmWidth), pDC->GetDeviceCaps( HORZRES ) );
    nGrayHt = min( (int)(4 * m_bmHeight), pDC->GetDeviceCaps( VERTRES ) );
        //      and create a gray-scaled bitmap to print
    hTargetBM = CreateBitmap( nGrayWd, nGrayHt, nPlanes, nBitPxl, NULL );
```

Our only restriction here is that we wish to ensure that the image we print is not larger that the output device supports. But we also need to make the output size 16 times larger than the original, providing space for a 4×4 gray pattern for each pixel in the original image.

Having calculated the necessary size, a temporary bitmap, hTargetBM, is defined with the necessary width and height and with the color planes (1) and bits per pixel (1) set for a monochrome image.

Next, if the bitmap creation fails, we simply abort the print operation with a minimal explanation. In your own applications, you would probably want to include a more informative explanation and some alternatives or suggestions for accommodations.

```
        if( ! hTargetBM )
        {
            ErrorMsg( "Bitmap creation error" );
            return;
        }
```

If the bitmap creation is successful, we proceed by calling the SelectObject function to select the (blank) target bitmap into the memory device context, which is compatible with the printer device.

```
    pDCMem->SelectObject( hTargetBM );
        // create a device context compatible with the
        //      (color) display context, not the printer context
    pDCSrc = new CDC();
    pDCSrc->CreateCompatibleDC( GetDC() );
        //      but select the gray-scaled bitmap to the context
    pDCSrc->SelectObject( m_hBitmap );
```

We also need a second, temporary device context, pDCSrc, which is compatible with the screen display. This context is provided by calling CreateCompatible-DC with GetDC as an argument to supply the display context. The original bitmap is selected here in the second device context, where we do not need to be concerned about compatibility.

At this point, we have a blank bitmap—four times wider and four times taller than the original—selected in the memory context, pDCMem, and the color bitmap selected in the temporary context, pDCSrc, which is also a memory device context. The actual conversion from color to gray-scale works between these two memory device contexts; that is, using pDCSrc as the source and writing the output to pDCMem.

```
for( i=0; i<m_bmHeight; i++ )
    for( j=0; j<m_bmWidth; j++ )
    {
        Color = pDCSrc->GetPixel( j, i );
        rVal = (unsigned char)( LOBYTE( HIWORD( Color ) ) );
        gVal = (unsigned char)( HIBYTE( LOWORD( Color ) ) );
        bVal = (unsigned char)( LOBYTE( LOWORD( Color ) ) );
```

Within a double loop (height and width), the color bitmap is scanned to determine R, G, and B values for each pixel. To convert these color values to a gray value, two algorithms are provided: a TrueGray algorithm and an unweighted conversion.

```
if( theApp.m_bTrueGray )
    Gray = (BYTE)( (UINT)(float)( ( rVal * 0.30 ) / 16 ) +
                   (UINT)(float)( ( gVal * 0.59 ) / 16 ) +
                   (UINT)(float)( ( bVal * 0.11 ) / 16 ) );
else
    Gray = (BYTE)( ( rVal + gVal + bVal ) / 48 );
```

The TrueGray algorithm produces a rather dark printed image; the unweighted algorithm results in a lighter printed image. For a screen display, the TrueGray algorithm offers the better match. For printed output, the unweighted one is preferable.

TIP   As an alternative, the application could use a logarithmic scale to keep blacks black and whites white but shift most colors toward the light end of the scale. You can try implementing this in the sample program if you're interested.

Once a color value has been converted to a gray intensity, the DWORD Mask, from the GrayPal array of predefined patterns, must be written to the output bitmap in pDCMem, as a 4×4 array, not as a linear string of bits. Remember that each pixel in the original is being written as a square of pixels in the output.

```
Mask = GrayPal[Gray];
    //=== write gray mask to color bitmap context =========
for( m=0; m<4; m++ )
    for( n=0; n<4; n++ )
    {
        if( ( Mask >> ((m*4)+n) ) & 0x0001 )
            pDCMem->SetPixel( (j*4)+m, (i*4)+n, 0x00FFFFFF );
        else
            pDCMem->SetPixel( (j*4)+m, (i*4)+n, 0x00000000 );
    }
```

To write the output pixels, which are still written as full RGB values, the Mask value is tested bit-wise. The true bits are written as white, and the false bits are written as black.

And, finally, after the output bitmap is prepared, the BitBlt operation copies the image from the memory context, pDCMem, to the printer device context, pDC, where Windows assumes the rest of the task of handling the actual output.

```
    }
    //=== now copy from color context to printer context =====
pDC->BitBlt( 0, 0, nGrayWd, nGrayHt, pDCMem, 0, 0, SRCCOPY );
    //===    the result is printed as black and white =========
DeleteObject( hTargetBM );
delete pDCSrc;
}
```

Once the BitBlt operation is handled, a minimum of cleanup is required. We only need to delete the target bitmap, hTargetBM, and the pDCSrc device context.

Overall, this may appear to be a rather roundabout fashion to map a color image to a gray-scaled equivalent. Still, this process does have several advantages, including these:

- There is no need for far long pointers to index bitmaps greater than 64KB.

- There is no need to convert palette color indexes into RGB values.

- On the whole, processing times are very fast.

Incidentally, as you may notice, the color-to-gray conversion itself tends to be considerably faster than the process of copying the gray image to the Print Manager.

Figure 32.2 shows an actual printout created using the process described here to convert the 256-color original Modern.BMP to a gray-scaled hard copy. The original output was executed on a 300-dpi laser printer.

FIGURE 32.2:

A true gray-scaled printout

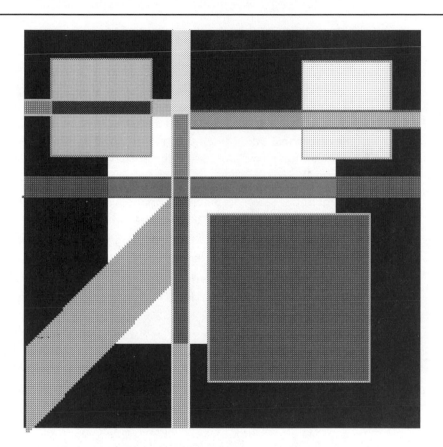

Improved Gray-Scale Printing

In the *GrayImage* demo (in the OnDraw method), the BitBlt API is used to copy a gray image to a monochrome printer. However, the BitBlt API does not include any provisions for resizing the image. As an alternative, you can use the StretchBlt API to create any size output image desired, and you might use CRect coordinates derived from the printer context to size the bitmap to fit the entire page. However, for several reasons, this may not always be an optimal choice. In actual graphics printing applications, you may want to improve the output in the following ways:

- Allow a specific size.

- Preserve the vertical and horizontal proportions.

- Avoid plaiding in the printed image.

Fortunately, all of these conditions are relatively easy to fulfill.

The first objective, a precise size, is simplicity itself. In the StretchDIBits operation, replace the page size with the desired image size. Just remember to convert from inches or millimeters (or whatever unit you're using) into logical-device coordinates (pixels or printer dots). For this purpose, device-resolution information is available using the GetDeviceCaps function (see Chapter 23).

The second objective, maintaining proportion, is equally easy. For the maximum image size, compare the horizontal and vertical size ratios, and then adjust the greater ratio to maintain image proportions.

Avoiding plaiding is perhaps the most difficult objective, simply because this provision is not completely compatible with either of the first two. Even so, in execution, it is not exceedingly difficult. In practice, the simplest solution is to size the image so that the dots in the output image are some multiple of the original pixel size (or, for gray-scales, some multiple of the gray-scaled pixel size). Thus, for a 200×200 pixel image converted into a 16-level gray-scale, the gray image is 800×800 pixels and could be printed as 800×800, 1600×1600, or 2400×2400 dots. Assuming a 300-dpi laser printer, the largest (2400-dot) image would be 8 inches wide.

NOTE For dot-matrix printers with lower resolutions, the choices and possibilities are more restricted. Typesetting printers and many of the newer laser printer designs offer more versatility.

The only real problem is found with devices that lack a 1-to-1 horizontal-to-vertical aspect ratio. For example, some dot-matrix printers might provide a horizontal resolution of 96 dpi, while their vertical resolution is 180 dpi, for a ratio of 96-to-180 or 8-to-15. This is not an easy ratio to fit without distorting the image proportions. Fortunately, most laser and ink-jet printers do have 1-to-1 aspect ratios.

Gray Images Printed in Color

In some cases, you might need to print a color hard-copy from a gray-scale original. For example, infrared photography images, particularly video images, are captured as gray-scale. In similar fashion, low-light (night-scope) images, NMR, and even CAT scan images do not have inherent color information but are gathered as images scaled by intensity, density, or a synthetic scale.

With infrared images, the problem is that we do not see in this portion of the spectrum, even if we did have printers or monitors capable of displaying these frequencies. But, at the same time, a black-and-white image is less informative than a color image.

In all of these cases, a common solution is to produce a false-color image in which colors are assigned (arbitrarily or otherwise) to various intensity ranges. How colors are assigned is subject to several considerations:

- What is the available range of information? How many gray, intensity, or other levels of information are available in the original image or data?

- How many colors can be displayed? Those who are working with more sophisticated forms of imaging equipment are rarely limited in their display capabilities and can usually assume at least a 256-color display capacity. However, printers may be more restricted in their color ranges.

- How large a range of color is actually needed? Do you need to use 256 colors or will a simpler palette of 16 colors serve just as well or even better?

- What color palette will best serve to display the information? In general, converting intensity to color is done to make certain characteristics stand out for easy identification and recognition.

As an example, one intensity-to-color development was done as a color printer driver for a company involved in infrared imaging The image was captured using a special (and expensive) video camera and capture board and held a wide range of intensity data (at least 256 levels). The limiting factor was not the video display but the printer, which supported only a 16-color palette. Also, the printer palette needed to accommodate a background color that was used for low-temperature areas in the image. The color chosen for the background was a light-blue palette entry for a neutral backgrounds. Black was used as a temperature threshold marker. Temperatures (intensities) below a certain level were mapped to violets, blues, and greens, advancing to black, and then to reds and yellows to show the higher intensities.

Color Images Printed in Color

In recent years, a variety of color printers have appeared on the market, ranging from paint-jet printers that produce medium-quality color images to dye-diffusion printers that produce more expensive but near-photographic-quality color images.

Unlike video displays, which use an RGB color scheme (as explained in Chapter 24), all printers use the complementary CYM (cyan-yellow-magenta) color scheme to print color. The complementary inks absorb everything except cyan, yellow, or magenta, respectively. But, by combining yellow and cyan, everything except green is absorbed, and the result is a green image. In like fashion, reds, blues, and all other shades are created by varying the combination and amount of each ink to leave only the desired color reflected. White, of course, is provided by the paper without ink; black uses all three inks to absorb all colors.

To the general relief of programmers, Windows supplies drivers for almost all printer types, including color printers. As for those printers that are not currently supported, most manufacturers are busy developing Windows drivers for them. Of course, there may be a few who are blithely attempting to ignore the new paradigm, but this may also be taken as a benchmark of their probable future and your own future expectations from such companies. Still, the usual cautions apply: Check available support before investing in a specialty printer, not after.

In general, printing a color image is quite similar to printing a monochrome image, as demonstrated in the *GrayImage* demo discussed in this chapter. The one difference is that no color palette is written to the output device context for monochrome images. For color printers, a palette must be supplied.

Before supplying a palette, you will need to ask the printer what its palette capacity is and supply a palette of the appropriate size. For limited palette sizes, you may need to construct an appropriate palette. Still, you can have a lot of fun simply experimenting, or if you're too busy, turn a teenager (or pre-teen) loose on the problem and see what he or she comes up with.

The *GrayImage* demo included on the CD accompanying this book provides default handling for a color printer as well as gray-scaled output to a monochrome device.

The description of graphics printing in this chapter brings us to the end of Part 4 of this book. In this part, we have explored all the topics related to handling graphics in Windows 98 applications. In the next chapter, we will begin our coverage of information exchange with a look at metafile operations.

PART 5

Exchanging Information between Applications

Metafile Operations

- ■ Advantages of metafiles

- ■ Metafiles written to a memory context

- ■ Metafile playback

- ■ Metafiles written to disk files

- ■ Temporary metafiles

- ■ The structure of metafiles

A *metafile* is a method of storing the operations used to create an image. After you create a metafile, you can replay the operations recorded in it to re-create the original image, in much the same fashion as you can replay a CD or tape to re-create a voice or a piece of music.

Although this may sound interesting, it does not seem particularly useful. Ergo, what good are metafiles?

As with all simple explanations, the preceding description was both accurate and misleading. We'll begin this chapter by talking about some possible applications of metafiles, and you'll see that they can be very useful. Then we'll go into the details of recording and playing back metafiles.

Metafile Uses

One of the principal purposes of metafile operations is to exchange images between applications. You can do this directly, using the clipboard operations (described in Chapter 34) or via file operations, as demonstrated in this chapter.

For example, an accounting program could construct a business graph while recording a metafile of the operations involved, then pass the resulting metafile to a text editor, where the image could be re-created for inclusion in a report. This same metafile can also be "played" directly to the printer, without first creating and copying a bitmap image for the purpose.

Another use for metafiles is to record a calculated graphic (image), permitting it to be re-created or duplicated without the need of repeating the calculations. As an intrinsically calculation-intensive example, consider applying this process to a fractal image. The metafile of the fractal could be replayed in a fraction of the time required for the original calculations.

Another advantage of metafiles lies in the storage space required for them versus image files. For example, a scant 150-byte metafile can easily replace a 3970-byte image file. Disk storage may not be not a consideration, but even with 33.6 and 56Kps modems, image-transmission times are still an important factor in more than a few circumstances.

In some cases, metafiles may be preferred over DIB (device-independent bitmap) files. Although DIBs have advantages over conventional image files, metafiles are even less device-dependent and adapt automatically to the device context where they are replayed.

Metafiles are not miracle solutions and will not immediately solve all of your programming problems. But metafiles do offer possibilities. And, perhaps this list of uses has already suggested a possibility or two relevant to your own applications? If you don't have any ideas yet, you may by the time you finish reading this chapter.

The PenDraw 6 Demo: Creating a Metafile

 Because metafile operations are easier to demonstrate than to explain, we'll go through the steps to record a process for a metafile, using an image and a process that should be familiar to you by now. The *PenDraw6* demo creates the same seven-pointed star that was used to illustrate fill and brush operations in the chapters in Part 4. This demo completes the image by enclosing the star with a circle provided by the Ellipse function.

NOTE   The *PenDraw6* demo is included on the CD that accompanies this book, in the Chapter 33 folder.

The Metafile Device Context

The initial requirement is to calculate a series of points describing the seven-pointed star.

```
for( i=j=0; i<7; i++, j=(j+3)%7 )
{
    pt[i].x = (int)( sin( j*PI2/7 ) * 100 );
    pt[i].y = (int)( cos( j*PI2/7 ) * 100 );
}
hdc = BeginPaint( hwnd, &ps );
hPen = CreatePen( PS_NULL, 1, OL );
SelectObject( hdc, hPen );
SelectObject( hdc, GetStockObject( LTGRAY_BRUSH ) );
Ellipse( hdcMeta, -100, -100, 100, 100 );
```

After calculating the points, we create and select a null pen and standard brush (these operations are covered in Part 4). We draw the enclosing circle first, using the null pen and filled by the light-gray brush, to complete the background portion of the image.

Next, still using the null pen, we swap the light-gray brush for a dark-gray one, select the fill mode, and call the Polygon function to draw the star inside the light-gray disk.

```
SelectObject( hdc, GetStockObject( DKGRAY_BRUSH ) );
    SetPolyFillMode( hdc, ALTERNATE );
    Polygon( hdc, pt, 7 );
    DeleteObject( hPen );
    EndPaint( hdc, &ps );
```

Finally, we delete the null pen.

Executing this same operation to record the process for a metafile is not much different but requires two new variables:

```
static HANDLE hMetaFile;
HDC           hdc, hdcMeta;
```

The two new variables are a static handle, hMetaFile, and a device-context handle, hdcMeta. The declaration of this latter variable, hdcMeta, may have already suggested a major element of the changes necessary: the substitution of the hdcMeta device context for the more usual hdc context.

But simply changing the device-context ID isn't enough. A more important change appears immediately following:

```
for( i=j=0; i<7; i++, j=(j+3)%7 )
{
    pt[i].x = (int)( sin( j*PI2/7 ) * 100 );
    pt[i].y = (int)( cos( j*PI2/7 ) * 100 );
}
hdcMeta = CreateMetaFile( NULL );
```

Replacing the familiar BeginPaint (or GetDC) instruction, the CreateMetaFile API function provides the metafile equivalent and, in similar fashion, returns a device-context handle. The big difference is that this handle is directed to a device context that is not associated with any physical device. At the same time, since the single parameter has been specified as NULL, the metafile created will exist in memory only; that is, as a temporary memory file.

NOTE   Later in the chapter, you'll see another form in which the metafile data is written to a physical (disk) file. But, even limited to a memory context, the metafile can still be written to and replayed.

Once the metafile device context has been created, the **hdcMeta** handle can be substituted for the earlier **hdc** handle in the drawing instructions, which now appear thus:

```
hPen = CreatePen( PS_NULL, 1, 0L );
SelectObject( hdcMeta, hPen );
SelectObject( hdcMeta, GetStockObject( LTGRAY_BRUSH ) );
Ellipse( hdcMeta, -100, -100, 100, 100 );
SelectObject( hdcMeta, GetStockObject( DKGRAY_BRUSH ) );
SetPolyFillMode( hdcMeta, ALTERNATE );
Polygon( hdcMeta, pt, 7 );
```

Except for the change in the device context, the drawing operations are precisely the same as those previously directed to the screen context. The image itself, however, has not been drawn to the screen; instead, only the GDI operations necessary to draw the image have been recorded.

Metafile Cleanup Operations

Rather than using the EndPaint (or ReleaseDC) instruction when you are finished using the device context, you use the CloseMetaFile instruction.

```
hMetaFile = CloseMetaFile( hdcMeta );
DeleteObject( hPen );
```

The call to the CloseMetaFile instruction, unlike an EndPaint or ReleaseDC instruction, returns a handle to the metafile itself (which is currently in memory), rather than to a device context. At this point, this metafile handle can be used to replay the same GDI instructions just calculated. But, unlike the original image, which would have been drawn to match the display context, the GDI instructions can be played back to any device context and will create an image appropriate to the device context.

Last, even though the metafile has been created only in memory, it is still a logical object and must be disposed of when no longer required (or, at the very least, before the application closes). In this case, the appropriate point is in response to the WM_DESTROY message, thus:

```
case WM_DESTROY:
    DeleteMetaFile( hMetaFile );
    ...
```

Metafile Playback Operations

Initially, the drawing instructions for our sample image were presented in the form that would have been used to draw to the screen, nominally in response to a WM_PAINT instruction. But, because these were intended for a metafile rather than a display, the instructions were executed in response to the WM_INITIALIZE instruction. But now that it's time to replay the metafile instructions, this operation will be carried out in response to a WM_PAINT operation, in the same fashion as any other screen refresh. However, before actually replaying the metafile, we need to add a few instructions.

Providing Mapping Mode and Extent Information

Because the metafile image was drawn to a memory context as GDI instructions, it lacks any physical device-context information, including mapping modes and viewport and window extents. Therefore, before replaying the metafile instructions, we need to provide a physical device-context handle, as well as mapping mode and extent settings.

```
case WM_PAINT:
    hdc = BeginPaint( hwnd, &ps );
    SetMapMode( hdc, MM_ANISOTROPIC );
    SetWindowExt( hdc, 1000, 1000 );
    SetViewportExt( hdc, cxWnd, cyWnd );
```

The fact that the metafile does not include mapping mode and extent settings is an advantage, not a disadvantage. Because these are not predefined within the metafile, before you play back a metafile, you can establish any mapping mode or window and viewport extents desired, and the metafile's GDI operations will be executed accordingly.

Changing Viewport and Window Origins

Of necessity, one element is predetermined: the origin point. When the graphics drawing operations were originally executed, the drawing was centered around a (hypothetical) 0,0 origin point, simply because it was convenient. Alternatively, the origin could have been located anywhere in the metaspace, and the resulting operations would be recorded at points relative to this new theoretical origin.

But, while the metafile's origin is known, the viewport and window extents and origins are still undetermined. Because of these two factors, you can control the position of the resulting image by changing the window origin when the metafile image is replayed.

For the present demonstration, we'll replay the metafile image a total of six times, changing the window origin point each time, to produce an image similar to the screen shown in Figure 33.1. (Because two of the resulting images use the same screen coordinates, only five images appear on the screen.)

```
for( i=0; i<3; i++ )
{
    SetWindowOrg( hdc, -200 -( i * 300 ), -500 );
    PlayMetaFile( hdc, hMetaFile );
    SetWindowOrg( hdc, -500, -200 -( i * 300 ) );
    PlayMetaFile( hdc, hMetaFile );
}
EndPaint( hwnd, &ps );
break;
```

In addition to the metafile drawing operations, other drawing operations could also be carried out, either before or after the metafile is replayed. Also, remember that this is not simply an image being copied to the screen; these images are drawn in the same fashion as any other object created by drawing instructions. You should also realize that the metafile may include ROP instructions governing how the recorded drawing operations will interact with existing screen images (see Chapter 25 for more information about ROP instructions).

Metafiles as Disk Files

The preceding fragmentary examples for both recording and playing back a metafile assume that the metafile exists only as a memory file. A memory metafile provides an acceptable format for transfer using clipboard functions. For other purposes, you may want to create a disk metafile, by writing the GDI operation instructions to an external disk file in a condensed binary format.

FIGURE 33.1:

Five images produced by a metafile

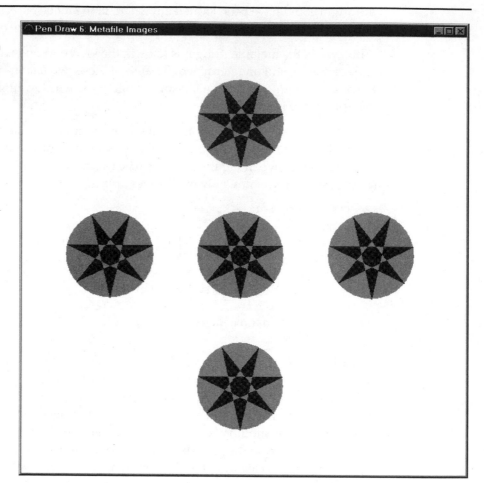

Conventional Disk Files

Writing metafiles to disk requires only a minor change in format and could be accomplished, using the preceding examples, by changing one line in the source code:

```
hdcMeta = CreateMetaFile( "D:\\METAFILE.WMF" );
```

Neither the filename nor the file extension used here have any particular significance, although the WMF extension (Windows MetaFile) does provide a convenient convention.

The CreateMetaFile instruction could also be written using an indirect reference:

```
hdcMeta = CreateMetaFile( (LPSTR) szMetaFileName );
```

In this form, szMetaFileName is a null-terminated string specifying the filename and, if desired, the drive and path specifications.

But, in either case, when the metafile is written to disk, the DeleteMetaFile instruction in response to the WM_DESTROY message (shown earlier in the chapter) does not affect the metafile disk file. The DeleteMetaFile instruction deletes only the local handle to the file. The file itself remains until explicitly erased by other instructions.

As another alternative, you can create a temporary file. This form of storage is more ephemeral than a conventional disk file, but less transitory than a memory file. This is the format used in the *PenDraw6* demo discussed in this chapter.

Temporary Files

To create a temporary file, the *PenDraw6* demo uses the GetTempFileName function to create a temporary filename and calls it in response to the WM_CREATE function, instead of supplying a string constant when calling the CreateMetaFile function. The GetTempFileName function is called as:

```
GetTempFileName( lpszDrivePath, lpszPrefixStr, wUnique, lpszTempFileName );
```

The function's parameters are as follows:

lpszDrivePath Points to a null-terminated string specifying the drive and directory where the temporary file will be located. If no drive and path are specified, the current drive and directory will be used. (If desired, a call to GetTempPath will return the path name of the system's predefined temporary file directory.)

lpszPrefixStr Points to a null-terminated string to be used as the prefix for a temporary filename. It is limited to three characters in length.

wUnique An unsigned short integer (WORD) that is used to generate the temporary filename. If this argument is 0, a unique number based on the system time will be generated and will also be returned by GetTempFile-Name. If a file already exists with the generated name, the number will be incremented and the new name tested for conflicts, continuing until a unique filename is found.

lpszTempFileName Points to a buffer that receives the temporary file-name. The return string consists of characters in the OEM-defined character set and should be at least MAX_PATH (260) characters in length to allow sufficient room for a complete drive/path/filename specification.

In actual practice (and in the *PenDraw6* demo), GetTempFileName can also be called as:

```
GetTempFileName( NULL, "MFT", 0, (LPSTR) szMetaFileName );
```

The *PenDraw6* demo includes a message box provision that reports the temporary filename generated. As you will observe, the temporary filename created begins with a tilde character (~), followed by the optional prefix ("MFT") and completed with a unique four-character hexadecimal value generated from the wUnique parameter. For example, the returned drive/path/filename might be C:\\Win98\\TEMP\\~MFT12F3.TMP. Notice that the path specification uses backslash characters, as required by C-language conventions.

Deleting Temporary Files

Because large numbers of temporary files tend to clog a hard drive (a fault that, unfortunately, is characteristic of too many existing Windows applications), any applications using temporary files should also include provisions to erase these files when they are no longer needed.

This task can be accomplished quite easily by minor provisions in response to the WM_DESTROY message.

```
case WM_DESTROY:
    DeleteMetaFile( hMetaFile );
    unlink( szMetaFileName );
    PostQuitMessage(0);
    break;
```

The unlink function erases the temporary file without requiring a file handle or other handling provisions. (Remember that read-only files cannot be unlinked.)

There is one flaw in this system: If an application is interrupted—because of a hang-up requiring a reset, a power interruption, or any other reason—any temporary files created will not be erased, and you will need to manually delete them from the hard drive. Of course, this can also be done to clean up after other, less-well-behaved applications, and this is also a good reason for using the `GetTempPath` function. With this last provision, all garbage files will remain in one convenient location where they're easily found and deleted—a small courtesy but also an appreciated one.

Accessing Temporary Metafiles

The principal reason for creating temporary metafiles is to allow other applications to access the information that they contain (an application also might need to access metafiles that it created earlier, but a temporary file format would probably not be used in this case). Thus, you need a provision to retrieve or create a metafile handle for a file that was not created by the application or that was previously discarded via the `DeleteMetaFile` function. This facility is provided by the `GetMetaFile` function, which is called as:

```
hMetaFile = GetMetaFile( (LPSTR) szMetaFileName );
```

Once the handle has been retrieved, you can access the metafile as before. And, when finished, you should discard the metafile handle using `DeleteMetaFile`.

If the metafile is being created by one application for use by another, the originating application should not call `unlink` to delete the disk file, but the recipient application definitely should.

Metafile Structures

Metafiles, whether in memory or on disk, are simply structured records using the `METARECORD` and `METAHEADER` structures or the `METAFILEPICT` structure for clipboard operations, which is discussed in Chapter 34.

You do not need to know how to read or decipher metafile instructions in order to use metafile operations. However, being able to do so may prove worthwhile, and they really aren't as difficult to understand as you might assume.

A metafile begins with an 18-byte record header described by the `METAHEADER` structure. This structure is followed by a series of `METARECORD` records, each consisting of a minimum of four `WORD` values, which describe the actual GDI operations.

The Metafile Header Structure

The METAHEADER structure is defined in WinGDI.H as:

```
typedef struct tagMETAHEADER
{
    WORD    mtType;             // metafile type
    WORD    mtHeaderSize;       // header size (bytes)
    WORD    mtVersion;          // version number
    DWORD   mtSize;             // metafile size (bytes)
    WORD    mtNoObjects;
    DWORD   mtMaxRecord;
    WORD    mtNoParameters;
} METAHEADER;
```

The Metafile Record Structure

The METARECORD structure is defined in WinGDI.H as:

```
typedef struct tagMETARECORD
{
    DWORD rdSize;       // record size
    WORD  rdFunction;   // function ID
    WORD  rdParm[1];
} METARECORD;
```

Each METARECORD record records a specific GDI function call and varies in length with the first DWORD value, rdSize, identifying the total size of the individual record. This value is expressed in lsw,msw order, with each word expressed in lsb,msb order.

The second record element, rdFunction, identifies the function to be executed. The low byte identifies the GDI function, and the high byte reports the number of parameters passed to the function. Thus, a hex value 0418 identifies the Ellipse function (18h or META_ELLIPSE), which receives four (04h) parameters, excluding the hdcMeta argument (which is understood).

Metafile operation constants are defined in WinGDI.H. Table 33.1 lists some representative metafile operations.

TABLE 33.1:   Representative Metafile Operations

Metafile Operation	Value	Op ID	Arguments
META_SETBKCOLOR	0x0201	01h	2
META_SETBKMODE	0x0102	02h	1
META_SETMAPMODE	0x0103	03h	1
META_SETROP2	0x0104	04h	1
META_SETRELABS	0x0105	05h	1
META_SETPOLYFILLMODE	0x0106	06h	1
META_SETSTRETCHBLTMODE	0x0107	07h	1
META_SETTEXTCHAREXTRA	0x0108	08h	1
META_SETTEXTCOLOR	0x0209	09h	2
META_SETTEXTJUSTIFICATION	0x020A	0Ah	2
META_SETWINDOWORG	0x020B	0Bh	2
META_SETWINDOWEXT	0x020C	0Ch	2
META_SETVIEWPORTORG	0x020D	0Dh	2
META_SETVIEWPORTEXT	0x020E	0Eh	2
META_OFFSETWINDOWORG	0x020F	0Fh	2
META_SCALEWINDOWEXT	0x0410	10h	4
META_OFFSETVIEWPORTORG	0x0211	11h	2
META_SCALEVIEWPORTEXT	0x0412	12h	4
META_LINETO	0x0213	13h	2
META_MOVETO	0x0214	14h	2
META_EXCLUDECLIPRECT	0x0415	15h	4
META_INTERSECTCLIPRECT	0x0416	16h	4
META_ARC	0x0817	17h	8

Continued on next page

TABLE 33.1 (CONTINUED):   Representative Metafile Operations

Metafile Operation	Value	Op ID	Arguments
META_ELLIPSE	0x0418	18h	4
META_FLOODFILL	0x0419	19h	4
META_PIE	0x081A	1Ah	8
META_RECTANGLE	0x041B	1Bh	4
META_ROUNDRECT	0x061C	1Ch	6

The final element in the METARECORD structure will be one or more bytes containing the arguments required by the GDI operation.

Sample Metafile Instructions

Using the metafile operations recorded by the *PenDraw6* demo, as written to a temporary (disk) metafile, a sample of metafile instructions is shown below. The sample code has been interlineated with the program instructions generating each metafile record, and the META_*xxxxxx* operation is named at the right. Notice also that, in some cases, a single source code line may generate more than one metafile instruction record.

```
0001 0009 0300 00000004B 0003 00000012 0000        METAHEADER Record

    hPen = CreatePen( PS_NULL, 1, 0L )
00000008 02FA 0005 0001 0000 0000 0000             META_CREATEPENINDIRECT

    SelectObject( hdcMeta, hPen );
00000004 012D 0000                                 META_SELECTOBJECT

    SelectObject( hdcMeta, GetStockObject( LTGRAY_BRUSH ) );
00000007 02FC 0000 C0C0 00C0 0000                  META_CREATEBRUSHINDIRECT
    (notice that LTGRAY_BRUSH is expressed as an RGB quad)
00000004 012D 0002                                 META_SELECTOBJECT

    Ellipse( hdcMeta, -100, -100, 100, 100 );
00000007 0418 0064 0064 FF9C FF9C                  META_ELLIPSE

    SelectObject( hdcMeta, GetStockObject( DKGRAY_BRUSH ) );
00000007 02FC 0000 4040 0040 0000                  META_CREATEBRUSHINDIRECT
    (again, DKGRAY_BRUSH is specified as an RGB quad)
```

```
00000004 012D 0002                                    META_SELECTOBJECT

    SetPolyFillMode( hdcMeta, ALTERNATE );
00000004 0106 0001                                    META_SETPOLYFILLMODE

    Polygon( hdcMeta, pt, 7 );
00000012 0324 0007 0000 0064 002B FFA6 FFB2 003E  META_POLYGON
         0061 FFEA FF9F FFEA 004E 003E FFD5 FFA6
    (includes 14 coordinates - 7 points - from pt reference)

    (A 3-byte null record terminates the metafile)
00000003 0000
```

> **NOTE**   If you compare the instructions in the metafile with the complete source code generating these instructions, you may notice a few discrepancies. Where the original instruction was `CreatePen`, the metafile equivalent has become `CreatePenIndirect`. Also, the `DeletePen` instruction in the original source code is not reflected in the metafile instructions. Neither of these are errors but, instead, are simplifications of the original code. Because the `CreatePenIndirect` instruction was used instead of `CreatePen`, the need for a `DeletePen` instruction has been eliminated as has been any requirement to restore the original pen. Thus, in brief—and in the interests of brevity—the metafile translation has improved on the original code.

Again, you do not need to know the structure of a metafile in order to use metafile operations, but the information may prove helpful. Besides, given the preceding breakdown, it really shouldn't be much of a challenge to write a utility to decipher and decode metafile instructions, should it? If you're interested, you can experiment on your own.

Metafile Cautions

Before leaving the subject of metafile operations, there are a few comments and cautions that are worth keeping in mind. Even a cursory awareness of these may assist in preventing future errors or at least in alleviating confusion.

The metafile device context is not a true device context in the sense that it does not correspond to any physical or logical device. As such, the metafile device context does not include a mapping mode, window sizes and origins, or viewport sizes and origins.

All parameters passed to metafiles are actual values, not formulas or references to variable values. Thus, variable references used in generating an application's source code are evaluated at the time the metafile is compiled and may or may not contain appropriate values when the metafile is replayed. Thus, an argument such as cxWnd/2 is recorded as the constant resulting from the calculation and, later, will not reflect changes in window size. (This specific conflict, despite the use of a similar reference, was avoided in the *PenDraw6* demo by using the isotropic mapping mode.)

TIP

The *PenDraw6* demo, which is included on the accompanying CD, provides a platform for experimentation with metafile operations. To further your expertise and understanding, you might also consider creating two new programs: the first to create a metafile as a disk file and the second to retrieve the metafile from disk, using the `GetMetaFile` instruction. Then you can replay the graphics under the same or different mapping modes.

Metafile instructions are always interpreted in terms of the existing mapping mode. Metafiles may, however, include instructions to select specific mapping modes.

Also, there are several classes of instructions that are not compatible with metafile operations. The following five categories of GDI instructions are invalid and will not be recorded as metafile operations:

- Any function treating the metafile device context as if it were a physical device context, including operations such as `CreateCompatibleBitmap`, `CreateCompatibleDC`, `CreateDiscardableBitmap`, `DeleteDC`, `PlayMetaFile` (self-referential), and `ReleaseDC`.

- Any function beginning with the form `Get...`, such as `GetDeviceCaps` and `GetTextMetrics`. All data contained in a metafile is preset, and the record structure cannot accommodate information returned by such functions.

- Any function designed to return information to the program, such as `DPtoLP` and `LPtoDP`. (However, macros, which are evaluated during compilation, are permitted.)

- Functions requiring handles to brushes, such as `FillRect` and `FrameRect`.

- A few of the more complex functions, such as `DrawIcon`, `GrayString`, and `SetBrushOrg`.

If you have any questions about which GDI function calls are permitted in a metafile operation, refer to the list of metafile constants defined in WinGDI.H. All constants begin with the prefix META_*xxxxxxx*. But, remember, some GDI functions do not appear, simply because when the compiler encounters these, it will automatically choose a more compatible variation. For example, a call for the CreatePen function appears in the metafile as META_CREATEPENINDIRECT.

One final caution involves saving the present device context before replaying a metafile and, when finished, restoring the original device context. Because a metafile can change device-context settings but cannot record or restore existing device-context settings, your applications should include their own provisions for this operation.

Remember, the metafile is free to change drawing and mapping modes, change colors, and make other changes. When the metafile is finished replaying, these changes will remain in effect. Therefore, to save the original device context, save the existing device context before executing the PlayMetaFile instruction:

```
SaveDC( hdc );
```

And, after the metafile has been replayed, restore the original device context:

```
RestoreDC( hdc, -1 );
```

Since neither of these instructions involve any operations forbidden to metafiles, and both are supported by metafile instructions, a well-behaved metafile could simply include these provisions within itself. Do remember, however, that every call to SaveDC must have a corresponding RestoreDC call using the −1 argument, and vice versa.

As you've seen in this chapter, metafile operations provide a powerful means to record and replay drawing operations. They can also be used to transfer graphics operations between applications or even between devices (such as from the screen to a printer). In the next chapter, you'll see how metafiles can be used with the clipboard as an alternative to physical (disk) file transfers. Also, the DDE functions detailed in Chapter 35 provide a useful means for requesting and confirming metafile transfers.

Clipboard Data Transfers

- Advantages of using the clipboard

- Clipboard data formats

- Clipboard access

- Private clipboard formats

The Windows Clipboard consists of two quite different entities: the clipboard viewer, Clipbrd.EXE, and the real clipboard. The real clipboard is a feature of the Windows User module. It provides a series of functions that facilitate the temporary storage of information in a form that permits applications other than the originating application to retrieve that information. Of course, the originating application is not prohibited from retrieving its own clipboard information, but the important item to remember is that data passed to the clipboard is public, which means that it is accessible to any application.

The clipboard provides a useful and convenient method for exchanging data of many different types between applications, as explained and demonstrated in this chapter.

Clipboard Uses

The clipboard consists of a series of facilities that provide a platform for the temporary (nondisk) storage of data. Data stored on the clipboard can be transferred between applications or simply retrieved by the application that put it there in the first place.

A source application can copy data to the clipboard using one of the predefined formats or using a custom format (clipboard file formats are discussed later in the chapter). As the data is transferred, the clipboard facilities allocate and manage memory to contain the data.

After the data has been transferred, any application can access the clipboard, inquire what type of data is present, and, if desired, retrieve a copy of the data from the clipboard.

When the clipboard viewer (Clipbrd.EXE) is active, the clipboard is queried regularly to determine if any data has been written to the clipboard and, if so, what data type is contained. If possible, the clipboard viewer then retrieves a copy of the data, displaying the data in its own client window. Note, however, that the clipboard viewer itself does not alter or erase the clipboard contents.

While the clipboard does work very well, it also has a few disadvantages:

- There is only one clipboard.
- All material written to the clipboard is public.

- Any material written to the clipboard is volatile.

Because there is only one clipboard, all applications that want to use the clipboard must share use of this single facility. And sharing can mean conflicts. For example, suppose that Application A writes a bitmap to the clipboard and then Application B writes a block of text data. However, because Application B, quite reasonably begins by clearing the clipboard, the bitmap written by Application A is erased. Now, if the bitmap destination, Application C, has already retrieved the image, everything is fine. But, if Application C has not gotten the bitmap before Application B replaces it with text data, the bitmap is lost.

The public nature of the clipboard also offers opportunities for error. Because the data element written to the clipboard cannot be addressed to a specific recipient, this data can be accessed, by mistake, by another application seeking data of the same type.

The clipboard can contain data of several different types, written by a single application or by different applications. If this is the case, the problem is how to distinguish between the blocks—for example, multiple blocks of text supplied by different sources. For this reason, applications normally begin by clearing the clipboard before writing new material to the clipboard.

These are factors to consider, but they are not serious problems demanding extensive worry and circumvention measures. And, in circumstances where these could become more serious considerations, DDE (Dynamic Data Exchange) techniques, discussed in Chapter 35, provide a more secure channel for the exchange of data.

The Clipboard Viewer

The Clipbrd.EXE program, which is distributed with all versions of Windows, is a clipboard viewer that provides a means of checking (viewing) data that has been copied to the User clipboard facilities. As such, the Clipbrd program can be used while testing your own clipboard routines.

The clipboard viewer can also be used to capture (or copy) material transferred to the clipboard facilities by other applications, saving the captured data to a disk file or simply viewing the data.

But, remember, the Clipbrd application is only a viewer, not the real clipboard. It cannot affect the contents of the clipboard.

Clipboard Operations

Basically, the clipboard operates by assuming control over globally allocated memory blocks that contain data supplied by applications, by altering memory allocation flags. To copy or write material to the clipboard, an application begins by using the GlobalAlloc function and the GHND flag (defined as GMEM_MOVABLE and GMEM_ZEROINIT) to initialize a memory block which, initially, belongs to the originating application instance.

Under normal circumstances, when the originating application exits or closes, the global memory allocated would be deleted (freed) by Windows. However, when the originating instance calls the SetClipboardData function, using the global handle to the memory block, Windows transfers ownership of the memory block from the application to itself—to the clipboard—by modifying the memory allocation flags for the global memory block.

Ownership of a global memory block is accomplished by the GlobalRealloc function, called as:

```
GlobalRealloc( hMem, NULL, GMEM_MODIFY | GMEM_DDESHARE );
```

Once this is done, the allocated memory no longer belongs to the original application and can now be accessed only through the clipboard using the GetClipboardData function. The GetClipboardData function grants the calling application temporary access to the clipboard data by providing a handle to the global memory block. Ownership, however, remains with the clipboard, not with the application accessing the data.

For this reason, clipboard data can be erased only by calling the Empty-Clipboard function. (One exception to this rule will be discussed presently but is not recommended.)

Clipboard Data Formats

Windows supports 14 standard clipboard data formats, defined in WinUser.H as the following:

CF_TEXT	CF_PALETTE	CF_BITMAP
CF_PENDATA	CF_METAFILEPICT	CF_RIFF
CF_SYLK	CF_WAVE	CF_DIF
CF_DIB	CF_TIFF	CF_UNICODETEXT
CF_OEMTEXT	CF_ENHMETAFILE	

An additional nine special formats or format flags are also defined, and any application is free to define its own custom clipboard data format. For most purposes, however, the standard formats should suffice.

Text Formats

The simplest clipboard data format is the CF_TEXT format, which consists of null-terminated ANSI character strings, each line ending with a carriage return (0x0D) / line feed (0x0A) character. The CF_OEMTEXT format is an OEM character set. The CF_UNICODETEXT format uses 32-bit Unicode characters.

Once the text has been transferred to the clipboard, the originating application cannot access the text further except by requesting access from the clipboard.

Bitmap Format

The CF_BITMAP format is used to transfer Windows bitmap images by transferring the bitmap handle to the clipboard. Once the bitmap handle has been transferred to the clipboard, the originating application cannot use the bitmap except by calling the clipboard for access.

Metafile Formats

The CF_METAFILEPICT format is used to transfer memory (not disk) metafiles between applications. This format uses the METAFILEPICT structure, defined in WinGDI.H as:

```
typedef struct tagMETAFILEPICT
{
    LONG      mm;
    LONG      xExt;
    LONG      yExt;
    HMETAFILE hMF;
} METAFILEPICT, FAR *LPMETAFILEPICT;
```

The first three fields show the differences between a clipboard metafile transfer and a disk metafile transfer. The first field, mm, identifies the preferred mapping mode (discussed later). The second and third fields, xExt and yExt, identify the height and width of the metafile image. The HMETAFILE field is simply a handle to the METAFILE structure introduced in Chapter 33. The use of this data is demonstrated later in the chapter.

The CF_ENHMETAFILE format is the same as the CF_METAFILEPICT format, except that it identifies a metafile using the enhanced metafile format instructions.

Once a metafile is transferred to the clipboard, the originating application should not attempt to use either the global memory block or the original metafile handle, except by requesting access through the clipboard.

DIB Format

The CF_DIB format is used to transfer DIBs (device-independent bitmaps) to the clipboard. The DIB is transferred as a global memory block, beginning with a BITMAPINFO header structure, followed by the bitmap image data. Bitmap structures were introduced in Chapter 26.

The **CF_BITMAP** format supported by Windows 2.x and 3.x identifies device-dependent bitmap formats is also supported by Windows 98 but not by Windows NT. However, the **CF_DIB** format is preferred, and is supported by Windows 98, Windows 95, and Windows NT.

After a bitmap has been transferred to the clipboard, the originating application should not attempt to use either the global memory block or the original bitmap handle except by requesting access through the clipboard.

Palette and Pen Formats

The CF_PALETTE and CF_PENDATA formats are used to transfer a handle to a color palette or a pen, respectively. The palette transfer is often used together with the CF_DIB format to define color palettes used by a bitmap.

Wave Format

The CF_WAVE format is used to transfer audio (waveform) information between applications.

Special-Purpose Formats

Three special-purpose clipboard formats provide support for data formats that were originally designed for use by and between specific applications:

- The CF_TIFF format uses a global memory block to transfer data using the Tagged Image File Format (TIFF). See Chapter 28 for more information about TIFF files.

- The CF_DIF format uses a global memory block to transfer data using the Data Interchange Format (DIF) created by Software Arts, originally for use with the VisiCalc spreadsheet program but now controlled by Lotus Corporation. The format is essentially an ASCII-string format with each line terminated by a CR/LF pair.

- The CF_SYLK format uses a global memory block to transfer data using the Microsoft Symbolic Link format, originally designed for data exchanges between Microsoft's Multiplan (spreadsheet), Chart, and Excel applications. The format is an ASCII string format with each line terminated by a CR/LF pair.

Clipboard Access

While many Windows facilities are designed to permit shared access, access to the clipboard is permitted to only one application at a time; this mechanism prevents conflicts among applications.

Opening and Closing the Clipboard

Before any application can access the clipboard to read, write, or clear it, the application must begin by calling the OpenClipboard function, requesting access. The OpenClipboard function returns a Boolean result, with TRUE indicating that the clipboard is available and access is granted or FALSE indicating that access is denied because another application currently holds access rights.

When the application is finished with the clipboard, the CloseClipboard function is called, relinquishing access and freeing the clipboard for access by other applications.

Remember that the **OpenClipboard** function is *always* matched with a **Close-Clipboard** call. Emphasis on the *always*! An application should never, ever attempt to hold the clipboard open, and should always relinquish control of the clipboard as quickly as possible.

Transferring Data to the Clipboard

The *ClipBoard* demo discussed in this chapter provides an example of a clipboard-transfer function that copies a memory block to the clipboard.

```
BOOL TransferToClipboard( HWND hwnd, HANDLE hMemBlock, WORD FormatCB )
{
    if( OpenClipboard( hwnd ) )
    {
        EmptyClipboard();
        SetClipboardData( FormatCB, hMemBlock );
        CloseClipboard();
        return( TRUE );
    }
    return( FALSE );
}
```

The TransferToClipboard function begins by requesting access (opening) the clipboard, then copying a single memory block to the clipboard. Last, the clipboard is closed, relinquishing further access.

The TransferToClipboard function is quite generic in design, accepting any type of handle (hMemBlock). However, it does require the FormatCB parameter to specify the format type (the type of data copied to the clipboard).

The term *memory block* does not refer to a specific size; the size of the memory block was set earlier by the GlobalAlloc function. A single memory block might contain paragraphs of text, multiple records, or any other data. Each memory block, however, can contain only one data type.

So, what if an application needs to transfer a bitmap, a metafile, a palette, and a text block? The solution is relatively simple. First, each block is copied separately to globally allocated memory, retaining a handle to each memory block as, for example, hBitmap, hMetafile, hPalette, and hText. With this done, the clipboard is opened and emptied, then each of the handles is transferred to the clipboard as:

```
if( OpenClipboard( hwnd ) )
```

```
{
    EmptyClipboard();
    SetClipboardData( CF_BITMAP, hBitmap );
    SetClipboardData( CF_PALETTE, hPalette );
    SetClipboardData( CF_METAFILEPICT, hMetafile );
    SetClipboardData( CF_TEXT, hText );
    CloseClipboard();
}
```

Last, the clipboard is closed, relinquishing further access to other applications.

In actual practice, the preceding example would be rather cumbersome; providing source code for every possible combination of data types would be more than a little frustrating. But, since the data type identifiers are all WORD values, and the memory block handles are simply that—handles—a simpler form would be to begin by assigning the data types and handle as arrays of WORD and HANDLE, and then calling the transfer function with a further parameter reporting the number of items to transfer. This done, the transfer could be handled as:

```
if( OpenClipboard( hwnd ) )
{
    EmptyClipboard();
    for( i=0; i<nCount; i++ )
        SetClipboardData( cfType[i], hData[i] );
    CloseClipboard();
}
```

Retrieving Clipboard Data

Before attempting to retrieve an item from the clipboard, the first step is to find out if the clipboard holds a particular type of data. Because different data types require different handling after they are retrieved, applications need to know what they're retrieving and to be prepared to handle the result before requesting retrieval.

One method is to simply ask for data of a desired type and see if anything is returned. But this approach does lack a certain elegance, not to mention efficiency.

The more efficient way to discover the clipboard contents is to use one of the two supplied functions: IsClipboardFormatAvailable or EnumClipboardFormats.

The IsClipboardFormatAvailable function returns a Boolean result to report if the clipboard contains a desired data format. IsClipboardFormatAvailable is called as:

```
if( IsClipboardFormatAvailable( CF_xxtypexx ) ) ...
```

The EnumClipboardFormats function queries all available clipboard formats. When you initially call EnumClipboardFormats with a NULL parameter, it reports the first available format. Each time you call the EnumClipboardFormats function, it returns a value reporting the next available format. Thus, to request a list of all available formats:

```
wFormat = NULL;
OpenClipboard( hwnd );
while( wFormat = EnumClipboardFormats( wFormat ) )
{
     ... code handling various formats ...
}
CloseClipboard();
```

The formats returned are reported in the same order as the originating application used to paste items to the clipboard. This ordering allows the querying application to respond to the first format acceptable. The originating application can post items in a recommended order; for example, in order of descending data reliability.

If no further formats are available, if the clipboard is empty, or if the clipboard has not been opened, the return result will be zero. The wFormat parameter could be reset to a specific value to repeat the list from that point. Also, the number of formats available in the clipboard can be retrieved by calling:

```
nFormats = CountClipboardFormats();
```

Once an application has determined that the clipboard contains data of a desired type, retrieving the clipboard data consists of two operations:

- Retrieving a handle to the clipboard data, the memory block

- Doing something with the data after retrieving the handle

The first is quite simple, as illustrated by the RetrieveCB function:

```
HANDLE RetrieveCB( HWND hwnd, WORD FormatCB )
{
    HANDLE hCB;

    if( ! IsClipboardFormatAvailable( FormatCB ) )
        return( NULL );
    OpenClipboard( hwnd );
    hCB = GetClipboardData( FormatCB );
    CloseClipboard();
    return( hCB );
}
```

This example offers a generic subroutine that returns an untyped handle to a clipboard memory block. If the requested type is not available, it returns NULL.

In actual practice, a slightly different format is used, as in the *ClipBoard* demo, where a request is made to the clipboard for a metafile object:

```
nClipRetrieve = 0;
if( IsClipboardFormatAvailable( CF_METAFILEPICT ) )
{
    OpenClipboard( hwnd );
    hGMem = GetClipboardData( CF_METAFILEPICT );
    lpMFP = (LPMETAFILEPICT) GlobalLock( hGMem );
    SaveDC( hdc );
    CreateMapMode( hdc, lpMFP, cxWnd, cyWnd );
    PlayMetaFile( hdc, lpMFP->hMF );
    RestoreDC( hdc, - 1 );
    GlobalUnlock( hGMem );
    CloseClipboard();
}
```

The *ClipBoard* demo includes several other examples of requesting specific data types, as discussed presently.

Restrictions on Clipboard Operations

There are a few restrictions on clipboard operations:

- Before you can copy an item to the clipboard, you must call EmptyClipboard to erase the present contents of the clipboard. Remember, simply accessing the clipboard does not transfer ownership of the existing contents. Use the EmptyClipboard function to assign ownership and, at the same time, to clear (release) any and all existing contents.

- Any application can access the contents of the clipboard, but only the clipboard owner—an application that has called the EmptyClipboard function—can write material to the clipboard. However, because the clipboard can have only one owner, the previous owner's contents are simply erased, even if the same application was the previous owner.

- Although you can copy multiple items to the clipboard, you must transfer all of them in a single operation. The clipboard cannot be opened, written, closed, and then reopened again to transfer another item (at least not without erasing the first item transferred).

TIP

If an application desires to preserve the original contents of the clipboard while adding new material, the simple solution is to copy the existing contents, clear the clipboard, and then replace the original contents together with whatever new material is desired.

- Only one item of each type can be transferred to the clipboard at any time. This is for the simple reason that there is no method to distinguish between multiple items of a given type. However, when multiple items of different types have been written to the clipboard, an application accessing the clipboard may request only one item, several items, or all items, but it must request each item separately.

The clipboard can be opened repeatedly to request different items or to request the same item a second (or third, fourth, and so on) time. But, in general, when requesting an item from the clipboard, the best option is to make a local copy of the desired item rather than attempting to request the same item more than once. Remember, there are no assurances that the data item requested will remain available locally.

The ClipBoard Demo: Reading and Writing Different Data Types

The *ClipBoard* demo demonstrates writing and reading the clipboard with three different data types: text, bitmap, and metafile. *ClipBoard* uses a simple menu with two primary options: Data To Clipboard and Data From Clipboard, each with a submenu listing equally unimaginative Write and Retrieve options.

The Write Bitmap option includes a simple provision that captures the entire screen (or at least a 640×480 section of the screen) as a bitmap, writing the image to the clipboard. The Write Metafile option uses the same metafile construct demonstrated in the *PenDraw6* demo (described in Chapter 33). The Write Text option copies a simple text string to the clipboard.

NOTE

The *ClipBoard* demo is included on the CD that accompanies this book, in the Chapter 34 folder.

Reading and Writing Text

Text operations may be the simplest type of clipboard operation, if only because text (string) operations themselves are comfortably familiar and require little explanation.

Writing Text

Because the *ClipBoard* demo will be both source and recipient, the first step is to transfer text information to the clipboard. The text chosen is brief, static string, declared as "The quick brown fox jumps over the lazy red dog." It's not very original, but it serves to demonstrate the principles involved.

The mechanism for handling the text transfer is provided by a subprocedure called with two parameters: a handle to the application (hwnd) and a pointer to the text string (lpText).

```
BOOL TextToClipboard( HWND hwnd, LPSTR lpText )
{
    int          i, wLen;
    GLOBALHANDLE hGMem;
    LPSTR        lpGMem;
```

Within the TextToClipboard subroutine, four local variables are required, although only the latter two need an explanation. The hGMem variable provides a global handle to a memory block that has not yet been allocated. The second variable, lpGMem, is used as a pointer into the memory block.

After the wLen variable is initialized with the length of the text parameter, hGMem becomes a pointer to memory globally allocated to hold a copy of the text. Notice, however, that wLen is one larger than the string, providing space allocation for a null terminator. Clipboard text is always stored as an ASCIIZ (or ANSIZ) format:

```
wLen = strlen( lpText );
hGMem = GlobalAlloc( GHND, (DWORD) wLen + 1 );
lpGMem = GlobalLock( hGMem );
```

Last, lpGMem receives the pointer to the memory block returned by the Global-Lock function. But, remember, the GHND specification has, properly, declared this memory block as movable. Also, in addition to returning an address (which could have been obtained several other ways), the GlobalLock function locks the memory block, temporarily preventing it from being moved by Windows.

The second feature provided by the GHND specification is to clear the memory block allocated, filling the memory block with zeros. Thus, the next step is to copy the local string, pointed to by lpText, into the memory block.

```
    for( i=0; i<wLen; i++ )
        *lpGMem = *lpText++;
    GlobalUnlock( hGMem );
    return( TransferToClipboard( hwnd, hGMem, CF_TEXT ) );
}
```

After copying the text information, GlobalUnlock is called to release the lock on hGMem, making it movable and relocatable. If, however, the memory block had been moved while the local text information was being copied, the lpGMem pointer would not have remained valid.

As a last step, the TransferToClipboard function (discussed earlier in the chapter), is called with the hGMem block, the flag CF_TEXT, and the application's window handle to complete the transfer process.

Memory Ownership and the Clipboard

Do not under any circumstances free memory after transferring a data object to the clipboard. For example, suppose that the text-to-clipboard operation were rewritten to include a GlobalFree instruction, thus:

```
    for( i=0; i<wLen; i++ )
        *lpGMem = *lpText++;
    GlobalUnlock( hGMem );
    GlobalFree( hGMem );
    return( TransferToClipboard( hwnd, hGMem, CF_TEXT ) );
```

The result of calling GlobalFree would delete the item from the clipboard. Instead, once a data item has been transferred, ownership of the item has also been transferred, and the local handle should not be used or tampered with further.

Likewise, when a data object is retrieved from the clipboard, the handle to the retrieved data may be locked and unlocked as necessary but should not be freed because the object itself still belongs to the clipboard.

Data objects placed on the clipboard are only freed when an application assumes ownership of the clipboard and calls the EmptyClipboard instruction. At this point, all data objects owned by the clipboard are freed by the clipboard itself.

Retrieving Text Retrieving text from the clipboard is almost as simple as writing it, but instead of a subroutine, the text-retrieval operations in the *ClipBoard* demo are included in the response to the WM_PAINT message. This allows the application to update the window as required. (Other applications may handle this in another fashion.)

Retrieval operations begin by opening the clipboard and using the Get-ClipboardData API call to return a handle to the clipboard memory block.

```
OpenClipboard( hwnd );
hTextMem = GetClipboardData( CF_TEXT );
lpText = GlobalLock( hTextMem );
```

Just as was done during the transfer to the clipboard, and for the same reasons, GlobalLock is called to lock the memory block, returning a pointer to the memory address held by lpText. This time, however, instead of a loop, the lstrcpy function is used to copy the string contents from the memory address (lpText) to the local variable, TextStr.

```
lstrcpy( TextStr, lpText );
GlobalUnlock( hTextMem );
CloseClipboard();
```

Last, GlobalUnlock releases the lock on the memory block; CloseClipboard completes the operation. It's important to remember that a memory block should never be left locked. Always call GlobalUnlock after calling GlobalLock.

Reading and Writing Bitmaps

The *ClipBoard* demo also includes a demonstration of bitmap transfer through the clipboard. This demonstration begins with provisions to capture the existing screen to provide a bitmap for transfer to the clipboard. The screen-capture process itself is peripheral to the present topic; it follows the general form demonstrated in the *Capture* demo (discussed in Chapter 28).

Figure 34.1 shows the *ClipBoard* demo window (lower right), together with the Windows clipboard viewer, Clipbrd (upper left), in a recursive situation following several screen captures. The current clipboard contents appear in both application windows.

FIGURE 34.1:

Two clipboard views

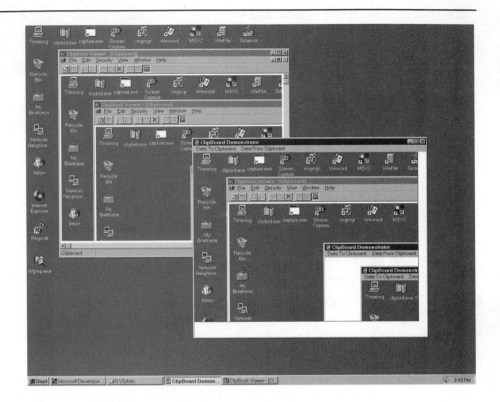

Writing a Bitmap The bitmap-to-clipboard transfer process begins by creating a compatible device context, hdcMem, in memory and then creating and selecting a compatible bitmap (also in memory).

```
hdc = GetDC( hwnd );
hdcMem = CreateCompatibleDC( hdc );
hBitmap = CreateCompatibleBitmap( hdc, 640, 480 );
SelectObject( hdcMem, hBitmap );
```

The next step is to copy the bitmap image from the original (source)—in this example, the screen—to the memory context before calling the TransferTo-Clipboard function to complete the transfer.

```
StretchBlt( hdcMem, 0, 0, 639, 479,
            hdc,    0, 0, 639, 479, SRCCOPY );
TransferToClipboard( hwnd, hBitmap, CF_BITMAP );
DeleteDC( hdcMem );
```

Last, the memory device context is deleted, leaving ownership of the bitmap image to the clipboard.

Retrieving a Bitmap   Retrieving the bitmap image from the clipboard is similar to copying the image to the clipboard. The process begins by opening the clipboard and retrieving a handle to the bitmap (from the clipboard):

```
OpenClipboard( hwnd );
hBitmap = GetClipboardData( CF_BITMAP );
hdcMem = CreateCompatibleDC( hdc );
SelectObject( hdcMem, hBitmap );
```

Again, a compatible device context is required. Then the `SelectObject` function selects the bitmap.

At this point, there are a few other tasks involved. First, the mapping mode needs to be set in the memory context for compatibility with the display context. And, second, before the bitmap can be copied, the size of the bitmap is needed. We obtain the bitmap size by copying the bitmap header into a local variable, `bm`.

```
SetMapMode( hdcMem, GetMapMode( hdc ) );
GetObject( hBitmap, sizeof(BITMAP), (LPSTR) &bm );
```

The `BITMAP` variable (`bm`) now contains the bitmap header information needed to copy the actual bitmap from the memory context to the device context, this time using the `BitBlt` function.

```
BitBlt( hdc,    0, 0, bm.bmWidth, bm.bmHeight,
        hdcMem, 0, 0, SRCCOPY );
ReleaseDC( hwnd, hdc );
DeleteDC( hdcMem );
CloseClipboard();
```

All that's left is a bit of cleanup before closing the clipboard, and the job is done.

NOTE   The clipboard could have been closed earlier—just as soon as a handle had been returned to the image memory block—because closing the clipboard doesn't delete the memory block.

Reading and Writing Metafiles

Metafile transfers introduce an element that is not present in text transfers. Although this element is present in bitmap transfers, it is not obtrusively visible (and in the previous examples, it was handled virtually without remark). The new element required for metafile transfers is information about the file: the mapping mode under which the metafile was originally created and the extent or size information. This data is not necessarily inherent in the metafile itself.

Writing a Metafile   With a text, metric, English, or TWIPS mapping mode, the mapping scale is fixed. The isotropic and anisotropic mapping modes, both of which have advantages for metafile operations, present a need for special information to accompany the metafile instructions.

For metafile clipboard transfers, the METAFILEPICT record is used. This record includes the mapping mode used, size information, and the metafile script itself.

The METAFILEPICT record structure is defined in WinGDI.H as:

```
typedef struct tagMETAFILEPICT
{
    LONG      mm;
    LONG      xExt;
    LONG      yExt;
    HMETAFILE hMF;
} METAFILEPICT, FAR *LPMETAFILEPICT;
```

The mm field contains the mapping mode. The hMF field is a handle to the metafile instructions. The remaining two fields, xExt and yExt, may contain two different types of information, depending on the mapping mode.

For text, metric, English, or TWIPS mapping modes, the xExt and yExt fields specify the horizontal and vertical size of the metafile picture in units appropriate to the mapping mode.

For the MM_ISOTROPIC or MM_ANISOTROPIC mapping modes, the xExt and yExt fields contain an optional, suggested size expressed in MM_HIMETRIC units, or may be zero if no suggested size is offered. Alternatively, if the xExt and yExt fields are negative, the information is provided as a suggested size ratio, rather than an absolute size.

In the *ClipBoard* demo, a metafile image is supplied by duplicating the metafile image code from Chapter 33, now in a subroutine titled DrawMetafile. Much of the DrawMetafile procedure should be familiar from previous examples, but it does begin with one new variable declaration:

```
BOOL DrawMetafile( HWND hwnd, int cxWnd, int cyWnd )
{
    LPMETAFILEPICT   lpMFP;
```

Aside from the variable lpMFP, which is used as a pointer to an instance of the METAFILEPICT structure, the DrawMetafile function proceeds by creating a metafile in memory as demonstrated in Chapter 33. But, after the metafile is created, the next step is to create a METAFILEPICT structure in memory and, using GlobalLock, to return a value to the lpMFP pointer.

```
hGMem = GlobalAlloc( GHND, (DWORD) sizeof( METAFILEPICT ) );
lpMFP = (LPMETAFILEPICT) GlobalLock( hGMem );
```

Now that the METAFILEPICT structure is allocated and locked, the next steps are to assign values to the mapping mode, provide a suggested size, and assign the metafile handle.

```
lpMFP->mm = MM_ISOTROPIC;
lpMFP->xExt = 200;          // suggested size in //
lpMFP->yExt = 200;          // MM_HIMETRIC units //
lpMFP->hMF = hMetaFile;
```

And, with the assignments completed, all that remains is to unlock the memory before transferring the handle to the clipboard.

```
GlobalUnlock( hGMem );
TransferToClipboard( hwnd, hGMem, CF_METAFILEPICT );
```

Retrieving a Metafile   Retrieving the metafile from the clipboard begins by opening the clipboard, asking for a handle to the memory block containing the metafile, and locking the block while returning a pointer.

```
OpenClipboard( hwnd );
hGMem = GetClipboardData( CF_METAFILEPICT );
lpMFP = (LPMETAFILEPICT) GlobalLock( hGMem );
```

At this point, the lpMFP variable contains a pointer to the metafile memory block or, more accurately, to the METAFILEPICT structure, which contains a pointer to the metafile proper.

But, before replaying the metafile itself, there are a couple of other tasks that require attention, beginning by saving the present device context (as suggested in Chapter 33).

```
SaveDC( hdc );
CreateMapMode( hdc, lpMFP, cxWnd, cyWnd );
```

After saving the present device context, the METAFILEPICT information is passed to a subroutine, CreateMapMode, for processing. This is done because deciphering the mapping mode and size/extent information is moderately complex.

CreateMapMode is called with four parameters, which specify the application's device-context handle, the METAFILEPICT pointer, and the application window's size.

```
BOOL CreateMapMode( HDC hdc,    LPMETAFILEPICT lpMFP,
                        int cxWnd, int cyWnd )
{
    long  lMapScale;
    int   nHRes, nVRes, nHSize, nVSize;

    SetMapMode( hdc, lpMFP->mm );
    if( lpMFP->mm != MM_ISOTROPIC && lpMFP->mm != MM_ANISOTROPIC )
        return( TRUE );
```

First, CreateMapMode sets the mapping mode specified for the metafile. If the mapping mode is anything except MM_ISOTROPIC or MM_ANISOTROPIC, the function simply returns, with nothing more required.

TIP

The image-size data could be extracted, but there really isn't any point in doing so in this demo. If desired, you could get the size information and use it to position the metafile image, in a fashion similar to that demonstrated in Chapter 24.

If the metafile mapping mode is MM_ISOTROPIC or MM_ANISOTROPIC, then the CreateMapMode function still has work to do. First, it proceeds by calling the Get-DeviceCaps function to query the horizontal and vertical size and resolution.

```
nHRes  = GetDeviceCaps( hdc, HORZRES );
nVRes  = GetDeviceCaps( hdc, VERTRES );
nHSize = GetDeviceCaps( hdc, HORZSIZE );
nVSize = GetDeviceCaps( hdc, VERTSIZE );
```

The next actions depend on the values passed in the xExt and yExt fields. These values may be positive or negative, or no values at all may be passed.

If the arguments are positive, the values are intended to suggest a size in MM_ HIMETRIC units. Therefore, the SetViewportExtEx function is called to set the viewport size appropriately.

```
        if( lpMFP->xExt > 0 )
            SetViewportExtEx( hdc,
                (int)((long) lpMFP->xExt * nHRes / nHSize / 100 ),
                (int)((long) lpMFP->yExt * nHRes / nHSize / 100 ),   NULL
    );
```

If negative values have been entered, the arguments are intended as a ratio rather than an absolute size. Therefore, the first step is to calculate a scale to fit the device context.

```
else
if( lpMFP->xExt < 0 )
{
    lMapScale = min( ( 100L * (long) cxWnd * nHSize / nHRes / -lpMFP->xExt ),
                     ( 100L * (long) cyWnd * nVSize / nVRes / -lpMFP->yExt ) );
```

Two scales are calculated: one to fit the x-axis and one to fit the y-axis. But the iMapScale value is chosen as the smaller of the two possible scales to ensure that the resulting image fits the display. And, once the mapping scale has been calculated, SetViewportExtEx is called again to size the viewport to fit.

```
    SetViewportExtEx( hdc,
        (int)((long) -lpMFP->xExt * lMapScale * nHRes / nHSize / 100 ),
        (int)((long) -lpMFP->yExt * lMapScale * nVRes / nVSize / 100 ), NULL );
}
```

The third possibility is that neither size nor ratio information was supplied. In this case, the solution is simply to set the viewport to match the window size.

```
        else
            SetViewportExtEx( hdc, cxWnd, cyWnd, NULL );
```

Once the CreateMapMode function returns, the remainder of the task is simple, requiring nothing more than a call to PlayMetaFile, almost exactly as shown previously.

```
        PlayMetaFile( hdc, lpMFP->hMF );
        RestoreDC( hdc, - 1 );
        GlobalUnlock( hGMem );
        CloseClipboard();
```

And, after replaying the metafile, the `RestoreDC` function is called with an argument of −1 to restore the original device context, the metafile memory is unlocked, and the clipboard is closed.

TIP   In the *ClipBoard* demo, only one item at a time is written to the clipboard. If you want to experiment, you can try adding a provision to copy multiple items.

Private Clipboard Formats

The three clipboard formats used in the *ClipBoard* demo demonstrate the general processes involved in working with the clipboard. Any of the other clipboard formats should present no special difficulties. However, there are a few clipboard formats that merit some explanation, not because they require special handling as much as because they are defined for special purposes.

Special Text, Bitmap, and Metafile Formats

Windows defines the "private" clipboard formats of CF_DSPTEXT, CF_DSPBITMAP, CF_DSPMETAFILEPICT, and CF_DSPENHMETAFILE. These correspond to the CF_TEXT, CF_BITMAP, CF_METAFILEPICT, and CF_ENHMETAFILE types, but with the one principal difference: Applications requesting the standard formats will not access these private formats.

There are two assumptions here:

- Data using one of these private formats is intended for exchange between two instances of the same application or two applications specifically designed to operate together.

- Such exchanges may include private information, such as formatting and/or font information used by the Windows Write program.

The term *private* could be misleading. There is nothing to prevent any application from requesting access to one or more of these private formats; these are not designed for security purposes, only to declare nonpublic clipboard transfers.

Although two instances of an application, or two related applications, should understand their own private formats, the use of one of these formats does not ensure that the originator is, indeed, another instance of the same application or a companion application. In other words, there is nothing to prevent another, totally unrelated application from using these same format designations.

However, provisions have been made for this circumstance, and you can obtain the originator of the clipboard contents by calling the `GetClipboardOwner` function, as:

```
hwndCBOwner = GetClipboardOwner();
```

When the `EmptyClipboard` function was called in preparation for copying materials to the clipboard, the calling application became the new clipboard owner. Other applications accessing the clipboard to retrieve material do not gain ownership of the clipboard, only access. Thus, only the clipboard owner is responsible for originating material on the clipboard, and an application cannot place material on the clipboard without first becoming the clipboard owner and erasing the previous contents. Therefore, any application accessing information in a private format should also query the identity of the clipboard owner to determine if this data is, indeed, in a common format.

Although the `GetClipboardOwner` function returns a handle identifying the owner, this handle doesn't really tell you very much. But, given the handle, you can make another call to query the application's class name:

```
GetClassName( hwndCBOwner, &szClassName, 16 );
```

Finally, you can compare `szClassName` with the current application's class name or to a list of companion application class names to identify the source of the clipboard information.

Delayed Rendering

Frequently, posting data to the clipboard involves passing a copy of the data to the clipboard while keeping the original intact, which means expending memory on duplicate data blocks. In many circumstances, this may be unimportant, particularly when the memory requirements are small. One obvious solution, which is used in the *ClipBoard* demo, is to transfer the data without keeping a copy, thus avoiding the problem entirely.

But, there is also another solution, which is particularly appropriate when large amounts of data are involved: delayed rendering of the clipboard data. In delayed rendering, only the format specification is posted to the clipboard and instead of a global memory block handle, the handle parameter is passed as a NULL:

```
SetClipboardData( wFormat, NULL );
```

When an application requests a data item that has been posted for delayed rendering, identified by the NULL in place of the data block, Windows recognizes the use of delayed rendering and calls the clipboard owner (the application that posted the material to the clipboard) with a WM_RENDERFORMAT message, with the requested format specified in wParam.

In response to the WM_RENDERFORMAT message, the application is expected to respond with a SetClipboardData call, accompanied by the global memory block handle and the format identifier (rather than responding with an Open-Clipboard and EmptyClipboard call). In this fashion, the actual data is posted only when the recipient is ready to accept it.

You may pass multiple items to the clipboard as a mixture of conventional data transfers and delayed rendering transfers.

Special-Circumstance Messages

When an application loses ownership of the clipboard, Windows does nothing to prevent this loss but does post a WM_DESTROYCLIPBOARD message to the previous owner, indicating that ownership has been lost. In response, an application can resume ownership and post the same material again, but this is not recommended except in special circumstances.

Also, if an application is ready to terminate itself but is also currently the clipboard owner and the clipboard contains NULL data handles, Windows will send a WM_RENDERALLFORMATS message, without any format specifications, before the application is permitted to terminate. In response, the owner application has two options: clear the clipboard entirely or complete the delayed calls.

Unlike the response to the WM_RENDERFORMAT call, however, the terminating application should not use the SetClipboardData call but should simply clear the clipboard and write new entries entirely, just as if delayed rendering had not been used at all.

Owner-Displayed Clipboard Data

Another, very private, clipboard format is declared as:

```
SetClipboardData( CF_OWNERDISPLAY, NULL );
```

The CL_OWNERDISPLAY type is always passed with the global memory handle specified as NULL, just as with the delayed rendering format. But, because the clipboard
owner is directly responsible for the display, Windows does not send a WM_RENDER-
FORMAT message when the data is requested. Instead, messages must be sent
directly from the clipboard viewer to the clipboard owner.

You can identify the clipboard owner using the GetClipboardOwner function,
as described in the earlier section about private text, bitmap, and metafile formats. Conversely, the clipboard owner can use the GetClipboardViewer function
to identify the viewing application.

To use this private format, the viewer application posts a request to the clipboard owner application, requesting the originating application to provide the
actual display and granting the originating application access to the destination
application's display. Five messages may be sent from the destination:

WM_ASKCBFORMATNAME This message is sent by the clipboard viewer to
request a copy of the format name from the clipboard owner. Remember,
the clipboard itself contains only the CF_OWNERDISPLAY identifier, and the
viewer application is still free to decide if it is interested in the actual data
type. The WM_ASKCBFORMATNAME message is accompanied by a specification
in wParam for the number of bytes to copy. lParam provides a pointer to the
buffer where the response should be posted.

WM_HSCROLLCLIPBOARD/WM_VSCROLLCLIPBOARD These messages are sent
when the viewer application contains a horizontal or vertical scrollbar and
a scrollbar event must be reported to the clipboard owner. The wParam argument contains a handle to the viewer's window. The lParam argument contains the same scrollbar messages as would accompany standard
WM_HSCROLL or WM_VSCROLL messages.

WM_PAINTCLIPBOARD This message is sent requesting a repaint of the
viewer application's display, probably in response to a WM_PAINT message
received by the viewer application. The wParam argument contains a handle to the viewer's window. The lParam argument is a global DDESHARE
handle which, when locked, points to a PAINTSTRUCT structure defining

the area requiring repainting. To determine if all or part of the client area requires repainting, the clipboard owner must compare the dimensions of the drawing area reported in the rcpaint field of the PAINTSTRUCT with the dimensions reported in the most recent WM_SIZECLIPBOARD message.

WM_SIZECLIPBOARD This message is sent to indicate that the clipboard viewer has changed size. The wParam argument contains a handle to the viewer window. The lParam argument is a global DDESHARE handle pointing to a RECT structure defining the area to be painted.

In response to any of these messages, the clipboard owner should use the InvalidateRect function or repaint the viewer as desired and reset the scrollbar positions appropriately.

User-Defined Private Formats

Applications may also define their own private clipboard formats, registering a new clipboard format by calling the RegisterClipboardFormat function:

```
wFormat = RegisterClipboardFormat( lpszFormatTitle );
```

The returned wFormat identifier will be a value in the range 0xC000 to 0xFFFF and can subsequently be used as the format parameter in SetClipboardData and GetClipboardData calls. Before another application or instance can retrieve clipboard data in this format, it will require the same wFormat ID. This value could be passed via the clipboard using the CD_TEXT format.

Alternatively, you could use the EnumClipboardFormats function, discussed earlier in the chapter, to return all format identifiers, after which you should call the GetClipboardFormatName function to return the ASCII name of the format:

```
GetClipboardFormatName( wFormat, lpszBuffer, nCharCount );
```

WARNING The format identifiers CF_PRIVATEFIRST (0x0200) and CF_PRIVATELAST (0x02FF) may also be used as a range of integer values for private format identifiers. Note that data handles associated with formats in this range will not be freed automatically when another application requests clipboard ownership. Instead, any data handles in this range must be freed by the owner application before the application terminates or when a WM_DESTROYCLIPBOARD message is received. Use these latter format IDs with care.

Finally, note that Windows does not require any information about the organization of the data transferred using a private format. It is the application's responsibility to understand the details of the transfer format. All that Windows requires is a format name and a handle to the memory block.

As you've seen in this chapter, a variety of standard and special-purpose clipboard formats are available. Applications can also define and register their own special formats.

The clipboard offers an easy way for applications to exchange information. In the next chapter, we'll talk about DDE (Dynamic Data Exchange), which is another method that applications can use to exchange information.

CHAPTER
THIRTY-FIVE

Dynamic Data Exchange Operations

■ DDE basics

■ Client/server transactions

■ DDE Management Library (DDEML) functions

■ Asynchronous and synchronous transactions

The previous chapter introduced Windows clipboard functions as a means of exchanging data between different applications. This chapter introduces another way to transfer information and instructions between applications: Dynamic Data Exchange (DDE).

DDE is not suitable for distributed processing or for intensive data sharing in a situation where speed is the first, second, and third consideration. Instead, the real strength of DDE is that independent applications can exchange data without necessarily having been written explicitly to share with each other. As long as both applications know how to communicate, can request compatible topics and items, and understand each other's formats, the two applications can communicate.

Unlike clipboard operations, DDE ensures that messages and data are passed directly between applications sharing a conversation without the data becoming public (accessible to every application) and without the possibility of data being lost (as can happen if the clipboard is preempted by another application). Furthermore, unlike clipboard transfers in which a single service resource must be shared, several DDE conversations can be carried on simultaneously between two or more applications, with each conversation independent of the others.

An Introduction to DDE

DDE is a message-based system, the interapplication equivalent of the internal messaging system integral to all Windows applications. As with internal messages, DDE messages are managed by Windows.

Through DDE, independent applications may exchange messages and data. DDE messages may be broadcast (sent to any other applications that may be listening) or may be posted directly to specific applications.

DDE message traffic is a conversation between two (or more) applications and, like a human conversation, includes both protocols and redundancies. But even though both protocols and the inherent redundancies result in a system that, theoretically, is less than 100 percent efficient, like human conversations, the results produce a high degree of surety.

There is one big difference between human conversations and DDE conversations: Unlike humans, applications can carry on multiple DDE conversations with different applications or multiple DDE conversations with a single application—without losing track of the conversations or becoming hopelessly confused. In this respect, instead of engaging in conversations, a more reasonable analogy would be playing multiple chess games by post, with one or more opponents. In this fashion, even a mediocre player can keep up several "conversations," which would be quite impractical in a more time-intensive situation such as a tournament.

And the chess-by-post analogy holds in other respects. As with posting letters (or e-mail), the transactions themselves require some overhead and lack the immediacy of a conversation. Furthermore, like the postal-chess players, applications normally are doing other things between reading and responding to messages.

DDE Conversation Identifiers

In order to carry on a conversation, DDE applications require three basic identifiers:

Application name or service name In a DDE application, the application name refers to a broad category of information that may be provided by the server. While some servers do supply only one type of information, others may provide several types of data and thus use several *application names*. To avoid confusion, the DDEML (DDE Management Library) uses the term *service name* instead of *application name*.

NOTE Broadcast messages may be addressed to anyone listening (if they choose to pay attention), rather than to a specific application name. This is the equivalent of shouting "Hey, Joe ..." or "Attention, everyone ...".

Topic Any DDE conversation must have at least one topic, even though a single conversation may switch between multiple topics or multiple conversations may be using different topics. In a human conversation, the topic would be the subject; but in a DDL conversation, the topic must be specified and recognized by both parties. The topic name is commonly a filename.

Item The item name is an identifier within a topic that specifies a particular item of data as the subject of the current exchange. If a member of the conversation does not recognize the topic, the exchange fails and the conversation falters, even though the conversation itself may not fail completely. An item name might identify a page, a string, a bitmap, a spreadsheet cell, or any other data that might be transferred from one program to another.

For example, a spreadsheet might support two service types: spreadsheet and chart. As topics, each of these services might use filenames to refer to specific spreadsheet data files. The items in the spreadsheet services could be cell ranges or labels used within the spreadsheet. Items in the chart service might be presentation formats such as pie or bar.

In the *DDE* demo discussed in this chapter, a relatively limited conversation is carried on between five instances and involves only a few topics and items. In other cases, the topics and items can be quite extensive. These are limited only by the vocabulary that the participants share. Also, like the clipboard data transfers described in Chapter 34, the data elements exchanged can be as simple as integer data, as extensive as a bitmap or metafile, or as complex as an array of record structures. The information may even be any custom data type that all the participants recognize.

Limiting a server to a single service has its own advantages. If the service and the server have the same name, a client who knows one also knows the other. Given the .EXE filename, a client could initiate a conversation.

If the server and service have different names or if there are several services, then client applications (and developers) need additional information before clients can initiate conversations. An alternative is for the server to provide one service, named something like system service, which simply reports the names of the available services to the client applications. See "The System Topic" later in this chapter.

Also, when the client application knows the server (program) name as well as the service name, the client can launch the server, using the CreateProcess function, for example, and resume links from the last session.

Types of Transactions

DDEML conversations consist of three types of transactions: link, poke, and execute.

Link Transactions

The link transaction is the most common type, in which the client requests a data item from the server. The link may be any of three types:

> **Cold link** This conversation is initiated by a client application that broadcasts a WM_DDE_INITIATE request, identifying both the called application and the type of data requested (either or both of these can be NULL if any available server or subject is acceptable). In turn, as appropriate, one or

more servers may respond, identifying themselves for further conversation. If the server does not match the requested name or does not recognize the topic, it will not respond; only affirmative responses are expected. The link ends immediately after receiving the data.

Warm link This conversation assumes that the client and server "know" each other and that the server has new information it believes the client will find of interest. Normally, the client will have sent a WM_DDE_ADVISE message to the server requesting updates on a topic (and item) as they become available. The server, aside from acknowledging the request, responds only when there is new information available.

Hot link This conversation is similar to a warm-link in that the client requests information, but differs in that the client expects acknowledgment and an immediate reply. If the server does not have information available immediately, it will simply respond that the data is not available and will wait for another request. For a hot-link conversation, the server does not volunteer information until the client places a request.

Elements of all three types of links may occur during a single conversation. Also, the types are quite mutable—so mutable, in fact, that it may be difficult to determine where one type starts and another ends.

Poke Transactions

A poke transaction is used to send an item from the client to the server or, more explicitly, to send an unsolicited data item as opposed to responding to a request for data.

Execute Transactions

A command or execute transaction allows the client to send the server a command or series of commands instructing the server to perform specific actions. Execute transactions are discussed presently.

DDE Data Exchange

Trying to explain how DDE exchanges work can quickly degenerate into a Marx Brothers' comedy routine, or perhaps more like the famous Abbot and Costello "Who's On First." A simple overview of a DDE conversation may be of more benefit.

A DDE exchange begins when a client application initiates a conversation and a server application responds. Once a conversation is initiated and until one party or the other terminates (disconnects) from the conversation, the client and server exchange data in one or more of the following fashions:

- The client requests data and the server fills the request.

- The client asks to be informed whenever a specific data item (or items) changes.

- The client requests an automatic update whenever a specific data item (or items) changes.

- The client transmits a command and the server executes the command.

- The client sends unsolicited data to the server.

An important point to remember is that a client application can also be a server, and vice versa. Any application may fill both roles at the same time. The distinction between client and server is artificial and a matter of momentary definition, because either machine can request or supply data.

The DDEML Functions

On its most basic level, a DDE conversation is a detailed and laborious process, involving exacting protocols and acknowledgments. However, because the most important element of programming is your results, not of how much code you slog through to get there, the DDEML provides an alternative. While concealing many of the details involved, the DDEML also conceals much of the labor.

The DDEML is a Windows-supplied library offering high-level API functions to simplify the DDE conversation process. The DDEML maintains a record for each conversation, using the CONVINFO structure, which includes the partners in the conversation, the topics and items requested, and the data format used, as well as type, status, errors, and other details concerning the conversation. Fortunately, most of these elements can simply be ignored by both the application and the programmer and left to the DDEML for handling.

Perhaps most important for developers is the simple fact that DDEML functions are far more transportable between Windows 3.x and Windows 98 (as well as Windows 95 and NT) than the native DDE functions that form the basis for the library routines.

The DDE Initalization Function

DdeInitialize is a DDEML function called to set up a callback function to DDE message traffic. Its use is demonstrated in the *DDE_Demo* demo described in this chapter.

When a program calls DdeInitialize, the DDEML notifies other programs by sending an XTYP_REGISTER to their callback functions. These XTYP_REGISTER messages are used by many clients to maintain a list of available services.

The use of an instance identifier in the DdeInitialize call places a new constraint on Windows programmers, because the instance identifier is local to a thread and is not inherited by a child process. Furthermore, because most of the DDEML operations require the instance identifier as a parameter, most of the program's DDEML operations for a specific service must be in the same thread where the DdeInitialize call was issued. In addition, the thread that initialized the DDE session must not terminate until the session ends; otherwise, there is no way to call DdeUninitialize and no graceful way to end the session.

The DDE Name Service Function

After initialization, server applications should also register the names of the services provided. The DdeNameService function is called with a handle to the string naming the service and an instance identifier for the service. From the instance identifier, the DDEML knows which callback procedure (and thread) supports the service.

```
HDDEDATA DdeNameService (
    DWORD dwInstID,      // instance ID
    HSZ   hsz1,          // string naming service
    HSZ   hszRes,        // reserved
    UINT  uFlags );      // service name flags
```

The value in dwInstID is derived from DdeInitialize. The flags in the uFlags parameter select registration/unregistration and blocking or receiving connection signals for the registered service:

DNS_REGISTER Registers the service name.

DNS_UNREGISTER Unregisters the service name. If the hsz1 argument is NULL, all services for this server are unregistered.

DNS_FILTERON Prevents the server from receiving XTYP_CONNECT messages for services that have not been registered.

DNS_FILTEROFF   Allows the server to receive XTYP_CONNECT messages whenever any DDE program calls DdeConnect.

The value returned by DdeNameService is actually a Boolean response of 0 for failure or nonzero for success, but it is typed as HDDEDATA to allow for possible future improvements in the return indicator.

If the application will support more than one service, each service must be registered separately. Also, it can be advantageous to use a separate thread for each service, maintaining the thread and the thread's instance handle while the service is in use.

The DDE Callback Function

The heart of each DDEML application is found in the DdeCallback function. The entry for this function is predefined, complete with a list of eight calling parameters, which will be supplied by Windows. However, DdeCallback is like the WndProc function in that the application is still responsible for filling in the responses. Table 35.1 lists the DdeCallback messages and the types of responses they expect.

TABLE 35.1:   DdeCallBack Message Types

Message	Response
XTYP_ADVSTART XTYP_CONNECT	Boolean: (TRUE or FALSE)
XTYP_ADVREQ XTYP_REQUEST XTYP_WILDCONNECT	Data handle (or NULL)
XTYP_ADVDATA XTYP_EXECUTE XTYP_POKE	Transaction flag: DDE_FACK, DDE_FBUSY, or DDE_FNOTPROCESSED
XTYP_ADVSTOP XTYP_CONNECT_CONFIRM XTYP_DISCONNECT XTYP_ERROR XTYP_REGISTER XTYP_UNREGISTER XTYP_XACT_COMPLETE	None; notification only

The DDE Client Transaction Function

Each call to the DdeClientTransaction function instructs the DDEML to send a message to the server. The message type differs according to the type of action requested by the client. The server's callback function deals with each message in an appropriate fashion. Table 35.2 summarizes the transactions for some message types, which are explained in more detail in the following sections.

TABLE 35.2: Transaction Types

Message	Transaction
XTYP_REQUEST	Cold link; send a single data item
XTYP_ADVISE	Warm or hot link; respond by sending data and updates
XTYP_POKE	Poke (receive) data from the client
XTYP_EXECUTE	Execute a command or perform an action

Request Transaction Handling

When the server receives an XTYP_REQUEST message, it reads the topic and item names from the two string handle parameters and checks the requested data format. If the server recognizes the item and supports the format, the server creates a data object for the item's current value and returns a handle to the data object (HDDEDATA). If the server does not support the item or does not recognize the format, the server returns NULL.

> **NOTE**   A server that does not support request transactions should set the CBF_ FAIL_REQUESTS flag in DdeInitialize to avoid receiving unwanted XTYP_ REQUEST messages.

The value supplied by the server is returned to the client as the response from the DdeClientTransaction call. Figure 35.1 diagrams a typical interaction in three steps:

1. The client sends a request to the server, via the DDEML.

2. The server deciphers the request and packages the requested data.

3. The client receives and deciphers the response.

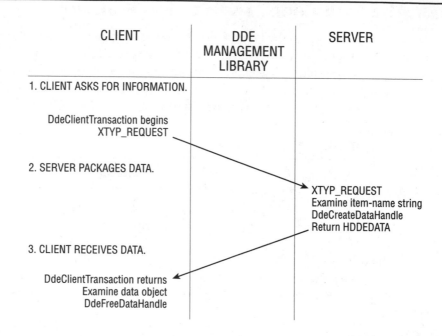

Advise Transaction Handling

When the client requests a link with updates, the server's callback procedure receives an XTYP_ADVSTART message. If the server recognizes the topic and item names and supports the requested format, the server returns TRUE to confirm the link; if not, it returns FALSE to prevent the link.

NOTE   The XTYP_ADVSTART message does not tell the server whether the link will be warm or hot.

Hot-Link Operations In a hot link, the server does not return data immediately; it sends data only when the requested data item next changes. In response to XTYP_ADVSTART, the server often sets a flag to remind itself that updates have been requested. Whenever an item changes, the server checks the state of the flag and, if it is set, calls `DdePostAdvise` to notify the DDEML that new data is available for an interested client.

The server does not need to remember which client has requested a particular item; the DDEML handles this task internally. Given the topic and item name, which are supplied by the server to identify the available item data, the DDEML determines which clients are linked and whether the links are hot or warm.

If the links are hot, the DDEML immediately sends the server an XTYP_ADVREQ message, receives the data from the server, and then posts it to the client in an XTYP_ADVDATA message. Figure 35.2 illustrates the steps in the process:

1. The loop is initiated by the client with the server acknowledging the request with a TRUE response.

2. The server advises the DDEML that new data is available. In turn, the DDEML determines this is a hot link and requests the data, then sends it to the client application. This step will repeat as often as the server has new data available.

3. The client terminates the hot link by sending an XTYP_ADVSTOP message, which the server acknowledges with a NULL response.

FIGURE 35.2:

Initiating, executing, and closing a hot link advise loop

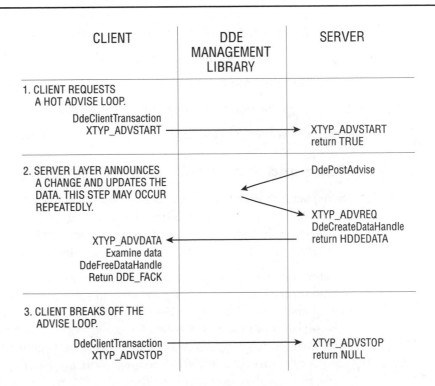

Warm-Loop Operations When a warm-loop advice operation is requested, the DDEML is still advised when the server's data changes for the requested item, but it does not send a data request message to the server. Instead, the DDEML sends an empty XTYP_ADVDATA message to the client with a NULL data handle.

NOTE   A server that does not support advise loops of any kind should set the CBF_FAIL_ADVISES flag in the `DdeInitialize` operation to avoid receiving unwanted XTYP_ADVSTART and XTYP_ADVSTOP messages.

To see the item's data (to receive a new value), the client must execute a request transaction. Figure 35.3 illustrates the steps in the process:

1. The server announces that new data is available.

2. The DDEML notifies the client but the client ignores the notification. In this case, notifications will be sent to the client each time the server data changes, but the client is free to ignore these notifications.

3. The server announces a change in the requested data item.

4. The client responds with a request for the data (XTYP_REQUEST).

5. The data request is passed by the DDEML to the server.

6. The server returns the requested data to the client.

Poke and Execute Transaction Handling

Some servers wish to accept data from the client, reversing the usual transfer direction. A client that intends to send data to the server needs an XTYP_POKE transaction. In response to this message, the server checks the topic and item, then if it wants the information, it reads the data object.

Some servers also accept commands from their clients, receiving the commands in the form of data handles. The server locks the object, parses, the command string contained in the data object, and then performs some action in response. The server must also free the data handle after parsing, but it may duplicate the data string if it will be needed later. Because clients generally expect commands to execute immediately and may expect confirmation, the server should, if possible, execute the command from the callback function prior to returning.

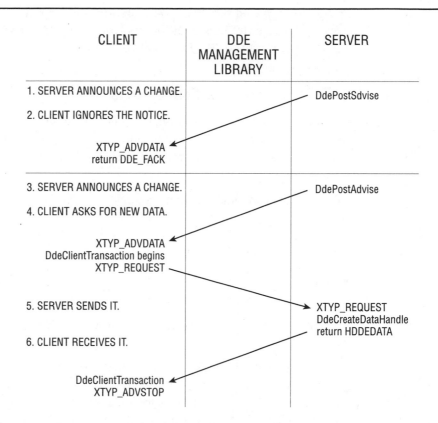

Initiating, executing, and closing a warm link advise loop

TIP

Both Microsoft Excel and Word accept execute messages where the item string is a command from the application's macro language. For example, a DDEML transaction addressed to the **winword** service on the **system** topic with the string [**file1**] in the data handle instructs Word to load its most recently used file.

In response to a poke or execute transaction, the server returns one of three values:

DDE_FACK The data is received and acknowledged.

DDE_FBUSY The server is too busy to process the data or instruction; try again later.

DDE_FNOTPROCESSED The data or instruction is refused.

Flags set in the DdeInitialize operation can filter out unwanted poke or execute messages for servers not supporting these. CBF_FAIL_POKES blocks poke transaction messages. CBF_FAIL_EXECUTES blocks execute transaction messages.

The DDE Disconnect Functions

To terminate a DDE conversation, the client or the server calls either DdeDisconnect to terminate a specific conversation or DdeDisconnectList to terminate all conversations. In both cases, an XTYP_DISCONNECT transaction is sent to the other application or applications.

For a single conversation, DdeDisconnect is called:

```
DdeDisconnect( hConv );
```

where hConv is the conversation handle returned from the DdeConnect function.

To disconnect all conversations, DdeDisconnectList is called:

```
DdeDisconnectList( hConvList );
```

where hConvList is the conversation handle returned from the DdeConnectList function.

When the DDEML receives the XTYP_DISCONNECT transaction message, any transactions still in progress for the given conversation(s) are abandoned. By convention, only clients are expected to break off conversations. Depending on circumstances, however, servers sometimes must disconnect, such as when the server application is closed.

WARNING   Clients and servers alike should be prepared to receive disconnect messages at any time during a conversation and should close data structures accordingly.

The DDE Uninitialize Function

When an application closes, or when it no longer wishes to converse with other applications, the application should uninitialize all DDEML callback procedures.

Calling DdeUninitialize removes a service from the DDEML tables, terminates any conversations still in progress, and sends XTYP_UNREGISTER messages to all DDEML callback procedures. Figure 35.4 shows the steps involved in breaking off a conversation and withdrawing from the DDEML.

FIGURE 35.4:

Closing down a client and a server

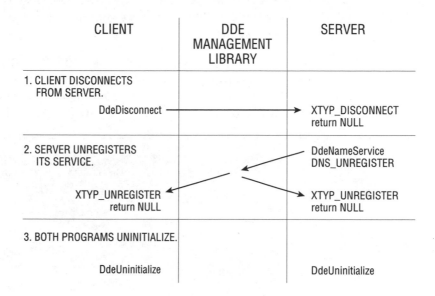

DDE Errors

Normally, when a DDEML function fails and returns either NULL or FALSE, extended error information can be retrieved by calling DdeGetLastError:

```
UINT DdeGetLastError( DWORD dwInstID );
```

Because DdeGetLastError requires an instance identifier, this function cannot be used to return error information if DdeInitialize fails. Therefore DdeInitialize returns its own extended error codes:

DWLERR_NO_ERROR Initialization succeeded.

DWLERR_DLL_USAGE The program is registered as a monitor and cannot use the DDEML for transactions.

DWLERR_INVALIDPARAMETER A parameter contained invalid information.

DWLERR_SYS_ERROR An internal error occurred in DDEML.

The DDE_Demo Demo: Using the DDML Functions

The *DDE_Demo* demo uses multiple instances of a single application, with each instance acting as both client and server to all other instances. Structurally, *DDE_Demo* is similar to the previous examples in this book, but it does introduce a few new elements.

Figure 35.5 shows an example of the *DDE_Demo* window, with five instances of the application communicating with each other. Individual instances could be minimized (reduced to an icon on the program bar) or even hidden, but despite changes in size, state, or Desktop visibility, they still remain active.

FIGURE 35.5:

Five instances communicating via DDE

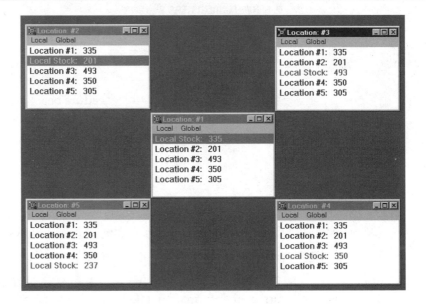

Each instance of *DDE_Demo* is communicating with each of the other instances. Each instance is maintaining a local data element which is listed in this simulation as *Local Stock*, with the label and amount appearing in red. At the same time, each instance also reports the stock level of all of the other instances, listing these in black.

In Figure 35.5, the instance identified as Location #5 has just updated its own stock level but has not yet reported the change to the remaining instances. Also, the instances identified as Locations #1 and #2 are currently inactive (paused). The window in Figure 35.5 reflects this by showing its stock level (locally) as a gray bar with light gray text. Also, even though these two instances are paused, they continue to report changes made by other locations.

The remaining active instances show their own stock levels in red and display the stock levels of other locations in black.

NOTE The *DDE_Demo* is included on the CD that accompanies this book, in the Chapter 35 folder. Keep in mind that this demo has been written simply to illustrate how DDE data exchanges work and how instructions can be passed between applications or application instances. It uses source code that is both relatively brief and sufficiently structured to allow you to understand what is happening. This is not intended as a practical application—in fact, it is a rather frivolous example.

DDE Application Initalization

Within the application, the `WinMain` procedure begins in a familiar enough fashion by initializing itself (by calling the `InitApplication` function from the Template.I include file). Once the application has been initialized, `DdeInitialize`, a DDEML function, is called to set up a callback function to DDE message traffic.

```
int WINAPI WinMain( HINSTANCE hInstance,
                    HINSTANCE hPrevInstance,
                    LPSTR     lpCmdLine,
                    INT       nCmdShow )
{
    ...
    if( DdeInitialize( &idInst, (PFNCALLBACK) DdeCallback,
                    APPCMD_FILTERINITS |
                    CBF_SKIP_CONNECT_CONFIRMS |
                    CBF_FAIL_SELFCONNECTIONS |
                    CBF_FAIL_POKES,
                    0 ) )
        return(FALSE);          // fail if error occurs
```

NOTE Under Windows 3.*x*, the `DdeCallback` procedure cannot be referenced directly but requires the use of a `MakeProcInstance` call. Although it is not required by Windows 98 (or Windows 95 or NT), `MakeProcInstance` is still defined, as a null macro, for compatibility with Windows 3.*x*.

While establishing the callback function, several conditions are also established. These are a series of filter conditions that restrict the types of message traffic handled:

APPCMD_FILTERINITS Filter out any applications except those with our own service name.

CBF_SKIP_CONNECT_CONFIRMS Don't bother to confirm connections.

CBF_FAIL_SELFCONNECTIONS Don't permit self-connections.

CBF_FAIL_POKES Don't allow XTYP_POKE transactions.

Additional filter conditions can be imposed (as defined in DDEML.H), but these conditions suffice for the present demonstration.

If the callback function cannot be established for some reason, the application returns FALSE and terminates (this is an unlikely event).

Next, the CreateWindow function is called in the customary fashion. An addition is that in case of failure, provisions are made to call the DdeUninitialize function before terminating.

```
hInst = hInstance;
hwnd = CreateWindow( szAppName, szAppTitle,
                     WS_OVERLAPPEDWINDOW,
                     CW_USEDEFAULT, CW_USEDEFAULT,
                     CW_USEDEFAULT, CW_USEDEFAULT,
                     NULL, NULL, hInstance, NULL );
if( ! hwnd )
{
    DdeUninitialize( idInst );
    return( FALSE );
}
```

The next provision is specific to the present demo. It looks for a command-line parameter, which will be used to identify the separate instances of the application (for our benefit only). Because the initial instance is not expected to have a command-line argument, a default of 1 is also supplied.

```
if( strlen( lpCmdLine ) )
    iInst = atoi( lpCmdLine );
else
    iInst = 1;
```

The supplied arguments have nothing to do with the DDEML and are used only for labeling purposes. The DDEML has other means of identifying each individual instance, using the identification handle supplied by Windows. The origin of the command-line parameters for all but the first instance will be apparent in a moment.

NOTE   If it occurs to you that the `hPrevInstance` argument could be used to determine if this is the first instance of the application, note that Windows 98 does not supply an `hPrevInstance` argument. Because each application under Windows 98 executes in its own virtual space, this argument is always supplied as NULL, irrespective of how many other instances of an application are executing. The customary test is supplied only for compatibility with Windows 3.x.

Pseudo-random number generators are used to supply data. Characteristically, these will always generate the same number sequence unless they are seeded (or initialized) to provide a different starting condition. For this purpose, Borland's `randomize` function accesses the system clock. However, because Microsoft C does not supply a `randomize` function, an alternative is supplied to ensure that each instance of the application will generate a different series.

```
#ifdef __BORLANDC__
    randomize();
#else
    srand( (unsigned)time( NULL ) );
#endif
```

The next task, if this is the first instance of the application, is to spawn the remaining four instances by calling the `WinExec` function and supplying the command-line parameter for each.

```
switch( iInst )
{                    // first instance calls four others
    case 1:   xLoc = 195;   yLoc = 125;
              WinExec( "DDE_DEMO 2", SW_SHOW );
              WinExec( "DDE_DEMO 3", SW_SHOW );
              WinExec( "DDE_DEMO 4", SW_SHOW );
              WinExec( "DDE_DEMO 5", SW_SHOW );   break;
    case 2:   xLoc = 0;      yLoc = 0;            break;
    case 3:   xLoc = 390;    yLoc = 0;            break;
    case 4:   xLoc = 390;    yLoc = 250;          break;
    case 5:   xLoc = 0;      yLoc = 250;          break;
}
```

Also, each instance of the application is supplied with separate xLoc and yLoc coordinates, spacing each around the screen for an optimum display. Again, these provisions are specific to the present demo, and have nothing to do with DDE functions or the DDEML.

Connection Preparations

Next, the ShowWindow and UpdateWindow functions are called in the usual fashion. However, before proceeding to the customary message loop, there are a few provisions that the DDEML requires.

```
hszAppName = DdeCreateStringHandle( idInst, szAppTitle, 0 );
```

The first step for this operation is to create a string handle for the application title. The idInst argument was supplied earlier by the DDEInitialize function and identifies this instance of the application. The final argument, CP_WINANSI, identifies the default code page. Alternatively, you would use CP_WINUNICODE if you wanted the Unicode version of the DDEML.

Next, a format handle is retrieved by calling the RegisterClipboardFormat function before the present instance attempts to connect to any other matching DDE applications by calling DdeConnectList.

```
hFormat = RegisterClipboardFormat( szAppTitle );
hConvList = DdeConnectList( idInst, hszAppName, hszAppName,
                            hConvList, NULL );
```

If there are no DDE applications matching the requested name and topic, that's okay; the conversation list (hConvList) simply remains empty until there is someone to talk to. (Remember, if this is the first instance, self-connection has already been prohibited.)

Last, the DdeNameService function is called to register the current instance. This function broadcasts to all other DDE applications that the present application instance is available, but it does not force a connection.

```
DdeNameService( idInst, hszAppName, 0, DNS_REGISTER );
```

Finally, with the DDE connections established, the usual message loop begins and continues until the application instance is ready to terminate.

```
while( GetMessage( &msg, NULL, 0, 0 ) )
{
    TranslateMessage( &msg );
    DispatchMessage( &msg );
}
```

When the application is ready to terminate, a couple of cleanup provisions are desirable. These provisions include a call to `DestroyWindow` and then to `UnregisterClass`.

```
DestroyWindow( hwnd );
UnregisterClass( szAppTitle, hInstance );
```

Transaction Message Responses

Although the application is responsible for handling `DdeCallback` responses, you are not required to respond to all possible transaction types. In the *DDE_Demo* demo, responses are limited to eight XTYP_*xxxx* transactions.

In the demo, the subprocedure `PostTransaction` is used to handle the details of the transaction (as discussed a bit later in the chapter), but still specifies the transaction type, as follows:

XTYP_REQUEST	Cold link	Transaction ends with receipt of data item
XTYP_ADVSTART	Hot link	Server sends new data in an **XTYP_ADVDATA** message whenever the item change
XTYP_ADV_START or XTYPF_ADVNODATA	Warm link	Server sends an empty **XTYP_ADVDATA** message whenever the data item changes

The first transaction is XTYP_CONNECT. However, because filtering has already been specified (in the `DdeInitialize` call), any connections that come through are for the present DDE application and can be accepted by returning TRUE.

```
case XTYP_CONNECT:            return( TRUE );
```

Also, because no provisions have been made for XTYP_WILD_CONNECT transactions, attempts at wildcard connections will fail automatically.

Despite the preceding, when an XTYP_ADVSTART transaction request is received to start a conversation, a test is applied to ensure that we are both (client and server) talking about the same topic and know who we're talking to.

```
case XTYP_ADVSTART:
    return( (UINT) wFmt == hFormat && hszItem == hszAppName );
```

If either calling argument fails, the result returned is FALSE, declining the conversation. Of course, the calling application is free to try again with a different topic (or maybe it really wanted to query a different application and was broadcasting the request).

Since new DDE applications can come in at any time, it would be impractical to attempt to synchronize everybody's initialization. The XTYP_REGISTER transaction notes the new arrival, updates the connection list (hConvList), and then posts a XTYP_ADVSTART transaction back—kind of a "Howdy, neighbor" conversation.

```
case XTYP_REGISTER:
    hConvList = DdeConnectList( idInst, hszItem, hszAppName,
                                hConvList, NULL );
    PostTransaction( NULL, 0, hFormat, XTYP_ADVSTART );
    UpdateWindow( hwnd );
    return( TRUE );
```

With a new DDE application in the loop, this is also an appropriate time to update the current instance's window. Alternatively, this could be left to wait for more information (such as a data transaction).

Another event that could occur is that somebody exits from our conversation. But when this happens, there isn't a great deal that the present demo needs to handle. A simple InvalidateRect instruction to repaint the window is quite sufficient.

```
case XTYP_DISCONNECT:
    InvalidateRect( hwnd, NULL, TRUE );
    break;
```

The next two transaction types are XTYP_ADVREQ (ADVise REQuested) and XTYP_REQUEST, both of which expect a response in the form of a data report. In many DDE applications, this would result in the data being rendered in text format (usually a delimited format) to fit the CF_TEXT format. Here, however, a custom format has been used and rendering is not required.

```
case XTYP_ADVREQ:
case XTYP_REQUEST:
    return( DdeCreateDataHandle( idInst, (PBYTE) &DataOut,
                                 sizeof( DataOut ),
                                 0, hszAppName, hFormat, 0 ) );
```

The DdeCreateDataHandle function is used to provide a handle to the data block. In this case, the data that will be transferred is a UNIT (32-bit unsigned integer), which has the source ID (iInst) in the high byte of the high word and the remainder of the data in the low-order word. Packing this custom format is handled in the WndProc procedure, as described a bit later in the chapter.

When the application is acting as a client rather than a server, the XTYP_ADVDATA (ADVise DATA) transaction handles the other end of the transaction, by calling `DdeGetData` and `DdeSetUserHandle` to render the data in a format accessible to the rest of the application.

```
case XTYP_ADVDATA:
    if( DdeGetData( hData, (PBYTE) &DataIn, sizeof(DataIn), 0 ) )
        DdeSetUserHandle( hConv, QID_SYNC, DataIn );
    InvalidateRect( hwnd, NULL, TRUE );
    return( DDE_FACK );
```

The `DdeGetData` function copies the data to a local buffer (`DataIn`) before the `DdeSetUserHandle` function is called to associate the local buffer with a conversation handle (`hConv`). This process simplifies asynchronous transactions (discussed later in the chapter) and is completed, in the `WndProc` procedure, when the `DdeQueryConvInfo` procedure is called in response to the `WM_PAINT` message.

Also, as you will note in the `WndProc` procedure, this transaction is initiated, within a loop calling all parties to the present conversation, in response to the `WM_PAINT` message. This transaction could be initiated for many different reasons under many different conditions—perhaps periodically by a timer or in response to a request for a recalculation of some type. The current handling was dictated only by the requirements of this demo.

One transaction type remains in the current demo: the XTYP_EXECUTE transaction (a request issued by another application or application instance for the present instance to take some particular action). The first step, before we can determine what action is requested, is to access the data by calling `DdeAccessData` to return a local pointer (local to this instance and procedure) to what is assumed to be string data.

```
case XTYP_EXECUTE:
    pszExec = DdeAccessData( hData, &dwSize );
    if( pszExec )
    {
```

Optionally, the `dwSize` parameter receives the size of the returned string. If the size of the returned data is not required, this argument may be supplied as NULL.

If `pszExec` is not NULL (it points to a string), the next step is to determine if the string instruction matches anything that we're prepared to respond to.

```
        if( ! stricmp( "PAUSE", pszExec ) )
            PauseAutomatic( hwnd );
        else
        if( ! stricmp( "RESUME", pszExec ) )
            ResumeAutomatic( hwnd );
```

Only two responses have been provided here, triggered by the key strings "PAUSE" and "RESUME" and each calling a subprocedure. As you will see in the WndProc procedure, these same subprocedures are also called in response to menu messages. Incidentally, notice that the string comparison used is case-insensitive.

What is immediately relevant here is that these instructions are received from another application or application instance. The instructions originate outside the application but are acted on by the application. In a moment, in the WndProc procedure, you will find the matching provisions that permit transmitting such instructions to other applications.

For the moment, however, because switch/case statements can only use integral arguments, we need a series of if/else statements for matching strings. And, if more than a few tests are required, this can result in a rather complicated structure.

As an alternative, you could use a loop to match string arguments against string-table entries with a following switch/case statement using the string-table entry number when a match is found.

DDE Performance Discrepancies under Windows 98

Although the DdeAccessData function performs correctly on a Windows NT system, under Windows 98 the execution string returned (pszExec) by the function is not correct. Instead, the returned string has a four-byte error, beginning 0x00, 0x20, 0x0C, 0xDC. To correct this discrepancy, a test routine has been added as follows:

```
case XTYP_EXECUTE:
    pszExec = DdeAccessData( hData, &dwSize );
    if( pszExec[0] <= 0x20 )
        pszExec += 4;
    if( pszExec )
    {
```

You can test this under Windows 98 by placing a break on the DdeAccessData call and using the watch window to examine the string value returned when issuing a global **Pause** or **Resume** instruction. Alternatively, if you comment out the test provision, the global **Pause** and **Resume** instructions will function locally (in the instance window where they are issued) but will not be recognized by any of the other processes.

Continued on next page

Also, the dwSize value returned by the DdeAccessData function under Windows 98 bears no connection to the actual string length nor to the arguments passed in either of the PostTransaction instructions:

```
PostTransaction( "RESUME", 7, 0, XTYP_EXECUTE );
PostTransaction( "PAUSE", 6, 0, XTYP_EXECUTE );
```

Because the dwSize argument is not used by the *DDE_Demo* demo, this error does not require correction in this case. The same, however, cannot be said to apply to all applications.

Although less critical, in *DDE_Demo*, breakpoints may not respond to events generated from the first instance of the five client/server instances but will respond to the same events generated by any of the remaining instances. This discrepancy has no effect on the actual instructions being passed between the five instances. It affects only attempts to debug operations. This particular idiosyncrasy applies equally under Windows using the Microsoft compiler.

DDE Elements in the WndProc Procedure

As usual, the WndProc procedure directs the principal activities of the *DDE_Demo* demo, with the obvious exception of responses to instructions received from another application (or instance of this application) via DDE links.

As each instance is created in the demo, the WM_CREATE message provides an opportunity to initialize a timer before sending a WM_SIZE message to size and position the application instance.

The WM_TIMER response is the first location where the DDE functions are actually invoked. It begins by updating the LocalStock variable:

```
case WM_TIMER:
    if( random( 2 ) )
        LocalStock += random( 100 );
    else
        LocalStock -= min( (UINT) random( 100 ), LocalStock );
    DataOut = ( iInst << 24 ) + LocalStock;
```

After the LocalStock variable has changed, the DataOut variable, which is used as the custom data format for the actual data transfer, is updated by packing the instance identifier (iInst) in the high byte of the high word with the Local-Stock value in the low-order word. In your own applications, you might prefer to use a record or data structure at this point. For the demo, this simpler format is sufficient.

Next, now that the data is ready, a DdePostAdvise message is issued to let other applications know that new data is available. This will be received by other parties to the conversation, in the DdeCallback function, as an XTYP_ADVDATA transaction.

```
DdePostAdvise( idInst, hszAppName, hszAppName );
SetRect( &rc, 0, 0, cxText, cyText );
InvalidateRect( hwnd, &rc, TRUE );
UpdateWindow( hwnd );
break;
```

Last, after the DDE transaction has been posted, the application instance issues instructions to update its own window to show the new value. As you can see in Figure 35.5 (shown earlier in the chapter), where Location #5 has been updated but the remaining instances have not, this does not determine which of the DDE clients will be first to update their screens.

The WM_PAINT message response also executes DDE link transactions. First, if hConvList is not NULL, indicating that the application does have conversation links with other applications or instances, DdeQueryNextServer is called to set hConv to the first conversation on the list.

```
case WM_PAINT:
    ...             // poll other locations and report
    if( hConvList )
    {
        hConv = DdeQueryNextServer( hConvList, 0 );
        while( hConv )
        {
            ciData.cb = sizeof(CONVINFO);
            DdeQueryConvInfo( hConv, QID_SYNC, &ciData );
```

Once we have a handle to a conversation, DdeQueryConvInfo is used to get the latest data. (The actual paint operations used to display this data are not particularly different from those demonstrated in earlier examples.)

Once we've finished with the present conversation, DdeQueryNextServer is called again, this time using the current conversation as an argument, to get the next conversation in the list. The loop continues until no further conversations are found.

```
            hConv = DdeQueryNextServer( hConvList, hConv );
        }
    }
```

Before an application can terminate, the WM_CLOSE message is always posted and, normally, responds by calling PostQuitMessage to terminate. In this application, however, before terminating, there are a few other tasks that need to be handled. These are primarily steps to clean up the DDE link, but also to kill the local timer. (Timers may not be the limited resource that they were under Windows 3.1, but they are still not a resource we should waste by leaving them active when no longer needed.)

```
case WM_CLOSE:
    KillTimer( hwnd, TRUE );
    DdeDisconnectList( hConvList );
    DdeNameService( idInst, 0, 0, DNS_UNREGISTER );
    DdeFreeStringHandle( idInst, hszAppName );
    DdeUninitialize( idInst );
    PostQuitMessage( FALSE );
    break;
```

As for the DDE link itself, the first step is to disconnect, then to unregister the service name and free the string handle before, finally, uninitializing the DDE link. And, with this done, the application is finally free to exit.

Other Provisions in WndProc

Aside from direct DDE provisions, the WndProc procedure also processes menu messages. The demo provides two pull-down menus: Local and Global. Each of these menus offers two options: Resume and Pause. The two Local menu options are used to instruct the local instance to either resume automatic operation or to pause automatic operation. The two Global menu options fall through to the local options.

Before falling though, however, the two Global options are used to broadcast messages to other conversation clients, instructing them to either resume or pause. This is accomplished by calling the PostTransaction procedure:

```
case WM_COMMAND:
    switch( LOWORD( wParam ) )
    {
        case IDG_RESUME:
            PostTransaction( "RESUME", 7, 0, XTYP_EXECUTE );
            // no break - falls through to local selection //

        case IDL_RESUME:
            ResumeAutomatic( hwnd );
            break;
```

```
                    case IDG_PAUSE:
                        PostTransaction( "PAUSE", 6, 0, XTYP_EXECUTE );
                        // no break - falls through to local selection //

                    case IDL_PAUSE:
                        PauseAutomatic( hwnd );
                        break;
            }
            break;
```

The `PostTransaction` procedure is a locally defined operation called with four parameters:

> **pScr** A pointer to the instruction string.
>
> **cbData** The length (size) of the instruction.
>
> **fmt** The data format identifier.
>
> **xtyp** The transaction type.

```
VOID PostTransaction( PBYTE pSrc, DWORD cbSize, UINT fmt, UINT xtyp )
{
    HCONV   hConv;
    DWORD   dwResult;
    int     iCheck = 0;
```

Locally, the `hConv` variable is a handle to a conversation. The integer `iCheck` is used to check if any new conversations have been established and, if so, to allow the local instance to update its display. The conversation loop is essentially the same as the one for the `WM_PAINT` message, described in the previous section. The type of conversation, however, differs.

In this situation, the `DdeClientTransaction` API function is called with the instruction, the instruction size (length), the application name (ID), the format, the transaction type, and the `TIMEOUT_ASYNC` instruction identifying this as an asynchronous transaction. Synchronous DDE transactions would specify a time-out in milliseconds.

Last, `dwResult` would receive the results of the transaction but, in this case, we really don't care about the success or failure of this transaction. Because we don't want to wait for a result to be reported, this is being sent as an asynchronous transaction that returns immediately (automatically returning TRUE). Although a subsequent transaction message would report success or failure, no provisions are included to handle or, in the case of failure, to send the instruction again. Therefore,

DdeAbandonTransaction is called to terminate this conversation without waiting for a response.

```
if( DdeClientTransaction( pSrc, cbSize, hConv, hszAppName, fmt,
                          xtyp, TIMEOUT_ASYNC, &dwResult ) )
    DdeAbandonTransaction( idInst, hConv, dwResult );
```

Presumably, however, the posted instruction will be received by the other application instances, in the DdeCallback function, and acted on accordingly.

Asynchronous versus Synchronous Transactions

DDEML clients have a choice between synchronous and asynchronous transactions. The *DDE_Demo* demo uses asynchronous transactions. The difference between synchronous and asynchronous operations matters only to the client programs. From the server's viewpoint, both types of transactions appear the same.

The advantages of synchronous transactions are that they are faster and easier to program. Asynchronous transactions are useful for busy programs that need to perform substantial amounts of processing while interacting with a DDEML server, or for programs that regularly interact with a particularly slow server and need to avoid remaining idle.

Synchronous Transactions

When synchronous transactions are used, the client application waits for an answer from the server after initiating a transaction, whether issuing a request for information or a sending a command for action. If the server makes the client wait longer than the client's time-out period, DdeClientTransaction cancels the transaction and returns.

In a synchronous transaction, you must make provisions for freeing data objects. The DDEML passes the data handle as a return value from DdeClient-Transaction and has no way of knowing when the data can be freed. The client owns the data objects received synchronously from DdeClientTransaction and must eventually call DdeFreeDataHandle to release them.

Asynchronous Transactions

For asynchronous operation, when calling DdeClientTransaction, set the time-out period to TIMEOUT_ASYNCH. In return, DdeClientTransaction will return TRUE immediately, returning a transaction ID in the dwResult field.

While the client application continues executing other operations, DDEML pursues the transaction in the background. Then, when the transaction is complete, the DDEML sends an XTYP_XACT_COMPLETE message to the client's callback procedure. This completion message includes the transaction ID in the dwData1 parameter, allowing the client to determine which transaction request is completed.

The DDEML also provides an alternative mechanism for identifying transactions from their completion messages. The client may register a DWORD value of its own to associate with each asynchronous transaction. DdeSetUserHandle accepts a conversation handle, an asynchronous transaction ID, and a custom DWORD value, storing these internally. When the XTYP_XACT_COMPLETE message is received, the client retrieves the private identifier by calling DdeQueryComplete.

While waiting for an asynchronous transaction to complete, DdeClient-Transaction enters a modal loop and polls for window messages, allowing the client to continue to respond to user input while waiting. The client may not, however, execute a second DDEML function during this period.

An attempt to call DdeClientTransaction also fails if another synchronous operation is already in progress for the same client.

To cancel an asynchronous operation before completion, call the **DdeAbandon-Transaction** function. The DDEML then discards all resources associated with the transaction and discards the result when the server eventually returns. (This is the same process that occurs when a synchronous transaction times out.)

In an asynchronous transaction, the DDEML delivers the data object handle to the client's callback function. When the callback function returns, the DDEML reasonably assumes that the data is no longer needed and frees the data object automatically. If the client needs to preserve the data, the client should make a copy of the data (using DdeGetData) before returning.

WARNING The client must not free data handles received asynchronously. Because the server is not aware that the data has been received, the server continues to assume ownership of the data package and will take the responsibility for freeing the data when notified that the data was received.

The System Topic

As explained earlier in the chapter, the customary sequence for initiating a conversation requires the client to know in advance which servers and/or topics are required. To make it possible for a client to survey available topics, DDEML servers sometimes include in each service a topic titled `system`.

Under the `system` name, support is provided for a set of standard informational items. Through the `system` topic, a client may obtain information about a specific service.

NOTE   A typical third-party server will normally document its service name(s), topic name(s), and item name(s).

Strings identifying standard system items are defined in DDEML.H and identified by constants. Three of these in particular should be supported by all server applications:

SZDDESYS_ITEM_FORMATS A list of strings, tab-delimited, indicating the clipboard formats supported by the server. (The item name string is `"Formats"`.)

SZDDESYS_ITEM_SYSITEMS A list of items supported by the server under the `system` topic. (The item name is `"SysItems"`.)

SZDDESYS_ITEM_TOPICS A list of topics supported by the server. (The item name is `"Topics"`.)

In addition to these three items under the `system` topic, a DDEML server should support another standard item under every topic:

SZDDE_ITEM_ITEMLIST A list of items from a topic other than `system`. (The item name is `"TopicItemList"`.)

In response to requests for these items, the server is expected to concatenate all of the topic, item, or format names into a single long string using tab characters as delimiters. The server creates a data object from the string, then passes the handle back to the DDEML as the return value in response to the XTYP_REQUEST message. The client then extracts the data from the object, parses the list, and displays the items for the user.

TIP   For an example of building an HDDEDATA list containing strings, refer to the TabList.C file on the accompanying CD.

Other DDE Examples

The *DDE_Demo* demo, discussed in this chapter and included on the CD that accompanies this book, demonstrates how the DDEML can be used for communications among applications. This program is limited to a single topic and two instructions, and forms little more than a sketch of DDE operations.

Two other demos, named *DBServer* and *DBClient*, are also included on the CD accompanying this book. The database server, *DBServer*, interacts only with DDEML clients and has a minimal user interface, possesses no menu, and remains permanently iconized. The only options provided to the user are to launch the server application and to close it. The *DBServer* application maintains a simple address/phone book, with all user interactions supplied by the client application.

The database client, *DBClient*, offers one menu and four dialog boxes. When you execute *DBClient*, the Connect option from the Database menu initiates a DDEML conversation with the server. Other menu options are Add, Delete, and Search, each of which brings up a simple dialog box to enter a name or phone number or both, as appropriate for the command. A fourth dialog box appears to show matching records located by the Search command.

This chapter has provided an introduction to DDE application development. For more details and more extensive examples, see the Windows 98 SDK. Keep in mind that these same DDEML functions are available to 16-bit applications under Windows 3.*x*, making them far more transportable than the low-level DDE functions themselves.

CHAPTER

THIRTY-SIX

OLE Client and Server Application Development

- OLE basics

- OLE library functions

- OLE server registration and selection

- OLE client development

- OLE server application development

You've learned about the clipboard and DDE in the previous chapters. Object Linking and Embedding (OLE) provides yet another way for applications to share data. OLE has the advantage of being virtually unlimited in its scope. An OLE application that you write now will work perfectly well even if it encounters a server that supplies data in a format Microsoft hasn't anticipated. Microsoft doesn't need to anticipate formats; if a server can handle the data, any client can receive it. A user may well apply OLE programs to tasks the developer never imagined.

An Introduction to OLE

OLE is a set of protocols and procedures proposed by Aldus Corporation in 1988 to simplify the creation and maintenance of compound documents. A *compound document* is a file belonging to one application (for example, a word processor) that also includes data created by another application (such as a graphics editor). Blocks of foreign data in a compound document are called *objects*. An application that receives data objects and builds compound documents is called an OLE *client*, and one that exports objects for other applications to use is called an OLE *server*. Whether an application is a client or a server depends on its role in a particular interaction. One application may act simultaneously as a client and a server in different interactions.

Application-Based versus Document-Based Environments

When Microsoft built OLE into Windows, it took a big step toward making the user's work center on documents rather than applications. Traditionally, the user invokes a single application for each new document. Changing from one data format to another—from text to numbers or from pictures to sounds—usually means quitting one application and starting another. Typically, in an application-based environment, a document makes sense only when read by the application that created it.

A document-based environment, on the other hand, lets several applications cooperate in creating a single document. No one application understands all the objects in the document, but as you move from piece to piece, the system automatically invokes the appropriate applications. You edit the pieces separately in their native applications, and the master document automatically receives updates from every contributor. You have more freedom to exercise creativity in combining sounds, video, pictures, numbers, and text in a single, integrated document. You can show pictures in your word processor or attach video clips to records in your database.

Compound documents existed in Windows before OLE, but their capabilities were limited. A user would create a compound document by copying data to the clipboard and pasting it into another application. In this common transaction, a data object moves from a server to a client program. But whenever the server subsequently edits its copy of the object, the cut-and-paste operation must be repeated *for all documents into which the object has been pasted.*

To create a document-based environment, the system must offer substantial facilities for coordinating applications. For example, the system must know which applications can operate on which kinds of data. As the user moves from object to object through a document, the system must recognize and support links to various other programs. In Windows, the OLE extension libraries assume these complex chores. The three libraries that implement OLE currently contain a variety of functions to help you create programs that handle virtually any kind of data object through a seamless cooperation with the program that created it.

Linking versus Embedding

An object is any set of data from one application treated as a unit. OLE applications create compound documents when they combine several objects in one file. The user sees all the objects from one document displayed together in a single window. To the client program, each object looks like a black box full of incomprehensible data. The program calls OLE functions to manipulate objects; it does not need to understand them.

When importing an object, a client chooses between linking and embedding. *Embedding*, just like pasting, gives the client a complete and independent copy of the data. An embedded object, however, remembers its origin, and the user can edit an embedded document by double-clicking it. The double-click invokes the server application, and the editing happens there. When the user closes the server, the client receives the updated object.

The second way of storing objects is to *link* them. Linking does not give the client its own independent copy of the data; instead, the client receives a live connection to a piece of the server's document—a kind of window opening into a view of the server's data. If the object is modified in the server, the modifications appear automatically in the client. If several clients link to the same object, an update in one place is visible in all the others.

In summary, when a document file contains all the data for an object, the object is *embedded*. When a document contains only a reference pointing to data in another document, the object is *linked*. Both methods produce the same result on the screen, but only linked objects receive updates. Embedded objects are transferred through the equivalent of a DDE cold link; when you copy them into your document, they become independent of their source. By contrast, if you link an object into several documents, changing the object in one place causes it to change in all the others.

Linked objects have the advantage of taking less space in the document file. Embedded objects have the advantage of being very portable; documents that contain only embedded objects can move from system to system. Because they carry all their data with them, they do not require the OLE server to reside on the destination system. The user can change linked objects into embedded objects at will.

OLE Clients versus OLE Servers

As mentioned earlier, OLE applications come in two basic types: clients and servers. If you embed a Paintbrush picture in a Write document, Paintbrush is the server and Write is the client. Write does not need to understand the data that makes up the image file. Write calls OLE functions to display the data. If the OLE system doesn't know how, it calls on the server, Paintbrush, to display data in the Write window.

Applications such as Word, WordPad, Excel, and Quattro Pro are both clients and servers. These applications both accept OLE objects supplied by other servers and act as OLE servers to other client applications. The Write editor and CardFile programs under Windows 3.x function only as OLE clients; they do not offer server services. (Few contemporary applications act as clients without also offering server capabilities.) In contrast, the Windows Paint program is an OLE server but incorporates no client capabilities. Instead, the Paint program limits itself to providing images and image-editing services to client applications.

Because Paint is a stand-alone application as well as an OLE server, Paint is a *full server*. In contrast, a *mini-server* does not operate as a stand-alone application; it does not contain any provisions to open or save files, but it does provide services to OLE client applications.

Servers of either type (full server or mini-server) may offer more than one type of service. Quattro Pro, for example, offers a choice of Quattro Pro Graph or Quattro Pro Notebook. Microsoft Word offers a choice of Microsoft Word Document or Microsoft Word Picture objects.

Object Classes and Verbs

The type of data a server exports is called an *object class*. Different classes contain different kinds of data. Paintbrush, for example, exports objects of the `PBrush` class. Excel supports the classes `ExcelWorksheet` and `ExcelChart`. Servers register their classes in the system registry. Only one server may handle each class.

For each of its object classes, a server also registers a set of verbs. A *verb* is something a server can do to an object. Two common verbs are `Edit` and `Play`. When the user selects an object in a compound document, the client application retrieves the list of verbs for that object class and makes the verbs available on one of its menus. The user manipulates objects by executing their verbs. Different objects respond to different verbs.

OLE Object Insertion

The process of adding an object to a container document is simple. From within the client application, the user chooses the type of object to insert. For example, a list box might offer picture data, spreadsheet data, and video clips; the list varies with the available servers.

Suppose that you're running Microsoft Word and decide to embed a drawing in your document. You start Paint, the registered server for bitmap objects. Then you open a .BMP file, select part of the image, and copy it to the clipboard. In Microsoft Word, you open the destination file and pull down the Edit menu. There you see a choice of three commands: Paste, Paste Link, and Paste Special. All of these commands bring the drawing into the text file. The simplest one, Paste, embeds the object. (If Paint did not support OLE, the Paste command would merely copy the object, not embed it.)

Object Packages

You can also embed .AVI or .WAV files (multimedia video or sound files) in a compound document. But what does a video clip or sound look like on the screen when you paste it? In this case, the application uses a graphical representation of the data, called a *package*.

A package is an icon that represents an OLE object. When you double-click the icon, the OLE libraries determine what data the object contains and perform the appropriate verb action.

For some data types, such as .WAV or .AVI files, only packages make sense. By default, the package icon comes from the program that created the data.

TIP Using the Object Packager program that comes with Windows, you can customize both the icon and the label of any package.

Activation of Inserted Objects

Once an object is in the client's document, the client provides ways to activate it. Usually, double-clicking activates an object. An activated object performs whatever action is appropriate to its format.

Figure 36.1 shows the process of linking a picture into a Microsoft Word document, where OLE provides in-place editing (editing the picture directly within the linked document) using the Paint program.

As illustrated, the Edit menu now contains a Bitmap Image Object submenu with three verbs—Edit, Open, and Convert—supplied by the Paint application. For a Paint drawing, the default is the verb Edit, which activates in-place editing. When you select in-place editing, the Paint menu, palette, and toolbars appear inside the Word document frame, allow editing without leaving the document. Selecting Open calls the Paint application with the embedded image, as shown in the lower half of Figure 36.1. Changes made using the Paint program will be reflected in the embedded object in the Word document when the Paint program exits, signaling on termination that the compound document should be updated.

Figure 36.2 shows a sound package and a video package pasted into a WordPad document. The Edit menu, under the Sound Recorder Document Object entry, offers three verbs associated with sound data: Play, Edit, and Open. Since more than one OLE object is embedded in this document, the Wave Sound object must be selected before the Object Properties and Sound Recorder menu options are enabled.

FIGURE 36.1:

Linking a picture into a text document and activating the picture to edit it

FIGURE 36.2:

A WordPad document
with embedded audio
and video clips

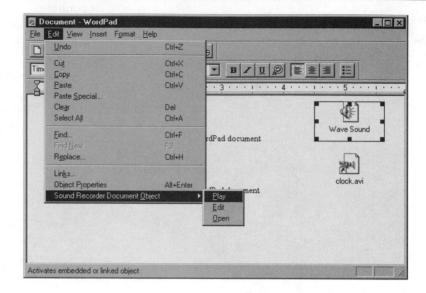

The Clock.AVI file is also an embedded object and, when selected, provides the same three verb entries in the Edit menu under the Linked Video Clip Object entry. Both the .AVI and .WAV files also respond to a double-click; the .AVI object plays the video in a separate .AVI window, and the .WAV object plays the sound waveform through the system sound card (assuming that a sound card is installed).

Eventually, with the help of some OLE functions, the client application saves the compound document. The document can then be transferred from user to user and read by the same client application on other computers. If the new system lacks some servers, all the objects will still display correctly. This is because the OLE system itself handles standard clipboard formats like bitmaps and metafiles in any client without calling a server. You cannot activate objects without a server, however. You can't do much with .WAV packages, for example, unless you have the Sound Recorder.

Presentation and Native Data Formats

Two of OLE's goals seem to place contradictory demands on data objects. In order to display the object in any application, whether or not the original server is present in the system, the object must contain data in some common, recognizable display format, such as a metafile or bitmap.

On the other hand, OLE also lets the user continue to edit objects even *after* they are pasted into a new application. In order for the server to edit objects, they must contain whatever data the server uses to represent them internally. Excel, for example, cannot continue to edit spreadsheet cells that have been converted for display as a metafile, but neither can client programs—or even the OLE libraries—be expected to understand Excel's internal data well enough to display the cells by themselves on systems where Excel is not installed.

The solution is to supply two copies of the data for every OLE object. You'll read more in a moment about how the server does this, but essentially every OLE object contains data in a *native* format, as the server created it, and in one of several standard *presentation* formats—usually a metafile—so anyone can display it.

The OLE Libraries

OLE gives you high-level functions to implement low-level data-sharing processes, similar to the DDE functions provided by the DDEML (discussed in Chapter 35). The OLE functions reside in three dynamic link libraries. OleCli32.DLL contains all the functions for an OLE client, and OleCvr32.DLL contains the functions for an OLE server. In OLE 1.0, these two libraries exchange data and commands through DDE messages. The third library, Shell32.DLL, maintains a database of servers and data types to ensure that requests for assistance are routed correctly.

OLE applications interact with each other through the libraries. When a client decides to edit a picture object, for example, it passes the request to the OleCli DLL. OleCli sends a message to OleSvr. OleSvr locates a server and asks it to begin an editing session. When the user activates an object, the OleSvr library must determine which server application corresponds to the given data format. To identify servers, OleSvr consults the Shell library. The Shell functions manage the system registry, which maps each data type to a server application name. Servers add their own names to the registry during their installation.

When the operation has completed, OleSvr passes the results back to OleCli, and OleCli passes them on to the client. The interaction of client and server through the OLE libraries is shown in Figure 36.3.

FIGURE 36.3:

How the three OLE libraries interact with client and server applications

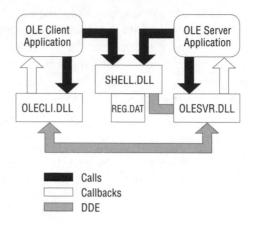

Like the DDEML, the OLE libraries work through the DDE protocol. OLE commands send DDE messages. The underlying DDE processes are invisible to an OLE application. Because Microsoft developed the DDEML and OLE systems in parallel, neither relies on the other.

Choosing between DDEML and OLE

To choose between the DDEML and OLE, consider what your application needs to do. For maintaining many links and updating them all frequently, choose the DDEML. One DDEML conversation can establish many links, but each OLE conversation transfers only a single object. Although OLE clients can initiate several conversations with one server, this incurs an overhead that the DDEML avoids. DDEML links, however, die when either participant terminates.

Choose OLE when you want to support any of the following:

- Persistent embedding and linking

- Rendering common data formats

- Rendering specialized data formats through the server

- Transferring data through the clipboard and through files

- Activating objects

OLE Information

As mentioned earlier, when an OLE server is installed on your system or is first executed, it registers itself with the Windows registry. This registration includes, among other elements, the name and location of the server, as well as the various types of services which it is prepared to supply.

In turn, an OLE client application can query the registry to find an appropriate server and service. You can also access the registry information directly by using the Registry Editor utility (RegEdit.EXE or RegEdit32.EXE, located in your \WINDOWS or \WINDOWS\SYSTEM directory), as explained in Chapter 17.

As an example, Figure 36.4 shows the Registry Editor after using the Edit ➤ Find function to locate the Excel application registry information. Actually, there are quite a few entries for Excel, but the one of interest is the class ID. This is found under the branch HKEY_CLASSES_ROOT\CLSID\ and identified by a unique (generated) class ID entry: 00020810-0000-0000-C0000-000000000046. (As with most registry entries, this same information can also be found under the entry: HKEY_LOCAL_MACHINE\SOFTWARE\Classes\CLSID, as well as in other locations; this duplication is not unusual.)

FIGURE 36.4:

The Registry Editor with information about Excel

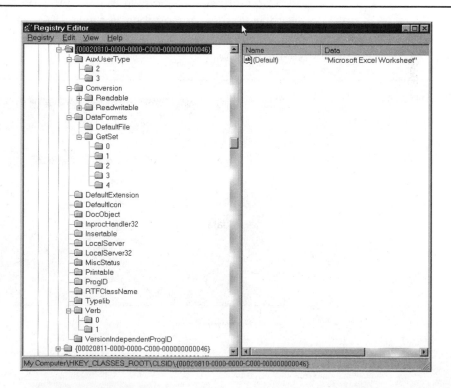

As you can see in Figure 36.4, the available information includes data formats, conversion options, the default extension(s) and icon, the program ID and, not least, which action verbs the OLE server supports.

TIP

Visual C++ includes an application titled OLE2View (located on the Visual C++ CD in the \MSDEV\Samples\MFC\OLE\OleView directory), which provides another way to view information about OLE applications. Despite the lack of documentation, the OLE2View application does provide an interesting view of a variety of OLE-support functions.

Most of the time, there is no need to access the registry directly. A number of mechanisms provide indirect access, such as the `COleInsertDialog` method (discussed later in this chapter), for safe (but restricted) access to registry information.

OLE Server Selection

Before an OLE client can use server services, the client application must select an OLE server. How a server is selected varies depending on how the client application chooses to set up the menu options. For the *Ole_Client* demo discussed in this chapter, the Edit menu's Insert New Object option calls the Insert Object dialog box, shown in Figure 36.5.

FIGURE 36.5:

The Insert Object dialog box

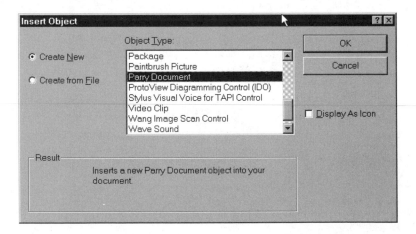

The list box in the Insert Object dialog box lists all of the registered OLE server object types. The Result box below offers a brief explanation of the selected item.

The Create New radio button is selected by default. If you select the Create from File radio button, the Insert Object dialog box changes to allow you to select a file of any type to insert as an OLE object, as shown in Figure 36.6. (Inserting a file does not guarantee that there is a supporting server for that file.) Here, you may enter path and filename information directly or click the Browse button to call the standard file-selection dialog box. If you select the Link checkbox, any changes to an OLE file object through external sources, such as when you edit the file through another application, are immediately reflected in the linked object.

FIGURE 36.6:

Inserting a file object

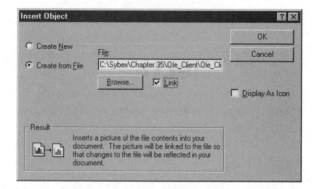

You can select the Display As Icon checkbox on the right side of the Insert Object dialog box to insert the object as an icon rather than as an active item. The advantage is that an iconized object does not require redrawing and remains inactive until selected. (Files are always inserted with icon representation, regardless of the selection made in the Display As Icon checkbox.)

NOTE   AppWizard supports full in-place editing only for OLE server objects, not for files. To fully support embedded or linked files, either the client application must be modified to provide support or the Edit menu's Packager option must be used to call the appropriate support utility.

OLE Server Registration

You've been introduced to the Registry Editor utility for viewing the registry and to the Insert Object dialog box for selecting a registered server. But how do you register an OLE server?

Full-server applications register themselves automatically the first time the server application is executed as a stand-alone process by invoking the COleServerRegister member. Furthermore, if the application was created using MFC and the AppWizard, the COleServerRegister function was installed in the InitInstance procedure as a call to the COleTemplate-Server::RegisterAll function. These processes are described later in the chapter.

For mini-server applications, which cannot run as stand-alone applications, a different approach is necessary. AppWizard provides for registering a mini-server by creating a REG script for the server application:

```
REGEDIT
; This .REG file may be used by your SETUP program.
;   If a SETUP program is not available, the entries below will be
;   registered in your InitInstance automatically with a call to
;   CWinApp::RegisterShellFileTypes and COleObjectFactory::UpdateRegistryAll.

HKEY_CLASSES_ROOT\Parry.Document = Parry Document
HKEY_CLASSES_ROOT\Parry.Document\protocol\StdFileEditing\server = PARRY.EXE
HKEY_CLASSES_ROOT\Parry.Document\protocol\StdFileEditing\verb\0 = &Edit
HKEY_CLASSES_ROOT\Parry.Document\Insertable =
HKEY_CLASSES_ROOT\Parry.Document\CLSID = {C6A0FC60-3173-11D0-93D7-BA6083000000}
HKEY_CLASSES_ROOT\CLSID\{C6A0FC60-3173-11D0-93D7-BA6083000000} = Parry Document
HKEY_CLASSES_ROOT\CLSID\{C6A0FC60-3173-11D0-93D7-BA6083000000}\DefaultIcon
    = PARRY.EXE,1
HKEY_CLASSES_ROOT\CLSID\{C6A0FC60-3173-11D0-93D7-BA6083000000}\LocalServer32
    = PARRY.EXE
HKEY_CLASSES_ROOT\CLSID\{C6A0FC60-3173-11D0-93D7-BA6083000000}\ProgId = Parry.Document
HKEY_CLASSES_ROOT\CLSID\{C6A0FC60-3173-11D0-93D7-BA6083000000}\MiscStatus = 32
HKEY_CLASSES_ROOT\CLSID\{C6A0FC60-3173-11D0-93D7-BA6083000000}\AuxUserType\3 = Parry
HKEY_CLASSES_ROOT\CLSID\{C6A0FC60-3173-11D0-93D7-BA6083000000}\AuxUserType\2 = Parry
HKEY_CLASSES_ROOT\CLSID\{C6A0FC60-3173-11D0-93D7-BA6083000000}\Insertable =
HKEY_CLASSES_ROOT\CLSID\{C6A0FC60-3173-11D0-93D7-BA6083000000}\verb\1 = &Open,0,2
HKEY_CLASSES_ROOT\CLSID\{C6A0FC60-3173-11D0-93D7-BA6083000000}\verb\0 = &Edit,0,2
HKEY_CLASSES_ROOT\CLSID\{C6A0FC60-3173-11D0-93D7-BA6083000000}\InprocHandler32
    = ole32.dll
```

Normally, when a finished application is installed, the Setup procedure also executes the REG script. For development purposes, you can also use the Registry Editor to execute this script directly. From the Registry menu in the Registry Editor, select Import Registry Files to open the file-selection dialog box. Select the application's REG script. A few seconds later, the Registry Editor should inform you that the registry information has been entered, which is all that is required.

OLE Applications

In the past, creating any OLE application was a long and involved process requiring hundreds of lines of code, simply to provide the most rudimentary client capabilities. The good news is that creating an OLE client application using MFC and the AppWizard (or their equivalent in other compilers) is almost trivial. Just as you can use MFC and the AppWizard to create an OLE client, these services also provide the means to create a basic OLE server.

> **NOTE**   If you are interested in developing OLE applications, you should refer to any of the many books devoted to the topic. For example, *Mastering OLE 2* by Bryan Waters (published by Sybex) provides more details about how to provide extended OLE support in your applications.

The OLE_Client Demo: Creating an OLE Client Application

Using MFC's AppWizard to build the skeleton for your client application, in Step 3 of the AppWizard process, you are presented with an option to include OLE compound document support in your application, as shown in Figure 36.7. (In Step 1 of the AppWizard process, you must select a multi-document application; OLE support does not function for single-document applications.) By default, the None option is checked. To provide OLE client support, simply select the Container option from the list. Following Step 3, continue to specify the remainder of the options required for your application.

FIGURE 36.7:

Adding OLE client support for an application

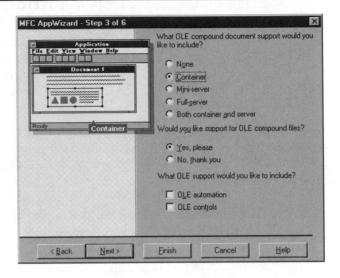

While you are experimenting, there is one restriction to observe in creating an OLE client application. Do not name the application "OLE Client" or "OLEClient" (however, "OLE_Client, with an underscore, is permissible). Using either of these proscribed names results in a `COleClientDoc` class being created as an application class, leading to a conflict with the library class of the same name, which is required to support OLE client operations.

When you complete the AppWizard specifications, MFC creates a multidocument interface with the usual object classes but includes one new object class: the client item, `COle_ClientCntrItem` (container item).

And—surprise!—you now have an OLE client application that is completely ready to compile, link, and execute. More important, the OLE client is ready to operate without any further provisions to support OLE. Granted, this simple application does not do much other than accept OLE support from server applications. However, given the complexity of creating an OLE client from scratch, this in itself is no small matter.

NOTE The *OLE_Client* demo is included on the CD that accompanies this book, in the Chapter 36 folder.

Client Support and Control Methods

When you create an OLE client application through the AppWizard, it provides classes and functions that handle client support and connections to embedded or linked OLE items.

The COle_ClientView Class

When you instruct AppWizard to provide OLE client support, the COle_Client-View class is created, with seven OLE client-support functions, which are already fully implemented. These functions are discussed in the following sections.

OnInitialUpdate This function includes a provision to set the member variable m_pSelection to NULL, where the m_pSelection member is a pointer to a COle_ContainerCntrItem object.

```
void COle_ClientView::OnInitialUpdate()
{
    CView::OnInitialUpdate();
    m_pSelection = NULL;    // initialize selection
}
```

The default provision shown is adequate for most purposes. However, if you are going to use something besides the default selection mechanisms for variant server classes, you will need to provide the appropriate initialization.

OnDraw This function, which should be familiar from earlier examples, is expected to draw application-specific data for the client window (the document window). For OLE objects, this is also where the server drawing operations are implemented. Now, according to the stated purposes of OLE, the server application is responsible for doing the actual drawing, right? So, why do we need special provisions in the client's OnDraw function?

The reason is that, before it can carry out its drawing instructions, the OLE server needs to know where to do the drawing operation.

```
void COle_ClientView::OnDraw(CDC* pDC)
{
    COle_ClientDoc* pDoc = GetDocument();
    ASSERT_VALID(pDoc);

    // TODO: add draw code for native data here
    // TODO: also draw all OLE items in the document
```

```
        if (m_pSelection == NULL)
        {
            POSITION pos = pDoc->GetStartPosition();
            m_pSelection = (COle_ClientCntrItem*)pDoc->GetNextClientItem(pos);
        }
        if (m_pSelection != NULL)
            m_pSelection->Draw(pDC, CRect(10, 10, 210, 210));
    }
```

In this default version, the selected OLE object is drawn at an arbitrary position using the rectangle returned by the `COle_ClientCntrItem` class and an arbitrary drawing rectangle.

When you create a real application, your application must be responsible for positioning the OLE object and for determining the area appropriate for the object's drawing operations (see the description of the `OnSize` function).

IsSelected This method performs a test to determine if a specific object corresponds to the `m_pSelection` object, returning either a TRUE or FALSE response.

```
BOOL COle_ClientView::IsSelected(const CObject* pDocItem) const
{
    // TODO: implement this function that tests for a selected OLE client item
    return pDocItem == m_pSelection;
}
```

As long as the selection is limited to `COle_ClientCntrItem` objects, no additional provisions are required. If, however, you are planning to handle other types of selection mechanisms, this implementation will require revisions.

OnInsertObject This method serves two functions. The first function is to invoke the standard Insert Object dialog box to select an OLE object (described earlier in the chapter).

```
    void COle_ClientView::OnInsertObject()
    {
        COleInsertDialog dlg;
        if( dlg.DoModal() != IDOK ) return;
```

If the Insert Object dialog box does not return IDOK, no selection has been made and no further action is necessary. However, assuming that an OLE object has been selected, `OnInsertObject` is responsible for connecting the item to the application document. It begins by declaring a new instance of the `COle_ClientCntrItem` class.

```
BeginWaitCursor();
COle_ClientCntrItem* pItem = NULL;
TRY
{
    // create new item connected to this document
    COle_ClientDoc* pDoc = GetDocument();
    ASSERT_VALID(pDoc);
    pItem = new COle_ClientCntrItem(pDoc);
    ASSERT_VALID(pItem);
```

Next, the OLE item must be initialized from the dialog box data.

```
if (!dlg.CreateItem(pItem))
    AfxThrowMemoryException();  // any exception will do
```

Assuming that the item was created from the class list (rather than from a file), the object's OLE server is launched to edit the item. In this case, however, editing is simply the method used to create the item's data rather than a process to change the object.

If there is a problem (because of a failure of the server or the system), an exception is thrown and the current TRY loop terminates before the CATCH response (following) takes over to report the failure.

NOTE   The term "throwing an exception" refers to intercepting an error condition and generating ("throwing") an exception condition to allow an exception handler to either correct the error or to recover from the error without terminating the application. See Chapter 18 for more information about handling exceptions.

Once the object has been created, the server is instructed to show the selected object.

```
ASSERT_VALID(pItem);
if (dlg.GetSelectionType() == COleInsertDialog::createNewItem)
    pItem->DoVerb(OLEIVERB_SHOW, this);
```

Notice that a number of ASSERT_VALID statements are included in the TRY... CATCH loop. These are present only for debugging purposes, and have no effect when the application is compiled for release. The TRY...CATCH loop, however, is active both in the debug version and the release version.

Last, the default provisions in the `OnInsertObject` method set the current selection (`m_pSelection`) to point to the last selected item before calling the document with an `UpdateAllViews` instruction, which will result in the document (and, therefore, the view) being refreshed.

```
    ASSERT_VALID(pItem);
    m_pSelection = pItem;   // set selection to last inserted item
    pDoc->UpdateAllViews(NULL);
}
```

If you don't want the last selected item to be the current selection, you can revise this portion of the code to create a different selection. However, regardless of how the default selection is made, clicking on an object in the document should still change the object selection.

The CATCH loop simply provides the standard error trapping when an error exception is generated.

```
    CATCH(CException, e)
    {
        if (pItem != NULL)
        {
            ASSERT_VALID(pItem);
            pItem->Delete();
        }
        AfxMessageBox(IDP_FAILED_TO_CREATE);
    }
    END_CATCH
    EndWaitCursor();
}
```

OnCancelEditCntr This method provides the standard keyboard UI (user interface) to cancel an in-place editing session, allowing the client, not the server, to deactivate the operation.

```
void COle_ClientView::OnCancelEditCntr()
{
    // Close any in-place active item on this view.
    COleClientItem* pActiveItem = GetDocument()->GetInPlaceActiveItem(this);
    if (pActiveItem != NULL)
    {
        pActiveItem->Close();
    }
    ASSERT(GetDocument()->GetInPlaceActiveItem(this) == NULL);
}
```

OnSetFocus This method provides the special handling required for an object being edited in-place.

```
void COle_ClientView::OnSetFocus(CWnd* pOldWnd)
{
    COleClientItem* pActiveItem = GetDocument()->GetInPlaceActiveItem(this);
    if (pActiveItem != NULL &&
        pActiveItem->GetItemState() == COleClientItem::activeUIState)
    {
        // need to set focus to this item if it is in the same view
        CWnd* pWnd = pActiveItem->GetInPlaceWindow();
        if (pWnd != NULL)
        {
            pWnd->SetFocus();    // don't call the base class
            return;
        }
    }
    CView::OnSetFocus(pOldWnd);
}
```

The OnSetFocus method provided is used to check selection and set the focus to the appropriate OLE object. Except for very unusual circumstances, this method should not require revision.

OnSize This method allows the user to resize an OLE object by selecting the object and dragging the object outline.

```
void COle_ClientView::OnSize(UINT nType, int cx, int cy)
{
    CView::OnSize(nType, cx, cy);
    COleClientItem* pActiveItem = GetDocument()->GetInPlaceActiveItem(this);
    if (pActiveItem != NULL)
        pActiveItem->SetItemRects();
}
```

Except for very unusual circumstances, this method should not require revision.

The COle_ClientCntrItem Class

The COle_ClientCntrItem class is derived from the COleClientItem class and is used to provide a connection to an embedded or linked OLE item. The COle_ClientCntrItem class created by AppWizard is a minimal implementation; the real functionality is supplied by the parent COleClientItem class.

There are more than 70 OLE-handling methods supplied by library and API functions. For details, refer to the online documentation.

The COleClientItem creation methods provide functions to create both embedded and linked items from the clipboard services, from selected files, or by launching an OLE server. The Implement_Serial macro generates the basic code required for a CObject-derived class, providing runtime access to the class name and base class name defining the class position within the hierarchy. The constructor and destructor methods provided for the derived COle_Client-CntrItem class are skeletal and provide no functionality beyond the derived functionality of the parent.

```
IMPLEMENT_SERIAL(COle_ClientCntrItem, COleClientItem, 0)
COle_ClientCntrItem::COle_ClientCntrItem(COle_ClientDoc* pContainer)
    : COleClientItem(pContainer)
{
    // TODO: add one-time construction code here
}


COle_ClientCntrItem::~COle_ClientCntrItem()
{
    // TODO: add cleanup code here
}
```

The default functionality should be sufficient for most purposes but, if you decide to add custom construction code to COle_ClientCntrItem, you need to include corresponding cleanup code in the destructor method.

OnChange Whenever an OLE item is being edited—whether the editing is occurring in-place or in a fully open server—OnChange notifications are sent to the client application to notify the client of changes in the state of the item or changes in the visual appearance of the content. The OnChange method allows the client application to update its own appearance.

```
void COle_ClientCntrItem::OnChange(OLE_NOTIFICATION nCode, DWORD dwParam)
{
    ASSERT_VALID(this);

    COleClientItem::OnChange(nCode, dwParam);
        // TODO: invalidate the item by calling UpdateAllViews
```

```
            // (with hints appropriate to your application)
        GetDocument()->UpdateAllViews(NULL);
            // for now just update ALL views/no hints
    }
```

Again, the default functionality will serve for most purposes. However, you may wish to alter the update performance for special circumstances.

OnChangeItemPosition This function is used during in-place activation to change the position of the in-place window. This may be done because changes to the data in the server document require a change in extent or may be a response to in-place resizing. The default operation is to call the base class COle-ClientItem::OnChangeItemPosition with the new in-place window rectangle. In turn, the COleClientItem::SetItemRects function is notified to move and/or resize the item to fit the specified rectangle.

```
BOOL COle_ClientCntrItem::OnChangeItemPosition(const CRect& rectPos)
{
    ASSERT_VALID(this);
    if (!COleClientItem::OnChangeItemPosition(rectPos))
        return FALSE;
        // TODO: update any cache you may have of the item's rectangle/extent
    return TRUE;
}
```

If you wish to provide your own resizing implementation, refer to the Set-Extent method for embedded OLE items.

OnGetItemPosition This method is called to determine the location of an item during in-place activation. The default implementation provided simply returns a hard-coded rectangle, which was defined by AppWizard.

```
    void COle_ClientCntrItem::OnGetItemPosition(CRect& rPosition)
    {
        ASSERT_VALID(this);
            // TODO: return correct rectangle (in pixels) in rPosition
        rPosition.SetRect(10, 10, 210, 210);
    }
```

For a more sophisticated approach, this rectangle should reflect the current position of the item relative to the view used for activation. To obtain the view, call COle_ClientCntrItem::GetActiveView.

OnActivate This function is used to activate an OLE item in-place by calling the `COleDocument::GetInPlaceActiveItem` function.

```
void COle_ClientCntrItem::OnActivate()
{
    COle_ClientView* pView = GetActiveView();
    ASSERT_VALID(pView);
    COleClientItem* pItem = GetDocument()->GetInPlaceActiveItem(pView);
    if (pItem != NULL && pItem != this)
        pItem->Close();
    COleClientItem::OnActivate();
}
```

Only one item (per frame) can be activated at a time.

OnDeactivate This function is called when an item that was activated in-place is to be deactivated. This restores the container application's user interface to its original state, hiding any menus and other controls that were created for in-place activation.

```
void COle_ClientCntrItem::OnDeactivateUI(BOOL bUndoable)
{
    COleClientItem::OnDeactivateUI(bUndoable);

    DWORD dwMisc = 0;
    m_lpObject->GetMiscStatus(GetDrawAspect(), &dwMisc);
    if (dwMisc & OLEMISC_INSIDEOUT)
        DoVerb(OLEIVERB_HIDE, NULL);
}
```

If `bUndoable` is FALSE, the container should disable the Undo command, in effect discarding the undo state of the container, because it indicates that the last operation performed by the server is not undoable.

Serialize This method is used to load or store data related to an OLE item within the client document. By default, the data contained within an OLE object is handled by the OLE server and does not require handling by the OLE client. Depending on the type of application you are designing, however, you may need to store references to the linked/embedded items as part of your document storage.

```
void COle_ClientCntrItem::Serialize(CArchive& ar)
{
    ASSERT_VALID(this);
    COleClientItem::Serialize(ar);
```

```
    // now store/retrieve data specific to COle_ClientCntrItem
    if (ar.IsStoring())
    {
        // TODO: add storing code here
    }
    else
    {
        // TODO: add loading code here
    }
}
```

Other Methods There are a host of methods supplied by the parent class, COleClientItem, which may be overwritten when your application needs special handling. Status methods provide functions to retrieve OLE item aspects, including the item's class ID, the view aspect, and the OLE type and descriptive string.

The clipboard services support drag-and-drop operations and allow items to be retrieved from the clipboard or passed to the clipboard. Additional methods allow items to be drawn, closed, released, or executed. Object activation is provided by a series of functions handing different aspects of activation. The Set-Extent and SetItemRects methods provide resizing. All in all, there are 20 or more functions for various aspects of OLE client operations.

Given these possibilities, you may be properly relieved to know that you do not need to write all of these yourself. For the most part, the default functionality for a client has been supplied. And, when necessary, you can override or extend the default methods.

An OLE Server

Just as you can use MFC and the AppWizard to create an OLE client, these services also provide the means to create a basic OLE server, offering a choice of a mini-server or full-server application.

OLE Server Types

OLE server applications are defined by four base classes: the COleServerDoc and COleServerItem classes used by all server applications, the COleServer class used by mini-servers, and the COleTemplateServer class used by full-server applications.

SDI (Single Document Interface) servers are probably the most common type of OLE servers as well as the simplest to implement. Each SDI server uses a single server object and a single document object but launches a new server instance for each client requesting service. Table 36.1 shows the SDI architecture characteristics. Because mini-servers do not support multiple links, an SDI mini-server offers only one item object. In contrast, a full server supplies multiple item objects when multiple clients are linked to the same document.

TABLE 36.1: SDI Server, Multiple Instances

Class Type	Classes	Mini-server Objects	Full-server Objects
Server	1	1	1
Document	1	1	1
Item	1	1	Many

MDI (Multiple Document Interface) servers are used when DGROUP (the default data segment) memory constraints preclude multiple-instance servers or when a full server needs to be MDI in stand-alone mode. For mini-servers, there is still only one item per document. Table 36.2 shows characteristics of the MDI server architecture for a single server type, single instance.

TABLE 36.2: MDI Server, Single Server Type, Single Instance

Class Type	Classes	Mini-server Objects	Full-server Objects
Server	1	1	1
Document	1	Many	Many
Item	1	Many	Many

Multiple-instance MDI servers include applications such as Excel or Quattro Pro, which provide both charts (graphic objects) and spreadsheets. Each server class has only one document class, and each server object has one document object. Since full servers support links, each document can provide multiple item objects, and each document class can support multiple item classes. Table 36.3 shows the MDI server characteristics for multiple instances.

TABLE 36.3: MDI Server, Multiple Instances

Class Type	Classes	Full-server Objects
Server	Many	Many
Document	Many	1
Item	Many	Many

The AppWizard Process

Just as you are presented with an option to include OLE support in your client application in Step 3 of the AppWizard process, this step also includes selections for a mini-server, full-server, or client/server application. In Figure 36.8, a full-server application has been selected.

FIGURE 36.8:

Adding OLE server support for an application

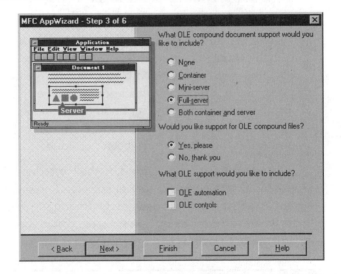

For OLE support, creating a mini-server and full-server application are essentially the same. However, it's easier to test a a full-server application during development because it can also run in stand-alone mode. The combined client/server option automatically selects a full server rather than a mini-server, because the client-side insists that the application must run in stand-alone mode (a mini-server cannot be a client without a user interface).

When you are creating a full-server application, keep in mind that just because the server works correctly in stand-alone mode, this is no guarantee that it also works as a server. Later, we will discuss at least one point of failure where an application works by itself but fails during client operations.

After you have finished creating your application skeleton, in addition to the application, mainframe, document, and view classes, the AppWizard has also created an in-place frame class, `CInPlaceFrame`, and a server class, `CxxxSrvr-Item`, derived from the `COleServerItem` class. For the *Parry* demo discussed in this chapter, the server class is named `CParrySrvrItem`.

The Parry Demo: A Simple OLE Application

The *Parry* demo is a relatively simple OLE application that is intended to demonstrate how an OLE application can provide embedded services. The embedded object offers a single menu option and a single toolbar option.

The menu and toolbar entries could be anything desired and could also duplicate the usual system menus, with File, Edit, and Help entries. Remember, however, that options provided by the OLE embedded menu and toolbar, which are presented in the client application when the embedded object is selected, must also be supported by the server application. Because the *Parry* demo does not offer File, Edit, or Help services in the context of the server application, no menu entries for these items have been provided.

The single service provided by the *Parry* demo is the Scan action, which, in true paranoid fashion, looks for enemies (and often finds them). No, this is not a serious application; it was designed with tongue firmly in cheek and for amusement as well as education. But even so, the principles demonstrated in the *Parry* demo still apply to serious server applications.

NOTE The *Parry* demo is included on the CD that accompanies this book, in the Chapter 36 folder.

Table 36.4 lists the main source files used in this demo. The following sections describe the classes used for the program.

TABLE 36.4: Principal Source Files in the Parry Demo

Source File(s)	Function
SrvrItem.CPP, .H	Source files for the `CParrySrvrItem` class
MainFrm.CPP, .H	Defines the `CMainFrame` class derived from `CMDIFrameWnd`; controls all MDI frame features
ParryDoc.CPP, .H	Document class files for the server document class; modify these source files to add special document features and implement serialization
IpFrame.CPP, .H	Source files for the in-place frame class derived from the `COleIPFrameWnd` class; controls all frame features when the object is activated in-place
Parry.CPP, .H	Source files for the `CParryApp` application class
ParryView.CPP, .H	Source files for the view class files creating the `CParryView` class; handles in-place editing capabilities
IToolbar.BMP	Bitmap for in-place toolbar
Toolbar.BMP	Bitmap for stand-alone toolbar
Parry.ICO	Icon for stand-alone operation
ParryDoc.ICO	Icon for embedded object
Parry.REG	Registration script used to register the server

The CParrySrvrItem Class

The `CParrySrvrItem` class is derived from `COleServerItem` and provides the link functionality between the server application and the client through the OLE system. The default functionality is provided by the parent class, but there are ample opportunities within the derived class to customize the server's behavior.

The first point where the server can be customized is found in the constructor and destructor methods. The default versions are functional, but they can be modified to provide, for example, additional clipboard formats specific to the item's data source.

```
CParrySrvrItem::CParrySrvrItem(CParryDoc* pContainerDoc)
    : COleServerItem(pContainerDoc, TRUE)
{
    // TODO: add one-time construction code here
}
```

```
CParrySrvrItem::~CParrySrvrItem()
{
    // TODO: add cleanup code here
}
```

Serialize This method is called by the framework when a data item is copied to the clipboard, an action that happens automatically though the OLE callback function OnGetClipboardData.

The default provisions expect the server object to be embedded and delegate serialization to the document's Serialize function. Notice that the IsLinkedItem is called and expects a negative response (FALSE) to identify an embedded object.

```
void CParrySrvrItem::Serialize(CArchive& ar)
{
    if( ! IsLinkedItem() )
    {
        CParryDoc* pDoc = GetDocument();
        ASSERT_VALID(pDoc);
        pDoc->Serialize(ar);
    }
}
```

For linked support, additional provisions are needed to serialize only a portion of the server data.

OnGetExtent This method is designed to check the drawing aspect, returning a CSize variable with the appropriate size information.

```
// CParrySrvrItem::OnGetExtent is called to get the extent in
//  HIMETRIC units of the entire item.  The default implementation
//  here simply returns a hard-coded number of units.

BOOL CParrySrvrItem::OnGetExtent(DVASPECT dwDrawAspect, CSize& rSize)
{
    if (dwDrawAspect != DVASPECT_CONTENT)
        return COleServerItem::OnGetExtent(dwDrawAspect, rSize);
```

If the drawing aspect is DVASPECT_CONTENT, the parent OnGetExtent method is called to retrieve the rSize variable. Otherwise, the default implementation provided by the AppWizard simply returns a hard-coded 3000 by 3000 units (in MM_HIMETRIC mode).

```
            CParryDoc* pDoc = GetDocument();
            ASSERT_VALID(pDoc);
                // TODO: replace this arbitrary size
            rSize = CSize(3000, 3000);    // 3000 x 3000 HIMETRIC units
            return TRUE;
        }
```

Normally, the server application is expected to handle drawing the content aspect of the item. To support other aspects, such as DVASPECT_THUMBNAIL, you need to override the OnDrawEx function and modify the OnGetExtent function to handle this additional aspect.

The drawing mode, identified by the dwDrawAspect parameter, may be DVASPECT_CONTENT, DVASPECT_THUMBNAIL, DVASPECT_ICON, or DVASPECT_DOCPRINT. To support any modes other than DVASPECT_CONTENT, additional provisions will be required both here and in the OnDraw method.

NOTE   Embedded or linked OLE items are always drawn using HIMETRIC units and a metafile device context. Of course, while the application is executing in stand-alone mode, any drawing mode is acceptable.

OnDraw This method is provided as a default implementation that sets up the mapping mode and extent in preparation for drawing in a metafile context. But, before you duplicate your entire application's drawing routines, realize that this is not the purpose of the server item's OnDraw method.

When the item is active, it is the View class that is called to provide the drawing operations. The function of the server item's OnDraw method is to act only when the OLE item is active, but the client screen still needs to be updated. It might provide instructions for a simple default drawing operation, for drawing an icon view, or for whatever is desired to provide an inactive display.

```
BOOL CParrySrvrItem::OnDraw(CDC* pDC, CSize& rSize)
{
    CParryDoc* pDoc = GetDocument();
    ASSERT_VALID(pDoc);

        // TODO: set mapping mode and extent
        // (the extent is usually the same as the size returned from OnGetExtent)
    pDC->SetMapMode(MM_ANISOTROPIC);
    pDC->SetWindowOrg(0,0);
    pDC->SetWindowExt(3000, 3000);
```

```
     // TODO: add drawing code here.  Optionally, fill in the HIMETRIC extent
     //  all drawing takes place in the metafile device context (pDC)

  return TRUE;
}
```

In addition to providing some form of drawing instructions here, the `Set-WindowExt` function call should be rewritten to use the `CSize` value returned by the `OnGetExtent` function. Of course, this also assumes that the `OnGetExtent` function has been rewritten to return something besides the hard-coded values supplied by the AppWizard.

Also, if you want the OLE server view to be drawn both when the item is active and when it is inactive, rather than attempting to provide duplicate code for each operation, a simpler approach is to provide a set of shared drawing functions that are called for both.

OnDraw and Drawing in a Metafile Context Although both the server item class's and view class's `OnDraw` methods are called with a pointer to a device context, the supplied device context is not the same in both cases. When the view's `OnDraw` function is called, the supplied device context is the screen device; when the server item's `OnDraw` method is invoked (while the item is inactive), the device context supplied is a metafile context.

There are several differences between a screen device context and a metafile context, but the difference you need to be most aware of when designing your OLE server is that a metafile context does not supply the same information as an active screen device context. The information supplied for a metafile context does not include any data that depends on the context actually being a window and an active element in the window hierarchy. This limitation means that functions such as `GetTextMetrics`, `GetDeviceCaps`, or many of the other `Getxxxxxxx` functions simply do not operate in a metafile context because there is no connection to any actual physical device context. In like fashion, functions such as `CreateCompatibleDC`, which might be used to create a bitmap memory context, simply do nothing.

In view of these limitations, the server item's `OnDraw` function must rely on `MM_ANISOTROPIC` mode with an extent defined in `MM_HIMETRIC` units. This selection is based on providing the highest resolution available.

This limitation means that both types of drawing operations must be carried out in `MM_HIMETRIC` units to make the normal drawing operations compatible with the inactive server drawing operations. Unfortunately, the `MM_HIMETRIC` mode is not necessarily ideal for this purpose. For example, consider that application fonts must be rendered using MM_HIMETRIC units. (An alternative in this situation is to use conversion functions such as the `CFont::CreateFont` or `CFont::CreateFontIndirect` to force a font match based on the relative font size instead of using a font sized according to the metafile context.)

Restrictions aside, most of the output functions, such as `MoveTo`, `TextOut`, and `DrawText`, still remain valid. Also, if necessary, the `CDC::HIMETRICtoDP` and `CDC::DPtoHIMETRIC` functions can be used to convert coordinates between the application's format context and device pixels.

The CParryView Class

The OLE application's view class, which is `CParryView` in this instance, provides the application view in both stand-alone mode and as an active OLE object. As usual, the `CParryView` class is derived from the `CView` class.

The AppWizard has included one provision in the `View` class to support server operations: the `OnCancelEditSrvr` method.

OnCancelEditSrvr This method parallels `OnCancelEditCntr` in the client application, providing the standard keyboard UI to cancel an in-place editing session. Here, the method allows the server, not the client, to deactivate the operation.

```
void CParryView::OnCancelEditSrvr()
{
    GetDocument()->OnDeactivateUI(FALSE);
}
```

OnDraw Because the *Parry* demo depends on a dialog box (or a series of dialog boxes) to present information as a pop-up service, the View's `OnDraw` method really doesn't have much to do besides displaying a text string announcing its services.

```
void CParryView::OnDraw(CDC* pDC)
{
    CParryDoc* pDoc = GetDocument();
    ASSERT_VALID(pDoc);

    CString csText = "Paranoid Scanning Services";

    pDC->TextOut( 10, 10, csText );
}
```

However, if you have any graphics information to display (or if you have a more conventional display), this is where the drawing operations would occur, just as they would in any conventional application. Keep in mind, however, that the inactive display for an embedded server item is not drawn in the same context as the active display (see the "OnDraw and Drawing in a Metafile Context" section).

OnScan In the *Parry* demo, this method is called by the server-supplied menu or the server-supplied toolbar and uses a random-number generator to select the advice message to display. Technically, this is a very minimal application and shouldn't require any particular explanation.

```
void CParryView::OnScan()
{
    CDialog *pDlg;
    UINT     nDlg;

        // Seed the random-number generator with current time so that
        //   the numbers will be different every time we run.
    srand( (unsigned)time( NULL ) );
    switch( ( rand() % 10 ) + 1 )
    {
        case 1:    nDlg = IDD_DIALOG1;    break;
        case 2:    nDlg = IDD_DIALOG2;    break;
        case 3:    nDlg = IDD_DIALOG3;    break;
        case 4:    nDlg = IDD_DIALOG4;    break;
        case 5:    nDlg = IDD_DIALOG5;    break;
        default:   nDlg = IDD_DIALOG6;    break;
    }
    if( nDlg != IDD_DIALOG6 )
        MessageBeep( MB_ICONEXCLAMATION );
    pDlg = new CDialog( nDlg, NULL );
    pDlg->DoModal();
    delete pDlg;
}
```

The CInPlaceFrame Class

The CInPlaceFrame class, derived from the COleIPFrame class, creates and positions the frame and control bars for the server window within the client application's document window. The CInPlaceFrame class also handles notifications for embedded COleResizeBar objects whenever an in-place editing window is resized. The parent class provides complete default functionality, but there are still possibilities for customization in the derived class.

The heart of the `CInPlaceFrame` class is found in two create functions: `OnCreate` and `OnCreateControlBars`.

OnCreate After calling the usual default method from the parent class, this method performs two tasks: setting up a `CResizeBar` instance to provide for in-place resizing and providing a default drop target.

```
int CInPlaceFrame::OnCreate(LPCREATESTRUCT lpCreateStruct)
{
    if (COleIPFrameWnd::OnCreate(lpCreateStruct) == -1)
        return -1;
    if (!m_wndResizeBar.Create(this))
    {
        TRACE0("Failed to create resize bar\n");
        return -1;        // fail to create
    }
    m_dropTarget.Register(this);
    return 0;
}
```

The default drop target does nothing for the frame window but it does prevent drops (as in "drag-and-drop" operations) from falling through to another class that does support drag-and-drop, such as the OLE client.

If your application will be supporting drop operations, then this registration will be necessary anyway—along with provisions to handle drops, naturally.

OnCreateControlBars This method will be called, as required, by the framework to create control bars for the container application's windows.

```
BOOL CInPlaceFrame::OnCreateControlBars( CFrameWnd* pWndFrame,
                                         CFrameWnd* pWndDoc )
{
    // set owner to this window, so messages are delivered to correct app
    m_wndToolBar.SetOwner(this);
    // create toolbar on client's frame window
    if( ! m_wndToolBar.Create(pWndFrame) || !
m_wndToolBar.LoadToolBar(IDR_SRVR_INPLACE) )
    {
        TRACE0("Failed to create toolbar\n");
        return FALSE;
    }
```

The pWndFrame argument is the client application's top-level frame window and is always non-NULL. The pWndDoc argument is the document-level frame window and, if the client is an SDI application, may be NULL. The server application may place control bars on either window but, in this case, the principal task is to create the toolbar and, by default, to dock the toolbar to the client's document window.

```
    // TODO: remove this if you don't want tooltips or a resizable toolbar
m_wndToolBar.SetBarStyle( m_wndToolBar.GetBarStyle() |
                        CBRS_TOOLTIPS | CBRS_FLYBY | CBRS_SIZE_DYNAMIC );
    // TODO: delete these three lines if you don't want the toolbar to
    //  be dockable
m_wndToolBar.EnableDocking(CBRS_ALIGN_ANY);
pWndFrame->EnableDocking(CBRS_ALIGN_ANY);
pWndFrame->DockControlBar(&m_wndToolBar);
return TRUE;
}
```

The toolbar docking and tooltips provisions, as well as the toolbar button assignments, provide operations only while the OLE item is active in-place. If the OLE item is not active, the toolbar (and menu) will not appear.

The CParryApp Class

The CParryApp class is derived from the CWinApp class. In earlier examples, we have paid little attention to any of the applications' CWinApp-derived classes. We've simply assumed that these classes were there and that they provided, by default, the essentials necessary for initializing and executing our application instances. For our OLE server application, however, the derived CParryApp class continues to supply the same functionality as previous examples but now also offers a few elements that non-OLE applications haven't needed. These elements are described in the following sections.

The CLSID Value This is the CLSID (CLaSS ID) value used by the system registry. The CLSID value is defined in the CParry.CPP file as:

```
static const CLSID clsid =
    { 0xc6a0fc60, 0x3173, 0x11d0, { 0x93, 0xd7, 0xba, 0x60, 0x83, 0x0, 0x0, 0x0 } };
```

The generated value, C6A0FC60-3173-11D0-93D7-BA6083000000, is statistically unique but may be changed if you want to substitute another identifier.

InitInstance This function begins by initializing the OLE libraries through a call to AfxOleInit, reporting failure if there is an error.

```
BOOL CParryApp::InitInstance()
{
    // initialize OLE libraries
    if (!AfxOleInit())
    {
        AfxMessageBox(IDP_OLE_INIT_FAILED);
        return FALSE;
    }
}
```

Next, as usual, the standard profile settings are loaded, and the document, window, and view class names are assigned.

```
LoadStdProfileSettings();
CSingleDocTemplate* pDocTemplate;
pDocTemplate = new CSingleDocTemplate( IDR_MAINFRAME,
                                RUNTIME_CLASS(CParryDoc),
                                RUNTIME_CLASS(CMainFrame),
                                RUNTIME_CLASS(CParryView) );
```

Now the InitInstance routine departs from the usual routine by calling the SetServerInfo function to identify server resources, including menus and accelerator tables, which are used by the server application when an embedded object is activated.

```
pDocTemplate->SetServerInfo( IDR_SRVR_EMBEDDED, IDR_SRVR_INPLACE,
                                RUNTIME_CLASS(CInPlaceFrame) );
AddDocTemplate(pDocTemplate);
```

The ConnectTemplate function is called to connect the server to the document template so that COleTemplateServer can use information in the document template to create new documents on behalf of OLE clients.

```
m_server.ConnectTemplate(clsid, pDocTemplate, TRUE);

    // note: SDI applications register server objects only if /Embedding
    //   or /Automation is present on the command line.

    // parse command line for standard shell commands, DDE, file open
CCommandLineInfo cmdInfo;
ParseCommandLine(cmdInfo);
```

Finally, after parsing any command-line instructions, a check is made to determine if the application instance is being launched as an OLE server and, if so, to register all of the OLE services as running (RegisterAll), allowing the OLE libraries to create objects from other applications.

```
if( cmdInfo.m_bRunEmbedded || cmdInfo.m_bRunAutomated )
{
    COleTemplateServer::RegisterAll();
    return TRUE;
}
```

If the application is being executed as a server rather than as a stand-alone application, the InitInstance routine returns TRUE here, so that the application's main window is not created or displayed.

On the other hand, if the application is being run as a stand-alone application, this is a good time to call UpdateRegistry to update the system registry with information about the OLE services before proceeding with normal operations (including starting the command processor and displaying the application window).

```
m_server.UpdateRegistry(OAT_INPLACE_SERVER);
if (!ProcessShellCommand(cmdInfo))
    return FALSE;
return TRUE;
}
```

This chapter has provided an introduction to programming OLE clients and servers. The next, and final, chapter takes a look at another intriguing and growing field for application development: multimedia.

37

Multimedia Operations

- ■ Windows multimedia features

- ■ Commands for playing waveform sounds

- ■ Multimedia control and file operations functions

- ■ A Sound Recorder demo for playing, recording, and mixing sounds

Integration has been a guiding principle behind the design of each version of Windows. Programs can exchange data, send each other messages and commands, and cooperate in combining linked and embedded objects to create compound documents. The various methods of linking communications and services has occupied the past several chapters. Now we conclude with a discussion of multimedia operations, which further the goal of integration by embracing new ranges of data.

Audio and video data in many formats now have a place in the general PC market. For about the price of a large hard disk, you can add a sound board and a CD-ROM drive to your computer and play audio CDs, watch movies, record sounds to the disk, and create animation sequences. Multimedia seems to promise the most for the education and entertainment fields, but business, too, will appreciate the new flexibility and variety of choices in presenting information.

This chapter explains the general support Windows provides for multimedia applications. You will learn the high-level commands for operating any multimedia device and the file I/O commands for reading and writing many kinds of multimedia data. You will also see how to play sounds, record them, change their volume, and combine them.

Windows Multimedia Support

Windows multimedia support is a collection of capabilities for dealing with audio and visual peripherals. Its purpose is to allow the integration of many different data formats in a single system environment. The Windows multimedia features include three different components: audio and visual hardware devices, drivers for those devices, and a generalized API that translates programming commands into instructions for any multimedia driver.

Multimedia Devices

Multimedia operations are data-intensive; they make great demands on the CPU to process large quantities of data rapidly. The devices that store the data must meet certain function and protocol standards in order to work effectively.

To encourage the proliferation of multimedia-capable systems, Microsoft consulted with a number of hardware and software companies to develop a Multimedia PC specification establishing minimum system capabilities for multimedia computing. Hardware and software products compatible with this standard carry the MPC trademark. For example, to carry the MPC mark, a CD-ROM drive must transfer data at a minimum rate of 150KB per second without utilizing more than 40 percent of the CPU's capacity. It must also have an average seek time of 1 second.

Windows 98 recognizes the multimedia device types listed in Table 37.1.

TABLE 37.1: Multimedia Device Types Recognized by Windows 98

Multimedia Type	Device Type
animation	Animation device
cdaudio	Audio CD player
dat	Digital audio tape player
digitalvideo	Digital video (not GDI) in a window
mmovie	Animation movie files
other	Undefined MCI device
overlay	Overlay device (analog video in a window)
scanner	Image scanner
sequencer	MIDI sequencer
videodisc	Videodisc player
waveaudio	Device that plays digitized waveform sounds

The list of drivers suggests the range of hardware and data formats that Windows now expects to encounter. These types of devices and data were formerly inaccessible to most Intel-based PC users. Besides these drivers, multimedia also brings enhanced display drivers for high-resolution adapters and gray-scale VGA, the Sound Recorder and Media Player applications, and several applets in the Control Panel for installing devices and setting system sounds.

Multimedia Services

Beyond the hardware and drivers, the multimedia services include a layer of software defining (predictably) a device-independent interface for programs to use multimedia. A single set of commands will, for example, play sounds on any waveform device. Under Windows 98 (and the other Win32 versions), the multimedia services reside in WinMM.DLL. The layer of Win32 that interprets multimedia commands is called WinMM.

> **NOTE** A program that uses the WinMM commands must include the Mmsystem.H header file and link with the Winmm.LIB library. Under Windows 3.1, the multimedia services reside in Mmsystem.DLL. When porting from Windows 3.1, be sure to change your Makefile to use Winmm.LIB instead of Mmsystem.LIB.

Four Command Sets

The system provides four different ways to manage multimedia services: two high-level command sets, one low-level command set, and a set of file I/O commands.

The low-level and the high-level commands control the same multimedia devices. The low-level commands are more powerful, and the high-level commands are more convenient. To record a sound, for example, the low-level functions make you repeatedly send the device an empty buffer and wait for it to come back full. But the low-level functions will also let you mix a new sound with an old sound as you record, scale the pitch and playback rates, change the device volume setting, record a MIDI song, and send custom messages defined by the driver. Also, since all the high-level commands are implemented internally through the low-level commands, you can get better performance by calling the low-level commands directly.

Low-level commands interact with drivers for particular devices. The more generalized high-level commands interact with drivers for logical devices. Windows 98 comes with three: a MIDI sequencer, a CD player, and a waveform audio player. These generic drivers translate high-level commands into low-level function calls for particular drivers. The high-level API defined by the generic drivers is called the Multimedia Command Interface (MCI). MCI commands shield you from many small details of managing data streams, but at the expense of some flexibility. The high-level commands give the same kind of control that, for example, `wsprintf` gives for string output. Sometimes you really do need low-level commands like `lstrcat` and `_fcvt`, but the high-level commands are usually much easier to use.

Only specialized programs require the low-level multimedia functions. The high-level functions can play MIDI files, movies, videodiscs, and CD-ROMs, and they can record as well as play waveform sounds.

The MCI supports two parallel sets of high-level MCI functions: a command interface and a message interface. Command strings and command messages do the same thing, but strings are useful for authoring systems where the user writes command scripts to control a device. The function `mciSendCommand` sends drivers messages like `MCI_OPEN` and `MCI_PLAY`. The parallel function `mciSendString` sends strings like `"open c:\sounds\harp.wav"` and `"play waveaudio to 500"`.

Besides the low-level commands, the MCI commands, and the MCI strings, a fourth command set facilitates reading and writing with multimedia data files. The Multimedia I/O (MMIO) commands understand the organization of files in the standard RIFF format (discussed later, in the "RIFF Files" section) and also perform buffering, a useful optimization for data-intensive multimedia programs.

The Multimedia Timer

Since timing is often critical in multimedia, particularly for playing MIDI music and for coordinating different devices during a presentation, WinMM also includes enhanced timer services. The multimedia timer does not send `WM_TIMER` messages; instead, it is based on interrupts. The CPU regularly receives interrupt signals from the computer's timer chip, and the multimedia timer invokes a callback function from your program during those interrupts.

Interrupt-driven timer signals are much more regular because no time is lost waiting for the application's message queue to empty. Furthermore, the multimedia timer is accurate down to about 10 (MIPS) or 16 (Intel) milliseconds, but the smallest effective interval for `SetTimer` is about 55 milliseconds, and even that resolution isn't guaranteed because of message queue delays. The timer resolution varies from system to system; you can determine the resolution by calling `timeGetDevCaps`.

NOTE	The drawback of real-time interrupt processing is that it can significantly slow other applications and degrade system performance.

Multimedia Animation

WinMM includes animation capabilities. By opening an `mmovie` device, you can play animation files called *movies.* Multimedia animation does not provide new GDI functions to create moving images. It works very much like the audio device, translating a data file into output. The movie player reads from a RIFF file (one containing RMMP format chunks).

Movie files can support casts, scores, inks, transitions, palette effects, audio, and other animation structures. You open the movie-player device with the `MCI_OPEN` command message, play the movie with `MCI_PLAY`, and finish with `MCI_CLOSE`. Some other command messages are specific to movie files; `MCI_STEP`, for example, changes the current position forward or backward a set number of movie frames. `MCI_WINDOW` sets or adjusts the window where the movie appears. But in general, the MCI commands for movies work the same way as the commands for sound, and when you have learned one set, you can easily learn the other.

NOTE	Creating movie files is more difficult than playing them. You need a high-level tool for designing animation. Microsoft's Video for Windows 3.1 is one choice; the MacroMind Director is another. Although the MacroMind Director runs on the Macintosh, its data files easily convert to Windows' multimedia format.

Sound Data Formats

Digitized sounds for the PC generally come in one of three common forms. One is the Compact Disc-Digital Audio format (also called *Red Book audio*). Commercial CDs use this data-intensive format to store high-quality digitized sound. Each second of sound consumes 176KB of disk space.

Another more compact storage format is defined by the Musical Instrument Digital Interface (MIDI). MIDI is a standard protocol for communication between musical instruments and computers. MIDI files contain instructions for a synthesizer to play a piece of music. MIDI sound files take up less room and produce good-quality sound, but recording them requires MIDI hardware.

A third format, waveform files, produces adequate sound without a synthesizer and consumes less disk space than the CD Digital Audio format. *Waveform audio* is a technique for re-creating sound waves by sampling the original sound at discrete intervals and recording a digital representation of each sample.

To store sound as waveform data, a digitizer measures the sound at frequent intervals. Each measurement forms a snapshot called a *sample*. With smaller intervals and more frequent samples, the sound quality improves. Sound travels in waves; by sampling frequently, you can plot more points on the wave and reproduce it more accurately. WinMM supports three sampling rates: 11.025 kHz, 22.05 kHz, and 44.1 kHz (1 kHz equals 1000 times per second; 44.1 kHz is 44,100 times per second). In a .WAV file digitized with a sampling rate of 11.025 kHz, each millisecond contains about 11 samples.

The human ear stops perceiving high-pitched sounds when they reach a frequency near 20 kHz. For a recording to capture a sound, it must sample at a rate at least twice the frequency of the sound, so a sampling rate of 44.1 kHz captures the full range of perceptible frequencies. Commercial audio CDs sample at 44.1 kHz. The lower sampling rates, which are fractions of 44.1 kHz, reproduce sound less well but take up less storage room.

Three Easy Ways to Play Sounds

Waveform files conventionally have the .WAV extension. To produce waveform sounds, most programs will rely on one of three simple commands, which work best with short .WAV files:

MessageBeep   Plays only sounds configured in the registry for warnings and errors.

sndPlaySound   Plays sounds directly from .WAV files or from memory buffers.

PlaySound   New in Win32, resembles sndPlaySound but differs in two respects: It does not play sounds from memory, and it does play sounds stored as resources of type WAVE.

MessageBeep

The MessageBeep command takes one parameter naming one of five system sounds configured in the Control Panel. By pairing every call to MessageBox with a MessageBeep, you can make your program play sounds the user selects to indicate different levels of warnings. If MessageBox displays the MB_ICONHAND icon, MessageBeep should pass MB_ICONHAND as its parameter. The sound produced depends on the SystemHand entry in the system registry.

TIP

You should allow the user to disable your program's message beeps. If many errors occur, the repeated sounds of yellow-alert sirens and broken dishes crashing may become irritating.

Table 37.2 lists the possible `MessageBeep` parameter values and their corresponding registry entries.

TABLE 37.2: MessageBeep Parameter Values

Parameter Value	Registry Entry
0xFFFFFFFF	Standard beep through PC speaker
MB_ICONASTERISK	SystemAsterisk
MB_ICONEXCLAMATION	SystemExclamation
MB_ICONHAND	SystemHand
MB_ICONQUESTION	SystemQuestion
MB_OK	SystemDefault

Through the Control Panel or the Registry Editor, the user may associate any .WAV file with these signals (see Chapter 17 for more information about the Registry Editor).

Like all the sound functions, `MessageBeep` requires an appropriate device driver in order to play a waveform sound. The normal PC speaker is not an adequate device for multimedia.

sndPlaySound

With the `sndPlaySound` command, you can play any system sound named in the registry and configured from the Control Panel (there may be others besides the standard five), or you can play .WAV files directly.

```
BOOL sndPlaySound( LPCTSTR lpszSoundName,  // file or registry key
                   UINT uFlags   );        // SND_ option flags
```

The first parameter names a registry entry such as `SystemStart` or `SystemQuestion`; alternatively, it may contain a full path name pointing to a .WAV file.

sndPlaySound requires enough memory to load the full sound into memory. It works best with sound files no larger than about 100KB.

The second parameter expects a flag controlling how the sound is played. Here are some possible values:

> **SND_MEMORY**   Identifies the first parameter as a pointer to an object in memory and not to a filename or system sound.

> **SND_SYNC**   Finishes playing sound before returning control to the program.

> **SND_ASYNC**   Returns control to the program immediately and plays sound in the background.

> **SND_ASYNC|SND_LOOP**   Return control to the program immediately and play the sound continuously in the background until the program calls sndPlaySound with NULL for the first parameter.

> **SND_NODEFAULT**   Instructs the function to make no noise at all if for any reason it cannot find or play the sound. Normally, sndPlaySound feels obligated to produce a noise of some sort on every call, and if all else fails, it will at least play the SystemDefault sound.

PlaySound

To play sounds compiled as resources, PlaySound is the best choice. (sndPlay-Sound can also play sounds from the program's resources, but only if you load them into memory first and set the SND_MEMORY flag.)

```
BOOL PlaySound( LPCTSTR lpszSoundName,    // file or resource name
                HANDLE hModule,           // source for resource sounds
                DWORD dwFlags );          // sound type and option flags
```

The function interprets the first parameter according to the option flags.

> **SND_ALIAS**   Plays a sound from the system registry. The first parameter is an alias from the registry, such as SystemAsterisk or SystemHand.

> **SND_FILENAME**   Plays a sound from a .WAV file, just as sndPlaySound does. The first parameter points to a filename.

> **SND_RESOURCE**   Plays a sound from a program's resources. The first parameter is a resource ID string, possibly returned from the MAKEINTRESOURCE macro.

These three flags are mutually exclusive. In addition to these flags, PlaySound recognizes some of the same flags defined for sndPlaySound, such as SND_NODEFAULT and SND_ASYNC. (It does not recognize SND_MEMORY.)

The second parameter, hModule, is ignored unless dwFlags includes SND_RESOURCE, in which case hModule identifies the program whose resources contain the wave data named in lpszSoundName. The handle may belong to an instance rather than a module and may be acquired, for example, from GetModuleHandle, LoadLibrary, or GetWindowLong.

Windows does not define a WAVE keyword to use in resource files the way you use ICON or BITMAP, but you can always define your own resource types.

```
<resname> WAVE <filename> // add sound to program's resources
```

<resname> is a name you choose for your resource, and <filename> points to a .WAV file. PlaySound always looks for resources identified as type WAVE.

PlaySound (and MessageBeep and sndPlaySound) is simple to use, but it has limitations. In order to control where in a sound the playback starts, to record sounds, to mix them and change their volume, and to save new sound files, you need more commands. The Media Control Interface is the easiest way to program for multimedia, as described in the next section.

Media Control Interface (MCI) Operations

MCI operations take the form of command messages sent to devices. Generally, you begin an operation by opening a device; then you send commands, such as MCI_PLAY or MCI_STOP, to make the device play, stop, record, or rewind, and finally you close the device.

The most important and most versatile of the MCI functions is mciSendCommand. This function is to multimedia what Escape is to printing: a route for sending any of many possible signals to a device.

`mciSendCommand` expects four parameters:

```
MCIERROR mciSendCommand( MCIDEVICEID mciDeviceID,
                                            // mm device identifier
                UINT uMessage,         // command message number
                DWORD dwFlags,         // flags modifying command
                DWORD dwParamBlock );  // info structure
```

The first parameter, `mciDeviceID`, addresses a particular device. When you open a device, `mciSendCommand` gives you a device ID; in subsequent commands, the device ID tells Windows where to deliver the message.

The second parameter, `uMessage`, is a constant like MCI_PLAY or MCI_STOP. *ShowWave*, the demo described in this chapter, sends the following messages:

MCI_OPEN   Opens a device (to begin an interaction).

MCI_CLOSE   Closes a device (to end interaction).

MCI_SET   Changes device settings.

MCI_PLAY   Begins playback.

MCI_STOP   Interrupts current action.

MCI_RECORD   Begins recording.

MCI_SAVE   Saves a recorded sound in a file.

Other messages might, for example, make the device pause, seek a location in the device element, or retrieve information about the device.

The third parameter, `dwFlags`, usually combines several bit flags that help Windows interpret the command. The set of possible flags varies for each message, but a few are common to all messages. For example, `mciSendCommand` normally works asynchronously. When it initiates a device operation, it doesn't wait for the device to finish. It returns immediately and the device continues to operate in the background. If you want to know when the operation ends, setting the MCI_NOTIFY flag causes WinMM to send you a termination message. You might, for example, want to close the audio device when a sound finishes playing. On the other hand, sometimes you don't want to proceed until you are certain the device operation succeeded. The MCI_WAIT flag forces the command to run synchronously. Program execution stops at `mciSendCommand` until the device finishes the requested task.

The final parameter for mciSendCommand, dwParamBlock, also varies from message to message. It is always a structured variable holding either information the device may need to execute the command or empty fields for information the device may return after executing the command. Here are the parameter block data structures needed for the *ShowWave* demo:

Data Structure	Associated Message
MCI_OPEN_PARMS	MCI_OPEN
MCI_SET_PARMS	MCI_SET
MCI_PLAY_PARMS	MCI_PLAY
MCI_RECORD_PARMS	MCI_RECORD
MCI_SAVE_PARMS	MCI_SAVE

The fields of these structures might hold a filename, positions in the file at which to start or stop playing, a device ID, or the address of a callback function to receive the asynchronous completion message. We'll consider each structure in more detail as we encounter it in the *ShowWave* demo.

NOTE   One consideration shaping the design of the MCI was clearly extensibility. As other devices and other technologies find their way into Windows PCs, the set of MCI command messages and parameter block structures can easily expand to accommodate them. New drivers can define their own messages and structures.

Multimedia File I/O Functions

Multimedia data files conform to the standard RIFF format. Multimedia programmers need to understand the structure of a RIFF file and to learn the MMIO functions for reading and writing them.

RIFF Files

The Resource Interchange File Format (RIFF) protocol is a tagged file structure, meaning that a file can be divided into a series of irregular sections marked off by *tags*, or short strings. The tags in RIFF files are four-character codes, such as

"RIFF", "INFO", and "PAL ". (The fourth character in "PAL " is a space.) Each tag begins a *chunk*. The most important chunks begin with the tag "RIFF". RIFF chunks are allowed to contain other chunks, sometimes called *subchunks*. RIFF files always begin with a RIFF chunk, and all the remaining data is organized as subchunks of the first one.

Every chunk has three parts: a tag, a size, and some binary data. The tag tells what kind of data follows. The size, a DWORD, tells how much data the chunk contains. At the end of the data comes the tag for the next chunk (if any). A waveform file always has at least two subchunks—one for the format and one for the sound data—and may have more. Some chunks might carry copyright and version information; others might hold a list of *cues*, locations in the file that coordinate with events in some other chunk or file.

RIFF chunks differ from most others in that their data fields—the binary data section—always begin with another four-letter code indicating the file's contents. The "RIFF" tag identifies a RIFF file, and the form code tells you to expect subchunks appropriate for a waveform ("WAVE"), a MIDI sound ("RMID"), a DIB ("RDIB"), a movie file ("RMMP"), or a palette file ("PAL").

Since RIFF files need so many of these four-character codes, there's a macro for creating them: mmioFOURCC. This command stores a "RIFF" tag in one field of a chunk-information structure:

```
MMCKINFO mmckinfo.ckid = mmioFOURCC( 'R', 'I', 'F', 'F' );
```

The MMCKINFO structure holds information describing a single chunk. When reading data, the system fills out fields describing the current chunk for you. When writing data, you fill out the information for the system to store.

```
typedef struct _MMCKINFO     /* RIFF chunk information data structure */
{
    FOURCC  ckid;                    // chunk ID
    DWORD   cksize;                  // chunk size
    FOURCC  fccType;                 // form type or list type
    DWORD   dwDataOffset;            // offset of data portion of chunk
    DWORD   dwFlags;                 // flags used by MMIO functions
} MMCKINFO;
```

FOURCC is a new data type based on the DWORD type. Each character in the code fills one of the 4 bytes in a DWORD. The third field, fccType, is the form tag that follows every "RIFF" tag. The fccType field is irrelevant for non-RIFF chunks because they don't have forms. Figure 37.1 illustrates parent chunks (or superchunks) and subchunks in a RIFF file.

FIGURE 37.1:

Structure of a RIFF file

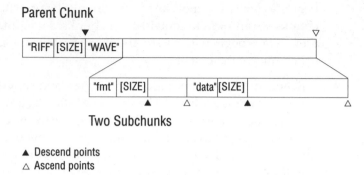

The Multimedia File I/O Functions

You've already encountered two sets of file I/O functions, one in the C runtime libraries and one in the Windows API. The WinMM API includes yet another set, which has special features for chunky RIFF files. The multimedia file I/O functions understand chunks better than other functions do. In addition, they allow buffered file access. (The Windows 95 system caches file I/O by default, but functions that do their own additional buffering can still improve performance.)

File Operations

The command that opens a file also controls the buffer settings.

```
HMMIO mmioOpen( LPTSTR      lpszFilename,  // name of file to open
                LPMMIOINFO  lpmmioinfo,    // place to put file info
                DWORD       fdwOpen );     // option flags
```

The first parameter names the file, and the second stores information about its current state. Unless you want to change a default setting, such as the size of the I/O buffer (8KB), lpmmioinfo should be NULL. The third parameter contains a variety of option flags. Here are some of them:

MMIO_READ   Allows reading only.

MMIO_WRITE   Allows writing only.

MMIO_READWRITE   Allows reading and writing.

MMIO_CREATE   Creates a new file.

MMIO_DELETE   Deletes an existing file.

MMIO_EXCLUSIVE   Prevents other programs from using the file.

MMIO_DENYWRITE   Prevents other programs from changing the file.

MMIO_ALLOCBUF   Enables buffered I/O.

In the C libraries, fopen begins buffered I/O and _open begins unbuffered I/O. The MMIO_ALLOCBUF flag makes the same distinction for the multimedia file I/O procedures. The system responds by allocating a default buffer of 8KB. (To make the buffer larger or smaller, set a value in the MMIOINFO structure or call mmio-SetBuffer.)

mmioOpen returns a handle of type HMMIO, meaning a handle to a multimedia file. Multimedia file handles are not compatible with other file handles; don't use them with the other C or Win32 file functions.

The functions mmioRead, mmioWrite, and mmioClose perform easily recognizable file operations.

Chunk Operations

A few other I/O functions deal specifically with RIFF data chunks. To put a new chunk in a file, call mmioCreateChunk. This command writes a chunk header, including the tag, the size, and, for RIFF and LIST chunks, a form code as well. It leaves the file pointer on the byte where you will begin writing the chunk's data with mmioWrite.

```
MMRESULT mmioCreateChunk( HMMIO hmmio,        // handle of RIFF file
                          LPMMCKINFO lpmmcki, // description of new chunk
                          UINT uOptions );    // creation options
```

To write a RIFF or LIST superchunk, set an option flag, either MMIO_CREATERIFF or MMIO_CREATELIST.

Moving the file pointer from chunk to chunk calls for mmioDescend and mmio-Ascend. *Descending* into a chunk means advancing the file pointer past the tag and size fields to the beginning of the chunk's binary data. *Ascending* from a chunk means advancing the pointer to the end of its data.

```
MMRESULT mmioDescend( HMMIO hmmio,              // handle of RIFF file
                      LPMMCKINFO lpmmcki,       // place to put chunk info
                      LPMMCKINFO lpmmckiParent, // optional parent struct
                      UINT uSearch );           // search option flags
```

```
MMRESULT mmioAscend(  HMMIO hmmio,           // handle of RIFF file
                      LPMMCKINFO lpmmcki,    // place to put chunk info
                      UINT uReserved );      // reserved; must be zero
```

After each descent, mmioDescend returns information about the chunk through the MMCKINFO parameter. You can also make mmioDescend search for a chunk of a certain type and descend into it. To initiate a search, the last parameter should contain MMIO_FINDCHUNK, MMIO_FINDLIST, or MMIO_FINDRIFF. The search begins at the current file position and stops at the end of the file. mmioAscend, besides advancing to the end of a chunk, helps build new chunks. mmioAscend is called after you write new data, when it pads the chunk to an even byte boundary and writes the data size in the chunk's header.

The PCMWAVEFORMAT Structure

Every waveform in a RIFF file is required to contain a chunk tagged "fmt". (Lowercase tags indicate subchunks in a larger form.) The PCMWAVEFORMAT structure defines the contents of the format subchunk. The *ShowWave* demo reads the format information to confirm that the sound is playable. It also remembers the sampling rate (nSamplesPerSecond) for calculating file positions and scrollbar ranges.

```
/* general waveform format (information common to all formats) */
typedef struct waveformat_tag
{
    WORD wFormatTag;            // format type
    WORD nChannels;            // number of channels (1 = mono; 2 = stereo)
    DWORD nSamplesPerSec;      // sample rate
    DWORD nAvgBytesPerSec;     // for buffer estimation
    WORD nBlockAlign;          // block size of data
} WAVEFORMAT;


/* specific waveform format structure for PCM data */
typedef struct pcmwaveformat_tag
{
    WAVEFORMAT wf;
    WORD wBitsPerSample;
} PCMWAVEFORMAT;
```

Currently, PCM (pulse control modulation) is the only format category defined for .WAV files, so the value in the wFormatTag field of a WAVEFORMAT structure should be WAVE_FORMAT_PCM.

The PCMWAVEFORMAT structure adds to the general wave data a single field for bits per sample; this describes the space required to hold the data for a single sound sample. The common values on personal computers are 8 and 16 bits. A monaural wave sound sampled for 1 second at 11 kHz and 8 bits per sample contains 11,000 different samples of 8 bits each, for a total of about 11KB. A stereo waveform samples in two channels simultaneously. If each channel records 8 bits at a time, a single full sample is 16 bits. A 1-second 11 kHz stereo waveform with a wBitsPerSample value of 8 would fill 22KB.

The ShowWave Demo:
A Sound Recorder Clone

The *ShowWave* demo imitates the Sound Recorder that comes with Windows 98 by reading and writing waveform files, playing and recording wave sounds, mixing sounds from several files, and adjusting the volume of a sound. Without a sound card, you can still run the program to open, close, mix, scroll through, and save sound files; however, the program will be deaf and dumb, unable to play or record anything.

ShowWave is made up of several modules. Here they are in the order in which we'll present them:

- Mci.C sends commands to the audio device.

- Mmio.C reads and writes waveform data.

- WinMain.C contains WinMain and the About box procedure.

- ShowWave.C responds to dialog box controls.

- GraphWin.C manages the custom control used for the program's graph.

The first two modules, Mci.C and Mmio.C, contain general procedures for performing basic sound operations, such as playback and record. WinMain.C registers and creates the program's window and runs the About box. The fourth module, ShowWave.C, calls the appropriate functions in response to input from the user. GraphWin.C manages the sound graph at the center of the program's window, visible in Figure 37.2. When the user scrolls with the scrollbar, the graph display shows the sound wave in different parts of the file. To paint the graph display, we create a custom control and write a window procedure for it. (Another solution would be to subclass a standard control.)

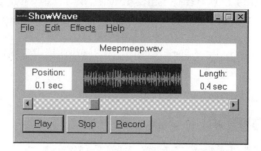

NOTE
The *ShowWave* demo is included on the CD accompanying this book, in the Chapter 37 folder.

The ShowWave Header Files and Resource Script

In the ShowWave header files and resource script (on the CD accompanying this book), you may notice a few oddities in the main dialog box's resource template. One difference is that the demos we've discussed in earlier chapters don't use the MENU keyword in a dialog box resource. However, dialog boxes may have menus, just as overlapping windows do.

Also, the dialog template refers to two custom window classes: GraphClass and ShowWaveClass. Defining new classes for a dialog box control and for the dialog box itself makes it possible to assign nonstandard properties to both windows.

The control in the center of the program window represents the current wave sound as a graph. When the user scrolls through the file, the graph changes to represent different parts of the sound. The custom class for the graph window lets us write the window's paint procedure for graphing the sound. The custom class for the main dialog window lets us assign the dialog box an icon to display when minimized.

The MCI Module

In the MCI module, we've isolated all the mciSendCommand function calls and built a separate routine for each command message. All the procedures are short and most follow this basic pattern:

1. Initialize a parameter block.

2. Send a command.

3. Check for errors.

4. Return a value.

The module's eight procedures are described at the top of the Mci.C file:

```
PUBLIC FUNCTIONS
     OpenDevice          open audio device
     CloseDevice         close audio device
     SetTimeFormat       choose millisecond time format
     BeginPlay           begin sound playback
     StopPlay            end sound playback
     BeginRecord         begin recording
     SaveRecord          save recording
```

Opening and Closing a Device

Opening a device is like opening a file; it announces your intention to exchange information with some piece of hardware and tells the system to create whatever internal structures are needed to manage the interaction. The system gives you a device ID number that, like a file handle, identifies your partner in the exchange. When the interaction ends, you close the device, the system releases any related memory resources, and the device ID becomes invalid.

All multimedia devices respond to the MCI_OPEN and MCI_CLOSE messages. (The other three messages to which all drivers must respond are MCI_GETDEVCAPS, MCI_STATUS, and MCI_INFO—all of which request information about the device.)

Every MCI_OPEN command is accompanied by an MCI_OPEN_PARMS structure, defined in Mmsystem.H:

```
    /* parameter block for MCI_OPEN command message */
typedef struct tagMCI_OPEN_PARMS
{
    DWORD dwCallback;               // window handle
    MCIDEVICEID wDeviceID;          // number identifying device
    LPCTSTR lpstrDeviceType;        // type of device to open
    LPCTSTR lpstrElementName;       // input element for device
    LPCTSTR lpstrAlias;             // optional
} MCI_OPEN_PARMS;
```

The dwCallback field appears in all the parameter structures. It works in tandem with the MCI_NOTIFY flag. Any mciSendCommand function call that asks for a notification message must include a window handle in the low-order word of the dwCallback field. This way, when the operation ends, the system can send an MM_MCINOTIFY message to the window we named. You'll see how to answer the notification message when we discuss the ShowWave.C module.

The wDeviceID field must be empty when you open a device; WinMM assigns an ID to the device you open and places the ID in the wDeviceID field. After opening any device, you will want to save the ID number.

NOTE

When Microsoft first released the Multimedia Extensions as a separate product enhancing Windows 3.0, the second and third fields were declared to be type **WORD**. In Windows 3.1 they changed to the polymorphic type **UINT**, and in Win32 the ID field changed again to the newly defined **MCIDEVICEID** type. For backward compatibility, however, both fields still incongruously retain the **w** prefix. In the transition from Windows 3.1 to Windows 98, the **MCI_OPEN_PARMS** structure has also lost an unused field, **wReserved0**.

The lpcstrDeviceType field names the sort of device you need for your data. The type name comes from the system registry, where you find entries like these:

```
AVIVideo : REG_SZ : mciavi32.dll
WaveAudio : REG_SZ : mciwave.dll
Sequencer : REG_SZ : mciseq.dll
CDAudio : REG_SZ : mcicda.dll
```

TIP

To find these multimedia device entries with the Registry Editor, go to HKEY_LOCAL_MACHINE and descend through SOFTWARE to Microsoft to Windows to CurrentVersion to MCI and MCI32.

ShowWave requests a device of type WaveAudio in order to play .WAV files.

The lpstrElementName field designates a data source for a compound device. Windows distinguishes between simple devices and compound devices. A *simple device* doesn't need the name of a file in order to operate; a *compound device* does. For example, a program cannot choose what a CD player will play; the player plays only whatever CD the drive contains. A CD player is a simple device. A waveform sound driver, on the other hand, might play any of many different files currently available in the system; you must specify the file. The waveaudio device is always a compound device.

A *device element* is whatever input or output medium your program connects with the device. The device element is usually a file, so the lpstrElementName field usually contains a filename.

The final field, lpstrAlias, allows you to provide a synonym for naming the device you open. Aliases matter only for the MCI string command interface.

You don't need to fill out all the fields in the parameter block. You might, for example, provide only the element name and let the system choose a matching device by looking at the file's extension—for example, a wave audio device for a .WAV file or a sequencer for an .MID file. Or if you just want information about the device, you might open it by supplying the type without any element. The flags parameter of the mciSendCommand function tells the system which fields to read. Here is an example:

```
/*------------------------------------------------------------------

OPEN DEVICE
Open a waveaudio device
----------------------------------------------------------------*/
BOOL OpenDevice( HWND hWnd, LPSTR lpszFileName,
              MCIDEVICEID *lpmciDevice )
{
    DWORD dwRet;
    MCI_OPEN_PARMS mciOpenParms;
        /* open the compound device */
    mciOpenParms.lpstrDeviceType  = "waveaudio";
```

```
            mciOpenParms.lpstrElementName = lpszFileName;
            dwRet = mciSendCommand( 0,                                 // device ID
                                    MCI_OPEN,                          // command
                                    MCI_OPEN_TYPE | MCI_OPEN_ELEMENT,  // flags
                                    (DWORD)(LPVOID)&mciOpenParms );    // param blk
        if( dwRet != 0 )
        {
            ReportMCIError( hWnd, dwRet );
            return( FALSE );
        }
            /* set return values */
        *lpmciDevice = mciOpenParms.wDeviceID;
        return( TRUE );
    }
```

The first parameter for `mciSendCommand` can only be 0 because the device is not open and has not yet been assigned an ID. The third parameter combines two flags. The first, `MCI_OPEN_TYPE`, tells the system to read the `lpstrDeviceType` field of the parameter block because we have put a string there. The second flag, `MCI_OPEN_ELEMENT`, says to read the `lpstrElementName` field as well. Because we have omitted the `MCI_OPEN_ALIAS` flag, the system will ignore any value in the `lpstrAlias` field.

Our `OpenDevice` procedure returns TRUE or FALSE to indicate its success; if it succeeds, it also returns the device ID in its third parameter. The device ID will be needed for subsequent operations; for example, closing the device:

```
/*------------------------------------------------------------------
   CLOSE DEVICE
   Close a multimedia device
   ----------------------------------------------------------------*/
void CloseDevice( HWND hWnd, MCIDEVICEID mciDevice )
{
    DWORD dwRet;

    dwRet = mciSendCommand( mciDevice, MCI_CLOSE, MCI_WAIT, (DWORD)NULL );
    if( dwRet != 0 )
        ReportMCIError( hWnd, dwRet );
    return;
}
```

`CloseDevice` expects a device ID as part of its input. No other input is needed; the MCI_CLOSE command doesn't even use a parameter block.

Setting the Time Format

When *ShowWave* asks the `waveaudio` device to play a sound, it always specifies a location in the file from which to begin. With the program's scrollbar, the user can move to any part of the file before starting playback. *ShowWave* and the driver need to agree on units for measuring the file.

The possible units for waveform files are bytes, samples, and milliseconds. Measuring files in bytes makes intuitive sense. As explained earlier in the chapter, a sample is a discrete instant of digitized sound. To measure a file in samples means counting each individual snapshot of the sound wave. Samples are taken at a constant rate, so every millisecond of sound contains the same number of samples. A sound recorded with a sampling rate of 22.5 kHz contains about 22 samples in every millisecond. Because milliseconds mean more to most users than do samples or bytes, *ShowWave* chooses the MM_FORMAT_MILLISECONDS format. Choosing a format means sending the MCI_SET command message with the MCI_SET_PARMS parameter block:

```
/* parameter block for MCI_SET command message */
typedef struct tagMCI_SET_PARMS
{
    DWORD dwCallback;               // window for MM_MCINOTIFY message
    DWORD dwTimeFormat;            // time format constant
    DWORD dwAudio;                 // audio output channel
} MCI_SET_PARMS;
```

`dwTimeFormat` may be MM_FORMAT_BYTES, MM_FORMAT_SAMPLES, or MM_FORMAT_MILLISECONDS. *ShowWave* doesn't play stereo, so we ignore the `dwAudio` field.

```
/*-------------------------------------------------------------------------
    SET TIME FORMAT
    Set time format.  Use milliseconds (not bytes or samples).
  -------------------------------------------------------------------------*/
BOOL SetTimeFormat( HWND hWnd, MCIDEVICEID mciDevice )
{
    DWORD dwRet;
    MCI_SET_PARMS mciSetParms;
```

```
      /* set time format to milliseconds */
   mciSetParms.dwTimeFormat = MCI_FORMAT_MILLISECONDS;
   dwRet = mciSendCommand( mciDevice, MCI_SET, MCI_SET_TIME_FORMAT,
                           (DWORD)(LPVOID)&mciSetParms );
   if( dwRet != 0 )
   {
       ReportMCIError( hWnd, dwRet );
       return( FALSE );
   }
   return( TRUE );                          // success
}
```

The MCI_SET_TIME_FORMAT flag tells the system to read the value in the dwTimeFormat field of mciSetParms.

Playing a Sound

For modularity, PlayBack makes no assumptions about the device settings. It resets the time format before each operation. The MCI_PLAY command initiates playback, and its parameter block is called MCI_PLAY_PARMS:

```
/* parameter block for MCI_PLAY command message */
typedef struct tagMCI_PLAY_PARMS
{
    DWORD dwCallback;                    // window for MM_MCINOTIFY
    DWORD dwFrom;                        // starting point
    DWORD dwTo;                          // ending point
} MCI_PLAY_PARMS;
```

By default, the Play command starts at the current position in the file and plays to the end, but dwFrom and dwTo, if they are flagged, direct WinMM to start and stop at other points. You may express the starting and stopping points in bytes, samples, or milliseconds, but you should tell the driver in advance which units to expect. (By default, drivers work in milliseconds.)

```
/*--------------------------------------------------------------------
   BEGIN PLAYBACK
--------------------------------------------------------------------*/
BOOL BeginPlay ( HWND hWnd, MCIDEVICEID mciDevice, DWORD dwFrom )
{
    DWORD dwRet;
    MCI_PLAY_PARMS mciPlayParms;
```

```
        /* set time format to milliseconds */
    if( ! SetTimeFormat( hWnd, mciDevice ) )
    {
        return( FALSE );
    }
        // The callback window will be notified with an MM_MCINOTIFY message
        // when playback is complete.  At that time, the window procedure
        // closes the device.
    mciPlayParms.dwCallback = (DWORD)(LPVOID) hWnd;
    mciPlayParms.dwFrom = dwFrom;
    dwRet = mciSendCommand( mciDevice, MCI_PLAY, MCI_FROM | MCI_NOTIFY,
                            (DWORD)(LPVOID)&mciPlayParms );
    if (dwRet != 0)
    {
        ReportMCIError( hWnd, dwRet );
        return( FALSE );
    }
    return( TRUE );                              // success
}
```

The MCI_FROM flag signals the presence of a value in the dwFrom field. The MCI_NOTIFY flag tells the system to send a message when the sound stops playing. Sounds can be quite long, so we let WinMM take over and continue to play the sound in the background while *ShowWave* moves on to the next procedure. When WinMM reaches the end of the .WAV file, it addresses an MM_MCINOTIFY message to the window named in the dwCallback field. Look for an MM_MCINOTIFY message handler when we reach ShowWave_WndProc. It is the completion routine for asynchronous multimedia operations.

The notify message won't arrive until after the wave device reaches the dwTo point or the end of the file. In its wParam, the message carries a result code indicating whether the operation finished normally, was interrupted or superseded by another command to the device, or failed from a device error. The low word of lParam carries the device ID.

Stopping a Sound

The MCI_STOP command interrupts an operation already in progress. If the user begins playing a long sound and then decides not to listen after all, clicking on the Stop button sends an MCI_STOP command to abort the playback. Like the MCI_CLOSE message, the MCI_STOP command uses no parameter block.

```
/*─────────────────────────────────────────────────────────────────────
   STOP PLAY
   Terminate playback
─────────────────────────────────────────────────────────────────────*/
void StopPlay( HWND hWnd, MCIDEVICEID mciDevice )
{
    DWORD dwRet;

    dwRet = mciSendCommand( mciDevice, MCI_STOP, MCI_WAIT, (DWORD)NULL );
    if( dwRet != 0 )
    {
        ReportMCIError( hWnd, dwRet );
    }
    return;
}
```

If you sent MCI_STOP with MCI_NOTIFY instead of MCI_WAIT, the window proce-dure would receive *two* notification messages. The first, MCI_NOTIFY_ABORTED, would tell you that playback ended before reaching the terminal point. The sec-ond, MCI_NOTIFY_SUCCESSFUL, would indicate successful completion of the Stop command.

Recording a Sound

Sound boards generally include a jack so you can plug a microphone directly into your computer and record straight to disk. The MCI_RECORD message directs the sound device to accept input from a microphone.

```
/* parameter block for MCI_RECORD command message */
typedef struct tagMCI_RECORD_PARMS
{
    DWORD dwCallback;              // window for MM_MCINOTIFY
    DWORD dwFrom;                  // starting point
    DWORD dwTo;                    // ending point
} MCI_RECORD_PARMS;
```

The dwFrom and dwTo fields name points in an existing file where the recorded information should be written. In a new file, only the dwTo field matters; new files must always begin at 0. Without the MCI_TO flag and a dwTo value, recording con-tinues until either the disk fills up or the driver receives a stop command. (To get a new file, give MCI_OPEN a null string, "", for the element name.)

```
/*-----------------------------------------------------------------
BEGIN RECORD
------------------------------------------------------------------*/

BOOL BeginRecord( HWND hWnd, MCIDEVICEID mciDevice, DWORD dwTo )
{
    DWORD dwRet;
    MCI_RECORD_PARMS mciRecordParms;

        /* set time format to milliseconds */
    if( ! SetTimeFormat( hWnd, mciDevice ) )
    {
        return( FALSE );
    }
        // Begin recording for the specified number of milliseconds.
        // The callback window will be notified with an MM_MCINOTIFY message
        // when recording is complete.  At that time, the window procedure
        // saves the recording and closes the device.
    mciRecordParms.dwCallback = (DWORD)(LPVOID) hWnd;
    mciRecordParms.dwTo = dwTo;
    dwRet = mciSendCommand( mciDevice, MCI_RECORD, MCI_TO | MCI_NOTIFY,
                        (DWORD)(LPVOID) &mciRecordParms );

    if( dwRet != 0 )
    {
        ReportMCIError( hWnd, dwRet );
        return( FALSE );
    }
    return( TRUE );                                // success
}
```

Saving a Recorded Sound

The MCI_SAVE command instructs a driver to save the current recording to disk. If you record and then close the application without sending MCI_SAVE, the data will be lost.

```
    /* parameter block for MCI_SAVE command message */
typedef struct tagMCI_SAVE_PARMS
{
    DWORD dwCallback;                    // window for MM_MCINOTIFY
    LPCTSTR lpfilename;                  // name of disk file
} MCI_SAVE_PARMS;
```

The string in lpfilename names the output file.

```
/*----------------------------------------------------------------------
   SAVE RECORD
   Save recording
-------------------------------------------------------------------------*/
BOOL SaveRecord( HWND hWnd, MCIDEVICEID mciDevice, LPSTR lpszFileName )
{
   DWORD dwRet;
   MCI_SAVE_PARMS mciSaveParms;

      // Save the recording to the specified file.  Wait for
      // the operation to complete before continuing.
   mciSaveParms.lpfilename = lpszFileName;
   dwRet = mciSendCommand( mciDevice, MCI_SAVE, MCI_SAVE_FILE | MCI_WAIT,
                         (DWORD)(LPVOID)&mciSaveParms );
   if( dwRet != 0 )
   {
      ReportMCIError( hWnd, dwRet );
      return( FALSE );
   }
   return( TRUE );                              // success
}
```

Handling Errors

The last function in the MCI module handles errors in any of the other functions. It displays a message box telling the user what happened.

The error procedure needs two strings. The first, the program title for the caption bar, it loads from the string table; the second, an error message, it gets directly from MCI. The mciGetErrorString function retrieves a string describing a WinMM error. mciSendCommand returns detailed error codes that *ShowWave* dutifully stores in its dwResult variable. If the return value is not 0, an error has occurred and *ShowWave* calls ReportMCIError. Given the dwResult error code, mciGetErrorString returns an appropriate string.

The Mmsystem.H file defines about 90 different error codes. Some of them, like MCIERR_INVALID_DEVICE_ID, can happen any time; others, like MCIERR_CANNOT_LOAD_DRIVER, arise only during a specific command (in this case, Open); still others are peculiar to one device. MCIERR_WAVES_OUTPUTSINUSE, for example, indicates that all waveform devices are already busy.

```
/*--------------------------------------------------------------------
   REPORT MCI ERROR
   Report given MCI error to the user
--------------------------------------------------------------------*/
static void ReportMCIError( HWND hWnd, DWORD dwError )
{
    HINSTANCE hInstance;
    char szErrStr[MAXERRORLENGTH];
    char szCaption[MAX_RSRC_STRING_LEN];

    hInstance = GetWindowInstance( hWnd );
    LoadString( hInstance, IDS_CAPTION, szCaption, sizeof(szCaption) );
    mciGetErrorString( dwError, szErrStr, sizeof(szErrStr) );
    MessageBox( hWnd, szErrStr, szCaption, MB_ICONEXCLAMATION | MB_OK );
    return;
}
```

The MMIO Module

If *ShowWave* only played and recorded sounds, it wouldn't need the MMIO module. Several of its functions, however, require the program to manipulate the data in sound files directly. Most obviously, to draw the sound wave, it must read samples from the .WAV file. Also, since the user can modify sounds in memory by mixing them or changing the volume, sometimes *ShowWave* must save data into a new file. The MMIO module contains one function to read wave data, one to write wave data, and one to handle file errors.

Reading the .WAV File

The ReadWaveData procedure loads all the data from a .WAV file into memory. It performs the following steps:

1. Open the file.

2. Find the WAVE chunk.

3. Locate the fmt subchunk and confirm that the sound is in a suitable format.

4. Find the data subchunk and load it into memory.

5. Close the file.

```
/*————————————————————————————————————————————————————————————
    READ WAVE DATA
        Read waveform data from a RIFF file into a memory buffer.

    RETURN
        TRUE if we successfully fill the buffer, otherwise FALSE.
        If the function returns TRUE, then the last three parameters
        return information about the new buffer.
————————————————————————————————————————————————————————————————*/
BOOL ReadWaveData( HWND hWnd,
                   LPSTR lpszFileName,
                   LPSTR *lplpWaveData,          // points to buffer
                   DWORD *lpdwWaveDataSize,      // size of buffer
                   DWORD *lpdwSamplesPerSec )    // sampling rate
{
    HMMIO           hmmio;              // file handle
    MMCKINFO        mmckinfoWave;       // description of "WAVE" chunk
    MMCKINFO        mmckinfoFmt;        // description of "fmt " chunk
    MMCKINFO        mmckinfoData;       // description of "data" chunk
    PCMWAVEFORMAT   pcmWaveFormat;      // contents of "fmt " chunk
    LONG            lFmtSize;           // size of "fmt " chunk
    LONG            lDataSize;          // size of "data" chunk
    LPSTR           lpData;             // pointer to data buffer

        /* open the given file for reading using multimedia file I/O */
    hmmio = mmioOpen( lpszFileName, NULL, MMIO_ALLOCBUF | MMIO_READ );
    if (hmmio == NULL)
    {
        ReportError( hWnd, IDS_CANTOPENFILE );
        return( FALSE );
    }
```

The `mmioOpen` command takes three parameters: a filename, a structure for extra parameters, and some operation flags. The extra parameters matter only for changing the size of the file I/O buffer, for opening a memory file, or for naming a custom I/O procedure to read the file. Since `ReadWaveData` does none of these, the parameter is NULL.

MMIO_ALLOCBUF turns on I/O buffering. The other flag, MMIO_READ, opens the file for reading only. `mmioWrite` will return an error for files opened with MMIO_READ.

```
        /* locate a chunk with a "WAVE" form type */
    mmckinfoWave.fccType = mmioFOURCC('W','A','V','E');
```

```
if (mmioDescend( hmmio, &mmckinfoWave, NULL, MMIO_FINDRIFF ) != 0)
{
    ReportError( hWnd, IDS_NOTWAVEFILE );
    mmioClose( hmmio, 0 );
    return( FALSE );
}
    /* find the format subchunk */
mmckinfoFmt.ckid = mmioFOURCC('f','m','t',' ');
if( mmioDescend( hmmio, &mmckinfoFmt, &mmckinfoWave,
                MMIO_FINDCHUNK ) != 0)
{
    ReportError( hWnd, IDS_CORRUPTEDFILE );
    mmioClose( hmmio, 0 );
    return( FALSE );
}
```

After opening the file, we next locate and verify the data. The first `mmioDescend` command looks for a "RIFF" tag followed by a WAVE code. If that works, the second command looks for the waveform's format subchunk.

To find the first chunk, we fill out only one field in the chunk info structure: `fccType`. The form type we seek is WAVE. The `ckid` (chunk ID) field should be RIFF, but the MMIO_FINDRIFF flag adequately describes that part of our target. The `Descend` command also recognizes three other flags: MMIO_FINDCHUNK, MMIO_FINDRIFF, and MMIO_FINDLIST. In effect, the FINDCHUNK flag says to search for whatever is in the `ckid` field, and the other flags say to match the `fccType` field with a RIFF or LIST chunk.

`mmioDescend` takes four parameters: an HMMIO file handle, a description of the target chunk, a description of its parent chunk, and some operation flags. RIFF chunks don't have parents, so we leave the third field NULL, but the format chunk is always a subchunk of some parent. Only RIFF and LIST chunks can have subchunks.

NOTE   Pardon the mixed metaphors for chunk relationships. The terminology comes from the Microsoft manuals. Perhaps *superchunk* would be clearer than *parent*.

To find the format subchunk, we put "fmt" in the target information structure and "WAVE" in the parent information structure. `mmioDescend` will stop looking for "fmt" if it reaches the end of the current WAVE chunk. In this case, the file is unusable, perhaps corrupted, because you cannot interpret a WAVE without its format specifications.

The second `Descend` command left the file pointer at the beginning of the data in the format subchunk. Next, we load the format information into memory for verification:

```
/* read the format subchunk */
lFmtSize = (LONG)sizeof( pcmWaveFormat );
if( mmioRead( hmmio, (LPSTR)&pcmWaveFormat, lFmtSize ) != lFmtSize )
{
    ReportError( hWnd,IDS_CANTREADFORMAT );
    mmioClose( hmmio, 0 );
    return( FALSE );
}

/* ascend out of the format subchunk */
if( mmioAscend( hmmio, &mmckinfoFmt, 0 ) != 0 )
{
    ReportError( hWnd, IDS_CANTREADFORMAT );
    mmioClose( hmmio, 0 );
    return( FALSE );
}

/* make sure the sound file is an 8-bit mono PCM .WAV file */
if( ( pcmWaveFormat.wf.wFormatTag != WAVE_FORMAT_PCM ) ||
    ( pcmWaveFormat.wf.nChannels != 1 ) ||
    ( pcmWaveFormat.wBitsPerSample != 8 ) )
{
    ReportError( hWnd, IDS_UNSUPPORTEDFORMAT );
    mmioClose( hmmio, 0 );
    return( FALSE );
}
```

`mmioRead` expects a file handle, a pointer to a memory buffer, and a byte quantity. `lFmtSize` contains the number of bytes in a `PCMWAVEFORMAT` structure, and `mmioRead` loads that many bytes from the disk.

The `Ascend` command advances the file-position pointer past the last byte of the format chunk, ready for the next file operation. `mmioAscend` takes only three parameters because it never needs to think about the enclosing superchunk in order to find the end of a subchunk.

For clarity, we've limited *ShowWave* to one-channel sounds with 8 bits per pixel. To allow other ratings, you could add a few variables and modify the scrollbar code (see "Scrolling while Playing or Recording" later in this chapter).

We've verified the data format. Now we can load it into memory. We'll find the data subchunk, determine its size, allocate a memory buffer for it, and read the data into the buffer.

```
    /* find the data subchunk */
mmckinfoData.ckid = mmioFOURCC('d','a','t','a');
if( mmioDescend( hmmio, &mmckinfoData, &mmckinfoWave, MMIO_FINDCHUNK ) != 0 )
{
    ReportError( hWnd, IDS_CORRUPTEDFILE );
    mmioClose( hmmio, 0 );
    return( FALSE );
}
    /* get the size of the data subchunk */
lDataSize = (LONG)mmckinfoData.cksize;
if( lDataSize == 0 )
{
    ReportError( hWnd,IDS_NOWAVEDATA );
    mmioClose( hmmio, 0 );
    return( FALSE );
}
    /* allocate and lock memory for the waveform data */
lpData = GlobalAllocPtr( GMEM_MOVEABLE, lDataSize );
if( ! lpData )
{
    ReportError( hWnd, IDS_OUTOFMEMORY );
    mmioClose( hmmio, 0 );
    return( FALSE );
}
    /* read the data subchunk */
if( mmioRead( hmmio, (LPSTR)lpData, lDataSize ) != lDataSize )
{
    ReportError( hWnd, IDS_CANTREADDATA );
    GlobalFreePtr( lpData );
    mmioClose( hmmio, 0 );
    return( FALSE );
}
```

Finding the data chunk is just like finding the fmt chunk. mmioDescend fills the mmckinfoData variable with information that includes the size of the data. lDataSize tells us how much space to allocate from memory and how many bytes to read from the file.

To finish ReadWaveData, we close the file and return through the procedure's parameters three values: a pointer to the new memory object, the number of data bytes in the object, and the sampling rate:

```
    /* close the file */
mmioClose( hmmio, 0 );
    /* set return variables */
*lplpWaveData = lpData;
*lpdwWaveDataSize = (DWORD)lDataSize;
*lpdwSamplesPerSec = pcmWaveFormat.wf.nSamplesPerSec;
return( TRUE );
}
```

WARNING

After closing the .WAV audio file, do not free the pointer to the retrieved data because the data is retained in memory for further use. When the audio waveform is replayed, instead of reopening the file to read the data again, the audio player plays from memory.

Writing the .WAV File

WriteWaveData transfers a wave sound from a memory buffer to a disk file. When the user modifies an existing sound or records a new one, WriteWaveData saves the result. It performs these steps:

1. Open the file.

2. Create the RIFF superchunk with a WAVE format type.

3. Create the format subchunk; fill in its size and data fields.

4. Create the data subchunk; fill in its size and data fields.

5. Ascend to the end of the file, causing the total size to be written in for the superchunk.

6. Close the file.

```
/*-----------------------------------------------------------------------------
    WRITE WAVE DATA
    Transfer waveform data from a memory buffer to a disk file          ·
------------------------------------------------------------------------------*/
BOOL WriteWaveData( HWND hWnd,                    // main window
                    LPSTR lpszFileName,           // destination file
                    LPSTR lpWaveData,             // data source buffer
                    DWORD dwWaveDataSize,         // size of data in buffer
                    DWORD dwSamplesPerSec )       // sampling rate
{
    HMMIO           hmmio;              // file handle
    MMCKINFO        mmckinfoWave;       // description of "WAVE" chunk
    MMCKINFO        mmckinfoFmt;        // description of "fmt " chunk
    MMCKINFO        mmckinfoData;       // description of "data" chunk
    PCMWAVEFORMAT   pcmWaveFormat;      // contents of "fmt " chunk
    LONG            lFmtSize;           // size of "fmt " chunk
    LONG            lDataSize;          // size of "data" chunk

        /* open the given file for writing using multimedia file I/O */
    hmmio = mmioOpen( lpszFileName, NULL, MMIO_ALLOCBUF | MMIO_WRITE | MMIO_CREATE );
    if( hmmio == NULL )
    {
        ReportError( hWnd, IDS_CANTOPENFILE );
        return( FALSE );
    }
        /* create a "RIFF" chunk with a "WAVE" form type */
    mmckinfoWave.fccType = mmioFOURCC( 'W','A','V','E' );
    if( mmioCreateChunk( hmmio, &mmckinfoWave, MMIO_CREATERIFF ) != 0 )
    {
        ReportError( hWnd, IDS_CANTWRITEWAVE );
        mmioClose( hmmio, 0 );
        return( FALSE );
    }
```

The mmioOpen command tells the system we want to buffer our file operations, write without reading, and create the file if it doesn't already exist. mmioCreate-Chunk expects three parameters: a file handle, a structure describing the new chunk, and an optional flag for creating superchunks.

The MMCKINFO structure has a field called dwDataOffset. mmioCreateChunk returns a value there telling where in the file the new chunk's data area begins. It also leaves the file pointer on the first byte of the new data area.

mmioCreateChunk cannot insert new chunks into the middle of a file. If the file pointer is not at the end of the file, old data will be overwritten.

Having established the main RIFF chunk, we next create and initialize the format subchunk:

```
    /* store size of the format subchunk */
lFmtSize = (LONG)sizeof( pcmWaveFormat );
    // Create the format subchunk.
    // Since we know the size of this chunk, specify it in the
    // MMCKINFO structure so MMIO doesn't have to seek back and
    // set the chunk size after ascending from the chunk.
mmckinfoFmt.ckid = mmioFOURCC( 'f', 'm', 't', ' ' );
mmckinfoFmt.cksize = lFmtSize;
if (mmioCreateChunk( hmmio, &mmckinfoFmt, 0 ) != 0)
{
    ReportError( hWnd, IDS_CANTWRITEFORMAT );
    mmioClose( hmmio, 0 );
    return( FALSE );
}
    /* initialize PCMWAVEFORMAT structure */
pcmWaveFormat.wf.wFormatTag      = WAVE_FORMAT_PCM;
pcmWaveFormat.wf.nChannels       = 1;
pcmWaveFormat.wf.nSamplesPerSec  = dwSamplesPerSec;
pcmWaveFormat.wf.nAvgBytesPerSec = dwSamplesPerSec;
pcmWaveFormat.wf.nBlockAlign     = 1;
pcmWaveFormat.wBitsPerSample     = 8;
    /* write the format subchunk */
if( mmioWrite( hmmio, (LPSTR)&pcmWaveFormat, lFmtSize ) != lFmtSize )
{
    ReportError( hWnd, IDS_CANTWRITEFORMAT );
    mmioClose( hmmio, 0 );
    return( FALSE );
}
    /* ascend out of the format subchunk */
if( mmioAscend( hmmio, &mmckinfoFmt, 0 ) != 0 )
{
    ReportError( hWnd, IDS_CANTWRITEFORMAT );
    mmioClose( hmmio, 0 );
    return( FALSE );
}
```

Remember that every chunk contains a tag, a size, and some data. mmioCreate-Chunk leaves a space for the size, but if the cksize field is 0, then the space remains blank until the next mmioAscend seals off the new chunk. Normally, mmioAscend must calculate the data size, move back to the size field and fill it in, and then move forward to the end of the data. By providing the size, we avoid the extra backward motion, saving the time of two disk accesses.

The value in the global variable dwSamplesPerSecond defaults to 22,050 (22.05 kHz), but it changes whenever ReadWaveData loads a new file. (Choosing New from the File menu resets the value.) Because *ShowWave* restricts itself to one-channel sounds with 8 bits per sample, every sample always contains 1 byte. This is why we can put the same value in the nSamplesPerSecond and nAvgBytesPerSecond fields of the pcmWaveForm variable.

The nBlockAlign field tells how many bytes one sample fills. The size of a sample must be rounded up to the nearest byte. A 12-bit-per-sample sound, for example, would align on 2-byte boundaries. Four bits would be wasted in each block, but when they are loaded into memory, the extra padding speeds up data access. The CPU always fetches information from memory in whole bytes and words, not bits.

You may wonder why we call mmioAscend when the write operation has already moved the file position to the end of the format data. Again, the answer has to do with alignment and access speed. A chunk's data area must always contain an even number of bytes so that it aligns on word (2-byte) boundaries. If the data contains an odd number of bytes, the final mmioAscend adds padding. Otherwise, it has no effect. mmioCreateChunk should nearly always be followed eventually by mmioAscend.

With the format chunk written, we next perform the same steps to create the data chunk:

```
    /* store size of the "data" subchunk */
lDataSize = (LONG)dwWaveDataSize;
    /* create the "data" subchunk that holds the waveform samples */
mmckinfoData.ckid  = mmioFOURCC( 'd', 'a', 't', 'a' );
mmckinfoFmt.cksize = lDataSize;
if( mmioCreateChunk( hmmio, &mmckinfoData, 0 ) != 0 )
{
    ReportError( hWnd, IDS_CANTWRITEDATA );
    mmioClose( hmmio, 0 );
    return( FALSE );
}
```

```
    /* write the "data" subchunk */
if( mmioWrite( hmmio, lpWaveData, lDataSize ) != lDataSize )
{
    ReportError( hWnd, IDS_CANTWRITEDATA );
    mmioClose( hmmio, 0 );
    return( FALSE );
}
    /* ascend out of the "data" subchunk */
if( mmioAscend( hmmio, &mmckinfoData, 0 ) != 0 )
{
    ReportError( hWnd, IDS_CANTWRITEDATA );
    mmioClose( hmmio, 0 );
    return( FALSE );
}
```

That mmioAscend command moves to the end of the data subchunk, but remember we are still inside the RIFF superchunk. We've called mmioCreateChunk three times but mmioAscend only twice.

```
        /* ascend out of the "WAVE" chunk—causes size to be written */
    if( mmioAscend( hmmio, &mmckinfoWave, 0 ) != 0 )
    {
        ReportError( hWnd, IDS_CANTWRITEWAVE );
        mmioClose( hmmio, 0 );
        return( FALSE );
    }
        /* close the file */
    mmioClose( hmmio, 0 );
    return( TRUE );
}
```

Before creating each subchunk, we put a size value in the cksize field, so that WinMM knew the chunk size from the beginning. But for the first chunk, the parent chunk, we provided only a format type (WAVE). The final mmioAscend completes the creation of the first chunk. It computes the size and records it right after the "RIFF" tag at the beginning of the file.

Handling Errors

mciGetErrorString works only with the error returns from mciSendCommand; the file I/O procedures have no equivalent function for error messages. We put our own messages in ShowWave.RC and wrote ReportError to display them.

```
/*--------------------------------------------------------------------------
    REPORT ERROR
    Report given error to the user
---------------------------------------------------------------------*/
static void ReportError( HWND hWnd, int iErrorID )
{
    HINSTANCE hInstance;
    char szErrStr[MAX_RSRC_STRING_LEN];
    char szCaption[MAX_RSRC_STRING_LEN];

    hInstance = GetWindowInstance( hWnd );
    LoadString( hInstance, iErrorID, szErrStr, sizeof(szErrStr) );
    LoadString( hInstance, IDS_CAPTION, szCaption, sizeof(szCaption) );
    MessageBox( hWnd, szErrStr, szCaption, MB_ICONEXCLAMATION | MB_OK );
    return;
}
```

The WinMain Module

WinMain registers window classes for the main window and the sound graph
control. The custom window classes let us paint the control window and assign
an icon to the dialog window. This module also contains the About box procedure.

The ShowWave Module

The MCI and MMIO modules provide a modular set of tools that any program
might use to manipulate .WAV files. The ShowWave.C module runs the program's main window and a modal dialog box. In response to commands from
the user, it calls functions from the other modules to play and record sounds.

ShowWave_WndProc mixes characteristics of a window procedure and a dialog procedure. Like a window procedure, it calls DefWindowProc and returns
an LRESULT; like a dialog procedure, it receives WM_INITDIALOG rather than
WM_CREATE. Because the window is launched by the DialogBox command, it
initializes like a dialog box. Because the window has its own custom window
class, it must have its own window procedure and does not use the default
DefDlgProc processing.

ShowWave stores newly recorded sounds in the temporary file until they have
names, so the dialog initialization handler generates a name for the file by calling GetTempPath and GetTempFileName. These commands generate a full path

with a unique filename suitable for storing temporary data. If the environment defines a TEMP variable, the path takes it into account. The second and third parameters of GetTempFileName are for alphabetic and numeric elements to be combined in the filename.

SWT stands for ShowWave Temporary. Since we haven't provided a number, Windows will append digits drawn from the current system time to create a unique name. The new name is returned in the final parameter.

Responding to Commands

Some of the WM_COMMAND messages come from the menu, some from buttons on the dialog box. A different procedure handles each command. StopPlay appeared earlier in the MCI module.

```
/*───────────────────────────────────────────────────────────────────

   SHOWWAVE_ONCOMMAND
       Handle WM_COMMAND messages here.  Respond to actions from
       each dialog control and from the menu.
   ──────────────────────────────────────────────────────────────────*/
static void ShowWave_OnCommand( HWND hDlg, int  iCmd, HWND hCtl, UINT uCode )
{
    switch( iCmd )
    {
       case IDM_NEW:                      // clear data buffer
           NewWaveFile( hDlg );
           break;

       case IDM_OPEN:                     // load a disk file
           OpenWaveFile( hDlg );
           break;

       case IDM_SAVE:                     // save to disk file
       case IDM_SAVEAS:
           SaveWaveFile( hDlg, (iCmd==IDM_SAVEAS) );
           break;

       case IDM_EXIT:                     // end program
           FORWARD_WM_CLOSE( hDlg, PostMessage );
           break;

       case IDM_MIXWITHFILE:              // mix two sounds
           MixWithFile( hDlg );
           break;
```

```
        case IDM_INCREASEVOLUME:            // make louder
        case IDM_DECREASEVOLUME:            // make softer
            ChangeVolume( hDlg, iCmd==IDM_INCREASEVOLUME );
            break;

        case IDM_ABOUT:                     // show About box
            DialogBox( GetWindowInstance(hDlg),
                    MAKEINTRESOURCE(DLG_ABOUT), hDlg, About_DlgProc );
            break;

        case IDD_PLAY:                      // play a sound
            PlayWaveFile( hDlg );
            break;

        case IDD_RECORD:                    // record a sound
            RecordWaveFile( hDlg );
            break;

        case IDD_STOP:                      // interrupt device
            if( mciDevice )
                StopPlay( hDlg, mciDevice );
            break;

        default:
            break;
    }
    return;
    UNREFERENCED_PARAMETER( hCtl );
    UNREFERENCED_PARAMETER( uCode );
}
```

Scrolling the Wave Image

Windows translates scrollbar input into one of eight SB_ notification codes delivered through the first parameter of a WM_HSCROLL message. The eight signals reflect the actions described in Figure 37.3.

Each program decides for itself what the signals mean. The SB_ signals are named for their most common application, paging through a document. SB_TOP and SB_BOTTOM indicate opposite ends of the data. SB_LINEUP and SB_LINEDOWN move through the data by the smallest permissible increment, usually 1. The page-scrolling messages move at whatever intermediate increment the programmer decides is convenient.

FIGURE 37.3:

Scrollbar commands

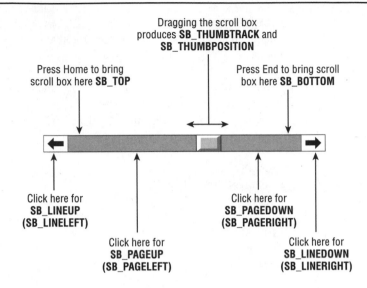

The range of ShowWave's scrollbar measures the current sound in hundredths of a second. Line commands scroll in tenths of a second; page commands scroll in full seconds. When the new position is reached, we store it in dwCurrentSample, move the scrollbar thumb, update the dialog text that says how many seconds we have progressed into the file, and call another procedure to repaint the wave graph. The value in dwCurrentSample measures the current position in samples. The assignment statement converts hundredths of a second to samples. It assumes each sample contains 8 bits.

```
/*─────────────────────────────────────────────────────────
    SHOWWAVE_ONHSCROLL
        Process WM_HSCROLL messages here.  Advance through the sound
        file according to the user's signals from the scrollbar.
    ─────────────────────────────────────────────────────────*/

static void ShowWave_OnHScroll( HWND hDlg,  HWND hCtl,
                                UINT uCode, int  iPos )
{
    int iMinPos, iMaxPos;

    ScrollBar_GetRange( hCtl, &iMinPos, &iMaxPos );
```

```
        switch( uCode )
        {
            case SB_LINEUP:        iHScrollPos -= 11;        break;
            case SB_LINEDOWN:      iHScrollPos += 11;        break;
            case SB_PAGEUP:        iHScrollPos -= 101;       break;
            case SB_PAGEDOWN:      iHScrollPos += 101;       break;
            case SB_TOP:           iHScrollPos = iMinPos;    break;
            case SB_BOTTOM:        iHScrollPos = iMaxPos;    break;
            case SB_THUMBPOSITION:
            case SB_THUMBTRACK:    iHScrollPos = iPos;       break;
            default:               return;
        }
            /* update scrollbar thumb */
        iHScrollPos = max( iMinPos, min(iHScrollPos, iMaxPos) );
        ScrollBar_SetPos( hCtl, iHScrollPos, TRUE );
            /* set current sample */
        dwCurrentSample = (iHScrollPos*dwSamplesPerSec) / 100;
            /* set position and length text */
        UpdateTimeText( hDlg );
            /* paint the waveform data */
        PaintWaveData( hDlg );
        return;
    }
```

While ShowWave plays or records a sound, we want the scrollbar thumb to move forward and the sound wave to scroll with it. As you'll see in a minute, ShowWave always begins a timer at the same time it begins playing or recording. ShowWave_OnTimer responds to the WM_TIMER messages.

```
/*─────────────────────────────────────────────────────────────────────

    SHOWWAVE_ONTIMER
        Handle WM_TIMER messages here.  Update display to show
        current position in sound file.
    ─────────────────────────────────────────────────────────────────────*/
void ShowWave_OnTimer( HWND hDlg, UINT uID )
{
    int   iMaxPos;
    HWND hwndScrollBar = GetDlgItem( hDlg, IDD_SCROLLBAR );
    if( uID == TMRPLAY )
            /* set the new scrollbar position */
        FORWARD_WM_HSCROLL( hDlg, hwndScrollBar, SB_LINEDOWN, 0, SendMessage );
    else
```

```
{       /* set the new waveform data */
    dwWaveDataSize += dwSamplesPerSec/10;
        /* set the new scrollbar range */
    iMaxPos = (int)((dwWaveDataSize*100) / dwSamplesPerSec );
    ScrollBar_SetRange( hwndScrollBar, 0, iMaxPos, FALSE );
        /* set the new scrollbar position */
    FORWARD_WM_HSCROLL( hDlg, hwndScrollBar, SB_BOTTOM, 0, SendMessage );
}
    return;
}
```

The timer messages arrive ten times each second. The uID value is set when the timer begins and will be either TMRPLAY or TMRRECORD. If the timer is marking progress during a Play operation, we send ourselves a scroll message to advance the thumb one-tenth of a second further into the sound wave.

While ShowWave records, the size of the file through which we're scrolling changes. The scrollbar thumb is always at the right end of the bar because we're always at the end of the recorded data, but as more data comes in, the file size increases and the scrollbar range must increase, too. First we update the global variable dwWaveDataSize, adding to it the number of bytes received every tenth of a second. (Remember that with 8 bits per sample, each sample adds 1 byte to the file size.) Then we convert the new file size into hundredths of a second and set that as the scrollbar's new maximum range. And again we send ourselves another scroll message to keep the thumb at the end of the bar.

Ending a Play or Record Operation

Playing and recording continue in the background until the user clicks on Stop or the device reaches the end of its input element. When the action ends, WinMM sends the MM_MCINOTIFY message that we requested with the MCI_NOTIFY flag. The Windowsx.H file does not include message-handler macros for any multimedia messages, so we wrote HANDLE_MM_MCINOTIFY and put it in ShowWave.H. When the notify message comes, we need to close the device and kill the timer.

```
/*----------------------------------------------------------------
    SHOWWAVE_ONMCINOTIFY
        Handle MM_MCINOTIFY messages here.  Clean up after a playback
        or recording operation terminates.
    ----------------------------------------------------------------*/

static void ShowWave_OnMCINotify( HWND hDlg, UINT uCode, MCIDEVICEID mciDevice )
{
    int  iMaxPos;
```

```
HWND hwndScrollBar = GetDlgItem( hDlg, IDD_SCROLLBAR );
if( uTimerID == TMRPLAY )
{       /* close devices */
    CloseAudioDevice( hDlg );
    CloseTimerDevice( hDlg );
    if( uCode == MCI_NOTIFY_SUCCESSFUL )
        FORWARD_WM_HSCROLL( hDlg, hwndScrollBar, SB_BOTTOM, 0,
                            SendMessage );
}
else
{       /* save recording and close devices */
    SaveRecord( hDlg, mciDevice, szTempFileName );
    CloseAudioDevice( hDlg );
    CloseTimerDevice( hDlg );
        /* set file dirty flag */
    bIsFileDirty = TRUE;
        /* read new waveform data */
    ReadWaveData( hDlg, szTempFileName, &lpWaveData, &dwWaveDataSize,
                  &dwSamplesPerSec );
        /* set the new scrollbar range */
    iMaxPos = (int)( ( dwWaveDataSize * 100 ) / dwSamplesPerSec );
    ScrollBar_SetRange( hwndScrollBar, 0, iMaxPos, FALSE );
        /* set the new scrollbar position */
    FORWARD_WM_HSCROLL( hDlg, hwndScrollBar, SB_BOTTOM, 0, SendMessage );
}
return;
UNREFERENCED_PARAMETER( mciDevice );
}
```

This time, we determine which action has stopped by testing a global variable, uTimerID, which we set when the timer started. If the device was playing sound and the sound ended successfully, we finish the scroll action by advancing the thumb to the end of the bar.

When ShowWave records a sound, the new data accumulates in a temporary file. When the recording ends, the program lifts the entire sound into a memory buffer so it can be the current sound. Since the user has not yet given the new sound a name and saved it, we mark the current file "dirty." And again we finish the scroll operation by updating the scroll range and moving the thumb to the end.

Ending the Program

The last few message-handling functions help the program close down without losing data or leaving objects behind.

```
/*--------------------------------------------------------------------

    SHOWWAVE_ONQUERYENDSESSION
        Handle WM_QUERYENDSESSION messages here.  Give the user a
        chance to save any open file before program ends.
    --------------------------------------------------------------*/
static BOOL ShowWave_OnQueryEndSession ( HWND hDlg )
{
    return( QuerySave(hDlg) );
}


/*--------------------------------------------------------------------

    SHOWWAVE_ONDESTROY
        Handle WM_DESTROY message here.  Close all devices.
    --------------------------------------------------------------*/
static void ShowWave_OnDestroy ( HWND hDlg )
{
    OFSTRUCT of;

    DeleteBrush( hbrBackgnd );
    FreeGlobalWaveData( );                      // release buffer
    CloseAudioDevice( hDlg );                   // close devices
    CloseTimerDevice( hDlg );
    OpenFile( szTempFileName, &of, OF_DELETE ); // delete temp file
    PostQuitMessage( 0 );                       // send WM_QUIT
    return;
}
```

To clean up, we delete the background brush created in ShowWave_OnInit-Dialog, release the buffer where the current sound is held, close the audio device if it's open, kill the timer if it's running, and delete the temporary file we opened on initializing.

```
/*----------------------------------------------------------------------
   QUERY SAVE
      Ask user to confirm loss of unsaved file before closing
----------------------------------------------------------------------*/
BOOL QuerySave ( HWND hDlg )
{
    HINSTANCE hInstance;
    char szText[MAX_RSRC_STRING_LEN];
    char szCaption[MAX_RSRC_STRING_LEN];
    char szFormat[MAX_RSRC_STRING_LEN];
    int  iRet;

        /* is file dirty? */
    if( ! bIsFileDirty )
        return( TRUE );
        /* see if user wants to save the modifications */
    hInstance = GetWindowInstance( hDlg );
    LoadString( hInstance, IDS_CAPTION, szCaption, sizeof(szCaption) );
    LoadString( hInstance, IDS_CONFIRMCLOSE, szFormat, sizeof(szFormat) );
    wsprintf( szText, szFormat, (LPSTR)szFileTitle );
    iRet = MessageBox( hDlg, szText, szCaption,
                         MB_YESNOCANCEL | MB_ICONQUESTION );
    if( iRet == IDYES )
        FORWARD_WM_COMMAND( hDlg, IDM_SAVE, NULL, 0, SendMessage );
    return( iRet != IDCANCEL );
}


/*----------------------------------------------------------------------
   FREE GLOBAL WAVE DATA
      Free storage associated with the global waveform data
----------------------------------------------------------------------*/
static void FreeGlobalWaveData( void )
{
    if( lpWaveData )
    {
        GlobalFreePtr( lpWaveData );
        lpWaveData = NULL;
    }
    return;
}
```

```
/*------------------------------------------------------------------
    CLOSE AUDIO DEVICE
        Close an opened waveform audio device
------------------------------------------------------------------*/
static void CloseAudioDevice ( HWND hDlg )
{
    if( mciDevice )
    {
        CloseDevice( hDlg, mciDevice );
        mciDevice = 0;
    }
    return;
}


/*------------------------------------------------------------------
    CLOSE TIMER DEVICE
        Kill an active timer; stop receiving WM_TIMER messages
------------------------------------------------------------------*/
static void CloseTimerDevice ( HWND hDlg )
{
    if( uTimerID )
    {
        KillTimer( hDlg, uTimerID );
        uTimerID = 0;
    }
    return;
}
```

QuerySave tests bIsFileDirty to see whether the current sound has been saved. If not, we put up a message box asking the user what to do. The user chooses Yes (to save), No (to end without saving), or Cancel (to avoid ending after all). The function returns TRUE unless the user cancels.

Displaying Information in Static Controls

The next procedures change static controls in the dialog box to make them show current information.

```
/*------------------------------------------------------------------
    PAINT WAVE DATA
        Repaint the dialog box's GraphClass display control
------------------------------------------------------------------*/

static void PaintWaveData ( HWND hDlg )
```

```
{
    HWND hwndShowWave = GetDlgItem( hDlg, IDD_SHOWWAVE );
    InvalidateRect( hwndShowWave, NULL, TRUE );
    UpdateWindow( hwndShowWave );
    return;
}

/*------------------------------------------------------------------------------
    UPDATE FILE TITLE TEXT
        Set a new filename in the dialog box's static filename control
  ----------------------------------------------------------------------------*/
static void UpdateFileTitleText ( HWND hDlg )
{
    Static_SetText( GetDlgItem(hDlg, IDD_FILETITLE), szFileTitle );
    return;
}

/*------------------------------------------------------------------------------
    UPDATE TIME TEXT
        Update the static dialog controls that show the scroll
        thumb's current position and the playing time for the
        current .WAV file
  ----------------------------------------------------------------------------*/
static void UpdateTimeText ( HWND hDlg )
{
    DWORD dwFrac;
    UINT  uSecs, uTenthSecs;
    char  szText[MAX_RSRC_STRING_LEN];
    char  szFormat[MAX_RSRC_STRING_LEN];

        /* get the format string */
    LoadString( GetWindowInstance(hDlg), IDS_TIMEFMT, szFormat, sizeof(szFormat) );
        /* update position text */
    dwFrac     = ((dwCurrentSample*100) / dwSamplesPerSec) / 10;
    uSecs      = (UINT)(dwFrac / 10);
    uTenthSecs = (UINT)(dwFrac % 10);
    wsprintf( szText, szFormat, uSecs, uTenthSecs );
    Static_SetText( GetDlgItem(hDlg, IDD_POSITION), szText );
        /* update length text */
    dwFrac     = ((dwWaveDataSize*100) / dwSamplesPerSec) / 10;
    uSecs      = (UINT)(dwFrac / 10);
    uTenthSecs = (UINT)(dwFrac % 10);
    wsprintf( szText, szFormat, uSecs, uTenthSecs );
    Static_SetText( GetDlgItem(hDlg, IDD_LENGTH), szText );
    return;
}
```

Resetting the Program

When the user chooses New from the File menu, the program must discard any current data and reset all its variables. NewWaveFile also updates the static dialog box controls and effectively disables the scrollbar by making its range very small.

```
/*─────────────────────────────────────────────────────────────

   NEW .WAV FILE
      Start work on a new .WAV file.  Reset variables and update
      display.  Called in response to the New command.
   ──────────────────────────────────────────────────────────────*/
static void NewWaveFile ( HWND hDlg )
{
    HINSTANCE hInstance;
    HWND hwndScrollBar = GetDlgItem( hDlg, IDD_SCROLLBAR );

        /* close the old .WAV file */
    if( ! QuerySave( hDlg ) )
        return;
        /* set filename and title */
    hInstance = GetWindowInstance( hDlg );
    LoadString( hInstance, IDS_UNTITLED, szFileTitle,
                sizeof(szFileTitle) );
    szFileName[0] = '\0';
    FreeGlobalWaveData();                   // delete old waveform data
    bIsFileDirty = FALSE;                    // set file dirty flag
    UpdateFileTitleText( hDlg );             // set filename text
        /* set the new waveform data */
    dwCurrentSample = 0;
    lpWaveData      = NULL;
    dwWaveDataSize  = 0;
    dwSamplesPerSec = 22050;
        /* set the new scrollbar range */
    ScrollBar_SetRange( hwndScrollBar, 0, 1, FALSE );
        /* set the new scrollbar position */
    FORWARD_WM_HSCROLL( hDlg, hwndScrollBar, SB_TOP, 0, SendMessage );
    return;
}
```

Getting a Filename

GetFileName calls the common dialog box for opening or saving files.

```
/*-----------------------------------------------------------------------
   GET FILE NAME
      Invoke the File Open or File Save As common dialog box.
      If the bOpenName parameter is TRUE, the procedure runs
      the OpenFileName dialog box.

   RETURN
      TRUE if the dialog box closes without error.  If the dialog
      box returns TRUE, then lpszFile and lpszFileTitle point to
      the new file path and name, respectively.
-----------------------------------------------------------------------*/
static BOOL GetFileName ( HWND hDlg,
                          BOOL bOpenName,        // open file or save as
                          LPSTR lpszFile,        // buffer for file path
                          int iMaxFileNmLen,     // max file path length
                          LPSTR lpszFileTitle,   // buffer for filename
                          int iMaxFileTitleLen ) // max filename length
{
    OPENFILENAME ofn;

        /* initialize structure for the common dialog box */
    lpszFile[0] = '\0';
    ofn.lStructSize      = sizeof( OPENFILENAME );
    ofn.hwndOwner        = hDlg;
    ofn.hInstance        = NULL;
    ofn.lpstrFilter      = szOFNFilter[0];
    ofn.lpstrCustomFilter = NULL;
    ofn.nMaxCustFilter   = 0;
    ofn.nFilterIndex     = 1;
    ofn.lpstrFile        = lpszFile;
    ofn.nMaxFile         = iMaxFileNmLen;
    ofn.lpstrFileTitle   = lpszFileTitle;
    ofn.nMaxFileTitle    = iMaxFileTitleLen;
    ofn.lpstrInitialDir  = NULL;
    ofn.lpstrTitle       = NULL;
    ofn.nFileOffset      = 0;
    ofn.nFileExtension   = 0;
    ofn.lpstrDefExt      = szOFNDefExt;
    ofn.lCustData        = 0;
```

```
    ofn.lpfnHook        = NULL;
    ofn.lpTemplateName  = NULL;
        /* invoke the common dialog box */
    if( bOpenName )                                // open a file
    {
        ofn.Flags = OFN_HIDEREADONLY | OFN_PATHMUSTEXIST |
                    OFN_FILEMUSTEXIST;
        return( GetOpenFileName(&ofn) );
    }
    else                                           // Save As...
    {
        ofn.Flags = OFN_HIDEREADONLY | OFN_OVERWRITEPROMPT;
        return( GetSaveFileName(&ofn) );
    }
}
```

Opening a Data File

When the user chooses Open from the File menu, the procedure asks the user to choose a file and then passes the name to ReadWaveData in the MMIO module. When the program loads new data, it resets the scrollbar range and pushes the thumb back to 0.

```
/*------------------------------------------------------------------------
   OPEN .WAV FILE
     Open a new .WAV file
   --------------------------------------------------------------------*/
static void OpenWaveFile ( HWND hDlg )
{
    int  iMaxPos;
    HWND hwndScrollBar = GetDlgItem( hDlg, IDD_SCROLLBAR );

      /* close the old .WAV file */
    if( ! QuerySave( hDlg ) )
     return;
        /* get a .WAV file to open */
    if( ! GetFileName( hDlg, TRUE, szFileName, sizeof(szFileName),
                    szFileTitle, sizeof(szFileTitle) ) )
       return;
    FreeGlobalWaveData();                    // delete old waveform data
    bIsFileDirty = FALSE;                    // set file dirty flag
    UpdateFileTitleText( hDlg );             // set filename text
```

```
    /* read new waveform data */
dwCurrentSample = 0;
ReadWaveData( hDlg, szFileName, &lpWaveData, &dwWaveDataSize, &dwSamplesPerSec );
    /* set the new scrollbar range */
iMaxPos = (int)(( dwWaveDataSize * 100 ) / dwSamplesPerSec );
ScrollBar_SetRange( hwndScrollBar, 0, iMaxPos, FALSE );
    /* set the new scrollbar position */
FORWARD_WM_HSCROLL( hDlg, hwndScrollBar, SB_TOP, 0, SendMessage );
return;
}
```

Saving New Data

With the procedures we've already defined, writing a .WAV file to disk is easy.
SaveWaveFile spends most of its time ensuring that we have a filename and that
we don't write over important data.

```
/*─────────────────────────────────────────────────────────────────
   SAVE .WAV FILE
      Save waveform data to disk.  If the second parameter is TRUE,
      or if the current data does not yet have a filename, this
      procedure will request a name.
   ────────────────────────────────────────────────────────────────*/
static void SaveWaveFile( HWND hDlg, BOOL bAskForName )
{
    HINSTANCE hInstance;
    BOOL bSave;
    char szText[MAX_RSRC_STRING_LEN];
    char szCaption[MAX_RSRC_STRING_LEN];
    int  iRet;

        /* anything to save? */
    if( ! lpWaveData )
        return;
        /* if renaming or no name, prompt user for name */
    if( ( bAskForName ) || ( szFileName[0] == '\0' ) )
    {     /* get the name of the .WAV file to save as */
        bSave = GetFileName( hDlg, FALSE,
        szFileName,  sizeof(szFileName),
        szFileTitle, sizeof(szFileTitle) );
    }
```

```
        else
        {     /* no new name; confirm overwriting old file */
            hInstance = GetWindowInstance( hDlg );
            LoadString( hInstance, IDS_OVERWRITE, szText, sizeof(szText) );
            LoadString( hInstance, IDS_CAPTION, szCaption, sizeof(szCaption) );
            iRet = MessageBox( hDlg, szText, szCaption, MB_YESNO | MB_ICONQUESTION );
            bSave = (iRet == IDYES);
        }

        /* save to the .WAV file */
        if( bSave )
        {
            bIsFileDirty = FALSE;      /* set file dirty flag */
            UpdateFileTitleText( hDlg );  /* set filename text */
                /* write out the waveform data */
            WriteWaveData( hDlg, szFileName, lpWaveData, dwWaveDataSize,
    dwSamplesPerSec );
        }
        return;
}
```

Mixing Two Sounds Together

ShowWave's Edit menu includes a Mix command. To mix one sound with
another, you average them; that is, you add together each pair of samples and
divide by two. When you play the combined sounds, you should hear both
components simultaneously.

```
/*--------------------------------------------------------------------

    MIX WITH FILE
        Mix a .WAV file into the current waveform data, combining
        the data from both into a single recording.  Mixing begins
        at the current point in the current file.  Mixing stops if
        we reach the end of the current file; it will not extend
        the current file.

----------------------------------------------------------------------*/
static void MixWithFile ( HWND hDlg )
{
    HINSTANCE hInstance;
    char   szMixFile[_MAX_FNAME];           // name of second .WAV file
    LPSTR  lpMix;                           // data from second file
    DWORD  dwMixSize;                       // size of new data
    DWORD  dwMixSPS;                        // samples per second
    char   szErrStr[MAX_RSRC_STRING_LEN];
    char   szCaption[MAX_RSRC_STRING_LEN];
```

```
LPSTR  lpDest, lpSrc;               // pointers for data transfer
DWORD  dw;                          // loop variable
int    iMaxPos;                     // scrollbar range
HWND   hwndScrollBar = GetDlgItem( hDlg, IDD_SCROLLBAR );

    /* get a .WAV file to mix with */
if( ! GetFileName( hDlg, TRUE, szMixFile,
                   sizeof(szMixFile), NULL, 0 ) )
    return;                         // no filename
    /* read waveform data */
if( ! ReadWaveData( hDlg, szMixFile, &lpMix, &dwMixSize, &dwMixSPS ) )
    return;                         // error reading data
    /* mix data */
if( ! lpWaveData )
{
    bIsFileDirty = TRUE;        /* set file dirty flag */
        /* set the new waveform data */
    dwCurrentSample = 0;
    lpWaveData      = lpMix;
    dwWaveDataSize  = dwMixSize;
    dwSamplesPerSec = dwMixSPS;
        /* set the new scrollbar range */
    iMaxPos = (int)((dwWaveDataSize*100) / dwSamplesPerSec );
    ScrollBar_SetRange( hwndScrollBar, 0, iMaxPos, FALSE );
        /* set the new scrollbar position */
    FORWARD_WM_HSCROLL( hDlg, hwndScrollBar, SB_TOP, 0, SendMessage );
}
else
{       /* for demo, use only matching frequencies */
    if( dwSamplesPerSec != dwMixSPS )
    {
        hInstance = GetWindowInstance( hDlg );
        LoadString( hInstance, IDS_BADFREQUENCY, szErrStr,
                    sizeof(szErrStr) );
        LoadString( hInstance, IDS_CAPTION, szCaption,
                    sizeof(szCaption) );
        MessageBox( hDlg, szErrStr, szCaption,
                    MB_ICONEXCLAMATION | MB_OK );
        GlobalFreePtr( lpMix );
        return;
    }
        /* mix new file into waveform at current position (lpDest) */
    lpSrc  = lpMix;
```

```
        lpDest = lpWaveData + dwCurrentSample;
        for( dw = 0; dw < (dwWaveDataSize-dwCurrentSample); dw++ )
        {
            /* merge one source and destination sample */
            *lpDest = (BYTE)(((int)(BYTE)*lpDest + (BYTE)*lpSrc) / 2);
            lpSrc++;                    // increment transfer pointers
            lpDest++;
            if( lpSrc >= ( lpMix + dwMixSize ) )
                break;                  // reached end of original data
        }
            /* clean up */
        GlobalFreePtr( lpMix );         // free memory
        bIsFileDirty = TRUE;            // set file dirty flag
        PaintWaveData( hDlg );          // paint the new waveform data
    }
    return;
}
```

MixWithFile begins by asking for the name of a .WAV file to open and reading the data into a second memory buffer, lpMix. If there is no current sound (the user has not already opened another file), the new "mix" sound simply becomes the current sound. We mark the new file as unsaved, set the global variables, and give the scrollbar new range values based on the length of the new sound.

But normally, the user will already have loaded a sound and we'll need to combine two sets of data. For demonstration purposes, *ShowWave* mixes only sounds that have the same sampling rate. To mix sounds with different rates, you would skip over some samples in the faster sound. For example, if one had a sampling rate of 11 and the other of 22, you would average every other sample from the second sound with one sample from the first.

The for loop that averages bytes together starts with the current position in the current sound. The user may already have played or scrolled partway through the file. The loop continues averaging bytes until it reaches the end of either sound and then stops. The new sound is cut off if it extends past the end of the old one. You could allow mixing to expand the current sound by calling GlobalReallocPtr to expand the lpWaveData buffer.

The line that averages two samples performs some type-casting to ensure that the compiler uses integers (which have 2 bytes) when it multiplies and divides. Even though the answer always fits in a byte, the intermediate product of two samples often overflows that limit.

Changing the Volume

The Effects menu lets the user make the current sound louder or softer. Like mixing, this effect involves modifying the samples mathematically. To understand the calculation, consider the diagram of a sound wave in Figure 37.4. The wave undulates above and below a middle point, called the *baseline*. When the wave swings very high and low, far away from the baseline, the sound it makes is loud. Quiet sounds have low peaks and shallow troughs. You can make a quiet sound loud by raising the peaks and lowering the troughs.

FIGURE 37.4:

A sound wave undulates around its baseline

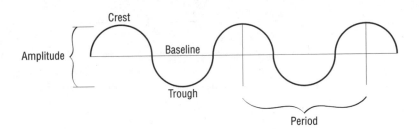

When a digitizer samples a sound wave, it notes where the wave falls in relation to the baseline at any given moment. When recording with 8 bits per sample, the range of the largest wave is divided into 256 different regions. Each sample names one of the regions. Sixteen-bit samples perceive 65,536 regions in the same amplitude and so record much finer distinctions. *ShowWave* works with 8-bit samples, so a value of 128 represents the baseline.

To change the volume of a sound sample, first determine its distance from the baseline:

$$WaveHeight = sample - baseline$$

Samples with values less than 128 produce negative heights, indicating a trough in the wave. To increase the volume by 25 percent, multiply each height by 1.25:

$$LouderHeight = (WaveHeight * 125) / 100;$$

Finally, we need to be sure the new value doesn't fall outside the possible range of 8-bit values. Amplitudes greater than 255 or less than 0 are not permitted.

$$LouderSample = LouderHeight + baseline$$

$$LouderSample = \max(\, 0, \min(\, LouderSample, 255\,)\,)$$

For 16-bit samples, make *LouderSample* type LONG and change the second calculation to this:

$$LouderSample = \max(\, -32768, \min(\, LouderSample, 32767\,)\,)$$

ShowWave can either increase or decrease the volume by 25 percent. To decrease the volume, multiply each height by 0.75.

```
/*----------------------------------------------------------------
    CHANGE VOLUME
        Increase/decrease the volume of the waveform data playback
----------------------------------------------------------------*/
static void ChangeVolume( HWND hDlg, BOOL bIncrease )
{
    LPSTR lp;
    DWORD dw;
    int   iTmp, iFactor;

        /* anything to change? */
    if( ! lpWaveData )
        return;
        /* change the volume of the waveform data */
    lp     = lpWaveData;
    iFactor = (bIncrease ? 125 : 75);
    for( dw = 0; dw < dwWaveDataSize; dw++ )
    {
        iTmp = (((int)(BYTE)(*lp) - MIDVALUE) * iFactor) / 100;
        *lp = (BYTE)max( MINVALUE, min(iTmp+MIDVALUE, MAXVALUE) );
        lp++;
    }
        /* set file dirty flag */
    bIsFileDirty = TRUE;
        /* paint the new waveform data */
    PaintWaveData( hDlg );
    return;
}
```

Playing a Sound

BeginPlay from the MCI module plays a sound, but PlayWaveFile performs some additional housekeeping chores before calling that core function.

```c
/*---------------------------------------------------------------------
   PLAY .WAV FILE
      Play waveform data
------------------------------------------------------------------*/
static void PlayWaveFile ( HWND hDlg )
{
    LPSTR lpsz;
    DWORD dwFrom;
    int   iMinPos, iMaxPos;
    HWND  hwndScrollBar = GetDlgItem( hDlg, IDD_SCROLLBAR );

        /* anything to play? */
    if( ! lpWaveData )
        return;
        /* get waveform file to play */
    if( ! bIsFileDirty )
        lpsz = szFileName;
    else
    {   /* temporarily store waveform data to disk for playing */
        WriteWaveData( hDlg, szTempFileName, lpWaveData, dwWaveDataSize,
                       dwSamplesPerSec );
        lpsz = szTempFileName;
    }
        /* if current position is end of sound, reset to beginning */
    ScrollBar_GetRange( hwndScrollBar, &iMinPos, &iMaxPos );
    if( iHScrollPos == iMaxPos )
        FORWARD_WM_HSCROLL( hDlg, hwndScrollBar, SB_TOP, 0, SendMessage );
        /* convert current sample position to milliseconds */
    dwFrom = (dwCurrentSample*1000) / dwSamplesPerSec;
        /* play waveform file */
    if( OpenDevice( hDlg, lpsz, &mciDevice ) )
    {
        if( ! BeginPlay( hDlg, mciDevice, dwFrom) )
        {
            CloseAudioDevice( hDlg );
            return;
        }
    }
```

```
        /* set timer to update display */
    uTimerID = TMRPLAY;
    SetTimer( hDlg, uTimerID, 100, NULL );
}
return;
}
```

Since `BeginPlay` must play from a disk file, first we need to decide which file to pass to it. If the sound in memory has not changed since the user loaded it, *ShowWave* reads from the sound's original file. But if the user has changed the sound by mixing it or adjusting its volume, *ShowWave* deposits the sound in the temporary file we created on initialization.

If the user has scrolled partway through the current sound, we should start playing at the current position. The static variable `iHScrollPos` remembers where the scrollbar thumb is. If the user has scrolled to the end of the file, `PlayWaveFile` sends a message to reset the thumb at the beginning. `ShowWave_OnHScroll` answers the message, updating both `iHScrollPos` and `dwCurrentSample` to reflect the new file position.

Having guaranteed that the starting point is not the end of the file, `PlayWaveFile` opens the audio device and calls `BeginPlay`. The sound starts, and `BeginPlay` returns immediately. The `SetTimer` command causes Windows to send us `WM_TIMER` messages every tenth of a second while the sound continues to play. You already saw how `ShowWave_OnTimer` responds to each message by advancing the scrollbar thumb and scrolling the wave graph.

Recording a Sound

The code for recording closely resembles the code for playing sound. The opening chores differ, however. Although the high-level audio commands allow you to insert newly recorded sound into an existing wave sound, not all devices support the `MCI_RECORD_INSERT` flag with the `MCI_RECORD` command. For simplicity, *ShowWave* insists on recording to an empty file, and the opening `if` statement enforces the restriction.

We have also somewhat arbitrarily limited the recording to 20 seconds. The user can interrupt the recording any time before that by clicking the Stop button. If you prefer to leave the recording time open-ended, modify `BeginPlay` by removing the `MCI_TO` flag. (Or you might conditionally remove the flag only if the `dwTo` parameter is 0.)

```c
/*------------------------------------------------------------------
   RECORD .WAV FILE
      Record waveform data
--------------------------------------------------------------*/
static void RecordWaveFile ( HWND hDlg )
{
    HINSTANCE hInstance;
    char szErrStr[MAX_RSRC_STRING_LEN];
    char szCaption[MAX_RSRC_STRING_LEN];

        /* for demo purposes, record only onto new .WAV files */
    if( lpWaveData )
    {
        hInstance = GetWindowInstance( hDlg );
        LoadString( hInstance, IDS_BADRECORDFILE, szErrStr,
                    sizeof(szErrStr) );
        LoadString( hInstance, IDS_CAPTION, szCaption,
                    sizeof(szCaption) );
        MessageBox( hDlg, szErrStr, szCaption,
                    MB_ICONEXCLAMATION | MB_OK );
        return;
    }
        /* record waveform data into a new file */
    if( OpenDevice( hDlg, "", &mciDevice ) )
    {
            /* set recording to stop after 20 seconds */
        if( ! BeginRecord( hDlg, mciDevice, 20000 ) )
        {
            CloseAudioDevice( hDlg );
            return;
        }
            /* set timer to update display */
        uTimerID = TMRRECORD;
        SetTimer( hDlg, uTimerID, 100, NULL );
    }
    return;
}
```

The GraphWin Module

The *ShowWave* demo uses a custom window class, GraphClass, to display the sound wave. The custom control is defined in the resource script thus:

```
CONTROL    "", IDD_SHOWWAVE, "GraphClass", 0x0000, 53, 22, 76, 23
```

GraphClass names a window class that *ShowWave* registers when it initializes. The Graphwin.C module contains the three procedures that support our Graph-Class window: RegisterGraphClass tells the system about the new class when the program begins, Graph_WndProc receives messages for the control, and Graph_OnPaint draws the sound wave.

```
/*─────────────────────────────────────────────────────────────
    REGISTER GRAPH CLASS
        Register the window class for the dialog box's wave graph
        control window.  The main dialog box's resource template
        names this window class for one of its controls.  This
        procedure must be called before CreateDialog.
    ─────────────────────────────────────────────────────────────*/

BOOL RegisterGraphClass ( HINSTANCE hInstance )
{
    WNDCLASS wc;

    wc.style         = 0;
    wc.lpfnWndProc   = Graph_WndProc;
    wc.cbClsExtra    = 0;
    wc.cbWndExtra    = 0;
    wc.hInstance     = hInstance;
    wc.hIcon         = NULL;
    wc.hCursor       = LoadCursor( NULL, IDC_ARROW );
    wc.hbrBackground = GetStockBrush( BLACK_BRUSH );
    wc.lpszMenuName  = NULL;
    wc.lpszClassName = szGraphClass;
    return( RegisterClass(&wc) );
}
```

```
/*—————————————————————————————————————————————————————
    GRAPH WNDPROC
        Receive messages for the main dialog box's sound graph window.
    ———————————————————————————————————————————————————*/


LRESULT WINAPI Graph_WndProc( HWND    hWnd,    UINT    uMsg,
                                WPARAM wParam, LPARAM lParam )
{
    switch (uMsg)
    {
        HANDLE_MSG( hWnd, WM_PAINT, Graph_OnPaint );
            // paint the green sound graph line
        default:
            return( DefWindowProc(hWnd, uMsg, wParam, lParam) );
    }
}
```

The window procedure intercepts only one message, WM_PAINT, and in every other case, the window accepts the standard message responses from the default window procedure. (Dialog box controls are not themselves dialog boxes, so they call DefWindowProc and not DefDlgProc.)

Our GraphClass window isn't really a full-blown control. Real controls must be careful with global or static variables because, unlike child windows, they do not have separate data segments for each window instance. Changing one static variable for one control would change that variable for all controls of the same class. Also, a control should answer the WM_GETDLGCODE message to tell the parent dialog box what keyboard input it wants. (GraphClass doesn't want any and would respond with DLGC_STATIC.)

TIP   A tightly designed custom control can be compiled into a DLL and made available to all applications, including a dialog box editor. To do this, you would need to write and export a small set of standard control functions.

Drawing the Sound Wave

Rather than connecting points on the wave curve, *ShowWave* represents each sample as a vertical line. The wave height indicated in the sample determines the height of the vertical line. Each line extends an equal distance above and below the baseline, coloring in the space over and under each wave. Solid shapes show up better in the small graph window than a single wave line could. In Figure 37.5, you can see how the vertical lines fill the wave.

FIGURE 37.5:

How ShowWave draws the sound wave

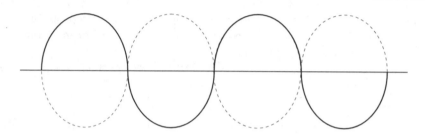

```
/*------------------------------------------------------------------
    GRAPH_ONPAINT
        Handle WM_PAINT messages for the Graph window.   Draw
        the green wave graph.
----------------------------------------------------------------*/
static void Graph_OnPaint ( HWND hWnd )
{
    PAINTSTRUCT ps;
    HDC    hDC;
    HPEN   hPen, hpenOld;          // green pen for drawing columns
    RECT   rClient;                // size of graph control window
    int    iBase;                  // vertical position of baseline
    LPSTR  lp;                     // points to one sample in wave data
    DWORD  dwMaxStart;             // maximum value for starting point
    int    iYScale;                // vertical scaling factor
    int    iCol;                   // horizontal position of a column
    int    iColHeight;             // height of a column

        /* begin paint processing */
    hDC = BeginPaint( hWnd, &ps );
        /* create a pen for drawing graph */
    if( GetDeviceCaps(hDC, NUMCOLORS) > 2 )
        hPen = CreatePen( PS_SOLID, 1, RGB_GREEN );      // color display
```

```
        else
            hPen = CreatePen( PS_SOLID, 1, RGB_WHITE );       // mono display
        if( hPen )
        {       /* select the pen */
            hpenOld = SelectPen( hDC, hPen );
                /* draw the waveform baseline */
            GetClientRect( hWnd, &rClient );
            iBase = RECTHEIGHT(rClient) / 2;
            MoveToEx( hDC, 0, iBase, NULL );
            LineTo( hDC, (int)rClient.right, iBase );
                /* graph waveform data */
            if( lpWaveData )
            {       /* set the current sample position in the waveform data */
                dwMaxStart = dwWaveDataSize - RECTWIDTH(rClient) - 1;
                lp = lpWaveData + min( dwCurrentSample, dwMaxStart );
                    /* determine the height scaling factor */
                iYScale = ( ( MAXVALUE - MINVALUE) + 1 ) /  // amplitude
                            ( RECTHEIGHT(rClient) - 4 );    // control height
                    // Subtracting 4 from the height ensures a small
                    // margin above and below the biggest waves
                    /* paint samples from the waveform data */
                for( iCol = (int)rClient.left; iCol <= (int)rClient.right;
                     iCol++ )
                {
                    iColHeight = ( (int)(BYTE)(*lp++) - MIDVALUE ) / iYScale;
                    if( iColHeight != 0 )
                    {       /* figure absolute value of column height */
                        if( iColHeight < 0 )
                            iColHeight = -iColHeight;
                            /* draw line from below base to above base */
                        MoveToEx( hDC, iCol, iBase - iColHeight, NULL );
                        LineTo( hDC, iCol, iBase + ( iColHeight + 1 ) );
                    }
                }
            }
                /* restore the DC and delete the pen */
            SelectPen( hDC, hpenOld );
            DeletePen( hPen );
        }
            /* end paint processing */
        EndPaint( hWnd, &ps );
        return;
    }
```

`Graph_OnPaint` represents the baseline with a horizontal line bisecting the graph window. The first vertical line on the left side of the control window will represent the current sample. If the user has scrolled to a point near the end of the file and only a few samples remain, the wave graph might not extend all the way across the window. To avoid leaving part of the graph empty, the program imposes a maximum value for the starting point. If the graph control is 50 pixels wide, for example, the graph must not begin less than 50 samples from the end.

The heights must be scaled to fit inside the window. A line extending the full height of the window must represent the maximum possible amplitude. With 8-bit samples, the maximum is 256. *ShowWave* calculates the line height with the following formulas:

Scale factor = maximum amplitude / window height

Column height = sample height / scale factor

To preserve a small margin of 2 pixels below and above the tallest waves, *ShowWave* subtracts 4 from the window height when figuring the scale factor.

The loop that draws each column begins by figuring the sample height and scaling it down to fit in the window. It draws each column by moving to a point below the baseline and drawing upward to a point an equal distance above the baseline. Because the columns extend on both sides of the baseline, the height of each column is twice the height of the sample.

We could call the C library function `abs` to get the absolute value of `iColHeight`, but then the compiler would add library code to the .EXE file. The `if` statement takes up less memory.

Some Improvements for the ShowWave Program

You might want to do some experimenting to see how you can improve the demo multimedia program. Here, we present some ideas, but you probably can think of some others.

Although the 8-bit sample size is common, you might want to allow *ShowWave* to work with 16-bit samples as well. We've described several places where *Show-Wave* makes calculations that assume 8-bit samples, such as in changing the volume, drawing the sound wave, and moving the scrollbar thumb. You would need to change any place that assumes a sample is a BYTE or refers to the manifest constants MINVALUE, MIDVALUE, and MAXVALUE. Sixteen-bit samples range in value from –32,768 to 32,767, with a midpoint of 0.

You also know enough to add stereo sound. MixWithFile and ChangeVolume would need to do everything twice—once for the left channel and once for the right. To draw the sound wave, you could average both channels together or let the user choose which channel to see. In a stereo data chunk, the channels are interleaved:

Sample one: channel 0 sample, channel 1 sample

Sample two: channel 0 sample, channel 1 sample

You might also modify MixWithFile to permit expanding the original sound. To do this, you would need to reallocate the buffer periodically.

The MCI_OPEN command reloads the waveaudio driver each time you open the device. From working with printers, you know that loading the driver causes a noticeable lag. *ShowWave* could load the driver once on opening and close it once at the end. In between, it would open and close individual device elements. The very first Open command would specify a device type but no device element; subsequent commands would open and close with an element name. The final Close command would again omit the element.

Several programs may open one device simultaneously, so holding it open won't cause trouble. (Whether different programs can share the same device *element* depends on the flags they use with MCI_OPEN.)

With EnableWindow and EnableMenuItem, you could disable buttons and menu commands not currently available. For example, all the buttons should be disabled until the user loads a sound. Stop should be disabled unless a playback or record message is in progress.

Finally, you could add MessageBeep commands to the program's error messages. Those who favor restraint in interface design will limit audio signals to the more critical errors or allow the user to choose whether and when to hear error sounds.

This chapter began with a general discussion of the hardware for multimedia applications and the WinMM translation layer that permits Windows programs to manipulate multimedia files in a device-independent manner. Windows works with files that contain data for wave sounds, MIDI music, animation, and analog video, among other formats.

WinMM was designed to be extensible. When other data types appear, new chunk formats can expand the RIFF standards. The MCI commands could send new messages, and their parameter structures could easily acquire new fields to accommodate more input. The high-level MCI commands establish a general protocol for opening and operating many different devices.

For the demo discussed in this chapter, we chose to work with waveform audio because its hardware requirements are less demanding; many machines now have inexpensive sound cards. The *ShowWave* demo demonstrates a full range of MCI command messages for opening and closing a device, playing and recording sounds, and interrupting operations. The MMIO module demonstrates the group of WinMM functions that facilitate reading and writing chunks of a RIFF file.

Having read this far, you have passed well beyond the beginning stages of Windows programming and have come to understand such advanced topics as threads, processes, synchronization, pipes, virtual memory, exception handling, enhanced metafiles, DDEML, and multimedia. Thorough as we have been, more remains. Windows 98 is too large a system for one book to explain everything.

However, you should now be well prepared to proceed into new fields on your own, exploring even more mysteries. After all, the best applications cannot be described here, because they are still waiting for you—not me—to think of them.

Finally, for those of you who are moving applications from Windows 3.x (Win16) to Windows 98 (or 95 or NT) systems (Win32), Appendix A provides an overview of the principal differences between the 16-bit and 32-bit systems and a few guidelines for converting your applications.

APPENDIX

A

From 16-Bit Windows to 32-Bit Windows

For many programmers, a topic of immediate interest will be how to transport existing applications originally written for the 16-bit Windows 3.*x* (Win16) to the 32-bit Windows 98 and Windows NT (Win32) environments. Fortunately, such conversions, although sometimes tedious, can be relatively simple.

Because both Windows 3.*x* and 98/95/NT follow the same general structural format, use the same messaging systems, and employ the same resource elements, the overall structure being moved from Windows 3.*x* to 98/95/NT does not change. For the most part, existing Windows 3.*x* applications will run directly under Windows 98/95/NT without requiring recompilation for the 32-bit environment.

This compatibility is provided by a translation feature in Windows 98/95/NT that interprets 16-bit API function calls and message structures into 32-bit formats, and translates 32-bit messages and data formats into their 16-bit equivalents. The result, as you might expect, is a less efficient program. And depending on the circumstances, the result may also be a slower execution, which may or may not be viewed as acceptable.

Alternatively, you can avoid such problems with 16-bit applications by converting and recompiling them using the Windows 98/95/NT format with a suitable 32-bit compiler. Still, transforming applications from Windows 3.*x* 16-bit formats to the 98/95/NT 32-bit format requires more than simply a change of compilers.

Although the tasks accomplished under Windows 3.*x* and under Windows 98/95/NT are essentially the same, the manner in which these are executed and the formats in which information is handled present several differences. These differences must be taken into account when you are converting an application from the 16-bit to the 32-bit environment.

This appendix provides an overview of some common programming changes you need to be aware of when you convert programs from Windows 3.*x* to 98/95/NT. It does not cover *all* the possibilities—just the more common ones you are likely to encounter. No single program can illustrate all the relevant changes necessary, so program fragments have been used to illustrate specific topics.

The WinMain Procedure

The entry point for any Windows application—3.*x*, 95, 98, or NT—is the `WinMain` procedure. Outwardly, this portion of an application has not changed, at least in most cases.

In any of these versions of Windows, the `WinMain` procedure is called as:

```
int PASCAL WinMain( HANDLE hInstance,           // 3.x, NT/95/98
                    HANDLE hPrevInstance,
                    LPSTR  lpszCmdParam,
                    int    nCmdShow  )
{
    ... same for Windows 3.x, Windows NT, Windows 98, et al ...
}
```

The body of the `WinMain` procedure also remains the same for these versions.

What is not apparent to programmers, however, is which definitions have changed. For example, under Windows 3.*x*, the data type HANDLE has a 16-bit value; under Windows 98/95/NT, it has a 32-bit value. Still, as long as the function parameters have not changed, these definition changes are handled by the compiler and, for the programmer, are not immediately relevant.

In other cases, however, the changes are relevant and are reflected in the format and parameter declarations. For example, in the `WndProc` procedure, which (under this or another name) forms the heart of every Windows program, the 3.*x* and 98/95/NT version declarations are similar, but not identical.

For Windows 3.*x*, the `WndProc` declaration appears as:

```
long FAR PASCAL WndProc( HWND hwnd,    WORD msg,     // 3.x
                         WORD wParam, LONG lParam )
```

For Windows 98/95/NT, the `WndProc` declaration is slightly different, appearing as:

```
long FAR PASCAL WndProc( HWND hwnd,    UINT msg,     // 98/95/NT
                         UINT wParam, LONG lParam )
```

In both cases, the `WndProc` procedure is called with four arguments: `hwnd`, `msg`, `wParam`, and `lParam`. The first of these, `hwnd`, has transparently changed from a 16-bit to a 32-bit argument, because the definition of HWND has changed. The second and third parameters, however, are declared as WORD values in Windows 3.*x*; for 98/95/NT, they become UINT, or 32-bit unsigned integer values. Only the fourth argument, `lParam`, remains unchanged as a LONG, or 32-bit signed value. Thus, where the `WndProc` procedure under Windows 3.*x* was called with a total of 80 bits (10 bytes) of information, under 98/95/NT, the calling arguments have expanded to a total of 128 bits (16 bytes).

Remember, however, even though the fourth parameter, lParam, remains unchanged and is defined, for consistency, as a long signed integer, this parameter does not determine how this data will be used or in what forms. Furthermore, except for the hwnd parameter, each of these 32-bit values may be interpreted as one or more individual arguments.

WndProc and MFC

If you are using MFC (Microsoft Foundation Classes), the WndProc procedure is effectively hidden within the CApp and CMainFrame classes and is not visible for editing and revision. Likewise, much of the message handling is also concealed, and many of the parameters accompanying messages are parsed before being passed to the derived functions.

These differences are too numerous to list in detail, but they should be relatively easy for you to understand. If you have difficulties, refer to the online documentation supplied with the Visual C/C++ compiler and Microsoft Developer Studio.

The Message-Handling Structure

Under Windows 3.x, a common practice in the message handling is to have all message cases end by returning a NULL or 0. Any messages that are not handled internally are returned via the DefWindowProc procedure. Here is an example of a skeleton WndProc message format:

```
switch( msg )                                    // 3.x
{
    case WM_PAINT:   ...    return( NULL );
    case WM_DESTROY:  ...    return( NULL );
}
return( DefWindowProc( hwnd, msg, wParam, lParam ) );
```

The preceding example is fairly simple. Only two case statements require handling, and all other messages (if any) receive default handling. However, under

98/95/NT, this specific handling has produced some conflicts in some cases. A slight variation, shown below, produces much cleaner results.

```
switch( msg )                                    // 98/95/NT
{
   case WM_PAINT:  ...     break;
   case WM_DESTROY:  ...   break;
   default:
      return( DefWindowProc( hwnd, msg, wParam, lParam ) );
}
return( FALSE );
```

This variation has the following differences:

- Rather than the individual cases returning immediately, each case response ends with a break.

- A default case explicitly returns all unhandled messages for processing by 98/95/NT.

- All messages that have been handled within WndProc do, in the end, return a FALSE result.

You might have expected a NULL return value here, assuming that NULL and FALSE would have the same value. In one sense, both are a 0 (zero) but, because these do not have the same type, you will get a compiler warning—not an error—by returning a NULL.

But remember, this handling is used only for the WndProc procedure. Other exported procedures, such as dialog box handlers and other child window procedures, even though these are called with similar parameters and provide similar message handling, do not use the DefWindowProc API call to return any messages. Instead, each message case handled returns TRUE to report having handled the message. Any unhandled messages, by default, return FALSE. The default message handling for all child window processes is just that—provided by default.

Child window message handling is illustrated by the following skeletal DialogProc procedure:

```
BOOL APIENTRY DialogProc( HWND hDlg,   UINT msg,    // 98/95/NT
                          UINT wParam, LONG lParam )
```

```
{
   switch( msg )
   {
      case WM_INITDIALOG:   ...   return( TRUE );

      case WM_COMMAND:
         switch( LOWORD( wParam ) )
         {
            case IDOK:       ...   return( TRUE );
            case IDCANCEL:   ...   return( TRUE );
         }
         break;
   }
   return( FALSE );
}
```

Alternatively, if the calling procedure doesn't really care about the response returned by this child window process, the three return(TRUE) provisions in the above example could be replaced by break statements.

In most cases, both the OK and Cancel buttons are used to close a dialog box, but only the OK button returns TRUE; the Cancel button returns FALSE. In this fashion, a TRUE result indicates that the actions or settings in the dialog box should be implemented, and a FALSE result indicates that no changes should be made.

Messages and Accompanying Arguments

Within the switch...case message structures, there are several important differences between Windows 3.x and 98/95/NT. As a reminder, under Windows 3.x, in response to a WM_COMMAND message, the usual response is a second switch...case structure using the wParam argument, appearing as:

```
case WM_COMMAND:                              // 3.x
   switch( wParam )
   {
      case IDD_FNAME: ...
      case IDD_FPATH: ...
```

Under Windows 3.x, the wParam value is a 16-bit argument identifying the menu item, accelerator entry, or dialog box control originating the message. In other cases, the wParam value does not originate with a control or accelerator entry but may simply be an application-supplied value used to direct a specific response.

Under 98/95/NT, the wParam argument is a 32-bit value. The item ID originating the message, which is still a 16-bit argument, is now contained in the low-order word of the wParam argument. Therefore, under Windows 98/95/NT, this item ID value must be extracted from the 32-bit argument, thus:

```
case WM_COMMAND:                                    // 98/95/NT
    switch( LOWORD( wParam ) )
    {
        case IDD_FNAME: ...
        case IDD_FPATH: ...
```

Under 98/95/NT, the high-order word of the wParam argument accompanying a WM_COMMAND message is one (1) if the message originates from an accelerator message or zero (0) if the message originated from a menu or control element. Likewise, if the message originates with a menu, the lParam argument is NULL. Alternatively, if the message originates with a control element, lParam contains the window handle of the control.

WARNING

There is a potentially hazardous habit among programmers of ignoring the need to use the LOWORD macro when employing a wParam message in a switch...case statement. Because the messages originating with menu or control elements contain a 0 in the high word, omitting this provision normally does not cause any problems. If, however, the message originated with an accelerator table entry (a hotkey definition), the high word would contain a 1, and this would prevent the correct case statement from being recognized ... unless, of course, you wished to distinguish between control/menu commands and hotkey entries.

The important element here is that the low-order word of the wParam argument must be explicitly used in response to the WM_COMMAND message; simply following the Windows 3.x format may or may not produce the appropriate response (depending on whether the high-order word is set or not). Also, in many cases, the high-order word of the wParam argument and the lParam argument can simply be ignored.

As an alternative, you could also use the high-order word to distinguish an application-generated message from a message generated by a menu or dialog box. For example, you could do this by setting the high word to 0x02. But, remember, this particular format applies only to WM_COMMAND messages. Also, it is not always completely valid, as you will see in a moment.

If you are using MFC, the same restrictions apply to the wParam and lParam arguments reported to the CWnd::OnCommand handler.

Continuing with the WM_COMMAND message, consider a message sent from a list box. Under Windows 3.x, the high-order word of the lParam argument is tested for the EN_CHANGE secondary message, which reports a change in the list box selection.

```
case IDD_FNAME:                                    // 3.x
    if( HIWORD( lParam ) == EN_CHANGE )
```

Under Windows 98/95/NT, however, the EN_CHANGE message has moved. It's now found in the high-order word of wParam, not lParam, thus:

```
case IDD_FNAME:                                    // 98/95/NT
    if( HIWORD( wParam ) == EN_CHANGE )
```

But this is only part of the information that will be extracted. Next, assuming the EN_CHANGE message was sent, the sample application needs to extract information from the list box, which is accomplished by sending a message back to the list box control.

```
EnableWindow( GetDlgItem( hDlg, IDOK ),    // 3.x
        (BOOL) SendMessage( LOWORD( lParam ),
                            WM_GETTEXTLENGTH, 0, OL ) );
```

Exactly which information is being used in the list box message is irrelevant at the moment. What is relevant is the list box handle which, for Windows 3.x, is found in the low-order word of the lParam argument, preceding. But in Windows 3.x, this handle is only a 16-bit value extracted from a 32-bit argument.

Under Windows 98/95/NT, the equivalent list box handle is a 32-bit argument and consists of the entire high- and low-order word values of the lParam argument.

```
EnableWindow( GetDlgItem( hDlg, IDOK ),    // 98/95/NT
        (BOOL) SendMessage( (HWND) lParam,
                            WM_GETTEXTLENGTH, 0, OL ) );
```

Comparing the two fragments immediately preceding, you should notice the differences in how the two version examples reference control handles. Note that in the second fragment, the (HWND) typecast is used simply to prevent the Microsoft C compiler from generating an irrelevant warning message.

Application Class Values

When a Windows application class is defined, normally within the `WinMain` procedure, several class values are assigned before the window class is registered. Under Windows 3.*x*, several of these are `WORD` values; under Windows 98/95/NT, `DWORD` values are used. Following is a fragmentary listing from a `WinMain` procedure that might belong to either a Windows 3.*x* or a 98/95/NT application.

```
wc.style          = NULL;
wc.lpfnWndProc    = (WNDPROC) WndProc;
wc.cbClsExtra     = 0;
wc.cbWndExtra     = 0;
wc.hInstance      = hInstance;
wc.hIcon          = LoadIcon( hInstance, APP_ICON );
wc.hCursor        = LoadCursor( NULL, IDC_ARROW );
wc.hbrBackground  = GetStockObject( WHITE_BRUSH );
wc.lpszMenuName   = APP_MENU;
wc.lpszClassName  = szAppName;
return( RegisterClass( &wc ) );
```

However, because the values used are assigned either as constants (`wc.lpsz-MenuName` and `wc.lpszClassName`) or by indirect reference (`wc.hIcon` and `wc.hCursor`), the question of whether a `WORD` or `DWORD` value is being used doesn't really come up—at least, not at this time. But there are other circumstances where an application may quite reasonably desire to change one or more of these window class elements. Under Windows 3.*x*, this is normally accomplished using the `SetClassWord` function, as:

```
SetClassWord( hwnd, GCW_HCURSOR, LoadCursor( hInst, HrGls[11] ) );
// 3.x
```

In this fragmentary example, the constant GCW_HCURSOR designates the `wc.h-Cursor` field as the element to be changed. The `SetClassWord` function, however, explicitly changes a `WORD` value and, for Windows 98/95/NT, the corresponding field is a `DWORD` or `LONG` value. Therefore, for Windows 98/95/NT applications, the `SetClassWord` function is replaced by a new function, `SetClassLong`, which is called as:

```
SetClassLong( hwnd, GCL_HCURSOR,
              LoadCursor( hInst, HrGls[11] ) );    // 98/95/NT
```

Notice also that the GCW_HCURSOR constant has been changed to become GCL_HCURSOR.

The danger—in this pair of functions and in converting applications from Windows 3.*x* to 98/95/NT—is that the SetClassWord function has not been totally superseded by the SetClassLong function. Instead, both forms continue to be supported, as are both the GCW_*xxxx* and GCL_*xxxx* constants. And, in some circumstances, the SetClassWord function remains valid and useful. However, any applications being translated into Windows 98/95/NT format that use the SetWindowWord function to change window class assignments should be particularly careful to translate these to SetWindowLong API function calls, and to replace the GCW_*xxxx* constants with the corresponding GCL_*xxxx* constants.

Child Window and Dialog Box Procedures

Child window dialog boxes are an integral feature of Windows applications, in both 3.*x* and 98/95/NT. Those converting applications from the older version to the newer versions will be happy to know that the DialogBox function can be used precisely as it has been in the past. The following subprocedure might be used by any version to call a resource dialog box titled SELECTFILE, with message-handling responses provided by the exported procedure: FileSelectDlgProc.

```
int DialogProc( HWND hwnd, HINSTANCE hInst )
{
    static FARPROC  lpProc;                    // 3.x, 98/95/NT
    int     iReturn;

    lpProc = MakeProcInstance( FileSelectDlgProc, hInst );
    iReturn = DialogBox( hInst, "SELECTFILE", hwnd,  lpProc );
    FreeProcInstance( lpProc );
    return( iReturn );
}
```

Windows 98/95/NT, however, introduces a few changes that make the preceding code not only unnecessarily verbose, but also wastefully redundant.

The first change is in the MakeProcInstance API function call. While this API call is both functional and necessary under Windows 3.*x*, under 98/95/NT, MakeProcInstance has become a macro. This macro, quite simply, returns the first argument ... and does nothing more. Thus, calling MakeProcInstance under 98/95/NT, aside from providing backward compatibility, has the singularly useless effect of making lpProc equal to FileSelectDlgProc.

Likewise, the FreeProcInstance function has also become a macro. However, in this case, the macro has even less real value, since FreeProcInstance does precisely nothing.

The upshot of this is that the lpProc variable can be replaced in the Dialog-Box API call with FileSelectDlgProc reference, without needing to declare the lpProc variable or call MakeProcInstance at all. And, of course, without calling FreeProcInstance afterward.

The second change has to do with the FreeProcInstance API call. Again, under Windows 3.x, this API function was necessary and operational, used to release memory allocated by the DialogBox API call for the child window dialog box. But under Windows 98/95/NT, the FreeProcInstance call has also been redefined, again to provide backward compatibility, as a macro that does precisely nothing.

Therefore, given these two revisions in MakeProcInstance and FreeProc-Instance, the DialogProc function can be rewritten:

```
int DialogProc( HWND hwnd, HINSTANCE hInst )
{
    int     iReturn;                            // 98/95/NT only

    iReturn = DialogBox( hInst, "SELECTFILE", hwnd,
                         FileSelectDlgProc );
    return( iReturn );
}
```

Given the modification shown, you could simplify this subprocedure even further by omitting the iReturn variable in favor of a direct return. Or, you could discard it entirely in favor of calling the DialogBox API directly, unless there were other tasks to be accomplished before or after calling the DialogBox function, as there often are. But, in either case, the process of calling a dialog box is much simpler in Windows 98/95/NT than in 3.x.

Remember, this revision is optional. Windows 3.x subprocedures will still compile and execute under 98/95/NT without changes.

File and Directory Operations

File operations have undergone a distinct change from Windows 3.*x* to 98/95/NT—perhaps, on the surface, the most distinct changes of all. The reasons for such drastic changes, as opposed to the relatively simple changes in many other areas, are a direct consequence of three major factors:

- Changes in the Windows NT file system, which supports both the DOS 16-bit FAT system and the new NT 32-bit file system.

- Changes in the Windows 98 file system, which supports both the DOS 16-bit FAT and the 32-bit FAT32 file systems (see the "FAT, FAT32, and NTFS File Systems" section later in this appendix).

- Changes in the FAT file system for both Windows 98 and NT (but not Windows 3.1), which now supports long filenames (see the "Long Filenames" section later in this appendix).

- The introduction of the 32-bit Unicode character system, which is available as an alternative to the familiar 16-bit ANSI character system. Also, the Unicode character system is responsible, in part, for the changes in string-handling operations.

Here, I'll present only a brief overview of the changes involved in moving file operations from Windows 3.*x* to 98/95/NT. What you need to keep in mind for now is that both file and directory operations have changed drastically, and for application conversions from Windows 3.*x* to 98/95/NT, you must take these changes into account.

NOTE The *FileView* demo on the CD accompanying this book demonstrates the Windows 98/95/NT file and directory operations. This demo is discussed in Chapter 12.

File Operations

Under Windows 3.*x*, the usual method of opening and closing a file consists of calling the same `fopen` and `fclose` procedures used under DOS:

```
hFil = fopen( szFName, "r+b" );                    // 3.x
if( hFil != -1 )
```

```
{
   FilSz = filelength( fileno( hFil ) );
   ...
   fclose( hFil );
}
```

In addition to opening and closing the file in this fragmentary example, the filelength function is also invoked to return the file size. This also should be a familiar function both from Windows 3.1 and from DOS applications, but it changes almost beyond recognition in its Windows 98/95/NT counterpart.

In the Windows 98/95/NT revision, which follows, very little has remained the same. The hFil variable is still used to retrieve a handle to the file opened, but virtually everything else is different.

```
hFil = OpenFile( szFName, &FileBuff,              // 98/95/NT
                  OF_CANCEL | OF_PROMPT | OF_READ );
if( hFil != -1 )
{
   FilSz = GetFileSize( (HANDLE) hFil, &FilSzHigh );
   ...
   _lclose( hFil );
}
```

As you can see, the fopen procedure has been replaced by the OpenFile API call, which uses a quite different selection of parameters. One of these parameters is a pointer to the FileBuff structure, which receives information about the file.

The GetFileSize function is also a major change from its predecessor, file-length. Instead of returning a long value with the file size in bytes, GetFileSize returns two DWORD values: FilSz and FilSzHigh. The reason for this particular change is simple: A signed long value can only report a file size up to about 2GB, but a signed double DWORD value (64 bits) can handle really large file sizes—up to 1.7×10^{308} bytes. Granted, it may be a year or two before mass-storage facilities provide any real need for reporting files of such size, but it will happen eventually.

The final difference—changing fclose to _lclose—is almost no change at all.

NOTE   There is no CloseFile instruction corresponding to the OpenFile API. Instead, the _lclose function is normally used to close a file.

Alternately, instead of using the _lclose instruction, the CloseHandle function can also be used to close files:

```
hFil = OpenFile( szFName, &FileBuff,              // 98/95/NT
                    OF_CANCEL | OF_PROMPT | OF_READ );
if( hFil != -1 )
{
    FilSz = GetFileSize( (HANDLE) hFil, &FilSzHigh );
    ...
    CloseHandle( hFil );
}
```

But opening and closing files are only one aspect of file operations. The previously familiar directory operations have also changed, although perhaps not as drastically.

Directory Operations

Under Windows 3.x, retrieving the current directory or changing directories was accomplished as:

```
getcwd( DirPath, sizeof( DirPath ) );              // 3.x
...
chdir( DirPath );
```

The equivalent operations under Windows 98/95/NT follow the same general formats, but with a change in the function names:

```
GetCurrentDirectory( sizeof( DirPath ), DirPath );  // 98/95/NT
...
SetCurrentDirectory( DirPath );
```

Notice that the order of the arguments has been reversed. The size of the buffer now precedes rather than follows the buffer variable.

Long Filenames

Windows 3.x, like DOS, limited filenames and directory names to eight characters plus a three-character extension for filenames. This 8.3 format became extinct when Windows NT (version 3.1) was released. That version of NT supported both long filenames and long filename extensions, and this change has continued with Windows 95 and now with Windows 98.

Unfortunately, many applications—including more than a few released by Microsoft—have continued to use file/directory utilities that report only the old-style 8.3 format. The only task required to be able to recognize the new, long-format filenames is a very simple matter of changing one parameter: the length of the field receiving the filename information. This topic is covered in Chapter 12, where we discuss the *FileView* demo (included on the CD), which has no difficulty displaying long directory names and filenames.

FAT, FAT32, and NTFS File Systems

Under DOS and Windows 3.*x*, disk drives (or partitions) commonly used the FAT (file allocation table) system for storing disk files. Because the original FAT used 16-bit cluster addressing, the FAT system itself imposed limitations on how hard drives were used. (For convenience, this original FAT system is referred to as FAT16.) Since the FAT16 could handle only 2^{16} (= 65,536) addresses, hard drives larger than 512MB needed to allocate file space in 16KB blocks.

The first break in the inefficient FAT16 file system appeared with Windows NT (version 3.1), which introduced the NTFS file system. Unlike FAT16, NTFS uses 32-bit addresses (2^{32} = 4,294,967,296) and is no longer limited to 16KB blocks. Additionally, the NTFS file system also supports long filenames; security-access restrictions; special flags governing file usage; and last-access, last-write, and file-creation date-time stamps.

The limitation of the NTFS system, however, is that it is only accessible under Windows NT and cannot be read or even recognized from DOS or Windows 3.*x*, 95, or 98. In effect, any partition organized using NTFS is effectively invisible to operating systems other than Windows NT.

With the introduction of Windows 98, another new file system has been introduced: the FAT32 file system. Like NTFS, the FAT32 file system also handles 32-bit addresses (2^{32}), again erasing the old limitations imposed by the FAT16 addressing. Using the FAT32 system, the old limitations on partition and cluster size are obsolete, and even multigigabyte hard drives can exist as single partitions using 4KB clusters. More important, wasted drive space can commonly fall to as low as 2 percent or less.

But, again, there is a downside. Like Windows NT and the NTFS file system, the Windows 98 file system is incompatible with other operating systems, including DOS and Windows NT. And, in contrast, unlike NTFS, the FAT32 file system does not support multiple date-time stamps or security-access restrictions.

This means that if you are planning on running dual-operating systems such as Windows 98 and NT, you are pretty well stuck with the FAT16 file system and all of its attendant shortcomings—this is not only the lowest common denominator but the only common denominator. Of course, since hard drives are relatively cheap, efficiency is not the primary concern it would have been just a few years ago. Also, you can maintain some efficiency by using multiple partitions, even though these have their own inconveniences.

As a slight ray of hope, the next version of Windows NT, Windows NT 5.0, is expected to support the same FAT32 file system as Windows 98. This will make it possible to have a dual-boot Windows 98/NT5 system using FAT32 without restrictions on drive access. (Currently, any dual-boot system is restricted to using FAT16 to maintain drive compatibility.)

> **NOTE**   See Chapter 1 for more information about file system differences and setting up a dual-boot system.

From the programming standpoint, the question of whether a system is using FAT16 or FAT32 addressing remains inconsequential. As long as application file I/O is carried out through the standard API functions, no special provisions are demanded or required.

String Operations

String operations are another area that simply relied on existing DOS C functions under Windows 3.x. Like the other operations we've discussed, Windows 98/95/NT string operations are supplemented by newer API functions, which are compatible with Unicode strings and with international character sets.

> **NOTE**   See Chapter 4 for more information about Unicode, ANSI, and MBCS characters.

These newer API string functions, however, have not superseded the familiar string functions. You should continue to use #include <string.h> for old-style string functions. However, applications using Unicode strings should employ the API string functions rather than relying on the conventional string functions. Of course, applications written using the API string functions remain compatible with both Unicode and ANSI strings.

The following two code fragments contrast conventional and Windows 98/ 95/NT-supplied string functions.

```
strupr( szFPath );                                          // 3.x
if( szFPath[ strlen(szFPath)-1 ] != '\\' )
    strcat( szFPath, "\\" );
strcpy( szFName, fileinfo.ff_name );
```

In most cases, the corresponding 98/95/NT string functions are distinguished by substituting the form lstr__ for the conventional str__. One exception is the CharUpperBuff function, which replaces the conventional strupr function.

```
CharUpperBuff( szFPath, lstrlen( szFPath ) );    // 98/95/NT
if( szFPath[ lstrlen(szFPath)-1 ] != '\\' )
    lstrcat( szFPath, "\\" );
lstrcpy( szFName, lpFileInfo->cFileName );
```

Again, these two fragments are provided as illustrations of differences that you may or may not need to take into account while converting applications from Windows 3.x to 98/95/NT.

On the other hand, if you are using the MFC CString class and member functions, the CString class members are already Unicode-compatible.

Obsolete Functions

As you might expect, functions in various categories that were used under Windows 3.x are now obsolete in Windows 98/95/NT.

Fonts and Character Sets

Under Windows 3.x and earlier, several different types of character fonts were supported. Some were bitmapped fonts, others were stroked fonts, and both types could include variant characters used for special languages or purposes. Today, in Win32 applications, you should not rely on old-style bitmapped fonts. Instead, using true-type (stroked and sizable) fonts and Unicode for non-English character sets is the contemporary standard.

Also under Windows 3.x, fonts were a recognized resource type and could be installed as application resources. Under Windows 98/95/NT, fonts as resources are no longer supported.

Also, Windows 98/85/NT supports a number of extended font specifications for typesetting purposes. These include an extensive series of Panose definitions. For further details on using these specifications, refer to the online documentation.

> **NOTE** See Chapter 27 for more information about old-style, true-type, and custom fonts and font functions under Windows 98/95/NT.

ANSI/OEM Character Support

Earlier versions of Windows provided a variety of functions to support conversions between and within the ANSI and OEM character sets. Examples include the `AnsiUpper`, `AnsiLower`, `AnsiUpperBuff`, and `AnsiLowerBuff` functions for conversion within the ANSI character set; the `AnsiToOem`, `AnsiToOemBuff`, `Oem-ToAnsi`, and `OemToAnsiBuff` functions for conversions between the ANSI and OEM character formats; and the `AnsiNext` and `AnsiPrev` functions provided for string-scanning operations.

In most cases, even though these functions are technically obsolete, newer versions of Windows supply backward compatibility in the form of macros that call the newer function versions. For example, the old `AnsiUpper` function is now implemented as a macro invoking the new `CharUpper` API function. In like fashion, `AnsiNext` now invokes `CharNext`, and `AnsiToOem` invokes the `CharToOem` API function.

Functionally, each of these operations remains essentially the same as in the earlier Windows version. The singularly important difference is that they are now Unicode-compatible, not just ANSI-compatible.

Cursors

One cursor is now obsolete. Although the `IDC_SIZE` and `IDC_SIZEALL` cursors are documented as producing the identical four-pointed arrow, the `IDC_SIZE` cursor is obsolete. Instead, for reliability, use `IDC_SIZEALL`.

> **NOTE** See Chapter 8 for details about cursor operations.

Multiple Application Instances

Occasionally, developers have written applications with the expectation that multiple instances of the program would be executed simultaneously or that one instance of the application might call other instances. When this occurred under Windows 3.x, you could use the hPrevInstance argument to determine if there was a previous instance of the application already executing.

Beginning with Windows NT, when each instance of an application was given a separate memory space for execution, the hPrevInstance argument became obsolete. Since each instance was operating in a separate, independent memory space, the hPrevInstance argument was always NULL. regardless of how many copies of the application were executing.

NOTE   For one alternative approach, see the *DDEML* demo, which is on the CD accompanying this book and discussed in Chapter 35. In this demo, the first instance of the application launches four additional instances, but equally important, these later instances do not launch additional copies.

Clipboard Operations

The CF_BITMAP clipboard format supported by Windows 2.x and 3.x for device-dependent bitmaps is now obsolete. Instead, use the CF_DIB format for device-independent bitmaps. Remember, even though the .BMP extension continues to be used for all types of bitmaps, the most common bitmap format is actually the device-independent bitmap (or DIB).

NOTE   See Chapter 34 for more information about clipboard operations.

Portable APIs

Thus far, you've read a lot about API functions that have changed—in major or minor respects—from Windows 3.x to 98/95/NT. We've also covered elements that, despite changes, have been retained in one form or another to provide backward compatibility. There are other API functions that are the same in both Windows 3.*x* and 98/95/NT, but which have not been generally used by Windows 3.*x* programmers, simply because other, parallel functions have been the accepted standards.

The following code fragment example is typical of a Windows 3.*x* application that is setting a graphics mapping mode, nominally in response to a WM_PAINT message.

```
SetMapMode( hdc, nCurMode );                          // 3.x
SetWindowExt( hdc, xWinAspect, yWinAspect );
SetViewportExt( hdc, xViewAspect, yViewAspect );
SetWindowOrg( hdc, xOrg, yOrg );
MoveTo( hdc, xPos, yPos );
```

Except for the first API function, SetMapMode, which remains the same under Windows 98/95/NT, none of the remaining API functions are supported by 98/95/NT. But each of the four unsupported API functions has a counterpart, portable API function that differs from the format shown in only minor respects.

The following code fragment shows the same code using the portable API functions and is compatible with both Windows 3.*x* and 98/95/NT.

```
SetMapMode( hdc, nCurMode );                    // 3.x, 98/95/NT
SetWindowExtEx( hdc, xWinAspect, yWinAspect, NULL );
SetViewportExtEx( hdc, xViewAspect, yViewAspect, NULL);
SetWindowOrgEx( hdc, xOrg, yOrg, NULL );
MoveToEx( hdc, xPos, yPos, NULL );
```

As you will notice, each of the four portable APIs has essentially the same function name; the only difference is the addition of the extension Ex to the name. They also have one additional argument, which, in this example, is NULL in each case.

The NULL arguments have been used for compatibility with the original functional intent, but they could be used as pointers to data structures that return previous settings. For example, for the SetWindowExtEx and SetViewportExtEx API functions, the final argument could be a pointer to a SIZE structure, which would return the previous window or viewport extents. In like fashion, the SetWindowOrgEx and MoveToEx API calls could use a pointer to a POINT structure, which would return the previous origin or the current position.

Remember that for either Windows 3.*x* or 98/95/NT applications, the final argument is optional in each of these API functions. If you do not need the return information, use the NULL argument.

The portable APIs described here are only a few of the portable APIs available, but they are representative of the ones most commonly encountered. When your conversion attempts encounter error messages reporting that a Windows 3.*x* function is no longer recognized, look for a similar API name. You will probably find a portable API with the same functionality, even though it may have slightly different parameters.

Memory Spaces

The differences in memory management between Windows 3.*x* and 98/95/NT are so extreme that no simple comparison is possible. Under DOS (and Windows 3.*x*), only the bottom 640KB of memory was readily accessible, and extended memory managers were required to use any memory beyond the first megabyte. Under both Windows 98 and NT, with 32-bit addressing, memory is effectively flat up to several gigabytes.

There is, however, one important difference between Windows NT and 98. Where NT works in an imagined logical address space of 4GB, Windows 98 is limited to a mere 2GB address space. However, since both of these are well beyond what we can reasonably expect to see physically installed on machines in the near future, these limitations are more imagined than real and, for most practical purposes, both 98 and NT can be assumed to use the same memory address limitations. Also, the memory management APIs for both systems perform essentially the same functions.

Where a difference is visible, however, is when an application attempts to address memory that does not belong to the application. Under Windows NT, where memory access is very tightly regulated, the effect of an invalid address is that the system kills the application. Under Windows 98, however, there are no such protections and an errant application can disrupt other applications or crash the system.

NOTE   See Chapter 19 for more information about the memory management API.

.INI Files versus the Registry

In Windows 3.x applications, a wide variety of application-specific and user-specific information was commonly stored in .INI files. While .INI files may still be used, the system and user registry files are the preferred methods.

Although Windows 3.x did support a registry and registry access APIs, this original registry contained only one unnamed value per registry key, always in a string format. In contrast, the Windows 98/95/NT registry keys may contain multiple, named values and these values may consist of many different types of data.

> **NOTE** See Chapter 17 for more information about using the registry.

Multimedia Changes

Under Windows 3.x, the multimedia services were supported by the Mm-System.DLL. Under Windows 98/95/NT, these services are now supported by Win32 WinMM and the WinMM.DLL library. If you are porting a multimedia application from Windows 3.x to 98/95/NT, be sure to include the MmSystem.H header and to link WinMM.LIB instead of MmSystem.LIB.

Also, the Multimedia Extensions were originally released as a separate product enhancing Windows 3.0 with the MCI_OPEN_PARMS structure used to access multimedia services. Later, under Windows 3.1, the MCI_OPEN_PARMS structure changed the second and third fields from type WORD to the polymorphic type UINT and then, for Win32, to the newly defined MCIDEVICEID type.

If you are porting multimedia applications, keep in mind that a number of type changes have occurred, even though the functions and structures remain similar across the several versions of the operating system.

> **NOTE** See Chapter 37 for more information about developing multimedia applications.

In this appendix, we've covered many of the more common Windows 3.*x*-to-98/95/NT conversions and what types of changes may be necessary. Of course, there are many other possible differences between Windows 3.*x* and 98/95/NT that can affect program conversion. These are discussed and illustrated throughout the chapters in this book.

INDEX

Note to the Reader: First level entries are in **bold**. Page numbers in **bold** indicate the principal discussion of a topic or the definition of a term. Page numbers in *italic* indicate illustrations.

C

G

H

I

O

P

Q

R

S

U

V

X

Z

Master Your
WINDOWS® 98
Destiny WITH THESE BESTSELLING SYBEX TITLES

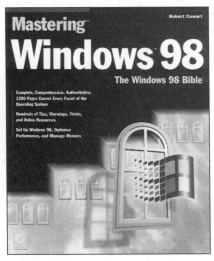

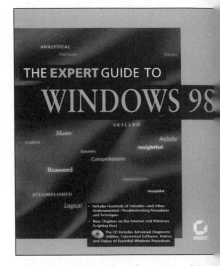

The best-selling *Mastering Windows 95* just got better in its latest edition. It not only covers Microsoft's new 32-bit operating system from beginning to end, but also includes new additions and enhancements. The new Explorer, installation, built-in applications, networking, optimization—it's all here in this absolutely essential guide to the newest version of the Windows operating system.

ISBN: 0-7821-1961-1
1,184pp; 7¹/₂" x 9"; Softcover; $34.99

This special Premium Edition is the complete solution for Windows users. It covers all of the essential topics, including an overview of the operating system, installation concerns, settings, and the file management system. Secrets of scripting, the Registry and other powerful features are explained. Also included are more than 400 pages of advanced customization and internet coverage for power users, as well as two CDs.

ISBN: 0-7821-2186-1
1,584pp; 7¹/₂" x 9"; Hardcover; $59.99

Based on Mark Minasi's seminar, this book is the Windows 98 troubleshooting bible for MIS professionals, consultants and power users. It's the most accessible guide to networking, installing, and supporting Windows 98. The companion CD includes animations of the book's procedures, and several commercial Windows antivirus, diagnostic, and troubleshooting utilities.

ISBN: 0-7821-1974-3
1,008pp; 7¹/₂" x 9"; Softcover; $49.99

SYBEX®
www.sybex.com

Windows 98 Developer's Handbook Companion CD

This companion CD contains:

- All of the code and examples described in this book

- Paint Shop Pro (shareware version)

NOTE Look just inside the front cover for a detailed list of all the unique examples included on the companion CD.

Some programs on this CD require Microsoft and Borland runtime libraries to function. Before installing the CD's sample programs and examples, copy everything in the Library directory to your PC's C:\windows\system directory. The \Library directory on the CD contains several runtime files you'll need to run some of the programs. Requirements for source code and .exes on the CD are listed here:

Chapter 3: PaintText2 requires that MFC42.dll be located in the Windows\System directory.

Chapter 15: To run the NMEDPIPE demo in Windows 98, you must compile it in Windows NT first.

Chapter 16: The Knob control is an OCX file. Chapter 16 includes installation instructions.

Chapter 17: You must run Special.reg before running any of the examples.

Chapter 21: WSock32.LIB is required for FindAddr and SendMail; Delphi is required for webview.exe.

Chapter 22: RPCNS4.LIB is required for RPCServ; RPCRT4.LIB is required for RPClient and RPCServ; WSock32.LIB is required for MacSock.

The readme.txt file contains more information about the CD.